# Contemporary
# Literary Criticism

# Guide to Gale Literary Criticism Series

| For criticism on | Consult these Gale series |
| --- | --- |
| Authors now living or who died after December 31, 1999 | **CONTEMPORARY LITERARY CRITICISM (CLC)** |
| Authors who died between 1900 and 1999 | **TWENTIETH-CENTURY LITERARY CRITICISM (TCLC)** |
| Authors who died between 1800 and 1899 | **NINETEENTH-CENTURY LITERATURE CRITICISM (NCLC)** |
| Authors who died between 1400 and 1799 | **LITERATURE CRITICISM FROM 1400 TO 1800 (LC)** <br><br> **SHAKESPEAREAN CRITICISM (SC)** |
| Authors who died before 1400 | **CLASSICAL AND MEDIEVAL LITERATURE CRITICISM (CMLC)** |
| Authors of books for children and young adults | **CHILDREN'S LITERATURE REVIEW (CLR)** |
| Dramatists | **DRAMA CRITICISM (DC)** |
| Poets | **POETRY CRITICISM (PC)** |
| Short story writers | **SHORT STORY CRITICISM (SSC)** |
| Asian American writers of the last two hundred years | **ASIAN AMERICAN LITERATURE (AAL)** |
| Black writers of the past two hundred years | **BLACK LITERATURE CRITICISM (BLC)** <br><br> **BLACK LITERATURE CRITICISM SUPPLEMENT (BLCS)** |
| Hispanic writers of the late nineteenth and twentieth centuries | **HISPANIC LITERATURE CRITICISM (HLC)** <br><br> **HISPANIC LITERATURE CRITICISM SUPPLEMENT (HLCS)** |
| Native North American writers and orators of the eighteenth, nineteenth, and twentieth centuries | **NATIVE NORTH AMERICAN LITERATURE (NNAL)** |
| Major authors from the Renaissance to the present | **WORLD LITERATURE CRITICISM, 1500 TO THE PRESENT (WLC)** <br><br> **WORLD LITERATURE CRITICISM SUPPLEMENT (WLCS)** |

Volume 169

# Contemporary Literary Criticism

Criticism of the Works
of Today's Novelists, Poets, Playwrights,
Short Story Writers, Scriptwriters, and
Other Creative Writers

**Janet Witalec**
PROJECT EDITOR

Detroit • New York • San Diego • San Francisco • Cleveland • New Haven, Conn. • Waterville, Maine • London • Munich

**Contemporary Literary Criticism, Vol. 169**

**Project Editor**
Janet Witalec

**Editorial**
Tom Burns, Jenny Cromie, Kathy D. Darrow, Jeffrey W. Hunter, Justin Karr, Lemma Shomali

**Research**
Sarah Genik, Tamara C. Nott, Tracie A. Richardson

**Permissions**
Shalice Shah-Caldwell

**Imaging and Multimedia**
Dean Dauphinais, Lezlie Light, David G. Oblender, Kelly A. Quin, Luke Rademacher

**Composition and Electronic Capture**
Gary Leach

**Manufacturing**
Stacy L. Melson

© 2003 by Gale. Gale is an imprint of The Gale Group, Inc., a division of Thomson Learning, Inc.

Gale and Design™ and Thomson Learning™ are trademarks used herein under license.

*For more information, contact*
The Gale Group, Inc.
27500 Drake Rd.
Farmington Hills, MI 48331-3535
Or you can visit our internet site at
http://www.gale.com

**ALL RIGHTS RESERVED**
No part of this work covered by the copyright herein may be reproduced or used in any form or by any means—graphic, electronic, or mechanical, including photocopying, recording, taping, Web distribution, or information storage retrieval systems—without the written permission of the publisher.

This publication is a creative work fully protected by all applicable copyright laws, as well as by misappropriation, trade secret, unfair competition, and other applicable laws. The authors and editors of this work have added value to the underlying factual material herein through one or more of the following: unique and original selection, coordination, expression, arrangement, and classification of the information.

For permission to use material from the product, submit your request via the Web at http://www.gale-edit.com/permissions, or you may download our Permissions Request form and submit your request by fax or mail to:

*Permisssions Department*
The Gale Group, Inc.
27500 Drake Rd.
Farmington Hills, MI 48331-3535
Permissions Hotline:
248-699-8006 or 800-877-4253, ext. 8006
Fax 248-699-8074 or 800-762-4058

Since this page cannot legibly accommodate all copyright notices, the acknowledgments constitute an extension of the copyright notice.

While every effort has been made to secure permission to reprint material and to ensure the reliability of the information presented in this publication, the Gale Group neither guarantees the accuracy of the data contained herein nor assumes any responsibility for errors, omissions or discrepancies. Gale accepts no payment for listing; and inclusion in the publication of any organization, agency, institution, publication, service, or individual does not imply endorsement of the editors or publisher. Errors brought to the attention of the publisher and verified to the satisfaction of the publisher will be corrected in future editions.

---

LIBRARY OF CONGRESS CATALOG CARD NUMBER 76-46132

ISBN 0-7876-6342-5
ISSN 0091-3421

---

Printed in the United States of America
10 9 8 7 6 5 4 3 2 1

# Contents

Preface vii

Acknowledgments xi

Literary Criticism Series Advisory Board xiii

**Nicole Brossard 1943-** ................................................................................... 1
 Canadian poet, novelist, essayist, director, editor, and playwright

**Elfriede Jelinek 1946-** ................................................................................... 67
 Austrian novelist, playwright, and screenwriter

**Ian McEwan 1948-** ....................................................................................... 156
 English novelist, short story writer, playwright, screenwriter, and
 children's writer

**Sam Shepard 1943-** ...................................................................................... 229
 American playwright, screenwriter, short story writer, director, and poet

**Elaine Showalter 1941-** ................................................................................ 311
 American critic, nonfiction writer, essayist, and editor

Literary Criticism Series Cumulative Author Index 381

Literary Criticism Series Cumulative Topic Index 471

*CLC* Cumulative Nationality Index 481

*CLC-169* Title Index 495

# Preface

Named "one of the twenty-five most distinguished reference titles published during the past twenty-five years" by *Reference Quarterly,* the *Contemporary Literary Criticism* (*CLC*) series provides readers with critical commentary and general information on more than 2,000 authors now living or who died after December 31, 1999. Volumes published from 1973 through 1999 include authors who died after December 31, 1959. Previous to the publication of the first volume of *CLC* in 1973, there was no ongoing digest monitoring scholarly and popular sources of critical opinion and explication of modern literature. *CLC,* therefore, has fulfilled an essential need, particularly since the complexity and variety of contemporary literature makes the function of criticism especially important to today's reader.

## Scope of the Series

*CLC* provides significant passages from published criticism of works by creative writers. Since many of the authors covered in *CLC* inspire continual critical commentary, writers are often represented in more than one volume. There is, of course, no duplication of reprinted criticism.

Authors are selected for inclusion for a variety of reasons, among them the publication or dramatic production of a critically acclaimed new work, the reception of a major literary award, revival of interest in past writings, or the adaptation of a literary work to film or television.

Attention is also given to several other groups of writers—authors of considerable public interest—about whose work criticism is often difficult to locate. These include mystery and science fiction writers, literary and social critics, foreign authors, and authors who represent particular ethnic groups.

Each *CLC* volume contains individual essays and reviews taken from hundreds of book review periodicals, general magazines, scholarly journals, monographs, and books. Entries include critical evaluations spanning from the beginning of an author's career to the most current commentary. Interviews, feature articles, and other published writings that offer insight into the author's works are also presented. Students, teachers, librarians, and researchers will find that the general critical and biographical material in *CLC* provides them with vital information required to write a term paper, analyze a poem, or lead a book discussion group. In addition, complete biographical citations note the original source and all of the information necessary for a term paper footnote or bibliography.

## Organization of the Book

A *CLC* entry consists of the following elements:

- The **Author Heading** cites the name under which the author most commonly wrote, followed by birth and death dates. Also located here are any name variations under which an author wrote, including transliterated forms for authors whose native languages use nonroman alphabets. If the author wrote consistently under a pseudonym, the pseudonym will be listed in the author heading and the author's actual name given in parenthesis on the first line of the biographical and critical information. Uncertain birth or death dates are indicated by question marks. Single-work entries are preceded by a heading that consists of the most common form of the title in English translation (if applicable) and the original date of composition.

- A **Portrait of the Author** is included when available.

- The **Introduction** contains background information that introduces the reader to the author, work, or topic that is the subject of the entry.

- The list of **Principal Works** is ordered chronologically by date of first publication and lists the most important works by the author. The genre and publication date of each work is given. In the case of foreign authors whose works have been translated into English, the English-language version of the title follows in brackets. Unless otherwise indicated, dramas are dated by first performance, not first publication.

- Reprinted **Criticism** is arranged chronologically in each entry to provide a useful perspective on changes in critical evaluation over time. The critic's name and the date of composition or publication of the critical work are given at the beginning of each piece of criticism. Unsigned criticism is preceded by the title of the source in which it appeared. All titles by the author featured in the text are printed in boldface type. Footnotes are reprinted at the end of each essay or excerpt. In the case of excerpted criticism, only those footnotes that pertain to the excerpted texts are included.

- A complete **Bibliographical Citation** of the original essay or book precedes each piece of criticism.

- Critical essays are prefaced by brief **Annotations** explicating each piece.

- Whenever possible, a recent **Author Interview** accompanies each entry.

- An annotated bibliography of **Further Reading** appears at the end of each entry and suggests resources for additional study. In some cases, significant essays for which the editors could not obtain reprint rights are included here. Boxed material following the further reading list provides references to other biographical and critical sources on the author in series published by Gale.

## Indexes

A **Cumulative Author Index** lists all of the authors that appear in a wide variety of reference sources published by the Gale Group, including *CLC*. A complete list of these sources is found facing the first page of the Author Index. The index also includes birth and death dates and cross references between pseudonyms and actual names.

A **Cumulative Nationality Index** lists all authors featured in *CLC* by nationality, followed by the number of the *CLC* volume in which their entry appears.

A **Cumulative Topic Index** lists the literary themes and topics treated in the series as well as in *Literature Criticism from 1400 to 1800, Nineteenth-Century Literature Criticism, Twentieth-Century Literary Criticism,* and the *Contemporary Literary Criticism* Yearbook, which was discontinued in 1998.

An alphabetical **Title Index** accompanies each volume of *CLC*. Listings of titles by authors covered in the given volume are followed by the author's name and the corresponding page numbers where the titles are discussed. English translations of foreign titles and variations of titles are cross-referenced to the title under which a work was originally published. Titles of novels, dramas, nonfiction books, and poetry, short story, or essay collections are printed in italics, while individual poems, short stories, and essays are printed in roman type within quotation marks.

In response to numerous suggestions from librarians, Gale also produces an annual cumulative title index that alphabetically lists all titles reviewed in *CLC* and is available to all customers. Additional copies of this index are available upon request. Librarians and patrons will welcome this separate index; it saves shelf space, is easy to use, and is recyclable upon receipt of the next edition.

## Citing *Contemporary Literary Criticism*

When writing papers, students who quote directly from any volume in the Literary Criticism Series may use the following general format to footnote reprinted criticism. The first example pertains to material drawn from periodicals, the second to material reprinted from books.

Alfred Cismaru, "Making the Best of It," *The New Republic* 207, no. 24 (December 7, 1992): 30, 32; excerpted and reprinted in *Contemporary Literary Criticism,* vol. 85, ed. Christopher Giroux (Detroit: The Gale Group, 1995), 73-4.

Yvor Winters, *The Post-Symbolist Methods* (Allen Swallow, 1967), 211-51; excerpted and reprinted in *Contemporary Literary Criticism,* vol. 85, ed. Christopher Giroux (Detroit: The Gale Group, 1995), 223-26.

## Suggestions are Welcome

Readers who wish to suggest new features, topics, or authors to appear in future volumes, or who have other suggestions or comments are cordially invited to call, write, or fax the Project Editor:

Project Editor, Literary Criticism Series
The Gale Group
27500 Drake Road
Farmington Hills, MI 48331-3535
1-800-347-4253 (GALE)
Fax: 248-699-8054

# Acknowledgments

The editors wish to thank the copyright holders of the criticism included in this volume and the permissions managers of many book and magazine publishing companies for assisting us in securing reproduction rights. We are also grateful to the staffs of the Detroit Public Library, the Library of Congress, the University of Detroit Mercy Library, Wayne State University Purdy/Kresge Library Complex, and the University of Michigan Libraries for making their resources available to us. Following is a list of the copyright holders who have granted us permission to reproduce material in this volume of *CLC*. Every effort has been made to trace copyright, but if omissions have been made, please let us know.

**COPYRIGHTED MATERIAL IN *CLC*, VOLUME 169, WAS REPRODUCED FROM THE FOLLOWING PERIODICALS:**

*America,* v. 170, April 30, 1994. Copyright 1994 America Press, Inc. Reproduced by permission of America Press, Inc., 106 West 56th Street, New York, NY 10019. http://www.americamagazine.org.—*American Historical Review,* v. 92, February, 1987. Reproduced by permission.—*American Literature,* v. 64, Spring, 1992; Reproduced by permission.—*American Theatre,* v. 14, July-August, 1997. Reproduced by permission.—*Bookforum,* Spring, 1998. © Bookforum 1998. Reproduced by permission.—*Canadian Literature,* n. 135, Winter, 1992 for "Installations," by Neil B. Bishop. Reproduced by permission of the author.—*Chicago Tribune,* December 20, 1992. © 1992 Tribune Media Services, Inc. All rights reserved. Reproduced by permission.—*Commonweal,* v. lxiii, February 14, 1986; December 6, 1991; v. 24, May 8, 1998. Copyright © 1986, 1991, 1998 Commonweal Publishing Co., Inc. All reproduced by permission.—*Contemporary Review,* v. 266, June, 1995. Reproduced by the permission of Contemporary Review Ltd.—*Contemporary Theatre,* v. 8, 1998. © 1998 OPA (Overseas Publishers Association) NV. Reproduced by permission of Taylor & Francis Ltd. http://www.tandf.co.uk/journals.—*Criticism,* v. xx, Spring, 1978. Copyright, 1978, Wayne State University Press. Reproduced by permission of the publisher.—*Critique,* v. xxxv, Summer, 1994; v. 42, Spring, 2001. Copyright © 1994, 2001 Helen Dwight Reid Educational Foundation. Both reproduced with permission of the Helen Dwight Reid Educational Foundation, published by Heldref Publications, 1319 18th Street, NW, Washington, DC, 20036-1802.—*Differences: A Journal of Feminist Cultural Studies,* v. 12, Summer, 2001. Copyright 2001 Indiana University Press. Reproduced by permission.—*English,* v. 44, Spring, 1995. © The English Association 1995. Reproduced by permission.—*Essays in Criticism,* v. xlii, October, 1992 for "American Patchwork," by Brenda Foglio Lyons. Reproduced by permission of the publisher and the author.—*Essays on Canadian Writing,* no. 70, Spring, 2000. © 2000 Essays on Canadian Writing Ltd. Reproduced by permission.—*The German Quarterly,* v. 74, Summer, 2001. Copyright © 2001 by the American Association of Teachers of German. Reproduced by permission—*Los Angeles Times Book Review,* September 2, 1990; December 16, 1990; December 20, 1992; April 27, 1997; January 25, 1998; November 17, 2000; November 8, 2000. Copyright, 1990, 1992, 1997, 1998, 2000, Los Angeles Times. All reproduced by permission.—*Maclean's,* May 20, 1991; November 17, 1997. © 1991; 1997 by Maclean's Magazine. Reproduced by permission.—*Modern Austrian Literature,* v. 23, 1990; v. 32, 1999. © copyright International Arthur Schnitzler Association 1990, 1999. Both reproduced by permission.—*Modern Drama,* v. 36, 1993; v. 41, 1998. Copyright © 1993, 1998 University of Toronto, Graduate Centre for Study of Drama. Reproduced by permission.—*Modern Fiction Studies,* v. 23, Winter, 1977-78; v. 45, Winter, 1999. Copyright © 1978, 1999 by Purdue Research Foundation, West Lafayette, IN 47907. All rights reserved. Reproduced by permission of The Johns Hopkins University.—*Modern Language Review,* v. 92, July, 1997; v. 95, April, 2000. Reproduced by permission of the publisher.—*Modern Philology,* v. 77, February, 1980 for "A Literature of Their Own: British Women Novelists from Bronte to Lessing," by Vineta Colby. Copyright © 1980 by The University of Chicago. Reproduced by permission of the author.—*Monatshefte,* v. 86, 1994. © 1994 by The Board of Regents of The University of Wisconsin System. Reproduced by permission.—*Mosaic,* v. 25, Fall, 1992. © Mosaic 1992. Reproduced by permission.— *The Nation,* New York, v. 252, March 18, 1991; v. 272, June 11, 2001. © 1991 The Nation magazine/The Nation Company, Inc. Reproduced by permission.—*National Review,* v. xlv, September 1, 1997. Copyright © 1997 by National Review, Inc, 215 Lexington Avenue. New York, NY 10016. Reproduced by permission—*The New Leader,* v. 85, March- April, 2002. © 2002 by The American Labor Conference on International Affairs, Inc. Reproduced by permission.—*The New Republic,* v. 194, January 27, 1986; v. 194, April 28, 1986; v. 207, November 16, 1992; v. 212, January 2, 1995; v. 215, July 15-22, 1996; v. 216, May 12, 1997; v. 226, March 25, 2002. © 1986, 1992, 1995, 1996, 1997, 2002. The New Republic, Inc. All reproduced by permission.—*New Statesman,* v. 96, July 21, 1978; v. 111, March 28, 1986; v. 126, June 13, 1997; v. 126, September 5, 1997; v. 127, September 11, 1998; v. 130, June 18, 2001; v. 130, July 23, 2001; v. 130, September 17, 2001. © 1978, 1986, 1997, 1998, 2001. Statesman & Nation Publishing Company Limited. All reproduced by permission.—*New Statesman & Society,* v. 2, July 28, 1989; v. 3, August 31, 1990; v. 4, March 29, 1991; v. 4, September 27, 1991; v. 6, June 18, 1993. © 1989, 1990, 1991, 1993. Statesman &

Nation Publishing Company Limited. All reproduced by permission.—*The New York Review of Books,* January 14, 1993; April 9, 1998; January 14, 1999. Copyright © 1993, 1998, 1999, Nyrev, Inc. All reproduced with permission from *The New York Review of Books.—NWSA Journal,* v. 10, Spring, 1998. Reproduced by permission.—*The Review of Contemporary Fiction,* Spring, 1992. Copyright, 1992, by John O'Brien. Reproduced by permission.—*Review of English Studies,* v. xlv, May, 1994 for a review of "Sister's Choice: Tradition and Change in American Women's Writing" by Navina Krishna Hooker. Reproduced by permission of the publisher and the author.—*Sewanee Review,* v. 100, Fall, 1992 for "Shepard's Plays: Stylistic and Thematic Ties" by Robert B. Heilman. © 1992 by Robert B. Heilman. Reproduced by permission.—*Signs,* v. 12, Winter, 1987 for a review of "The New Feminist Criticism: Essays on Women, Literature and Theory," by Linda Kauffman; v. 19, Winter, 1994 for a review of "Sister's Choice: Tradition and Change in American Women's Writing," by Elaine Hedges. Copyright © 1987 by The University of Chicago. Both reproduced by permission of the authors.—*Skeptical Inquirer,* v. 21, September-October, 1997. Reproduced by permission.—*South Atlantic Quarterly,* v. 91, Spring, 1992. Copyright © 1992 by Duke University Press. Reproduced by permission.—*The Spectator,* v. 266, April 6, 1991; v. 277, November 16, 1996; v. 279, August 30, 1997; v. 281, September 12, 1998; v. 286, June 30, 2001; v. 291, January 25, 2003. © 1991, 1996, 1997, 1998, 2001, 2003 by *The Spectator.* All reproduced by permission of *The Spectator.—Theater,* v. 25, Spring-Summer, 1994. Reproduced by permission.—*Times Literary Supplement,* July 21-27, 1989; November 2, 1990; November 15, 1991; September 3, 1993; September 30, 1994; May 16, 1997; September 12, 1997; September 4, 1998; August 10, 2001. © The Times Supplements Limited 1989, 1990, 1991, 1993, 1994, 1997, 1998, 2001. All reproduced from *The Times Literary Supplement* by permission.—*Tulsa Studies in Women's Literature,* v. 12, Spring, 1993. © 1993, The University of Tulsa. Reproduced by permission.—*Women's Review of Books,* v. ix, November, 1991 for "The Anatomy of Culture," by Florence Boos; v. 18, July, 2001 for "Unparalleled Lives," by Brenda Wineapple. Both reproduced by permission of the authors.—*Women's Studies,* v. 13, 1987. © Gordon and Breach Science Publishers. Reproduced by permission.—*Women's Studies International Forum,* v. 14, 1991. Reproduced by permission.—*World Literature in Review,* v. 70, Autumn, 1996. Reproduced by permission.—*World Literature Today,* v. 52, Winter, 1978; v. 70, Autumn, 1996; v. 72, Autumn, 1998; v. 75, Spring, 2001; v. 76, Winter, 2002. Copyright 1978, 1996, 1998, 2001, 2002 by the University of Oklahoma Press. All reproduced by permission.

**COPYRIGHTED MATERIAL IN *CLC*, VOLUME 169, WAS REPRODUCED FROM THE FOLLOWING BOOKS:**

Brossard, Nicole. From *The Politics of Poetic Form: Poetry and Public Policy.* Edited by Charles Bernstein. Roof, 1990. Copyright © 1990 by Charles Bernstein. Reproduced by permission.—Brossard, Nicole, and Beverley Daurio. From *The Power to Bend Spoons: Interviews with Canadian Novelists.* Edited by Beverley Daurio. The Mercury Press, 1998. Copyright © 1998 by Beverley Daurio. All rights reserved. Reproduced by permission.—Brossard, Nicole with Janice Williamson. From *Sounding Differences: Conversations with Seventeen Canadian Women Writers.* University of Toronto Press, 1993. © University of Toronto Press 1993. Reproduced by permission.—Gould, Karen. From *Writing in the Feminine: Feminism and Experimental Writing in Quebec.* Southern Illinois University Press, 1990. Copyright © 1990 by the Board of Trustees, Southern Illinois University. All rights reserved. Reproduced by permission.—Knutson, Susan. From *Narrative in the Feminine: Daphne Marlatt and Nicole Brossard.* Wilfrid Laurier University Press, 2000. © 2000 Wilfrid Laurier University Press. All rights reserved. Reproduced by permission.—Wilson, Ann. From *Modern Dramatists: A Casebook of Major British, Irish, and American Playwrights.* Edited by Kimball King. Routledge, 2001. Copyright © 2001 by Kimball King. All rights reserved. Reproduced by permission publisher and the author.

**PHOTOGRAPHS AND ILLUSTRATIONS APPEARING IN *CLC*, VOLUME 169, WERE RECEIVED FROM THE FOLLOWING SOURCES:**

Brossard, Nicole, photograph by John Reeves. Reproduced by permission of John Reeves.—McEwan, Ian, photograph. © Jerry Bauer. Reproduced by permission.—Shepard, Sam, photograph by Jakub Mosur. AP/Wide World Photos. Reproduced by permission.—Showalter, Elaine, appearing at the Edinburgh International Book Festival, photograph by McPherson Colin. Corbis Sygma. Reproduced by Corbis Corporation.

# Literary Criticism Series Advisory Board

The members of the Gale Group Literary Criticism Series Advisory Board—reference librarians and subject specialists from public, academic, and school library systems—represent a cross-section of our customer base and offer a variety of informed perspectives on both the presentation and content of our literature criticism products. Advisory board members assess and define such quality issues as the relevance, currency, and usefulness of the author coverage, critical content, and literary topics included in our series; evaluate the layout, presentation, and general quality of our printed volumes; provide feedback on the criteria used for selecting authors and topics covered in our series; provide suggestions for potential enhancements to our series; identify any gaps in our coverage of authors or literary topics, recommending authors or topics for inclusion; analyze the appropriateness of our content and presentation for various user audiences, such as high school students, undergraduates, graduate students, librarians, and educators; and offer feedback on any proposed changes/enhancements to our series. We wish to thank the following advisors for their advice throughout the year.

**Dr. Toby Burrows**
Principal Librarian
The Scholars' Centre
University of Western Australia Library

**David M. Durant**
Reference Librarian, Joyner Library
East Carolina University

**Steven R. Harris**
English Literature Librarian
University of Tennessee

**Mary Jane Marden**
Literature and General Reference Librarian
St. Petersburg Jr. College

**Mark Schumacher**
Jackson Library
University of North Carolina at Greensboro

**Gwen Scott-Miller**
Fiction Department Manager
Seattle Public Library

# Nicole Brossard
## 1943-

Canadian poet, novelist, essayist, director, editor, and playwright.

The following entry presents an overview of Brossard's career through 2001. For further information on her life and works, see *CLC,* Volume 115.

## INTRODUCTION

One of the most outspoken and innovative figures of late-twentieth-century Québécois literature, Brossard is an experimental and avant-garde writer, numbered among the foremost representatives of literary *modernité,* and regarded as a leading theoretician of *écriture au féminin*—women's writing—in French-speaking Canada. Openly and unapologetically political, Brossard's writing stresses her radical feminist beliefs, embracing her lesbianism and offering a literary celebration of the woman's body while promoting a sustained attack against the traditional orthodoxies of the dominant, patriarchal language, social systems, and cultural values. Additionally, Brossard's strong reaction against conventional views of poetry and fiction as mimetic representations of objective reality has become a central and defining theme in her writing—which values transgression and forbidden feminine desire—viewing these as integral elements in the creation of a radical, utopian, modern, and woman-centered vision of literature and society.

## BIOGRAPHICAL INFORMATION

Brossard was born in Montreal, Quebec, Canada, in 1943. Educated at the Collège Marguerite-Bourgeois in her youth, she later attended the Université de Montréal, graduating with a bachelor of arts degree in literature in 1965. That same year, Brossard published her first collection of verse, *Aube à la saison,* in the volume *Trois*—which included poetry by Michel Beaulieu and Micheline de Jordy—and co-founded the literary journal *La Barre du jour,* which published poetry by the significant figures of the avant-garde poetry scene in Quebec, including Brossard's own experimental verse. Brossard continued her education into the late 1960s and early 1970s, obtaining pedagogical certification and teaching briefly at secondary schools before opting to devote her full attention to a literary career. The birth of her daughter Julie and a new awareness of her lesbianism in the early 1970s shaped Brossard's emerging literary identity and helped to define the political motivations that would characterize her subsequent career as a writer and activist. She began to publish a steady stream of poetry and prose, which expanded upon the ideas suggested in her novel *Un livre* (1970; *A Book*) and her poetry collection *Le Centre blanc* (1970). In 1976 she co-created the radical feminist magazine *Les Têtes de Pioche*. By this time, Brossard had joined a community of avant-garde feminist writers and activists in Quebec, which included Marthe Blackburn, Marie-Claire Blais, Odette Gagnon, Luce Guilbeault, Pol Pelletier, and France Théoret. Among the products of this artistic collective was the theatrical production *La Nef des sorcières* (1976; *A Clash of Symbols*), for which Brossard contributed "L'Écrivain," a monologue on the creative process of the writer. In 1977 she co-directed the documentary film *Quelques féministes américaines* (*Some American Feminists*) with Luce Guilbeault and Margaret Wescott. Later that year, Brossard was elected to the first executive board of the Union des Écrivains Québécois, a literary organization designed to define and protect the ethical and economic rights of its constituents. She subsequently served as the group's vice-president between 1983 and 1985. Meanwhile, Brossard continued her increasingly prolific literary output in the 1980s with such novels as *Picture Theory* (1982) and *Le Désert mauve* (1987; *Mauve Desert*). By the 1990s, Brossard had become an icon of the radical, urban feminist movement in Quebec, and continued to write, edit, and speak about such issues as postmodern literature, semiotic theory, and the awakening of feminine consciousness and lesbian desire.

## MAJOR WORKS

Among Brossard's early collections of poetry, *Aube à la saison* and *Mordre en sa chair* (1966) are thought to reflect the influence of contemporary poets Hector de Saint-Denys Garneau, Alain Grandbois, and Anne Hébert, although they also demonstrate Brossard's movement away from the landscape focus then prevalent among Québécois writers. Her third volume, *L'Écho bouge beau* (1968), exhibits a more assured and individual control of poetic language, introducing many of the erotic and body-centered themes that Brossard has subsequently explored throughout her literary oeuvre. The collection also demonstrates her developing interest in semiotics and linguistic signification associated with such French poststructuralist theorists as Roland Barthes and Jacques Derrida. Beginning with *L'Écho bouge beau,* Brossard also began a process of experimentalism in her writing, seeking to divorce her work from the misrepresentation of dominant ideologies, particularly those linked with patriarchy and its manifestations in language. In her subsequent poetic works, including *Suite logique* (1970), *Le Centre blanc,* and *Mécanique jongleuse* (1973; *Daydream Mechanics*), Brossard continued to expand and develop this effort. *Le Centre blanc* endeavors to displace the conventional ordering of syntactic elements such as subject, verb, and predicate in order to multiply and expand the range of signification and meaning in poetic language. Additionally, these works demonstrate Brossard's interest in the seductive and desire-laden dimensions of writing, as well as its subversive potential. *Installations: Avec et sans pronoms* (1989) and the prose poem *La Nuit verte du Parc Labyrinthe* (1992; *Green Night of Labyrinth Park*) offer thorough examinations of language, sexuality, subjectivity, and representation and uses such themes to suggest multivalent layers of meaning.

Brossard's narrative texts, which often feature a mélange of poetry and prose, generally dismiss traditional plotting and schemes of characterization. *Un livre* focuses on a small group of acquaintances and lovers whose movements, actions, and gestures form the structural center of the work and contribute to its themes of liberation, autonomy, and simultaneity. Brossard's second novel, *French Kiss: étreinte/exploration* (1974; *French Kiss; or, A Pang's Progress*), shows more of a concern with the emotions and physical sensations of the main characters, rather than conforming to traditional notions of plot or narrative. The novel follows Marielle and four other underground revolutionaries who create a short-lived utopian community, successfully staving off outside reality and Montreal's authorities before their experiment is destroyed by police intervention. Evidencing the influence of the French *nouveau roman* and other experimental fiction of the twentieth century, *French Kiss* subverts traditional modes of psychological characterization, instead offering a deep focus on the characters's movements, smell, texture, skin, and hair. Brossard's lesbian-feminist viewpoint and its consequent critique of patriarchal society is the driving force behind *L'Amèr ou, le chapitre effrité: fiction théorétique* (1977; *These Our Mothers; or, the Disintegrating Chapter*), a work that probes the psycho-social dynamics of the relationships between mothers and daughters. Another defining element of Brossard's prose is its focus on sexuality, particularly in the novels *Amantes* (1980; *Lovhers*) and *Le Sens apparent* (1980; *Surfaces of Sense*). *Lovhers* ostensibly takes place at the Barbizon Hotel for Women in New York City, though the work itself is more specifically a mixture of erotic poetry and utopian prose focused on the lesbian body. Drawing upon technology for its central image, *Picture Theory*—the term is borrowed from the theoretical work of the Austrian philosopher Ludwig Wittgenstein—nevertheless critiques and transgresses notions of linear, scientific logic. Its central focus is the daily repression and potential liberation of feminine desire, which Brossard visualizes in the symbolic contexts of the hologram—a construct that employs laser light to create a seemingly animate, three-dimensional image in space. Brossard uses this image as an abstracted reference to the mystery of the feminine and of a woman's limitless potential for interpretation. In a departure from Montreal, the setting of most of her fiction, Brossard favors the symbolically suggestive desert of the American Southwest in her postmodern novel *Le Désert mauve,* a text that plays with categories of writing, reading, and translation. Its first portion recounts the adventures of an alienated and rebellious fifteen-year-old girl, Mélanie Kerouac, detailing her high-speed drives through the deserts of Arizona and New Mexico. In the novel's second section, Mélanie's narrative is transformed into a book written by an author named Laure Angstelle. In the third and final section of the volume, a woman named Maude Laures discovers Angstelle's long forgotten work and decides to translate and rework the story under the title *Mauve, l'horizon.* More fictionally accessible than Brossard's earlier novels, *Baroque d'aube* (1995; *Baroque at Dawn*) explores the theme of feminine imaginative desire as it follows the efforts of three women—a writer, a photographer, and an oceanographer—to understand and interpret the creative process.

## CRITICAL RECEPTION

Since the early 1970s, Brossard has been widely recognized as a principal figure among North American feminist intellectuals and writers. Her unique poetic voice, radical politics, and provocative interpretation of lesbian poetics have positioned Brossard as a central figure in the avant-garde movement in late-twentieth-century Québécois literature. While some commentators have criticized her fiction for its experimental and non-traditional treatment of plot and character as well as its heavily meta-literary content, many contemporary critics have praised Brossard's writing as demanding, multifaceted, and richly suggestive. Amid those undisturbed by Brossard's open challenge to existing social, cultural, literary, and political institutions, her creative and theoretical work has been regarded as among the most esteemed in contemporary Francophone literature.

## PRINCIPAL WORKS

*Aube à la saison* (poetry) 1965
*Mordre en sa chair* (poetry) 1966
*L'Écho bouge beau* (poetry) 1968
*Le Centre blanc* (poetry) 1970
*Suite logique* (poetry) 1970
*Un livre* [*A Book*] (novel) 1970
*Narrateur et personnages* (radio play) 1971
*Mécanique jongleuse* [*Daydream Mechanics*] (poetry) 1973
*Sold-out: étreinte/illustration* [*Turn of a Pang*] (novel) 1973
*French Kiss: étreinte/exploration* [*French Kiss; or, A Pang's Progress*] (novel) 1974
*Mécanique jongleuse suivi de masculin grammaticale* (poetry) 1974
*La Partie pour le tout* (poetry) 1975
*\*La Nef des sorcières* [*A Clash of Symbols*; with Marthe Blackburn, Marie-Claire Blais, Odette Gagnon, Luce Guilbeault, Pol Pelletier, and France Théoret] (play) 1976
*L'Amèr ou, le chapitre effrité: fiction théorétique* [*These Our Mothers; or, the Disintegrating Chapter*] (novel) 1977
*Quelques féministes américaines* [*Some American Feminists*; director; with Luce Guilbeault and Margaret Wescott] (documentary film) 1977
*D'Arcs de cycle la dérive* (poetry) 1979
*The Story So Far 6/Les Stratégies du réel* [editor] (prose) 1979
*Amantes* [*Lovhers*] (novel) 1980
*Le Sens apparent* [*Surfaces of Sense*] (novel) 1980
*Picture Theory* (novel) 1982
*Double Impression: poèmes et textes 1967-1984* (poetry) 1984
*Journal intime; ou, Voilà donc un manuscrit* (journal) 1984
*Domaine d'écriture* (poetry) 1985
*L'Aviva* (poetry) 1985
*La Falaise* (radio play) 1985
*La Lettre aérienne* [*The Aerial Letter*] (essays) 1985
*Mauve* [with Daphne Marlatt] (poetry) 1985
*Character/Jeu de lettres* [with Daphne Marlatt] (poetry) 1986
*Souvenirs d'enfance et de jeunesse* (radio play) 1986
*Correspondence* [with Michèle Causse] (radio play) 1987
*Le Désert mauve* [*Mauve Desert*] (novel) 1987
*Sous la langue/Under Tongue* (poetry) 1987
*À tout regard* [with Daphne Marlatt] (poetry) 1989
*Installations: Avec et sans pronoms* (poetry) 1989
*La Subjectivité des lionnes* (poetry) 1990
*Typhon Dru* (poetry) 1990
*Anthologie de la poésie des femmes au Québec (1677-1988)* [editor; with Lisette Girouard] (poetry) 1991
*Langues obscures* (poetry) 1992
*La Nuit verte du Parc Labyrinthe* [*Green Night of Labyrinth Park*] (poetry) 1992
*Baroque d'aube* [*Baroque at Dawn*] (novel) 1995
*Vertige de l'avant-scène* (poetry) 1997
*Elle serait la première phrase de mon prochain* [*She Would Be the First Sentence of My Next Novel*] (poetry) 1998
*Au présent des veines* (poetry) 1999
*Musée de l'os et de l'eau* (poetry) 1999
*Hier: Roman* (novel) 2001

\*Brossard contributed the monologue "L'Écrivain" ("The Writer") to this collaborative drama.

## CRITICISM

**Nicole Brossard (essay date 1990)**

SOURCE: Brossard, Nicole. "Poetic Politics." In *The Politics of Poetic Form: Poetry and Public Policy*, edited by Charles Bernstein, pp. 73-82. New York: Roof Books, 1990.

[*In the following essay, Brossard outlines her views on writing, desire, language, and reality, considering the political element of each.*]

I have divided my presentation into two parts. The first part has to do with the body of writing, its motivations, its energies. The second part has to do with the references and values that surround us and the kinds of linguistic reaction they call for when we disagree with them. I say *when we disagree with them* because I don't believe that one becomes a writer to reinforce common values or common perspectives on reality.

I would like, in this talk, to make space for questions regarding different rituals, different approaches, different postures that we take in language in order to exist, fulfill our needs to express, communicate, or to challenge language itself: hoping that by playing with language it will reveal unknown dimensions of reality. I have been writing for more than 20 years. I have written poetry, novels, texts, essays. Today, I am still fascinated by the act of writing, the processes, the trouble, the pain, and the joy that we go through in order to put in words what we feel, what we recall vaguely but which insists on being recalled, what we envision whether it is full-length images or enigmatic flashes running through our brain like a storm of truth.

Those who are familiar with my work will know that one of most recurrent words in my texts is *body* (*corps*). This word is usually accompanied by the words *writing* (*écriture*) and *text* (*texte*). The expression *Le Cortex exubérant* summarizes my obsession with body, text, and writing. For me the body is a metaphor of energy, intensity, desire, pleasure, memory, and awareness. The body interests me in its circulation of energy and the way it provides, through our senses, for a network of associations out of which we create our mental environment, out of which we imagine far beyond what we in fact see, feel, hear or taste. It is through this network of associations that we claim new sensations, that we dream backward in accelerated or slow motion, that we zoom in on sexual fantasies, that we discover unexpected angles of thought.

I have always said that writing is energy taking shape in language. Sexual, libidinal, mental, and spiritual energies give to us the irresistible need to declare things, to make new propositions, to look for solutions which can unknot social patterns of violence and death, to explore unknown territories of the mind, to search for each of our identities, to fill the gap between real and unreal. In other words, energy motivates us to write but it also needs to find its *motive* to be able to do this. Energy has to go out and has to come in. The body is its channel. But the body claims to be more than a channel: it thinks of strategies to regularize the flow of energy. The body alone cannot process all energy, it needs language to process energy into social meaning. Among the uses that we make of language, there is a privileged one called creative writing. It is in this sense that I say that writing is shaping figures and meanings within the merry-go-round of energy that traverses us. Filtered by language, this energy finds a rhythm, becomes a voice, transforms itself into images and metaphors. Energy that is too low keeps you silent, energy that is too high makes noise instead of meaning—even though silence and noise can eventually by interpreted as an historical momentum.

Sexual, libidinal, mental, and spiritual energies provided with a *motive* or an *object of desire,* or both, engage us in a creative dimension. When these energies synchronize they offer a privileged moment to a writer. Most of the time we call this "inspiration." These energies can also work alone or in combination. Sexual energy produces a multiplicity of images and scenarios. Libidinal energy creates projects and goals. Mental energy provides for sharpness and for abstraction. Spiritual energy links us to a global environment. Yet all these energies can stagnate or make you mad if they don't meet their object of desire, or organize themselves in such a way that they can at least dream of—or figure out—their object of desire.

Now let me make a distinction between the motive and the object of desire. The motive is something that whatever the situation eternally returns in the work of an artist. The motive is roots, flesh and skin. It is *incontrovertible*. It is inscribed in us as a first and ultimate memory. It is carnal knowledge. All good writers have a strong motive. The motive is most of the time hidden in the core of a work, hidden but recurrent as a theme. It seems to me that motive (a good reason and a pattern) is a personal, existential question that makes one endlessly repeat: why or how come? It is a three-dimensional question caused by a synergetic moment, this moment being either traumatic or ecstatic. With the synergetic moment gone, we are left with this three-dimensional question, a question to which we can only respond with a two-dimensional answer—that is, a partial answer that obliges us to repeat the question and to try other answers. We answer in two dimensions because we think in a chronological way, one word at the time, one word after the other, while the body experiences life synchronously. Writing, we have to make choices, to separate things. Naming is separation, it portions out reality. Dreams are 3-dimensional but we forget about them or cannot understand them.

As for the object of desire, it is probably always the same one mediated by different people we fall in love with, by books we cannot recover from, by situations to which we respond passionately. For me, a good writer or a good painter always repeats the same motive, the same question, the same statement in all her or his works. Think of Kandinsky, Rothko, Betty Goodwin. Great artists are always driven by a motive while fairly good creators have to rely on their objects of desire: if the object isn't there, then nothing happens but sweat.

It is well known that people give and take energy from one another; that blame, insult, humiliation take away energy; that praise, love, and respect multiply energy. The principle is very simple. But it gets complicated when it applies to the way men and women are positioned in regard to language's patriarchal values. We cannot avoid questioning this cultural field of language, which both provides us with energy or deprives us of it. What I call the cultural field of language is made of male sexual and psychic energies transformed through centuries of written fiction into standards for imagination, frames of references, patterns of analysis, networks of meaning, rhetorics of body and soul. Digging in that field can be, for a creative woman, a mental health hazard.

This second part is more personal. What I propose to discuss is a kind of trajectory in my writing. I would like to show how my politics of poetic form—my Poetic Politics—have been shaped within a sociocultural environment as well as through private life. But I would also like to talk in general terms of the behaviors that we encounter in writing while we make space for ourselves as well as for ideas that we value and themes that we privilege.

Since in principle language belongs to everyone, we are entitled to reappropriate it by taking the initiative to intervene when it gives the impression of closing itself off, and when our desire clashes with common usage. Very young, I perceived language as an obstacle, as a mask, narrow-spirited like a repetitive task of boredom and of lies. Only poetic language found mercy in my eyes. It is in this sense that my practice of writing became at once a practice of intervention and of exploration—a ludic experience. Very early I had a relationship to the language of transgression and of subversion. I wanted strong sensations: I wanted to unmask lies, hypocrisy, and banality. I had the feeling that if language was an obstacle, it was also the place where everything happens, where everything is possible. That I still believe.

I have often said that I don't write to express myself but that I write to understand reality, the way we process reality into fiction, the way we process feeling, emotion and sensation into ideas and landscapes of thought. After all, the difference between a writer and a nonwriter is that the writer processes life through written language and by doing so has access and gives access to unexpected, unsuspected angles of reality—which we commonly called fiction.

What about expressions like *strong sensations, transgression, subversion,* and *ludic experience*? Let's start with "strong sensations" and "ludic experience." What do these expressions oppose? For me, they oppose boredom and daily routine; in a word: *linearity*. Behind that there is obviously a statement something like: "I am not satisfied with what society offers me as a future or imposes on me in the present because if I was to follow its directives, it would mean that I would have to lead a boring, middlebrow, puritan life." This means that I value research, intelligence, and pleasure. It also means that I cannot function with cliches and standard values that somehow seem to narrow the possibilities of life: life of the mind as well as life of the emotion. Indeed, our emotional and our critical spirits are more and more eroded.

To be more concrete, let's say that I started to write, in the early 60s in a Quebec, which was at a turning point of our history, a period that we have called the "quiet revolution." Yes, everything was being questioned: education as well as social, political, religious, and cultural life. To my generation, the dream of an independent, French, socialist, secular Quebec provided for audacities, transgressions, and a quest for collective identity. But underneath these changes was essentially the question of identity. Who were we? Who are we? We have a Canadian passport but our soul and tradition are not Canadian, we speak French but we are not French, we are North American but we are not American. As a young person and as a young writer there were three kinds of institutions that had a sour taste to me:

First: *The Catholic Church* because it had a strong influence in almost every field of Quebec society and mainly because of its control on education and sexual life (marriage, contraception, abortion, homosexuality).

Second: *The Canadian Confederation* and all its British and Canadian symbols. I resent profoundly how as French Canadian we were despised and discriminated against by Anglo Canadian politics. I have always made the language issue a personal thing. Today I am still vividly hurt when someone who is living or has been living in Montreal for many years addresses me in English.

Third: *The literary establishment.* When you write you write with and against literature. You write out of inspiration from writers and books, but you also write against mediocrity and the cliches the literary establishment promotes. Maybe it has been unfair to some writers of the generation that preceded mine, but I was fed up with poems talking about landscapes, snow, mountains, and the tormented rhetoric of love and solitude. At the same time, I felt deeply for Quebec literature which the generation of *La Barre du Jour* and *Les Herbes rouges* were about to rediscover and to renew at the same time.

So all together those three realities set up for me a social and literary field that I could oppose and later on transgress and subvert. Very early my poetry was abstract, syntactically nonconventional; desire with its erotic drives had a great part in it. Part of what I was writing was consciously political, at least at the level of intention. Let's say that my "basic intention" was to make trouble, to be a troublemaker in regard to language but also with values of my own embodied by a writing practice that was ludic (playing with words), experimental (trying to understand processes of writing), and exploratory (searching). You see, it brings us back to my values: exploration (which provides for renewal of information and knowledge), intelligence (which provides the ability to process things), and pleasure (which provides for energy and desire).

So from 1965 to 1973, I can say that I would see myself as a poet—an avant-garde poet, a formalist poet. Being a woman was not at stake, didn't seem to be a problem. Of course it was not a problem because in some way I was not identifying with femininity nor with other women, with whom I felt I had nothing to share. I could understand and talk about alienation, oppression, domination, exploitation only when applied to me as a Quebecer. I was a Quebecer, an intellectual, a poet, a revolutionary. Those were my identities. They were all positive and somehow they were valued in those years of cultural changes and counterculture. So in some way by transgressing I was still on the good side.

But in 1974, I became a mother and about the same time fell in love with another woman. Suddenly, I was living the most common experience in a woman's life which is motherhood and at the same time I was living the most marginal experience in a woman's life which is lesbianism. Motherhood made life absolutely concrete (two bodies to wash, to clean, to move, to think of) and lesbianism made my life absolute fiction in a patriarchal heterosexual world. Motherhood shaped my solidarity with women and gave me a feminist consciousness as lesbianism opened new mental space to explore.

All this to say that my body was getting new ideas, new feelings, new emotions. From then on my writing started to change. It became more fluid, though still abstract and still obsessed with language, transgression, and subversion; but this time I had "carnal knowledge" of what I was investing in words. My frame of references started to change and new words (words that I had never used) started to invest my work: vertigo, cliff, amazon, sleep, memory, skin. I started to use new metaphors to understand things: the spiral, the hologram, metaphors which would help me to drift away from a linear and binary approach. Questions started to flow about identity, imagination, history, and more and more questions came about language and the incredible fraud I was discovering in the accumulated layers of lies told about women through centuries of the male version of reality. Which is to say that I also had to deal with contradictions, paradoxes, double binding, tautology in order to understand what I would call "the father knows best" business. Patriarchy being a highly sophisticated machine, it takes time and energy to understand how it works.

Now I would like to try to answer more precisely the questions raised in this series of lectures on "The Politics of Poetic Form." While writing this essay, I found myself saying: "It is not in the writing that a poetic text is political, it is in the reading that it becomes political." I knew something was true and wrong at the same time with this statement and therefore I decided to divide it in two affirmative statements which are:

A. It is in the writing that a text shows its politics.

B. It is in the reading that a text has a political aura.

I believe that a text gives subliminal information on how it wants to be read. Its structure is itself a statement, no matter what the text says. Of course, what the texts says is important but it is like body language. Body language tells more about yourself and how you want to relate with someone than does your words. I would like to point out three aspects in which a text shows politics: its perspective, its themes, its style.

The perspective. What I call the perspective is an angle from which we orient the reading of a text before it is even read. This can be done by *quotations* beginning or inserted in the text, for example from Virginia Woolf, Marx, Martin Luther King, etc. This can also be done by *dedication* of a poem to someone whose name will ring a political bell. For example, dedicating your poem to Che Guevara, to Valerie Solanas, to Paul Rose, or to even to Ben Johnson. The third way is to *title* your poem or your book in such a way that it will suggest some political metaphors. For example: *Chili's Bones Flowers, Clitoris at Sunset, The Color Purple* (in which we read subliminally "people of color") or *Give Em Enough Rope* (which can be understood "give them enough rope to hang themselves" or "give him enough rope to do want he wants"). Quotations, dedications, and titles provide for immediate references or statement. They tell a state of mind, they point out literary, cultural, or political networks.

Themes. There are themes that are bound to have if not ideological at least a troubling effect: *Sexuality,* eroticism, homosexuality, lesbianism—something is always at stake with eroticism because it deals with limits, moral, and the unavowable. *Language*—writing about language, pointing out how language works or giving feedback on how what is being read has been written can also imply politics of awareness because it takes away the "referential illusion" of the reader.

Postures. *Disqualifying symbols of authority* by uncovering the lies and the contradictions on which they have been constituted—God, Pope, President, Man, or little man (as in husband, lover, or father). *Valuing marginal experiences*—valuing people who are inferiorized, for example valuing women as subjects.

Style. Shaking the syntax, breaking grammatical law, not respecting punctuation, visually designing the text, using the white space, typesetting as you choose, using rhythms to create sounds: All of these have a profound effect on readers, offering a new perspective on reality through a global formal approach as did for example the impressionists, the cubists, and the expressionists, in painting and as did, in literature, the surrealists, *le nouveau roman,* the post-moderns. Among writers we can name Gertrude Stein, James Joyce, and Monique Wittig for *The Lesbian Body.*

So by changing the perspective, the themes, or the style, somehow you deceive the conformist reader in her or his moral or aesthetic expectations and you annoy her or him by breaking the habits of reading. At the same time, you provide for a new space of emotion and you make space for new materials to be taken into account about life and its meaning; you also offer the non-conformist reader a space for a new experience—travelling through meaning while simultaneously producing meaning.

These interventions send a message in which the poet says: I don't agree with prevalent moral or aesthetic values. I am not respecting the status quo. There is more to life than what we are thought to believe, there is more to language than what we are used to expecting.

While the statement "It is in the writing that a text shows its politics" repels or seduces the reader (most of the time belonging to the dominant culture), the second statement "It is in the reading that a text becomes political" calls for a process of identification from the reader belonging to a minority or treated as such.

I believe that a lot of writers belonging to minorities whether sexual, racial, or cultural, or writers who belong to groups who live or have lived under colonization, oppression, exploitation, or a dictatorship, are bound to have a highly loaded personal memory out of which they express themselves as individuals. But inevitably their personal story converges with the one of thousands who have felt and lived the same experience. Memory, identity, and solidarity are at stake when *reading* is taken as political; just as transgression, subversion, and exploration are at stake when *writing* is taken as political.

Anyone who encounters insult and hatred because of her or his differences from a powerful group is bound, soon or later, to echo a *we* through the use of *I* and to draw the line between *us and them, we* and *they.*

WE triggers emotions based on solidarity, memory, identification, complicity, proudness, or sadness.

THEY triggers emotions based on anger and revolt. Hatred also: THEY cuts the relation.

YOU (in the plural *vous*) triggers accusations, blame, reproach. It maintains the relation because it is a direct address. *You* calls for negotiation just as *they* calls for struggle.

We all have a I/We story and a We/They story. If you belong to a dominant group, they is either laughable, insignificant, or used as a scapegoat. If you belong to an oppressed group, they is targeted as enemy because they have proven to be a real threat or danger to your collectivity or your group. As an example, I could draw a personal chart which would read like this:

| | | |
|---|---|---|
| I/we a writer | you non-writers | politically non-pertinent |
| I/we poets | you prose writers | politically non-pertinent |
| I/we women | you men | politically pertinent |
| I/we feminists | you sexists | politically pertinent |
| I/we lesbians | you heterosexuals | politically pertinent |
| I/we Quebecers | you Canadians | politically pertinent |

People from groups who have been politically, economically, and culturally silenced or censored have expectations that one of them will speak about them and for them. Women have those expectations, feminists, lesbians, Indians, blacks, Chicanos have those expectations. Those readers want so much to hear or see things about themselves that they can even overestimate the political involvement of a writer. That is why writers from those groups are often asked the question: Are you a political writer? *Etes-vous un écrivain engagé?* A question that embarrasses them and which they will be tempted to avoid by saying that they write what they write because they are creative. Which is true, but not as simple as it seems. For example, while writing a feminist article, I questioned myself wondering who is writing my text: the poet, the feminist or the lesbian. I came up with this answer: The feminist is moral, responsible, fair, humanist, has solidarity. The lesbian is audacious, radical, takes risks, strictly focuses on women. The creative person has imagination and is able to process ambivalent emotion and contradictions as well as transforming anger, ecstasy, desire, pain, and so on, into social meaning.

So altogether, I would say that one's Poetic Politics shapes itself within the weaving movement of personal motive with energy, identity, knowledge, and the ability to process emotions, ideas, sensations into a meaningful response to the world. As for myself, my poetic is essentially to make space for the unthought. As a woman, I am left with a language that has either erased or marginalized women as subjects. Therefore in my poetic I perform what is necessary to make space for women's subjectivity and plurally, to make space for a positive image of women. This task engages me to question language—symbolic and imaginary, from all angles and dimensions.

In conclusion, I would like to say that a good part of my life has gone into writing and it probably will continue to be like that. In the desire and the necessity to reinvent language, there is certainly an intention for happiness, a utopian thrust, a serious responsibility. It is because I feel both profoundly in me that I continue my course of writing. Voyage without end, writing is what always comes back to seek me out in order to distance death and stupidity, lies and violence. Writing never lets me forget that if life has a meaning, somewhere it is in what we invent with our lives, with the aura of streams of words that, within us, form sequences of truth. There is a price for consciousness, for transgression. Sooner or later, the body of writing pays for its untamed desire of beauty and knowledge. I have always thought that the word beauty is related to the word desire. There are words, which, like the body, are irreducible: To write I am a woman is full of consequences.

## CODA

*Poetry*: For me poetry is the highest probability of desire and thought synchronized in a meaningful voice. Poetry is a formal and semantic intuition that is brought forth by our desire, this desire not knowing the laws that motivate it.

*Text*: The text is a thoughtful reflexive approach of the processes of writing and reading. When we play the text against the poem, it is as if we would like to tame the irrational of the poem. A text can be written without "inspiration", without a story. To write a text, you only need a "motive" to trigger the pleasure of writing and to perform or to explore in language.

Now I would like to establish the rapport—the connection—I have with poetry, prose, writing, and language. This I can say now, but even five years ago I would have been unable to identify this rapport.

A) My rapport with poetry has to do with the voice finding its way at the very moment of synchronization of thought and emotion. It is the rapport of intelligence in the sense of comprehension (to take with one self).

B) My rapport with prose and novels resembles my rapport with reality as it is in daily life. I find prose and daily life so boring that I can only exist in these two realities by making ruptures in the sentence or in the discourse, by seeking surprises and discoveries, by expending meaning. Writing prose, I need to explode the narrative, the anecdotal, the linearity of time, the normal mumbling of characters. That is why my novels are anti-novels that challenge traditional novels.

C) My rapport with writing has to do with desire and energy. This rapport is essentially ludic and about exploration. The body and the act of the eyes are mainly involved.

D) My rapport with language is a matter of perspective on patriarchal knowledge and on its symbolic hierarchal/dualist field. It calls for *vision* rather than for subversion. It calls for awareness, concentration, sharpness. Vision goes beyond transgression because it brings forth new material.

### Karen Gould (essay date 1990)

SOURCE: Gould, Karen. "Nicole Brossard: Beyond Modernity or Writing in the Third Dimension." In *Writing in the Feminine: Feminism and Experimental Writing in Quebec,* pp. 52-107. Carbondale: Southern Illinois University Press, 1990.

[*In the following excerpt, Gould evaluates Brossard's poetry volumes* Suite logique *and* Le Centre blanc, *and particularly her novel* Un livre, *as key texts in the formulation of a new, experimental literary modernity in Quebec.*]

> To imagine a language means to imagine a form of life.
>
> Wittgenstein, *Philosophical Investigations*

> Political liberation of sexuality: this is a double transgression, of politics by the sexual, and conversely. But this is nothing at all: let us now imagine reintroducing into the politico-sexual field thus discovered, recognized, traversed, and liberated . . . *a touch of sentimentality*: would that not be the *ultimate* transgression? For, after all, that would be *love*: which would return: *but in another place.*
>
> Roland Barthes, *Roland Barthes by Roland Barthes*

> Women whirling in be-ing shift the center of gravity.
>
> Mary Daly, *Gyn/Ecology*

The writing of Nicole Brossard lies at a unique historical and cultural juncture between a literature of modernity that has consciously broken with the past and an experimental women's writing that has added a gender specificity and an unavoidably political dimension to some of the more radical practices of textual modernity in Quebec. The link between Brossard's work and modernity has been the subject of much recent critical commentary. Among Quebec intellectuals (whether feminists or not), Brossard and *modernité*—that "radical impulse"[1] to sever with tradition and become *résolument moderne*—have often been uttered in the same breath. Brossard herself has distinguished between Rimbaud's etiquette, "Il faut être absolument moderne" ("One must be absolutely modern"), which she reads as the urgent modernist necessity to risk all, including sanity, and the more contemporary version, "Il faut être résolument moderne" (resolutely modern), which shifts the writer's focus away from the exploration of intensely personal experience and toward the vigorous pursuit of new avenues in textual production.[2] For Brossard, this resolve to be modern was initially conceived as a political and literary stance of defiance, an open challenge to the ideological forces that had helped shape and perpetuate social norms and conventional literary forms in Quebec.

Although currently regarded as one of the leading theoreticians of *écriture au féminin,* Nicole Brossard was one of the emerging voices of modernity in Quebec literature during the late 1960s.... Her early works (1964-73) clearly exemplified modernity's ostensibly gender-neutral preoccupations with rupture, deconstruction, and transgression, notions that have forged much of the direction of literary experimentation in Quebec since the late 1960s. However, with the move toward a self-consciously gender-marked writing in the mid-1970s, Brossard's forward-looking gaze has lost all vestiges of neutrality, having entered the realms of the forbidden and the repressed with the particular knowledge, force, and pleasure of her own experience as a woman.

More so than any other writer in Quebec, Brossard has attentively mapped the crucial points of intersection and divergence between literary modernity and contemporary feminist practices of writing and reading. Indeed, the theoretical aspects of her work provide the pivotal link between the projects of *modernité* and radical feminism in the francophone province. Brossard's early poetry and theoretical efforts to chart the direction of Quebec's avant-garde during the late 1960s had already given her a solid literary reputation long before her move toward the experimental forms of gender-marked writing that began to surface in 1974. Moreover, it is likely that at least some of the critical attention accorded her more recent feminist-inspired texts is due in part to her prior work and association with the project of literary modernity in Quebec. Brossard's ability to theorize on the connections and distinctions between a writing of modernity and a more emphatically women-centered writing as well as her own success in spanning these two cultural currents in Quebec are impressive indicators of the centrality of her work in contemporary Quebec literature and are also of considerable consequence for the project of feminist writing elsewhere and for recent American discussions of feminism and postmodernism in particular.

With the publication in 1970 of two volumes of poetry, *Suite logique* (*Logical Consequences/Succession*) and *Le Centre blanc* (*The White Center*), along with a first novel bearing the insistently auto-referential title of *Un livre* (*A Book*), Nicole Brossard confirmed her compelling presence on the modern stage of Quebec letters. In these relatively early writings, Brossard formulated as well as conveyed the new mood of experimental writing in Quebec—what has been described by many contemporary critics and writers alike as an emerging "crisis" of confidence in the representational powers of language and a mounting mistrust regarding the organic wholeness, the ostensibly unified sign system, and the presumed signification or predetermined meaning of the literary text. Quebec critic and poet Philippe Haeck, whose own poetry has been influenced by both Brossard's early formalism and subsequent *body writing,* credits her with circulating two key ideas in the work of her initial formalist period, "the death of the author and the death of meaning."[3]

The texts Brossard published in 1970 also echoed an increasing weariness on the part of a number of Quebec intellectuals with the nationalist themes and overtly political forms of nationalist writings that had dominated the literary scene in Quebec during the early 1960s. The appearance of important experimental works by Brossard and others at *La Barre du jour* called attention to the gap between the revolutionary themes of Quebec's nationalistic literature of the 1960s and the revolutionary nature of experimentations in form that were beginning to take place in some of the formal constructions of the avant-garde. Determinedly modern in her outlook, Brossard challenged the prevailing belief in representational literature, in the ability of words to name effectively the sociopolitical reality of Quebec or, for that matter, any other social reality.

Brossard's writing practice in *Un livre* called into question the very notion of the "real" in a way that both delighted and shocked her reading public. As Quebec critic and writer Claude Beausoleil has noted, the appearance of *Un livre* was a major literary event and a sign that the Quebec novel had lost its endearing innocence and had finally "come of age."[4] Brossard's first novel is marked with all of the textual self-consciousness, implied narrative distance, and heightened incredulity regarding language that this new age seemed to elicit. For Brossard and her contemporaries, Nathalie Sarraute's "age of suspicion" was perhaps dawning a little later in Quebec, but it was dawning nevertheless.[5] By 1970, there seemed little chance of turning back.

Even prior to the appearance of *Un livre* and *Le Centre blanc,* Nicole Brossard had already asserted substantial influence on the development of the notion of *modernité* in Quebec through her editorial work and writing for the avant-garde review, *La Barre du jour* (1965-77). . . . Brossard's emphasis at *La Barre du jour* on the materiality of language brought with it a new sense of how words, linguistic structures, and literary forms may be viewed as sociocultural constructions rather than as fixed objects of predetermined meaning. As was the case for a number of intellectuals in her generation, Brossard's theoretical positions during her formative years with *La Barre du jour* were nurtured by the formal experimentation of new novelists such as Sarraute, Robbe-Grillet, Butor, and Duras in France and by Aquin and others in Quebec as well as by the new criticism in France of Barthes, Ricardou, and the Marxist formalist review *Tel Quel*. The structuralist and formalist preoccupations of many of these writers called attention to the act of writing as process rather than as mimetic enterprise moving inevitably toward closure. By exposing the complex interplay of syntax, grammar, and formal structures that provide the actual matter for the text's own genesis, their writings underscored the autoreferential and internal generating properties of the text.

The impact of Brossard's initial concerns with the nature of textual production and with language as a forever new space of ecstatic, if nevertheless solitary invention, can in fact still be traced in even her most radically women-centered writing. In ***Picture Theory*** for example, which she published in 1982, we find repeated evidence of Brossard's earlier transgressive efforts to reverse the linear logic of mastery, undermine anticipated structures of meaning, confront the void or dense "whiteness," as she initially termed it, of unnarratability, and demonstrate how the text works—how it proceeds, falters, is condensed, and overflows the recognizable semantic field. From formalism to radical feminism, Brossard's extreme literary self-consciousness and fundamental questioning of virtually every aspect of the writing process have never really ceased, even though the act of writing itself has also become a way of exploring feminist consciousness, as well as a way of articulating her own desire for other women and for other ways of organizing reality. "What form can a contemporary thought best take that would give words another cast of mind, for the body has its reasons," writes Brossard in ***Picture Theory***. "How does she keep her distance with words without by the same token relinquishing her place, without reaching the point of neutralizing herself in the text, without losing sight of an image of self liberated at last from negativity, without neglecting what reflects it (women and the sense of honor, as Adrienne Rich would put it) and also what always transforms it and reveals its meaning."[6]

With its emphases on undermining traditional writing conventions and on dismantling the authority of the author and the word, literary modernity in Quebec gave Brossard a crucial theoretical basis from which to explore and develop a new theory and practice of women's writing.

### Le Centre Blanc or Writing from the Zero Point

In an interview with some of the writers and editors working at *La Nouvelle Barre du jour* in the 1980s, Hugues Corriveau cites the 1972-73 Montreal seminars of Hélène Cixous as the birthplace of modernity in Quebec. He also notes two other works of major significance for Quebec's literary modernity: Brossard's ***Le Centre blanc*** and ***Un livre***.[7] *Le Centre blanc* was certainly a key text for Brossard in her own development as a poet, and as the title suggests, its publication immediately placed her work in the resolutely modern camp of Blanchot's "writing without writing," what he describes in the works of Mallarmé, Beckett, and others as the movement of writing away from literature as convention and ideological practice, toward the point of its absence, the point as it were where literature observes its own dissolution or erasure and ultimately "disappears."[8] Brossard has explained her incorporation of Blanchot's neutral literary space in the following manner:

> Blanchot was very important for me. What was involved in the question of neutrality was the white space, which was linked to the question of ecstasy, to the present, the place where the "I" is dispersed to make room for the science of being, its contemplation. Neutrality also meant putting a halt to lyricism and to romanticism, to inspiration, in the ways in which I of course understood these words. Needless to say, neutrality was undoubtedly a fine displacement allowing me to forget that I was a woman, that is to say that I belonged to that category of non-thinkers. Feminist consciousness would de-neutralize me, by that I mean it would allow for an integrative formal presence rather than a formalist presence, so to speak.[9]

Brossard's notion of a *centre blanc* as a space of absolute nakedness, ecstasy, and concentrated meanings functions as a unifying concept in much of her early poetry. Already in 1968 in ***L'Echo bouge beau*** (***The Echo Moves Beautiful***), there is constant visual attention to whiteness, blackness, nudity, emptiness, and shadows. While the exterior world is characterized as a space of solitude and contradiction, "nu désolé et aspire quand même"[10] ("naked desolate yet still aspiring"), Brossard's poetic eye moves nostalgically inward in the hopes of regeneration, intoxication, and some kind of elevation. Her voice draws us toward the mysterious center of ourselves, to words seemingly still in formation, tremulous words that reach for the obscure origins of desire and indulgence: "sans mémoire deviner au zéro dans le blanc / faire le chiffre le mot extrême" (109) ("without memory imagine the zero in white / figure the extreme word").

In *Suite logique* and *Le Centre blanc,* the exploration of a language of neutrality and excess is intensified. Brossard conveys an increased bareness of vision here as she strips away the last traces of realistic description and empties her poems of conventional punctuation and syntax. The key verb in both texts is, in fact, *dénuder* with its sense of stripping, of laying bare, and, of course, of uncovering: "dénuder le sens sa non-évidence" (194) ("strip/uncover meaning its unclearness"). While commonly anticipated meanings are neutralized, formal structures are repeatedly fractured or erased altogether. In place of continuity, solidity, and certainty, we confront a discourse of instability and rebellious doubt in which "l'exil s'impose radical / la certitude n'est que vérifiable / en ce moment la démesure renverse" (155) ("exile is radically imposed / certainty is only verifiable / at this time excess overthrows"). For Brossard, these calculated efforts to destabilize meaning and identity are both destructive and fascinating; indeed, she marvels at the ruins:

> rien ne se confirme
> c'est
> ce qui ruine
> ruine et merveille
> du pareil au même
> l'éclosion se fait mal
> laissant croire qu'un jour
> elle se fera divine
> éclosion de rien pourtant
>
> (150)

> nothing is confirmed
> that is
> what ruins
> ruins and marvels
> all the same
> the opening hurts
> letting us believe that one day
> it will make itself divine
> the opening of nothing however

Brossard's approach to language at this point is not only to strip it bare but to split it open as well, to hollow it out and thereby create a space of entry into meanings that are as yet uncharted, undetermined. She beckons us to press inside these spatial openings without conventional preconceptions, to move and become excited by them: "les ouvertures font bondir et trembler" ("the openings make us leap and tremble"). Quebec critic Pierre Nepveu has argued that for Brossard and for those affiliated with *La Barre du jour* during the late 1960s, to be modern meant to "look lucidly into the hole" and to refuse to fill it with anything in particular. In so doing, he argues, they sought to reject the lure of myth, ideology, and nostalgia.[11]

In *Le Centre blanc,* however, this hole in the writing of modernity is not entirely empty. On the one hand, Brossard describes it as an interior magnet, a space where everything converges: "choses devinées lentement éprouvées de l'intérieur qui convergent" (185) ("conjectured things experienced from the inside which converge"). It is a space of extreme contradiction as well where desire and lack of desire, pleasure and pain, ecstasy and death, movement and calm coexist and intermingle in the color white—the only color to contain all the visible rays of the spectrum. *Le centre blanc* is the place in which Brossard's poetic voice maintains its "pure vigilance," an internal space of concentrated attention to the infinite and contradictory possibilities of language itself.

Prior to 1970 Brossard's literary inspiration appears to be uniformly grounded in the internal, in the depths of her own interior consciousness, a direction that in many ways seems to contradict the more outward-looking and politically motivated perspectives of her more recent women-centered texts. Yet the inward movement of her early poetry also reflects a refusal of imposed values from the outside, a literary posture central to the project of a thoroughly modern writing in Quebec, but not without a certain influence on feminists searching for other ways to write self-consciously as women. *Le Centre blanc* reads as an affirmatively modern quest for those inner sources of contemplation and energy that bring words into writing *autrement*—a key word that both French and Quebec feminists have invested with new meaning in recent years: "Je écrire (autrement) fissure renouveau aboli refaire or ce mutisme comblé verbal autrement"[12] ("I write [otherwise] fissure renewal abolished recommence now this silence overwhelmed verbal otherwise").

Although physicality is evoked only in the most abstract of terms rather than particularized in any way as female, Brossard already understands in *Le Centre blanc* that writing is both a form of seduction and a powerful release of desire. Thus she revels in her interior descent into whiteness, which she characterizes as the primary source of her own physical and intellectual vitality. The orgasm her writing unleashes during this insistently modern descent is autoerotic in nature, even though also portrayed at a careful distance:

> rien le moment venu se fondre à la source de sa propre vitalité s'isoler l'impression l'action d'être hors de soi figée paisible un aboutissement immobile à l'accueil des forces inaccessible de toute part blanche seule la croissance interne s'accomplissant ou l'irradiation la joie diffusant hors d'atteinte si intensément là cet état et d'abriter pendant un temps d'arrêt extase ou sourire
>
> (203)

> nothing at the right moment melt into the source of one's own vitality isolate oneself the impression the action of being outside oneself stiff peaceful a result unmoved by the greeting of forces inaccessible from all

sides white alone the internal growth taking place or the irradiation the joy becoming diffuse out of reach so intensely there this state and to screen during an interim ecstasy or a smile

With **Le Centre blanc** and **Suite logique,** Brossard brings our attention to the functioning of language, to its initial formlessness, to the "doubt" of modernity that results in a displacement of words and meanings outside the realm of the expected, and to a discourse of desire that remains excessively abstract yet undeniably subversive. The notion of the unrepresentable is perceptible throughout this early poetry and its increasingly experimental form refuses to allow us the accustomed conventional pleasures of reading. Brossard has said that her move from poetry to prose in the early 1970s was the result of a need to "intervene more directly in everyday scenes" and the result also of a desire to look at herself from a greater distance.[13] As we shall see in **Un livre, French Kiss,** and **L'Amèr ou le chapitre effrité,** this new interest in prose is also indicative of a growing fascination with the problematic place of language in society, with the relationships Brossard was beginning to discern between fiction, theory, and everyday life, between gender and urbanity, between politics and writing.

Thus, while not without contradictions for the subsequent project of writing through a feminist consciousness, the move to inscribe modernity in Quebec, as Brossard herself had originally promoted it, would bring language to the foreground without attaching it to a specific political agenda per se the way nationalist writers had frequently done. Rather, Brossard viewed language as a site of rupture and continually new beginnings and as a source of abstract pleasure in the infinite possibilities of creativity itself—even if the traces of gender were to a large extent obfuscated and even if the text did not appear to be historically grounded. The demandingly modern ethic to "inaugurate" rather than to "repeat," which Quebec critic Suzanne Lamy aptly associated with the most innovative examples of *écriture au féminin,* certainly has its roots in the deconstructive moves and radically experimental positions that Brossard and others wanted modernity to assume in Quebec.[14] From the outset, then, Brossard's emphasis on theorizing about her own personal writing practice prepared the way in Quebec for the subsequent integration of various theoretical discourses within feminism into women's writing. Ultimately, the literary project of *modernité* provided Brossard with much of the theoretical grounding for her subsequent experimentation with *écriture au féminin* and, perhaps more importantly, strengthened her affinity for the unexpected, the unexplored, and the vitally new.

### Filling in the Gaps: Reading Un livre

Although **Un livre** reads in many ways like a prototype for the Quebec *nouveau roman,* the issues of modernity that Brossard underscores so vigorously in this text have left their unmistakable traces on her subsequent and more markedly feminist work as well. In **Amantes** (1980) and **Picture Theory** (1982), for example, we still find the rejection of realism and traditional notions of characterization, an emphasis on exploring the nature and limits of textuality and its relationship to the real, and numerous reflections on the process of writing. Moreover, opposition to the laws of tradition (especially patriarchal tradition) continues to be expressed through the dislocation of conventional language and through efforts to suspend meaning as a way of bringing attention to the gaps or fissures in the narrative construction. All of these textual strategies are already dynamically at work in **Un livre** although they have not yet been incorporated into Brossard's rigorous feminist designs for a writing of difference. While decidedly modern in its discourse on the text and the invention of its own internal codes, many of the raw materials of **Un livre** thus reveal themselves to be the rudiments for a writing of the future as well.

Brossard's perspectives on the positions the Quebec woman writer occupies in language and in society differ significantly over the decade and more that separates **Un livre** from **Amantes** and **Picture Theory.** In more recent years, and particularly since the appearance of **Amantes** in 1980, her own relationships to language and to the act of writing itself have undergone dramatic, if not altogether unanticipated changes. In line with an ever-increasing commitment to feminist politics and a lesbian identity, Brossard's language has become emphatically gender-marked, intensely physical, and more radically expectant. By 1980, the space between fiction and reality, between the female writer and her words, is no longer the seemingly immeasurable gulf found in **Un livre.** Instead, we find a "marée spirale amoureuse"[15] ("loving spiral tide"), a passionate and integrative space in which fiction and everyday life, sexuality and discourse, literary theory and literary practice continually converge in a whirling spiral, through what Quebec writer and critic Louise Dupré has appropriately termed "a practice of excess."[16]

From the very beginning, **Un livre** demands multiple readings. On the level of what we might loosely refer to as plot, the text offers a discontinuous series of poses, gestures, and events from the lives of two female characters, O. R. and Dominique C., and three males, Dominique, Henri, and Mathieu. We learn little about these characters individually, with the exception of O. R. and Henri. Their respective activities as writer and political activist, however nominally described, are directly linked to the book's major themes. The five characters come together as lovers and friends in various configurations and with varying degrees of freedom and initiative. But Brossard's narrator is quick to relegate them to a secondary role in the unfolding narrative process:

> Des personnages dans le texte, mais qui passent en second lieu. Qui sont là à titre de prétexte pour que le texte puisse continuer sans autre but que celui de raconter sa génèse au fur et à mesure que la vie apparaît. Etrange narration mais plausible.[17]
>
> Characters who are in the text, but who remain backstage. Who are there as a pretext for the text to continue with no other goal than to keep telling of its own genesis as life gradually takes form. Strange but plausible narration.[18]

On the level of form, Brossard's first attempt at fiction produces a discourse that is both self-reflexive and self-directing. Using a remarkably restrained number of words, images, and themes, the novel progresses from one page to the next and from one word to the next through the active, almost self-indulgent contemplation of its own formal genesis. This narrative movement, however, is not necessarily linear or chronological. Scenes, phrases, words, are continually repeated, reviewed, and redistributed throughout the text. Indeed, the text appears to fetishize itself with the continual marking of its own progression or lack thereof. We find no noticeable movement toward epiphany or resolution in *Un livre* since, as one character puts it, "words and days look alike" (6). In an exemplary modern fashion, Brossard demystifies not only the characters in *Un livre* but, in a broader context, both her literary predecessors and her own fictional project as well:

> L'exécution d'un texte.
>
> Très peu différent de ceux qui précèdent mais unique, sans pareil. Le texte d'une seule page, inscrit dans la continuité d'un mode de composition qui en rappelle d'autres, qui en prépare d'autres.
>
> La mise à mort d'une chose au profit d'une autre. Le texte devant l'insolite du texte. Des mots qui s'expliquent les uns par rapport aux autres aux dépens des personnages, ébauches d'hommes et de femmes faites pour demeurer telles.
>
> (31)
>
> The production of a text.
> Not much different from existing ones, but unique, unmatched. A single page of text. Written in the continuity of a mode of composition resembling others in the past, suggesting others to come.
> The cancellation of one thing for the benefit of another. The text confronting the text's precipitousness. Words which take their meaning from other words at the expense of the characters, sketches of men and women made to remain as such.
>
> (31)

Brossard's writing here is terse, even dry. Sentences frequently lack verbs, and there is extensive use of the present participle. Such syntactic strategies result in a necessarily immediate temporal mode and heighten our sense of simultaneous impressions and occurrences:

> O. R. et Dominique à cinq heures. Vers le métro. Sous la pluie. La foule compacte. Envahissante. L'odeur des vêtements humides. Le regard inquiet (seulement inquiet) de Dominique.
>
> La foule.
>
> (62)
>
> O. R. and Dominique at five o'clock. Towards the métro. In the rain. The crowd compact. Crushing. The smell of wet clothes. Dominique looking uneasy (only uneasy).
>
> The crowd.
>
> (62)

Clearly, *Un livre* reads like a prototype for a new novel, a text whose primary subject is itself. A book about a book in the process of being written as we read it. This is, of course, a fictionalized genesis, since the entire book is already written before we actually begin to turn its pages—a fact the narrator rather cleverly notes when she acknowledges that the act of reading is the only "real" event of the novel. But this too has been fictionalized since the act of reading itself also functions as a thematic generator for the text's own internal development: "Le seul [événement] qui soit actuel est cette lecture en train de se faire, la seule chose réelle, qui fasse bouger imperceptiblement quelques muscles et qui rende conscient de sa respiration" (15) ("All that is happening is this reading being done, the only real thing, causing a few muscles to move imperceptibly and making one conscious of his [or her] own breathing" [15]).

Like the daily reality outside the text, words themselves are problematic in *Un livre,* rendering the writer's role in society more contradictory and at the same time, Brossard suggests, more honest. Yet *Un livre* does call attention to certain politically charged circumstances and culturally specific themes in the narrative. This is accomplished, however, through opaque references and ellipses rather than through direct elaboration. In fact, Brossard's narrator repeatedly speaks to us (*vous*) while drawing our eyes to what is being left out:

> Le texte et les espaces. Car les mots ne peuvent tout combler pour vous: O. R., Dominique, Mathieu, Dominique C., Henri, vous, les autres.
>
> (97)
>
> The text and the spaces. For the words cannot sum up everything for you: O. R., Dominique, Mathieu, Dominique C., Henri, you, the others.
>
> (97)

Between the words and the lines, we are told, the blank spaces reveal more of the essential text than the words themselves could ever do. This narrative clue appears worth pursuing. For the gaps in Brossard's text constitute an invisible subtext of considerable, if undetermined, significance. As investigative readers, we want to know what is being left out here and, more importantly, why these narrative holes remain. Brossard's enigmatic tone provokes us to ask questions such as these and to formulate our own readings in response. The implied subtext of *Un livre* evokes at least three fundamental concerns that emerge in various shapes in Brossard's later theoretical fiction and poetry as well: the frustrated aspirations of the body politic, the liberating power of the female body, and the essential identification of the woman writer with a female character who also writes. Over the twelve years that separate *Un livre* from *Amantes* and *Picture Theory*, these particular preoccupations will become more visibly present.

Although schematic at best, references to the political climate in Quebec in 1970 are not infrequent in this novel. A bomb goes off at midnight, for instance, and Mathieu smiles. Is this complicity or merely a nod of approval? Numerous other bombings are also mentioned. The summer heat is oppressive. People fill the streets at night, and eventually, a discernible crowd assembles. In fact, the crowd becomes a kind of sixth character in *Un livre* from which the five fictional characters originally emerge and to which they also presumably return beyond the space of the text. Moreover, this crowd has a definite political character. It forms along la rue Saint-Hubert, an area known for its firm support of the Parti Québécois in the early 1970s. The formation of the crowd is therefore indicative of some alternate vision of society. And in fact, the five characters wait for and mingle with the crowd much the way they wait for and arrange to meet with one other. This insistence on waiting and meeting becomes the textual evidence of a political collectivity that calls for change well beyond the boundaries of the text. Moreover, these comings and goings in Brossard's narrative suggest that her characters are themselves interchangeable with others—part of the larger crowd.

A change in the order of things is also alluded to within the confines of the text as the five characters anxiously watch election results that will not satisfy their hopes. But the political present "outside the text" is once again relegated to silence until we read of Henri's arrest and provisional release in September. His political incarceration operates as a form of textual prelude to the mass arrests of writers and activists that we know took place in Montreal under the War Measures Act of October 1970. This attempt by Trudeau's federal government to intimidate the nationalist left in Quebec occurred in response to prior political bombings, to the kidnappings of James Cross and Pierre Laporte in particular, and to the general social unrest of the period. As a gesture of support for the hundreds of activists and intellectuals who were arbitrarily rounded up and incarcerated without bail or legal representation for as long as three months, Brossard and Roger Soublière organized a conference to protest the reactionary nature of these arrests. While none of this autobiographical information nor the specific political events leading up to and during the enactment of the War Measures Act are evoked in anyway, the explosive and repressive climate of the period is clearly established. Brossard's highlighting of the date reminds us of the reality behind the reality of fiction.

As a novel about its own genesis, *Un livre* may well be as ordinary as any other, a point the narrator reiterates on several occasions. There is, however, nothing ordinary about the political subtext of this narrative: the real battle over Quebec identity in 1970 that is taking place outside on the streets. And Henri is, in many ways, the key to this political subtext. His words are not given in the text itself, we are told, because they speak directly to the political turbulence of the real world outside and carry with them the full weight of political commitment. Yet despite their intentional omission, the political nature of Henri's words is described, and we are left to imagine them carrying more force than those encountered anywhere else in the text.

> *Les mots d'Henri.*
>
> Peu nombreux, mais lourds de conséquences. Parce que politiques. Des mots à la portée de tous. Clairs et précis. Qui révèlent l'escroquerie, qui font réagir le meilleur et le pire. Henri au-delà des mots problématiques. En ce sens, engagé dans l'histoire, dans la trajectoire des gestes démesurés.
>
> Des mots qui n'ont rien à voir avec ce texte: des mots nécessaires, des prérequis qui demandent à être continuellement répétés.
>
> (34)
>
> *Henri's words.*
>
> Few, but full of consequence. Because political. Words within everyone's reach. Clear and precise. Exposing corruption, provoking reactions for better or worse. Henri beyond problematical words. In this sense, engaged in history, in the trajectory of inordinate actions.
>
> Words which have nothing to do with this text: necessary words, prerequisites which need continually to be repeated.
>
> (34)

Henri's words are anything but poetic, anything but the stuff of fiction. Yet in their textual absence, his words are even more strangely present—an ironic political twist for Brossard's feminist readers, given the insignificance and virtual disappearance of male words in her later works. The apparent contradiction in *Un livre* between the language of fiction and the language of politics is itself a strikingly modern consideration. Henri's discourse of violent political action and radical social change is both indispensable to and necessarily outside of the realm of the describable in Brossard's fictional construction. Yet while Henri's discourse speaks about revolution and radical change *in* society and *outside* the text, the exploratory nature of Brossard's own words in **Un livre** is no doubt more subversive and revolutionary in terms of the construction of an alternate discourse than the words of the activist himself. It is worth mentioning that the lines drawn here between the revolutionary in literature and the revolutionary in politics are notably more restrictive than the relationships Brossard establishes between politics and literature in her more recent feminist-inspired writing.

The coming of age of women's sexual independence and explicit desire for pleasure is another thematic component in Brossard's political subtext that leaves its occasional traces throughout the narrative. Primarily associated with O. R., women's sexuality in **Un livre** is beautiful, "scandalous," and continually in search of new modes of expression. And, like Henri's subversive discourse and political acts, O. R.'s naked body is both provocative and unnarratable:

> O. R., à cinq heures de l'après-midi, devant une tasse de café. Les mains autour. Présente. Nue. La chaleur écrasante. Décrire: peut-être, mais O. R. n'en sortirait pas vivante. Plutôt morte (pareille à autre chose).
>
> (7)

> O. R., at five o'clock in the afternoon, with a cup of tea. Her hands around it. Attentive. Naked. Crushing heat. Description: perhaps, but O. R. would not emerge from it alive. Dead rather (like something else).
>
> (7)

Ironically, her glimpsed nudity on the balcony on a hot summer day provokes numerous words of approval or condemnation from passersby, "trop belle, laide, vulgaire, putain" ("too pretty, ugly, vulgar, whorish"), but the words themselves only accumulate—they signify nothing. O. R.'s nakedness, which the narrator later associates with "le scandale de la liberté" ("the scandal of freedom"), is in effect assigned both meaning and power as a result of its untranslatable force in reality. It also becomes clear that, although brief in its description, the open-ended, unrestricted nature of sexuality in **Un livre** can be read as another legitimate form of revolt, another effort to formulate a future of radical difference and euphoric freedom.

O. R.'s body in the act of love is the symbolic key to a sexual polyvalence that erupts with considerable force amid an otherwise relatively neutral narration. She is alternately viewed in the intimate company of Dominique, Dominique and Mathieu, her female friend Dominique C., or Henri and Dominique C. As such, she becomes the pivotal sexual presence, the only sexualized body whose physicality inspires all of the other characters and both sexes. Moreover, in these few short passages of explicit sexual intimacy, Brossard's text comes closest to evoking the kind of language of desire so prevalent in a text such as **Amantes**.

Finally, Brossard's novel presents us with a narrative persona who is visibly engaged in the act of writing and in the contemplation of herself in the process of writing the book that **Un livre** will ostensibly become. Indeed, the woman writer in Brossard's text is a subject-in-process, searching for herself in and through writing. And while avoiding any use of the first person pronoun, Brossard continually reminds us of her own creative presence as the writer of the text by situating her search for words and for herself in the present tense:

> Ecrire le passage présent. Un passage qui s'ouvre sur nulle autre chose qu'une attitude de la main et de l'oeil vis-à-vis du papier. Le passage des mots désirés aux mots écrits. Un geste qui attire l'attention et qui la concentre à l'intérieur de quelques phrases, espérant par là, quelques dimensions inédites pour le regard.
>
> (28)

> To write the present passage. A passage which opens on nothing but the relative positions of a hand and eye and some paper. The passage from desired words to written words. A gesture which draws attention and concentrates it within a few sentences, hoping thus to attain various new dimensions in seeing.
>
> (28)

This emphasis on the woman writer's presence is also reinforced by the figure of O. R. herself who appears to duplicate many of the poses, reflections, and applied understanding of the writer of **Un livre**. Although all of the characters appear excessively attentive to language—whether personal, political, or literary, O. R. is nevertheless the only character who writes. O. R. writes words on a page late at night, searches for words in the dictionary, writes an open letter whose subject is open letters for the newspapers and, likewise, an anonymous letter whose subject is anonymous letters. O. R.'s writing is clearly self-referential as well as undecipherable according to the conventional rules of grammar. More fascinating still in terms of its thematic duplication, a crucial discursive transformation takes place when, for a moment, O. R. imaginatively becomes a reader of the text rather than a character in it. Like Brossard's own narrative voice, O. R.-as-reader brings pleasure and knowledge to the text of her own making through the intensity of her reader's gaze:

> A supposer ainsi, O. R. devient lectrice et ne se cache plus sous l'apparence d'un personnage. O. R. face aux mots, appliquée devant la page comme si elle tenait elle-même le stylo qui prolonge indéfiniment les phrases et qui les enligne sur des perspectives différentes à chaque fois que la chair pense son plaisir et le formule ainsi, de manière à ce que, tout autour, les choses restent en suspens.
>
> (73)

Supposing that O. R. also becomes a reader and is no longer hidden in the guise of a character. O. R. with the page before her, diligently confronting the words as if she herself held the pen that indefinitely lengthens the sentences and arranges them in different perspectives each time the flesh conceives of its pleasure and thus formulates it, with the result that, all around, things remain suspended.

(73)

As well as any in her work, the passage above highlights Brossard's thoroughly modern attention to the internal dynamics of writing. At the same time, it establishes a visionary fusion of the woman writer-reader-character, for O. R. is precisely the kind of reader Brossard has become and wants for her texts, particularly the more recent ones: a reader who actively writes the text through what can only be called an intense physical involvement, "lire comme s'il s'agissait d'écrire au fur et à mesure que les mots dessinés par un autre avancent sous le regard" (II) ("reading as though you were writing another's words as they appear and move through your vision" [II]). Brossard's ideal reader in *Un livre* is one who takes pleasure in the text at that moment when, as Barthes poetically characterized it, the body "pursues its own ideas."[19] Yet like Brossard, O. R. continues to acknowledge the inescapable distance between the words and her reader's gaze, between O. R. as reader and the fictional character of her own text. Her initials have become the enigmatic code for that distance: "O. R.: la distance qui sépare ses initiales de son personnage, son personnage d'elle-même. O. R. lectrice" (74) ("O. R.: the distance separating her initials from her character, her character from herself. O. R. the reader" [74]).

Thus, at the center of *Un livre* and of Brossard's entire literary project lies the woman writer—at work in fiction and reality—whether as narrator or as fictional character or both. What Louise Forsyth has noted as Brossard's splitting or *dédoublement* of the woman writer into both artist and the artist observed in the 1976 production of *La Nef des sorcières*[20] can, as we have seen, be traced back to *Un livre*. Admittedly, this *dédoublement* is even more striking in recent texts such as *Amantes, Le Sens apparent* and *Picture Theory,* due to the heightened erotic quality and lesbian positioning of these works. While Brossard's exploration in *Un livre* does not insist upon gender specificity as such, however, the initial elements are already in place for further contemplation of the woman-writer-as-she-writes—a woman who will eventually explore her difference through the words she writes for other women.

*Notes*

1. I borrow the term from Paul de Man, *Blindness and Insight* (Minneapolis: University of Minnesota Press, 1971), 147.

2. For her thoughts on the innovations and traps of *modernité*, see Nicole Brossard, "L'Epreuve de la modernité ou / et les preuves de modernité," *La Nouvelle Barre du jour* 90-91 (1980): 57-63.

3. Haeck, *La Table d'écriture,* 165.

4. See Claude Beausoleil's "Présentation critique," *Un livre,* by Nicole Brossard (Montreal: Quinze, 1980).

5. See Nathalie Sarraute, *L'Ere du soupçon* (Paris: Gallimard, 1956).

6. Nicole Brossard, *Picture Theory* (Montreal: Nouvelle Optique, 1985), 51. Subsequent references to this edition will appear parenthetically in the text.

7. See "La NBJ: le lieu du risque" (interview with Hugues Corriveau, Louise Cotnoir, Lise Guèvremont), *Voix et images* 10.2 (1985): 104.

8. Maurice Blanchot, *Le Livre à venir* (Paris: Gallimard, 1959), 303. Blanchot's influence was extensive among Quebec's literary avant-garde during the 1960s.

9. Brossard, "Ce que pouvait être, ici, une avant-garde," 80.

10. Nicole Brossard, *Le Centre blanc* (Montreal: L'Hexagone, 1978), 89. This edition includes Brossard's major volumes of poetry published from 1965 to 1975. All further references to poems originally published in separate editions of *L'Echo bouge beau, Suite logique,* and *Le Centre blanc* will be to this edition and will be included in the text.

11. Nepveu, "BJ/NBJ: difficile modernité," 163. This essay indicates the extent to which Nepveu is ill at ease with the amount of critical attention already devoted to Brossard and others affiliated with the literature of *la modernité* and *la nouvelle écriture.* He characterizes most readings of Brossard's work as "euphoric and romantic" (161).

12. Brossard, *Double Impression,* 32.

13. André Roy, "La Fiction vive: entretien avec Nicole Brossard sur sa prose," *Journal of Canadian Fiction* 25-26 (1979): 31.

14. Suzanne Lamy, *d'elles* (Montreal: L'Hexagone, 1979), 56.

15. Nicole Brossard, *Amantes* (Montreal: Quinze, 1980), 29. Subsequent references to this edition will appear parenthetically in the text.

16. Louise Dupré, "Les Utopies du réel," *La Nouvelle Barre du jour* 118-19 (1980): 86.

17. Nicole Brossard, *Un livre* (Montreal: Quinze, 1980), 21. *Un livre* was first published in Montreal in 1970 by Editions du Jour. Subsequent references to the 1980 edition will appear parenthetically in the text.

18. Nicole Brossard, *A Book,* trans. Larry Shouldice (Toronto: Coach House Press, 1976), 21. Subsequent references to this edition will appear parenthetically in the text.

19. Roland Barthes, *The Pleasure of the Text,* trans. Richard Miller (New York: Hill and Wang, 1975), 17. Brossard herself cites this passage from Barthes: "Le plaisir du texte, c'est ce moment où mon corps va suivre ses propres idées—car mon corps n'a pas les mêmes idées que moi," in *Le Plaisir du texte* (Paris: Seuil, 1973), 30. See Brossard, "L'Avenir de la littérature québécoise," 391.

20. Louise Forsyth, "Regards, Reflets, Reflux, Réflections: exploration de l'oeuvre de Nicole Brossard," *La Nouvelle Barre du jour* 118-19 (1982): 221. Forsyth observes: "In order to celebrate her solidarity with other women more effectively, she watches herself write" (22).

**Neil B. Bishop (review date winter 1992)**

SOURCE: Bishop, Neil B. "Installations." *Canadian Literature,* no. 135 (winter 1992): 158-60.

[*In the following review, Bishop offers a positive assessment of* Installations, *calling the work "a joy."*]

It is paradoxical but stimulating to read these two books [*Installations* and *Corps de glorie*] together. The authors seem to share little either as poets or individuals, with the exception of Montreal (and while Brossard is a long-time Montrealer, Juan Garcia lived there only from 1957 to 1967, although he has continued to publish there since). And although metaphysical preoccupations are present in some of Brossard's large body of work, they are not nearly as religiously-oriented as in Garcia's poems, where references to a monotheistic religion and mystical elements often clearly related to Christianity are thematically predominant. Stylistically also, the two books diverge so markedly as to signify profound ideological differences.

While Nicole Brossard's work is well-known among Anglophone Canadian literature aficionados, Juan Garcia's probably is not. Some English-Canadian readers will be intrigued to know how this immigrant writer from Morocco achieved such prestige in Quebec as to have this retrospective and quasi-complete collection of his work (1963-1988) published by one of Montreal's leading publishers. While it would be tempting to answer "the quality of his poetry," that answer would fall short. Garcia's work shows certain characteristics—its religious preoccupations, the stylistic conservatism of many (though not all) pieces—which have ensured its acceptance by influential members of the Quebec literary establishment. More important still has been the way Garcia's poetry and life have fitted in with the myth of the "poète maudit à la québécoise." His publisher, Editions de l'Hexagone, has exploited and reinforced this mythical status, by emphasizing that Garcia not only stayed in a monastery but also has spent a good deal of time in a psychiatric hospital where he wrote "la plupart de ses poèmes qui seront publiés dans des revues québécoises." Garcia has thus been able to appear as a new Nelligan in terms both of certain thematic and stylistic features (religion, the personal past, death; innumerable aquatic images, extensive use of rhyme and of regular line length, especially the *alexandrin*), and of his biography (the shared psychiatric hospital experience). Garcia's status as "poète maudit à la québécoise" is further reinforced by certain thematic similarities with the work of Saint-Denys Garneau, notably the theme of metaphysical uncertainty and resulting anguish, and also the theme of dichotomy and opposition between flesh and soul, the former being perceived, in much of Garcia's work as in much of Saint Denys Garneau's, as thwarting the poet's spiritual quest.

But while there are some fine poems in this volume, especially those of *Alchimie du corps* (1967) so warmly and rightly praised in Jacques Brault's moving and beautiful essay, "Juan Garcia, voyageur de nuit" (1971), many are weak (and some of them make quite superfluous the publisher's emphasis that these texts were written by a mentally distressed individual; such persons can write admirable poetry, and some of Garcia's post-1967 poems are excellent, but many others are slight indeed). It would have been fairer to Garcia to publish a less complete, more selective, edition of his poetry—and to let the poems speak for themselves.

*Installations* is excellent Brossard. The general tone of the volume is set by the epigraph from Clarice Lispector: "Je suis douce mais ma fonction de vivre est féroce." Less ferocious, however, than energetic, as suggested in this marvellous line from **"Acte sexuel"**: "un oui à l'infini qui va son energie." As the title of this poem suggests, Lispector's "fonction de vivre" often takes the form, in *Installations,* of eroticism; this book makes use of Lispector's "douce," too, for the subject persona knows how to be gentle with/to herself, as in a hotel where, she says, "je m'étends et prépare de longs touchers." Writing, language, the body and various facets of feminism, always major themes in Brossard, are not neglected here and are inter-related, as in **"Réplique,"** where the "e muet mutant" of Brossard's justly celebrated 1975 essay becomes, when "tu étires la voix / au fond de la gorge une syllable / calme et somptueusement valable." Or again, as in **"Installation"**: desire, the female body, mobility and the semiotic,

> je m'installe dans mon corps
> de manière à pouvoir bouger
> quand une femme me fait signe.

Feminism goes hand in hand with linguistic transgression in **"Chapitre,"** in which the masculine noun "ventre" is followed by the feminine adjective *"réelle"* (Brossard's italics), thus emphasizing the central importance of the female "ventre" in Brossard's universe, a feminine and feminist one. What is most interesting is the tone of euphoric contemplation (as in "calme et somptueusement") with which these themes are treated. "Contemplation" does not contradict the energy that animates this volume, for ***Installations*** is radiant with a sort of dynamic serenity. Some sad moments do surface, particularly in the poem **"Pays"** which, far from celebrating Québec as did so many "poèmes du pays" of the sixties, observes that

> au québec [. . .]
> mourir est bien facile, très souvent
> on retrouve une femme blessée
> au niveau du bonheur.

**"Mourir"** can be tragically "facile" in Quebec as elsewhere: all a woman need do is go to an engineering school or for a jog. Whence, no doubt, the androphobia of **"Partie des fesses,"** although Brossard does here specify that she is attacking a collective "homme," which allows one to hypothesize that she may be able to view some individual men positively. But the main theme of ***Installations*** is happiness, that of a female subject settling into happiness who well might be talking about herself when she describes a woman who is "insatiable / heureuse et infiniment amazone."

These short, carefully constructed poems are jewels. ***Installations*** is a joy.

### Irving Malin (review date spring 1992)

SOURCE: Malin, Irving. Review of *Mauve Desert*, by Nicole Brossard. *Review of Contemporary Fiction* 12, no. 1 (spring 1992): 158.

[*In the following review, Malin comments favorably on Brossard's "subversive, otherworldly" novel* Mauve Desert, *admiring its play with perception, language, and reality.*]

The epigraph to this wonderfully constructed novel [***Mauve Desert***] is by Calvino: "Reading is going toward something that is about to be, and no one yet knows what it will be." The epigraph suggests that reading is an "adventure"—an approach to some final meaning. But it also implies that this adventure is somehow dangerous—there may not, after all, be a complete disclosure, an ultimate truth. The epigraph hints at uncertainty, misdirection, indirection.

When we first read the novel we don't know how to summarize and interpret it. The novel consists of at least three parts—Mélanie travels across the desert to escape her mother and the ordinary life in the motel in which they live. There is a sudden change. We are given part of another novel in which another heroine, Maude Laures, also seeks adventure and knowledge. Maude is a reader of Mélanie's life story. In effect, the two women merge, so that we are not completely sure who is *author* and *character*. Does Mélanie create Maude or vice versa? And, to complicate matters, we are given an apparent *translation* by Maude of Mélanie's journey.

The three sections are, at first, discrete and separate, but then they seem to merge into the very novel we are reading. We note the paradoxes and we recognize that Brossard consciously twists us; she destabilizes our perceptions so that we wonder about the very nature of perception. What is the relationship of words to life? What exactly is the nature of creation? Do we create the novel as we read it? Perhaps the oddest pages of the novel are those which contain shadowy pictures of objects—pictures which are almost out of focus. We are not sure of their relationship to the text. We assume that they also suggest that any representation of matter is uncertain. And then we remember this remarkable passage about "suspected presence": "It can for a second be mistaken for image or mirage, an illusion as can occur when from moment to moment altostratus formations alter the depth of field and the color all around."

***Mauve Desert*** is an interpretation of misinterpretation, a text of countertexts, a brilliant presence of absence. It is suspect, subversive, otherworldly.

### Nicole Brossard and Janice Williamson (interview date 1993)

SOURCE: Brossard, Nicole, and Janice Williamson. "Nicole Brossard: 'Before I became a feminist, I suppose I was an angel, a poet, a revolutionary. . . .'" In *Sounding Differences: Conversations with Seventeen Canadian Women Writers,* by Janice Williamson, pp. 59-72. Toronto: University of Toronto Press, 1993.

[*In the following interview, Brossard discusses her feminism and political motivation in relation to her literary works.*]

[*Williamson*]: *Would you reflect on a comment you made during a 1975 Quebec conference on women and writing? You said, 'For that which speaks wants at the same time to condemn the law that calls for its repression, that which is forbidden desires and that which desires writes propelled by the very law it transgresses.' What do you mean by transgression and desire?*

[Brossard]: The notion of transgression has always been important in my writing. In books, mainly those published in the seventies, transgressing meant taking risks, making trouble in language and the bourgeois mentality, going over the limits of what is expected in a poem or a novel. Very often, I made a connection between transgression and desire because you transgress the permissible social space in order to make space for your desire. Transgression is defiance and can also be read as an attempt at renewal. If we talk in terms of feminist transgression, it is more complicated because the goal is not to make trouble for the sake of it, but to change the law and the authority to which it refers. Therefore transgression might not be enough. If we accept that transgression marginalizes those who do it, then we must ask the question: since the feminine is already marginalized in a patriarchal society, how can we transgress the law without marginalizing ourselves more? Personally, I can say that writing a feminist consciousness—which means somehow having to sort out and rethink values, patterns of behaviour, identities, fiction and reality—brought me to shift from the word 'transgression' to the word 'vision.'

*You talk of accomplices in your project of feminist 'vision.' Elizabeth Meese claims that because of women's marginalized relation to discourse, all women who write are in a sense 'feminist.' Does this perspective tend to elide the differences between women and the discursive privileges certain women enjoy?*

I don't think so. I wish that discursive analysis would not be considered a privilege. I believe that a feminist is a woman who can claim this title for herself because she is convinced within and beyond her own personal experience that this reality has to be changed in order for women to be able to breathe without further fear and humiliation. There is a difference between a woman complaining about woman's destiny in a man's world and a woman fighting for a change of values in mentality and the laws as a result of her understanding of patriarchal tricks and lies. I also believe that a feminist consciousness changes your perspective on reality and therefore your relation to people, to social attitudes, to morality, to art and language.

*Would you describe the development of your own feminist consciousness?*

Before I became a feminist, I suppose I was an angel, a poet, a revolutionary, which I still am [laugh], but I was definitely not identifying with women. In fact, I became a feminist when I became a mother. Almost at the same time I fell in love with another woman. Suddenly I was living the most common experience in a woman's life, motherhood, and at the same time, I was living the most marginal experience in a woman's life, lesbianism. Motherhood made life absolutely concrete for me, and lesbianism made my life absolute fiction in a patriarchal heterosexual world. Motherhood shaped my solidarity with women and gave me a feminist consciousness just as lesbianism gave me new ideas about almost everything and opened new spaces for me to explore. I read feminist and lesbian books. I surrounded myself with other women for the pleasure of being together but also to share some projects like the feminist magazine *Les Têtes de pioche*, the film **Some American Feminists,** and the collective play **La Nef des sorcières.** Lesbianism has affected my writing in the sense that it raised new questions, clarified others. It definitely changed my *rapport d'adresse*. It multiplied my senses, energized my body in a new way. It offered me new metaphors; for example, the spiral and the hologram. In other words, lesbianism gave me new feelings and new ideas about life, love, power, memory, identity. It gave another rhythm to my voice and therefore to my sentences. It stimulated me to look for the missing link between what we call fiction and reality.

*Your writing and language are anything but 'the expected.' There is a very dramatic moment when you write in* **L'Amèr ou,** *'I have murdered the womb and I am writing it.' It's a passage of great violence, which is shocking to the reader.*

It certainly is. Here you have the kind of sentence that comes out when you don't yet understand how you have been cheated. Without doubt, that phrase says that to a certain degree maternity makes women infirm. In writing that sentence, I wanted to signify how maternity in a patriarchal society makes women extremely vulnerable. The day I gave birth I became mortal and understood that it was necessary for me to stay alive in order to care for this new life. I don't know if I still agree with that sentence. It is a sentence of despair, but at the same time it communicates the information that the subject of the verb resists producing children for patriarchy. The sentence resists clichés about the docile patriarchal mother.

*You write about your disinterest in modes of 'authentic' self-expression.*

Well, I write because I believe that there are things which can only be said or conceived because of what we encounter in the process of writing, in the act of writing. I write to discover things which cannot be thought in the natural stream of thinking or in speech. I don't write what I know; I write what through language I process of my emotions, sensations, ideas, knowledge. I would rather believe more in an authentic voice than in an authentic self-expression. In life I am authentic in my self-expression. In writing I search for my voice in the 'authenticity' of words.

*In your* **Journal intime,** *you define the journal form as 'propaganda of the everyday.' Traditionally the journal has been a significant privatized writing practice for many women.*

Yes, well, I know I can be harsh on prose, the novel, anecdotes, *journal intime.* I mean the novel in general. I don't like novels because I associate them with anecdotes. I know this is unfair and that it is a very personal point of view. Yet I like my resistance to narrative prose because it has permitted me to question the novel from different angles. It is certain that there is a women's tradition in the use of *journal intime,* letters, and autobiography and even of novels if we think of it. In fact, it is interesting to notice that it is women who very often wrote influential novels like *Gone with the Wind, The Tale of Genji* [Murasaki Shibiku], *La Sage de Gösta Berling* [Selma Lagerlöf], *Frankenstein, La Princesse de Clèves.* Women are great tellers. But to come back to the *journal intime,* let's say that the more women's values and experience are socialized, the more they will be displaced into 'fiction.' If we come to think of it, journals and letters have been expressing the underground of reality. Your question reminds me of what Gertrude Stein says in the *Autobiography of Everyone.* She says that in the nineteenth century, men, when they were writing, were inventing all sorts of other men. On the other hand, women were unable to invent other women but were always creating women in their image. I think this is a great way to mock the idea of a hierarchy of inventiveness between men and women.

*You quote Monique Wittig advising us that we must invent what we don't remember. Is this the impetus for your lesbian love poems* **Lovhers,** *the suppressed history of lesbian writing?*

**Lovhers** is a work of love inspired by one woman and conveying the continent of women. When I wrote that book, I invested words in a different way—words like 'memory,' 'sleep,' 'vertigo.' Lesbian love brought in a new set of feelings and knowledge which expanded words in a different way. Love has a very interesting effect on your minds. It makes us travel in our past, present, and future. That is why very often people have the impression that they have always known the loved one. Love brings, along with pleasure, a capacity to see reality in three dimensions; it brings details to our attention. In our excitement and enthusiasm we create new metaphors. I like Wittig's sentence because in fact lesbian love calls for a re-membering—the way Mary Daly uses the word—which can only be achieved by the way we invent what we know from an ancient memory which tells us about the ever so good feeling of that woman's soft keen skin.

*Memory as a strategy of writing is central to Elly Danica's 'autofiction'* Don't: A Woman's Word. *You were sent the text in manuscript form when you participated in the West Word women writers' retreat. How does memory as recovery relate to memory as environment and invention? What was your experience of working with Elly on the manuscript?*

In 1988, at the Third International Book Fair, I gave a presentation in which I said that without an inner narrative [*un récit intérieur*], without a narrative lighting [*un éclairage sur les événements que donne tout récit*], memory is an eater of destiny. In other words, if you don't narrate the story of your life to yourself, this story might eat you from the inside. All the time I was preparing that paper, I thought of Elly Danica's book since after reading her manuscript, it became clear to me how much women's memory is occupied by males through the marks of terror and violence they have left on women's body and soul. The younger you are when men's terrorism destroys your integrity, the longer it takes you to clear your territory. When men introduce themselves in our life through physical or verbal violence, they literally break our inner clock; they stop our life, stealing both our time and energy. Narrative is a key element to bridge memory and the present. Narrative is a way to put our inner clock back to the present, and that is why a lot of women use it even in their poetic texts.

*You create character out of the urban environment in* **French Kiss** *where the bodies of cars are fleshy. 'Georgraphy' spatializes character. What is the significance of the city and the body in your work?*

Especially in **French Kiss,** there is a metaphoric network among the city, the body, the streets, the veins. The city has a nervous and erotic system just as the tongue and language are movement in the kissing or speaking mouth. The pleasure given by city life is associated with the pleasure given by the complexity of language.

*I was interested in how you remapped the city so that it was no longer a space of male aggression where women are at risk on the streets. Instead of a place of potential violence and agoraphobia, it is playful, joyous, and explosively pleasurable.*

Cities are a reservoir of differences, contrasts, contradictions. They can be monstrous as well as sumptuous. Because of their eccentricities they keep you alert in thinking. They remind you of solitude and togetherness, of fun and suffering. They offer their past, present, and their future/no-future at the same time. They make you travel. I know that I travel in Montreal just as I would in a foreign city. I rediscover my city every time I go downtown. The city makes my senses work, it makes me wonder about human species. In fact, very often cities will reverberate your feelings: if you are scared, the city will seem more dangerous; if you feel good, the city will be gorgeous; if you feel bad the city will be hell. You say that cities are a space of male aggression against women, but isn't home also a place of male aggression?

*You're right. The domestic can be dangerous. Your revision of the city tampers with the symbolic in a way which differs from other postmodern writers. Gail Scott writes about gender specific postmoderns. What is your sense of this specificity?*

It seems to me that woman 'derives,' diverts, or shifts meaning in such a way that meaning can be curved and redirected towards her experience and to *what matters.* In other words, postmodern women writers seem to re-route words in such a way that words will provide new meaning rather than a jab in grammar or the syntax. Marcelle Desjardins, a Quebec woman poet of the sixties, writes in one of her poems: 'do I say the truth or do I write a poem?' I believe that this has been and is still at stake for a lot of women in their writing. To me this also explains why women will link narrative fragments, poetical prose, autobiographical passages, and poetry in the same piece of writing. Because women's experience is marginalized in life as well as in literature, women's subjectivity needs all genres at the same time. The way we re-route words to our own experience opens up entire zones of unknown and unspoken dimensions of reality. It seems that while women re-route language, men sink into a kind of 'deroute.' On the other hand, in recent Quebec poetry I can sense that the younger women seem to 'neutralize' their writing. No more anger, utopias, great passions, just a quiet tone to talk about love, childhood, the disaster at the end of the century. But we have to wait and see what happens in the next future of women's writing. In any case, this convinces me that the work accomplished by postmodern women's writing with a feminist consciousness is the most stimulating.

*So young Quebec women write 'neutralized' texts.*

Yes, most of them. For young women, feminism is taken for granted. They have managed their lives to be nice and cool and don't focus any more on the questions of feminist consciousness and the combat.

*Is this a positive and inevitable progression? Or is it dangerous to not continually ask how we as women are positioned in this culture? Is this 'quiet tone' a refusal to take up the class interests of impoverished women?*

It is dangerous in the sense that we lose our focus. In a certain way, it neutralizes us again. Since feminist subjectivity is already marginalized, it seems, unfortunately, that either we keep focused on the feminine subject, risking repetition—as if men never repeated themselves—or we neutralize ourselves into the poetic subject. While I say that, I am trying to understand this horrible double bind into which the feminine gender is *enfermé.* For example, I know that, as a writer, I cannot always use the word *woman* in a poem, but I also know that when, as a reader, I see the word *woman* in a poem, it does have a positive effect on me. I still believe that to write *I am a woman* is full of consequences. I also think that patriarchal meaning cannot stand the visibility of women as a radical subject. It's like parents who accept their daughter's lesbianism as long as she doesn't use the word *lesbian.* In women's writing we are asking, 'What's reality,' and 'What's fiction?' because the reality we live in is a fiction for women since we didn't participate in creating it. Reality has been created through men's fictions, through the imaginary men projected of themselves on reality. If women had built our cities, the architecture would be totally different, because we would have projected part of our bodies as men projected their penis in military arsenals and guns. We would have projected the shapes of our bodies, our minds, and our emotions in the way we light up our cities, in architecture and painting. The question for women in playing with language is really a matter of life and death. We're not just playing for fun in a kind of game. We're finding our own voice, exploring it, and making new sense where the general sense has lost its meaning and is no longer of use. If you want to grow, you've got to be at the origin of new meaning, somehow you have to honour your gender.

*Some feminist critics have taken on the notion of authenticity in writing. Elaine Marks suggested in one essay that the more numerous the oppressions, the more 'authentic' the writing. Could you comment on this as a lesbian writer in Quebec?*

A good writer can only be authentic in the way he or she uses language. The authenticity of a work of art is in the style, which is to say, no one other than this writer can write about the same subject in the same way. In painting, no one can draw a flower like Georgia O'Keefe. Usually the more numerous the oppressions, the more people are unable to talk about their oppression, not because of the social aspect of it, but because the suffering, the humiliation, and the negation have silenced them. I would also say that exploitation and domination call for revolt and that colonization calls for a quest of identity. You can be exploited but not colonized. You can be exploited and still be proud of what you are. But if you are colonized, you don't even know who you are because being colonized means adopting the dominant devalued perspective of yourself. Fighting exploitation is talking about the facts; finding out about your identity is talking about values, memory, and desire. Now it is certain that feminism has made space for women to testify about their lives. This is very important because previously the same testimonies have been denied their 'authenticity.' Furthermore, we now know that these testimonies have a political impact. In fact, one of the main achievements of feminism is that validating women's experience and subjectively has given women self-confidence in their own evaluation of reality as well as in their creativity. As a lesbian and a Québécoise, I belong to minorities, but I always write as if the world belonged to me, allowing my desire to shape around me the space I need to be what I am.

*As you know there have been important discussions in the community of feminist writers about racism. How do you relate to these conversations?*

Sexism and racism can be found in little details as well as in obvious aggression and rejection. I think that Black women have made their points in showing White feminists where the subtleties of racism are hiding in everyday life, spoken or written language. Now, in terms of writing, I don't believe in such a thing as being 'politically correct.' I say that my politics have brought me as far as I could dream, but being politically correct never improved my writing. Either you question reality, language, cliché, alterity, and difference, or you don't and simply rely on what people tell you to think. The same thing applies to me as a lesbian, a feminist, or a Québécoise. On the other hand, I believe strongly in being 'politically connected,' which means—sisterhood, solidarity.

*You worked with other Quebec authors to develop a politicized analysis of aesthetics during what anglophone Canada called the FLQ crisis. You spoke of the necessity of changing discursive forms in order to communicate radical change.*

I have always been fascinated by patterns of discursive relations developing between the dominator and the dominated. From the dominant group one can see a chain reaction that goes from 'you're talking nonsense,' to paternalistic listening, to guilt or irritability, then negotiation, then either acceptance, rejection, or neutralization of the dominated. From the dominated group: a burst of anger, followed by the shaping of an identity and solidarity, empowerment, then negotiation, then autonomy, resistance, or integration. Most of the time guns interrupt the process, and the discursive forms are simplified by a cycle of violence-revenge arguments. Most of the time dominator and dominated have their own culture, values, and traditions, but in the case of women opposing men's domination, we have to consider that, because women live in the same culture as those they oppose, most of the time they are already 'integrated' or 'neutralized' by institutions such as marriage or heterosexism. What interests me in those patterns is when the dominated responds to the dominator's 'you're talking nonsense' with 'you're lying' and from that moment starts to uncover the lies. Uncovering lies makes space for a new sense and thereby transforms meaning. This is where I believe radical change can occur because then one has to take into account that new meaning. The new meaning also starts to produce new metaphors which change the way we see things.

*In feminist discourse the notion of 'identity politics' has been criticized as having authorized only White women to speak. Do the tensions which have developed between Quebec nationalism and the Native desire for sovereignty during the Meech Lake debates and the blockade at Oka suggest a problematic effect of privileging Quebec identity over other collective identities?*

I sense that your question has two directions: one dealing with Native interest and another about why an independent Quebec. On the first subject, a recent survey [November 1990] shows that a majority of Quebeckers would support the political and legislative autonomy of Natives in Quebec. The second direction deals with nationalism and feminism, which is actually for me a great source of questioning. In a recent text I wrote: 'The country which enters into us through the memory of arrogant winner and through the suffering of the losers is a country which divides us.' Nationalism is like heterosexuality; it makes women stick to their men. Now in a feminist context, women have to stick together, don't they? But in what language, on the ground of what tradition, what history? In our attempts to change all patriarchal forms of domination over women, the only ground where I believe we can stick together is the ground of each of our herstories and of a mutual political validation. There is a lot we can teach each other if we don't start by promoting our mutual males' traditions.

*In your work, you find risk and exploration pleasurable. Can you talk about your process of writing?*

It is a difficult question. Risks, I take by exploring. I take risks by phrasing inner radical certitudes which can be offensive to common sense. But on a larger scale writing is full of risks because you don't know where it will take you. After all, we write with that *fragile coherent system full of contradictions* which we call the self. It is always frightening to think that a writer has no rest in dealing with a question such as the meaning of life. It is also difficult for me to answer your question because poetry calls for one process while prose as well as a 'text' calls for another process. Writing poetry, you need to hear an inner voice; writing a 'text' you simply need words + words; writing a novel you need time, patience, and a story. Sometimes I see words in a very material way (sounds, etymology, shape of letters), sometimes I see words through tears, sometimes they are flat, sometimes in 3-D. I have written texts in cold blood, others with a lot of tears, others out of pure sexual energy. Most of them with the dictionaries beside me, some of them on a café, most of them believing that they were worth sharing because something was happening in language.

*Could you describe a politics of reading your texts?*

When you read a book, it is always a very serious thing. A book should always bring you more consciousness about life and about yourself. It should make you ask questions. I write to explore, to understand more, and to discover. And I want the reader to do the same—to stop, to question, to explore with me while reading the text. If my writing is elliptical and full of rupture, it is not because I want to be nasty to the reader. It is my way of creating new spaces for new meaning which would not appear if I wrote in a linear way.

*In making these new textual spaces for the reader's pleasure, how do you deal with criticism about inaccessibility or élitism?*

I don't believe in élitist writing. When you read a book, you have the choice of whether to take it or leave it. If you take it, you have to be willing to do some work on your own part as a reader. You also have to develop a habit of reading. With experience you can read 'difficult' books more easily. Through *le nouveau roman* and post-modernism there has been a kind of education in reading. The more you are able to follow what the writer has been doing with language, the more you enjoy your reading, because you also are playing and recreating the game which gives you pleasure. The more a text has layers of reading, the more it is exciting. There are two kinds of pleasure in reading. One is the pleasure of recognizing. For example, if I write a novel in which the action takes place in cities which you, the reader, have lived in, it will give you a kind of pleasure to recognize those places. That pleasure reinforces your identification with characters and your interest in the story. The other kind of pleasure comes strictly from the writing itself. Because of the way language is being used, you have to wander between the meanings even though you may intuit what the sentence means. This is both intellectual and mental pleasure, while the first example is about emotional pleasure.

*How do you distinguish between 'mental' and 'intellectual' inquiry?*

For me, the mental recognizes shapes, patterns, abstraction, lines. The intellectual deals with value, knowledge, morals, discursive posture. The mental is visual—it intuits patterns; the intellectual is verbal—it searches meaning and 'truth' among words.

*In Dorothy Hénault's NFB film on your writing in the* Firewords *trilogy, she develops an interesting reading of your work which emphasizes the intellectual and, except in one scene, tends to diminish the sensual, erotic, visceral quality of your writing.*

It's hard for me to tell. I only know that I cannot think properly without emotions and that I would hate to be just a garden of emotions. The best moments of writing are when memory, emotions, desire, thought, sensations, and knowledge all synchronize in the act of writing. In *Firewords* I believe that Dorothy saw what she needed to see in my writing. This process is about reading. A reader always focuses on what she or he needs. This is usually the part that we underline as if the writing belongs to us from now on. It would be an interesting experience to give a book to one hundred readers, see all the passages they underline (take with them), and see what's left for the author, which indeed would be the part where the author's subjectivity did not encounter the reader's subjectivity.

*Your work has been translated and made available to anglophone readers, and you have worked very closely with your translators. How does the translation process vary with each book?*

First, I have to say that I have been very lucky in having as translators women like Barbara Godard, Patricia Claxton, Marlene Wildeman, and Susanne de Lotbinière-Harwood for two reasons: these women are familiar with my writing, and most of all they are creative in their way of approaching translation. Indeed, the translation process varies with each book. Translating **French Kiss** or **Picture Theory** calls for different approaches because of the writing. **Mauve Desert** calls for rhythm and sensuality; **French Kiss** obliges the translator to shift very quickly from one pun to another, etc. Personally, I have always been fascinated by translation, as I am usually writing about acts of passage, whether it is passage from fiction to reality, from reality to fiction, or from one language to another. I wrote **Mauve Desert** because it blows my mind to think that someone can conceive a reality in their language while I can't in mine and vice-versa. I remember one day Patricia Claxton was asking me about the word *sapin*. I asked her to draw what a *sapin* was for her . . . ; while I drew mine. . . . One meaning, two images in the back of the mind. I like to work with translators because it keeps me alert in my own language, for which my fascination has no rest, as well as alerting me to other languages. The way we see and construct reality depends so much on the language which we are given at our birth.

*Daphne Marlatt writes language-centred poetry and prose. Was this an advantage in working on the 'tranceformation' of each other's work? What affinities and differences did you encounter?*

Working and speaking with Daphne is always a great pleasure for many reasons. I like the way Daphne thinks, feels, and writes. I am curious about her language (English and the poetic tradition that comes with it), and she is also curious about mine. Both of us know the weight of language. Both of us were, in the sixties, the only woman poet among male poets. As for our differences, there are just enough differences that we can recognize ourselves in them and be curious to know more about the part that we don't recognize. To be honest with you, I would say that I take Daphne and her writing for granted. There are people to whom you know that you will always be faithful. Daphne is one of them for me.

*You take pleasure in the slipperiness of language.*

Yes. Because changing the course of meaning is one of the greatest pleasures in writing. I like to be surprised by language. Sometimes the surprise pops out haphazardly. Sometimes it is the result of a difficult crafting; sometimes it is the result of a 'coherent contradiction.' Slipperiness has also to do with the aura of the words, their connotations. In fact, the life of a language takes place with the aura of words—their connotations; it is there that the meaning displays and renews itself. I also believe that there is a memory in language which leads to reconstituting patterns of ancient meaning. Once I wrote a text with the words *star, mirror,* and *speculum.* I went to look up the word *speculum* in order to be certain of its meaning, and there I found that the speculum was in earlier times a small mirror used to look at the stars. Without knowing, I had reconstituted a memory already at work in the language. This is exciting. Some writers say that writing is painful for them. I know sometimes it can be difficult, but writing definitely brings its own pleasure, even physically.

*What is your fascination with the multi-dimensions of holograms, which figure in* **French Kiss** *and are made central in* **Picture Theory***?*

When I wrote **Picture Theory,** I had completely forgotten that the hologram was already there in **French Kiss**. So it means that for almost ten years I had been bearing this word in my mind. But why was it only explored ten years later? As well, Arizona and the desert, which are central in **Mauve Desert,** are already present in **Picture Theory**. But why the hologram in **Picture Theory**? Well, I think that my questioning about woman, women, the real, the symbolic, the imaginary, and the notion of fiction versus reality, all came together in such a way that only the metaphor of the hologram could account for them. The hologram deals with a 'real' object, which through 'virtual' image produces a 'fictive' image. It is as if using 'real' characters through imagination—which is the virtual part of the real—I wanted to envision a symbolic woman, fictive but yet changing the perception of womanhood. I have often said that writing **Picture Theory** was making a synthesis of my world, a synthesis like a conclusion which simultaneously opens up on a new horizon. It is hard for me to talk about the state of mind I was in when I wrote **Picture Theory,** but I know that this is the state of mind which I value most. Probably because it embodies certitudes, questions, and utopias in an enigmatic encounter of fiction and reality.

### Maria Green (review date autumn 1996)

SOURCE: Green, Maria. Review of *Baroque d'aube,* by Nicole Brossard. *World Literature in Review* 70, no. 4 (autumn 1996): 905-06.

[*In the following review, Green discusses the plot and thematic content of Brossard's novel* Baroque d'aube, *noting its glorification of women and dismissive depiction of male characters.*]

At daybreak, Cybil Noland, the middle-aged *écrivaine,* heroine, and narrator of **Baroque d'aube,** brings to orgasm an unknown woman, picked up in the hotel's elevator. She learned in her youth to look straight into the eyes of women, and the beautiful young girl responded. Reader, don't put down the book after this first paragraph! The novel is not about lesbian love but rather the gestation of a novel, the intricate problems of the creative process, and the many questions it raises. The girl exits from Nicole Brossard's novel after the first chapter but emerges as the dramatis persona of the *écrivaine*'s book. She turns out to be a gifted violinist with an adventure-filled life.

Daybreak intonates the novel and enlightens the second word of the title, while *baroque* has many ramifications. Cybil has a baroque heart, a baroque imagination, and above all a baroque, exuberant style. Brossard cannot suppress the poet of her innermost being. Clusters of images sprint forth irrepressibly from her fertile imagination. They are always original, striking, and often memorable.

The main body of the novel deals with an unusual sea voyage, undertaken by three creative women: our *auteure,* a surrealist photographer, and an equally surrealist oceanographer. The last worries that the abstractions of science will eventually empty the sea of its symbolic significance. She wants to celebrate the still-existing symbolism with an album, created by the three of them. She counts on the two artists to nourish the symbols. The writer and the photographer spend a few days in the ship's library, filled to the brim with novels, engravings, and magazines dealing with seafare. After this first stage, the two artists are immersed into the sea. Actually, they are watching underwater life on a computer screen; but, with the help of the latest technology, they are treated to a lived experience of visual and tactile sensations. At this point, Cybil gives free rein to her baroque imagination, transforming the sea fauna and flora into stunning images.

The women in Brossard's universe are creative, articulate, generous, endowed with a superb, analytic intelligence. On the other hand, the few men who flit in and out of the novel are disgustingly hairy or have a protruding Adam's apple. They are silent or inarticulate. When one of them turns out to be a good conversationalist, he is likened to a shark. Another man eyewitnessed a gang rape and remarks airily that it was good fun for the boys, although it did not suit the girls. Mothers are loving, giving, admirable, and adorable beings; fathers, however, are just playing the role of being a father. When Cybil scrutinizes the old engravings in the library, she observes that women are depicted either as mysterious, fertile creatures or as prey. Men, on the other hand, with their well-sculpted genitals pointed toward heaven, seem to implore God to cleanse the female sexual organs of all impurities.

In a circular motion, *Baroque d'aube* started with daybreak and ends with it: "Montréal scintille, grand tatouage mauve entre la nuit et les premières lueurs de l'aube." The light of daybreak and the light of words fuse in the eyes of the young translator who translates Cybil's completed fiction.

## Nicole Brossard and Beverley Daurio (interview date 1998)

SOURCE: Brossard, Nicole, and Beverley Daurio. "Patriarchal Mothers: Nicole Brossard." In *The Power to Bend Spoons: Interviews with Canadian Novelists,* edited by Beverley Daurio, pp. 42-8. Toronto: Mercury Press, 1998.

[*In the following interview, Brossard discusses her feminist theory of writing and explains the linguistic effects she created in her novel* Mauve Desert.]

[Daurio]: *Among others, you have often referred to Djuna Barnes and Gertrude Stein in your work. Who else has influenced your writing, and who do you think people should be reading?*

[Brossard]: I make a distinction between people who have influenced you and people who are accompanying you in the writing. In the beginning when you are writing, you are much more impressed by other texts. For me, the main influences were Mallarmé, Maurice Blanchot, and then, in terms of women's writing, when I was much older: Adrienne Rich in her feminist essays; Mary Daly; Ti-Grace Atkinson and Kate Millet were important to me at the time that I read them; Clarice Lispector, a Brazilian writer who is stimulating and exciting.

*It has been twenty-five years since your first book of poetry,* **Aube à la saison,** *came out. What have been the major changes in your approach to writing during that time?*

You can see Nicole Brossard in my first two books, but as with most first books, especially if the writer is twenty or twenty-one when they are written, you don't know exactly who you are, and therefore you assimilate influences, sometimes quite well; you are only beginning to design your own individuality or style. With the third book I tried to be more Nicole Brossard the way people have read me for a long time, until 1973-74, when, with *These Our Mothers,* there was a shift in the writing because of a shift in feminist consciousness and the lesbian experience. After *Picture Theory* came a novel like *Mauve Desert,* which is again very different. If I try to be objective, I think that my writing has become more lyrical. In my new book of poetry, *Installations,* the poems have many layers of meaning, but you can understand them on first reading. Superficially, the writing seems more linear, but the questioning remains: about writing, value, philosophical questions.

*In her introduction to* **Lovhers,** *Barbara Godard said the subtitle of* **These Our Mothers,** *"The Disintegrating Chapter," "points to the effect this feminist fiction has in dissolving the authority of the male tradition of the book." How large a part of your writing project is that dissolution? Or are you more interested in building a new vision?*

In feminist writing, it has to be both. You have to write two kinds of pages almost at the same time: one on which you try to understand and uncover the patriarchal lies; and another on which you try to give your new values, your utopias, and everything you find positive about yourself and about women. You have to write an unedited version, something that is totally new, to shape it. You bring in thoughts that have never been thought, use words in ways they have never been used. You want to bring your anger but also your utopia and your connection and solidarity with other women.

*For me, reading* **Le Sens apparent** *was like having my skin removed and entering another woman's body, seeing and experiencing without those usual signposts of narrative. You have spoken elsewhere about the lack of outer reality which confirms women in their experiences; was part of the intention in writing this book the desire to chart an inner and recognizable reality for women?*

I don't know if there was any specific project when I wrote *Le Sens apparent,* as you would find in *Picture Theory* or even *Mauve Desert.* I wanted to fall in love and so I had to write a book. In society we think that things have clear meanings, but things aren't clear for women, because we haven't produced that reality; it is only an appearance. The work of the writer is to dig at those appearances and into the real meaning of what we experience in a strong and sometimes frustrating way.

*One of the most profoundly interesting aspects of your work is the way in which theory and emotion, wildness and discipline, randomness and intellectual concentration intersect in it. In part, this has meant vast violence to the distinctions between poetry, fiction, and theory. Was this intentional or is this just the way it worked out?*

I cannot think properly or deeply if emotion is not there in the thought itself. At the same time, I wouldn't want to just express emotion, because I know that I wouldn't be able to visualize and envision things I am writing about. I don't think it's an intention; it's a necessity. There are two sides here: I have always loved science, discipline, order, but also the imagination, ecstasy.

*Do you think theory has become more important in feminist and lesbian writing because of the whole project of making new visions?*

It is the theory that I make which interests me; of outside theory, I will only take the parts that stimulate me. I do not follow any theory; there would be no point in writing fiction if you were just a civil servant. For me, theory is a way of being able to mentally visualize and to read the patterns of the way people relate in life, patterns in creative work, patterns of rain or snow. Theory has true value when it comes from the subjectivity of someone who values awareness in movement.

*In* **The Aerial Letter,** *you wrote: "Reality has been for most women a fiction, and women's reality has been perceived as fiction." This seems to pose an incredible paradox for writing for women.*

The reality we live in is fictional for women because it is only the fantasy of men throughout history who have transformed their subjectivity into laws, religion, culture, and so on. Nobody believes what women live in their reality, whether it is about motherhood or rape or incest, good *or* bad things. What women were experiencing or saying was always understood as a result of "she fantasizes," whereas men's fantasies are there and are supposed to be the reality, in architecture and everywhere. Women's perspective is a territory which has not yet been mapped. We are the only ones who can do it, but sometimes we don't have the appropriate words. The words which were available would always push us back into madness or fantasy. The way we think when no-one knows about it is called "fiction," but when everybody agrees, it is called reality. In terms of women's texts, all the doors are open. Memory is one of the things we have to use, and it explains a lot about the way we go from narrative to prose to poetry. Women's memory is very loaded with narratives which have not been told, and it is important to tell those stories no-one wanted to tell or hear. Poetry is inner certitude, but without narrative yet, before narrative. Out of each verse you could start a novel.

*You have said: "The origin is not the mother, but the sense I make of words." What did you mean by that?*

That relates to the virtuality of the creative potential in each of us. It's too late to go to mythology. I can't believe in god so I can't believe in a goddess, either. Most of our mothers were very traditional, patriarchal mothers, so we cannot go to that concrete origin in real life. Maybe this generation of writers can become symbolic mothers to another generation; and if we are not patriarchal mothers, maybe we can have a continuity.

*Does that mean you are disappointed in the women of the past?*

I don't know what to do with the word "disappointed." We all know the pressure that the women of the past were under, the intimidation, the fact that they were deprived of many things. The process of fictionalizing the heroine that is where you can envision a process of validation of women, whoever they are. One of the problems of feminism is that we are moral: we don't belittle men, and we don't overestimate women. So it's hard to create a validating mythology.

*Your novel* **Mauve Desert** *is set in Arizona. Have you ever spent time in the desert?*

I wanted the book to take place in a North American desert, and that is the desert where they exploded the first nuclear bomb. It is a place where you can find high technology and also the greatest decadence: extremely rich people and extremely poor people. The desert is important as a symbol of highly spiritual life; and it is also a place of death, where everything can be dangerous. It is a place where life has to find very tricky ways to survive, and it's very beautiful how nature finds ways to remain alive. The horizon has always been important for me. I like open spaces, and the horizon is always open. It can be frightening, because we don't know where it ends, but you can project on it whatever you want.

**Mauve Desert** *is a mystery, in some senses, and it is written in three parts: first, "Mauve Desert," the short novel by Laure Angstelle about fifteen-year-old Mélanie Kerouac; second, a section written through the eyes of the older Maude Laures, who is obsessed with Laure's text; and the third, which is Maude's homolinguistic translation of "Mauve Desert," "Mauve Horizon." This structure gives the feeling of a book that has been expertly taken apart and surgically reassembled, so that all the parts can be examined. Do you think that's a valid way of looking at it?*

I knew that I would be writing a novel set in a very hot place. I knew that I would like to have that challenge of translating myself from French to French. I wrote the first section, Laure's novel, and then I asked myself, as the fictional translator of "Mauve Desert," *what do you* find in a novel? You find characters, you find objects, you find ideas, you find dialogue. And so I wrote those things, but in a different order. I liked the way the translator started to imagine those characters, to try to visualize the faces, the bodies, how they moved, the places and the people; and, in fact, Maude, as translator, does what we normally do as readers. I also enjoyed imagining the dialogue. I didn't know I could write dialogue. I didn't talk about anecdotal things, I went to the heart of the relationship between the daughter and the mother, between the two women lovers, between the translator and the author. In Maude's conversation with Angela Parkins, Angela wants to know why the author is killing her. The author replies, *I'm not killing you, he's killing you.* The ending seems very surprising, even gratuitous, but it's exactly what happened at the École Polytechnique, it's exactly the same kind of hatred. So I haven't imagined anything, I have only decoded a pattern which does not explode all the time, but which is there all the time. In the book, the act comes from a physicist, a man of knowledge, who's got everything; in our society he's "the perfect guy."

*Is it possible now to write a more traditional book, as in* **Mauve Desert,** *and have it carry the weight of feminist and lesbian ideas, without it having to be so radical in the way the language works?*

Writing **Mauve Desert,** sometimes I would pretend I didn't have the kind of knowledge that I have, because I needed that kind of innocence to go on with the characters and make them alive. If I, as the writer, knew everything, then I could not have created the characters. There are many things that I know because of the difficult work of **These Our Mothers,** of **Picture Theory,** and of **The Aerial Letter,** difficult work that you pay for. If you look at things from a lesbian and feminist point of view, reality has no more meaning, because we are not part of that meaning in the symbolic. It's as if you have to do the whole world again. So you have to be careful. There's a limit where you don't know if you are making sense.

*What do you mean by "pay for"?*

Some books that you write cost you more than others. Some books I have written in cold blood, some books I have written with tears in my eyes . . . but the result is not that one book is better than another. The price you pay is in terms of psychological energy, emotive energy, mental energy, intellectual energy. The more difficult questions call for more energy at all levels.

*Laure Angstelle's version of "Mauve Desert" seems younger and more fiery than Maude's, which is more fine-tuned and optimistic. Is the second version of that text there only because of Maude's obsession with it, or is it also there in order to provide a more mature version of the first text?*

The second version, the translation, is the result of the crafting of the first text. In the first version I found myself being very passionate; in the second version I had to craft very carefully. It was a different rapport with words; I could not choose or let myself go because I had to check on the sentences in the first version. In the middle section, where Maude Laures is re-imagining the characters and so on, I had a lot of freedom, because I was still inventing through the information I got in the first book, where very little had been said about the characters and spaces. That explains why the third part is less fiery but more precise, because I was also considering the structure of the whole book. I had to be very properly attuned to everything that was going on, each word and each sentence. Writing the third section—because I was not learning more, though I was learning the pleasure of crafting new sentences—I remember, I said, Nicole, you'd better go along and go through that whole project; otherwise, I'm not talking to you any more.

## Lianne Moyes (essay date spring 2000)

SOURCE: Moyes, Lianne. "Nothing Sacred: Nicole Brossard's *Baroque at Dawn* at the Limits of Lesbian Feminist Discourses of Sexuality." *Essays on Canadian Writing,* no. 70 (spring 2000): 28-63.

[*In the following essay, Moyes examines how* Baroque at Dawn *uses the baroque genre to "explore new vocabularies and new discourses of lesbian sexuality."*]

### RESISTING THE BAROQUE

Although the term "Baroque" surfaces occasionally in interviews with Nicole Brossard and in her essays and fiction from the mid-1970s onward, she resisted using the term to qualify her writing until she published the novel **Baroque at Dawn**[1] in 1995. In an effort to understand the meanings accrued to the baroque across the discourses of Brossard's oeuvre and to discern the terms of her initial resistance to the baroque, I begin this analysis of **Baroque at Dawn** with a brief discussion of three earlier texts: a 1982 interview with Brossard, the 1982 fiction **Picture Theory,** and the 1975 essay **"E Muet Mutant."** This gesture of doubling back helps to situate her use of the term within the field of Québécois literary discourse as well as within the broader field of baroque aesthetic practice. First used by late-eighteenth-century European art critics to refer to conventions and practices from the seventeenth and early eighteenth centuries that were out of fashion and considered grotesque, the term "baroque" has come to refer in the twentieth century to conventions and practices (associated with the Baroque period) that *recur throughout history* (see d'Ors).[2] Clearly, Brossard's lesbian feminist project sits uneasily within the religious fervour of the Counter-Reformation so crucial to the Baroque period. But the Baroque was also a period of substantial cultural transformation, including radical changes in conceptions of the subject; a period preoccupied with passion, with making the material (paint, marble, language, fabric, flesh) yield to signs of emotion; a period whose overelaborated surfaces are heavy with multiple, even contradictory, significations; a period fascinated with the ecstasy of the martyr; a period given to allegory, to representations that disrupt the eternal by yoking it to the historical; and a period associated with ornament, detail, and other categories identified as feminine. In this sense, whether they resist, mobilize, or recontextualize the baroque, Brossard's texts certainly have a stake in exploring it.[3]

In an interview in 1982 in *La Nouvelle barre du jour*, Brossard mentioned Claude Gauvreau.[4] Well known as a cosignatory of the 1948 manifesto *Refus global*, Gauvreau has also received attention for his engagement with the baroque, particularly in his 1952 novel *Beauté baroque*. According to Jacques Marchand in his study of Gauvreau's writing, the term "baroque" was used widely in the 1950s and 1960s in the sense of "uneven," "excessive," "unusual," and "exaggerated." Gauvreau considered "baroque" a work marked by the rush of life's impulses, by the erratic texture of desire (84-85).[5] His is a twentieth-century baroque that exists through form and abstraction infused with emotion. Curiously, when Brossard spoke of Gauvreau's work in 1982, she spoke not of the baroque but of a rejection of description and figuration in favour of a vital abstraction; she also spoke of a drive to generate meaning where there seems to be only nonsense (**"Entretien" ["Entretien avec Nicole Brossard sur *Picture Theory*"]** 192-93). She associates Gauvreau with her project of recomposing letter by letter, fragment by fragment, "the woman through whom everything could happen" (***Picture Theory*** 147).

Picking up on Brossard's reference to Gauvreau, the interviewers asked her if she would characterize ***Picture Theory*** as a baroque novel (Brossard, **"Entretien"** 193). She answered no and explained that precision, not the imprecision of shifting perspectives, is key to her sense of the holographic image of a woman at stake in ***Picture Theory*** (193-94). Yet the term "baroque" surfaces in ***Picture Theory***, precisely in the context of a meditation on eyes—and their excesses—in a section entitled "Perspective": "Claire Dérive pushes our sexes to the ultimate / encounter. Baroque eyes, clarity excessive / the pupil barely repetitive to wonder" (60). As I have argued elsewhere, this section bears the traces both of the narrator's reading of Djuna Barnes's novel *Nightwood* and of the narrator's encounter with her lover, Claire Dérive. Through the repetition of details from Barnes's text and the accumulation of different points of view, this section frames writing/reading as an erotic activity and throws into relief the lesbian embrace that remains hidden in the whorls of *Nightwood* (Moyes, "Composing" 212-13). When the interviewers reminded Brossard of the baroque work of "repetition, accumulation and shifting angles of vision" in her text (Brossard, **"Entretien"** 194), she warned them of the danger of associating sensory phenomena of the twentieth and twenty-first centuries (e.g., holography) with sensory phenomena that stem from "an entirely different practice of bodies, of the eye and therefore of the imaginary" (195).

I would agree with Brossard that ***Picture Theory*** is more a novel of clarity, light, and the *integration* of different angles of vision than a novel of ambiguity, shadow, and proliferating perspectives. ***Picture Theory*** emphasizes the role of lucidity in the process of women writing and in what Brossard has since described as "the projection of a mythic space freed of inferiorizing patriarchal images" ("Interview" 118). At the same time, there is in ***Picture Theory*** a certain engagement with the baroque. That Brossard played down this engagement betrays an ambivalence toward the baroque, an ambivalence that would intensify and permeate ***Baroque at Dawn***.

If, as Brossard argued, ***Picture Theory*** is a product of the late twentieth century, ***Baroque at Dawn*** is marked by more than one period, by movement *between* periods. Insofar as the baroque can be understood as a recurring aesthetic or tendency—often associated with moments of cultural transformation—and not simply as a fixed historical period, it is possible to apply the term "baroque" to twentieth-century sensory phenomena (see Bertrand 17-22). ***Baroque at Dawn*** explores the contemporary shift from a culture of print media to one of electronic media, a shift as radical as that from manuscript to print culture in the sixteenth and seventeenth centuries (see Guardiani 132-35; Moyes, Introduction 9-11). ***Picture Theory***, too, is concerned with this contemporary shift. However, whereas in ***Picture Theory*** words and visuals operate in tandem to produce a coherent image of a virtual woman, in ***Baroque at Dawn*** words and visuals are locked in "fearsome combat" (35), and the virtual experience generated by wearing a visiohelmet and dataglove overwhelms rather than invigorates (171; see McPherson 89-90).

Brossard is not the only one to characterize her writing prior to ***Baroque at Dawn*** in terms other than baroque. In an article published in the same issue of *La Nouvelle barre du jour* as the 1982 interview discussed above, François Charron calls Brossard a "peculiarly classical writer" (75). That one set of critics asks Brossard about the baroque while another describes her work as "peculiarly classical"—in the same issue of a magazine—is symptomatic of a tension within her writing. This tension is made explicit in *Baroque at Dawn* in the liaison between the characters Cybil Noland, a classical figure, and La Sixtine, a figure for a Christian chapel whose ceiling frescoes anticipate the baroque. Exploring the peculiarity of Brossard's classicism in further detail, Louise Dupré identifies a contradiction in Brossard's work between the desire for unity, for the perfection of the absolute, and the practice of writing through which that desire must be achieved (149-51), a practice "rooted in time and space, in history and subjectivity, in ideology and the unconscious" (150-51). In seeking unity through fragmentation, in generating a utopian image of a woman through broken syntax and multiple perspectives (151-52), Dupré suggests, Brossard's writing "reinvents classicism" (149).[6]

Brossard's 1975 essay **"E Muet Mutant"** offers another context in which to explore the ambivalence in her discourse toward the baroque. In that essay, the term "baroque" describes the spoken discourse of women:

> Women's speech is quickly exhausted. Supremely censored. Confined. Condemned to turn in circles, to close in on itself insofar as it doesn't become part of history, yet where history enters in by default. Speech of the detail and the insignificant (for the other). . . . Repetitive speech, based on the zero degree of tradition propagating itself, that's life. Baroque, rococo speech, with plenty of trimming: which expends itself in pure loss of energy that transforms nothing. Speech which contradicts itself.
>
> (47)

Brossard's essay manifests not so much a resistance to the baroque as a feminist resistance to the way in which prevailing culture views women's speech. The essay goes on to contrast women's *writing* with women's speech and to suggest that writing allows women to make themselves visible, to impose their gaze and their own subjectivity within the public sphere—in short, to enter history (49, 51).

In the twenty years between the publication of **"E Muet Mutant"** and that of *Baroque at Dawn,* Brossard found ways of mobilizing the nonlinear movement, excess of form, and spending of meaning so often used to dismiss women's speech. As Caroline Bayard points out in a discussion of **"E Muet Mutant,"** "what initially appeared to be a disadvantage became a tool, a means to transform the very nature of creativity" (184). Both at the level of textual practice and at the level of theoretical inquiry, a text such as *Picture Theory* is preoccupied with the relationship between sense and nonsense: "Fiction then foils illysybility in the sense that it always insinuates something more which forces you to imagine, to double. To come back to it again" (28). Inhabited by a sibyl, the word *illysybility* (*illisibilité* or "unreadability") suggests that there is always something to be made of the apparently illegible and that doubling back to make sense of what at first seems to be unintelligible is potentially transformative. In *Baroque at Dawn,* the baroque is more than the endless repetition of that which is deemed insignificant, without sense; it offers Brossard a conceptual framework in which to explore further the oscillation between sense and nonsense. In the words of the text, "baroque thought taken as a whole . . . hesitates between Chaos and Cosmos" (151). This movement between chaos (formlessness) and cosmos (form) structures Brossard's fictions from the mid-1970s onward.

The "sibyl" of *Picture Theory*'s "illysybility" becomes an important character in *Baroque at Dawn*: Cybil Noland. Sibyls are women of equivocal yet prophetic texts, whose power lies in their capacity to decode the present and to intervene in contemporary culture even more than in their capacity to foretell the future. Throughout Brossard's 1995 novel, Cybil bears witness to the transition from a culture of books to a culture of proliferating images and information. At times in *Baroque at Dawn,* the oscillation between sense and nonsense takes the violent form of "speedy visuals that gobble up meaning as fast as it appears" (59). Within this context, Cybil struggles to decipher and decode, to work with signs and generate meaning, and thereby to sustain the productive tension between chaos and cosmos, sense and nonsense, so crucial for Brossard to the transformation of the cultural imaginary.

In addition to mobilizing formal elements associated with the baroque, *Baroque at Dawn* returns to the issue of women's speech raised by **"E Muet Mutant."** Like all of Brossard's texts, *Baroque at Dawn* eschews the kind of anecdotal speech associated with the baroque in **"E Muet Mutant."** However, more than other novels to date, *Baroque at Dawn* foregrounds the question of dialogue between women (see Brossard, **"Energy"** 57-58). *Baroque at Dawn* opens with a sexual encounter between two women, an encounter that gives way to a conversation. Asked by La Sixtine (the younger of the two) "whether she's in the habit of 'taking the elevator' with perfect strangers," Cybil responds: "If possible yes. . . . In the sexual meeting of two stranger-women there's a temporal break that allows abstraction of the background baggage carried by each. Less of the past benefits an immediate presence" (18). The sexual energy that arises from the difference between the two women, from the fact that they are strangers to one another, is arguably the source of this extraordinary conversation. Insofar as the latter conversation is published, it locates the words of these women in history and allows their energy to transform the public sphere.

The exchange between Cybil and La Sixtine invites reflection about why, to borrow the words of Lynne Huffer in conversation with Brossard in 1993, it is so difficult "for women playwrights to create dialogue between women outside of the mother-daughter relationship," why, "Most of the time, female characters interact through monologues" ("Interview" 119). Brossard's tentative response, "Is it because of a feminist ethic that won't allow for power relations or hierarchical roles among women?" (119), is suggestive for my reading of *Baroque at Dawn*; the response troubles the notion that relations among women are always, or should always be, egalitarian, a contentious issue, for example, in feminist debates about lesbian sadomasochism in the 1980s.[7] In Brossard's novel, female characters confront, even play out, relations and roles that the discourses of lesbian feminism might otherwise dismiss. In what follows, taking my cue from Brossard's text, I examine ambiguities and contradictions within the discourses of the novel that open the possibility for further discussion and debate. What is at stake in the novel's fascination with Baroque religious art? How does the novel manipulate the slippage between the spiritual and the historical, the sacred and the profane, made available by that art? Within lesbian feminist discourses of sexuality, what remains "sacred"? In which ways do the novel's playful rereadings of the baroque—particularly the baroque's preoccupation with passion, with the ecstasy of the martyr, and with relations of domination and submission, sadism and masochism—push the limits of the latter discourses?

Whereas in **"E Muet Mutant"** the baroque is a descriptive term for a kind of discourse, in *Baroque at Dawn* it is a way of writing the ambivalence of the text's relationship to technology, violence, passion, ritualized suffering, Christianity, queer culture, S/M, and relations of power among women. Brossard's 1995 text draws on the potential in religious painting and sculpture, particularly in Baroque religious painting and sculpture, for reading the sublime and the ecstatic in terms of the homoerotic. *Baroque at Dawn* finds in Michelangelo's gesture of bringing pagan prophets and prophetesses (sibyls) within the sphere of a Christian chapel an important precedent for its own baroque conjunctions. Brossard's text restages his gesture as a sexual encounter between two women, Cybil and La Sixtine. Yoking together classical and Christian figures, lovers of different generations, radical lesbian feminist culture and queer culture, lesbians and *pietà*s, Jesuit martyrs and leathermen, *Baroque at Dawn* explores an erotics of incongruity. One minute, an encounter between women has the tenderness and tranquillity of a *pietà*; the next, it has the violence and intensity of baroque bodies clenched toward ecstasy. Each unexpected adjacency, each apparent incongruity, raises unsettling but nevertheless productive questions about lesbian feminist discourses of sexuality, about definitions, values, and attitudes that seem to be indisputable, inviolable, almost "sacred."

WOMEN OF DIFFERENT AGES: THE COMING TOGETHER OF THE CLASSICAL AND THE CHRISTIAN

Cybil Noland and La Sixtine, *Baroque at Dawn* makes clear, are of different ages, different epochs. They meet in Los Angeles, the city of angels. The first night the two women take the elevator together in the Hotel Rafale (18), Cybil's lover, a woman described as "a musician and young," insists that she is not sixteen (9). Cybil immediately christens her "La Sixtine," the French name for the Sistine Chapel (named after Pope Sixtus IV). The chapel is mentioned in a subsequent paragraph and again later in the novel, both times in conjunction with the five sibyls of Michelangelo (another of the text's angels). The second night the two women take the elevator together, Cybil is described, this time from the perspective of La Sixtine, as "the grey-haired woman" (38). Cybil is older than La Sixtine in more ways than one. The prophetesses of antiquity, sibyls were charged with the task of making known the pronouncements of the gods. Incorporated into the Christian narrative of the Sistine Chapel paintings, these women of words and books are evidence of the Renaissance will to reconcile classical culture and Christianity, "to see all antiquity . . . [as] 'preparation for the Gospel'" (O'Malley 116). Sibyls were of particular interest for this Renaissance project because they were alleged to have prophesied the coming of a Christ-like figure (116). They are of particular interest for Brossard's text because of the relative importance that Michelangelo gave them and their books within his representation of Genesis.[8]

In Brossard's novel, Michelangelo's sibyls thematize the problematics of framing, perspective, origins, and incongruity. In a chapter entitled "Sibyls and *Ignudi*," *Baroque at Dawn* reads the Sistine Chapel paintings in some detail. The scene is a ship called *The Symbol* engaged in oceanographic research off the coast of Argentina. Cybil has been hired by an oceanographer named Occident des Rives to write the text of a book about the sea, a book that will include photographs by another character, Irène Mage. *Padré* Sinocchio, the priest aboard ship, mentions Rome, and Occident takes the opportunity to give everyone a tour of the Sistine Chapel. A figure of power, Occident speaks continuously, without pausing to hear the stories of others. Her narrative, like the narrative of Creation presented in the ceiling's central tableaux, is apparently seamless. Nevertheless, the narrator, the one who selects what to report and what not to report, finds a way to intervene; she focuses on Occident's account of the *ignudi*[9] and the sibyls, the massive, three-dimensional figures that, along with the prophets, frame the two-dimensional tableaux representing various scenes from Genesis. The narrator also reminds the reader of the impact of perspective—of where one stands in the chapel and how one tells the story—on how one reads the relations between the nine central tableaux and the sibyls and *ignudi*. Most often, the latter are seen merely to punctuate the biblical narrative. However, the narrator intimates that, insofar as they disturb the centrality of the tableaux and draw attention to those positioned along the edges, the sibyls and *ignudi* play a larger role (134). From the perspective of Brossard's narrator, for whom the bare right arm of the Cumaean sybil is "as muscular as God's" (134), women of books play a key role in (the representation of) Creation.

Michelangelo's Creation narrative, the narrator observes, would not be possible today "because according to the rules of narrative you have to point at infinity with one hand and exploit it with the other" (134). This sibylline comment—in part a reference to Adam's arm outstretched toward that of God in Michelangelo's *Creation of Man*—has to do with myths of origins and with the way in which such myths are framed. *Padré* Sinocchio's impassioned response to Occident's presentation of the scenes from Genesis provides a context for reading the narrator's cryptic comment about the Infinite. Aware of the seas rising around them, he asserts that there can be no doubt about the phenomenon of the Flood: "Noah, the Ark and all that could not be merely the fruit of our imaginations" (135).[10] In the French text, use of the word *l'arche* is particularly revealing: *l'arche* refers to the ark but also to the arch, the curved structure of the ceiling on which scenes from Genesis are painted; in Greek, *arche* means first principle, primal element, origin. Taken as a whole, the discussion of the chapel's paintings poses the problem of beginnings, of priority. In the paintings, the *ignudi* and pagan sibyls appear to take precedence over the Creation. They draw attention to the illusory architectural structure that supports the central tableaux rather than to the Creation narrative. By emphasizing that which lies outside the narrative of God's Creation, that which precedes the formulation of Christian myths of origins, Brossard's text raises questions about the status of the narrative and about the privileged God-man connection. If God is the Creator, then who creates the structure, the framework in which God is represented creating? How can man represent God creating man? The Infinite, the Creator, the text suggests, is a retrospective construction that lends coherence to the biblical narrative and, at the same time, primacy to man.

The image of one hand gesturing toward the Infinite while the other assumes the creative powers of the Infinite also refers to the framing devices of ***Baroque at Dawn***. Cybil, the main character, turns out to be a narrator and perhaps even a writer of the novel; she refers in an ongoing way to writing a novel that resembles, even overlaps with, ***Baroque at Dawn***. As character, narrator, and writer, Cybil occupies a space inside and outside the fictional frame simultaneously; she has one hand in the realm of the Infinite (writing) and another in the realm of character (the written). In this way, she is able to intervene in the process of her own creation.

In bringing Cybil and La Sixtine together, ***Baroque at Dawn*** makes a gesture not unlike that of Michelangelo's frescoes: it accommodates difference, incongruity. Brossard's novel reads the relationship between the chapel and the frescoes, specifically the sibyls, as a liaison between two women. As Alice Parker has pointed out, "names in the novel are so pointedly symbolic that the text reads in part like a fable or an allegory" (195). The sexual encounter between Cybil and La Sixtine might be read as allegorical[11] of erotic ties between lesbians of different generations, different discourses of desire, different modes of self-presentation, and so forth. (It is not so much that Cybil and La Sixtine stand for two identifiable groups as that their coming together makes it more possible to imagine various unexpected conjunctions.) In the context of twentieth-century lesbian literary culture, classical figures such as amazons, eumenides (furies), and sibyls are not often found between the same covers as martyrs, madonnas, and Christian chapels. In this sense, the encounter of Cybil and La Sixtine is no less dramatic than the coming together of the classical and the Christian worlds. Lesbian literature and criticism arguably privilege classical figures such as Medusa, Leda, Demeter, and Persephone over Christian figures. In fact, so important are amazons to this body of literature and criticism that Elaine Marks's 1979 notion of "lesbian intertextuality" is recast as "amazon intertextuality" in a 1993 essay by Jeffner Allen. Moreover, the ancient Greek poet Sappho, key to Marks's discussion of intertextuality, is a recurring figure in readings of early-twentieth-century writing by lesbians (see Benstock; Marcus), a body of writing to which Brossard's oeuvre has important links (see Meese; Moyes, "Composing").

As Raymond-Jean Frontain observes in *The Gay and Lesbian Literary Heritage,* to date the Bible has provided far fewer inspirational figures (99). There are important reasons for this preference for the classical over the Christian, among them the greater susceptibility of figures such as amazons and Sappho to lesbian utopian and homoerotic readings (Griffin Crowder 25), the construction of women's bodies and regulation of women's sexuality within Christianity, and the difficulty that women have experienced in acceding to positions of discourse and authority within the Church. In the words of Cybil in ***Baroque at Dawn,*** "sacred books . . . have always endangered the lives of women" (68). In Marks's estimation, "There is no one person in or out of fiction who represents a stronger challenge to the Judeo-Christian tradition, to patriarchy and phallocentrism than the lesbian-feminist" (369). This is not to say that there are no works that draw on the Christian tradition. Christina Rossetti's *Goblin Market,* Radclyffe

Hall's *The Well of Loneliness,* Alice Walker's *The Color Purple,* Jeanette Winterson's *Oranges Are Not the Only Fruit,* poems such as "Immaculate, Inviolate: *Como Ella,*" "Holy Relics," and "My Black *Angelos*" in Gloria Anzaldúa's *Borderlands/La Frontera: The New Mestiza,* and titles such as "Passion Play" in *Coming to Power* (Samois), "Virgin's Request" in *The Second Coming: A Leatherdyke Reader* (Pat Califia and Robin Sweeney), and "Jesus Taught Me to Bottom" in *Some Women* (Laura Antoniou) are a few that come to mind. However, the postures that these texts adopt in relation to Christianity—from earnest affirmation or conversion to parodic recontextualization to playful, sacrilegious eroticism—are various enough and in some cases controversial enough to thwart, or at least to slow down, efforts to map the intertextual relations.

That Brossard's 1995 text associates its turn from classical to Christian subjects with the baroque is not surprising. There is an important precedent for such an association in art historical readings of the shift in the work of Michelangelo and other male painters in the second half of the sixteenth century, the earliest phase of the period that would come to be known as the Baroque. In an essay entitled "Homosexuality in the Renaissance: Behaviour, Identity, and Artistic Expression,"[12] James M. Saslow observes that "Succumbing to the ascetic Counter Reformation, each [painter] turned from the pagan subjects forbidden by the Council of Trent toward exclusively religious imagery" (102). He goes on to suggest that, "Although Judeo-Christian myth officially offered less material for homosexual identification, many artists' treatment of religious heroes suggests a veiled or half-conscious sensitivity toward male beauty and emotion" (102). *Baroque at Dawn* exploits this potential in Christian iconography for homoerotic—and specifically lesbian—readings. Working with language rather than with paint, and writing as a woman, a lesbian, and a feminist at the end of the twentieth century, Brossard has a relationship with such iconography different from that of the painters whom Saslow discusses. What they share, however, is the appropriation of seemingly "inappropriate" images to open representational spaces for sensibilities and sexualities that do not have the sanction of the Church.[13]

PASSION PLAYS

What is at stake for Brossard's text in staging an encounter between the classical and the Christian? Why is Cybil, a figure for the writer of *Baroque at Dawn,* involved with La Sixtine, a figure for Christianity? Why does this novel attend more to angels, martyrs, and *pietà* than to the classical figures that typically appear in Brossard's work?[14] One possible response is that *Baroque at Dawn* is (among other things) a meditation on women's relationship to suffering and, particularly, to images of suffering in Christianity that Cybil had known as a child in Montreal. A conversation between Cybil and "Nicole Brossard," who is described as "a novelist she [Cybil] had met in London at a conference on autobiography" (47), hints at this possibility. Asked by Cybil why she "so often gathered her characters around a restaurant table or desk," Brossard replies: "I don't know enough about suffering to know what's going on in people's hearts" (48). At another scene around a restaurant table, Cybil and Jasmine, another writer, worry "over the heavy cords of suffering around the world, a world tied up like Christo's packages" (60). The question of women's relationship to suffering is not a new one in Brossard's writing. In the 1983 essay **"Kind Skin My Mind,"** for example, Brossard writes that "The lesbian rejects *mortification* as a way of life. The lesbian suffers because of the mortification of women" (121). What is new in ***Baroque at Dawn*** is the engagement with Christian icons such as martyrs and *pietà*s. In this section, I suggest that Brossard's text reconfigures the *pietà* in ways that refuse the narrative of transcendence through sacrifice that subtends Christ's Passion. The latter passion, with its shades of martyrdom and suffering, is reread as ardent affection between women.

Throughout ***Baroque at Dawn,*** La Sixtine is associated with intense suffering as well as with intense pleasure. Her response to media coverage of a massacre in front of a cathedral in the former Yugoslavia, for example, is to adopt a "terribly awkward, limb-numbing *pietà* pose" (17), the posture of the one who bears the suffering of the world in her arms. Clinging "to a *passion* for life" (17; emphasis added), Cybil searches for a way of touching La Sixtine and of derailing the litany of atrocities that has overtaken her. The focus of the *pietà* in this scene is on death, a focus that leaves Cybil no point of intervention. Several chapters later, during a day spent with the writer Jasmine, Cybil visits a cemetery—one of many such visits in the text—and remarks on a monument depicting the Virgin and Christ. After dinner, as she drives back along the river St. Laurent to Rimouski, Cybil imagines La Sixtine coming and sitting on the end of the bed, "her back glistening with dancing drops of water" (60). She takes La Sixtine in her arms, and, "With a series of slow, deliberate movements, she [draws] La Sixtine's head against her breast so that their bodies [form] a huge *pietà* in the middle of the room" (60). Here the text reinterprets the *pietà* as an embrace. Insofar as La Sixtine (the Christ figure) is alive, this second *pietà* shifts the emphasis from Christ's Passion to the passion of two women. A simple identification of the two women with Christ or with the Virgin would potentially bind them to an all too familiar sainthood. An embrace, on the other hand, emphasizes relations of touch and contiguity and imagines roles other than those of the sorrowing and the sacrificed.

The two *pietà*s share a sculptural quality; they explore the relationship between the bodies of Cybil and La Sixtine, their postures, gestures, three dimensionality, and arrangement in space. In emphasizing the contrast between the "limb-numbing" posture of the first *pietà* and the movement of the second, the text effectively stages the transition from Renaissance to Baroque sculpture, from frozen image to unity in motion.

The cover image of the original French version of ***Baroque at Dawn***[15] also reinterprets the *pietà* as an embrace between two women, again in the context of a shift from Renaissance to Baroque aesthetic practice. The two faces that appear in the upper right corner of the text's cover are taken from a painting by Botticelli dated around 1490 entitled *Pietà* or, in English, *Lamentation over the Dead Christ with St. Jerome, St. Paul, and St. Peter*. They are the faces of Christ and an unknown woman who cradles his head (while his body lies across the knees of the Virgin in the centre of the painting). The cover image makes a number of important alterations to this detail from Botticelli's painting. In addition to inverting the faces, it crops them: that is, it cuts away the woman's halo along with the hand of the Virgin that hangs between the two faces, but it retains the luminous effect of the woman's veil and of Christ's shroud. In this way, the emphasis is on the two faces, their proximity to one another, and the rapturous elsewhere of their half-closed eyes and slightly parted lips. The cover image also alters the effects of lighting and colour. In the Botticelli painting, the lighting is general. According to convention, it falls slightly more intensely on the face and body of Christ and on the face of the Virgin. On the cover of ***Baroque at Dawn***, the two faces emerge from semidarkness by virtue of the fairly strong light that shines on them (and on the water) as if from a direct source. This effect of *tenebroso*, of situating bodies in shadow and using light to give them form, to give them a fleshy quality, is more typical of Baroque painting, particularly of the painting of Caravaggio, than of the Renaissance painting of Botticelli (Wittkower 54). Certainly, the frank eroticism and the bold use of few colours—in this case, ochre, olive green, and a deep, luminous blue—are reminiscent of Caravaggio. By way of these various alterations, the cover image of the original version of ***Baroque at Dawn*** opens the possibility of reading the two faces from Botticelli's *Pietà* as the faces of (female) lovers.

Facial expressions are not specifically an issue in ***Baroque at Dawn***'s presentation of the two *pietà*s involving La Sixtine and Cybil. However, the initial encounter between the two women prompts a reflection by Cybil about the ways in which "an orgasm will recompose the lines of the mouth and chin, make the eyelids droop, dilate the pupils or keep the eyes shining" (11-12), on the ways in which a face describes "its own aura of ecstasy, beginning with the light filtering through the enigmatic slit between the eyelids when they hover half-closed halfway between life and pleasure" (12). That these words could easily serve as a description of the face of Christ in the *pietà* on the book's cover further opens the possibility of reading the face on the cover as that of a woman transported, not by the elsewhere of suffering, indeed death, but by the elsewhere of pleasure. Importantly, whether they focus on faces (the text's cover) or on the postures of bodies (the text), the *pietà*s of ***Baroque at Dawn*** displace the role of suffering in Christian narratives by reconfiguring signs of suffering (or death) as signs of erotic intensity between women.

At the same time, Brossard's text grapples with the ambiguity that resides in such a reconfiguration or re-signification. What does it mean to read the faces or postures of suffering as those of pleasure? What are the ethical limits of such a reading? As Brossard points out in a 1990 essay, "There are themes that are bound to have if not an ideological at least a troubling effect: *Sexuality*, eroticism, homosexuality, lesbianism—something is always at stake with eroticism because it deals with limits, the moral, and the unavowable" (**"Poetic Politics"** 79). She goes on to explain that "A creative person has imagination and is able to process ambivalent emotion and contradictions as well as transforming anger, ecstasy, desire, pain, and so on, into social meaning" (81).

As if to test the point at which this process of transforming emotion and sensation into social meaning breaks down, ***Baroque at Dawn*** returns to the topic of a face reconfigured by a limit experience several pages after the initial encounter between Cybil and La Sixtine. As they walk in the streets of Los Angeles, the women hear shots in the distance. Pretending "that she [knows] violence and cruelty to be perennial" (30), La Sixtine mentions an old French writer (Georges Bataille) who appeared recently on television and "described the torture death of Leng-Tch'e" (30), which he had witnessed as a boy in the streets of Peking early in the century. Cybil says that she knows the pictures of this famous torture death, pictures "first published in 1923 in a psychological treatise [Georges Dumas], then again in 1961 by an author [Bataille] who gave them an erotic dimension" (30). Disturbed by the use of "ecstatic" and "erotic" (Bataille 237-39) "to portray the bewildered expression graven by extreme pain on the tortured man's face," Cybil quickens her pace and begins "muttering words whose sense escape[s] La Sixtine" (30). This breakdown in meaning, which takes the form of too many words rather than of silence, suggests that Cybil cannot make sense of torture; she has difficulty reading the elsewhere of a face marked by pain as the elsewhere of pleasure. Her mutterings are "interrupted by the cries of a woman standing in the middle of the street waving her arms and displaying her blood-stained bosom" (30), a sign that, in the terms of the text, there is a danger in confusing violence and suffering with the erotic. The immediate concern, this scene suggests, has to be the destructive effects of this confusion in the lives of women.

Both as a character and as a writer, Cybil is distressed by representations of violence and suffering; in effect, she "suffers because of the mortification of women" (Brossard, **"Kind Skin"** 121). In *Baroque at Dawn,* Cybil's response to Bataille's reading of the tortured face as erotic (30-31) is similar to her response to La Sixtine's "terribly awkward, limb-numbing *pietà* pose" (17). In both cases, Cybil is overwhelmed by a profusion of words and of "media-borne" images of death and violence (17). In both scenes, she asks herself questions about "the volcano of violence erupting in cities" (15) and about her reasons for writing "this violent book" for which she has "no special gift . . . or vocabulary or experience" (16). That Cybil repeatedly confronts scenes of violence suggests that the reference to "this violent book" is also a reference to *Baroque at Dawn.* Insofar as the book is of her own construction, a book that she is in the process of writing, she cannot distance herself from its scenes of violence and suffering; she has to acknowledge a certain complicity. Sitting with her coresearchers Irène and Occident on a terrace in Buenos Aires, Cybil suddenly hears a voice that speaks to her situation: *"You think keeping your distance will protect you from repeating yourself, help you understand the hidden side of your characters. Admit it you'd like to touch bottom without dirtying yourself too much"* (103).

In the sections that follow, I explore "the hidden side" of Cybil's character. In particular, I consider the role that she plays in fantasies that she might otherwise condemn and the pleasure that she takes in a vocabulary of violent or extreme sexuality that she might otherwise resist. This ambivalence within Cybil is symptomatic of tensions within Brossard's text—and within feminism—between fighting violence against women, fighting ritualized suffering, and exploring discourses and practices of sexuality that have the passion and intensity of the baroque.

### CYBIL'S BAROQUE HEART

An interest in Baroque religious art makes it difficult for Brossard's text to keep its hands clean. In addition to being susceptible to homoerotic rereading, such art frequently entails references to self-sacrifice and suffering. After all, martyrdom was to the Baroque what miracles were to the Renaissance (Hartt 688). Representations of martyrs and saints, designed to give individual viewers the illusion of a limit experience of the divine and thereby to heighten the emotional impact of religious art and Church architecture, played a key role in the Counter-Reformation project of intensifying individual conviction (688). Given that the same codes were used for sacred and secular works (Lucie-Smith 79), and given the preoccupation with representing the body in states of extremity, Baroque representations of martyrdom move ambiguously between the ecstatic and the erotic. As Saslow observes, "Sodoma's Saint Sebastian, bound to a tree and pierced with arrows, writhes in ostensibly religious ecstasy open to multiple personalized interpretations, from the epitome of sadomasochism to the artist's comment on his own public 'martyrdom'" ("Homosexuality" 102).

In *Baroque at Dawn,* the most vivid instance of homoerotic reframing of religious ecstasy is a fantasy that Cybil constructs while in conversation with *padré* Sinocchio aboard *The Symbol.* The priest is speaking to her about the role of the Jesuits in promoting Baroque art and architecture in Argentina and is trying to impress on her the fact that she "will never know boredom" if she heeds "her baroque heart" (151). Dissociating momentarily from the conversation, Cybil wonders at which moment a priest may be said to be Jesuitical (151). She imagines the priest tied to a tree in the forests of Quebec, tormented by mosquitoes and black flies. His skin, where it comes in contact with a necklace of burning stones, blisters, "ready to burst out like an identity" (151).[16] Fog envelops the martyr, and when he reappears it is "with wrists bound together and held over his head by an iron hoop" and his body "pierced everywhere" (151). In front of him stands a huge man, "partly clad in black leather" (151), who carefully calculates the pain needed to bring the man to orgasm. Chasing from her mind this image of man cultivating "his pain like an art" (151), Cybil returns to *padré* Sinocchio, a man depicted as "eagerly circling his god of deliverance with all imaginable baroque torments" (152). Yet, significantly, it is Cybil who has just finished conjuring up "all imaginable baroque torments"; it is *her* daydream or reverie.

The scene of Jesuit martyrdom from Cybil's reverie surfaces a second time in the context of a painting that Cybil dreams about seeing in Montreal's Mary Queen of the World Cathedral (172-73). The painting, *The Martyrdom of the Jesuit Fathers J. de Brébeuf and G. Lalemant in the Land of the Hurons 1649,*[17] allows *Baroque at Dawn* to comment on received modes of representing Jesuits martyred at the stake.[18] In her dream, Cybil takes the Jesuit in the foreground to be *padré* Sinocchio. She is particularly struck by the absence of signs of suffering or aggression in the painting: "Their faces show no trace of pain, hatred or cruelty. Sinocchio is intent, his gaze turned patiently toward Heaven. The Indians have the peaceful and peaceable look of people basking in the first days of spring" (173). The Jesuit, Brossard's text reminds us, bears witness to his faith in Christ by displaying forbearance in the face of extreme pain. The description of the Iroquois as "peaceful and peaceable" is more puzzling. The painting of Cybil's dream turns out to be one in a series of paintings by Georges Delfosse portraying Montreal's beginnings that Cybil has visited in the cathedral. Curiously, the Iroquois of the actual painting, with their burning pokers, pans of boiling water, and collars of red-hot axe heads, are far more aggressive than the dream suggests. In fact, Father Elie J. Auclair, in Delfosse's 1910 publication of photographs of the paintings, writes of the striking contrast between the serenity of the Jesuit and the "ferocious features of his executioners" (27). In playing down the agency and ferocity of the Iroquois, Brossard's text emphasizes two other forms of violence: first, the aestheticization of torture and suffering; and second, the construction of a founding myth of Montreal that simultaneously glorifies the trials of the Jesuits and rationalizes the spiritual conquest of the Iroquois.

Cybil's relationship to the scenes of martyrdom and sadomasochism in her dream and in her daydream is ambiguous. While Cybil takes a certain revenge upon the priest and critiques the Jesuits' cult of suffering, she is also fascinated by this cult of suffering. Toward the end of **Baroque at Dawn,** she explains: "I couldn't resist the urge I had to see the Delfosse paintings again. I don't know why these pictures have so long remained so deeply graven in my traveller's memory" (211). Her daydream, her dream, and her waking desire are interconnected yet somewhat contradictory manifestations of the same fantasy, something that I will return to after considering the ways in which the scenes of martyrdom and S/M are framed and the different ways in which they might be read.

Cybil's priest-turned-Jesuit-turned-leatherman is as open to, and as much a product of, multiple interpretations as Sodoma's Saint Sebastian (Saslow, "Homosexuality" 102). Reading the priest's passion for the baroque as Jesuitical, Cybil's daydream deidealizes the experience of the Jesuits, subjects the priest to torture, and details the effects of that torture in his body. Then, in yoking the Jesuit martyrdom to the leather scene, the fantasy sexualizes the passion of the priest/Jesuit. Once again, **Baroque at Dawn** plays with the slippage within the notion of passion between ardent affection or joyous enthusiasm and self-sacrifice or suffering. Passion, the text suggests, is a state of being subjected to or acted on by something outside oneself. The text's strategy of reading the Jesuit as a leatherman is not unlike that of reading the *pietà* as a lesbian embrace and not unlike reading the relationship between Michelangelo's sibyls and the Sistine Chapel as a liaison between women of different ages. In each case, the text reframes the Christian subject in homoerotic terms and demonstrates the incoherence of absolute categories such as the sacred and the profane.

Nevertheless, a reading that suggests radical continuities in the suspended subjectivities of martyr and masochist has a different status in Brossard's text from a reading that transforms a subject such as God's Creation or the Virgin lamenting the death of Christ into a liaison between women. A lesbian *pietà* for example, is easily integrated into lesbian feminist discourses of sexuality and, more particularly, into the network of positive associations that accrue to the arms of women in Brossard's texts (see Moyes, "Composing" 215-19). Whereas the women's embrace shifts the focus of the *pietà* from suffering and lamentation to bodies in pleasurable contact, the leathermen repeat the Jesuits' gesture of cultivating the art of pain; ecstasy, in the latter case, continues to be derived from and associated with suffering. Cybil's appropriation of the lesbian *pietà* and her rejection of the martyr-turned-leatherman says a great deal about what is safeguarded and held in high regard in lesbian feminist culture—what becomes "sacred"—and what offends.

Mary Daly's *Pure Lust: Elemental Feminist Philosophy* (1984), a text that reads scenes of Jesuit martyrdom in the context of an analysis of sadomasochistic elements in Western society, is an important intertext for **Baroque at Dawn.**[19] Daly's text finds in written descriptions of such scenes the same message that Brossard's text finds in the paintings: "The noble christians do not fight back" (38). From Daly's perspective, "Although these descriptions of the jesuit 'martyrs' do not explicitly name the *sexual* component of asceticism, they obviously reflect the male flight from lecherous obsessions. The fanaticism both of the missionaries and of the over-zealous author of these descriptions belongs to the province of sado-hagiology" (38). In a sense, in juxtaposing the martyrs and the leathermen, **Baroque at Dawn** makes explicit "the *sexual* component of asceticism" to which Daly alludes. Just as *Pure Lust* takes S/M "to be essentially a phallic phenomenon, inherently directed toward the destruction of the other" (60), Brossard's text limits its representation of S/M practice to men. Daly contends that, "when women, whether heterosexual or lesbian, . . . proclaim themselves pro-sadomasochism, pro-pornography . . . , they may be exercising 'free speech,' but they are speaking neither *as* feminists nor *for* feminists" (66).[20] Brossard's text is more playful than Daly's and allows for ambivalence where Daly's does not. However, the logic that subtends Daly's analysis of the "sadosociety" and the "sadospirituality" that legitimates it (35) also subtends Cybil's reverie. Read in the light of Daly's analysis, the representation of S/M practices in the reverie is more a mechanism for denouncing Christian ritual than for homoerotically reframing it.

The negative connotations of S/M in **Baroque at Dawn** are reinforced by parallels between the body style of the leathermen and that of the women and men whom

Cybil and La Sixtine happen upon in the streets of Los Angeles. Brossard's text associates the accoutrements of S/M—tattoos, body piercing, black leather, and shaved heads—with the grammatical tyranny of the masculine over the feminine:

> Another street. Here and there, women with tattooed biceps and men with bare chests and pierced nipples strolled about in black boots, heads shaven. Equipped with a new vocabulary, they were leaving walls alone in favour of more direct statements in their own flesh. The men carried fear and danger in their bodies, arming themselves only for sexual encounters when the electricity of a single shot would emerge from their bodies with much noise.
>
> (31)

Rather uncharacteristically, Brossard's text quickly loses sight of the women with tattooed biceps and refers to the group as men. This gesture of allowing the masculine to take precedence over the feminine—even more pronounced in French, in which "they" is gendered masculine[21]—is unexpected in light of Brossard's 1973 statement that "a grammar having as a rule: the masculine takes precedence over the feminine must be transgressed" (**"Vaseline"** 14). In allowing the rule to stand, Brossard's text associates the practice of marking signs in the flesh with an economy of representation that obscures women. That women might take sexual pleasure in such marking remains relatively unthinkable in the terms of the text. Furthermore, that feminist ends might be well served by queer culture, by a culture that exposes the incoherence of (and thereby destabilizes) categories such as "woman" and "man," is also relatively unimaginable.[22] Wedged between the conversation about the torture death of Leng-Tch'e (30) and a meditation on "Death" (31), the executioner, the passage cited above invites a comparison of the master of the S/M scene and the torturer/executioner. There are differences in the text's characterization of the two—notably, the difference between a man "wrapped in thought," "calculating" pain carefully in the direction of pleasure (151), and a man who "does not count the drops of blood on his free, lonely brow" but simply kills (31). Nevertheless, the spectre of torture that appears early in the text haunts the male-male S/M scene of Cybil's fantasy.

If, as Brossard's text suggests, sadomasochism is potentially dangerous within a feminist context, then what is it doing in Cybil's fantasy? The obvious answer is that the text uses the S/M fantasy to reinforce its feminist critique of religious asceticism and ritualized suffering. The less obvious answer is that S/M is as much a part of Cybil and her feminist critique as the scenes of martyrdom that she finds "deeply graven" in her memory (211). The S/M fantasy speaks of feminism's troubled yet necessary engagement with issues of sexuality, power, and violence. It speaks, for example, of an unconscious or repressed desire for mastery, a desire to make the priest suffer, which cannot be acknowledged or acted on but which can be translated into a scene of martyrdom, even a scene of S/M, and *watched*. The absence of a master or torturer in Cybil's dreams of Jesuit martyrdom, an absence made more noticeable by the presence of a master in the S/M scene (and in the actual painting by Delfosse), is a symptom of this repression and, at the same time, a reminder of Cybil's role in staging the martyrdom of *padré* Sinocchio.

In *The Language of Psycho-Analysis,* J. Laplanche and J. B. Pontalis define fantasy as an "imaginary scene in which the subject is a protagonist, representing the fulfilment of a wish (in the last analysis, an unconscious wish) in a manner that is distorted to a greater or lesser extent by defensive processes" (314). Cybil's fantasy plays itself out at various levels: Cybil sees the martyrdom of *padré* Sinocchio in a daydream and reframes it as masochistic, later she dreams the martyrdom of the *padré* represented in a painting, and even later she feels an inexplicable urge to see the painting that figured in her dream. Drawing on the work of Teresa de Lauretis on the forms and effects of fantasy, I would situate Cybil's urge, expressed in the first person, toward the conscious end of the "fantasy spectrum" and her daydream toward the unconscious end (143-48). The daydream, the form of the fantasy that in this instance requires the most analysis, is the focus of my reading.

In **Baroque at Dawn,** significantly, Cybil is not a protagonist in her daydream; she disavows the scenes of martyrdom and S/M as representations of herself. What is more, she does not appear to derive pleasure from the fantasy; immediately following her reverie, she joins Irène, Occident, and the divers, "relieved to have escaped Sinocchio's enthusiasm and particularly the *morbid* images it has raised" (152). Nevertheless, in imagining *padré* Sinocchio suffering in the forests of New France and in substituting his face for that of one of the Jesuits in the painting, Cybil plays the role of master in the scene of Jesuit martyrdom. In fact, her daydream is in keeping with the priest's own suggestion that she use "her baroque heart" to free herself from boredom—in this case, the boredom of the priest's own discourse. Although Cybil does not seem to derive pleasure from her reverie, there is a certain poetic justice and a certain satisfaction generated by it. Her desire to see the painting of Jesuit martyrdom over and over again suggests as much.

One might argue that the fantasy in question is not Cybil's but the priest's, that Cybil does little more than actualize the priest's fantasy of martyrdom and then expose its "*sexual* component" (Daly 38). However, this reading would deny Cybil's "baroque heart," a heart in evidence in discourses of sexuality elsewhere in the novel, and it would forget the continuities between her day dream, her dream, and her waking desires. Her fantasy cannot be reduced to a condemnation of the practices of martyrdom and S/M represented within it. The fantasy arguably plays out her (feminist) desires, albeit in oblique and distorted ways; in fact, the level of distortion or obliqueness is a measure of the danger that those desires pose for feminism. That the two scenarios present exclusively male protagonists and appear to fulfil the desires of men rather than those of Cybil is not simply a symptom of what Daly calls the "sadosociety." Feminist anxiety about women repeating patterns of desire that oppress women[23] makes it relatively unthinkable for women to be players in Cybil's S/M fantasy. As Julia Creet points out in an article on the ways in which feminism figures in the economy of lesbian S/M fantasy, this anxiety has structured feminism's internal struggles since the late 1970s:

> Charges on both sides of the "sex wars" are strikingly similar: both the charge of repression (by the "pro-sex" side) and the charge of replicating masculine desire (by the "anti-sex" side) carry with them the symbolic weight of the father. The ambivalence in assuming the power of either of these positions has to do with the monopoly that men have held over them. We are afraid of collapsing into the very system from which we struggle to liberate ourselves.
> 
> (138)

Creet goes on to observe that "a movement built on the repudiation of sexual objectification has had a very difficult time re-embracing sex and its inherent complexity without questioning the tenets of the movement itself" (139).

Transposed to Brossard's text, feminism's "anti-sex" and "pro-sex" arguments run as follows: to present women as participants in scenes of martyrdom or S/M is to replicate masculine desire; to deny women's participation in scenes of martyrdom or S/M is to repress aspects of their subjectivity and sexuality. Cybil's fantasy ostensibly makes the first (antisex) argument. Yet, read symptomatically, it also demonstrates the second (prosex) argument: that is, it betrays the workings of repression. The priest's asceticism, for example, can be read as a figure for the disciplining and regulating of sexual fantasies within the context of feminist antisex discourses. If the leather scene says something about the erotic intensity of the priest's regime of abstinence and self-discipline, it also says something about desires that are not allowed representation within certain discourses of feminism (see Creet 141-45). The desire for mastery mentioned earlier, the desire to make the priest suffer, is perhaps the safest and most representable of these desires because it can be understood as a form of feminist resistance.

Cybil's daydream, which positions Cybil as a voyeur at a male-male leather scene, not only transgresses the very stance against S/M (and pornography) that it sets up but also renegotiates the "turn" in the 1980s among some lesbians, notably among S/M dykes such as Pat Califia, "toward [gay] men as instructors and playmates in the world of sex practices" (Creet 148).[24] It is possible, indeed helpful, to read *Baroque at Dawn* as a meditation on the paradoxes of women's relationships to, and resignification of, the fantasies of gay men. Cybil's and La Sixtine's repeated encounters with eroticized rituals of violence and domination, for example, remind us that women's history of struggle against such rituals informs the lesbian feminist critique of S/M. Women's relationship to the queer culture that Cybil and La Sixtine happen upon in Los Angeles is equally specific. In tracing the ways in which women are effaced by masculine grammars, *Baroque at Dawn* expresses concern that queer culture will give way to a seemingly neutral and ultimately masculine construction of the subject. Yet, importantly, Brossard's text also recognizes that gay men have opened critical, representational, and erotic spaces for women. The liaison between Cybil and La Sixtine is an effect of such a space, a space imagined and designed by Michelangelo, a man whose principal sexual and emotional ties were with other men. Of course, Brossard's text reimagines the space between Cybil and La Sixtine in terms of a specifically lesbian sexuality and desire. For example, it appropriates details such as the muscular arms of the sibyls—which Saslow takes to be signs of Michelangelo's "obsession with the ideal nude male form" ("Veil" 78)—for its own inquiry into female figures of passion and cultural authority: "The urge to write comes on strong, as muscular as a seductive woman who wants to take her to bed" (143). Nevertheless, the erotics of incongruity that inspire the relationship between Cybil and La Sixtine also inspire that between Brossard's text and Michelangelo's frescoes.

### Veritable Torments of Pleasure

Why has S/M figured so centrally in lesbian feminist debates about sexuality since the 1970s? Discussing this question, Susan Ardill and Sue O'Sullivan speculate that, "in the vacuum of lesbians speaking and writing about sex, the language of sexual excitement used in, for example, *Coming to Power: Writings and Graphics on Lesbian SM,* resonates with a great many women who are not, technically speaking, into SM" (40). That a language of lesbian S/M might be used to explore and to convey sexual intensity is suggestive for my reading of Brossard's text. Although physical pain does not produce pleasure in the sexual encounters between women in *Baroque at Dawn,* pleasure is registered poetically on a number of occasions through metaphors of violence, suffering, and physical extremity: the novel opens with La Sixtine's injunction to Cybil to "devastate me, eat me up" (5); in a subsequent liaison, "bodies immolate, immobilize, are a hair's breadth from ecstasy"

(36); listening to La Sixtine's violin, Cybil weaves "veritable torments of pleasure" (37); the strident sounds make her think of "Luciano Fontana's paintings which, lacerated with a single stroke, open up, slash at the heart, and pose heartbreak as a fundamental question" (37); later in the narrative, Cybil imagines a woman's "[b]urning lips unbridled on her neck" (143). Through a brief consideration of the discourse of several of the scenes listed above, this final section returns to questions raised throughout the paper regarding the text's appropriation of (and resistance to) the baroque.

Much is made early in Brossard's text of the fact that the two women in the hotel room are strangers to each other, that they have exchanged only two or three sentences before having sex. Although this circumstance is framed in terms of Cybil's resistance to the biographical, it is significant as a departure from lesbian feminist discourses of sexuality of the late 1970s and 1980s. B. Ruby Rich observes that, within the latter discourses, "love replaces marriage as a prerequisite for sex" (529). In representing a sexual encounter between women outside—or on the edges of—an established relationship, the opening scene of *Baroque at Dawn* marks a departure from such discourses. What is more, the exchange between Cybil and La Sixtine about the former's "habit of 'taking the elevator' with perfect strangers" (18) makes an issue of promiscuity, another in a string of "unrespectable issues" that, according to Ardill and O'Sullivan, have led to coalition building among "sexual radicals" (40). Lesbian feminist subculture, they go on to argue, has tended to hang all of "these overlapping issues" from the peg of S/M (40).

The sexual encounter that opens *Baroque at Dawn* foregrounds—and confounds—postures of submission and domination in the relations between Cybil and La Sixtine. In that encounter, the command to "Devastate me, eat me up" (5), comes from the one who wants to lose herself in a limit experience with another. What Creet calls "the play of power between women" (139), or what Ardill and O'Sullivan call "the sexual dramatization . . . of power relations" (40), is even more ambivalent in the French text, in which Cybil hears La Sixtine's command to "Dévaste-moi, mange moi" as "Dé, vaste moi, m'ange moi" (13). This densely poetic enunciation, translated as "Day, vastate me, heat me up" (5), emphasizes the instability of relations of power and address within the scene. "Dé," seemingly addressed to Cybil by La Sixtine, is followed by a noun in apposition, "vaste moi," which is most easily read as a reference by La Sixtine to herself. Similarly, "m'ange moi" sounds like an imperative addressed to Cybil by La Sixtine but one with the marks of a reflexive verb—that is, something that one does to oneself. The sense of exquisite balance required to sustain the fever pitch of the opening scene is recaptured later in the description of a pair of dancers doing the tango:

> Staccato, saw-toothed beats and harmonics command each approach step and separation of the bodies, prolong the pact. Broken rhythm, broken pact. The woman turns about face, the slit of her dress opening from ankle to curve of thigh. The beauty of the coded, fetish movements where equilibrium is both unquestionably perfect and precarious.
>
> (114)

The tango, like the women's sex practice, is a performance subject to strict rules yet susceptible to endless resignification. Both scenes flirt with the contracted roles and ritualized violence of S/M. More specifically, the language of Brossard's text emphasizes movement or *play* among roles, positions, and modes of address. Power, the text implies, is carefully negotiated and always in flux; it is the angel ("l'ange") that Cybil hears in La Sixtine's command.

The second time the two women take the elevator together, Cybil watches while La Sixtine painstakingly applies makeup for her evening performance. Watching this ritual produces highly contradictory responses in Cybil: one minute she questions "the tools and strategies devised for facing up" and associates face painting, tattooing, and body piercing with "sensual overkill" (35); the next she takes pleasure in the spectacle and appropriates for a sexual encounter between women lips that glisten red "like a thousand scenarios in the story of women" (36). The reflections prompted by the spectacle of "facing up" help to explain Cybil's ambivalence toward images of torture and suffering in this scene as well as throughout the novel:

> Imagination used to give life another twist, implying that life had meaning. When the impression was of happiness, meaning froze. When suffering showed its face, meaning made a comeback, instigated prodigious faiths and terrible altercations in the world of the living. Each altercation generated new words and forced meaning the way you twist an arm.
>
> (35)

Cybil's reflections suggest that suffering, far more than happiness, stimulates the imagination and produces culture. In *Baroque at Dawn,* suffering helps to generate the vocabulary necessary to write "this violent book" (16) and to explore the intensity of the women's passion. At the same time, the meaning generated by suffering is coercive. Cybil finds herself in a baroque age of cultural transformation in which there are too many aesthetics, "too many feelings, too many bodies of knowledge. Too many signs" to analyse and interpret (145). In spite of this diversity, there is "too much of the same kind of life" (145). Cybil's principal avenue of resistance against this numbing repetition of the same in the guise of difference is to "Decode; evaluate life's chances in view of all the signs. In each sign calculate an added value that lets one dance amid the questions and justify happiness" (35). The text's reimagining of La Sixtine's initial *pietà* pose as an embrace between Cybil and La Sixtine is a vivid example of this work with signs. In fact, the *pietà*s of **Baroque at Dawn** invert the effects of suffering and happiness outlined in the citation above: pleasure produces a living sculpture, whereas suffering produces a frozen statue. Part of what fascinates and disturbs Cybil about the Delfosse painting (as she sees it in her dream) is the peaceful look on the faces in what is, fundamentally, a scene of torture. In the painting of Cybil's dream, "suffering show[s] its face," and "the impression [is] of happiness."

The scene in which Cybil watches La Sixtine put on makeup turns out to be an elaborate ritual of foreplay. Cybil's meditation on suffering leads to a sexual encounter: "Everything becomes hazy. The moves are different from the day before. Other words, other caresses. The room fills with a very virgin energy. The bodies immolate, immobilize, are a hair's breadth from ecstasy" (36). If, early in the scene, Cybil qualifies face painting as "sensual overkill," the scene's climax suggests that Cybil is not immune to the arm twist of spectacle. What is more, the discourse of her sexual pleasure is derived from a vocabulary of extremity shared with Christianity. Like representations of martyrdom in Baroque painting, and like Cybil's fantasy later in the novel, the excerpt above moves ambiguously between the sexual and the religious. In a discussion of feminism's relationship to fantasies of erotic domination, Jessica Benjamin associates continuities between sexual and religious eroticism with the "secularization of society" and the erosion of "previously existing forms of communal life that allowed for ritual transcendence" (296). In her view, "erotic masochism or submission expresses the same need for transcendence of self . . . formerly satisfied and expressed by religion" (296). Although there are hints of nostalgia in her discourse that have no currency in Brossard's text, Benjamin's insights help to explain why—from painters such as Sodoma to writers such as Brossard—discourses of religious ecstasy are so easily appropriated for discourses of sexual ecstasy (see also Bataille 239). Less clear, of course, is how to negotiate the tension between the narrative of transcendence through sacrifice implied by the words *immolate* and *ecstasy* and the resistance to such a narrative elsewhere in the text, particularly in the resignification of the *pietà*.

As I have suggested at several points in this paper, Cybil is not without her complicities and her contradictions. She is able to analyse the mechanisms by which suffering generates a spectacular array of signs with little possibility for meaningful intervention in culture. For example, when she hears a former member of the Hell's Angels telling other members of her Spanish class about several gang rapes that he had witnessed, she observes that "Any evildoer capable of telling his story with hand over heart indicating confidentiality can sidetrack the subject every time, opening the way for an emotional intimacy that leads one to 'understand' the worst crimes and taste the bite of senses sharpened by violence" (101). Yet Cybil herself is susceptible to a poetics of suffering and to "the bite of senses sharpened by violence." As she listens to La Sixtine's violin, for example, she wonders, "Who has made me this happy in a world of horrors?" (37). In the words of the narrator, "The word horror diverts Cybil's attention briefly but the present returns the stronger for it, brings her back to the raw pleasure of the sounds and heat of the bar" (37). The fact that "the present returns the stronger" for the use of the word *horror* implies that Cybil participates in a culture in which experience is intensified by suffering. In the sequence of texts that concludes the novel, she suggests as much as she reflects on her urge to see the Delfosse paintings: "It could be, after all, that we're able to reproduce a joie de vivre by introducing as decorative motifs our torments and the odd weak argument not too far off joy" (211).

Cybil's contradictions and complicities are crucial to an understanding of how Brossard's text appropriates and resists the baroque. Cybil is a reluctant participant in the construction of "this violent book," **Baroque at Dawn.** Her reluctance stems from a critical awareness of tendencies in a range of discourses—from Christianity to Western science—to aestheticize and eroticize pain. Cybil is also a passionate participant in the projects and relationships in which she engages with other women. Alive to the exuberance and embodied sexuality of the baroque, she nevertheless balks at its rampant spectacle of ritualized violence. For if the baroque is a theatre of sexual intensity, it is also a theatre of pain. The fashioning of the baroque body, especially the cutting and marking of flesh, sits uneasily with a lesbian feminist ethic that "rejects *mortification* as a way of life" (Brossard, **"Kind Skin"** 121) and with a lesbian feminist politics loath to risk the appearance of a passionate attachment to the terms of its own subjection (Butler 6). Yet in **Baroque at Dawn,** a text of unexpected and uneasy conjunctions, it is possible for a meditation on face painting, tattooing, and body piercing—what the text calls "sensual overkill"—to end in a crescendo of lesbian passion.

In resisting an electronic culture that pushes the production of signs to the point of "sensual overkill," of meaningless repetition that "transforms nothing" (Brossard, **"E Muet Mutant"** 47), **Baroque at Dawn** might be said to resist the baroque. However, Brossard's text also turns to the baroque, particularly the subjects of Baroque religious art, to explore new vocabularies and new discourses of lesbian sexuality. Baroque religious art furnishes subjects susceptible to appropriation and resignification (Michelangelo's sibyls, the *pietà*) and others more susceptible to resistance and critique (Jesuit martyrs). Significantly, in spite of these strategies of resignification and critique, the poetics of suffering and self-sacrifice that subtends images of *pietà* and martyrs has considerable currency in the text's representations of pleasure, whether sexual pleasure or the pleasure of listening to music or watching a tango. If feminism has a moralizing side, it also has a baroque side. In a sense, Brossard's **Baroque at Dawn** has it both ways; the text leaves the reader wondering where to draw the line between passion and pain, leatherman and torturer, exuberance and overkill, lesbian feminist resignification and age-old cliché. In the face of such ambivalence—ambivalence so key to the baroque—the reader has little choice but to follow Cybil's injunction to decode.

*Notes*

I would like to thank Nancy Roussy for assisting me in the process of researching this paper, translating citations, and thinking through the contradictions of Brossard's text. I am also grateful to Domenic Benventi for his research on the baroque, Robert K. Martin for his dialogue, and to Ian MacKenzie for his editorial suggestions. The research for this paper was enabled by grants from Fonds pour la formation de Chercheurs et d'Aide à la Recherche, Québec, and the Social Sciences and Humanities Research Council of Canada.

1. Throughout the essay, I cite the English translations of Brossard's texts where translations are available. All other translations are mine.

2. I use the term "baroque" to refer to practices and preoccupations that surface in twentieth-century contexts and reserve the term "Barque" for the art historical period from 1580 to 1750.

3. For further discussion of the ways in which the baroque has been appropriated by contemporary Canadian and Québécois women writers and artists, see Moyes, Introduction.

4. Gauvreau is associated with *les Automatistes,* the group of Québécois poets and painters of the late 1940s and 1950s whose nonfigurative use of words and paint paved the way for the experimental writing and counter-culture of Brossard and other young artists in the late 1960s and 1970s.

5. For André G. Bourassa, Gauvreau uses the term "baroque" in the sense of profusion, generosity, and absolute liberty (29). Michel Peterson's reading of *Beauté baroque* analyses the baroque as a site of the sublime, a site of the constitution of the self-contradictory subject (363). The term "baroque" does not entirely disappear in the 1970s and 1980s; it surfaces, for example, in the work of Bourassa and Marchand in the late 1970s and in that of Louise Dupré in the late 1980s. With the resurgence of interest in the baroque in the 1990s, the term is used more frequently. See, for example, Robert Richard's 1990 discussion of Hubert Aquin, Claudine Bertrand's 1993 discussion of new tendencies in Québécois writing, Pierre L'Hérault's 1994 discussion of Antonio D'Alfonso, and Peterson's 1994 discussion of Gauvreau.

6. Gauvreau's "beauté baroque" arises in Dupré's study in a reflection on indeterminacy in the writing of Brossard's contemporary, Madeleine Gagnon: "Is this indeterminacy not founded in the refusal of control which results in a warping of taste? As if the proper, classical 'style' . . . were endlessly overextended by exaggeration. As if the poetry showed too much: alternately too lyrical, too theoretical, too allegorical, too anecdotal, too painful, too fragmented. As if from this exacerbation comes a 'beauté baroque' to take up Claude Gauvreau's title" (224).

7. As B. Ruby Rich observes in her discussion of the evolution of feminist attitudes toward sexuality in the late 1970s and 1980s, "the defense of lesbian sadomasochism is linked to an attack on 1970s lesbian feminism and its assumed orthodoxy (nonexploitation, equal power relations, and so forth)" (532).

8. Significantly, the image that appears on the cover of the *Oxford Dictionary of the Bible* (Browning) that I consulted from time to time as I wrote this paper is that of Michelangelo's prophet Zechariah. At the present juncture, an image of one of Michelangelo's five sibyls on such a cover is unlikely—both because a sibyl is pagan and because she is a woman.

9. The *ignudi* are naked figures that hold up the series of medallions and tablets bearing the names of the prophets and sibyls. Because their function is primarily architectural, Michelangelo had a certain freedom in depicting them (O'Malley 100). Like the captives or slaves whom he carved around the same time, the *ignudi* prefigure the arrested motion, contorted shapes, and intense facial expressions of baroque sculpture and painting (Blunt 374; O'Malley 101).

10. In French, "Noé, l'arche, tout cela ne pouvait pas être le fruit de notre imagination" (141).

11. Allegory, a form associated with the baroque by Walter Benjamin (166) and Christine Buci-Glucksmann (68), allows for movement between historical moments but also between the mythic and the historical, the spiritual and the material, Michelangelo's frescoes and contemporary lesbian lovers.

12. In spite of the title's emphasis on the Renaissance, the first line of the abstract refers to the "Renaissance and Baroque periods" (90).

13. In his reading of Michel Marc Bouchard's play *Les Feluettes* (adapted in the film *Lilies* by John Greyson), Robert K. Martin comments helpfully on the tension between a church "founded on the hatred of the body and the repression of desire" and a church which "makes a place . . . for the homoerotic."

14. I do not want to give the impression that classical figures dominate Brossard's texts or that there are only two possible discourses, classical and Christian. In an effort to disrupt prevailing codes and symbols, Brossard's writing ranges widely—from literature to economics to physics to popular culture—and intercalates such discourses in unexpected ways.

15. In conversation at the 1997 Women and Texts conference in Leeds, England, Brossard explained to me that she had asked the artist in charge of designing the cover to collage a *pietà,* a bridge, and turbulent water; the specific choices and the intense light had been the artist's idea.

16. The accounts of the torture deaths of Jesuits such as Brébeuf and Lalement in the *Relations des Jésuites* give similar details.

17. Painted by Georges Delfosse (1869-1939) between 1908 and 1909, this painting is not of the Baroque period, but it does depict a seventeenth-century religious subject, the Jesuit martyrs of New France.

18. In his history of the Jesuits, Jean Lacouture finds in the work of nineteenth-century historian Jules Michelet a relevant critique of the art inspired by the Jesuits and their "spirit of death" (2: 102). Michelet writes of the irony of Jesuits whose desire to be represented as beautiful and appealing (rather than twisted or tortured) in their martyrdom ultimately translates into ridiculous images of eyes rolling skyward in contrived beatitude and smiles so forced that they verge on grimaces (2: 102).

19. Daly thanks Brossard in her acknowledgements for being an encouraging and faithful colleague. There are numerous parallels in the discourse of the two texts. For example, "Males have tried to rid themselves of their impurities by subliming themselves into 'God'" (Daly 73); "All this time, the sexes of men were being carved to point straight at the sky, imploring God to do the dirty work of cleansing women's sexes of all impurities so that sons could step over the present and ride off on the stars" (Brossard, *Baroque* 145).

20. Daly's is part of a wider feminist discourse that considers S/M to be "*intrinsically antagonistic to the goals of feminism*" (Wilton 53). One finds versions of the discourse against S/M, for example, in works by Sheila Jeffreys; Bev Jo, Linda Strega, and Ruston; Robin Linden et al.; and Irene Reti. Gayle S. Rubin, in her groundbreaking 1984 commentary on the struggle between Women against Pornography and lesbian sadomasochists, expresses the concern that antiporn rhetoric "criticizes non-routine acts of love rather than routine acts of oppression, exploitation, or violence" and "directs legitimate anger at women's lack of personal safety against innocent individuals, practices, and communities" (28). For further discussion of feminism's relationship to S/M, particularly lesbian S/M, see Ardill and O'Sullivan; Califia; Creet; Rich; and Wilton.

21. In French, "Armés d'un vocabulaire neuf, *ils* laissent les murs tranquilles, préférant dans leur chair des signifiants plus directs" (39; emphasis added).

22. For a helpful overview and excellent bibliography of the much debated relationships among queer theory, feminism, and lesbian and gay sexualities, see Wallace.

23. Judith Butler's response to "the insistence that a subject is passionately attached to his or her own subordination," one of the sources of this feminist anxiety, is that "the attachment to subjection is produced through the workings of power, and that part of the operation of power is made clear in this psychic effect, one of the most insidious of its productions" (6).

24. Rubin anticipates such a turn when she argues that feminism is not—and should not be—"the privileged site of a theory of sexuality" (32) and that lesbians might explore a theory of sexuality in conjunction with gay men and other sexual minorities as well as with feminists. In her terms, "lesbian feminist ideology has mostly analysed the oppression of lesbians in terms of the oppression of women. However, lesbians are also oppressed as queers and perverts, by the operation of sexual, not gender, stratification. Although it pains many lesbians to think about it, the fact is that lesbians have shared many of the sociological features and suffered from many of the same social penalties as have gay men, sadomasochists, transvestites, and prostitutes" (33).

## Works Cited

Allen, Jeffner. "Poetic Politics: How the Amazons Took the Acropolis." *Sexual Practice, Textual Theory: Lesbian Cultural Criticism.* Ed. Susan J. Wolfe and Julia Penelope. Cambridge, MA: Blackwell, 1993. 307-21.

Antoniou, Laura, ed. *Some Women*. New York: Masquerade, 1995.

Anzaldúa, Gloria. *Borderlands/La Frontera: The New Mestiza*. San Francisco: Aunt Lute, 1987.

Ardill, Susan, and Sue O'Sullivan. "Upsetting an Applecart: Difference, Desire, and Lesbian Sadomasochism." *Feminist Review* 23 (1986): 31-57.

Barnes, Djuna. *Nightwood*. 1936. New York: New Directions, 1961.

Bataille, Georges. *Les Larmes d'éros*. 1961. Paris: Pauvert, 1971.

Bayard, Caroline. *The New Poetics in Canada and Quebec: From Concretism to Post-Modernism*. Toronto: U of Toronto P, 1989.

Benjamin, Jessica. "Master and Slave: The Fantasy of Erotic Domination." *Powers of Desire*. Ed. Ann Snitow, Christine Stansell, and Sharon Thompson. New York: Monthly Review, 1983. 280-99.

Benjamin, Walter. *The Origin of German Tragic Drama*. Trans. John Osborne. 1963. London: Verso, 1985.

Benstock, Shari. "Expatriate Sapphic Modernism: Entering Literary History." *Lesbian Texts and Contexts: Radical Revisions*. Ed. Karla Jay and Jane Glasgow. New York: New York UP, 1990. 183-203.

Bertrand, Claudine. "Voix nouvelles de la littérature québécoise." *Écrits du Canada français* 79 (1993): 15-34.

Blunt, Anthony. *Art and Architecture in France 1500-1700*. 1953. New Haven: Yale UP, 1993.

Bourassa, André G. "Gauvreau et la critique baroque." *Voix et images* 3.1 (1977): 19-31.

Brossard, Nicole. *Baroque at Dawn*. Trans. Patricia Claxton. Toronto: McClelland, 1997. [Trans. of *Baroque d'aube*. Montréal: Hexagone, 1995.]

———. *Baroque d'aube*. Montréal: Hexagone, 1995.

———. "*E Muet Mutant*." Trans. M. L. Taylor. *Ellipse* 23-24 (1979): 44-63. [Trans. of "*E muet mutant*." *La Barre du jour* 50 (1975): 10-28.]

———. "Energy, Emotion, and Perspective: An Interview with Nicole Brossard." With Nathalie Cooke. *Arc* 32 (1994): 55-61.

———. "Entretien avec Nicole Brossard sur *Picture Theory*." With Louise Cotnoir et al. *La Nouvelle barre du jour* 118-19 (1982): 177-201.

———. "An Interview with Nicole Brossard." With Lynne Huffer. *Yale French Studies* 87 (1993): 115-21.

———. "Kind Skin My Mind." *The Aerial Letter*. Trans. Marlene Wildeman. Toronto: Women's, 1988. 121-23. [Trans. of "Kind Skin My Mind." *La Lettre aérienne*. Montréal: Remue-ménage, 1985. 107-09].

———. *Picture Theory*. Trans. Barbara Godard. Montréal: Guernica, 1991. [Trans. of *Picture Theory*. 1982. Montréal: Hexagone, 1989.]

———. "Poetic Politics." *The Politics of Poetic Form: Poetry and Public Policy*. Ed. Charles Bernstein. New York: Roof, 1990. 73-86.

———. "Vaseline." *La Barre du jour* 42 (1973): 11-17.

Browning, W. R. F. *Oxford Dictionary of the Bible*. New York: Oxford UP, 1997.

Buci-Glucksmann, Christine. *La Raison Baroque: de Baudelaire à Benjamin*. Paris: Galilée, 1984.

Butler, Judith. *The Psychic Life of Power: Theories in Subjection*. Stanford: Stanford UP, 1997.

Califia, Pat. "Feminism and Sadomasochism." *Public Sex: The Culture of Radical Sex*. San Francisco: Cleis, 1994. 165-74.

Califia, Pat, and Robin Sweeney, eds. *The Second Coming: A Leatherdyke Reader*. Los Angeles: Alyson, 1996.

Charron, François. "Nicole Brossard, écrivain classique." *La Nouvelle barre du jour* 118-19 (1982): 71-75.

Creet, Julia. "Daughter of the Movement: The Psychodynamics of Lesbian S/M Fantasy." *Differences* 3.2 (1991): 135-59.

Daly, Mary. *Pure Lust: Elemental Feminist Philosophy*. Boston: Beacon, 1984.

de Lauretis, Teresa. *The Practice of Love: Lesbian Sexuality and Perverse Desire*. Bloomington: Indiana UP, 1994.

Delfosse, Georges. *Le Canada héroïque: Tableaux de la Cathédrale de Montréal peints par Georges Delfosse, 1908-1909*. Montréal: Morrissette, 1910.

d'Ors, Eugenio. *Du baroque*. 1935. Paris: Gallimard, 1968.

Dumas, Georges. *Traité de psychologie*. 2 vols. Paris: Alcan, 1923-24.

Dupré, Louise. *Stratégies du vertige: Trois poètes: Nicole Brossard, Madeleine Gagnon, France Théoret*. Montréal: Remue-ménage, 1989.

Frontain, Raymond-Jean. "The Bible." Summers 92-100.

Gauvreau, Claude. *Beauté baroque*. 1952. *Oeuvres créatrices complètes*. Montréal: Parti pris, 1971. 379-500.

Griffin Crowder, Diane. "Amazons." Summers 24-25.

Guardiani, Francesco. "Notes: Baroque and Neobaroque: The Great Retrievals." *Forum Italicum* 30.1 (1996): 129-35.

Hall, Radclyffe. *The Well of Loneliness*. 1828. London: Virago, 1982.

Hartt, Frederick. "The Baroque." *Art: A History of Painting, Sculpture, Architecture*. New York: Abrams, 1989. 687-779.

Jeffreys, Sheila. "Sadomasochism: The Erotic Cult of Fascism." *The Lesbian Heresy*. London: Women's, 1994. 171-89.

Jésuites (lettres des missions). *Relations des Jésuites, contenant ce qui s'est passé de plus remarquable dans les missions des Pères de la Compagnie de Jésus dans la Nouvelle-France*. 1858. Montréal: du Jour, 1972.

Jo, Bev, Linda Strega, and Ruston. "S/M = Sadism and Masochism = Heterosexism." *Dykes-Loving-Dykes: Dyke Separatist Politics for Lesbians Only*. Oakland: Battleaxe, 1990. 190-206.

Lacouture, Jean. *Jésuites*. 2 vols. Paris: Seuil, 1991-92.

Laplanche, J., and J. B. Pontalis. *The Language of Psycho-Analysis*. 1973. London: Karnac, 1988.

L'Hérault, Pierre. "Figurations spatiales de l'altérité chez Antonio D'Alfonso, Gabrielle Roy, et Jacques Ferron." *Protée* 22.1 (1994): 45-52.

Linden, Robin, et al., eds. *Against Sadomasochism: A Radical Feminist Analysis*. San Francisco (East Palo Alto): Frog in the Well, 1982.

Lucie-Smith, Edward. *Sexuality in Western Art*. 1971. New York: Thames, 1991.

Marchand, Jacques. *Claude Gauvreau, poète et mythocrate*. Montréal: VLB, 1979.

Marcus, Jane. "Sapphistory: The Woolf and the Well." *Lesbian Texts and Contexts: Radical Revisions*. Ed. Karla Jay and Jane Glasgow. New York: New York UP, 1990.

Marks, Elaine. "Lesbian Intertextuality." *Homosexualities and French Literature: Cultural Contexts/Critical Texts*. Ed. George Stambolian and Elaine Marks. Ithaca: Cornell UP, 1979. 353-77.

Martin, Robert K. "Performing Nationality, Performing Gender: The Plays of Michel Marc Bouchard." Paper presented at the Third Solitude: Canadian Minority Writing Conference, Université de Montréal, 20 Mar. 1997.

McPherson, Karen S. "Archaeologies of an Uncertain Future in the Novels of Marie-Claire Blais." *Quebec Studies* 25 (1998): 80-96.

Meese, Elizabeth A. *(Sem) Erotics: Theorizing Lesbian: Writing*. New York: New York UP, 1992.

Moyes, Lianne. "Composing in the Scent of Wood and Roses: Nicole Brossard's Intertextual Encounters with Djuna Barnes and Gertrude Stein." *English Studies in Canada* 21.2 (1995): 206-25.

———. Introduction. *Tessera: Contemporary Feminist Baroque/Baroque féministe contemporain* 24 (1998): 8-23.

O'Malley, John. "The Theology behind Michelangelo's Ceiling." *The Sistine Chapel*. London: Harmony, 1986. 92-148.

Parker, Alice. *Liminal Visions of Nicole Brossard*. New York: Lang, 1998.

Peterson, Michel. "*Beauté baroque* de Claude Gauvreau: Les Apories de l'esthétique exploréenne." *Voix et images* 19.2 (1994): 363-73.

Reti, Irene, ed. *Unleashing Feminism: Critiquing Lesbian Sadomasochism in the Gay Nineties*. Santa Cruz: Herbooks, 1993.

Rich, B. Ruby. "Review Essay: Feminism and Sexuality in the 1980s." *Feminist Studies* 12.3 (1986): 525-61.

Richard, Robert. *Le Corps logique de la fiction: Le Code romanesque chez Hubert Aquin*. Montréal: Hexagone, 1990.

Rossetti, Christina. *Goblin Market*. 1862. *The Complete Poems of Christina Rossetti*. Ed. R. W. Crump. Vol. I. Baton Rouge: Louisiana State UP, 1979. 11-26.

Rubin, Gayle S. "Thinking Sex: Notes for a Radical Theory of the Politics of Sexuality." *The Lesbian and Gay Studies Reader*. Ed. Henry Abelove, Michele Aina Barale, and David M. Halperin. New York: Routledge, 1993. 3-44.

Samois, ed. *Coming to Power: Writings and Graphics on Lesbian S/M*. 3rd ed. 1981. Boston: Alyson, 1987.

Saslow, James M. "Homosexuality in the Renaissance: Behavior, Identity, and Artistic Expression." *Hidden from History: Reclaiming the Gay and Lesbian Past*. Ed. Martin Duberman, Martha Vicinus, and George Chauncey. 1989. New York: Meridian, 1990. 90-105.

———. "'A Veil of Ice between My Heart and the Fire': Michelangelo's Sexual Identity and Early Modern Constructs of Homosexuality." *Genders* 2 (1988): 77-90.

Summers, Claude J., ed. *The Gay and Lesbian Literary Heritage*. New York: Holt, 1995.

Walker, Alice. *The Color Purple*. New York: Washington Square, 1982.

Wallace, Robert. "Signifying 'Lesbian'/Strategizing Error." *Resources for Feminist Research/ Documentation sur la recherche féministe* 25.3-4 (1997): 82-91.

Wilton, Tasmin. "Do You Always Love the One You Hurt? Lesbian Sado masochism." *Finger-Licking Good: The Ins and Outs of Lesbian Sex*. New York: Cassell, 1996. 41-77.

Winterson, Jeanette. *Oranges Are Not the Only Fruit.* 1985. London: Vintage, 1991.

Wittkower, Rudolf. *Art and Architecture in Italy 1600-1750.* 1958. New Haven: Yale UP, 1982.

## Susan Knutson (essay date 2000)

SOURCE: Knutson, Susan. "Text: *In Which* the Reader Sees a Hologram in Her Mind's Eye." In *Narrative in the Feminine: Daphne Marlatt and Nicole Brossard*, pp. 155-68. Waterloo, Ont.: Wilfrid Laurier University Press, 2000.

[*In the following essay, Knutson studies Brossard's feminist vision of woman as it is symbolized by a three-dimensional, holographic image in her novel* Picture Theory.]

> La langue est ce qui nous permet d'acheminer l'image mentale vers la pensée.
>
> —Nicole Brossard, *Accès à l'écriture*

The first edition of ***Picture Theory*** (1982) has a design on the bottom right-hand corner of page 97, showing the corner of the page lifting to reveal a three-dimensional city, its highrises modelled in shimmering white outline against a dark grid. "Enter this book/city," suggests the picture, "and enter a virtual and three-dimensional world." The image corresponds to a densely written passage describing the vacationers' last night on the island, during which they negotiate the ninth and richest turn of the spiral: "une nuit parfaite"[1] (112):

> À l'autre bout de la nuit, j'allais ouvrir une bouteillle. Les cités convergeaient dans nos verres. Des femmes émergeaient de partout, l'architecture; la somme des lois tournait dans leurs yeux, la vélocité de leur vie, les formes qu'elles s'apprêtaient à prendre: chiffres, herbes, livres, lettres, spirale, première neige.[2]
>
> (112-13)

The scene contrasts two Brossardian conceptions of the modern city, two urban realities which co-exist. The first, defined in a 1981 text entitled **"Pré(e),"** is the "la ville . . . patriarcale jusqu'aux dents"[3] (5). The second is the urban environment in which radical lesbian women come together. "[L]es cités convergeaient une à une, convoquées par la fulgurante intuition que nous avions traversant l'histoire de l'art, sagittaires aériennes en voie de transformations"[4] (***PT*** [***Picture Theory***] 113). Gazing into their glasses as if they were crystal balls, the five travellers witness Universal Man in the form of straight red arrows which inundate the patriarchal city, wounding women in their bodies and in their vision:

> chaque ville était un document qui abondait en flèches . . . l'homme-flèche. . . . Les villes, l'orbe lunaire, black out, il nous fallait apprivoiser l'énergie pour éviter que s'installe dans nos membres et surtout dans nos regards, une mortelle immobilité pouvant faire croire à un renoncement.[5]
>
> (113)

Still in the virtual world of their glasses, the horizon is opened by a flash of lightning, and the women walk calmly, in spite of the arrows in their souls, into the virtual city of their feminist desire:

> Dans nos verres, un coup d'éclat ouvrant l'horizon sous nos yeux, à même mos corps en état de pensée, dans une position de tir, anticipation mentale, la flèche dans l'eau de l'âme, nous avancions calmement dans les rues désertes.[6]
>
> (113)

The flash of lightning that opens the horizon links this spatial traversal to the night voyage across the continent to the island, identifying it with the primary event. Louise Forsyth argues that the city, like the human being, is a transformative *topos* of concentrated energy: "la rencontre des femmes fait lever la page sur la cité des femmes"[7] (*Préface* [Louise Forsyth's "Préface" to *Picture Theory*] 23. See also "Deconstructing Formal Space" ["Deconstructing Formal Space/Accelerating Motion in the Work of Nicole Brossard"] 337). The city of women is the virtual site of freedom *to be* for the "[t]raversières, urbaines radicales, lesbiennes"[8] (105) of ***Picture Theory.*** The women walk into the city on page 97, which rises like a hologram above the streets of New York, Montréal, Buenos Aires, Cairo or Paris—its hieratic metonymy evoking the textual three-dimensionality of Brossard's vision.

Three-dimensionality is an important figure in Brossard's work of this period, and not only in association with the virtual three-dimensionality of the hologram. Everyday, ordinary reality also has three dimensions, and Brossard celebrates every woman's effort to live fully, at any given moment, in all three of them. She writes in the dedication to ***La lettre aérienne*** of her desire to understand patriarchal reality and its functions, "non pas pour elle-même mais pour ses conséquences tragiques dans la vie des femmes, dan la vie de l'esprit"[9] (9). In relating this dedication to the figure of three-dimensionality, we remember the patriarchal limitation of women's physical freedom, not only by extreme practices such as foot-binding and purdah, but wherever the ability of girls and women to exercise freely in three dimensions is constrained by regulations of propriety, safety and morality. In ***Picture Theory,*** the character of Judith Pamela accepts patriarchal law, unlike the five protagonists who practise extending women's horizons. Brossard writes,

> Il y a dans ***La Lettre aérienne*** dix ans de combat contre ce qui fait écran à l'énergie, à l'identité et à la créativité des femmmes. Dix ans de courbes, de graffiti, de

ratures et d'écriture afin d'exorciser "le mauvais sort."
Il a fallu me "colleter aux mots" pour que naissent de
la bagarre bigarrée des émotions, le flamboiement des
spirales et les femmes tridimensionelles qui alimentent
mon désire et mon espoir.[10]

(9)

These three-dimensional women who nourish desire and hope are related not only to the characters in *Picture Theory* but also to actual women fighting for women's rights and freedoms around the world. To such women, Brossard offers a mirror which, while it is as provisional as any other representation, is relatively accurate and a welcome relief from the unrelentingly negative portrayals of feminists in mainstream culture. In fact, *Picture Theory* is full of rather ordinary mirrors which reflect what is: as Brossard puts it, "si le patriarcat est parvenu à ne pas faire exister ce qui existe, il nous sera sans doute possible de faire exister ce qui existe"[11] (*RI* ["**De radical à intágrales**"] 87).

The figures of the mirror and of three-dimensionality are related to those of the hologram and the three-dimensional text. Narratology describes as three-dimensional any narrative text that includes discourse, or citation, because it implies multiple narrative levels or textual depth. The feminist reader of *Picture Theory* will see herself repeatedly in the mirror texts of the "discours autour de la table quotidienne"[12] (95). But *Picture Theory* extends narrative three-dimensionality by signifying holography in all three registers of fabula, story and text. Perspective becomes a function of reading and writing, while mirrors and embedded mirror texts play a key role as part of the holographic mechanism.

Mirror texts share important elements with the primary fabula, signifying the fabula to the reader as to the characters (*N* [*Narratology*] 146). An important contrasting mirror text is the fragment of Richard Wagner's *Die Walküre,* which serves also as a footnote to Oriana's operatic career. Wagner articulates clearly the principles of European patriarchy: the daughter is subject to patriarchal authority on the four levels of her body, her family, her state and her religion: she is dominated by her husband, father, king and god. Because she has rebelled, she is isolated from any community, even the natural one of her siblings:

*Wotan*

Did you not hear what I ordained?
J'ai exclu de votre troupe la soeur infidèle;
à cheval avec vous elle ne traversera plus les airs;
la fleur virginale se fanera,
un époux gagnera ses faveurs de femme;
désormais elle obéira à son seigneur et maître,
et, assise devant son foyer filant la quenouille,
elle sera la cible et l'objet de toutes les moqueries.

Si son sort vous effraie, alors fuyez celle qui est perdue!
Ecartez-vous d'elle et restez loin d'elle.
Celle d'entre vous qui oserait demeurer auprès d'elle
celle qui me braverait, prendrait le parti de la misérable,
cette insensée partagerait son sort: cette téméraire doit le savoir![13]

(54)

The narratological requirement that a mirror text share a common element with the main fabula is fulfilled by the rebellious figures of the outcast sister and the other, bold woman who stays close to her. Wotan's ordained punishment of isolation images in reverse the feminist community of *Picture Theory.*

The talk around the daily table is the central mirror text and sign of the novel, as Claire Dérive herself points out early in "L'émotion": "Nous étions assises autour de la table et Claire Dérive disait que de nous voir ensemble et ici retrouvées au bord de la mer, c'est un signe"[14] (96-97). The women seated together in the house by the sea are a sign of the book and a sign of social change, signifying that the break from patriarchal meaning has been effected, and the second stage, the creation of the imaginary territory or "vacance" to be filled with women's energies, is in progress. The embedded conversations impact causally on the main fabula, producing the energy essential to the primary event. The narrative technique of free indirect discourse blurs hierarchical embedding and underlines the importance of feminist discourse as the irreplaceable model and strategic occasion for the collective feminist practice of semantic divergence in the spiral of political and personal change.

The overarching topic of conversation is, of course, women's trajectory out of patriarchy, making the embedded conversations argumentative and mirroring the intentions of the book as a whole. The conversations move rapidly over a range of theoretical issues associated with the radical feminism of the 1980s, including the concept of matriarchy, the nature of patriarchy and the role of the patriarchal mother, and the resocialization of women's sexual desires. Claire is thinking about a key condition for the creation of the hologram:

Bien qu'elle affirmait que le mot abstraction se glisse quelque part dans sa pensée, elle admettait pour le moment qu'il lui était difficile d'établir un lien direct entre le fait d'être cinq femmes dans une île et la notion même de ce que peut être une abstraction.[15]

(97)

Her intuition of an abstraction refers to "l'abstraction vitale" (88) of May 16, which, I have argued, corresponds to Brossard's concept of turning away from negative memory in order to build on what is ecstacy, and new. It also recalls the abstraction through which women, as subjects of language, "lay claim to universality," as Wittig argues in "The Mark of Gender" (6). Claire develops her ideas further, relating *being* to *utopia*:

> à la source de chaque émotion, il y a une abstraction dont l'effet est l'émotion mais dont les conséquences dérivent la fixité du regard et des idées. Chaque abstraction est une forme potentielle dans l'espace mental. Et quand l'abstraction prend forme, elle s'inscrit radicalement comme énigme et affirmation. Avoir recours à l'abstraction est une nécessité pour celle qui fait le projet, tentée par l'existence, de traverser les anecdotes quotidiennes et les mémoires d'utopie qu'elle rencontre à chaque usage de la parole.[16]
>
> (105)

The "je suis" of "La perspective" (76) and "des phrases complètes et abstraites liant la vie et la parole"[17] (96) are also Brossardian responses to this key issue of language and the access to undivided subjectivity.

While Claire's friends don't respond theoretically to her point, they respond in practice, each woman offering her own being, preoccupations and thought:

> Oriana se mit alors à parler du temps tout en cherchant ses mots en français pour dire comment elle l'imaginait. Elle dit ne pas comprendre pourquoi, chaque fois que des femmes sont réunies, dans les films par exemple, le temps semble s'arrêter autour d'elles après les avoir figées ou changées en statues de sel chargées de symboles. Oriana, après que Danièle Judith l'eût interrompue pour dire matriarcat, continuait sa description du temps.[18]
>
> (97)

In speaking of the deathly effect of the patriarchal gaze on the bodies of women, Oriana refers to the myths of Lot's wife and Eurydice, each woman paralyzed by her husband's gaze. These classical myths, rewritten by Brossard as well as by Marlatt and Wittig, are central to lesbian rewriting of patriarchal mythology. The lesbian is able to lead her lover out of hell—unlike the male lover who betrays her and incorporates her death into a religious symbology. In *Picture Theory,* the taste of salt is a motif associated with the memory of ancient betrayal. Danièle interrupts Oriana with the talisman of matriarchy to charm away damage to the body and imagination. Later, however, she corrects herself, disassociating the concept of matriarchy from that of utopia: "Danièle Judith disait que le matriarcat est un mot d'anthropologie et qu'il ne peut pas être utilisé d'une manière contemporaine pour exorciser le patriarcat. Ce mot ne pouvait non plus servir à élaborer quelque utopie qui aurait rendu les femmes à leur genre"[19] (101). The developing political critique of lesbian utopianism, discussed in chapter 1, lies behind Danièle's qualifications of the word "matriarcat" as well as Michèle's and Claire's programmatic interventions with respect to ecstasy: "Je voulais dire que l'extase est une réalité en soi qui rend le temps éternel. Claire Dérive affirmait qu'il ne fallait pas confondre la nuit des temps, le temps patriarcal et l'extase"[20] (97).

In *Picture Theory,* ecstasy is related to utopia, and both are feminist issues. As Brossard explains, *La lettre aérienne* addresses a feminist question to the heart of "des séquences utopiques qui traversent nos pensées, nos paroles et nos gestes"[21] (9-10). The timelessness of ecstasy, Claire specifies, has nothing in common with the timelessness of women's non-being in patriarchal systems, as patriarchal darkness has nothing in common with night. To imagine otherwise is to identify pleasure with a masochistic annihilation: "de cette confusion naissaient des femmes suspendues et immobiles dans l'espace"[22] (97). Ecstasy is part of the utopian program because it is forward looking; it can provide a match for our glimpses of what is not, but what could be. Even Oriana's search for words corresponds to the creation of a screen sufficiently imbued with ecstatic elements that it will be able to interact eventually with the utopian screen. At issue is a quality of emotion:

> Nous étions assises autour de la table. . . . Je disais, avec dans la bouche un goût de sel, à propos de l'utopie en commençant par le mot femme que l'utopie n'allait pas assurer notre insertion dans la réalité mais qu'un témoignage utopique de notre part pouvait stimuler en nous une qualité d'émotion propice à notre insertion dans l'histoire. Avant que Claire Dérive parle d'abstraction, j'ajoutais que nous devions socialiser nos énergies de manière à n'en être point victimes ou encore pour éviter que nos ventres seuls soient méritoires comme une virilité mentale pouvant servir par la suite à meurtrir les corps pensants.[23]
>
> (101-102)

Michèle argues that women's energies must be resocialized in order for them to cease to live as victims—a radical argument made convincingly by Monique Wittig in "La pensée straight." Michèle might have added that such resocialization, if it is possible at all, could never take place in isolation but would require the complicity of others doing the same. Michèle's words metonymically interpellate the reorganized subjectivity of which she dreams. In order to effect the transformation of individual utopian experience into a new symbolic and historical organization of gender, women must generate a new libidinal economy. The ideal point of departure for such an enterprise is exactly where these characters are, around the table sharing language and energy. The repetition of the phrase "nous étions assises autour de la table"[24] (96, 101, 105, 107, 109), with its feminine "assises," underlines the round-table discussions as a motif in the novel, and a mirror for the readers who find themselves participating in a virtual reality there.

The circle around the table is also a healing circle, for the long-term destructive effects of the formation of female identity in the patriarchal family is also a feminist issue, as the characters' tearful memories of childhood make clear. Women are paralyzed in "le temps patriarchal," betrayed in many ways, as Mary Daly elaborates in chapter 4 of *Gyn/Ecology,* often by their own mothers who initiate them into patriarchal law. In the morning light of **Picture Theory,** Claire Dérive denounces the patriarchal mother:

> Le temps patriarcal ne s'est-il pas arrêté autour d'elles pour les confondre morbidement à la folie, à la mort et à la soumission. La mère est partout quand le temps s'arrête, la mère est pleine de secrets qui angoissent les filles laissées à elles-mêmes dans les ruines patriarcales: autos, pneus, ascenseurs, métros, verres brisés. L'âme en ruine, l'esprit de l'homme ne peut plus *se concevoir* autrement qu'en projetant la perte de sa déité dans les corps abstraits de quelques femmes isolément réunies, l'âme en ruines. Il y a là un manque à imaginer qui bien que n'étant pas nôtre, nous accable dans l'exercice même de nos fonctions mentales.[25]
>
> (97-98)

But the narrator testifies to the changing times: "Pour la première fois, comme ce matin devant la mer, je n'ai pas peur d'entendre les mots d'une autre femme"[26] (98). After ***L'amèr,*** in the transformative world of **Picture Theory,** Michèle can listen without fear to the words of another woman because, in this world, women no longer have anything to gain by initiating other women into patriarchal law.

In "L'émotion," the characters reach for words adequate to a shared experience of utopia/ecstasy freed from the patriarchy, and they depend on each other for a linguistic community that understands words the way they do. In Brossard's thought, the women are speaking with the same accent, having undergone a parallel process of semantic deviation so that, by the time they reach the spiralling world of **Picture Theory,** they are practised at articulating reality from multiple perspectives. "La perspective," which follows "L'ordinaire" but precedes the virtual production of "L'émotion," prepares the reader to participate in "L'émotion" by developing the double perspective first suggested in the fragmentary *scènes blanches.*

"La perspective" presents two scenes: the scene of the book, which reads Djuna Barnes's *Nightwood* as mirror text/intertext, and the love scene, which carries forward the abstraction and which reveals the narrator to herself. Claire's arrival, announced with great anticipation at the close of "L'ordinaire," is the beam of coherent light that transforms the holographic plate, the incoherent record of the first exposure, into the virtual three-dimensionality of the holographic image. The love scene between the narrator and Claire Derive puts "L'ordinaire" into a new perspective.

Perspective is traditionally thought to formalize a relationship between a work of art and an observer. The mathematical principles of one-point or central perspective, known to the architects of classical Greece but lost during the Middle Ages, were rediscovered by Renaissance architect Filippo Brunelleschi, and Leon Battista Alberti theorized and applied Brunelleschi's discovery of the vanishing point in his thesis *Della pittura* (1436). According to his "picture theory," all parts of a painting were to be constructed in rational relationship to each other and to the observer. The ideal observer's height and distance from the painting are established by the artist during the perspective construction, thus placing the viewer in a fixed position. This traditional one-point perspective is made obsolete by the three-dimensionality of the hologram, which permits a multiplicity of points of view.

**Picture Theory** interpellates a viewer/reader who develops new perspectives while engaged in the ongoing activity of reading. Whereas traditional perspective effectively transforms three-dimensional objects and spatial relationships in order to represent them on a two-dimensional plane or in flat relief, in **Picture Theory,** the printed page, imagined as a shallow relief of paper and ink, functions as a relay-transistor or screen for the reconstitution of a utopian and three-dimensional image. Brossard creates a place for the reader in the textual perspective, but it is no longer necessary for this place to be fixed because a hologram, like a "real" object, can be regarded from any situation without distortion of its vital characteristics.

The difficulties encountered in reading **Picture Theory** are guides for the developing perspectives of the reader. The hologram is to appear in the mind's eye of the reader, not as an image of woman, for images of women are everywhere and entirely co-opted, nor as a hologram of a woman, for such holograms already exist, and have changed nothing. The hologram is to appear like a wave of emotion evoked by the memory of utopia; it is to appear as interacting wave formations in the cervical cortex, resulting in a three-dimensional consciousness/memory/picture of "la femme intégrale": a generically female human being, with all ensuring consequences. In order to produce this desired effect, **Picture Theory** assembles the necessary elements: Claire Dérive, the love scene, the narrator who reconstitutes nothing, the mirror and the beam of coherent light which is split into two. The love scene will be holographed, and at the right moment, the hologram will be activated by the reader.

The split beam of light, necessary for three-dimensional perspective, is figured in a variety of ways. In *la scène blanche* and "La perspective" the text is diffracted into the parallel scenes of the carpet or love scene, the holographed scene (43) and the book (43). Concurrently, a double perspective on time is elaborated through alternate use of the present tense with the imperfect or the passé composé (65), and through the correlation between *changing consciousness* and *crossing the threshold*. The motifs of the "hall d'entrée" and the room filled with light, familiar from *la scène blanche*, guide the reader through the transformations of "La perspective." The split scene corresponds to the split beam of light; the passages in the present tense correspond to the reference beam and the passages in the past tense have been reflected off the love scene and carry that information forward to the future. Claire's cheek, offered to her lover, is a "mise en abyme" (65), but, as the section continues, the perspective appears more and more to be based on a vanishing point of light (88). The rose of light which Dante saw in paradise appears in aerial perspective: "posture aérienne / l'apparence d'une rose double dans la clarté"[27] (69). Claire enters "le hall d'entrée," and then the forest, and the images turn to Dante, Wittig and the Joycean event of the book.

Parallel linguistic strategies model wave-front interaction throughout *Picture Theory*. Just before the achievement of the hologram, "Screen Skin Utopia" evokes the polysemy of words in the first-person, present tense: "La langue est fiévreuse comme un recours polysémique. Le point de non-retour de toute affirmation amoureuse est atteint. Je suis là où commence 'l'apparence magique,' la cohérence de mondes, trouée par d'invisibles spirales qui l'activent"[28] (188). The second paragraph, written in the pluperfect and imparfait tenses and in the third person, looks at the scene from a position in the future: "M. V. s'était redressée, avait lentement tourné la tête le regard pris entre le rebord de la fenêtre et l'horizon. Le poème hurlait opening the mind"[29] (188). As the mind opens, Michèle's gaze traverses the boundary of the window to reach that of the horizon. The temporal gymnastics implicate the deixis inherent in verb tenses, analyzed by Benveniste as one of the primary means through which subjectivity is created in language. . . . *Picture Theory* uses every tense in the French language to invoke every conceivable relationship a subject may have to time.

In addition, the text moves between English, French, Italian and sometimes Spanish. This is characteristic of Brossard's work, as testified by her long interest in linguistic plurality and translation, her fascination with what can be richly present in one language, yet absent from another. Translation, like thought, is understood to be "a complex act of passage which inflame[s] the mind" (**"Nicole Brossard"** 53). Because translation is always the site of an encounter between language, thought and meaning, it suggests the transcendent figure of the white centre, that sudden illumination of the mind which transforms consciousness.

Since the characters of *Picture Theory* are Québecoise, American and Italian-American, the encounter of languages in *Picture Theory* is realistically motivated; Claire, for example, speaks English as her mother tongue. But Brossard's "literary bilingual consciousness" is creative because, as Bakhtin suggests, in the encounter of languages, "two myths perish simultaneously: the myth of a language that presumes to be the only language, and the myth of a language that presumes to be completely unified" (62, 68). In *Picture Theory*, the confusion of tongues is related to the creation of new discourse based not on the single origin of patriarchal law but on a double origin and all that it might represent for the development of a non-binary symbolic:

> Claire revenait avec le vin, hors d'elle, parlait bitch, dyke, sentait l'américaine à plein nez, ultra modern style new-yorkais. Stop it, Michèle, watch it, disait Florence très énervée pendant que je savais vouloir réaliser la fameuse synthèse de l'eau et de feu qui brûle la langue. I know, ça me trahit cette synthèse de la double origine, I kn*e*w, I kn*o*w.[30]
>
> (112)

"I kn*e*w, I kn*o*w" enacts the strategies of parallel verb tenses and the use of English, while naming the new perspective. "Cette synthèse de la double origine" is opposed to the single logos of phallogocentric vision. The creative chaos of circulating language elements is underlined by Oriana's speech, which slips from French to English to Italian to German: "Elle était tout genre à la fois d'une langue à l'autre"[31] (111). Oriana, who of the five women is the character most marked by patriarchy, is helped in her progress towards a generically feminine mind by her polyglot origins.

*Picture Theory* ends on page 188 where it begins again in a new book, *Hologramme,* another figure of translation and another mirror text, a sign of utopia which re-enacts *Picture Theory* on the level of the hologram. The translation and re-enactment of a text within a text is a technique that Brossard has explored in ***French Kiss*** (1974), ***Le Désert mauve*** (1987) and ***Aviva*** (1985), exploiting, as she has explained, the "abundant use of synonyms, homonyms . . . rhymes and rhythm" (**"Nicole Brossard"** 54). Activating musically symbolic associations between words and things, Brossard creates an intertextual magnetism within her texts and from one text to the next. Certain words tend to evoke others as they do in translation or in any act of interpretation. Reading Brossard reading Brossard makes virtual both the musicality of her language and the flexibility of the intertextual alliances (*les connivences*) between the dominant figures in her work, including a radical reading of reading. Brossard has qualified the enthusiastic claims made for "écriture feminine" by specifying that writing which is "traversé," or "crossed," by feminist consciousness simply permits "another *reading* of reality and self" (personal interview with Nicole Brossard, June 8, 1988). Feminist desire to "metamorphose mental space" (43, 58) and "open the mind" (188) can result in the cortical realization of a three-dimensional virtual reality. This hologram will not be found in a holography museum, but between the leaves of a book, where it waits for the readers' gaze to illuminate lovingly or boldly traverse the body/screen/text, seeking the perspective that will reconstitute feminist desire.

*Notes*

1. a perfect night (84).

2. At the other end of the night, I was going to open a bottle. The cities were converging in our glasses. Women were emerging from everywhere, architecture: the sum(ma) of laws revolving in their eyes, the speed of life, the forms they are preparing to take on: numbers, grasses, books, letters, spiral, first snow (85).

3. the city . . . patriarchal to its teeth." (My translation.)

4. The cities were converging one by one, called forth by the flashing intuition we had passing through the history of art, aerial sagittarians en route to transformation (85).

5. Each city was a document abounding in arrows . . . arrow-man. . . . The cities, lunar orb, black out, we needed to tame energy in order to avoid the installation in our limbs and especially in our gazes, of a moral immobility able to make one believe in renunciation (85).

6. In our glasses, a flash opening the horizon under our eyes, our very bodies in a state of thought, in firing position, mental anticipation, the arrow in the water of the soul, we were advancing calmly through the deserted streets (85).

7. The encounters between women lift the page on the city of women. (My translation.)

8. Border crossers, radical city dwellers, lesbians (76).

9. not for its own sake, but for its tragic consequences in the lives of women, in the life of the spirit (35).

10. Ten years of anger, revolt, certitude, and conviction are in *The Aerial Letter*; ten years of fighting against that screen which stands in the way of women's energy, identity, and creativity. Ten years of curves, graffiti, erasures, and writing, in order to exorcise that "curse." I had to "come to grips with words," in order that, from the heated emotional struggle, the three-dimensional women who nourish my desire and my hope would spiral forth (35).

11. If patriarchy can take what exists and make it not, surely we can take what exists and make it be (103).

12. Talk around the daily table (67).

13. Did You Not Hear What I Ordained?
J'ai exclu de votre troupe la soeur infidèle;
No more will she ride her horse through the air with you;
the virginal flower will wither,
a husband will win her womanly favours;
henceforth she'll obey her lord and master
and, seated at her hearth will ply the distaff,
she'll be the target and object of all mockery.
If her fate frightens you, then flee her who is lost!
Distance yourself, keep away from her.
One of you women who dare to stay near her
who will bravely defy me, take the side of the miserable wretch,
that rash woman will share her fate: that bold one must know it!

(33)

14. We were seated around the table, and Claire Dérive said that to see us all here together again, meeting at the seaside, was a sign (69).

15. Even though she asserted that the word abstraction slipped its way somewhere into her thought, she admitted for the moment that it was difficult to establish a direct link between the fact of being five women on the island and the very idea of what could be an abstraction (69).

16. at the source of each emotion, there is an abstraction whose effect is the emotion but whose consequences derive from the fixity of the gaze and ideas. Each abstraction is a potential form in mental space. And when the abstraction takes shape, it inscribes itself radically as enigma and affirmation. Resorting to abstraction is a necessity for the woman who, tempted by existence, invents the project of going beyond routine daily anecdotes and the memories of Utopia she meets each time she uses language (77).

17. complete sentences, abstract ones, linking life and speech (69).

18. Oriana then began to talk about time and the weather all the while searching for the words in French to say how she imagined it. She said that she did not understand why, each time certain women got together, in films for example, time seemed to stop around them after having frozen them or changed them into pillars of salt, loaded (with) symbols. After Danièle Judith had interrupted her to say matriarchy, Oriana continued her description of time (69).

19. Danièle Judith was saying that matriarchy is a word from anthropology and it cannot be used in a contemporary way to exorcize patriarchy. This word could not be used either to elaborate some Utopia that would have restored women to their gender (73-74).

20. I wanted to say that ecstacy is a reality in itself which makes time eternal. Claire Dérive affirmed that we mustn't confound time out of mind, patriarchal time and ecstacy (69).

21. the utopian sequences which traverse our thoughts, words and deeds (36).

22. from this confusion were born women suspended and immobile in space (69).

23. We were sitting around the table.... I said, with a taste of salt in the mouth, on the subject of Utopia beginning with the word woman that Utopia was not going to ensure our insertion into reality but that a Utopian testimony on our part could stimulate in us a quality of emotion favourable for our insertion into history. Before Claire talks about abstraction, I added that we ought to socialize our energies so that we would in no way be victims or again to avoid having our wombs alone praiseworthy as mental virility able to serve afterward for the murder of thinking bodies (73-74).

24. We were seated around the table (69, 73, 77, 78, 81).

25. Didn't patriarchal time come to a stop around them merging them morbidly in madness, death and submission. The mother is everywhere when time stops, the mother full of secrets that cause anguish to girls left to themselves in the patriarchal ruins: cars, tires, elevators, subways, broken windows. The soul in ruins, the mind of man can no longer *conceive itself* differently except by projecting the loss of his deity on the abstract bodies of a few women reunited in isolation, soul in ruins. There is a lack of imag(in)ing in this which, although not ours, overwhelms us in the very exercise of our mental functions (70).

26. For the first time, as this morning in front of the sea, I was not afraid to hear the words of another woman" (70).

27.     [A]erial posture
    the appearance of a double rose in the clarity
                                                    (45)

28. Langu age is feverish like a polysemic resource. The point of no return for all amorous affirmation is reached. I am there where "the magical appearance" begins, the coherence of wor(l)ds, perforated by invisible spirals that quicken it (153).

29. M. V. had straightened herself up, slowly turned her head her gaze caught between the window ledge and the horizon. Le poème hurlait opening the mind (153).

30. Claire came back with the wine, beside herself, saying bitch, dyke, feeling American to the tip of her nose, ultra-modern New York style. Stop it, Michèle, watch it, said Florence very worked up while I knew I wanted to real-ize the celebrated synthesis of water and fire that burns the tongue. I know, that synthesis of the double origin betrays me, I kn*e*w, I kn*ow* (84).

31. She was all genders at once in one language or another (83).

*Abbreviations*

*A*: Daphne Marlatt's *Ana Historic*.

*HHS*: Daphne Marlatt's *How Hug a Stone*.

*IASR*: Roland Barthes's "Introduction à l'analyse structurale des récits."

*MG*: Monique Wittig's "The Mark of Gender."

*N*: Mieke Bal's *Narratology*.

*NBBW*: Alice Parker's "Nicole Brossard's Body Work."

*Préface*: Louise Forsyth's "Préface" to *Picture Theory*.

*PT*: Nicole Brossard's *Picture Theory*.

*RI*: Nicole Brossard's "De radical à intágrales."

*RM*: Hélène Cixous's "Le rire de la Mèduse."

*Touch*: Daphne Marlatt's *Touch to My Tongue*.

*WG*: Robert Graves's *The White Goddess*.

*Bibliography*

Adrados, Francisco Rodriguez. "The Archaic Structure of Hittite." *The Journal of Indo-European Studies* 10, 1-2 (Spring/Summer 1982): 1-35.

Alberti, Leon Battista. *Della pittura*. 1436. *On Painting*. Trans. and intro. John R. Spencer. Westport, CT: Greenwood Press, 1966.

Alighieri, Dante. *The Divine Comedy of Dante Alighieri*. Trans. and comment John D. Sinclair. 3 vols. New York: Oxford University Press, 1961.

Althusser, Louis. *Lenin and Philosophy*. Trans. Ben Brewster. London: Monthly Review Press, 1971.

Anzaldúa, Gloria. *Borderlands/La Frontera: The New Mestiza*. San Francisco: Spinsters/aunt lute, 1987.

Bakhtin, M. M. *The Dialogic Imagination*. Trans. Michael Holquist and Caryl Emerson. Ed. Michael Holquist. Austin: University of Texas, 1981.

Bal, Mieke. *Narratology: Introduction to the Theory of Narrative*. Trans. Christine van Boheemen. Toronto: University of Toronto Press, 1985.

———. *On Story-telling: Essays in Narratology*. Sonoma, CA: Polebridge Press, 1991.

Barbizet, Jacques. *Human Memory and Its Pathology.* Trans. D. K. Jardine. San Francisco: W. H. Freedman, 1970.

Barnes, Djuna. *Nightwood.* New York: New Directions, 1937.

Baron, Denis. *Grammar and Gender.* New Haven, CT: Yale University Press, 1986.

Barthes, Roland. "Introduction à l'analyse structurale des récits." *Communications* 8 (1966): 1-27. "Introduction to the Structural Analysis of Narratives." In *Image—Music—Text.* Trans. Stephen Heath. New York: Hill and Wang, 1977.

———. *S/Z.* Trans. Richard Miller. New York: Hill and Wang, 1974.

Beck, Evelyn Torton, ed. *Nice Jewish Girls: A Lesbian Anthology.* Watertown, MA: Persephone Press, 1982.

Belenky, Mary Field, Blythe McVicker Clinchy, Nancy Rule Goldberger and Jill Mattuck Tarule. *Women's Ways of Knowing: The Development of Self, Voice, and Mind.* New York: Basic Books, 1986.

Bersianik, Louky. *L'Euguélionne.* Montréal: La Presse, 1976.

Benveniste, Emile. *Problémés de linguistique générale.* Paris: Gallimard, 1966. *Problems in General Linguistics.* Trans. Mary Elizabeth Meek. Coral Gables, FL: University of Miami Press, 1971.

Black, Maria, and Rosalind Coward. "Linguistic, Social and Sexual Relations: A Review of Dale Spender's *Man Made Language.*" *Screen Education* 29 (1981): 69-84.

Blake, William. *Milton.* Boulder, CO: Shambala, 1978.

Blau DuPlessis, Rachel. *Writing beyond the Ending: Narrative Strategies of Twentieth-Century Women Writers.* Bloomington: Indiana University Press, 1985.

Booth, Wayne. *The Rhetoric of Fiction.* 2nd ed. Chicago: University of Chicago Press, 1983.

Bourgeois, Louise. *Destruction of the Father, Reconstruction of the Father.* Ed. Marie-Lauare Bernadac and Hans-Ulrich Obrist. Cambridge, MA: MIT Press, 1998.

Brémond, Claude. *Logique du récit.* Paris: Seuil, 1973.

Brosman, Paul. "Designation of Females in Hittite." *The Journal of Indo-European Studies* 10, 1/2 (Spring/Summer 1982): 65-70.

———. "The Development of P.I.E. Feminine." *The Journal of Indo-European Studies* 10, 3/4 (Fall/Winter 1982): 253-72.

———. "The Hittite Gender of Cognates of P.I.E. Neuters." *The Journal of Indo-European Studies* 6, 1/2 (Spring/Summer 1978): 93-106.

———. "The Semantics of the Hittite Gender System. *The Journal of Indo-European Studies* 7, 3/4 (Fall/Winter 1979): 227-36.

Brossard, Nicole. "Accès à l'écriture: rituel langagier." In *La lettre aérienne.* Montréal: Remue-ménage, 1985. 131-42. "Access to Writing: Rites of Language." In *The Aerial Letter.* Trans. Marlene Wildeman. Toronto: The Women's Press, 1988. 139-47.

———. *Amantes.* Montréal: Quinze, 1980. Rpt. in *Amantes suivi de Le sens apparent et de Sous la langue.* Montréal: Hexagone, 1998. *Lovhers.* Trans. Barbara Godard. Montréal: Guernica, 1986.

———. *Baroque d'aube.* Montréal: Hexagone, 1995.

———. "De radical à l'intégrales." In *La lettre aérienne.* Montréal: Remueménage, 1985. 87-105. "From Radical to Integral." In *The Aerial Letter.* Trans. Marlene Wildeman. Toronto: The Women's Press, 1988. 103-20. "From Radical to Integral." Trans. Lise Weil and Miranda Hay. *Trivia: A Journal of Ideas* 5 (Fall 1984): 6-16.

———. "Djuna Barnes de profil moderne." In *Mon héroïne.* Montréal: Remue-ménage, 1981. 206.

———. *French Kiss: étreinte/exploration.* Montréal: Quinze/présence, 1974.

———. *Installations.* Trois Rivières: écrits des Forges, 1989.

———. "Interview with Nicole Brossard on *Picture Theory.*" Trans. Luise von Flotow-Evans. *Canadian Fiction Magazine* 47 (1983): 122-35.

———. *L'amèr ou Le chapitre effrité: théorie/fiction.* Préface de Louise Dupré. 2nd corr. ed. Montréal: Hexagone, 1988. *These Our Mothers or: The Disintegrating Chapter.* Trans. Barbara Godard. Toronto: Coach House Quebec Translations, 1983.

———. *La Nuit verte du Parc Labyrinthe.* Laval, QC: Éditions Trois, 1992.

———. "La plaque tournante." In *La lettre aérienne.* Montreal: Remueménage, 1985. 11-28. "Turning-Platform." In *The Aerial Letter.* Trans. Marlene Wildeman. Toronto: The Women's Press, 1988. 37-51.

———. "La tête qu'elle fait." *La Barre du jour* 56-57 (mai-aôut 1977): 83-92.

———. *L'Aviva.* Montréal: nbj, 1985.

———. *Le désert mauve: roman.* Montréal: Hexagone, 1987.

———. "Mais voici venir la fiction ou l'épreuve au féminin." *La Nouvelle Barre du jour* (mai 1980).

———. "Mémoire: hologramme du désir." *La parole métèque* 7 (1988): 6-8.

———. "Nicole Brossard." Trans. Susanne de Lotbinière-Harwood. In *Contemporary Authors Autobiography Series,* Vol. 16. Ed. Hal May and Susan M. Trotsky. Detroit: Gale Research Company, 1993.

———. *Picture Theory.* Montréal: Nouvelle Optique, 1982. 2nd ed. Préface de Louise H. Forsyth. Montréal: Hexagone, 1989. *Picture Theory.* Trans. Barbara Godard. Montreal: Guernica, 1991.

———. "Pré(e)." *La femme et la ville, la Nouvelle Barre du jour* 102 (avril 1981): 5.

———. *Sous la langue/Under Tongue.* Trans. Susanne Lotbinière-Harwood. Montréal: L'Essentielle; Charlottetown: Gynergy Books, 1987.

———. "Synchronie." In *La lettre aérienne.* Montréal: Remue-ménage, 1985. 79-85. "Synchrony." In *The Aerial Letter.* Trans. Marlene Wildeman. Toronto: The Women's Press, 1988. 71-101.

———. *un livre.* Montréal: Quinze, 1980.

Brossard, Nicole, with Daphne Marlatt. *Character/Jeu de lettres.* Montréal: nbj/writing, 1986.

———. *Mauve.* Montréal: nbj/writing, 1985.

Brugmann, Karl. *Grundriss der vergleichenden Grammatik der indogermanischen* [*Outline of the Grammatical Comparison of the Indo-European Languages*]. Berlin, 1893; 2nd ed. Vol. 2 Strassburg: Trubner, 1906-11.

Bruner, Jerome. *Actual Minds, Possible Worlds.* Cambridge, MA: Harvard University Press, 1986.

———. "The Narrative Construction of Reality." *Critical Inquiry* 18, 1 (Autumn 1991): 1-21.

Bucher, Cornelius J. *Three Models on a Rocking-Horse: A Comparative Study in Narratology.* Tübingen: Gunter Narr Verlag Tübingen, 1990.

Butler, Judith. *Gender Trouble.* New York: Routledge, 1990.

Butling, Pauline. "'From Radical to Integral': Daphne Marlatt's "Booking Passage." In *Inside the Poem.* Ed. W. H. New. Toronto: Oxford University Press, 1992. 167-73.

Cameron, Deborah. *Feminism and Linguistic Theory.* London: Macmillan, 1985.

Carman, Bliss. *Sappho: One Hundred Lyrics.* London: Chatto & Windus, 1921.

———. *Vision of Sappho.* [New York?]: Bliss Carman, 1903.

———. "Re-casting the Steveston Net: Recalling the Invisible Women from the Margins." *Line* 13 (1989): 83-95.

Caulfield, John H. "The Wonder of Holography." *National Geographic* 165, 3 (March 1984): 364-77.

Causse, Michèle. *Lesbiana.* Paris: Nouveau Commerce, 1980.

Cayley, David. *Prison and Its Alternatives.* In *Ideas.* The Canadian Broadcasting Corporation. June 17-28, 1996.

Chamberlain, Lori. "Consent after Liberalism? A Review Essay of Catharine MacKinnon's *Towards a Feminist Theory of the State* and Carole Paterman's *The Sexual Contract.*" *Genders* 11 (Fall 1991): 111-25.

Chevalier, Jean-Claude, Claire Blanche-Benveniste, et al. *Grammaire Larousse du français contemporain.* Paris: Larousse, 1964.

Chodorow, Nancy. 1985. "Gender, Relation, and Difference in Psychoanalytic Perspective." In *The Future of Difference.* Ed. Hester Eisenstein and Alice Jardine. New Brunswick: Rutgers University Press, 1985. 3-19.

Chow, K. L., and Leiman, A. L. "Aspects of the Structure and Functional Organization of the Neocortex." *Neurosciences Bulletin* 8 (1970): 157-219.

Cixous, Hélène. "Le rire de la méduse." *L'arc* 61 (1975): 39-54. "The Laugh of the Medusa." Trans. Keith Cohen and Paula Cohen. In *New French Feminisms.* Ed. Elaine Marks and Isabelle de Courtivron. New York: Schocken, 1981. 245-65.

———. "Ô grand-mère que vous avez de beaux concepts! C'est pour mieux vous arrièrer, mon enfant! un colloque féministe à New York: le second sexe trente ans après." *des femmes en mouvements, hebdo* 1 (9-16 novembre 1979): 11-12.

———. "Poésie, e(s)t politique?" *des femmes en mouvements* 4 (novembre-décembre 1979): 29-32.

Cixous, Hélène, and Catherine Clément. *La jeune née.* Paris: Union Générale, 1975. *The Newly Born Woman.* Trans. Betsy Wing. Minneapolis: University of Minnesota Press, 1986.

Clarke, George Elliott. *Whylah Falls.* Winlaw: Polestar Press, 1990.

Conley, Katharine. "The Spiral as Möbius Strip: Inside/Outside *Le désert mauve.*" *Québec Studies* 18 (Spring/Summer 1994): 149-58.

Cook, Theodore Andrea. *The Curves of Life.* London: Constable, 1914; New York: Dover, 1979.

Corbett, Greville. *Gender.* Cambridge: Cambridge University Press, 1991.

Cornillon, Susan Koppelman, ed. *Images of Women in Fiction: Feminist Perspectives.* Bowling Green, KY: Bowling Green University Press, 1972.

Cortazar, Julio. *Blow Up and Other Stories*. Trans. Paul Black. New York: Collier, 1968.

Cotnoir, Louise. "S'écrire avec, dans et contre le langage." *Tessera 1/Room of One's Own* 8 (1984): 47-49.

Cranny-Francis, Anne. *Feminist Fiction: Feminist Uses of Generic Fiction*. New York: St. Martin's Press, 1990.

Culler, Jonathan. *The Pursuit of Signs: Semiotics, Literature, Deconstruction*. Ithaca, NY: Cornell University Press, 1981.

Daly, Mary. *Gyn/Ecology: The Metaethics of Radical Feminism*. Boston: Beacon Press, 1978.

Dames, Michael. *The Avebury Cycle*. London: Thames and Hudson, 1977.

Davey, Frank. *From There to Here*. Erin, Ontario: Press Porcepic, 1974.

———. "Words and Stones in *How Hug a Stone*." *Line* 13 (Spring 1989): 40-46.

De Beauvoir, Simone. *Le deuxième sexe*. 2 vols. Paris: Gallimard, 1949.

de Lauretis, Teresa. *Alice Doesn't: Feminism, Semiotics, Cinema*. Bloomington: Indiana University Press, 1984.

———. *Technologies of Gender: Essays on Theory, Film, and Fiction*. Bloomington: Indiana University Press, 1987.

———. "The Essence of the Triangle or, Taking the Risk of Essentialism Seriously: Feminist Theory in Italy, the U.S., and Britain." *Differences: A Journal of Feminist Cultural Studies* 1, 2 (Summer 1989): 3-37.

Delgado, Richard, ed. *Critical Race Theory: The Cutting Edge*. Philadelphia: Temple University Press, 1995.

Delphy, Christine. "The Invention of French Feminism: An Essential Move." *Yale French Studies* 87 (1995): 190-221.

Derrida, Jacques. *Of Grammatology*. Trans. Gayatri Chakravorty Spivak. Baltimore: Johns Hopkins University Press, 1984.

Des femmes. "Pour la premiere fois, peut-être, en vacances." *des femmes en mouvements* (juin 1978): 41-42.

———. "la difference internée." *des femmes en mouvements* 2 (mai 1978): 13.

———. "la situation et notre politique." *le quotidien des femmes* (3 mars 1975): 1-3.

Des Filles homosexuelles à Marseille. "La Foret." *Les femmes s'entêtent, Menstruel* 1 [1975?]: 4.

Dragland, Stan. *The Bees of the Invisible: Essays in Contemporary English Canadian Writing*. Toronto: Coach House Press, 1991.

Duff, Gail. *Country Wisdom: An Encyclopedia of Recipes, Remedies and Traditional Good Sense*. London: Pan Books, 1979.

Dumond, Val. *Sheit: A No-Nonsense Guidebook to Writing and Using Nonsexist Language*. Tacoma, WA: Dumond Publications, 1984.

Dupré, Louise. "Du propre au figuré." Introduction to Nicole Brossard, *L'amèr ou le chapitre effrité*. Montréal: Hexagone, 1988.

———. *Stratégies du vertige: trois poètes: Nicole Brossard, Madeleine Gagnon, France Théoret*. Montréal: Remue-ménage, 1989.

Dyer, Gwynne. "Millennium." In *Ideas*. The Canadian Broadcasting Corporation, June 17-28, 1996.

Editorial Collective of *Questions féministes*. "Variations on Some Common Themes." *Feminist Issues* 1, 1 (Summer 1980): 3-22.

Engels, Frederick. *The Origin of the Family, Private Property, and the State, in the Light of the Researches of Lewis H. Morgan*. Moscow: Progress Publishers, 1968.

Epstein, Julia. "Either/Or—Neither/Both: Sexual Ambiguity and the Ideology of Gender." *Genders* 7 (Spring 1990): 99-142.

Fallon, Mary. *Working Hot*. Melbourne: Sybylla Press, 1989.

Fenn, Ann, Ingeborg Hoesterey and Maria Tatar, eds. *Neverending Stories: Toward a Critical Narratology*. Princeton: Princeton University Press, 1992.

Forsyth, Louise. "Deconstructing Formal Space/Accelerating Motion in the Work of Nicole Brossard." In *A Mazing Space: Writing Canadian Women Writing*. Ed. Shirley Neuman and Smaro Kamboureli. Edmonton: NeWest, 1986. 334-44.

———. "Errant and Air-Born in the City." Introduction to Nicole Brossard, *The Aerial Letter*. Trans. Marlene Wildeman. Toronto: The Women's Press, 1988.

———. Préface to Nicole Brossard, *Picture Theory: Théorie/Fiction*. 2nd ed. Montreal: Hexagone, 1989.

Freud, Sigmund. *The Standard Edition of the Complete Psychological Works of Sigmund Freud*. Trans. James Strachey in collaboration with Anna Freud. London: Hogarth, 1959.

Fuss, Diana. *Essentially Speaking: Feminism, Nature & Difference*. New York: Routledge, 1989.

Gallant, Corinne, ed. *La philosophie . . . au féminin*. Moncton: Éditions Acadie, 1984.

Gelfand, Elissa D., and Virginia Thorndike Hules. *French Feminist Criticism: Women, Language, Literature: An Annotated Bibliography*. New York: Garland, 1985.

Genette, Gérard. "Discours du récit: essai de méthode." In *Figures Trois*. Paris: éditions du Seuil, 1972. *Narrative Discourse: An Essay in Method*. Trans. Jane E. Lewin. Ithaca, NY: Cornell University Press, 1980.

Gilbert, Sandra, and Susan Gubar. "Sexual Linguistics: Gender, Language, Sexuality." In *The Feminist Reader: Essays in Gender and the Politics of Literary Criticism*. Ed. Catherine Belsey and Jane Moore. New York: Basil Blackwell, 1989. 81-99.

Gilligan, Carol. *In a Different Voice: Psychological Theory and Women's Development*. Cambridge, MA: Harvard University Press, 1982.

Gimbutas, Marija. "An Archaeologist's View of P.I.E in 1975." *The Journal of Indo-European Studies* 2, 3 (1974): 289-307.

———. "The First Wave of Eurasian Steppe Pastoralists into Copper Age Europe." *The Journal of Indo-European Studies* 5, 4 (1977): 277-338.

———. *The Goddess Civilization: The World of Old Europe*. San Francisco: HarperCollins, 1991.

———. *The Gods and Goddesses of Old Europe 7000-3500 B.C.* London: Thames and Hudson, 1974.

———. *The Language of the Goddess*. With a Foreword by Joseph Campbell. San Francisco: Harper & Row, 1989.

———. "The Social Structure of Old Europe, Parts 2 & 3." *The Journal of Indo-European Studies* 18, 3/4 (Fall/Winter 1990): 225-84.

Godard, Barbara, ed. *Collaboration in the Feminine: Writings on Women and Culture from Tessera*. Toronto: Second Story Press, 1994.

———. "Essentialism? A Problem in Discourse." *Tessera* 10 (Summer/été 1991): 22-39.

———. "Theorizing Feminist Discourse/Translation." *Tessera* 6 (Spring/printemps 1989): 42-53.

———. "Translating Translation." Introduction to France Théoret, *The Tangible Word*. Trans. Barbara Godard. Montréal: Guernica, 1991.

Gould, Karen. *Writing in the Feminine: Feminism and Experimental Writing in Quebec*. Carbondale and Edwardsville: Southern Illinois University Press, 1990.

Graves, Robert. *The Greek Myths*. 2 vols. Harmondsworth: Penguin, 1957.

———. *The White Goddess: A Historical Grammar of Poetic Myth*. London: Faber and Faber, 1961.

Grillo, Trina, and Stephanie M. Wildman. "Obscuring the Importance of Race: The Implications of Making Comparisons between Racism and Sexism (or Other -isms)." In *Critical Race Theory: The Cutting Edge*. Ed. Richard Delgado. Philadelphia: Temple University Press, 1995. 564-72.

Groult, Benoîte. *Le féminisme au masculin*. Paris: Denoël/Gonthier, 1977.

———. "Rencontre du dimanche 24 november 1985 avec l'écrivaine Benoîte Groult." *Dialogue de Femmes*. Privately printed (12 rue Georges Berger, 75017, Paris, France).

Gubar, Susan. "Sapphistries." In *The Lesbian Issue: Essays from Signs*. Ed. Estelle Freedman et al. Chicago: University of Chicago Press, 1982. 91-110.

Hacker, Marilyn. *Love, Death, and the Changing of the Seasons*. New York: Arbor House, 1986.

Hanafi, Rhoda. "When 'I' Speaks to 'You': The Literary Subject as an Effect of Pronominal Play in Two Works by Contemporary Women Writers." Master's thesis, University of British Columbia, 1987.

Handy López, Ian F. "White by Law." In *Critical Race Theory*. Ed. Richard Delgado. Philadelphia: Temple University Press, 1995. 564-72.

Heidegger, Martin. *Poetry, Language, Thought*. Trans. Albert Hofstadter. New York: Harper & Row, 1971.

Hendricks, William. "Methodology of Narrative Discourse." *Semiotica* 7 (1973): 163-84.

*Houghton Mifflin Canadian Dictionary of the English Language, The*. Ed. William Morris. Markham, ON: Houghton Mifflini, 1982.

Huld, Martin E. "The Linguistic Typology of the Old European Substrata in North Central Europe." *The Journal of Indo-European Studies* 18, 3/4 (Fall/Winter 1990): 417-23.

Irigaray, Luce. *Ce sexe qui n'en est pas un*. Paris: Minuit, 1977. *This Sex Which Is Not One*. Trans. Catherine Porter. Ithaca, NY: Cornell University Press, 1985.

Jacobson, Roman. *Selected Writings*. 8 vols. The Hague: N.p, 1971-88.

Jagose, Annamarie. *Lesbian Utopics*. New York: Routledge, 1994.

Jardine, Alice, and Anne Menke, eds. *Shifting Scenes: Interviews on Women, Writing, and Politics in Post-68 France*. New York: Columbia University Press, 1991.

Jelinek, Estelle, ed. *Women's Autobiography*. Bloomington: Indiana University Press, 1980.

Johnson-Laird, Philip N. "How Is Meaning Mentally Represented?" In *Meaning and Mental Representations*. Ed. Umberto Eco, Marco Santambrogio and Patrizia Violi. Bloomington: Indiana University Press, 1988. 99-118.

Katz, Wendy. *Her and His—Language of Equal Value: A Report of the Status of Women Committee of the Nova Scotia Confederation of University Faculty Associations on Sexist Language and the University,* 1981.

Knutson, Susan. "Challenging the Masculine Generic." *Tessera 4/Contemporary Verse* 11, 2/3 (Spring/Summer 1988): 76-88. Rpt. *WS 200A: Women in Society: Past and Present.* Victoria, BC: University of Victoria, 1993.

———. "'Imagine Her Surprise': The Debate over Feminist Essentialism." In *Collaboration in the Feminine: Writings on Women and Culture from Tessera.* Ed. Barbara Godard. Toronto: Second Story Press, 1994. 228-36.

———. "Nicole Brossard's Elegant International Play." In *Canada: Theoretical Discourse/Discours théoriques.* Ed. Terry Goldie, Carmen Lambert and Rowland Lorimer. Montréal: Association for Canadian Studies/Association d'études canadiennes, 1994. 187-202.

———. "Paleo-linguistics and Feminist Theory: Reading between the Lines in The Journal of Indo-European Studies." In *Centre for Language in Social Life Working Papers.* Ed. Sally Johnson and Jane Sunderland. Lancaster, U.K.: Lancaster University, 1998. 1-13.

———. "Protean Travelogue in Nicole Brossard's *Picture Theory*: Feminist Desire and Narrative Form." *Modern Language Studies* 27.3, 4 (Winter 1997): 197-211.

———. "Reading Nicole Brossard." *Ellipse* 53 (Spring 1995): 9-19.

———. "Writing Metanarrative in the Feminine." *Signature: A Journal of Theory and Canadian Literature* 3 (Summer 1990): 28-43.

Kristeva, Julia. *La révolution du langage poétique: l'avant-garde à la fin du XIX$^e$ siècle: Lautréamont et Mallarmé.* Paris: Seuil, 1974. *Revolution in Poetic Language.* Trans. Margaret Waller. New York: Columbia University Press, 1984.

Labrosse, Céline. *Pour une grammaire non-sexiste.* Montréal: Remue-ménage, 1996.

Leach, Edmund. "Fishing for Men on the Edge of the Wilderness." In *The Literary Guide to the Bible.* Ed. Frank Kermode and Robert Alter. Cambridge, MA: Harvard University Press, 1987.

Le Doeuff, Michèle. "Colloque féministe à New York: *Le deuxième Sexe* trente ans après." *Questions féministes* 7 (février 1980): 103-109.

Leith, Emmett N., and Juris Upatnieks. "Photography by Laser." *Scientific American* 212, 6 (June 1965): 24-35.

*Le livre au féminin: les réponses à vos questions.* Boucherville, QC: Éditions Proteau, 1983.

Lemire Tostevin, Lola. "Daphne Marlatt: Writing in the Space that Is Her Mother's Face." *Line* 13 (Spring 1989): 32-39.

Lenin, V. I. *The State and Revolution.* Moscow: Foreign Languages Publishing House, 1917.

Lerner, Gerda. *The Creation of Patriarchy.* New York: Oxford University Press, 1986.

Lévi-Strauss, Claude. "Structural Study of Myth." *Journal of American Folklore* 68 (1955): 428-43.

Libreria delle Donne di Milano [Milan Women's Bookstore]. *Non credere di avere dei diritti: la generazione della libertà femminile nell'idea e nelle vicende di un gruppo di donne* [*Don't Think You Have Any Rights: The Engendering of Female Freedom in the Thought and Vicissitudes of a Women's Group*]. Turin: Rosenberg & Sellier, 1987. Cited in de Lauretis, 1989.

Linke, Uli. "Blood as Metaphor in Proto-Indo-European." *The Journal of Indo-European Studies* 13, 3/4 (Fall/Winter 1985): 333-76.

Lorber, Judith, and Susan A. Farrell, eds. *The Social Construction of Gender.* New York: Sage, 1991.

Lorde, Audre. "An Open Letter to Mary Daly." In *This Bridge Called My Back: Writings by Radical Women of Color.* Ed. Cherríe Moraga and Gloria Anzaldúa. New York: Kitchen Table Press, 1993, 95.

Lotman, Jurij. "The Origin of Plot in the Light of Typology." *Poetics Today* 1, 1-2 (1979): 161-84.

Lowry, Glen. "Risking Perversion & Reclaiming Our Hysterical Mother: Reading the Material Body in *Ana Historic* and *Double Standards.*" *West Coast Line* 5, 25/2 (Fall 1991): 83-96.

Lyons, John. *Introduction to Theoretical Linguistics.* London: Cambridge University Press, 1977.

Lyotard, Jean-François. *La condition postmoderne: rapport sur le savoir.* Paris: Éditions de Minuit, 1979. *The Postmodern Condition: A Report on Knowledge.* Trans. Geoff Bennington and Brian Massumi. Manchester: Manchester University Press, 1984.

Mackenzie, D. A. *Scottish Folklore and Folk Life* (1935); cited in Dames 1977, 86.

Mallarmé, Stéphane. *Un coup de dés jamais n'abolira le hasard.* Neuchâtel: Messeiller, 1960.

Marks, Elaine, and Isabelle de Courtivron, eds. *New French Feminisms.* New York: Schocken, 1981.

Marlatt, Daphne. *How Hug a Stone.* Winnipeg: Turnstone, 1983. Rpt. in Ghostworks. Edmonton: NeWest, 1993. 129-87.

———. "In the Month of Hungry Ghosts." *The Capilano Review* 16/17, 2-3 (1979): 45-95. Rpt. in *Ghostworks.* Edmonton: NeWest, 1993. 75-128.

———. Letter to Frank Davey, June 15, 1966. "Correspondences: Selected Letters." *Line* 13 (Spring 1989): 32-39.

———. "Narrative in Language Circuits." *The Dinosaur Review* 7 (1986): 60-61.

———. *Salvage*. Red Deer, AB: Red Deer College Press, 1991.

———. *Touch to My Tongue*. Edmonton: Longspoon, 1984.

———. "When We Change Language . . ." In *Sounding Differences*. Ed. Janice Williamson. Toronto: University of Toronto Press, 1993. 182-99.

———. "Writing Our Way through the Labyrinth." *Tessera* 2/nbj (1985): 45-49.

Marlatt, Daphne, and Betsy Warland. *Double Negative*. With negative collages by Cheryl Sourkes. Charlottetown: Gynergy Books, 1988.

Marlatt, Daphne, and Nicole Brossard. *Character/Jeu de lettres*. Montréal: nbj/writing, 1986.

———. *Mauve*. Montréal: nbj/writing, 1985.

Marlatt, Daphne, Barbara Pulling, Victoria Freeman, Betsy Warland and Ann Dybikowski, eds. *In the Feminine: Women and Words/Les femmes et les mots, Conference Proceedings 1983*. Edmonton: Longspoon Press, 1985.

Marlatt, Daphne, Sky Lee, Lee Maracle and Betsy Warland, eds. (The Telling It Book Collective). *Telling It: Women and Language Across Cultures*. Vancouver: Press Gang, 1990.

Martin, André, and Henriette Dupuis. *La féminization des titres et les leaders d'opinion: une étude exploratoire*. Québec: Gouvernement du Québec, 1985.

Matejka, Ladislav, and Krystyna Pomorska, eds. *Readings in Russian Poetics: Formalist and Structuralist Views*. Cambridge: M.I.T. Press, 1971.

McDermott, Patrice. *Politics and Scholarship: Feminist Academic Journals and the Production of Knowledge*. Chicago: University of Illinois Press, 1994.

McIntosh Snyder, Jane. *Sappho*. New York: Chelsea House, 1995.

Mehta, Gita. *A River Sutra*. New York: Vintage Books, 1993.

Meigs, Mary. *The Medusa Head*. Vancouver: Talon Books, 1983.

Miller, Casey, and Kate Smith. *The Handbook of Non-Sexist Writing*. London: Women's Press, 1980.

Miranda, Rocky V. "Indo-European Gender: A Study in Semantic and Syntactic Change." *The Journal of Indo-European Studies* 3, 3 (Fall 1975): 199-215.

Moi, Toril. *Sexual/Textual Politics: Feminist Literary Theory*. London: Routledge, 1985.

Moraga, Cherríe, and Gloria Anzaldúa, eds. *This Bridge Called My Back: Writings by Radical Women of Color*. Watertown, MA: Persephone Books, 1981. Rpt. New York: Kitchen Table Press, 1993.

Mordecai, Pamela, and Betty Wilson, eds. *Her True-True Name: An Anthology of Women's Writing from the Caribbean*. London: Heinemann, 1989.

Morgan, Lewis H. *Ancient Society, or Researches in the Lines of Human Progress from Savagery through Barbarism to Civilization*. London: Macmillan, 1877.

Nicholson, Linda J., and Nancy Fraser. "Social Criticism without Philosophy." In *Feminism/Postmodernism*. Ed. Linda J. Nicholson. New York: Routledge, 1990. 19-38.

Nourbese Philip, Marlene. *She Tries Her Tongue, Her Silence Softly Breaks*. Charlottetown: Ragweed, 1989.

———. "Whose Idea Was It Anyway?" *Tessera, Vers une narratologie féministe/Toward Feminist Narratology* 7 (Fall/automne 1989): 45-54.

Olson, Charles. *Selected Writings*. Ed. Robert Creeley. New York: New Directions, 1966.

Paglia, Camille. *Sexual Personae: Art and Decadence from Nefertiti to Emily Dickinson*. New York: Vintage Books, 1990.

Parker, Alice. *Liminal Visions of Nicole Brossard*. New York: Peter Lang, 1998.

———. "Nicole Brossard's Body Work: *Le corps impair*." Paper presented to N.E.M.L.A., Montréal, April 20, 1996.

Penelope, Julia. [a.k.a. Julia P. Stanley]. "Gender-Marking in American English: Usage and Reference." In *Sexism and Language*. Ed. Alleen Pace Nilsen et al. Urbana, IL: National Council of Teachers of English, 1977. 43-76.

———. "Paradigmatic Woman: The Prostitute." *Linguistic Society of America* (1973).

———. *Speaking Freely: Unlearning the Lies of the Fathers' Tongues*. Elmsford, NY: Pergamon Press, 1990.

Penelope, Julia [Stanley], and Cynthia McGowan. "Woman and Wife: Social and Semantic Shifts in English." *Papers in Linguistics* 12, 3-4 (1979): 491-502.

Penelope, Julia [Stanley], and Susan J. Wolfe [a.k.a. Susan Wolfe Robbins]. "Linguistic Problems with Patriarchal Reconstructions of Indo-European Culture: A Little More than Kin, a Little Less than Kind." *Women's Studies International Quarterly* 3 (1980): 227-37.

Penelope, Julia [Stanley], and Susan Wolfe Robbins. "Sex-Marked Predicates in English." *Papers in Linguistics* 11, 1-2 (1978): 487-516.

Pribram, Karl. *Languages of the Brain: Experimental Paradoxes and Principles in Neuropsychology.* Englewood Cliffs, NJ: Prentice-Hall, 1971.

Propp, Vladímir. *Morphology of the Folktale.* Ed. Louis A. Wagner. Trans. Laurence Scott. Intro. Alan Dundes. 2nd ed. rev. Austin: University of Texas, 1968.

The Province of British Columbia. *Communicating Without Bias: Guidelines for Government.* Victoria: Government of British Columbia, 1992.

———. *Gender Neutral Language: Interim Guidelines for Government Communications.* Victoria: Government of British Columbia, 1991.

Raoul, Valerie. "Women and Diaries: Gender and Genre." *Mosaic* 22-23 (Summer 1989): 57-65.

Rich, Adrienne. *The Dream of a Common Language: Poems 1974-1977.* New York: Norton, 1978.

Ricouart, Janine. "De la spirale au baroque our La spirale de Nicole Brossard at-elle perdu le Nord?" Paper presented to N.E.M.L.A., Montréal, April 20, 1996.

Riley, Denise. "Commentary: Feminism and the Consolidations of 'Women' in History." In *Coming to Terms: Feminism, Theory, Politics.* Ed. Elizabeth Weed. London: Routledge, 1989. 134-39.

Robinson, David. *Sappho and Her Influence.* New York: Cooper Square, 1963.

Russ, Joanna. "What Can a Heroine Do? Or Why Women Can't Write." In *Images of Women in Fiction: Feminist Perspectives.* Ed. Susan Koppelman Cornillon. Bowling Green, KY: Bowling Green University Popular Press, 1972.

Shaktini, Namascar. "Displacing the Phallic Subject: Wittig's Lesbian Writing." In *The Lesbian Issue: Essays from Signs.* Ed. Estelle Freedman et al. Chicago: University of Chicago Press, 1982. 137-52.

Silveira, Jeanette. "Generic Masculine Words and Thinking." *Women's Studies International Quarterly* 3 (1980): 165-78.

Silverman, Kaja. *The Subject of Semiotics.* New York: Oxford University Press, 1983.

Spender, Dale. *Man Made Language.* 2nd ed. London: Routledge and Kegan Paul, 1985.

Spivak, Gayatri Chakravorty, with Ellen Rooney. "In a Word: Interview." *differences* 1, 2 (Summer 1989): 124-56.

Stein, Gertrude. *Bee Time Vine and Other Pieces* (1913-1927) New Haven, CT: Yale University Press, 1953.

Stephens, Donald. *Bliss Carman.* New York: Twayne, 1966.

Stukeley, William. *Stonehenge, a Temple Restor'd to the British Druids: Abury, a Temple of the British Druids: Myth & Romanticism: A Collection of the Major Mythographic Sources used by the English Romantic Poets.* Ed. Burton Feldman and Robert Richardson. Rpt. New York: Garland, 1984.

Théoret, France. *Entre raison et déraison.* Montréal: Les Herbes Rouges, 1987.

———. "Speech in Defense of Women's Right to Existance!" In *The Tangible Word.* Trans. Barbara Godard. Montríal: Guernica, 1991.

Tomashevsky, Boris. "Thematics." In *Russian Formalist Criticism: Four Essays.* Trans. with intr. Lee T. Lemon and Marion J. Reis. Lincoln: University of Nebraska Press, 1965.

Tostevin, Lola Lemire. "Daphne Marlatt: Writing in the Space that Is Her Mother's Face." *Line* 13 (1989): 32-39.

Valverde, Mariana. *Sex, Power and Pleasure.* Toronto: The Women's Press, 1985.

Van Gennep, Arnold. *The Rites of Passage.* Trans. Monika Vizedom and Gabrielle Caffee. Intr. Solon Kimball. London: Routledge & Kegan Paul, 1960.

Vatcher, Faith, and Lance Vatcher. *The Avebury Monuments.* The Department of the Environment Official Handbook. London: Her Majesty's Stationery Office, 1976.

Wagner, Richard. *Die Walküre: Erster Tag aus der Trilogie: Derring des Nibelungen.* Mayence: B. Schott's Söhne, 1882.

Weed, Elizabeth. "Introduction: Terms of Reference." In *Coming to Terms: Feminism, Theory, Politics.* Ed. Elizabeth Weed. London: Routledge, 1989. xi-xxxi.

Weir, Lorna. "Anti-Racist Feminist Pedagogy, Self-Observed." *Resources for Feminist Research/Documentation sur la recherche feministe* 20, 3/4 (Fall/Winter 1991).

Weir, Lorraine. "From Picture to Hologram: Nicole Brossard's Grammar of Utopia." In *A Mazing Space: Writing Canadian Women Writing.* Ed. Shirley Neuman and Smaro Kamboureli. Edmonton: NeWest Press, 1986. 345-54.

Wildman, Stephanie, with Adrienne D. Davis. "Language and Silence: Making Systems of Privilege Visible." In *Critical Race Theory: The Cutting Edge.* Ed. Richard Delgado. Philadelphia: Temple University Press, 1995.

Williamson, Janice. "Sounding a Difference: An Interview with Daphne Marlatt." *Line* 13 (1989): 47-56.

Wilson, Thomas. *Arte of Rhetorique.* 1553. Rpt. Gainesville, FL: Scholars' Facsimiles and Reprints, 1962.

Wittig, Monique. "La pensée straight." *Questions féministes* 7 (février 1980): 45-54. "The Straight Mind." *Feminist Issues* 1, 1 (Summer 1980): 103-11.

———. *Le corps lesbien.* Paris: Minuit, 1973. *The Lesbian Body.* Trans. David Le Vay. London: Peter Owen, 1975.

———. *Les guérillères.* Paris: Minuit, 1969. *Les Guérillères.* Trans. David Le Vay. Boston: Beacon Press, 1985.

———. *L'opoponax.* Paris: Minuit, 1964. *L'Opoponax.* Trans. Helen Weaver. New York: Simon and Schuster, 1966.

———. "On ne naît pas femme." *Questions féministes* 8 (mai 1980): 75-84. "One Is Not Born a Woman." *Feminist Issues* 1, 2 (Winter 1981): 47-54.

———. "The Mark of Gender." *Feminist Issues* 5, 2 (1985): 3-12.

———. *Virgile, non.* Paris: Minuit, 1985. *Across the Acheron.* Trans. David Le Vay. London: Peter Owen, 1987.

Wittig, Monique, and Sande Zeig. *Brouillon pour un dictionnaire des amantes.* Paris: Bernard Grasset, 1976.

———. *Lesbian Peoples: Materials for a Dictionary.* New York: Avon, 1979. *Women's Review of Books, The.* Special Issue: *The French Connection* 3, 6 (1986).

Wolfe, Susan J. "Amazon Etymology." *Sinister Wisdom* 12 (Winter 1980): 15-20.

———. "Constructing and Reconstructing Patriarchy: Sexism and Diachronic Semantics." *Papers in Linguistics* 13, 2 (1980): 321-44.

———. "Gender and Agency in Indo-European Languages." *Papers in Linguistics* 13, 4 (1980): 773-94.

Woolf, Virginia. *A Room of One's Own.* 1929. Rpt. London: Granada, 1981.

———. "The Intellectual Status of Women." *The New Statesman* (London, October 16 1920): 45-46. (Woolf is responding to Desmond MacCarthy's ["Affable Hawk"] review of Arnold Bennett's *Our Women* and Otto Weininger's *Sex and Character, The New Statesman* [London, October 9, 1920]).

———. *Women and Writing.* Ed. Michèle Barrett. New York and London: Harcourt Brace Jovanovich, 1979.

Wright, Ellea. "Text and Tissue: Body Language: Interview with Daphne Marlatt and Betsy Warland." *Broadside: A Feminist Review* 6, 3 (1986): 4-6.

Yeats, William Butler. *The Variorum Edition of the Poems of W. B. Yeats.* Ed. Peter Allt and Russell Alspach. New York: Macmillan, 1957.

Zavalloni, Marisa, ed. *L'emergence d'une culture au féminin.* Montréal: Saint-Martin, 1987.

Zimmerman, Bonnie. "The Politics of Transliteration: Lesbian Personal Narratives." *Signs* 9, 4 (Summer 1984): 663-82.

**Susan Holbrook (essay date summer 2001)**

SOURCE: Holbrook, Susan. "Delirium and Desire in Nicole Brossard's *Le Désert mauve/Mauve Desert.*" *Differences: A Journal of Feminist Cultural Studies* 12, no. 2 (summer 2001): 70-85.

[*In the following essay, Holbrook explores the suggestive relationships among reading, writing, translation, interpretation, and desire illustrated in Brossard's novel* Mauve Desert.]

> "le ravissement" dit L. pour saisir
>                       le sens
> d'une expérience mentale où
>                fragments et delire
> de l'éclat traduisent une pratique
>                     de l'émeute
> en soi comme une théorie de la réalité
> . . . . . . . . . . . . . . . . .
> JE N'ARRÊTE PAS DE LIRE
>
>                     (Brossard, *Amantes* 11)

> "the rapture" said L. to grasp the sense
> of a mental experience where
>                fragments and delirium
> from the explosion translate and
>                    experiment on riot
> within the self as a theory of reality
> . . . . . . . . . . . . . . . . .
> I DON'T STOP READING/DELIRING
>
>                     (Godard, *Lovhers* 16)

Hurtling home on the C-train, Calgary's rapid transit car, I read Nicole Brossard's ***Amantes***. Actually, I am reading Barbara Godard's translation, ***Lovhers***. Actually, I am reading them both, one book planted on the fingers of my left hand, the other planted on the fingers of my right. Reading this poetry means looking back and forth. That phrase tumbling in French, how does Godard spin it in English? What shifts between this and that French word, this English, that French? And more often, what does that word mean? Sometimes a French-English dictionary triangulates my field of reading, so that interpretation is a juggle: three texts spinning, aerial. Fingers slipping in and out of contiguous pages, head moving back and forth as if in a slow shake of amazement, eyes tracing transformations in shape, sound, sense. French lessons, English lessons. The train stops before I can extricate my hands from ***Amantes*** and *Lovhers,* and I rise abruptly, fingers in spastic collusion with books, making delirious signals. The yellow sign at the C-train tracks announces "Look Both Ways for Trans."

The vertiginous act of reading back and forth has skewed my vision, absenting the "i" from "Trains." But perhaps my error springs not from bleary eyes but from a wish—Octavio Paz tells us, "as always when we talk about accidents, we also talk about desire" (qtd. in Honig 153)—for what I am faced with is a bold-face imperative, black on yellow, to embrace the unusual hermeneutic I practiced on the train. Reading a translation does not necessarily entail looking back and forth; many translations are read as if original, as if the original had been borne whole through a field of linguistic equations. But to read the action, the across, you need to look both ways. You may swing your jaw slowly from left to right and back or, as in the apprehension of a pun, there might be a frenzied shake between meanings. Perhaps it is even possible to look both ways at once, left eyeball going one way, right another. This may be the poet's cross-eyed gift.[1]

Barbara Godard's translation of *Amantes* emerges out of a complex back-and-forth traffic of sounds, signs, nodes of associative potential. Brossard's writing, with its neologisms, polyvalencies, puns, and indeterminacies, demands an attentive, creative translator. In her translator's preface, Godard comments on how her interaction with such an experimental poetic results in the asymmetrical distribution of linguistic play across texts. While some associative clusters arise only out of the English incarnation—Godard cites as an example her spinning out of "sinks" and "ink" in "Igneous Woman"—a pun central to *Amantes,* "deliré," appears in English as ramified paraphrase (11). "Délire" appears in Brossard's text both as a single word and in the recurrent, punning statement, "JE N'ARRÊTE PAS DE LIRE" (11). The pun, a notoriously untranslatable figure, is spelled out in *Lovhers* as "I DON'T STOP READING/DELIRING" (16). In the French, *délire* (or *de lire*) signifies variously as "reading," "delirium" and, as Godard points out, "*dé-lire,* to unread or unfix reading" (11). Working in English, unable to accommodate this particular semantic cluster within one word, Godard concretizes the bipolar constitution of the pun by placing "reading" and "deliring" on either side of a virgule. This slashed construction (compelling the reader to look both ways) marks the operation of translation, not only in its bifurcation of the pun, but also in its exhibition of what appears to be an anglicized French word resulting in an English neologism. Indeed, "deliring" is nowhere to be found in dictionaries of contemporary English usage, and thus functions as an instance of foreignness, a nod both to the linguistic specificity of the first version and to the translator's labor. An etymological dig, however, reveals that the verb "delire" was once in English circulation, losing ground only at the end of the seventeenth century. Delire meant "to go astray, go wrong, err," and was derived, like the French, from the Latin *delirare* which originally meant "to go out of the furrow, to deviate from the straight." When Brossard deploys *délire* in its unbroken form, Godard translates it literally as "delirium," a word that is also derived, like the French and English delire, from *delirare* and signifies a "frenzied rapture."

Brossard invokes *délire/de lire* in order to convey the momentous stimulation, excitation, and creative response a woman experiences when reading the text of another woman. The first section of *Amantes,* "(4): AMANTES/ÉCRIRE," includes multiple citations from other women writers; the words of Mary Daly, Monique Wittig, Sande Zeig, Michele Causse, Adrienne Rich, Louky Bersianik, Djuna Barnes, and others designated by initials, are honored by the refrain, "JE N'ARRÊTE PAS DE LIRE." The following section, "juin le fièvre," makes explicit the productive response provoked by a lover's text; it is a letter of straying response, a writing, which never abandons the imperative of reading: "si j'écris aujourd'hui, c'est afin de te lire mieux comme une provocation . . ." (18), insists the speaker, "if i am writing today it is so i can read you better provocatively" (24). The process celebrated here is not a progression from reading to writing but an energizing circuit of mutual ignition. In her preface to *Lovhers,* Godard proposes a translation strategy that resonates with Brossard's poetic. Moving away from a model of translation that aligns translation acts with vanishing acts, her strategy "would insist on translation as an act of reading, as an interpretation, one among many possible. Translation here is a practice of reading/writing . . ." (7).

Emergent in the poetic models of both Brossard and Godard is a network of agents—translator, reader, writer—all engaged in the production of text. For all, these roles are shared attentions, so that Godard's translating Brossard's book, the poet responding to her lover's letter, my reading the books and writing this essay—all these acts entail at some level reading, writing, translation. All entail looking both ways, refusing the single function, exploding the single meaning, stepping out of the straight furrow, deliring. Exploring the generative interconnectedness of these functions has been a lasting passion of Brossard's. In an interview with Janice Williamson, she says:

> *Personally, I have always been fascinated by translation, as I am usually writing about acts of passage, whether it is passage from fiction to reality, from reality to fiction, or from one language to another. I wrote* **Mauve Desert** *because it blows my mind to think that*

> *someone can consider a reality in their language while I can't in mine and vice-versa. . . . I like to work with translators because it keeps me alert in my own language.*
>
> (70-71)

**Le Désert mauve/Mauve Desert,** in fact, represents Brossard's most explicit demonstration of the metonymic, rather than metaphoric, relations among translation, reading, and writing. The deliring figure in this poetic novel is Maude Laures, who comes across Laure Angstelle's novel, *Le Desert mauve*[2] (comprising the first part of Brossard's book) in a second-hand bookstore; reading it, she is seduced into rewriting it, translating it into *Mauve l'horizon* (comprising the last section of Brossard's book). Laures's "act of passage" can be suggestively articulated through the invocation of a mode of interpretation Julia Kristeva names "delirium" ("délire" in the original French). After contextualizing Kristeva's delirium within the European tradition of thought around *délire,* I will introduce her provocative notion into my discussion of the several acts of passage at work in the production of **Le Desert mauve/Mauve Desert.** Several bodies, some more textualized than others, participate: the fictive Maude Laures translates Laure Angstelle homolinguistically, the living Susanne de Lotbinière-Harwood translates Brossard across languages, and I read **Le Desert mauve** and **Mauve Desert** together, in effect reading four novels simultaneously. I opened this section with an account of my encumbered hands, with Brossard's play on *de lire/ délire,* and now proceed to Kristeva's notion of delirium with a wish to highlight, rather than isolate, the function of reading as it joins translation and writing to comprise the cluster of energies propelling **Mauve Desert** and, more generally, Brossard's poetic.

*Délire,* or delirium—Jean-Jacques Lecercle favors retaining the French in his discussion of this complex term—is a prevalent concept in European (particularly French) philosophy, linguistics, and psychoanalysis. Lecercle's *Philosophy through the Looking Glass* traces the various traditions and incarnations of *délire/* delirium, arriving at some definitions that are as consistent as such a critical text, which adopts a method informed by its own delirious object, can allow. Focusing on certain disjunctive writers (Raymond Roussel, Jean-Pierre Brisset, Louis Wolfson), case-studies of schizophrenia (notably that of Daniel Paul Schreber), and unconventional critics (Gilles Deleuze), Lecercle characterizes *délire*/delirium as "a form of discourse . . . where the material side of language, its origin in the human body and *desire,* are no longer eclipsed by its abstract aspect (as an instrument of communication or expression)" (6). *Délire*/delirium is consistently referred to in Lecercle as "the other side of language" (65), a phrase that suggests this discursive mode's deviations from protocols of syntax, grammar, phonotactics, logic. Attending the uncertain distinction in Lecercle between the poet and the schizophrenic patient is a contradiction through which the issue of agency, or mastery, percolates. On the one hand, Lecercle submits that "*délire* is a perversion which consists in interfering, or rather taking risks, with language" (16); he can also assert, however, that "in the case of delire, language is master" (9). Perhaps such an uncertainty surrounding the question of how the subject is disposed to language springs from Lecercle's notion (borrowed from Deleuze) that "*délire* is the linguistic manifestation of desire" (165). Desire can always be imagined, produced, theorized in complex, oblique, and contradictory relation with the subject; we speak of desire as an unconscious drive, a conscious motivation and, indeed, a consciousness.[3] Consonant with Lecercle's ambivalence, Kristeva's delirious subject hovers over a distinction between being overwhelmed by the discursive mode of *délire*/delirium and employing it as a vehicle of transgression. Her important departure within a psychoanalytic tradition, however, lies in her refusal to reserve delirium for certain types of subjects, a refusal to fantasize, in other words, delirium as proper only to schizophrenic patients.

In "Psychoanalysis and the Polis," Kristeva focuses on interpretation, compensating somewhat for the underplayed role of the reader in *Revolution in Poetic Language* as she differentiates between ways of reading and their implications for both subject and societal formations. Kristeva begins her article with a critique of what she calls "political interpretation" (304). The word "political" here is apparently deployed, as Toril Moi suggests, in "its original Greek sense of 'popular' (*politikos*) discourse, or discourse for and of the citizens (*polites*) of the city-state (*polis*)" (301). Indeed, the hermeneutic designated as "political" in Kristeva's article is that which institutes the irrefutability of singular, delimited meanings; she points to Fascism and Stalinism as totalitarian outcomes of political interpretation. Such an interpretive mode arises, she argues, from "the simple desire to give a meaning, to explain, to provide the answer," and this desire in turn springs from the "subject's need to reassure himself of his image and his identity faced with an object" (304). She views the project of psychoanalysis as offering an antidote to such an interpretive mode, as it is founded on the notion of a cloven subject, in whom the presence of an unconscious precludes the possibility of conscious mastery and thus of singular meaning. Also underlining the energy of desire, psychoanalysis becomes both inspiration and privileged example of the interpretive mode Kristeva advocates, a mode characterized by delirium. Her focus on the delirious interpreter (or analyst) can be read as a fruitful response to Gilles Deleuze and Félix Guattari's critique, in *Anti-Oedipus,* of a psychoanalytic tradition of imposing reductive, pre-ordained interpretations on the rich, transgressive, and fantastical discourse of the delirious patient. Addressing the problem of subjective insecurity, of the threat semantic incoherence poses to the coherence of the subject, Kristeva emphasizes the "lucidity and ethics" (304) promised in the complex and unpredictable results of the new interpreter's delirium.

Kristeva argues that the interpreter should submit to the undeniable and exciting fact that "the knowing subject is also a desiring subject, and the paths of desire ensnarl the paths of knowledge" (307). The desire propelling Maude Laures's reading of *Le Désert mauve* is made explicit. When that book falls into her hands it "arous[es] the throbbing desire that never quit her" and for two years she "stretche[s] herself through the pages" (51). While *Le Désert mauve* has "seduced her" (62), it is her own desire that extends the production of that book. The erotics thematized here points to a dynamic of intersubjectivity wherein the reader makes as many passes as there are passages. "Ensnarled" with desire, the reader's knowledge is subject to desire's unconscious realms, its changeability, vagaries, idiosyncracies. Knowledge, giving way to delirium, proves neither a passive replica of its object nor the inevitable result of a predetermined interpretive schema that evacuates its object of possibility. What the delirious reader produces instead, Kristeva suggests, is "a fiction, an uncentred discourse, a subjective polytopia" (306). Certainly this is the outcome of Maude Laure's desiring, deliring interpretation. Stretching herself through the pages, sleeping on it often, she finds that it "is not always possible to dream without having to follow through on the images" (55), and she writes her own delirious "fiction," *Mauve, l'horizon.*

A useful analogue to Kristevan delirium can be found in *The Pleasure of the Text,* written by Roland Barthes, one of Kristeva's contemporaries in the *Tel Quel* group. Barthes proposes an "erotics of reading" (Howard v) for which the ideal text to read is clearly a "modern" one (Barthes 12), one that "unsettles the reader's historical, cultural, psychological assumptions, the consistency of his tastes, values, memories, brings to a crisis his relation with language" (14).[4] While privileging such defamiliarizing, polylingual "texts of bliss" (21), Barthes maintains his emphasis on the reader's role, suggesting that even when encountering a traditional narrative, we can transform or derail the intended experience by leafing through, jumping around. "Our very avidity for knowledge," he claims, "impels us to skim or to skip certain passages" (11). This "avidity" speaks to the desirous knowledge of delirium, and to the skipping and flipping I do as my fingers work among the four novels which make up **Le Désert mauve/Mauve Desert.** Yet I don't flip to get past the expositions, explanations, and descriptions of linear narrative prose; **Le Désert mauve/Mauve Desert,** foregrounding the problematic of translation, invites flipping back and forth, looking both ways. In her novel, Brossard has presented us with a striking testament to the erotics of reading; Barthes claims that a text of bliss can only be "reached through another text of bliss" (22), and Laures's *Mauve l'horizon* is that answering "text of bliss." Similarly, Susanne de Lotbiniere-Harwood's translations, *Mauve Desert* and *Mauve, the Horizon* are themselves further texts of bliss.

Barthes locates textual pleasure in a bustling *entre*: "Between two onslaughts of words, between two imposing systematic presences, the pleasure of the text is always possible, not as respite, but as the incongruous—dissociated—passage from another language . . ." (30). While the disjunctive "modern" text, favoring juxtaposition and interruption over normative syntax, occasions pleasurable readings of between, I note that translation, the "passage from another language," functions here as privileged template. Translation is the spectral figure haunting Barthes' book from the onset, where he insists that "the subject gains access to bliss by the cohabitation of languages *working side by side*: the text of pleasure is a sanctioned Babel" (4). Indeed, the between of translation is exemplary, when visible. (Its magnitude can also extend into virtual invisibility, rendering either original or translation a speck in that distance.) In **Mauve Desert,** both original and translation appear, constituting and concretizing a between which, dense with the meditations of Maude Laures, occupies more space than both novels put together.

The force of a between is celebrated in Elizabeth Meese's *(Sem)erotics,* a study that inflects Barthes' interleaving of desire, text, and reading with the particularity of a lesbian poetics. *(Sem)erotics* posits "the lesbian love letter" (26) as genre and as amorous paradigm through which to consider many of the lesbian experimental works of this century as well as the relationships among author, text, reader. In choosing the love letter as paradigm, Meese initiates an elaboration of the interstitial, the "energetics" (123) between sender and receiver, text and reader, and letters both epistolary and alphabetical.[5] The back-and-forth traffic of love letters ensures a certain repetition she deems imperative to the survival of lesbian culture:

> Saying it, over and over, in our own ways helps make it so: L, L, L, L. Dear L, we need to play it again and again and again, patiently recording the variations in our tunes.
>
> (128)

The interstices between "the variations in our tunes" and between the variations on **Le Désert mauve** dilate and contract, enabling Barthesian blissful readings of repetition's stray.

*Re-belle et Infidèle/The Body Bilingual* is the title of Susanne de Lotbiniere-Harwood's account of her own bilingualism, her particular history as a translator, and her theorizations on translation as feminist practice. The French half of her title, *Re-belle et Infidèle,* reworks the traditional tag "belles infidèles" (unfaithful beauties), an expression indexing the imperial practice of skewing the sense of foreign language texts to confirm target-culture ideologies. Because Lotbinière-Harwood brings to her translations a particularly language-centered feminist ethic, an ethic that assumes her medium is compromised by the sedimentation of misogynist bias, skewing text can prove an act of renewal and survival. She comments on her title: "My addition of the prefix re-changes the beauties into rebels and implies repetition with change" (99). This "change" could be seen to result from the desire innervating delirium, a state in which, Kristeva says, "the speaking subject is presumed to have known an object, a relationship, an experience that he is henceforth incapable of reconstituting accurately" (307). The sense of delire as "err" and the idea of accuracy as casualty of desire raise questions about the role of voluntarism, or conscious rebellion—questions that Brossard engages in **Mauve Desert.** Close to the beginning of *Un Livre à traduire,* the elaborate "between" of Brossard's book, appears the phrase, "Elle plonge, est-ce erreur ou strategie" (57). ("She dives in, is this mistake or strategy. (53).) Further down the page we find a word that might have occasioned that question, "l'auteure." In French "auteur," author, is gendered male; Brossard's erroneous addition of an "e muet," or silent "e," which marks the feminine in French grammar, makes visible the exclusionary function of grammatical structures and mobilizes the *e muet* with a view to feminist resignification. The author is embodied differently, transgendered, through a mistake in spelling that has been foreshadowed as strategic. The inaccurate reconstitution of "auteur," one that has been widely deployed by Quebec feminists, is indeed a grammatical error, yet an intentional one, one that attempts to makes sense of "the non-sense patriarchal reality constitutes for us" (Brossard, **Aerial Letter** 112).

When Susanne de Lotbinière-Harwood embarked on the English translation of **Le Désert mauve,** she was faced with the dilemma of how to feminize "author" in a target language framed by different grammatical schemata. Feminist translators are aware that because of the "technical difficulties" between the two languages, English translations can neutralize feminist subversions that exploit the gender-marking of French. The force of error in its more delirious guise is evidenced in Lotbinière-Harwood's anecdote about her translation of "auteure":

> How it came about: my colleague Marie-Cecile Brasseur and I were drafting a work-related letter on computer. She was inputting as I dictated. Instead of typing "author" she slipped and wrote "auther." "Eureka," I gasped, "that's it!"
>
> (131)

This instance of rebellion (which "repeats with change" both "auteure" and "author") illustrates the potential of the cleavage in the subject discovered by psychoanalysis. Brasseur's "slip" is apparently unconscious, yet it is consonant with the desires of a feminist poetic to the extent that Brasseur's collaborator, Lotbinière-Harwood, regards it as a gift and a textual solution. Delirium, that state where "the imaginary may join interpretive closure" (Kristeva 307), produces such gifts-"e" slips over "o" to create "auther" and "i" slips from trains to make "trans." More important than the quest to distinguish between the strategic and the erratic (and their respective value) is perhaps the ability to welcome moments when, in the rapturous state of delirium, the two are productively interlined.

The complex "auteure"/"auther" is the result of collaboration, not only between Brasseur and Lotbinière-Harwood, but between Lotbinière-Harwood and Brossard. The reader/translator's desire to find a feminized "author" is excited by Brossard's subversion, and that subversion is extended through translation. Pertinent here is a description of the generative bivalence Kristeva observes in delirium:

> . . . the object may reveal to the interpreter the unknown of his theory and permit the constitution of a new theory. Discourse in this case is renewed; it can begin again: it forms a new object and a new interpretation in this reciprocal transference.
>
> (306)

"Reciprocal transference" could serve to characterize the acts of passage carried out among the various readers/writers/translators I've been discussing. Replacing a notion of the unidirectional flow of knowledge (from intending author, from source language, from original), delirium's "reciprocal transference" acknowledges the traffic between readers, languages, versions, words. In *Le Désert mauve,* Laure Angstelle writes, "Lorna dit qu'elle aimait le moly et la mousse de saumon" (12). Noting the turbine of alliteration here, Maude Laures translates, "Lorna s'émerveilla a propos de la mousse au sommet des montagnes, douce sur les mollets" (182), moving *m*'s off of the kitchen range and onto a mountain range. This is truly "literal," letteral translation.[6] "Mousse" has survived the transfer physically intact, yet semantically skewed, or expanded; the second "mousse" whips moss into its antecedent, salmon mousse, conferring on it the pleasure of a homonym. A further instance of reciprocal transference is inaugurated by Lotbinière-Harwood, when she reads Maude Laures's translation as, "Lorna marveled over the moss on the mountaintops, soft against the shins" (168). Although "douce sur les mollets" means "soft against the calves," Lotbinière-Harwood delires it as "soft against the shins"; in doing so she welcomes the alliteration of the original's *m*'s and *s*'s while moving meaning beyond. Given a leg up, she twists it around for the sound of it, for a new sense. Here is a moment that demonstrates Lecercle's notion of *délire*/delirium as exposing "the material side of language, its origin in the human body."

A dynamic of reciprocal transference supposes the active presence of the interpreter. In the world of **Mauve Desert**, where translation is the dominant figure of interpretation, this means making visible an agent traditionally obscured, the translator. The construction of **Mauve Desert** honors the vision Lotbinière-Harwood articulates in *Re-belle et Infidèle*, that of a "co-authorship" between writer and translator (155). Confronted with Angstelle's compelling book, Laures imagines herself to be a "minimal presence. . . . A marker perhaps between this book and its becoming in another language. This remained precisely to be seen" (51). The deictic, "this," in the last sentence might refer to the eventual translation, that text which remains to be seen. The "perhaps" of the preceding sentence, however, points to another possible antecedent; "this" can refer to "minimal presence" and "A marker," indexing the conventional invisibility of translators and denying it as *a priori*. It is "precisely" the translator and her labor that, historically, remain "to be seen." In this particular context, what remains "precisely to be seen is whether the translator will indeed only act as "marker." The rest of the book demonstrates that she moves far beyond that; *A Book to Translate*, the 116-page narrative and record of Laures's creative process, stages a remarkable translative labor.

Delirious readings, Kristeva suggests, exhibit "a transforming power" (307). Clearly, the syntax, drift, and noise shift among versions, but what or who has been radically transformed in **Mauve Desert**? Here, I recall the cloven scaffolding of "Psychoanalysis and the Polis" and attempt to unsettle Kristeva's opposition of political interpretation and delirium. Transforming her sense of the "political" into the sense deployed in contemporary feminist and poetic communities, I want to pull it into delirium's realm; delirium, as it is played out through **Mauve Desert**, is crucial to a "political" that, in direct contradiction to Kristeva's use, can inspire Brossard to state: "I don't believe that one becomes a writer to reinforce common values or common perspectives on reality" (**"Poetic Politics"** 73). Brossard's delired "auteure" or Lotbinière-Harwood's answering neologism "auther," for example, are motivated by the assumption of an interdependence between linguistic and social structures, and thus gesture toward political transformation. But Brossard's ethic of creating a more hospitable, even compelling, language for women is not always marked by neologism. More often, in fact, Brossard chooses to repeat certain words over and over, threading them through various contexts in an effort to resignify. Any reader familiar with her work will already register the charge of the words "horizon," "vertigo," "reality."

In *Un Livre à Traduire/A Book to Translate*, Maude Laures interprets and imagines aspects of the source text, elaborating on settings and characters and composing conversations. She also elaborates on what she calls "Dimensions," and their names prove to be the words that are repeated in this book to the point of shimmering: desert, dawn, light, reality, beauty, fear, civilization. The first appearance of "civilization," for example, is modified by a reference to atom bomb testing, "the civilization of men who came to the desert to watch their equations explode like a humanity" (13). Brossard already begins, then, from the point of negative resignification Adrienne Rich initiated in her article "Disloyal to Civilization," which interrogates the misogyny and racism implicated in what passes for "civilized." Later appearances of the word are inflected, alternatively, as positive or negative, with the leap between often overlapping the translative gap. Laure Angstelle has Mélanie describe herself as "civilization in reverse" (19), while Maude Laures translates the self-portrait, "I was speed, civilization, in the distance, city, lost gaze, ruin in reverse" (175). The substitution of "ruin" for "civilization" in the final phrase invites the pessimistic consideration of the mutuality of these terms, while in its new syntactical position, the second "civilization" assumes a hopeful cast. In another case, a utopic deployment of the word is delired into a use of "civilization" that, again, resonates with Rich's argument:

*Some day I would know the silence and the secret that lives on inside beings so that other civilizations may be born.*

(36)

. . . . . . . . . . . . . . . . . . . . . . . .

*Some day I would experience everything in synchrony, ecstasy, the secrets which from within undermine dear civilization.*

(192)

There is no simple progression, in **Mauve Desert**, from a negative to a positive inflection of "civilization." Rather, its persistent "repetition with change" compels the reader to perform the defamiliarizing act of looking both ways, and arouses in her, all at once, suspicion, critique, hope.

The "transforming power" of Kristeva's delirious mode of interpretation, then, should not be conceived as one that shapes words into static conclusions. The transformation of language, or "resignification" (to use Judith Butler's term), is a process rather than a task, as can be observed in the drama of the word "horizon" in **Mauve**

*Desert.* "Horizon" emerges as a highly invested term in Brossard's book, as is signaled by the translation of Laure Angstelle's title, *Le Désert mauve/Mauve Desert,* into Maude Laures's title, *Mauve, l'horizon/Mauve, the Horizon.* On a mundane level, the horizon is that ever-shifting contour of land toward which Mélanie races in her Meteor. Suggestively in flux, shifting with vantage point and atmosphere, a limit to the seen that promises a beyond, the figure of the horizon takes on the rhetorical significance here of a permeable line between reality and fiction, between the sayable and the unsaid, between the imagined and the unimaginable, between the normative and the perverse. Along this line, Brossard martials words that resonate with a potential world where a lesbian reality is no longer considered fictional, where patriarchal fictions disperse, where knowledges are "ensnarled" with a woman-centered desire. The horizon itself, in other words, functions as a figure for the dynamic of resignification operant on language in the novel, including that very word, "horizon." Resignification entails the unfaithful citation of "horizon," its deployment in varying contexts. Laure Angstelle writes of the "vanishing horizon" (18) while Laures translates that as "the repeated horizon" (174). At times "the horizon is a mirage" (28), while at other times it is something of which you can be "certain" (23). It can be set in threatening language, as in "*crazy cracks horizons horrible zones of laughter*" (28), and also be characterized as "magical" (23), "beautiful" (184) and "immediate" (179). "The horizon is curving," notes Mélanie on her way back to the Motel (24); and, indeed, the word "horizon" *is* "curving." *Mauve, l'horizon* is not a translation into anything so final as a "target" language, rather it joins *Mauve Desert* to produce a "horizon" language, where familiar terms warp and curve.

While Judith Butler's *Bodies That Matter* proceeds on assumptions that the improper constitutes the proper and the abject constitutes the normative, her "political" contribution to these deconstructive commonplaces lies in her interrogation of limits, of the surety of distinctions between what counts and what is relegated to an outside. She argues that "the task is to refigure this necessary 'outside' as a future *horizon,* one in which the violence of exclusion is perpetually in the process of being overcome" (53 my emphasis). According to Butler, this process of overcoming exclusion, silence, and oppression is driven by the engine of citation or, rather, the instability of that engine, which allows for an emancipatory ripple in the horizon. Maude Laures's unstable citation, or "repetition with change," of Angstelle's *Mauve Desert,* agitates signification in the places, things, characters, scenes, and dimensions of Mélanie's desert, Mélanie who has "eyes that seek to get ahead of the horizon" (120). Laures's motivation for reading/translating *Mauve Desert* is clear; she undertakes it for the "approach and possibility of some transformations" (54). She is like the woman in *Amantes/Lovhers,* who experiences "all her senses . . . working for her to give her pleasure and to make her think up a version of existence which takes a displacement of the horizon for granted" (80).

The "transforming power" Kristeva attributes to delirious reading is affirmed by Brossard's belief that "it is in the reading that a text has a political aura (**"Poetic Politics"** 78). In Barbara Godard's reading of **Amantes,** in Lotbinière-Harwood's reading of *Le Désert mauve,* in Maude Laures's reading of Laure Angstelle's novel, the transformative effects of the "two-way passage" (*Mauve Desert* 57) are vital, radical. It is Brossard's radical reading of Brossard, however, that I would like to acknowledge at this point. Perhaps it is time, in other words, to dismantle her fiction (one I have maintained in my discussion) that *Le Désert mauve* is written by two people. While this novel's pretense of dual authership offers a crucial critique of conventional notions of originality and translative invisibility, as well as dramatizing the energy and erotics made possible through the textual meeting of two women, *Le Désert mauve* is, in fact, written by Brossard. This novel is a more theatrical incarnation of a compositional process Brossard engages in all her writing, a delirous self-reading, a poetics of autotranslation. Dismantling the fiction of dual authership entails dismantling somewhat the generative fiction of translation that propels the book. In "Reading Nicole Brossard," Susan Knutson articulates the dynamic function of translation in Brossard's poetic:

> As in **L'Aviva,** Brossard in **Le Désert mauve** *translates Brossard from French into French, and again, she points clearly to translation not so much as an exploration of the physical frontiers of languages and cultures—although these are still present as fictions, as metaphors, as incitations—but rather as the drive to reach the internal horizons of meaning and the consciousness or construction of reality.*
>
> (12)

While I would use the term metonym, rather than metaphor, to characterize translation's intimate relation to her poetics—thus my inclusion of the Godard and Lotbinière-Harwood material—I take as paramount Knutson's observation that it is the "internal horizons" that are at stake. Internal horizons comprise the field of action in a translative poetic; one writer reads her own language over, looking behind and ahead of words, looking deliriously both ways, so that language chafes at itself and at the realities it both reflects and envisions.

### Notes

1. Peter Quartermain deems it significant that Robert Duncan, who often published several incarnations of a single poem, was cross-eyed: "How, if you're cross-eyed, can reading not be revision? And how can revision ever stop" (109)?

2. For the sake of clarity, the titles of Brossard's and Lotbinière-Harwood's books will remain italicized while the novels *within* those novels will be underlined in the remainder of this text.

3. Lesbian performance artist Holly Hughes recalls discovering her desire as an experience "that the expression 'coming out' doesn't quite cover. In my case, it was more a question of . . . coming to" (191).

4. Godard honors his deliring theory in her preface to *Lovhers* when she declares, "Reader, the pleasure of the text is now yours" (12).

5. The love letter is especially pertinent to the composition of *Le Désert mauve/Mauve Desert*; Laure Angstelle wrote her novel during a time when she was reading and rereading a lesbian love letter she found in a geology book (83). In a sense, *Le Désert mauve* reads that letter and writes back.

6. My use of "literal" here favors the OED definition, "expressed by letters of the alphabet." Louis and Celia Zukofsky's translation of Catullus is founded on this definition, as their preface indicates: "This translation of Catullus follows the sound, rhythm, and syntax of his Latin—tries, as is said, to breathe the 'literal' meaning with him" (n. pag.).

### Works Cited

Barthes, Roland. *The Pleasure of the Text*. Trans. Richard Miller. New York: Hill and Wang, 1975.

Brossard, Nicole. *The Aerial Letter*. Trans. Marlene Wildeman. Toronto: The Women's P, 1988.

———. *Amantes*. Montréal: Les Quinze, 1980.

———. *Le Désert mauve*. Montréal: l'Hexagone, 1987.

———. *Lovhers*. Trans. Barbara Godard. Montreal: Guernica, 1986.

———. *Mauve Desert*. Trans. Susanne de Lotbinière-Harwood. Toronto: Coach House P, 1990.

———. "Poetic Politics." *The Politics of Poetic Form*. Ed. Charles Bernstein. New York: Roof, 1990. 73-86.

Butler, Judith. *Bodies That Matter*. New York: Routledge, 1993.

de Lotbinière-Harwood, Susanne. *Re-Belle et Infidèle/The Body Bilingual*. Montréal: Les editions du remue-menage/Women's P, 1991.

Honig, Edwin. *The Poet's Other Voice: Conversations on Literary Translation*. Amherst: U of Massachusetts P, 1985.

Howard, Richard. Introduction. *The Pleasure of the Text* by Roland Barthes. New York: Hill and Wang, 1975. v-viii.

Hughes, Holly. "Clit Notes." *Clit Notes: A Sapphic Sampler*. New York: Grove P, 1996.

Knutson, Susan. "Reading Nicole Brossard." *ellipse* 53 (1995): 9-21.

Kristeva, Julia. "Psychoanalysis and the Polis." Trans. Margaret Waller. *The Kristeva Reader*. Ed. Toril Moi. New York: Columbia UP, 1986. 301-20.

Lecercle, Jean-Jacques. *Philosophy through the Looking Glass: Language, Nonsense, Desire*. La Salle: Open Court, 1985.

Meese, Elizabeth. *(Sem)erotics: theorizing lesbian: writing*. New York: New York UP, 1992.

Moi, Toril, ed. *The Kristeva Reader*. New York: Columbia UP, 1986.

Quartermain, Peter. "Duncan's Texts." *Sulfur* 40 (1997): 108-121.

Rich, Adrienne. "Disloyal to Civilization: Feminism, Racism, Gynephobia." *On Lies, Secrets, and Silence: Selected Prose 1966-1978*. 275-310.

Williamson, Janice. Interview with Nicole Brossard. *Sounding Differences: Conversations with Seventeen Canadian Women Writers*. Toronto: U of Toronto P, 1993. 57-74.

Zukofsky, L., and C. Zukofsky. *Catullus (Gal Catulli Veronensis Liber)*. New York: Grossman, 1969.

---

# FURTHER READING

### Criticism

Brossard, Nicole. "Interview with Nicole Brossard on *Picture Theory*." *Canadian Fiction Magazine*, no. 47 (1983): 122-35.

> Brossard discusses the form and major themes of *Picture Theory* and the novel's relationship to her entire body of work.

Brossard, Nicole, and Daphne Marlatt. "Only a Body to Measure Reality By: Writing the In-Between." *Journal of Commonwealth Literature* 31, no. 2 (1996): 5-17.

> Brossard and Marlatt discuss their thoughts and observations on the centrality of the body in relation to their writing.

Diehl-Jones, Charlene. Review of *Green Night of Labyrinth Park*, by Nicole Brossard. *Books in Canada* 22, no. 5 (summer 1993): 38-40.

> Diehl-Jones lauds Brossard's fascination with subjectivity and sensitivity to language in the poetry of *Green Night of Labyrinth Park*.

Godard, Barbara. "Producing Visibility for Lesbians: Nicole Brossard's Quantum Poetics." *English Studies in Canada* 21, no. 2 (June 1995): 125-37.

> Godard considers Brossard's application of quantum theory to her discussion of visualization and lesbian poetics in *Picture Theory*.

Huffer, Lynne. "From Lesbos to Montreal: Nicole Brossard's Urban Fictions." *Yale French Studies,* no. 90 (1996): 95-114.

> Huffer explores Brossard's writing in *French Kiss, Amantes, The Aerial Letter,* and other works as they define a prototype of the urban, radical feminist.

Kaganoff, Peggy. Review of *Picture Theory,* by Nicole Brossard. *Publishers Weekly* 238, no. 17 (12 April 1991): 53.

> Kaganoff faults Brossard's forays into feminist theorizing and anti-narrative in the poetry and prose of *Picture Theory,* calling the work flat, fragmentary, and narcissistic.

Parker, Alice A. Review of *Picture Theory* and *Mauve Desert,* by Nicole Brossard. *Belles Lettres* 9, no. 3 (spring 1994): 6-7, 9.

> Parker presents a thematic summary of Brossard's literary works and approvingly evaluates her ambitious, postmodern novels, *Mauve Desert* and *Picture Theory*.

Prieto, René. "In-Fringe: The Role of French Criticism in the Fiction of Nicole Brossard and Severo Sarduy." In *Do the Americas Have a Common Literature?,* pp. 266-81. Durham, N.C.: Duke University Press, 1990.

> Prieto compares the influence of James Joyce and contemporary French critical theory—from such writers as Julia Kristeva, Jacques Derrida, and Roland Barthes—on Brossard and the Cuban writer Severo Sarduy.

Siemerling, Winfried. "The Visibility of the Utopian Form in the Work of Nicole Brossard." In *Discoveries of the Other: Alterity in the Work of Leonard Cohen, Hubert Aquin, Michael Ondaatje, and Nicole Brossard,* pp. 173-204. Toronto: University of Toronto Press, 1994.

> Siemerling examines the utopian method of Brossard's fiction—particularly of her novel *Picture Theory*—within the framework of a full-length, poststructuralist and feminist analysis of visibility and otherness.

Review of *Mauve Desert,* by Nicole Brossard. *University of Toronto Quarterly* 62, no. 1 (fall 1992): 109-10.

> The critic comments specifically on the status of translation in Susanne de Lotbinière-Harwood's English rendering of *Le Désert mauve* in relation to the thematic focus on author, translator, and text in Brossard's original version of the novel.

Verwaayan, Kimberly. "Region/Body: In? Of? And? Or? (Alter/Native) Separatism in the Politics of Nicole Brossard." *Essays on Canadian Writing,* no. 61 (spring 1997): 1-16.

> Verwaayan highlights the theme of separatism and an analogous commitment to Quebec nationalism in the writings of Brossard.

---

**Additional coverage of Brossard's life and career is contained in the following sources published by the Gale Group:** *Contemporary Authors,* **Vol. 122;** *Contemporary Authors Autobiography Series,* **Vol. 16;** *Contemporary Canadian Authors,* **Vol. 1;** *Contemporary Literary Criticism,* **Vol. 115;** *Contemporary Women Poets; Contemporary World Writers,* **Ed. 2;** *Dictionary of Literary Biography,* **Vol. 53;** *Feminist Writers; Gay & Lesbian Literature,* **Ed. 2;** *Literature Resource Center;* **and** *Reference Guide to World Literature,* **Ed. 3.**

# Elfriede Jelinek
## 1946-

Austrian novelist, playwright, and screenwriter.

The following entry presents an overview of Jelinek's career through 2002.

## INTRODUCTION

One of Austria's most prolific and political writers, Jelinek is best known for her outspoken feminism and sharp criticism of capitalist patriarchy. Although openly admitting to a feminist agenda, Jelinek is primarily concerned in her writing with the material conditions of the working class in a capitalist society, paying particular attention to its effects on the position of women. Her works typically feature female protagonists who become victims of male-perpetrated abuse, such as domestic violence or sexual exploitation. Heavily influenced by the works of dramatist Bertholt Brecht, Jelinek often uses graphic depictions and crude, deliberately shocking language to lampoon cultural assumptions, conventions, and taboos.

## BIOGRAPHICAL INFORMATION

Jelinek was born on October 20, 1946, in Muerzzuschlag, Steiermark, Austria. Raised in Vienna by her Romanian-German mother and Czech-Jewish father, Jelinek struggled under a rigorous schedule of academic studies and musical training. She was enrolled concurrently in a local parochial school and the Viennese Conservatory of Music, where she studied piano, organ, viola, and composition. While she was in secondary school, her father became mentally ill and was placed in a mental institution. Following her graduation, with distinction, from the Albertsgymnasium in 1964, Jelinek also suffered an emotional breakdown. During the two years following her collapse, Jelinek became interested in writing. She continued to write while studying art history and drama at the University of Vienna, and while completing her study of the organ at the conservatory. In 1966 Jelinek received her first critical recognition and encouragement for her writing after submitting some of her poetry to the Austrian Society for Literature. In 1969 she received prizes for both poetry and prose at the Twentieth Austrian Festival of Youth and Culture in Innsbruck. After the publication of her first two novels—*Lisas Schatten: 7 Gedichte* (1967) and *Wir sind lockvögel baby!* (1970; *Wonderful, Wonderful Times*)—Jelinek was commissioned to write several radio plays, receiving the Radio Play Award of the West German War Blind in 1973. She moved to Berlin in 1972 and later lived for extended periods in Rome and Paris. Her involvement with the student and feminist movements as well as her affiliation with the Marxist Party led to Jelinek's public break with bourgeois values, a process she chronicled in a series of essays published between 1970 and 1971. In 1974 she married Gottfried Huengsberg. Jelinek has received several awards for her work, including the Interior Ministry of West Germany award for best screenplay in 1979, the Heinrich-Böll award in 1986, and the Honorary Award for Literature of Vienna in 1989.

## MAJOR WORKS

Although most of Jelinek's novels are set in a fictitious rural Austrian village, her books typically are not concerned with regional characters or issues. Instead, Jelinek's narratives use a variety of verbal images borrowed from the media, television, and comic strips to deconstruct societal myths of family, love, self-determination, and free will. In *Die Liebhaberinnen* (1975; *Women as Lovers*) two young Austrian girls, Brigitte and Paula, struggle to find personal and financial independence. While both aspire to find true love, Brigitte settles for a financially stable marriage with an electrician. Paula, however, refuses to compromise her lifestyle and begins to work at a local factory. She later marries an alcoholic who beats her and her children. *Die Klavierspielerin* (1983; *The Piano Teacher*) chronicles the story of Erika Kohut, a shy, thirty-year-old piano instructor at the Vienna Conservatory of Music. When a young student named Walter Klemmer shows an interest in her, Erika begins to rebel against her domineering mother, indulging in voyeurism and a sadomasochistic sexual relationship with Klemmer. When her emotional and physical demands become too extreme, Klemmer attacks Erika and leaves. In *Lust* (1989) Jelinek portrays the impossibility of female desire through the wife of a factory owner who is treated as property by her husband.

Jelinek's plays address many of the same themes as her novels, focusing heavily on the injustices in capitalist societies and the marginalization of women. Her play *Was geschah, nachdem Nora ihren mann verlassen hatte* oder Stutzen der Gesellschaften (1979; *What Happened after Nora Left Her Husband or the Pillars of Society*) was written as a sequel to Henrik Ibsen's *A Doll's House,* using Ibsen's protagonist, Nora, to show how a small capitalist elite is able to control political and economic institutions and, through them, the destinies of the many. In Jelinek's play Nora frees herself from her upper-class role as a wife and mother to become a factory worker. *Clara S.: Musikalische Tragödie* (1982; *Clara S.: A Musical Tragedy*) portrays a fictional meeting in 1929 between nineteenth-century German composer Clara Schumann and Gabriele D'Annunzio, a late nineteenth/early twentieth-century Italian author and political leader. Jelinek attracted public controversy with her play *Burgtheater* (1985), which depicted a selection of sordid scenes from private lives of well-known actors at the Burgtheater, Austria's national theater. Jelinek reveals the actors as shallow, petty tyrants and makes allegations about the theater's past collaboration with the Nazi regime. *Krankheit oder Moderne Frauen* (1987; *Illness or Modern Women*) is a graphic farce about gender relations that follows a woman named Emily and her friend Carmilla and their two husbands. Carmilla dies during childbirth, but is then turned into a vampire by Emily. Jelinek contrasts Emily and Carmilla's vampirism—a condition that leaves them neither dead nor alive—with the exaggerated vitality of Carmilla's husband, Dr. Benno Hundekoffer. Jelinek has also authored a number of radio plays, including *Untergang eines tauchers* (1973; *Demise of a Diver*), *Die Bienenkönige* (1976; *The King Bees*), and *Erziehung eines Vampirs* (1986; *Bringing up a Vampire*).

## CRITICAL RECEPTION

Jelinek's unique narrative style has been the subject of much critical attention. Feminist critics have praised her examinations of the exploitation of women in patriarchal societies and her commitment to exposing the violence perpetrated against women. Nevertheless, some female scholars have argued that Jelinek's plays and novels work against feminist causes because of their brutal depictions of female sexuality, masochism, and self-mutilation. Several male critics have concurred with this assessment, citing the cold and overly analytical nature of Jelinek's prose. Such criticism has caused the Austrian media to frequently refer to Jelinek as the nation's "best-hated author." Commentators have also debated Jelinek's use of Marxist theory in her writing, noting the firm sense of class-consciousness in *Die Liebhaberinnen* and other works. *Lust* has attracted a great deal of critical controversy, with many reviewers arguing that the novel is a work of pornography. Still, Jelinek has been consistently praised throughout her career for her skill with satire and political commentary, earning comparisons to such authors as Johann Nestroy, Karl Kraus, and Elias Canetti.

## PRINCIPAL WORKS

*Lisas Schatten: 7 Gedichte* (novel) 1967

*Wir sind lockvögel baby!* [*Wonderful, Wonderful Times*] (novel) 1970

*Michael: Ein jugendbuch für die infantilgesellschaft* [*Michael: A Children's Book for the Infantile Society*] (novel) 1972

*Wenn die Sonne sinkt ist für manche auch noch büroschluss!* [*For Some, the Setting Sun Means the End of a Working Day*] (radio play) 1972

*Untergang eines tauchers* [*Demise of a Diver*] (radio play) 1973

*Kasperl und die dicke Prinzessin oder Kasperl und die dünnen bauern* [*Kasperl and the Chubby Princess or Kasperl and the Skinny Peasants*] (radio play) 1974

*Die Liebhaberinnen* [*Women as Lovers*] (novel) 1975

*Die Bienenkönige* [*The King Bees*] (radio play) 1976

*Was geschah, nachdem Nora ihren mann verlassen hatte oder Stutzen der Gesellschaften* [*What Happened after Nora Left Her Husband or the Pillars of Society*] (play) 1979

*Die Ausgesperrten* (novel) 1980

*Clara S.: Musikalische Tragödie* [*Clara S. A Musical Tragedy*] (play) 1982

†*Die Klavierspielerin* [*The Piano Teacher*] (novel) 1983

‡*Theaterstücke* (plays) 1984

*Burgtheater* (play) 1985

*Oh Wildnis, oh Schutz vor ihr* (novel) 1985

*Erziehung eines Vampirs* [*Bringing up a Vampire*] (radio play) 1986

*Krankheit oder Moderne Frauen* [*Illness or Modern Women*] (play) 1987

*Lust* (novel) 1989

§*Malina* (screenplay) 1990

*Wolken.Heim* (play) 1990

*Totenauberg* (play) 1991

*Die Kinder der Toten* [*The Children of the Dead*] (novel) 1995

*Ein Sportstück* (play) 1998

*Macht Nichts: Eine Kleine Trilogie des Todes* (play) 1999

*Gier: Ein Unterhaltungroman Elfriede Jelinek* (novel) 2000

‖*Das Lebewohl: 3 kl. Dramen* (plays) 2000

#*In den Alpen: Drei Dramen* (plays) 2002

*This work has also been translated as *We're Decoys, Baby!*

†This work has also been translated as *The Piano Player.*

‡Includes *Clara S.: Musikalische Tragödie, Was geschah, nachdem Nora ihren mann verlassen hatte oder Stutzen der Gesellschaften,* and *Burgtheater.*

§The screenplay was based on the novel by Ingeborg Bachmann.

‖Includes *Das Lebewohl, Das Schweigen,* and *Der Tod und das Mädchen II.*

#Includes *In den Alpen, Der Tod und das Mädchen III/Rosamunde,* and *Das Werk.*

# CRITICISM

## Michael Hulse (review date 21-27 July 1989)

SOURCE: Hulse, Michael. "Brute Encounters." *Times Literary Supplement*, no. 4503 (21-27 July 1989): 802.

[*In the following review, Hulse discusses the satiric elements and disturbing subject matter of* Lust.]

The main characters in Elfriede Jelinek's new novel *Lust* are the managing director of an Austrian papermill and his much-abused wife Gerti. The man is referred to as "der Direktor", much as one might refer to "der Führer"; his attitude to women matches that expressed in Hitler's table talk. Hermann is Schiller's "Ewig-Gestrige" with a vengeance, a man whose life is spent in the pursuit of power.

His exploitation of Gerti's body is rendered in formidably horrible terms. In the age of AIDS, the Direktor has reluctantly decided that gratification begins at home, and he uses his passive wife to satisfy his needs. There is nothing mutual about this satisfaction: Gerti is merely a machine for fornication, and she no longer even attempts to express her wishes. Deploying a repertoire of familiar images for the genitals and the sexual act, Jelinek gives us many that are singularly degrading. Those who found *Die Klavierspielerin* painful to read will find *Lust* altogether repugnant.

But then, that is the point. Elfriede Jelinek has said that she set out to write an erotic, indeed pornographic novel from the woman's point of view but found it impossible because the brutalized language used to describe sex was a purely male language of exploitation. If the unrelenting, nasty sameness here reminds us of "the inescapable monotony of pornographic writing" (in George Steiner's phrase), that too is part of Jelinek's intention.

Gerti, who has taken to drink, wanders out for a winter stroll, where she has a brute encounter with a self-centred student who then discards her for the younger women he routinely seduces. Gerti, however, mistakes this for love, has her hair done, and goes to find Michael on the ski-slopes he frequents; there he abuses her physically before a giggling crowd of youngsters. If the lonely middle-aged wife thought she had found the archangel to deliver her from her sorrows, she was pathetically wrong. The novel ends on a despairing note reminiscent of the infanticide dramas (written by men) of the *Sturm und Drang*: Gerti suffocates her son, already grasping and domineering, and sinks the child's corpse in the stream. The killing is the inevitable outcome of a growing abhorrence of the self-perpetuating male principle.

There are no new insights into sexuality, language and power in *Lust*. Jelinek avoids originality and achieves her satiric effects through pastiche and misprision. As in *Die Ausgesperrten,* she is still keen to *épater les bourgeois,* and is particularly scathing on sports, cars and savings banks. But her more searching scrutiny is reserved for the old gods of male culture; and textually, her satire is impressively rich. Her sardonic approach to "Natur", with its exaggerated sense of concomitant savagery, often reads like a commentary on Goethe's "Wie ist Natur so hold und gut, / Die mich am Busen hält!" In the processes of assimilation and absorption that underpin power in her world-view, Jelinek seems to be restating the gist of Elias Canetti's *Masse und Macht* in a form that exposes the limits of its maleness. Above all, Jelinek's obsessive subtext is the history and teachings of Christ, for her apparently the archetype of male domination.

With twenty years of fiction, theatre and a little poetry behind her, Elfriede Jelinek has now attracted a wide readership. Like *Die Ausgesperrten* and *Die Klavierspielerin*, *Lust* is written in a vigorous, metaphoric prose unlike anybody else's in German. Her wit, contempt, satiric observation, and taste for the distasteful, are all impressive. But for a writer who does not intend to remain an *enfant terrible*, these gifts may not suffice.

## Carole Morin (review date 28 July 1989)

SOURCE: Morin, Carole. "Dreamed of Depths." *New Statesman and Society* 2, no. 60 (28 July 1989): 33-4.

[*In the following review, Morin praises* The Piano Teacher *as a "dramatic" and "seriously comic" work of fiction.*]

Good books, like haircuts, should fill you with awe, change your life, or make you long for another. Elfriede Jelinek's *The Piano Teacher* manages to fulfil at least two of these demands in a reckless recital that is difficult to read and difficult to stop reading. The racy, relentless, consuming style is a metaphor for passion: impossible to ignore.

Of course, thwarted passion and unrequited love have been themes of fiction for centuries but the repressed piano teacher, Erika, and her "averagely handsome, averagely talented" pupil, Klemmer, reach dreamed of depths of mutual humiliation and dashed hopes.

These dashed hopes are expected, longed for, engineered and dreaded by Erika from the first signs of desire in her young pupil; but her middle-aged familiarity with pain, and her knowledge that "vice is basically the love of failure" makes the pain no less painful, this time.

By day Erika teaches piano, at night she watches TV with her attentive mother, whose love for her child is another selfish and all-consuming passion that "provides security, and security creates fear of uncertainty". Mother and Erika are seldom apart. They have shared the same bed since "delivering the feeble-minded . . . disoriented father to the sanitarium in Lower Austria".

Walking home from lessons, Erika rebels against Mother by buying vivacious dresses to hide in her closet, visiting peep shows, and observing copulating couples with fear and longing through the long grass of an infamous Viennese field.

The pupil Klemmer, who identifies with Nietzsche, is a debonair young Walter (who should be played in the forthcoming movie by Crispin Glover). He first pounces upon his teacher in a toilet, but Erika—afraid of losing the affection he hasn't yet given her—reacts to his advances by writing him a masochistic letter detailing perverse desires that she secretly hopes he will reject in the name of love.

Walter can't believe that "a woman who plays Chopin so marvellously" could long for these base acts, but he eventually complies by breaking her nose and cracking a couple of ribs while Mother—hilariously—is locked in the adjoining bedroom.

Because as well as being disturbing and dramatic, *The Piano Teacher* is seriously comic, even during the appalling scene when Erika inserts broken glass into the pocket of a pretty 18 year old piano student who has been smiled at by Klemmer. Because Erika knows that "ultimately the only things that count are creases, wrinkles, cellulite, grey hair, bags under the eyes, large pores, artificial teeth, glasses and loss of the figure".

The most grotesque scene in this spiritually reckless book is not when Erika, during some rare time alone, nonchalantly slashes her genitalia with a razor blade; but the moment when frustration and desperation lead her to make a shameful pass at ugly old Mother, showering her with promiscuous kisses in the middle of the night, "sucking and gnawing on her big body" because the closest Klemmer comes to sensuality is to "keep barking Erika's name (which she knows anyway) into her mouth".

The morning after Walter breaks her nose, Erika walks the streets of Vienna wearing one of the vivacious dresses, now ridiculously short and tight, with a blade in her handbag. When she spots her pupil laughing on distant steps with his young student friends in the sunlight the piano teacher has a choice. She knows that "only death is free, and even death costs you your life".

## Dagmar C. G. Lorenz (essay date 1990)

SOURCE: Lorenz, Dagmar C. G. "Elfriede Jelinek's Political Feminism: *Die Ausgesperrten*." *Modern Austrian Literature* 23, nos. 3-4 (1990): 111-19.

[*In the following essay, Lorenz explores Jelinek's attitudes toward feminism and the role of women in* Die Ausgesperrten.]

While Elfriede Jelinek addresses women's issues she rejects the epithet "Feminist." Her works focus on sexual politics, the socioeconomic plight of women to which she subordinates the theme of the female body and sexuality.[1] Jelinek's literary tool, satire, is an oddity in the post-Holocaust literary scene in Austria and Germany, according to Jelinek, "weil die Juden nicht mehr leben." Jelinek identifies with the Viennese Jewish tradition mentioning, among others, Kraus's and Canetti's method of dissection as a major influence.[2] She places herself in the tradition of political and aesthetic antifascism.

Jelinek believes that the answer to the question about the meaning of life and women's opportunity for gainful employment are immediately connected. In her opinion, the position of a woman working at a conveyer belt is preferable to that of a housewife because the former has an economic basis on which to develop some measure of self-esteem, whereas the latter depends financially on her husband.[3] When in the 70s feminist debates tended to deal with feminist separatism, an autonomous women's culture, women's history, and gender specificity, Jelinek demonstrated little interest in such issues isolated from the entire social system.[4] She is rooted in the Marxist Feminist tradition, in the 1968 student movement. She herself experienced life in a Berlin Maoist commune,[5] and she is a member of the Austrian Communist Party.

In the nineteenth century Marxist and bourgeois feminism evolved side by side, however, representing different interests. The former was political, the latter cultural. The names Zetkin and Bäumer exemplify the two opposite poles.[6] Marxist-based feminism was concerned with systems, means of production, and gender roles resulting from social conditioning. Middle-class feminism with its theoretical link to anthropology and psychology stressed genetic and psychological differences between men and women. Jelinek's aversion to the term feminist may indicate distance from cultural feminism as institutionalized in Women's Studies Programs as well as from feminist critical debates which address predominantly white middle-class women's concerns.

Jelinek's feminism is political. It originated with her criticism of postwar Austrian culture and does not exclusively focus on women. Her topic is oppression.

In keeping with Engels' *Origin of the Family, Private Property and the State* she portrays women and children as the most oppressed of all classes. Individualism is no longer possible.[7] Jelinek does not regret the demise of this favorite bourgeois ideal. In the unegalitarian systems she describes, men and women are incapable of working together because they have been raised to view each other as different. Indoctrination about gender roles prevents communication. All males consider themselves potential owners of all females. Jelinek's characters are prisoners of reactionary language patterns and stimuli reinforced by media and popular culture, a situation that Marcuse analyzed as follows:

> The toleration of the systematic moronization of children and adults alike by publicity and propaganda, the release of destructiveness in aggressive driving, the recruitment for and training of special forces, the impotent and benevolent tolerance toward outright deception in merchandising, waste, and planned obsolescence are not distortions and aberrations, they are the essence of a system which fosters tolerance as a means of perpetuating the struggle for existence and suppressing the alternatives. The authorities in education, morals, and psychology are vociferous against the increase in juvenile delinquency; they are less vociferous against the proud presentation in word and deed and pictures, of ever more powerful missiles, rockets, bombs—the mature delinquency of a whole civilization.[8]

Jelinek's ***Die Ausgesperrten*** is based on an actual criminal case. In 1965 Wunderer, a seventeen-year-old high school student, killed his parents and brother with a handgun, an ax, and a bayonet inflicting 180 injuries.[9] But the novel is not intended as a documentary. Details of the incident were changed to develop a dialectic historical perspective. The names Hans Sepp and Sophie Pachofen recall *Der Mann ohne Eigenschaften,* the "great" K. and K. tradition, and its bourgeois critic Musil to indicate that there is a continuity from the turn of the century into the post-Holocaust republic. Witkowski and Sepp's mother, the former Nazi perpetrator and the widow of a victim of fascism, a proletarian murdered at Mauthausen, establish the connection with the Nazi past. The novel is set in the 1950s, the years of Austria's culture crisis and its inability to come to terms with Austrofascism.[10] Jelinek's discourse links the collapsing Danube monarchy and its bourgeois values with the misguided individual anarchy of the pop culture.

The youthful gangster and killer in ***Die Ausgesperrten***—here his name is Rainer Witkowski—continues the legacy of the mass murderers in the concentration camps. For this purpose Jelinek changed Wunderer's father, an unresocialized World-War-I officer, into the former SS officer Witkowski. Other characteristics of Wunderer senior, such as his sadism and his compulsion to make pornographic photos of his wife, needed no change. The disabled veteran's preoccupation with pornography calls to mind Hitler's drawings of Geli Raubal, his fiancée who committed suicide, and literary figures such as Canetti's "Good Father" in *Die Blendung,*[11] a protofascist sadist and pervert. Jelinek's interest in women's issues is evidenced by the fact that she replaced Wunderer's brother by a sister, Anna, and by the well-developed mother characters as well as Sophie Pachofen.

Anna is by no means a contrast figure to Rainer. Womanhood or femininity in Jelinek's discourse denote no alternative to the status quo. As the child of a wife abuser and a codependent mother, Anna is as incapable as her brother of resolving the conflicts inherent in her environment. Her mother—martyr and masochist—is a negative role model. Jelinek smashes the myth of the potential of femininity by virtue of its "otherness." Anna represents more of the same: she is more brainwashed and less functional than her brother. Socialized as a female she does not even have the option of aggression as a form of rebellion. Internalized gender stereotypes as propagated in popular culture, but no less in the literature and art that represent high culture, make Anna's situation even more hopeless than her brother's. Rainer, much like Sepp, envisions sex as a means of social advancement, an illusionary notion, to be sure, because Sophie has no intention of accepting either boy's advances.

Anna accepts emotions and sex as an end in itself. She turns her aggression inwards. The results are a speech impediment and an eating disorder. Even when she demonstrates defiance, for instance in the sexual encounter in the toilet with a fellow student she abhors, she turns against herself by acting against her own values. To Anna love is the ultimate woman's fate, her fate. She submits to it after having become sexually involved with Hans who, in keeping with her society's standards, is her inferior. For Hans and Rainer, on the other hand, love is an issue only with Sophie, the girl who impresses them because of the opportunities she can provide them. Anna is a sex object to Hans, a substitute, useful until a better opportunity arises. Anna, on the other hand, becomes fixated on him, unable to envision an alternative. While the males have been trained to distinguish between sex and love, subject and object, women—and that also applies to Sophie—are indoctrinated to believe in the unity of body and mind, which makes them controllable.

Although the external circumstances of the women's lives differ, common to all of them is their passivity. Having no options, they are not involved in decision-making processes. Worse yet, they would be unable to recognize options if there were any. The most Anna is capable of is inflicting pain on defenseless victims under the watchful gaze of Rainer and Hans. "Anna hat einen Zorn auf alle Menschen, was schlecht ist, weil es den

Blick vernebelt und den Zugang verstellt. Allerdings hat Anna ohnedies wenig Zugang zu den schönen Dingen, die es so gibt, weil man sie mit Geld kaufen muβ," the narrator comments sarcastically.[12]

"Das positive Gegenmodell läβt sich mit meinen iterarischen Techniken nicht vereinbaren," stated Jelinek.[13] Indeed, there is not one hope-inspiring character in her novel. Sophie Pachofen is free of the illusions that blind her proletarian and lumpenproletarian acquaintances—after all, it is her own class that fabricates the mass-media dreams to keep the underprivileged ignorant. She is, however, little more than her family's pawn in the capitalists' power play. Her carefully cultivated image of impeccable cleanliness and her sexual frigidity are her selling points for a later marriage. The closest she comes to showing interest in sexual matters is when she has Sepp—in the hierarchy of the gang he represents the body—masturbate while she watches and worries about spots on her upholstery. Her mother's hypochondria and drug abuse foreshadow Sophie's adult years, the existence of a luxury object. In her own way she may be a time-bomb like Rainer. Her involvement with Sepp and the Witkowskis is a field trip, a privileged woman's study of the lower classes, yet not without a hint of exploitation: Sophie without fail has her poor friends pick up the tab for her.

While there is an instinctive acknowledgement of class differences, none of the characters has a political awareness except for Mrs. Sepp. Her Marxist class-consciousness is a leftover of the Austrian workers' movement, which, like the German Left, was destroyed by the Nazis. To an extent reflecting the author's own ideological predicament, Jelinek belongs to the KPÖ, a small party, almost an anachronism on the political scene, and yet the only one with an alternative program, and historically with a theoretical commitment to women's equality. The satirical stance taken toward Mrs. Sepp corresponds with Jelinek's dissatisfaction with any existing socialist society.[14]

Mrs. Sepp remains loyal to the party whose meetings her son rejects in favor of the jazz clubs[15] and his vague hopes of making Sophie a vehicle for his social advancement. Rather than admirable, however, her clinging to an ideology without a future is pathetic. She is no less caught up in a misleading discourse than the other characters, rendered no less incapable of learning. Despite the murder of her husband, the never ending drudgery and poverty, and the movement's failure in the 30s and in the present she repeats her litanies of struggle and suffering as lessons to her son[16] who is "a worker, degenerated from Marx to Elvis," as Sichrovsky puts it.[17]

Yet Hans' mother is the only character with some kind of integrity, some kind of historical perspective and commitment to an antifascist program, ineffective as it may be in the era of postmodernity, a euphemism for post-Holocaust as far as the Austrian and German scene is concerned.

The placement of the gang's activities in the 1950s implies a connection between its anarchism and that of contemporary artistic movements, the *Wiener Gruppe* and *Aktionismus*. Jelinek is familiar with both movements, which in spite of their self-proclaimed progressiveness took no political course of action nor attempted to come to terms with fascism. Their protest, which in all likelihood was sparked by desperation over the past, remained diffuse at best, and at worst became an imitation of Nazi terror. Rainer Witkowski's atavistic bloodbath is *in nuce* fascist rage which Theweleit termed "the white terror," only Rainer is unaware of it because he never analyzes anything as profane as politics or history.[18] Much less does Anna, who is stuck somewhere in Schoenberg's pre-atonal phase and would-be elitist irrationality. Both twins' intellectual claims are pretense, originating in the unarticulated outrage at having been given a raw deal and in their impotence to understand and change their situation. In that respect they reproduce their parents' dilemma. Their *Mittelschul*-education alienates them from social and economical reality, teaching them that their needs are actually not their needs, and their desires not their desires. Sepp, in contrast, states his aspirations bluntly without sentimental and pseudointellectual embroidery.

*Die Ausgesperrten* establishes a complex net of interactions between individuals of different social strata, of both genders, and of different generations. While the young people are at the center of the work, older individuals provide the historical and social background and foreshadow the insurmountable rift between the social classes after the school years are over. Through the parents it becomes manifest that for the postwar children as well—for each class in a different way—there is no way out. All possibilities are limited, even if popular culture suggests the opposite. Birth determines the future. Postwar culture is shown as fascist in an insidious way: no external force is necessary to keep people in their place. Indoctrination through schools, pop culture, and homes creates concentration camps of the mind. Rainer seems to have vaguely sensed this reality while committing an Existentialist *acte gratuit*.[19] It is no accident that he slaughters his family after the fateful Five O'Clock Tea at school with his parents, who destroy Rainer's debonnair façade.[20]

While the twin brother turns to murder, Anna and her mother are killed in passing, as it were, for Rainer's foremost hatred is directed against his father. As in warfare women and children are the incidental victims, so is Anna the victim of her brother's private revolution. While Rainer survives, she dies as his last victim.

Jelinek's narrator is omniscient in a fundamental way. She is cognizant of all events and not only interprets and psychology of the individual characters but also articulates the values of society. As the mouthpiece of the collective subconscious, a quasi chorus, the narrator makes transparent the dynamics that direct the behavior of the characters. The narrator has an intimate knowledge of her time's metalanguage, the ideology of postwar Austrian capitalism. As a hidden blueprint it determines social patterns by suggesting individualism, freedom, equal chances, and paying lip service to education and intellectual endeavors. In the final analysis all of these are mechanisms to keep the oppressed divided: the apparent chances are no chances, the education is communication of useless information to ensure that no social change will occur.

Yet that there is a voice from outside the prison of the mind that exposes and criticizes the mass culture is a sign of hope in a novel without heroes. Although Jelinek's characters have no chance—after all, they are representative of the norm—they are made transparent from a detached point of view. The discrepancy between each individual's self-image and his or her actual situation is laid open.

The narrator's cynicism equals that of the directors of the totalitarian mass culture. She avoids getting caught up in the sentimentality that comprises the foremost barrier to understanding. She exposes a disabling collective discourse that determines actions by prescribing feelings and reactions even before the occasion for them arises.

Short of a revolutionary change of all existing conditions, but most of all, of all existing language habits, breaking out of the prison of the mind is the best that can be hoped for. The realistic assessment of social facts and an unsentimental approach to basic social phenomena are a first step, hence the brutal unmasking of family and sexual relationships as conveniences based on economic conditions, of feelings as manufactured by the media. Hence the iconoclastic assault on the collective's "holy cows": disabled veterans, mother- and fatherhood, the home, love, and friendship.

Women as the most immediate victims of brainwashing by oppressive discourses ranging from Genesis to Freud, Weininger, and Elvis, have the greatest need for a revolutionary change—such is implied in Jelinek's novel. That for them such a liberation is the least likely is implied as well. There is hope in Jelinek's novel, and no hope.

### Notes

1. *Die Liebhaberinnen* became a feminist cult book. Cf. Donna Hoffmeister, "Access Routes into Postmodernism: Interviews with Innerhofer, Jelinek, Rosei, and Wolfgruber," *Modern Austrian Literature,* 20 (1987) 97-130. Jelinek believes that a man could not have written *Die Liebhaberinnen.* "Es wäre nicht richtig, mich als Feministin zu bezeichnen," (Hoffmeister, p. 116). Jelinek holds that male critics do not forgive her for writing about female sexuality from a woman's perspective. Interview with Sigrid Löffler, "Jedes ihrer Werke ist eine Provokation," *Brigitte Sonderhefte Bücher,* 23, (1983) 27.

2. Hoffmeister, "Access Routes into Postmodernism," 109 and 111. Jelinek believes that "durch die Faschisten wichtige literarische Traditionen gewaltsam abgebrochen worden sind."

3. Ibid., 113.

4. On the contrary, as Jacqueline Vansant, *Against the Horizon. Feminism and Postwar Austrian Women Writers* (New York, Westport, London: Greenwood, 1988), p. 129, points out about *Die Liebhaberinnen,* the protagonists never discover their communality, "the critical stance of the author points to the mechanisms that keep women apart and the consequences of encouraging rivalry."

5. Beyond her aesthetics rooted in the Austrian satirical tradition as well as the experimentalism of the *Wiener Gruppe* there is the political component of the 1968 student movement. Jelinek lived in Berlin in the early 1970s, considered herself a Maoist, and has been a member of the Austrian Communist Party (KPÖ) since 1973. However, she does not consider any existing socialist society a valid alternative. (Hoffmeister, "Access Routes into Postmodernism," 112) Aesthetically she has no link with social realism, with which she associates most of the contemporary women authors.

6. Gertrud Bäumer was the exponent of the middle-class women's movement that found it possible to coexist with Nazism.

7. "Literatur muß dem Rechnung tragen, daß der Individualismus nicht mehr möglich ist." Hoffmeister, "Access Routes into Postmodernism," 115.

8. Herbert Marcuse, "Repressive Tolerance," in "*A Critique of Pure Tolerance* (Boston: Beacon, 1965) p. 83.

9. Heinz Sichrovsky, "Die Ausgesperrten," *Arbeiter Zeitung, Wien,* 17. November 1979, pp. 8-9.

10. Joseph McVeigh, *Kontinuität und Vergangenheitsbewältigung in der österreichischen Literatur nach 1945* (Wien: Braumüller, 1988). "Zur sogenannten 'Kulturkrise' der 50er Jahre," pp. 117ff.

11. Elias Canetti, "Der gute Vater," *Die Blendung* (Frankfurt: Fischer, 1963), pp. 326-335. Michael Zeller, "Haß auf den Nazi-Vater," *Frankfurter Al-*

lgemeine, 4.6.80, beobachtet korrekt "haßerfüllte Abgrenzungsversuche der Zwillinge gegen den Nazi-Vater" und ihre letztliche Hilflosigkeit, da sie selbst vom Elternhaus geprägt sind.

12. *DA,* p. 11.

13. Hoffmeister, "Access Routes into Postmodernism," 111.

14. Jelinek does not consider any existing socialist society a valid alternative. Cf. Hoffmeister, "Access Routes into Postmodernism," 112. For Jelinek the father's proletarian, Jewish-atheist background was the decisive ideological influence. Hoffmeister, ibid., 109.

15. Elfriede Jelinek, *Die Ausgesperrten* (Hamburg: Rowohlt, 1985), p. 27.

16. Ibid., pp. 26-27.

17. Heinz Sichrovsky, "Die Ausgesperrten," p. 9.

18. Klaus Theweleit, *Männerphantasien,* Band II, "Zur Psychoanalyse des weißen Terrors" (Hamburg: Rowohlt, 1980).

19. *DA,* p. 263.

20. Ibid., pp. 249ff.

## Carole Morin (review date 31 August 1990)

SOURCE: Morin, Carole. "Triumph of the Will." *New Statesman and Society* 3, no. 116 (31 August 1990): 38.

[*In the following review, Morin offers a mixed assessment of* Wonderful, Wonderful Times, *calling the novel "a flawed triumph."*]

My husband gave up guilt for Lent. He says guilt, like masochism, can be a subtle pleasure. And S&M is now in fashion the way bisexuality was in the early eighties.

Elfriede Jelinek wrote **Wonderful, Wonderful Times** before she perfected her unique voice, which combines the immediacy of the first person and the detachment of the third, in the brilliant **Piano Teacher.** Her publisher is not doing her any favour in failing to mention that this is not a new book. While it is undeniably powerful, it lacks the beauty and wit of the later book, and the echoes of last year's masterpiece make it disappointing: like the unavoidable dismay you might feel admiring the Sistine Chapel fresco after witnessing the Resurrection.

Every character in this book is grotesque. They are all masochists, sadists, or both: designed to bring out the sado-masochistic Nazi in all of us. The lurid lives of individuals full of bitterness, failure, weakness and hatred are an obvious metaphor for bourgeois Austria's Nazi past and (possible) neo-Nazi future. Jelinek's fear of decay, decline and death, is described in a simultaneously brutal and subtle poetic flow.

Her concern with Taikyoku, the great emptiness, is shown through consistently revolting characters uncompromisingly presented without any appeal or hidden charm. The four teenagers, who relieve their insecurity and sexual tensions by beating random victims senseless, are the Nazis. Their mothers "swaddled in the human tea-cosy of the murdered, the hanged, the gassed" are the Jews. The father of the violent teenage twins is an ex-SS officer with one leg who takes degrading pictures of his decaying wife's genitalia and rapes her on the dirty kitchen floor, then beats her with his crutch.

This is one vision of an endless march in unforgettable images: the father masturbating in his car while being driven home by his son; the worker Hans "spitting a thick gobbet of phlegm" into his broken mother's soup; the speechless anorexic female twin Anna shrinking from a maternal embrace while practising piano.

Her brother Rainer, the self-proclaimed gang-leader—a nihilist existentialist ex-altar boy virgin who writes down boasts to say in school—believes in the triumph of his will. Jelinek's ironic striptease scorns the notion that "you can create your own light if none is available."

Nevertheless, the ecstatic violence of the final scene challenges any celluloid holocaust and **Wonderful, Wonderful Times** is a flawed triumph.

## Angela McRobbie (review date 2 November 1990)

SOURCE: McRobbie, Angela. "A Universe of Pain." *Times Literary Supplement,* no. 4570 (2 November 1990): 1183.

[*In the following review, McRobbie examines the depraved and bleak world portrayed in* Wonderful, Wonderful Times.]

Elfriede Jelinek's Vienna is a city of sexual squalor. Its post-war population—men, women and children—is taking revenge on its once noble or dignified past. These people bear no resemblance to the voluptuous, sexually satisfied creatures of Klimt's paintings. Nor are they the sexually curious but refined patients who filled Freud's consulting-room. Jelinek's men and women inhabit a universe of pain for which there is no "talking cure". They are victims so given over to intensifying their suffering, to pursuing their own degradation, that we can feel no sorrow, no sympathy. In *The Piano Teacher* (published in Britain last year), Erika, the novel's central character, is brought up by a refined but insane mother, her madness masked by respectability and love of the arts. Erika's mother jealously protects her daughter's musical talent by cutting her off from humanity. She even shares a bed with her. Erika's will is broken, her talent takes her no further than a modest teaching job at the conservatoire. Her sexuality is not so much extinguished as deflected. She stalks the Prater park, spying on prostitutes and their clients. She visits peep-shows and takes delight in the sperm-filled tissues which litter the floor. She also cuts herself. Sex is an opportunity only for confirming everything that is rotten. It is the ultimate act of self-hatred.

*Wonderful, Wonderful Times* is set in Vienna in the early 1950s. It was written before *The Piano Teacher,* and, although it is just as brutal, its concern with literary precedents (Sartre, Camus and even Cocteau) bestows on it a hint of playfulness. It is not quite as stripped, not quite as anguished as Jelinek's more recent writing (including the as yet untranslated *Lust*). The forces of history and those of the unconscious come together in the four young teenagers who represent the Austrian version of the age of affluence. Rainer and Anna have an ex-SS father who looks back with longing to the wonderful times of the title, when he could boot to death Polish peasants with impunity. Now with a wooden leg, an invalidity pension and a job as a night porter, he turns his attention to "art" photography. His only model is his wife, whom he forces to pose for full frontal nudes. He tries to capture something of the style of the porn magazines by having her "caught unaware" with nothing on but an apron. He complains when she doesn't look right, when her hair isn't clean and silky as it should be, when her body is more like a "piece of mouldy cheese" than that of a proper photographic model. When she objects he abuses her.

Rainer is psychically battered. He is clever and seeks in art not so much solace as guidance. He reads French literature and finds what he needs in 1950s existentialism. Like his sister, Anna, he more often resorts to violence. Anna periodically cannot speak. They are disturbed children for whom some allowances are made at the city Gymnasium. Sex is another of their weapons. Anna offers herself to a classmate in the school toilet and watches Gerhard losing his virginity with only a flicker of interest. Later, on the tram home, a man pushes his penis against her. When she doesn't move away he thinks he's in luck. Anna then signals to the gang who rifle his pockets as he edges closer.

Anna and Rainer are the leaders because they have the least to lose. Sophie is rich, which seems to give her something to live for, but in reality she too is already lost. Hans is a working-class youth whose mother is a communist and whose father died in the camps. Together this foursome rob, steal, drown cats, and eventually plant an incendiary device in the school cloakroom. Only Rainer aspires to truly psychopathic status. On achieving this he quickly and willingly turns himself in.

*Wonderful, Wonderful Times* is spartan in style and Jelinek's tone is dry and laconic. So debased is her world, so full of loathing, that there can be no beauty in language. That would be to veer too close to the version of art so valued by the various mother figures who crop up in her inner landscape of hate. If art, in Vienna, has been seen as something better, something out of the ordinary, something majestic, Jelinek will make of it something worse. She will insist that flat, unadorned and even ugly writing is what is required.

Jelinek writes as the child who has not recovered, the victim of abuse who has never made the transition to being a "survivor". Like the child who fantasizes playing with its own excrement, Jelinek discovers humour only in moments of complete perversity. In Jelinek's world, pop culture, especially porn films and horror movies, offer something of a relief. Now celebrated as a major writer in France as well as in German-speaking Europe, Jelinek said of her writing in a recent interview in *Die Zeit*, "Yes. I am that in my hatred of myself."

### Richard Eder (review date 16 December 1990)

SOURCE: Eder, Richard. "A Cuckoo Clockwork Orange." *Los Angeles Times Book Review* (16 December 1990): 3

[*In the following review, Eder notes the "black irony and jarring distortion" in* Wonderful, Wonderful Times, *comparing Jelinek to Austrian author Thomas Bernhard.*]

Since *Wonderful, Wonderful Times* is set in the 1950s gloom of postwar Vienna; since everyone in it is crass, corrupt or distorted; and since it ends in a horrible blood bath, the title could justifiably be taken as gallows humor of the crudest kind.

It is, in fact. Jelinek's characters, and the voice she uses to tell of them, are fashioned with black irony and jarring distortion. Yet the ultimate effect is grace, a dark image delivered in terms appropriate to it, but in a draftsmanship that conveys a hint of delicacy and lyricism, as if these had been ejected from the room but continued to haunt it. We think of George Grosz.

Like Thomas Bernhard, her older Austrian compatriot, Elfriede Jelinek writes of the still-unsettled accounts of the 20th Century. Austria is the place to do it, of course;

with the dismemberment of her one-time empire, the bitter chaos following World War I, her acceptance of the Nazi version of being German, and her abdication of a version of her own.

The unhealed guilts were never confronted the way they largely were in Germany. Avoidance is paid for in the figure of an internationally shunned president whose history is as unclear as that of his country. And in the harsh, surreal denunciation by such writers as Bernhard and Jelinek.

The sleep of memory, like that of reason, produces monsters. Rainer, his twin sister Anna, and their buddies Hans and Sophie, are monsters of a sort, as they rampage around Vienna. They are teenagers for whom the word *wilding* would be invented 30 years later; they waylay passersby, rob and savagely beat them.

But Jelinek does not write of this violence as we write of American wilding—as awful and arbitrary acts afflicted upon a troubled but still coherent society. It is Vienna, and the society that emerged from its past without naming it, that is awful and arbitrary. Monstrosity is the history that the four young people breathe. And because it is, Jelinek can endow them with a measure of perverted innocence. Fleetingly, we perceive the innocence along with the perversion.

When we meet them at the start, the four are at work upon an unfortunate innocent who happens to be walking through the park. Anna, thin and perpetually raging, concentrates on scratching his face and eyes. Hans, a factory worker, punches stolidly away. Sophie, from a rich family, keeps her distance and uses the points of her expensive boots. Rainer, the intellectual, does little actual damage; he concentrates mainly on fumbling for the wallet.

I referred to the victim as "an innocent," but Jelinek's narrator does not altogether agree. Its voice suggests that to have a wallet is already not to be altogether innocent. It is a disembodied voice, sardonic, amused, nihilistic, with an occasional moralizing phrase that parodies respectability, like a teenager trying on his aunt's hat.

We hear it describing the initiation of Sophie into the gang. Rainer—whose mother named him after the poet Rilke—is an existentialist, an admirer of Camus and Sartre. When he sits with the others in a cafe, something they do a lot of, he tries to practice Sartrean "nausea," though he only manages queasiness. Sophie, he decides, must commit an existential free act, so they all go off to the Vienna Woods carrying a sack that twitches:

> In Jean-Paul Sartre's *The Age of Reason* is a character who wants to drown his acts, and so today they are planning to drown this cat too, though this cat also has a right to live. Rainer says that he himself has an equal right to nonexistence, just as this cat does, this cat which he is going to assist on its way to nonexistence before it can count to three. The cat has its suspicions. Hence the brouhaha in the sack.

Sophie gets her designer dress muddy and botches the job. Hans smacks her on the mouth. Both the mud and the smack are piquancies for her; she hangs out with the others as a diversion from her privileged life. She brings the gang home mainly to annoy her mother; she makes Hans strip and masturbate but won't let him touch her. She has the coldness of the rich and powerful, and will leave the others at the end to go to school in Switzerland.

Hans, son of the widow of a Communist labor leader, rebuffs his mother's efforts to make him socially conscious. He burns her pamphlets; he wants to be a rock star; he is besotted with Sophie. Since he can't have her, he has energetic sex with Anna.

She, like her brother, is an intellectual, or tries to be. In fact, her philosophical fury masks perfectly conventional longings; she falls helplessly and romantically in love with Hans. As for Rainer, he too is obsessed with Sophie and tries to win her from Hans by talking incessantly. After one of the gang's sorties, he begs her to stay with him. "I need someone to explain everything to," he says, imagining himself a fashionable savant to whom beautiful women are bound to flock the way they do—he has heard—in Paris.

If the gang's maraudings and arguments are narrated with a sardonic lightness, the comedy is grimmer when it comes to Anna's and Rainer's parents. The father is a former SS man, now crippled and working at a humdrum job. He is as filled with rage and fantasies as Anna is, but his are real and deadly.

"His one-time enemies got away through the chimneys and crematoria of Auschwitz and Treblinka," the narrator savagely tells us. He can't kill Jews, but he can beat his wife. He interrupts her cooking to make her strip and pose for pornographic photographs; it is hard, he tells himself, for a man to be satisfied with one naked alive woman when he has seen piles of naked dead ones. For real arousal, he pulls out his pistol and rushes into the kitchen to "rape" his wife. She is wearily submissive, but it is necessary for him to think of it that way.

Hans, with his rock-star fantasies, represents the corruption of the working class; Rainer's father, the corrupt history of the middle class; Sophie's all-but-invisible parents, the continuing corruption of the wealthy and powerful. Their grotesquerie fills gradually with horror.

Rainer's intellectual fantasies, which have protected him from his own and the world's rage, give way in a scene of wild bloodiness. Until then, except for the manipulative Sophie, the young people were like frail and jaunty paper boats floating in a sewer. Its contents—Austria's unpurged history of denial—is backed up. Of course, it will rise and engulf them.

**Tobe Levin (essay date 1991)**

SOURCE: Levin, Tobe. "Jelinek's Radical Radio: Deconstructing the Woman in Context." *Women's Studies International Forum* 14, nos. 1-2 (1991): 85-97.

[*In the following essay, Levin examines the gender and feminist themes explored in a selection of Jelinek's radio plays.*]

> Australian expert in bioethics, Paul Gerber, commenting on the possibility of using braindead women as incubators for implanted fertilized eggs and as storage for donor organs, stated that this development would not only be ethically sound but in fact "progressive" and "a great" idea. The professor from the University of Queensland made his views known at a recent conference on medical ethics.
>
> (Brutkästen, 1988, p. 8)

At their international conference in July, 1985, FINRRAGE (Feminist International Network of Resistance to Reproductive and Genetic Engineering) issued a statement deploring the "expropriation" of "the female body," its dissection "as raw material for the technological production of human beings." Warning against the power relations informing the new technologies, the delegates declared: "We do not need to transform our biology, we need to transform patriarchal, social, political, and economic conditions" (Spallone & Steinberg, 1987, p. 211).

Central to any analysis of this threatening phenomenon is the context: In whose interest is the current "externalization of conception and gestation" occurring? Not in the interests of women. Technocrats claim they are helping the sterile. But desire to give birth at any cost betrays a suspect origin in male dominance. Patriarchy's control of female fertility has been a cornerstone of disempowerment; in a phallocratic world, genetic manipulations further cement women's exclusion from power.

In the 1980s, reproductive technologies have witnessed an astonishing rate of development. But the destructive logic behind such macabre procedures as fishing for eggs or grafting of species could have been foreseen earlier and appears in fact in a little known but startlingly revealing radio play by Austrian Marxist Elfriede Jelinek, broadcast on March 27, 1976, *The King Bees*. In it Jelinek addresses issues central to feminism—power relations between the sexes and who controls fertility—in a poetic language that unmasks the motives of the dominant discourse and, through displacement, irony, and emphasis on the context of an utterance, offers tools for resisting manipulation, hence of defying, as the FINRRAGE women do, the hegemony of the technocrats. In the most effective sense, *The King Bees*, because it addresses itself to a well-schooled audience conversant in these issues, can perhaps challenge the seeming inevitability of increasing power differentials between females and males that threaten to result from the reign of "male mothers."

We can more easily understand how Jelinek's project works if we focus a deconstructive lens on it. More recently than their European counterparts, American feminist literary critics have turned to the French theorists for insight into the fundamental questions of subjectivity and language. In an issue of *Feminist Studies* devoted entirely to feminism and deconstruction, Mary Poovey sets the tone when she asks whether deconstruction constitutes an adequate methodology for feminist critics, pointing on the one hand to the theory's "antihumanist premises" that undermine "a feminism . . . [whose] epistemology and practice [build] on women's experience" (Poovey, 1988, pp. 51-52). In this view feminism is "simply another deluded humanism" (Poovey, 1988, p. 52). At the same time, poststructuralist theory is an "endeavor . . . to imagine some organization of fantasy, language, and reality other than one based on identity and binary oppositions" (Poovey, 1988, p. 56), although, admittedly, this is difficult: Images of utopian future(s) often elude the pen.

Jelinek's work has been discussed in terms of a similar conflict, between her humanism, inspired by Marxist/feminism, and her aesthetic, variously described as elitist, esoteric, inaccessible, but mainly faulted with negativity. Irony, her principal tool, reverses, opening up the void between expectation and fulfillment, emphasizing what is not. Similarly, deconstruction seems to feed into reaction: Its refusal of identity and its engagement in endless unravelings of meaning, while challenging the economy of the One, do not empower the Other. Insight into the mechanics of domination does not per se erase it. Yet, as a methodology, deconstruction has been held by some to be a useful arm in the radical's arsenal. Specifically, by destablizing the dyad male/female, uncoupling the sexual signifier from its anatomical referent, it may increase the range of options for "women" and "men."

This explosion of the sign, an important dimension in Jelinek's novels, is perhaps even more striking in her radio plays. If a prose work like *Michael: A Children's Book for the Infantile Society* (1972a) functions as a take-off on the consciousness industries like radio and television, how much more cutting is the parody within those media themselves. Critiquing her form in her content while undermining content in her form, Jelinek refuses to participate in the illusionist tradition sucking an audience into the very structures that silence them. Instead her radio drama makes hierarchies the object of her radical reversals. If deconstruction offers a method of reading the individual's relation to the system, so Jelinek's metaproject would seem to be offering an inspired opportunity for deconstructive thinking.

To take an introductory example from *The King Bees*: Post-structuralism emphasizes moving beyond the production of meaning(s) dependent entirely on linked elements in a closed system. Jelinek sets up and explodes such a system. In Terrana I after the maximum holocaust, language, literally the same as that used in the contemporary world, is radically dislocated as soon as the context is invoked. One particularly macabre illustration is an ordinary "patriotic text"—the perennial discussion concerning relations between the individual and the state:

MALE VOICE 4:

(*very affected, almost gay*) That [soldiering] is a wonderful thing for a young person.

MALE VOICE 3:

(*enthusiastic*) When I was young I would have given my right arm for a job like that.

(Jelinek, 1982a, p. 29)

*Dulce et decorum est pro patria mori*: Such sentiment serves the ruling class. Here, however, the euphemism of sacrifice is unmasked by the context. The ruling technocrats, after discovering a life-prolonging substance, have determined to exterminate their younger male rivals and store their organs for future transplants, initiating an economy to harvest human beings. The figurative subjunctive statement—I would have given my right arm—must now be taken literally, and the interested ideology behind it is revealed. Similar pious language—"We'll think about them always, they'll live on in us"—is equally inverted by repartee perfect in this context: "Maybe even in the form of a kidney or a heart!" (Jelinek, 1982a, p. 29)

To continue the illustration, a second important moment in Jelinek's project is her deconstruction of the term "woman." In Terrana, those with the power to name call themselves King Bees, a type that, significantly, does not exist at all in nature. Women they divide into the Mutas or incubators and the Hetis or courtesans. Because the Mutas have been isolated in cubicles like honeycombs, they have been styled euphemistically Queen Bees. Now, in Poovey's words, breaking the concept of "woman" into "independent variables . . .

show[s] how consolidating all women into a falsely unified 'woman' has helped mask the operations of power that actually divide women's interests as much as unite them" (Poovey, 1988, p. 59). If the feminist task includes mitigating the political ramifications of essentialism or biologism, then a deconstructive vision can reveal the interests served by the ruling ideologies of "woman."

At the same time, however, Jelinek's myth risks essentializing "man": The patriarchy appears so seamless, so monolithic, that it suggests a "natural" marriage of masculinity and dominance. But a deconstructive reading discourages this impression: Women are not alone in their exclusion from power. Nor are all women equally far from the governing circles. In a gesture of Marxist inspiration, Jelinek links the Mutas to the technocrats and the Hetis to the sons, these new political alignments exploding "sex" as a marker of class. This, too, recalls post-structuralism: Disconnecting anatomical sexuality from gender, it might be possible, as Poovey notes, to cease "relegating all biological variants into the two categories, 'male' and 'female' (with 'abnormal' absorbing everything that is 'leftover'), [and] enable us both to multiply the categories of sex and to detach reproduction from sex" (Poovey, 1988, pp. 59, 60). I see a similar projection in Jelinek's work.

READINGS IN CONTEXT

Unmasking the context of veiled brutality is Jelinek's metaproject in two early radio plays, *Demise of a Diver* (1973) and *Kasperl and the Chubby Princess or Kasperl and the Skinny Peasants* (1974). Both offer an acoustical mirror of the early prose work *Michael: A Children's Book for the Infantile Society* (1972a) laced with the cartoon brutality of *We're Decoys, Baby!* (1970). Like the novel, they parody "die heile Welt," the unsullied world of television and mass media. Written mainly in cliché, the platitudes of "performance" and "place" are revealed as antithetical to the interests of those for whom they are broadcast, mainly the powerless. As Jelinek explains in a 1978 interview, she is concerned with "this society of minors infantilized by a gigantic consciousness industry functioning like the Super-ego of psycho-analysis, like all-powerful fathers. . . . Models to emulate are placed so far above the norm, taken from the level of wealthy sports car drivers and lottery winners that people never even consider making any political demands. . . . Nobody thinks of questioning, let alone dismantling, the dominant structures" (Levin, 1979, p. 130).

Her principal theme is subjectivity: how the majority has come to think as it does, and how the sedative effect of ideology is to be counteracted. *Demise of a Diver* (1973), inspired by the bourgeois myth of individualism, suggests several answers. A caricature of the modern citizen, the title figure, with a wife and two children, is a professional snorkler despite old war wounds and has set out on holiday in hopes of encountering some famous person to adulate. Lassie and Flipper soon appear, emissaries of the "realm of the children's laughing eyes" who, however, reward expectations of kindness with brutality. Gratuitously, the television dolphin tells his "speechless" admirer, "I'll bite off two of your fingers and throw them in the trash" (Jelinek, 1973, p. 6). Threatened by this misfortune, the diver responds with the time-worn adage, "I'll pull myself back up by my own bootstraps" (Jelinek, 1973, p. 8) but the bourgeois promise of success and humanist view of the worthy idol are disappointed time and again. In fact, the radio drama translates the slogans of the status quo, like those of working yourself up, into literal catapults and stressful climbs, and the "diver," although he surfaces for air, is headed straight down, doomed to experience the "demise" of his entire class, prey to its internalized illusions.

This radical critique extends to the very idea of the "Mensch," the concept of the human being used to sedate suspicion and deflect awareness away from inequalities of power. The respected television personalities, parodied by Lassie or Flipper, constantly deny the possibility of differences in both essence and position, spouting such pieties as "There are no winners or losers, there are only people" (Jelinek, 1973, p. 41); or relying on the liberal illusion: "Wars would be superfluous with only a little understanding" (Jelinek, 1973, p. 29). Hence the call for "a little more kindness from mensch to mensch to mensch to mensch to mensch" (Jelinek, 1973, p. 20). The repetition heightens our awareness of the utterance as cliché and, while seeming to broaden the field of individuals designated "mensch," it actually collapses distinctions, particularly in the context of brutality Jelinek presents, sparing no one. Extending from child abuse through rape to medieval methods of torture, the radio's play-by-play descriptives redefine *menschlichkeit* (humaneness) as cruelty. For example, the job interview à la Jelinek: "The boss is merely going to finish listening to Mozart's Symphony in G-minor. Then he'll be ready to crush your fingers and toes" (Jelinek, 1973, p. 32) Clearly, in this world of systemic violence, the "humanities" also fail.

Ute Nyssen, in her "Afterword" to the Prometh edition of Jelinek's plays, writes of the author's "overriding method," that her reliance on "a pastiche of quotations from the media and advertising" evidences not only a satiric impulse, but perhaps more importantly constitutes an attack "against strategies of obfuscation" (Nyssen, 1984, p. 156). This is clearly the case in **Kasperl and the Chubby Princess or Kasperl and the Skinny Peasants** (Jelinek, 1974). An allegory in which the obese noblewoman represents the propertied class and her suppliers the working majority, the tale focuses once again on the myth of mobility and, in its didacticism, offers intellectual tools for unmasking it. The gourmand's royal father makes a proclamation in fine fairy-tale tradition: Whoever can help his daughter lose weight and regain her health will be rewarded with her hand. The effect is not unlike the appeal of a lottery, to individualism, for hypothetically, anyone can win. In fact, rigid material distinctions are maintained. The mystification this implies warrants such a clear lesson in political economy as the following:

SPEAKER:

> If somebody wants more than anybody else, then he has to take it away from them. Of course it may happen that the others don't even notice that anything's being taken away, or else they think its O.K. to lose out if the person doing the taking is a powerful man or if he has a pretty face or simply drives a fat car or has a gigantic castle or even a private airplane and so forth.

(Jelinek, 1974, p. 32)

The icons of wealth identify the idols of the meek who are trained in self-effacement by those placing themselves above others. Here Jelinek attempts to disassociate the symbol from the emotion it evokes, to bring the powerful down to the level of selfish children for whom Kasperl is king. He in turn holds the discourse of the status quo: "Industry and sacrifice make the good child" (Jelinek, 1974, p. 8); "We always want to obey our King . . . by not eating too much and not drinking too much and not snacking too much and not playing too loud." And "whoever gives up his lunch for a day makes the King particularly happy" (Jelinek, 1974, p. 7). The interests propagating "sacrifice" as a civic virtue are visible in this fable despite the masquerade: Motivated by fear of authority, the "altruistic" spirit is omnipotent Father State internalized by the infantile. Only the "common sense" of that underestimated outsider, the kitchen maid, breaks into the closed discourse of mystification.

If the princess—a woman—seems at first a dangerous choice to represent privilege, another female stands for the counterpart of sceptical resistance, creating an effect that makes biological sex far less significant as an indicator of status than type of work and distance from power. If the first remains a ruling class accomplice whose interests differ markedly from those females of the unpropertied group, the character called Gretel is the single questioning voice. The person in charge of the kitchen, who knows first when the pot is empty and whose stomach knots with what has been taken away, she is less easily duped, more strategic in her "morality," the type of down-to-earth mother courage capable of rippling the smooth flow of jargon with her irreverence: "I didn't really hear that, did I? And you really believe all that junk your teachers stuffed your heads with?" (Jelinek, 1974, p. 7).

## Deconstructing Woman

The silence of women (and the disempowered of both sexes) is a commonplace of feminist literary criticism, and, in fact, the princess in Kasperl never speaks. But slapstick disfigures the voice of the powerful also, treating it like white noise against which Gretel's "common sense" stands out. As the stage directions make clear, the king's language, for example, is incomprehensible apart from the key words: "Crisis, work, hard work, heavy work, love, the well-being of the people, sacrifice, work . . . ballet dancer . . ." (Jelinek, 1974, p. 18) while his sidekick Pezi echoes the ends of Kasperl's sentences. Thus floating freely without anchor in a comprehensive discourse of authority, the terms are easily deflated by the pinprick of audience complicity.

This manipulation of a sign's context is a strategy applied to portraits of biological women in a number of the radio plays and can be viewed as an attack on essentialist interpretations. Specifically in *For Some, the Setting Sun Means the End of a Working Day* (1972b), *What Happened after Nora Left Her Husband or the Pillars of Society* (1982b), and *Bringing up a Vampire* (1986). This reorientation is effected either by clearly equating "female" with "function"—no matter who, male or female, is subordinate, that is the "woman"—or by transgressing the boundaries of "sex," exaggerating the exclusivity of the label "woman," inadequate to cover the multiplicity of incompatible characteristics associated with anatomically female characters or, in the case of Emily, with disembodied female anatomies, the ultimate in reversal and absence.

Function, not biology, defines the female in Jelinek's prize-winning radio play *For Some, the Setting Sun Means the End of a Working Day* (1972b) where we encounter the familiar pastiche modus and self-conscious broadcast. Gaby, a dreamy teenage department store clerk, accepts the advances of Markus, an established man in his late thirties. He courts her gently, in the fashion of romance heroes, with suspense stemming from his frequent disappearances and reappearances in the company of a mystery woman. At last we learn she is his doctor; he is stricken with a fatal illness that he wishes to hide from Gaby in order to live out his last days in idyllic harmony. All the soporific appeal of the soaps is here, impinged on, however, by the media's self-reflection: This tale is itself a radio soap whose performance is frequently interrupted by a parody of audience involvement. After Gaby and Markus have exchanged good-byes, a professional announcer's voice initiates the "dialogue." First with a hypothetical female listener:

> Whom did you say I should ask your?—husband.— What do you think is important, that a woman should make herself pretty for her?—husband. You can tell what by looking at whom your?—that. husband. . . . What do you have that's the most beautiful in the world?—profession. Who always suffers when the mother works the?—children.
>
> (Jelinek, 1972b, p. 8)

Then with a man:

> What's your profession?—butcher. . . . What is it after all that men don't have the? children.—What is your ideal your?—work.
>
> (Jelinek, 1972b, pp. 11, 12)

This takeoff of the magazine quiz parodies biologism as it informs the pedagogic impulse of the media and the slogans of the everyday. Prejudice thus becomes conscious. The catechism of female submission is sabotaged by turning declarative statements into interrogatives, the resulting broken clichés to be mended by the listener whose participation lends new meaning to the hackneyed phrases. They appear as the binary oppositions on which deconstructive critics find Western culture to be based and as such contain the source of their own displacement. That is, the man's ideal can be his work only so long as anatomy, and specifically the birthing of children, places "women" in a wholly separate category. This in turn is the case neither in the listeners' world nor in the radio play whose women also work, one as a sales clerk, the other as a doctor, even though marriage and motherhood represent the illusion in which Gaby is trapped. But as parts of a system dependent on each other, the wage-earning male implying the child-bearing female, challenge to one will also undermine the other and the system. Thus anatomy, the fact of women's bearing children, is significant only as part of a system of ideas, one also confronted by Jelinek's Nora (1982b).

In this radio play Jelinek continues to deconstruct the concept of "woman" by disassociating anatomy from social category in a gesture moving well beyond the ending of Ibsen's masterpiece, as implied by the title: *What Happened after Nora Left Her Husband or the Pillars of Society.* Similar in inspiration to Jean Rhys' *Wide Sargasso Sea* (1982), which exposes the Victorian repressed by exploring the insanity of Jane Eyre's double in the attic, Jelinek deflates her model's upbeat implications by revealing the futility of various positivistic theories of women's advancement, in particular emancipation through entry into the wage economy. Instead the bourgeois woman's attempt to escape domination by men lands her in the working class where differences among women are highlighted, thereby calling the category itself into question. The factory workers stand by their men, against Nora's advice: "You've got to burn whatever makes you unfree. If you have to burn your men, too, so what? They've put machines in your hands and doubly and triply exploited you without giving you anything in return" (Jelinek, 1982b, p. 189). Nora, distinguished by her background and verbal skills, appears to be more radical than her colleagues in naming and denouncing sexism, going so far as to employ a deconstructive lens herself. But she ultimately reverts to a type of bourgeois individualism that allows events in context to cement and not dismantle gender and class hierarchies.

The context is the plot. In forsaking the security of bourgeois marriage, Nora drops in status but only temporarily. In a skillful parody of Ibsen's entertainment scene, she is selected from among the troupe of women workers to amuse the industrial bigwigs on their factory tour. Her tarantula seduces the politician Weyland who courts her with the material goods she has begun to miss, the "long done-without," namely furs. The remainder of the action merely underscores the impotence of her feminist theory: As Weyland's consort, she gains privileged knowledge of secret plans to construct a nuclear power plant but cannot parley that information into any kind of constructive opposition. Instead, after having maneuvered her ex-husband Helmer out of a fortune, she rejoins him as a petit-bourgeois shopkeeper.

Staged in the twenties, events in the play occur under the sign of Hitler's and Mussolini's pronouncements on gender, which ironically encourage an equal-rights feminist response. The educated Nora quotes both men:

> "A majority of the people are supposedly so feminine that its thought and action results less from cool reasoning and much more from emotionality," says Mr. Hitler.
>
> (Jelinek, 1982b, p. 174)

and

> "The moment a woman touches a machine she loses her femininity, unmans the man at the same time and discourages him by taking the break out of his mouth," says Mr. Mussolini.
>
> (Jelinek, 1982b, p. 174)

Both statements lift the term "woman" from its exclusive application to female anatomies by including less powerful males in the category. Yet no female anatomy is freed from the stigma of "womanhood." Difference means inferiority.

Historically there have been two responses to this, the equality vs. difference debate in which neither answer seems adequate. Illustrative of the latter, the contemporary radical feminist project, according to Chris Weedon, "is not to deconstruct the discursive processes whereby certain qualities come to be defined as feminine and others as masculine nor to challenge directly the power relations which these differences guarantee. It is rather to revalue the feminine the patriarchy devalues" (1987, p. 81). The women in the factory lean toward this position. Jelinek's Nora, however, begins by taking the former, but equally impotent, track, turning away from difference to claim political equality with men in an economy that makes a mockery of her pretensions. Claiming, "by working for wages I wanted to transform myself from object to subject. . . . And most importantly, . . . to become my own person" (Weedon, 1987, p. 171) she echoes the humanist school whose bankruptcy becomes even clearer as both terms, "person" and "woman," are emptied of meaning.

This occurs in the political discussion among Nora, her former colleague Eva, and other women on the assembly line, Nora having dropped by the factory because she is experiencing a crisis "touching upon her existence as a feminine being" (Jelinek, 1982b, p. 159). Management's motives in having just agreed to provide the workers with both a library and a child care facility are being debated. Some of the workers take the liberal bourgeois line: This is progress, as woman worker number 2 suggests, "Since the French Revolution equality and justice have shimmered through the branches of the tree of enterprise" (Jelinek, 1982b, p. 198). But Eva, armed with Bebel and Marx, warns against cooptation. And Nora cuts in as an amazon:

> If I have to listen to you for another minute I'll go crazy! I'm a woman. The history of women to this day has been a history of gynocide, and you're talking about your ridiculous books! I don't see how murder can ever be balanced out if not through another act of violence.
>
> (Jelinek, 1982b, p. 197)

"Violence" is the key word here: Nora understands the present context as the result of force but experiences the dilemma of the intellectual whose insights are unacceptable to the women workers attached to husbands and their identities as mothers. Nora's statement that "a woman's refusal to please is the first step toward emancipation. A kick against the pyramid of covert violence" (Jelinek, 1982b, p. 199) is irrelevant to them because it is applicable to another class of creatures. Even though Eva claims, "I'm a woman, too! A woman like Nora here! I hop around with little cries of joys" (Jelinek, 1982b, p. 199) the consequences of her womanhood are so different as to belie the accuracy of the common label. When Nora admonishes the workers—"Anything's better than a sexual parasite, which I refuse to be any longer" (Jelinek, 1982b, p. 198)—it is clear that bourgeoise and laborer are not participating in the same discourse. Working women are hardly sexual parasites. And finally, when Nora claims that: "Woman has been decapitated and dismembered. Allowed to be only body, she's had her head knocked off" (Jelinek,

1982b, p. 198) her words apply not only to women but to the entire silenced working class. Only when she declares: "I want to find out what it means to be a woman because as yet nobody knows" (Jelinek, 1982b, p. 198), does she speak exclusively for women without regard to class, and although she may appear to universalize, her terms are so close to post-structuralist thought that this danger is avoided: "Woman stands in the place of the secret, that which cannot speak nor be spoken about" (Jelinek, 1982b, p. 178). Ultimately there are no "women."

Jelinek's attacks on essentialist views of "woman" culminate in **Bringing up a Vampire** (1986) for in this very figure we have a complex transgression of sexual categories. In a gothic take-off of Emile Brontë's famous work, Jelinek literalizes aspects of the Victorian repressed suggested by the original, particularly the defiance of female sexuality. After all, Emily has visited the dentist and gynecologist Heidkliff—the vagina dentata inspiring this combination—to receive some extraordinary and transparently symbolic bridge work. She wants her incisors "to be made expandable. . . . They should be able to lunge forward and then disappear. Like me. I need an apparatus like men have! I want to impress! I want to be able to demonstrate my lust! I have juices, but they don't count for much in daily life. I want to be allowed to function according to a principle, too!" (Jelinek, 1986, p. 17).

This principle is elucidated in an article, "A Vampire in the Mirror: The Sexuality of Dracula," (1988) by John A. Stevenson, which sheds light on the Austrian writer's project. After noting that Dracula makes "blood and semen interchangeable," Stevenson points to a discrepancy in that "the 'vital fluid' is being withdrawn from women, . . . the nightly visitor [being] a man." And he concludes:

> Clearly, in the vampire world traditional sexual roles are terribly confused. Dracula penetrates, but he receives the "vital fluid"; after Lucy becomes a vampire, she acts as a "penetrator" (and becomes sexually aggressive), but she now receives fluid from those she attacks.
>
> (p. 146)

These liquids also include milk, as in one of Stoker's scenes Dracula forces his victim's face onto "'his bosom,'" the couple's "'attitude . . . [bearing] a terrible resemblance to a child forcing a kitten's nose into a saucer of milk . . .'" (Stevenson, 1988, p. 146). This breast-feeding combined with oral sex in a single tableau leads Stevenson to ask: "What is going on? Fellatio? Lactation? It seems that the vampire is sexually capable of everything, [and] like Tiresias, . . . has looked at sex from both sides . . . [thus making] it difficult to say, simply, that [Stoker's] novel is hostile to female sexuality." Rather, "the nature of the 'female' has itself been made problematic" (Stevenson, 1988, p. 146).

That radio should be an especially appropriate medium for exploring these sex/gender fluidities and disconnections has been noticed by others. Frances Gray, for example, in her article "The Nature of Radio Drama" (1981) chooses Angela Carter's *Vampirella* (1976) to highlight this. She writes:

> The play explores the attempts of reality and myth to come to terms with each other. The hero sensibly offers his beloved vampire-countess a context in which to be loved; he wants to take her to Vienna—where presumably Freud, who destroyed one lot of myths only to set up another, would psychoanalyze her out of existence after a dentist had fixed the fangs that deter the hero from taking her straight home to mother.
>
> (Gray, 1981, p. 57)

The heroine, however, refuses. She will stand by her negativity, disparaging any comfortable identity: "I am not a demon, for a demon is incorporeal; not a phantom for phantoms are intangible. I have a shape; it is my own shape; but I am not alive, and so I cannot die. I need your life to sustain this physical show, myself" (Carter cited in Gray, 1981, p. 57). And Gray concludes, "Only on radio can this kind of nonbeing be given, a body without any kind of filmic illusion to falsify its nature" (Gray, 1981, p. 57).

Because "radio's ambiguity is its major strength" (Gray, 1981, p. 57), the "physical show" of which the vampire speaks is pure discourse, especially well suited to exploring sexual difference and alterity as a product of language. This would also appear to be Jelinek's foreground project in **The King Bees** (1982a).

## Not Found in Nature: *King Bees*

"Irony," writes Michael Seidel, "is a kind of subversive allegory, a doubling that cancels . . ." (1986, p. 14). Like science fiction generally, **The King Bees** stages such an allegory, its secondary "plot" implicating those citadels of unabridged male power, business and government colluding in the nuclear industry.

The tale of Terrana is narrated by one of the "boys" who survives a revolution directed by the Hetis or courtesan class of women. But leading up to liberation is a complex history. With the world's population having reached 35 billion and raw materials exhausted, the fear of increasing totalitarianism proves justified: "In an unprecedented economic and technical effort involving all the world's governments, they succeeded in centralizing energy production" (Jelinek, 1982a, p. 9). The docility of the masses has been assured by strict control of resources: "At that time, the fact that people had nothing left to drink, eat, or breath made them peaceful" (Jelinek, 1982a, p. 11).

At the south pole, a reactor complex is thus constructed on several levels underground, with male personnel assigned to the safer, lower regions, wives and children housed closer to the dangerous surface. This both literalizes and inverts organizational hierarchy, while also parodying that archetypal literary form, the descent into hell.

Due to their increased exposure, the women are more devastatingly affected by the catastrophe—a melt-down—which leads to a scarcity of females and a reproductive crisis. The population now consists of 250 males and 18 females, 8 fertile and 10 infertile women, divided according to the classic mother/whore dichotomy into Mutas and Hetis. The former however are unable to carry normally to term. Instead they expel two months' children four times per year. This requires construction of artificial wombs. Yet an additional problem remains: All the foetuses are male. Now, if Hélène Cixous (1981) is right, this eradication of the female has been at the base of Western phallocratic discourse all along:

> In the extreme the world of "being" can function to the exclusion of the mother. No need for mother—provided there is something of the maternal; and it is the father then who acts as—is—the mother. Either the woman is passive; or she doesn't exist. What is left is unthinkable, unthought of. She does not enter into the oppositions, she is not coupled with the father (who is coupled with the son).
> 
> (Cixous cited in Marks and Courtivron, 1981, p. 92)

Jelinek merely translates the poorly repressed desire into "fact."

***The King Bees*** then explores the consequences of this demographic fluke. On the one hand, a daughter is needed for humanity's survival, but experimental efforts to produce one vie for priority with genetic engineering. Ultimately, having discovered both a means to considerably prolong their lives and youth while also exercising "positive" eugenics, the ruling technocrats recognize to their dismay that the too perfect male offspring being run off the assembly line can be expected to rival and displace their "betters."

> Question: Once it has a monopoly on technological power and knowledge, as well as having achieved a quasi-immortality, what does a kingly society do with a generation, many generations of growing sons, of maturing young men, who perhaps can be expected someday to challenge their rulers?
> 
> (Jelinek, 1982a, p. 27)

In this scenario echoing Freud's "primal horde," the answer is "Auswahlverfahren"—to initiate a selection process equivalent to castration, to remove the rival sons from the very category of "men."

They are unmanned in two ways: denied access to women and put in charge of raising babies, a task linking them to the Heti's or courtesans. Both restrictions are highly significant. Lévi-Strauss has pointed out how the exchange of women is central to patriarchal status; without this power, even possession of the phallus does not confer the title "man." This is implied in the discussion among the male technocrats assessing the situation in the early years after the melt-down. At issue is how to deal with the women:

MALE VOICE 3:

> (*enthusiastic*) It's not enough to have men who conquer the world; you've got to have the world made pleasant for the men by self-subordinating women.
> 
> (Jelinek, 1982a, p. 20)

A tautology, this argument slots both "men" and "women" into their classic places as active and passive, their positions mutually dependent. The reflexive pronoun, however, is suspect: It leaves the women their complicity, making them also active in their passivity. This seriously destabilizes the dyad by deferring closure. An additional threat proceeds from the others eliminated from the category—males without access to women. Like members of racial minorities, they remain "boys." The meaning of gender is thus derived not from anatomy but from function and context.

Unmanning is a further consequence of shared parenting. Relevant here is Nancy Chodorow's hypothesis concerning the preoedipal stage of psychic development, in *The Reproduction of Mothering* (1978), linking differences in gender formation to the near-universality of the female parent with whom girls may identify strongly while boys feel compelled to separate. The conclusion for Chodorow's followers who wish to disrupt this order is precisely to disband the female monopoly on child care. This happens in Terrana: The socialization of women and introduction of "boys" as caregivers appear indeed to have initiated revolutionary consequences. The technocrats, no longer interested in perpetuating individual names and bloodlines through marriage, are content to engineer survival of the species with allegiance offered only to their own elites. This, too, functions ironically to unmake "men."

Now the fact that, although all the powerful are males, not all males are powerful, marks a break between anatomy and sign, while power itself would seem to be no longer "phallocratic" but some other kind. Neither the Marxist nor as yet any feminist theory can define what it is, but coming closest is probably the deconstructive view for which it may comfortably remain unknown.

There are a significant number of other unknowns in the piece, among them the nature of "woman." In ***Nora*** Jelinek has written: "Woman and nature together aren't necessarily natural. They can be separated" (Jelinek, 1982b, p. 186). *The King Bees* continues that disruptive project. Elsewhere Jelinek has pointed out the political folly of relying on procreative power as a route to empowerment. As Regine Friedrich notes in her "Afterword" to *Illness or the Modern Woman*:

> The feminist movement has spread like a bacterial invasion, one of its varieties having landed in the same trap it had just broken out of. It sings in a witch's chorus of the mysterious link to nature, of the wonder of female biology . . .
>
> (Friedrich, 1987, p. 85)

*The King Bees* takes the wonder of female anatomy to its logical conclusion, as the opponents of genetic engineering under male control have warned. Isolated from one another in cells like honeycombs, hooked up to "surveillance, feeding and impregnating systems" maintained in a twilight world of sedativa, biology becomes even more functional, legs atrophy and some women are no longer women but "Mutas," mutations, allies of the Kings who, all together, are smothered in their cells when the Hetis and the sons revolt; inspired by the honeycomb, they seal all entrances/exits with wax as the entire ruling class assembles to celebrate the long-waited birth of daughters.

Clearly then it is not anatomy but function that determines class, although the seduction of essentialism is hard to resist. One heti, for example, is tempted to see herself and the mothers as allies: Female voice 5: "They're women like us." But the others disagree:

FEMALE VOICE 4:

We can't expect any help from the birthing women.

FEMALE VOICE 5:

They are happy with a happiness reserved only for mothers.

(Jelinek, 1982a, p. 42)

This tautology mirrors the mutas' ideological entrapment. Declared "Queen Bees," "bestowers of life," "most precious possessions" (Jelinek, 1982a, p. 19) they receive compliments camouflaging condescension that create a seductive double bind. In sum, maternal subjectivity is the kings' creation: "They think with the heads of the kings" and must therefore be killed. "If you want to kill something, the head must die first" (Jelinek, 1982a, p. 43).

The attack on conventional thinking about "men" and "women" continues on a semantic plain. The "head" to be severed is a metonymy for the chain of signifiers bound into the binary opposition rational/emotional or scientific/mystical (which, as Cixous notes, leads back to the male/female dyad: "the fact that logocentrism subjects thought—all the concepts, the codes, the values—to a two-term system [is] related to 'the' couple man/woman . . ." (Cixous cited in Marks & Courtivron, 1981, p. 91). Jelinek clearly challenges the hegemony of instrumental thinking, but without denying its importance. When asked in an early interview to comment on trends revaluing the female body, she agreed with the benefits of raising individual women's confidence but moved quickly on to the collective, warning: "If they are really going to spend ten more years concentrating on their bodies, that will mean ten more years in which men rule the world. They are the ones studying nuclear physics and biology and so forth and are running things, while the women go on with their consciousness-raising." (Münchner Literaturarbeitskreis, 1978, p. 174).

Although linking science with power, this is neither a plaidoyer for "equality" nor a defense of technocracy. It does, however, open up a void, expressing that negativity for which Jelinek is known. "Her engagement is directed against the ruling class," explains Roland Heger in *Austrian Radio Drama*. "What she is working FOR, in her books as in her radio plays, remains unclear" (Heger, 1977, p. 221).

Actually, it isn't a lack of clarity the critic notes but a staging of the indefinable, that empty space between irony and understanding. To illustrate, a child has died but its hobby horse survives. Comment: "The horse is fine because I suppose it's made of such resistent stuff" (Jelinek, 1982a, p. 16). A mother's collapsed rib elicits the following: "She apparently wanted to throw herself over her son, to protect him with something as unperfected as her own body" (Jelinek, 1982a, p. 16). Irony is the discrepancy between expectation and delivery: Here we are waiting for a focus on the human. Instead, material is emphasized. But far from having our humanism reconfirmed, it too is undermined, the chain of metonymies for "human being" having already exploded the concept: People are spoken of as "simple organic compounds," "copies," "female hosts," "relics of women and children" (Jelinek, 1982a, p. 15). Deconstruction would read these terms not as a human tendency to cruelty but as creating the context for cruelty, a sadistic language paving the way for increasingly exploitative circumstances. And these lead to revolt.

Jelinek's final scene attempts to confirm the absence of "women," "men," and "Menschen" from the world. Cultural values have been erased. The hetis and sons emerge on a terra nova offering a sensuous counterpart to critic Elizabeth Meese's view of "deconstruction's utopic projection . . . assert[ing] its motion toward the unthinkable, unknowable point(s) beyond the system it deconstructs" (Meese, 1986, p. 87). Jelinek's "so-called landscape," "bottomless," is indeed an unstructured space, not yet bearing the imprint of human subjectivity. But as Seidel notes of exile, ". . . supplemental spaces conceived are supplemental spaces controlled . . ." (Seidel, 1986, p. 13). Like artists, poets, and mathematicians, the voices inscribe their need for markers on the unscarred land:

YOUNG MALE SPEAKER 3:

Like the beaten yolk of an egg.

YOUNG MALE SPEAKER 4:

The sun is like a drop of cream in a bowl of water.

FEMALE 4:

The horizon meets the so-called landscape in a far distant line.

YOUNG MALE SPEAKER 4:

Shouldn't we try to move toward the horizon which is an imaginary, not a real line?

YOUNG MALE SPEAKER 3:

It's like an egg-yolk being beaten in a bowl of milk.

YOUNG MALE SPEAKER 4:

Namely the sun.

YOUNG MALE SPEAKER 3:

It's like a draft in this deserted landscape. Everything is pulled away, it's like vacuumed off.

(Jelinek, 1982a, pp. 45-46)

This dialogue disrupts the economy of binary opposites, splits the sex/gender dyad, and levels the linguistic barrier between the poetic and the technocratic. First, Jelinek sets up oppositions staged throughout the piece: male/female, sciences/arts, truth/fiction. She then inverts these. For example, the male and female speakers are distinguished by their discursive fields but not in the way we have been lead to expect, the women in the arts, the men in sciences. Instead, the men parody literary creativity (while at the same time engaging in it), domesticating their strange new world with their culinary similes, thereby exhibiting a sensuousness in contrast to the women's mathematical approach.

And both subvert the approaches they have chosen. Specifically, the vocabulary of the sciences—of navigation ("coastline"), cartography ("distance"), surveying ("horizon"), and mathematics ("line")—is used to negate the matter to which the terms refer. For example, the "imaginary line" as well as the "horizon" are at the same time mathematically calculable realities and mirages, ever-receding illusions. Thus, art and technology are no longer opposites but subversive dimensions in a larger project. For the current sweeping across this canvas is the seduction of the not-yet-inscribed and on this terrain, male and female meet not as themselves, but as others. Of course the threat of old history remains. Females voice the danger:

FEMALE 4:

. . . At some point our lives will have woven themselves once again into a destiny.

FEMALE 5:

Female and male destinies.

(Jelinek, 1982a, p. 47)

A destiny reflects the urge of human subjectivity to tell its story, and narratives have, thus far, included heroines and heroes, men and women.

But perhaps the decentering of the human subject will effect a change:

FEMALE 4:

But do we dare weigh down the emptied earth with women's and men's destinies?

FEMALE 6:

Do we dare take our goal orientation to prop up the landscape's goallessness?

FEMALE 5:

Whose only goal is an imaginary line.

FEMALE 4:

While our goals are more grounded in reality.

(Jelinek, 1982a, pp. 47-48)

The drama concludes with this tension. Facing the empty landscape that seems to beg for a signature, and tempted to exercise artistic mastery, Jelinek's characters give in to another vision. It is no longer a question of humanity imposing itself on the wilderness but rather of "reality" accommodating humans:

FEMALE 4:

Can we trust something as empty as the earth to something as full as ourselves? . . . do we dare weigh down the emptied earth with women's and men's destinies?

FEMALE 5:

That is very much the question.

(Jelinek, 1982a, p. 48)[1]

NOTE ON TRANSLATION

None of the Jelinek texts discussed are available in English. All quotations are therefore the author's translations. All quotations from German language texts listed in the Reference section have also been translated by the author.

ACKNOWLEDGEMENTS

The author would like to thank Josefine Carls for her translation of this article into German.

*Note*

1. Since this piece was written, Jelinek has become a *cause célèbre* with her latest work, *Lust* (Rowohlt, 1989). Attempting to take Georges Bataille as the model for an experiment in female pornography, the author asking whether heterosexual women become aroused by certain images and texts, Jelinek admits "failure" to critic Sigrid Loffler (1989, "Die Hose Runter im Feuilleton," [Pants dropped in the culture section] *Emma*, May, 4-5): "I wanted to find a female equivalent of obscene language. But the very writing of such a text destroyed me—as a subject and in my intention to write pornography. I came to recognize that a woman can't do this, at least not given the contemporary social situation."

*Works Cited*

"Brutkasten [Incubators]." (1988, September). *Emma*, 8.

Chodorow, Nancy. (1978). *The Reproduction of Mothering*. Berkeley: University of California Press.

Cixous, Hélène. (1981). "Sorties." In Elaine Marks & Isabelle de Courtivron (Eds.), *New French Feminisms*. New York: Schocken.

*Feminist Studies*. (1988). 14(1).

Friedrich, Regine. (1987). "Nachwort [Afterword]." In Elfriede Jelinek. *Krankheit oder Moderne Frauen [Illness or the Modern Woman]*. Köln: Prometh Verlag.

Gray, Frances. (1981). "The Nature of Radio Drama." In Peter Lewis (Ed.), *Radio Drama*. New York: Longman.

Heger, Roland. (1977). *Das Österreichische hörspiel [Austrian Radio Drama]*. Wien: Wilhelm Braunmüller Universitätsbuchhandlung.

Jelinek, Elfriede. (1970). *Wir sind lockvögel, baby! [We're Decoys, Baby!]*. Reinbek bei Hamburg: Rowohlt.

Jelinek, Elfriede. (1972a). *Michael: Ein jugendbuch für die infantilgesellschaft [Michael: A Children's Book for the Infantile Society]*. Reinbek bei Hamburg: Rowohlt.

Jelinek, Elfriede. (1972b). *Wenn die Sonne sinkt ist für manche auch noch büroschluss! [For Some, the Setting Sun Means the End of a Working Day]*. Süddeutscher Rundfunk Archivexemplar, 1470. (First broadcast 16 November.)

Jelinek, Elfriede. (1973). *Untergang eines tauchers [Demise of a Diver]*. Süddeutscher Rundfunk Archivexemplar, 1506. (First broadcast 22 November.)

Jelinek, Elfriede. (1974). *Kasperl und die dicke Prinzessin oder Kasperl und die dünnen bauern [Kasperl and the Chubby Princess or Kasperl and the Skinny Peasants]*. Süddeutscher Rundfunk Archivexemplar, 1541. (First broadcast 10 November.)

Jelinek, Elfriede. (1982a). *Die Bienenkönige [The King Bees]*. In Helga Geyer-Ryan (Ed.), *Was geschah, nachdem Nora ihren mann verlassen hatte? [What Happened after Nora Left Her Husband?]*. München: DTV.

Jelinek, Elfriede. (1982b). *Was geschah, nachdem Nora ihren mann verlassen hatte oder Stutzen der Gesellschaften [What Happened after Nora Left Her Husband or the Pillars of Society]*. In Helga Geyer-Ryan (Ed.), *Was geschah, nachdem Nora ihren mann verlassen hatte? [What Happened after Nora Left Her Husband?]*. München: DTV.

Jelinek, Elfriede. (1983). *Die Klavierspielerin [The Piano Player]*. Reinbekbei. Hamburg: Rowohlt.

Jelinek, Elfriede. (1986). *Erziehung eines Vampirs [Bringing up a Vampire]*. Süddeutscher Rundfunk Archivexemplar, 2039. (First broadcast 12 June.)

Levin, Tobe Joyce. (1979). *Ideology and Aesthetics in Neo-feminist German Fiction: Verena Stefan, Elfriede Jelinek, Margot Schroeder*. Ph.D. Dissertation. University Microfilms: Ann Arbor.

Marks, Elaine, & de Courtivron, Isabelle. (1981). *New French Feminisms*. New York: Schocken.

Meese, Elizabeth, A. (1986). *Crossing the Double-cross. The Practice of Feminist Criticism*. Chapel Hill: University of North Carolina Press.

*Münchner Literaturarbeitskreis*. (1978). *Gespräch mit Elfriede Jelinek [Talking with Elfriede Jelinek]. mamas pfirsiche* 9/10, 170-181.

Nyssen, Ute. (1984). "Nachwort [Afterword]." In Elfriede Jelinek. *Theaterstücke [Plays]*. Köln: Prometh Verlag.

Poovey, Mary. (1988). "Feminism and Deconstruction." *Feminist Studies*, 14, 51-65.

Rhys, Jean. (1982). *Wide Sargasso Sea*. New York: W. W. Norton.

Seidel, Michael. (1986). *Exile and the Narrative Imagination*. New Haven: Yale University Press.

Spallone, Patricia & Steinberg, Deborah Lynn (Eds.). (1987). *Made to Order. The Myth of Reproductive and Genetic Progress*. Oxford: Pergamon Press.

Stevenson, John Allen. (1988). "A Vampire in the Mirror: The Sexuality of *Dracula*." *PMLA* 103 (2), 139-147.

Weedon, Chris. (1987). *Feminist Practice and Poststructuralist Theory*. London: Basil Blackwell.

## Charlotte Innes (review date 18 March 1991)

SOURCE: Innes, Charlotte. "Death in Vienna." *Nation* 252, no. 10 (18 March 1991): 346-48.

[*In the following review, Innes compliments Jelinek's exploration of fascism in* Wonderful, Wonderful Times, *noting that the novel is "a comedy of the absurd."*]

In the summer of 1962, I spent a vacation in Austria with my family. One night, in a small village on the Danube, my father went to a Bierkeller with some friendly locals, who before long were singing Nazi songs and reminiscing about the good old days. I was only 11 years old, but I remember that it really spooked my father, who was not just an English tourist who spoke good German (and whom they oddly assumed to be sympathetic) but a German-Jewish refugee. Clearly, there was more to Austria than beautiful scenery—a suspicion that, thirty years later, is more than confirmed by two remarkable Austrian novels newly translated into English.

*Malina* by Ingeborg Bachmann and ***Wonderful, Wonderful Times*** by Elfriede Jelinek show us, in their different ways, that fascism is not a temporary madness, easily stamped out by allied victory, but a continuing presence—in the relationships between parents and children, men and women, those in authority and those who are not. Fascism, they say, is another word for patriarchy.

This tracing of dark undercurrents in the routines of daily life places Jelinek and Bachmann firmly in the company of other Austrian postwar writers, whose work is often fragmentary and introspective in nature and skeptical of taking on large subjects. Though not as internationally well-known as some of their peers (like Peter Handke, Elias Canetti or Thomas Bernhard), the two women have long struck a chord in German-speaking countries. *Malina* was a best seller when it came out in 1971, despite the disapproval critics had for Bachmann's discursive prose style—critics who had earlier applauded her tightly written, aesthetically beautiful poetry. Today, eighteen years after her death at the age of 47, Bachmann's prose is back in critical favor, having influenced writers like Günter Grass and Christa Wolf—and Elfriede Jelinek, who wrote the screenplay of the film version of *Malina* just released in Germany. Jelinek was born twenty years later than Bachmann and is more overtly political; she is the 1986 winner of the Heinrich Böll Prize for her contributions to German literature, which include five novels. . . .

If the Vienna of *Malina* is more a state of mind, the city in ***Wonderful, Wonderful Times*** is equally removed from its tourist-bureau image as a citadel of culture that carries echoes of Haydn, Mozart, Freud and Schnitzler. Set in the late 1950s, this Vienna is a poverty-stricken place of sexual sadists and youthful delinquents. Austria's impending "economic miracle" hangs over the book, but there is no sense of renewal, only a weary repetition of the past, which weaves like a snake through the lives of the characters, depositing a venom that isn't classifiable in a historical sense but clearly marks its victims. This is somewhat reminiscent of ***The Piano Teacher*** (1988), the only other of Jelinek's novels to appear in the United States; in that, the three main characters were caught in a web of love and torture that could also be seen as a brilliant if grim exploration of fascism, in which a woman, like the "I" in *Malina,* could take control of her life only by being a victim. ***Wonderful, Wonderful Times,*** for all its sickening images, is more a comedy of the absurd, yet it keeps the relationship between the powerful and the powerless central.

Sometimes painful, sometimes ludicrously comic in tone, the story concerns four teenage rebels and their efforts to assault citizens and relieve them of their wallets, not for money but for existentialist kicks. The more they rebel, the more they fall into patterns already laid down for them by society: The two middle-class would-be intellectuals find their books of little help; the working-class boy cannot break out of his groove; the rich girl reaps the benefits of her wealth; parents and children hate each other with a vengeful fury.

Their self-described leader is Rainer Witkowski, named for the Austrian lyric poet Rainer Maria Rilke. Obsessed with Camus's hero in *The Outsider* (an early title of *The Stranger* in English), stuck in an existential literary rut, Rainer performs an act of meaningless violence to prove he exists—the powerless man's attempt at power. His twin sister, Anna, a brilliant young pianist who prefers difficult modernist works by Berg and Webern to traditional Austrian composers, struggles to keep her autonomy in a country that wants women to stay home and cook. She remains mute for long periods. When she falls in love with a muscular young worker, Hans, sex is her downfall. We see that she is repeating the pattern of her mother, a teacher from a "superior background" who suddenly found herself one half of a couple copulating on the floor; the man, Herr Witkowski, became her husband. This one-legged former S.S. officer is the most obvious symbol of continuing fascism in the book. He makes up for his demotion to the lowly position of porter by beating, raping and taking pornographic pictures of his protesting but compliant wife.

The only winner in this oppressive setup is Sophie, the rich girl. Between tennis games, she amuses herself with both Rainer and Hans—Sophie has a voyeur's interest in the social underclass—but really she cares for no one but herself. Chillingly uninvolved, a "will-o'-the-wisp" and a "white mirage," wealthy Sophie is simultaneously the ghost of Austria's past—of the bourgeoisie that welcomed Nazism—and a sign of the prosperous future. Like fascist acolytes, Rainer and Hans are drawn toward her aura of power.

Clearly sympathetic to socialism and feminism, Jelinek nevertheless has no political ax to grind; in particular, she echoes Ilse Aichinger, whose 1946 "Call for Skepticism," a magazine article that urged artists to reject all dogma, so influenced Handke and Bachmann. Her goal is to examine society with a cool, analytical eye. Youth, love, art, political systems, memory, religion, intellectualism and even nature are placed on the Jelinek operating table and stripped of all our most treasured notions. Her method, more that of a lunatic researcher than a novelist, involves presenting each chapter as a different cross section of the same bundle of themes; this may be as artificial a technique as any, but Jelinek knows it and has fun with it.

It can be said without qualification that after Bachmann and Jelinek, Austria will never seem quite the same. The remarkable winding beauty of Bachmann's prose and the crazy logic of Jelinek's make some familiar themes fresh and new. And as the world stumbles through yet another major war, their profound pessimism seems unnervingly on target.

Back in 1962, after my family left the village of nostalgic Nazis, we drove past Mauthausen, an Austrian concentration camp overlooking the Danube. As a child, I thought naïvely that the presence of such massive monuments to human cruelty would prevent the occurrence of further atrocities. Now I am not so sure. Perhaps we are all a little like Jelinek's Herr Witkowski, who "often thinks of the dark skeletons of people he killed. The white and immaculate snow of Poland turns bloody and maculate. But snow goes on falling, again and again, and by now it bears no trace of those who disappeared there."

**Barbara Kosta (essay date 1994)**

SOURCE: Kosta, Barbara. "Inscribing Erika: Mother-Daughter Bond/age in Elfriede Jelinek's *Die Klavierspielerin*." *Monatshefte* 86, no. 2 (1994): 218-34.

[*In the following essay, Kosta analyzes the mother-daughter relationship in* Die Klavierspielerin.]

> Before they were mothers Leto and Niobe had been the most devoted of friends.
>
> —Sappho

While the Oedipal battles that have informed much of Western literature continue to rage on, the figure of the mother, traditionally less visible, slowly begins to take her place among the dramas of identity. Only recently has the mother become a prominent presence in contemporary literature as well as in many psychological and critical studies. This figure's increasing appearance in contemporary texts stems largely from the women's movement and its focus on the private sphere and women's lives. In literature, the mother takes on a central role once daughters begin to map and assess their lives. For many women authors, dealing with the mother usually entails grappling with the internalization of the mother's voice. In essence, it represents a daughter's investigation of her own identity.

Recent examinations of the mother in texts by women authors, often autobiographical, have moved from a rejection of the mother as a model which stood for a dramatic performance of separation and the desire for autonomy in the early phases of second-wave feminism, to beginnings of a dialogue and an exploration of the constraints which have informed traditional mothers' lives. In both cases, the complexity of these representations opens up many questions about the configurations of female identity and about the mother's function in its formation.

At a time when the mother-daughter relationship has begun to constitute a "new psychic geography of feminist discourse," Austrian writer Elfriede Jelinek presents her novel *Die Klavierspielerin,* published in 1983.[1] Unlike her contemporaries whose autobiographical descriptions of the mother-daughter dyad are often infused with a desire for the lost mother and based upon a continuing search for her (the realm of the pre-Oedipal bond), Jelinek describes a pathogenic symbiotic relationship that in effect entombs the daughter.[2] A nightmarishly devouring mother is portrayed, one who never releases the daughter, Erika Kohut, from her attachment. She is a beast, the narrator reveals, "eine Niobe in Pension" (157), "Inquisitor und Erschießungskommando in einer Person, in Staat und Familie einstimmig als Mutter anerkannt" (5).[3]

Given this portrait of the mother, could it be that Jelinek's caustic narrative of the mother-daughter relationship places her at odds with the feminist literature of her time? Is *Die Klavierspielerin* matrophobic in the way in which Adrienne Rich defines it as a daughter's desire to free herself from the mother's control, with the "mother standing for the victim in ourselves?"[4] Or does Jelinek, like so many autobiographical narrators of the 1980s, attempt to come to terms with her own mother by initiating a dialogue?

With *Die Klavierspielerin* Jelinek takes a different tack. Rather than presenting a personal account, she ironically stages the psychodynamics of the mother-daughter relationship in order to inflate and pervert them to the point of their collapse. With her two Kohut women, mother and daughter, Jelinek looks at the cultural figuring and the socially inscribed structures that perpetuate a relationship of domination and subservience. At the same time, Jelinek targets the mother-daughter relationship to show how this relationship potentially lays the ground for female masochism, dependency, and the repression of female sexuality. She illustrates the daughter's masochistic disposition prepared, as I will argue, by the oppressive proximity of the maternal, and thereby rouses a discussion of female masochism which has received little attention in most theoretical discussions of this topic.

Psychoanalyst Gilles Deleuze's conceptualization of masochism sheds light on the very complex relationship Jelinek represents.[5] Deleuze sees masochism as a pre-Oedipal phenomenon rooted in an infantile ambivalence toward the mother as love object and controlling agent, and recognizes the mother's vast influence as a cultural *body* on the child's psychic development. It is the mother to whom the infant surrenders to receive gratification and pleasure, and it is the mother who controls its denial. The mother, therefore, does not lack, as Freud's model implies. She is the imago of the oral mother, the nurturing mother associated with the critical oral stage as sustaining, yet threatening. Unfortunately, Deleuze discusses masochism only in terms of the male protagonist. But by interweaving his understanding with object-relation theory's complex interpretation of female dependency, Deleuze's model can lend insight into the mother-daughter and later the daughter-lover relationship Jelinek constructs.

In **Die Klavierspielerin,** the mother appears at the center of the narrative, overbearing and ever-present, just as she resides at the center of her daughter's life. Significantly, she plays the role of primary caretaker; she tends the private sphere, provides nourishment and security, and has full reign over the daughter; she stands as a replica of the oral mother. The mother is also the cold mother, who, "in Deleuze's construct," Gaylyn Studlar observes, "becomes the familiar dual symbol of creation and death who crystallizes infantile ambivalence in the masochistic ideal of 'coldness, solicitude and death.' She is the figure of the cold oral mother who represents the good mother from the infantile stage of imagined dual unity or symbiosis between mother and child."[6] While nourishing her daughter, the mother simultaneously denies her daughter the possibility of separation.

The novel opens with Erika Kohut, the piano teacher, entering like a wild storm the apartment she shares with her mother. Her movements and the reference to her as "child" evoke the image of an adolescent. As the narrator, however, soberly points out: "Erika geht auf das Ende der Dreißig zu" (5). Indeed, the introduction portends an unnaturally prolonged symbiosis between mother and daughter and suggests a dialectic of control in which one party ceases to exist. The mother is marked by a "large" presence that overshadows and engulfs the daughter to the point of her obliteration.

In addition to Deleuze's assertion that the primary function of the oral mother is to stimulate the masochist's active search for submission, object-relations theory and research compellingly illustrate how women develop relationships of dependency which confine them in what may be called masochistic bondage. Psychologist Nancy Chodorow discusses the effects of separation and individuation processes on gender arrangements. In contrast to male children's right to independence, she suggests, the daughter's autonomy is discouraged and the profound emotional bond never surrendered. For the daughter, this scheme has asserted itself widely through the social structures of Western society. Because girls are of the same gender as their mothers, they are less encouraged than sons to separate, to go off into the world, and to assert their difference. Consequently, for the daughter, the mother represents regression, inhibition, and lack of autonomy. Contrary to Freud's belief that daughters gain a sense of femaleness when they turn toward their fathers in search of a heterosexual love object, Chodorow ascertains that girls draw their sense of identity from the mother throughout their adolescence.[7]

The deep bond, whether it negates or affirms the daughter, results from the social conceptualization of the mother-daughter relationship. This configuration in Jelinek's narrative produces an intricate interweaving of psyches in which the daughter inevitably emerges as the effect of the mother. Jelinek describes the symbiotic merger with the mother as follows: "Mutter und Kind stecken die Köpfe ineinander, als wären sie nur ein einziger Mensch . . ." (127). Under the mother's strict tutelage, the child's psychic organization is molded to conform to the mother's, making the border between mother and daughter virtually intangible. Jelinek exaggerates these psychological maneuvers to show how ego boundaries dissipate through the mother's relentless imposition of her will onto the "other." Frau Kohut, whose name suggests "caring for" (*hüten*) incessantly transgresses the boundaries essential for the daughter's assertion of herself as subject. As the more powerful voice, the mother authors the daughter; she determines Erika's identity and inscribes her laws and needs onto her daughter's body to the extent that Erika is fixed within the matrix of maternal control, where she stagnates. Even though Erika struggles to break away from the mother, she paradoxically longs for pre-Oedipal intimacy, to sit and watch television in the evenings in their cozy apartment, and—"sanft im warmen Leibwasser schaukeln" (76).

Erika's containment in a "pre-Oedipal" situation and the continued symbiosis with her mother manifests itself as perversion climactically portrayed when she turns to her mother in their shared bed and overwhelms her with infantile, though explicitly sexual overtures of intimacy. The pseudo-incestuous undercurrent emphasizes the claustrophobic confines of the relationship and the scarce possibilities of movement outward. An aggressive struggle for control takes place in which the child wishes to devour the mother to fulfill her insatiable oral needs. While Erika's gestures of domination indicate an attempt to seize power, a regression to the mother occurs in which the daughter tries to still her libidinal needs after being rejected by Walter Klemmer, her student and intended lover:

> Erika drückt ihren nassen Mund der Mutter vielfach ins Antlitz und hält die Mutter eisern mit den Armen fest, damit sie sich nicht dagegen wehren kann. . . . Die Mutter wirft ihren Kopf wild herum, um den Küssen entkommen zu können, es ist wie bei einem Liebeskampf, und nicht Orgasmus ist das Ziel, sondern die Mutter an sich, die Person Mutter. . . . Erika saugt und nagt an diesem großen Leib herum, als wollte sie gleich noch einmal hineinkriechen, sich darin verbergen. Erika gesteht der Mutter ihre Liebe, und die Mutter keucht das Gegenteil, nämlich, daß sie ihr Kind ebenfalls liebe, doch solle dies Kind sofort aufhören!
>
> (235)

"The Mother per se" ("die Mutter an sich") as essence functions to soothe instinctual desires. She represents the oral mother, the nurturing mother associated with the masochist's desire for submission. As we will see, Frau Kohut leaves her daughter with few channels for her own desire independent of the mother's. Like the door that Walter Klemmer tries to open, Erika "bleibt kalt und stumm. Sie gibt keinen Millimeter nach, weil sie versperrt ist" (125).

Among the reasons which figure into a daughter's failed separation and subsequent inhibited independence are the social positioning of the mother within various dependencies and, historically, women's exclusive role as mother. Within traditional white, middle-class Austrian culture, particularly within the generations like that of the mother in *Die Klavierspielerin,* the mother is economically powerless, isolated and without social recognition. Even though the daughter's social situation is meant to resemble the mother's, the daughter provides a means for the mother's own empowerment. By virtue of possessing the child, the mother gains control, purpose, and a heightened sense of herself as subject within the mother (subject) and daughter (object) dyad. Thus the power relations within the mother-daughter relationship confine the daughter within the mirror image of the mother as sameness, instead of expressing the simultaneity of sameness and difference. A relationship of mutual recognition, as envisioned by Luce Irigaray in *And the One Doesn't Stir without the Other,* is impeded and patriarchy, which constructs the mother to perpetuate in her transmission of powerlessness, remains intact.[8] In *Die Klavierspielerin,* the mother is reduced to the most basic descriptor "die Mutter" or represented as "Frau Kohut," placing her in a dual tradition, one of a namelessness that anchors woman in a patriarchal lineage, and the other that scripts her as the "oral mother."

As a constant companion, the mother influences the child's subject formation by laying much of the groundwork for the course of later psychological growth. She also inevitably exercises unconditional power over the child. To contain the daughter, in order to enforce their continuing bond, Erika learns to submit and obey. The term "dressieren" ("to train"), normally used in reference to animals, graphically emphasizes the tyrannical methods of discipline in child rearing. Her mother vanquishes Erika's will, and thus acquiescence, as the narrator notes, becomes second nature to her: "Doch das ist ihr dermaßen in Fleisch und Blut übergegangen, daß sie es nicht mehr merkt" (199). The child, moreover, is treated like an object, a piece of property, that is, the mother's private domain. By contrast the "modern mothers" which Jelinek introduces allow their children "eine längere Leine." Despite more leniency, their children desert them later on just the same (90). In response to children's penchant for straying, Frau Kohut frantically tries to contain her daughter by keeping Erika pre-Oedipally bound: "Das Hauptproblem der Mama besteht darin, ihr Besitztum möglichst unbeweglich an einem Ort zu fixieren" (7). The daughter is the mother's working capital. Frau Kohut, therefore, invests her life in her daughter, which guarantees her daughter's indebtedness. Jelinek skillfully represents the complex double bind of exchange. Since the mother lives only for her child, the child, without recourse, ends up owing her life to the mother. The narrator wittingly points out the underlying terms of this contract: "Das Kind ist der Abgott seiner Mutter, welche dem Kind dafür nur geringe Gebühr abverlangt: sein Leben" (28). Frau Kohut ensures the bond through self-sacrifice, which serves as the ultimate instrument to emotionally harness the daughter. The narrator sarcastically refers to the mother as an aging saint, "die alte Frau Heilige," which assigns martyrdom as well as divinity to her position (268).

Elisabeth Badinter reveals the ideological underwriting of motherhood, which contains the discourse of self-denial and sacrifice, a type of masochism associated with the institution of motherhood rarely articulated:

> Indeed, motherhood, as it was conceived in the nineteenth century, in close harmony with Rousseau, was understood as a holy office, a happy experience that necessarily brought with it pain and suffering, a literal sacrifice of oneself on the altar of devotion.[9]

*Die Klavierspielerin* exemplifies the narrative of "das grausame Land der Mutterliebe" (156). Jelinek unmasks devotion and self-sacrifice as a tactic of oppressive manipulation meshed with the mother's own interests. While this representation of the mother judicially absolves her of "wickedness" or even "sadism," as opposed to many other literary representations of the "bad mother," it points to the complex forms of interaction and negotiation that develop when emotional deficits and insufficiencies constitute the foundation of relationships. The relationship of power becomes more fragile.

To offset the potential loss of control, the mother targets the daughter's body, which is cautiously kept within close range through the unremitting surveillance of Erika's every move with the mother's so-called built-in radar system. When Erika enters puberty, for instance, mother and grandmother, together sardonically referred to as the "female brigade," stand between Erika's emerging sexuality and any potential male stalker, ready to throw themselves into battle in order to protect their young against repossession.

The grandmother, as an accomplice, personifies a lineage of sexual repression: "Die beiden älteren Frauen mit ihren zugewachsenen verdorrten Geschlechtsteilen werfen sich vor jeden Mann, damit er zu ihrem Kitz nicht eindringen kann. Dem Jungtier sollen nicht Liebe, nicht Lust etwas anhaben können" (35). Jelinek's aggressive language describes mother and grandmother, whose own bodies have atrophied, killing Erika's budding sexuality by building a shield around the pubescent female body. She is robbed of her body through its denial, with the mother, as Jessica Benjamin points out, acting as "the restrictive prohibitor of desire" which stems from the experience of her own body.[10] At night, we learn, Frau Kohut watches her daughter's hands, which are only meant for piano playing—a means of social mobility and recognition for the mother.[11] Erika is denied her own sexuality because it represents a process of maturation and separation. Under the mother's panoptic regime, Erika's body atrophies too. Over and over again she is described as a corpse, a shell, a hole: "Sie ist Nichts" (199). She is detached from her body and left without the slightest feeling.

Undoubtedly, Erika is a prisoner of her body while the mother stands guard. Tyrannically shielding the daughter from the male gaze, the mother hovers over Erika, her possession. For the mother, men connote nothing but an intrusion into the sphere of the mother-daughter relationship and the potential loss of the daughter, in Erika's case, to heterosexual love. She chastises Erika for her elaborate attire, which she construes as her wish to attract men. Adornment not only becomes an economic issue of luxury, since the money Erika earns should be put toward a new apartment, but it simultaneously stands for individuation and for rejection of the mother. The clothes Erika illicitly buys, her desire for high-heel shoes, scarves and accessories, reflect her defiant attempts to assert her own boundaries. Yet these substitutes for her own sexuality remain limp in the closet, never worn.

To maintain sole property of the daughter, the mother conceals the daughter from men though simultaneously, Erika serves as a male-substitute, as provider. Jane Flax offers one symptomatic reading of the multiple roles that overburden daughters which seems to resonate in Jelinek's novel:

> Oftentimes the daughter and not the father is the primary source of nurturance for the mother. . . . Daughters serve as confidants, friends, and even lovers in a way that is often confusing and inappropriate to the daughter's developmental process.[12]

Erika shares the marital bed with the mother. They are referred to as a couple, "das Ehepaar Erika/Mama," with Erika's name notably appearing first, and their relationship, as Jelinek taunts, will last until "der Tod sie scheidet" (32). "Scheidet" functions as an unmistakable homology of "schneidet," to cut, which plays upon Erika's later acts of self-mutilation. Finally, Erika financially supports the mother, which points to the mother's social powerlessness, her ultimate dependence and confined living situation.

The mother's power and influence increase with the absence of the father, who is admitted to an asylum and spatially exiled. Aside from the fact that the exclusive bond between mother and daughter remains uninterrupted and maternal domination unobstructed, his displacement suggests the cause for Erika's failed separation from the mother and her excessive masochistic drive.

The narrative implies that the absent father within the nuclear family and the mother's traditional role as primary caretaker both contribute to Erika's dysfunctional development.[13] Viewed as such, Jelinek's text appears aligned with feminist texts that see the father (or similar caretakers other than the mother) as a necessary agent in the child's process of separation. He provides additional possibilities for detachment and distance from the child's primary relationship. Jessica Benjamin discusses the importance of the father in his representation of difference, of agency, excitement, and otherness.[14] He not only embodies a point outside of the mother, but more significantly, he represents the outside world and mobility. Within the traditional family romance, the father facilitates movement from inside to outside, a necessary step in the individuation process typically frustrated by the mother. Like Deleuze, Benjamin roots women's masochistic disposition in the pre-Oedipal relationship, but then goes a step further to explain its persistence in the female's adult life. The "missing father," exemplary of a girl's paternal relationship in Western culture, is the "key to [women's] missing desire," Benjamin declares, "and to its return in the form of masochism" through the creation of an ideal love.[15] In Benjamin's scheme, the female surrenders herself to the male in order to vicariously gain recognition and to experience agency through the male. Paraphrasing Chodorow and other object relations theorists, Coppelia Kahn problematically rewrites the daughter's desire for her own space outside of the mother as the daughter's desire for a penis:

> Because she [the daughter] is of the same sex as her mother and thus is more profoundly attached to her than the boy is, she desires a penis as a crucial sign of difference, to serve as a defense against the undertow of merger with the mother and, as a symbol of power, to establish herself against the woman she has known as all-powerful.[16]

Yet rather than abet the misconception of a classical syndrome of penis envy, it is necessary at this juncture to distinguish between the child wanting a penis and the symbolic value she attributes to the phallus. Desiring the phallus does not mean equating the female body with lack, but rather signifies the daughter's desire to gain distance from the powerful oral mother. The phallus symbolically facilitates access to the outside world, the possibility of becoming actively desiring, instead of being confined to maternal domination and power. In Janine Chasseguet-Smirgel's words, the phallus provides a means "to beat back the mother" which the daughter is often denied. Through her alliance with her student Walter Klemmer as well as through her secret excursions, Erika seizes chances to evade the mother.

Jelinek alludes to the loss of the paternal symbol in the Kohut family when she has the local butcher philosophizing about the costs of life (or "Wurst") while transporting the father to the asylum. Erika and Frau Kohut agree that everything has its price, which Jelinek describes as: "Die Damen K. stimmen ihm etwas wehmütig zu, weil ihnen ein Glied der Familie abgeht." In the course of the conversation, the butcher inquires: "Welches spezielle Stück denn. . . ." (98). Later Erika appears to fetishize precisely this missing "member."

Significantly, Erika escapes maternal control by standing in for the father in her regular visits to Vienna's Prater, described as a carnival sphere of lust. Equipped with her binoculars (inherited from her father), she prowls the area looking for scenes of sex in order to satisfy her scopophilic urges—the only way she can engage her body without risking distance. She becomes the voyeur par excellence, illicitly watching what is forbidden her: "Sie muß und muß schauen. Sie ist für sich selbst tabu. Anfassen gibt es nicht" (56). At peep shows, Erika explores the female body, albeit visually. Yet, within this arena, her position as spectator remains ambiguous. She not only occupies a "male" space, the cabin of the peep show, but assumes the male role of voyeur, since voyeurism is the property of the masculine spectator (the binoculars she uses belong to her father as well). Erika performs the act of looking, with woman as spectacle and the exhibitionistic object constructed for male pleasure.[17]

The gaze here is exploitative, just like the sexual relations Erika observes in porno films or between the male "guest worker" and an Austrian woman in the bushes. On one level, appropriation of the male gaze allows her to maintain a distance and relieves the threat of engulfment. Throughout the narrative Erika shuns proximity: "Man sagt gern von einer solchen Person, sie sei unnahbar" (93). On another level, occupying a male space perpetuates a "negative" female identity and further removes Erika from the possibility of finding a confirming, mirroring response in her confrontation with woman constructed as object or as other who is void of agency and her own desire. Female sexuality, or "the dark continent," remains hidden, despite Erika's wish to see inside the female body, to gain "insight" or "Einblick" (109). The narrator chidingly reminds the reader that Erika pays for what she could view in the mirror at home.

Still, she perceives herself as an aberration of nature. In an allusion to creation stories, the narrator describes Erika's visit to the peep show: "Auch Erika will nichts weiter als zuschauen. Hier, in dieser Kabine, wird sie zu garnichts. . . . Die Natur scheint keine Öffnungen in ihr gelassen zu haben. . . . Dafür stolziert Erika als Herrin herum." (53).[18] The German word "Herrin", a compound of male and female signifier, essentially marks her as a genderless oddity, neither here nor there.

Erika, however, finds few avenues of exploration outside of the maternal realm. As a result, she cuts or gouges herself in reaction to her inability to separate and as an expression of wishing to penetrate the cast that encases her. The daughter defiles the female body not only as an aggressive retaliation against her entrapment, but symptomatically attempts to cut through the ice (as one critic suggests, the German word for ice "EIS" is the mirror image of "SIE") that envelops her and leads to dissociation from her body.[19] Erika consequently punishes and negates herself as daughter and symbolically severs the umbilical cord in an effort to control her life.

Particularly after encounters with men who unleash her discordant desire to feel her own body and to separate from the maternal aegis, Erika, wielding a razor blade or knife, initiates her private rituals of self-mutilation. The narrator comments: "Die Klinge lacht wie der Bräutigam der Braut entgegen" (45). The bridegroom (the male), an ambiguous emblem of liberation (since he repossesses the daughter), takes the bride away from the mother. He, so to speak, "penetrates" the bond. Yet as Jelinek illustrates in ***Die Klavierspielerin,*** as well as in other works, the male picks up where the mother leaves off. The mother essentially prepares the daughter for masochist submission and further "bond/age."

Jelinek graphically describes Erika's masochistic destruction of the body that imprisons her. In one scene, as soon as she hears her mother leave the house, the daughter attempts to extend an opening in herself by cutting the vagina with the father's all-purpose razor blade. Again, it is the fetishized "missing father" who provides the instrument of separation:

> SIE setzt sich mit gespreizten Beinen vor die Vergrößerungsseite des Rasierspiegels und vollzieht einen Schnitt, der die Öffnung vergrößern soll, die als Tür in ihren Leib hineinführt. . . . SIE schneidet sich jedoch an der falschen Stelle und trennt damit, was Herr Gott und Mutter Natur in ungewohnter Einigkeit zusammengefügt haben. Der Mensch darf es nicht und es rächt sich. Sie fühlt nichts. Einen Augenblick lang starren die beiden zerschnittenen Fleischhälften einander betroffen an, weil plötzlich dieser Abstand entstanden ist, der vorher noch nicht da war. Sie haben viele Jahre lang Freud und Leid miteinander geteilt, und nun separiert man sie voneinander! Im Spiegel sehen die Hälften sich auch noch seiten-verkehrt, so daß keine weiß, welche Hälfte sie ist.
>
> (88-89)

Implied is that the mother and daughter, as the same sex, are biologically connected. Within Erika's mirror no differentiation exists; they are interchangeable. Unlike Irigaray's positive description of the female genitals as autoerotic and self-contained, which resists the Freudian inscription of deficiency, punned in Jelinek's reference to "Freud und Leid," Erika's genitals are mute.[20] Just like her body, they too are besieged by the mother.

In Erika's relationship to Walter Klemmer, Jelinek shows how the mother-daughter relationship initiates Erika into asymmetrical power relationships of domination and subservience. The mother's authority, which does not recognize the daughter outside of her domain, veritably erases the daughter as subject. Consequently, Erika only knows submission, self-abnegation and obedience. For her, love translates into dependence and submission to another's will. Advertisements for pornographic movies that reinforce erotic fantasies of female subordination and male rule find fertile ground in the psychology prepared by the mother, but more importantly, they allude to the pervasive expression of this power structure. It is not surprising then that the dramaturgy of "love" that Erika directs with her student is masochistically choreographed. In a detailed letter to Klemmer, Erika finely outlines the stages of her abuse and humiliation: she wishes to be chained, beaten and gagged to the point of self-annihilation. As the letter shows, the masochist yields yet paradoxically exerts control by determining her own punishment.

Through slavery and obedience, the daughter attempts to attain freedom; through pain, she hopes to be reached and touched—as long as she stipulates the parameters. Jessica Benjamin speaks of submission as "the desire for independence and the desire for recognition" and ultimately the desire for love.[21] She continues: "But current psychoanalytical theory appreciates that pain is a route to pleasure only when it involves submission to an idealized figure."[22] According to Benjamin's model, Walter Klemmer becomes the idealized figure who potentially liberates Erika from the mother and offers her a means of obtaining self-worth. Benjamin claims that "woman loses herself in the identification with the powerful other who embodies the missing desire and agency."[23] Klemmer is always described as healthy, athletic, "intakt und unbeschwert" (114); "Klemmer ist die Norm" (216). However, a second voice emerges in this masochistic fantasy of denial and humiliation that confers another dimension upon Erika's declaration of subjugation.

The daughter secretly hopes that Klemmer resists violating her—as an ultimate expression of love. This other voice resists penetration, contrary to Benjamin's prediction, and impedes orgasm or closure. Erika even recommends that their erotic exchange remain textual, i.e. fantasy: "Erika spricht nicht, sie schreibt" or "Nebst Brief ist sie eigentlich wunschlos" (218; 233). Since the masochist draws pleasure from postponement, such delays are intrinsic to masochistic desire. "Hence," as Gaylyn Studlar concludes, "the need to control desire and suspend consummation."[24] At the same time, the masochist "depends upon separation to guarantee a pain/pleasure structure."[25] In other words, the masochist's pleasure is at stake if the boundaries between subject and object are violated, since the masochist's ego boundaries are too weak to sustain herself. It is the possibility of acting out obedience that belongs to the fantasy world of the masochist rather than pain.

Erika's three sexual encounters with Walter Klemmer illustrate the pinings and power of the masochistic text. Their first erotic confrontation takes place in a lavatory stall. Erika allows Klemmer access to her body, described as a discarded instrument—she remains remarkably passive during Klemmer's passionate outburst and energetic demonstration of agency. Upon taking Klemmer's penis into her hand, Erika takes command and regains power. With this gesture, she also initiates a delay and postpones consummation. The narrator comments: "In der Geschichte der Musik und auch nirgendwo sonst wird der werbende Mann aus dem Geschehen einfach entlassen" (79). Inactivated and reduced to "Liebeswörter," Erika informs Klemmer that she will write him a letter, the pact of the masochist's madness, as Deleuze suggests.[26]

The second encounter takes place in a janitorial closet. Amidst antiseptic cleaners and brooms, Klemmer remains impotent (sterile). Finally, they meet inside the Kohut apartment "von Nahrungsmittel umgeben" which imperils the realm of the (oral) mother. It is here that Erika produces the letter in which she details the mechanics of her subjugation (211). Marking the longest single scene in the novel, she entreats Klemmer to participate in her masochistic fantasy. Full of delays and circuitous, descriptive meanderings, the masochistic fantasy evolves as an aesthetic expression of desire. During the fourth encounter, however, his feelings of agency violated once again, Klemmer's sense of frustration and humiliation climaxes. Disgusted by the role of dependence imposed upon him in Erika's fantasy, he wantonly retaliates. He returns to the Kohut apartment late at night seeking to annihilate the object of his degradation. By brutalizing and raping Erika, Klemmer reinstates his masculinity and the traditionally gendered power relationship: "Er geht nicht ohne Lohn" (276). Contrary to the belief of the intricate complementarity of sadistic and masochistic desire, Erika's desire finds no articulation at the sadist's hand. Abused and violated, she returns to the mother.

In *Die Klavierspielerin,* the mother represents the culprit. Undoubtedly, there are autobiographical shadings in Jelinek's novel. In an interview in *Die Zeit,* she admits: "*Die Klavierspielerin* ist ja nicht nur gegen mich, sondern auch gegen meine Mutter gerichtet. . . . Ich habe mir den Haß gegen meine Mutter lange nicht eingestanden."[27] Yet despite the author's personal investment, it should not be forgotten that the mother, a caricature in this novel, primarily embodies a perspective of the institution of motherhood, of structures and not persons. Jelinek neither represents individual psychologies, nor produces a first-person confessional narrative. Rather, she banters with continuously shifting viewpoints and creates puppet-like figures which perform the conditions set by Anglo-European culture. She artfully exposes their contours in the same subversive manner as Irigaray, whose provocative reading of Freud's texts dissects the cultural fears and desires that underpin Western culture.[28] With scathing wit, Jelinek moves her figures through the scripts prepared by patriarchy to induce some of the monstrous personality structures they evoke. She depicts mother and daughter as caricatures who perform the inhibiting social structures that significantly enforce their exclusive bond.[29] At the same time, Jelinek brings behavioral norms that have entrenched themselves in Western culture into a play of excess.[30] She explains her writing:

> Was mich, glaube ich, von vielen Autoren unterscheidet, ist, daß bei mir keine Menschen agieren. Es sind Kunstfiguren, die auf das Archetypische und Reliefartige wie bei einem Holzschnitt reduziert sind, oder ausschließlich Vertreter ihrer Klasse. Mir wird oft vorgeworfen: wo bleiben Psychologie, Subtilität und Differenzierungen? Ich halte es für absolut legitim, diese vergröbernde, ironisierte, satirische Darstellung zu verwenden, wenn man polemisch und agitatorisch wirken will.[31]

Jelinek wields language to provoke, agitate and unsettle. In her transgression of the boundaries of realism, it is clear that she distorts the socially choreographed notion of the mother-daughter relationship to such an extent that it must collapse and expose its operations. As Marlies Janz remarks, this narrative strategy characterizes many of Jelinek's works: "Jelinek begegnet den patriarchalisch geprägten Weiblichkeitsbildern nicht mit der abstrakten Behauptung weiblicher Alterität, sondern mit der Aneignung und Sinnentleerung dieser Bilder. Sie bleiben, absurd geworden, schließlich als leere Hülle zurück."[32] The inner dynamics which Jelinek lays open have been affixed by discourses that over the years have invented motherhood and continuously reconfigured women to meet what was thought to be the needs of the child.[33] Within this configuration the daughter is left defenseless.

Erika, therefore, never breaks out of the mother's realm. At the end, she is seen returning to the mother's lair with a self-inflicted wound as a mark of her guilt. In fact, the beginning and end of the narrative share a common destination, namely the mother. The mother-daughter relationship within the bounds of its existent structure is doomed in its compulsion to repeat the dependencies cast by the mother-imago.

Unlike the autobiographical accusations which appeared in numerous protocols and published letters written during the 1970s in West Germany that blamed the mother for the daughter's social position as victim, Jelinek's novel depersonalizes the relationship. In contrast, she dissects a social arrangement. Neither mother nor daughter can be cured or salvaged in her work. They stay within the hermetically sealed world of the mother-daughter bond and do what they are destined to do, namely to perform the injunctions of Western culture and the epistemologies that negate them both.

Not interested in creating a utopian literature, Jelinek breaks into the sacrosanct territory of motherhood and critically exposes its cultural structuring. She allies herself with the notion that the family structure must be remodeled. As it stands now, the "family romance" in sociopolitical and psychological terms inscribes and perpetuates women's dual role of power/powerlessness. It promotes a social structure that is no longer tenable, if it ever was, especially in view of the psychic mapping that Jelinek describes.

The conclusions put forth by numerous feminist researchers that motherhood as an institution may be viewed as "the root cause of the oppression of women" is underscored by Jelinek, who shows how such a maternal voice promotes female masochism.[34] Here motherhood is defined as the mother-involved, father-absent nuclear family that perpetuates traditional notions of gendered identities. The mother who must be dealt with in such a case is what Irigaray refers to as the traditionally phallic mother—an all-powerful/powerless mother for whom the child becomes the first and only love object for a considerable duration. This is not the woman in the mother, but the phallic mother within patriarchy. Irigaray asserts:

> More of us have suffered from over-protection by our mothers which paralyzed them, as their own mothers were already. Because this investment corresponds to a guilty and prescribed motherhood, abstract function whose power is then without limits. Whence the threatening fantasms attached to the maternal functions. The fear of being engulfed by an abyss, of sinking into darkness.[35]

The mother's "love" ends up suffocating, (s)mothering the body she once nourished. Many contemporary feminists subscribe to the necessary separation between mother and daughter—especially on the part of the daughter in order to re-identify—and call for a heightened involvement of other caretakers. Picking up from there, other feminist scholars have strongly proposed that "maternal subjectivity must be erased for a daughterly subjectivity to develop."[36]

Numerous texts written by women during the 1970s and 1980s in Germany attest to the early confrontations with the mother figure and the recognition of her internalization. Separation in these texts is a precondition for the daughter's selfhood, since leaving the "mother" implies not only growing up, but, more important, leaving the terms that have defined and thus confined the traditional dutiful daughter, impelling her to uphold the existing social practices.

So where does this leave the mothers, particularly in a social, political climate that reinforces the role of mother as primary caretaker? Perhaps when mothers' voices begin to contribute to the knowledge of the mother-child relationship, then daughters will be able to enter into a dialogue with their mothers as recognized subjects. Mutual recognition of each other as subjects in their own right comprises an essential step in the process of differentiation. Also, once the obstacles to mothering are reduced through additional support systems for parents, then the terms of motherhood can change.[37] In the meantime, Jelinek turns the mother-daughter relationship into a cannibalistic ritual that devours itself, so that, in its present form, it will one day go away.

### Notes

1. Marianne Hirsch, *The Mother/Daughter Plot: Narrative, Psychoanalysis, Feminism* (Bloomington: Indiana UP, 1989) 130.

2. The mother/daughter relationship has been the central theme of many German women writers and filmmakers alike. See such novels as Gabriele Wohmann, *Ausflug mit der Mutter* (Darmstadt: Luchterhand, 1976); Jutta Heinrich, *Das Geschlecht der Gedanken* (München: Frauenoffensive, 1976); Brigitte Schwaiger, *Wie kommt das Salz ins Meer* (Reinbeck: Rowohlt, 1977); Helga Novak, *Die Eisheiligen* (Darmstadt: Luchterhand, 1979); Waltraud Anna Mitgutsch, *Die Züchtigung* (München: Deutscher Taschenbuch Verlag, 1985). In films, see Jutta Brückner, *Hungerjahre—In einem reichen Land* (1980); Helma Sanders-Brahms, *Deutschland, bleiche Mutter* (1980) and *Flügel und Fesseln* (1984); Jeanine Meerapfel, *Malou* (1981). In addition to these texts, a plethora of protocols and interviews appeared during the 1970s. Among them are Barbara Franck, *Ich schau in den Spiegel und sehe meine Mutter: Gesprächsprotokolle mit Töchtern* (Hamburg: Hoffmann und Campe, 1979); Roswitha Fröhlich, *Ich und meine Mutter: Mädchen erzählen* (Ravensburg: Otto Maier, 1980); Erika Schilling, *Manchmal hasse ich meine Mutter* (Ravensburg: Otto Maier, 1981); Monika Sperr, ed., *Liebe Mutter Liebe Tochter: Frauenbriefe von heute* (München: Rogner und Bernhard, 1981). For further discussions of the mother-daughter relationship, see *Mütter-Töchter Frauen: Weiblichkeitsbilder in der Literatur,* ed. Helga Kraft and Elke Liebs (Stuttgart: Metzler, 1993).

3. All references are taken from Elfriede Jelinek, *Die Klavierspielerin* (Hamburg: Rowohlt, 1986). *Die Klavierspielerin* has been translated into English as: *The Piano Teacher,* trans. Joachim Newgroschel (New York: Weidenfeld and Nicolson, 1988). This edition was reviewed in the *New York Times* by Michiko Kakutani (17 December 1988).

4. Adrienne Rich, *Of Woman Born: Motherhood as Experience and Institution* (New York: Bantam Books, 1976) 238.

5. My analysis of masochism is motivated, in part, by Gilles Deleuze's discussion of this perversion. His studies are based on Sacher-Masoch's novels in *Masochism: Coldness and Cruelty* (New York: Zone Books, 1991).

6. Gaylyn Studlar, *In the Realm of Pleasure: von Sternberg, Dietrich and the Masochistic Aesthetic* (Urbana: U of Illinois P, 1988) 16.

7. See Nancy Chodorow, "Family Structure and Feminine Personality," *Women, Culture and Society,* ed. Michelle Zimbalist Rosaldo and Luise Lamphere (Palo Alto: Stanford UP, 1974) and *The Reproduction of Mothering: Psychoanalysis and the Sociology of Gender* (Berkeley: U of California P, 1978).

8. Luce Irigaray, "And the One Doesn't Stir without the Other," trans. Helene Vivienne Wenzel, *Signs* 7.1 (1981): 67-68.

9. Elisabeth Badinter, *Mother Love: Myth and Reality* (New York: Macmillan, 1980) 215.

10. Jessica Benjamin, *The Bonds of Love: Psychoanalysis, Feminism and the Problems of Domination* (New York: Pantheon Books, 1988) 97.

11. A similar scene occurs in Jutta Brückner's film *Hungerjahre* (*Years of Hunger*, 1980). The daughter in the film resorts to self-mutilation and even suicide through pills in order to break through the vigilant regime of the mother. The social context is the 1950s in Germany, when sexual repression in the name of postwar stability was at a peak.

12. Jane Flax, "Mother-Daughter Relationships: Psychodynamics, Politics, and Philosophy," *The Future of Difference,* ed. Alice Jardine et al. (Boston: Halo, 1980) 31.

13. With the increasing focus on the mother during the 1970s, interest in the father figure diminished. It is interesting that men play a marginal role in much of the literature written by German women during the 1970s.

14. Benjamin 125.

15. Benjamin 107.

16. Coppelia Kahn, "The Hand That Rocks the Cradle: Recent Gender Theories and Their Implications," *The (M)other Tongue: Essays in Feminist Psychoanalytic Interpretation,* ed. Shirley Nelson Garner, et al. (Ithaca: Cornell UP, 1985) 76.

17. See E. Ann Kaplan, ed. *Psychoanalysis and Cinema* (New York: Routledge, 1990); Judith Mayne, *The Woman at the Keyhole: Feminism and Women's Cinema* (Bloomington: Indiana UP, 1990); Constance Penley, ed. *Feminism and Film Theory* (New York: Routledge, 1988).

18. The German word "Herrin" may also be seen as a word play connoting a combination of male and female in one person that negates both male and female. Even though the power/superiority implied in the term "Herrin" tenuously proceeds from Erika's narcissistic image as artist, the incompatibility of woman and artist that Jelinek often thematizes but especially in her play *Clara S.,* is alluded to here as well. In a video interview prepared by the Austrian consulate, "Elfriede Jelinek—Von der mangelnden Tragfähigkeit des Bodens," Jelinek briefly and sarcastically comments on Freud's attitude toward women artists, which seems to influence her representation of the character Erika Kohut. The following quote has been transcribed from the tape: "Nach der freudschen Kulturtheorie sind Frauen zu künstlerischen Leistungen nicht fähig. Der hat recht, denn ich glaube, Frauen können sich doch durch künstlerischen Leistungen keineswegs die Liebe der Männer erringen, sondern im Gegenteil, sie werden vor den Männern eher etwas unheimlich. Ich habe die Erfahrung gemacht, daß das Künstlerische oder die intellektuelle Leistung die Frau sexuell nicht aufwertet, sondern im Gegenteil, sie fast abwertet oder sie zumindest zu einem Neutrum macht." See also the interview in *Die Tiefe der Tinte,* ed. Harald Friedl (Salzburg: Verlag Grauwerte im Institut für Alltagskultur, 1990) 27-51.

19. Hedwig Appelt, *Die leibhaftige Literatur: Das Phantasma und die Präsenz der Frau in der Schrift* (Weinheim: Quadriga, 1989) 118.

20. See Irigaray 67-68; *This Sex Which Is Not One,* trans. Catherine Porter (Ithaca: Cornell UP, 1985); "Le corps-a-corps avec la mere," *Zur Geschlechter differenz,* trans. Xenia Rajewsky (Wien: Wiener Frauenverlag, 1987).

21. Benjamin 52.

22. Benjamin 60.

23. Ibid.

24. Studlar 27.

25. Ibid.

26. Deleuze 74-78.

27. Elfriede Jelinek, "Ich lebe nicht," interview with Andre Müller, *Die Zeit* 22 June 1990: 55. As in most of his interviews, Müller intrudes on the intimate sphere of his guests, performing a type of intellectual sensationalism. In the interview with Jelinek, he drives her to a confession, although in her case it is difficult to distinguish between exposure and self-stylization.

28. Irigaray describes the suffocating merger between mother and daughter that restrains the daughter's experience of herself and the mother as two separate subjects differently than Jelinek's rendition, but with the same underlying critique. Rendered completely dependent, according to Irigaray, the symbolically paralyzed daughter appeals to the mother: "And look at me. I would like us to play together at being the same and different. You/I exchanging selves endlessly and each staying herself. Living mirrors" (61). See also Jane Gallop, "The Father's Seduction," *The (M)other Tongue: Essays on Feminist Psychoanalytic Interpretation,* eds. Shirley Nelson Garner, et al. (Ithaca: Cornell UP, 1985).

29. Donna Hoffmeister, "Access Routes into Postmodernism: Interviews with Innerhofer, Jelinek, Rosei and Wolfgruber," *Modern Austrian Literature* 20.2 (1987), 107-17. Here Jelinek discusses her perspective on the modern novel. She comments: "Die persönliche Identität des Einzelnen ist durch die Festigkeit und die Geschlossenheit des Systems kaum mehr zu verwirklichen. Das ist auch einer der Gründe, und das wird mir ständig vorgeworfen, daß meine Figuren keine Menschen mehr sind. Sie sind Schablonen, Bedeutungsträger, nur Repräsentanten. Der psychologische Roman ist tot. Wer versucht, den psychologischen Roman zu schreiben, kann nur scheitern. Es ist nicht mehr möglich. Die Literatur muß dem Rechnung tragen, daß der Individualismus nicht mehr möglich ist" (115).

30. In Jelinek's novel *Lust* (Reinbeck: Rowohlt, 1987), the sexual relationship between man and wife is reduced to a performance of male pleasure and female erasure. Here the violent interplay of subject and object is stripped to its barest and most brutal expression.

31. Josef Hermann Sauter, "Interviews mit österreichischen Autoren," *Weimarer Beiträge* 27.6 (1981) 113.

32. Marlies Janz "Falsche Spiegel: Über die Umkehrung als Verfahren bei Elfriede Jelinek," *Gegen den schönen Schein*, ed. Christa Gürtler (Frankfurt a.M.: Verlag neue Kritik, 1990) 136.

33. See Badinter's discussion of the historical conceptualization of motherhood and the changing attitudes that are effected by science, philosophy, literature or myth in *Mother Love: Myth and Reality*. She reinforces the perspective of mother love as a social, historical institution, that is, a construct, and thereby questions the ideological appropriation of maternal instinct.

34. Kahn 73.

35. Irigaray cited in Elizabeth Grosz, *Sexual Subversions* (Sydney: Allen and Unwin, 1989) 122.

36. Irigaray puts it in terms of learning to speak to the mother and not at her; "to talk to one's mother as a woman presupposes giving up the idea of maternal omnipotence. . . . To accept that one's mother is not all protective, the ultimate amorous recourse, the refuge against abandonment. Which then allows us to establish with her ties of reciprocity, where she could eventually also feel herself to be my daughter. Cited in Grosz 122: Luce Irigaray, "Meres et filles vues par Luce Irigaray," *Liberation* (1979): 13.

37. In Juanna Malamud Smith, "Mothers: Tired of Taking the Rap," *The New York Times Magazine* (June 10, 1990): 32-38, she emphasizes psychology's grotesque form of mother-bashing in its blaming of the mother for any form of a child's disorder ranging from the emotional to the physical realm. In all of these "studies," she writes, "the social context of mothering is largely left out of any account of parenting" (32).

## Elfriede Jelinek and Gitta Honegger (interview date spring-summer 1994)

SOURCE: Jelinek, Elfriede, and Gitta Honegger. "The German Language: An Interview with Elfriede Jelinek." *Theater* 25, no. 1 (spring-summer 1994): 14-22.

[*In the following interview, Jelinek discusses the influence of philosopher Martin Heidegger on her work, her role as an artist, and writing within the Austrian literary tradition.*]

On a home movie screen a middle-aged woman carrying a suitcase wanders along a mountain path. Hannah Arendt is returning, after the war, to visit Heidegger in *Todtnauberg*, his beloved Black Forest country retreat. For her play's title, Austrian writer Elfriede Jelinek extracts the root words hidden in the village's name. It only takes a slight adjustment to create ***Totenauberg, Mountain/Meadow of the Dead***, to highlight what's in a (compound) name, and set up the ironic context for its most famous inhabitant and the central tenets of his philosophy. In that philosophy, *Nature/home/habitation* function like Duchampian "hinges" in a construct that enshrines the native and excludes the foreign—with catastrophic consequences, as the play points out.

On stage, the frail old man is stuck in an odd contraption, the literal rendering of Heidegger's famous term, *Gestell*, academically translated as "enframing," a kind of existential walker that supports man on his intellectual hikes through the dark forests and dizzying peaks of abstraction. The woman sits on a bench, watching her former-lover-turned-Nazi-ally from the perspective of the Jewish refugee. Philosophically, she is an emigrée from the flights of German idealism to the more concrete grounds of Anglo-Saxon rationalism. Out of Heidegger's metaphysical speculations, with their monumental linguistic arches between Greek genius and its self-proclaimed Germanic double, arise the new myths of a self-consciously New Age: a new motherhood devoted to the birthing of a perfect generation, new philosophies of ethnic hygiene, the renewal of nature in perfectly controlled national parks, where tourists resembling refugees are the new game to be hunted and devoured.

At age 47, Elfriede Jelinek has been finally acknowledged as a leading, if controversial, figure. Over the years, her works—including some ten prose pieces, eight or so texts for the theater, countless radio plays, and several filmscripts—have gathered a respectable group of followers: intellectuals, mostly women and students. But until recently their eruptive potential has simmered just below the surface of serious recognition, thanks to a unique and historically tested Viennese strategy summed up in the term *totschweigen*—the act of killing someone through silence. This is a sophisticated act of self-preservation: rather than letting the ripples of outrage and contempt in Vienna's quasisophisticated circles escalate to the point where they ricochet exactly off their intended target, they are marvelously drowned in silently agreed-upon silence.

Each of Jelinek's works aims at demolishing social and sexual conduct, historic pride and shame, aesthetic and erotic tastes, as they are perpetuated or infected by the dominant male culture. She called a recent play ***Sickness or Modern Woman***. Her fierce intelligence, her superb command of language, and the wicked humor of the outraged make her heir to a long line of Vienna-based literary malcontents such as Karl Kraus, Elias Canetti, and Thomas Bernhard. With ***Totenauberg***, produced by the Vienna Burgtheater a season ago, she has finally staked out her territory, right between the two undisputed masters of contemporary German-language literature and theater: Bernhard and Peter Handke.

No mean achievement, particularly for a woman—as she is quick to point out. The wrath with which she smashes the icons and taboos of Austrian self-esteem is not the only thing that connects her to Bernhard. More important is the power of her language, exploding the linguistic cornerstones of her culture. With savage wit, Jelinek's play ***Burgtheater*** tore the Olympian masks off Austria's most revered actor-family (all members of the venerable Burgtheater, Austria's National Theater, instituted by the Kaiser himself). Out of the rubble of their domestic battles, in what would usually be considered the charming lilt and picaresque turns of Viennese dialect, emerge grotesque fragments of provincial Nazism. Her latest novel, ***Lust***, appropriates the strategies of the pornographic novel in its monotonous repetition of graphic details, calmly demonstrating the husband's brutal, mechanical use of his wife as a sexual household appliance.

***Wolken.Heim***, a theater text, does not read like a play at all. There are no characters, not even distinct speakers. Variations on excerpts from Kleist, Hölderlin, Heidegger, Hegel, and Fichte, and letters from the Baader-Meinhof group, coalesce in a powerful dirge, a dramatized ode to the German language's self-destructive collision with history. Her theater pieces do not examine characters through their interactions. Rather, they illuminate how language itself generates actions and realities. A character must first be held accountable for his language—not just at the moment of actual speech, but as a cultural legacy that must be examined and challenged at all times.

In view of the obsession with language, it isn't surprising that Jelinek tackled Heidegger, one of the most controversial philosophers of language. In describing her dramaturgy, Jelinek speaks of "planes of language" as opposed to dialogue. Her stage characters turn almost literally into "figures of speech." Their long speeches, devoid of psychological distinctions, spread like huge verbal canvases. It is up to the director to place them against each other and let the images emerge in the spaces between them. As the old man lectures, ruminates, stumbles, and pants across the landslides of his thoughts, specters of Auschwitz emerge from the cultural rubble among the severed limbs and bloody corpses of mountain climbers, skiers, and multicultural refugees. ***Totenauberg*** juxtaposes the philosopher guru of ecologically pure New Age proselytizers surprisingly quick to ignore his Nazi past, and his former student and lover Hannah Arendt, the Jewish emigrée intellectual. Jelinek's portrayal of the strenuously pontificating old man is mainly taken from his essay *The Question Concerning Technology*, written after World War II, in which he summons up all his linguistic tricks to come to terms with his Nazi utopia. His etymological obsessions permit endless transformations of words, especially compound words, so dear to the German language, and perversion of meaning. It is a fatal process, leading not only to the philosopher's personal tragedy but contributing to the moral collapse of an entire culture. With merciless humor and piercing intelligence, Jelinek demonstrates how the rhetoric of the most self-consciously politically, morally, religiously, and fashionably correct picks up on philosophical and linguistic "Heideggerisms," which easily convert into the slogans of a newly emerging elite of nativism, evolutionary perfectionism, ethnic chauvinism. The insipid mutations of Heidegger's word games lead right into the present, a present that cheerfully exonerates itself from any guilt or moral responsibility by exploiting its bona fide status *post*: after the Holocaust, after Chernobyl, after the Wall.

[*Honegger*]: *How did you get involved with Heidegger?*

[Jelinek]: In quite an abstract way, originally. I always thought one should connect this "my land, my blood, my soil" kind of fascism to the thought processes in which it originated. Two years ago I wrote ***Wolken.Heim***, which deals with the philosophy of German Idealism, with Hegel, Fichte—quite a few quotes—with Hölderlin, the poet who inspired them. I wanted to continue from those roots to Heidegger, who immersed himself in Hölderlin. I was interested in a nativist philosopher who wanted to guide the *Führer*—to lead the leader as it were—this thinker in his own misguidedness. One can't breathe spirit into *unspirit,* just as one can't breathe Christianity into the Antichrist. How could thinking be so deluded as to believe that it could influence a fascist state?

*That's what he wanted?*

Yes, that's a quote: he wanted to lead the leader, and the *Führer,* naturally devoid of spirit, wasn't interested at all in being led by a thinker; he had destroyed thinking together with German culture, an entire culture. That was Heidegger's immense delusion, and he never renounced it, not even after the war. Many actually tried to get him to do that, to find one word of regret about the crimes of the Third Reich and he always refused. Paul Celan hoped he would, Ingeborg Bachmann hoped he would. He wanted her and Celan to contribute to some kind of commemorative publication, I don't know for which of his birthdays, and both declined, because he wasn't ready to renounce, so to speak. Which, I think, shows character. On the other hand, there is this awful passage in a letter to Jaspers, I believe, in which he attributes the destruction of the European Jews to a kind of natural process, comparable to the pollution of the environment or the phosphorization of the ocean.

I was interested in confronting that kind of wrongheadedness with a woman who was led to political thinking, to political philosophizing, by her forced life in emigration. Those two figures. Not arguing with each other—that would have been another possibility, an argument between the two, the obvious solution. But I wanted to transform philosophical talk into poetic speech, to juxtapose those planes of speech.

Of course I am dealing with what is happening in Austria and Germany today, the repression. The new, socially acceptable right—I call it white fascism—this renewed respectability of thinking along the rightist margin, that's what I tried to show, otherwise it would have made no sense to write a history play. I tried to denounce what's happening along the margin of the Green movement, this obsession with health, this claim to health for oneself and one's children, this claim to physical intactness, while in the Third World everyone's dying. Well, I simply try to show where these new rightist thinkers are located.

*This continuation of the right reveals itself through language?*

I am trying to show it only through language. I don't try to set contents against each other, but rather husks of speech: the nativist thinking of Heidegger against the ironic, precise thinking of Hannah Arendt; however, she knows, right from the beginning, that she is fighting a losing battle and that she will always be fighting a losing battle. The European left, for example, is finished, finished as a moral authority, because of what's happened in the Eastern bloc, the actual political practices of the real socialist countries. The left is also finished as an intellectual force. I let all this converge in the figure of Hannah Arendt—this loss of belief in one's political effectiveness. And God knows, Hannah Arendt was no leftist.

Heidegger was quite active as a linguist. It's no coincidence that he devoted himself mainly to poets. He had these tendencies to appropriate Hölderlin's biography for himself to the point of grotesque correspondences, which are also in the play: the stable, where his grandfather was born among the sheep, it's the same with Hölderlin. Heidegger himself wrote little texts which are unbelievably kitschy, they're really bad literature—just like Hegel, by the way, who also wrote awful poems. Well, when philosophers write poetry, it's a disaster, most of the time.

Furthermore, there is the exclusion of women from philosophy, which made me approach the subject from another plane of thinking, in a poetic, literary way.

*It's pretty amazing, how outstanding women are preoccupied with Heidegger; there is Arendt . . .*

Of course, Arendt was his lover, she was the great love of his life, and she was very young when she met him. She visited him after the war and—what I sensed when I wrote the play but didn't know then—she was also deeply moved by the widespread disappointment over his unwillingness to admit his political mistakes. She was deeply moved *for* him, as well. Shortly after the war, in 1946-47, she wrote an essay in which she deals with his existential philosophy, and she says explicitly that one mustn't take him that seriously: it's all right to laugh about him, this pathos of the self rooted in the soil has its comic aspects as well. I also tried to show that in the play.

*In most plays one wonders what happens next. But in* **Totenauberg** *one is always in suspense about what will happen to a given word—the way you start with one word and play around with the root until something quite different comes out at the end of an unbelievable play of verbal transformations.*

Yes, I don't work with alliterations, but with the word itself, all the way to the cheapest pun.

*Your critique manifests itself in Heidegger's language itself.*

Yes, yes. Oskar Maria Graf also wrote a text ridiculing Heidegger; that's very easy, one can expose Heidegger's most serious philosophical texts as ridiculous.

That would have been too cheap for me. It wouldn't have been appropriate in view of the enormity of the subject—how German thinkers, that is to say a large part of German thinkers, let themselves be corrupted by the Nazis, by—as I said before—*unspirit* personified. One has only to look at the history of German philosophy: all philosophy departments were brought into line. The Jews were thrown out and the institutions changed over seamlessly to nativist, nationalist stuff. It wasn't just Heidegger. He happened to be the most famous, there were many more.

*When one asks, how was it possible, there is the temptation to look for a psychological explanation.*

That's something everyone has to do for himself. Psychology doesn't exist in my work. I mean, those texts are written in a way that everyone can draw his own conclusions as to where the danger is. I see it coming—and I show it in the play—I see the danger coming from someone like Peter Singer, from this health mania. Suddenly the notion appears again that there is life which has no value; seriously damaged infants can be killed, children can be aborted only because they would be born handicapped. In many of his passages Heidegger appears a forerunner of the ecology movement. There is one passage which I quote, "you don't have to be afraid of nuclear power, we'll be killed by cars," he said. One has to become very aware of what's so horrendous, creepy about this home/land way of thinking, but one must not just throw out his thinking altogether, one has to acknowledge him, that is to say acknowledge him as dangerous, because something that's put aside or repressed or hidden becomes all the more dangerous.

*How did Heidegger arrive at his perception of the foreign?*

It's rural. I think the Catholic farming tradition brings about disaster—it excludes what it doesn't understand. I think this is also one of the tragedies of the Yugoslavian catastrophe. A very rural society—Karadzic is a farmer's son who came to Sarajevo to study—has always had this hatred against urban socialization. That's how it was during the Nazis, the hatred of Jews as the carriers of an urban, intellectual cultured bourgeoisie, completely at ease with the cultural accomplishments of the Germans—Goethe, the museums, the philharmonic concerts on Sundays. There are many concentration camp documents about this love for German culture—Jews had it more than the Germans. Anger is directed against that urbanness—women in makeup, elegant people, as opposed to the unmade-up ideal of the German girl. There is a hatred of the urban, educated class that has interests beyond itself, while the farmer is interested only in himself, his animals, his closer surroundings. Whenever Catholicism and the farming tradition, or orthodoxy and rural life, come together I notice an inferiority complex towards any interests that could further human development outside their own immediate sphere. That's dangerous.

*You talked about Arendt coming back and saying one has to look at Heidegger ironically also. Could this be the influence of an Anglo-Saxon perspective?*

In the case of Hannah Arendt, certainly. There is a soberness—which she always had, to be sure—in some very early interviews, she comes across as a quite resolute person, a very resolute philosopher of "common sense" one would call it; but as I said, it's a development she didn't choose voluntarily. If she had stayed in Germany, she might have spent her whole life devoted to the most abstract ways of thinking. But this wasn't possible and that is precisely what interests me: her thinking didn't evolve that way voluntarily; through emigration she was forced to politicize herself.

*Language also affects the direction of thinking, doesn't it?*

Yes, "whereof one cannot speak, thereof . . . ." That's early Wittgenstein, of course, who was a strong influence on the entire postwar literature in Austria—beginning with the Vienna Group, it is a literature whose preoccupation with the word is much stronger here than in Germany, zeroing in on the word and ironicizing it.

*Wittgenstein also helps us get a clearer picture of Heidegger.*

Wittgenstein always searches for the utmost precision, while Heidegger is cloudy—it is this haze which always rejects the foreign. There is *us* rooted in our soil, and what's foreign is always a threat. It's something very real again today in Austria and Germany, where foreigners are set on fire, houses are set on fire. By defining what's native in a genetic manner, the foreign has to remain outside, and this is certainly a German tragedy which doesn't exist in North American society; they may not have always been able to assimilate the foreign, but they always accepted it—for example, Americans probably wouldn't understand that people, Turks for example, who have worked and lived in Germany for 20 years, are still called Turks. I guess I have quite an idealistic image of the United States, and I am sure there's a terrible Nazism against the blacks, but still an unbelievably integrative force is at work. You have those famous rightist extremists such as the Ku Klux Klan and their hate crimes, but there also is this fetishization of the First Amendment, that one can say everything but just say it and not carry it over into actions. Society is not as unhealthy and repressive as in Germany.

*How does one survive here as an artist?*

By fighting against repression, by talking about it incessantly—that is what I consider my task as a writer—by always pointing to it. Writers like me do not develop their literary strengths through formulating a positive utopia or describing subtle nuances, but through polemics, through exposing things. That's when the writing works.

*From an American perspective your position seems quite enviable; at least people are listening.*

It's all right to generate some friction here. Still, there is a Toni Morrison in the U.S., there are great black women writers and filmmakers, who assert themselves as such powerful artists precisely because they write from the position of the oppressed, because the language of the oppressed is always more on target than the language of the oppressors, that metalanguage which is always inexact and deceitful.

*As women, are we still speaking the language of the oppressed? You are the rare woman who has been acknowledged as a serious writer—there are scholarly texts about you, the whole works.*

But I am not acknowledged the way I would be if I were a man. I am absolutely certain about that and every writing woman will agree with me. Even if one has been recognized more or less and that is what I have finally accomplished—I am not that young, after all—a female work is not treated with the same respect as a man's—Handke, Bernhard, or Jandl for example. I think every woman writing in America will confirm this. Female works, female products are met with a benign form of contempt.

*We are about the same generation, the first who have made it as a larger group.*

There are quite a few in the preceding generation—Ingeborg Bachmann, Ilse Aichinger. Perhaps Bachmann was the most successful, but she also knew that in her private life she was the image of the very feminine, very vulnerable little darling, while in fact she was very intelligent and not at all like that. Many women who knew her say that she was quite able, quite strong in matters of practical living. But her biography shows that she was crushed between the claim to femininity in her private life and the male, phallic presumption to write art, and that this simply is not possible. That's what Bachmann's novel *Malina* is about, which I adapted as a screenplay: that it is not possible for a woman to be a female sexual being and a male-writing Ego, a phallic entity, to develop a phallus that says "I," that speaks. Many women have been crushed by that. It doesn't happen to me, because I voluntarily pulled back from life, I forsook life, life as the darling little female, and made it my subject matter instead.

*Is that possible?*

Well, of course we do have it easier. Of course, we do have a broad feminist movement today—reading *Malina* now, one can only be totally amazed that this was written without a feminist context. In the '60s and early '70s, that's when feminism had just started, really, and Bachmann wasn't part of the student generation, she was an older woman, a middle-aged woman. And reading the reviews at that time, it's obvious that the male critics couldn't stomach it at all.

*That happens to you, too, doesn't it—at least it used to?*

It still does, but I find myself protected within an international women's movement. When men hit me too strongly, there are always women placing themselves in front of me or joining me to fight back. Even though feminism didn't achieve much, at least one feels in a better place connected to other women. Bachmann certainly didn't have that, she had no female network, especially since she increasingly sought the closeness of men much more than of women.

*That way she also was able to maintain the position of the only woman—that's no longer possible either.*

I am afraid one loses perspective if men become too important in one's life. In certain ways one has to become like a nun in order to preserve one's integrity, one's broader view.

*How does one reconcile this with one's sexuality?*

One has to split oneself in two. According to Freudian cultural theory women are not able to produce cultural creations, aside from braiding and weaving, for the simple reason that their superegos are not strong enough to fight those oedipal conflicts. A man doesn't have to do what a woman has to do. She first has to accomplish the intellectual task of creating a superego for herself, out of which she produces her works, be they scientific or artistic—and then there is this femininity in her sexuality. A man doesn't have to do this—he doesn't have to split himself in two, he can always remain whole, he can fuck his mother all his life, he will always find mothers who can take care of him, and he never has to change his primary object, while a woman has to change her primary object.

*Then thinking, intellectuality are male by definition?*

It looks like it in practice. As long as society doesn't change and as long as a new consciousness of different values isn't developed, womanness and women will still get lost for the most part. Once social norms begin to change, then female speech will also come through.

*Handke talks about finding a language that heals.*

Handke has this desperate wish for the positive. But it's not that different from me, basically. He sees it as quite different, but it's not that different from my wish to tear open the negative over and over again, to make it visible. These are always the two sides of one coin, I think.

*A Native American writer once said, "before healing can take place, the poison must first be exposed."*

Yes, that certainly goes for me. While Handke's wish to create a harmony is also legitimate. Only, as a man, he might have less personal suffering. For women, because of the contempt for their work, the pressure of their pain and what to do about it is different than for a man—I also see this wish for harmony as tragic for Handke. But at least during the last years he has been very articulate politically—for example during the Waldheim campaign he expressed himself very decidedly, or now during the Yugoslavian crisis when he came out with very clear political statements. That's something he didn't do before.

*In your work there is this incredible wrath—*

Yes, yes.

*One could call it a Biblical wrath—and that's what creates the controversy, also the rejection of your work. Yet following your career from the outside, I would have thought that your work represents "literature" and that you would no longer be categorized and rejected as a "woman writer."*

It hasn't changed. For example, a collection of critical texts about my work is coming out in the U.S., including only one man, writing about **Lust,** and that essay has already been published in the German *Text und Kritik.* I regret that, because I'm interested in how men receive my work. Can a man accept a "battle between sexes" no longer fought with brutality and force, but as an intellectual competition between men and women? If well-fought it could be very interesting, just like a well-played game of chess, which also has certain aggressive features. Men don't find it necessary to deal with a work by a woman.

*Well, I'd say that* **Lust** *would be a bit difficult for them to accept.*

**Lust** isn't even unrealistic. I mean, many people say relationships like that don't exist. That's nonsense. Of course they exist. The use of women for daily, monotonous consumption, especially in rural areas where women do not yet have escape routes, that's everywhere. Duras wrote about it too.

*You write within a typically Austrian tradition—out of this anger, this wrath, which seems absolutely necessary to survive here. This connects you to Thomas Bernhard, wouldn't you say?*

Oh yes. Only Bernhard's tirades are rhythmical—with Bernhard it's not so important what he had to say, it's his stylistic mastery, those repetitions which pull you in almost hypnotically. My theory is that this is a prosodic phenomenon—a phenomenon of his prose rhythm, which gets you to breathe along with his tirades, which means you have to alter your own breath, which gets you into an almost hypnotic, trance-like state. One develops a kind of addiction, an addictive behavior, as if—quite literally—inhaling the other person's breath, the breath of the spoken word. As if he had dictated his texts. Maybe he did.

He himself was an obsessive talker. I know a very good friend of his, a woman; she said that after ten hours talking she was dead, and then he said, well, let's round it up to 12 hours and he went on talking for two more hours.

He was a manic talker; that really was his greatness, wasn't it? This bachelor-machine that keeps on going.

*I didn't have that kind of anger. I wasn't strong enough. I had to run away from here.*

I have to confess, I'd love to go to England, to live in a little house in the country—that is, in a country with an older democratic tradition. That's a big temptation.

All those lords of the provinces here, those Jörg Haiders [the youthful leader of Austria's right-wing Freedom Party who has gained considerable support for his populist, nativist-nationalist platform]—I'd move far away to get away from that scene. On the other hand, my writing, its polemics depend on the collision with these figures. As long as that's productive—what's the name of the classic hero who received new strength every time he touched the soil?—as long as I receive strength for my work from touching this soil I'll stay here. But it doesn't have to be forever. I have the feeling if I got to New York I'd never leave.

*What was most important for me in New York, what really shaped me as the "American" I have become, was the culture of the Jewish emigrants, the Hitler refugees.*

Of course. And that is precisely the culture I come from—the Eastern-Jewish world, the tradition of language critique, Karl Kraus. Think of Handke, in comparison, coming from such a poor, rural background—the only picture on the wall was a calendar from the local grocer. He had to acquire language, speech out of speechlessness. It happened in the Catholic boarding school he attended. Consequently, language to him is a unique treasure; therefore also the exquisiteness of his language. I, by contrast, coming from an urban cultured middle class, have the desire to smash language, to strip it to the bone, to tear the last bits of truths out of it, to rip open its chest. It's a destructive process, whereas for Handke, whose speech originated in speechlessness—this rural speechlessness, out of which his mother ultimately killed herself—language is what saved him. Canetti speaks of the "rescued tongue"; that also goes for Handke. I think, in his way he wants to preserve the "rescued tongue."

*Canetti, Bulgarian born, also had to acquire the German language.*

Yes. In this country, which destroyed the Jews, in the Burgtheater—his parents regularly took him to performances there and they gave him the gift of the German language as mother tongue. He never came back to Vienna after the war to live, he only visited.

*You talk of smashing language—is this why you often write for the theater? Does the destruction become more visible?*

Yes. I was fascinated by theater because of the artificiality of language that's possible there, quite unlike in the movies, for example, where one has to write more realistic dialogues, unless one is Fassbinder. In the theater, language is put on a pedestal and exhibited, language gets bigger, and one can write big language—that's what interested me. But, I should add, until now the productions of my plays were not successful. Perhaps I haven't yet found the right director, one who wanted to follow me to the utmost stylization.

*In your work you examine—quite critically and angrily—the notion Heimat, home, the place one comes from. What does Austria mean to you, is it Heimat?*

Yes, it is, but only in its great ethnic and cultural diversity. Especially eastern Austria. I'd say Vienna is home, this Eastern Slavic-Jewish culture I come from, my family comes from. With authors who come from the western states, it's a different tradition. That scepticism towards language, also that burlesque playing with language practiced in Jewish cabaret, those are brilliant language games; a Karl Farkas, for example, produced word games that went on for hours, he was a genius of language; or Fritz Grünbaum, the great comic who was murdered in a concentration camp. That's a language tradition I feel very close to—it goes all the way to the Marx Brothers, the way Groucho shoots off obscenities in his maniacal machine-gun-like rounds.

*The other day I mentioned to a colleague that the Groucho Mask comes pretty close to Heidegger's face.*

Yes, that little mustache.

*Thomas Bernhard, who comes from small rural circumstances, also has this longing for the cultured urban bourgeoisie.*

Yes, and he studied it like someone else would study medicine—I think Zuckmayr was his most important socializer—where to get his shirts custom-tailored, where to get his shoes custom-made, all those rites of the cultured upper middle class. In his case it also is a reaction against the pressure of provincial, rural fascism.

*In this small country there are Bernhard and you and Handke, and all its contrasts and contradictions are reflected within the triangle of your works.*

Handke doesn't live here anymore, you know; he has jumped ship. He got arrested in Salzburg—I mean, it's unbelievable, the greatest poet in the country, arrested by some village cops. All he did was shout at the guys because they were carrying on unbelievably—rednecks, of course, hurling these horrific insults at him; they must have known who he was. This is exactly what I've been saying—the hatred against someone, because they sense his impact goes far beyond their world; others listen to him, he is acknowledged even in other countries. There is a saying, what the farmer doesn't know . . .

*. . . he doesn't eat . . .*

That's also a great truth, isn't it? Everything outside his own sphere of experience is rejected. These farmers are also terribly brutal to their animals and their farmhands. I have been involved in this issue, I made a TV film about it—the way they treat their servants, it's absolute, naked, cruel bondage. I'm familiar with the farming environment, we had a farmhouse in the country where I spent all my summer vacations. I studied the rural proletariat very, very carefully; that's how I got to understand fascism.

*I feel that the writing of all three of you is about how to find language again, after the Holocaust.*

This German language—I know of French people, former concentration camp inmates who recited Hölderlin's poems in Auschwitz . . . it's not just that this German language . . .

*Exactly at this point the tape stopped: a technical coincidence proving Wittgenstein's point, "Whereof one cannot speak thereof one must be silent."*

### Susan L. Cocalis (review date autumn 1996)

SOURCE: Cocalis, Susan L. Review of *Die Kinder der Toten,* by Elfriede Jelinek. *World Literature Today* 70, no. 4 (autumn 1996): 946-47.

[*In the following review of* Die Kinder der Toten, *Cocalis argues that Jelinek's prose style and subject material are enjoyable in "small doses," but are too excessive and overwhelming in novel form.*]

While reading Elfriede Jelinek's latest novel *Die Kinder der Toten* (*The Children of the Dead*), one cannot help thinking that Ingeborg Bachmann is not the only postwar Austrian woman writer who was obsessed with death and ways of dying (*Todesarten*). In the tradition of Bachmann's prose works, Jelinek relates her meditations on death to the legacy of Austro-fascism, but she goes far beyond Bachmann in her merciless scrutiny of Austrian pop culture, consumerism, and middle-class values. She also outdoes her literary predecessor in her graphic descriptions of the brutality of male-female relations. But for Jelinek, the women are the predators as often as the men. Since the female characters are already dead in Jelinek's text, they are free to die multiple "deaths" at the hands of exploitative men but also to engage in orgiastic cannibalistic and vampiristic escapades à la *Krankheit oder Moderne Frauen*. Although Jelinek's heterosexual relationships may be abominable, the interactions between the women are even worse, especially her renditions of the mother-daughter bond (age). Welcome to Jelinek's Austria, the realm of the living dead.

Against the backdrop of an Alpine village located at the "outskirts of Austrian tourism," the author plays with "death" as a trope for the way her country (wo)men have repressed the fascist past (itself both dead and alive) and embraced sports, sex, pop culture, and consumerism as a way of staying young and denying death. Jelinek accomplishes this end by tracing the "lives" of three main characters, all of whom have died and now exist, like so many Austrians, as the "living dead": Gudrun Bichler, a student of the humanities, who slit her wrists; Edgar Gstranz, a downhill skier destined for the Austrian national team, who was killed in a car accident; and Karin Frenzel, a middle-aged widow (with a demanding mother!), who plunged to her death in an Alpine gorge. Although they are already dead, they are resurrected into the same or different identities, only to die all over again. It is not clear, however, if these deaths are sequential, since there is no linear progression of a narrative charted through time. The narrator tells stories but also deconstructs them and reconstitutes them arbitrarily, so that the reader must abandon any pretense of chronological time, logical causality, or individual character development.

If one accepts the three main figures as "themes," then Jelinek's compositional technique might be described as themes with variations. The reader learns in graphic detail about their various identities, clothes, diets, possessions, families, deaths, sexual encounters (before and especially after death), cannibalism, vampirism, and what is left of their bodies (with a focus on their penises, vaginas, and labia). Over and over again. Over hundreds of pages. This is not to say that there is no progression in the narrative, for if you last that long, Jelinek does build up to an allegorical climax, a phantasmagoric image of the hair of millions of dead people invading the idyllic Alpine landscape. There is also an attendant message, a vision of how the ashes of the dead enter the flesh of the living so that the dead can "be themselves" again.

*Die Kinder der Toten* is not for the faint of heart or stomach, or for those who like their books with a plot or a clear narrative line. While reading the novel, I savored Jelinek's style, which can be delightfully rich in its playful linguistic sophistication, satiric detail, and black humor; but her style is rich like a fine chocolate truffle, which for me is best enjoyed in small doses. Many of the individual segments of the novel had this effect on me, and I found them delectably malicious. However, taking it as a whole—i.e., as a novel of 667 pages—I soon felt surfeited. By the end of this forced feeding, I had binged to excess and was myself more dead than alive.

### Brigid Haines (essay date July 1997)

SOURCE: Haines, Brigid. "Beyond Patriarchy: Marxism, Feminism, and Elfriede Jelinek's *Die Liebhaberinnen*." *Modern Language Review* 92, no. 3 (July 1997): 643-55.

[*In the following essay, Haines utilizes the theories of feminist theorist Luce Irigaray to delineate the relationship between Marxist and feminist thought in* Die Liebhaberinnen.]

Despite their common roots in enlightenment discourses of liberation, Marxism and feminism have always regarded each other with a degree of friendly exasperation. The central problem of Marxism from a feminist point of view is its failure to theorize adequately either subjectivity or gender. In addition, though Marxism explains the workings of capitalism with great conviction and, when pushed, can comment on women's place within capitalism (this is broadly what Marxist-feminists have attempted to do)[1] it has not thrown significant light on the *origins* of the oppression of women endemic to most known societies.[2] Indeed, it has often been convenient for Marxists to overlook the oppression of women since that oppression serves the interests of men (Hartmann, p. 5). From a Marxist point of view on the other hand, feminism has often been perceived to incline towards ahistoricism and essentialism in its claims to speak for and about women as a group. Feminism has arguably never theorized patriarchy as convincingly as Marx theorized capitalism[3] and, as a consequence, has lacked a coherent political programme.

Marxism and feminism seemed to find common ground in the seminal statement by Simone de Beauvoir that 'one is not born a woman, one becomes one', which laid the basis for the sex/gender distinction, and provided a meeting-point for Marxism, feminism, and psychoanalysis on the all-important question of subjectivity.[4] Generations of students on gender studies courses felt the penny drop when they heard it argued that while biology is immutable (we are born male or female), the acquisition of gender identity depends on a complex mix of psycho-sexual, historical, political, and cultural factors mediated through the family and through Althusser's other Ideological State Apparatuses.[5] Thus the materialism of Marxism was harnessed for feminism in a model that also included insights drawn from psychoanalysis, and a theory of (gendered) subjectivity could be added to a Marxist analysis of society (though as Terry Lovell and others were quick to point out, Althusser's theory left little room for resistance and agency).[6]

Since those days of lively debate in the 1970s and early 1980s Marxist-feminism has, as a movement, to some extent run out of steam, with theorists such as Hartmann and Barrett arguing for an alliance between the projects rather than a merger,[7] but that Marxism and feminism still need each other, many take to be self-evident: a revolutionary theory that does not seek to end the oppression of women is clearly deficient, while feminism continues to find Marxist theories of historical change, value, and ideology, to name some of the more obvious ones, of enormous relevance to its own concerns, not least in the field of literary studies.

Recently, of course, both Marxism and feminism have been challenged as master discourses by post-structuralism, post-colonialism, and post-Marxism. Western feminists, for example, have been made conscious of the imperialism inherent in the gesture of attempting to speak for women,[8] and a question mark has been placed against some Marxist categories such as the social totality.[9] Even the seemingly obvious sex/gender distinction so dear to feminists has been deconstructed by Judith Butler and others and shown to be an historically produced binary division that serves as a regulatory fiction to perpetuate heterosexuality.[10] It has been argued that clinging to the sex/gender distinction has prevented feminists from historicizing sex.[11] However, some important work has come out of precisely the encounter between post-structuralism and Marxist-feminist debates, such as in the work of Gayatri Spivak, Seyla Benhabib, Drucilla Cornell, Rosemary Hennessey and in Michéle Barrett's recent post-Marxist account of ideology, *The Politics of Truth,* which moves beyond Althusser's 'scientific' and epistemological definition of ideology to a more Foucauldian view of ideology as discourse.[12]

The theorist on whose work I draw might seem at first sight to owe more to radical feminism than to either Marxism or post-structuralism, though I believe this not to be the case.[13] The liberatory project developed by the feminist philosopher Luce Irigaray picks up some of the threads of de Beauvoir's argument, though with a difference of emphasis. While de Beauvoir demanded equality for women and conceded sexual difference reluctantly, Irigaray proclaims sexual difference as the first stage in changing the symbolic order in order to effect real change for both men and women. As a philosopher she sees her own role in this to lie in speaking as a woman in order to show up the masculine bias in all Western systems of thought. Since we cannot speak from outside the phallogocentrism of culture, however, Irigaray adopts the tactic of strategic mimicry:

> To play with mimesis is thus, for a woman, to try to locate the place of her exploitation by discourse, without allowing herself to be simply reduced to it. It means to resubmit herself [. . .] to 'ideas', in particular to ideas about herself that are elaborated in/by a masculine logic, but so as to make 'visible' by an effect of playful repetition, what was supposed to remain invisible: recovering a possible operation of the feminine in language.
>
> (Irigaray, quoted in Whitford, p. 71)

Irigaray's project inaugurates, claims Jean-Joseph Goux, a new moment in the history of feminism.[14]

Irigaray's strategic mimicry is one aspect of her work that I consider in relation to Jelinek's text ***Die Liebhaberinnen*** (Reinbek bei Hamburg: Rowohlt, 1975). The other is the theory, developed in her article 'Women on the Market', of the exchange of women in patriarchal economies.[15] While her starting-point here is Marx's theory of the law of value, she works with a deliberate conceptual imprecision which, while it might irritate purists, allows for many fruitful interdisciplinary associations to be made (Whitford, p. 37). Other modern theorists have also developed Marx's law of value away from a strictly Marxist context. For example, Spivak, whose work crosses the boundaries of Marxism, feminism, deconstruction, and post-colonialism, has described it as Marx's most enduring legacy but pleaded that it should be liberated from its narrow use:

> 'Value' is the name of that 'contentless and simple [inhaltslos und einfach]' thing by way of which Marx rewrote not mediation, but the possibility of the mediation that makes possible in its turn all exchange, all communication, sociality itself. Marx's especial concern is the appropriation of the human capacity to produce, not objects, nor anything tangible, but that simple contentless thing which is *not* pure form; the possibility of mediation (through coding) so that exchange and sociality can exist. Marx's point of entry is the economic coding of value, but the notion itself has a much more supple range.[16]

Irigaray's use of Marx's theory of value and the exchange of commodities is indebted to Gayle Rubin's feminist theory of patriarchy, which also derives insights from anthropology. In her influential 1975 essay, 'The Traffic in Women' (see note 3), Rubin develops Lévi-Strauss's theory that the essence of kinship systems lies in the exchange of women between men. These systems are based on the gift, which creates a social link between the partners of an exchange, and the incest taboo, which is 'less a rule prohibiting marriage with the mother, sister, or daughter, than a rule obliging the mother, sister, or daughter to be given to others. It is the supreme rule of the gift' (Lévi-Strauss, quoted in Rubin, p. 173). The sex/gender system, which Rubin defines as 'the set of arrangements by which a society transforms biological sexuality into products of human activity, and in which these transformed sexual needs are satisfied' (p. 159), leads to the division of labour by sex, a device 'to insure the union of men and women by making the smallest viable economic unit contain at least one man and one woman' (p. 178). The importance of Rubin's theory is that it places the oppression of women within social systems rather than in biology (p. 175) and shows how gender, obligatory heterosexuality, and the constraint of female sexuality underwrite social organization under patriarchy (p. 179).

Irigaray's analysis of the exchange of women, to which I shall return in my reading of *Die Liebhaberinnen,* places this exchange in a still wider context: not just within capitalism or societies based on kinship but also within the symbolic order and indeed the whole of western metaphysics. In brief she argues that under patriarchy, which she defines as a hom(m)o-sexual economy (that is, an economy of relations between men), women, like commodities, are valued according to an exterior system of value. This places them in competition with each other, subjects them to a schism between private use and public, social use, and renders them liable to fetishization as a manifestation of the power of the phallus.

Elfriede Jelinek is a Marxist-feminist writer and this fact is consistently reflected in her work.[17] Jelinek's project, as Allyson Fiddler has shown in the first full length study of her *œuvre,* is to 'rewrite reality' in a Brechtian sense, to 'expose the way in which patterns of oppression—particularly those of a class or sexual nature—are masked by the ruling ideology of patriarchal capitalism and represented as immutable facts about the "natural" world'.[18] Jelinek seeks to 'demystify': 'Ich wollte ja immer die Wahrheit hinter einem Schein oder die politische Geschichte hinter einem unschuldigen Bild hervorholen. Das ist das, was als roter Faden durch meine Texte hindurchgeht',[19] and to suggest that 'the "reality" of life is more accurately portrayed by her own very negative and exaggerated picture of brutality, ignorance and perversion' (Fiddler, *Framed by Language,* p. xii). Jelinek's works thus aim to enlighten and mobilize the reader through presenting a negative picture. As one interviewer remarked, her texts do, however, contain, in their continued faith in language, a utopian element,[20] but I would add that the heavy negativity marks her off from the Brecht of the 'Lehrstücke', who provides an explicitly upbeat political message to the audience, and also, I believe, in some respects from the later Brecht. The question I want to raise at this stage is whether the negativity in Jelinek might spring from a feminist awareness that the causes of women's oppression lie much deeper than merely in capitalism, and that something far more radical than the overthrow of capitalism is therefore required to liberate them. While *Die Liebhaberinnen* may demonstrate (in a Brechtian way) the partnership of capitalism and patriarchy, it also reveals (in a confirmation of Irigaray) that patriarchy is based on the exchange of women, and in its aesthetic it illustrates (in an Irigarayan way) the need to subvert and change the symbolic order.

Jelinek's characteristic 'aesthetics of exaggeration' (*Rewriting Reality,* p. 126) and her Marxist-feminist principles are used to great effect in this 1975 work. Telling the story of two young women who set out to do what patriarchal capitalist ideology tells them to do (namely, to secure themselves husbands and thus legitimacy as women through motherhood) but who nevertheless fail to achieve happiness, this story provides in microcosm a picture of the deadly, exploitative power structures of capitalism, which work hand in hand with those of patriarchy, and also shows how these power structures reproduce themselves so that capitalism continuously creates the submissive and compliant subjects it requires.

The type of employer—worker relations depicted are those prevailing in the rural Austria of the 1970s, where many features have changed little since the nineteenth century. Work is scarce and competition for it fierce; the contract between worker and employer is not freely entered into. Working conditions for all workers are harsh and have a brutalizing effect;[21] nevertheless fear of unemployment is a major motivating factor.[22] All profit disappears into the hands of invisible capitalists. For some families the husband's earning power is sufficient to allow the wife not to work, but for most the depth of poverty is such that women are obliged to work too: the concept of the family wage has barely penetrated to this isolated corner of rural Austria. Nevertheless the work that women do is less well paid and of lower status than that of the men, which ensures that men's control over women is maintained.[23]

The major locus for the exploitation of women is, however, not the workplace but the family. According to Donna Haraway, the three major stages of capitalism (commercial/early industrial, monopoly, and multinational) are related dialectically to specific forms of family, and this is borne out by *Die Liebhaberinnen,* where, corresponding to the capital depicted (which is primarily a mix of Haraway's first stage and to a lesser extent her second), we see the patriarchal nuclear family, structured by the dichotomy between public and private, and, but only to a very limited extent, 'the modern family mediated (or enforced) by the welfare state and institutions like the family wage'.[24] In such a society opportunities for women are extremely limited; they are absolutely subject to the institutions of marriage and the family. Marriage is equated with death for both men and women: 'schrecklich, dieses langsame sterben. und die männer und die frauen sterben gemeinsam dahin' (p. 17). Family life is brutal in the extreme, the stress resulting from exploitation at work leading to domestic violence, shown in particular detail through the depiction of Erich's violent family.[25] Paid work thus oppresses and also makes the (male) worker complicit in an hierarchical social system in which men have power over women. This, in addition to the deadly effect of women's (unpaid) work in the home which, in a Marxist-feminist analysis, contributes to the economy by servicing male workers and producing new workers (see Barrett, pp. 208-26), means that life is one stage worse for the women than it is for the men.[26]

If men have a better deal than women, this raises the question of why women allow it to be so. The book contains, as does much of Jelinek's work, a searing indictment of the role of the media and the culture industry generally in serving the interests of patriarchal capitalism, which bears witness to Jelinek's reading of Frankfurt School theory. Like Friedrich Engels before her, Jelinek believes in the importance of paid employment, however menial or low paid it might be, as a first stage in a women's emancipation.[27] Nevertheless her female protagonists are blind to the liberatory potential of work, and seek marriage as a way to escape from its constraints. It does not occur to them to see work as a way of achieving independence from men, as it might have been, particularly for Paula, who starts an apprenticeship as a seamstress, thus breaking out of the pattern of choice for local women between sales assistant or housewife. Brigitte seeks marriage as a way to escape her work in the underwear factory and share in Heinz's earning power as businessman. Susi feels superior to Brigitte in that she finds a husband who can support her, whereas in her eyes Brigitte merely swaps a menial job for a better one: after marriage she still has to work in Heinz's business (their married life consists of 'arbeit arbeit arbeit' (p. 143)). After the failure of her marriage Paula ends up where Brigitte began, on the assembly line in the underwear factory, condemned to work away her life.

The reason for the women's blindness is the fact that, to use Althusser's term, they have been successfully interpellated by the ideology of love and marriage perpetuated by the media. This suggests that Jelinek holds an epistemological view of ideology as false consciousness that places the author/narrator and the reader outside it, though, as I shall show later, this is only partly the case. Paula, the only 'character'[28] towards whom the narrative voice displays sympathy, is depicted as a victim of the romantic ideology of love and marriage that blinds her to the (slim) liberatory potential of work and the truth about Erich.[29] In the first sexual encounter between Paula, 'die dumme kuh' (p. 71), and Erich, we are not told of the love between them because, as the narrator tells us in an uncharacteristically serious moment, there was no love, 'es war wie ein loch, in das man hineinstolpert, und nach dem man wieder weiterhumpelt. gebrochen ist nichts, außer einem menschenkinde in der blüte seiner jahre' (p. 91). Nevertheless Paula believes that her dreams can come true (p. 51), and even after she has been beaten up by her mother she can think of nothing other than the romantic wish-fulfilment that has claimed her and she has made her own:

> in paula klingt ein lied, aber sehr schwach.
> statt der wunden ein bodenlanges weißes spitzenkleid samt schleier.
> keine seifenlauge, sondern eine schöne blumenhaube.
> keine aborte, sondern eine gute hochzeitstorte.
> kein toter embryo kein, sondern ein guter braten vom schwein.
>
> (p. 97)

The pathos aroused by Paula's silent song is very different from that aroused by the moment in *Der kaukasische Kreidekreis* when, though they have remained true to each other, Gruscha and Simon are separated by circumstances.[30] Unlike Gruscha and Simon, Paula has no inner core to which she can remain true, her core *is* the ideology of love out of which she has been constructed.

True to the 'modellhaft' construction of the story, 'immer abwechselnd mit dem guten beispiel brigittes schleppt sich das schlechte beispiel paulas dahin' (p. 26), the ruthless Brigitte prospers while Paula is brought down. And though Paula is not a 'real character' but a demonstration piece, the reader is left with a sense of waste as strong as that conveyed at the end of *Effi Briest* (whose heroine's downfall is also caused by her 'Schritt vom Wege'), made explicit by the narrator's final, condemnatory comment:

> aus dem hoffnungsvollen lehrmädchen der schneiderei im ersten lehrjahr ist eine zerbrochene frau mit ungenügenden schneidereikenntnissen geworden.
>
> das ist zu wenig.
>
> (p. 154)

Thus far, then, we see an exaggerated Marxist-feminist account of life under capitalism, in which men and women are exploited and alienated by capitalism, women are further oppressed by men as a result of capitalism, and all go along with the system because they have been socialized into so doing through economic competition for jobs and through Ideological State Apparatuses, in particular the media and the family. But this is not the whole picture. I suggested above that women function under patriarchy (not just capitalism) as objects of exchange between men, and I want to show now how this is depicted in Jelinek's text following Irigaray's formulation of this phenomenon in her essay 'Women on the Market'.

First, and fundamentally, in Irigaray's account women, like commodities, are valued according to an exterior system of value. The system is set by men, for patriarchy is a hom(m)o-sexual economy, an economy of relations between men:

> The law that orders our society is the exclusive valorization of men's needs/desires, of exchanges among men. What the anthropologist calls the passage from nature to culture thus amounts to the institution of the reign of hom(m)o-sexuality. Not in an 'immediate' practice, but in its 'social' mediation. From this point on, patriarchal societies might be interpreted as societies functioning in the mode of 'semblance.' The value of symbolic and imaginary productions is superimposed upon, and even substituted for, the value of relations of material, natural, and corporal (re)production.
>
> In this new matrix of History, in which man begets man as his own likeness, wives, daughters, and sisters have value only in that they serve as the possibility of, and potential benefit in, relations among men. The use of and traffic in women subtend and uphold the reign of masculine hom(m)o-sexuality, even while they maintain that hom(m)o-sexuality in speculations, mirror games, identifications, and more or less rivalrous appropriations, which defer its real practice. Reigning everywhere, although prohibited in practice, hom(m)o-sexuality is played out through the bodies of women, matter, or sign, and heterosexuality has been up to now just an alibi for the smooth workings of man's relations with himself, of relations among men. Whose 'sociocultural endogamy' excludes the participation of that other, so foreign to the social order: woman.
>
> (pp. 171-72)

In Irigaray's analysis value does not inhere in the object (a woman), but appears only in exchange. Three fetishized roles are imposed on women in relation to value: that of mother, who has (been) withdrawn from exchange, of virgin, who represents pure exchange value, and of prostitutes, explicitly condemned by the social order but implicitly tolerated because the break between usage and exchange is less clear-cut (p. 186).

Jelinek makes explicit the commodity function of women in both main protagonists' quest for marriage, making repeated use of the vocabulary of capital and the market: Brigitte, for example, is described as 'austauschbar und unnötig' (p. 12), all that she has to offer being a body, which is, however, only one of many on the market: 'brigitte hat brüste, schenkel, beine, hüften und eine möse. das haben andre auch, manchmal sogar von besserer qualität' (p. 13). Her market value is declining with her age, 'brigitte wird immer älter und immer weniger frau, die konkurrenz wird immer jünger und immer mehr frau' (p. 13). In a nice piece of Jelinekian irony, Heinz's choice between the two commodities, Susi, Brigitte's rival, and Brigitte, though disavowed, is laid out for the reader:

> susi ist etwas feines, brigitte nicht.
> man kann die beiden nicht gegenüberstellen. das ist unmöglich.
> man kann das eine mögen oder das andre, entscheiden muß heinz.
> hat er das lieber oder das.
>
> (p. 63)

The commodification of women could not be clearer. And after marriage and motherhood Brigitte's transformation from object of exchange to one withdrawn from exchange is made complete when she loses her name and is now referred to as 'mama' (p. 149).

The course of Paula's life is also related in terms of her relative value. At first she is aware that she must not allow her 'marktwert' (p. 30), measured in terms of her virginity, to diminish by sleeping around, a fate that does in fact befall her when she becomes pregnant by Erich:

> paulas mickriger bauch, der bald schon dick aufgeschwollen sein wird, sodaß man für das gleiche geld plötzlich viel mehr kilogramm paula bekommen könnte, steht zur versteigerung. aber keiner will ihn haben. bei einem schwein wäre das ein enormer wertzuwachs. bei paula ist es ein zeichen, daß sie leicht zu haben war, zu leicht, und jetzt umso schwerer anzubringen ist.
>
> (p. 100)

Paula's status as commodity is underlined again when she confronts Erich in the bar, and the narrator makes an extended play on the word 'Wert':

> alle meinen, daß erich, wenn er schon nachgeben muß, erst nachgeben soll, wenn das kind schon anwesend, und so die wertreduzierung paulas zu einer entwertung geworden ist.
>
> wenn einer so abgewertet ist, dann sind sie alle dadurch ein wenig aufgewertet. die demütigung paulas entschädigt sie für ihre eigenen, manchmal viel schrecklicheren demütigungen.
>
> plötzlich sind sie alle wieder personen gegenüber einer unperson geworden.
>
> (p. 120)

Indeed, as the narrator points out in an unusually unambiguous didactic moment, 'dieser roman handelt vom gegenstand paula' (p. 130), and the object Paula finds herself in an hierarchical structure of domination: 'über den gegenstand paula bestimmt erich, über dessen körperkräfte wieder andre bestimmen, bis sich seine eingeweide einem frühen tod entgegenzersetzen, bei dem der alkohol das seine leistet' (p. 130).

Interestingly, when Paula, working as a prostitute, is spotted by one of Erich's friends, even though she claims that her motives were to support her family, her actions are seen as a betrayal not only of her husband but also of the local hom(m)osexual economy, for she is caught with a stranger:

> paula hat ihren mann verraten. paula hat ihren mann mit einem oder mehreren andren männern betrogen.
>
> es war noch dazu ein ortsfremder. keiner von den hiesigen burschen. ein ortsfremder hat ihnen ins nest geschissen.
>
> (p. 153)

Paula's descent into prostitution means of course total devaluation and consequent exclusion from the social group.

Brigitte and Paula are defined in terms of what they represent to men for 'they are the manifestation and the circulation of a power of the Phallus, establishing relationships of men with each other' (Irigaray, p. 183).[31] Brigitte becomes a mother, Paula a prostitute, and even Susi, who tries to live femininity positively, will have to submit to the violence of patriarchy, as Heinz observes to himself with a characteristically obscene turn of phrase, 'susi wird den schwanz fest in die möse und das familienleben fest in den kopf gepflanzt bekommen' (p. 83).

Secondly, in Irigaray's account, the exchange of women means certain things for them: that they are in competition with each other; that, as a result of this, far from rebelling, they speak to and are anxious to confirm their value; that they are subject to a schism between private use and public, social use; that they have no right to their own pleasure; that, unlike men, they have no access to the symbolic. This last point is crucial, for in both Irigaray's analysis and Jelinek's text the symbolic provides positive symbolization only of the power of the phallus and of relationships between men, not of those between the sexes, the maternal/feminine, or of relationships between women. The competition between Brigitte and Susi for Heinz thus represents a systemic competition between women, based on the defence of what they see as their property: 'es ist ein allgemeines hassen im ort, das immer mehr um sich greift, das alles ansteckt, das vor keinem halt macht, die frauen entdecken keine gemeinsamkeiten zwischen sich, nur gegensätze' (p. 29); women who are 'herrenlos' are seen by other women to be a threat (p. 92). Nowhere is this lack of solidarity more striking than in the relations between mothers and daughters, where mothers wish the worst for their daughters, for 'warum soll die tochter nicht verbraucht werden, wenn die mutter auch verbraucht worden ist?' (p. 16). Paula, indeed, receives no support from her mother when she becomes pregnant, but rather violence.

Far from showing solidarity with each other, the women assert their legitimacy through their men, their only access to the power of the phallus: Brigitte's main concern is to obtain Heinz's name for herself; Heinz's and Erich's mothers want to protect them from the predatory girls; when talking of their men, the women of the village use one word only, 'MEINER': 'sonst nichts, nicht mein mann, nur meiner [. . .] paula beobachtet das siegerlächeln, wenn die mutta oder die schwestern sagen: meiner. die einzige gelegenheit, wo die besiegten ein siegerlächeln im mundwinkel haben' (p. 31). The women all aspire to motherhood (in Irigarayan terms this represents speaking to their value) though Susi resists it for a while and Brigitte hates babies. Motherhood brings justification, jubilation ('sie hats geschafft' (p. 37)) and security (though not for Paula, since Erich does not earn enough to support a family). Motherhood is, however, condemned by the narrator as monotonous drudgery, a series of useless tasks that weigh on the individual like a 'zentnergewicht, das einen letzten endes zu brei schlägt' (p. 88). Paula's status as commodity on a market means that she is subject to a schism she visualizes in terms of two bodies:

> frühzeitig lernt paula, ihren körper und das, was mit ihm geschieht, als etwas zu betrachten, das einem andren passiert als ihr selbst. einem nebenkörper gewissermaßen, einer nebenpaula.
>
> alles material aus paulas träumen, alle zärtlichkeit geschieht mit paulas hauptkörper, die prügel, die vom vatter kommen, geschehen dem nebenkörper.
>
> (p. 31)

That women have no right to their own pleasure is shown graphically through the description of Brigitte's sexual encounters with Heinz, which fill her with disgust (pp. 55-56), and of Paula's with Erich, which bear no relation to the amorous exchanges she has read about in magazines (p. 91). Men's sexuality is symbolized positively (though mocked by the narrator) in imagery of panthers (p. 41), sunsets, and natural catastrophes (p. 56), and male promiscuity and lust are implicitly condoned:

> als holzarbeiter hat er einen schweren und gefährlichen beruf, von dem schon oft einer nie mehr zurückgekommen ist. daher genießen sie ihr leben unheimlich, solange sie jung sind, ab 13 ist kein mädchen mehr sicher vor ihnen, das allgemeine wettrennen beginnt, und die hörner werden abgestoßen, von welchem vorgang das ganze dorf widerhallt. der vorgang hallt durchs tal.
>
> (p. 15)

Women's desire, by contrast, is simply left unfigured and a woman's attractiveness defined solely in terms of her 'sauberkeit' (p. 53) and 'häuslichkeit' (p. 65). Similarly, the only supportive and positively symbolized relationships are those between males: between Erich and his companions in the pub, for example (p. 20), or between Heinz's father and his son: 'der opa kann dir auch beibringen, was ein mann wissen muß, wie man auf bäume klettert [. . .] weil der opa auch ein mann ist, weißt du' (p. 142), whereas supportive relations between women are impossible.

Jelinek thus shows that women's exploitation, their alienation from each other, from desire, and from the symbolic order are not explicable by the mechanics of capitalism alone but can also be explained in terms of their status as commodities within a patriarchal economy. That these often overlap (the regulation of women's sexuality is a key part of Marxist-feminist analysis) shows that capitalism has taken over and reinforced pre-existing practices. This takes us beyond a Marxist analysis and back into the realm of the symbolic and makes Jelinek's picture more bleak, for the practical advice suggested to her female readers (that women's liberation might start with the financial independence afforded by employment) is undermined by the other factors stacked against them.

If Jelinek, like Althusser, in dwelling on their constructedness as subjects, seems to deny her characters the possibility of resistance, and if, like Irigaray, she backs this up by showing how patriarchy exerts its powerful hold through the symbolic, in her aesthetic she is less 'scientific' and less negative. Unlike Irigaray she does not explicitly seek to speak as a woman, but she does have in common with her a desire to attack and subvert language in order to expose its role in oppressive power structures and thus hint at the possibility of change. For Irigaray this is in direct contradiction to the tactics of Marxism.[32] Jelinek, as I have shown, does present for her readers a Marxist view of the deadly functioning of capitalism and exposes the harmful effects of patriarchal capitalist ideology, particularly for women. Capitalism, it is clear, must be changed. But her attacks on language show that this is not in itself enough. As she said in a recent interview: 'Ich zwinge sofort den Ideologiecharakter der Worte hervor. Ich lasse die Sprache sich nicht ausruhen. Ich reiße sie immer wieder aus ihrem Bett heraus. [. . .] man muß die Sprache foltern, damit sie die Wahrheit sagt' (Meier, p. 73).

Jelinek's narrator in *Die Liebhaberinnen* does violence to the discourses that do violence to people through ruthless mimicry, whether it be of the discourse of the idyllic Austrian 'Heimat' (pp. 5-7), or of the human face of capitalism (p. 9), the clichéd discourse of 'common sense' or of course the powerful discourse of romance that leads Paula astray. Thus when the reader reads that Brigitte's hair shines like chestnuts (p. 21), or hears of 'die heilsamen schmerzen des kinderkriegens' (p. 28), or meets Heinz's mother, 'die heinzmutter, von natur aus gutmütig' (p. 33) and finds her to be anything but goodnatured, or hears that 'alles ist in ordnung' (p. 147) when what is actually being described is Paula's miserable circumstances, what comes through is the mismatch between language and truth and yet also the very real power invested in ideologically loaded language.

It is at this point that the narrator's standpoint becomes crucial. Margret Brügmann has analysed the difference between Brecht's inbuilt comments on the action of his 'Lehrstücke' and the comments of Jelinek's narrator in *Die Liebhaberinnen,* which is that while Brecht's comments show the false consciousness depicted to be correctable, Jelinek's narrator speaks from a position much closer to her protagonists and deliberately refrains from stating the essence of what is being depicted, thus making the reader work harder and denying him/her the catharsis resulting from a clear analysis.[33] I would add that the narrative voice shifts, sometimes appearing complicit in patriarchal ideology, thus turning the reader into a voyeur ('susi ist kein kleines mädel mehr, sondern schon eine richtige frau, was man beim räkeln genau merkt' (p. 65)), sometimes directly mimicking it in order to open it up to scrutiny ('heinz und brigitte erschrecken vor der größe dieses gefühls. brigitte erschrickt mehr als heinz, weil gefühle mehr weiblich sind' (p. 23)), sometimes achieving the same effect by use of a rhetorical question ('seit brigitte heinz kennt, drängt es sie dazu, ein kind zu gebären. wenn das kein gefühl ist, was ist dann ein gefühl?' (p. 106)), and occasionally drawing an unambiguous moral, as in the key passages above concerning Paula. That close attention should be paid to the shifting positions of her narrative voice was confirmed by Jelinek in a recent interview: 'Bei mir gibt es oft diese objektivierenden Kommentare. Wenn ich über mich eine Doktorarbeit schriebe, würde ich wahrscheinlich die Bedeutung des Wir, des auktorialen Kommentars in der Erzählung, analysieren, der ja ständig seine Perspektive ändert' (Meier, p. 28). The constant shifting of narrative position in relation to the language used and the repeated drawing attention to the ideological character of language suggest a different relationship on the part of the Brecht of the 'Lehrstücke' and Jelinek to ideology and to truth, with both viewing ideology as false consciousness but Jelinek less ready to identify her own position outside it. Jelinek's position here is post-Foucauldian, and implicitly post-Marxist: she is aware that truth, like ideology, is also discursively constructed.

Jelinek does not propose a way out of the impasse of women's role in symbolic exchange because an alternative is literally unimaginable. Paula and Brigitte are nothing outside this economy, they have no being. Jelinek showed in this 1975 work that women are excluded from the symbolic order, not just from economic power. Nevertheless, she saw hope for change: her technique in *Die Liebhaberinnen*, while indebted to the (masculine, Marxist) Brechtian tradition of uncovering and demonstrating false consciousness from outside, also has affinities with Irigaray's feminist and post-structuralist strategic mimicry, which speaks from a position within ideology and allows for resistance by 'make[ing] "visible" by an effect of playful repetition, what was supposed to remain invisible: recovering a possible operation of the feminine in language'.[34]

### Notes

1. The best introduction to this topic remains Michèle Barrett's influential *Women's Oppression Today: The Marxist/Feminist Encounter*, revised edn (London: Verso, 1988).

2. Friedrich Engels's early contribution to this debate is seen as flawed, though interesting: see *The Origin of the Family, Private Property and the State* (Harmondsworth: Penguin, 1986). Heidi Hartmann has shown how patriarchy underlies capitalism in her essay 'The Unhappy Marriage of Marxism and Feminism: Towards a More Progressive Union', in *The Unhappy Marriage of Marxism and Feminism: A Debate of Class and Patriarchy*, ed. by Lydia Sargent (London: Pluto, 1981), pp. 1-41.

3. Gayle Rubin, 'The Traffic in Women: Notes on the "Political Economy" of Sex', in *Towards an Anthropology of Women*, ed. by Rayna R. Reiter (New York: Monthly Review Press, 1975), pp. 157-210 (p. 160).

4. Simone de Beauvoir, *The Second Sex* (Harmondsworth: Penguin, 1972).

5. Louis Althusser, 'Ideology and Ideological State Apparatuses (Notes Towards and Investigation)', in *'Lenin and Philosophy' and Other Essays* (London: New Left Books, 1971), pp. 127-186.

6. Terry Lovell, *Pictures of Reality: Aesthetics, Politics, Pleasure* (London: BFI, 1980), p. 40.

7. Indeed, Michèle Barrett no longer felt able to use the term 'Marxist Feminist', which she had used only eight years earlier, in her 1988 revised edition of *Women's Oppression Today*: 'The confident combination of "Marxist Feminist", a common phrase in the late 1970s when the book was written, uncomfortably reminds us of an attempt to bring together two world-views that have continued to go their separate ways in spite of our efforts at marriage guidance' (p. v).

8. See, for example, Adrienne Rich, 'Compulsory Heterosexuality and Lesbian Existence (1980)', in *Blood, Bread, and Poetry: Selected Prose 1979-1985* (London: Virago, 1987), pp. 23-75; Chandra Talpade Mohanty, 'Under Western Eyes: Feminist Scholarship and Colonial Discourses', *boundary 2*, 12:3, 13:1 (1984), 333-58; Gayatri Chakravorty Spivak, 'French Feminism in an International Frame', in *In Other Worlds: Essays in Cultural Politics* (New York: Routledge, 1988), pp. 134-53.

9. Ernesto Laclau and Chantal Mouffe, *Hegemony and Socialist Strategy: Towards a Radical Democratic Politics* (London: Verso, 1985).

10. Judith Butler, *Gender Trouble* (London: Routledge, 1990), and *Bodies That Matter: On the Discursive Limits of 'Sex'* (London: Routledge, 1993).

11. Donna Haraway, '"Gender" for a Marxist Dictionary: The Sexual Politics of a Word', in *Simians, Cyborgs, and Women: The Reinvention of Nature* (London: Free Association Books, 1991), pp. 127-48 (p. 136).

12. Gayatri Chakravorty Spivak, *In Other Worlds: Essays in Cultural Politics* (London: Routledge, 1987); *Outside in the Teaching Machine* (London: Routledge, 1993); *The Post-Colonial Critic: Interviews, Strategies, Dialogues* (London: Routledge, 1990); *Feminism as Critique: Essays on the Politics of Gender in Late-Capitalist Societies*, ed. by Seyla Benhabib and Drucilla Cornell (Cambridge: Polity Press, 1987); Rosemary Hennessey, *Materialist Feminism and the Politics of Discourse* (New York: Routledge, 1993); Michèle Barrett, *The Politics of Truth: From Marx to Foucault* (Cambridge: Polity Press, 1991).

13. My account of Irigaray's ideas is heavily indebted to Margaret Whittord's book, *Luce Irigaray: Philosophy in the Feminine* (London: Routledge, 1991).

14. Jean-Joseph Goux, 'Luce Irigaray Versus the Utopia of the Neutral Sex', in *Engaging with Irigaray*, ed. by Carolyn Burke, Naomi Schor, and Margaret Whitford (New York: Columbia University Press, 1994), pp. 175-89 (p. 184).

15. In *This Sex Which Is Not One*, trans. by Catherine Porter with Carolyn Burke (Ithaca, NY: Cornell University Press, 1985), pp. 170-92.

16. Gayatri Chakravorty Spivak, 'Poststructuralism, Marginality, Postcoloniality and Value', in *Literary Theory Today*, ed. by Peter Collier and Helga Geyer-Ryan (Cambridge: Polity Press, 1990), pp. 219-44 (p. 226).

17. For example, Allyson Fiddler argues that it is Jelinek's attachment to the master narratives of Marxism and feminism which, despite her leanings towards post-modernism, makes her work

differ from it ('There Goes That Word Again, or Elfriede Jelinek and Postmodernism', in *Elfriede Jelinek: Framed by Language,* ed. by Jorun B. Johns and Katherine Arens (Riverside, CA: Ariadne Press, 1994), 129-49). See also, in the same volume, Linda C. DeMerritt, who argues that, even in her most autobiographical and psychoanalytically informed work, *Die Klavierspielerin,* Jelinek's main theme 'is the submission of everyone, regardless of sex, to the accumulation of capital and their resultant alienation' ('A "Healthier Marriage": Elfriede Jelinek's Marxist Feminism in *Die Klavierspielerin* and *Lust',* pp. 107-28 (p. 115)).

18. Allyson Fiddler, *Rewriting Reality: An Introduction to Elfriede Jelinek* (Oxford: Berg, 1994), pp. xi-xii.

19. Riki winter, 'Gespräch mit Elfriede Jelinek', in *Elfriede Jelinek,* ed. by Kurt Bartsch and Günther A. Höfler (Graz: Droschl, 1991), pp. 9-19 (p. 11).

20. Sigrid Berka, 'Ein Gespräch mit Elfriede Jelinek', *Modern Austrian Literature,* 26 (1993), 127-53 (p. 138).

21. This is stressed on every occasion: Paula's mother's overreaction to the news of her daughter's pregnancy (she beats her up) is occasioned by the stress of work: 'zu dieser wahnsinnigen arbeit jeden tag auch noch schande und spott' (p. 95). An appeal to the reader's sympathy, or at least understanding, is made even on behalf of the violent, stupid, and drunken Erich, the woodman, when Paula, not interested in him as a person but merely as father to her child, tries to trap him into marriage, catching him on his way home from work, when he is exhausted to dropping point (p. 103). Work for him is 'das schlimmste [. . .], was einem passieren kann' but nevertheless a stark fact of life: 'sie muß aber gemacht werden' (p. 113). Both men and women are alienated and physically and mentally worn out by their work, whether they work on the land, like Erich, a woodman, as 'Beamte', like Heinz's father, or in the factory producing women's underwear, like Brigitte.

22. Both Heinz's father and Erich's stepfather are ill as a result of work (pp. 25, 41), which fact is measured in the heightened economic insecurity of the families and the fact that they both fear losing their working sons to potential wives who are perceived as a threat (pp. 36, 79). To stress the debilitating effects of work, both fathers are referred to metonymically by the narrator in terms indicating their ill health: Heinz's father is called 'bandscheiben', since his discs have suffered as a result of his work as a long-distance lorry driver, a job he in fact loses during the course of the novel (p. 99), while Erich's stepfather is called 'asthma', his condition a result of his work on the railways (p. 41).

23. Hartmann makes the point that along with the development of the family wage in the twentieth century, the allocation of low-status and low-paid work to women allows patriarchal relations to remain intact (p. 25).

24. Donna J. Haraway, 'A Cyborg Manifesto: Science, Technology, and Socialist-Feminism in the Late Twentieth Century', in *Simians, Cyborgs, and Women,* pp. 149-81 (p. 167).

25. His stepfather derives his authority and his ability to give orders from the fact that he was a 'beamter' (p. 101). The violence in the family, which may have caused Erich to suffer brain damage as a child (pp. 38, 42, 115), becomes a cycle as he extends the pleasure he gets from secret petty cruelties towards animals or children (p. 89) to the officially sanctioned cruelty against Paula: 'erich erfaßt, daß auf einmal seine entschlüsse und handlungen für einen andren wichtig geworden sind. daß jemand von ihm ABHÄNGIG ist. daß jemand ihm in gewisser weise AUSGELIEFERT ist. das gibt ein schönes neues gefühl' (p. 104). When his stepfather 'Asthma' dies, the effect of his authoritarian character on that of his wife is revealed. She experiences 'eine unglaubliche leere' in the absence of his barked out orders (p. 127) and finds herself confused by being asked to make a decision about whether her son may marry, so unused is she to being agent of her own actions. As the narrator caustically phrases it, 'einer ist schon weggestorben, wer bleibt denn übrig? gar niemand' (p. 129).

26. Heinz's mother, even though her husband's job meant that she did not have to go out to work (p. 12), is called a 'leiche' (p. 100); Erich's mother spent most of her life in service, had four children by different men before finding one who would marry her, and is chronically sick (pp. 39, 78); Paula's mother, described ironically as 'wunschlos glücklich' because it is too late for her to desire anything, has cancer, which may be a result of self-induced abortions (p. 75); Paula has her first child 'in mühevoller kleinarbeit' (p. 122), and her prostitution, engaged in so that she can support her family, is also described as 'arbeit' (p. 153). To be without a man is, however, worse, as Brigitte's unmarried mother is aware (p. 24). This is also the case for Erich's old, silent grandmother, who is 'nur mehr geduldet', and whose existence 'hängt an einem seidenen faden' because, being human, she has to be fed, and is thus a drain on the family's resources (p. 79).

27. 'Arbeit ist eine Möglichkeit der Frau, zum Subjekt zu werden, indem sie ökonomische Unabhängigkeit vom Mann erwirbt' ('Elfriede Jelinek im Gespräch mit Adolf-Ernst Meyer', in Elfriede Jelinek, Jutta Heinrich; and Adolf-Ernst Meyer, *Sturm und Zwang: Schreiben als Geschlechterkampf* (Hamburg: Klein, 1995), pp. 7-74 (p. 57)).

28. Jelinek's characters are not meant to be 'realistic' bourgeois subjects: '[das bürgerliche Subjekt] existiert nicht nur in meinem Werk nicht mehr, es existiert überhaupt nicht mehr. Aber es ist natürlich die Illusion eines gigantischen Marktes, den Menschen zu suggerieren, sie wären einmalig und unverwechselbar und imstande, individualistisch zu handeln' (Winter, p. 14).

29. 'zu ihrer schneiderei sagt paula nie: meine arbeit. zu ihrer arbeit sagt paula nie: meine. auch innerlich nicht. die arbeit, das ist etwas, das von einem losgelöst ist, die arbeit das ist doch mehr eine pflicht und geschieht daher dem nebenkörper. die liebe, das ist eine freude, eine erholung, und geschieht daher dem hauptkörper' (p. 32).

30. 'Der Eid ist gebrochen. Warum, wird nicht mitgeteilt.
    Hört, was sie dachte, nicht sagte:
    Als du kämpftest in der Schlacht, Soldat
    Der blutigen Schlacht, der bitteren Schlacht
    Traf ein Kind ich, das hilflos war
    Hätt' es abzutun nicht das Herz.'

    (*Der kaukasische Kreidekreis* (Berlin: Suhrkamp, 1955), p. 75)

31. The question of defining 'woman' causes particular difficulty to the mentally challenged Erich in a passage that reveals that definitions of femininity are man-made. Relating Erich's ponderings on the difference between the two kinds of women he knows (the summer guests whom he services sexually, and motherly types who service his physical needs, both of whom disqualify themselves as women), the narrator laconically observes that 'erich denkt also an frauen, die für ihn keine frauen sind, weil sie ihm wie die geschlechtslose mutta dauernd fressen und trinken hineinschieben, und an frauen, die für ihn keine frauen sind, weil sie für ihn keine frauen sein dürfen, weil sie es mit jedem machen, ohne mit ihm verliebt, verlobt oder verheiratet zu sein und überhaupt unmöglich ein ganzes haus sauberhalten könnten' (p. 58).

32. 'Contrary to the implications of Marxism [. . .] in order to change the economic structure, it is necessary to change the structure of language' (Irigaray, quoted in Whitford, pp. 20-21).

33. *Amazonen der Literatur: Studien zur deutschsprachigen Frauenliteratur der 70er Fahre* (Amsterdam: Rodopi, 1986), pp. 156-57.

34. In the meantime, however, it seems that Jelinek has become more pessimistic, as her comments on one of her most recent plays, *Totenauberg,* make explicit. She describes *Totenauberg* as 'mein resignativster Text [. . .] ein bitterer Text, da nicht nur alle Hoffnungen auf Veränderung zunichte gemacht wurden, sondern für mich auch klar wurde, daß die Frau nicht ins Denken Eingang finden kann'. Even Hannah Arendt, a figure in the play, cannot achieve 'die Souveränität des reinen Ontologisierens [. . .] Gleichzeitig sollte dieser Text auch mein letzter Versuch sein, als Frau in die männlichste aller Bastionen, das Denken, einzudringen, allerdings mit dem Wissen, daß dies nicht möglich ist' (Winter, p. 17).

### Christine Kiebuzinska (essay date spring 1998)

SOURCE: Kiebuzinska, Christine. "Elfriede Jelinek's *Nora* Project: Or What Happens When Nora Meets the Capitalists." *Modern Drama* 41, no. 1 (spring 1998): 134-45.

[*In the following essay, Kiebuzinska discusses how* Was geschah, nachdem Nora ihren Mann verlassen hatte oder Stützen der Gesellschaften *functions as both a deconstruction and re-appropriation of Henrik Ibsen's* A Doll's House.]

The distinguishing feature of the creative output of the contemporary Austrian writer Elfriede Jelinek is the unmasking of the illusion perpetuated by misreadings of canonical texts. In her play **Was geschah, nachdem Nora ihren Mann verlassen hatte oder Stützen der Gesellschaften,** written in 1979 as a reflection upon the centennial of Henrik Ibsen's *A Doll's House,* Jelinek superimposes a strong materialist feminist reading on a range of contemporary issues: the demythification of canonical texts that adhere to the fictions of everyday life, the continuity of patriarchal structures in capitalist market economies, and the limitations of utopian individualism in feminist myths.[1] Jelinek recognizes that a critique of the appropriation of Ibsen's classic simultaneously necessitates a demystification of the modes of representation most successful in the dissemination of ideologies. In her deconstruction of Ibsen's *A Doll's House,* Jelinek transposes the action of the play to reveal "what happened after Nora left her husband and met the pillars of societies."[2]

Ibsen's *A Doll's House* is continually present in **Nora,** particularly in Jelinek's deconstruction of its idealistic implications, the heroic strength of the heroine and the utopian hopes for the equality in the partnership of the married couple; however, in Jelinek's version the psychological depth of the characters has disappeared and utopian dreams of gender equality are undermined by her use of the clichés that continue to surround the reception of Ibsen's play. Throughout Ibsen's play, we see Torvald carefully creating the terms and appropriate postures of his fictive world out of the moral maxims on debt, responsibility, the telling of lies, the aesthetic differences between knitting and embroidery, and even on eating macaroons. Nora in turn has become an accomplished actress in sustaining her fiction of youthfulness and irresponsibility by acting out the prettifying, self-deluding fiction of innocence for the eight years of their marriage. When the "wonderful" does not happen, Nora's and Torvald's fictions collapse and they are left, as in theatre, only with the appearance of a marriage.[3] Nora discards her dancing-girl costume and assumes the adult costume essential to her new recreation of self as an uncompromising and strong-minded heroine capable of taking on all society. It is in this somewhat frayed adult "costume" from the last scene of *A Doll's House* that Nora wanders into Jelinek's script looking for a self-fulfilling job in a factory in order to test her quest for self-realization.

In Jelinek's play, Nora's "redefinition" occurs in the time space of the Germany of the 1920s, as it is undergoing economic collapse following the economic crash and hyperinflation leading to the rise of Hitler's National Socialism. Simultaneously, Jelinek also projects the action into the time space of the late 1970s, a time space that represents the accelerated economic development in West Germany as well as the emergence of Germany's feminist movement. Jelinek sets the play within these time spaces in order to demonstrate the ideological continuities between National Socialism and the contemporary German *Wirtschaftswunder,* or economic miracle, brought about through market deregulations and highly sophisticated take-over maneuvers, behind which the unseen power of the multinational corporations conspires to overcome political and legal constraints. In her play Jelinek reveals the mechanism of "the linguistic cover-up of what a capitalist knows and thinks, but doesn't express publicly,"[4] and this was the reason that Jelinek wrote her *Nora* "as a kind of *Wirtschaftskrimi* (business crime novel)."[5]

Since the very title of Jelinek's play refers to both Ibsen's *A Doll's House* and *The Pillars of Society,* it might be fruitful to examine how Ibsen's texts function as pretexts to *Nora. A Doll's House* provides the entire ensemble of characters with the exception of Dr. Rank; from *The Pillars of Society* Jelinek borrows the motive of land speculation, for the source of Konsul Weygang's characterization in *Nora* as a speculator, capitalist and profiteer is not difficult to recognize in the figure of Konsul Bernick from Ibsen's play. At the same time, Jelinek playfully changes the "pillars of society" to "pillars of societies,"[6] the plural suggesting a dispersal of power structures in the form of multinational banks and corporations. Jelinek also replaces the railroad project, so symbolic of nineteenth-century capitalist expansion, with the much more deadly enterprise of an atomic power plant on the site of a profit-losing cotton mill. Ultimately, Jelinek's reliance on the ethical dilemma rather than the actual characters or situations of Ibsen's *Pillars of Society* invests contemporary issues with archetypal attributes that bring the continuities of the cultural past into play.

Jelinek's declaration that "plays by women should not deal with emotions"[7] provides a means of interpreting her *Nora,* for the play serves as an example of her critique of the subjective fictions perpetuated by the many interpretations of Ibsen's drama of Nora's quest for self-realization. In Jelinek's play, however, Nora's search for meaning takes place within a context wherein the mechanism of patriarchal capitalism subverts Nora's striving for selfhood to its own purposes. Jelinek eliminates the subtextual depth of Ibsen's characterizations by flattening out characters to mere surfaces in order to show how Nora's aspirations for selfhood must be tested in the reality of the cutthroat jungle marketplace of corporate takeovers, diversions of funds and the corruption of all traces of moral order.

According to Jelinek, in a society dominated by crude materialism and the predatory pursuit of success, personal self-realization is the ultimate fiction. In re-imagining Nora as an innocent who wanders into the text of *The Pillars of Society,* Jelinek reveals that Nora's conditioning as consumer of her own myth is perfected to the point where individual identity is indistinguishable from societal role. Thus any attempt on Nora's part to change her life by slamming shut the door to the "doll's house" is sabotaged from the outset because it is conceptualized from within the power framework Nora tries to escape, refracted in Jelinek's version in the many "societies" she encounters as she proceeds from millworker to a capitalist's mistress and back to the entrapment of the "doll's house."

Jelinek's method depends on the deconstruction of signification systems by means of a montage or collage that juxtaposes quotations from the canonical texts to linguistic "readymades" from popular scandal sheets, advertisements, television talk shows, soap operas and popular film. She accomplishes this by means of selecting, transposing and dispersing fragments of metaphors from canonical texts and mixing them up with contemporary clichés about individualism and self-realization drawn from these sources. Ultimately *Nora* reflects Jelinek's experimentation with an intertextual collage of "readymades" from Ibsen, Hitler, Mussolini, Wedekind, women's magazines, pulp fiction and market analysis, as well as quotations from her own interviews and critical articles in which she comments on the limitations of liberal feminism. Though these elements coexist in a single textual space, the relation of these discourses with each other is often in conflict. At the same time, Jelinek's subversive use of both temporal and ideological doubleness challenges the spectator into reflecting on the usual representation of the feminine. Thus Jelinek's play self-consciously "rewrites" already scripted texts in order to display how ideological myths are perpetuated from Ibsen's time frame into the contemporary, with the two world views coexisting in the "repetition" of archetypes.

The intention of Jelinek's distorted mimicry of Ibsen's pre-texts is to foreground and estrange aspects of the original's style and message, while ensuring that the origins of the new imitation are still recognizable. Allyson Fiddler mentions that the success of Jelinek's eclecticism and mixing up of codes depends on the intertext being recognized. "[P]arody is not just an internal relation between the work and its model, but is necessarily pragmatic, in that it assumes the audience will "get" the reference, and appreciate the double coding."[8]

In foregrounding her explicit references to Ibsen's two classics, Jelinek depends on the audience's knowledge of both *A Doll's House* and *The Pillars of Society,* as well as a familiarity with the ideological debates surrounding contemporary feminism, capitalist market economies, and residues of fascist myths in contemporary politics. However, the fragments from Ibsen and contemporary media are frequently decontextualized, and characters seem to quote from Ibsen's text as second-rate performers rather than characters. Ultimately, the assembly-line language that the characters have appropriated from Ibsen saps them of their strength to think through and to articulate their situation. As a result, Jelinek's characters occupy a distinctly postmodern space, what Rosalind Krauss calls a "paraliterary space . . . of debate, quotation, partisanship, betrayal, reconciliation; but . . . not the space of unity, coherence, or resolution that we think of as constituting the work of art."[9]

Quotations from both of Ibsen's texts are marked as if from a *chambre d'échos,* for even before the spectator views the play, the title alone signals that this is a sequel or "what happens next." Similarly the first line sets up the identifying relationship to Ibsen's text: "I'm Nora, the same as in the play by Ibsen" (8). The intertextual relationship is thus based on the use of self-reflexive references, as later we are reminded of the relationship to the original when Weygang identifies Nora as "the central character with the same name as in Ibsen" (20). Jelinek calls attention to the fact that her play is a parody of Ibsen, when for example Torvald condescendingly acknowledges to Krogstad that Frau Linde is now his housekeeper: "We all know from the theatre, that you had once loved this woman, the one now in the kitchen" (47). The self-reflexive quotations function to alert the spectator to watch for the follies in the original.

Jelinek transforms Nora by focusing entirely on the surfaces of Ibsen's character, for her Nora becomes a performing squirrel whose qualifications for the marketplace include the dancing of the tarantella as well as performing gymnastic exercises such as splits, back bends and leaps to show her "flexibility." Various references to the flying and jumping animal world such as "my little lark" or "my squirrel" are exaggerated. At the same time, allusions to Nora's willful little-girl impudence and obstinacy become parodies of Ibsen's Nora as she threatens to stamp her "little foot" and thump her "little fist" if she doesn't get her way (*Was geschah* 30). In this manner, actions are not so much "performed" as "announced" to reveal Nora's unconscious appropriation of her familiar role of performing squirrel and chirping lark. Similarly, the other characters from *A Doll's House* are presented as one-track speech machines. For example, Anne Marie quotes automatically her cloyingly sentimental platitudes on motherhood, Frau Linde enacts her one-track spiel on care and devotion, and Torvald flatly pronounces his robotic clichés on fiscal and moral responsibility. Ultimately, these quotations reveal that the characters are merely acting out on an already previously-scripted life text, for it is important to remember that for Jelinek her characters "exist only in language, and as long as they speak, they are present, when they don't speak, they disappear."[10] In Jelinek's version,

> Nora epitomises the exploitation of woman as a sexual object, changing hands several times during the course of the action. But it must be noted that Nora collaborates in this process, for she uses her sexuality both subtly, by making herself attractive to Weygang, and overtly, to wheedle information from Helmer. In order to shatter the conventional connotations of love and marriage, Jelinek confuses these with the connotations of money and economics by having the former talked about in a style or jargon which would normally be used for the latter, and vice versa: "When one speaks of love, it should be presented completely in an objective manner, and when the conversation turns to economics the tone should be quite sentimental and sensual."[11]

Jelinek explains that anyone who at this time believes that it is still possible to present characters who act as individuals is strongly mistaken. "Instead, one can only present characters as zombies, or as holders of constructed ideology or significance, but not as fully developed individuals with joy or sorrow and all that garbage; that is gone, once and for all times."[12]

***Nora*** also presents the contradictions between bourgeois and working-class women's emancipation, and for this purpose Jelinek introduces Eva and the other women workers in the mill factory as the only truly new characters. In particular, Eva serves as Jelinek's skeptical mouthpiece, who in her radicalism, as Ute Nyssen comments, has strong affinities to Ulrike Meinhof.[13] Through Eva, Jelinek condemns Nora's romantic notions of individualism, particularly when the price for Nora's self-realization comes at the cost of the other working women's continuous exploitation, for Eva is the only one to understand that the sudden prettification of their working place with curtains, flower boxes, a library and even a children's crèche does not represent improvement but is instead a "cheap" cover-up for the unemployment that threatens once the factory changes hands.

Jelinek parodies the language of the contemporary women's movement from the play's first lines as Nora explains that she's left the comforts of her middle-class home so that she can develop herself from "object to subject" in the workingplace (7). Thus, Nora's "search for self" (9) clashes with the personnel manager's cynical observation that it is the task of employers to "promote and protect" the "full development" of the personality of their employees (7). While Nora's middle-class assumption is that emancipation comes through self-realization in work, for the mill-factory working women their "productive labor" in the factory is a necessary evil. The scenes in the factory illustrate not only Nora's naïveté but also her insensitivity to the plight of the other women workers, and Jelinek foregrounds this in the slight changes of vocabulary that separate the working women and Nora's vocabulary of 1970s women's liberation. As she tries to explain her abandonment of a husband, children and the comforts of her middle-class home to Eva and the other working women, it becomes evident that Nora's language, as the only medium of defining herself, is also what distances her from the other women, who cannot understand her pursuit of her self-determination as *Lebensaufgabe* (life's work), since for them the dehumanizing dailiness of clock-punching, piecework and quality control has more to do with *Leben aufgeben* (to surrender life). While Nora promotes her complexity in referring to her *Verteilung* (inner split) of personal desires, Eva and the others fear *Zerteilung* (dismemberment) by the machines. And while Nora attempts to convince them that marriage and children represent the "falsehood" that prevents women from exploring their innate destiny, Eva counters that for her and the other factory workers "the machine is the false part" (10).

Through these linguistic juxtapositions Jelinek illustrates that Nora's clichés drawn from the vocabulary of liberal feminism are nothing more than middle-class self-indulgences in the face of the working women's painful struggle with "self-alienation" and "self-estrangement" from love in marriage, the rearing of children and the comforts of home. The hypocrisy of Nora's middle-class values in the factory surfaces when within moments she recognizes that she has met the best that can be attained in Weygang and adopts the exaggerated discourse of sentimental love from pulp fiction. Ultimately, Jelinek's characterization of Nora represents her settling of accounts with liberal and radical feminism of the 1970s, and she focuses on the images that the Nora figure has assumed that exhibit the contradictions between her quest for self-realization and such helpless, dependent, feminine expressions as, "I frighten more easily than you do, since feelings are more feminine" (20). Nora's feminism, insofar as Nora understands it, is perverted into a deteriorated myth of the essential difference between the nature of a man and that of a woman.

Thus the whole repertoire of Nora's observations about the "essential feminine" (24) is drawn from social Darwinism (23) or biological determinism (23), and the theories from the turn of the century as well as the feminist theories of the 1970s ultimately appear as unhistoricized and unpoliticized reified myths, subsumed equally to the purposes of the radical left as well as the reactionary right, to terrorists or fascists. Therefore it is with extreme awareness of irony that Jelinek has Nora announce that she refuses to be "a sexual parasite" (52). Familiar quotations from Freud, Hitler and Mussolini on the woman's role are juxtaposed to equally recognizable phrases such as "the history of women until recently was the history of their murder" (51) from the radical feminist movement. In defending her use of these ready-mades, Jelinek explains that as an author she can present her meaning in her own words. However, she writes that "most things have been said so frequently that it's unnecessary to create something that has already been said elsewhere much better." Her main focus is not on the characters, who are, as Jelinek explains, mere self-conscious fictions, but on the nature of discourse as she probes language and its ability to reformulate, reiterate and translate the already spoken.[14]

Nora easily confuses such women's-movement-generated phrases as "pornography murders women" (18) with those from the pulp fiction clichés on love. As a result, when later in the play she is turned into an S&M Dominatrix figure from pornography, she does not recognize her situation. Similarly, she is reduced to a stereotype of a *femme fatale* (32), *femme fragile* (33), Wedekind's Lulu (40) or a flapper (57). Nor can she recognize misogynistic stereotypes when her new lover Weygang and his friends quote Freud or imitate Wittgenstein: "A woman is that which does not speak and about which one cannot speak . . . Precisely. This Freud says that first one has to experience what it means to be castrated before one can begin to speak" (24). Indeed, Nora unfortunately illustrates this point of view when she speaks: "My husband wanted me to be at home and closed up, since the wife should not look to the sides, but primarily into herself or her husband" (7).

What Jelinek shows is that Nora fails to develop a critical distance on her marriage with Torvald and instead appropriates the language of the 1970s feminists on the woman's role in marriage. In other words, one stereotype supplants another.

Thus feminist discourse does not liberate Nora but instead makes her a collaborator in the perpetuation of misogynistic stereotypes concerning the feminine. She uses Freud on "penis envy" to explain the inferior creative output of women (12) as readily as her references to "women's solidarity" which she interprets by the fact that "women . . . by nature have a stronger bond to each other" (13). Solidarity is thus made into another myth, which collapses in her confrontation with the manager's secretary, a scene that illustrates that class and status are in opposition to notions of solidarity:

NORA:

Are you not also a woman . . . ?

SECRETARY:

Of course, isn't that obvious?

NORA:

Why don't you look like a woman then, I mean cheerful? Why do you look so joyless?

SECRETARY:

When one's a private secretary to the manager one doesn't need to keep a grin on one's face all the time, particularly since one's personal life circumstances aren't necessarily pretty.

NORA:

Don't you feel some solidarity with me?

SECRETARY:

At most we have in common similar pain in childbirth. Although I suspect that I'll feel these pains more strongly than you.

(15)

The painful juxtapositions of Nora's rhetoric to the working women's reality are balanced with highly comical effects, as Nora tries out her rhetoric of liberal feminism and as she moves into the milieu of the "pillars of societies." Nora's movement into that world has to do with her "artistic" talents, which are soon put to good use by the personnel manager of the factory in which she now works to provide "classy" entertainment in the form of two choral arrangements for mixed voices and a short but "cultured" tarantella dance interlude for distinguished visiting dignitaries, among whom is Konsul Weygang. Indeed it is obvious that Jelinek's Nora has absorbed exceedingly well Torvald's guidance of the "talent" to please him as the spectator in their private theatre in *A Doll's House*. She reminds herself, in Jelinek's version, "to repeat the movements once more, as my husband taught me, sensually, but not too sensually" (18). Despite this she throws in acrobatic tricks and makes a backbend, thereby "deforming" her body. The manager of the factory takes up Torvald's former paternalistic position and scolds Nora for dancing so "tempestuously," for she might "hurt herself," and hence not be able to fulfill her piece-work quota. Weygang, however, is attracted by her grand leaps, twists and back bends. For the manager Nora's movements appear "uneconomical" (18), but for Weygang, Nora's body interprets the capitalistic rhetoric of "risk taking" capitalism, and her painful acrobatic exhibition serves as an ideal model of "flexibility" as she explains that "my husband wanted me sensual but not too sensual" (18).

To set off Nora's desirability on the market, Weygang foregrounds his total devotion and overwhelming desire for "my Nora my sunshine and my precious possession." However, though he is quite taken with his new possession, he shows that he is also interested in her exchange value before it turns into a loss: "What is significant about women is that they present easily damaged goods, quality before quantity" (26). The progress of the not-so-subtle buying and selling of Nora occurs when he tempts the Minister, who too would like to possess her, for "she could also be my sunshine as easily":

WEYGANG:

She not only has a face and body, but also a considerable general education.

MINISTER:

You're a good businessman, Fritz, one has to give you credit for that, you know how to sell.

WEYGANG:

Yes, I love her and am totally committed to her.

MINISTER:

I too could love her.

(26)

The Minister is excited by the description of Nora's market qualities of incomparable skin, body and charm, and Weygang entices him further by mentioning that her most significant asset is her childlike innocence which borders on perversion, almost exactly like Wedekind's Lulu, for like Lulu, Nora has no discernible moral standards. Since for Weygang Nora's sexuality is an abstract commodity, it can be traded in a similar manner as contracts for "futures" in the financial markets. Though Weygang puts the finishing touches to his deal with the Minister by proclaiming that he will live faithfully with Nora into old age "like Philemon and Baucis," he soon qualifies this sentimental allusion by letting the Minister know that once his passion wanes, Nora will become available for the minister's pleasure:

WEYGANG:

> In general, that's been my experience, the greatest passion lasts only a short while. If you wait until my passion has played itself out, you can take her.

MINISTER:

> Done.

WEYGANG:

> Losing Nora will be like a knife in the heart.

MINISTER:

> You shouldn't give her away for nothing. The administrations of three countries are tearing themselves to pieces over the deal, and I have the key to it.

WEYGANG:

> It's a deal. Let's say in three weeks.

(27)

Jelinek provides several perspectives from which to view Nora's body, for Weygang sees it as both a source for the regeneration of new energy and, simultaneously, an expensive investment. Nora too views her body as objectified goods or capital: "I've always taken care of my body" (19). In fact Nora's body provides an access to further riches, and both Weygang and Nora acknowledge that a business transaction has taken place as Weygang watches her perform the tarantella: "Don't I have the right to see my newest most expensive *property*," and Nora replies, "but I hope you also own many more expensive *properties*" (19). By showing the similarity of the language of market economies and love, Jelinek thus subjects the semantic romantic language of "you are precious to me" to examination. Thus *love* becomes a cover-up for the fact that the financially potent Weygang is going to help Nora in her climb up the social ladder. When Nora leaves the factory on Weygang's arm, Eva observes that behind their manifested love lies the "shadow of speculation" (22). In this manner Nora becomes property for the second time.

To enhance her own investment in her body, Nora's acrobatic exercises become a means of making her market value as a woman. However, with increasing age and decreasing attractiveness, her exercises become less pliable, less graceful and show her off to a disadvantage, and Weygang cold-bloodedly evaluates his investment and its diminishing returns: her aging body with its drooping ass, flabby arms and orange-like cellulose skin (55-6). When Nora's body is no longer of any use for Weygang, he accepts it as a market loss. In reflecting on the difference between capital and Nora's body, Weygang comes to the conclusion that unlike the spreading of a woman's body, "capital never decreases in attractiveness when there's more of it" (26), for "it's greatest attraction is that quite simply there's more" (28).

Many of the quotations from *A Doll's House* are distributed to Nora and Weygang, particularly Torvald's discourse on frugality and financial solidity. The quotation from Ibsen, "what's the name of the bird that eats up money," when it is placed into the context of a major speculation by Weygang, no longer represents Torvald's lecture on the bourgeois family ideal of fiscal responsibility. Instead, in the new context, the quotation functions as an expression of "exchange," for Nora can't just "eat up money" without paying for her keep. Weygang, the capitalist, can make out of money more money without producing anything. But Nora must literally give of herself; "otherwise buying and selling, trade and exchange come to a standstill" (30).

In Weygang's interests and the interests of capitalism Nora is completely dispossessed of her voice to make decisions about her body. Assuming her voice, Weygang speaks out both his and her part (32), and Nora remains standing benumbed (33). Wegang shows how well he knows Ibsen's *A Doll's House* by appealing to her to become his "partner" instead of his "little lark." And Nora has nothing with which to resist him but her whole repertoire of arabesques, backbends and splits. "Often," Weygang explains, "cruelty is a sign of love," as he convinces her in her own voice to seduce Torvald, for the entire enterprise depends on her: "Your big bear would jump around and do all kinds of funny pranks," he promises, disguised by her voice. He patiently explains that the situation at the factory resembles precisely that of Ibsen's *Pillars of Society* since in order for the "railroad" to be built for "the good of mankind," one must have information that will make it possible, for the construction of the "railroad" would make it possible to build "new, bright, and friendly apartments for the workers" which he will name the "Nora-Weygang Blocks." "Oh beloved of course," he concludes in her voice, "for now I belong to you entirely and truly" (29-33).

Despite Nora's illusions about the power of her love over Weygang, Weygang is the embodiment of absolute power that determines her sinking value in the sinking of her ass and hanging breasts. When initially Weygang invests in Nora, he offers his financial acceptability, and Nora in exchange offers her body. When later Nora attempts to create an even exchange once more by expressing her interest in his financial deals and so agreeing to play the S&M Dominatrix to get information out of Torvald, she doesn't understand that the exchange is uneven, and that Weygang looks upon her body as a subject perceiving an object, or the owner upon his property. It is a relationship in which Weygang has complete control over his goods. He can throw them away, sell them, conduct transactions and exchange, or whatever he chooses: "That's what one does with property, my little lark" (33).

Even as a Dominatrix, Nora's role is only one in appearance, for as Jelinek explains, fashion subjugates women particularly insidiously by means of that role. The costume of a Dominatrix is sadomasochistic, for the black leather and metal on naked flesh are imposed by the desire of men who must subjugate women even as they receive pleasure from the exchange. The reason, according to Jelinek, that the current fascination with the costume of the Dominatrix has become so strong is that men must break the resistance of women with renewed brutality. The Dominatrix in her thigh-high leather boots must ultimately be brought to her knees. And men who seek out a Dominatrix are overwhelmingly those in power positions, for they seek chastisement in torture chambers as a means of arousing their renewed feelings of innocence in the marketplace. However, business is transacted as usual, and Nora is not among the competitors, as usual (48). It is Weygang's power that "whips" Torvald into obedience; Nora is simply his whip. And even the words she uses to assault Torvald are not hers, for she is merely "reproducing" the already established relationship in *A Doll's House*.

The sentences that Jelinek sticks into Nora's mouth to accompany the lashes of the whip appear in Ibsen's text as affectionate endearments such as "Is that my little squirrel that's chattering . . . Is that my finch that is chirping?" (41-6). Thus, Nora holds Torvald to the same level of significance as he did her in Ibsen. She pokes fun at the ideal of his prudence and frugality. He can sell the factory grounds to Weygang "so that he won't have to borrow in the future" (46). Jelinek takes these passages, distorts them and pits them one against the other in order to show that these familiar discourses are the producers of myths of power relationships easily reproducible even by the powerless.

Despite her transitory participation on the side of power in the games that Weygang had initiated, all Nora has to defend herself against patriarchal power is the whole rage of clichés about "true love," the kind that is revealed in expressions such as "Your look pierces me like lightening" (19). Jelinek's dialogue debases each sentimentalized emotional moment, moving by turns from playfulness to mockery, and on to total undermining of all myths of love. Jelinek parodies the pattern of the romance novels in which falling in love is made part of the process of social ascent that ultimately culminates in marriage. But instead of "happiness" Jelinek makes visible the calculations that are part of the process, the addition and subtraction of market value. Since Nora's market value has fallen, Weygang pensions her off by giving her a choice of typical spheres of female entrepreneurship: a stationery store or a fabric store.

Using her skills as a composer of texts Jelinek brings the spectators back to the doll house "idyll" and Nora's new/old marriage with Torvald. Another reversal has occurred, for it is now Nora who works all day at the fabric store, while Torvald, having lost his job at the bank, does the accounts. As he pores over the daily receipts, he lectures Nora that the first stage of capitalist enterprise necessitates above all "the accumulation of capital" (60). All vestiges of middle-class manners and decorum disappear from the once genteel Helmer household as Torvald commands Nora "to shut your mouth," and Nora, in turn, screams at the returning children, "Shut your traps, you wretched brats. Can't you hear that your father wants to listen to the business news?" (61). The only trace of Nora's quest for self-realization is her complaint that Torvald "left her sexually unsatisfied last night" (60).

The evening news on the blaring radio reveals that the cotton mill and the adjoining housing projects have mysteriously gone up in flames during the previous night. It is further reported that the fate of the mill is presently unknown, though Consul Weygang, as chairman of the corporation with controlling interest in the mill, has given assurances that a speedy reconstruction is being considered in order "not to endanger the situation of the workers" (62). As Torvald speculates that most likely it was "the Jews that had ignited the fire," the news broadcast fades into a spirited march evoking the memory of early German fascism. Torvald's expression of delight, "I love to hear this music," ends the play (62). With the audible lingering strains of the "quoted" march, Jelinek illustrates how the mechanism of the historical process has been set into motion in re-enactment of the past.

*Notes*

1. See Elfriede Jelinek, *Was geschah, nachdem Nora ihren Mann verlassen hatte oder Stützen der Gesellschaften*, in *Theaterstücke* (Köln, 1984), 7-78, Subsequent references appear parenthetically in the text.

2. Quotations from German texts are given in translation. This and all subsequent translations from the German are mine.

3. Henrik Ibsen, *A Doll's House*, in *Six Plays by Henrik Ibsen*, trans. Eva Le Gallienne (New York, 1951), 79.

4. Elfriede Jelinek, "Ich schlage sozusagen mit der Axt drein," *Theaterzeitschrift,* 7 (1984), 14.

5. Elfriede Jelinek, "Gespräch mit Elfriede Jelinek," interview by Riki Winter, *Dossier über Elfriede Jelinek,* ed. Kurt Bartsch and Günther A. Höfler (Graz, 1992), 15.

6. Henrik Ibsen, *Pillars of Society,* in *Henrik Ibsen: Four Plays,* trans. Michael Meyer (London, 1990).

7. Elfriede Jelinek, quoted in Brigitte Landes, "Kunst aus Kakanien: Über Elfriede Jelinek," *Theatre heute,* 27:1 (1968), 7.

8. Michael Newman, "Revising Modernism, Representing Postmodernism," in *Postmodernism,* ed. Lisa Appignanesi (London, 1986), 48, quoted in Allyson Fiddler, "There Goes That Word Again, or Elfriede Jelinek and Postmodernism," in *Elfriede Jelinek: Framed by Language,* ed. Jorun B. Johns and Katherine Arens (Riverside, CA, 1994), 135.

9. Rosalind Krauss, "Poststructuralism and the 'Paraliterary,'" *October,* 13 (1980), 37.

10. Elfriede Jelinek, "Wir leben auf einem Berg von Leichen und Schmerz," interview by Peter von Becker, *Theatre heute,* 33:9 (1992), 4.

11. Allyson Fiddler, *Reviewing Reality: An Introduction to Elfriede Jelinek* (Oxford, 1994), 80, quoting Elfriede Jelinek as quoted in Stefan Makk, "Ein politisches Stück, ein Stück übers Kapital," *Kleine Zeitung,* 6 October 1979.

12. Yvonne Spielmann, "Ein unerhörtes Sprachlabor: Feministische Aspekte im Werk von Elfriede Jelinek," in *Dossier über Elfriede Jelinek,* 36, quoting Elfriede Jelinek in Barbara Alms, ed., *Blauer Streusand* (Frankfurt am Main, 1987), 41.

13. Ute Nyssen, afterword to Jelinek, *Theaterstücke,* 155. See note 1.

14. Jelinek, "Ich schlage sozusagen," 15. See note 4.

## Gregory H. Wolf (review date autumn 1998)

SOURCE: Wolf, Gregory H. Review of *Ein Sportstück,* by Elfriede Jelinek. *World Literature Today* 72, no. 4 (autumn 1998): 823-24.

[*In the following review, Wolf praises the lack of plot-driven action in* Ein Sportstück, *contending that the long passages of dialogue and monologue "allow Jelinek to diagnose and criticize directly society's ills."*]

**Ein Sportstück,** the latest drama from the controversial Austrian writer Elfriede Jelinek, is a brutally graphic condemnation of contemporary society's obsession with sports, the athletes who compete, the narcissistic attitude bred by athletics, and the language used to describe competition and victory. Stretching the bounds of dramatic form, Jelinek creates a work with very little action; she even admitted in a recent interview that there is none (*Der Spiegel,* 6 February 1998). Instead, she relies on long dialogic passages, and employs her command of language to portray a society in which the desire for competition, the indiscriminate use of violence, and the ultimate victory have created a new set of ethical and moral norms. The "athlete," a metaphor for the individual who, because of fame, power, and money, does what he pleases regardless of the feelings and welfare of others, pursues an agenda of immediate gratification, and, in doing so, debases humanity.

Jelinek organizes the drama around a group of core figures, including Electra, Achilles, and Hector from Greek mythology, who discuss the role of sports and humanity while kicking and torturing a sack which holds an unidentified individual. The faceless victim serves as a leitmotif throughout the drama. The athlete, lauded for his ability to crush and maim opponents, is analogous to the soldier who is trained to kill and wreak destruction upon his enemies. With a command of contemporary cultural symbols and pop culture, Jelinek compares these two modern gladiators and suggests that sports have led to the militarization of society and are directly responsible for the all-pervasive machismo attitude and increased violence. She employs expressionistic, indeed grotesque elements to underscore the propensity to commit acts of violence against faceless victims.

The long passages in *Ein Sportstück* allow Jelinek to diagnose and criticize directly society's ills. She uncovers male atrocities toward women, gross abuse of power, and a lack of communication between the sexes. Parts of the drama read, in fact, as essays condemning everything from television and the mass media to sports in general. With a postmodern approach, Jelinek creates an image which simultaneously alienates the reader while capturing his or her attention. The appearance of the author onstage underscores her desire to speak directly to the reader and to deconstruct the notion of literature as solely entertainment. By addressing current events such as the war in Yugoslavia and the bullish stock market, Jelinek forces the reader to reflect on his or her behavior within the larger framework of society.

Sports, like the military, rob the mother of her son and teach the son how to die without purpose. Whereas birth and life are associated with the realm of the mother, death and destruction are the man's. Due to these domains, the sexes have an inherent inability to communicate meaningfully with one another. Because of her willingness to create and preserve life, the woman is reduced to a weak being, not just incapable of competing but also possessing the status of an unworthy victim. Sports enable the male to act without reason and responsibility ("Sport ist die Organisation menschlicher Unmündigkeit"), and the necessity for competition leads to more victims.

With *Ein Sportstück* Jelinek suggests that the language of destruction, specifically the language of the military and war, has determined and framed the language of sports and, as such, has glorified violence, power, and individual bravado and degraded humanity. The "sportification" of society—e.g., the statistics of the dead in Yugoslavia and the nightly recap of murders in Rwanda—has numbed our senses to the victims and their suffering. Jelinek, who appears at the end of the drama, leaves the reader with a subtle reminder of life and death: "Wenn einer tot ist, dann kommt er nicht wieder."

### Rebecca S. Thomas (essay date 1999)

SOURCE: Thomas, Rebecca S. "Subjectivity in Elfriede Jelinek's *Clara S.*: Resisting the Vanishing Point." *Modern Austrian Literature* 32, no. 1 (1999): 141-58.

[*In the following essay, Thomas explores the theme of female subjectivity in* Clara S., *contending that "Clara's usurpation of power and will separates this drama from Jelinek's other works."*]

"Nur die Frau gibt es nicht und darf es nicht geben."[1] This dictum reflects Elfriede Jelinek's view that women are impossible as subjects in what she frames as a fascist, patriarchal, postwar, capitalist society. Work, love, marriage, motherhood, and art, all western institutions in which self-fulfillment has traditionally been sought and glorified, are systematically unmasked by Jelinek as delusion-filled prisons in which women are erased as subjects in dehumanizing power relationships. Jelinek's oeuvre functions as a prism, with each work acting as a facet through which one of these institutions is refracted, broken down into the constituent parts which individually undermine female potential.

In the early work, *Was geschah, nachdem Nora ihren Mann verlassen hatte* (1977), Jelinek picks up the tale of Ibsen's Nora. The open ending of Ibsen's drama has long been viewed as an invitation to see positive potential for Nora's self-development after she leaves her oppressive and infantalizing marriage. While Ibsen's Nora has become a symbol of female awakening and liberation, Jelinek's Nora must confront the exigencies of her reality as a woman trying to survive in the world of male-dominated capital and machines. She enters the work-world full of hope that income and career will be the path to "persönliche Verwirklichung:"[2] "Ich wollte mich am Arbeitsplatz vom Object zum Subjekt entwickeln."[3] However, instead of economic liberation, Nora discovers "daß Arbeit einen Menschen töten kann."[4] Women cannot actualize themselves "im Schatten des Kapitals."[5] Nora ultimately returns to Helmer, undoing the liberating gesture of her initial departure. The consequences for Nora's development as a subject are clear: "Noras selbst bleibt ein blinder Fleck . . . nichts sonst."[6]

The stultifying effects of capitalism and patriarchy on women's "Selbstverwirklichung" are similarly exposed in the novel *Die Liebhaberinnen* (1975), in which the deformation of women through labor and culture is symbolized in their work in a brazier factory and concretized in the misogynist relationships that fill their leisure time. These women are shaped physically and emotionally by outside forces. They are interchangeable parts reproducing culturally dictated norms. The "Trivialliteratur" that Jelinek parodies on the formal level of the work also creates "das falsche Bewußtsein"[7] that forms these women's consciousness and prevents any potential for authentic will or desire.

The female protagonist Erika Kohut in *Die Klavierspielerin* (1983) is likewise derailed in her attempts at self-becoming, this time by the duo of an abusive mother and classical music, both of which serve to stunt any growth or relation to self. Whereas Nora looks for the building blocks of a self in work only to discover the imprisoning qualities of capitalized labor, Erika seeks her substance and authenticity in culture, that is, in developing the inner life through music. However, as Jelinek deconstructs the hero-worship of such German holies as Goethe, Bach, Schubert and Brahms and systematically undermines the idea of "das befreite bürgerliche Subject"[8] that they represent, it becomes clear that art does not liberate, but rather it destroys Erika's life. She is left the numb and passive victim of abuse by men, mother and self.

Jelinek continues to dismantle the ideas of individualism and personal development in *Die Ausgesperrten* (1980) as she parodies the tradition of "Bildungsroman." The "Mythos der 'Einzelpersönlichkeit'"[9] and the cult of genius that is its extreme form, are revealed as faschistoid and particularly lethal to women. Although Jelinek's male characters are also victims of this culture, they nonetheless maintain a power relationship over women who remain in a worse situation. As Marlies Janz notes, this is "eine Formulierung, in der Frauen als 'Einzelpersonen' gleich zweifach ausgelöscht sind."[10]

In an interesting twist to the theme of female subjectivity, *Krankheit oder Moderne Frauen* (1987) presents female figures who are transformed into vampires. The vampire embodies the un-dead life of female existence that is echoed in the portrayal of women artists in *Clara S.* Within existing socio-political parameters, women are both there and not there. On closer inspection this means that women are present always as objects of abuse but never as subjects in creating themselves or their world. They are imprisoned by patriarchy, capitalism, and the culture industry, all of which unite to deprive them of agency in their own existence.

"Nur die Frau gibt es nicht und darf es nicht geben." This recurring refrain of Jelinek's work overall is the stated subtext of *Clara S.,* a drama that reveals the mechanism of this oft-posed negation but juxtaposes it against Clara's refusal to signify nothing. In fact, Clara's liberating moment comes in her refusal to signify anything other than her self, the one who is supposedly not there. Clara's usurpation of power and will separates this drama from Jelinek's other works by allowing her a moment of self-actualization that is denied Nora, Erika, and Jelinek's other female protagonists.

*Clara S.* (1981) explodes time continuity to bring together Clara Schumann (1819-1896) and Gabrielle D'Annunzio (1863-1938) in a scathing denunciation of individualism in its most extreme expression. The cult of genius, born in German Romanticism, culminating in Hitler and perpetuated in an underconstructed postwar society has manifestations in both art and politics.[11] Jelinek joins her critique of artistic and political traditions in the character of Gabriel D'Annunzio, the author and paramilitary leader who seeks fame and immortality in both arenas, and who embodies the abusive power relationships that are manifest in military conquest and covert but present in bourgeois art, according to Jelinek. By conflating the historic time frame within the drama, Jelinek emphasizes what she views as the link between nineteenth-century idealist traditions and their culmination in twentieth-century fascism.

The drama is set in 1929 at Il Vittoriale, D'Annunzio's palatial villa. Here, he has surrounded himself with women who depend on him for basic financial support: the Venetian pianist Luisa Baccara, the dancer Carlotta Barra, the painter Tamara de Lempicka, the housekeeper Aelis Mazoyer, a prostitute from the area, and finally "die Fürstin," D'Annunzio's wife whom he married to gain a title. Except for his wife, whom he generally disregards, D'Annunzio uses these women as sexual objects while holding out the promise of financial support and career advancement which is never quite forthcoming. Their conversations form a background of dependence and abuse that provide the context for the main action of the drama.

Clara Schumann has brought her husband Robert to Il Vittoriale to plead for D'Annunzio's aid and support. Robert is already mentally ill by this point, and the fact that he is attended by an "Irrenwärter" contributes to the subliminal impression that the action is set in an asylum, a trite but accurate metaphor for Jelinek's view of the nineteenth and early twentieth-century world. In Jelinek's revaluation of Clara Schumann, she paints an alternative portrait to the standard view of Clara as the model of wifely devotion and renunciation. Jelinek's Clara rises up to empower herself, a process she initiates by taking revenge on the husband who has thwarted her dreams and artistic aspirations.

Jelinek sets her negation of the feminine in the context of post-modernism, which augments her political critique of individualism with the view that any character constructed as an individual is untenable. In the modernist drama, dialog was reduced to existentialist monologue signaling the failure of inter-subjectivity in the modern era.[12] In the postmodern drama, dialog has been transformed again into a collage of cultural and linguistic clichés that is supposed to reflect the disappearance of the subject as origin and of subjectivity per se. In this paradigm, the self is reduced to "a shallow artifact of cultural production."[13]

While Jelinek's formal approach and the ideological statements she places in the mouths of her characters proclaim the end of subjectivity in general and of female subjectivity in particular, the drama contains tensions that undermine both of these claims. In order to discover where her radical critique of subjectivity breaks down it is first necessary to note the techniques Jelinek employs to lay bare the alleged destruction of the subject.

Jelinek illustrates the demise of the individual along the coordinates of postmodern decentering and Marxist culture critique, which together govern both form and content of *Clara S.* Jelinek reproduces the decentered ego of postmodernism through an extensive use of quotation, which supplants authentic dialogue. By displacing herself as the originator of her characters' dialog, Jelinek formally illustrates her denunciation of originality as elevated in the cult of genius. In a broader sense, this technique is meant to undermine the notion of origins per se. If the technique is successful, the *dramatis personae* do not appear as individuals asserting a Cartesian will and ego. They are not the origin of their own words and actions, rather they are the locus of intersecting discourses and desires. They are constructs of language, culture and the unconscious.

Frank Farrell describes this view of the world, in which everything but discourse disappears, in theological terms: "It is as difficult to find a space for human activity over against the formative power of the cultural economy as it was to find a space of genuine human agency over against the absolute freedom and predestining power of the divine will."[14] Farrell notes a huge "gap" between the observations made by postmodernists about cultural phenomena and the "radical philosophical conclusions that are thought to follow from them."[15] Although it is surely necessary and desirable to reconsider subjectivity within the context of cultural forces, we must not necessarily conclude that the self recedes totally in their sway. Indeed, "very much of what was important to the modern notion of autonomous, self-willing selves survives the disenchantment of subjectivity."[16] In other words, the issue of selfhood is not an absolute proposition: either totally autonomous Cartesian will or a totally deterministic culture monopoly. It is within this context that I will speak of subjectivity and selfhood in *Clara S.*

Jelinek's use of quotation to decenter dialog has been widely noted and analyzed, particularly as it reveals the impact of this formal gesture on our reading of the figure of Clara.[17] It has been noted that a ventriloquist's voice often seems to be speaking through Clara's character, emitting strains of the alien discourses that combine in and through her.[18] The ventriloquist, I might add, is Jelinek, the *origin* of these juxtapositions, and a kind of auctorial voice who has, herself, somewhat transcended the power of discourse to become a controlling agent in its production. This paradox in the metatext is mirrored within the drama as Clara also resists and ultimately transcends the political and linguistic constraints on subjectivity that Jelinek posits as universal.

Although critics have focused primarily on the effects of discourse on Clara and the other female characters, we must be clear that in the world of this particular drama, if there is a "prison-house of language" it is a gender-neutral confinement. The question of quotation and its effect on our reading of the male characters is, however, scarcely discussed. That Jelinek quotes Robert Schumann's letters and Gabrielle D'Annunzio's correspondence and novels in constructing their characters carries a heavy implication for a predominantly feminist critique: both men and women are displaced as subjects, both are located within linguistic-cultural structures that guide their behavior and speech. In this sense, Jelinek illustrates Barthes' dictum "Die Sprache spricht" and gives shape to her own claim that "der Individualismus nicht mehr möglich ist,"[19] a claim that sweeps across the borders of gender and class.

The universal revocation of selfhood that is suggested on the formal level stands in contrast to the exclusive nullification of the female subject that is sustained on the thematic plane. In her critique of the material power structure which is informed by her stance as a communist[20] Jelinek focuses heavily on the relationships of gender and patriarchy. Although she rejects the feminist label,[21] she is aggressive in disclosing the impact of material conditions on women's lives. Her critique of male behavior and its consequences for individual women is scathing and unabating. This theme dominates such early works as *Die Liebhaberinnen* (1975) and *Wir sind lockvögel baby!* (1970) as well as the more recent novel *Lust* (1989), and it is a driving moment in *Clara S.*

Thus, the unilateral revocation of the feminine ("*Nur die Frau gibt es nicht . . .*" my emphasis) is primarily a function of the political landscape Jelinek paints, and it is juxtaposed against the wholesale negation of the individual through discourse. The discursive power that D'Annunzio holds is primarily a function of this political reflex. D'Annunzio, the Italian fascist writer and soldier, enunciates the negation that the women artists residing at the Vittoriale depict and experience: "Wahrscheinlich ist die Frau doch eher das Nichts" (84). His dual role as warrior and writer form the link of power and language that Jelinek posits. He controls the female characters' physical and material conditions and thus limits their access to self-determination and actualization. He has the power to deny female existence through his rhetoric thus mirroring on the discursive level the material destruction of women's lives within the patriarchal order that forms the backdrop of the drama. D'Annunzio's abuse and oppression of the female residents represents the social context and conditions that allow Robert to ruin Clara's life by denying her the opportunity for self-realization: "Komponieren durfte ich nie selber. Obwohl ich es so sehr wollte" (80).

As might be expected, the questions of sexuality and domestic responsibility play key roles in Jelinek's critique of patriarchy and its role in manipulating female experience. Jelinek circumscribes the conditions that govern the male-female dynamic in stark terms. D'Annunzio's power, which he derives from financial wealth, is played out in his sexual and emotional abuse of the female residents who are financially dependent on him, and who therefore have no recourse or defense against his advances. Corina Caduff describes Jelinek's characterization of these conditions clearly when she notes that within the drama she has made the "Vittoriale zum Bordell, D'Annunzio zum Zuhälter, die Künstlerinnen zu Prostituierten . . ."[22] Clara alone refuses to relinquish control of her sexuality to the Commandante: "Mein Künstlerinnenkörper, der früher sogar selbsttätig komponiert hat, als er noch Zeit dafür hatte, wird von Ihnen nicht geschändet werden" (68). She withholds the sexual act as a decree of independence, as a protection of the boundaries of her self.

Predictably, D'Annunzio meets her failure to acquiesce with a violent emotional response. Not only does he harm Clara vicariously by molesting her daughter, he also fantasizes that Clara herself wants to be raped: "Wie in einem Blitz sehe ich Sie hingestreckt. Jetzt sind Sie müde und dürsten voll Begierde, genommen und durchrüttelt zu werden. Kommen Sie, das machen wir jetzt gleich! Anschließend werde ich Ihnen beschreiben, was den kühnen Eroberer von einem ebenfalls kühnen Künstler unterscheidet. Nichts im Prinzip" (69). The rape motif that lingers ready to erupt at the border of bodily "Hingabe" is the violent conquest of anyone who will not willingly surrender her "self." By equating the conqueror and the artist, D'Annunzio's remark underscores again the power inherent in the world of signs/language. Although Clara's refusal to give herself to D'Annunzio signals the germination of her rebellion, she nonetheless remains trapped in her domestic obligation to Robert until the final act of the drama. Her alienation and resistance to norms is an undercurrent throughout.

In a further political commentary Clara describes how, in the exclusively domestic role, her self, and particularly her creative self, has been consumed. She has become a living sacrifice to Robert's productivity, both in his idealization of her as muse and in her domestic labor which freed his time for the creative act: "Ich bin im sakralen Raum deiner Genialität geopfert worden, Robert" (93). Male-artist and female-muse are inextricably intertwined: "Meist aber ist die Frau dann schon eine verdorrte Wurzel, während der männliche Künstler noch voll im Saft steht" (75). The sacrifice of female subjectivity is symbolized in the withering of the body: "Dieser Wahn der Selbstverwirklichung. Die Frau bezahlt es. Es zahlt die Künstlerfrau. Ist sie ebenfalls Künstlerin, verfaulen ihr die Gliedereinzeln bei lebendigem Leib unter der Kunst-produktion des Mannes" (75). Jelinek links her portrayal of material and domestic power with illustrations of male control over the language and discourse that creates and maintains norms of female experience. This formative power of the image maker is augmented by the Olympian power to grant and revoke existence through language.

In the confluence of material and discursive power in the persons of Robert and D'Annunzio, the notion that none of the characters controls language begins to break down. The Commandante clearly uses it to define and limit female experience and expression. It is not simply the case that the feminine doesn't exist and that the Commandante describes this pre-existing condition. It is rather the case that the feminine has been denied through male speech and political will, that is, through the speech acts and behavior of particular men who presumably could have chosen otherwise but elected to abuse their power. This is the root of Jelinek's critique of patriarchy. We encounter here a pointed political comment, not an existentialist cry against an immutable linguistic fate.

Jelinek illustrates male control over discursive power within the realm of art, the unabashed province of signs, in which men create, and women are created as ideals, muses or the work of art itself. With the exception of Clara, the women of the drama are objects that become interchangeable with and indistinguishable from art. Their function is to be viewed and admired. This sublimation of individual women into aesthetics guarantees their disappearance into "nichts," as their subjectivity is displaced by their function as works of art. The extreme idealization of women in art can only be fulfilled through total abstraction from the social or real, that is, by draining the woman from her image. The reduction of women to a purely instrumental role in aesthetics amplifies and augments D'Annunzio's and Robert's use of women as the objects of conquest and inspiration. It is precisely the question of who controls discourse that is at stake in this power play.

In the political and aesthetic realms, which clearly co-define each other, the end of female subjectivity is signaled in women's reduction to roles, abstractions and ciphers that change their significance according to male needs. Jelinek expresses the insubstantial quality of her female characters through repeated images of incorporeity. The loss of body has the varying functions of expressing loss of self and general invisibility within the culture. Each of these is the expression of a void or "nichts" where there should be a woman.

Jelinek's choice of female artists for her collage underscores this conflation of women and art. Except for Clara, the women artists who populate Il Vittoriale only perform art; they do not write, compose, choreograph, or paint. Their artistic production is in fact reproduction, and thus immediately related to their bodies: "Luisa: Sängerin müβte man sein. Die Leute staunen bei einer Frau noch viel mehr, wenn sie die jeweiligen Töne ausschlieβlich mit dem Körper ohne Aushilfenahme von Geräten hervorbringt" (79).

The singer's voice (body) *is* her art in which she becomes symbolic and disappears. Carlotta, the dancer, also uses her body as medium: "Ich drücke Kunst ausschlieβlich mit Hilfe des Körpers aus, wobei ich imstande bin, jeden Millimeter von mir auf das Unwahrscheinlichste zu verbiegen, beziehungsweise zu verdrehen" (83).

Her body is her language, with which she defines what she cannot express verbally. Her specific identity is absorbed into the abstraction of her art, and she ceases to be: "Ich bin sozusagen die Kunst in Person" (83). In her role as art, her subjectivity is engulfed and disappears. As art, she becomes a signifier, pointing beyond herself, a self that is both there and not there. She does not have access to language because she *is* language, raw symbol. These women artists document the social transformation of women into "things of beauty," aesthetic artifacts.

The woman's body is dislocated from her other attributes as the first step in aesthetic commodification. The women artists of the drama are not "Künstlerinnen," they are "Künstlerinnenkörper" and "Tänzerinnenkörper" (68). As such, they lose all individuation and become interchangeable within the dehumanizing mass-culture represented by the Commandante: "Wir haben hier noch mehr Künstlerinnenkörper außer Ihrem im Haus. Hier kommt zum Beispiel gleich ein Tänzerinnenkörper angewirbelt" (68).

Paradoxically, when the woman is reduced to all-body, she becomes no-body. The body itself is subsumed in the abstraction and becomes incorporeal: "Carlotta: Wir Tänzerinnen sind mehr als alle anderen Menschen Flaumfedern. Unsere Körper sind durchsichtig von Licht und Luft. Am Boden hält uns nichts. Manchmal sind wir weniger Licht und Luft als ekstatische Priesterinnen unserer Kunst. Wie jetzt soeben. Man sucht uns auf wie ein Pilger ein fernes Altarbild!" (69). The dancer is no longer a woman but an idealized projection. Art has become a pseudo-religion leading to transcendence. The women, however, do not experience transcendence, rather they are priestesses who point the way for others. By cultivating themselves as the objects of worship and dedication, the women artists participate in their own destruction. Their role is to be viewed and admired, "im Auge eines Mannes schön zu sein" (71). This objectification neutralizes them as subjects.

The religious icon refers to a transcendental being. Moreover, like the secular work of art, its function is by definition metonymous. Now as a symbol for both the holy and the aesthetic, woman stands in for an already symbolic artifact referring beyond and away from herself. As either an art work or religious icon, she attracts attention to herself in order to deflect that attention immediately away to a deferred meaning other than herself. In this depletion of self, she becomes "ecstatic," in the sense of being separated from her body, which becomes "Licht" and "Luft" as she loses it. This loss occurs at the altar, where devotion also requires a sacrifice.

Jelinek allows Clara to resist these images of incorporeity and absence when she remarks on the Commandante's response to the ethereal conception of women he himself has invoked: "Das mit der Körperlosigkeit zieht bei ihm nicht so recht. Soll ich lieber sagen, die Frau ist ein schweigsames, aber faulendes Loch?" (85). Clara attempts to bring substance back to the idea of woman by invoking an image to replace or fill the "Körperlosigkeit." Ironically, she chooses the image of a "Loch," a void that cannot be filled without destroying itself, and the substance of which is by definition that which is not there. The "Loch" is, however, like the woman, not nothing. Its meaning lies precisely in the circumscription of the presence of an absence. Insistence on this presence, however tenuous, characterizes Clara throughout. This insistent presence is paradigmatic for Jelinek's portrayal of women in culture, and she consistently seeks ambiguous figures to represent the dual nature of this existence that is not one. Sigrid Berka's analysis of ***Krankheit oder Moderne Frauen*** in which she speaks of the female vampires in terms of "present absence" and "undead life" echoes this point.[23] The "Loch" and the vampire are both there and not there, real and unreal.

In ***Clara S.,*** this present absence is located in the sociocultural arena where women are denied potential as subjects. Jelinek's critique of the cultural fetishization of the female body parallels her parody of the overemphasis on the male intellect, specifically as the alleged origin of subjectivity, genius, and artistic production. Disproportionate attention to the female body in the drama is set in relief against the exaggerated significance ascribed to the male head. The artificial polarization of male-mind versus female-body necessarily results in the polarization and alienation of mind and body within each individual. In Clara's opening line she laments: "Mein Inneres kämpft so stark gegen mein Äußeres an. Das Äußere hält die vergeistigte Frau für unwichtig" (64). Because she has crossed the border of gender-appropriate behavior, she has become alienated from her body, and the other women remark on her "Körperfeindlichkeit." Because women are socially constructed through their relationship to body-nature, this estrangement from the physical is in fact alienation from the self.

Drawing out the parallels, Jelinek contrasts women losing their bodies to males losing their heads; in each case the threat is against the defining attribute: "Clara: Robert, die Bestie, fantasiert die ganze Zeit, daß er seinen Kopf verliert . . . Diese ungeheuerliche Angst vor dem Verlust des Kopfes! Da er doch weiß, daß darin seine Genialität haust wie der Wurm im Apfel" (65). Jelinek is unsubtle in her use of the castration metaphor: "Natürlich ist das eine Verlagerung von unten nach oben" (72). Robert Schumann's mental infirmity lends itself to ample word play on this topic, as his "losing his head" can be alternately interpreted as going insane and losing male potency. In this word play, the idea of specifically male intellect is enhanced by the phallic reference. The antithesis of this deduction also obtains: in Jelinek's theatrical asylum, women, who have been culturally defined and limited as all-body have no capacity for intellect or creativity because they lack the crucial "head."

Jelinek attacks the institution of genius and creativity as a self-deception (Robert is unaware that the themes running through his head have all been composed years before). Robert and D'Annunzio's grandiose claims to greatness appear ludicrous in light of the banality of their accomplishments as drawn by Jelinek. It is nevertheless clear that Jelinek finds the exclusion of women from the maligned realm of creativity reprehensible. The critique of patriarchy's attempted monopoly on genius is clear throughout the drama. The latent valuing of this realm, even in its imperfect or deluded state, sets the ethical tone of the drama: women's exclusion from cultural activity, which Clara continually bemoans, is clearly viewed as unjust. The desire for participation and the sense of injustice that lingers in the accusations against Robert and D'Annunzio undermine Jelinek's devaluation of the artistic tradition and in fact elevates the longing for inclusion to a moral principle.

Although this is evident in the portrayal of the secondary tier of female artists who have been reduced to objects of male will, it is even more evident in Clara's resistance to this exclusion. Clara alone among her female peers transcends the social parameters that would deny her access to intellect and creation. In her art she goes beyond acting as a medium, beyond performing works created by her male counterparts: she moves from re-production to production. Her desire to compose for herself is an attempt to break out of the nothingness, to countermand the ban on female selfhood and become a subject through action. Even her extraordinary performing talent is driven by the desire to be "selbstschöpferisch" (96). She refuses to be constructed solely by the gaze of the spectator, or to perpetuate the silence of the object. Her composition is an act of individuation. She acts as a subject when she has been constructed as object; she exercises her mind when she has been constructed as body. Her defiance of the "nichts" comes in her refusal to signify nothing.

Clara's ability to break the bonds of negation is predicated on two conditions: first, on her ability to escape Robert's controlling grasp, and second on her ability to appropriate the supposedly male-symbolic universe for herself, that is, to find a way to control and manipulate language. She can only reclaim her self for her self in the context of Robert's demise because she must create a space for her existence. She cannot simply leave the villa and seek a more congenial atmosphere because she, like the other women, depends on the Commandante for financial support: "Ich brauche das Geld!" (85). In addition, she must rid herself of Robert's specter. His personality and the sense of duty she feels as his wife are dominating forces in her mind. As long as he is alive, she will exist only in relationship to him, and in this relationship, she will always be a shadow.

The murder scene symbolically delivers the death-blow to the established hierarchy. As in many traditional works (Hebbel's *Judith* for example), the decay of male efficacy is accompanied by the cessation of female submission. In each case, women gain stature and control proportional to the weakness of their male counterparts. Robert, the representative of decrepit male culture, has passed on his infirmity to his children, indicating the progressive nature of the decline, particularly in the male line of succession: "Clara: Söhne! Söhne! Wenn ich Ihnen doch sage, Gabriele, meine Söhne waren in der Qualität noch miserabler als die Mädchen, mit Ausnahme Maries . . . Ansammlungen von schwersten Krankheiten, meine Söhne" (81). As the masculine figures degenerate, female characters become proportionally more vigorous and powerful. Clara's development from acquiescence to action is predicated not only on her own inner drive but also on the power-vacuum created by the decline of masculine potency.

Jelinek's fantasy of subversion is melodramatically acted out when Clara strangles Robert (with hands ironically made strong by piano playing) and then climbs the phallic mountain, thus claiming the symbolic universe for herself: "Ich habe jetzt keine Angst vor weiblicher Radikalität mehr und erklimme soeben ein phallisches Symbol. Und *du* kannst gar nichts dagegen machen" (99 my emphasis).

This is a revolutionary moment that requires the agency of a subject. In fact, this act of liberation and appropriation has been Clara's goal and the impetus behind her creative endeavors all along. Until this time she has been thwarted by repeated pregnancies and Robert's meddling in her composition. Now, after Robert's death, as she climbs the mountain, she claims language without becoming it. In claiming language she transcends her female counterparts whose identity with the mode of signification precluded their control over it. In this context, one might usefully recollect the oft pilloried claims of Freudian and Lacanian psychology that define women as "lack" (lacking the phallic signifier, hence true access to signification). The inevitable outcome of this definition is Lacan's negation of woman per se[24] that echoes Clara's lament "Nur die Frau gibt es nicht und darf es nicht geben" (103). By climbing the mountain, appropriating the means of signification, Clara countermands this edict. Although she cannot escape the system of language, she can, like Jelinek, momentarily attain an Olympian stance (symbolized in her ascent) that allows her to manipulate the structure, molding it to her will.

Clara uses the symbolic tools she gains to compose her life plot to create the text for her own life that will be completely self-referential and absolutely hers: "Ein vollkommen neues Gefühl kommt über mich, das *ich selbsttätig* hervorrief. Was der Künstler erlebt, setzt er gleich in ein Werk um" (98 my emphasis). When Clara goes to the piano, she authors her own death through music. This "Werk," which she emphatically declares is the product of her independent will, refers not away from her but always back to her: she is creator and created. Clara's death highlights a valid critique of the western canon which is littered with the corpses of women sacrificed for men and ideals. This moment of cultural critique does not, however, nullify her moment of being.

Clara's final transformation in music recalls the drama's distinctly Nietzschean subtitle: "musikalische Tragödie." Despite Jelinek's attempt to break fully with the western tradition which she criticizes, certain elements that do not allow themselves to be fully deconstructed into culture critique persist in *Clara S.* Although one can only suppose an ironic intent behind labeling a work "Tragödie" when it is built around characters who are presupposed to be without subjective qualities hence incapable of experiencing or portraying the heroic or the tragic, Clara's "development" within the drama does in fact lead to the formation of a tragic knot: the vehicle for her self-becoming is also the mechanism of her self-destruction.

In the *Geburt der Tragödie aus dem Geiste der Musik,* Nietzsche develops the Apollonian-Dionysian polarity. This tension is central to the question of subjectivity in *Clara S.* Nietzsche defines the Appolinian as the *principium individuationis* and the Dionysian as the dissolution of individuation in the communal rite. In the Nietzschean world view, tragedy lives in the dialectic of these two forces.[25]

On the formal level of *Clara S.*, Clara is portrayed as fundamentally non-individuated. The myriad voices speaking through her for much of the drama might be viewed as a type of post-modern chorus, multi-vocal, representative of the community, often in the role of commentator. However when Clara ascends the mountain, emphasizing the first-person pronoun over against Robert's distinct "du," she achieves a moment of Appolinian individuation which, in Nietzsche's lexicon, is also linked to the heroic a status which Clara achieves after the demise of male heroes. In the context of Jelinek's postmodern cynicism, the idea of the hero seems to strike a dissonant, even ridiculous chord. Yet the hero in the Nietzschean sense, an individual with the strength to rise above the "Massenmenschen" and stand alone, is specifically what is required on the political-revolutionary axis of Jelinek's critique and what is delivered in the person of Clara. The reference to the heroic here is thus made in full recognition that "Ironie auch der Rezeption dieser [Jelineks] Texte eingeschrieben."[26] In this case, however, reading against the grain leads back to undeconstructed traditional paradigms.

Clara's new subjectivity is not absolute or permanent. It is the momentary harmonization of the fragmented self in the moment of action. This self is subject to change and reconfiguration, but there is clearly a moment of consistency in the tension between the two poles from which issues the agency of will and self-determination. Clara's will and arising awareness of self derive specifically from her emerging cognizance that she has been dislocated from her self in the past. Consequently, the experience of this Dionysian non-individuation as depicted in her creation out of quotes and in her function as a "generic" woman is the precondition for her momentary becoming. Her autonomy is an achievement (hence the appeal to the heroic), not a "metaphysical given."[27] While it is true that even notions of the desirability of a self who values freedom arise within the context of cultural discourse, there is nonetheless a moment of "discovery . . . as we come to understand better . . . the worth of a self that can relate to itself as something to be worked upon and chosen . . ."[28] This moment of discovery is made apparent in Clara's action.

Viewed through the prism of the *Birth of Tragedy,* it becomes a matter of some consequence that Jelinek has chosen a musical "heroine" who dies in a "Rausch" of music. The Appolinian principle of individuation gives way to dissolution. But in authoring her own death, Clara transcends the subject-object dualism of politics, art, and discourse: she creates a musical text of herself in death. Consequently, Clara's death includes and maintains both the moment of individuation and its transcendence, the tension that Nietzsche prescribes as constitutive of tragedy. The text thus reveals a certain unity in fragmentation, a dialectic of self which, in moments of mediation between the Appolinian and Dionysian, has the capacity to overcome dissolution and become a navigating force in the maelstrom of opposing discourses.

Most analyses of *Clara S.* accept the view that when it comes to Clara's character "nichts Erkennbares, keine weibliche Substanz . . . verbirgt sich unter den Zitaten,"[29] that there is, in effect, no authentic woman behind the curtain. Annette Doll, for example, claims that Jelinek builds her figures out of "vorgefertigte . . . Weiblichkeitsbilder" that leave "keine Vision einer weiblichen Künstlerin."[30] Walter Klier sees "nichts Eigenes . . . das dem zitathaft eingesetzten trivialen Material übergeordnet wäre."[31] Günther A. Höfler asserts "der reine Objektstatus der Figuren und ihre absolute Dezentrierung in gesellschaftliche Determinanten."[32] In this view, feminine absence is viewed as a prefiguration of post-modernism and becomes theoretically avant-garde.[33] Indeed, according to this model, women's failed access to bourgeois subjectivity and authenticity has prevented them from indulging in the search for self that Jelinek laments and lampoons as naive.[34] By forfeiting their claim to authenticity, women have pre-figured the post-modern age, and "In diesem Sinne wäre die weibliche Künstlerin von jeher eine postmoderne Autorin."[35] Presumably this would apply to both Clara and Jelinek.

Despite both textual and critical assertions to the contrary, there is indeed not a nothing but rather a woman behind the curtain, even as that curtain is drawn by Jelinek. While Jelinek attacks as fascistic and destructive what she characterizes as the specifically nineteenth-century male drive for subjectivity, it is precisely the prohibition against women's participation in this quest that creates the bitterness with which she portrays her male characters. Within the plot of the text, denial of access to these arenas engenders the longing and ultimately the outrage that motivate Clara out of her prescribed negation into action. Although the originality inherent in the genius ideal is viewed as a destructive force, the text reveals as deplorable the exclusion of women from the arenas in which the potential for creativity and authenticity is located. The desirability of striving for selfhood and individuality lingers in the implicit critique of patriarchy's suppression of women's voices and bodies. The longing to recover the aura of self is not only sanctioned but championed by the implications of *Clara S.* in which feminine subjectivity refuses to be nullified as Clara refuses to portray a silent absence.[36]

Finally, let me return to the questions raised in the rift between Jelinek's theoretical approaches. While the postmodern sensibility postulates the diffusion of subjectivity and the fragmentation of intentionality, the politically engaged theory that informs Jelinek's feminist stance demands personal responsibility and social change through individual action. Throughout the drama, Robert and D'Annunzio are not portrayed as mere victims of oppressive discourses which they unwittingly though lamentably carry out and reproduce. Instead they are depicted as co-producers of the system that destroys all women in its wake. They are portrayed as personally liable and reprehensible.

The implicit critique of patriarchal behavior *Clara S.* demands change, requires acknowledgment. However, by undermining the concept of the individual with even limited or contingent autonomy, Jelinek destroys the very target of her critique, namely, a responsible party, an entity with the capacity to do otherwise. This conflict within the theoretical matrix diminishes Jelinek's pointed critique to a blind rage, a senseless anger directed at people who are not responsible for their actions but are, instead, pawns in a reified system of culture without human intention.

In investigating the fissures pulling at the drama's form and content, it becomes clear that despite Jelinek's self-definition as a postmodern writer, the text does not unequivocally embrace the postmodern moment of anti-subjectivity that it illustrates. While the peripheral characters in *Clara S.* do unmask the mechanism of enforced feminine absence and Jelinek's formal techniques are designed to dislocate all subjects, Clara acts to clear a space in which she can create herself, a space in which she can say "I."

*Notes*

1. Elfriede Jelinek, *Clara S.: Musikalische Tragödie: Theaterstücke* (Hamburg: Rowohlt, 1992), p. 81. All further references to the text will be cited by page number in the text.
2. Elfriede Jelinek, *Was geschah, nachdem Nora ihren Mann verlassen hatte: Theaterstücke* (Hamburg: Rowohlt, 1992), p. 7.
3. Ibid., p. 8.
4. Ibid., p. 55.
5. Ibid., p. 60.
6. Ulrike Haβ, "Grausige Bilder. Große Musik: Zu den Theaterstücken Elfriede Jelineks." *Text und Kritik* 117 (1993), p. 23.
7. Marlies Janz, "Mythendestruktion und 'Wissen': Aspekte der Intertextualität in Elfriede Jelineks Roman *Die Ausgesperrten*," *Text und Kritik* 117 (1983), p. 38.
8. Elizabeth Wright, "Eine Ästhetik des Ekels: Elfriede Jelineks Roman *Die Klavierspielerin*," *Text und Kritik* 117 (1993), p. 52.
9. Janz, p. 41.
10. Ibid., p. 40.
11. Marlies Janz, *Elfriede Jelinek* (Stuttgart: Metzler, 1995), p. 53.
12. Peter Szondi, *Theorie des modernen Dramas* (Frankfurt: Suhrkamp, 1959), p. 62.
13. Frank B. Farrell, *Subjectivity, Realism, and Postmodernism—The Recovery of the World* (Cambridge: Cambridge UP, 1994), p. 245.
14. Ibid., p. 250.
15. Ibid., p. 247.
16. Ibid., p. 243.
17. Birgit R. Erdle, "'Die Kunst ist ein schwarzes glitschiges Sekret.' Zur feministischen Kunst-Kritik in neueren Texten Elfriede Jelineks." *Amsterdamer Beiträge zur neueren Germanistik* 29 (1989)p. 327-333.
18. Ibid., p. 327.
19. Donna Hoffmeister, "Access Routes to Postmodernism: Interviews with Innerhofer, Jelinek, Rosei, and Wolfgruber," *Modern Austrian Literature* Vol. 20, No. 2 (1987), p. 115.
20. Dagmar Lorenz, "Elfriede Jelinek's Political Feminism: *Die Ausgesperrten*." *Modern Austrian Literatur* Vol. 23, Nos. 3/4 (1990), p. 111.
21. Ibid., p. 111.

22. Corina Caduff, *Ich gedeihe inmitten von Seuchen: Elfriede Jelinek—Theatertexten.* (Bern: Peter Lang, 1991), p. 106.

23. Sigrid Berka, "'Das bissigste Stück der Saison': The textual and sexual politics of Vampirism in Elfriede Jelinek's *Krankheit oder Moderne Frauen,*" The German Quarterly Vol. 68, No. 4 (1995), p. 373.

24. Jacques Lacan, *Encore: Das Seminar Buch XX* Trans. Norbert Haas et. al. (Weinheim: Quadriga, 1986).

25. Friedrich Nietzsche, *Die Geburt der Tragödie. Werke.* Ed. Karl Schlechta (Frankfurt/M: Ullstein, 1980), p. 21.

26. Ingeborg Hoesterey, "Postmoderner Blick auf österreichische Literatur: Bernhard, Glaser, Handke, Jelinek, Roth," *Modern Austrian Literature* 23:3-4 (1990), p. 72.

27. Farrell, p. 243.

28. Ibid., p. 275.

29. Erdle, p. 329.

30. Annette Doll, *Mythos, Natur und Geschichte bei Elfriede Jelinek: Eine Untersuchung ihrer literarischen Intentionen* (Stuttgart: M & P Verlag für Wiss. und Forschung, 1994), p. 64.

31. Walter Klier, "In der Liebe schon ist die Frau nicht voll auf ihre Kosten gekommen, jetzt will sie nicht auch noch ermordet werden." *Merkur* 41 (1987), p. 424.

32. Günther A. Höfler, "Sexualität und Macht in Elfriede Jelineks Prosa." *Modern Austrian Literature* Vol. 23, Nos. 3/4. (1990), p. 103.

33. Erdle, p. 333.

34. Ibid.

35. Ibid.

36. Moreover, from the extrinsic view, one must be skeptical of the apparent coincidence that subjectivity is decried as a hoax and a fraud at just the historical moment in which women and other marginalized groups are becoming equipped to make their claims on self-definition and self-expression. Women cannot look back on the days of the eminence of the self-evident subject with nostalgia, and hence cannot cast aside the potential for their own self-becoming as a relic of a bygone age.

## Erika Swales (essay date April 2000)

SOURCE: Swales, Erika. "Pathography as Metaphor: Elfriede Jelinek's *Die Klavierspielerin.*" *Modern Language Review* 95, no. 2 (April 2000): 437-49.

[*In the following essay, Swales delineates the effects of Jelinek's "fierce pathography" through a close reading of* Die Klavierspielerin, *contending that her stridency generates "a sense of tensions that invite the reader to be not reductive but reflective."*]

Whatever kind of reputation Elfriede Jelinek may have, it is not that of a subtle, thoughtful author. Indeed, for many readers and critics, the stridency of her writing is the most defining characteristic, a stridency that has been variously applauded or condemned. Yet even stridency can generate its own dialectically complex echo. I begin this article by indicating some of the tensions that mark Jelinek's relation to the literary marketplace. Then, I consider one of her most strident texts, **Die Klavierspielerin** (1983).[1] Nothing can diminish the fierce pathography of this work, but I shall endeavour to show that far from being monolithic, the novel generates, by virtue of its aesthetic configuration, a sense of tensions that invite the reader to be not reductive but reflective.

The case of Jelinek epitomizes one of the ironies of late capitalist culture: here is an end-game Marxist writer, whose work denounces the all-pervasive power of the free market system that disfigures our material and cultural reality. Yet this very market has consistently absorbed her voice of outrage. The early novel **Wir sind lockvögel baby!** (1968), with its rebellious pop-art energy, was successfully processed by the public relations department of Rowohlt. In **Oh Wildnis, oh Schutz vor ihr** (1985), Jelinek mocks the mechanisms of the literary market ('Herrliche Prosa! Wertvolle Preise!'), only to be awarded the 'Heinrich Böll-Preis der Stadt Köln' in 1986 and the 'Literaturpreis des Landes Steiermark' in 1987. Similarly, the corrosive anger of **Lust** (1989) is honoured by the 'Preis der Stadt Wien für Literatur'. Nowadays, her writing in the critical margin enjoys editions and reprints into the thousands.

The contradictions inherent in Jelinek's relation to the dominant system show up most tangibly in the fact that she has published her major works with Rowohlt, whose *rororo* series epitomizes the interlinking of artistic creativity and the world of finance: in a full-page advertisement, the voice of the stock exchange is allowed to disrupt the literary text. Thus, for example, Jelinek speaks of the 'streng genommen marxistischer Ansatz'[2] of **Die Ausgesperrten** (1980), yet this very analysis is crossed through by the customary injunction to the reader to invest in 'Pfandbrief und Kommunalobligationen'. Equally tension-ridden is Jelinek's homepage on the Internet Here: a curtsying teddybear on strings invites us to enter the hidden chamber. The allusions to the iconography of the porn industry are perfectly clear, yet inside are extracts from her literary work and some highly demanding articles. This latest development again demonstrates that for Jelinek the literary text is not sacrosanct. It interlinks with all other texts of capitalist culture and only by openly acknowledging that dependency can it hope to negotiate a relative degree of autonomy.

Within the aesthetic economy of Jelinek's *œuvre*, such negotiations can prove knife-edged, precisely in texts that appear most uncompromising. As critics commonly acknowledge, the hallmark of her writing is one of all-pervasive aggression, 'von geballter Wut'.[3] In structural terms, it manifests itself in a fiercely sustained narratorial control which, in the name of a Marxist-cum-feminist analysis, makes no apology for a hard-line viewpoint and reduces events and characters to functional particles.[4] Stylistically, the 'geballte Wut' finds its most typical expression in sharply cutting formulations. But precisely this compositional mode (one thinks, for example, of **Die Liebhaberinnen**)[5] proves tantalizingly ambiguous: its aim is of course that of critical exposure, but in its sheer aggressiveness it comes close to replicating the grip of the control system it sets out to criticize. In particular, the hard-hitting rhetoric can be said to overlap all too closely with the slogans and soundbytes of capitalist culture. In this sense, Jelinek's work exemplifies the familiar complexities of critically inflected mimicry.[6] Furthermore, her ironically fractured intertexting, which since **Die Ausgesperrten** has become such a prominent feature, entails another set of contradictions. For this technique is grounded in, and expects from the reader, a considerable degree of 'Bildung'. **Lust,** for example, and above all **Wolken- .Heim** are in fact dependent on that high-bourgeois culture whose institutions and mechanisms Jelinek regularly debunks.[7]

I would, then, argue that such texts, for all their impressive moments, are ultimately entrapped in internal and external contradictions. By contrast, **Die Klavierspielerin** is in my view composed in such a way that the ferocity of the foregrounded statement constantly modulates into a richness of parallel intimations. Pathography is not allowed the last word.

In the first instance, of course, **Die Klavierspielerin** also comes across as a fiercely closed textual system. In terms of representation, the narrative stands as a merciless psychological case study, an autobiographically rooted account of a self deformed and destroyed by the all-powerful mother figure. The precisely observed (and explicated) power struggles between mother and daughter, between Erika and Walter Klemmer, and the narratorial close-ups that brutally magnify Erika's psycho-sexual pathology, her acts of self-mutilation, speak for themselves. Furthermore, the text repeatedly, albeit on occasion ironically, points to its own interpretative frame, a Marxist perspective coupled with the psycho-analytical theories of Freud and Lacan,[8] and thus would seem to kill off any interpretative reflectivity. As Janz warns, a psycho-analytical interpretation 'verdoppelt nur den Text, ohne ihm noch einen latenten Sinn abgewinnen zu können' (p. 72).

Nevertheless, we owe valuable insights to studies that have focused on the mother—daughter relationship. One thinks of Sigrid Weigel, who discusses the link between the tyranny of the mother and Erika's alienation from her own body, her voyeurism and sado-masochistic fantasies.[9] Allyson Fiddler, in her key study, follows similar lines of enquiry: invoking Juliet Mitchell's concept of psychosis, she argues convincingly that Erika, unable to break free from the mother, fails to attain subjectivity, sexual identity.[10] Janz shares this reading, but in addition suggests that whilst the text, like the protagonist, remains trapped in classical psycho-analytical models of femininity, as formulated by Freud and Lacan, it also unmasks them in part as 'Spiegelung der Geschlechterhierarchie und des Gewaltverhältnisses unter den Geschlechtern' (p. 81).

Such readings clearly help us to reflect on the place of **Die Klavierspielerin** within the genre of women's autobiography which since the 1970s has made a striking impact in the German-speaking countries. Yet they tend to isolate the text from the rest of Jelinek's work.[11] In consequence, the novel would seem to lack the socio-critical edge that is the hallmark of her writing, and to move alarmingly close to the genre of confessional autobiography whose general lack of 'gesellschaftliche Analyse' Jelinek herself finds deeply unsatisfactory.[12] In particular, psycho-analytical readings are rather restrictive as regards the evaluation of the novel's aesthetic organization. Thus Annegret Mahler-Bungers, who does discuss this issue, subsumes the aesthetic under a strictly psycho-analytical agenda: on her reading, the (self)destructive compulsion of the protagonist, the process of 'Abtötung', also informs the narrative, which systematically excises all emotion and warmth (p. 194). This undialectical alignment of theme and form on the part of the critic harbours considerable dangers: the force of the aesthetic is marginalized by being identified with the foregrounded thematic statement, and the question whether it might deviate from, and differentiate that statement, is simply not allowed to arise.[13] Thereby we are deprived not only of a decisive criterion by which to arrive at a balanced critical assessment (and that is urgently needed, given the polarized reception of Jelinek) but also of the possibility of defining the novel's place in the overall *œuvre*.

Recently, Ricarda Schmidt has addressed the aesthetic modality and rhetorical strategies of **Die Klavierspielerin.**[14] Whilst there are a number of points where my account coincides with hers, we come to rather different conclusions. Schmidt argues that the novel is a firmly closed textual system within which a number of almost predictable, ideologically underpinned devices can be traced. Overall, Schmidt is critical of the all-pervasive 'übergeordnete Erzählinstanz' (p. 355), a 'richtende Erzählerin' (p. 356). As I hope to show in the following, I share this reading only in part; viewed in its entirety, the textuality of *Die Klavierspielerin* strikes me as far more complex than Schmidt allows.

True, the foreground is dominated by the psycho-sexual drama, which, as I have suggested, is so self-explanatory that critical reflectivity can add very little. However, there are other sections to do with life in the city, and these raise the critical question of the extent to which the personal drama relates to the representation of that public life. It is here that the aesthetic, the compositional mode of the novel, comes into play. It is in fact far more complex than the foregrounded psycho-sexual drama first suggests: the text shifts between irony and pathos, the stylistic registers range from the crudely immediate to the intensely poetic, and, overall, Jelinek works here with a multiplicity of representational means. Paradoxically, the aggressive overtness of the textual foreground generates narrative strategies of subtle, yet powerful indirection. In particular, as I shall show, the novel is driven by constant shifts between the literal and figurative. Precisely this disposition lends the text a conceptual and cognitive force that extends well beyond the personal drama of mother and daughter, Klemmer and Erika. In consequence, the autobiographically rooted case study acquires a socio-critical and, ultimately, existential dimension that enriches the text's import at every turn. It is in its profusion of significances, and in its sense of the interplay between them, that the power of *Die Klavierspielerin* resides.[15]

On the overt level, then, Jelinek's Marxist-cum-feminist voice unleashes its anger in unashamedly overt fashion. Here, totally crude patternings, be they of images or of codes, dominate and drive home their polemic point. Take her use of the economic code: its all-pervasive presence flaunts the authorial perception of society as one gigantic market place and stock exchange. Accordingly, Erika's artistic ambition is expressed in the code of finance: 'So wartet SIE ungeduldig, daß ihr Wert als künftige Spitzenkraft der Musik an der Börse des Lebens steigen möge' (p. 87). For her pupils, the pursuit of music signals the 'Aufstieg aus den Tiefen der Arbeiterschaft in die Höhen künstlerischer Sauberkeit' (p. 30). Economizing is of course the overriding imperative in the petty-bourgeois Kohut household, and Jelinek mercilessly brings this pattern to bear upon Erika's relation to her own body, comprehending it as 'Kleingeld' and 'Sparschwein' (p. 241). Similarly, there are countless allusions to the world of mechanization, which reduce human relations to automated processes and capture the dehumanizing grip of the surrounding system. Again, the patterning here is predictable, but it does generate moments of grim humour. Hence, in the peep-show, male masturbation is represented thus: 'Zehn kleine Pumpwerke sind unter Volldampf in Betrieb' (p. 55). As the code of labour invades the representation of porn films, the male is likened to a 'gelernte Mechaniker' hammering away at the 'kaputte Auto, das Werkstück Frau'. Wryly, the narrator concludes: 'In den Pornofilmen wird allgemein mehr gearbeitet als im Film über die Welt der Arbeit' (p. 108). To take a final example from the specifically feminist sphere: biting satire pervades the representation of the power struggle between Erika and Klemmer. Sexual pursuit is constantly couched in terms of the hunt, 'Jagd', 'Jäger', 'Jagdbeute' are key motifs in this familiar design of the battle of the sexes.

As these few examples suggest, on this level of the narrative, Jelinek's ideological control would seem to be total; the text is not allowed to generate an aesthetic force of its own, but figures in fixed correlation to the author's ideational system. This aspect is well analysed by Ricarda Schmidt, but she confines the import of *Die Klavierspielerin* to such instances of totalizing aesthetic and ideological control. It is, however, precisely at such points that *Die Klavierspielerin* as a textual system fractures under its own monolithic pressure and generates spaces of much freer signification. This emerges most vividly if the constant allusions to the world of economics, labour, and power relations are contrasted with the countless images of animals that pervade the text. True, some may be predictable: Erika's disgust at her body is captured in the 'wanzige Ratte [. . .] die sich ihr Geschlecht nennt' (p. 86), and in her pathetic fantasies, the power of male sexuality parade as 'Wolf' (p. 46), 'Jungstier' (p. 80), 'Gemsbock' (p. 87), 'Panther' (p. 106). But for the most part, beasts of all shapes and sizes freely roam the textual landscape: 'Hirschkäfer' (p. 35), 'Kreuzspinnen' (p. 38), 'Walfisch', 'Seehund' (p. 42), 'Taube' (p. 46), 'Nachtschmetterlinge' (p. 52), 'Lämmer', 'Kuh', 'Affen' (p. 70), 'Schwan' (p. 71), 'Igel' (p. 100), 'Ochsenfrosch' (p. 111), 'Kaffernbüffel' (p. 145), and many more. This carnivalesque assembly of beasts is quite beyond the underlying ideological control system.[16] As a textual breakaway, it is reminiscent of the narrator's comment in *Die Liebhaberinnen*: 'Jedes noch so rigide system hat irgendwo eine lücke, durch die man schlüpfen kann' (p. 87). Whilst the protagonists' attempts to escape are doomed, in *Die Klavierspielerin* the aesthetic force is able to exploit the gaps within the text's ideological frame. This is in sharpest contrast to, say, the utterly monolithic writing of Jelinek's compatriot Werner Schwab, whose 'Fäkaliendramen' are driven by a similar loathing for the petty-bourgeois world.

The double aspect of a claustrophobic textual system that yet exploits its own 'Lücke' is crucial for an understanding of the structural principles that are at the centre of the narrative: circularity and repetition. They inform the overall story line, every step within it, and they reverberate, as I shall show, in precise textual details. At one level, they assert that all attempts by Erika to break out from the mother/daughter dyad are futile, and she ends up where she started.[17] Ideationally, these fundamental configurations mirror Jelinek's conception of the social world as a closed system. Circularity and endless repetition crystallize, in other words, her conviction that 'alles ist ausdeterminiert. Die Gesellschaft, wir in ihr, Trieb-, Räder-, Walzwerk. Automatisierte Fabrik'.[18] To this degree, the compositional principle prefigures the reductivism of Schwab's *Der reizende Reigen* (1995), which extends the Viennese focus of Arthur Schnitzler's play into a social criticism of bourgeois society. At another level, however, Jelinek's use of circularity and repetition acquires a poetic energy of its own whereby the narrative turns into a web of interconnected literal and metaphorical intimations. It is here that the private story of Erika is constantly made to link with a much more public and differentiated narrative. On a purely psychological reading, the combination of circularity and repetition amounts to sheer pathography; coercion and violence, the patterns of Erika's childhood, spent in the straitjacket of piano practice under ruthless maternal supervision, replicate themselves in the scenes at the music school where Erika now presides over her pupils. Likewise, the power struggle between mother and the adult daughter doubles in Erika's relationship with Walter Klemmer. But, within the overall context of the novel, this private psychological drama acquires a metaphorical force; its compulsively repetitive patterns link throughout with the pathology of the social world. Thus, the coercion that marks Erika's life turns into a generalized social pattern; one thinks, for example, of the young victims at the music school: 'Ihre Eltern zwingen zur Kunstausübung. Und daher kann das Fräulein Professor Kohut ebenfalls die Zwinge anwenden' (p. 13). Erika's compulsions, above all her imperative need for 'Gehorsam' (p. 104) and 'Besser sein als andere!' (p. 16), magnify general, socio-cultural 'Wiederholungszwänge'. The deadly monotony of the Kohut life links with the utterly fixed order of the surrounding world. Here the text covers, in varying degrees, the span of Viennese society. At the top end, there is the cultural system of 'Wien, Stadt der Musik' with her 'fetten Bauch der Kultur' (p. 14), and as one of its subsets is the aristocratic Polish family with their merciless routine of Kammermusik (p. 62). Here, the narrative is informed by a hilarious sense of irony. But whenever the text tracks lower down the social scale, the tone becomes fierce. The Prater scene captures the dreary routine of family outings, their patterns of mental and physical violence within the hierarchical structure. The tensions are thrown into ironic relief by the 'Hochschaubahn' whose circular motion temporarily inverts the order of 'Unten und Oben' (p. 130). Or take the vision of Vienna by night, its popular culture. Here a poetically heightened register articulates a deadly monotony: 'Es brausen Ströme von Neonlicht in Eiseskälte durch Eissalons, durch Tanzhallen. Es hängen Trauben von summendem Licht an Peitschenmasten über Minigolfanlagen. Ein flimmernder Kältestrom' (p. 58). The perpetuum mobile of alienated life informs most powerfully the scenes set in the dismal suburbs 'die man nicht aufsucht, wenn man nicht muß' (p. 47). In their monotony, they connect strikingly back to the Kohut routine of dinner followed by favourite television programmes: 'Die Fassaden werden zu flächigen Bühnenkulissen, hinter denen nichts zu vermuten ist; alles ist gleich und gesellt sich zu gleichem' (p. 49). It is in this dreariness, underneath the arches of the transport system, that the peep-show is located, and its clients are the marginalized, the Turkish workers. The key motifs of this scene link explicitly back to the macro-structure of the narrative, to circularity and repetition: the women on show rotate 'auf einer Art Töpferscheibe' a 'Drehscheibe' (pp. 55-56). Later on in the novel, a simile reduces the Turkish workers, too, to mere 'Pappfiguren' mounted on the circular belt of the shooting galleries in the Prater (p. 123).[19]

As these examples show, the narrative constantly shifts between the metonymic and the symbolic, and it is precisely by virtue of this overall connectivity that quite specific details of the personal drama link with the conditions of public life and set up a complex reflectivity in the reader. Thus the motif of 'Kette' and its variants range from the 'Mutterbänder' (p. 75) of maternal coercion via Erika's collection of bondage items and Klemmer's ambition to 'jede Frau an sich ketten' (p. 65) to the 'Kette' (p. 113) of the conservatory and beyond to the tramway system: 'Das sind Ketten, die nie abreißen' (p. 17). Jelinek's representation of the conservatory is particularly telling, for it figures as an unending conveyor-belt within the machine of Vienna's culture industry:

> Nach dem letzten der Schüler läuft die Kette nachtsüber rückwärts, um sich ab neun Uhr früh erneut, mit frischen Kandidaten besteckt, voran auf den Weg zu machen. Die Zahnräder klicken, die Kolben boxen, die Finger werden an-und wieder abgestellt. Etwas erklingt.
>
> (p. 113)

Viewed within this network of literal and figurative significations, Erika's psycho-sexual pathology, her bodily alienation, acquires a strong metaphorical function: 'Es war ihr eigener Körper, doch er ist ihr fürchterlich fremd' (p. 89) captures Erika's condition as much as the sense of alienation that pervades the scenes of public life, in particular family relations. Violence, so central to the personal drama, extends to generalized patterns of brutality. Motifs such as 'treiben', 'Zwang', 'Gewalt', 'Wut', and 'Angst' dominate. The 'Sprache der Gewalt' (p. 48) finds concrete shape in the motif of 'schlagen'. At its most specific, it is the hallmark of maternal tyranny: she regularly threatens to 'erschlagen' (p. 83) the child Erika, just as she assaults her husband

(p. 156) so that, once infirm, he 'fleht, nicht geschlagen zu werden' (p. 97). But in the course of the novel the motif is generalized. There are regular instances of children being beaten by their mothers, most mercilessly so in the suburban scene of deprivation:

> Der Kopf einer etwa vierjährigen wird von einer mütterlichen Orkanwatsche in das Genick zurückgeworfen und rotiert einen Augenblick hilflos wie ein Stehaufmännchen [. . .]. Endlich steht der Kinderkopf wieder senkrecht, wo er hingehört und gibt schauerliche Laute von sich, worauf er von der ungeduldigen Frau sogleich wieder aus der Lotrechten befördert wird.
>
> (p. 48)

All such references finally culminate in the closing pages of the novel when, over some ten pages, Klemmer batters Erika.[20]

These passages are admittedly marked by a clarity of patterning, but one that is complexly mediated, reflective, rather than simply denunciatory. There are other major areas where the text creates much more subtle yet equally compelling links. I am thinking here of the aspect of space: On a purely feminist reading, *Die Klavierspielerin* takes back the gist of Virginia Woolf's text *A Room of One's Own*, 1929, a cornerstone of the literary feminist movement. Erika has a 'kleine[s] Zimmer' (p. 7), but as there is no lock and the mother constantly invades, her private space is minimal. This factor is of course central to the psychological drama engulfing mother and daughter and symbolizes Erika's disempowerment: 'Erika hat keine Geschichte und macht keine Geschichten' (p. 15). This echoes literally *Die Liebhaberinnen*, where Brigitte and Heinz, too, 'haben keine geschichte' (p. 10). But in *Die Klavierspielerin* the insignificance of Erika's fate connects with all those groups that lack space of their own and have no history, men and women who live in the dreary suburbs or the 'Ausländer' who make a living in the Prater by flogging cheap goods 'direkt aus der Fabrik' (p. 136). Once again, the peep-show scene, where the disempowered Turkish workers meet, is crucial. The narrator makes a direct and explicit link between their living conditions and the booths of the peep-show:

> Die Kleinheit der Kästchen ist direkt proportional zur Kleinheit ihrer privaten Behausung, in denen sie manchmal nur ein Eck bewohnen können. Sie sind die Enge also gewohnt und können sich hier sogar mittels einer Trennwand von anderen separieren. Es darf in jede Boxe nur einer zur selben Zeit hinein. Dort ist er mit sich selbst allein.
>
> (pp. 52-53)

It is a measure of Jelinek's compositional skill that this scene not only links back to Erika's cramped space but also prefigures the most devastating instance of spatial deprivation: the nursing-home where father Kohut is stashed away. Here, Jelinek reworks the code of the fairy tale *Schneewittchen*: the cosy form of diminutives indicts the living conditions of the infirm, the real dwarfs of society: 'Das Zimmer ist in Einzelbetten säuberlich unterteilt, jedem gehört ein eigenes Bettchen, und diese Bettchen sind klein, desto mehr gehen davon in den Raum hinein' (p. 96). The motif of cramped space runs through the novel and acquires increasingly critical importance. To recall the issue of feminist aesthetics: Jelinek acidly reinterprets central feminist configurations (for example, caverns as metaphorical sites of femininity) and charges them with socio-critical energy, turning them into ciphers of material deprivation. In the 'achte Bezirk', where Erika and mother live, dingy flats house the forgotten lives of the old and the poor: 'Manchmal kommt in diesem Bezirk eine Mordserie vor und ein paar alte Weiberln sterben in ihren mit Altpapier völlig zugewachsenen Fuchsbauten' (p. 32). Or take the discreet but sustained modulation of the sexual motif of 'Loch' whereby it comes to denote housing conditions in the impoverished suburbs, life in 'den Löchern [. . .] die man hier Wohnungen nennt' (p. 49), and finally figures as the 'schwarze Loch' (p. 118) of the deadly Kohut routine.

This transvaluation, whereby sexual motifs modulate along a sliding scale of signification into socio-economic and cultural patterns and then back again, applies above all to the figuration of Erika's voyeurism. Generally, critics comment on it in purely psychological terms. Whilst such accounts are of diagnostic interest, it seems to me that the literary resonance of this theme deserves more attention. It is, for example, worth noting that Erika's compulsive yet emptied 'Schauen' radically reinterprets a key theme in German twentieth-century writing. Repeated intertextual allusions point above all to Rilke and his theme of alienated, unhoused selfhood, the division into spectating and spectated subject. Fractured references to his poem *Herbsttag* pervade the scene at the peep-show, and indeed, Jelinek's representation here, with its insistent motif of 'schauen', 'zuschauen', 'Vorhang' (p. 55), points painfully back to the fourth *Duineser Elegie*, its sense of facing the void:

> Ich will nicht diese halbgefüllten Masken,
> lieber die Puppe. Die ist voll. Ich will
> den Balg aushalten und den Draht und ihr
> Gesicht aus Aussehn. Hier. Ich bin davor.
> [. . .]
> Ich bleibe dennoch. Es giebt immer Zuschaun.[21]

Seen within the more recent context of women's writing, Erika's voyeurism figures as a disillusioned version of the highly charged 'Sehen' motif, which in the work of Christa Wolf or Ingeborg Bachmann encapsulates visionary aspirations.[22] Clearly, *Die Klavierspielerin* invokes this tradition, but, crucially, divests the theme of all transcendent force and links it to a social argument. Erika's personal compulsion of 'will nur schauen' and 'Sie muß und muß schauen' (pp. 55-56.) connects with the fate of the marginalized who, deprived of all agency, are reduced to mere spectating: 'Der Tölpel glotzt nur und tut nichts' (p. 55).[23] Beyond the peep-show, this aspect reverberates in the recurrent motif of shop-windows and the television screen that clearly function as the up-market version of desire: 'Auslagen' (p. 32), 'Auslagenscheiben' (pp. 79, 129), 'Schaufenster' (p. 107), 'gläsernen Bilderkasten' (p. 101).

I hope the above examples suffice to illustrate the complex connective disposition of *Die Klavierspielerin.* Overall, the text traces, within both the personal and public frame, central aspects of human agency, the interplay of constraint and compulsion, of lack and desire. At its most succinct, it does so through sharply angled configurations of such modal verbs as 'müssen', 'können', 'wollen'. An early prefiguration is to be found in *Die Liebhaberinnen,* where the chapter *anfang* typically ends: 'Diese kleine episode soll nichts weiter zeigen, als daß brigitte arbeiten *kann,* wenn es sein muß. und es muß sein' (p. 14). But in *Die Klavierspielerin* the patterns are particularly prominent. The juxtaposition of 'wollen' and 'müssen' recurs in numerous variations. Take, for example, the representation of Klemmer's sexual failure, typically sited in the stifling 'Kabinett' of the conservatory's cleaners. His malfunction, we are told, is due to constraint: 'Klemmer will eigentlich gar nicht, aber er muß' (p. 243), and 'Er MUSS jetzt and KANN daher nicht [. . .]. Klemmer kann nicht, weil er muß' (p. 244). Again, the sexual nucleus generates a wider meaning, the novel's central concern with social entrapment, the vicious circle of 'müssen' and 'nicht können'. It is in this context that Erika's letter acquires a crucial function.

Clearly, the letter is the culmination of Erika's pathology: it is an extended and detailed exercise in masochistic fantasy and as such is an utterly scandalous document. Its shock-effect is reinforced by Jelinek's concern to generate suspense in time-honoured manner: from page 181 onwards, there are insistent references to the letter, but the contents of the 'geheimnisvollen Brief' (p. 192) are kept secret. Tension grows irresistibly so that when revelation finally comes, it exerts an overwhelming force. Jelinek undoubtedly runs a considerable risk here: the horrendous details of Erika's sado-masochistic fantasies (and the subsequent nemesis of reality when Klemmer literally hits back) displace at first sight the context of complex metaphorical intimation in which the letter is embedded.[24]

It is therefore not surprising that critics have homed in on this section (see Fiddler, pp. 146-53). In a psychoanalytical reading, Elizabeth Wright argues along the lines of Lacan's and Kristeva's concept of abjection and concludes that Erika's pleasure in disgust is ultimately also the condition of the text overall: 'Poetic language is thereby deprived of its "normal" aesthetic, and instead assumes the form of a hysteric-aesthetic language where pleasure is taken in disgust.'[25] This strikes me as a profound misreading because it overlooks the fundamental distinction throughout the text between the narrative voice and the protagonist. Erika is irretrievably trapped in the psycho-sexual pathology that culminates in her letter.[26] By contrast, the narrator figures that pathology and invites reflectivity from the reader: through cognitively shifting configuration of the literal and metaphorical, she not only traces Erika's history of violence and humiliation but, as I have shown, widens it into a fierce, Swiftian onslaught on the repressions of social life in Vienna and of human existence in general.

The letter, then, belongs structurally and discursively within the totality of statement that is *Die Klavierspielerin,* a narrative that consistently brings into congruence discourses of sexuality and discourses of culture and society. Crucially, the key motifs of the letter are powerfully prefigured: all the preceding references to 'Ketten', 'Fesseln', to woman as a 'Paket' (pp. 176, 202) culminate here. The dwelling on moments of confinement, subjection, and dominance reverberate both within the pathology of Erika's consciousness and within the broader diagnostic purpose of the text.[27] In this sense, the letter functions as an extended coda that brings together precisely the codes of the psycho-sexual and the socio-cultural. In other words, *Die Klavierspielerin* is a text *about* abjection, not *of* abjection. It refers recurrently to Erika's 'Verwesung', 'Zerfall' (p. 116), 'Verrotten' (p. 39), to mindscapes of 'Steinlawine' (p. 44), 'Schutthalden' (p. 200): in short, to waste lands beyond the confines of civilization. But, crucially, it does not give in to the allure of the abject that informs the Kristeva project and harks back to Rilke's problematic validation, both aesthetic and metaphysical, of the 'Fortgeworfenen'.

As in the work of Thomas Bernhard, human desolation figures without solace; it is overarched only by brute temporality. Recurrently, *Die Klavierspielerin* points back to *Die Liebhaberinnen,* where the narrative voice ruminates 'schrecklich, dieses langsame sterben, und die männer und die frauen sterben gemeinsam dahin' (p. 17). The theme of transience is stated at the very start of the novel. Here, the decline of the father immediately after Erika's birth is formulated thus: 'Sofort gab der Vater den Stab an seine Tochter weiter und trat ab' (p. 5). Psychological accounts conclude that Erika 'wird von der Mutter phallisch besetzt' (Janz, p. 71; see also Fiddler, pp. 129-40). Whilst this reading is undoubtedly pertinent, it does foreclose the metaphorical resonance of the phrase, which is spelt out later on in the novel when Erika 'gibt diesen Willen [. . .] jetzt wie einen Stab beim Stafettenlauf an Walter Klemmer weiter' (p. 208). Clearly, metaphorical signification here combines the sexual with an ontological dimension whereby human life, in a modern variation on a Baroque theme, figures as a frantic, but ultimately futile race. As the narrator comments in the opening section of the novel: 'Die Zeit vergeht, und wir vergehen in ihr' (p. 15). And so, again in a kind of radically secularized Baroque vision, both personal and public life figure as that vanity fair symbolized in the Prater scene. Admittedly, such passages may be precariously poised on the parodistic brink, alluding to the central theme of transience in Austrian thought and writing. Yet there is a piercing quality to the writing whenever Erika is seen not in the grip of her pathology but in the grip of time itself. Propped up by the 'gipsernen orthopädischen Kragenresten der Zeit um ihren dünnen Hals' (p. 9), she ages mercilessly into the void: 'Erika zieht dahin. [. . .] Nichts hat sie erreicht. Nichts, was vorher nicht da war, ist jetzt da, und nichts, was vorher nicht da war, ist inzwischen angekommen' (p. 57). This wry pathos of transience is also created by recurrent patterns of repetition, as in: 'Und es rinnt immer weiter. Es rinnt und rinnt und rinnt und rinnt' (p. 45) and 'Sie geht und geht und geht' (p. 140).

Jelinek frequently conjoins such variations on the theme of transience with the modality of farce. Repeatedly, *Die Klavierspielerin* generates at one and the same time a sense of total paralysis, futility, and a Bergsonian sense of convulsively mechanical comedy. As she comments: 'Die Welt läuft auf der Stelle. Und der Text schreibt, treibt ihr nach' (quoted in Meyer, p. 45). Manic motion informs Jelinek's staging of the battle for supremacy between the mother, Erika, and Klemmer, and throughout these sections she employs stock-in-trade devices of farce: eavesdropping, doors, opening and shutting, the chase, and phallic slap-stick comedy.

To register the element of farce in *Die Klavierspielerin* is to come full circle, back to the issue of 'Gewalt'. Farce as a genre is a form of violent authorial control, and as such raises the question of the extent to which *Die Klavierspielerin* as a text ultimately replicates the system it sets out to expose, the 'geballte Wut' (p. 82) that marks the life of both Erika and the city. As we know, in general Jelinek stands by the aggressive mode of her writing. She argues both in feminist terms that writing by women is *per se* a violent act, given the exclusion of woman from the symbolic order, and in Brechtian terms that the system is so closed that it can be answered only by violence.[28] As regards *Die Klavierspielerin,* she speaks of 'musische Ironie zum Sarkasmus vorangetrieben' (Bartsch, p. 10).

This certainly applies to the overt level of the text, where the ideational and the aesthetic figure in strict correlation. However, as I have attempted to demonstrate, on the latent level, the narrative unfolds in associative metaphorical patterns that widen and enrich the foreground statement. This structural tension is crystallized in the fact that the text consistently interrogates its own modality of sarcastic control. The comparison with the earlier novels is illuminating here: the narrative voice of *Die Liebhaberinnen* keeps the characters on an extremely tight rein. They are not individualized figures but paradigmatic ciphers: they merely serve to illustrate the determining power of the socio-economic system. But above all, they are totally at the mercy of authorial control: 'Da wir das schicksal brigittes in der hand halten, können wir es auch an jeder beliebigen stelle wieder abreißen' (p. 105) and:

dieser roman handelt vom gegenstand paula.

über den gegenstand paula bestimmt erich, über dessen körperkräfte wieder andre bestimmen, bis sich seine eingeweide einem frühen tod entgegensetzen.

(p. 130)

Throughout, the fiercely determined and determining narrative replicates the control system of the surrounding world, but it does not reflect on the difficulties of this duplication: it simply radicalizes Kafka's comment that language 'nur vom Besitz und seinen Beziehungen handelt'.[29] This largely applies also to Jelinek's second novel, *Die Ausgesperrten.* But through the figure of Rainer, addict of existentialist philosophy and literature, the text begins to generate a growing degree of self-reflectivity in so far as it thematizes the bad faith of reading and writing, the destructive clutches of art.

Such critical self-interrogation is much more developed in *Die Klavierspielerin.* It is no coincidence that Part I of the novel ends on critical ruminations about the issue of control. Nor is it by pure chance that the motif of 'Papier' increasingly comes to dominate: the motif of a city-scape, strewn with crumpled paper, epitomizes a throw-away culture and thus inscribes transitoriness into the very fabric of the text.[30] As Erika reflects: 'Jeden Tag stirbt ein Musikstück, eine Novelle oder ein Gedicht, weil es keine Berechtigung in heutiger Zeit mehr hat' (p. 92). But above all there is the complex relationship between the narrator and her protagonist. On the one hand, narratorial representation overlaps with the perspective of Erika, who coldly observes and judges the world around her. Thus the comment 'mit einem kleinen Hammer klopft sie die Wirklichkeit ab, eine eifrige Zahnärztin der Sprache' (p. 59) applies self-reflectively also to Jelinek's sharp narratorial stance.[31] On the other hand, however, the narrator distances herself regularly from her protagonist whose identity is fractured in such varying terms as 'sie', 'Erika K', 'Frau Professor', 'die K.', 'die Frau'. On this level, the negativity of Erika's viewpoint is defined as 'beinahe zwanghaft' as she 'sieht nur selten, daß etwas wächst und gedeiht' (p. 92). Whilst this comment in part may ironize bourgeois reader expectations of positivity, it does in fact echo Jelinek's admission in interview that her perspective is limited: 'Ich kann nichts Positives schildern. Das ist ein Unvermögen, weil ich wirklich die Verhältnisse eigentlich sehr schwarz sehe—ich hoffe natürlich auf eine Veränderung.'[32] To this degree, the narrative is, then, precariously balanced. In so far as it both overlaps with yet interrogates the perception of a pathologically impaired protagonist, it reflects dialectically back on its own modality, the presumption of a superior viewpoint.[33]

> Jeder Phrase vermag sie den vorherbestimmten Ort zuzuordnen. Nur sie allein kann jegliches Gehörte an die richtige Stelle schieben, wohin es gehört. Sie packt die Unwissenheit dieser blökenden Lämmer in ihre Verachtung und straft die Lämmer damit. Ihr Körper ist ein einziger großer Kühlschrank, in dem sich die Kunst gut hält.
>
> (p. 23)

It is at such points that the self-reflectivity of *Die Klavierspielerin* moves beyond the bulk of Jelinek's *œuvre*: the novel both posits and relativizes itself as merciless pathography, it both validates and disparages itself as art. The upshot is a work that challenges us to reflect on how, within a field of signification that extends from pornographic pathology on the one hand to virtuoso metaphorical sophistication on the other, the text is to be read.

## Notes

1. Elfriede Jelinek, *Die Klavierspielerin* (Reinbek bei Hamburg: Rowohlt, 1983, 1986). All page references are to the later, paperback edition.

2. Marlies Janz, *Elfriede Jelinek* (Stuttgart: Metzler, 1995), p. 52.

3. Yvonne Spielmann, 'Ein unerhörtes Sprachlabor. Feministische Aspekte im Werk von Elfriede Jelinek', in *Dossier 2: Elfriede Jelinek,* ed. by Kurt Bartsch and Günther A. Höfler (Graz and Vienna: Droschl, 1991), p. 24.

4. In this sense, Jelinek argues: 'Ich habe ja immer, wenn man will, realistische Literatur geschrieben, nur ist das eine Art Hyperrealismus oder Überrealismus' (interview with Riki Winter, in Bartsch, p. 12).

5. Elfriede Jelinek, *Die Liebhaberinnen* (Reinbek bei Hamburg: Rowohlt, 1975). All page references are to this edition.

6. See, for example, Inge Stephan and Sigrid Weigel, *Die verborgene Frau, 6 Beiträge zu einer feministischen Literaturwissenschaft* (Berlin: Argument, 1983); Judith P. Butler, *Gender Trouble: Feminism and the Subversion of Identity* (New York and London: Routledge, 1990); *Feminists Theorize the Political,* ed. by Judith P. Butler and Joan W. Scott (New York and London: Routledge, 1992); Judith P. Butler, *Bodies that Matter* (New York and London: Routledge 1993).

7. See Margarete Kohlenbach, 'Montage und Mimikry. Zu Elfriede Jelineks *Wolken.Heim,* in Bartsch, pp. 12-53. For Janz, the relentless intertexting of *Lust* constitutes a 'Tortur' of the reader (Janz, p. 113), and *Die Kinder der Toten* (1995), is no less demanding.

8. On this aspect, see Annegret Mahler-Bungers, *Der Trauer auf der Spur. Zu Elfriede Jelineks 'Die Klavierspielerin',* in *Freiburger literaturpsychologische Gespräche,* VII *Masochismus in der Literatur,* ed. by Johannes Cremerius and others (Würzburg: Königshausen & Neumann, 1988), pp. 80-95; Hedwig Appelt, *Die leibhaftige Literatur. Das Phantasma und die Präsenz der Frau in der Schrift* (Weinheim and Berlin: Quadriga, 1989); Maria-Regina Kecht, '"In the Name of Obedience, Reason, Fear": Mother—Daughter Relations in W. A. Mitgutsch and E. Jelinek', *German Quarterly,* 62 (1989), 357-72.

9. *Die Stimme der Medusa* (Dülmen-Hiddingsel: tende, 1987), pp. 193-95.

10. *Rewriting Reality: An Introduction to Elfriede Jelinek* (Oxford and Providence, RI: Berg, 1994), pp. 129-40.

11. See Janz: 'Einzigartig in Jelineks Oeuvre steht *Die Klavierspielerin* auch insofern da, als der Roman durchaus psychologische Charaktere kennt' (p. 71).

12. See Fiddler, pp. 139-40, also Frank W. Young, '"Am Haken des Fleischhauers". Zum politökonomischen Gehalt der *Klavierspielerin',* in *Gegen den schönen Schein,* ed. by Christa Gürtler (Frankfurt a.M., 1990), pp. 75-80.

13. See also Janz, whose study views stylistic features throughout in terms of 'das mythendestruierend-ideologiekritische Verfahren' (for example, p. 113).

14. 'Die böse Mutter. Zur Ästhetik sadomasochistischer Mutter-Tochter-Beziehungen in literarischen Texten aus dem Kontext der Frauenbewegung', in *Mutter und Mütterlichkeit. Wandel und Wirksamkeit einer Phantasie in der deutschen Literatur. Festschrift für Verena Ehrlich-Haefeli,* ed. by Irmgard Roebling and Wolfram Mauser (Würzburg: Königshausen & Neumann, 1996), pp. 347-58).

15. On Jelinek's playing with language in general, see Yasmin Hoffman, '"Hier lacht sich die Sprache selbst aus". Sprachsatire—Sprachspiele bei Elfriede Jelinek', in Bartsch, pp. 41-55.

16. For Schmidt, who also discusses the animal imagery, there is no such freedom (Schmidt, pp. 350-51).

17. This pattern of circularity, so reminiscent of Kafka, yet critically charged, is the hallmark of Jelinek's work overall. Time and again, her texts turn on figures who strive in vain to escape from the vicious circle of precise cultural settings. See, for example, *Die Liebhaberinnen, Die Ausgesperrten, Oh Wildnis, oh Schutz vor ihr,* and *Lust.*

18. Anja Meyer, *Elfriede Jelinek in der Geschlechterpresse* (Hildesheim: Olms-Weidmann, 1994), p. 45.

19. See also the motif of 'Drehscheibe' and 'Kreislauf' in *Die Liebhaberinnen,* p. 15.

20. In many ways, the motif of 'schlagen', which is so central to the work of Christa Wolf and Ingeborg Bachmann, finds here its most brutal concretization. See also the portrayal of battered children in *Die Liebhaberinnen,* p. 88.

21. See also Janz on *Sonette an Orpheus* as one of the intertexts in *Lust* (Janz, p. 116).

22. On various versions of the (male and female) gaze, see Sabine Wilke, '"Ich bin eine Frau mit einer männlichen Anmaßung": Eine Analyse des "bösen Blicks" in Elfriede Jelineks *Die Klavierspielerin'*, *Modern Austrian Literature,* 26 (1993), 115-44.

23. Typically, the 'Schmalfilme und Video-Kasetten" that are also on sale are out of their economic reach: 'Der Kunde hat das dazugehörige Gerät nicht bei sich zu Hause stehen' (p. 51).

24. The problem is acute in *Lust,* where the pornographic sections tend to take centre-stage in the reader's mind, yet they constitute only a quarter of the text (see Meyer, p. 119). More generally, the issue also arises in respect of Jelinek's plays, where stage business tends to muffle the import of the spoken text.

25. Elizabeth Wright, 'An Aesthetic of Disgust: Elfriede Jelinek's *Die Klaverspielerin'*, *Paragraph,* 14 (1991), 184-93.

26. See Margarete Mitscherlich, *Die friedfertige Frau* (Frankfurt a.M.: Fischer, 1987). She notes that sado-masochistic fantasies are more prevalent in women than in men, and she argues that such fantasies can have an enabling function in so far as they change 'passiv erlittene Unterdrückung in kontrollierbare Situationen'. Yet they inevitably harbour the danger of turning the subject into a 'Sklave seiner Phantasien' (pp. 141-42).

27. Note, for example, the dialectical link between the imposed claustrophobia of the tram scene (pp. 16-25) and the desire for confined spaces in the Prater scene (pp. 130, 139).

28. 'Schon der phallische Anspruch, Kunst machen zu wollen und mich in dieser Weise zum Subjekt zu machen, wird mir verübelt' (Gürtler, p. 120).

29. Franz Kafka, *Tagebücher 1910-1923* (Frankfurt a.M.: Fischer), p. 248.

30. The motif culminates of course in the 'Papierfabrik' of *Lust.*

31. Such comments remind us that Jelinek sites her criticism of ideology and language very much in the tradition of Nietzsche and, within the Austrian context, of Karl Kraus.

32. Quoted in Fiddler, p. 29. Even if interview statements must be treated with caution, it seems to me that time and again one senses that *Die Klavierspielerin* longs for another story that cannot be written. The notion of 'Erlösung' (p. 214) can appear only in fractured form, in Erika's deluded flights beyond facticity into the realm of music and love, into visions of some ultimate significance.

33. In this sense the text differentiates the common feminist claim that precisely by virtue of her exclusion from the symbolic order, woman perceives and articulates the truth, a view Jelinek at times shares: 'Die Frau ist das Andere, der Mann ist die Norm. Er hat seinen Ort, und er funktioniert, Ideologien produzierend. Die Frau hat keinen Ort [. . .]. Auf diese Weise ist sie aber dazu verurteilt, die Wahrheit zu sprechen und nicht den schönen Schein. "Die Wahrheit ist dem Menschen zumutbar", sagt Ingeborg Bachmann' (quoted in Gürtler, p. 8).

## Gregory H. Wolf (review date spring 2001)

SOURCE: Wolf, Gregory H. Review of *Das Lebewohl: 3 kl. Dramen,* by Elfriede Jelinek. *World Literature Today* 75, no. 2 (spring 2001): 369.

[*In the following review of* Das Lebewohl: 3 kl. Dramen, *Wolf compliments the social commentary in Jelinek's three dramas, but notes that without a firm understanding of Austrian politics, "one will not catch their poignant political critique."*]

Elfriede Jelinek's latest work, **Das Lebewohl,** a collection of three short dramas, problematizes the serious political developments and situation in Austria since Jörg Haíder's ascension to a position of prominence in national, indeed European politics. The phenomenon of Haider, the young, charismatic, wealthy governor of the province of Carinthia (Kärnten), has been well documented over the last two years. As the head of the right-wing Austrian Freedom Party (Freiheitliche Partei Österreichs, or FPÖ), he transformed the party from political obscurity to national significance within a matter of fifteen years. In the national election of autumn 1999, the FPÖ garnered 28 percent of the public vote, and in the spring 2000 entered into a coalition government with the liberal Austrian People's Party (Österreichische Volks Partei, or ÖVP).

Haider and his party are characterized by their anti-European, anti-immigrant, xenophobic platform, and ran campaign advertisements such as "Stop der Uberfremdung, "Stop dem Asylmiβbrauch," and "Gerade jetzt FPÖ" After the European Union passed sanctions against Austria, Haider resigned as chairman of the FPÖ, but he still retains his position as governor of Carinthia. It is within this context of increased political extremism that Elfriede Jelinek, one of Austria's most politically active writers and intellectuals, has published her latest work. At one point, Jelinek threatened to prohibit any of her dramas from being performed while the FPÖ was in national power.

The three short dramas in this volume could be characterized as *Ideendramen* that are to be read and not performed, but without an understanding of the political developments in Austria, one will not catch their poignant political critique. The first drama, **Das Lebewohl,** is a long monologue spoken by an unnamed individual. In fact, Haider is not mentioned in the works, and considering his legal successes with libel suits against his critics, Jelinek acted wisely. The monologue is alienating, with aggressive language, often choppy and skewed syntax, and filled with hyperbole and cliché. The speaker exalts himself as a type of a savior, a father-figure, whose concern is the welfare of Austria and Austrians. Like Haider, whose parents were early members of the Nazi Party and who has publicly defended Nazi atrocities, the speaker refers to history with a certain blank deafness: "wir warens nicht, und unsre Väter warens auch nicht." The drama suggests that the *Vergangenheitsbewältigung,* the coming to terms with one's past, specifically during the period of the Third Reich, a topic that has dominated public and political discourse in the Federal Republic of Germany during the last two decades, has not yet been addressed in Austria. The speaker acknowledges that he is the reason that other countries suddenly take notice of the small alpine republic which has been ignored hither-to, but does not realize his extremism is the cause of the newfound attention. Finally, the speaker claims victory when he departs from the national stage so that he can control his party from behind the scenes.

In the next short drama, **Das Schweigen,** Jelinek offers an esthetic counter to the cliché-laden first monologue. An unnamed speaker suggests that (s)he expected more of a public outcry against the developments, and wonders what (s)he can do, if anything. Are words enough, or are more (unarticulated) measures necessary?

The third drama is a modern version of Sleeping Beauty titled **Der Tod und das Mädchen II.** The princess, symbolizing the slumbering country of Austria, is suddenly awakened by her magical prince, symbolizing Haider. The princess asks, "Sind Sie überhaupt der, auf den ich warten soll, bis er mich küsst?" The drama affords Jelinek more artistic freedom than do the first two, and she takes full advantage of it to craft witty, forceful, and artful situations. While the princess attempts to gain an answer and to discover the true identity of her prince, he identifies himself as the incarnation of power: "Ich bin die Macht. Wer sich gegen mich stellt, verliert sich selbst." In the grotesque ending, the prince puts on an animal costume with an exaggerated penis, the princess dresses herself in one with an exaggerated vagina, and they begin to have aggressive sex. The ending suggests the situation that exists in Austrians but one for which some Austrians are themselves responsible and indeed wanted. The slogan "BESUCHEN SIE OSTERREICH, ERST JEIZT RECHT" recalls the slogans during Haider's political campaign and, as wordplay (*recht*/right), signals the country's political leanings.

### Eva Ludwiga Szalay (essay date summer 2001)

SOURCE: Szalay, Eva Ludwiga. "Of Gender and the Gaze: Constructing the Disease(d) in Elfriede Jelinek's *Krankheit oder Moderne Frauen.*" German Quarterly 74, no. 3 (summer 2001): 237-58.

[*In the following essay, Szalay investigates the influence of the theories of French philosopher Michel Foucault on Jelinek's* Krankheit oder Moderne Frauen.]

> Weiβt du, einer sagt, die Geschichte beruhe in letzter Instanz auf dem Körper des Menschen.[1]

In staging what might be called the symbolically or metaphorically diseased condition of modern women, Elfriede Jelinek's **Krankheit oder Moderne Frauen** sets out to radically deconstruct the integral body, identity, and language. In the above quote, one of the play's main figures alludes to Foucault's compelling notion that history ultimately rests on the human body. That Jelinek's play would allude to Foucault is hardly surprising, since his analytics of power and processes of subjection offer feminist poststructuralists a useful framework for conceptualizing the body as site of political struggle. In "Nietzsche, Genealogy, History," *Discipline and Punish, The Birth of the Clinic,* and *The History of Sexuality* (volume 1), Foucault posits the body as a locus upon which the rules, hierarchies, and metaphysical commitments of society are inscribed and reinforced.[2] Although Foucault's influence has been duly noted in a few readings of this play, these references are brief and invariably tangential to a different interpretative focus.[3] The Austrian playwright does acknowledge several other sources in her credits, yet Foucault is never mentioned by name.[4] Nevertheless, it is impossible to avoid hearing unmistakable echoes of his account of power relations and subjection in Jelinek's dramatic enactment of sickness/disease-or-modern women. Indeed, both Jelinek's and Foucault's focus on the power of perception, its force in subjection, and their attention to the creation of matter in (medical) discourses, specifically, to the constitution of bodies as illness at the microlevel, merit exploration. How Jelinek and Foucault—in striking convergences—represent the body and how it functions as metaphor for cultural and social crises presents one of the significant sites in contemporary critical work where the interactions of representation and power are made visible. Yet, surprisingly, despite the Foucauldian resonance throughout the play, scholarship on ***Krankheit*** has not established substantial connections between this play and Foucault's influence, nor has this commentary drawn on Foucauldian thinking in any extensive and meaningful way to examine power relations. Only a few studies deal explicitly with sexuality and power (Höfler), language and power (Luscher), and politics and power (Wigmore) in ***Krankheit.***

The body's centrality for the analyses of subjection both in Jelinek's ***Krankheit*** and in Foucault is a function of its role in constituting a central tool through which post-structuralists launch their strike on classical thought and its linchpin, the rational subject or cogito. Through the body post-structuralism deconstructs the Cartesian body/mind opposition, undermining Western civilization's prioritization of rational thought, spirit, and objectivity over emotions, passions, needs, and subjectivity. For an author like Jelinek whose œuvre disrupts common sense beliefs and practices and rigorously detaches itself from the assumption that there are essences to uncover, Foucault is useful for assessing whether it is strategically sound to speak of feminine subjectivity as "ill" or "diseased," and for considering the consequences and implications such a proposition might hold for an examination of gender relations. Though *The Birth of the Clinic* concentrates on particular historical conjunctures, Foucault's formations nonetheless provide analytic paradigms of wider applicability to other eras and contexts: *The Birth of the Clinic* is about seeing and naming human disease in the eighteenth century—and, *if* modern woman is, metaphorically speaking or symbolically, ill or disease(d), then reading Foucault and ***Krankheit*** in conjunction with one another promises insight into the reasons for which the self-evident—whether this applies to sexed bodies or to sick bodies—appears as "the given."[5] By making sense of the "Ich bin krank, daher bin ich"-utterance by Carmilla (***K*** [***Krankheit oder Moderne Frauen***] 44) from perspectives articulated in *The Birth of the Clinic, The History of Sexuality* (vol. 1), and from inquiries into discursive formations, the image construction of "sickness or modern women" assumes a new meaning in a way that problematizes the more essentializing dimensions of this work and its interpretation. In the analysis of key scenes, I contend that we have much to gain by allowing a certain paradox in Jelinek's parodic method to obtain, namely, that ***Krankheit*** not only deconstructs, but also partially reconstructs the original Foucauldian thought through its self-reflexive intertextuality. I suggest, specifically, that the parody Jelinek employs in referencing Foucault draws on the Greek *paròdia,* meaning "counter-song," whereby the critical distance to the original (Foucault) engages far more in a respectful echo and considerably less in belittling mockery (as it has been read to date) to create a substantially deeper level of social critique.

The more reflexive, inquiry-oriented perspective I offer attends a general turn in more recent feminist scholarship and follows from a period of critical attention focused on feminine subjectivity that has made rather generalizing assumptions about Jelinek's position on power as Marxist.[6] A consequence of this assumption is that gender relations in this author's œuvre, with power repressing, blocking, concealing, and with male subjects dominating and oppressing female subjects. Though this approach has had considerable influence in Jelinek's reception, it strikes me as inadequate and dangerously one-sided. One of the reasons we have as yet failed to adequately consider the essentialistic propositions of power/gender relations in ***Krankheit*** is that the scholarship has neglected to account for the play's more differentiating take on power and the tensions by which this representation is informed, tensions which point to the constraining, repressive force of power, as well as to its productive, creative aspect. Therefore, in addition to pointing to the affinities of ***Krankheit*** with Foucauldian positions, my analysis seeks to move beyond the strictures that have influenced various readings of this drama to date and interpretations that have contained or recuperated elements of the narrative's radical critique and ignored the unrelenting pessimism that imbues this work as well as the play's refusal to resolve the disturbing contradictions. The play's pessimism shares much with Foucault's deep, abiding skepticism in the way it endorses a view of the contemporary era that suggests an ever-increasing refinement in processes of domination, a continuity of power plays leading, to speak with Adorno, from the slingshot to the megaton bomb.[7] But where the Frankfurt School critics would hold out hope for the emergence of a few autonomous individuals within the totally administered society, the drama's positioning much more closely approximates Foucault's profound pessimism in the refutation of modern belief in the free, agential subject.

Foucault's critique of essentialist conceptions of sexuality assists in examining the paradoxical notion upon which Jelinek's drama rests: whereas the play's approach to the body is materialist and insists on confrontation with the real oppression of women and the domination of women's biological bodies, its treatment of embodiment is also anti-essentialist in that it seeks to disabuse its audience of the notion that women and men constitute natural anatomical categories. A differentiating conceptualization of power that accounts for its exercise at the microlevel—that is, at local, individual points—without enabling some bodies to stand external to power by virtue of a raw anatomical core, can be useful in making more explicit the irreducible residue of essentialism informing Jelinek's drama. It can, further, serve as a means for exploring this dramatic representation of the contemporary institutions and practices that appear as given and natural, but are, in fact, contingent constructs of power and domination.

That Jelinek's drama strives to resist prevailing dramatic-performative conventions is beyond contention.[8] However, the degree to which her work also participates, uncritically at times, in all-too-familiar image constructions even while it aspires to radically subvert the representational tradition, is an issue that has been raised by some commentators. Dagmar Lorenz's reading of works prior to *Krankheit,* for example, finds Jelinek's humorous attacks affirmative of the hierarchical structures of Western society and not a fundamental revision of ideology.[9] Beatrice Hanssen, who focuses on Jelinek's engagement with violence and (anti-)pornography, asserts that Jelinek's "writings appear to be informed by seemingly conflicting intentions" and concludes that the author's "appropriation of representational violence may seem too assured of its critical, even redemptive, power."[10] Luscher, in a similar vein, has pointed out the difficulty in separating the satirical enunciation of preexisting myth from the creation of counter-myth in *Krankheit.*[11] The point they make, implicitly or explicitly, is that *Krankheit* appears too self-assured for its critique to be understood by its audience: *Krankheit* depends upon a highly sophisticated appreciation of the diverse intertexts that open up the more complex, at times antithetical readings available to this parodic-satiric text. Like those critics, I shall call our attention to a related issue here, but rather than focus primarily on an analysis of the drama's critical potential or exclusively on the text's reappropriation of specific patriarchal discourses and images (e.g., porn, fascism, sado-masochism), I shall address more generally the play's treatment of power in relation to subjectification and the medico-scientific discourses.

\* \* \*

A useful starting point for the analysis of power's inscription on the body is the scene in *Krankheit* in which the four main figures—Carmilla, Emily, Dr. Benno Hundekoffer and Dr. Heidkliff—converge in Dr. Heidkliff's medical practice, depicted in the set description:

> Die Bühne ist zweigeteilt, und zwar so, daß ein Teil in den anderen übergeht. Links: Eine Art Arztpraxis mit einem Stuhl, der eine Mischung aus Zahnarzt- und Gynäkologenstuhl darstellt. Dazu ein Tisch, auf dem ein Sortiment Blutkonserven steht. Die Praxis geht rechts in eine wilde Heidelandschaft mit Felsblöcken über. In der Ferne Hügel, Wasser etc. Auf kleinen Bühnen kann die Landschaft durch ein Kinderplanschbecken dargestellt werden.
>
> (*K* 6)

This dramatic staging, which frames a significant part of the play's action, merits close attention since the scenes set in the *Arztpraxis* provide much of the explicit material for the exploration of power's operation in gender relations. The avant-garde staging of the scenes has thus far been accorded attention primarily for the manner in which the play draws on a variety of dramatic traditions, including the popular horror genre of the *Grand Guignol* spectacle, the allegorical mode of the Surrealist-derived Theater of the Absurd, and the Artaudian "Theater of Cruelty."[12] What has been overlooked to date is how the staging also sets up a focus on the naming, visualization, and spatialization of disease in relation to the (gendered) subject. The conscious use in the set and set description of the combination dentist's-gynecological chair and the *Arztpraxis* setting implies a principle of selection that indicates a specific designated significance, a meaning that becomes clearer as the figures assume their positions and perform their functions. In limiting character description to the roles that define these figures on the basis of their social position and sexual identity (nurse, lesbian, housewife, writer, doctor, tax consultant), the play foregrounds to some extent the economic determinism inhering in these power relations, and, far more subtly, the knowledge/power differential. Dr. Heidkliff, gynecologist and dentist, is introduced as nurse/writer Emily's fiancé; Dr. Benno Hundekoffer, a tax consultant, is Carmilla's husband. The bonds of engagement and marriage are commodified, determined by financial exigencies, and the partnership of man and wife is—as are all familial relations—seemingly prostituted to the demands of contemporary Austrian consumer society. From a less transparent Foucauldian perspective, these modern figures are also the subjects of normalization, whereby specific technologies, or knowledges, are directed at producing a thoroughly normed subject: healthy, well-functioning, docile. By representing male characters not only of superior socio-economic status, but also in a differential relation to knowledge/power (Dr. Heidkliff—nurse Emily; tax consultant Dr. Hundekoffer—housewife Carmilla), an imbalance more complex than that of the (male) dominator over the dominated (female) becomes manifest.

Much as these figures are devoid of traditional, coherent psychological character development and lack any real history or substantive motivational force, so too does their language evince little, if any, development and progression. In my view, this is suggestive of a Foucauldian take—in its fragmentary, disruptive nature—on power's instantiation of subjects. Utterances jump about in seemingly random association in rambling dialogues, forming a textual construct of sentences and parodic imitations of patriarchal language, making it difficult to establish a narrative continuum.[13] This appears underscored in what one critic views as the consistent disjunction between words (verbal signs) and action throughout the play,[14] a disjunction I find not nearly as complete or manifest, particularly since the play's parodic-satiric effect often also requires the meaningful association of speech and action to make its point. Although these figures derive their inspiration from the Theater of the Absurd, the male figures are often interpreted differently from their female counterparts, figures that are *generally* treated both more sympathetically and unequivocally as expressing the drama's social critique. This is not to say that the female and male figures have been viewed only in positive and negative, black and white terms, but to emphasize that their relative complexity, within the frame of their construction as "Sprachflächen" and "Sprachschablonen,"[15] has been overlooked by much of the scholarship on **Krankheit**. Indeed, the pronouncements of the male figures articulate a kind of one-foot-in-the-asylum style of speech, but their parroting back an utterance is not the work of mindless fools. According to critics, Heidkliff derives his name from Emily Brontë's Heathcliff in *Wuthering Heights*. Heathcliff's monomania (clinically, a form of mental illness) imbues him with pariah status and has undoubtedly occasioned critics to dismiss Heidkliff's utterances as mindless babble.[16] A noteworthy aspect of this condition, often forgotten or ignored, is that monomaniacs can reason logically and coherently and, in some instances, display the highest intellectual powers (Tytler). Careful consideration of Jelinek's ingenious use of such intertexts would render more nuanced and balanced interpretations of Heidkliff (and Hundekoffer). I will show how this form of language has been implicated in the general tendency among critics to disregard Heidkliff and Hundekoffer's utterances, to dismiss their talk as babble, pure rubbish. Indeed, the humorous, asylum-like aspect of the satire produced by these two figures appears to belie the drama's scathing critique of contemporary Austrian gender and social relations.[17] Ultimately, the schematic quality of the main figures makes them representative of dimensions of the human condition, whereby their stereotypical qualities serve to generalize this particular configuration for the broader postwar Austrian society. This satire of the darkest sort—even in its unevenness—succeeds precisely because it points its audience to issues beyond the narrative that include the subjection of individuals in the production of "truths" and the emergence of disease and the sick patient in discursive regimes.

The scene unfolding in the *Arztpraxis*—with Dr. Heidkliff initially absent—shows Carmilla first being "invited" by her husband to assume a comfortable position in the upholstered chair ("Vorerst darfst du dich sicher ohne seine Erlaubnis in diesen netten gepolsterten Stuhl setzen" [*K* 13]), and then getting shackled with increasing force into the gynecological chair ("Benno fesselt sie immer fester an den Stuhl" [*K* 14]). In preceding Act I's fifth scene in which Emily positions herself, also as patient, in the dentist's-gynecological chair, this spectacle from scene two has vital implications for how we are to make sense of power's operation in gender relations. To Emily I shall return later. First, I want to point out that several critics have used this scene with Carmilla and Benno to draw attention to the violence perpetrated against woman,[18] and to assert that "women are present always as objects of abuse but never as subjects creating themselves or their world,"[19] i.e., as victims.[20] In my view, this focus on the depiction of the oppression of women is influenced by misreading the quote from Derridean critic Eva Meyer, which frames the play:

> In chinesischen Legenden steht geschrieben, daß große Meister in ihre Bilder hineingingen und verschwunden sind. Die Frau ist kein großer Meister. Deshalb wird ihr Verschwinden nie vollkommen sein. Sie taucht wieder auf, beschäftigt wie sie ist, mit dem Verschwinden.
>
> (*K* 5)

Often taken as the programmatic beginning of the drama, literal readings of Meyer's epigraph impede consideration of what I perceive to be a more differentiated dramatic representation, and frustrate appreciation of the play's more radical critique with respect to the subjectification of female *and male* subjects.[21] The passage's prominent placement has been used to validate a type of essentializing analysis ("Die Frau ist kein großer Meister") that refuses an examination of power to consider how concepts like femininity, masculinity, and sexuality, for example, are understood in particular cultural contexts. Furthermore, this treatment invokes what one critic of essentialist feminism terms the "great animating myth," namely that a poor man (class) always and everywhere has it better than a rich woman.[22] This approach deflects attention from the point that meanings ascribed to femininity (masculinity, sexuality) vary significantly along the lines of race, ethnicity, nationality, class, and sexual orientation, among other axes (Fuss). Moreover, Jelinek's references to Meyer's epigraph when discussing this drama and her œuvre in interviews have enabled, and have likely encouraged, a reading of the text that "personalizes" the message for women as it supports their viewing themselves as victims, made ill by a male system.[23] We will see this most clearly at those points where *Krankheit*—despite its generally rigorous assault on "truths" awaiting revelation—implies that knowledge of the female condition (as diseased/sick/ill) was actually "discovered." The play also suggests in places that women always and everywhere have been constituted as ill/sick/diseased by man-made constructions of the female/feminine, ignoring momentarily that this notion is as much a product of distinct sociohistorical factors as the search itself that lays such evidence bare. Although a few readings acknowledge that Jelinek's drama exposes unequal gender relations, that men and women are subjected to the full force of Jelinek's attack,[24] that both sexes are "victims of ideology in the play,"[25] the overwhelming focus, nevertheless, has remained on the female figures, with the consequence that consideration of masculine subjectivity is rendered parenthetical, as a questionable "inclusion" in which the masculine functions as an expendable afterthought. Lanyon's reading presents a typical example: "[t]he play ***Krankheit oder Moderne Frauen*** engages with social and cultural constructions of female (and male) subjectivity [. . .]."[26]

By emphasizing authorial intent commentators elevate Jelinek to the vaunted position of the drama's authoritative interpreter and meaning maker. As Ingeborg Hoesterey points out, due in part to the dialogicity of our media culture, the autobiographical presence of the interviewed author has permitted structuring of her works' reception, a dynamic that arises after the publication of *Lust* in 1989.[27] I think a similar case can be made for *Krankheit*'s reception, particularly since the drama was "exiled" on the grounds of its radicality to German stages in Bonn, Hamburg, and Koblenz prior to its performance in Austria in 1990. The influence of the author on her works' reception has been well documented: Konstanz Fliedl, for example, notes that Jelinek's approval of critic Michael Scharang's commentary on *Lust* legitimizes this particular mode of reading.[28]

The many implications of this approach need not be revisited in detail, suffice it to say that the reliance on the "design" or "intention" of the author is problematic. For one, studies impelled by feminist and Left-intellectuals' hopes that at some point Jelinek will receive the recognition she deserves, and those who ally the oppressed figures in *Krankheit* with the author's personal message to women, are not inclined to consider the play as a site of ideological struggle in which the female figures play highly ambivalent roles. The elevation of Jelinek to the status of one of the premier avant-garde postmodern authors, internationally celebrated in the main by feminists and left-wing intellectuals as Austria's literary exponent of the ethical; anti-fascist line, has not likely enhanced critical propensity to make sense of *Krankheit* in the manner I advocate here. Secondly, this author-intent driven interpretive mode detracts much from the play's more radical, culturally-critical message and its most pessimistic implications. The trouble, specifically, with such interpretations is their tendency to deflect from the examination of processes of subjectification from which there is no liberation or escape, a critique implied and explicit in this drama.[29] These readings overlook a vital dimension of Jelinek's social analysis that I make more explicit by drawing on Foucault's studies of modern medicine and sexuality in the analysis of individual scenes and performative events.

That the *Arztpraxis* scene in particular is perceived to represent the violence of men and medicine against women derives its force in part from Benno's behavior vis-à-vis Carmilla, and in part from Heidkliff's "doctoring." Upon entering the *Arztpraxis,* Benno is seen as the active perpetrator, as he "*zwingt seine Frau in den Gynä-Stuhl, zwingt ihr die Beine fröhlich auseinander, befestigt sie in den Steigbügeln [. . .]. Benno fesselt sie immer fester an den Stuhl, Carmilla kämpft gegen die Fesseln*" (*K* 14). In decontextualizing this particular action by focusing exclusively on Benno's use of force and on Carmilla's inability to resist Benno's efforts, these actions can readily be reduced to a parodic act of violent male aggression. Although Luscher, like other critics in this vein, acknowledges the aesthetic-distancing influences of the Artaudian "Theater of Cruelty" in framing her interpretation of this scene, she lapses into a literal reading of the performance's mimetic intent, exemplified by her assertions that "the message communicated by the scene relies on [. . .] the meaning of Carmilla's posture which, in its obvious reference to bondage and submission, is part of the discourse of pornography."[30] Luscher makes valuable points, but her approach neglects the text's multivalence and indeterminacy in representing power relations.

Readings that ignore the productive quality of power overlook, furthermore, that Carmilla has been conveyed to Dr. Heidkliff's gynecological practice by her husband ("*Der Steuerberater Dr. Benno Hundekoffer kommt herein. Er führt liebevoll seine Frau Carmilla mit sich*" [*K* 12]), and disregard, too, Carmilla's investment in the capacities of mother, caregiver, and consuming citizen, roles for which Carmilla manifests explicit ambition. Carmilla has, in fact, come to the practice in the first place in her role as productive Austrian citizen, in order to deliver her *sixth* child. Her first utterances, once she occupies the gynecological chair, relate her concerns about her having perhaps forgotten to turn off the gas at home and the high energy costs involved in using light, a scene offering—on one level—a parodic look at the sadistic stranglehold consumerism exerts. As a consumer of material goods and products, and as producer of "products" (children), Carmilla is clearly complicit in upholding the status quo. That Carmilla "voluntarily"[31] goes to the *Arztpraxis* by no overt coercion also suggests that she has internalized messages about the "good mother," compelled by a variety of coherent discourses the drama plays on to become an active participant in scientific practices, notably the medicalization of motherhood.[32] The subject position and identity of contemporary mothering depends on a series of coherences implied by the human chain links of children that here bind Dr. Benno Hundekoffer and his wife Carmilla ("*An dem Paar hängt eine Menschenkette dran* [. . .]." [*K* 12]), including: the female anatomy; the desire, propensity, and ability to bear and raise children; the preference for reproduction in a secure heterosexual setting; a nurturant orientation; and the predilection for domestic issues.[33] This scene continually invokes the puissant force of the structural and ideological pressures exerted in producing the "good mother" and is expressed in the thinking and speech of the main figures.[34] That Carmilla's willingness to go the practice in the first place, and that her influence on the health of her future child is determined by her socio-economic circumstances (social class, place of residence, level of education) are much more implied here does not detract in the least from what is clearly a staging of a power network in which subtle constraints and coercions figure prominently in these characters' subjectification. Furthermore, the play unambiguously underscores Carmilla's implication in the exploitation of her husband's economic productivity, as Benno Hundekoffer declares in one of the play's decidedly less ironic passages: "Ihr ehrgeizigen Frauen! Woher kommt dieser Druck, den ihr auf eure Männer auszuüben versteht? Warum wollt ihr uns immer in die gesellschaftliche Höhe hinaufgestellt wissen? [. . .]. Ich bin Steuerberater. Dorthin hast du mich gestellt, damit du dich neben mich stellen konntest. Geld muss arbeiten. Der Mensch auch" (*K* 16). Here and in other passages, the play exposes Carmilla's investment in motherhood and the *Hausfrau* existence that typifies a postwar Austrian society in its material pursuits and conformity with dominant images of status and success. Just as Carmilla produces children, not out of a sense of personal fulfillment or love, but to solidify and enhance her social status, so too does she compel her husband to perform and produce. These aspects here, as well as the parodically violent acts Carmilla and Emily perpetrate later throughout the play (for example, as lesbian vampires, biting the throats of the Hundekoffer children; Carmilla's Medea-like murder and devouring of her children), point more to an active negotiation of Foucault's "fine meshes of the web of power" (*Power/Knowledge* 116) than to woman's putative inability to exist and create meaning beyond the male constructed images of femininity.

There is, undoubtedly, something to the notion that Jelinek's drama implies the force of violence and oppression in the play's construction *in places,* at least, of passive, victimized female subjects. Like works of art (famous paintings), these female figures are fashioned into image-objects (Emily: "Ich spreche in der Kunst. Ich bin international. Ich bin abstrakt," [*K* 21]), who have all but completely disappeared into the patriarchal myths constructed to contain them (Emily: "Reine Natur bin ich, erinnere daher oft an Kunst" [*K* 8]). Even within the explicitly parodic framing, relations between the sexes appear at points as aggressive and violent in nature, suggesting an emphasis on these behaviors' roots in sexuality. Sexuality at its core appears so thoroughly saturated with aggression, that the male (body) seems fashioned into a weapon or recalls an instinctive creature (dog), a depiction leaving little room for the consideration of social influences. Similarly, the female body is characterized tendentiously at points as a physiological given: woman's behaviors are shown to relate to this given in that the female's natural submissiveness in the sexual act is both the effect of her biology and an artifact culturally co-opted by society as "natural." This constitutes a move that does little in ***Krankheit*** to neutralize, much less to counter, female passivity and woman's submissive masochism as pathological.[35] In these instances, Jelinek's play produces Carmilla as a passive cipher of power, unable to escape the ineluctable flow of discipline and normalization, and consequently incapable of subversive activity. Yet, given the broader context of the drama's performances of power, which includes male subjectification and the popular feminist fiction of the lesbian vampire, it seems disingenuous to assert, as have several critics,[36] that only the female protagonists are so caught up in the myths propagated by society that they are able to envision themselves only within the narrowly circumscribed parameters of the man-made and art-like construction of woman in iconography.

Foucault's analysis of processes of "subjection" (*assujettissement*) in *Discipline and Punish* illustrates how power relations permeate interpersonal relations and target *all* subjects, as power circulates in the social body and emanates from every point in the social field.[37] Together with *The Birth of the Clinic,* Foucault's later "interpretive analytics"[38] suggest how the social practices and institutions critiqued in ***Krankheit*** instantiate the bodies of subjects by means of the medicine of pathology and its discourses. Even assessments that acknowledge the drama's critical engagement with male and female subjectivities fail to delineate how men *and* *women* are complicit in securing and upholding dominant power relations.[39] Clearly, some measure of responsibility needs to be shared by those critics who have failed to maintain the requisite critical distance from their subject, and have more consistently cast the relationship of the genders in regressive and superficial terms: in the language of male perpetrators and female victims.[40] As a consequence of this at times implicit valorization of the oppressed, victimized female subject, Carmilla and Emily attain paradigmatic status as *the* oppressed: Carmilla as mother-figure and as Emily's marginalized lesbian-vampire lover; and Emily as writer-vampire, whose "in-between" status has been read as a "positive" force,[41] and whose feminist consciousness appears developed sufficiently enough for her to enlist Carmilla in joining forces "against women's entrapment in a male system."[42] Such readings tend to highlight the "subversive potential" of the defiant female vampire, often employing a feminist perspective that focusses—sometimes to the point of denying the pessimism in Jelinek's work—on empowerment, efficacy, and agency. While a great deal more critical commentary by comparison has addressed how these female figures are subjugated and compelled to signify motherhood and the oppressed through the discourses of "nature," "woman," and "femininity," we would do well to consider how the male figures are constituted in the discursive practices that structure the examination of the sick patient: the "medical look" (*le regard médical*) or "gaze" (*le regard*).[43]

Before I explore in further detail the play's performance of subjectification by means of the clinical-medical discourses, it will be necessary to examine how Jelinek's drama constructs the gaze, not merely, as some would have it, as instrument and proof positive of male oppression of females, but as instrument of production in processes of subjectification. Interpretations of the *Arztpraxis*-scenes of Act I often see in Heidkliff's patriarchal "male gaze" the gaze that projects its fantasies and myths onto the female figure. In this reading, women are both looked at and displayed, with their appearance coded for strong visual and erotic impact so that they connote that certain *to be looked-at-ness*.[44] This reading perceives in the male's dominating perspective the play's critique of women's oppression. Consequently, the emphasis is consistently on Heidkliff's acting upon, on the imposition of his will as a central moment in the staging of woman's oppression.

As doctor, gynecologist and dentist, Heidkliff is, in fact, more so invested with the signifying processes that make him as "doctor" the point of articulation of medicine's scientific institutional discourses, an aspect to which the play alludes and explicitly refers on several occasions: Heidkliff: "Jetzt bin ich Beruf. Ganz in weiß [. . .]. *Er setzt sich entschlossen auf einen Hocker zwischen Carmillas Beinen. Der Ehemann kommt sofort neugierig herbei, schaut in den Unterleib*" (**K** 25). On an almost imperceptible level the varied elements of the doctor's practice underscore the making of Heidkliff-the-doctor and the production of modern medicine: the *Blutkonserven*; the properly elevated examination chair itself, a hybrid dentist's-gynecological chair (*Gynä-Stuhl*); and the chair's gynecological stirrups. The *Arztpraxis* subtly foregrounds the accumulated knowledge of the past: the blood containers and the chair itself—in its design to maximize a probing, atomizing, and detailing vision—enhance the efficiency and productivity of the medical gaze.[45] To interpret Heidkliff reductively, only as male oppressor, and not more expressly as bearer of the medical-scientific gaze, is to overlook that the gaze of this doctor-figure is *productive* of a certain subject, a subject produced by a certain "labour in thought" that has been historically required.[46] Indeed, to read Dr. Heidkliff as primarily or exclusively the object of the play's attack on patriarchy, males, and the male medical establishment, is to ignore that the boundlessly self-absorbed, "pretentious," and "utterly trivial" discourse of the doctor is not godlike merely in its parodic function, which is to deride the omniscience and omnipotence of science.[47] Rather, this inflated medico-scientific discourse is significant for the drama's critique of processes of subjectification through this very discursive regime. Heidkliff's medical-discourse is part of what differentiates doctors from mere mortals, for whom all the old rules hold; it is unquestionably neither a discourse Heidkliff has created, one of which he is Master, nor is it one turning on the fact that some give commands and others obey. As the drama ingeniously insinuates, the medical discourse—and the manner in which Heidkliff (in places, together with Hundekoffer) articulates it—enables the religious and moral dogma about sexuality "to be" in the first place, as through this discourse, in godlike fashion, doctors are empowered to bridge moral and technological obstacles, that is, to "see" what mere mortals cannot. In a more profound sense, then, Heidkliff is made, produced and shaped by this discourse more than he can possibly "voluntarily" deploy it to elevate himself.

To understand this gaze, then, not simply as a patriarchal or male gaze, but as a clinical gaze, is vital to an appreciation of Jelinek's staging of the diseased state that afflicts modern women, for it is through Foucault that we can understand the technology of control in the form of medicine and the medical exam in fabricating modern individuality as one of its products. It is to this gaze's role in the constitution of subjectivity that I now direct our attention. To deepen appreciation for the nuances in the critical force of Heidkliff's performance of the medical gaze and the manner in which the drama exploits Foucauldian insights, I will briefly contextualize the gaze's significance for the drama's staging. This clinical gaze is the look Foucault perceives to emerge in the writings of French pathologist Marie Francois

Xavier Bichat (1771-1802), the gaze that would become definitive for modern medicine (*The Clinic,* esp. 124-48). The era Foucault refers to as "the age of Bichat" witnessed the emergence of a new mechanism of power and subjection, possessed of highly specific procedural techniques and radically different apparatuses. Bichat's exhortation to "open a few corpses" ushers in a new era, for prior to Bichat's. "Treatise on Membranes" (in *Anatomie Générale,* 1801-1802) and other histories by French physicians (including Laennec, Corvisart, Cabanis, Pinel, and Broussais), diseases were not conceptualized in terms of anatomical origin. The previous focus had centered on visible surfaces and symptoms, but with the opening of bodies and the auscultation of the hidden noises of disease in cadavers, specifically, with the beginnings of the eighteenth-century post-mortem exam, the clinic arises as an examining apparatus, a site of production of a certain kind of knowledge, with its own mode of perception and discourse. Thus, the older form of medicine gives way to a more penetrating gaze into the internal organic landscape, effecting in new ways the continued search for an "invisible visibility" (*The Clinic* 165).[48]

As is characteristic of Foucault's complexity, his study of modern medicine, in answering certain questions, raises contradictions that lend even deeper irony to Jelinek's staging of the diseased state of female subjectivity. In *The Birth of the Clinic*'s exploration of the forces that dictate what a doctor sees and does not see in his examination when he looks at a patient, a dichotomization of patient and disease begins to take shape:

> Paradoxically, in relation to that which he is suffering from, the patient is only an external fact; the medical reading must take him into account only to place him in parentheses. Of course, the doctor must know the "internal structure of our bodies" (Clifton 213); but only in order to subtract it, and to free to the doctor's gaze "the nature and combination of symptoms, crises, and other circumstances that accompany diseases" (213). It is not the pathological that functions, in relation to life, as a *counter-nature,* but the patient in relation to the disease itself [. . .]. Hence the strange character of the medical gaze; it is caught up in an endless reciprocity.
>
> (8-9)

In order to render disease visible, the medical gaze must factor out the subject with illness: seeing the patient as an embodied subject emerges not only as inconsequential but as counterproductive. If Heidkliff can be said to bear the special gaze, *le regard médical,* then this backgrounded material suggests the extent to which the experts (doctors) are unequivocally subjectified in the discourses of medicine and caught up in the gaze's "endless reciprocity," a reciprocity that has the disease and the gaze at its center, and its subjects (doctor and patient) the objectives of this control. It is a degree of irony that lends considerable depth to Jelinek's production of "sickness or modern women," but that finds little exploitation of its most radical implications. One significant implication of these Foucauldian insights for the staging of **Krankheit** is the suggestion here that the gaze and its discourses, and not the male doctor himself, objectify. It is an aspect that remains exploited, but generally in a more essentializing manner. Presumably, a female "made" doctor in these regimes of medical knowledge/power/discourses would also assume *le regard médical* and proceed to objectify her patients. The problem posed in this dramatic enactment is that there are only female patients and male doctors.

In several other ways, nevertheless, Jelinek's drama exploits this deployment and placement of female and male bodies characteristic of the modern era, possible only after Bichat "opens up a few corpses." As I noted, according to *The Birth of the Clinic,* the gaze produces individuality, uniqueness, and particularity. Further, if, as a specialized mode of perception, the gaze only "sees" what is obvious, then, for what is only obvious to become visible or significant in the first place, a certain "labour in thought"—the labor-intensive fabrication of clinical medicine itself—has been historically required. This very process of fabrication and of subjectification in clinical medicine is brought into play in Act II when Benno asks: "Wo, meinst du, Heidkliff, war das Geschlecht, bevor man darüber gesprochen hat?" Heidkliff responds, "Die Klinik ist geboren. Und das Geschlecht ist dann auch irgendwann einmal geboren" (*K* 53). As is characteristic of the play's pastiche and (de)montage, phrases drawing on intertexts like *The Birth of the Clinic* and *The History of Sexuality* (vol. 1) are placed into a new context, altered to offer new meanings, and through ironic juxtaposition produce that knowing amusement in the audience. Although the dialogue between Hundekoffer and Heidkliff appears through this shift and apparently offhanded treatment as little more than a parodic gesture—as it has often been read—designed to belittle and mock, the subject of ridicule here is neither Foucault nor his analyses of the phenomenon of power.[49] Though parody's target may usually be the creator of the original work or its style, Heidkliff and Hundekoffer's echoic mention of Foucauldian notions requires this approximation to the original source so that its ironic twist functions. The doctors, in their casual, imprecise thinking ("Und das Geschlecht ist dann auch irgendwann einmal geboren") seem unaware of the implications of these significant thoughts, whereby Heidkliff's metonymy "das Geschlecht" can be subsumed into the canon of standard metonymy, a metonymy of content: as crown for monarch, so "das Geschlecht" for woman/(modern) women. The drama's satirical presentation of the male figure as split, sometimes the wise, godlike master and other times the *ignotus,* enhances the critical force of this scene, which is to foreground the constructed nature of sex/sexuality and, by extension, of woman's construction as sex. The ironic-parodic positioning of Heidkliff and Hundekoffer involves a role-play of pretense, in which these figures appear as ignorant and injudicious as complete fools, but the audience sees through this ploy, and assumes a self-reflexive position to fully appreciate the multivalent utterances.

By means of Heidkliff's reference to "the clinic" in this exchange, the play alludes most apparently to *The Birth of the Clinic*. According to this analysis, the medical look (or gaze) and the words or pictures used to name or represent what is seen (discourse) were altered by 18th century morbid anatomists who made statements about death in their considerations of disease. In that century medicine took a detour through death in the form of pathological anatomy (*The Clinic* 124-48), in the sense that the code of knowledge changed what could be seen and determined the path of medicine for centuries to come. But what was historically a detour through death via pathological anatomy is recast in **Krankheit** as a highly charged logic of inversion that derives in part from Nietzsche's technique of reversal.[50] This inversion builds upon a chain of replacements whereby vision (produces) illness/disease (which stands in for) modern women. The drama's central meanings pivot upon precisely this chain. In this sequence, the medical gaze (*le regard médical*) produces illness, and here "illness," "sickness" and/or "disease" can be metonymically, metaphorically substituted with, or symbolic for, modern women. As Heidkliff and Benno's exchange relates, the clinic's birth and the birth (or production) of sex are intimately intertwined, particularly insofar as the clinic's gaze creates "disease," which, according to **Krankheit,** *is* sickness or modern women. This investment of medical discourse in making the body diseased appears in the scene where the doctors rummage through Carmilla's "dead" body. It also surfaces in the doctors' seemingly nonsensical pronouncements, for example, when Heidkliff proclaims: "Sie bieten einen köstlichen Anblick dem, der in ihnen zu lesen versteht. Ich. Sie duldén Raketen! Sie sind Geschlecht" (**K** 22). In the play's enactment the patient Carmilla represents women, who, categorically, as defined by their very sex, *are* "disease(d)"—countering to some degree the constructed quality of disease and the patient, but also suggesting how the medico-scientific discourse lends concepts and ideas an essence of timelessness, universality, and a self-evident foundation. That Heidkliff and Hundekoffer rummage through Carmilla's "dead" body after her "death" in childbirth (she is soon thereafter reanimated by Emily's vampire bite) serves as compelling insinuation of Foucault's analysis of pathology and of pathology's contributions to modern medicine. The play parodies this analytic insight by having the doctors extract visual props and performance elements from Carmilla's body, including inflatable toys and objects, suggesting that the establishment of pathology or a pathological condition involved little or no science, inasmuch as women were *de facto* always already disease itself (an essentializing proposition indeed!). Thus, as the play mockingly insinuates, medicine could dispense with the scientific establishment of that "fact."

The somewhat more oblique reference in this exchange between the doctors ("Die Klinik ist geboren") is to the theoretical orientation underpinning *The Birth of the Clinic,* namely, the archaeological method of identifying the conditions for the possibility of knowledge. The clinic's "being born" alludes to power's operation in constituting the materiality of the subject, and its operation in the principle which simultaneously forms and regulates the subject of subjectification. In *The Birth of the Clinic* Foucault refers not only to the materiality of the clinic patient's body, but also to the materiality of the clinic itself. This materiality is established in the clinic's creation as a vector and instrument of power (*Discipline* 30). It is in the product of his genealogical method, the first volume of *The History of Sexuality* and not *The Birth of the Clinic,* that Foucault explores the social mechanisms that create "sex." In a fundamental inversion, a counterintuitive reversal much like those we find characterizing Jelinek's techniques of "Umkehrung" and "Ver-kehrung," Foucault claims that instead of assuming that human sexuality derives from a pre-given biological "sex," sexuality (in the sense of a network of power and regulatory regimes) should be construed as operating primarily on bodies by investing bodies with the category of sex. In other words, sexuality makes bodies into the bearers of a principle of identity: sex.[51] That these insights are a function of distinctive historical processes that involved the creation (or birth) of disease by means of *le regard* (the gaze) adds substantial force to the drama's de-construction, to the un-making of self-evident contents and to the destruction of pre-given meanings.

\* \* \*

I have sought to show thus far that the processes of subject constitution and, specifically, the roles assumed by the male figures should not be underestimated if we are to appreciate the broader implications of the play's critique and its particular deployment of power in gender relations. Next, I direct our attention to a different dimension in the exercise of power in processes of subject constitution, brought into play when Heidkliff articulates the vital link between *voir* (seeing), *savoir* (knowledge), and *pouvoir* (power).[52]

In this scene, part of Act II's change in setting, the *Arztpraxis* has disappeared and in its place is a bedroom decorated in a Camp gesture at pop art in 1950s *Kitsch*. The replacement of the gynecological-dentist's chair with a bed(room) fashioned into a coffin serves to extend the *Arztpraxis* in the continued dramatic exploration of the gaze's power. Both settings, medical exam room and bedroom, illustrate the gaze's role in the construction of pathology, sexual practices, and "the truth" in the constitution of identity. Heidkliff and Hundekoffer, having returned from "sportieren" and outfitted in hunter's garb with guns and dogs, are now outside the bedroom, and are aggressively "communicating with" united lovers Emily and Carmilla, who are shut off from them by a closed door. Heidkliff bellows, "Nur mehr der Blick gilt jetzt. Ich sehe dich ganz objektiv. Ich verschaffe mir Zutritt rein als Zuschauer. Ich bin gewiss von meiner Macht verführt" (*K* 53). Once more, the godlike bridging of technological objects enabling the doctor to see what the average human, un-informed and shaped by the medical gaze, cannot, is satirically reintroduced in Heidkliff's inflated style. Ironic is Heidkliff's assertion that he is "gewiss" seduced by *his own* power, particularly when this content is juxtaposed with "Nur mehr der Blick gilt jetzt." Heidkliff's reference to "only" the gaze's "counting any more" (signifying) echoes Foucault's assessment of sight in constituting medical knowledge and of mankind's limitless faith in visual evidence. Heidkliff's apparently hyperbolic statements (for example, "Ich verschaffe mir Zutritt rein als Zuschauer") speak to the objectifying and subjectifying power of *le regard médical* as delineated extensively in *The Birth of the Clinic* and, to a lesser extent and with different emphases, in Foucault's later œuvre. This power is underscored in the doctors' declaration of visual power's ability to penetrate the door, through which Heidkliff and Hundekoffer continue to broadcast loudly.[53]

The men's attack on the door, coupled with Heidkliff's surveying, penetrating gaze, is suggestive of how control over sexuality itself is inscribed in architecture itself: the bedroom door and walls speak the struggle against homosexuality (cf. "The Eye of Power" 148), as Emily and Carmilla cower in fright in their coffin-beds just on the other side the door. Heidkliff and Hundekoffer's seemingly senseless behavior might, of course, be interpreted away as mad rantings, typifying the godlike posturing of the male medical establishment. But this interpretation would reduce this scene's dark ironic effect by relying exclusively on the levity of farcical ridicule and by not more fully exploiting the context. It is as if Jelinek assumes Foucault's art of eluding all commentators' predictions of what the author was to be: "[. . .] no, no, I'm not where you are lying in wait for me, but over here, laughing at you" (*Archaeology/Knowledge* 17). Indeed, the drama's staging here appears the work of nothing less than a literary black humorist for whom the condition of universal absurdity no longer needs to be demonstrated. To accept this interpretation is to acknowledge this brand of humor's satirical form of social instruction. This scene actually constitutes an imaginative transformation of medical discourses, a transformation intended to make the audience grasp the imitative gesturing at Foucauldian insight, serving as a homage to Foucault, as well as a derisive thumbed nose at a male-dominated medical science, as the play seeks through parodic incorporation to come to terms with the complex backgrounded material provided in Foucault's account of vision as the dominant cognitive sense.[54] Here, the language of doctors is parodied in a satire of medicine's power as a subjectifying discourse. In this sense, the real subject matter of this parody-satire is medical knowledge's ocularcentrism.[55] Foucault had already emphasized the sinister implications of ocular primacy in an analysis of the history of madness in his earlier work of 1961, *Madness and Civilization*. There he details that the sciences of man, intended to assist in the macrological normalizing of individuals, drew on a mixture of the gaze and discourse Foucault then identifies with psychoanalysis in 1963's *The Birth of the Clinic*. Although Foucault later in his investigations of sexuality also stressed the power of discourse, such as that of confession in creating the very notion of sexuality, he insisted on the importance of spatial and visual controls in policing sexuality and disease (homosexuality, masturbation). Jelinek's staging derides this notion of the primacy of vision as the dominant means of ascertaining reliable knowledge about the external world, but acknowledges its impact in the noxious internalizing mechanisms and social conditions afflicting gender relations.

Similar references to vision and the power of the gaze occur throughout the second act, including at the drama's conclusion, as Heidkliff and Hundekoffer hunt down Emily and Carmilla. In the last scenes, the two female figures emerge from hiding in a restroom, reconstituted as a *Doppelgeschöpf*, sewn together into one giant Siamese twin doll. In the midst of the men's diatribe against the merged monster-figure, Heidkliff interjects a seemingly nonsensical "Die Sprach und die Anschau gehören zusammen" (*K* 74). Hardly the ridiculing deflation of Foucauldian insight, the allusion to the gaze here and in other exchanges references the visual power-discourse connection in processes of subjection, assigning a central role to speech and language in naming bodies, even in abjection, in the very act of expelling and excluding that which is nevertheless constitutive of the self (cf. Kristeva).[56] This highlights a vital aspect in the play's representation of power relations: a central point on which Foucault's account of power and Jelinek's drama converge is in the gaze's force, not as merely reductive, repressive, but as a productive mode of perception. The gaze is, as Jelinek's play continually performs it, *productive* of individuality and the discursive constitution of sexuality. The gaze's force in the production of the modern individual is noted in Hundekoffer's explicit linkage of desire, body, and conscience, whereby the speech of confession produces the subject of desire/subjectification: "Wohnt nicht auch die Lust im Körper, fällt mir jetzt ein? Und wird der Körper nicht schon vom Blick durchbohrt? Jetzt beißt mein Gewissen irgendwo" (*K* 51). This statement extends the notion that the body is transformed over time by technologies (e.g. sexual mores, penal systems) to include other dimensions of pastoral power such as confession, self-examination, and the guidance of the conscience. The Christian preoccupation with the sinful nature of the flesh and its desires hardly, as intended, eradicated that desire through the bite or sting of guilt, but produced it, a function of a specific gaze directed at the body.

That not only Heidkliff articulates the subject's seduction in this circulation of power ("Ich bin von meiner Macht verführt" [*K* 53]), but that Emily, too, declares: "Die Macht ist ein Kreislauf wechselseitiger Verführung" (*K* 54), serves to underscore the infinite impossibilities for the modern subject: the impossibility of escape, of taking control over the signification of bodies, of refusing one's construction as sexuality. This point returns us to Emily's positioning in the medical gaze in Act I, scene five, to which I briefly alluded during my discussion of Carmilla and of Benno's use of force. Emily's assertion, in its parodic gesture of speaking as lesbian vampire, is to suggest that feminine subjects *are part of* power's circulation. To understand the complex psychological investment subjects make in gender conventions,[57] I suggest we make sense of Emily's parodic attempt to "assume the mantle of the Phallus"[58] by means of an approach that acknowledges power's permeation of all aspects of social relations. This perspective resists facile conceptualizations that ignore that even the seemingly "independent" standpoints are implicated in the disciplinary establishments of modern society. Emily's wish—as she expresses it to Heidkliff—in having retractable teeth installed, is ostensibly to be able to demonstrate, to produce, to show ["vorzeigen"] Phallic desire ["Lust"] (*K* 34-35). Through this violent insertion Emily seeks to insert herself into the Phallic law/order/discourse. Her desire, construed as "need," in mimicking the expandable penis, is to become (like) the subject of Phallic power/desire. Emily's actions—her request and her undergoing the operation by having Heidkliff violently insert the retractable teeth—parodically mimic the collapse of the representational symbol (the phallus) and the anatomical organ (the penis). This performance, moreover, can be read as a parody of Lacan's assertion that somehow the phallus as non-object, non-fantasy, non-diminishable symbol can never be reduced to the penis itself, and, therefore, is *always prior to* the penis. Emily's demand to acquire retractable teeth suggests that although the phallus is not the penis in any straightforward sense, the metaphor as signifying chain is never at far remove from the very object it symbolizes. By demanding from Dr. Heidkliff the insertion of retractable teeth, Emily inscribes the phallus upon the vampire's body itself, and creates a representation that must appear ambiguous to the audience with respect to the play's position in undermining the dominant order.[59]

How are we to interpret Emily's actions in the contexts of gender/power relations—as Emily's attempt to identify with the phallogocentrism of the prevailing order, that is, with the law of the father? Or, are we to see Emily's actions as subverting the (symbolic) order by satirizing, mocking, and parodying the complicity of subjects with the forces of domination? Although the black humor in this case lies in a critical disjunction (a lesbian vampire cannot assume a Phallic position), this scene offers us several readings, none of which entirely excludes or invalidates the others. It can, for example, be seen as a satire on the phallocentric order, or, perhaps, as a pure parody of Lacanian concepts and terms. Irrespective of what one concludes, I contend that the overarching effect is to dramatize through performance power's permeation of all relations. Even though Emily's attempts to gain entry into the Phallic order bodily deploy the masculinist-patriarchal show of desire and can be considered, through mimicry, parodic of the dominant system, her desire to invest herself with the ultimate authority of the Master (phallic) signifier does not undermine the hegemony of the discourse she seeks to imitate. For a subject to represent herself as literally speaking the Master's words and assuming his desire/subject position is to expose the split subjectivity that, in rational discourse, is covered up by metaphor. Emily's insistence that the Master/Phallus speak through her as she assumes its position (bodily) literalizes the key metaphorical assumption on which the Cartesian *cogito* is based. That is, when she, as fiancée/writer/lesbian vampire declares, "Ich wünsche mir diese beiden Zähne ausfahrbar gemacht! Sie sollen hervorlugen und wieder verschwinden können. Wie ich ja auch. Ich brauche einen ähnlichen Apparat wie ihr Männer ihn habt! Ich möchte imponieren können. Ich möchte Lust vorzeigen können!" (*K* 33), Emily usurps the position of the masculine *cogito*. This can hardly be said, however, as **Krankheit** implies through the forces of subjection, to constitute "liberation." In a Foucauldian sense, Emily's very need to assume the position of Phallus/Master ("Ich brauche einen ähnlichen Apparat wie ihr Männer ihn habt!") can only reproduce dominant power relations, because this "need" or "demand" is itself constructed, a "political instrument meticulously prepared, calculated, and used" (*Discipline* 26). Emily's desire/need, then, can be viewed as a function of hegemonic power's influence: it may be impossible to unequivocally deny that her oppositional, "in-between" position has internalized the hegemonic position here, and been absorbed and incorporated.[60] Emily's actions suggest more the opposite of power as an exclusively repressive force, as working solely to censor, block, exclude, and repress: her voluntary move to the gynecological/dentist's chair—just as Carmilla's movement into the *Gyna-Stuhl* in the second scene—suggests that she accepts the meanings and adopts the practices that reflect the exercise of a hegemonic medico-scientific power.

The inability of feminine subjects to resist or escape is further underscored in the play in Carmilla's expression of her self-investment in illness, once more underscoring power's ineluctable circulation: "Die Krankheit ist schön. Sie ist mir unentbehrlich. Ich bin krank, daher bin ich [. . .]. Ich bin krank, und es geht mir gut. Ich leide, und ich fühle mich sehr sehr schlecht. Gesundheit ist nicht alles, und mein Körper hält sie nun gar nicht aus [. . .]. Ich bin schön krank! Krank! Krank! Krank!" (*K* 44-45). Her seemingly nonsensical rejoinder to Emily's declaration "Weißt du, einer sagt, die Geschichte beruhe in letzter Instanz auf dem Körper des Menschen" (*K* 44) expresses not only Carmilla's investment in illness, but also her finding self-expression by means of this condition, made explicit in other places: "Ich genieße meine Krankheit ja auch!" (*K* 47). This utterance relativizes Carmilla's "Ich bin krank, daher bin ich"-pronouncement by revealing that woman-as-sickness is not exclusively a function of a man-made, diseased state of gender relations, but created through female subjects' negotiation of their condition. Repeatedly and insistently, these figures make sense of their state in ways that undermine what would be their static representation as the victims of a male-defined medical discourse which extends to Freud and Charcot: "Die Krankheit ist schön. Sie ist mir unentbehrlich. Ich bin krank, daher bin ich [. . .]. Ohne Krankheit wäre ich nichts" (*K* 44). These figures are not simplistically "trapped" in a static state of illness and disease, in a universal *conditio feminina* ostensibly created by males expressly for oppressing females—even though the drama comes close to suggesting this in places. As I mentioned at the outset, through its framing with Eva Meyer's quote about *woman* not being like the great masters who command the ability to disappear in their great works, and its title **Krankheit oder Moderne Frauen,** Jelinek's narrative does presume to an extent upon the unity of its gendered subject of presentation and performance (i.e., modern women), just as it does presume upon a unity for male subjects, even when the drama is at pains to demonstrate, and deconstruct, the differences within these admittedly generalizing and imprecise categories. What I have sought, further, to pose as significant questions and central contradictions in this reading of **Krankheit** is that certain interpretations of the play have not merely involved a question of seeing things differently, but also of suppressing, overlooking, and/or misreading vital and radical aspects of the drama's social critique. Significant to the critical force of this analytic-dramatic enactment is the female figures' appropriation of the vocabulary of the "experts" Drs. Heidkliff and Benno Hundekoffer, for it is through *this* vocabulary, its terms, concepts, and its distortions [women (as sex) = illness], that these figures interpret their experiences and construct themselves. By viewing the subjectification of the genders from a more differentiating perspective on power (as productive, a network), and recognizing this perspective's enactment in all its pessimism in **Krankheit oder Moderne Frauen,** we can more precisely apprehend the diseased state that characterizes contemporary gender relations.

*Notes*

Research for this article was made possible by a faculty research award from Weber State University's Dean for the Arts and Humanities: I am indebted to June K. Phillips for granting me the support to research and write this essay in the summer of 2000. I am, further, grateful to Michael Wutz for calling this opportunity to my attention in the first place. For their insights on Jelinek and thoughtful comments, I thank Dagmar Lorenz, Lilian Friedberg, and the *German Quarterly* reviewers.

1. Elfriede Jelinek, *Krankheit oder Moderne Frauen,* ed. Regine Friedrich (Köln: Prometh, 1987): 44; hereafter referred to as *K* and followed by page number(s).

2. References to Foucault will be cited here parenthetically by (abbreviated) title and page number(s).

3. E.g., Lanyon 87; Janz 91-92. Hanssen's analysis of the language of violence engages critically with poststructuralist and postmodern feminist strategies in reading *Krankheit,* drawing more on feminist appropriations of the French school of theories, particularly Lacan, Derrida, and, to a lesser extent, Foucault.

4. Among the personalities and media Jelinek salutes, several in mock deference, on the cast of characters page in *Krankheit* are Baudrillard, Robert Walser, Barthes, Bram Stoker, Joseph Sheridan Le Fanu, Goebbels, *Der Spiegel,* "Der Hörfunk," and "Das Fernsehen" (*K* 5).

5. A note on the translation: the play's German title is not unambiguously translatable. Meyer, for example, renders *Krankheit oder Moderne Frauen* as *Sickness or Modern Women* (116), and Poole as *Illness or Modern Women* (252). For the purposes of my analysis "Krankheit" can be variously translated as "sickness," "illness," and/or "disease." In instances where I employ the slash ("/"), I seek to emphasize that the two (or three) terms are not to be considered separately. In these ("/") cases, there seems little point in belaboring the relationship between sickness, illness, and disease, since these are not so readily distinguishable to the untrained eye. To a disciplined clinical eye, however, they are, and significantly so.

6. E.g., the contributions by Janz, Fiddler, Wigmore.

7. Adorno 312.

8. As Heiner Müller noted in a panel discussion before the premiere of *Krankheit*: "Was mich interessiert an den Texten von Elfriede Jelinek, ist der Widerstand, den sie leisten gegen das Theater, so wie er ist" (Friedrich 98).

9. Lorenz 35.

10. Hanssen 80, 112; see also Fiddler, "Problems with Porn: Situating Elfriede Jelinek's *Lust*."

11. Luscher 174.

12. See Janz 82; Hoffmann 198; Hoesterey; Hoffmann 198; Luscher 173.

13. Cf. Hiebel.

14. Hoesterey 156.

15. Jelinek, "Ich möchte seicht sein" 157.

16. See for example Janz 91-92.

17. Cf. Lorenz esp. 31-33, 35.

18. Hoesterey 153-57; Luscher esp. 167-79; Spielmann esp. 27.

19. Thomas 142.

20. Hoffmann 195.

21. Scholars and critics who draw more substantively on Meyer's framing quote in their analysis include Berka ("'Das bissigste Stück'"), Haß (esp. 25-26), Hoesterey (esp. 152-58), Hoffmann, and Janz.

22. Lentricchia 188.

23. See, for example, Berka's "Ein Gespräch mit Elfriede Jelinek" and Jelinek, Heinrich, Meyer. Support for assuming a "personalizing" approach to *Krankheit* stems from passages in Jelinek interviews, such as, for example: "Für alle Frauen versuche ich den Kampf gegen die normenbildende Kaste aufzunehmen, denn die schreckliche Ungerechtigkeit ist ja nicht die wirtschaftliche Unterdrückung der Frau, die auch entsetzlich ist und längst behoben werden müßte, sondern das Schlimme ist dieses männliche Wert- und Normensystem, dem die Frau unterliegt, und zwar so unterliegt, daß sie eben immer anders sein muß und die ihr zugeschriebenen Eigenschaften wie Sanftmütigkeit, Gefühlsseligkeit und Freundlichkeit ja nur das andere zu dem der Männer sind, daß man gar nicht weiß, was die Frau ist" (Presber 114).

24. Schmid-Bortenschlager 119; Lanyon 80.

25. Lanyon 88.

26. Lanyon 88.

27. Hoesterey 151.

28. Fliedl 65. See also Meyer (esp. 122-25) and Barthofer in this regard.

29. Cf. Meyer 117.

30. Luscher 173-74.

31. With "voluntarily" I wish to emphasize that there is much in human self-understanding that is not exactly voluntary, though to call it *in*voluntary, to my mind, is by far the greater misrepresentation, for it misses the extent to which subjects form their identities by conforming themselves over time to tacitly understood norms and generally accepted practices.

32. Cf. Nettleton; Simons.

33. Cf. Simons 199.

34. Benno: "Was soll ich dem Arzt sagen, wenn er kommt? Woran genau leidest du? [. . .] Gleich kommt der Arzt. [. . .] Wie gern säße ich an deiner Stelle! Ich Kümmere mich einstweilen in meiner sanften Art um unsere Kleinen [*K* 13]. [. . .] Ich schaue ein wenig auf unsere Kinderschar, und schon kann ich dir nicht mehr böse sein. Diese Kinder werden Nachfolger der großen Klassiker werden" (*K* 16); Carmilla: "Ich hoffe, der Arzt kommt bald zu mir und macht dein Werk fertig. [. . .] Ich werde an dich denken, wenn das Kind herauskommt. Ich danke dir, daß du mich erneut vollgefüllt hast" (*K* 17); Heidkliff "*wühlt in Carmilla, wirft Gummitiere*: Ich bin nichts so sehr gewöhnt wie den Anblick von Frauen. Bei mir ist die Frau Patientin und sonst nichts [*K* 29]. [. . .] Kinder fernhalten! Wegbringen! Staub saugen! Meine nächsten Patientinnen warten schon" (*K* 30).

35. Cf. Ockenfuss 75.

36. See for example Claes 82-126; Hoesterey 153, 157; Lanyon 75-76; Luscher 171-72; Janz.

37. "Two Lectures" 96.

38. Dreyfus and Rabinow 115.

39. E.g., Hoffmann esp. 199; Roeder 16-18.

40. E.g., Lanyon, Claes.

41. Fiddler, "Reading Elfriede Jelinek" 303.

42. Hoesterey 153. See in this regard Lanyon (esp. 83-84, 89); Claes 82-126; Haß, who reads Emily as breaking with the central construction in that "[s]he decides for herself" (27); and Berka, who claims that Jelinek "engage[s] in an affirmation of vampirism among women" ("'Das bissigste Stück

der Saison'" 373). Berka views *Krankheit*'s representation of female vampires—a medium of ideological critique—as addressing "violence against women, their resistance to being exploited or vampirized, to the one-way pornographic aspects and consequences of one dominating sexuality, and their affirmation of gender inversion and a revaluated status for women in society" (373).

43. Although Foucault deals extensively with the discourses of clinical medicine in *The Birth of the Clinic*, he treats this theme only briefly in the preface to *The Order of Things: An Archaeology of the Human Sciences* and in *The Archaeology of Knowledge* (50-55). *The Birth of the Clinic* has been called an "extended postscript" to *Madness and Civilization*, a particularly fitting description, as Martin Jay notes, if one acknowledges its concentration on the complicity of visual domination with the rise of modern medicine ("Empire of the Gaze" 181).

44. Cf. Mulvey 436.

45. This could apply to the audience too, as, like the viewers behind a surgeon in a clinic, we witness a performance, transfixed by the surgeon's gaze. After Carmilla's "death" in the gynecological chair where Benno Hundekoffer had "assisted" her in childbirth, Dr. Heidkliff declares: "Es macht mir nichts aus, Rezitator und horchendes Publikum zu sein" (*K* 31). His statement relates to the role of the clinician as researcher-gaze and teacher vis-à-vis his students, a role that has been prepared in Hundekoffer's description of Dr. Heidkliff's role. Earlier, Benno in speaking had "prepared" his wife in the gynecological chair: "Dieser Arzt ist nach allen mir zugänglichen Quellen jedoch auch Zahnarzt und kann deine [Carmilla's] Wurzel jederzeit extrahieren. Er kann wo er will etwas aus dir herausnehmen. Er wird dann rezitieren und Publikum sein" (*K* 16). The implicit image with which *Krankheit* confronts the audience is that of the "speaking eye," specifically the discursive constellation of the gaze that makes it possible for the act of instruction to take place at the operating table-examination chair.

46. Althusser 45; Foucault, *The Birth of the Clinic*. While there is clearly a derisive element in Jelinek's parodic treatment of males as doctors and of medicine, as, for example, when Heidkliff enthusiastically exclaims: "Ja! Ja! Ja! Ja! Das Knirschen des Pfahls beim Eindringen in den Knochen, der sich windende Leib, der blutige Schaum vor dem Mund, das Erbrochene. Wir dürfen uns daran erinnern: *Es muss sein. Es dient der Menschheit. Wie ich als Arzt.*" (*K* 48—emphasis mine), the juxtaposition of medicine's service in the betterment of the human condition with vampire hunting belies a serious content. This points to the compelling constraint of the subjectification of subjects in discourses of science and medicine: "*Es muss sein. Es dient der Menschheit. Wie ich als Arzt.*" The performance here requires that the audience maintain multiple representations that specify, for one, what the character Heidkliff doesn't really know, and, second, the satire that results from the audience's considering the broader social issues of culture and socialization, specifically, Foucault's insight into the fabrication of subjects compelled to serve discursive regimes.

47. For the play's attack on patriarchy Luscher 167; Lanyon 84; Hoesterey 156; for critique of "self-absorption" Luscher 173; for pretentiousness and triviality, Hoesterey 156.

48. Cf. Jay, "In the Empire of the Gaze" 182.

49. E.g., Hoesterey 156; Janz 91-92. Janz's otherwise incisive analysis is in several respects representative of readings that tend to reduce the male figures to producers of nonsense, such as when, for example, Heidkliff *drivels* ("faselt") the statement "Ich bin gewiß von meiner Macht verführt" (91) and Hundekoffer poses *imbecilic* questions ("So fragt Benno Hundekoffer blöde [. . .]" [*K* 92]). Janz in effect reads the male figures as idiots, who—at best only accidentally—experience an occasional flash of insight, whereby she misreads the more complex allusions to Foucault: "Was hier wie eine unfreiwillige Foucault-Parodie erschient, zeugt doch zugleich auch von Einsicht, allerdings in Gestalt der Idiotensprache. Zumindest dämmert hier die Einsicht, daß es im Grunde gar nicht geht um das tatsächliche Geschlecht der Frau, sondern um den *Diskurs* über die Frau als Geschlechtswesen, der ihre Ausgrenzung legitimiert und als angebliche weibliche 'Natur' festgeschrieben hat" (92). There are instances where *Krankheit* subverts an author's position (e.g., the misogyny of Otto Weininger; see Luscher 168-69; Hoesterey 157-58), but Foucault's insights are generally used to deepen the drama's social critique. As profound as his analyses are, Foucault is also said to have playfully suggested that there has been "sex" only since the 19th century and that we would have been better off not wanting to "have sex." See Hoy, "Power, Repression, Progress" (133).

50. Cf. Eigler; Hanssen 97.

51. Cf. Butler, "Sexual Inversions" esp. 66-67; Foucault, *History of Sexuality* 155-56.

52. Cf. Jay, "In the Empire of the Gaze" 178.

53. [. . .] brüllt unartikuliert durch die verschlossene Tür, hinter der die Frauen in ihren Sargbetten entsetzt aneinandergeklammert sitzen (*K* 52). [. . .] Schlägt wütend gegen die Tür" (*K* 53).

54. Cf. Hutcheon 211.

55. Jay, "In the Empire of the Gaze" 180-93. My discussion on ocularcentrism is indebted to Martin Jay's compelling analysis of Foucault's fit and continuity with 20th century philosophy, specifically with the interrogation of sight carried out by a disparate number of French intellectuals beginning roughly with Henri Louis Bergson. See also Jay's *Marxism and Totality: The Adventures of a Concept from Lukács to Habermas*.

56. In another Act II scene with the bedroom setting and two male figures, Benno declares: "Selbst ist der Mann! Er führt sein Geschlecht lauthals vor. Wie ein Dokument. Er hat es ja bekommen! Alles soll produziert werden. Alles soll lesbar sein. Alles soll man sehen können" (*K* 50). At a later point in this exchange, Heidkliff responds: "Es ist auch gefährlich hier drinnen. Es ist gefährlich im Sichtbaren wie im Unsichtbaren, wo die große Verführung stattfindet" (*K* 50).

57. Cf. Lanyon 89.

58. Lanyon 81.

59. Cf. Lorenz; Kohlenbach.

60. Cf. Berka, "Das bissigste Stück" 373.

*Works Cited*

Adorno, Theodor. *Negative Dialektik*. Frankfurt a.M.: Suhrkamp, 1996.

Althusser, Louis. *Reading Capital*. London: Verso, 1970.

Barthofer, Alfred. "Vanishing in the Text: Elfriede Jelinek's Art of Self-Effacement in *The Piano Teacher* and *Children of the Dead*." Meyerhofer 138-63.

Bartsch, Kurt, and Günther Höfler, eds. *Elfriede Jelinek*. Graz: Droschl, 1991. 57-77.

Berka, Sigrid. "'Das bissigste Stück der Saison?' The Textual and Sexual Politics of Vampirism in Elfriede Jelinek's *Krankheit oder Moderne Frauen*." *The German Quarterly* 68.4 (1995): 372-88.

———. "Ein Gespräch mit Elfriede Jelinek." *Modern Austrian Literature* 26.2 (1993): 127-55.

Bichat, Marie Francois Xavier. *Anatomie Generale (1801-1802). Selected Reading in Pathology from Hippocrates to Virchow*. Esmond R. Long. Springfield, IL: Charles C. Thomas, 1929. 130-39.

Butler, Judith. *Bodies that Matter: On the Discursive Limits of "Sex."* New York: Routledge, 1990.

———. "Sexual Inversions." Hekman 59-75.

Claes, Oliver. *Fremde. Vampire: Sexualität, Tod und Kunst bei Elfriede Jelinek und Adolf Muschg*. Bielefeld: Aisthesis, 1994.

Clifton, Francis. *État de la médecine ancienne et moderne*. Paris: n.p., 1742.

Dreyfus, Hubert L., and Paul Rabinow. "What is Maturity? Habermas and Foucault on 'What is Enlightenment?'" Hoy 109-21.

Eigler, Friederike. "'Gewissenlose Erkenntnis': Frauen-Bilder und Kulturkritik bei Elfriede Jelinek und Friedrich Nietzsche." *Seminar* 30.1 (1994): 44-58.

Fiddler, Allyson. "Problems with Porn: Situating Elfriede Jelinek's *Lust*." *German Life and Letters* 44.5 (1991): 404-15.

———. "Reading Elfriede Jelinek." *Post-War Women's Writing in German: Feminist Critical Approaches. A Study of Women's Writing in the Federal Republic, the German Democratic Republic, Austria and Switzerland*. Ed. Chris Weedon. Providence: Berghahn, 1997. 291-304.

———. *Rewriting Reality. An Introduction to Elfriede Jelinek*. Oxford: Berg, 1994.

———. "There Goes That Word Again, or Elfriede Jelinek and Postmodernism." Johns and Arens 129-49.

Fliedl, Konstanz. "'Echt sind nur wir!' Realismus und Satire bei Elfriede Jelinek." Bartsch and Höfler 57-77.

Foucault, Michel. *The Archaeology of Knowledge and the Discourse on Language*. Trans. A. M. Sheridan Smith. New York: Pantheon, 1972.

———. *The Birth of the Clinic: An Archaeology of Medical Perception*. Trans. A. M. Sheridan Smith. New York: Vintage, 1973.

———. *Discipline and Punish: The Birth of the Prison*. New York: Pantheon, 1977.

———. "The Ethic of Care for the Self as a Practice of Freedom: An Interview with Michel Foucault on January 20, 1984." Interview by Raul Fornet-Betancourt et al. Trans. Joseph D. Gauthier. *The Final Foucualt*. Ed. James Bernauer and David Rasmussen. Cambridge: MIT P, 1988. 1-20.

———. "The Eye of Power," *Power/Knowledge: Selected Interviews and Other Writings, 1972-1977*. Ed. Colin Gordon. Trans. Colin Gordon et al. New York: Pantheon, 1980. 146-65.

———. *The History of Sexuality*, vol. 1: *An Introduction*. Trans. Robert Hurley. New York: Pantheon, 1978.

———. *Madness and Civilization: A History of Insanity in the Age of Reason.* Trans. Richard Howard. New York: Vintage, 1988.

———. "Nietzsche, Genealogy, History." *Language, Counter-Memory, Practice: Selected Essays and Interviews.* Ed. Donald F. Bouchard. Trans. D. F. Bouchard and Sherry Simon. Ithaca: Cornell UP, 1977. 139-64.

———. *The Order of Things: An Archaeology of the Human Sciences.* New York: Random House, 1970.

———. *Power/Knowledge. Selected Interviews and Other Writings 1972-1977.* Michel Foucault. Ed. Colin Gordon. Trans. Gordon et al. New York: Pantheon, 1980.

———. "Two Lectures." *Power/Knowledge. Selected Interviews and Other Writings 1972-1977.* Michel Foucault. Ed. Colin Gordon. Trans. Gordon et al. New York: Pantheon, 1980. 78-108.

Friedrich, Regine. Nachwort. *Krankheit oder Moderne Frauen.* Ed. Friedrich. Köln: Prometh, 1987. 84-93.

Fuss, Diana. *Essentially Speaking. Feminism, Nature and Difference.* New York: Routledge, 1989.

Gorsky, Susan Rubinow. "'I'll cry myself sick': Illness in *Wuthering Heights.*" *Literature and Medicine* 18.2 (1999): 173-91.

Gürtler, Christa, ed. *Gegen den schönen Schein: Texte zu Elfriede Jelinek.* Frankfurt: Neue Kritik, 1990.

Hanssen, Beatrice. "Elfriede Jelinek's Language of Violence." *New German Critique* 68 (1996): 79-112.

Haβ, Ulrike. "Grausige Bilder. Groβe Musik. Zu den Theaterstücken Elfriede Jelineks." *Text + Kritik* 117 (1993): 21-30.

Hekman, Susan J., ed. *Feminist Interpretations of Michel Foucault.* University Park: The Pennsylvania State UP, 1996.

Hiebel, Hans H. "Elfriede Jelinek's Satirical 'Prose-Poem' *Lust.*" Johns and Arens 48-72.

Hoesterey, Ingeborg. "A Feminist 'Theater of Cruelty': Surrealist and Mannerist Strategies in *Krankheit oder Moderne Frauen.*" Johns and Arens 151-65.

Höfler, Günther A. "Sexualität und Macht in Elfriede Jelineks Prosa." *Modern Austrian Literature* 23.3-4 (1990): 99-110.

Hoffmann, Yasmin. "'Noch immer riecht es hier nach Blut': Zu Elfriede Jelineks Stück *Krankheit oder Moderne Frauen.*" *Cahiers de l'Etudes Germaniques* 20 (1991): 191-204.

Hutcheon, Linda. "Parody without Ridicule: Observations on Modern Literary Parody." *Canadian Review of Comparative Literature* 5 (1978): 201-11.

Hoy, David Couzens, ed. *Foucault: A Critical Reader.* Oxford: Basil Blackwell, 1986.

———. "Introduction." Hoy 1-25.

———. "Power, Repression, Progress: Foucault, Lukes, and the Frankfurt School." Hoy 123-47.

Janz, Marlies. "Falsche Spiegel. Über die Umkehrung als Verfahren bei Elfriede Jelinek." Gürtler 81-97.

Jay, Martin. "In the Empire of the Gaze: Foucault and the Denigration of Vision in Twentieth-century Thought." Hoy 175-204.

———. *Marxism and Totality: The Adventures of a Concept from Lukács to Habermas.* Berkeley: U of California P, 1984.

Jelinek, Elfriede. "Elfriede Jelinek im Gespräch." *Valie Export and Elfriede Jelinek im Spiegel der Presse. Zur Rezeption der feministischen Avantgarde Österreichs.* Ed. Margarete Lamb-Faffelberger. New York: Peter Lang, 1992.

———. "Ich möchte seicht sein." Gürtler 157-61.

———. "Ich will kein Theater. Ich will ein anderes Theater." Interview with Anke Roeder. Roeder 141-57.

———. *Krankheit oder Moderne Frauen.* Ed. Regine Friedrich. Köln: Prometh, 1987.

Jelinek, Elfriede, Jutta Heinrich, and Adolf-Ernst Meyer. "Elfriede Jelinek im Gespräch mit Adolf-Ernst Meyer." *Sturm und Zwang. Schreiben als Geschlechterkampf.* Hamburg: Ingrid Klein, 1995.

Johns, Jorun B., and Katherine Arens, eds. *Elfriede Jelinek: Framed by Language.* Riverside: Ariadne, 1994.

Kohlenbach, Margarete. "Montage und Mimikry." Bartsch and Höfler 121-47.

Kristeva, Julia. *Powers of Horror: An Essay in Abjection.* Trans. Leon S. Roudiez. New York: Columbia UP, 1982.

Lamb-Faffelberger, Margarete. "Austria's Feminist Avant-Garde: Valie Export's and Elfriede Jelinek's Aesthetic Innovations." *Out from the Shadows: Essays on Contemporary Austrian Women Writers and Filmmakers.* Ed. Margarete Lamb-Faffelberger. Riverside: Ariadne, 1997. 229-41.

Lanyon, Jenny. "The De(con)struction of Female Subjectivity in Elfriede Jelinek's Play *Krankheit oder Moderne Frauen.*" *Centre Stage. Contemporary Drama in Austria.* Ed. Frank Finlay and Ralf Jeutter. Amsterdam: Rodopi, 1999. 73-89.

Lentricchia, Frank. *Ariel and the Police: Michel Foucault, William James, Wallace Stevens.* Madison: U of Wisconsin P, 1988.

Lorenz, Dagmar C. G. "Humor bei zeitgenössischen Autorinnen." *The Germanic Review* 62.1 (1987): 28-36.

Luscher, Jean A. "Myth, Language and Power in Elfriede Jelinek's *Krankheit oder Moderne Frauen*." Johns and Arens 166-75.

Meyer, Imke. "The Trouble with Elfriede: Jelinek and Autobiography." Meyerhofer 116-37.

Meyerhofer, Nicholas J., ed. *The Fiction of the I: Contemporary Austrian Writers and Autobiography*. Riverside, CA: Ariadne, 1999.

Mulvey, Laura. "Visual Pleasure and Narrative Cinema." *Feminisms: An Anthology of Literary Theory and Criticism*. Ed. Robyn R. Warhol and Diane Price Herndl. New Brunswick, NJ: Rutgers UP, 1993. 432-42.

Nettleton, Sarah. "Wisdom, Diligence and Teeth: Discursive Practices and the Creation of Mothers." *Sociology of Health and Illness* 13.1 (1991): 98-111.

Ockenfuss, Crystal Mazur. "Keeping Promises, Breaking Rules: Stylistic Innovations in Elfriede Jelinek's *Lust*." Johns and Arens 73-88.

Poole, Ralph J. "'Ich gebäre nicht. Ich begehre dich': The Lesbian Vampire as Mother/Artist in Elfriede Jelinek." *Queering the Canon: Defying Sights in German Literature and Culture*. Ed. Christoph Lorey and John L. Plews. Columbia: Camden House, 1998. 248-71.

Presber, Gabriele, ed. "Elfriede Jelinek." Interview. *Die Kunst ist weiblich*. München: Knaur, 1988. 108-13.

Roeder, Anke, ed. *Autorinnen: Herausforderungen an das Theater*. Frankfurt: Suhrkamp, 1989.

Schmid-Bortenschlager, Sigrid. "Der analytische Blick." *Frauenliteratur in Österreich von 1945 bis heute: Beiträge des internationalen Kolloquiums in Mulhouse, 21.-23. Februar 1985*. Ed. Carine Kleiber und Erika Tunner. Bern: Peter Lang, 1986. 109-29.

Simons, Jon. "Foucault's Mother." Hekman 179-209.

Spielmann, Yvonne. "Ein unerhörtes Sprachlabor. Feministische Aspekte im Werk von Elfriede Jelinek." Bartsch and Höfler 21-40.

Thomas, Rebecca S. "Subjectivity in *Clara S.*: Resisting the Vanishing Point. *Modern Austrian Literature* 32.1 (1999): 141-58.

Tytler, Graeme. "Heathcliff's Monomania: An Anachronism in *Wuthering Heights*." *Brontë Society Transactions* 20.6 (1992): 331-43.

Wigmore, Juliet. "Power, Politics and Pornography: Elfriede Jelinek's Satirical Exposés." *Literature on the Threshold: The German Novel in the 1980s*. Ed. Arthur Williams, Stuart Parkes, Roland Smith. Providence: Berg, 1990. 209-19.

**Stephan Atzert (review date winter 2002)**

SOURCE: Atzert, Stephan. Review of *Gier: Ein Unterhaltungroman Elfriede Jelinek,* by Elfriede Jelinek. *World Literature Today* 76, no. 1 (winter 2002): 184.

[*In the following positive review of* Gier, *Atzert calls Jelinek "one of the few established* and *interesting authors in the German-writing world."*]

In nine numbered but untitled sections [in *Gier*], Elfriede Jelinek tells a story of violence, set in rural Austria. The police officer Kurt Janisch is interested in women and houses. His wife watches TV serials in their home, while the elderly original owner slowly disintegrates psychologically, uncared for in her upstairs flat. By means of the power he yields as a police officer, Janisch identifies, courts, and soon abuses Gerti, a middle-aged homeowner, with a view toward obtaining her villa. While Gerti is caught up in her hopeless dependency on him, Janisch maintains sexual relations with Gabi, an underage teenager. At the end of the book Gabi and Gerti are dead and Janisch inherits Gerti's house. According to the grossly misleading cover text provided by the publisher, *Gier* (Avarice) is a combination of detective story, pornography, and penny novel.

Arguably, the plot as outlined above takes second place to Jelinek's literary style. The narrator's relentless monologue incorporates voices from multiple sources. It does not limit itself to being self-reflective and to presenting different aspects of the characters. In effect, the characters and their statements become blurred against the domination of the narrator, who interrupts her own narrative to question and even mock herself, her narrative strategies, and her characters. Another feature of Jelinek's style is the provocative use of clichés. The narrator's monologue makes use of commonplace views on every imaginable topic. Such views are contextualized so as to expose them as clichés. Ordinarily, such views are invoked to provide coherence to the fabric of existence, but under the narrator's treatment they become highly disturbing. Apart from obvious commonplaces, the narrator's sources include the advertising world as well as less obvious intertextual references.

All these elements are held together by the plot, and the apparent digressions follow a logic of their own before they return, either in a labored way or effortlessly, or not at all, to the main story line. While challenging to the reader, these carefully organized diversions form the interesting and engaging centerpiece of the text. Elfriede Jelinek is well known for her literary protests, and the unique textual sphere she creates in *Gier* is no exception. Her writing here shows yet again that she is one of the few established *and* interesting authors in the German-writing world.

## FURTHER READING

### Criticism

Jelinek, Elfriede, and *Index on Censorship.* "Viennese Whirl." *Index on Censorship* 29, no. 5 (September-October 2000): 170-74.

Jelinek discusses Austrian right-wing political activist Jörg Haider's Freedom Party, her dramatic works, and issues surrounding tourism in Austria.

Olson, Steven E. Review of *The Piano Teacher,* by Elfriede Jelinek. *Antioch Review* 48, no. 2 (spring 1990): 258.

Olson offers a generally positive assessment of *The Piano Teacher.*

Rocamora, Carol. "The Germans Call It 'Vergangenheitsbewaltigung.'" *New York Times* (13 May 2001): AR10.

Rocamora examines Jelinek's public criticism of Jörg Haider in her play *Das Lebewohl.*

---

**Additional coverage of Jelinek's life and career is contained in the following sources published by the Gale Group:** *Contemporary Authors,* **Vol. 154;** *Dictionary of Literary Biography,* **Vol. 85;** *Feminist Writers*; **and** *Literature Resource Center.*

# Ian McEwan
## 1948-

(Full name Ian Russell McEwan) English novelist, short story writer, playwright, screenwriter, and children's writer.

The following entry presents an overview of McEwan's career through 2002. For further information on his life and works, see *CLC*, Volumes 13 and 66.

## INTRODUCTION

One of the most celebrated British writers to come of age during the 1970s, McEwan emerged onto the literary scene at age twenty-seven with the short story collection *First Love, Last Rights* (1975). Riddled with graphic depictions of rape, incest, and murder—all rendered in detached, forensically precise first-person narration—*First Love, Last Rights* and its follow-up, *In Between the Sheets* (1978), earned McEwan both critical acclaim and scorn for his macabre preoccupations. While his later novels, including *The Innocent* (1990), *Enduring Love* (1998), and *Amsterdam* (1999), display considerable growth in the range and depth of his work, McEwan's prose still focuses heavily on gothic predilections and shocking subject material. McEwan has also written several notable screenplays, which include some of his most pointedly political work, as evident in *The Ploughman's Lunch* (1983). Although his fiction is generally conventional in terms of narrative structure, McEwan's unique prose style, technical skill, unusual characterizations, and satiric wit have earned him acceptance in both traditional and postmodernist literary circles.

## BIOGRAPHICAL INFORMATION

McEwan was born on June 21, 1948, in Aldershot, England. His father, David, was a career Army officer, and McEwan spent most of his childhood years in Singapore and Libya. When he was twelve, McEwan's family returned to England, and he attended a boarding school in Suffolk, where he developed a fondness for English Romantic poetry and modern American and English fiction. He worked briefly in London as a garbage collector before enrolling at the University of Sussex in Brighton, receiving his bachelor's degree in English literature with honors. In 1970 McEwan was accepted into the creative writing program at the

University of East Anglia, where the teaching faculty included novelists Malcolm Bradbury and Angus Wilson. After completing his master's degree, McEwan toured Afghanistan and soon began publishing stories in literary magazines. In 1975 McEwan published a selection of short stories he had written for his master's degree under the title *First Love, Last Rights,* which later received a Somerset Maugham Award. McEwan began writing radio scripts and screenplays and soon had two produced—*Conversations with a Cupboardman* (1975) was produced for British Broadcasting Company (BBC) radio, and *Jack Flea's Birthday Celebration* (1976) was produced for BBC television. In 1978 he published a second collection of stories, *In Between the Sheets,* and his first novel, *The Cement Garden.* Controversy arose, however, when critics noticed plot similarities between *The Cement Garden* and *Our Mother's House,* a 1963 novel by Julian Gloag. McEwan denied having read Gloag's work and no formal charges of plagiarism were filed. McEwan was again the subject of scandal in 1980 when BBC television decided at the last minute to cancel the production of *Solid Geometry,* a teleplay he adapted from his short story of the same title. The story features a protagonist who keeps a chemically preserved penis in a jar on his desk. Throughout the 1980s, McEwan concentrated primarily on writing screenplays for television and motion pictures, including *The Imitation Game, The Ploughman's Lunch, The Last Day of Summer* (1984), and *Soursweet* (1988), as well as the stage play, *Strangers* (1989). During this period, McEwan also wrote two novels, *The Comfort of Strangers* (1981) and *The Child in Time* (1987), which was awarded the Whitbread Award. McEwan married Penny Allen in 1982; the couple would later divorce in 1995. McEwan was on the short-list for the Booker Prize for *The Comfort of Strangers* and *Black Dogs* (1992), and was awarded the Booker for his novel *Amsterdam.* McEwan published *Atonement* in 2001, which was also short-listed for the Booker Prize, and later received the W. H. Smith Award.

## MAJOR WORKS

In McEwan's first two short story collections—*First Love, Last Rights* and *In Between the Sheets*—he establishes several of the recurring motifs that would become hallmarks of his fiction, most notably, the exploration of the effects of power and obsession on the human psyche. The eight stories in *First Love, Last Rights* are primarily concerned with coming-of-age, though within the collection's grim worldview, maturity is tantamount to corruption. In "Homemade," the protagonist recounts his first sexual experience—the rape of his younger sister. "Butterflies" also centers on a tale of sexual predation, made even more horrifying by the inclusion of a matter-of-fact murder, while "Disguises" tells of an embittered actress who schools a young nephew in debauchery. *In Between the Sheets* covers similar subject material, but the collection exhibits a more fabulistic, Kafkaesque tone, indulging heavily in black humor. In "Pornography" two nurses plot to castrate a man who has sexually abused them both, and "Reflections of a Kept Ape" centers on a woman who initiates a sexual relationship with a pet monkey—narrated from the point-of-view of the monkey. McEwan uses these specific episodes of violence and cruelty to investigate how obsession can shape human desires. McEwan continued to examine similar themes in his novels, such as *The Cement Garden.* The novel follows a group of four children who, after the sudden deaths of their parents, decide to live without adult supervision, presenting a scenario that resembles William Golding's *Lord of the Flies.* The older children try to master the power necessary to fill the adult roles, but ultimately fail, sending the broken family into chaos. *The Comfort of Strangers* revolves around a married English couple on an ill-fated vacation in Venice. After a seemingly chance encounter, they become involved with a man who has a psychotic thirst for sexual dominance. In the opening pages of *The Child in Time,* a man discovers that his young daughter is missing. His daughter is never found, and McEwan traces the man's downward spiral into alcoholic infantilism. By making his protagonist a minor government functionary, McEwan is able to work in themes of political as well as emotional helplessness. In *The Innocent,* the protagonist is an Englishman working in postwar Germany who, after being recruited by the English intelligence service, discovers that as his power over others increases, so does his desire to exercise it.

McEwan revisited postwar continental Europe in *Black Dogs,* a dense, multilayered story which explores the effects of power on morality. The novel follows a couple whose marriage begins to crumble after an encounter with a pair of feral dogs. The dogs symbolize not only the evil that humans are capable of, but also the extraordinary acts that people can accomplish when confronting such evil. *Enduring Love* is a darkly comic tale of two men, Joe Rose and Jed Parry, who meet at the site of a hot-air balloon crash. Jed succumbs to an obsessive love for Joe and begins stalking him. Meanwhile, Joe finds it nearly impossible to convince his wife and friends that Jed is obsessed with him. *Amsterdam* also centers upon a relationship between two men, a composer and a newspaper editor, who, at the funeral of a mutual friend, initiate an euthanasia pact. The complex and comic plot eventually puts the characters at odds, climaxing in Holland where euthanasia can be easily arranged. *Atonement* recounts the story of a novelist who, in her youth, gave damning testimony that led to a working-class boy's false conviction for rape. Subsequent sections of the novel follow the boy's post-prison experiences during the British retreat from Dunkirk during World War II, and the novelist's experiences as a nurse during the Battle of Britain. While his dramatic works have received considerably less critical attention than his fiction, *The Ploughman's Lunch* is often noted as one of McEwan's strongest works. Set during the Falkland Islands War of the 1980s, the tale centers on a cynical journalist who is writing a revisionist history of the Suez crisis of the 1950s—one which defends British attempts to retain control of the canal, and thereby the Middle East. By juxtaposing the two crises, McEwan displays how fictional gamesmanship can have very real—and very dire—consequences.

## CRITICAL RECEPTION

McEwan's preoccupation with disquieting subject matter has garnered him a great deal of public notoriety in England, but it has also polarized the critical assessment of his work. While some critics have maintained that McEwan is a serious literary writer who addresses challenging issues in his work, others have asserted that he is merely a glorified horror writer who is solely concerned with producing gratuitously shocking prose. Despite these disagreements about the topics of his novels, short stories, and screenplays, McEwan has been consistently praised for his storytelling, characterizations, and adept handling of metaphor and symbol. Several reviewers have noted the publication of *The Child in Time* as the beginning of a more mature stage in McEwan's writing career. These critics have argued that McEwan's novels published after *The Child in Time*—including *Enduring Love* and *Atonement*—focus much more heavily on elements of psychological depth, moral complexity, and political awareness than his earlier works. While many commentators have suggested that McEwan's Booker-winning novel *Amsterdam* was not his strongest work, most have agreed that McEwan had been long overdue for serious literary recognition. However, a number of reviewers have found McEwan's schematic moral and philosophical oppositions distracting, particularly in *Black Dogs*, and have complained that his later plot-driven fiction too easily falls prey to the demands of narrative movement. Additionally, several critics have suggested that McEwan abandoned the subversive and experimental elements of his earlier work—as seen in the stories "Reflections of a Kept Ape" and "To and Fro" from *In Between the Sheets*—to obtain more mainstream acceptance. Although many postmodern critics have maintained that McEwan's later work has not lived up to the promise of his early short stories, McEwan is still often compared to such avant garde authors as Martin Amis and J. G. Ballard.

## PRINCIPAL WORKS

*Conversations with a Cupboardman* (radio play) 1975
*First Love, Last Rites* (short stories) 1975
*Jack Flea's Birthday Celebration* (screenplay) 1976
*The Cement Garden* (novel) 1978
*In Between the Sheets* (short stories) 1978
*The Imitation Game* (screenplay) 1980
*The Comfort of Strangers* (novel) 1981
\**The Imitation Game: Three Plays for Television* (screenplays) 1981
*Or Shall We Die?* [music by Michael Berkeley] (oratorio) 1983
*The Ploughman's Lunch* (screenplay) 1983
*The Last Day of Summer* (screenplay) 1984
*Rose Blanche* [illustrations by Roberto Innocenti] (juvenilia) 1985
*The Child in Time* (novel) 1987
*Soursweet* (screenplay) 1988
*Strangers* (play) 1989
*The Innocent* (novel) 1990
*Black Dogs* (novel) 1992
*The Good Son* (screenplay) 1993
*The Innocent* (screenplay) 1993
*The Daydreamer* [illustrations by Anthony Brown] (juvenilia) 1994
*Enduring Love* (novel) 1998
*Amsterdam* (novel) 1999
*Atonement* (novel) 2001

\*Includes *Jack Flea's Birthday Celebration, The Imitation Game,* and *Solid Geometry.*

## CRITICISM

**Wendy Lesser (review date 16 November 1992)**

SOURCE: Lesser, Wendy. "The Heart of the Matter." *New Republic* 207, no. 21 (16 November 1992): 41-2, 44.

[*In the following review, Lesser discusses the two phases of McEwan's career commonly identified by critics, examining such elements as plot, characterization, and style in* Black Dogs.]

Ian McEwan's career is sometimes seen by his critics as falling into two distinct clumps. The first, in this view, consists of his first three books: the stories in *First Love, Last Rites* (1975), the early novel called *The Cement Garden* (1978), and a second set of stories called *In Between the Sheets* (1978). The turning point is either just before or just after *The Comfort of Strangers* (1981), which in any case is seen as the transitional novel. And then, in this saga of the divided author, we have the "mature" McEwan: *The Child in Time* (1987), *The Innocent* (1989), and, now, one presumes, *Black Dogs.* The difference between early and late McEwan is supposed to be that the young writer, though enormously talented, was mainly interested in visceral shocks and thrills, while the older one is interested in ideas; the young man focused on sex, the older ponders love; the young one indulged in spectacularly horrific Grand Guignol effects, the older settles for more muted violence.

I don't subscribe to the myth of the two McEwans. I say this as someone who can barely hear the difference between early and late Henry James, and who cannot for the life of me distinguish a Graham Greene entertainment from a Graham Greene novel, so you may not feel inclined to trust me. But when an author is as obsessed with his themes as McEwan is (or James or Greene was), then petty niceties of subject matter and style do not alter his essential nature. These petty niceties are crucial to our interest in each novel; they are what enable him to go from one novel to the next without writing the same book over and over again, without boringly repeating himself. But they do not break his world in half.

The world of a great novelist—and McEwan is a great novelist—is continuous not only with our daily, lived world, but also with the slightly distorted, hyperreal, eerily patterned but surprisingly free world he has populated with all his fictional characters. When he sits down to write a new novel, he returns again as a traveler to that world, and the novel is the letter he posts out to us. The great novelist (unlike the clever, tricky novelist—I will refrain from naming names among McEwan's British contemporaries) does not construct an entirely new fictional world each time he writes a novel. He cannot choose to do that, as his inferiors can, because the world he visits in his fiction has a reality for him that is not entirely of his own willed making.

From the beginning, McEwan's world has been one in which sexual love holds both great allure and great peril; in which violence is a weapon of intimates; in which the self-enclosure of family life can be both comforting and terrifying; in which childhood, though seductive, must be escaped from; in which innocence is a danger to itself and others; in which one relies on the kindness of sometimes sinister strangers; in which time flows backward and forward, with last things influencing first as well as first last. McEwan's is a world informed by mass historical movements from totalitarianism to Thatcherism, but in his world these abstractions always take a human, immediate, personal form. His is a world where the rational mind struggles with madness, superstition, and faith—a fair struggle, in which we're not sure whose side to back. It is a world where the horrifying, the sad, and the comic intermingle; and it is a world where fear and its henchman, suspense, generally play leading roles. One reviewer described McEwan's last book as the kind of novel that would result "if Stephen King could write like Henry James," and in a way this is true of all his books. The horror lies precisely in the delicate turn of the screw.

In each novel from *The Comfort of Strangers* onward, McEwan has been fiddling with the nature of suspense—that is, with the relationship between fear and time. *The Comfort of Strangers* is pure foreboding. We feel throughout that something awful is going to happen, and in the end it does. (If you have only seen the movie, forget it. Pinter's idiosyncratic screenplay flattens the texture of the novel, making morbid nonsense out of what seems compelling and inevitable in the book.) *The Child in Time* creates nearly unbearable suspense out of an incident that took place before the novel opened: that is, the abduction of the main character's 3-year-old daughter. In *The Innocent,* McEwan locates most of the suspense within a historical fait accompli. By giving us a doomed love story set around the discovery of an Anglo-American spy tunnel in Berlin in the 1950s, he makes us fruitlessly hope for an outcome that actual history has already defeated.

And now, in *Black Dogs,* Ian McEwan pushes the limits of suspense even further. After telling us at the beginning of the novel that its two main characters lived into the late 1980s, he asks us at the novel's end to feel suspense as he unravels something that happened to them in 1946. He asks us, that is, to fear the past. The central debate in *Black Dogs* is the same one that surrounds McEwan's career: whether we are continuous with our own past or divorced from it. "We" in this case includes not only novelists and readers, but citizens of real life; and "our past" is not just the one we have lived for ourselves, but the one history has lived for us.

Jeremy, the narrator of *Black Dogs,* is a passive, evasive, only marginally literary fellow who nonetheless bears an oddly explicit resemblance to his author. Both men, Jeremy and Ian, are well-traveled Britons who have reached their mid-40s by the early 1990s; each has four children; Jeremy is married to a Jenny, Ian to a Penny. But Jeremy (no last name given) is no more the "real" McEwan than Marcel (no last name given) is the "real" Proust. Perhaps it would be more accurate to say that Jeremy is no more his author's stand-in than Colin was in *The Comfort of Strangers,* or Stephen in *The Child in Time,* or Leonard in *The Innocent.* No more, and no less. One of McEwan's insidiously powerful qualities as an author is the way he seeps inside other people—not just his youngish men, but also his women, his aging parents, his madmen, his scientists, his government officials, his small children. He has the gift, or the curse, of unwilled empathy.

The narrator of *Black Dogs* has it too, as we learn early in the novel when Jeremy goes to visit his dying mother-in-law, June Tremaine, in a Wiltshire nursing home. At the threshold of the visit, he finds himself already falling into someone else's existence:

> A shortage of oxygen made me yawn; did I have the energy for the visit? I could as easily have passed the untended reception desk and wandered the corridors until I found an empty room and a bed made up. I would slip between the institutional sheets. Check-in formalities would be concluded later, after I had been woken for my supper, brought on a rubber-wheeled trolley. Afterward, I would take a sedative and doze again. The years would slip by. . . .
>
> At this, a minor flutter of panic restored me to my purpose.

Panic is the galvanizing emotion for McEwan's characters—often, as in this case, panic brought on by an intense but unintentional act of imagination.

Jeremy's purpose, as he repeatedly reminds us, is to write a memoir about June, or perhaps about June and her husband, Bernard—a memoir of their painful but enduring marriage: their initial shared political idealism, their passionate love, his rationalism, her mysticism, his socialist agenda (first Communist, then Labour), her religious faith, their consequent inability to live together, their equally powerful inability to let each other go. Their son-in-law has been selected, or self-selected, to record their tale. "Ever since I lost mine in a road accident when I was 8," Jeremy tells us in the first sentence of his preface, "I have had my eye on other people's parents." Despite the parent-borrowing that began in adolescence, he remained an orphan, essentially familyless, until he met his wife, Jenny, and became part of *her* family: not only the family they created together ("the simplest way of restoring a lost parent was to become one yourself"), but also the family she was born into, the estranged but still married Bernard and June.

Jeremy is not the only one in the novel to reach beyond his birthright. *Black Dogs* is filled with things and people and ideas crossing their natural boundaries, taking over territory that does not officially belong to them. On the largest scale this notion pervades the background plot of the Second World War, in the Nazi invasions of France and Poland. Less chillingly, the idea of broken boundaries emerges in the contemporary reference to the Berlin Wall coming down—an event that Jeremy and Bernard excitedly rush to witness. And on the level of detail it appears over and over in the metaphors throughout the book—for instance, in Jeremy's assertion that his older sister "Jean had spread her beautiful limbs—to adapt Kafka's formulation—across my map of the world and obliterated the territory marked 'sex,' so that I was obliged to voyage elsewhere," or in his musing comment about whether it was always raining when he visited June in the Wiltshire nursing home: "Perhaps there was only one such day, and it has blown itself across the others."

He may have his shortcomings as a meteorologist, but Jeremy is in general a persuasive guide. Just as he immediately and effectively conveyed the essence of nursing-home-induced passivity, so does he elsewhere seize on the one or two or three determining details that define a place, a time, a person. Reporting on the morning the Berlin Wall came down, he says: "We stood in the living room in our dressing gowns with mugs of tea, staring at the set. It did not seem right to sit. East Berliners in nylon anoraks and bleached-out jean jackets, pushing buggies or holding their children's hands, were filing past Checkpoint Charlie, unchecked." Elsewhere, in a few sentences, he gives us the 1960s in an upper-middle-class London household (the home of two of the parents the adolescent Jeremy has borrowed):

> Toby was at my place . . . while I was at his, comfortable on the chesterfield in front of an open fire, a glass of his father's single malt warming in my hand, under my shoeless feet the lovely Bokhara that Toby claimed was a symbol of cultural rape, listening to Tom Langley's account of a deadly poisonous spider and the death throes of a certain third secretary on the first landing of the British embassy in Caracas, while across the hall, through open doors, we heard Brenda at one of Scott Joplin's lilting, syncopated rags, which at that time were being rediscovered and had not yet been played to death.

There is something lilting and syncopated in Jeremy's prose as well—the off-rhyme of "staring at the *set* . . . right to *sit*"; the little joke in "Checkpoint Charlie, unchecked"; the ironic counterpoint of the third secretary's "death throes" and the Scott Joplin "played to death." If such precision can be enormously pleasing, it can also risk seeming finicky or precious at times, but this too Jeremy takes account of. In the paragraph that immediately follows the Scott Joplin set piece, he admits that

> in describing this period of my life I have unconsciously mimicked not only, here and there, the superior sounding attitudes of my adolescent self, but also the rather formal, distancing, labyrinthine tone in which I used to speak, clumsily derived from my scant reading of Proust, which was supposed to announce me to the world as an intellectual.

Admits it, and thereby gets away with it.

If Proust is evident in the sentences of *Black Dogs,* Graham Greene is the shadowy eminence who colors the plot, visible not only in the central choices made by the two older characters (June's in favor of spiritual faith, Bernard's of politics), but also in the very notion of a crucial moment of choice. "Turning points are the inventions of storytellers and dramatists," Jeremy interrupts the plot to tell us, "a necessary mechanism when a life is reduced to, traduced by a plot, when a morality must be distilled from a sequence of actions, when an audience must be sent home with something unforgettable to mark a character's growth."

Jeremy, as usual, mocks the tactic and then continues to use it. He builds the whole story of June and Bernard's marriage, of June's life, around the moment in 1946 when, walking ahead of her husband in Provence, she meets on the path two vicious black dogs. June decides (or "realizes," or "imagines"—the nature of the thought process is part of what's in doubt) that these dogs are the incarnation of evil; at the same moment, she has a sudden apprehension of an infinite, invisible, but salvational good. This, in her own view, is the significant turn in her life's plot. And her family, though they fight her mysticism, unavoidably find themselves adopting the metaphor, the explanation, of the black dogs. It becomes family shorthand for incomprehensible evil, and also for a crucial turning point, a moment in history so powerful it can never be reversed. "Black dogs," mutters Jenny—incomprehensibly to Jeremy, who has only just met her—when they visit the site of a Polish concentration camp.

Only at the end of the novel do we finally get June's encounter with the dogs rendered directly, from her viewpoint (though we know from the context that this is actually Jeremy *imagining* her viewpoint; nothing in this novel can ever be rendered "directly"). I had thought—erroneously, as it turned out—that for once in McEwan's work the novel would not have a suspenseful ending. After all, Jeremy has by this time told us just about everything we need to know, several times over. It would be churlish of me to give away the few factual details that do remain hidden until the end. They do not, in any case, account for the power of the story. What accounts for the power—what produced the suspense, the fear—is that at the end of all the third-hand information-gathering and secondhand relaying, we are actually going through the experience with June. We are there, in her world, in the recently liberated Provence of 1946, on a hot, dry path, a couple of hundred yards and a hairpin turn away from her husband, who misses the whole incident because he has crouched down to scrutinize and sketch a train of unusual caterpillars. (Bernard is, and remains, a passionate entomologist.)

If this moment sounds comic rather than horrifying, it is because I have succeeded in conveying only half of McEwan's technique. All the best scenes in his books are both comic and horrifying. Think of the heroine's dead German ex-husband being messily dismembered and stealthily removed by the protagonists of *The Innocent*; think of the car accident in *The Child in Time*. In McEwan, as in Hitchcock, the comic makes way for the terrifying, softens us up, gets us to loosen our hold on rationality. If he can get us to snort or giggle, McEwan knows he'll be halfway toward making us gasp or cry out.

We do not, I think, quite feel June's fear of absolute evil, nor do we fully absorb her revelation about absolute good. In that sense, *Black Dogs* is doomed to fail. But the novel so understands and collaborates in its own doom, so cunningly and intelligently sets itself up for this unachievable moment, that the effect can hardly be called a failure. *Black Dogs* proves to us what it set out to prove: that we can only by great effort and under special circumstances be made to fear a past that is over and done with; and that we are doomed—as individuals, and as individuals in history—*unless* we can fear the past. We need to think about history, but we also need to feel it. Neither June's mysticism nor Bernard's rationalism will alone be enough to save us.

And yet this makes the book sound too apocalyptic, as if its whole point lies only in its ending (which is also its beginning, and its center). There is, besides all the politics and philosophy, the texture of daily life. At one point June accuses Bernard of living only in the future, waiting impatiently for the social and economic improvement of mankind's welfare, thereby slighting the present. Bernard, in turn, might accuse her of living too deeply in the past, deriving her present too wholly from a single vanished moment. But *Black Dogs* itself, while attracted to both those perspectives, does neither. It lives in its own present: in the experience of "companiable lovemaking that is the privilege and compromise of married life"; in the feel of a house that has been empty for months and now has a single inhabitant, preparing for his family's arrival; in the blood-thirsty satisfaction of fist meeting face as a bystander knocks down a brutal child-beater; in the warmth of a summer day in empty, innocent, rural France. *Black Dogs* calls into question the whole distinction between a novel of ideas and a novel of sensation, for one of its important realizations is that sensation *is* an idea, and thought a sensation.

**Frances Padorr Brent (review date 20 December 1992)**

SOURCE: Brent, Frances Padorr. "Seeing the 'Debased Imagination' That Shapes History." *Chicago Tribune Books* (20 December 1992): 3.

[*In the following review of* Black Dogs, *Brent commends McEwan's unsettling depiction of domestic violence, but finds his political commentary lifeless.*]

As we approach the year 2000, it is not surprising to find a number of American and European novelists evoking apocalyptic imagery in order to express the conflicting forces of a receding century.

British novelist Ian McEwan has summoned the images of wild dogs [in *Black Dogs*], with their age-old association to the vengeance of the Lord, to examine the way that history and the imagination are intertwined. The epigraph to the novel comes from the words of the Renaissance Platonist, Marsilio Ficino: "In these times I don't, in a manner of speaking, know what I want; perhaps I don't want what I know and want what I don't know."

The "black dogs," emblems for that which is sinister at heart, are only perceived by those few individuals who permit themselves to recognize what they have seen. The novel begins with the specter of those dogs, which for 40 years have haunted McEwan's protagonist, June Tremaine. In the summer of 1987 she is dying of cancer in a Wiltshire nursing home, and her son-in-law Jeremy visits with the intention of writing a memoir of sorts. He commences with the description of a photograph that sits on the chest by her bed. Taken in the spring of 1946, the picture commemorates the day that June and her young husband, Bernard, joined the British Communist Party, only a week before they were to embark on a honeymoon tour of the Northern Europe.

The story comes in fragments as the narration crosses through time and geography, moving from the British countryside to Berlin, the concentration camp in Majdanek and the region of Southern France where June encountered the dogs. In the novel's brief final section, the pieces of the plot are put together.

Late in the summer of 1946, two weeks before they were due back in England, June and Bernard embarked on a walking tour of the rocky tableland facing the French Mediterranean. Along the way they stopped at an ancient burial site, the Dolmen de la Prunarede, and something in the prehistoric stones triggered an anxiety within June that would not go away.

The following day, June's uncertainty redoubled. In an attempt to counteract the strange mood that was settling upon her, she walked ahead of Bernard and he, therefore, never saw how she stabbed one of the "waist high" dogs who sprang at her with foaming black mouths, open sores and a cloud of flies or the "luminous penumbra" that floated over her head. Later the mayor of the village where they spent the night disclosed that the dogs had been trained by Nazis who had lived there during the winter of 1942.

The dogs remain for June a symbol for the evil that exists all around us: "It takes hold in an individual, in private lives, within a family, and then it's children who suffer most. And then, when the conditions are right, in different countries, at different times, a terrible cruelty, a viciousness against life erupts, and everyone is surprised by the depth of hatred within himself." All the assumptions about past and future that June had previously held were undermined by this experience.

While the premise of McEwan's novel, the "debased imagination" that ultimately shapes history, is quite interesting, *Black Dogs* is not entirely successful. Sometimes the telling seems held back, and the account of contemporary politics often comes across academically. By far the most compelling incidents in the book have to do with domestic violence, the abuse of children.

In an extended preface to the book, McEwan describes the pain of his own childhood. After he was orphaned at age 8, he lived with his sister, her husband and their small child, Sally. He was witness to their bouts of alcohol and brutality and felt a natural bond to his little niece, who was alternately neglected and abused by her parents.

Likewise, the most startling scene in the novel involves the abuse of another child, a 7- or 8-year-old boy whose parents strike him viciously in the dining room of a hotel. It is in the cruelty of private life that the agony of the dying century seems most authentic here.

### Ariel Swartley (review date 20 December 1992)

SOURCE: Swartley, Ariel. "Fissures under the Crust." *Los Angeles Times Book Review* (20 December 1992): 3-4.

[*In the following review, Swartley presents a plot synopsis of* Black Dogs, *asserting that the character portraits of Bernard and June Tremaine and the attack on June by a pair of feral dogs both reflect McEwan's penchant for examining humanity.*]

The anticipatory chill begins with the title, ***Black Dogs.*** Fans of Ian McEwan's fiction know better than to envision cuddly house pets. Hounds of the general size and ferocity of the Baskerville beasts would be more likely. In four previous novels and two short-story collections, the 44-year-old Briton has proven himself to be a master of menace, an excavator of the jagged fissures that lie just under civilization's crust. McEwan's menaces often take the form of actual dismemberment and sexual perversity. The civilization is all in his prose: an eminently British combination of lucid syntax and detached compassion.

***Black Dogs,*** however, begins with disconcerting gentleness. A pleasantly tweedy narrator, who in the superficial details of gender, age, nationality, profession and number of children resembles McEwan, reminisces about his adolescent fascination with other people's parents by way of introducing his main subject: a portrait of his in-laws. In previous novels, ***The Child in Time*** and ***The Innocent,*** McEwan evoked contemporary genres like "missing-child thriller" or "anti-hero spy novel" before bending them to his own purposes, in ***Black Dogs,*** the writing is simple and confessional, the apparent frankness disarming.

Described by their son-in-law, Bernard and June Tremaine are admirable, articulate and infuriating—a kind of Everyparent, elder variety. Their oddity lies in their decades-long marriage, a union at once loving and irreconcilable, fruitful and desolate. Bernard, who became a communist as a young man, is now an Establishment figure, a former Member of Parliament and Labour Party stalwart. He is a rationalist, a secular humanist, a man who collects and mounts insects with scientific precision and still believes in the perfectibility of systems that deliver social welfare.

June, when the novel opens in 1987, is bedridden in a suburban English nursing home, suffering from an obscure form of cancer. In the solitude imposed by uncongenial surroundings, she reads and writes, trades wildflower lore with her doctor and dispenses pointed advice to her children, all with the serene authority of her spiritual mentor, Lao tzu.

In 1946 she had been as eager as Bernard to join the Party, but her faith was shattered by a traumatic experience during their honeymoon tour of France. One effect of the trauma was that she discovered God, and in time it became apparent that not only her politics but her life with Bernard could not survive her religious conversion.

To an activist and intellectual like Bernard June's retreat into spirituality (amid the rustic comforts of a French farmhouse) is evidence of either massive self-indulgence or an elective lobotomy. To June, Bernard's life of sound and fury has resulted in the predictable emptiness: The suffering still suffer. Meanwhile, his plummy elder-statesman manner drives her wild.

No one is less forgiving of another's point of view than someone who hoped to change the world. But no one is more persistent, either. And so despite 35 years apart, their marriage survives—in a fashion. Instead of speaking to each other, they constantly lecture their family and anyone else who will listen on each other's errors of temperament and philosophy.

And the menacing dogs of McEwan's title? They're there from the beginning, slavering at the edges of the narrative pounding through June's consciousness as she drops to sleep each night, the agents of her trauma, symbol of her satori—although, as McEwan's narrator warns, she would disagree: "No, you clot. Not symbolic! . . . Literal, anecdotal, true. Don't you know I was nearly killed!"

Unlike Henry James, who, abhorring banality, once described a neighbor's pet, also a black dog, as "something dark, something canine," McEwan finds the bald statement, the literal truth full enough of ambiguity.

Banality in fact fascinates McEwan, in particular the banality of evil, and part of the chill of his books comes from his ability to recount the most grisly events in cool and meticulously observed detail. Yet his is not the scientific detachment that collapses polarities, allowing good to become indistinguishable from evil. Rather he seems anxious to identify the cracked steps, the crucibles of experience that jolt individuals, for better or worse, out of their moral skins.

June's black dogs are one such crucible—a half-starved, feral legacy from the Gestapo whose forces—only two years before the Tremaines' honeymoon in the Languedoc—had terrorized these quiet villages.

"You wait until you come to make sense of your life," June tells the narrator in their last interview. "You'll either find you're too old and lazy to make the attempt, or you'll do what I've done, single out a certain event, find in something ordinary and explicable a means of expressing what might otherwise be lost to you—a conflict, a change of heart, a new understanding." Part of McEwan's fascination in *Black Dogs* is also reserved for people like Bernard who are not changed by circumstances. Even his beating at the hands of an angry Berlin mob is defanged by his protective coating of rationalism and self-esteem. In Berlin to celebrate the opening of the Wall, he springs to the defense of a red-flag-waving youth.

"It wasn't his red flag, you know," Bernard says the next day. "I don't think they even saw it. You heard what they were shouting? Foreigners out!"

In the novel's preface, McEwan's narrator outlines the reasons for his obsession with his in-laws, calling the elder Tremaines "the extremities, the twin poles along whose slippery axis my own unbelief slithers and never comes to rest." But his obsession has a more personal cause as well. Orphaned in childhood, he is acutely aware that all children are in a sense a reconciliation of opposites, a synthesis between two points of view that in his case remain unknown. "Nor will it do," he warns, "to suggest that both . . . are correct. To believe everything, to make no choices, amounts to much the same thing, to my mind, as believing nothing at all."

By the book's end one thing is certain to rationalists and mystics alike: June's dogs come between people. Forty years later they're still causing arguments among neighbors in a French village. Was an earlier victim of the dogs—when their German masters were still on the scene—an informer, as some of the villagers suspected, or a pretty woman whose aloofness offended her male neighbors? The arguments, like the schism in a marriage, go way beyond a single incident or a pair of beasts, go beyond intellectual opposites to fundamental polarities including gender. And McEwan's preoccupation with menace is revealed as part of a larger preoccupation with humanity.

## Kerry Fried (review date 14 January 1993)

SOURCE: Fried, Kerry. "Criminal Elements." *New York Review of Books* 40, nos. 1-2 (14 January 1993): 36-7.

[*In the following excerpt, Fried examines various aspects of* Black Dogs, *such as its handling of domestic violence, the importance of Jeremy in comparison to protagonists June and Bernard, its portrayal of the post-World War II period, and the events surrounding the fall of European communism in 1989.*]

The narrators in Ian McEwan's earlier books tend to live in rarefied, nightmarish domestic situations rather than in precise locations or times. His explorations of solitary lives and domestic futility, and particularly the ruin of childhood, occasionally can seem conceits, as with a boy who has been literally infantilized for eighteen years. There were also potential moral underpinnings in the horror of his stories, and there were, too, the wit and strangeness of his prose.

But his more recent work is very different, carefully grounded in a particular time, and preoccupied with recent history. Indeed, in **Black Dogs** two historical periods—the immediate post-World War II period with its illusions about communism, and 1989 during the collapse of European communism—crowd the foreground. The novel's narrator, Jeremy, and his wife hear the news that the Berlin Wall has come down while they are making love: "We were doing our best to keep its full importance at arm's length. . . . But the spell had been broken. Cheering crowds were surging through the early morning gloom of our bedroom."

**Black Dogs** purports to be Jeremy's memoir of his mother-in-law, June Tremaine. In 1946, June and her lover, Bernard, have just been married and quit their wartime jobs in British intelligence. Full of confidence in the future, they have joined the Communist Party. Their illusions of love and politics are dangerously linked. "We'd founded a private utopia, and it was only a matter of time before the nations of the world followed our example," June wryly tells Jeremy forty years later.

But while she and Bernard, on their honeymoon, are walking in the Languedoc, looking forward to "a new Europe" and their first child. June is set upon and terrorized by two feral dogs: "They moved slowly. They seemed to be working together to some purpose." She is paralyzed by fear for several minutes, but feels herself suddenly surrounded by an energy, a trust in survival, or God, perhaps, she thinks, and is determined to fight and survive.

> The big dog was down, ready for the spring, waiting for one moment's inattention. The muscles in its haunches quivered. A back paw scrabbled for better purchase. She had seconds left, and her hand was around her third rock. . . . In a delirium of abandonment, she attacked. She had passed through fear to fury that her happiness, the hopes of the past months, and now the revelation of this extraordinary light were about to be destroyed by a pair of abandoned dogs.

While the dogs stalk June, Bernard, an amateur entomologist, has fallen behind and stopped to examine a group of caterpillars. The separateness of the two experiences will pull them apart. Though he is capable of minute observation when it comes to insects, Bernard fails to take in the bite marks and saliva on June's knapsack and never quite believes that June was in danger, let alone that she had a vision. Even though the villagers at St. Maurice verify June's encounter with the dogs, telling the couple that in 1944 the Gestapo had brought them to the village in order to intimidate the inhabitants, and they have been roaming about wild for months.

The attack by the dogs becomes part of family lore, but forty years later Bernard is still denying the experience: "'Face to face with evil'?" he prods Jeremy, "I'll tell you what she was up against that day—a good lunch and a spot of malicious village gossip!"

The couple drifts apart. June loses her interest in politics, becoming solitary and mystical, as Bernard becomes "a public man," a Labour politician, and then TV spokesman for the "certainties" of science and left-wing politics. Indeed, the novel can at times read like a symposium between the mystical June and the pragmatic Bernard, with Jeremy as their skeptical acolyte: "Statements and counter-statements chased their tales. . . . It was a drone that would not be banished." Two years after June dies, Jeremy finds himself becoming increasingly irritated with Bernard's complacency and aware of its destructiveness:

> What struck me then was not simply the injustice of Bernard's remarks, but a wild impatience at the difficulty of communication, and an image of parallel mirrors in place of lovers on a bed, throwing back in infinite regression likenesses paling into untruth.

The book shifts in time back and forth between the late Eighties and 1946, and in place between Wiltshire, Berlin, and the south of France. Although in the very opening of the narrative, when Jeremy goes to visit June, now dying in a nursing home, he hears the familiar story of the black dogs, the event itself is not described until the last section. This scene is paralleled, and in a way confirmed, by an event that takes place forty years later, in Berlin, where Jeremy has taken Bernard just after the Wall has come down. A group of young neo-Nazis sets upon Bernard, but he is rescued when

> out of the crowd there sprang a figure who whirled about us, lashing the boys with staccato sentences of piercing rebuke. It was a furious young woman. Her power was of the street. . . . The force of her disgust was sexual.

Here McEwan invokes June's spirit all too neatly, but the parallel manages to make the menace of the scene seem less gratuitous.

Exploring politics and history in Europe through very isolated and violent moments is, of course, a risk, and the connections between Bernard's encounter with the neo-Nazi youths in 1989 and June's moment of terror in 1946 can seem schematic, the events themselves forced. But each scene is brilliantly lit, and has a characteristically strange fascination as Ian McEwan juxtaposes "huge and tiny currents" to show the ways in which individuals react to history. Jeremy first hears of the black dogs in Poland in 1981, when he and June's daughter Jenny Tremaine are visiting a concentration camp. It is here, too, that their love affair begins, and they spend the next three days in bed together in the shadow of the Majdenek camp. This scene comes dangerously close to being obtrusive, grotesque, but McEwan is so deft a writer that again the violence does not, finally, seem gratuitous.

While June and Bernard are the central characters, the novel subtly revolves around the bleak figure of Jeremy, an outsider, a man of great loneliness and guilt. "Ever since I lost mine in a road accident when I was eight, I have had my eye on other people's parents," **Black Dogs** arrestingly begins. Jeremy has grown up living with his older sister and her husband, and, later, their daughter, Sally.

> Harper had a gift for violence. . . . But there were also times when I went into the kitchen and found Jean at the table reading a magazine and smoking while Harper stood at the kitchen sink, naked but for his purple jock strap, with half a dozen bright red weals across his buttocks, humbly washing the dishes.

Unable to distinguish between guilt and love or to overcome his own sense of abandonment, Jeremy seeks out other families. He eventually discovers that "the simplest way of restoring a lost parent was to become one yourself." He has married happily and has four children—who are virtually absent from the novel. Even his wife, Jenny, though described in physical detail (down to an amputated sixth finger), is only dimly present—Sally's loneliness and misery are far more realized. Jeremy is haunted by leaving his niece behind and by his inability to help her when she repeats her parents' history. And in spite of his assertions about love's power, Jeremy admits, "It is the black dogs I return to most often. They trouble me when I consider what happiness I owe them."

In the middle of the novel Jeremy witnesses a French couple gratuitously beating their son. In a rage, he challenges the father, wanting, he thinks, to ennoble himself and somehow atone for his having abandoned Sally. Instead he finds himself dangerously exhilarated: "I think I might have kicked and stomped him to death if I had not heard a voice. . . . Immediately I knew that the elation driving me had nothing to do with revenge and justice." This revelation does not require the fall of the Berlin Wall for its force. Ambitious as **Black Dogs** is in its time and setting, it comes to life in such moments of intense domestic violence.

## Joseph J. Feeney (review date 30 April 1994)

SOURCE: Feeney, Joseph J. Review of *Black Dogs*, by Ian McEwan. *America* 170, no. 15 (30 April 1994): 22-4.

[*In the following excerpt, Feeney offers praise for* Black Dogs, *lauding its "scope, depth, and unity," and its treatment of such themes as politics, religion, the quest for family, and European political oppression.*]

London booksellers are brave: They display works of quality along with best sellers. Not too long ago, on their laden tables, I found three superb new novels—one British, two Irish—that are now available in American editions and deserve an American audience.

Ian McEwan's **Black Dogs** is brilliant, with a scope, depth and unity that belie its brevity. Beginning as a quest for family, the novel gradually encompasses England, Berlin, Poland and southern France, brings in politics, rationalism and religion, involves mythic dogs and ancient dolmens, and ends as a symbol of Europe from World War II to the 1989 collapse of Communism. In a similar expansion, the black dogs begin as horrid memories, develop into painfully real beasts of attack and, by the end, symbolize European political oppression on the right and on the left. The novel's movement from realism to symbol is seamless, and McEwan faultlessly balances sensuous detail—the "scent of thyme crushed underfoot"—with the resonance and scope of myth.

A novel of memory, **Black Dogs** has a disarmingly simple plot. The middle-aged Jeremy, orphaned when he was eight, finds family in his wife's parents—June and Bernard Tremaine—and tries to piece together their life-stories. The novel is a "memoir" of his discoveries: how June was attacked by dogs during her Languedoc honeymoon, how she and Bernard reject English Communism, how their affection outlives their marriage and how June turns to religion and Bernard to rationalism. Jeremy also has his own memories: visiting a Polish concentration camp in 1981, experiencing Berlin in 1989 as the Wall was being pulled down, hiking to the dolmens—the sacred altars—of Languedoc, where June fended off the dogs in 1946. McEwan smoothly weaves all this together—self and family, 1946 and 1989, dogs and dolmens, history and politics, England and Europe—into a resonant myth of politics, rationalism, religion and "the chasm of meaninglessness." By the end, Jeremy has found a family, yet feels a foreboding: In 1946, the black dogs of fascism—"spirit hounds" of "the savagery beyond"—ran away from June, yet lived on as "black stains in the grey of the dawn, fading as they move into the foothills of the mountains from where they will return to haunt us, somewhere in Europe, in another time." Gliding so suavely from realism to symbol, ***Black Dogs*** is a remarkable feat, an extraordinary performance. With this novel, McEwan becomes a major writer. . . .

All three novelists, I might note, are experienced and well regarded. Ian McEwan (British, b. 1948) has done T.V. plays, a film script and six novels, including the celebrated ***The Comfort of Strangers*** (later filmed), ***The Child in Time*** and ***The Innocent.*** Patrick McCabe (Irish, b. 1955) has published two novels, a children's story and several short stories. Roddy Doyle (Irish, b. 1958) is known for his fictional trilogy, *The Commitments*, *The Snapper* and *The Van*, two stage plays, and the screenplays for films of *The Commitments* (1991) and *The Snapper* (1993).

In these new novels, each writer is at his best, probing memory, self and family, worrying about love and permanence and crafting inventive stories with verbal skill. The booksellers of London were right: The novels are superb, and have all won prizes. Happily, American readers can now enjoy them also.

## Jack Slay, Jr. (essay date summer 1994)

SOURCE: Slay, Jack, Jr. "Vandalizing Time: Ian McEwan's *The Child in Time*." *Critique* 35, no. 4 (summer 1994): 205-18.

[*In the following essay, Slay examines the connections between children and the passage of time in* The Child in Time, *drawing attention to parallels between the loss of the protagonist's child and the theme of time as the destroyer of youth and, alternately, as a mode of recovery and rejuvenation.*]

At first, ***The Child in Time*** seems to be a radical departure from the violence and shock of Ian McEwan's earlier work. The novel is certainly a departure from the blood, pus, and semen that inundate his stories and previous novels; gone are the incest of ***The Cement Garden*** and the mindless violence of ***The Comfort of Strangers*** and such stories as **"Butterflies"** (in which a man sexually abuses, then murders a young girl) and **"Pornography"** (in which a man is emasculated by a couple of his girlfriends). ***The Child in Time*** is, as some critics would have it, embarrassingly affirmative.[1] Whereas ***The Cement Garden*** ends in the destruction of the family unit, ***The Child in Time*** ends with family unity; whereas ***The Comfort of Strangers*** uncovers only death and the destruction of love, ***The Child in Time*** discovers life and the resurrection of love. Indeed, McEwan's third novel reads as a magical work, filled with warmth and hope and love. However, McEwan warns that this optimism is not necessarily a brighter view of contemporary society: "Maybe [it is] because I feel more alarmed about the world that I feel a responsibility to locate what is good. . . . I cling to the idea that people are always better than the systems in which they live" (Muchnick 102).

McEwan's novel concerns a child's sudden and mysterious disappearance and the painful ordeal that the parents must endure to accept their daughter-less, and seemingly hopeless, lives. ***The Child in Time,*** however, is much more than a missing-child novel. With the intricate images of children and the complexities of time that recur, McEwan portrays the search for—and the importance of recognizing and accepting—the child that exists in every individual. As Richard Locke says, "The theme is—clearly—the remembrance of things past: recovery, re-creation, redemption or reconciliation to the loss of children, childhood, time itself" (30). The search for the child in time—both Stephen's and Julie's daughter Kate as well as each individual's youthful essence—is an often warm and poignant, a sometimes wild and humorous romp through time itself. McEwan creates a sense of time that is malleable, wondrous, infinitely complex. Time is a vandal: it is the essence that can make one forget the inner child, that innocent and youthful joy of life. Simultaneously, time is also vandalized: characters experience periods that stall in slow motion, that pass in a blur of quickness, that are even altered, with the past coming round to the present. These motifs of the child and of time unify the novel, intricately connecting the various episodes while simultaneously accentuating the delicate relationship between childhood and adulthood and the need for every individual to discover that child within him- or herself.

Images of children and of time dominate the novel. For instance, immediately after the experience of seeing his parents "out of time," Stephen relives his mother's decision not to abort him, imagining himself as a fetus:

> His eyes grew large and round and lidless with desperate, protesting innocence, his knees rose under him and touched his chin, his fingers were scaly flippers, gills beat time, urgent, hopeless strokes through the salty ocean that engulfed the treetops and surged between their roots; and for all the crying, calling sounds he thought were his own, he formed a single thought: he had nowhere to go, no moment that could embody him, he was not expected, no destination or time could be named; for while he moved forward violently, he was immobile, he was hurtling round a fixed point.
>
> (66)

Later, when Stephen rescues the driver from a wrecked lorry, the man emerges in a parody of birth (112). Similar to these more complex images are numerous brief references to children and childhood. For example, Julie lives in a house "such as a child might draw" (74); Stephen finds boyish pleasure in railroads (54); Charles Darke is his wife's "difficult child" (42).

Through these images of the child, McEwan emphasizes the innocence and purity of childhood, something that is quickly and almost completely forgotten in adulthood. Rarely do adults abandon themselves to childish pleasures, as do Stephen and Julie when they become joyfully captivated in building a sand castle with Kate: ". . . soon, and without quite realizing it was happening, they became engrossed, filled with the little girl's urgency, working with no awareness of time beyond the imperative of the approaching tide" (121). Unfortunately, the adult must throw off the spell and return to the world of responsibilities and appointments. Stephen later thinks that "if he could do everything with the intensity and abandonment with which he had once helped Kate build her castle, he would be a happy man of extraordinary powers" (122). McEwan, though, suggests that happiness can be achieved in a compromise—but only if the adult is willing to recognize the child within.

Like the image of the child, images of time also serve to unify the novel. McEwan sets the novel in the near future. As with many contemporary novels—Angela Carter's *Heroes and Villains* (1969), J. G. Ballard's *High-Rise* (1975), Russell Hoban's *Riddley Walker* (1980), Kathy Acker's *Empire of the Senseless* (1988), Martin Amis's *London Fields* (1989)—a near-future is envisioned in order to demonstrate the results of our own chaotic present; in some instances, the future is so near that, for all practical purposes, it is *now*. In his vision of the future, McEwan portrays an England controlled by a post-Thatcher conservative extremism. This is a society guided by a government that has offered schools for sale to private investors, that has commissioned a child-care book so that the nation can be "'regenerated by reformed child-care practice'" (191), that has regulated its beggars, forcing them to wear begging badges and to beg in allotted areas only. Time, though, is more than a structural motif; it also has the tendency to govern each character's individual life. Stephen is constantly slipping into the past of memories through his "structured daydreams." Throughout the novel, then, there is a continuous shift from the present to the past and back again. Likewise, there are many references to the seeming instability of time and how it often shifts according to perception; Stephen is especially susceptible to the shifting qualities of time. For instance, thinking about his aging parents, he feels "the urgency of constricting time" (50); as he is traveling to visit Julie, his sense of time disappears (55); he feels as if "time had fixed him in his place" (117); when he pursues the girl whom he thinks is Kate, time "had a closed-down, forbidden quality" (166). These constant references to time and childhood help to unify McEwan's novel, complementing both theme and structure.

The images of time and childhood are inexorably linked in Kate, the missing daughter of Stephen and Julie Lewis; through her mysterious evanescence, she becomes just one of the many children in time who populate the novel. Kate's disappearance is a terrifyingly beautiful passage. McEwan poetically captures the sheer terror of a parent's worst nightmare, describing how Stephen's uneasiness quickly becomes blind panic; how the city's anonymity crumbles; and the lost child becomes "everyone's property" (15); how Stephen attempts to distance himself in order to cope with the loss of his daughter. Long after her disappearance, Stephen—in a desperate, pathetic attempt to save Kate, to prevent his daughter from forever vanishing from his life—seeks to alter time. He vainly strives to re-enter the past but discovers only that time "monomanically forbids second chances" (10); he struggles to see through the veil of time, hoping to discover the person who might have stolen her:

> [He] tried to move his eyes, lift them against the weight of time, to find that shrouded figure at the periphery of vision, the one who was always to the side and slightly behind, who, filled with a strange desire, was calculating odds, or simply waiting. But time held his sight forever on his mundane errands, and all about him shapes without definition drifted and dissolved, lost to categories.
>
> (12)

Unable to penetrate the past, Stephen resists the impulse to surrender, remaining adamant in his battle against time, the ultimate kidnapper of his only child. Perceiving himself as "the father of an invisible child" (2), he vehemently maintains the hope that Kate may indeed exist somewhere; to cope, he allows her to continue growing, to continue aging within his own mind:

> There was a biological clock, dispassionate in its unstoppability, which let his daughter go on growing, extended and complicated her simple vocabulary, made her stronger, her movements surer. The clock, sinewy like a heart, kept faith with an unceasing conditional: she would be drawing, she would be starting to read, she would be losing a milk tooth.
>
> (2)

This mental child that Stephen nurtures eventually enables him to accept his pain and, through the course of two events, helps him to continue with his own life.

The first incident occurs two and a half years after Kate's disappearance, during the week that she would have turned six years old. Stephen wants to celebrate her birthday but fears that to "buy a toy would undo two years of adjustment, it would be irrational, indulgent, self-destructive; and weak, above all weak" (145). However, he soon justifies his need to celebrate for Kate, saying to himself that this "would be an act of faith in his daughter's continued existence" (146); moreover, he sees the action as an act of joy as well as a plea for Kate's return:

> To buy a present would demonstrate that he was not yet beaten, that he could do the surprising, lively thing. He would purchase his gift in joy rather than sorrow, in the spirit of loving extravagance, and in bringing it home and wrapping it up he would be making an offering to fate, or a challenge—*Look, I've brought the present, now you bring back the girl.*
>
> (146)

As he embarks on his shopping spree, Stephen mentally creates through "magical thinking" the image of Kate as a growing, maturing child and buys birthday toys to match her ever-changing needs:

> He needed to test her reactions. She was a reticent girl, in company at least, with a straight back and dark bangs. She was a fantasist, a daydreamer, a lover of strange-sounding words, a keeper of secret diaries, a hoarder of inexplicable objects. . . . She preferred soft toys to dolls, and he dropped into his wire basket a lifelike gray cat. She was a giggler with a taste for practical jokes. He took the cushion and a flower that squirted water. . . . She liked to dress up. He reached for a witch's hat. . . . Beyond all question she was a graceful child, but she was hopeless with a ball and it was time she knew how to throw. He took from the shelves a plastic sock of tennis balls.
>
> (148)

Kate's birthday eventually brings more dismay than relief; Stephen ends his celebration—at once one of the most touching and absurd scenes in the novel—by singing "Happy Birthday" to his missing daughter through a child's walkie-talkie set. Though momentarily upsetting for Stephen, the event is the beginning of a capitulation; for the first time he realizes that Kate is fading and that he has no control over his lost daughter:

> He brought to mind the three-year-old, the springy touch of her, how she fit herself so comfortably round his body, the solemn purity of her voice, the wet red and white of tongue and lips and teeth, the unconditional trust. It was getting harder to recall. She was fading, and all the time his useless love was swelling, encumbering and disfiguring him like a goiter. He thought, I want you. I want you back. I want you brought back now. I don't want anything else. All I want to do is to want you to come back. . . . *It hurts.*
>
> (151)

Ultimately, with time, Stephen's pain reaches a nadir, triggering the second incident, which directs him toward acceptance and recovery.

Stephen's fanatical search for his daughter eventually ends in finding Kate—however, it is the wrong Kate. Passing a schoolyard filled with children while *en route* to a lunch meeting with the prime minister, Stephen encounters Kate:

> The first girl was closest to him. The thick bangs bobbed against her white forehead, her chin was raised, she had a dreamy appearance. He was looking at his daughter. He shook his head, he opened his mouth without making a sound. She was fifty feet away, unmistakable.
>
> (165)

Confronting the girl, he notices that "what was most strikingly new was a brown mole high on her right cheekbone" (172). The child is, then, obviously not Kate, but Stephen refuses to accept this. His unending search for his daughter and the confrontation with the "false" Kate exhibit the degree of his obsession and desperation; Stephen, in order to survive the madness of his situation, realizes that he must keep Kate alive—even if only in his own mind, for if Kate continues to exist, then he can continue to survive. Eventually, Stephen is convinced by the school principal and by himself that this is not Kate; once he admits this to himself, the likeness of Kate fades from the girl: ". . . the girl crossing the reception area was taller, more angular, especially about the shoulders, and sharper in her features" (177). The false recognition concludes in a purging that, in turn, results in Stephen's release from his obsession, his maniacal search:

> He was beginning to face the difficult truth that Kate was no longer a living presence, she was not an invisible girl at his side whom he knew intimately remembering how Ruth Lyle [the false Kate] did and did not resemble his daughter, he understood how there were many paths Kate might have gone down, countless ways in which she might have changed in two and a half years, and that he knew nothing about any of them. He had been made, now he felt purged.
>
> (179)

Stephen never completely abandons the hope that Kate may indeed be alive and that she may someday return; however, the two confrontations with "Kate" succeed in helping him comprehend the danger of his obsession. Essentially, Stephen realizes that he must continue his own life without Kate; he must remain whole in order to keep Kate as a part of himself.

***The Child in Time,*** however, is more than Stephen's search for his lost daughter; it also presents the search for the lost child that exists within every adult. The appearance of adulthood necessitates, more often than not, the disappearance of innocence and, consequently, the loss of one's childish pleasure in life itself. Commenting on the adult's denial of the child-self, McEwan says,

> It's been a current in my fiction for a long time that we carry about with us our childhood selves. We deny that self at our peril. . . . It was both inevitable and desirable that my own range or preoccupation should change and that my emotional range should increase. Having

children has been a major experience in my life in the last few years. It's extended me emotionally, personally, in ways that could never be guessed at. It's inevitable that that change would be reflected in my writing.

(Smith 68)

The search for Kate, then, reintroduces Stephen to his own child-self in time; and Kate, as John Bemrose says, becomes a "metaphor for the vanished freshness of youth. The book suggests that only by getting back some of the glorious vitality of childhood can people live to the fullest" (52).

Charles Darke, one of the few characters in the novel who willingly seeks out the child within himself, tells Stephen that "childhood is timeless" (32). Attempting to persuade Stephen to market his novel *Lemonade* as a children's book, Charles says that the book has "spoken directly to children. . . . you've communicated with them across the abyss that separates the child from the adult and you've given them a first, ghostly intimation of their mortality. . . . This is a book for children through the eyes of an adult" (33). As Charles explains, the best of the "so-called children's books" are "those that spoke to both children and adults, to the incipient adult within the child, to the forgotten child within the adult" (30). Stephen reluctantly agrees to this marketing scheme and, then, inadvertently, becomes "famous among schoolchildren" (25). Not only does Stephen succeed in communicating with children—including his own inner child, but he also *becomes* metaphorically a child, another of the novel's many children in time. Throughout the novel, Stephen is portrayed as a child or in childlike terms; both Charles and the assistant secretary to the prime minister speak to him "as though to a child" (30, 154); he is mothered by Thelma when he goes into a catatonic state shortly after Kate vanishes; at the thought of nuclear war he is "suddenly, childishly, afraid" (193); on his final visit to Julie's, he fulfills a "boyhood dream" by riding in the cab of a train (247). While on the trail of the false Kate, Stephen reverts to a childlike state when he enters a classroom and finds himself participating in an art class: when the teacher instructs the children to draw a picture of a medieval village, Stephen earnestly, obediently jumps to the task, "imparting to his row of huts a degree of perspective they had never had in previous attempts" (169); years after leaving grade school, he is still eager to impress the teacher. Through the novel, Stephen is unashamed, even willing, to express his child-self, succumbing to the youthful innocence, the harmless naiveté that dwells within him. By doing so, McEwan suggests, the adult-self is better able to survive the turmoil and chaos of adult society. Accepting the child within himself helps him to bear the loss of his daughter; in essence, the child within him is an embodiment of Kate, allowing her to live and grow always beside her father.

Although the acceptance of the inner child is more often life-affirming, McEwan warns that complete submersion into this child-self can be anything but a positive, healthy experience. Charles Darke, for example, is yet another of the novel's many children in time. Several of McEwan's characters—Tom in *The Cement Garden* and David in the television film *Jack Flea's Birthday Celebration*—regress into childhood in order to temporarily escape the difficulties of their lives. Charles, however, seeks to escape the confusion and chaos of his world by regressing wholly into the serenity and security of childhood. Because of this regression, his wife Thelma is forced into the role of surrogate mother. Thelma, however, finds this role of motherhood comfortable, even natural, accepting the regression of her husband as "'quite ordinary'" (240), happily complying with her new role as mother.

Stephen, however, finds Charles's regression disturbing. When he first encounters Charles in his new state, Stephen thinks that he is, indeed, a little boy: ". . . this was just the kind of boy who used to fascinate and terrify him at school" (122). Stephen is shocked that Charles has so totally transformed himself into a "successful prepubescent" (125); nonetheless, he feigns acceptance and follows the forty-nine-year-old child into his world of innocence and treehouses. The climb to Charles's treehouse accentuates the chasm between their states: Stephen is, momentarily, the terrified adult, the frightened realist, clinging with desperation to the tree; Charles is the carefree, innocent child, scampering from limb to limb, heedless of the danger. Charles's metamorphosis into a child is total. He has built a treehouse, made his own lemonade, and stuffed his pockets with all the paraphernalia of childhood. Stephen views Charles's regression as a calculated move. Examining the contents of Charles's pockets, he is "impressed by what appeared to be very thorough research. It was as if his friend had combed libraries, diligently consulted the appropriate authorities to discover just what it was a certain kind of boy was likely to have in his pockets" (130). Later, cryptically explaining himself, Charles tells Stephen that "it's a matter of letting go. . . ." (132). His regression, then, is an escape, a freedom from the pressures of politics, a freedom from the chaos of contemporary society.

Thelma, however, explains her husband's regression differently; she tells Stephen, "He's completely mad" (140). As a result, the consequences of Charles's fantasy are dire indeed, eventually leading to his death. Torn between his need "'to be famous, and have people tell him that one day he would be prime minister . . .'" and his desire "'to be a little boy without a care in the world, with no responsibility, no knowledge of the world outside'" (238), Charles eventually surrenders, giving up on the world and his life simultaneously. However, even in the end, his child-self dominates; like a little boy he commits suicide in a "'petulant and childish'" way, immaturely lashing out at Thelma, his wife/mother, by putting himself out in the snow, stripping off most of his clothing, and dying of hypothermia. After his death, Thelma attempts to explain her husband's torment, explaining that his regression "was an overwhelming fantasy that dominated all his private moments" (238). For Charles, childhood was not only timeless, but was also a "mystical state" (238); as Thelma explains, he "'wanted the security of childhood, the powerlessness, the obedience, and also the freedom that goes with it, freedom from money, decisions, plans, demands'" (238). However, the regression becomes more and more difficult to maintain; soon Charles "'was sitting up all night agonizing [over his adult responsibilities], and he was still out in the woods during the day, trying to maintain his innocence. . . . He was in his treehouse in his short trousers wondering whether he should style himself Lord Eaton and whether anyone else had taken the name'" (240-41). His agony of indecision eventually leads to another breakdown that, in turn, leads to his death. Through Charles's regression into childhood, McEwan suggests that although it is important, even crucial, for the adult to accept the child that resides within him- or herself, it is dangerous, even suicidal, to become wholly that child-self or to surrender entirely to that desire. Acceptance and acknowledgement of the child-self can lead to a greater joy of life; submersion in that child can lead to a breakdown of the adult spirit.

2

Like so many of the characters and elements in *The Child in Time,* science (especially in its associations with the entity of time), too, is seen metaphorically as a child. Thelma envisions this particular child as "on the point of growing up and learning to claim less for itself" (45). The science of time is also one of the keys to discovering the child that dwells within each adult; as Roberta Smoodin writes, this lost childhood remains in the mature adult "not only in memory but in a kind of time that spirals in upon itself, seems to be recapturable in some plausible intermingling of Einstein and Proust, quantum physics and magical realism" (19). Time, then, plays a major role in Stephen's rejuvenation; through his course of recovery, he experiences several episodes in which time seems to slow, to elongate, or to warp completely out of context.

For example, while journeying to visit Charles and Thelma, Stephen narrowly escapes a serious automobile accident. When a lorry overturns in front of his car—forcing him to veer dangerously between the wreck and a road sign—Stephen experiences a "slowing of time" (106), one in which time itself seems to stall momentarily, allowing him to record events with unnatural clarity. Dodging the lorry but coming so close to the road sign that it shears away his door handle and side mirror, Stephen is at first elated by the near miss and then stunned by the fact that the entire incident had "lasted no longer than five seconds" (108). Later, after being rescued by Stephen, the lorry driver also expressed having experienced a similar slowing of time; asking "'How long was I in there? Two hours? Three?'" He finds it incredible when Stephen replies, "'Ten minutes. Or less'" (114). Time, inexplicably, is apparently malleable, a concept that Stephen has difficulty in understanding; nonetheless, it is an idea—like the mysterious child within himself—that he accepts as an ordinary aspect of an extraordinary world.

An even more astonishing distortion of time occurs when Stephen encounters a flaw in time. In an episode of magical realism, Stephen steps into the past and meets his parents. Walking through the countryside, in a place he has never before been, Stephen experiences an overwhelming familiarity, an eerie sense of *déjà vu.* Coming across an old tavern, he senses that "the day he now inhabited was not the day he had woken into. . . . He was in another time . . ." (63). Seeing a young couple through the tavern window, he experiences "not recognition so much as its shadow, not its familiar sound but a brief resonance . . ." (64). When the young woman looks out and stares intently at Stephen, he suddenly, inexplicably, realizes that she is, "beyond question," his mother (65).

Stephen is baffled by this incident, uncertain about how to accept seeing his parents in a time before he existed. Not until his mother relives the event, through the "timelessness of memory" (195), does Stephen begin to understand the repercussions of his experience with time.[2] Claire tells her son of the courtship between her and his father,[3] and the dilemma that they faced when she became pregnant. It was at the small tavern—where Stephen experienced his contortion of time—that Douglas had indirectly suggested an abortion. Before answering her husband-to-be, before considering the implications of marriage or abortion, Claire looked out the tavern window and experienced her own distortion of time:

> I can see it now as clearly as I can see you. There was a face at the window, the face of a child, sort of floating there. It was staring into the pub. It had a kind of pleading look, and it was so white, white as an aspirin. It was looking right at me. Thinking about it over the years, I realize it was probably the landlord's boy, or some kid off one of the local farms. But as far as I was concerned then, I was convinced, I just *knew* that I was looking at my own child. If you like, I was looking at you.
>
> (207)

From that point in time, she says, the baby "was suddenly flesh" (207); it was not "an abstraction. . . . It was . . . a complete self, begging her for its existence, and it was inside her, unfolding intricately, living off the pulse of her own blood" (207). Thus, Stephen himself becomes a child in time, magically appearing forty-four years later as the face his mother sees just weeks after his conception. In a sense, then, Stephen confirms his own existence. However, the full significance of his experience is not revealed until the end of the novel; when he has his interlude with the past, Stephen is just hours away from creating his own child in time.

Stephen continually ponders his seemingly preternatural experiences with time as well as the mysterious nature of time itself. Thelma, a theoretical physicist, offers scientific explanations, speaking to him as she would a classroom full of scientists, revealing that "there's a whole supermarket of theories these days" (135). For example, she lectures, one possibility "'has the world dividing every infinitesimal fraction of a second into an infinite number of possible versions, constantly branching and proliferating, with consciousness neatly picking its way through to create the illusion of a stable reality'" (135). Another theory states that "'time is variable. We know it from Einstein, who is still our bedrock here. In relativity theory, time is dependent on the speed of the observer'" (136). Yet another theory suggests that time is a separate entity in and of itself: "'In the big-bang theory, time is thought to have been created in the same moment as matter, it's inseparable from it'" (136). The only certainty about time, Thelma says, is its uncertainty: "'. . . whatever time is, the common-sense, everyday version of it as linear, regular, absolute, marching from left to right, from the past through the present to the future, is either nonsense or a tiny fraction of the truth'" (135-36). *The Child in Time* exemplifies how time is not a certainty, not a reality of the world; rather, as in Stephen's experience, time is a magical essence of life, an inexplicable entity that allows Kate to grow and exist within her father, that allows the ephemeral childhood of each person to continue existing throughout life, that enables Stephen to encounter his mother's decision to let him live. Time, then, is as ambiguous and as difficult as life itself.

Uniting the complex images of time and childhood, the problems of contemporary society, the complicated issues of love and heartache is the relationship between Stephen and Julie. Before Kate vanishes, Stephen and Julie share a powerful love: ". . . she loved him fiercely and liked to tell him. He had built his life round their intimacy and come to depend on it" (18). However, their daughter's disappearance brutally disrupts their relationship. In the aftermath of their tragedy, Stephen "anesthetize[s] himself with activity," searching desperately for Kate, while Julie collapses into a numbness of inactivity, spending day after day in a listless daze. They become embittered toward one another, their opposing reactions opening a rift in their marriage.

Their sorrow increases, pain multiplies, forcing them further and further apart. Ultimately, even their love falters and, like Kate, disappears: "If there was a love it was buried beyond their reach" (58). To save themselves, the two separate, with Julie fleeing to a retreat and Stephen immersing himself in the meaningless, everyday life of television and committee meetings. Surprisingly, it is this separation that saves their marriage and preserves their love for one another. As is the case in so many of McEwan's portraits of relationships, it is the female who provides the strength that sustains the alliance. By leaving—but not abandoning—the marriage, Julie is able to preserve (although at first unwittingly) the love that allows them to reunite; her time alone is a healing process that enables her to accept Kate's disappearance and to recognize her need and love for Stephen. When Julie leaves, Stephen recognizes, in turn, what he believes to be the essential difference between men and women: their "attitudes to change" (59). Most men, he concludes, after a certain age "froze into place" (59); women, on the other hand, forced to live several lives at once (motherhood and a "professional life on men's terms," for example), are more agile in the face of change and, therefore, more complete. Julie's ability to change through time and her insistence upon a change keep her spirit whole and her love intact.

The love that Stephen and Julie once shared and, for much of the novel, believe to be buried beyond recovery is, nevertheless, always between them, ready to resurface at the slightest coaxing. When Stephen visits Julie at her retreat, they find it easy to fall momentarily in love again; reunited, they become "their old, wise selves" (71). As they make love, Stephen connects this immediate experience to the incident in which he broke through time to see his parents: to him there is no "doubt that what was happening now, and what would happen as a consequence of now, was not separate from what he had experienced earlier that day" (70). Not until nine months later does he discover the full fruition of his premonition; his brief tryst with Julie results in a pregnancy that in turn reignites their spirit of love. However, their reunion in the present is short-lived as Kate comes irrevocably, inevitably between them. Stephen and Julie realize that each as an individual must learn to accept Kate's disappearance before they can accept that perpetual emptiness in their lives as a couple, a whole.

Shortly after Charles's death, Thelma tells Stephen that the solution to all of his problems has been in front of him all along: "'. . . think back over the last year and all *your* unhappiness, all the floundering about, the catatonia, when right in front of you was . . . Julie. . . . Julie was in front of you" (242-43). Journeying to rejoin his wife, Stephen imagines that the ghosts of his parents accompany him, for just as they were trodding this same path forty-four years before, on the verge of crossing the threshold into marriage and family, Stephen, too, is about to be reinitiated into the rites of marriage and love with the news that Julie is pregnant. Likewise, he discovers that all his sorrow, all his wasted and empty days have actually been "enclosed within meaningful time, within the richest unfolding conceivable" (251). During their second reunion, Julie explains to her husband that she "'came out here to face up to losing Kate. It was my task, my work, if you like, more important to me than our marriage, or my music. It was more important than the new baby. If I didn't face it, I thought I could go under. . . . I had to go on loving her, but I had to stop desiring her'" (254-55). With the knowledge that they will survive, that their love and need for each other are as strong as ever, they unite in their grief for the first time, mourning "the lost, irreplaceable child who would not grow older for them, whose characteristic look and movement could never be dispelled by time" (256). In their "wild expressiveness" of sorrow

> they undertook to heal everyone and everything, the government, the country, the planet, but they would start with themselves; and while they could never redeem the loss of their daughter, they would love her through their new child, and never close their minds to the possibility of her return.
>
> (256)

Their release of inner grief frees them and cleanses them; once again, they are a couple, a marriage, a unified whole.

Through the life that they have created, Stephen and Julie are given a second chance; essentially, they, too, are reborn with this child. Speaking of the seeming inevitableness of the conception, Julie says, "'. . . it did seem extraordinary, the ease with which it happened. . . . There had to be a deeper patterning to time, its wrong and right moments can't be that limited'" (254). As the baby is born, there is a "shock, a jarring, a slowing down as [Stephen] entered dream time" (261); again, time closes upon Stephen, but this time it slows in joy and wonderment. As the baby—the final child in time of the novel—emerges, it seems to say, "*Had you forgotten me? Did you not realize it was me all along? I am here*" (261). Helping the baby into the world, Stephen is suddenly struck with the simpleness of life: "This is really all we have got, this increase, this matter of life loving itself; everything we have has to come from this" (261). Life itself, he realizes, is the answer to the questions of life. As this family of three huddles together between the sheets revelling in the joy of love, outside their window can be seen the planet Mars, the lone "reminder of a harsh world" (263); for the moment, though, this harsh world is held at bay. The novel closes as Julie slips her hand beneath the covers to determine the sex of the baby. McEwan, however, does not reveal the sex because at this moment for this reborn family, it is not important—for this instant in time, there is only unqualified love, life, family.

In comparison with McEwan's earlier works, *The Child in Time* appears incredibly sentimental; McEwan has certainly abandoned the dirt, scum, and murder that proliferate in his earlier stories and novels. One must be careful, though, in this assessment, for underlying much of the brutality, violence, and chaos of McEwan's canon is a subtle yet prevailing optimism. In the story **"In Between the Sheets,"** a father's paternal love and concern conquer his sexual longings for his daughter; in **"First Love, Last Rites,"** a young couple remain united and hopeful despite the filth and chaos of an encroaching city; in *The Cement Garden,* Jack and Julie are drawn into their incestuous union through their need for comfort, for love. For the first time, however, with *The Child in Time,* McEwan allows this sentimentality to dominate. With the birth of the new child and the rejuvenation of Stephen's and Julie's relationships, McEwan allows sentimentality aptly to prevail.

Commenting on the optimism prevalent in McEwan's conclusion, Roberta Smoodin says,

> The ending . . . amazes one with its rightness, but more than this, allows McEwan to transcend the bounds of his style and to leap with abandon, into new territory. This territory is the possibility of happiness, the continuation of fragile, tenuous life, and even more improbable: love. The gloriousness of this ending, in all its faces . . . is masterful, even more so because it is so deeply felt, so perfectly crafted.
>
> (19)

McEwan has certainly moved beyond the shock and solipsism of his earlier fiction, but this "leap into new territory"—although it is a guarded optimism—is as well a culmination of his previous work, a coming together of his major themes and concerns. Throughout his canon, McEwan presents the endless struggle of men and women attempting to establish relationships that will sustain, nourish, and strengthen them in the chaotic world of contemporary society. In large part, these adult alliances are strengthened by the acknowledgment of the inner child, by an acceptance of the innocent joy of life and love that dwells within each individual; thus, in *The Child in Time,* the ever elusive fulfilling relationship is joyfully discovered and disclosed as to be quite permanent. Without doubt, *The Child in Time* is a fully grown novel.

*Notes*

1. McEwan, however, is far from alone among his British contemporaries in this kinder, gentler literature. Compare, for instance, Martin Amis's

*Einstein's Monsters,* Fay Weldon's *The Life and Loves of a She-Devil,* or J. G. Ballard's *Empire of the Sun* to their earlier works.

2. As Claire recounts her story, the narration slips into the past, with the narrator telling the story as it happened forty-four years ago; however, Claire's intrusions upon the story bring us back to the immediate present. Interestingly, then, there are two simultaneous presents: the present of Claire and Douglas and their courtship, and the present of Claire relating the story to her son. In essence, time has warped yet again in the novel.

3. Even the courtship is filled with amusing references to time; for instance, Claire works in the clock section of a department store, and Stephen's father, Douglas, meets his future wife when he returns a broken clock.

### Works Cited

Bemrose, John. "A Welcome Literary Invasion." *Maclean's* 25 April 1988: 51-52.

Locke, Richard. "Shades of Dickens and Woolf." *The Wall Street Journal* 15 Sept. 1987: 30.

McEwan, Ian. *The Child in Time.* 1987. New York: Penguin, 1988.

Muchnick, Laurie. "You Must Dismember This." *The Village Voice* 28 Aug. 1990: 102.

Smoodin, Roberta. "The Theft of a Child and the Gift of Time." *The Los Angeles Times Book Review* 20 Sept. 1987: 19.

## Phil Baker (review date 30 September 1994)

SOURCE: Baker, Phil. "Studies in Solipsism." *Times Literary Supplement,* no. 4774 (30 September 1994): 25.

[*In the following review, Baker offers praise for* The Daydreamer, *lauding the characterizations, wit, and attention to detail in the work.*]

***The Daydreamer*** is a children's book, containing seven stories about the adventures of young Peter Fortune. Peter is a "difficult" child, not because he is badly behaved but because he is so quiet and dreamy. Throughout these stories, he slips in and out of reality, crossing the threshold with a just perceptible shift.

Alone with his sister's dolls, he feels their uncanny little eyes watching him. Then one doll—a particularly ugly one called the Bad Doll, which is missing an arm and a leg and has only a single hank of hair left in its scalp holes—begins to question him. "Its tone was very polite, but there were titters in the crowd, and Peter knew he was being set up." Before long, the dolls move in on him, twisting his leg off for a spare part, "and instead of blood there was a little torn spring poking out through his torn trousers". Just as the mere presence of another person protects him from nightmares, so this awful transformation evaporates when his sister arrives. Peter's imagination is solitary enough for another's presence to break the spell, and yet it is through imagination that he empathizes with others and even shapes them. After overhearing some older children talk about solipsism, he proceeds to undream the school bully, Barry Tamerlane, dispelling the consensus of fear and reducing Tamerlane to a ridiculous plump boy with glasses.

Other metamorphoses include making his family vanish with vanishing cream, exchanging bodies with his cat, and changing into his baby cousin. Being a baby fills him with wonder; he enters a world of Mount Rushmore faces, booming orchestral voices and hands that lift him fifty feet in the air. Orange juice has an "itchy tangy noisy taste", and when mashed banana starts arriving in his mouth: "This food was so good he was *proud* to wear it in his hair, and on his hands and face and chest." He comes back to his own body with a new enthusiasm for his puling little cousin. Being a temporary adult extends his emotional range even further, giving him a taste of romance. Peter is a doubly liminal being, on the borders of adolescence as well as of reality, and the stories follow him from ten to twelve. "He'd been just a kid then", he realizes:

> Nine! What could he have known? If only his ten-year-old self could go back and tell that innocent fool what was what. When you got to ten, you began to see the whole picture, how things connected, how things worked, an overview.

Written with great understated intelligence and wit, the book is rich in captured perceptions like this. But it is here that the psychology stops; perhaps happily so. Given McEwan's reputation for perversity, guignol and gothic, the temptation on first reading is to be too alert for sinister detours into the Vienna Woods or the Bloody Chamber—"ever since he could remember, Peter had shared a bedroom with Kate", for example, or (playing with the cat) "Perhaps, Peter thought, I'll see his heart beating. . . . Peter wanted to part the skin to peep inside."

But instead, this is a very good-tempered and charming book, entirely trustworthy and safe; even the expletives of the Bad Doll have a kind of charm ("Filthy custard"). ***The Daydreamer*** is a benevolent celebration of childhood as adults see it; it is, in other words, entirely suitable for children.

**Paul Edwards (essay date spring 1995)**

SOURCE: Edwards, Paul. "Time, Romanticism, Modernism and Moderation in Ian McEwan's *The Child in Time*." *English* 44, no. 178 (spring 1995): 41-55.

[*In the following essay, Edwards considers McEwan's evocation of Romantic and Modernist conceptions of time, experience, and natural order in* The Child in Time, *especially as such motifs underscore the novel's literary critique of British social and political reality.*]

Ian McEwan's *The Child in Time* tells the story of a couple whose lives (and marriage, it would seem) have been blighted by the abduction of their child, and depicts an England which has been blighted by a government even more 'Thatcherite' than that which was in power at the time of the novel's first publication.[1] The blights are not unconnected, and the governmental attitude towards children, child-rearing and education continually emerge into the foreground of the novel. Each chapter is prefaced by an epigraph supposedly taken from the government-issued *Authorised Childcare Handbook,* and Stephen, a children's author and the father of the abducted child, serves on a Government Commission that is enquiring into such issues. But the connections are established also by more subtle means. At the opening of the book, Stephen, always on the look-out for his five-year-old daughter Kate, abducted two years ago, is accosted by a 'licensed beggar', a foul-mouthed little girl with a 'standard-issue' begging bowl (8-9). This victim of government social policy is slightly too old to be the lost child, but she is emblematic of a possible future for her. Placed at the opening of the book she is also emblematic of the novel's own procedure. It, too, represents an imagined, but not distant, future; what England would be if, at crucial forking points in time, it went in one direction rather than another. Stephen sees the girl again, after he has realised that such unpredictable forks in time have now taken his own daughter irrevocably away. He sees her one frozen morning seated among a group of badged beggars at a railway station, and gives her his coat, only to find that she is dead; the moment of futile charity represents also that moment where he is released from the obsession of his lost daughter.

The fate of specific children, then, enforces the novel's critique of a certain set of social and political values, and this critique is extended by a more general opposition between the phenomenology of childhood and that of a rather chilly variety of adulthood. The opposition is a familiar one, and the implicit moral of the novel—that we need to integrate both the qualities of childhood and the unregarded aspects of feminine experience into our notion (and practice) of adulthood—is perhaps trite when torn from the narrative that constructs it. The chief exemplar of a failure to integrate in this way is Charles Darke, Stephen's publisher. He embodies the opposition in his own character. Responding to the representation of childhood in Stephen's novel *Lemonade,* he insists that it is a book for children, and he later gives up a brilliant but haphazard career to return to the countryside and live out a second childhood. An amusing but nightmarish chapter has him, in *Just William* fashion, urging Stephen up a perilous climb to a treehouse, from which he can command the surrounding area with his catapult and refresh himself with swigs of cloudy lemonade. In terms of the traditional contrast between adulthood and childhood, Charles's valuation of Stephen's *Lemonade* should put us on our guard, however:

> . . . *Lemonade* is a message from you to a previous self which will never cease to exist. And the message is bitter. . . . You've spoken directly to children. Whether you wanted to or not, you've communicated with them across the abyss that separates the child from the adult and you've given them a first, ghostly intimation of their mortality. . . .
>
> (33)

Whatever the qualities of Stephen's book, this negative emphasis contrasts starkly with the message of hope drawn from even the most threatening moments of childhood experience by Wordsworth in the poem Charles's phrase alludes to:

> Blank misgivings of a Creature
> Moving about in worlds not realized,
> High instincts, before which our mortal Nature
> Did tremble like a guilty Thing surprised . . .

Our mortal nature might tremble, but Wordsworth takes such moments as intimations not of mortality but immortality. Charles sees only mortality (". . . it can't last, that sooner or later they're finished, done for, that their childhood is not for ever . . ."), but there is reason to suppose that his perception of Stephen's book is skewed by his own pessimism. His judgement is a self-fulfilling prophecy of the end of his own attempt to live as a child, and is recalled by his widow (". . . Your book . . . was a warning of mortality . . ." [201]) when she explains his suicide to Stephen near the end of the novel.

The character of Charles Darke is radically divided; his 'child' self is truly separated by an 'abyss' from the adult self that flourishes erratically but successfully in the public world. Before dropping out he has been an up-and-coming government minister, a protégé of that Prime Minister whose policies are shown as inimical to those human qualities that childhood represents. Indeed he is not merely a protégé, but diligently contributes to her (?—the novel coyly obscures the Prime Minister's sex) policies, and is revealed to be the author of the back-to-basics *Authorised Childcare Handbook* from which the novel's epigraphs are drawn. Darke writes this in a spirit directly contradictory to that sense of the mystery of childhood expressed in his subsequent attempted regression:

> Make it clear to him that the clock cannot be argued with and that when it is time to leave for school, for Daddy to go to work, for Mummy to attend to her duties, then these changes are as incontestable as the tides.
>
> (27)

The fatalistic subservience of 'him' (the child) and his parents to mechanical time (the clock) and to their gender-roles is surreptitiously smuggled into the order of nature by the final simile. But again we can turn to Wordsworth's *Immortality Ode* to see that imagery of the ocean need not lead in such a discouraging direction, that it can hint at eternity rather than servitude to a mechanism:

> Hence, in a season of calm weather,
>   Though inland far we be,
> Our souls have sight of that immortal sea
>   Which brought us hither,
>   Can in a moment travel thither,
> And see the children sport upon the shore,
> And hear the mighty waters rolling evermore.

Charles has a conception of childhood ('timelessness . . . a mystical state' [201]) that is close to Wordsworth's, but his attempt to live this state is simply an imitation of Richmal Crompton books. This character, then, functions as the carrier of a false or unsatisfactory version of the novel's value-system. Therefore, like the surrogate-daughter, he must die before Stephen can recognise that value-system manifested through his own experience. His morbid obsession with childhood is a version of the morbidity (at least adequately motivated in Stephen's case) that blights Stephen's life and marriage after Kate's abduction. Hence Stephen's cry, when weighed down by the corpse of Charles (which he has carried in from the tree which held his tree-house), 'For God's sake get him off me!' (199). The value-system of the novel is, then, roughly based on a conviction of the sustenance that we may derive from 'childhood' (properly understood) when we are adults.

For Wordsworth, as later for Yeats, this sustenance could be explained in terms of the Platonic myth of a form of 'existence' before birth in eternity; the clouds of glory that we trail in childhood are traces of this state. In the Kantian terms that were familiar to his friend Coleridge, childhood would be seen as an at least partial penetration through the ideal categories of space and time—especially time—to the 'thing-in-itself'. And since Wordsworth's time, the perceptual manifold of space and time has often been seen as the complement of the Newtonian mechanics that have created the industrial societies governed by inhuman clock-time rather than 'organic' time, and of the psychology that represents us as units behaving according to predictable patterns.[2] One strand of what we call 'Modernism' is predicated on the superiority of types of experience and forms of representation that subvert the Newtonian-Kantian manifold of our common-sense world. Except to lofty mythologers like Yeats, the Platonic system is no longer an adequate vehicle for such subversion. Besides, science itself now seems to be escaping from the Newtonian straitjacket that also confined our human nature. And this transformation of science is an explicit (perhaps too explicit) topic in *The Child in Time*.

Charles Darke's wife Thelma is a physicist who has worked on the theory of time and is now attempting a theoretical synthesis that will explain the consequences of such scientific revolutions as quantum mechanics. In a light-hearted, but serious enough, 'Two Cultures' style, she execrates Stephen (and other writers) for their ignorance of modern science. This, she claims, is becoming more feminine and is 'growing up' and overcoming the 'frenetic, childish' egotism of its 'Just William' obsession with commanding viewpoints, catapults and control. It accommodates such anti-Newtonian concepts as 'backward flowing time' and shows that our common experiences of time, space and matter are 'intricate illusions'. The conclusion of her harangue is ignorant but effective: 'As far as I can make out, you think that some local, passing fashion like modernism—modernism!—is the intellectual achievement of our time. Pathetic!' (43-45). It is, in fact, a leading characteristic of Modernism that it seeks to accommodate and realise the metaphysics implicit in modern scientific revolutions. *The Child in Time* itself is based on a metaphor of alternative universes that develop from the choices not taken in this one, and within the novel the attempts of that arch-Modernist miniaturist, Borges, to accommodate physical theories of time are unmistakably alluded to: 'Their hesitation was brief, delicious before the forking paths' (63; cf. 'The Garden of Forking Paths'). Thelma's vision, also, of a grand theory referring to an 'order of reality, a higher ground, the ground of all that is, an undivided whole of which matter, space, time, even consciousness itself, would be complicatedly related embodiments, intrusions which make up the reality we understood' (119) has been anticipated in metaphysical systems such as that of Alfred North Whitehead, expounded in the twenties and thirties, and thence found its way into such intransigently Modernist and experimental works as Charles Olson's *The Maximus Poems* in the fifties and sixties. Yet in relation to such works, which implicitly raise the question of the possibility of connecting 'the ground of all that is' to the world of common sense through language, the refusal of McEwan in this work to violate the form of the realist novel (while allowing it to encompass apparently non-realist content which I shall discuss) reminds us of the continuous relegation to eccentricity by British culture of any writer who wholeheartedly practises formal innovation in a Modernist tradition. The only major Modernist that McEwan invokes is the T. S. Eliot of *Four Quartets* (118)—a poem that eschews the more radical formal invention and disruption of Eliot's most 'Modernist' work. And many of the experiences of 'time' incorporated into McEwan's novel can be accounted for within the terms of the philosophy of Henri Bergson, which was so popular and influential before the First World War. The subjective experience of a few seconds (of clock-time) in which Stephen manages skilfully to avoid a lorry which is crashing in front of his car is characterised as 'duration shap[ing] itself round the event', for example. Bergson's philosophy, as expressed in *Time and Free Will,* distinguished between intensive, psychological duration (*durée*), which is unique and creative, and extensive clock-time as homogeneous and repeatable.[3] Where Bergson's philosophy inspired the early Modernists to radical formal innovation, however, McEwan remains faithful to a moderate English eschewal of extremism—though fortunately exhibiting its strengths rather than its weaknesses.

But there is a politics that accompanies these questions of form, which is ultimately related to the more explicit political characterisation of England that occurs in McEwan's book. Its terms were set out towards the close of the increasingly desperate period of post-war 'consensus' by Donald Davie, in his book *Thomas Hardy and British Poetry.*[4] Davie was writing before 'extremism' and Englishness could be thought of as a possible hegemonic combination; before Thatcherism, in other words, Davie's artistic (and cultural) predilections are to artistic extremism, (even, and far more than any other respectable critic, to the extremism of Charles Olson), but ultimately, on political grounds, it is to 'moderation' that he gives his support, even in the arts. This constitutes a conscious lowering of sights on Davie's part, and is consonant with Britain's role as a second-class power and (inglorious) welfare state. McEwan's moderation in the face of Thatcherism is a quite different thing from Davie's exasperated and wounded moderation in the face of Heath-Wilson, but Davie's book retains its relevance, not least, to McEwan's novel.[5]

The central, redemptive experience of 'time' in the novel (actually of a process that violates clock-time), initiating a hidden development unrevealed until the novel's closing pages, occurs in Chapter Three. Stephen visits his virtually estranged wife Julie in her cottage in a Sussex village. Before seeing her he has a strange disorientating *déjà vu* experience of seeing his parents through a pub window. But the scene he witnesses evidently occurred before his own birth, and his young mother gives no sign of recognition when he meets her gaze. In a state of shock, he appears to lose consciousness, and wakes to find himself in his wife's cottage, in their old marital bed, clasping a tepid hot-water-bottle. Almost as a matter of course, he and Julie make love, but their lost child again reminds them of their unhappiness, and the fresh start the moment could have led to seems aborted. Stephen returns to London. In a later chapter he recounts the experience to Thelma (omitting mention of the love-making, which 'was not Thelma's business' [116]) and asks for a scientific explanation. Her response is humorously derisive: 'You come cap in hand to the oracle you quietly despise. Why don't you go and ask a modernist?' (117). Perhaps the event could be accounted for in general terms by analogy with the 'backward flowing' of time that Thelma has already mentioned, for it turns out to have had an apparent influence upon the past. But, it seems to me, Thelma's mock advice, though misleading, suggests the correct affiliations for this experience; it needs to be understood in a literary context. Not a Modernist context, primarily, but one derived from the subject of Donald Davie's literary criticism.[6]

Several aspects of the chapter will need examination in order to bring out this context, and this will be easier if I explain what I take to be the significance of the incident in the value-scheme of the novel. It has two 'results', one in the past, and one in the future. Stephen later learns from his mother that his conception had been unplanned, and that his father (for whose sake she had lost her job selling clocks), had been in favour of aborting the foetus. Discussing this in the Sussex pub (in just such a scene as Stephen witnessed), his mother was swayed by the apparently pleading face of a child at the window to carry the pregnancy through to fruition. For Stephen himself, the quasi-noumenal experience is the crucial determinant in his choosing to make love with his wife rather than turn his back on her. The fruit of this is not revealed until the close of the novel, when he is suddenly summoned again to her cottage, and assists her in giving birth to their second child. The nine months interval had for Stephen been apparently no more than a halting but pointless reconciliation to loss. Approaching the village again, he suddenly realises why he has been sent for, and a pattern becomes clear to him:

> It was then that he understood that his experience there had not only been reciprocal with his parents', it had been a continuation, a kind of repetition. He had a premonition followed instantly by certainty . . . that all the sorrow, all the empty waiting had been enclosed within meaningful time, within the richest unfolding conceivable.
>
> (211)

This 'meaningful time' had been initiated as a result of Stephen's acknowledgement of, and guidance by, qualities he genders as feminine—'a faith in endless mutability, in remaking yourself as you came to understand more' (54). Men, on the other hand, take a line and stick to it. When Stephen makes love with his wife, however, he does so despite having so far taken the line that their relationship is now finished.

> Had he not seen two ghosts already that day and brushed against . . . the times and places in which they occurred, then he would not have been able to choose, as he did now, without deliberation and with an immediacy which felt both wise and abandoned.
>
> (63)

Reality itself, in this novel, follows the 'feminine' patterns of cyclical time, time in which alternative ghostly events may seem causative, or time which may reverse itself. It may, through childhood, overcome the seemingly inevitable progression of determined, (masculine) clock time.

In its schematised form, this value system sounds petty trite, perhaps, but that is the fault of my summary rather than McEwan's writing, which is vivid yet tactful, and deploys narrative suspense in such a way that the values are revealed through Stephen's own appealingly childish surprise at the end of the novel. Looking abstractly for the moment, though, we seem to have here an attempt to naturalise a set of values, and to ground them in biology and (to a more debatable extent) in physics. The extent of the naturalism is debatable because the precise status of Stephen's experience of temporal regression is left undetermined by the narrator. It in fact borders on the metaphysical. The narrator, in telling us that the noumenal experience is prior to, and determined, the love-making ('Had he not seen . . . he would not have . . .') grounds those 'biological' natural values on this ambiguously natural (real? hallucinatory? physical? metaphysical?) experience.[7] As well as seeming schematic, the values may be criticised for their consonance with gender-roles that are ideological and oppressive rather than natural ('There's no such thing as nature'); and, in the context of a supposed critique of Thatcherite tendencies in society, unduly quietistic and apolitical. The first charge can, at least provisionally, be fairly simply answered. The novel, after all, appears to argue for an integration of the various gendered characteristics, not for irreconcilable differences or social roles determined by difference. But it is, in broad terms, the political that I wish to address, and for this a closer commentary on Chapter Three is necessary.

It begins with a railway journey. Railways are themselves, the novel slyly reminds us at one point, the stuff of politics: 'The Prime Minister . . . was known to despise railways' (186). In terms of the opposition between Thatcherite politics and the values of childhood, this has a significance that is playfully indicated in the narrative when Stephen makes his way down to Sussex after the pregnant Julie's urgent summons. Arriving too late for the final train (he has no car, again in opposition to the 'great car economy'—Baroness Thatcher's phrase—that is shown as choking the city in the novel), he persuades a train driver to give him a lift in the cab of the engine. The line, with its cathedral-like tunnels, will shortly be closed and replaced by a motorway. We already know that Stephen still nourishes a boyhood ambition to ride in a railway engine cab (191). The journey thus becomes emblematic of the fortuitous (but how else can it occur?) integration of the boy within the man, and thus forms a contrast with Charles Darke's willed and artificial second childhood. Within Chapter Three itself a brief passage of recollection has already made the association between childhood and trains, as well as linking both to a sense of wonder that subtly prepares for the ghostly experience at the pub. As a child, standing on the footbridge over the railway, Stephen had asked his father why the lines grew together as they got further away. His father had explained that this was because

> the trains got smaller and smaller as they moved away, and that to accommodate them the rails did the same. Otherwise there would be derailments. Shortly after that an express shook the bridge as it shot beneath their feet. Stephen marvelled then at the intricate relation of things, the deep symmetry which conspired to narrow the rail's gauge precisely in keeping with the train's diminishment; no matter how fast it rushed, the rails were always ready.
>
> (51)

His father's explanation is a fiction, of course, a story to be told to a child, but it is a fiction which expresses truth and reveals it to the child. It thus forms a miniature apologia for the form of the novel itself.

But railway trains and train journeys also have a particular place in the English poetic tradition, where they serve to define a certain sense of the nation, from Edward Thomas's 'Adlestrop', Auden's 'Night Mail' to Philip Larkin's 'The Whitsun Weddings' and 'Here'.[8] The Larkin poems are both central exhibits in Donald Davie's discussion of the 'lowered sights' of post-war British poetry in *Thomas Hardy and British Poetry*. Both of these poems also seem to me to lie behind Chapter Three of **The Child in Time**. Davie makes what is now a common point about the English landscape that appears in Larkin's poems; that its heterogeneous confusion of the industrial, suburban, post-industrial and pre-industrial reflects for the first time in English poetry both the bare fact of that landscape and the manner in which we take its degradation for granted. McEwan's description of the landscape is clearly in the tradition that Larkin initiated. Mildly infected with a Larkinesque misanthropy, Stephen shuts himself away from the other 'customers' in a first-class compartment:

> They ran along the rear gardens of Victorian terraces whose back additions offered glimpses through open

doors into kitchens, past Edwardian and pre-war semis, and then they were threading through suburbs, southwards then eastwards, past encampments of minute, new houses with dirty, well-thumbed scraps of country in between. The train slowed over a tangle of junctions and shuddered to a halt. In the abrupt, expectant silence exuded by railway lines he realised how impatient he was to arrive. They had stopped by a new housing estate of raw, undersized semi-detached houses, starter homes for first time buyers. The front gardens were still rutted earth; out the back, fluttering white nappies proclaimed from diagrammatic, metal trees a surrender to a new life. Two infants, hand in hand, staggered beneath the washing and waved at the train.

Shortly before his stop it began to rain.

(50)

The passage (and I have quoted only a part of it) is a beautiful set of variations on 'The Whitsun Weddings': 'We ran Behind the backs of houses . . . the next town, new and nondescript, Approached with acres of dismantled cars . . . now fields were building plots . . . And as the tightened brakes took hold, there swelled A sense of falling, like an arrow-shower Sent out of sight, somewhere becoming rain.' Larkin's poem is not simply about landscape, of course. It is about weddings, and the mixed values and emotions that marriages (and by implication, parenthood) imply. Its conclusion, like many of the better moments in Larkin's poetry, represents a triumph over the small-minded misanthropy shown in the descriptions of the wedding parties themselves. And that triumph (in absolute terms not much more than an acceptance of the reality of other people's emotional lives, whose field will be the continuation of the species) is expressed largely in terms of transformed pastoral. The syntactic complementarity in 'Now fields were buildings plots' (carrying its ghostly equivalent: now building plots were fields) is realised in the famous and still startling lines:

> I thought of London spread out in the sun,
> Its postal districts packed like squares of wheat . . .

Davie's comment deserves quoting:

> . . . The collision between the organicism of wheat and the rigidity of 'postal districts' is calculated. It is the human pathos of the many weddings he has seen from the train which spills over to sanctify, for the poet, the postal districts of London, the train's destination; the human value suffuses the abstractly schematized with the grace of an organic fertility.[9]

The same might be said of the image of rain, which, as well as evoking the dreariness of a wet day indoors with bored children, plays its part in the natural cycle which culminates in the grown wheat. Like Larkin, McEwan assimilates the natural to the human in the passage quoted above, in his image of the metal trees bearing white nappies. This assimilation is a process that, in its accurate replication of the condition of post-war England (the reduction of a sense of the landscape as something other than merely human) Davie protests against, understandably, I think. Davie does not really address the question of how far it is actually possible to avoid some form of anthropomorphism in any representation of nature, and is presumably aware that the matter is one of degree: Larkin in some poems, and the English in their land, have tamed and humanised nature too much. McEwan's metal trees, representing (proclaiming, indeed) a surrender to the exigencies of the fertility of the species, are themselves a sardonic emblem of what Davie is objecting to. The 'natural' image, and nature itself, become 'abstractly schematized' to fit the schematization of our human lives; and we and nature both suffer diminishment on that account.

Davie recognises that this is a result of a historical process, while objecting that to think of people as merely the victims of such a process (rather than its perpetrators) adds to the diminishment. But Davie was writing his discussion as long ago as 1963,[10] and McEwan's novel is suffused with a sense that the processes Davie describes have progressed almost beyond what could have been imagined at that time. The countryside of his alternative present, through which Stephen walks after leaving the train, is dotted with hypermarkets, car parks and motorways. 'Real, open country' is a concrete track traversing symmetrical conifer plantations. The closest thing to an animal (a counterpart to the metal trees), a 'grey beast languidly lifting its blunt, heavy head with a steady purr', is a nodding donkey engine pumping at a small oil-well (51). From a perspective derived from Davie's discussion, what might be most depressing about this is Stephen's apparent acquiescence in the substitution of this landscape for the less schematized land that preceded it. Stephen feels 'light-hearted' now he is in open country. I take it that it is the double diminishment that Davie is concerned about. Human, not solely environmental, diminishment distresses him. This, also, is McEwan's subject, it seems to me. Stephen is in danger of losing a more nourishing sense of wonder than what a tidied and industrialised environment can provide: the 'flashing parallax as one row [of the geometrically arrayed conifers] cede to the next, a pleasing effect . . .' We can connect this with Stephen's rather indifferent and at times cynical acquiescence in the political fraud of the child-care commission on which he serves. Despite his beliefs, he is capable of simply shrugging his shoulders at the whole business, so impoverished are his political expectations in this England.

What Davie objects to is that such a diminished sense of both nature and human nature—the last refuge of liberal humanism—should be considered and adequate basis for a worthwhile life. Larkin, in his poetry, appears to think it is; but Davie has a Modernist revulsion from such a surrender."[11] McEwan, also, in apparently grounding his values naturalistically on human fertility itself (admittedly with all the concomitant values that inhere in the more tender forms of sexual intercourse) might be held to be vulnerable to Davie's criticism. But I have already suggested that the value-system of *The Child in Time* is not simplistically naturalistic, and might be said to be grounded on the borderline between nature and metaphysics. This can also best be approached through a Larkin 'railway' poem: 'Here', which Davie severely criticises for its apparent disparagement of the natural (on account of the way the 'otherness' of nature is defined solely as a negation of the human, rather than as a value in itself). *The Child in Time*'s 'housing estate of raw, undersized semi-detached houses' is surely one of the 'raw estates' of Larkin's poem, and its 'halt for commuters' (50) is Larkin's, 'harsh-named halt'. It may be that my reaction to 'Here' has been affected by what I take to be the use made of the poem by McEwan, but it seems to me that Davie does less than justice to the poem's final verse. This continues the sweep of the railway journey (though we are now past the terminus) out beyond Hull, over the countryside until it arrives before what it cannot reach, the sea:

> . . . Here silence stands
> Like wheat. Here leaves unnoticed thicken,
> Hidden weeds flower, neglected waters quicken,
> Luminously-peopled air ascends;
> And past the poppies bluish neutral distance
> Ends the land suddenly beyond a beach
> Of shapes and shingle. Here is unfenced existence:
> Facing the sun, untalkative, out of reach.

It seems to me that Davie is determined not to hear the (faint enough) note of wonder before the unbounded and out of reach ocean in these lines. He might well, after all, welcome the negation of the merely human, as much as bemoan the fact that it is the human that provides the positive term from which the negation is effected. The same note of wonder before the unbounded is struck when Stephen, on his walk to his wife's cottage, emerges from the pine plantation:

> The pine forest gave way abruptly to an unbounded prairie of wheat. Stephen rested against an aluminium five-barred gate. The only indication that the yellow field, which resembled a desert, was finite was a line on the horizon where the plantation resumed. Perhaps it was a mirage . . . He set off, and within minutes found satisfaction in this new landscape. He was marching across a void. All sense of progress, and therefore all sense of time, disappeared. The trees on the far side did not come closer . . . The lack of hurry, the disappearance of any real sense of a destination suited him.
>
> (51-52)[12]

Wheat is the most human of plants—a result of man's 'improvement' of nature—and the boundless prairie has been created by agri-business for ease of mechanical harvesting. The landscape Stephen walks through can be found already in parts of East Anglia; it is the product of the economic and political forces (which I have called in shorthand Thatcherism, though more than that limited ideology is at stake here) that are responsible for the social disintegration depicted in the novel. Yet it is not, surely, a sign of Stephen's limitations that he responds positively to the experience of traversing this vast wheatfield. In a sense the infinite wheat is cognate with the ocean (as it is to some extent in 'Here'), the closest phenomenon in nature to the unbounded and eternal experience of the noumenal itself, as in Wordsworth's Ode. Both time and space are abolished in Stephen's experience; he crosses a 'void' and time disappears. I shall argue that, as also in Wordsworth's poem, this noumenon is associated with origins and (mediated through childhood) with sustaining value. In terms of the environmental politics of Davie's discussion, what the novel is asserting is that even in a landscape apparently violated and schematised beyond recognition, we may still have sight of that immortal sea which brought us hither, so that our humanity need not be as diminished as our politics. And if our humanity is not diminished, (the novel implies) it remains open to us to invent a politics that does justice to our values.

Again the summary betrays a complex literary creation. I can only briefly indicate how the links are made, and the values established. The strange, noumenal experience on the prairie removes Stephen from space and time. This results in his finding himself in the village (which, with its bicycles, pub, and 'magnificent trees' [57], is the 'timeless' England of Georgian poetry recently evoked in a tepid speech by England's current Prime Minister), where he witnesses his parents discussing whether he should be born. Immediately afterwards he undergoes a regression through birth and beyond, back to the nothingness of pre-existence. Oceanic images are evoked (ontogeny here recapitulating phylogeny and substituting a scientific perspective for Wordsworth's Platonism). He is 'hurled through . . . muscular sluices';

> his knees rose under him and touched his chin, his fingers were scaly flippers, gills beat time, urgent, hopeless strokes through the salty ocean . . . he formed a single thought: he had nowhere to go, no moment which could embody him, he was not expected, no destination or time could be named . . .
>
> (60)

The lack of destination and time link this passage (already linked by narrative sequence) to the experience of crossing the prairie. It is not by any means a benign experience, but is fraught with the terrifying sense of the contingency of one's own existence (sensed more through parenthood in this novel than through childhood), just as Wordsworth's sense of the noumenal is fraught with the 'Blank misgivings of a Creature Moving about in worlds not realized'. Stephen is brought to the borders of what is out of reach of language, so far beyond the identity that is contingent on the perceptual manifold of time and space and the sign systems with which we label it that 'Nothing was his own, not his strokes or his movement, not the calling sounds, not even the sadness, nothing was nothing's own' (60). I have suggested that this takes us beyond naturalism to the metaphysical. Yet of course the novel cannot argue across that boundary. And the logical generation of all our categories out of the simple given, 'Being', is, compared with those experiences that novels explore, a barren-seeming procedure. In the human terms of novels, the boundary is conception itself—terrifying when seen, as Stephen sees it, from the perspective of the foetus regressing into nothingness, but from another perspective the origin of a faith that life is fundamentally benign. Stephen makes love with his wife:

> Not governments, or publicity firms or research departments, but biology, existence, matter itself had dreamed this up for its own pleasure and perpetuity, and this was exactly what you were meant to do, it wanted you to like it . . . Surely then, he thought, as he fell backwards into the exquisite, dizzy emptiness and accelerated down the irresponsibly steep slope, surely at heart the place is benevolent, it likes us, it wants us to like it, likes itself.
>
> (64-65)

The novel by no means claims that these values are in themselves a victory over the unhumanity and unnaturalness of the political system that prevails in the England of *The Child in Time*; children do die or are abducted, 'Authorised Childcare Handbooks' are written. But it suggests that only through a sense of these values can any political opposition become possible. My aim here, however, is literary-critical, not political. It seems to me that *The Child in Time* reveals its deepest meaning when viewed in the literary and cultural perspectives that I have attempted to outline in this essay.

### Notes

1. Ian McEwan, *The Child in Time*, (1987) rpt. (London: Picador, 1988).

2. For a fuller discussion of this topic, and some of the modern attempts to avoid these consequences of this side of Kantianism, see the editorial 'Afterword' in Wyndham Lewis, *Time and Western Man*, ed. P. Edwards (Santa Rosa: Black Sparrow Press, 1993), pp. 466-74.

3. Henri Bergson, *Time and Free Will: An Essay on the Immediate Data of Consciousness*, tr. F. L. Pogson, (London: G. Allen and Unwin, 1910).

4. Donald Davie, *Thomas Hardy and British Poetry*, (London: Routledge and Kegan Paul, 1973).

5. A discussion following the session on 'Englishness and English Art' at the 19th Annual Conference of the Association of Art Historians (The Tate Gallery, April 1993) found itself addressing the same issues as those raised twenty years ago in Davie's book, though the parallel was probably unknown to most participants.

6. This does not mean that there are no connections with Modernism. The allusion to Borges already mentioned occurs in this chapter. It is also just possible that the 'time hallucination' that Stephen enters was in part suggested by the time hallucination of old England into which the ghosts, Pullman and Satterthwaite, stray in Wyndham Lewis's representation of the afterworld (*The Childermass: Section I* [London: Chatto and Windus, 1928], pp. 83-103). Also, after Stephen's hallucination, in the period of semi-consciousness, it is just possible that his sensation of being like a fish with flippers and gills recalls the 'strange fishes withouten heads' in Joyce's *Ulysses* (ed. J. Johnson, [Oxford: OUP, 1993], p. 370) mentioned at that point to point up the parallel between the development of English and the development of the foetus. But both parallels are doubtful, and reveal the distance, rather than any closeness, of *The Child in Time* from high Modernism.

7. By definition the noumenal must logically precede natural phenomena, of course. But Stephen's experience is not directly classified in the novel as quasi-noumenal or noumenal; that description is mine.

8. The tradition can be said to begin with Wordsworth's opposition to the encroachment of the railway on the Lake District; a reminder of the shifting significance of this (it now seems) most human of industrial forms of transport in the poetic sense of the country and its landscape.

9. Davie, op. cit., p. 66.

10. See ibid., p. 73.

11. The Modernist point of view is expressed by Wyndham Lewis in a way that brings out the dilemma (but squares the circle), in a passage discussing the liberal-humanist attitudes to meat-eating and capital punishment, written around 1925: 'At the root of both of these questions it is advisable to place the not necessarily inhuman proposition that life is in itself not important. Our values make it so: but they are mostly, the important ones, non-human values, although the intenser they are the more they imply a supreme, vital connotation'. *The Art of Being Ruled* (1926),

rpt., ed. R. W. Dasenbrock (Santa Rosa: Black Sparrow Press, 1989), p. 59.

12. 'The Whitsun Weddings' is also still present in the writing at this point: 'all sense of being in a hurry gone'; and, of course, wheat is a central image in that poem as it is in 'Here'.

**Christina Byrnes (essay date June 1995)**

SOURCE: Byrnes, Christina. "Ian McEwan—Pornographer or Prophet?" *Contemporary Review* 266, no. 1553 (June 1995): 320-23.

[*In the following essay, Byrnes provides an overview of McEwan's artistic and thematic development through the publication of* The Daydreamer, *drawing attention to his explorations of sexual obsession and psychic integration.*]

Considering that Ian McEwan won the Somerset Maugham award for his first book, a collection of short stories entitled *First Love, Last Rites,* there is surprisingly little written about him. In the eighteen years that he has been writing, he has often been misunderstood and plagued by controversy. The BBC first commissioned a play by him and then in March 1979, four days before he was due to record it, the management called a halt. McEwan was told the play was 'untransmittable' and the BBC put out a press notice that announced the ban and referred to 'grotesque and bizarre sexual elements of the play'. In fact, *Solid Geometry,* published in play form in *The Imitation Game* (1982) and as a short story in *First Love, Last Rites* (1991) is the least bizarrely sexual of McEwan's early work and he was hugely disappointed that it was not given a fair trial (see the introduction to *The Imitation Game*). Several people in the BBC strongly supported McEwan and were subsequently sacked for objecting to the ban. McEwan was labelled as 'dirty' and it is this reputation that many people still recall when his name is mentioned. However, there are also those who consider McEwan a great writer and see him as one of the most significant post-war authors.

McEwan is careful to research his subject matter very thoroughly as can be seen from the gruelling descriptions of dissection in *The Innocent* (1990) for which he acknowledges the help of Dr. M. Dunhill, University Lecturer in Pathology, Merton College, Oxford. It comes as some relief to the reader of his early works, which deal with the subject of sexual deviation and emotional immaturity, that he does not write from personal experience—despite a most convincing use of first person narrative. McEwan describes sex in explicit detail from the perfectly individual experience of the narrator and manages to create startled surprise but never incredulity in the reader. He gives an experience of horror and perversion beyond ordinary fantasy that is so skilfully integrated with the character's life situations that we reluctantly identify with them. We are forced to face, in ourselves, those aspects of the unconscious which we might have preferred to remain unaware of, but which must, in the last analysis, be part of our human heritage. McEwan himself describes this process in his preface to *A Move Abroad*:

> There it is this man again, a version of yourself . . . someone you might have become if your luck had been really atrocious.

The shock of his work is in the recognition that he manages to communicate what you would otherwise consider impossible to talk about.

McEwan makes the connection between how situations look and how they feel. He changes the reader's perspective from being on the outside (objective) to one of being on the inside (subjective), unable to react rationally to events. His identification is so compelling that he leads us gradually further and further into the depth of a character and thus enables us to get 'in touch' with the feelings that would lead to the 'grotesque and bizarre sexual' acts committed by the characters in his short stories. Themes such as incest, cross-dressing, sado-masochism and death are captured in tiny but perfect fragments and McEwan explores each idea in an utterly convincing way.

These themes are revisited in his shorter novels: *The Cement Garden* (1980) and *The Comfort of Strangers* (1982). Here they are set in a background of ongoing, long-term relationships so that we can more fully appreciate the conditions which facilitate these perversions. We have much more detail about the physical environment in which the characters live and move. The complex sequence of events and actions reveal the underlying and implicit motives. In *The Cement Garden* for example, the metaphor contained in the title, a garden stifled by cement, expresses the condition of the children in the book. They are first repressed by their rigid father and then bound by their dead mother's wishes. They are prevented from 'growing', like the flowers in the garden and are forced 'underground' by the distorting limitations of the script they feel obliged to live out. We fully understand the characters, as we did in previous works but we are now able to step back from them. We still experience their feelings first hand but at the same time we can distance ourselves into a position of sympathetic judgement. We are able to observe as well as experience the action. In this way, McEwan is able to become even more disturbing. In *The Comfort of Strangers,* realization dawns on Mary and the reader that she and Colin are in serious danger but neither she, nor the reader are prepared for the obscene horror of what actually takes place.

Following the incredible creativity of his early works, there is a gap of six years in McEwan's novels between 1981 and 1987. Despairing temporarily of his ability to reconcile 'the specific' that makes novels so powerful with 'hard ideas, social theories, axes to grind, persuasive intentions or the determination to be right' (Preface to *A Move Abroad*), he began to experiment with other media. He achieved his goal by giving open, straight forward expression to his beliefs in the words of an Oratorio. The Oratorio ends with questions that should, according to McEwan, preoccupy us all:

> Shall there be womanly times or shall we die?
> Are there men unafraid of gentleness?
> Can we have strength without aggression,
> without disgust,
> strength to bring feeling to the intellect?
> Shall we change or shall we die?
>
> *(Or Shall We Die?)*

The film *The Ploughman's Lunch* (produced by Simon Relph and Anne Scott for Greenpoint Films Ltd., 1983, shown on Channel 4), continues to portray these preoccupations and adds the danger of distorting history in the interests of politics by giving an 'official version of events'. These two works: the Oratorio *Or Shall We Die?* and the film *A Ploughman's Lunch* are published as *A Move Abroad*; the title serves as a metaphor for McEwan's departure into drama. He also wrote three plays: *Jack Flea's Birthday Celebration, Solid Geometry* and *The Imitation Game.*

There is a marked change in breadth between his earlier and later works. There is an expansion in scope to include McEwan's preoccupations with the Cold War, the nuclear threat, the women's movement, environmental pollution etc., and reflect his interest in the work of psychologist Carl Jung. The gap between the highly personal experience of the narrators in the early stories and complex sophistication of the later novels is bridged by the plays, which gives McEwan an opportunity to have many characters speaking for themselves as well as telling a story. He adapts this scheme in his later fiction by skilfully introducing both narratives and narrators. Characters begin to speak for themselves instead of being observed only through an unreliable narrator.

In the later novels, the protagonists or principal narrators are adults. They live in a complex, contemporary world, are set in precise time and geographical space and it is easy to identify them if not identify with them. We recognise them as 'normal', mature and reasonably well adjusted people. The unconscious, so transparent in the narrators of the early stories, now seems to have moved into the background of politics, global events and changes in the philosophy of science. This shift does not cause McEwan to stray from the theme of sexuality, since he uses this very vehicle to develop the idea of the division or splitting of the wholeness of the human psyche into the opposites of male and female. The characters could imaginably lead ordinary, successful and conventional lives, were it not for the events of external reality which shatter the reasonable life plans they made for themselves. Stephen, for example, the main narrator in *The Child in Time* is set to have a perfectly enjoyable life with his wife until somebody steals their three-year-old daughter at a supermarket. This loss deals an inevitable blow to their lives and their relationship which they only barely learn to accept with time.

Leonard Marnham, the main character in *The Innocent* is well educated and socially upwardly mobile. His world is the masculine world of power, competition and technology. Ambiguous loyalties, secret machinations and betrayal figure large here and he is enmeshed in high level politics but maintains the role of a trusting innocent until he can no longer sustain these unrealistic fictions. The secrecy and spying, first touched on in *The Imitation Game,* together with the symbolic equivalents between underground tunnels (where Otto's body eventually ends up), the unconscious and the sea (from which Buster Crabbe's headless body is recovered by fishermen) serve McEwan to bury the shadow aspects of human evil.

The hallmark of the later characters is their competence in coping with the full complexity of life. The developmental phases progress through the mid-life crisis to a gradual involution in old age and a preparation for death. There is, in later life, a shift of emphasis from the striving for erotic experience to emotional relationship and adjustment to one partner, who becomes 'the other half' of one's self. Gradually, both sides of the sexual polarity are experienced within the self and a stage of psychic wholeness is reached, which does not preclude love but rather makes a deeper love possible. The other person's wholeness and difference is valued. During mid-life crisis, as in adolescence, there can be temporary instability and a reassessment and restructuring of the value systems and life scripts. McEwan's preoccupation with the topics of sex and sexuality reflects the contemporary obsession with eroticism and the dilemma created by the failure to integrate masculine and feminine consciousness. His efforts to clarify these issues most surely rank as a major contribution to late twentieth century literature.

McEwan's latest novel *Daydreamer* marks his debut into children's fiction and represents another change in direction for him. The book, intended for children, has as much, if not more, relevance for the adult reader.

McEwan has turned his attention to the child, the symbol of the unification of opposites. But that, of course, is another story . . .

## Anita Brookner (review date 30 August 1997)

SOURCE: Brookner, Anita. "Desire and Pursuit." *Spectator* 279, no. 8822 (30 August 1997): 28-9.

[*In the following review, Brookner praises* Enduring Love *for its effective use of "psychological terrorism," McEwan's patient building of conflict and suspense, and the book's ultimate portrait of disintegration.*]

De Clérambault's syndrome, named after the French psychiatrist who first isolated and identified it in 1942, describes that state of would-be possession which is now tamely known as stalking. De Clérambault's most famous patient was in love with King George V, and was convinced that the curtains of the upper windows of Buckingham Palace delivered messages of regard, concern, or warning which only she could perceive. There are a lot of single-issue fanatics out there, lonely lobbyists for some hopeless personal cause who perceive persecution as legitimate in the crazed circumstances which they have devised and who conceive of love as a form of assault. Some of them, regrettably, discern God's hand guiding them in their quest. Their victims, employing every form of common sense in their resistance to this obsession, will be shaken by it, progressively convinced that they are in some way responsible, and finally terrified, their own lives neglected and atomised by the need to keep the madness at bay. Some of them may never recover.

In Ian McEwan's clever, even brilliant novel [*Enduring Love*] victim meets executioner in highly unusual circumstances: both are witnesses to an incident in which a hot-air balloon is driven off course by a high wind and drifts into the distance, or would do, if rescuers were not valiantly clinging to the ropes. One by one they drop away; a body, that of the most persistent, falls to the ground, shattered by the impact. Joe Rose, our hero, races to see if he can help. He is joined by Jed Parry, another of the rescuers, who pleasantly suggests that they get down on their knees and pray. Joe, just as pleasantly, or so he thinks, refuses. That is his mistake. It is obvious to Parry that Joe needs persuading, that God's love is also Parry's love. This may, indeed will, necessitate certain crucial changes in Joe's life, but instructions will come from Parry in the form of constant telephone calls, letters, attendance outside Joe's flat in Maida Vale, and loving assurances of attention at all times. The police can do nothing because in their book Parry has not committed an offence.

If the hairs are already rising on the back of the reader's neck this is entirely in order. Ian McEwan, in solemn, sober prose, is a past master at psychological terrorism, overlaid with courtesy and a genuine curiosity. *The Comfort of Strangers* is still a worrying book, demonstrating the dangers of instant friendship and offers of hospitality. *Enduring Love* is in the same vein, but far outdoes the earlier novel, which is brief, lapidary, and devoid of judgment. *Enduring Love* is, in fact, even more alarming, as Joe's behaviour, his love affair, and his way of life collapse under the weight of Parry's insistence. Joe is a likeable fellow; he is a scientist, a rationalist, and a journalist, three callings which should provide proof that he is not easy to frighten, not susceptible, not in the last analysis mad himself. The ardent Parry, no less than the woman who watched the curtains at Buckingham Palace, is as unrelenting as the love of God, with whose purposes he claims to be familiar and whose radiance he believes he shares.

No outline of the plot will be given here; the narrative must be read word by sinister word. What impresses in this novel is not only the author's care but his extreme patience with a story targeted at disintegration. His protagonist, Joe, is a freelance scientific populariser, whose unstructured days give him plenty of opportunity for observation, so that he is usually aware of the figure on the opposite pavement, is available to note telephone calls, even when he has switched off his answering machine. This is clearly an affair between men; it is erotomania disguised as concern, religion without morality, loving kindness designed as endless pursuit, and in the final analysis a will to extinction. It is almost a miracle that the novel holds up under the strain.

But hold up it does, and the author's control is impressive. The direction of the novel is only a little marred by three diversions, almost but not quite believable, accepted only later, when the book has been closed. In these episodes McEwan's direction seems to have been adapted from one of his more extraneous character's dicta: Always win, always cheat. But these are minor quibbles, objected to only when they diverge from the main theme. In Parry, the hunger artist, the man first glimpsed in a field in the Chilterns clinging on to the rope of an escaping balloon, McEwan has created his most terrifying archetype, the inimical lover whose desire and pursuit of the whole outdistance the amorous behaviour of any normally constituted person.

In Joe he has given us a patient, scrupulous, likeable character whose world reveals itself to be as fragile as a drifting balloon. In *Enduring Love* McEwan has contrived a marvellous fiction on the basis of fact (references are given), yet it remains an imaginative reconstruction of a superior kind. This is the writer as stalker, agent and patient in a delusional system that bestows anxiety to the very last page.

## Amanda Craig (review date 5 September 1997)

SOURCE: Craig, Amanda. "Out of the Balloon." *New Statesman* 126, no. 4350 (5 September 1997): 43.

[*In the following review of* Enduring Love, *Craig criticizes the novel's schematic opposition of science and religion.*]

Is love the subject or object? Is it love that endures or love that must be endured which preoccupies the protagonist of Ian McEwan's latest novel [*Enduring Love*]?

It gets off to a splendid start. Joe and Clarissa are having a picnic in the Chilterns. Suddenly they notice a balloon with a child in it floating off despite the desperate attempts of the child's grandfather to hang on. The child seems certain to be electrocuted on the nearby pylons. The narrator, and several others, race towards the balloon and try to anchor it. Only one, however, has the courage to keep trying; as the balloon soars upwards, he falls to his death.

The child is safe, but the narrator finds he has attracted the affections of a mad-man, Jed. The latter obtains his telephone number and address with ease, and is soon making telephone calls, stalking, and sending letters which combine protestations of passion with religious argument. Joe is driven to the brink of his own sanity. He can get neither the police nor his own wife (who leaves him) to take Jed seriously, even when two hit men shoot a man similar to himself at a neighbouring table in a restaurant.

Jed, as Joe comes to realise, has "de Clerambault's syndrome", an erotomaniac state in which the subject has the intense delusional belief that the object of their passion is in love with them. Tragic for both sufferer and victim, the syndrome mimics real love although the victim has usually never met the sufferer, or done so only briefly. This is a novel idea, and one which gives rise to many trains of thought on love—was Dante, for instance, a sufferer?—few of which are taken up. What McEwan seems intent on doing is showing how deranged Jed is, and by extension, Christianity. Joe is a successful science writer; his mind is a cornucopia of rationalist arguments, including one (unacknowledged by the author) lifted straight from Harold Bloom on the authorship of the Old Testament. Presented with the outpourings of a born-again nut, "generally aligned to the culture of personal growth and fulfilment" he reacts as many feel like doing: he reaches for a gun.

From *Middlemarch* to *Brazzaville Beach*, novelists have mined science for metaphor and, perhaps, intellectual respectability. The trouble is, most of us have now read the same books, and we are not overly excited by having rationalist arguments repeated at third-hand in a work of fiction.

The clash between Joe's scientific rationalism and Jed's Christianity is merely symbolic, as between the sane and the mad; the novel would have been deeper and stronger for being more impartial, less schematic. Ever since his first collection of short stories, McEwan has displayed a fascination with the scientific and the supernatural—an interest which scaled peaks of absurdity in *Black Dogs.* You cannot fight a cast of mind, yet it is frustrating when one greatly admires a writer to see a kind of silliness creep into their work— even if this particular book is a rejection of credulity. The observations remain telling. Joe's description of how certain women of his generation have all the same mouths from "a lifetime of putting out, as they saw it, and getting nothing back . . . a Cupid's bow of loss" has an undeniable authenticity; but it is not followed through into a rounded characterisation.

In outline, McEwan has written a good psychological thriller, without the squamous sex'n'violence that characterises his earlier work. He is the maestro at creating suspense: the particular, sickening, see-sawing kind that demands a kind of physical courage from the reader to continue reading. McEwan will rise higher, though, if he lets go of the half-baked ideas.

## Oliver Reynolds (review date 12 September 1997)

SOURCE: Reynolds, Oliver. "A Master of Accidents." *Times Literary Supplement*, no. 4928 (12 September 1997): 12.

[*In the following review, Reynolds proposes that each of McEwan's novels follows a template of three parts revolving around a male-female relationship, an external threat to that relationship, and a definite focus on language. However, Reynolds faults* Enduring Love *for its asides on scientific theory and the vagaries of love, and its use of multiple narrative points of view.*]

Early in his second novel, *The Comfort of Strangers* (1981), Ian McEwan calls up Mozart to usher in the theme which virtually dominates all his work. Colin, who is on holiday with Mary, hears a man singing in the shower: "tra-la-ing the forgotten words, bellowing out the orchestral parts, '*Mann und Weib, Und Weib und Mann,* together make a godly span.'" If one were to produce a template for the McEwan novel, its three essential features would be a relationship between a man and a woman, an external threat which clarifies the nature of that relationship, and a prose style equal to that of any writer in English today. The template would not fit McEwan's one book for children, *The Daydreamer* (1994), but it would serve for all his novels, from the first, *The Cement Garden* (1978)—the couple there is an incestuous brother and sister—to his latest. Its title, *Enduring Love,* explicitly announces McEwan's perennial romantic theme, but the effortful pun—love that lasts may also have to be suffered—reminds us that, although some of his couples may live to enjoy "a godly span", all of them go through hell.

Joe and Clarissa are a happy couple. He is a science journalist and she is an academic. McEwan's first two novels seemed to issue direct from an imagination complete in itself, diamond-hard, exact and exacting. His third, *The Child in Time* (1987), mentions three non-fiction books on its acknowledgements page; storytelling has broadened out into an engagement with political and cultural forces. *Enduring Love* acknowledges ten books and also includes a list of twenty medical papers. One has a sense of fiction threatened by background reading, of the novelist's bookcase toppling on top of him. As if to counteract the danger of the book's being hobbled by its themes, there are thriller-like injections of action: a high-speed drive, two shootings, a hostage. These follow on from the book's central triangle; Joe and Clarissa may be in love, but someone else is obsessed with Joe. He has a stalker or, as his researches tell him, he is being pursued by someone with "de Clérambault's syndrome".

A significant moment in *The Comfort of Strangers* has a woman asking Mary about her relationship with Colin: "Are you in love?" It seems an innocuous question, until the woman reveals what it means to her: "If you are in love with someone, you would even be prepared to let them kill you, if necessary." Jed Parry, the man obsessed with Joe, is another example of an extreme manifestation of love, and one which is meant to throw light on what it means for people like Joe and Clarissa to be in love, but not pathologically so. There is something rather predetermined in McEwan's use of de Clérambault's syndrome as a kind of rabid stalking-horse, behind which he can approach more ordinary forms of love. Jed's continual presence under Joe's window and his repeated phone calls and letters lead to a breakdown of trust between Joe and Clarissa. For the science journalist, reconciliation is a matter of checking references and collating information. The way to regain his lover is to understand Jed: "For there to be a pathology there had to be a lurking concept of health. . . . Sickness and health. In other words, what could I learn about Parry that would restore me to Clarissa?" The novel has two appendices. The second is another letter from Jed, unrepentant and ecstatic to the end; the first rounds up the medical background, finishing with a quotation from the *British Journal of Psychiatry*: "the pathological extensions of love not only touch upon but overlap with normal experience, and it is not always easy to accept that one of our most valued experiences may merge into psychopathology."

Joe and Jed are brought together by chance when they are caught up in a ballooning accident, the superb scene with which the novel begins. McEwan is a master of accidents and the procedures of mayhem, the stretching of time that occurs as brain and body are doused in shock (the car crash in *The Child in Time* or the killing of a man and his dismemberment—partly for love—in *The Innocent*). He specializes in graphic stillness, in a charged attention to the immediate detail which prefigures a larger emotional or psychological truth. In *The Cement Garden* there is a moment when the brother and sister "looked at each other knowingly, knowing nothing", and this is emblematic of the disturbing ambivalences of McEwan's style, of its ability to be both scrupulously neutral and pulsing with psychological energy. In *Enduring Love,* the balloon accident causes a man's death, and when Joe visits the man's widow, an academic living in North Oxford, she is created for the reader by a description of her home:

> No colours but brown and cream. No design or style, no comfort, and in winter, very little warmth. Even the light was brownish, at one with the smells of damp, coal dust and soap. . . . There was lino, and grimy electrical piping on the walls, and from the kitchen, the sour scent of gas, and a glimpse of laminated shelves on metal brackets supporting bottles of brown and red sauce. This was the austerity once thought appropriate to the intellectual life, unsensually aligned to the soul of English pragmatism, unfussy, honed to the essential, to the collegiate world beyond the shops. In its time it might have appeared to strike a blow at the Edwardian encumbrances of a older generation. Now it seemed a perfect setting for sorrow.

Is it significant that one of the best passages in the book should be devoted to a secondary character?

*Enduring Love* is narrated by Joe, who describes himself as "a large, clumsy, balding fellow". Extending this clumsiness to some of the novel's methods may be a gain in verisimilitude (name three great novels by science journalists), but the book suffers too much as a result. Joe is determined to understand things—the accident, his relationship with Clarissa, Jed's obsession with him—and, as a result, the narrative is constantly diverted by his need to analyse. The opening sentence is one of a number that proclaims a self-aware narrative, a story as experiment, one where the telling will distance us from what is told: "The beginning is simple to mark." More disabling, though, than this verbal tic ("I see us from three hundred feet up . . . I'm holding back the information . . . let me freeze the frame. . . .") is the way Jed and Clarissa are not really granted their own inner lives. Rather awkwardly, Chapter Nine is told from Clarissa's point of view, because, as Joe tells us, "It would make more sense."

Soon, however, he is back to seeing her from outside and at risk of reducing her to little more than a mood and an eye-colour: "She drew her breath sharply and shot me a beam of angry green."

Jed's obsession with Joe is intensified by religious mania. The instructions on his answering machine give some measure of the man: "Please leave your message after the tone. And may the Lord be with you." There is a fractured comedy in his first approaches to Joe and in Joe's baffled response, the funnier for the absence of any cues to suggest that the scene is meant to be funny. (Conversely, when Joe buys a gun from some hippies, McEwan's busy signalling of the scene's hilarity—one hippy has a comic moustache which gives Joe the giggles—is rather desperate.) We learn most about Jed from his letters to Joe. However, the epistolary mode is rarely as engaging as dialogue or soliloquy, and Jed can seem as much a function of the novel's thriller-like conventions (the Threat) as a fully realized character. McEwan may have set out to invoke certain genres by having two chapters end with threatening phone calls or by naming a virtuous character Bonny Deedes, but *Enduring Love* lacks the singleness of narrative vision required by these sorts of model. The divagations into scientific theory and the mysteries of love, although they have an intellectual reach fitting for the literary novel, occur too obtrusively for theme and story to have a complementary wholeness (as in *The Child in Time*). Ian McEwan's career is testament to his readiness to extend his immense gifts by dealing with an ever-larger range of subjects. *Enduring Love* opens with an over-buoyant balloon carried off by the wind; the novel's problems are of an opposite kind: too much ballast.

## Brian D. Johnson (review date 17 November 1997)

SOURCE: Johnson, Brian D. "Of Human Bonding." *Maclean's* (17 November 1997): 106, 108.

[*In the following review, Johnson extols the descriptive opening portions of* Enduring Love, *praising McEwan's ability to delineate events with precision.*]

As a storyteller, British author Ian McEwan is something of a pathologist. His narratives tend to circle around a single terrifying event, a moment of panic that casts a long and malignant shadow over a character's life. Using spare, ruthless prose, McEwan magnifies the event and dissects it with clinical precision, slowing motion and stopping time to let strange and inappropriate thoughts float to the surface.

In his Whitbread Award-winning novel, *The Child in Time* (1987), the event is the abduction of a writer's three-year-old daughter in a supermarket, a loss that leaves the man's marriage devastated and sends him reeling back through his own childhood. In the Booker-nominated *Black Dogs* (1992), it is the ordeal of a woman who is cornered by two vicious mastiffs in the French countryside while, out of earshot down the path, her husband examines some caterpillars. And in *Enduring Love,* McEwan's seventh novel, the event is a bizarre ballooning accident in which a man falls to his death while trying to rescue a child. The tragedy sets the stage for an obsessive relationship—and a rivetting showdown between faith and logic. *Enduring Love,* a novel as profound and playful as the double entendre of its title, is one of the most original, compelling works of McEwan's career.

The story begins with a meticulous reconstruction of the ballooning accident. The novel's first-person narrator, Joe Rose, is sitting down to a picnic in a field with his wife, Clarissa, a happy reunion after spending six weeks apart. Then, he hears a shout, and suddenly he is running across the field to a balloon the size of a house that is about to blow away with a child trapped in the basket. Pulling on ropes, he and several other bystanders frantically try to bring the balloon back to earth. During the rescue attempt, Joe encounters a man named Jed Parry, who becomes convinced that a cosmic bond has passed between them. Jed develops an obsessive love for Joe, a kind of religious passion. And in the weeks that follow, he stalks him incessantly, threatening to ruin his marriage and his life.

As Joe becomes increasingly aggravated, his wife, a scholar investigating the love life of poet John Keats, refuses to take his situation seriously. Clarissa cannot see the evidence of Jed's harassment firsthand, and assumes her husband is overreacting. Gradually, from a "fine crack of estrangement," a rift opens up in their marriage, which McEwan describes with startling lucidity: "We were lying face-to-face in bed, as though nothing was wrong," recounts Joe. "The silence appeared to have a visual quality, a sparkle or hard gloss, and a thickness too, like fresh paint. . . . We were hardly at war, but everything between us was stalled. We were like armies facing each other across a maze of trenches. We were immobilized. The only movement was that of silent accusations rippling over our heads like standards."

Joe is a scientist who fears he is losing his grip on the truth. Having abandoned serious research for a career as a magazine journalist popularizing science, he worries that he has become "parasitic and marginal." Now, tenaciously, he clings to scientific rationality in the face of his demented stalker. He conducts exhaustive research into erotomania, concluding that Jed suffers from a religious version of de Clérambault's syndrome. (The novel offers a bibliography of 20 psychiatric texts.) But Joe's attempt to shake off his stalker becomes an obsession in its own right. And his rationality becomes so precarious that the reader, like his wife, begins to wonder if his observations can be trusted.

In fact, for a first-person narrative, the novel has a peculiar omniscience—Joe's voice is laminated with layers of inquiry and innuendo. In one chapter, for the sake of balance, he narrates an episode from Clarissa's point of view. He offers up letters from Jed. And in the opening chapter, as he reconstructs the balloon accident in magnified detail, he views himself with uncanny detachment: "Like a self in a dream, I was both first and third persons. I acted, and saw myself act. I had my thoughts, and I saw them drift across a screen. As in a dream, my emotional responses were non-existent or inappropriate."

It is hard for the rest of the novel to live up to the drama of the balloon accident. Focusing on the "pinprick" instant when he first heard a man shouting across the field, Joe unfurls the event like a vast map of time, noting that "whole books, whole research departments, are dedicated to the first half minute in the history of the universe." It is a brilliant scene. As it gathers momentum, the suspense is unbearable. And although it falls right at the beginning of the story, it is in some sense the climax—the epicentre—and its shock waves radiate through the rest of the narrative.

Late in the novel, as the conflict reaches a violent resolution, Joe explains his numbed state: "The narrative compression of storytelling, especially in the movies, beguiles us with happy endings into forgetting that sustained stress is corrosive of feeling. It's the great deadener." McEwan, instead of compressing the event, just keeps expanding it. In the spirit of fearless postmortem, he turns it over in his mind, backwards and forwards, finding illumination for the soul in the darkest places.

**Richard Eder (review date 25 January 1998)**

SOURCE: Eder, Richard. "Twitching Curtains." *Los Angeles Times Book Review* (25 January 1998): 2.

[*In the following review, Eder finds major flaws in the uneven narrative energy and invented case study in* Enduring Love.]

It begins [in *Enduring Love*] with dazzling cinematic bravura. Joe and Clarissa, his live-in lover, are having a spring picnic in Britain's Chiltern Hills. About to uncork the wine, they hear a man shout.

"We turned to look across the field and saw the danger. Next thing I was running towards it," Joe relates. Then for an instant, like a bright lure seized by a bottom fish and dragged under, the dazzle yields to leaden hindsight. "What idiocy, to be racing into this story and its labyrinths, sprinting away from our happiness among the fresh spring grasses by the oak."

Narrator's hindsight and reader's foreboding: Ian McEwan weights them on before surfacing back into the immediacy of what is taking place. "There was the shout again, and a child's cry, enfeebled by the wind that roared in the tall trees along the hedgerows. I ran faster. And there, suddenly, from different points around the field, four other men were converging on the scene, running like me."

McEwan, author of *The Cement Garden* and *The Child in Time,* shapes this dramatic opening with breathtaking dexterity. Alternating between Joe's dazed, camera-like perceptions and his subsequent settled narration, we get the transformation of picnic idyll into disaster.

A balloon carrying a child and piloted by his uncle had landed in the field without incident. Getting out of the basket, the uncle tangled his legs in the lines, and a sudden gust began dragging the balloon, the child and the uncle to the edge of a promontory falling steeply to the Oxfordshire plain hundreds of feet below.

Joe and the four other men who spot the danger manage to grab the lines. They work at confused cross-purposes, though, and a violent updraft begins lifting them into the air. Had they all held on they might have maneuvered the balloon down, but one panics and lets go. Feeling themselves jolted upward and afraid of being carried off, Joe and two others release their hold, falling a dozen feet.

Only one, a doctor named Logan, holds on, counting on the others until it is too late. At 300 feet, his grip loosens, and he plummets to his death. (The balloon eventually drifts down, and the child in the basket is unharmed.)

McEwan, one of Britain's finest writers, renders it all with a characteristic skill: peacefulness changing in a flash to panicked horror and then to shock's slow, disabling tide. It is bound together by a grim moral reflection on how panicked animal reflexes instantly obliterate social cooperation. "Someone said 'me' and then there was nothing to be gained by saying 'us,'" Joe says.

It is a wild racehorse of a start. Immediately, though, McEwan hitches it to a dray cart. Joe's initial words about "sprinting away from our happiness" do not refer to the tragedy and its consequences for him and Clarissa—consequences on whose exploration we seemed to be launched in such fire and style. It refers to an entirely tangential development.

One of Joe's fellow would-be rescuers is a weird young man, Jed Parry. A solitary, possessed of a certain amount of money, he is convinced that he has a vaguely Christian religious mission. His deep, wasting mental disorder, though, is the conviction that Joe has fallen in love with him and that it is their destiny to be together.

Most of the rest of *Enduring Love* tells of Parry's obsessive pursuit and—as if the sick mind spreads contagion—of Joe's near undoing, both in himself and in his relationship with Clarissa. It is a creepy story and told with skill, but its mismatch with the beginning is disconcerting. This is true not just because it wanders narratively but because of its decidedly inferior level of fictional energy and expansiveness.

Parry phones repeatedly, stations himself in front of Joe's front door, pursues him down the street weeping. If he were simply proclaiming his love, it would be bad enough, the true horror lies in his insistence that Joe loves him, has incited him and simply feigns indifference in order to exercise power. Parry leaves as many as 33 messages in the course of a single day. He writes long letters to Joe, picturing their life together and urging that they sitdown with Clarissa to work out a fair arrangement.

Nothing could be worse, of course, than to be conscripted into the mind of a solipsist, particularly one with a deranged obsession. It is like being pursued by an enormous molasses jar, lid flapping hungrily. For Joe, who has his own insecurities—a sense of failure at throwing away a career in science to become a best-selling popularizer—the siege is disabling. Particularly it disables his relations with Clarissa, and McEwan writes a masterly scene in which their two sets of jitters go into a fibrilation that comes close to being lethal.

Parry's pursuit goes from entreaty to threat, and there is a series of melodramatic scenes of near-lethal violence before the police are persuaded to take action. At one point, Joe visits a household of former hippie drug dealers to buy a pistol; the scene has its piquancy, but it seems quite detached in style or effect from everything else.

McEwan is unable to be dull, and his detail is invariably sharp and well-managed. But *Enduring Love* is seriously flawed. The author has researched a psychological disorder known as De Clerambault's Syndrome, named after the author of a study of a French-woman who haunted the sidewalk in front of Buckingham Palace, convinced that King George V was sending her love signals. One signal, she claimed, was a periodic twitching of the upstairs curtains. Twitching curtains, in fact, are part of Parry's delusion.

The author, in effect, has written a fictionalized version of a case history, which he appends at the end in the form of a study printed in a psychiatric journal. The study is itself made up, although the reader may not realize it, as I did not until a perceptive editor checked up.

This is confusing, to say the least; furthermore, why invent a case history to bolster a story of manic obsession unless the author is unsure of making it convincing? Until the melodramatic ending, in fact, Parry's obsessive pursuit is credible, however grisly.

Confusion apart, to turn *Enduring Love* into a tale of a sick mind and the contagion it spreads is to narrow sharply the beginning's expansive promise of a fictional and moral exploration with an open road in front of it.

Instead, the reader is shunted indoors to something much less: a storified lecture, graphic and well-illustrated.

### Jonathan Taylor (review date March 1998)

SOURCE: Taylor, Jonathan. Review of *Enduring Love*, by Ian McEwan. *Artforum* 36, no. 7 (March 1998): S20.

[*In the following review, Taylor offers an unfavorable assessment of* Enduring Love, *asserting that McEwan's style and structure in the novel is overbearing and repetitive.*]

"The pathological extensions of love not only touch upon but overlap with normal experience," goes the neatly summarizing thesis of *Enduring Love* (quoted, apparently, from an actual *British Journal of Psychiatry* article), a statement that evokes the irritatingly schematic quality Ian McEwan's books sometimes have. It's fair to say that he intends, as the cover of *First Love, Last Rites* nicely synopsized, to "compel us to confront our secret kinship with the horrifying." Yet in execution this mission has often seemed overdetermined, making the rounds of the taboo: incest (***The Cement Garden***), sexual murder and sadism (**"Pornography,"** ***The Comfort of Strangers***).

*Enduring Love* replaces the specter of taboo sexual practice with a menace whose creepiness is not titillatingly transgressive. It's just crazy, or, more to the point, delusional; it even has an interesting medical literature. Less predisposed to the superficially risque, the novel taps a deeper undercurrent where love and insanity do flow together. Joe, the narrator, and his girlfriend, Clarissa, are, respectively, a science journalist and a Keats specialist. Love's pathological extension takes the form of Jed, a loner Jesus-freak who begins stalking Joe. The overlap, these characters' abundantly fertile common ground, is "how dishonestly," as Joe learns, "we can hold things together for ourselves."

A freak ballooning accident in the countryside brings Joe and Jed together in an effort to rescue a child, an attempt in which another man falls to his death. In the dazed aftermath, Jed locks onto Joe instantly, almost randomly, it seems. His particular insanity, Joe later finds, is known as de Clerambault's syndrome, which features a belief that the object of obsession has initiated a love affair and is cruelly toying with the subject by sending secret signals of encouragement while overtly denying the shared passion. Jed's fervor is especially disturbing because, in a '90s kind of way (Jed speaks with the young American habit of intoning statements as questions), it is so unconvincing either as religion or sexual attraction. His Christianity is vague; asked what he really wishes to do with Joe, he squeaks, "I want to see you?" In fact, his letters and phone calls, which turn rapidly from jubilant gratitude to mocking threats, bear no connection to any actual quality pertaining to Joe, who notes, "If I had written him a letter declaring passionate love, it would have made no difference."

Meanwhile, Clarissa, who has her own worries to deal with, believes that Joe is inventing the whole thing. Joe, stunned by this, diagnoses her "self-persuasion," a handy bit of evolutionary psychology from his files. And as if immediately catching it, he ransacks the letters in her study for an ulterior motive—"some hot little bearded fuck-goat of a post-graduate," perhaps—while acting out the lame pretext, even though he's alone in the house, of locating his stapler.

It's all downhill from there. McEwan's grasp of how strange people will always be to each other, in "love's prison of self-reference," seems to undermine the postulate that Joe and Clarissa's relationship had been, before Jed's intrusion, "without a trace of complication." The stalemate of two intimate but still alien mentalities becomes the meticulously observed drama, as facilitated by McEwan's talents in the narration of consciousness: a clinical ability to evoke "the usual flotsam" of thought, to supply the banal details of contemporary living in just the way one's eye ridiculously falls on them in moments of crisis.

"Our love," Joe and Jed both repeat throughout, like a mantra, for their divergent, desperate purposes. This meaningless repetition gradually corrodes the tender noun; by the end, it seems little more than a proxy for wishful thinking. And it is Jed, safely ensconced forever in his prison of self-reference, who uses the word last: "Thank you for loving me, thank you for accepting me, thank you for recognizing what I am doing for our love."

## Rosemary Dinnage (review date 9 April 1998)

SOURCE: Dinnage, Rosemary. "So Alert with Love." *New York Review of Books* 45, no. 6 (9 April 1998): 32-3.

[*In the following review, Dinnage argues that* Enduring Love *is an efficient, gripping examination of such themes as "guilt and love and fear."*]

After six previous novels and two books of short stories, Ian McEwan's reputation as a writer of small, impeccably written fictions is secure. His gift for the cold and scary is well established, too: among the critical praise that festoons his book jackets, the word "macabre" crops up more than once. But his books are more than tales of suspense and shock: they raise issues of guilt and love and fear, essentially of what happens when the civilized and ordered splinters against chaos. There can be something of Greek myth in his narratives—man casually overthrown by the indifferent Fates. At the same time he is the quietest and most lucid of stylists, with never a word wasted or fumbled. It is a pity his surname is resistant to adjective (as in "Kafkan"): it would have a quite recognizable meaning by now.

*Enduring Love* is as satisfying in the menace and tension departments as any of the previous books, and less unforgiving than, some—his best, perhaps, since *The Child in Time*. The plot is simplicity itself: a loving and well-matched couple, Joe and Clarissa, are split apart by a deranged stalker who believes that instant mutual love has struck himself and Joe. One kind of enduring love meets another and (to Jed, the stalker, just as real), and the result is disaster. So what is love, anyway: what real, what illusory, what benign, what destructive?

The opening of the story is a Verdi overture: sweet tunes are played, ominous notes struck, and the curtain rises on a baritone voice. Clarissa and Joe are having a celebratory picnic after a six-week separation during which Clarissa has been researching letters of Keats to Fanny Brawne (obsessive love!). The baritone voice comes from the pilot of a helium balloon heading for a smash in the field below.

McEwan excels in presenting the single moment frozen in time. Clarissa has handed Joe the wine bottle, his palm has just touched the neck, and the frightened shout comes from across the grass.

> We were running toward a catastrophe, which itself was a kind of furnace in whose heat identities and fates would buckle into new shapes. At the base of the balloon was a basket in which there was a boy, and by the basket, clinging to a rope, was a man in need of help.

There is a horrible accident: a man dies gruesomely. It is not certain whether it could have been prevented, whether someone let it happen (did Joe?). Everyone who saw the event is affected; together, and with friends, Joe and Clarissa talk it out and try to exorcise it. At the moment of the accident, in a marvelously described state of manic shock, Joe has thrown a wildly cheerful glance at one of the other bystanders. And so it begins.

Jed Parry is youngish, ponytailed, in denims and red-laced trainers. No sooner has the glance found him than he is coming up to Joe, falling to his knees, and asking Joe to pray with him. "You shouldn't, you know, think of this as some kind of duty. It's like, your own needs are being answered? It's got nothing to do with me, really. I'm just the messenger. It's a gift." With distaste Joe disentangles himself, goes home with Clarissa for mutual comfort, forgets Jed. After midnight, the phone rings with a message of love from him. It will go on ringing: a relentless pursuit has begun.

McEwan's cunning as a narrator is in the hint of a suggestion as the story develops, that Jed may not be as mad as he seems. The two names, Jed and Joe, even suggest alter egos. Joe is, after all, disgusted with his job as popular science writer, recycling current materialisms into whatever shape pleases the public. ("Might there be a genetic basis to religious belief, or was it merely refreshing to think so? . . . What if it bestowed strength in adversity, the power of consolation, the chance of surviving the disaster that might crush a godless man?") Perhaps for him prayer *could* be a gift; the reader is tantalized. And McEwan has Jed write rather beautiful love letters:

> I'm sitting at a small wooden table on a covered balcony that extends from the study and looks out over the inner courtyard. The rain is falling on two flowering cherry trees. The branch of one grows through the railings, so that I am close enough to see how the water, forms into oval beads tinged by the flowers pale pink. Love has given me new eyes, I see with such clarity, in such detail. The grain of the old wooden posts, every separate blade of grass on the wet lawn below, the little tickly black legs of the lady bird walking across my hand a minute ago. Everything I see I want to touch and stroke. At last I'm awake. I feel so alive, so alert with love.

If the letters were mad and silly, we would have just a run-of-the-mill suspense story.

Ambiguity is carried further when it becomes clear that nice Clarissa really hardly believes Joe's story of persecution, or at least finds it hard to sympathize. The handwriting on the love letters is not unlike his own! For the first time, a rift is growing in their own well-established love, so good and true up until now. (McEwan has the rather rare gift of convincingly describing homely felicity.) She shows signs of catching the paranoia virus from the stalker. The police offer little help. Under Jed's relentless gaze, Joe is more and more alone. "It was as if I had fallen through a crack in my own existence, down into another life, another set of sexual preferences, another past history and future." From one minute to the next, evil transformation spreads and strengthens.

Meanwhile the hunter is inside his own bubble of aloneness:

> He crouched in a cell of his own devising, teasing out meanings, imbuing nonexistent exchanges with their drama of hope or disappointment, always scrutinizing the physical world, its random placements and chaotic noise and colors, for the correlatives of his current emotional state—and always finding satisfaction. He illuminated the world with his feelings, and the world confirmed him at every turn his feelings took.

To his prey, the hunt seems to be getting closer. At one moment Jed's bubble—religion? fantasy? love, even?—is clearly pathological: at another, his critique of Joe's godless writings seems to be hitting home: "Never deny my reality, because in the end you'll deny yourself," he writes to him.

Then while Clarissa and Joe, out to lunch with friends are in the middle of a discussion of imagination and destructiveness (Wordsworth snubbing the young Keats), physical attack comes very close. Joe becomes terrified, acquires an illicit gun, and in no time at all is using it to save Clarissa from a dangerous Jed. Jed's "love," and his despair, have exploded into violence at last.

Tension is so important a part of McEwan's method that it would be criminal of the reviewer to give away every last turn in the narrative. Does Clarissa repent her unjust doubts of Joe, thank him for his swift action, fall into his arms? Has *their* enduring love, in sum, been destroyed by Jed's? Reader, you must find out for yourself. To do this, the so-called "Appendix I" at the end of the book must not on any account be skipped. This purports to be—perhaps is—a paper from *The British Review of Psychiatry* entitled "A homoerotic obsession, with religious overtones: a clinical variant of de Clerambault's syndrome." In 1942, it reports, de Clerambault first distinguished his syndrome from other *psychoses passionelles*. The patient, usually a woman,

> has the intense delusional belief that a man, "the object," often of higher social standing, is in love with her. The patient may have had little or no contact with the object of her delusion. The fact that the object is already married is likely to be regarded by the patient as irrelevant. His protestations of indifference or even hatred are seen as paradoxical or contradictory; her conviction that he "really" loves her remains fixed. Other derived themes include beliefs that the object will never find true happiness without her, and also that the relationship is universally acknowledged and approved.

By creating a full intrapsychic world, such erotomania may act as a defense against loneliness, the authorities suggest. The case of the middle-aged Frenchwoman who was unshakably convinced that King George V was in love with her is quoted; and then—of course—that of the religiously obsessed young man who happened to be at the scene of an accident involving a helium balloon . . . For this young man, appropriate medication and psychotherapy were prescribed, but in vain; and in view of his occasional violence, indefinite incarceration in a secure unit was the only solution.

This is the last of repeated confrontations between scientific and imaginative explanations throughout the book. The composition of water, the search for DNA, future space colonization are topics that legitimately weave in and out of the narrative through Joe's work as a scientific journalist. The very helium in the unleashed balloon is "that elemental gas forged from hydrogen in the nuclear furnace of the stars, first step along the way in the generation of multiplicity and variety of matter in the universe, including our selves and all our thoughts."

Opponents of this view of a ruthlessly materialist universe have been, in their different ways, both Jed and Clarissa. Why reduce a baby's smile to neo-Darwinism or evolutionary psychology? she queried. "It's the new fundamentalism. . . . Twenty years ago you and your friends were all socialists and you blamed the environment for everyone's hard luck. Now you've got us trapped in our genes, and there's a reason for everything!" Jed's approach has come from another angle. "Life has been very good to you. . . . It probably never crosses your mind to give thanks for what you have. It all happened by blind chance? You made it all yourself? I worry for you, Joe. I worry for what your arrogance could bring down on you."

Letters from Jed do not stop. "Appendix II" is from the case file of J. Parry at the end of his third year after admittance.

> . . . It was a cloudless day and what rose up above the treetops ten minutes later was nothing less than the resplendence of God's glory and love. Our love! First bathing me, then warming me through the pane. I stood there, shoulders back, my arms hanging loosely at my sides, taking deep breaths. The old tears streaming. But the joy! The thousandth day, my thousandth letter, and you telling me that what I'm doing is right!

The patient writes daily, the case notes record. His letters are collected by staff but not forwarded, in order to protect the addressee from further distress.

**Valerie Sayers (review date 8 May 1998)**

SOURCE: Sayers, Valerie. "Up, Up and Away." *Commonweal* 125, no. 9 (8 May 1998): 24-6.

[*In the following review, Sayers offers a positive assessment of* Enduring Love, *but notes that the novel's philosophical ideas and thematic tensions ultimately give way to the demands of narrative movement.*]

Ian McEwan's elegant, unsettling novels seek out the dangers that lurk, waiting to disrupt everyday lives: child snatchers, accidents, vicious animals, stalkers. These threatening motifs are connected, often implicitly, to questions of political and philosophical belief. In *Enduring Love* this connection is explicit: from the opening scene onward, it is clear that McEwan means to balance his usual Gothic elements with complex explorations of the ideas they represent. The novel opens in a field in the Chilterns, where five men see a balloon descend and race to help the inept pilot anchor it. Inside the passenger basket crouches a terrified young boy who may be swept away at any moment. The men grab ropes and are themselves carried off, dangling from the balloon, by a violent gust. In the agonizing seconds that follow, they must decide whether to hold on together or to save themselves by dropping, singly, to the ground. The narrator and protagonist of the novel, Joe Rose, explores the accident's connection to notions of selfless love, community, and self-preservation. The balance between dramatic scene and philosophical narrative, between exterior reality and interior struggle, is beautifully achieved; this is as stunning and promising a novel opening as I have read.

Joe is one of the men who chooses to drop to the ground, and so must face his own ordinary cowardice, but that is only the beginning of his dilemma. As the plot progresses, it appears that so, too, will the tensions between the rational and the irrational. Joe is a science writer who has abandoned the academic world for the life of the free-lance popularizer. His belief in the rational is absolute. His wife Clarissa, a Keats scholar, is more interested in the intuitive and the emotional. ("You're so rational sometimes," she tells him, "you're like a child.") This standard assigning of sex roles might be irritating were it not for the casting of Keats's long romantic shadow in the novel—and were it not for a third principal character, Jed Parry, who disrupts all notions of assigned sex roles. Parry is another of the men who drops to the ground with Joe Rose in the failed rescue attempt. At the scene of the accident, he falls instantly and pathologically in love with Joe and begins to disrupt his life: phoning, writing, stalking, and finally attacking him.

Part of Jed Parry's disturbance is religious belief, and one of the novel's early promises is the possibility that Joe's rationalism will be seriously challenged by religious faith. But Jed's religion, as Joe points out, is "dreamily vague on the specifics of doctrine. . . . a self-made affair, generally aligned to the culture of personal growth and fulfillment." It is also the belief of a madman, and as such Parry's challenges are hardly taken seriously, either by Joe or by the novel. Parry's affliction is identified as de Clerambault's syndrome, in which the sufferers believe that the objects of their desire return the love and send secret signals of reciprocation. Parry's religious belief, as hopelessly deluded as his erotic fixation, is a variant of the syndrome.

It's an interesting notion, this coupling of erotic and religious delusion, but because the religious aspect is expressed only in Jed Parry's melodramatic pronouncements, it can't be explored physically (or for that matter philosophically) in the same way that the idea of human love can be. One of the principal tensions of the novel, then, is eased out early, and it becomes clear that rationalism will not be tested by religious faith but by faith in human love, the possibility of "enduring love" that Joe Rose believes he and Clarissa can achieve.

Clarissa, though, is seriously disturbed by Joe's response to Parry. At first she believes Parry's only a pathetic character; later she wonders whether Joe is in fact inventing his obsessive presence. The novel moves from another interesting tension (why can't the sensitive, intelligent Clarissa understand that Joe's terror is in fact a completely rational response?) to a more predictable movement of plot (will she believe him in time to save them from Parry's violence?). Clarissa's role in the novel, though key, is not explored in nearly as much depth as Joe's or Parry's. She is sketched, believably, as Keats scholar and as a maternal figure who cannot bear children (the motif of children—especially as objects of selfless love—is one of the most successful), but her lack of faith in Joe is not entirely convincing. It seems more plot-driven than it does character-driven: it is necessary for the story to progress, therefore it exists.

The same complaint might be made of the last scenes of the novel, thrilling, amusing, and unsettling though they are. Joe buys a gun in a funny and depressing scene that seems to come out of another (naturalistic) novel, then sets out to rescue Clarissa. The story has begun, of course, with a bungled rescue, and one of the novel's concerns is the strange movement of narrative itself: narrative in science, narratives of grief, narratives of the imagination. It is fitting, then, that narrative might loop back on itself this way, but the story floats away as quickly as the balloon which set Joe Rose's ordeal in motion, and the current carrying it is plot. The ideas trying to anchor that plot drop one by one to the ground. Some of its most disturbing suggestions (this is not the first time McEwan has used homosexual desire as his central threat) are never fully explored. The story ends with the notion of forgiveness, but it's a partial resolution, for poor Jed Parry is locked away with his delusions, and neither narrator nor narrative is concerned with what forgiveness or peace might be offered him.

This is not to say that *Enduring Love* is not engaging throughout—it is more than engaging, it is clever and compelling—but rather that it is considerably lightened at the end of its journey, that its balance tips, finally, toward the pleasures of unburdened plot.

**Phil Baker (review date 4 September 1998)**

SOURCE: Baker, Phil. "Comfy Conspiracies." *Times Literary Supplement*, no. 4979 (4 September 1998): 9.

[*In the following review, Baker judges* Amsterdam *to be an entertaining examination of such favorite McEwan themes as "grotesque private behaviour, the violation of privacy, and a couple threatened by circumstances."*]

Hailing a cab outside the Dorchester one day, the gorgeous restaurant critic and photographer, Molly Lane, feels a tingling in her arm. It is the beginning of events that neither she nor anyone else could have foreseen. First comes the appallingly rapid progress of a disease that reduces her to an abject state before it kills her. And then comes a far more extraordinary chain of events following her death, which forms the substance of Ian McEwan's implausibly elegant black comedy [*Amsterdam*].

Four of Molly's lovers are present at her funeral. There is the rich old publisher, George, her final partner. There is the Foreign Secretary, Julian Garmony, who is a likely future Prime Minister. And there are two old friends, Vernon Halliday, the broadsheet newspaper editor, and the famous modern composer, Clive Linley, who is working on a "Millennial Symphony" to crown his career. Something of a hypochondriac, Clive is so shocked by the speed with which Molly's condition shelved into a state where she was incapable even of killing herself, that he asks a favour of Vernon: if anything similar should happen to him, he would like Vernon to arrange euthanasia. (There are, they both know, people in Holland who will take care of these things.) Vernon agrees, if Clive will do the same for him.

George, meanwhile, is now in possession of some extraordinary photographs of Julian, and shows them to Vernon. Initially undescribed, they are "Incredible", and Vernon feels "waves of distinct responses: astonishment first, followed by a wild inward hilarity". At first, McEwan lets the reader imagine them (like the unknown contents of the mysteriously shocking box in Buñuel's *Belle de Jour*), although later in the book they are revealed. Since Garmony is rather right-wing, Vernon feels entirely justified in publishing them, and the newspaper brushes up Garmony's obituary in case he should kill himself.

It is the beginning of the end for the friendship between Clive and Vernon. Clive is so disgusted that he sends Vernon a card telling him he deserves to be sacked. Arriving after Vernon actually has been sacked, it now reads as gloating instead of outraged: "You deserve to be *sacked*" has become "You *deserve* to be sacked"—a neat slippage that typifies the clockwork neatness of the book. Their annoyance with each other escalates, until Clive invites Vernon to Amsterdam with a murderous plan in mind. Of course, plans often go wrong. Clive has a glass of champagne in each hand: "Vernon's in the right, his own in the left. Important to remember that." Should we be alerted to an impending disaster, or is it a red herring? Perhaps the salient line is instead: "he saw Vernon coming towards him with a big smile . . . he had two full glasses of his own."

Clive, although preferable to Vernon, is the book's chief comic butt. Egregiously middle-class, he is solidly sent up by McEwan whenever we are made party to his sentimental, self-deluded, preeningly fatuous thoughts. He finds the police to be splendid fellows: "To think he had once called them pigs and argued, during a three month flirtation with anarchism in 1967, that they were the cause of crime. . . . They seemed to like him, these policemen, and Clive wondered if there were not certain qualities he never knew he possessed—a level manner, quiet charm, authority perhaps." He also finds the Dutch to be truly civilized, although not everybody comes in for his approval; people who don't share his love of the Lake District, for example: "Surely they could not claim to be fully alive."

It is while Clive is up creating music among the Lakes that he sees a woman hiker having trouble with a man. Unknown to Clive, the man happens to be the notorious Lakeland Rapist, but he doesn't get involved because he doesn't want it to interfere with his musical inspiration: "this was his business, and it wasn't easy, and he wasn't asking for anyone's help." Later, he looks back on the responsibilities which his gift has imposed on him, and realizes he was entirely justified in being prepared "to sacrifice an anonymous rambler" for his music.

McEwan has plenty of fun at the expense of Clive's romantic belief in his genius, and he treats the reader to a good deal of material about musical composition. This mockery of artistic ambition complements the relatively slight nature of the book, which is unashamedly a five-finger exercise in comparison to the aspirations of some of McEwan's earlier work, such as **The Child in Time**. There is something rather comfortable about it, which extends to the satire. "It's time we ran more regular columns", says a newspaper editor:

> they're cheap, and everyone else is doing them. You know, we hire someone of low to medium intelligence, possibly female, to write about, well, nothing much. . . . Goes to a party and can't remember someone's name. Twelve hundred words.

McEwan's earlier interests are still here: grotesque private behaviour, the violation of privacy, and a couple threatened by circumstances (Garmony's survival is largely due to his formidable trouper of a Tory wife). The interest in privacy extends to the deceit shown by almost every character in the book, where rottenness is universal; even a music critic with a walk-on part turns out to be a paedophile, and the saintly Mrs Garmony describes Molly as "a friend of the family" who took the photos "rather in a spirit of celebration", while being privately glad that the woman who indulged Julian's "grotesque cravings" is dead. The one character whose mind we are hardly shown inside is the supremely manipulative George. If there is sometimes a sense that Vernon and Clive are being indicted as representatives of a caste or generation, George remains his own evil agent.

*Amsterdam* is a consummately well-orchestrated performance, and the feel of a major artist operating at something less than full blast gives it a smoothness and a sense of capacity in reserve. If, like Graham Greene, McEwan divided his books into "novels" and "entertainments", then there is no doubt into which category this one would fall.

### Stuart Burrows (review date 11 September 1998)

SOURCE: Burrows, Stuart. "Lost Promise." *New Statesman* 127, no. 4402 (11 September 1998): 47-8.

[*In the following review, Burrows provides an unfavorable assessment of* Amsterdam, *deriding McEwan's tendency toward melodrama and forced symbolism in his novels.*]

Ian McEwan lays claim to a world of terrifying violence and desire uncharted by the polite talking shop of the postwar British novel. "Angus Wilson, Iris Murdoch, Kingsley Amis . . . they all seemed to come from a world and a social milieu that I had nothing to do with," he has said. "I guess the stories I was writing were a lunge at another territory."

McEwan's new work, *Amsterdam,* unfortunately signals yet another retreat from this new aesthetic territory, offering in its place the world of gossip columnists, newspaper editors and cabinet ministers tediously familiar to readers of contemporary British fiction. Bestseller lists notwithstanding, his most interesting work now seems far behind him.

For at least a decade, McEwan has preferred the easy consolations of narrative suspense to the hard work of aesthetic experimentation. His early stories posed the moral dilemmas at the heart of all his fiction at the level of form rather than content, exploring language's complicity in the appalling crimes of his stunted protagonists through a fidelity to the interior monologue reminiscent of Beckett. But his most recent work, such as the widely praised *Enduring Love,* substitutes narrative pace for the moral complexities raised by its dazzling opening chapter. Ethical dilemmas, specifically the question of the relationship between art and morality, are also at the heart of *Amsterdam,* but any interest they might hold is brutally swept away by McEwan's weakness for melodrama.

Other McEwan failings surface repeatedly in his new work: events are recorded in the manner of a historical textbook; crude biographical summaries pass themselves off as characterisation. And *Amsterdam* offers several new stylistic lapses, including a cumbersome narrative intervention in the manner of *Vanity Fair.* McEwan is left with only his fine eye for detail and the familiar staccato style that holds the attention but fails to move. *Amsterdam* is certainly readable, but readability may be precisely McEwan's great failing.

His recent work, like that of Martin Amis, forsakes literature for the adolescent pleasures of the thriller or detective novel. Language is the victim. The thrills of the murder plot in *Amsterdam,* or the descent into madness of Jed Parry, the gay stalker in *Enduring Love,* disappoint when set against the exploitation of language in McEwan's first work, the short story collection *First Love, Last Rites* (1975). What is so remarkable about the unnamed narrator of the opening story, **"Homemade,"** is less his sexual desire for his sister than his relationship to language itself: "[I] listened to who and how the dustmen fucked, how the Co-op milkmen fitted it in, what the coalmen could hump, what the carpet-fitter could lay, what the builders could erect, what the meter man could inspect, what the bread man could deliver, the gas man sniff out, the plumber plumb, the electrician connect, the doctor inject, the lawyer solicit, the furniture man install."

Here seemingly innocuous verbs are transformed into synonyms for the narrator's incestuous longings. Innocence—its loss and the possibility of regaining it—has long been McEwan's subject. His early stories feature a series of first-person narrators whom we choose to label innocents, animals, adolescents, the mad, the old. To be innocent, in his world, is to lack self-consciousness, yet we see these bewildered characters struggling towards consciousness even as they deliberately choose the term innocent for themselves. The narrator of **"Homemade,"** for example, rejoices "in innocent bliss worthy of the Prelude" as he roasts a budgerigar over an open flame; the phrase is disturbing not so much for its grotesquely amusing distance from the act of burning alive a pet, as for the knowing reference to Wordsworth.

The idea of spoiled innocence resurfaces in *Black Dogs,* where the narrator, Jeremy, declares that "it is photography itself that creates the illusion of innocence". Yet the idea is left unexplored, lost amid the novel's clumsy symbolism and deadening dichotomies.

The success of *First Love, Last Rites* led to McEwan retaining the short simple sentences and adolescent first-person narrator in his first novel, *The Cement Garden* (1978). But the experiment was not a success; the book has the feel of a project undertaken for a creative writing seminar, as language succumbs to melodrama, whose festering body lies beneath the surface of all McEwan's work.

The decline was immediately arrested with the publication that same year of a second (and sadly final) collection of stories, *In Between the Sheets.* **"Reflections of a Kept Ape"** is particularly fine, recording the anguished confessions of the eponymous hero, the former lover but now merely pet of a famous writer, Sally Klee. Like Sterne's Uncle Toby, the ape whistles "Lilliburlero" at times of stress; and with his owner suffering a severe case of writer's block, opportunities for whistling are very much on the increase. McEwan incorporates passages from Sally Klee's one successful novel into the ape's narrative, a novel she is busy retyping as a substitute for her inability to write something new.

The story never completely escapes misogyny—a woman becoming a writer seems as likely here as a pet becoming a lover—but the suggestion that all novels merely ape former ones, in this case *Tristram Shandy,* is compelling.

The lesson, however, seems to have been lost on McEwan himself, whose next three novels were all attempts to escape the interiority of his earlier work. Only one, *The Child in Time* (1987), can be deemed a success. *The Comfort of Strangers,* short-listed for the 1981 Booker Prize, and *The Innocent* (1989) quickly succumb to the demands of plot, offering sensational murders and lumbering symbolism in place of character development and metaphorical elaboration. *The Child in Time* succeeds despite a melodrama of its own—a rather foolish political entanglement—because McEwan offers the reader his one completely successful character study, a missing child called Kate. She is snatched from a supermarket at the beginning of the novel. The episode, a model for the balloon sequence in *Enduring Love,* is beautifully controlled, allowing McEwan to display the same techniques that made his short stories so successful; he may indeed ultimately be a short story writer rather than a novelist, in that his understanding of the circular structure of consciousness can, in the shorter form, compensate for an absence of metaphor.

We believe in Kate as we do not believe in Clive Linley and Vernon Halliday, the dual protagonists of *Amsterdam—because she is a creation of her father Stephen's memory, both outside time and time's victim. Stephen struggles to hold on to an innocence that is necessarily absent: what he fears yet knows he is powerless to prevent is his daughter's fall into another narrative altogether, that of a life completely separate from her real parents. Writing, even though it is described at one point as "nothing less than a banishment from the Garden", is the one thing we depend on to offer us faith in the existence of Eden. The novel survives even McEwan's need to burden his work with long and wearying scientific explanations, integrating its moral paradoxes within the narrative through the simple device of making Stephen a writer of children's books, the most famous of which, *Lemonade*, teaches its 10-year-old readers that "they are finite as children".

All this is a long way from *Amsterdam*, which is itself mercifully finite at 178 pages. The characters are all too present here; one, the foreign secretary, appears to be a dead ringer for Michael Portillo. And McEwan's interest in innocence is now purely a legal or moral matter, not a function of language. *Amsterdam* offers us a world without metaphor, necessitating the triumph of melodrama. Sally Klee's ape would be disappointed.

### Anita Brookner (review date 12 September 1998)

SOURCE: Brookner, Anita. "All Good Pals and Jolly Bad Company." *Spectator* 281, no. 8875 (12 September 1998): 39.

[*In the following review, Brookner criticizes* Amsterdam, *faulting the plot for being underdeveloped, lacking female characters, and weak characterizations.*]

When three old friends—well, two friends and one intimate enemy—meet at a former lover's funeral and offer their glum condolences [in the novel *Amsterdam*] to the deceased's uninteresting husband, George, they set in train a revenge tragedy which is ludic, heartless, and oddly lightweight. The friends are Clive Linley, a composer who is working on a symphony for the Millennium, Vernon Halliday, editor of a newspaper entitled *The Judge,* and Julian Garmony, a politician expected to challenge the Prime Minister for the leadership. All are shaken by Molly's last illness, which began, sinisterly, with a tingling in the left arm before developing rapidly into full-blown helplessness.

In the days following the funeral both Clive and Vernon experience distressing, but possibly illusory, symptoms: a numbness in the arm in one case, on the right side of the head in the other. Braced by his all-purpose composure, Garmony seems most likely to ride out the storm. All are united by their indifference towards the widower, with his 'pleading' eyes. He happens to have an interest in Halliday's newspaper, but this does not seem important enough to win him any sort of respect. The friends disperse thankfully, each to his own concerns. Clive and Vernon trust each other well enough to beg a service of the other: rather than descend into Molly's condition they will see to it that a better end is ensured when the ultimate moment is perceived. Garmony has no such qualms. He is, he thinks, invulnerable.

The end, or what is to be the end in this oddly twilit narrative, can probably be intuited here, and is indeed indicated by the title. In Holland respectable doctors can be persuaded to administer the fatal dose. In Amsterdam Clive's symphony is due for rehearsal. So far, so equable. Then matters deteriorate with increasing momentum. The action is punctuated by intemperate phone calls, and the one moment of tension in the book comes as Clive, within reach of his final variation and coda, is interrupted by calls from Vernon who is on to a story. Did Clive, on a walking tour in the Lake District, hear the voice of a woman in distress and fail to come to her assistance? Is this suspicious? (It may be.) But of greater significance are the repeated telephone calls. For the elusive theme continues to be just within reach, and there are only a few days to the rehearsal. A change of heart weakens Clive's resolve, or perhaps it is a genuine aberration: the symphony is doomed to remain unfinished, and with it Clive's crowning achievement. His revenge is to break with his friend, by means of an unforgivable postcard accusing him of moral turpitude as a journalist. Some photographs have been found, and of course they are compromising. Molly is the photographer; George has them in his possession. Vernon will publish them and Clive will never speak to him again.

But all is not well with Clive. He may be slipping into madness. Certainly his light-hearted way with policemen and orchestral conductors does not inspire confidence. His downfall is well within the reader's sights, as is Vernon's dismissal from his post. What brings the two former friends to Amsterdam is anybody's guess. We know about the rehearsal: that accounts for Clive's presence. But Vernon's? This denouement seemed to me singularly weak. But then the whole text is surprising from a writer like McEwan, drab where it should have been authentically nasty. *Amsterdam* reads as if it were something to be got out of the way before another important novel in the making. It is about blackmail, into which former allies can enter with surprising self-justification. But blackmail here is not based on bad faith and envy, as it usually is, but on a sudden whim, on the crudest of assessments.

For readers in search of a happy ending, and mindful of George's pleading eyes, there is a resolution of sorts. But—perhaps because of the book's odd length—much material is wasted. Characters are not properly defined, there are few landscapes apart from that of the Lake District, which is meticulously itemised; more important (though this fact should not be important), there are few women. *Amsterdam* reads like a barely outlined plot summary, the sort that can be elaborated in a single session. Only that inconvenient telephone bell conveys an authentic note of horror, as a grand conception is jeopardised by the insistent ringing. These competing sounds might have created something more compelling than that part of the narrative which races towards its conclusion. McEwan is a master of even-paced nightmare. *Amsterdam* is little more than a brief bad dream.

### Peter Bien (review date autumn 1998)

SOURCE: Bien, Peter. Review of *Enduring Love,* by Ian McEwan. *World Literature Today* 72, no. 4 (autumn 1998): 830-31.

[*In the following review of* Enduring Love, *Bien commends McEwan's literary skill, but finds the novel weakened by its dependence on plot for its impetus.*]

One does not appreciate how cynical Ian McEwan's novel *Enduring Love* is before reaching "Appendix I," purportedly a scientific paper on de Clerambault's syndrome (a homoerotic obsession with religious overtones), where one reads, "A review of the literature . . . suggests that this is indeed a most lasting form of love, often terminated only by the death of the patient." Only then does the "enduring love" of the title leap out as, alas, that of the madman Jed Parry, whose protestations of attachment to the hapless Joe Rose never waver, whereas all the "normal" people in the novel suffer ups and downs, suspicions, and anguish in their relationships. A secondary theme, equally cynical, is the impossibility of objective knowledge. Joe Rose is a journalist who researches everything carefully and who prides himself on "scientific" accuracy, yet he—like everyone else except the monomaniac who acts out de Clerambault's syndrome—misunderstands most of what is happening.

These themes need to be emphasized, since, on the surface, the novel seems mostly a whodunit that captures our attention by making us yearn to know who is going to kill whom, and why. More deeply, however, McEwan examines so-called normalcy versus abnormalcy, so-called rationality versus lunacy. Everything is set in motion by a freak accident that brings Parry and Rose together; everything begins to be "resolved," strangely, by an attempt to murder the wrong victim. Yet until Parry's obsession leads to violence, his insane form of "enduring love" is considered inoffensive not only by the police but also by its victim's partner, a woman ironically fascinated by the "abnormal behavior" of Keats and Wordsworth! Clearly, the categories by which we think we understand human phenomena are arbitrary and ineffective.

*Enduring Love* is Ian McEwan's seventh novel. Both *The Comfort of Strangers* and *Black Dogs* were short-listed for the Booker Prize, whereas *The Child in Time* won the Whitbread Novel of the Year Award. It is hardly surprising that skill at narration, description, dialogue, characterization, and especially suspense is evident throughout *Enduring Love,* making it hard to put down. But is this a novel that one will want to reread? Probably not, since too much hinges on the plot. Once the story's outcome is known, not enough remains to be compelling in its own right.

For an American reader, perhaps the trouble is the novel's failure to be distinctively British. Yes, certain very British elements are present, such as the difficulty of securing a handgun. But generally the characters, situations, and environment could just as easily be those of educated, urban America, and the writing just as easily the pleasing blend of the intellectual and the colloquial that we know from our own novelists. Has the Americanization of Britain gone so far as to eliminate even class as an element in fictionalized British life?

### Judith Seaboyer (essay date winter 1999)

SOURCE: Seaboyer, Judith. "Sadism Demands a Story: Ian McEwan's *The Comfort of Strangers.*" *Modern Fiction Studies* 45, no. 4 (winter 1999): 957-86.

[*In the following essay, Seaboyer examines the significance of psychic trauma, violence, and the cultural landscape of Venice in* The Comfort of Strangers.]

Ian McEwan's *The Comfort of Strangers* operates on two levels. It is an *unheimlich* tale of gothic horror that turns on sadomasochism and ritualized murder, but at the same time—and I will focus on this aspect of the novella—it is an engaged meditation on the historical, cultural, and psychoanalytic narratives that uphold an economy Kaja Silverman terms the "dominant fiction [that] solicits our faith above all else in the unity of the family, and the adequacy of the male subject" (*Male Subjectivity* 15-16). This fiction, Silverman explains, manifests itself as "the ideological system through which the normative subject lives its relation to the symbolic order and [quoting Ernesto Laclau (24)] it is the mechanism by which a society 'tries to institute itself as such on the basis of closure, of the fixation of meaning, of the non-recognition of the infinite play of differences'" (*Male Subjectivity* 54). It is a narrative pattern that Laura Mulvey famously recognizes as sadistic in "Visual Pleasure and Narrative Cinema," her influential 1975 essay on film and the objectifying male gaze (14-26).

In an early review Christopher Ricks draws a particularly telling link between McEwan's position as author and that of Mary, one of his protagonists, grieving over the body of her dead lover:

> The last page of the book grants access to Mary bewilderedly "in the mood for explanation." "But she explained nothing." There is a great pathos in this ending, and it comes from the coinciding—perfectly honourable—of Mary's doubleness with McEwan's. He too is in the mood for explanation, but is willing, at least for now and at least in the face of the pain which he has imagined, to explain nothing.
>
> (14)

My aim is to engage the ongoing critique of the political role of psychoanalysis in feminist theory by extending and explicating what McEwan—perfectly honorably and perfectly appropriately—chooses not to explain, and so the essay that follows is a close reading of *The Comfort of Strangers* as an exploration of the violent psychic dreams through which we imagine ourselves into existence as gendered subjects. In line with this psychoanalytic perspective, I read McEwan's decision "to explain nothing," mirrored as it is in Mary's inability to articulate her argument, as a traumatic breaking off of the text in the face of the unnameable horror that has occurred.

My critical framework is the Freudian account of the family romance and the shaping force of sadomasochism as they are foregrounded by McEwan, and also Lacan's remapping of Freud's psychic topography. That topography is, I suggest, significantly mirrored in the mysterious topography of Venice, the city in which the novella is set. McEwan's text is exemplary for my purposes because it self-consciously inscribes the "dominant fiction" with a sadistic savagery that unmasks its origins in psychic structures and exposes the dangers of failing to recognize the role of the psyche in the formation of social reality.[1] My point of departure is psychoanalysis, but I have found myself "looking back" (Rich, "When" 35) not only to Mulvey's "Visual Pleasure," itself a discussion of the Oedipus complex, but also to another seminal essay, Adrienne Rich's "When We Dead Awaken: Writing as Re-Vision," that also shares McEwan's concern with gender and violence and that was also published in the decade before *The Comfort of Strangers*. Rich, whose poetry provides McEwan with his epigraph, sees the "re-visioning" of the past as a means of restructuring a male-dominated and self-destructive culture, while Mulvey sees the narrative of psychoanalysis as a political weapon for exposing the sadistic force of "the unconscious of patriarchal society" (14).[2] McEwan's story, culminating in a sadomasochistic murder in which perverse perpetrators and "innocent" victims are alike complicit, is an expression of what Freud terms the "merciless violence" the superego can come to exercise over the ego, a violence which can spiral into "a pure culture of the death instinct" (Freud, *Ego* 53). The driving force behind the sadomasochistic violence of his story is oedipal, and—despite its overt "nastiness"[3]—it is a move toward understanding that opens up the possibility of rereading the Oedipus with all the polemical force of Rich's rereading as a political "act of survival" ("When" 35).

Drucilla Cornell's feminist project, like Mulvey's and Silverman's, emphasizes the importance of psychoanalysis as well as of semiotics. It also rethinks legal interpretation as an act of "recollective imagination" which, while it recognizes the power of an already given reality, views the past not as a prison that prevents change but as a storehouse of signification always open to rereading, "open to the invitation to create new worlds" (*Transformations* 23).[4] McEwan's allusive text functions as just such an act of "recollective imagination," an invitation to recognize that for all their force, the psychic realities that underlie the narratives that make us what we are have their foundation in fantasy, and so they are open to being rethought, reshaped, reformed. With this in mind, I will read McEwan's novella as a parable for gender relations and examine his use of intertextual repetition together with the broader structuring dreamlike and theatrical qualities of his narrative. These elements allude to the fact that, although we may be shaped by powerful "ancient dreams" (McEwan 125) that favor sameness over difference, we nevertheless have agency. The trajectory of McEwan's skillfully constructed narrative seems fated, but he makes us aware that the actors on his oedipal stage could have extemporized. Had Colin and Mary, or, for that matter, Robert and Caroline, understood the script in its historical, cultural, and psychic complexity, things might have ended differently.

The actors in McEwan's psychodrama play out prescribed roles precisely because the script that structures their behavior is invisible to them; psychic space proves as unmappable as the city of Venice, which I suggest is the perfect mirroring backdrop, at once a museum and a historical map for western culture. Unnamed yet unmistakable,[5] Venice underpins the narrative at every level. Like Fredric Jameson in his discussion of Kevin Lynch and cognitive mapping, McEwan draws an analogy between the inability to map urban space and the inability to map social structure (Jameson 416). *The Comfort of Strangers* is about the repercussions attending the failure to read and negotiate a city, but more importantly it is about the failure to read and negotiate, to reread, renegotiate, and revision the culture for which Venice stands as a kind of museum. McEwan's Venice, like the London of Conrad's *Heart of Darkness,* is "one of the dark places of the earth," and the "meaning" of his narrative, like Marlow's, is "not inside like a kernel but outside, enveloping the tale which [brings] it out only as a glow brings out a haze, in the likeness of one of these misty halos that sometimes are made visible by the spectral illumination of moonshine" (Conrad 5). Conrad's city is the dark heart of the British Empire but, given McEwan's echoes of Conrad in the unnamableness of his city and its landmarks and the unspeakable horror he uncovers at its heart, it is interesting that Marlow's direct reference is not to the modern commercial metropolis but to the settlement on the banks of the Thames "when the Romans first came here, nineteen hundred years ago" (5). There is a striking similarity between Marlow's fantasized description of London's river and historical reconstructions of the Venetian lagoon, when the refugees of the old cities of Altino, Aquileia, Concordia, and Padova fled there in the fifth century. John Julius Norwich wonders "who in their senses [. . .] would leave the fertile plains of Lombardy to build a settlement—let alone a city—among these marshy, malarial wastes, on little islets of sand and couchgrass, the playthings of current and tide?" (Norwich 40), and Marlow imagines "[s]andbanks, marshes [. . .] precious little to eat fit for a civilized man [. . .] cold, fog, tempests, disease, exile, and death—death skulking in the air, in the water" (Conrad 6). The emotional responses of Marlow's conjured Roman commander, too, could be attributed to the early Venetians (or, for that matter, to McEwan's tourists), who may well have felt themselves to be "in the midst of the incomprehensible," faced with "[t]he fascination of the abomination [. . .] the growing regrets, the longing to escape, the powerless disgust, the surrender, the hate" (Conrad 6). McEwan's gothic "tale" is a waking dream of corruption, imprisonment, mutilation, and death whose extrapolated "meaning" is an exposition of the shaping power of the sexual imagination, and of social structure as it finds its expression in contemporary sexual politics—the "dominant fiction." The "horror" he exposes at the heart of the unnameable lies not so much in human cruelty and ritualized murder, or even in the passive collusion of its alienated victims, as in the uncanny precision of the mirroring of the first narrative by the second, of the "tale" by the "meaning." The sadism that has demanded the tale of Robert and Caroline and Colin and Mary at once explains and is explained by the psychopathology of western patriarchy.

McEwan's Venice serves as a metaphorical map against which to read and interpret not only western history and culture but also our modernist and postmodernist understanding of the psyche, and at the same time it is a figure for ancient narratives of the labyrinth, that impenetrable space which resists mapping or topographical survey. For reasons that include its decaying beauty and watery, labyrinthine topography, Venice in all its seductive otherness has long been read as a figure for death and for the feminine body, hallucinatory object of and liminal obstacle to the hero's desire. In the second half of the twentieth century that narrative topography accommodates the psychic topography mapped by Freud and redrawn by Lacan: the centrality of death and the woman to the Venetian narrative and to psychoanalysis makes them a perfect fit. The fragmentation of the city, which has been reflected in that of fictional Venetian protagonists and culture alike since the Renaissance, is intensified as the crumbling Venetian stage bears witness to allegories of psychic disintegration expressed in bodily mutilation and murder and also in a wider politics of social disintegration and environmental degradation. McEwan's Venice, material enough for all that it is an unnamed fantasy city, is alternately a clearly articulated space, all sunlit, glittering surface as it opens out from the Piazza San Marco onto the Lagoon and the Adriatic, and an illegible labyrinth, confusing and sinister as it collapses back into a womblike enclosure of narrow streets and canals. A perfected, contained medieval/Renaissance city, whole and unchanging, Venice may be read as a figure for the Lacanian Imaginary, but at the same time it is a figure for the end of everything as it slowly loses the battle against time, pollution, and rising water levels and returns to the Real of the Lagoon from which it was created. From this perspective, too, the Venetian stage is an ideal site for McEwan's story of Colin and Mary, English tourists in Venice, and Robert and Caroline, who live there: the dark, pure perversity of Robert and Caroline's relationship is the overt expression of that which, repressed, structures the somewhat dishonest, somewhat dull, occasionally passionate, largely comfortable normalcy of Colin and Mary's.

From the beginning, as Colin and Mary are drawn into the liminal space of the labyrinth and toward death, a sense of fatal inevitability is reinforced through echoes of a second modernist novella: *Death in Venice*.[6] Mann was candid about the autobiographical aspects of this work. He said his experiences on holiday there in 1911 provided much of the material, and that he found the novella difficult to complete (qtd. in Reed 153-54). McEwan admits in an interview with John Haffenden that "something" of a visit to Venice with his partner in 1978 "found its way into the book" (qtd. in Haffenden 177). It goes without saying that Colin and Mary are no more Ian McEwan and Penny Allen than Gustav von Aschenbach is Thomas Mann, but McEwan has said he found the writing "painful" (qtd. in Haffenden 170), and in writing Colin's death, he felt as if he were writing his own (qtd. in Haffenden 183). In the construction of his narrative, McEwan takes up Mann's juxtaposition of the Apollonian and the Dionysian, his references to Platonic thought, and his anxieties surrounding sexuality and the power of the repressed ancient myth of Dionysus within the contemporary sexual imagination. Mann's expressed concern is with the place in society of art and the artist at the beginning of the century;

McEwan's is with Platonic oppositional logic—Mary's "organizing principle" (125) is that which shapes western metaphysics.

McEwan's text by no means mirrors Mann's, but a series of elliptical and increasingly *unheimlich* doublings and echoes accrue as the protagonists lose their bearings. Both narratives are driven by the homoerotic attraction of an older man to a beautiful younger one,[7] through whom some kind of transcendent state is to be achieved. The sense of material decay that pervades Mann's Venice is almost entirely metaphorical in McEwan's and the only plague is high-season tourists, yet there is a sense of threat ("It's like a prison here," Mary complains to Colin [50]), and in spite or, unconsciously, because of it, the visitors, like Aschenbach, choose not to leave. It is as though, like him, they "[share] the city's secret, the city's guilt" (Mann 65). An unpleasant yet somehow alluring "Dionysian" stranger entices them into the labyrinth until all escape routes are shut off, and Aschenbach's quiet death in the presence of his "pale and lovely Summoner" (73) is replaced by a horrifying parody of the Maenadic frenzy and bloody mutilation of his bacchantic dream (Mann 65-67) as Colin is murdered by Robert and Caroline (McEwan 121).

Other repetitions from Mann have less to do with the overall structure of the text, but are nonetheless forceful. It is a commonplace that Venetians, and even Venetian tourists, dress elegantly—Joseph Brodsky (who was a regular visitor for twenty years and is buried in Venice) wryly suggested it is as though visitors take up a challenge to match the city's constructed beauty (*Watermark* 24-28). Like Aschenbach, McEwan's tourists spend a good deal of time in "self-obsessed" (13) narcissistic grooming. Each dresses with infinite care, Aschenbach, because "[l]ike any lover, he desire[s] to please" (Mann 67), and Colin and Mary, "as though somewhere among the thousands they were soon to join, there waited someone who cared deeply how they appeared" (McEwan 13). The hotel barber daubs Aschenbach's lips "the colour of ripe strawberries" (Mann 68); Colin's lips, too, will be carefully rouged, but with spilt blood. Of Aschenbach's self-mastery, "a nice observer once said [. . .] 'Aschenbach has always lived like this'—here the speaker closed the fingers of his left hand to a fist—'never like this'—and he let his open hand hang relaxed from the back of his chair" (Mann 9). In light of this, Colin's dangling wrist as he lounges on the hotel balcony, and as he is later mimicked by Robert, is telling. Mann's "laughing song," performed by a strolling player who uncannily evokes the mysterious "horned" figure Aschenbach saw outside the mausoleum in Munich just before he was overwhelmed by the fatal urge to visit Venice (4-5), is echoed in an attenuated contemporary version Colin and Mary hear played over and over on a jukebox in Robert's dismal gay bar. On the Lido, they watch adolescents play aggressive games at the water's edge, recalling the "rather lawless and out-of-hand" fight between Mann's Tadzio and Jaschiu (72), but in McEwan's text the game centers on a young man and a young woman, underscoring that what is at stake in *The Comfort of Strangers* is not lawlessness but the maintenance of a violent patriarchal law that insists on the centrality of heterosexuality.

In his earliest writings on sadism and masochism, Freud notes that their most remarkable feature is that they oscillate. They "are habitually to be found to occur together in the same individual. [. . .] A sadist is always at the same time a masochist" (*Three Essays* 159). Not only are they "[t]he most common and the most significant of all the perversions" (157) but, he suggests, they are culturally serviceable, since they encompass attitudes to masculine activity and aggression and feminine passivity and compliance that are compatible with normative heterosexuality. Later (and this relates to Robert's psychic reality) Freud recognizes that they could be more overtly dangerous (*Ego* 53). McEwan draws attention to the deadly persistence of sadomasochism within the late-twentieth-century western sexual imagination; for all that death is central, the driving force that pushes the subject beyond the pleasure principle is not the desire for death, but the normative production of gendered subjectivity, which Freud explains by means of the Oedipus.

Colin and Mary lose their way in a multilayered liminal space that is at once a physical labyrinth and a maze of constructs whose roots are in western culture's distant social and psychic past—and McEwan's *hypocrite lecteur* must negotiate the equally complex space of the mirror construction that is the text itself. In terms of a Lacanian psychic topography, it is not surprising, given the associations that exist between sadism and looking (Lacan, *Four Fundamentals* 181-84), that in this most to-be-looked-at of cities, the Imaginary, with its fantasies of cohesion and mirror likeness, holds sway. Further, the Imaginary contaminates the Symbolic so that language, rather than disrupting Imaginary cohesion by introducing the possibility of difference and change, upholds the mask that disguises at the same time as it disavows the presence of the Real. The division between vision and language, looking and speaking (underscored by the fact that twentieth-century Venice exists to be admired, and that Colin and Mary don't speak the language that surrounds them, as well as the link between sadism and language and masochism and silence[8]), can be plotted according to the text's division into chapters. In the first two, Colin and Mary are "not on speaking terms" (11). Foregrounded against this absence of language, against its failure, are a plethora of concepts that are linked to the field of vision: narcissism, exhibitionism, voyeurism, performance, and audience, together with such signifiers as mirrors, cameras, binoculars, photographs, and the "screen" of the retina. Scopophilia persists, but there is a marked increase in speech beyond the second chapter. Chapter three, for example, is a lengthy confessional monologue recited before a captive audience, and it is followed by a series of dialogues, cross-examinations, and confessions that continue until the final pages, when the text subsides back into speechlessness. Chapter seven seems almost a celebration of linguistic exchange. The standard methods of argument of the western rhetorical tradition that have dominated Colin and Mary's conversations until now are "re-visioned" and displaced by what appear to be more open-ended exchanges that move toward recognizing, articulating, and analyzing desires that threaten Imaginary identity and unity. Up to this point,

> [t]he unspoken assumption [. . .] was that a subject was best explored by taking the opposing view, even if it was not quite the view one held oneself; a considered opinion was less important than the fact of opposition. The idea, if it was an idea and not a habit of mind, was that adversaries, fearing contradiction, would be more rigorous in argument, like scientists proposing innovation to their colleagues.
>
> (80)

Topics begin to be "explored" rather than "defensively reiterated, or forced into elaborate irrelevancies" (81) that maintain and protect the rigid mask of the Imaginary, but by the next chapter Colin and Mary have lapsed into resistance and reticence, recognizing that, oxymoronically, all the talk of the past few days has been an extension of the "unacknowledged conspiracy of silence" (91) that has allowed the unspeakable to remain unspoken. The horror that lies beneath the mask of language they have created is revealed to be the "merciless violence" of the novella's structuring sadism. Unnamed, it retains its terrible power to control and subjugate, to punish or to forgive, and thus to drive the narrative. "Sadism demands a story," as Mulvey says (22).

This brings me back to Venice and its role in McEwan's exploration of the "dominant fiction." For all its labyrinthine confusion, this city is in many ways a clearly articulated space, its medieval construction rendered still more legible through Renaissance town planning. Henri Lefebvre has said that "Venice, more than any other place, bears witness to the existence [. . .] of a unitary code or common language of the city" (73), but codes and common languages have to be deciphered and assimilated before they can provide a key. Pattern eludes Colin and Mary. They persistently leave behind the easily read tourist areas of San Marco and Dorsoduro for the labyrinthine alleys of Castello and Cannaregio, but "the fine old churches, the altarpieces, the stone bridges over canals" (12) remain alienated illegible fragments rather than taking on shape as individual parishes that have, over the centuries, coalesced into a complex but unified whole. By day they distractedly experience the city as a series of jumbled images projected in rapid succession against the screen of the eye as they are swept along on a tide of tourists. At night, after the crush subsides, instead of actively plotting a course on a map or choosing a path according to the logic of the city's configuration, they are led, passively, by their senses. They dip into what is for them an unmappable, invisible city after the manner of the flaneur, responding randomly to the tantalizing curve of a street, the smell of frying fish, the comforting sight of a distant stranger.

That this failure to map urban space proves deadly suggests by extension the careful attention that must be paid to the negotiation of cultural space, and also of McEwan's mirroring *textual* space. On the occasions Mary and Colin do resort to maps they find them to be either badly printed, incomplete, or a series of disconnected fragments, and they find, like McEwan's readers, that it is easy "to get lost [walking] from one page to another" (20). Colin and Mary move impulsively, their failure to read or to remember almost willful; we may of course choose to do the same, but for all the labyrinthine complexity of McEwan's text, it is possible to move back and forth within it, literally or by means of memory, recognizing and misrecognizing, remembering and misremembering, noting a repeated phrase or image, interpreting now this piece of the puzzle and now that, until pattern and meaning are gradually revealed. It is possible to make links between his images, words, and silences, and also to move beyond the bounds of the text itself, since if culture and the role of the "dominant fiction" are to be understood and interpreted, it will be necessary to extrapolate an allegorical "mental map of city space [. . .] to that mental map of the social and global totality we all carry around in our heads in variously garbled forms" (Jameson 415).

McEwan plays on a Venetian sense of enclosure and claustrophobia by introducing only four characters. Three of them are alien to Venice. Mary and Colin move through a museumlike space in which one may look at a culture through its artifacts, skimming across the surface without the need to go deeper. Caroline is Canadian, and has been imprisoned within the house since her arrival with Robert several years earlier. Although Robert grew up in London, he inherited his grandfather's Venetian palazzo and functions within a milieu of local people as the other three do not. Of the four, only he has the key, the controlling power that comes from a knowledge of the city that enables him to co-opt it as a stage for the drama by means of which he will transform psychic reality into real event—although by the end of the text it is apparent that Caroline has been directing from the wings.

Mary and Colin have been lovers for seven years. We learn little about her life and even less of his, but significantly, given the text's theatrical aspect, and the place in it of the voyeurism/exhibitionism binary, they have both been actors. McEwan alludes, directly or indirectly, to three dramatic tragedies that turn on family romance and violence and its painful corollary, the getting of wisdom—*The Bacchae, Oedipus Rex,* and *Hamlet*—and Mary and Colin will each be assigned specific roles to play in the restaging of Dionysian passion that is at the same time a restaging of the Freudian family romance and the culmination of a drama at once absurd and tragic, contemporary and ancient. Theirs is "no longer a great passion" (18) but they insist they are so close they feel like "misted mirror" images of each other (18). Reinforcing this, Caroline remarks that they look "almost like twins" (67). Such a superficially attractive ease of resemblance disguises a perilous denial of difference that fixes them within the static realm of illusion, narcissism, and the Imaginary, and outside language and the Symbolic. The Imaginary city they glide across is similarly illusory and similarly dangerous.

From the beginning, their holiday proves exhausting. They sleep badly and suffer recurrent nightmares of infantilization, passivity, and helplessness. Mary's suggest she feels trapped by her family and incapable of protecting her children, and Colin's are pure Freud—"of flying [. . .], of crumbling teeth, of appearing naked before a seated stranger" (12).[9] These dreams of helplessness and exposure are relentlessly realized until, immobile, Mary will watch Colin bleed to death before her.

Each morning they allow themselves to be swept along with thousands of other visitors, "dutifully fulfill[ing] the many tasks of tourism the ancient city imposed" (14). It is a passive, even masochistic, routine from which they return exhausted to sleep away the afternoons before rising to set out again as night falls. All this is, of course, normal enough behavior for people on holiday, but in the context of the whole it is disturbing. Not only are they somewhat sleep-deprived but they sleep and dream during the sunlit, "rational" part of the day, and wake to occupy an irrational dream space at night. Sleeping and waking, dream and reality, blend into a waking dream, until they begin to sleep not just at inappropriate times but in inappropriate places—first in the street, and then in the house of a far from comforting stranger.

They lose themselves, but instead of taking pleasure in the aimlessness of the flaneur as might have been possible had each been alone (the flaneur is, after all, necessarily a solitary figure), they spend hours exasperatedly retracing their steps. The closeness of their relationship, artificially intensified by their isolation in a foreign city, leads to an unspoken stultifying identification with the other's desire, and thus to compromise and resentment. From the beginning there is a sense that more than just their holiday is out of kilter. Arguments are "resolved" without ever being articulated. Mary feels as though she is sleepwalking not just through the labyrinth of Venice but through her life, and longs for the "comfort" of the ordered existence of her childhood, "for time and events to be at least partially subject to control" (19). Things are critically out of balance, but McEwan is at his most coolly witty in these opening pages, and his protagonists' situation is amusing in its familiarity, for all that it is disquieting. By such means complicity is from the opening pages extended from McEwan's victims to include his reader.

Late in the evening, Colin and Mary are lost and hungry and bickering when their path is suddenly blocked by the third actor in the drama, who offers to guide them to a restaurant. From the beginning, Robert is obnoxious. His machismo and misogyny are undisguised, yet Colin and Mary follow him deeper into the labyrinth, farther and farther from the brightly lit legibility of San Marco and Dorsoduro to a gay bar, probably somewhere in Cannaregio. The bar is full of chainsmoking silent young men, the music supplied by the juke-box is "chirpily sentimental" (29), and there is no food, but, beguiled at finding themselves amongst local people in this city of visitors, they stay, a captive audience for Robert's long, patently rehearsed confessional monologue about his childhood, an ugly case study of oedipal desire, paternal violence, sibling hatred, and revenge. He stops only as the bar closes, and leaves Colin and Mary, hungry, tired, and now slightly drunk, to make their own way back to Dorsoduro. Still hopelessly lost, they wander on until dawn, snatching an hour's sleep in a narrow street near the Ospedale Civile on the Fondamenta Nuove, about as far away from their hotel as they could possibly be. In the morning, they take the vaporetto to San Marco, returning to the area of the city they know, whose code is easily deciphered. When they meet Robert a second time—or rather, as later becomes clear, when he shows himself to them a second time—they are no match for his insistence that he offer them further "hospitality." He carries them off to his house, uncannily close to the *calle* in which they had fallen asleep a few hours before.

Again they sleep during the day, to wake in a room whose walls are barred by the rays of the setting sun shining orange through shutters, recalling Mary's earlier feeling of imprisonment. She wakes first and spends a long time staring at Colin, her mirror twin. Her gaze slowly catalogues the parts of his naked body in terms that suggest a sculpted beauty that is iconic, not quite real in its androgyny. He has a narrow waist, slender, hairless legs, and "abnormally" small feet. She "move[s] closer to examine his face as one might a statue's" (56). The skin of his ears is "so pale and fine" as to be "almost translucent," their construction so intricate as to be "impossible." His eyebrows are dark and straight, his lashes long and thick, and his "unnaturally" fine dark hair curls on his slender, womanly neck. His nose in profile lies classically "flat, along the face," its nostrils no more than sculpted "commas" (56). The description could be of a classical sculpture, or, looking forward to the photographs Robert takes and their immobilizing two-dimensionality, the eroticized, horizontally posed male nudes of late-eighteenth-, early-nineteenth-century French neoclassical painting[10]—for example, Anne-Louis Girodet's *The Sleep of Endymion* or Pierre-Narcisse Guérin's *Aurora and Cephalus*. A childlike physical flawlessness and vulnerability and an ambiguous sexuality are emphasized by the fact that "his arms [are] crossed foetally over his chest" (55) and he lies face down with only the upper part of his body "twisted a little awkwardly towards [Mary]" (55), so that neither pubic hair nor genitals are visible. There is in such an image of androgyny, as Francette Pacteau has pointed out, the promise of the (impossible) erasure of sexual difference as the resolution of the narcissistic desire for pregendered completeness and self-sufficiency (Pacteau 63). In the light of their unspoken sense of entrapment within their "mirror" relationship, it is telling that Mary moves to stroke Colin but, rather than wake him, chooses instead to gaze without touching.[11]

This lengthy construction of Colin as the object of the gaze is the first description we have of him, and it is telling that it is framed by the first overt reference to a structuring scopic regime that has been foregrounded from the beginning. Robert, described in some detail on his first appearance, is Colin's physical antithesis. The oppositionality of the representation of the two men, as arresting as the mirroring that exists between Colin and Mary, begs to be read in iconographical terms: naked and clothed, supine and upright, passive and active, innocent and knowing, spectacle and spectator, masculine and feminine, and so on. At their first meeting Colin is dressed in white, and Robert wears a black shirt (26) that is both a declaration of his machismo and, in the light of his politics and his nostalgia for the way the world was during his father's and grandfather's lifetimes, a sinister nod toward Italian fascism and the reinscription of the patriarchal values that accompanied it. Robert projects an immediacy and a worldliness that contrast with Colin's somewhat petulant passivity. Colin is confined, immobilized by the camera, while Robert is actively *present,* a Mulveyan three-dimensional figure in the landscape, alert, moving surely across the feminine space of the city, manipulating his surroundings and the people he comes across. His is a performance of masculinity that declares his virility. In one nice juxtaposition, Colin cannot get the attention of a waiter in the Piazza, but a few minutes later the water-taxi drivers squabble for Robert's custom. The contrast becomes even more striking when Colin is described in sleep in Robert's house. Contained and displayed within the feminine space of a shuttered bedroom, he is beautiful, passive, prone, oblivious. Each man is portrayed as other than human; Colin's slender beauty causes Mary to liken him to a god and Robert to liken him to an angel, and this accentuates Robert's brutishness. He is almost simian: stocky, with long muscular arms, large hairy hands, and a carefully exposed "pelt" of chest hair (26).

From the moment Colin wakes, the carefully staged direction of the drama becomes clearer. Since the one piece of clothing to be found is a woman's dressing gown, it falls to Mary to venture out of the enclosure of the bedroom. She finds herself in a gallery that is more like a museum than a lived-in house. Like Pandora, or Bluebeard's bride, with all that those figures conjure up of forbidden secrets and spaces, female sexual curiosity, and guilt, she tries to open a sideboard, "a monstrosity of reflecting surfaces whose every drawer ha[s] a brass knob in the shape of a woman's head" (60), but all the drawers are locked, the knowledge they might contain denied her.

The fourth actor is introduced. Caroline has been watching Mary's breach of etiquette from a balcony, and now she questions her about her life, continuing to stare, adding a twist to the increasingly complicated field of vision when she owns to having watched Colin and Mary as they slept. This admission of voyeurism is the more peculiar not only because they were naked but because of its juxtaposition to Mary's observation of her sleeping lover. With what we already know of Colin and Mary's mirror relationship, Caroline's confession nudges Mary's narcissistic delight in her lover's beauty from an uncomplicated pleasure in looking toward something abnormal, perverse. Mary is uncomfortable but barely responds to Caroline's disclosure and when Colin hears, he merely asks Caroline if she's American, as if that would explain either her unusual behavior or her remarkable lack of embarrassment. The relative ease with which they both accept this objectification recalls their self-obsessed preparation before stepping into the city as though onto a stage.

For all this looking, the stream of language continues as Caroline presses Mary to confess her feelings for Colin and her views on sexual love. She is comically confused by Mary's ironic description of a women's theater group she had belonged to and the problems they'd had working together, and she is stunned by the idea of a play without male characters, since without an active (sadistic) masculine figure to create the action, "what could *happen?*" (68).

In keeping with the pattern of display and vision, Robert acts as cicerone for Colin in a tour of the "family museum" (59)—furniture, paintings, books, sculpture, and such prosaic items as brushes and razors, a riding crop and a fly swat (70-71)—that are his paternal legacy. A collection of memorabilia, it parodies the cultural authority and validation offered by the museum—doubly resonant in the context of this city, which is itself a museum to the past—for not only does it prove to be a collection of fragments shored against the ruins of patriarchal culture, but the things are valued less for themselves than for their associations with his father and grandfather, who inhabited a golden time when men were men and women knew their place. A series of "murky," artistically insignificant paintings are prized first because his grandfather collected them, and second because his father showed that "certain brushstrokes were those of a master" (71); opera glasses are revered because both men witnessed particular performances through them. He delivers a banal homily on gender politics, philosophizing that we are confused and unhappy because men don't believe in themselves and "[w]omen treat them like children, because they can't take them seriously" (72). For all that women talk of freedom, they want masculine aggression and dream of captivity. Colin, "affable, but strained," responds with mocking banter about "the good old days" (73). It is an encounter between strangers establishing the boundaries of small talk, but Robert has no conception of boundaries, social, bodily, or psychic. His transgressive behavior is more tangible than his wife's, and he punches Colin in the stomach so that he falls to the floor. No one else sees what has happened and nothing is said.

Colin and Mary's response to this unpleasant encounter is as odd as the encounter itself: they retreat to their hotel room, and make love for days. Conversation is renewed along with sexual passion. They discuss their lives and rework old arguments about gender and class politics from a personal rather than from their usual detached, analytical perspective, and each actually tries to listen to the other. They also—playfully—invent sadistic fantasies, but neither the fantasies nor what might underlie them ever enters into the intense conversations they conduct outside sex. They barely refer to the experience at Robert and Caroline's that marked the shift in their relationship; they speak neither of the sadomasochism each later admits they recognized in the other couple, nor of the coercion to which they each acquiesced.

After three days, Mary, a little self-consciously and for the first time since their jouissant idyll began, slips downstairs to have breakfast alone, and when she sees Colin smiling down from the balcony, she is jarred by an uncanny sense of unease "at the back of her mind, just beyond her reach, [. . .] like a vivid dream that cannot be recalled" (84). The anxiety persists and the next day she wakes at dawn, struggling out of a horrifying nightmare she doesn't explain, except to say she realizes that seeing Colin on the balcony had reminded her of a photograph Robert had shown her. It was blown up and indistinct, but she now knows the man in the picture was Colin. At first Colin placates her, but as she begins to formulate her thoughts and to face what is happening, he cuts her off and falls asleep—this time the hour and the place are appropriate for sleep, but the circumstances demand wakefulness. Mary doesn't name the unnameable, and the moment is lost.

Later the same day they escape to the Lido and the open Adriatic. At the edge of the ocean, they begin to speak about the photograph, recognizing it now as evidence of Robert's predatory voyeurism. They admit they were aware of Caroline and Robert's sadomasochism, and Colin confesses Robert had hit him. This is a second moment when they might have recognized themselves as enabling elements within Robert's brutal fantasy and refused the roles he allocated them. Because they do not, the Lacanian scopophilic loop remains intact[12] and Robert and Caroline will be able—jointly—to take up the position of sadistic subject, and experience a *jouissance* beyond the pleasure principle. Colin and Mary no sooner begin to talk than their mode of conversation relapses into adversarial detachment, and instead of being discovered and examined, their appalling fascination is repressed, allowed to retain its power. Their passionate talk and lovemaking now seem to have been "nothing more than a form of parasitism, an unacknowledged conspiracy of silence" (91). Sickened, they return to their mode of irritable taciturnity, papering over the glimpsed violence that lies at the heart of their relationship. On the way back to the vaporetto, Colin returns to the question of Robert and the photograph, but this time Mary forestalls discussion, shrugging it off as though she has forgotten the horror glimpsed only a few hours before. Their silence on the return journey is broken by an apparently casual agreement to walk back across the island to the hotel from the Ospedale Civile stop instead of going on to San Marco, because "[i]t will be quicker" (98). With their record for negotiating the city, it's hardly a convincing reason, and when Caroline waves from her balcony they wordlessly walk toward her.

Robert leads Colin back to his bar. The women remain at the house, and at Mary's insistence it is now Caroline's turn to talk, to confess. By the time Caroline has described the development of her relationship with Robert, his "deep loathing" for her (for all his play-acting, she explains, "[i]t wasn't theatre" [109]), the pleasure she came to take in the pain as well as in her feelings of guilt and helplessness, Mary has drunk the spiked tea Caroline has prepared, and her silence is no longer voluntary. Like Bluebeard's bride, her curiosity is satisfied and, like her, she is in no position to retreat to take stock of her newfound knowledge. The men return, and Mary, her still gaze fixed on the scene being enacted before her, takes up the role of Hitchcockian "made-to-order-witness" (Silverman, *Threshold* 126; n. 6, 243) to the ritualistic murder of her lover. Like Pentheus manipulated by Dionysus, she is forced to watch what she has refused to see. It is, and it is not, theater.

The matching pieces of the textual puzzle coalesce around the vision/language division: the first is the photograph Mary recalls in her nightmare, a grainy blowup of Colin standing on the hotel balcony;[13] the second, the oedipal story within the story Robert narrates to Colin and Mary. The photograph is, like Venice itself, a figure for the text's structuring scopophilia; at the same time, and again like Venice, it is a figure for reading and interpretation and the role of memory. Associated with the photograph that frames Colin as "spectacle" is an enfilade of gazes that extends to include Robert, Caroline, and Mary, and the reader, in a complex structure of fascination and complicity. Mary's uncanny experience of seeing Colin on the balcony nudges her memory and she struggles to recall what turns out to be the forgotten photograph. She remains within the narcissistic economy that applied when she looked at his sleeping body, but now she occupies Robert's line of vision, and this results in a subtle shift, actual and metaphorical, in her perspective. She sees as though through the lens of his camera, her gaze contaminated by his, rather as earlier her pleasure in looking at Colin's sleeping body was corrupted by its juxtaposition with Caroline's voyeurism. She is inserted into the position of the bearer of the gaze as Colin has been placed in the position of its object. This does not make her a voyeur, but it does further align her with Robert and Caroline on their side of the voyeur/exhibitionist binary, and foreshadows her role as coerced witness to Colin's murder.

Caroline, too, gazes at the photographic image of Colin from Robert's perspective. Confined within his house, the only perspective available to her is the one he chooses. The camera becomes her eye, and the photograph of Colin provides what she lacks: access to a world in which she can make something happen. As she looks, she crosses from the position of masochistic object to share the visually active role of voyeur and begins to plan with Robert how to transform sadomasochistic fantasy into deadly reality. "It's like stepping into a mirror," she explains to Mary (114).

In this way, the field of vision comes to encompass the reader, *hypocrite lecteur* and mirror witness to the unfolding drama. Just as Mary struggles to recall the photograph and to interpret the circumstances surrounding its existence, so the reader must remember and bring together a series of random textual and intertextual elements surrounding the same image, metaphorically narrowing his or her eyes until the *unheimlich* fragments achieve their terrible clarity. Mary's gaze is fascinated and complicit; her desire to know leads her into the trap Robert and Caroline have set. The reader's desire to know suggests a similar complicity.

McEwan's textual staging distracts attention from the blown up photograph when it is first mentioned, so that it is as easy for readers to overlook its importance as it is for Mary. Dinner at Robert and Caroline's apartment is over. Caroline and Colin are center stage as she hints at her imprisonment and insists Colin promise that he and Mary will visit again. Mary overhears, moves upstage away from the conversation, and suggests it is time to leave. She glances first at a magazine and then at the photograph, in what appears to be no more than stage business. She is curious enough to take the picture in her hand and can make out a man smoking on a balcony, but like the thousands of other images that have "fallen dully on her retina, as on a distant screen" (12) over the past few days, it holds no meaning for her. Robert takes it from her after a few seconds, but not until the noose is drawn tight does McEwan let us know that Mary did not pick up the picture by chance, that Robert showed it to her. He does, however, provide a number of textual "clues" to the photograph's provenance and to its importance, clues that weave the image back into the text. It is a visual reprise of the early linguistic description of Colin smoking a joint on the hotel balcony, and photography has been foregrounded from the beginning by its presence and by its absence. By the time the picture is mentioned, seemingly disconnected references to lenses, cameras, and photography have become a kind of leitmotif. A camera is an instrument of domination and torture in Mary's nightmares: she dreams her ex-husband has cornered her and for hours relentlessly explains the operation of his camera as she sighs and moans and begs him to stop. She is bleached to photographic "silver and sepia" (22) by street lighting, becoming the living embodiment of Robert's gaze as he stalks and photographs them. In a shop window "a single camera lens [is] mounted on a velvet plinth," (24) accorded the kind of reverence usually reserved for works of art or precious jewelry, and in this city of tourists, where "[t]wo-thirds, perhaps, of the adult males [carry] cameras" (47), Colin, as object rather than bearer of the gaze, takes no pictures. Before they leave the hotel, he watches tourists capturing the city and each other on film and recounts an anecdote about it to Mary, as a man in a small boat on the Giudecca Canal returns binoculars to their case.[14] The binoculars chime uncannily with the suggestions of theatricality, and more particularly with those of voyeurism, recalling the description a few pages earlier of Colin and Mary's "exhibitionist" ritualized toilet preparations. When they encounter Robert later that evening, he is carrying a camera, although it is quite dark, and he still has it with him the next day when he runs them to ground in the Piazza. None of these references is accorded particular attention: not until Caroline sits Mary down before the record of Robert's perverse looking in the form of the collage of photographs of Colin, framed and cropped, reduced to two-dimensionality, do they shift into focus.

A second key to the textual puzzle is the embedded story that explains Robert's careful orchestration of Colin's murder in terms of childhood trauma and the effort to master it by reproducing the sadistic experience in all its painful horror. Robert's perverse barroom soliloquy may have its basis in the real events of his childhood, but it is an expression of his *psychic* reality.[15] He prepares himself as an actor might, pausing, adjusting his body and breathing—going into character. There is neither opportunity nor need for a response from Mary and Colin, who are set up as audience rather than as interlocutors; this may be a self-telling, but there is to be no talking cure. There is something of Browning's technique in what is essentially an interior monologue, in that it is as though in spite of itself psychologically revealing of Robert and incriminating of the feared and respected father he longs to emulate. For all that he professes only admiration and respect, the paternal portrait is that of a vain, manipulative, petty tyrant, complete with Hitlerian moustache, whose inner sanctum deserved to be defiled by his powerless son.

Just as the photograph may be read as a figure for scopophilia in the text, Robert's family narrative is a figure for the Oedipus complex, with its foundations in violence, eroticism, and guilt. Robert's account circulates around fantasies of possession of the mother, and paternal retribution for his forbidden desire to be the father and for his failure to measure up to the father, to be *like* the father (Freud, *Ego* 34). He describes fantasies of humiliation and punishment that are echoed in the wider structuring violence of the "dominant fiction" that informs the text as a whole. Although his behavior is sadistic, what demands his story is not "simple" sadism but its oscillatory other, an unconscious primary masochism that will ensure his public punishment and humiliation. The unconscious desire to master the trauma of childhood betrayal and punishment at the hands of his father leads to the reproduction of his psychic reality in an effort not to bind it, but to shatter the guilty ego once and for all, and in so doing to achieve a *jouissance* that can only be attained with the complete destruction of the self. This will be effected beyond the bounds of the text, when he will step onto the juridical stage and become the object of the gaze of society.

Robert is the youngest of five siblings, the only son and, according to his monologue (31-40), not merely his stern father's favorite, but "his passion" (32). When his father is away, Robert shares his mother's bed until, at the age of ten, he meets Caroline and transfers his love to her. His father is a terrifying figure ("even the ambassador was afraid of [him]" [32])[16] who pits his daughters against their brother. His sisters, too, are "frightening": a more or less undifferentiated Medusan "tangle of ribbon and lace and curls" (40), and they turn their castrating fury on their little brother. His oldest sisters—tellingly named Eva and Maria—will be punished for reaching sexual maturity while he, as the male heir and "the next head of the family" (33) is set up by his father in a false position of power over them. His father pretends to allow Robert to infantilize his sisters, forbidding them to go out unchaperoned or to exchange girlish socks for silk stockings. But, as he discovers, the dangerous female body is not so easily contained, and in their parents' absence his sisters flaunt their outlawed sexuality before his spellbound gaze, transforming themselves from "tall schoolgirls" into "real women" (34) as they put on the fascinating and threatening masquerade of femininity in the form of their mother's clothes and makeup. As they pose narcissistically for each other, he follows them, "looking at them all the time, just looking" (34). At dinner that night, Robert betrays his sisters, and in his father's study, a forbidden, secret place of gold leaf, chandeliers, and red velvet, he witnesses his sisters being beaten.

They take their revenge by persuading him to swallow castor oil before gorging on the chocolate that is forbidden him because it was "bad for boys. It made them weak in character, like girls" (35). As the room begins to swim, Eva and Maria bind him and lock him in his father's tabooed study ("Bravo Robert! [. . .] Now you are big Papa" [37]), where he throws up and defecates on the precious rugs. Before his father's return, the sisters untie their brother and leave him to his fate (37). Now it is his turn to be beaten, for failing to measure up to his paternal inheritance, for proving to be no better than a weak-willed girl.

Freud explains this kind of fantasy in terms of the negative Oedipus and "moral masochism" ("Masochism" 161, 165); the split subject turns upon itself, the superego hounding and punishing the ego. He describes "an unconscious sense of guilt" (166) which drives the subject "to seek punishment at the hands of a parental power" (169). The ego, which is after all, as Silverman reminds us, "first and foremost a bodily ego,"[17] becomes "the erotogenic zone of choice, the site where [the moral masochist] seeks to be beaten" (Silverman, *Male Subjectivity* 188-89). In the case of the female subject, masochism is more or less acceptable within the formations of normative heterosexuality, in keeping with the binaries that define woman as the gentle, passive, childlike, weak, evil, lacking, guilty complement of man. The positive resolution of the Oedipus complex, which validates the little girl's willingness to subordinate herself to the masculine subject, means such fantasy may be acknowledged consciously. She identifies with her (powerless, passive) mother and "loves" her (powerful, active) father. With maturity she will "become" the mother and transfer her love for the father to a patriarchal husband. However pathological her behavior may be, Caroline recognizes her love of suffering and her desire to be destroyed; Robert has had to repress the homosexual desire to be beaten/loved by the father, so that his desire to be destroyed is unavailable to consciousness. Misrecognized, it is outside his control, even more dangerous than his sadism or Caroline's desire for self-destruction.

She describes their marriage, which proceeded smoothly enough until they were unable to conceive a child. Robert, anxious to step into his father's position, "was desperate to be a father, desperate to have sons, but nothing came of it" (108). Further proof of his "castration" was exposed as doctors discovered there was "something wrong with his sperm" (108). Unable to be the father, he began to hurt Caroline as they had sex, punishing in her a femininity he feared in himself. They found their roles irresistible, and after they moved to Venice the level of violence and the pleasure they took from it escalated until Robert broke Caroline's back. They had stepped into the Real, and according to Caroline, they were at once frightened and thrilled, and "the idea of death [. . .] wouldn't go away" (110). "We had arrived at the point we had been heading towards all the time" (109)—that "point" is also, of course, the geographical, topographical space of Venice as figure for the body of the woman and as the Real of fragmentation, horror, and death.

At a physical level, Robert is in control, but at the level of the psyche, the power relation is less definite. It becomes clear that Caroline takes Robert "seriously" only within the frame of her bodily pain: for the rest (and tellingly, given Robert's sermon to Colin about gender roles), she describes him as a child who makes up stories and is obsessed with his father and grandfather and his "little museum" of their possessions (111). His desire may be unavailable to his consciousness, but it is all too available to being manipulated by Caroline's desire.

Robert must prove that he is not weak like his sisters; indeed he must show that he is like the father, and he must *be* the father, whom he introjects as the sadistic superego. His conscious drive to destroy Colin, who is for him exemplary of the gender "confusion and unhappiness" (73) that pervades and undermines patriarchal culture, masks an unconscious drive toward his own humiliation and destruction. The murder ensures the annihilation of his castrated self, and makes "real" the father of his psychic reality. In "punishing" Colin, he is able at last to step into his father's shoes and punish his failed, effeminate self once and for all, and this ultimate transgression will guarantee the ego's exposure and destruction at the hands of the law, as the symbolic father. Part of Robert and Caroline's planning includes escape, but because the unconscious aim of Robert's desire is to engineer a repetition of his childhood trauma, he ensures he will be caught and punished by leaving a legible trail. Air tickets are booked in their own names; before Robert kills Colin he parades him through the streets leading to his bar, telling everyone they meet they are lovers; and Mary is set up as a witness. In the wake of his crime, he defiles the patriarchal house as he had once defiled his father's study, smearing it with the blood of his victim that is the guilty and abject trace of his own feminized aberrance.

I have spoken of the structure of McEwan's text as a negotiation of two textual zones, the "tale" and the "meaning," against the mental map of Venice as a figure for culture. A tale of gothic horror informs a discussion of our "dominant fiction," and an individual capacity for "map reading," the negotiation of urban space, is a figure for the negotiation of social structure. The trauma faced by patriarchal culture at the end of the twentieth-century is vividly figured in Robert's personal trauma. The disruption of the "dominant fiction" by feminism and the development of gender politics reflect Robert's after-the-event construction of his childhood, and each threatens his Imaginary relation with the phallus. His museum, reflecting the role of Venice as a museum to western culture, is a defense against chaos, a collection of fragments he has shored against the ruins of a society he views as undermined by a feminizing force that is bringing him, and patriarchy as a whole, face to face with loss.

His sisters tricked him into exposing his weakness for sugar, and by analogy, his femininity. For all that he appears to have succeeded in hobbling and imprisoning his wife where he was unable to control his siblings, she too views him as infantile, and he has been unable to make her the bearer of his sons. Robert explains to Colin that in his father's and grandfather's time, men "understood themselves clearly. They were men, and they were proud of their sex. [. . .] There was no confusion" (72). But now men are filled with self-doubt and women "treat men like children because they can't take them seriously" (72-73). Nobody, it would seem, benefits. His "recital" could be reworded: "I am confused. I don't believe in myself as a man, and Caroline treats me as a child because, for all that she is terrified of me, she cannot take me seriously." Robert must perform a masquerade of masculinity in order to retain the fantasy of the phallus as signifier of masculine potency in the face of the appalling abyss of the fantasy of the feminine. Constructed by castration and lack, he rigidly, as it were, maintains an active, sadistic position while unconsciously being drawn toward that of the passive masochist. Such a response has terrible repercussions: for all that Colin colludes in what happens, he dies because the misrecognized aim of Robert's unconscious drive is his own discovery and punishment.

In the last lines of the text, Mary sits beside her lover's body in the hospital mortuary, and begins to explain the story Caroline told her on the afternoon of the murder, and to extrapolate from that "her theory, tentative at this stage, of course, which explained how the imagination, the sexual imagination, men's ancient dreams of hurting, and women's of being hurt, embodied and declared a powerful single organizing principle, which distorted all relations, all truth" (125). But she loses the thread of her argument, rather as she repeatedly lost her way in the city. She lapses into silence and so any examination of the violence that underlies the trauma she has experienced is cut off, the possibility of change blocked. The text literally becomes silent too—it ends—but the challenge of McEwan's text is that *we* do not lose the thread, that we recognize the patterns by which we have narrated ourselves into being, since only then will we be able to undertake the task of "re-vision." Adrienne Rich states that we must recognize that a change in the concept of sexual identity is essential if there is to be a real shift in the old political order, and insists that for this to happen, we must reread and revision the past that has constructed us:

> Re-vision—the act of looking back, of seeing with fresh eyes, of entering an old text from a new critical direction—is [. . .] more than a chapter in cultural history: it is an act of survival. Until we can understand the assumptions in which we are drenched we cannot know ourselves. And this drive to self-knowledge [. . .] is part of our refusal of the self-destructiveness of male-dominated society. A radical critique of literature, feminist in its impulse, would take the work first of all as a clue to how we live, how we have been living, how we have been led to imagine ourselves, how our language has trapped as well as liberated us [. . .]. A change in the concept of sexual identity is essential if we are not going to see the old political order reassert itself in every new revolution. We need to know the writing of the past, and know it differently than we have ever known it; not to pass on a tradition but to break its hold over us.
>
> ("When" 35)

**The Comfort of Strangers** breaks off too, but McEwan's polemic is as urgent as Rich's or Mulvey's or Cornell's. Although he is writing fiction and "meaning" is veiled behind his gothic "tale," the narrative structure that foregrounds the violence of the "single organizing principle" that is patriarchal law and that equates remembering and revision with survival, means that it would be fatal to ignore the narratives of psychoanalysis; as Cornell insists ("What" 76), they provide a collection of "analytic tools" by means of which it is possible to critique and reimagine those aspects of social reality that have their basis in psychic fantasy.

*Notes*

1. In an interview a couple of years after the book was published, McEwan discussed at length eroticism and sadomasochism in relation to *The Comfort of Strangers* itself and also in the wider context of political theory and practice. He explained that in the novella he was attempting to address issues of the unconscious and the role of sadism and masochism, "which act out the oppression of women in patriarchal societies but which have actually become related to sources of pleasure," since to view relationships of power from a purely rational position as the effect of social forces alone means we are vulnerable to manipulation at the irrational, psychic level (qtd. in Haffenden 178). Lacan recognized the central importance of masochism to the psychic economy when he wrote ironically in his introduction to the seminar he called *The Ethics of Psychoanalysis* that "it would be a definite sign that we have really arrived at the heart of the problem of existing perversions, if we managed to deepen our understanding of the economic role of masochism," adding that "it is useful to give oneself a task that is unattainable" (15).

2. The epigraph McEwan chooses for *The Comfort of Strangers* comes from Rich's "Sibling Mysteries," published in *Dream of a Common Language* (1978): "how we dwelt in two worlds / the daughters and the mothers / in the kingdom of the sons" (*Dream* 49). (In a 1985 interview McEwan said of *Comfort*, "People of our generation, who grew up in the 1950s, grew up in the time of the fathers" [qtd. in Haffenden 179].) Rich's essay, a 1971 address to the MLA published in 1972, is not a direct intertext, but it was a central influence on feminist thinking at the time. It was reprinted in 1976, and collected in *On Lies, Secrets, and Silence* in 1979. Mulvey's "Visual Pleasure and Narrative Cinema" was first published in *Screen* in 1975.

3. When McEwan was his student, Angus Wilson said he especially liked his writing's "nastiness" (qtd. in Lawson 45). Reviewers have tended to respond less positively, and an almost prurient interest in his text's nastiness and the possibility that they mirror his own behavior has dogged him since his first volume of short stories was published in 1975. In a 1990 interview, McEwan exasperatedly pointed out how often reviews of his work focus on, and misread, a short violent scene as though it were the whole novel and, with an apparent refusal to take into account the power of the novelistic imagination, McEwan himself is portrayed by interviewers as "a trembling ghoul, who's just stepped away from some unspeakable

act." He gives as an example the dismemberment of a body in *The Innocent*, which is read neither in the context of the whole novel nor, metaphorically, in the context of a century of violence that has resulted in the dismemberment of Europe itself (Johnson 16).

4. Cornell's fascinating discussion of the indeterminacy of the sign is based on the semiotic theory of Charles Sanders Peirce (*Transformations*, esp. Ch. 2).

5. For McEwan it is the sense of Venice rather than the reality that counts, and he manipulates the city and its topography to suit his purpose: "The unnaming of Venice gave me, I thought at the time, a degree of descriptive freedom. I think I rotated parts of the city to catch the sunset. I also wanted to be set free of the place-name tedium that can bog down fictions set in real cities. Finally, an unnamed city was a better sink for C and M's vulnerability" (personal communication, 1 September 1996). He told John Haffenden in 1983 that from the beginning he found himself "to be describing the city in terms of a state of mind, and vice versa" (177). But, as Gaetano d'Elia and Christopher Williams note in discussing his deliberate decision to avoid topographical connotations, this is "senza ombra di dubbio la città di Venezia" (without a shadow of a doubt the city of Venice) (233): the Zattere, Palladio's Redentore church viewed from Colin and Mary's hotel on the Giudecca, the Fondamenta Nuove, the Piazza and Basilica of San Marco, the Lido and the island of San Michele are rendered with meticulous realism. And, as d'Elia and Williams note (233-36), he quotes, almost verbatim, the famous description of the domes and west facade of the Basilica from Ruskin's *The Stones of Venice* (2: 67; McEwan 49), but in keeping with the namelessness of the rest, he excises a reference to the Lido, and doesn't credit Ruskin. Interestingly, when Colin and Mary are not literally lost, their position in the city is clear to the reader—in their hotel on the Zattere, trying to get a glass of water in the Piazza San Marco—but when they are lost in the labyrinth, so is the reader. The area around Robert's bar, for example, seems to be Cannaregio but could as easily be Castello or even San Polo.

6. Intertextual repetition is a marked characteristic of twentieth-century Venetian fictions in general: in *The Passion* (1987), Jeanette Winterson's Henri recalls the French madman of Shelley's *Julian and Maddalo*; in *The Book of Mrs Noah* (1987), Michèle Roberts's narrator's fantasized underwater experiences in Venice recall the boundless crystal caverns imagined by Radcliffe's Emily during her visit to Venice in *The Mysteries of Udolpho*; the hero of Caryl Phillips's *The Nature of Blood* (1997) is a rereading of Shakespeare's Othello; and Coover's Pinocchio (*Pinocchio in Venice* [1991]) is wickedly reminiscent of Mann's Aschenbach. Each of these repetitions serves a particular purpose, but what is fascinating about McEwan's allusions to *Death in Venice* is a shared focus on the shaping influence of ancient tragedy, which he extends to an engagement with psychoanalysis's rereading of the oedipal narrative.

7. Mann's Tadzio is of course a child; Colin is adult, but he is repeatedly infantilized.

8. As Susan Suleiman puts it, "since all fantasy is ultimately *textual* [. . .] the subject of Sadean fantasy can be none other than the speaking subject of the Sadean sentence" (66).

9. The dreams Colin lists are even mentioned on the same page in *The Interpretation of Dreams*: "There is a fair amount of agreement, however, over the interpretation of various forms of dreams that are described as 'typical', because they occur in large numbers of people and with very similar content. Such are the familiar dreams of falling from a height, of teeth falling out, of flying and of embarrassment at being naked or insufficiently clad" (*Interpretation* 37).

10. My reading of Colin's body in terms of iconography employed in French neoclassical painting is influenced by Thomas Crow's work on that subject, including his paper "Observations on Style and History in French Painting of the Male Nude, 1785-1794," which uses these paintings as illustrations of shifts that occurred in the period in the depiction of classical subjects.

11. For Freud, of course, scopophilia is foreplay and properly should lead to intercourse; anything else risks perversion (*Three Essays* 156-57).

12. Lacan discusses Freud's insight that the sadomasochistic drive is directed toward the active sadistic subject. "*At what moment,* says Freud, *do we see the possibility of pain introduced into the sadomasochistic drive?*—the possibility of pain undergone by him who has become, at that moment, the subject of the drive. It is, he tells us, at the moment when the loop is closed, . . . when the subject has taken himself as the end, the terminus of the drive" (*Four Fundamentals* 183. The italics are Lacan's.). The loop to which he refers is the circular path of the drive which, rather than moving from sadistic subject to masochistic object, begins and ends with the subject.

13. The image has something of the haunting effect of the photographs in Cortázar's short story "Blow-Up" and, even more particularly, of the photographs in Antonioni's film of the same name.

14. The man in the boat is probably Robert, who has just taken the photograph he later shows to Mary.

15. Caroline emphasizes this point when she says that while Robert's childhood was "weird," he "exaggerates a lot, and turns his past into stories to tell at the bar" (108).

16. True to the Browningesque nature of his monologue, Robert casually reveals in this fantasy of hierarchies of power that his father was not actually an ambassador; he was not at the top of the diplomatic pecking order (108).

17. The ego is first and foremost a bodily ego; it is not merely a surface entity, but is itself the projection of a surface." Strachey's footnote to Freud's text adds: "I.e. the ego is ultimately derived from bodily sensations, chiefly from those springing from the surface of the body. It may thus be regarded as a mental projection of the surface of the body" (*Ego* 26).

## Works Cited

Brodsky, Joseph. *Watermark*. New York: Farrar, 1992.

Conrad, Joseph. *Heart of Darkness*. 1902. New York: Norton, 1971.

Coover, Robert. *Pinocchio in Venice*. London: Heinemann, 1991.

Cornell, Drucilla. *Transformations*. New York: Routledge, 1993.

———. "What is Ethical Feminism?" *Feminist Contentions: A Philosophical Exchange*. Ed. Seyla Benhabib, et al. New York: Routledge, 1995.

Cortázar, Julio. "Blow-Up." *Blow-Up and Other Stories*. 1967. Trans. Paul Blackburn. New York: Pantheon, 1985. 114-31.

Crow, Thomas. "Observations on Style and History in French Painting of the Male Nude, 1785-1794." *Visual Culture: Images and Interpretations*. Ed. Norman Bryson, Michael Ann Holly, and Keith Moxey. Hanover, NH: UP of New England, 1994. 141-67.

d'Elia, Gaetano, and Christopher Williams. *La Nuova Letteratura Inglese: Ian McEwan*. Fasano, Italy: Schena, 1986.

Freud, Sigmund. *The Standard Edition of the Complete Psychological Works*. 18 vols. Ed. and trans. James Strachey. London: Hogarth, 1953-74.

———. Beyond the Pleasure Principle. (*SE*) 1920. 18:1-64.

———. "A Child Is Being Beaten." (*SE*) 1917-19. 17:177-204.

———. "The Economic Problem of Masochism." (*SE*) 1924. 19:157-70.

———. *The Ego and the Id*. (*SE*) 1923. 19:1-66.

———. *The Interpretation of Dreams*. (*SE*) 1900. 4 and 5.

———. *Three Essays on the Theory of Sexuality*. (*SE*) 1905. 7:123-245.

Haffenden, John. *Novelists in Interview*. London: Methuen, 1985.

Jameson, Fredric. *Postmodernism, or, The Cultural Logic of Late Capitalism*. Durham: Duke UP, 1991.

Johnson, Daniel. "The Timeless and the Timely Child." *The Times Saturday Review*. 8 December 1990: 16-17.

Lacan, Jacques. *The Four Fundamentals of Psychoanalysis*. 1977. Ed. Jacques-Alain Miller. Trans. Alan Sheridan. Harmondsworth, England: Penguin, 1979.

———. *The Ethics of Psychoanalysis 1959-1960: The Seminar of Jacques Lacan Book VII*. Ed. Jacques-Alain Miller. Trans. Dennis Porter. New York: Norton, 1992.

Laclau, Ernesto. "The Impossibility of Society." *Canadian Journal of Political and Social Theory* 7.1 and 2 (1983): 21-24.

Lawson, Mark. "Innocent Victim." *The Independent Magazine*. 28 April 1990: 44-45.

Lefevbre, Henri. *The Production of Space*. Trans. Donald Nicholson-Smith. Oxford: Blackwell, 1991.

Lynch, Kevin. *The Image of the City*. Cambridge, MA: Technology, 1960.

Mann, Thomas. *Death in Venice and Seven Other Stories*. Trans. H. T. Lowe-Porter. 1954. New York: Vintage, 1989.

McEwan, Ian. *The Comfort of Strangers*. 1981. London: Picador, 1982.

———. Letter to Judith Seaboyer. 1 Sept. 1996.

Mulvey, Laura. "Visual Pleasure and Narrative Cinema." 1975. *Visual and Other Pleasures*. Bloomington: Indiana UP, 1989.

Norwich, John Julius. *A History of Venice*. 1982. London: Penguin, 1983.

Pacteau, Francette. "The Impossible Referent: Representations of the Androgyne." *Formations of Fantasy*. Ed. Victor Burgin, James Donald, and Cora Kaplan. London: Methuen, 1986. 62-84.

Phillips, Caryl. *The Nature of Blood*. New York: Knopf, 1997.

Reed, T. J. *Thomas Mann: The Uses of Tradition*. London: Oxford UP, 1974.

Rich, Adrienne. *The Dream of a Common Language.* New York: Norton, 1978. 33-49.

———. "When We Dead Awaken: Writing as Re-Vision." 1972. *On Lies, Secrets, and Silence: Selected Prose 1966-1978.* 1979. London: Virago, 1980.

Ricks, Christopher. "Playing with Terror." *London Review of Books.* 21 Jan.-3 Feb. 1982: 13-14.

Ruskin, John. *The Stones of Venice.* 1851-53. 3 vols. London: George Allen, 1905.

Silverman, Kaja. *Male Subjectivity at the Margins.* London: Routledge, 1992.

———. *The Threshold of the Visible World.* London: Routledge, 1996.

Suleiman, Susan Robin. *Subversive Intent: Gender, Politics, and the Avant-Garde.* Cambridge: Harvard UP, 1990.

Winterson, Jeanette. *The Passion.* 1987. New York: Vintage, 1989.

**Gabriele Annan (review date 14 January 1999)**

SOURCE: Annan, Gabriele. "Wages of Sin." *New York Review of Books* 46, no. 1 (14 January 1999): 7-8.

[*In the following review, Annan commends* Amsterdam, *praising it as a "savage farce" and an "indictment of human nature." Annan also lauds McEwan's descriptive skills, scientific acumen, and portrayal of children.*]

Ian McEwan is a prize winner. His novels and stories have won the Somerset Maugham Award and the Whitbread Prize, and have been shortlisted for Britain's most hyped trophy, the Booker Prize. This year he won it with *Amsterdam.* When the award was made in October, there were murmurs that it must have been an act of reparation by this year's Booker judges for their predecessors' mistake: the 1997 prize should have gone to McEwan for *Enduring Love,* which was thought to be a much meatier, longer and more profound novel. *Amsterdam* is an intricate satirical *jeu d'esprit* and topical to the point of Tom Wolfeishness. It is also funnier than anything McEwan has written before, though just as lethal.

Death always figures in his work. In his heart-rending (but ultra-cool) first novel, *The Cement Garden,* a mother dies and her four young children bury her in a box of cement in the basement: their father died some time before, and they realize that if her death becomes known, they will be separated and sent to orphanages. In *The Innocent,* a couple of lovers accidentally kill the woman's violent divorced husband in self-defense. McEwan devotes many pages to their methodical dismembering of the body ("There was a glutinous sound which brought him the memory of a jelly eased from its mould") and the difficulties of its disposal. Reviewing *Enduring Love* (which opens sensationally with a man killed falling from a balloon) in these pages last April, Rosemary Dinnage remarked that "among the critical praise that festoons his book jackets, the word 'macabre' crops up more than once." But until *Amsterdam,* McEwan's macabre has not been merely "grim, gruesome" (OED); not been like, say, Genet's. There have been hints of the supernatural. His novels are spooky—particularly *Enduring Love* and *The Child in Time,* which is, among other things, about second sight.

So what happened when McEwan won this year's Booker Prize seemed as strange as one of his own plots—as though he himself had second sight, in fact. On the very day it was announced, a ministerial scandal broke in the British press and the subsequent events developed along lines uncannily like the story of *Amsterdam.* In fact as in fiction, a government minister resigned because of a harmless sexual indiscretion. The real-life minister went home with a stranger he met on Clapham Common, a known homosexual beat. He was robbed at knife-point and blackmailed. He informed the police, the affair became public, and he chose to resign. In *Amsterdam,* McEwan's foreign secretary is forced to resign because photographs of him in drag appear on the front page of a national paper. What makes the coincidence even stranger is that as the real-life events in Britain faded from the front page, a story broke about the birth of Siamese twins: it happens in *Amsterdam* as well.

Julian Garmony, the foreign secretary in *Amsterdam,* is a bland right-wing monster, a hanger and flogger who wants to keep immigrants and asylum seekers out of Britain. (McEwan usually manages to introduce an element of anti-Thatcherism, most notably in *The Child in Time,* where each chapter is preceded by an excerpt from a spoof Thatcherite, ultra-disciplinarian "Authorised Childcare Handbook"). There is a danger that Garmony might be the next prime minister. So Vernon Halliday, the editor of a national paper, decides to use the photographs to ruin his career: he convinces himself that this is a noble cause. But his motives are mixed: he needs to raise a falling circulation, and the Garmony scoop would make it zoom.

There is a lot of opposition from the old-guard journalists on the paper, who feel that Vernon has been dragging it down-market since he took over after, the previous editor was sacked. They are dismayed at the proposed invasion of Garmony's privacy. (In Britain at this moment, you couldn't find more topical subjects than invasion of privacy and the vulgarization of the press. Vernon is frantic with indecision, and seeks the advice of his oldest friend. Clive Linley: Clive sides with the older journalists. Besides, he points out, publishing the photographs would be a betrayal of the adorable woman who took them. She is called Molly, and the book begins with her funeral. The wife of the millionaire George Lane, a shareholder in Vernon's paper, she died in her forties of a degenerative disease.

George owns the photographs, is keen to sell them, and urges Vernon to publish them. Molly had had a great many affairs, including twice each with Vernon and Clive, and once with Garmony, she remained on the warmest terms with all three. Sentimental nostalgia for her affects them all. The plot here is pure Feydeau, except for Molly's horrible death, which is pure McEwan, who is given to dwelling on physical horrors especially deterioration, decay, decomposition, putrefaction. It is not the only plot, though: *Amsterdam* is a thriller as well as a farce, with a plot whose extreme convolution and plethora of unlikely coincidences reads as a sendup of the thriller genre.

It is also an ethical duel between Clive and Vernon, neither of whom is ethically motivated at all, though both like to think they are. Clive is a composer of independent means, and his morality is actually the fat-cat fastidiousness of a spoiled, conceited man who thinks he may be a genius. He is currently absorbed in a commission for a "Millennial Symphony" to have its premiere shortly. As for Vernon, the general view of him is that he does "not fully exist. Within his profession Vernon was revered as a nonentity." Neither Clive nor Vernon is likable or even charming. Both are hypochondriacs, and thoughts of Molly's grisly demise bring on suspicious tingling sensations and feelings of numbness in both of them. Without disclosing their disquieting symptoms to each other, they make a suicide pact: each promises that if his friend becomes incapacitated, he will make the necessary arrangements with a euthanasia specialist in Holland.

But their argument about the photographs turns nasty; they fall out, and each seizes a chance to stab the other in the back, with the result that Vernon gets the sack. As for Clive, rage at Vernon's perfidy destroys his concentration and he fails to get together the finale for his symphony—which therefore later turns out to be a flop. Its première, by a British orchestra, is only a week ahead. The orchestra is currently performing in Holland, so Clive flies to Amsterdam for rehearsals. Vernon follows him, and the suicide pact turns into a reciprocal murder by medical syringe. One isn't, of course, meant to believe in this far-fetched scenario. *Amsterdam* is a savage farce about horrible people, whose every motive is flawed—and that goes for the minor characters as well, except the dead Molly. They are all hypocrites, adept at finding ways of living with any bad conscience they might have. The old-guard journalist who overcomes his objections and finally backs Vernon about publishing the photographs is typical of all the rest. After Vernon is fired, "he was heard to say in the canteen that once his misgivings were not listened to, he did his best to be loyal. By Monday they had all remembered their misgivings and how they had all tried to be loyal." McEwan is a super-sleuth when it comes to digging up bad motivation.

*Amsterdam* is an indictment of human nature, with special reference to the Sixties generation to which Clive and Vernon belong—and all the other players too (except for the ruthless young journalist who steps into Vernon's shoes).

> Nurtured in the postwar settlement with the state's own milk and juice, and then sustained by their parents' tentative, innocent prosperity, to come of age in full employment, new universities, bright paperback books, the Augustan age of rock and roll, affordable ideals. When the ladder crumbled behind them, when the state withdrew her tit and became a scold, they were already safe, they consolidated and settled down to forming this and that—taste, opinion, fortunes.

Because *Amsterdam* is cast as a farce, McEwan can be even more judgmental than usual. Moral judgment is a built-in component of his stories, which often feature a woman whose wisdom and exemplary behavior show up the callousness or just the wetness and confusion of the men. His women are also much better at loving than their partners. McEwan can write about love with a rare combination of delighted surprise and specificity that gives it an unusual sheen; and he is brilliant at writing about children—though when he writes about babies, especially dead, unborn, or aborted ones, the pathos can be excessive.

There is no scope for any of this in *Amsterdam,* or really for the lyrical evocation of nature that is, another of McEwan's specialties. Perhaps that is why a longish Wordsworthian interlude doesn't come off. Clive goes to the Lake District to seek inspiration for the finale of his symphony, and his walk in the hills turns out rather tedious—overlong and overloaded with the names of mountains and dales that can't evoke much for anyone who hasn't been there. On the other hand Clive's compositional problems and tactics are made so clear that one can almost hear the score as well as see it go down on the ruled paper. McEwan knows about composing music: he wrote the words for Michael Berkeley's oratorio *Or Shall We Die?* And he enjoys displaying his expertise. In *The Innocent* it was electronic engineering and tunneling; in *The Child in Time,* relativity theory; and in *Enduring Love,* evolutionary genetics, psychiatry and physics. In *Amsterdam* one gets not only music but also journalism: the daily hypertension of the editorial meeting.

McEwan is among the most idiosyncratic of British novelists, even if he doesn't seem interested in experimental writing. His prose is precise and revelatory, and whatever he writes about comes up fresh, luminous, and surprising, like a familiar painting recently cleaned. An example: Clive glimpses an old black woman "folded double" with osteoporosis. If she were just "bent" double, one wouldn't notice her; "folded" evokes her pathos and makes her visible. She gets only one sentence for her walk-on appearance, but she fulfills her purpose, which is to evoke pathos at that point in the story. The contrast between McEwan's superclean prose and lay-preacher stance on the one hand, and his steamy, ghoulish, tender, sometimes even mawkish subject matter and moods on the other, make him dangerously attractive and repellent at the same time.

## Jago Morrison (essay date spring 2001)

SOURCE: Morrison, Jago. "Narration and Unease in Ian McEwan's Later Fiction." *Critique* 42, no. 3 (spring 2001): 253-68.

[*In the following essay, Morrison examines aspects of time, gender identity, and historical memory in* Black Dogs *and* Enduring Love, *particularly as informed by Paul Ricoeur's* Time and Narrative *and the feminist theory of Julia Kristeva.*]

For a generation of well-established postmodernist writers in Britain, the exploration of narrative as the containment and control of temporal experience is of central importance. What makes Ian McEwan's writing especially worthy of attention is the way in which his experimentation with time and narrative is interlinked with the rethinking of gender identity. The early stories *First Love, Last Rites* (1975) and *In Between the Sheets* (1979) contained troubled and claustrophobic examinations of emergent masculinity. However, his novels from the 1980s onward contain an increasingly confident investment in gender as the central problematic through which the agency of the male writer can be reimagined in relation to both time and social space.

Perhaps the starkest example of this strategy can be traced in McEwan's anti-nuclear oratorio *Or Shall We Die?* (1983). Here the key mother-and-child image iconic to the oratorio form is set up directly against the paradigm of "mastery" and war. A working opposition is clearly established between a masculine-identified trajectory toward destruction, epitomized by the experience of the Cold War, and the promise of salvation in "womanly times" (23), characterized as an amalgamation of maternal empathy and (in an unexamined paradox) the post-positivistic Einsteinean legacy in science. Femininity, however, is not naturalized through conventional characterization but is broadened and abstracted as an alternate paradigm of temporal and social understanding. Thus gender becomes the focus in McEwan's work for a distinctive response to existing political and historical conditions:

> Shall there be womanly times, or shall we die?
> [. . .]
> Can we have strength without aggression,
> without disgust,
> strength to bind feeling to the intellect?
>
> (23)

In *The Child in Time* this stylized use of gender as an approach to the political is developed much further, with the ideological obsessions of the Thatcherite right ironically reduced to the pathos of prepubescent male anxiety. In this novel again, a feminine principle of empathy or insight and the New Physics are clearly conflated, most obviously through the figure of Thelma, a woman scientist. In a far more complex way than was possible in the oratorio, however, the quantum notions of complementarity and relative time have in this text become an organizing principle for the rethinking of masculinity in relation to the dissolution of the nuclear family. For example, the key confrontation between the protagonist Stephen and his mother is narrated at a moment before his own birth, when he is both adult and foetus combined. The loss of Stephen's daughter at the beginning of the novel and the subsequent breakup of his marriage are similarly framed around themes of temporal disjunction: catatonia, obsession, and infantile regression on the part of the male-identified characters, contrasted with a therapy through music, landscape, and study schematically identified as a "womanly" alternative. *The Child in Time,* therefore, can be seen as establishing very clearly in McEwan's work the development of a gendered framework for understanding social and personal time, with this negotiation written through the experimental form of the narrative itself as well as through its particular thematic foci.

In this essay I explore the way in which McEwan extends this distinctive engagement with time, narrative, and gender within his texts in two of his most recent novels, *Enduring Love* and *Black Dogs.* In *Enduring Love,* with Joe Rose's precious picnic of focaccia, black olives, and 1987 Daumas Gassac, we are aware almost immediately that here the stake in McEwan's wager on narrativity will be the constitution of a moneyed, successful masculinity. Indeed, the novel opens with the symbolic emasculation of its protagonist, his heroic impulses immediately revealed as banal and redundant in a bungled attempt to save a child from a ballooning accident. Like McEwan's earliest writings, the focus of *Enduring Love* is personal and claustrophobic. In *Black Dogs,* however, McEwan's canvas is much larger. With a narrative that spans the experience of two generations, there is a much stronger concentration here on the notion of femininity as a possible response to the vaster impasse of time and historicality associated with the postmodern. Moving alternately in and out of the linear writing conventions of biography, history, and chronology, the structure of McEwan's writing in this novel forms a spiral of meaning as much as it forms the familiar continuity of linear narration. At the same time, as the novel draws on the postmodernist thematics of dislocation and fragmentation, however, there is also an assertion of the risks or the costs implied by the epistemological breakdown and relativity with which postmodernist writing seems often to be so comfortable. Thus in the postwar setting of McEwan's novel, the all-too-canonical suggestion of amnesia as a defining feature of the postmodern condition is at the same time thrown into sharp and uncomfortable relief against the political and historical imperatives of the Holocaust and of neo-Nazi resurgence in Europe.

I

In contrast to the explicit political engagement of some of his earlier works, *Enduring Love* is striking for what seems like a loss of confidence in relation to the broad discourses of politics and history, a narrowing of narrative horizons and a return to personal obsessions. Certainly, in its negotiation of narrative form and of masculinity alike, *Enduring Love* is not a text of affirmation. Instead, its articulation of unease about the efficacy of both is everywhere apparent within the novel. The focus is on a successful writer whose comfortable family and professional life is challenged by the attentions of a fanatical male admirer. Above all, the novel depicts a scrabbling for security, as the protagonist seeks to bring the force of the law and of psychiatric medicine to bear on his unwelcome pursuer. However, the surge of panic that structures and consumes this text does not arise from any threat to his material security. Rather, the intruder needs to be seen as the catalyst for a panic that emerges from the more basic crisis that the novel discloses in the relationship between its privileged male subject and the public narratives of science, medicine, and law that are supposed to constitute and to defend his embattled masculinity.

At the end of the text, McEwan appends case notes and a fully reproduced and referenced journal article on de Clérambault's syndrome, the condition with which the "fanatic" Parry is ultimately identified. With its trappings of medical-scientific legitimacy, this appendix seems, on one level, to provide a sense of security and closure for the text. Such scientifically ratified documentation should represent an epistemological anchor for the narrative, locating its exploration and confirmation of masculine identity within the real. Approaching this documentation from our retrospective position as readers, we see the function and meaning of McEwan's novel very clearly on one level. Within the legitimizing discourse of science, both the standard of a "normal" masculinity and narrativity as a privileged mode of its articulation have been secured.

On another level, however, the text specifically invites our incredulity toward this grand narrative of male affirmation. As Umberto Eco suggests in his commentary *Reflections on "The Name of the Rose,"* it is necessary to distinguish between the possibility of what we might call the naïve and informed readings simultaneously facilitated by postmodernist writing. In Eco's scheme, the more informed reader might usefully be thought of as a "meta-reader," who reads not only through the text but also above it, who is alive to quotation, intertextuality, self-reflexivity, and epistemological insecurity. To read *Enduring Love* in this sense, then, is first of all to identify the spuriousness of McEwan's appended documentation. From the moment we start to dig around in the text, the very specificity of the references in McEwan's appended article invites the realization that these case notes and this entire academic journal are dissimulated continuations of the main fiction. In that sense *Enduring Love* mirrors directly the "scholarly" appendix that concludes Margaret Atwood's novel *The Handmaid's Tale,* which invites us to consider both the problematic status of Offred's account as a document and the violence implicit in her "historicization" within academic discourse. Similarly, the insertion of these fake fragments of psychiatric medicine in *Enduring Love* appears to an informed reader as a strangely overdetermined gesture of legitimation. With a characteristic postmodernist duplicity, McEwan's protagonist himself has already explicitly allowed for this possibility: "De Clérambault's syndrome was a dark, distorting mirror that reflected and parodied a brighter world of lovers whose reckless abandon to their cause was sane. [. . .] In other words, what could I learn about Parry that would restore me to Clarissa?" (128).

Taking those reading possibilities together, McEwan-Joe's appendices must be considered as presenting us *both* with the neutrality of information *and* with the knowledge of its duplicity. On a simple level, the novel educates us about a pathology of gender. As Joe suggests: "For there to be a pathology there had to be a lurking concept of health" (128). In that sense, these discursive fragments work to articulate in reverse the notion of a stable and healthful masculinity, a hegemonic narrative of gender identity within which the protagonist is able to reappear as the privileged subject. On a second level, however, in relation to his domestic status as a successful heterosexual male, the citation of a spurious psychiatric discourse in McEwan's text illustrates the instrumentality of that discourse in resecuring the privileged professional male as the standard of psycho-sexual normalcy. In terms of our informed reading, the reverse side of this coin is the destabilizing effects those appended fragments introduce into the narrative fabric of the novel. Understood in Eco's first sense, they seem to represent within the broader structure of the text a confirmation of the fruitful continuum between the writing and reading of literary narrative and the understanding of the world of the real. In Eco's second or "meta" reading, however, by disclosing the epistemological crisis on the underside of narration, they seem rather to display the opposite. Over the shoulder of the narrator, against the grain of their own intentionality, they precipitate a knowledge of narrative dislocation, mirroring exactly the dislocation of a privileged masculinity with which the novel is centrally concerned.

Throughout McEwan's text, narrative, symbolized and encapsulated in the appended, concentrated text of this case study, is clearly foregrounded as the means through which rationality, identity, and especially a sense of temporal coherence repeatedly try to establish themselves. At the beginning of the text, as Joe and Clarissa attempt to come to terms with the ballooning accident and death they have witnessed, there is an instant tension between the forces of narration and those of meditation or repetition, specifically polarized along gender lines. Narrativization is implicitly posed as the means of containment and control that represents one half of this dichotomy: "so much repetition that evening of the incidents, and of our perceptions, and of the very phrases and words we honed to accommodate them that one could only assume that an element of ritual was in play, that these were not only descriptions but incantations also" (28). In a refiguration of the gendered opposition set up in McEwan's earlier work, moreover, we can see in place here, from the outset, the idea of a schism between the (male) protagonist's reliance on a therapy through narrative and his (female) partner's quite different desire to envision an encapsulating image:

> A little later we were back in our seats, leaning over the table like dedicated craftsmen at work, grinding the jagged edge of memories, hammering the unspeakable into forms of words, threading single perceptions into narrative, until Clarissa returned us to the fall, to the precise moment when Logan had slid down the rope, hung there one last precious second, and let go. This was what she had to get back to, the image to which her shock had attached itself.
>
> (30)

Narrativity is strongly identified as the medium through which Joe articulates his own masculine knowledge and agency. A science writer, his journalistic work is alternately a narration of scientific advances for popular understanding and an exploration of the death of narrative in science. Through narrative, very consciously, he both succeeds and fails to address the disruption precipitated by the fanatic Parry. Indeed, the text presents itself on a literal level as the record of that highly self-conscious struggle of narrativization. At the same time, however, the instability and disjunction potentially implicit in narration are constantly foregrounded: "I've already marked my beginning, the explosion of consequences. [. . .] But this pinprick is as notional as a point in Euclidean geometry [. . .]" (17). In Joe's intricate attempts to defend and justify his hegemonic subject positioning through narrative, we witness at the same time the increasing erosion and destabilization of his psychic and social world.

This text, then, is engaged in unpacking the assumption of a continuity between the socially legitimized grand-narratives of legality and medicine and the positioning of the privileged male subject. The public discourse of criminality, Joe painfully discovers, is not invoked as easily as he presumed against a diffuse and enigmatic threat to his person. The narrative of psychiatric knowledge requires articulation and ratification within the overdetermined frameworks of case study, public record, and predictability before it can be deployed as a weapon of policing and confinement. Instead, in the ironic twist of the novel's main text, we unwillingly discover that only the banal narrative of male violence can be engaged with ease. In *The Innocent* (1990) McEwan plays with and discards the genre of the spy thriller, with a tunneling project in postwar Berlin whose sexual overtones become increasingly and alarmingly apparent within the novel; in *Enduring Love* the generic quotation we encounter is that of the hard-boiled investigator, of a masculinity that is both orthodox and marginal, operating on the edge of the social, whose legality and stability are constantly in question:

> Clarissa thought I was mad, the police thought I was a fool, and one thing was clear: the task of getting us back to where we were was going to be mine alone.
>
> (161)

The very banality of this pivotal plot line—Joe rescues his frightened partner from the clutches of the knife-wielding erotomaniac by blowing off his elbow with a handgun—foregrounds what we might usefully denote as the postmodernist dynamics of this text, in relation to which our assent as readers is simultaneously demanded and withdrawn. At the moment we are encouraged to empathize, we are also encouraged to recoil and critique. On a simple level, *Enduring Love* narrates the triumph of an orthodox masculinity in restoring the protagonist's own identity and position within the nuclear family. At the same time, however, it also illustrates the breakdown within a text of the narratives of legality and mental health of which the professional, rational, solvent male is supposed to be the subject.

## II

For Paul Ricoeur in *Time and Narrative,* the function of narrative in relation to the everyday living of social and personal lives is to reflect and to affirm the coherence of temporal experience. Thus, according to Ricoeur, "time becomes human to the extent that it is articulated through a narrative mode, and narrative attains its full meaning when it becomes a condition of temporal existence" (1:52). Between the vast scheme of cosmic time, the meaning-laden scale of the historical, and the private, fluctuating experience of personal time, there is the potential for discordance. The task of narrative is to cement a continuum between those three orders of time perception. It could be argued that narrative in Ricoeur's scheme has a fundamentally conservative function. Arising out of "a pre-understanding of the world of action, its meaningful structures, its symbolic resources" (54) and mediating between those and the experience of the reader, narrative over and over rehearses and reproduces the hegemonic time frame. It ensures a comfortable continuum between our understanding of the cosmic or absolute, our sense of our historical placing, and the texture of our everyday experience.

Ricoeur's analysis becomes a problem in terms of the relatively unreconstructed commitment he frequently retains both to the universalistic properties of literature and to a notion of the author as *auteur,* self-determined designer of a work and of the readerly experience. Both of those critical tendencies emerge strongly, for example, in the analysis of *Mrs Dalloway* in volume 3. By the same token, there is little admission of the possibility that literary texts might also be deemed valuable and important for their articulation of ruptures, shifts, and discontinuities within the cultural and ideological fabric. Considering the negotiation of time in ***Enduring Love,*** however, it is nevertheless possible to see the usefulness of Ricoeur, not least in terms of his tripartite structure of understanding for time. The challenge posed by Parry to the security of the protagonist Joe can certainly be read on three levels, broadly mirroring the analysis proposed in *Time and Narrative.* First, Parry's stalking and harassment disrupt the fabric of Joe's personal life, in terms of his habitual work patterns and day-to-day routines. That threat on the one hand erodes his capacity to deploy the hours of the day usefully and, as important, on the other hand threatens his capacity to escape this level of consciousness into that other fundamental temporal experience, a necessary, undistracted state of intellectual concentration, "the high-walled infinite prison of directed thought" (48). Second, Parry's insistent intrusion precipitates pivotal crises in the larger narratives of Joe's family life and particularly in his professional life, the level at which personal experience interfaces with the public sphere. The stable relationship with Clarissa breaks down, and Joe finds himself compelled to re-assess the direction and value of his vocation as a writer. Finally, on a third and higher level, Parry's powerful imposition of a Christian teleology functions as a direct challenge to the temporal constitution of Joe's larger scientific and evolutionary belief system.

The response Joe's narrative initially articulates toward this complex onslaught, moreover, can be seen as an attempt at a closer marriage between the levels of his temporal consciousness. That appears most obviously in the move to abandon his career as a journalist—a mere mediator of knowledge—in favor of a re-entry into the metanarrative of scientific research, "carrying my own atomic increment to the mountain of human knowledge" (75). The continuum between his science-defined cosmic understanding and the narrative of his professional life is thus to be cemented more firmly. As a journalist, Joe's meditation on the role of narrative in science has raised some uncomfortable questions, not only about the sanctity of scientific knowledge in relation to the history of the cosmos, but also about the status and meaning of his own career in relation to the history of science. The attempt to abandon that and to re-enter the research community offers an easy refusal of both those sets of questions, precisely because it offers the possibility of re-establishing a narrative coherence between the different levels of his temporal world.

The ultimate failure of Joe's attempt at ontological self-defense, through the failure of his research bid, leads to the necessity for the alternate strategy that dominates McEwan's text—the more violent narrativization of Parry himself. It is in this sense that ***Enduring Love*** is "about" de Clérambault's syndrome. Through the syndrome, the novel identifies the power of medical-scientific discourse as a guarantor of temporal and epistemological security. In a social sense, the appended documents are significant because they cast Parry into a ratified linear-narrative framework that carries the force of juridical and disciplinary power. On a personal level, moreover, what de Clérambault offers Joe is a surrogate solution to his own sense of temporal dislocation:

> The name was like a fanfare, a clear trumpet sound recalling me to my own obsessions. There was research to follow through now and I knew exactly where to start. A syndrome was a framework of prediction and it offered a kind of comfort. I was almost happy. [. . .] It was as if I had at last been offered that research post with my old professor.
>
> (124)

Nevertheless, it is within this process that the affinity between the urges of narrativization and those of obsession is gradually and inexorably suggested in the text. In his journalistic role, Joe's own discursive practice involves a deployment of narrative as mediation: "People say I have a talent for clarity. I can spin a decent narrative out of the stumblings, back-trackings and random successes that lie behind most scientific breakthroughs. It's true, someone has to go between the researcher and the general public, giving the higher-order explanations that the average laboratory worker is too busy, or too cautious, to indulge" (75). In the course of the text, however, that professional penchant for the ordering and rationalization of the disordered becomes radically extended. While Joe labors with the enigmatic and allusive discourse of Parry's letters, cutting and pasting them into the deepening narrative of a threat (which he can then take to the police), the parallel suggestion is developed of the symbiotic relationship between Parry's intrusion and the neurosis implicit in Joe's own consciousness. For Joe, Clarissa's perception of Parry is cast in precisely those terms. "He was the kind of phantom that only I could have called up, a spirit of my dislocated, incomplete character, or what she fondly called my innocence" (102). Parry needs to be assimilated and contained within the narrative of criminality, and later of psychiatric disorder, before he can be policed and contained on a bodily level. On one level, the novel is the story of Joe's success in that endeavor. What emerges in his attempts to articulate Parry's deviancy is, nevertheless, as strong a conviction of his own obsessionality:

> Three times I crossed the street towards him with my hidden tape recorder turning, but he would not stay.
>
> "Clear off then!" I shouted at his retreating back. "Stop hanging around here. Stop bothering me with your stupid letters." Come back and talk to me, was what I really meant. Come back and face the hopelessness of your cause and issue your unveiled threats. Or phone them in. Leave them on my message machine. [. . .] I daydreamed violent confrontations that always fell out in my favour.
>
> (143-44)

### III

In her essay "Women's Time," Julia Kristeva offers a critical perspective for understanding time and narrative through gender, providing a clear context to the narrative strategies that we see in McEwan's writing. In parallel with the experimentation, we can identify in *The Child in Time* and *Enduring Love,* Kristeva develops a clear association between the notion of narrative linearity and the notion of obsession. She argues that feminists have articulated a problem with the dominant "conception of linear temporality, which is readily labelled masculine and which is at once both civilizational and obsessional" (447). Outlining the possibility of a number of alternative feminist responses to hegemonic ideas of national and personal identity, she sets out a clear gender framework for understanding temporal organization. In relation to *Black Dogs* in particular, Kristeva's implied schematic opposition between intuition, mystical vision, and female subjectivity on the one hand and "male-stream" linear rationality on the other—an opposition she finds in need of significant renegotiation—offers clear lines of critical engagement:

> In return, female subjectivity as it gives itself up to intuition becomes a problem with respect to a certain conception of time: time as project, teleology, linear and prospective unfolding; time as departure, progression and arrival-in other words, the time of history. It has already been abundantly demonstrated that this kind of temporality [. . .] renders explicit a rupture, as expectation, or an anguish which other temporalities work to conceal.
>
> (446)

For Kristeva the understanding of Europe in particular needs to be reconsidered in terms of its constitution in memory and historicality. Just as we can see with McEwan's protagonists, Kristeva suggests that for a new generation of feminists there is a need to negotiate *between* the time of narrative and history associated with the male and the problematic of the matrix space and the temporalities of repetition and eternity associated with the female.

In novels such as ***Black Dogs*** and ***Enduring Love,*** which center on the epistemological and existential problems of masculinity, the kind of gendered understanding of narrative, history, and biography that Kristeva proposes is highly applicable. With a far broader narrative scope than that of ***Enduring Love,*** McEwan's novel ***Black Dogs*** can be read directly in terms of its exploration of the problematic of historical memory through an explicitly gendered framework. More specifically, we see again in this novel an oscillation between the poles of intuition and rationalism, personified through the relationship of two of its central characters. Characteristically for McEwan's fiction, a male narrator becomes the focus of the text's attempt to negotiate a new understanding of personal and social time by mediating between these feminine- and masculine-identified modes of seeing and remembering:

> Rationalist and mystic, commissar and yogi, joiner and abstainer, scientist and intuitionist, Bernard and June are the extremities, the twin poles along whose slippery axis my own unbelief slithers and never comes to rest.
>
> (19)

The ability of narrative itself to articulate successfully and to preserve what needs to be remembered, as in both ***The Child in Time*** and in ***Enduring Love,*** is explicitly questioned in ***Black Dogs.*** Through the medium of a memoir, the novel follows its narrator Jeremy and his struggles to find or force coherence between radically disparate strands of temporal understanding: not only the biographical past of his mother-in-law June and the larger historical frame of World War Two but also the Holocaust and its legacy, the deterministic historicism of her postwar socialism and the universalist, visionary consciousness that remains her final, most defining feature. As Angela Rogers argues in "Ian McEwan's Portrayal of Women," to read McEwan's treatment of femininity in terms of authenticity of characterization may well be to find his work wanting—indeed Rogers's essay is oriented toward precisely such a conclusion. The serious limitation of that critical approach, however, is that it fails to recognize fully the role and use of gender in McEwan's writing, not as the medium of naturalistic narration but rather as the structural focus for a broader spiral of temporal and historical concerns. The strategy of McEwan's text is to pivot a plurality of narrative threads on a clear central moment. Indeed, **Black Dogs** turns on the simplest of parables, a girl frightened on a country path by a pair of dogs; all other narrative concerns are twisted and woven around that central motif.

Drawing again on Ricoeur, I have already implicitly characterized the task of narrative here, of Jeremy's memoir, as that of needing to find simplicity, security, and coherence between the dislocated levels of the temporal—the historical, the cosmic, and the personal. McEwan's text continually discloses something less reassuring: not the ease and potency of narrative as a guarantor of memory and of knowledge, but rather that it is barely adequate for this task. According to Ricoeur, historical narrative itself needs to be understood only as a "knowledge by traces" (3: 120). The construction of historical meaning must be conceived as the retrospective inscription of causal sequence on otherwise enigmatic marks of passage, a summary appropriation of traces or vestiges of something that has passed or is past. In **Black Dogs** even more strongly than in **Enduring Love,** we see in Jeremy's memoir the problems and the labor of forming that narrative chain, as well as the enigmatic quality of the trace itself.

First, the articulation of June's life as a linear development is constantly frustrated by the complexity and discontinuity of her consciousness, within which not biographical or historical causality but the coordinating force field of a central image or parable, the black dogs, dominates the alignments of her life and understanding as powerfully as a magnet under paper:

> As far as June was concerned, it was to be the centrepiece of my memoir, just as it was in her own story of her life—the defining moment, the experience that redirected, the revealed truth by whose light all previous conclusions must be rethought.
>
> (50)

Within the distinctive mode of June's understanding through insight and revision is an attempt to encapsulate in the central parable or vision something that is simultaneously meaningful on a personal, historical, and cosmic level. But the success of that endeavor is never clear. Second, in Bernard's Berlin experience we find an attempt to negotiate between those same elements, between the historicality of the Wall's demolition, the mystic identification between the young girl Greta and his dead wife, and the personal consummation represented by his courage in standing against racism at the close of an era. His experience is not offered as one of affirmation, however, but one closer to humiliation.

The progression of the various episodes of the novel, from Berlin in 1989 to Majdanek in 1981 to the Bergerie in 1989 to St Maurice de Navacelles in 1946, offers not a chronological or even a coherent narrative progression but rather a spiraling reorientation of temporal perspectives, through the disparate connections of history, of family, of intuition and recollection. In the midst of that complex or spiral of concerns in **Black Dogs,** moreover, only through the motif of the dogs, only in a vision or a dream, is any suggestion of closure found or durability, any possibility of encapsulation of the novel's vast concerns—on a historical level of racism's resurgence in Europe, on a political level of the danger of institutional and governmental complicity, on a biographical level of the possibility for making meaning out of an individual life, and on a spiritual or even visceral level of the understanding of evil. Paradoxically, nevertheless, part of the basic quality of that encapsulating vision or dream is to remain both transparent and enigmatic:

> They are running down the path into the Gorge of the Vis, the bigger one trailing blood on the white stones. They are crossing the shadow line and going deeper where the sun never reaches, and the amiable drunken mayor will not be sending his men in pursuit for the dogs are crossing the river in the dead of night, and forcing a way up the other side to cross the Causse; and as sleep rolls in they are receding from her, black stains in the grey of the dawn, fading as they move into the foothills of the mountains from where they will return to haunt us, somewhere in Europe, in another time.
>
> (174)

Within the text of **Black Dogs,** the framing of narrative in relation to the multilayered fabric of the temporal, refracted through the prism of gender, is a central concern. Around the axis of feminine identification, the dissident temporality of dreamtime is celebrated and privileged within the time-gender framework of the novel. However, that mode of seeing and understanding is also presented as problematic. June's consciousness is trenchant and visionary in its convictions but also fractured and riven with amnesia and the threat of temporal vacancy. "She cleared her throat. 'Where was I?' We both knew she had peeped into the pit, into a chasm of meaninglessness where everything was nameless and without relation, and it had frightened her. It had frightened us both" (49). By the same token, moreover, the novel offers a strong articulation of the inadequacy of conventionally ordered narrative, schematically identified with the male, for the task of social and personal remembering. On the opposite axis of McEwan's gender divide, the male-identified investment in a leftist historicism is presented as equally problematic. Against what are presented as the scientistic and deterministic contours of socialism in the postwar era, the mediation of historical time itself here precipitates a sense not of affirmation but of disillusionment and dislocation: "The news we didn't want to hear was trickling through. [. . .] Finally the contradictions are too much for you and you crack" (89).

As in Kristeva's essay, the novel presents us not with a choice between linear rationality and the temporalities of repetition and eternity but rather the need for a third way, or to put it differently, the challenge of imagination posed by the insufficiency of plot or of vision alone. In June's struggle for coherent understanding and in Bernard's, along both of these axes of McEwan's gendered scheme, the problem of incoherence, framed again as a disjuncture between the levels of temporal understanding, is central. On the one hand, the novel is enthralled and disturbed by June's investment in the immutable and her oscillating disclosure of vision and amnesia; but, on the other hand, there is an unwillingness to relinquish the sense of agency and the different promise of redemption held and withheld by Bernard's socialist and scientific rationality. Against the enormity, the vast backdrop of that schism of understanding, what we seem to understand is the weediness of words in the novel, a sense of inadequacy around the writing of narrative, which surely will not be able to effect its task of synthesis and reconciliation. What finally anchors the novel, however, despite that canonical suggestion of narrative insecurity or inadequacy, is the presence of a balancing imperative, represented by the quiet and dominating presence of the Holocaust and the reality of neo-Nazi resurgence in Europe. Within the duplex and discordant framework of the novel, therefore, both the problem of historical memory and its absolute necessity are forced into our consideration.

In the Berlin section of *Black Dogs,* we see a self-conscious transposition of the parable of the black dogs from its place in June's visionary understanding to a scenario of concrete historicality in which Bernard becomes the protagonist. The decommissioning of the Berlin Wall in 1989 and the accompanying citywide celebrations are only the background for an attack on the elderly Bernard by a group of young neo-Nazis. These skinheads, bunched in a pack with their hot breath and lolling tongues, are explicitly paralleled with June's dogs. The connection is clearly drawn between the central vision of the dogs, who attack and are wounded but then are ultimately reprieved by public complacency or complicity, and the continuing threat of neo-Nazism. In a characteristic strategy of resolution, not the Berlin authorities but a highly sexualized representation of young femininity—Greta, explicitly revisioned as June herself "the one on the left. Didn't you see?" (84)—is alone able to force a transformation of violence into impotency, reducing the racists to the status of "naughty children" (98). "She was a contemporary, an object of desire and aspiration. [. . .] The force of her disgust was sexual" (98).

Later in the text, after June's honeymoon attack, the thematic importance of patriarchal complacency and complicity is most clearly foregrounded in relation to the challenge of femininity, with the inaction of the local authorities in St Maurice to the black dogs, whose wildness and ferocity stand both symbolically and actually as a reminder of their fugitive Gestapo owners. There is a persistent rumor of their use during the war in the sexual humiliation of an independent, unmarried woman in the village; now in the war's aftermath, the text suggests an unspecified reluctance on the part of the Maire and his men to eliminate this threat by having the dogs exterminated. Similarly, in the scene in Berlin in 1989, there is an undertow not just of inaction but of complicity within the public sphere in relation to the violence of the young neo-Nazis, who first attack a young communist revolutionary before turning their attentions to the respectable establishment figure of Bernard. Two "business types or solicitors" (96) begin the violence and whet the appetite of the crowd and of the young Nazis for a beating. Moments later, "amazed by what their own violence had conjured up [they] had retreated deeper into the crowd to watch" (97). A hatred marginalized on one level is conceived and endorsed at another by the faces of a public and respectable masculinity. Moreover, not institutionalized authority but the moral-sexual force of the young Greta-June alone offers the possibility of its negation. In a scene whose focus and anchor should apparently be the weight of historicity itself, suggested jointly through the breaching of the wall and through the signal appearance of the neo-Nazis, McEwan's text instead becomes polarized between the sense of a more elusive and diffuse and recurring danger, suggested on a broader level than simply the presence of a few underprivileged thugs, and the insurgence of a specifically feminine agency that seems to provide its only effective counter-argument.

IV

In the Berlin section of *Black Dogs,* the text does not invite us to witness the historical confirmation of the end of Nazism's legacy and of the Cold War, with the decommissioning of the Wall and a concomitant moment of liberation. Instead there is a clear suggestion of historicization itself as a dissolution of meaning. As Jeremy and Bernard encounter the city's excavation of the Nazi terror, the idea of digging up the Gestapo headquarters, like framing an extracted fingernail in a museum case, renders each not so much preserved as "neutralised" (93). Similarly, in McEwan's portrayal, the excitement and expectation of the masses around the Brandenburg Gate dissolve to a recognition that "nothing was going to happen" (88). The threat and the confrontation are not here but elsewhere. Only the symbolic face-off between the young woman Greta and the pack of Bernard's neo-Nazi assailants provides any possibility of closure to this event, whose historical monumentality McEwan's text works systematically to resist and deny.

For Ricoeur in the third volume of *Time and Narrative,* what makes this whole notion of the monument open to suspicion is precisely its pretension to finality, and the elision of its imbrication with politics and power. In **Black Dogs,** all of Nazism's legacy as a "warning from history" is seen as subject to mutation, dissolution, and appropriation. The integrity of the monument is supposed to reside in its brave immutability, as Ricoeur suggests. But what if that appearance of immutability and integrity turns out to be a chimera? In the section "Majdanek, Les Salces and St Maurice de Navacelles 1989" not the Berlin wall but the concentration camp at Majdanek becomes most illustrative of this sense of the duplicity and mutability of the monument that is supposed to be a stand against history.

As Jeremy and his partner Jenny approach the gates of the concentration camp, their first confrontation is with an official sign in commemoration of the dead. But this monument, this publicly legitimized document, provides a sense not of security or of affirmation or even absolute condemnation of "our universal reference point of human depravity" (37) but rather a sense of threat and unease, a clear suggestion of the imbrication of the place with politics, institutional complicity, and power:

> "No mention of the Jews. See? It still goes on. And it's official." Then she added, more to herself, "The black dogs."
>
> These last words I ignored. As for the rest, even discounting the hyperbole, a residual truth was sufficient to transform Majdanek for me in an instant from a monument, an honourable civic defiance of oblivion, to a disease of the imagination and a living peril, a barely conscious connivance with evil.
>
> (109-10)

In Berlin, as we have seen, historicization becomes neutralization, with the symbolic demolition of the legacy of World War Two painted in terms not of euphoria but of blankness. The attempt by neo-Nazism symbolically to appropriate Germany's reunification is neutralized by the insurgence of a feminine agency that is simultaneously moral and sexual. At Majdanek, on the other hand, the distortion and appropriation of the monument are offered with even darker implications. Each, it is implied, contains within it a different form of connivance that subverts and appropriates the possibility of a benign historicality. Each contains a threat that we cannot afford to ignore.

Within and around the questioning of the historical monument comes a necessary questioning of the narrative fabric that constitutes and surrounds it. It is easy to see that, through the motif of Jeremy's memoir, **Black Dogs** constantly foregrounds its own status as a document in preparation, a negotiation, and an articulation. Clearly, a potential paradox exists between the novel's disclosure of itself as a made text, as something both compromised and unfixed, and the sense of the need to witness something more absolute—for the preservation or encapsulation of a point of durable meaning in relation to the threat of Nazism and its legacy. For Ricoeur, the critique of the monument is also that of the document, whose status is no less suspect and compromised in relation to power and knowledge:

> Conversely, the document, even though it is collected and not simply inherited, seems to possess an objectivity opposed to the intention of the monument, which is meant to be edifying. [But f]or criticism directed against ideology [. . .] documents turn out to be no less instituted than documents are.
>
> (118)

In a sense that is precisely the problem with which McEwan's text is grappling self-reflexively. Through June's memory and dream of the black dogs, instituted as it is into the family memory, through the witnessing of Nazi depravity first hand at the site of the concentration camp and the recognition of the continuing and institutionalized complicity in its project, through the documentation of the end of the Berlin Wall and the signal presence there of young neo-Nazis, what is at stake is the possibility of capturing in a document, through narrative, some durable sense of a threat that we should and must continue to take seriously.

The compromised status of the historicized past is a crucial part of the way in which that threat is constituted. On a different level of temporal perception, moreover, the possibility of a biographical discourse framed around June's life founders on Jeremy's difficulties in negotiating between the security of a linear-rational exposition and the more enigmatic and ungraspable structures of meaning disclosed within her vision and amnesia. In Ricoeur's scheme the classical function of narrative is clearly that of a guarantor of ontological and epistemological security. Its task is to mend discordance and to supply a structure of coherence that affirms the order and meaning of social and personal life. On a variety of levels, McEwan's text bears witness not to that process of coherence but rather to the insecurity or discordance of the biographical, historical, and metaphysical themes of which it is woven. Whether its central narrative motif of the black dogs is able to transfigure that discordance into a moment of durability or encapsulating meaning remains radically in question.

Both *Enduring Love* and *Black Dogs* are concerned with the struggle of narration. Each reveals in the center of its focus the craftedness of narrative and the difficulty with which narrative may be constructed as a coherent chain of meaning. To that extent McEwan's writing can be seen as symptomatic of a broad tendency in contemporary fiction. The unusualness of his work, however, is its distinctive use of gender as a focus for renegotiating those well-established concerns. For Julia Kristeva, the opposite pole to "women's time" of repetition, eternity, and the matrix space has often been seen as a masculinist temporality characterized by linearity, control, and obsessionality; and the task for a newer feminism becomes to transcend that kind of limiting dichotomy. In *Enduring Love* and *Black Dogs,* similarly, it is possible to see the ways in which an alternative to either of those gender polarities is explored on a number of different levels. McEwan's texts characteristically involve close identification with the problems and perceptions of their male narrators, but what we see in them is far from an attempt to rehabilitate some older, masculinist mode of authorship. On the contrary, McEwan's fiction might be better characterized in terms of its struggle to articulate the possibility of a narrative voice that is self-conscious in its refusal of full coherence or control and unable or unwilling to disguise the extent of its own instability and unease.

## Works Cited

Atwood, Margaret. *The Handmaid's Tale.* 1985. London: Vintage, 1996.

Eco, Umberto. *Reflections on "The Name of the Rose."* Trans. William Weaver. 1983. London: Secker, 1985.

Kristeva, Julia. "Women's Time." *Feminisms.* Ed. Robyn R. Warhal and Diane P. Hernde. New Brunswick, NJ: Rutgers UP, 1991. 443-62.

McEwan, Ian. *Black Dogs.* London: Cape, 1992.

———. *The Child in Time.* London: Pan/Picador, 1987.

———. *Enduring Love.* London: Cape, 1997.

———. *First Love, Last Rites.* London: Cape, 1975.

———. *In Between the Sheets.* London: Cape, 1978.

———. "Or Shall We Die." *A Move Abroad.* 1983. London: Pan/Picador, 1989. 1-24.

Ricoeur, Paul. *Time and Narrative.* Vol. 1. Trans. Kathleen McLaughlin and David Pellauer. 1983. Chicago: U of Chicago P, 1984.

———. Vol. 3. Trans. Kathleen Blamey and David Pellauer. 1985. Chicago: U of Chicago P, 1988.

Rogers, Angela. "Ian McEwan's Portrayal of Women." *Forum for Modern Language Studies* 32 (1996): 11-26.

### Robert Winder (review date 17 September 2001)

SOURCE: Winder, Robert. "Between the Acts." *New Statesman* 130, no. 4555 (17 September 2001): 49.

[*In the following review, Winder offers a mixed assessment of* Atonement, *praising McEwan's literary skill but finding the novel's narrative leaps and omissions unsatisfying.*]

Ian McEwan's new novel [*Atonement*], launched smoothly into the slipstream of the autumn rush, presents us with a puzzle. On one level, it is manifestly high-calibre stuff: cool, perceptive, serious and vibrant with surprises. It will probably be on the Booker shortlist, and might even win. So it is probably silly to waste time pointing out that the most glaring aspects of the book are its weaknesses and omissions. As usual, McEwan has contrived a good story; but he seems weirdly reluctant to tell it. The title—thematic rather than dramatic—feels like the idea you have before you have an idea, and what follows also seems incomplete. There are fine episodes, but it feels, in the end, not so much a novel as a description of a novel, a selection of scenes from some much larger project. The best we can say is that it will be marvellous when it is finished.

McEwan has certainly mellowed, as the saying goes. His reputation was forged by a succession of stories written with a scalpel: icy, calculated, elegant and hair-raising. They had a subversive edge, and prickled with a sense of danger. But recently, in the Booker-winning *Amsterdam* and now in *Atonement* (whatever else, no one can say he is merely working his way through the alphabet), he has settled in milder country, in an antique, upper-class England more usually associated with the Iris Murdochs of this world. *The Comfort of Strangers* sent plain old Colin and Mary to Venice to be savaged; now he prefers people called Vernon and Cecilia, Leon and Briony. They are composers or diplomats with Firsts from Cambridge and priceless Ming vases, and live in stately homes. Their misadventures are subtle.

There's nothing wrong with that, and McEwan's senses are as alert as ever. A glug of warm wine, damp earth, a violent word, the hiss of breeze over water, a dismembered leg in the fork of a tree . . . the novel is alive with physical shocks. But he is an obstinate storyteller and plugs the flow of his ample saga by dividing (and condensing) it into three tidy set pieces. In a languid pre-war country pile, a precocious 13-year-old girl, Briony, utterly misreads the nature of the goings-on between her older sister and the boy next door, Robbie. Driven by a bravura compulsion to star as the heroine in her own melodrama, she falsely accuses him of raping a guest, and sends her sister's one true love off to prison.

It is rather terrific. There's a frisson of class conflict (the boy in question is the son of the cleaner—a ruffian, in other words) and all sorts of interesting things seem about to happen. So it's more than a little disappointing when—cut!—we jump forward and rejoin Robbie in the retreat to Dunkirk. It is as if the author flinched at the thought of describing Robbie in prison, or the vain efforts of his lover to save him. So a couple of years have passed, and now we're in the middle of a new tableau, as Robbie trudges across France with Stukas shrieking overhead. Not surprisingly, he is still obsessed by the injustice done him in those halcyon days before the war, but for now he has more immediate worries. Somehow he makes it to the famous beach, and joins the swarm of dejected troops waiting to be rescued.

Again, it's pretty exciting. Will he make it? What kind of revenge (or atonement) will he be able to exact when he returns? Will his love be able to withstand the shock of war and separation? Once again, we begin to tilt towards the edge of our seats.

So it's more than a little disappointing when—cut!—we jump forward again, and find ourselves back with Briony, in a hospital in London, lugging bedpans to and fro and trembling before the matron. She is grown-up now, and wrestling with her conscience at last. She wants to make amends. For a few pages, all of the book's plates are spinning on the same pole. The protagonists revolve towards a showdown and—oh no, not again, cut!—we jump to Briony in old age. She is now a feted author, brooding on the nature of fiction in a way intended to suggest that nothing we have read so far is quite what it seems.

It's clever. But so are people who can solve crosswords in five minutes. McEwan has taken the classic ingredients of the bodice-ripper—a quivering love story set against a backdrop of war—and, striving for ingenuity, declined to make the most of them. This is not really a criticism. McEwan is sufficiently modern to renounce "character in action" in favour of "character lost in thought". He wants, as he says of Briony, to free himself from "the cumbrous battle between good and evil, heroes and villains", and simply present, without judging, the friction between different minds, fogged as they are with apprehension and conceit. He even invents a letter written by Cyril Connolly, the editor of *Horizon*, to Briony. It's an admiring rejection of her first effort, urging her to have more respect for the "childlike desire to be told a story, to be held in suspense, to know what happens".

McEwan tries to heed this advice, and offers plenty of suspense. But it is suspense of a thin sort, since it relies not on our ignorance of what might happen next, but simply on our not being told what is happening right now. McEwan deals out information cautiously, as if it were common to say too soon that the girl at the beginning of the book is 13, or that the year is 1938, or that many years divide some new chapter from its predecessor. McEwan carries on narrating in his shrewd and natural way, and it's up to us to figure out what he has neglected to mention. This is certainly a cunning way to keep us guessing, but the result is not mystery: it just feels blurred and out of focus.

None of this would matter if the author wasn't so obviously top-flight. And I might have got it completely wrong: perhaps the problem is not that McEwan is too tight-fisted with his booming emotional plot, but that he has leaned too far towards the love-war formula in the first place. Perhaps there is a fictional Gresham's Law, by which trashy ideas drive out good; maybe the fireworks of the underlying saga simply squelch his more delicate effects. McEwan once wrote a lovely children's book, ***The Daydreamer***, which captured the gulfs between children and grown-ups more vividly than he does here. So perhaps there are not too many gaps, but too few. It's a terrible confession, because I know that reviewers are supposed to be thoroughly adept at snap judgements, but . . . I'm baffled. As I said, it's a puzzle.

## James Wood (review date 25 March 2002)

SOURCE: Wood, James. "The Trick of Truth." *New Republic* 226, no. 11 (25 March 2002): 28.

[*In the following review, Wood commends* Atonement *as one of McEwan's finest novels, lauding the large scope of the plot and a feeling of "spaciousness" that is in contrast to McEwan's other works which, Wood asserts, have at times seemed "artificial" and contrived.*]

Ian McEwan is one of the most gifted literary storytellers alive—where storytelling means kinesis, momentum, prowl, suspense, charge. His paragraphs are mined with menace. He is a master of the undetonated bomb and the slow-acting detail: the fizzing fact that slowly dissolves throughout a novel and perturbs everything in its wake, the apparently buried secret that will not stay dead and must have its vampiric midnight. These talents, which are enabled by a penetrating intelligence and a prose style far richer and more flexible than most contemporary writers dream of, have made McEwan an anomalous figure in Britain: perhaps the only truly literary best-selling novelist in that country.

The cost has been high, however. McEwan's work is very controlled, but its reality is somewhat stifled. More often than not, one emerges from his stories as if from a vault, happy to breathe a more accidental air. In his careful, excessively managed universes, in which everything is made to fit together, the reader is offered many of the true pleasures of fiction, but sometimes starved of the truest difficulties. McEwan's fictions have been prodigies: they do everything but move us. In his world what is most important is our secrets, not our mysteries.

In other words, McEwan's fiction has sometimes felt artificial. It should be said, in his favor, that most contemporary novelists feel artificial because they are not competent enough to tell a convincing or interesting story; it is a peculiar excess of proficiency and talent, like McEwan's—or like Robert Stone's, W. Somerset Maugham's, or Graham Greene's—that produces a fiction so competently told that it also feels artificial. Still, one has tended to read McEwan with the sense that he is beautifully constructing and managing various hypothetical situations rather than freely following and grasping at a great truth. (That this latter mode is also an artifice is only a banal paradox.) In particular, McEwan's characters, while never less than interesting, lively, and sometimes interestingly weird, have tended not to be quite human. Many of them have neither pasts nor futures, but are frozen in the threatening present. Many of them have parents who died when they were young. They rarely refer to their childhoods, and seem not to have the use of deep memory as such. McEwan, unlike most writers, has not seemed to need any kitty of childhood detail on which to draw. This absence of past stories, of loitering retrospect, allows him to polish the clean lines of his stories. Since his writing rarely dips into the reflective past, it can exist the better as pure novelty. This is the key to McEwan's extraordinary narrative stealth. His fictions, like detective stories, are always moving forward. They seem to shed their sentences rather than to accumulate them.

*Atonement*, perhaps following the claim of its title, is a radical break with this earlier McEwan, and it is certainly his finest and most complex novel. It represents a new era in McEwan's work, and this revolution is achieved in two interesting ways. First, McEwan has loosened the golden ropes that have made his fiction feel so impressively imprisoned. His new book is larger and more ample than anything he has done before, and moves from an English country house in 1935 to an extraordinary description of the British army's retreat at Dunkirk and a chapter set in wartime London. And second, McEwan uses his new novel to comment on precisely the kind of fiction that he himself has tended to produce in the past. It may be going too far to see *Atonement* as a kind of atonement for fiction's untruths—not least because *Atonement* is ultimately, I think, a defense of fiction's untruths. But it is certainly a novel explicitly troubled by fiction's fictionality—its artificiality—and eager to explore the question of the novel's responsibility to truth.

Of course, confessing to a sin is not the same as abstaining from it, and *Atonement* might easily have been no more than an over-controlled novel that sought to apologize for being over-controlled. But from the beginning the book has a spaciousness that is new in this writer. Significantly, *Atonement* is chiefly about a child, a little girl named Briony Tallis. The novel opens in 1935; she lives in a large country house in Surrey. Her elder sister, Cecilia, has just come down from Girton College, Cambridge. Her mother, who is subject to migraines, spends much of the time lying in her bedroom. Her father, a civil servant, is a distant presence, usually away in London. Around the house, in addition to the usual staff, is a young man named Robbie Turner, who has also just come down from Cambridge. Robbie's status is ambiguous: he is the son of the Tallis family's cleaning lady, and lives with his mother in a nearby cottage, but as a child he was taken under the family's wing, and his education was paid for by them. He practically grew up with Cecilia, who is in love with him. Alas for Robbie, young Briony, who is thirteen years old, is also in love with him, and Briony will ultimately take her revenge on him, the revenge of the child who feels tempted by, but still exiled from, adulthood.

The novel opens as a house party is about to begin. Briony's elder brother Leon and his friend Paul Marshall are coming from London. Briony's young cousins Pierrot, Jackson, and Lola Quincey have just arrived. Briony has always dreamed of writing, and she is eager for her three cousins to act the parts of her new verse play, *The Trials of Arabella. Mansfield Park,* with its staged play in a country house, and its reflection on the dangerous excesses of the theater, is an obvious progenitor. McEwan has an epigraph from *Northanger Abbey,* and he clearly wants to perform that most difficult literary task, the simultaneous creation of a reality that satisfies as a reality while signaling itself as a fiction. The characters, for instance, have obviously theatrical and outlandish names (Pierrot, Lola, Leon, Briony), which are simply incompatible with verisimilitude.

One of the ways in which McEwan does endow this fictive world with a reality is by genuinely interesting himself in the ambitions and the follies of a little girl.

Briony Tallis, a prim, yearning, intelligent child with a rage for order and a tendency to judge before comprehending, is one of the novel's achievements. McEwan is funny about Briony's pretentious habit of stealing complicated words from the dictionary, so that her verse melodrama, *The Trials of Arabella,* opens thus:

> This is the tale of spontaneous Arabella
> Who ran off with an extrinsic fellow.
> It grieved her parents to see their first born
> Evanesce from her home to go to Eastbourne
> Without permission . . .

We follow Briony's furies and daydreams, as her plans for the staging of her play are slowly thwarted (as in *Mansfield Park,* the play is never successfully performed). McEwan is especially acute in his conjuring of the aimlessness and solitude of childhood. In one typical scene, we watch Briony as she sits and plays with her hands:

She raised one hand and flexed its fingers and wondered, as she had sometimes before, how this thing, this machine for gripping, this fleshy spider on the end of her arm, came to be hers, entirely at her command. Or did it have some little life of its own? She bent her finger and straightened it. The mystery was in the instance before it moved, the dividing moment between not moving and moving, when her intention took effect. It was like a wave breaking. If she could only find herself at the crest, she thought, she might find the secret of herself, that part of her that was really in charge. She brought her forefinger closer to her face and stared at it, urging it to move. It remained still because she was pretending, she was not entirely serious, and because willing it to move, or being about to move it, was not the same as actually moving it. And when she did crook it finally, the action seemed to start in the finger itself, not in some part of her mind. When did it know to move, when did she know to move it?

From here, Briony goes on to consider her own sense of reality: "was everyone else really as alive as she was? For example, did her sister really matter to herself, was she as valuable to herself as Briony was? Was being Cecilia just as vivid an affair as being Briony? Did her sister also have a real self concealed behind a breaking wave, and did she spend time thinking about it, with a finger held up to her face?" If the answer is yes, Briony thinks, then "the world, the social world, was unbearably complicated, with two billion voices, and everyone's thoughts striving in equal importance and everyone's claim on life as intense, and everyone thinking they were unique, when no one was." But if the answer is no, she thinks, then Briony "was surrounded by machines, intelligent and pleasant enough on the outside, but lacking the bright and private inside feeling she had."

So we follow the vain drift of a child's logic over a page. A universal experience is evoked, and McEwan subtly makes the banal and childish dilemma—when do I control my fingers?—the spur to those larger frustrations of childhood, the questions of authority, agency, importance. What child has not selfishly thought: is anyone else as real as I am? And McEwan traces this mental discussion with an exemplary tact, the language having the poise and the exactitude of the adult novelist while inhabiting the imperfect simplicity of the child ("the bright and private inside feeling she had").

Briony is about to discover that her sister Cecilia does indeed feel as "valuable to herself" as Briony does. Or, rather, Briony is about to ignore this truth, in a moment for which the rest of her life will be an atonement. Staring out of the window, she sees Cecilia and Robbie standing by the large fountain. Suddenly, Cecilia strips down to her underwear while Robbie watches her, and steps into the deep fountain to retrieve something. Cecilia emerges, puts her clothes back on, picks up a vase of flowers that had been hidden by the fountain, and walks into the house. Robbie also walks away. The scene stirs the little girl, who had once confessed her love to Robbie. She has the sense that she has witnessed some adult mystery, perhaps a scene of obscure erotic domination. Briony does not know what McEwan has told us, namely that Cecilia dipped into the fountain to retrieve a piece of the broken vase, and that Cecilia's provocative stripping had more to do with erotic challenge than submission or fear.

Briony is aware that her dim comprehension of what she has witnessed burdens her with an obligation not to race to judgment. Indeed, after her witnessing, she decides to abandon melodrama (which has been her habitual literary genre) and begin the more difficult task of writing truthfully and impartially. She could write the scene from three different perspectives, she excitedly realizes, from three points of view; her excitement was in the prospect of freedom, of being delivered from the cumbrous struggle between good and bad, heroes and villains. None of these three was bad, nor were they particularly good. She need not judge. There did not have to be a moral. She need only show separate minds, as alive as her own, struggling with the idea that other minds were equally alive. . . . And only in a story could you enter these different minds and show how they had an equal value.

Six decades later, McEwan tells us, when Briony Tallis is a celebrated author of fiction "known for its amorality," she will recall this year, in newspaper interviews, as a turning point in her literary development.

But in fact Briony ignores her own caveats, and vandalizes the wise perspectivism that she claims to have discovered. Over the next few hours, the idea that Robbie is an erotic menace, an outsider or even a predator, grows in Briony's mind. She interrupts Robbie and Cecilia having hurried sex in the library, and again infers from their position that Robbie is forcing Cecilia into something unpleasant. (McEwan tells us that actually the lovers were equally sexually inexperienced and mutually attracted.) When, later that night, Briony's fifteen-year-old cousin Lola is sexually attacked in the garden, Briony assumes that the shape she saw in the darkness, running away, was Robbie. (Lola was attacked from behind, and seems unable to identify her molester.) Briony tells the police that she is sure that she saw Robbie, and she has other information too, all of it damning to Robbie's case.

Her determination to accuse Robbie is bound up with her literary impulses. She needs to make a story of it:

> Surely it was not too childish to say there had to be a story; and this was the story of a man whom everybody liked, but about whom the heroine always had her doubts, and finally she was able to reveal that he was the incarnation of evil. But wasn't she—that was, Briony the writer—supposed to be so worldly now as to be above such nursery tale ideas as good and evil? There must be some lofty, god-like place from which all people could be judged alike, not pitted against each other. . . . If such a place existed, she was not worthy of it. She could never forgive Robbie his disgusting mind.

In part, Briony has been unable to shed her old melodramatic impulses, and is merely showing her age, even as she strives to get beyond it. But in part what is at work in her is the excitement of shaping a story that fits, that makes too much sense. McEwan surely wants us to reflect on the dangerous complicities of fiction, not just of melodrama but of form itself, which insists on sealing and plotting. What Briony saw was in truth plotless, because it could not be made to mean. Yet a plot is exactly what she imposes. Fiction, even very good fiction, often tends to notarize the incomprehensible simply because it insists on its readability. This is exactly the kind of fiction that McEwan has tended to produce in recent years; his last two novels, **Enduring Love** and **Amsterdam,** both begin with mysteries that they then efficiently lay bare. Formally and stylistically, both begin novelistically and accelerate into the neat, jig-sawed domain of the thriller. **Atonement,** by contrast, seems to want to ponder the deformation of tidiness in such fiction, and to propose instead an enriching confusion. McEwan, as Chesterton has it, chooses reality's battered truth over form's perfected error.

The paradox, of course, is that it is only through fiction itself that we can see how mistaken Briony is. McEwan's own wise perspectivism enables us to inhabit that "lofty, god-like place from which all people could be judged alike." Thanks to his own novel, we discover how terribly Briony misjudged the moment in front of the fountain. Thus **Atonement** is both a criticism of fiction and a defense of fiction; a criticism of its shaping and exclusive torque, and a defense of its ideal democratic generosity to all. A criticism of fiction's misuse; and a defense of an ideal. And this doubleness, of apologia and celebration, could not be otherwise, for art is always its own ombudsman, and thus healthier than its own sickness. Art is the foundation of its own anti-foundationalism, and the anti-foundation of its own foundationalism. And from this comes a further paradox: McEwan's perspectivism, whereby we see all the characters equally, cannot avoid having a shaping torque of its own. There is no such thing, really, as a confused or truly messy fiction; distortion is built into the form like radon underneath sick buildings. The greatest, freest, truest, most lifelike fiction is nothing like life (though some is closer to it than others). McEwan certainly knows this.

So innocent Robbie is arrested, and as Robbie is put into the police car Briony again watches from a window: "The disgrace of it horrified her. It was further confirmation of his guilt, and the beginning of his punishment. It had the look of eternal damnation." This is a fine example of how subtly McEwan follows the self-serving theatrics of Briony's mind. The idea that being arrested by the police is confirmation of guilt is a non sequitur indulged in by many people, often to disastrous effect, and probably no more so than to a child, who has rarely if ever seen the police doing their work. It is the final non sequitur from a girl who has consistently allowed the unfinished picture to finish her judgment, who has taken wonders for signs.

In its second and third parts (each about sixty pages long) **Atonement** leaves behind the Tallises' country house, but it cannot leave behind the shadow of Briony's false incrimination. In Part Two, we have advanced by five years, and are following Robbie Turner as he retreats, with the rest of the British Expeditionary Force, through northern France to Dunkirk. We gather that he has been in prison, that he and Cecilia have been corresponding, and that a remorseful Briony, now eighteen, wants to retract her statement to the police so that Robbie's name might be cleared. Cecilia, we learn, has not spoken to her parents or brother since 1935 (they sided with Briony against Robbie); and of course there has been no communication between Cecilia and her younger sister.

But in some ways this information is incidental to McEwan's extraordinary evocation of muddled warfare. I doubt that any English writer has conveyed quite as powerfully the bewilderments and the humiliations of this episode in World War II. After more than twenty years of writing with care and control, McEwan's anxious, disciplined richness of style finally expands to meet its subject. This section is vivid and unsentimental, and most importantly, though McEwan must have researched the war, there is no inky blot of other books: his details have the vividness and body of imagined things, they feel chosen rather than copied.

There is marvelous writing. Robbie has been wounded; he feels the pain in his side "like a flash of colour." Day after day, the British soldiers make their weary, undisciplined way to Dunkirk. They can see where they are supposed to be going, because miles away a fuel depot is on fire at the port, the cloud hanging over the landscape "like an angry father." They are not marching, but walking, slouching. Order has broken down, and a tired anarchy rules. McEwan captures the fatigue—which invades even eating—very well: "Even as he chewed, he felt himself plunging into sleep for seconds on end." Into this obscure, thudding chaos, discrete and vile happenings explode and then disappear. Occasionally the Luftwaffe's planes strafe the straggling infantrymen. And one day Robbie turns to hear behind him a rhythmic pounding on the road:

> At first sight it seemed that an enormous horizontal door was flying up the road towards them. It was a platoon of Welsh Guards in good order, rifles at the slope, led by a second-lieutenant. They came by at a forced march, their gaze fixed forwards, their arms swinging high. The stragglers stood aside to let them through. These were cynical times, but no one risked a catcall. The show of discipline and cohesion was shaming. It was a relief when the Guards had pounded out of sight and the rest could resume their introspective trudging.

As the soldiers near Dunkirk, Robbie crosses a bridge and sees a barge pass under it. It is like the boat in Auden's "Musee des Beaux Arts": ordinary indifferent life continues while Icarus falls. "The boatman sat at his tiller smoking a pipe, looking stolidly ahead. Behind him, ten miles away, Dunkirk burned. Ahead, in the prow, two boys were bending over an upturned bike, mending a puncture perhaps. A line of washing which included women's smalls was hanging out to dry." Finally, when the soldiers come upon the beach, they taste the salt—"the taste of holidays"—and then they see the remarkable formlessness of an army waiting to be shipped back to England. Some of the men are swimming, others playing football on the sand. One group is attacking a poor RAF officer, blaming him for the Luftwaffe's superiority. Others have dug themselves personal holes in the dunes, "from which they peeped out, proprietorial and smug. Like marmosets. . . ." But the majority of the army "wandered about the sands without purpose, like citizens of an Italian town in the hour of the passeggio."

In a novel so concerned with fiction's relation to actuality, this amazing conjuring cannot but fail to have the weird but successful doubleness of the novel's first section: it has a grave reality, while at the same time necessarily raises questions about its own literary rights to that reality. Was Dunkirk really like this? Stephen Crane's evocation of Antietam was so vivid that one veteran swore that Crane (who did not fight) was present with him. Like Crane's descriptions, McEwan's gather their strength not from the accuracy of their notation but from the accumulation of living human detail, so alive that we are persuaded that such a thing might have occurred even if no one actually witnessed it. The soldiers dug into their own little holes in the dunes, like marmosets, has just such a fictive reality, so that it becomes irrelevant to us were a veteran to say: "this never happened." McEwan has made it seem plausible, because alive. This is what Aristotle meant when he said that a convincing impossibility is preferable in literature to an unconvincing possibility. Yet this great freedom shows how dangerous fiction can be, and why its transit with lies has historically been subversive and threatening. Again, McEwan wants us to reflect on these matters. He has Robbie ponder: "Who could ever describe this confusion, and come up with the village names and the dates for the history books? And take the reasonable view and begin to assign the blame? No one would ever know what it was like to be here. Without the details there could be no larger picture." It is fiction, and McEwan's fiction, which provides "the details" that history may miss. But—and this is a gigantic but, surely, which this novel acknowledges—those details may be invented, may never have happened in history.

In Part Three, we see Briony working as a trainee nurse at a London hospital. We learn that she is terribly sorry for what she did in 1935 and that, in a gesture of atonement, she has forsworn Cambridge, and dedicated herself to nursing. Late in the section, she visits her estranged sister in Clapham, and finds her living with Robbie, who has briefly returned from his army service in France. Again, McEwan writes superbly well, especially in his evocation of Briony's nursing experiences. Soldiers arrive, looking identical in their dirt and torn clothes, "like a wild race of men from a terrible world." One of them has had most of his nose blown off, and it falls to Briony to change his dressings. "She could see through his missing cheek to his upper and lower molars, and the tongue glistening, and hideously long. Further up, where she hardly dared look, were the exposed muscles around his eye socket. So intimate, and never intended to be seen." There is great tenderness in this description of the poor soldier's eye muscles, "so intimate and never intended to be seen." We may even think of another moment, earlier in Briony's life, when she also witnessed something "intimate and never intended to be seen." But the mark of the true writer, the writer who is really looking, really witnessing, is that notation of the soldier's exposed tongue as "hideously long"—something worthy of Conrad.

*Atonement* ends with a devastating twist, a piece of information that changes our sense of everything we have just read. It is convincing enough, but its neatness seems like the reappearance of the old McEwan, unwilling to let the ropes fall from his hands. In an epilogue, set in 1999, we learn that Briony, now a distinguished old novelist, wrote the three sections—the country house scene, the Dunkirk retreat, and the London hospital—that we have just read. Moreover, Robbie and Cecilia were never together, as the third section suggested. Robbie was killed in France in 1940, and Cecilia died in the same year in London, during the German bombing. The conjuring that we have just witnessed has been Briony's atonement for what she did. She could not resist the chance to spare the young lovers, to continue their lives into fiction, to give the story a happy ending.

This twist, this revelation, further emphasizes the novel's already explicit ambivalence about being a novel, and makes the book a proper postmodern artifact, wearing its doubts on its sleeve, on the outside, as the Pompidou does its escalators. But it is unnecessary, unless the slightly self-defeating point is to signal that the author is himself finally incapable of resisting the distortions of tidiness. It is unnecessary because the novel has already raised, powerfully but murmuringly, the questions that this final revelation shouts out. And it is unnecessary because the fineness of the book as a novel, as a distinguished and complex evocation of English life before and during the war, burns away the theoretical, and implants in the memory a living, flaming presence.

## Lynne Sharon Schwartz (review date March-April 2002)

SOURCE: Schwartz, Lynne Sharon. "Quests for Redemption." *New Leader* 85, no. 2 (March-April 2002): 23-5.

[*In the following excerpt, Schwartz praises the engaging fictional world of* Atonement, *but objects to the novel's concluding postmodern conceit.*]

Good news: In a world turned surreal, realism in literature lives on, at least in Britain. Both Ian McEwan, prolific and experienced, and Andrew Miller, a young author of two previous novels, offer new works that seduce, absorb, illuminate, and comfort. By "comfort," I'm not suggesting that their visions are complacent or reassuring—far from it. But their painstaking exploration of private dilemmas in the midst of public turmoil validates the struggle to find coherent meaning. That remains a worthy aspiration, both writers remind us, even if the results are forever out of reach.

McEwan, with eight novels, two story collections and several prizes to his credit, is always fresh and arresting. Whether his theme is political, philosophical or domestic, he brings to it moral consciousness and educated skepticism, in shapely, intricate sentences George Eliot would have admired. *The Child in Time* (1987) presented a delicious dissection of the hypocrisies of Margaret Thatcher's government, and *Black Dogs* (1992) examined, with enviable objectivity, the usefulness of belief systems as embodied in a married couple—a religious mystic and a liberal positivist who can't live with or without each other. McEwan's finger is always on our pulse, so to speak: The narrator of *Black Dogs* ponders "whether our civilization at this turn of the millennium is cursed by too much or too little belief," a question that at this pass appears to have been answered.

*Atonement* is a dense, unsettling meditation on the interplay of imagination and reality, uneasy partners that need yet injure each other as grievously as the couple in *Black Dogs.* The story is set in 1935 at an ugly English country house built on the site of an older, beautiful one. In residence is the Tallis family. The father is away in London doing something obscurely connected with the approaching war and being unfaithful, and the mother is a patient Griselda, accepting, ineffectual and migraine-ridden. Thirteen-year-old Briony, the youngest child, consumed by a literary imagination (she goes on to become a successful novelist), causes the damage that requires atonement. Its victims are her older sister, Cecilia, and Cecilia's lover, Robbie, a former servant's gifted son whom the Tallises have taken under their wing. The first half of the book dwells on Briony's ambiguous accusation against Robbie and its immediate, devastating consequences; the second half leaps ahead five years to the War and the ignominious British retreat from Dunkirk.

At the start, to celebrate her adored older brother's return from London, Briony, the family's gifted darling, has written a play. A genre romance with typical heroine, villain and rescuer, it is to be performed by three visiting cousins—15-year-old Lola, already sexually wily, and her younger twin brothers. In between rehearsals, Briony spies from a window the incomprehensible scene that changes her life forever. She sees Cecilia and Robbie standing at a fountain. All at once, seemingly at Robbie's command, Cecilia removes her skirt and blouse, steps into the fountain, ducks under, then quickly walks away. As the huge enigma of adult behavior is borne in on her, "Briony had her first, weak intimation that for her now it could no longer be fairy-tale castles and princesses, but the strangeness of the here and now, of what passed between people, the ordinary people that she knew, and what power one could have over the other. . . ."

Instantaneously, she is transformed from a childish scribbler of hackneyed romance into a realist. She imagines writing the scene she's witnessed: "Her excitement was in the prospect of freedom, of being delivered from the cumbrous struggle between good and bad, heroes and villains. . . . There did not have to be a moral. She need only show separate minds, as alive as her own, struggling with the idea that other minds were equally alive. It wasn't only wickedness and scheming that made people unhappy, it was confusion and misunderstanding; above all, it was the failure to grasp the simple truth that other people are as real as you."

The meaning of the scene that brings about such transformation is simple. Cecilia and Robbie have grown up together and have just finished their years at university, where they avoided each other, finding their easy childhood friendship turned awkward in a setting where class barriers—that perennial ingredient of British fiction—are divisive. Back home, the awkwardness remains. At the fountain, they argue over filling a vase of flowers, he trying to help, she refusing the help. When the vase, a precious heirloom, breaks, Cecilia hunts for the pieces underwater. The tussle signals the opening moves of a love both are scarcely aware of. Yet only a few hours later it is consummated ardently, if not ideally, against a shelf of books in the library. Briony bursts in and once more is baffled, imagining the worst.

Class divisions cast a dark shadow when the oldest brother returns with a guest: stupid, pompous, but attractive Paul Marshall, a budding business tycoon thanks to his Amo chocolate bars, soon to become a staple of the British troops. Paul has his eye on the seductive Lola (shades of Lolita?), but when she's raped at night in the woods, no one suspects so rich and innocuous a stranger. Instead Briony accuses Robbie, the social upstart: She "thinks" he is the man she sees running away. Her thinking is a blend of inference, conjecture, envy, and self-dramatizing—all the elements of an overheated adolescent imagination. On her mistaken testimony Robbie goes to prison; his plans for medical school are over, his life ruined.

In 1940, having been released to serve in the infantry, Robbie, embittered but valiant, trudges through the French countryside to reach the Channel and home. Strictly speaking, this long section is not essential to the moral tale of injury and atonement, but it is narrated with such fierce verisimilitude—the wretched, bedraggled, fearful, hungry soldiers (their Amo bars long consumed) running from the strafing of German planes—that it justifies itself. And its vividness is exemplary, a brutal contrast to the serene country estate of Part I, where Briony has mused in privileged, sheltered leisure over how best to portray reality.

Cecilia and Briony, estranged from each other and their family since the debacle of Robbie's alleged crime, work as war nurses in London. McEwan's description of Briony's student training, especially her trial by fire when a convoy of wounded soldiers arrives at the hospital, is magnificent. After Dunkirk, the repentant Briony seeks out Cecilia and Robbie, still steadfast lovers, in an attempt to right her wrong and clear his name. She grasps her own early "confusion and misunderstanding." She has learned, to her sorrow, that "the simple truth that other people are as real as you" applies to life as well as to fiction. The specific acts of reparation are self-evident—recanting to the authorities, explaining to her family—but not until decades later can she find a way to make genuine atonement.

Then comes the one flaw: a 17-page epilogue in the voice of Briony at age 77, which is an unwarranted excursion into postmodernism. To wit: To atone at last for my awful deed, dear reader, I wrote the novel you have just read. . . . McEwan even drops a few words recalling the final page of Charlotte Bronte's *Villette*: "It is only in this last version," says Briony, "that my lovers end well, holding hands. . . . What purpose would be served if . . ." No purpose would be served if I told, either. (Briony, with her dry-ice nature, is not unlike Bronte's heroine, Lucy Snowe, except she pursues her dreams more aggressively.) "I know there's always a certain kind of reader," Briony goes on, "who will be compelled to ask, But what really happened?"

Not fair. I relish literary sleight-of-hand as much as the next one, but with a novel which for 330 pages gives no hint it is that kind of game, I become "a certain kind of reader." Why would McEwan spin such a rich and splendid story this way? I hope he has not decided realism no longer suffices. More likely the process of novel-writing, the way life contorts into fiction, intrigues him as it does Briony. Or else he means to illustrate Briony's desperate, guilty need to force a happy ending in the one realm she can control. Either way, his own process has been so successful that the reader is too invested in the story to care, so belatedly, about its armature.

Never mind. Forget the ending fillip. The rest is unforgettable.

# FURTHER READING

## Criticism

Bethune, Brian. "Look Back in Melancholy." *Maclean's* (14 January 2002): 45.

    Bethune discusses the ways that *Atonement* and W. G. Sebald's *Austerlitz* use the setting of the past and how both authors use events from history to comment on the art of writing.

Breslin, John B. "Lies and War." *America* 187, no. 2 (15 July 2002): 22.

    Breslin offers an overview of *Atonement*, extolling McEwan's narrative abilities as well as the novel's overall scope and ironic twists.

Charles, Ron. "Friends Strike Out in Dark Comedy." *Christian Science Monitor* (17 December 1998): 21.

    Charles evaluates the strengths and weaknesses of *Amsterdam*.

Dugan, Lawrence. Review of *Black Dogs*, by Ian McEwan. *National Review* 45, no. 1 (18 January 1993): 57-8.

    Dugan praises the humanizing elements in *Black Dogs* and McEwan's ability to present "stark dichotomies" at the heart of his story.

Lacayo, Richard. "Twisted Sister." *Time* 159, no. 12 (25 March 2002): 70.

    Lacayo comments favorably on *Atonement*, remarking that McEwan is a subtle and skilled writer.

McEwan, Ian, and Jeff Giles. "Luminous Novel from Dark Master." *Newsweek* 139, no. 11 (18 March 2002): 62-3.

    McEwan discusses his literary reputation, his influences, winning the Booker Prize, and the creation of *Atonement*.

Mesic, Penelope. "Fountain of Youth." *Book* (March-April 2002): 67.

    Mesic lauds *Atonement,* asserting that it contains descriptive prose, intricacy, and a detailed examination of a child's point of view in contrast to an adult world view.

Messud, Claire. "The Beauty of the Conjuring." *Atlantic Monthly* 289, no. 3 (March 2002): 106.

    Messud focuses on the role of Briony Tallis in *Atonement*, noting McEwan's evocation of war, his descriptions of the human psyche, and the suspenseful aspects of the novel.

Roberts, Rex. "Quite Write." *Insight on the News* 18, no. 19 (27 May 2002): 25.

    Roberts comments on the critical reaction to *Atonement,* noting the unusually positive reception of the work.

---

**Additional coverage of McEwan's life and career is contained in the following sources published by the Gale Group:** *Bestsellers,* **Vol. 90:4;** *British Writers Supplement,* **Vol. 4;** *Contemporary Authors,* **Vols. 61-64;** *Contemporary Authors New Revision Series,* **Vols. 14, 41, 69, 87;** *Contemporary Literary Criticism,* **Vols. 13, 66;** *Contemporary Novelists,* **Ed. 7;** *Dictionary of Literary Biography,* **Vols. 14, 194;** *DISCovering Authors Modules: Novelists;* *Literature Resource Center;* *Major 20th-Century Writers,* **Eds. 1, 2;** *Reference Guide to Short Fiction,* **Ed. 2;** *St. James Guide to Horror, Ghost, and Gothic Writers;* *Supernatural Fiction Writers,* **Vol. 2; and** *Twayne's English Authors.*

# Sam Shepard
## 1943-

(Born Samuel Rogers Shepard) American playwright, screenwriter, short story writer, director, and poet.

The following entry presents an overview of Shepard's career through 2002. For further information on his life and works, see *CLC,* Volumes 4, 6, 17, 34, 41, and 44.

## INTRODUCTION

Shepard is considered one of the foremost playwrights writing for the off-Broadway stage, having won eleven Obie Awards, the New York Drama Critics' Circle Award, and a Pulitzer Prize in 1979 for *Buried Child* (1978). His works, including over forty one-act and full-length dramas, convey a surreal vision of contemporary American society in which myth frequently collides with reality. Shepard's plays examine a wide range of topics, most notably the spiritual dissolution of the family, the corruption of the artist by commercialism, the disintegration of the American dream, and the vanishing Western frontier and its culture. His interest in the legends and myths of the American West dominate his dramas, as do references to jazz, song lyrics, drugs, Hollywood films, and other components of American popular culture.

## BIOGRAPHICAL INFORMATION

Shepard was born on November 5, 1943, to Samuel Shepard and Elaine Rogers in Fort Sheridan, Illinois. His father was in the Army Air Corps and, after World War II, the family shuttled between various military bases before settling in Duarte, California. Shepard began his acting career in California, but in 1963, he moved to New York City and became involved with several off-off-Broadway theater groups. His first one-act dramas, *Cowboys* and *The Rock Garden,* were part of the first Theatre Genesis show at St. Mark's Church-in-the-Bowery in 1964. Although virtually dismissed by critics, the plays attracted a sizable cult following. Between 1965 and 1970, Shepard continued to write prolifically, completing more than fourteen plays. In 1971 Shepard moved to London where he pursued his interest in music, directed several productions of his own plays, and wrote a number of new works, including *The Tooth of Crime* (1972). In the mid-1970s, Shepard resettled in California, becoming the playwright-in-residence at the Magic Theatre in San Francisco. He was awarded the Pulitzer Prize in 1979 for *Buried Child,* which also won an Obie Award. Eleven of Shepard's plays have won Obie Awards, including *Chicago* (1965), *Icarus's Mother* (1965), *La Turista* (1967), *The Tooth of Crime,* and *Curse of the Starving Class* (1976). *A Lie of the Mind* (1985) won the New York Drama Critics' Circle Award, the New York Drama Desk Award, and the Outer Critics' Circle Award for outstanding new play. Shepard was elected to the American Academy of Arts and Letters in 1986, and in 1992, he received the Gold Medal for Drama from the Academy. In 1994 Shepard was inducted into the Theatre Hall of Fame. A revised version of *Buried Child* opened on Broadway in April 1996 and was nominated for a Tony Award for Best Play. Shepard has also worked as an actor, screenwriter, and director in several motion pictures. His screen acting career began in 1970 with the film *Brand X.* He was nominated for a best supporting actor award from the Academy of Motion Picture Arts and Sciences in 1983 for his performance in *The Right Stuff,* and later appeared in several films, including the screen adaptation of his play *Fool for Love* (1983), *Country* (1984), *Thunderheart* (1992), and *Black Hawk Down* (2001). Shepard has written and directed two films—*Far North* (1988) and *Silent Tongue* (1993)—and has written a number of screenplays, most notably *Paris, Texas* (1984; with L. M. Kit Carson), which won the Grand Jury Prize at the 1984 Cannes Film Festival.

## MAJOR WORKS

Shepard's early one-act plays—such as *Cowboys, The Rock Garden,* and *Chicago*—are abstract and absurdist explorations that have been compared to the works of Samuel Beckett and Harold Pinter. The plays are marked by their disjointed structure, visual imagery, and long monologues typically loaded with obscenity. For example, *The Rock Garden* culminates in a verbal outburst by a teenager who details his sexual techniques to his dumbstruck father. These works combine wild humor, grotesque satire, myth, and a sparse, haunting language to create a subversive pop art vision of America. Shepard continued to explore various combinations of sight and sound in his early full-length dramas as well. His first full-length play, *La Turista,* is a comedy about a couple who fall prey to intestinal illness while vacationing in Mexico. *Operation Sidewinder* (1970)—which satirizes the social and political upheavals of the 1960s—features a giant rattlesnake-shaped computer as the central figure and ends with a prolonged burst of machine gun fire.

Theatre scholars often mark Shepard's move to London in 1971 as the beginning of the second stage of his playwriting career. Shepard's most notable work from this period is *The Tooth of Crime*, which Shepard later revised as *The Tooth of Crime (Second Dance)* in 1996. The play tells the story of two rock musicians, Hoss and Crow, whose battle for prominence in the music industry resembles the actions of gunfighters in the Old West. Language plays a crucial part in the play, as Shepard employs urban slang, rock lyrics, and other pop idioms in place of the conventional weapons of gunfighters. At the conclusion, Hoss, realizing that the language he uses for "dueling" is dated, commits suicide, leaving Crow in command until the next challenger comes along. Shepard's residency at the Magic Theatre in San Francisco began a new stage in his career—the plays from this period typically focus on an artist's pursuit of identity and creative freedom, as well as the struggles that result from this search. *Suicide in B-Flat* (1976) suggests the stifling of creativity in the life of a jazz musician, while *Angel City* (1976) satirizes the film industry and the corruption of young writers.

Shepard's major plays of the late 1970s and 1980s are domestic dramas in which working-class families become victims of self-perpetuated violence, guilt, and abnormal fantasy. These works reject the cartoonish imagery in Shepard's earlier works in favor of more realistic plot lines and characterizations. Shepard uses the dissolution of a southern California family in *Curse of the Starving Class* to symbolize the demise of the Western frontier and American society in general. The action in *Buried Child* unfolds when a man named Vince returns to his midwestern home after a long absence. He is confronted with a dangerously unbalanced cast of relatives who harbor secrets of incest and murder. Eventually, these secrets are discovered along with an unwanted infant buried in the backyard years earlier. *True West* (1980) highlights the struggle between the dual natures of two brothers, Austin and Lee. Austin, a reserved screenwriter, has returned to their mother's house to finish a long overdue script for his Hollywood contact, Saul. Lee is a charismatic and violent criminal who lives in the desert and surprises Austin by arriving unannounced. After impressing Saul with stories from his sordid past, Lee pitches Saul his own idea for a movie. Saul immediately buys the idea and breaks his agreement with Austin. The thematic concerns in several of Shepard's later plays culminate in *Fool for Love,* which examines obsession, betrayal, myth and truth. The plot develops through alternating submission and rejection between two lovers who may be half-brother and half-sister. *A Lie of the Mind* continues Shepard's exploration of American families in emotional distress. The work centers on a married couple, Beth and Jake, whose violent relationship both destroys and redeems their families. Beaten to the point of brain damage by Jake, Beth is slowly recuperating under the watchful eye of her loveless parents and her vengeful brother. Jake, thinking that he has killed Beth, hides in his boyhood home under the care of his over-protective mother. Although the two characters become geographically distant, they remain emotionally bonded by their obsessive love for each other. Throughout the course of the play the true nature of both families is probed and revealed.

Shepard's plays dating from 1990 to 2000 continue his examination of the American family, the nature of father-son relationships, and the search for love and personal identity. In *States of Shock* (1991) a nameless American colonel and an amputee soldier named Stubbs arrive at a restaurant to celebrate the anniversary of the death of the colonel's son. *Simpatico* (1994) follows the tensions between two ex-partners, Vinnie and Carter, who once made a fortune by fixing a horse race. Years later, Vinnie threatens to blackmail Carter, now a successful horse breeder, with evidence of their past crime. In *Eyes for Consuela* (1998)—a two-act play based on the short story "The Blue Bouquet" by Octavio Paz—a vacationing American is assaulted by a knife-wielding Mexican named Amado, who wishes to present his lover Consuela with a bouquet of blue eyeballs. In *The Late Henry Moss* (2000), two brothers return home to confront each other and their violent past after the unexpected death of their father.

Shepard has published several collections of prose and poetry in addition to his plays. *Hawk Moon* (1973) and *Motel Chronicles* (1982) each contain a variety of prose pieces, poems, and speeches, while *Rolling Thunder Logbook* (1977) reprints a journal based on Shepard's experiences traveling with musician Bob Dylan's Rolling Thunder Revue tour. *Cruising Paradise* (1996) and *Great Dream of Heaven: Stories* (2002) contain short stories exploring themes of solitude and loss. Shepard has also written a number of screenplays, including the award-winning *Paris, Texas, Far North,* and *Silent Tongue.*

## CRITICAL RECEPTION

Overall, Shepard's work has received largely enthusiastic reviews, although critics have at times had difficulty clearly delineating the merits of his unconventional methods. His initial plays have often been dismissed as poor imitations of the works of earlier absurdist playwrights, with detractors complaining about the obscure nature of his work. Others have since championed Shepard's plays, recognizing them as part of the postmodern departure from traditional literary modes. Works such as *The Tooth of Crime* and *Cowboy Mouth* have been commended for imaginatively employing elements of popular culture and for critiquing the American obsession with fame and celebrity. Likewise, the nonrealistic elements of Shepard's dramas have been acclaimed for focusing attention on the act of performing and on the audience's role in the artistic process. In general, his later works have received positive responses and have been touted for their greater emphasis on content rather than form. However, the preponderance of masculine characters and archetypes in Shepard's plays have led some critics to question his ability and desire to portray strong female characters. Despite these reservations, reviewers have frequently granted Shepard a pivotal role in contemporary American theater, applauding his ability to create accessible dramas while pioneering nontraditional techniques.

## PRINCIPAL WORKS

*Cowboys* (play) 1964
*The Rock Garden* (play) 1964
*Chicago* (play) 1965
*Icarus's Mother* (play) 1965
*Red Cross* (play) 1966
*Cowboys #2* (play) 1967
*Forensic and the Navigators* (play) 1967
*La Turista* (play) 1967
*The Holy Ghostly* (play) 1969
*The Unseen Hand* (play) 1969
*Operation Sidewinder* (play) 1970
*Zabriskie Point* [with Michelangelo Antonioni, Tonino Guerra, Fred Graham, and Clare Peploe] (screenplay) 1970
*Back Bog Beast Bait* (play) 1971
*Cowboy Mouth* [with Patti Smith] (play) 1971
*Mad Dog Blues* (play) 1971
*Blue Bitch* (screenplay) 1972
*The Tooth of Crime* (play) 1972; revised as *The Tooth of Crime (Second Dance)*, 1996
*Hawk Moon* (prose, poetry, and speeches) 1973
*Action* (play) 1974
*Geography of a Horse Dreamer* (play) 1974
*Killer's Head* (play) 1975
*Angel City* (play) 1976
*Curse of the Starving Class* (play) 1976
*The Sad Lament of Pecos Bill on the Eve of Killing His Wife* (play) 1976
*Suicide in B-Flat* (play) 1976
*Rolling Thunder Logbook* (journal) 1977
*Buried Child* (play) 1978
*Seduced* (play) 1978
*Tongues* [with Joseph Chaikin] (play) 1978
*Savage/Love* [with Joseph Chaikin] (play) 1979
*True West* (play) 1980
*Motel Chronicles* [photographs by Johnny Dark] (prose and poetry) 1982
*Fool for Love* (play) 1983
*Superstitions* (play) 1983
*Paris, Texas* [with L. M. Kit Carson] (screenplay) 1984
*A Lie of the Mind* (play) 1985
*The War in Heaven* [with Joseph Chaikin] (radio play) 1985
*True Dylan* (play) 1987
*Far North* [director and screenwriter] (film) 1988
*Joseph Chaikin and Sam Shepard: Letters and Texts, 1972-1984* [edited by Barry V. Daniels] (letters) 1989
*States of Shock* (play) 1991
*Silent Tongue* [director and screenwriter] (film) 1993
*Simpatico* (play) 1994
*Cruising Paradise* (short stories) 1996
*When the World Was Green (A Chef's Fable)* [with Joseph Chaikin] (play) 1996
†*Eyes for Consuela* (play) 1998
*The Late Henry Moss* (play) 2000
*Great Dream of Heaven: Stories* (short stories) 2002

*The screenplay was adapted for the stage in 1973.

†Based on the short story "The Blue Bouquet" by Octavio Paz.

# CRITICISM

**Robert Brustein (review date 27 January 1986)**

SOURCE: Brustein, Robert. "The Shepard Enigma." *New Republic* 194, no. 3706 (27 January 1986): 25-6, 28.

[*In the following review, Brustein offers a mixed assessment of* A Lie of the Mind, *noting that the "plotting is a little too undisciplined."*]

*A Lie of the Mind* is Sam Shepard's most ambitious play to date, the closest he has come to entering the mainstream of American drama. Directed by the playwright in association with professional producers, it has been mounted at the Promenade Theatre with a strong cast. Like David Rabe's *Hurly-Burly,* which also played that off-Broadway theater with box-office actors, it stands a good chance of moving later to a Broadway house. Thus Shepard seems to be following the pattern of all serious American dramatists since O'Neill—beginning with a small but passionate coterie of devoted admirers, and then achieving popular support and media recognition. In Shepard's case, this recognition has been enhanced, and complicated, by his celebrity as a movie actor, which has exacerbated the tension between his public and private careers. A similar tension was partly responsible for that neglect suffered by most reputable American playwrights after their greatest success (followed perhaps by a revival of interest when the playwright died or reached some venerable birthday). Clifford Odets got smothered by Hollywood; Arthur Miller ran out of usable material; Tennessee Williams lost control of his form; William Inge turned to increasingly hysterical plots; Edward Albee sacrificed his absurdist power for mythical drawing-room comedies modeled on T. S. Eliot. On the other hand, O'Neill, with whom Shepard is most frequently compared, wrote his greatest plays years after Broadway had abandoned him.

For that reason, any cautionary remarks about Shepard's future are premature, though I must admit I found *A Lie of the Mind* disappointing—a big canvas on which the colors run in smeared, sometimes slipshod fashion. True, Shepard's play writing has never been neat, but then it has never been very accessible either. What is strange for Shepard enthusiasts is how closely this one resembles a play by Lanford Wilson or Tennessee Williams. Ever since *Curse of the Starving Class,* Shepard has been moving away from extravagant characters, dream actions, and hallucinatory riffs into a more domestic style. With *Buried Child,* arguably his finest work, he managed to make the family play a structure for subterranean probes into the American nightmare. Now, however, those relationships between violent and sensitive brothers, loony mothers and children, fathers and alienated sons, husbands and estranged wives, have increasingly moved to the center of his plays, while whatever was fantastic and demonic has gone to the fringes. *A Lie of the Mind* goes delightfully haywire in the last of its three long acts, but for most of its four-hour length the action and the characters are relatively recognizable, even endearing eccentrics.

In short, Shepard is beginning to domesticate himself as a writer—ironically at the very moment when, as a movie actor, he is being catapulted into legend as the iconic lonely Westerner. Composing more and more out of his actual as opposed to his dream experience, Shepard is moving inexorably toward the heart of American realism, where audiences have the opportunity to identify him as a family member like themselves—son, brother, lover, husband. This has advantages: greater clarity, concentration, and recognition. It also has disadvantages, in that Shepard is now displaying what he has in common with the spectator rather than what the spectator unwittingly shares with him. Another disadvantage is that as Shepard's life gets increasingly familiar from interviews, his work seems to get increasingly biographical—and confined. The brothers in *A Lie of the Mind* remind us of the ones in *True West*; the husband and wife recall the brother and sister in *Fool for Love.* The California family comes from *Curse of the Starving Class,* the Montana family from *Buried Child.* Worse, one finds oneself speculating about more personal links: whether the enmity between the dead father and his son is based on Shepard's own published filial feelings, whether the hero's jealousy over his actress wife has any bearing on his relationship with Jessica Lange, whether the character's brain-damaged dialogue has been influenced by that of his close friend Joseph Chaikin, a recent stroke victim. One is tempted, in short, to confuse fiction with reality, imaginative creation with biographical gossip.

*A Lie of the Mind* begins with a frenzied telephone call from Jake to his brother Frankie, saying that he has killed his actress wife, Beth. Objecting to the way she identified with her roles, Jake imagined that, Method-like, she was sleeping with her leading man, and beat her about the head. Beth, however, is alive, though the assault has damaged her brain; hospitalized and visited by her own brother, Mike, she can speak only nonsense syllables ("I'm above my feet. . . . How high me? How high up?"). Jake is having his problems too; he refuses to believe Beth has survived and suffers catatonic fits. His mom, a menopausal vamp, tries to cure him by feeding him cream of broccoli soup, but he is in a fever of jealousy over a past affair he imagines between his brother and his wife.

Meanwhile, Beth has moved from a California hospital to her Montana home, where her father spends his days hunting venison. When Frankie arrives to try to reconcile Beth to Jake, her father, Baylor, mistaking him for a deer, shoots him in the leg. ("In my prime, you'd have been dead meat, son.") Beth's family, particularly Mike, is primed for vengeance. Beth, alternating between moments of clarity in which she confesses her love for Jake and periods when she thinks they cut out her brain, dresses up like a hooker and tries to seduce the wounded Frankie, while Mike gleefully hauls in the hind end of a deer and drops the carcass on the living-room floor.

Back in California, Jake is preoccupied with the ashes of his own father, an alcoholic Air Force officer who had abandoned the family. In a long revelation scene, Jake confesses his responsibility for the death of his father, whom he led from bar to bar, then encouraged to run down the middle of the highway. When Jake finally goes to Montana to find Beth, Mike trusses him like a horse, putting an American flag in his mouth for a bit. (Baylor is mighty upset by this desecration of the "flag of our nation.") While Baylor and his dotty wife carefully fold the flag, Jake announces his love for Beth—"I love you more than this earth. . . . Everything lied—you—you're true. I love you more than life." Then to prove it, he delivers her to his brother Frankie and leaves in the snow.

This is essentially the plot of the play, though there are dozens of other scenes, many irrelevant, including one in which Jake's mom leaves home with her daughter and, in order to avoid packing, sets fire to the house. (In Montana, Beth's mother thinks she sees a fire in the snow.) It may seem odd to describe such idiosyncratic characters and bizarre behavior as normal or domestic. Yet the eccentricities, while often amusing, sometimes seem willed, like the studied gothic in Beth Henley or Tennessee Williams, and at the heart of this work is a rather conventional, even somewhat banal, love story. "I love you more than this earth" is not a line one would ever expect to find in a Shepard play.

Nor would one expect to find such crude symbolism as the flag business at the end. Even his title lacks the customary, instinctual Shepard resonance. What *A Lie of the Mind* could use is a really exacting editor, one who might have persuaded the playwright to pare away irrelevancies and obesities from his rather bloated text, while encouraging him to examine more closely its themes and situations. This is a director's function; and much as I admire some of Shepard's work with the actors, I think it was a mistake for him to stage his own play. The setting, for example, apart from being crude and unsuggestive, leaves the central area of the stage virtually unused, with most of the scenes being staged in the two rooms on the sides.

I did not see Harvey Keitel play the part of Jake; perhaps to counteract his image as a woman-beater (following a similar role in *Hurly-Burly*), he was away with his own wife as she gave birth to a child. Instead, his understudy, Bill Raymond, performed Jake, script in hand, in a display of guts and talent that drew cheers, though it made one attend more to the achievement than the play. People have a tendency to miscast Amanda Plummer, and she seemed to me again miscast as Beth, too spiritual and stentorian to capture the steamy voluptuousness of the character. As Frankie, Aidan Quinn adds to his growing stature as an intelligent performer. Will Patton is a strong, vaguely simian Mike, roaring out the fury of an unsatisfied revenger; and James Gammon brings a hoarse crude authority to the deerstalker, Baylor, whether having his bare feet rubbed with an ointment made to soften leather boots or giving his wife her first kiss in 20 years.

But the acting honors of the evening belong to the two moms, Geraldine Page as Jake's mother and Ann Wedgeworth as Beth's. Her talent and control increasing with her age, Miss Page is a fearless and accomplished actress. She brings a bleary dissociation to the role—her belly swollen into a pot, bobby socks on her feet, a flower in her ear, whining like a fire siren—that tells us more about Jake's genetic disorders than Shepard's writing. As for Miss Wedgeworth, equally amnesiac about the facts of her past—demure, wan, trembling on the edge of hysteria—she emerges somehow as the most delicate member of the family, and the sanest too, for all her flakiness ("Please don't scream in this house; this house is very *old*").

But ultimately, despite the felicities of the acting and the writing, this play wears you down rather than works you up. The dialogue is a little too declarative, the plotting a little too undisciplined, the characters a little too unforgettable, to persuade you that the motor energies come out of inspiration rather than will. Critics are saying that Shepard's double role as playwright and movie actor is providing that missing link in American culture between high and popular art. I wonder. It must be very hard to write plays when people are staring at your hands to see if your nails are dirty. How does one perform the private act of creation under the blinding glare of publicity? How do you base your work on experience without making it a subject of gossip or speculation? How can Shepard find the freedom to separate himself as a writer from the role determined for him as a movie star? Perhaps those Pirandellian questions might form the subject of his next play.

## Gerald Weales (review date 14 February 1986)

SOURCE: Weales, Gerald. "Great Divide: Shepard's *Lie of the Mind*." *Commonweal* 63, no. 3 (14 February 1986): 86-7.

[*In the following review, Weales criticizes* A Lie of the Mind, *objecting to the "cartoon atmosphere" of the play.*]

Sam Shepard's new play, *A Lie of the Mind,* runs for more than four hours, but its length does not herald structural innovation in his drama. He is still working in short scenes, as he has been since he turned up off-off-Broadway in the 1960s. In the new play, he cuts back and forth between two families and their homes on opposite ends of the stage, jumping from one painful or comic sequence to the next. The play, as one expects with Shepard, is absorbing, but a kind of attenuation has set in. It has no images as sharp and compelling as the corn shucking in *Buried Child* or the nude man with the lamb in *Curse of the Starving Class*; nor does it manage the intensity of *True West* or *Fool for Love,* even though many of the scenes are two-person encounters.

Shepard is on familiar ground in *A Lie of the Mind,* dealing once again with the disintegration of the American family, as in *Curse* and *Child,* and with the violence and mutability of sexual love, as in *Fool for Love.* The event that triggers the minimal action of *Lie* is Jake's jealous beating of his wife, which sends him back to his home thinking he has killed Beth, and sends her, brain-damaged but slowly recovering, to her family. Both homes are loveless, Jake's father having long since walked out on his mother and died in a drunken accident for which Jake may have been responsible. Beth's mother is servant and burden to her husband, a Montana rancher who seems to prefer the deer he hunts to his family. Jake's mother dotes on him and tries to return him to the womb of his childhood room, evicting his sister in the process. When I used the adjective *minimal* with *action,* I intended to suggest that there was no dramatic development of importance. There is incident aplenty. Beth's father shoots Jake's brother, mistaking him for a deer, when Frankie comes to see if Beth is alive or dead; Beth, who perceives in fragmentary ways, decides to marry Frankie and gets herself tarted up for the occasion. Jake has made his way from California to Montana—that is, has crossed the stage—where, after having been tortured by Beth's brother, he begs everyone's pardon and gives Beth to Frankie.

The play is sprinkled with moments in which a character displays love, affection, protectiveness toward another, but the effect of the play as a whole is to suggest the impossibility of a happy relationship between a man and a woman or a healthy closeness within a family. At the end of the play Jake's mother, on one side of the stage, is burning her house down and getting ready to go to Ireland with her daughter to visit probably non-existent relatives; on the other side, Frankie and Beth embrace in an ending that would be a more comforting final clinch if her parents were not laboriously folding an American flag into the triangle that suggests a funeral; and the mutilated Jake and his mutilator are somewhere in between, each self-exiled from his uncongenial family circle. In the final moment, Beth's mother looks across the stage and comments on the fire which is presumably burning hundreds of miles away, thus providing the connection-disconnection image which indicates that the lie of the mind is not simply the false promise of love, but the geography of shared loss.

The most startling thing about *A Lie of the Mind* is the broad comedy in it. Vincent Canby, reviewing the movie version of *Fool for Love* (*New York Times,* December 15, 1985), called the original play "a live-action Maggie and Jiggs cartoon for which there is no exit," a label that he intends as descriptive, not pejorative, since he admires the play in preference to the film. I had not thought of *Fool for Love* in those terms, although the comedy in it, as in the other Shepard plays, is often center stage. With *A Lie of the Mind* the cartoon quality of the characters becomes pervasive, so much so that the knockabout often robs the play of the kind of powerful image that Shepard so often comes up with when a potentially comic situation or character turns suddenly painful or lyric. Since Shepard directed *Lie* and presumably chose the performers, the excessiveness in the production must be what he wants. Will Patton, as Beth's brother, gives a frenetic physical performance as though the character's anger has gone to the actor's nerve ends. At one point, he stiffens like a board and falls flat on his back; at another he throws himself on the ground and drags himself under the step in a single fine sweep of exasperation. All of the characters are overstated, but none of them has quite the flamboyance of the two mothers. Shepard has been having a run on peculiar mothers—in *Curse,* in *Buried Child,* in *True West*—but the two in *A Lie of the Mind* win blue ribbons for eccentricity. Ann Wedgeworth plays Beth's mother as a gently demented women, nervously upright in her fluffy mules. Geraldine Page, as Jake's mother, mugs and punches relentlessly, as though she were finally getting a chance to perfect her Marie Dressler imitation, a reading which should suit Shepard. After all, he seems to have built his performance as Eddie in the *Fool for Love* film out of bits and pieces of Gary Cooper.

On the night that I saw *A Lie of the Mind,* Harvey Keitel was out of the cast. His replacement as Jake was Bill Raymond, who had just been hired as understudy and had to work with script in hand. He knew the business, he knew the character, he even knew most of the lines, and the pages he carried interfered with his performance only once. Jake throws a tantrum, knocking a bowl of soup out of his mother's hand and ripping his bed apart; in the process, Raymond lost script as well as bed linen and had to scramble around to retrieve the pages, which he did without ever losing Jake or his histrionic bad temper. It is possible, I suppose, that

Raymond's presence disoriented the production to some extent, but the disconcerting broadness in so much of the show was clearly a deliberate decision of Shepard and his cast.

A major new Shepard play is always an occasion, but *A Lie of the Mind* seems to have extended Shepard's staying power without enriching his art. In the past, he has used his taste for caricature in the interest of dramatic or visual truth. Here the serious side of the play is so compromised by the cartoon atmosphere that Shepard sometimes seems to be mocking the themes that have given substance and force to so much of his recent work.

**David Wyatt (essay date spring 1992)**

SOURCE: Wyatt, David. "Shepard's Split." *South Atlantic Quarterly* 91, no. 2 (spring 1992): 333-60.

[*In the following essay, Wyatt explores the ambivalence of the characters and the world view in Shepard's body of work.*]

Sam Shepard does not write dramas of recognition. His characters renounce insight and resist growth; they seem, instead, the scene for their author's projection of violent, contradictory, inchoate emotions. Shepard's language remains acutely aware of this, but it is an awareness in which the characters scarcely participate. Few of the characters believe in any existence apart from a role, and one purpose of the plays is to explore this. Yet it also seems a limit by which the characters are bound, a repetitive irony through which the playwright asserts his superiority over his players. The conception of life is essentially dramatic, as Richard Gilman argued about Shepard in 1981:

> [W]e either take our places in a drama and discover ourselves as we act, or we remain unknown (as some indeed choose to do). In the reciprocal glances of the actors we all are, in our cues to dialogue, the perpetual agons and denouements that we participate in with others, identities are found, discarded, altered but above all *seen*. Not to be able to act, to be turned away from the audition, is the true painful condition of anonymity. But to try to act too much, to wish to star, the culmination and hypertrophy of the common desire, is a ripeness for disaster.

This seems so brilliantly right as nearly to forestall the need for future criticism. If it speaks to the basic thematic tension in the work, it also reveals a stance *toward* tension, Shepard's stubborn—almost willful—ambivalence. Ambivalence has been less his subject than his mode: his imagination craves what it spurns. "I think we're split in a much more devastating way than psychology can ever reveal," he has said. This torn mind has given his work its thrilling and irritating air of irresolution; he seems to like being split. "To be right in the middle of a conflict—right exactly in the middle—and let it play itself out where you can see . . . well, that's where things begin to get exciting. You can't avoid contradictions." Only in the most recent work for the stage does he begin to move beyond this habitual ambivalence toward a vision of resolution, of a world offering the possibilities of change and even choice.

\* \* \*

Shepard's plays explore the troubled relation between our fear of performance and our lust for attention. They do so by taking the careful measure of the spaces between us; there is nothing casual about the physical positions of the bodies on his stage. The blocking explicit in his stage directions and implicit in his scene dynamics advances a complex argument about the possibilities for character and action in his world. Exits and entrances reveal themselves as perilous moments of definition or self-loss. Characters seek without knowing it an instant of distinction or notice. Shepard's management of "where we stand" in respect to others reveals his conception of life as an unending and often unwilling competition for space and love.

Shepard's most celebrated play, which won the Pulitzer Prize in 1979, takes its power as much from how the actors move as from what they say. The subject of *Buried Child* could be called "the stark dignity of entrance." The phrase is from the William Carlos Williams poem in which he imagines the way a new shoot shoulders the earth crumbs and pushes up into the light. *Buried Child* ends with Halie's great speech about how shoots and people come into the world:

> Good hard rain. Takes everything straight down deep to the roots. The rest takes care of itself. You can't force a thing to grow. You can't interfere with it. It's all hidden. It's all unseen. You just gotta wait til it pops up out of the ground. Tiny little shoot. Tiny little white shoot. All hairy and fragile. Strong though. Strong enough to break the earth even. It's a miracle, Dodge. I've never seen a crop like this in my whole life. Maybe it's the sun. Maybe that's it. Maybe it's the sun.

If Shepard ends the play with this appeal to a sustaining natural order, it is because the cultural space of the family has so utterly botched the task of nurturance. What makes us grow, draws us out? The play foregrounds such questions by focusing on the birth of each character into the space of the stage. The moment of truth is the one of coming on to the set.

A set summary of *Buried Child* might read like this:

> Lights come up on a living room, with stairs upward to the left and a screen porch to the right. Wife Halie begins speaking upstairs, unseen, and husband Dodge

talks back from his seat on the couch at center stage. Dodge yells for son Tilden and Tilden "*enters from stage left, his arms loaded with fresh corn.*" Halie finally enters slowly, down the stairs, and "*continues talking.*" She does so after introducing by report another character we will never see, dead son Ansel. Near the end of act 1, son Bradley drags himself in on his wooden leg. He slips, enters from the screen porch "*laboriously,*" shaves and bloodies his father's scalp. Act 2 begins with Shelly's offstage laughter. She and her boyfriend, long-lost grandson Vince, enter the house unnoticed. The final entrance is effected by Tilden as he again carries something on, the bundle of the buried child, the last character to be granted entrance.

If kinds of entrance bespeak types of character, we get this reading of the play: Halie is the perpetually absent mother, a voice that speaks without loving or noticing. Dodge is the present but absent father, the paternal force who never leaves the stage and whose death occasions no notice. Memory-ridden Tilden carries the family burdens. Ansel exists only as rumor, the fantasy child who replaces the one his mother actually conceived and buried. Bradley's noise and violence measure his actual impotence. Stranger Shelly sneaks on and off, and so will fend off this uncanny family by finding it temporarily "familiar." Vince must revise his unremarked first entrance with a second, forcing the recognition—only Halie briefly grants it—his initial homecoming fails to evoke. The buried child appears in the play's last scene—its father presents it to its mother—so as to bring an end to the repressions set in motion in the first scene.

The major interruption in the play is Vince's second entrance; as act 3 winds down he cuts his own door through the screen and climbs, knife in mouth, into the central space. By doing so he also cuts short the recognition scene, Dodge's articulation of the story of the buried child. But interruption may be too strong a word. No one picks up the dropped stitch of Dodge's narration; attention simply shifts to Vince. An interruption can best occur during a continuing and focused act of attention, and this is what Shepard's plays do not provide. Instead, the inattentiveness of character quickly schools the audience to expect a series of arresting distractions. I once attended a production of **Buried Child** in a theater in the round, a space with fewer than two hundred seats. At the end of act 1, as Bradley began to shave Dodge's head, a man in the front row fell into a seizure, his breath short, his head tipped back. The audience soon noticed him, called for the lights. The lights came up and the house manager announced a ten-minute pause. A policewoman strolled in; the man's wife stroked his head. The house went dark; the lights came up on act 2. Nothing felt lost—only added. Asked to accommodate an unlooked-for interruption, the play did so as it had its other entrances, by revealing that its very structure was built out of whatever next thing managed to make us watch it.

"Me to play": Hamm's first line in Beckett's *Endgame* might well be the motto for Shepard's people. They insist on playing, on keeping the performance alive, without any solid faith or even interest in being comprehended or known. Attention without recognition; this is what they unhappily, desperately want. In **Buried Child**, "recognize" proves the operative verb. The verb gets attached to Vince, the unremembered son and grandson, but it extends to everyone, from the Halie who "*doesn't really notice the two men*" in her living room to the death of Dodge, "*completely unnoticed,*" against the TV. "I recognize the yard," Vince says. "Yeah but do you recognize the people?" Shelly replies. Tilden's answer to the question "Do you recognize him" refuses Vince any fatherly recognition: "I had a son once but I buried him." Shelly persists in forcing the issue with Dodge, but he turns it into a comic interrogation:

DODGE:

(*watching T.V.*) Recognize who?

SHELLY:

Vince.

DODGE:

What's to recognize?

To learn, see, know again—this is the burden of the verb. Shelly insists on keeping alive the fiction of recognition in a world in which no original cognition occurred. Recognition is the promise of drama, the experience Aristotle thought distinguished it from other literary genres. Shepard's conception of drama is so pure that his characters have been reduced to the desire to perform in spite of the absence of an action to be imitated. The outcome is no outcome, no *anagnorisis* or *cognitio*. The recognition that would lead to catharsis and hence to the end of drama and the need for drama—this is what Shepard's plays do not give.

While watching a Shepard play we are not present, then, to a world of character isolated by a deed. Things happen; there is plenty of noise and motion on the set. The scenery is relentlessly domestic or mundane; we are not allowed the escape hatch of thinking the action merely an allegory or a dream. Props play an abundant part. The major elements onstage at the end of **Buried Child** are less the actors than a wooden leg, a blanket, a rose bouquet. It is as if in the moment of discovering the expressive possibilities of the physical space of the stage this playwright had lost faith in the conventions of drama. The surviving given is the impulse to perform. Shepard's theater thus becomes not a space for the imitation of an action but one for acting out.

The space beyond roles, beyond the imperative "to act," is the unknown space within the self, the frightening realm of the "personal." This is the space Shepard has recently begun to explore. Jake uses the word "personal" in *A Lie of the Mind* (1985) to describe the part of himself he would never tell. It is a space he can conceive, yet one he refuses, consciously, to inhabit. He does this by refusing to remember. Through a recovery of Jake's lie of the mind, Shepard goes beyond the staging of behavior into his first sustained analysis of the motives for why we stage it. This inquiry into his characters' reasons for acting is made possible by his own deepening understanding of his reasons for writing.

* * *

Shepard's longest play, *A Lie of the Mind,* takes four hours to produce onstage. Its three acts trace the collision of two families linked by marriage. Each family has four members. Lorraine absentmindedly mothers sons Jake and Frankie and daughter Sally. The father is mysteriously dead. Meg and Baylor maintain a Montana ranch where their son Mike still lives, and to which their daughter Beth returns to convalesce from one of her husband Jake's near-fatal beatings. The action follows the two brothers, Jake and Frankie, as they work their way back toward Beth and into a forgotten past. At the play's end, the major characters have assembled around Beth, and, as they slowly exit, she is left in the arms of her brother-in-law, Frankie.

Repression is the lie of the mind, and Shepard's play turns upon the words "forget" and "remember." The story features two crimes Jake *could* keep in mind: his beating of his wife Beth, and his "murder" of his father. The first crime is as much "in" Jake's mind as the second is out of it. "You remember the night he died too, don't ya?" his sister asks Jake about his father. Jake answers: "That's the part I forgot." It is possible to wonder whether Jake abuses Beth because he killed his father, thereby submerging the taboo role of parricide into that of wife beater. (In his "Notes on Scenes" for *A Lie of the Mind,* Shepard himself asks the leading question: "What's the connection between Jake's break up with Beth & his quest for his dead father?"). Forgetting—hiding a part of the mind from the whole—is what people do in this play, how they get by, live onward. Both mothers forget that their children have married. Baylor triumphs over anger and ennui by remembering how to fold a flag. "HOW COULD I KNOW SOMETHIN' THAT I DON'T KNOW?" This is Jake's rhetorical question, and Shepard's emerging definition of the human. To know what we don't know, to be perpetually threatened by the irruption of memory—this is the painfully anxious state that energizes performance and drives people deeper into their roles.

Except Beth. Through an irony so violent that it may be intolerable, she has had forgetting knocked out of her head. Jake has beaten her into a permanent state of remembering, a mind, perhaps, without an unconscious. She is returned to the eloquence of primary process; her work now is to "never forget." And she knows it, or at least says it. "This is me. This is me now. The way I am. Now. This. All. Different. I—I live inside this. Remember. Remembering. You. You—were one. I know you. I know—love. I know what love is. I can never forget. That. Never." Beth lives "in" the permanent presence of her once and future feelings—in a state of terrifying mental health. It is a freedom we might also call madness, one no doubt purchased at too great a price.

Beth's oneness with her mental state defines by contrast the nature and necessity of performance in her play and in Shepard's work as a whole. Beyond pretending, she can speak now about its pleasures. "Pretend. Because it fills me. Pretending fills. Not empty. Other. Ordinary. Is no good. Empty. Ordinary is empty." Frankie responds to this with "You liked acting, huh?" and reminds us that the action of the play is set in motion by the response to a play. Jake claims that he beat up Beth because she had fallen in love with an actor she was "in love" with in a play: "I know what that acting shit is all about," he tells Frankie.

FRANKIE:

What?

JAKE:

They start doin' all the same stuff the person does!

FRANKIE:

What person?

JAKE:

The person! The—whad'ya call it? The—

FRANKIE:

Character?

JAKE:

Yeah. The character. That's right. They start acting that way in real life. Just like the character.

So, according to Jake, Beth goes crazy before he makes her lose her mind. This is madness for Shepard: to believe and become one's part. Yet it is also the way of life; it is nearly impossible to locate a "person" in his plays who does not mistake himself for a "character," who does not reduce and perfect himself in a role. Shepard's people mount performances that presume a massive act of forgetting; they become lost in what they "pretend" to be.

So is self-hate at the bottom of it all, and is the action of the mind a sort of guilty hiding? Yes, in part. Shepard's plays about families and their psyches operate to expose a secret, a buried child. Not the one out in the backyard, but the one within, the angry and therefore guilty and therefore repressed survivor of early loss. The plays are remarkable not in their grasp of this human pastime but in their sense of the vigor and variety of performances that lying minds can conjure up.

Shepard's play about lying turns upon an act of physical abuse, a chillingly beatifying exercise of male power, and yet its basic fantasy is of a confusion of family and even gender roles. Sally takes Jake's place in bed; Mike claims Frankie and Jake are "the same person"; Frankie even stands in for a deer. Baylor maintains that "a deer is a deer and a person is a person," but he's just shot the one for the other. Identity can so easily be mistaken because it is so haplessly confined to the role words—"brother" "daughter" "wife" "son"—ticked off by Frankie in act 3, scene 2. But the one division Shepard most diligently explores is that between woman and man.

Beth imagines something one hasn't seen before in Shepard, a "woman-man." She does so in her pretending with Frankie, the man whose wounded thigh has left him in her care:

BETH:

Pretend to be. Like you. Between us we can make a life. You could be the woman. You be.

FRANKIE:

What was the play you were in? Do you remember?

BETH:

(*Moving toward* FRANKIE) You could pretend to be in love with me. With my shirt. You love my shirt. This shirt is a man to you. You are my beautiful woman. You lie down.

Beth tries to push Frankie down on the sofa; he resists, and tells her he's come on Jake's behalf:

BETH:

Your other one. You have his same voice. Maybe you could be him. Pretend. Maybe. Just him. Just like him. But soft. With me. Gentle. Like a woman-man.

(BETH *starts moving slowly toward* FRANKIE. FRANKIE *stands awkwardly, supporting himself by the sofa, on his bad leg.*)

FRANKIE:

I need to find some transportation out a here! I need to find my car! I can't hang around here, Beth.

BETH:

(*Moving toward* FRANKIE) You could be better. Better man. Maybe. Without hate. You could be my sweet man. You could. Pretend to be. Try. My sweetest man.

This is an astonishing scene from a writer so concerned to shoulder the burden of American manhood, for better or for worse. *A Lie of the Mind* can shock in the way Hemingway's *The Garden of Eden* did, an unlooked-for outcry against the cost of the performance of being male. Yet both careers leave many signs of uneasiness along the way. Here, Shepard projects a fantasy, in the voice of a battered woman, that ought to become central to his future work. (It will not become so by simply clearing the decks of testosterone and then asking, as he does so endlessly in *Far North,* "Where's all the men?") But it is also a fantasy so embattled that he conjures here as its nemesis one of his most scary self-characters, Beth's brother Mike.

Mike inhabits the stage as the insane playwright, staging a revenge that requires Jake to memorize his lines. He compels performance and respects only roles. He lives within the myth of a solidarity (a family) that can be "betrayed." "I'm the only one who's loyal to this family!" he screams, and one hopes that, after Mike, Shepard himself will let his own loyalty lapse. His plays present the family, in Robert Stone's phrase, as "an instrument of grief," and yet he remains on record as stubbornly attached to it:

> Family—in the truest sense of people related by blood, knowing they are in a relationship with one another from birth to death—that's unbelievably awesome. . . . There's no way you can deny it. If a person denies it, he only ends up like Faust, you know?
>
> No matter what your family situation is—whether it's wonderful or chaotic—you have to accept it as part of the process of life. You can't jump out of it and say, "I'm free. I'm an individual." If the family exists in some kind of hell, that means you have to live in hell. Family is the soil you're born into. You gotta use it. You got to get through it. You can't run away from it.

Whatever Shepard's future take on the family, he has exposed in *A Lie of the Mind* the limits of a structure in which men "protect" women, brothers avenge sisters. Here Beth speaks to her brother Mike:

BETH:

(*Stiffens, stands back*) No! You make—you make a war. You make a war. You make an enemy. In me. In me! An enemy. You. You. You think me. You think you know. You think. You have a big idea.

Mike is a male who forces entry; he has no respect for Beth's "in." He thus becomes the double of what he sets out to punish, abusing what he is "tryin' to protect." Yet if the brother-avenger is merely an extension of the husband-abuser, it remains the case that Beth has been put into the position to be avenged and hurt and inspired by a man. Jake's act has "killed" her, as he says, but it has also created her, shifted her into a new vision and language. Upon this unresolved irony the play terribly turns, and so continues to betray Shepard's ambivalence about the fruits of male power.

The manuscript versions of *A Lie of the Mind* suggest that Shepard has become committed to revision of his work as well as to the revisions of lives within it. If early on Shepard thought that revision was "cheating," by the 1980s he had become fully committed to its possibilities. *True West* (1980) was revised thirteen times. The papers on deposit at the University of Virginia contain at least five manuscript versions of *A Lie of the Mind,* from the "Notes on Ideas for Plays" he sketched on 10 May 1984 to the final script from November 1985, one in which the pencilled cuts and revisions make their way into the typed text of the play. Two complementary motions of mind are revealed by these versions: one away from the "expository," and one toward the fusion of the themes of repression, revenge, and manhood. An examination of these manuscripts shows a writer hard at work changing both his stance and style.

Shepard's working drafts make much more room for a discursive imagination than does his finished work. In June 1984 he jotted down a list of "intrinsic necessities of the play." Foremost was "the need to allow the thing to tell its own story without bothering it with asking its meaning every step of the way." He didn't want the play to ask obvious questions: "What scenes are too expository right now?" Yet it seemed useful to ask about meaning at the start. A handwritten list of characters reduces them to themes:

> Repentance—(Jake)
>
> Transformation—(Beth)
>
> Insanity—(Meg, Lorraine)
>
> Betrayal—(Lorraine)
>
> Revenge—(Sally, Mike)
>
> Time, Tradition—(Baylor)
>
> Love—(Lyle)
>
> Fear—(Lou-Ann)

Lyle and Lou-Ann would get discarded; Frankie, the pivot man, is missing here. The earliest list of characters included Frankie, but not as Jake's brother. It is dated 10 May 1984:

> The Man
>
> The Woman
>
> The Friend of the Man
>
> The Brother of the Woman

Translated into the play's final terms, this list would read: Jake, Beth, Frankie, Mike. Here character gets reduced to gender or relational roles. Shepard begins with the function each character will essentially express. A third list can be found among Shepard's notes for the play:

> Imaginary Roles
>
> HEART SICK
>
> REAL LIFE
>
> Imitation
>
> Play Acting
>
> The War in Heaven
>
> Pretending to Die
>
> FRACTURED
>
> Broken
>
> On the Borderline
>
> A LIE OF THE MIND
>
> PROTECTION
>
> Believing a Lie

These proposed titles are handwritten on a piece of white typing paper. Shepard made the right choice; none of those discarded pose themselves as a kind of riddle that governs the play without explicating it.

If *A Lie of the Mind* explores the logic of the unconscious, Shepard chose not to make that easily plain. In act 1, scene 3, Jake insists upon Beth's hanky-panky as an actress: "I knew what she was up to even if she didn't." Frankie responds: "So, you mean you're accusing her of somethin' she wasn't even aware of?" In the "First Version" of the play (dated May-August 1984), the reply read this way: "You mean this was all unconscious on her part?" Strike the analytical term when everyday words will do. A more substantial revision involves the original act 1, scene 9, a scene eventually removed from the play. Why did Shepard cut it? First, because it contains the discarded character Lou-Ann. Lou-Ann is an actress who was to have replaced Beth when she is forced by Jake to drop out of her play. Second, the scene is relentlessly thematizing: in Shepard's words, "too expository." In it, Lou-Ann does a monologue from the part she has inherited from Beth, and what she talks about is something called "a lie of the mind." The play within the play here becomes too obviously an exemplum of the whole, and Shepard decides, unlike Hamlet, not to have his "mousetrap" snap so sententiously shut.

A final example suggests how Shepard allowed the play, in his words, "to tell its own story." In act 2, scene 3, Shepard reaches for the most radical emotion of the play, Beth's attempt to convert Frankie into her "woman-man." In what he labels the "True Second Version" (dated 5 November 1984), Beth tries to get Frankie to remember "making love to me." He cannot, because she has imagined it. She then says: "Nobody needs to have brain damage to wipe things out. You just chop it off. You just take someone in your arms and if it doesn't work you chop it off. You cancel the whole thing out like it never happened." These lines are crossed out by Shepard's pen. If repression is a kind of self-castration, as these rejected lines suggest, it was a case Shepard chose to make through staging and action rather than through strict exposition.

Shepard sought to protect his themes from his own literal intelligence; he did not stint, however, from amplifying them through the careful elision and revision of scenes. Three major scenes—they are the three on which my reading has focused—had to be invented or substantially altered after he had completed the first version of the play. These scenes were to become:

| Act/Scene | Date |
|---|---|
| 1.7 Jake and Lorraine: "How was it he died?" | 24 August 1984 |
| 2.1 Beth, Mike, Baylor, Meg: "You make a war." | 5 November 1984 |
| 2.3 Frankie and Beth: "Like a woman-man." | November 1985 |

The order in which these scenes compelled his attention suggests that Shepard had to work his way through many versions to his deepest and most original material.

The Jake we see onstage represses nearly everything about his father's death. "How was it he died?" he asks his mother. He does remember one thing, about the ashes. "Where's that box?" The focus here is on the fetishized remains. The end of the scene, where, in the original stage production, Harvey Keitel blows lightly into the box and sends his father's ashes up into a beam of light, has been called by Frank Rich the "play's most overwhelming theatrical moment." All that can be remembered is that remains remain. In the original version of the scene, the reach of memory does not stop with the ashes (Mrs. Willis will become mother Lorraine):

JAKE:

Where's he?

MRS. WILLIS:

He's gone. He's been a long time gone.

JAKE:

Dead? I remember him. [handwritten]

MRS. WILLIS:

Yeah.

J:

He's dead. [handwritten]

MRS. WILLIS:

Yes, he is. [handwritten]

Jake's active remembering here—his volunteering of the word "dead," a word Shepard typed and then crossed out—does not prove compatible with the emerging pattern of his lying mind. So Shepard adds the business with the ashes, and the talk about the father's unremembered death. The theme of repression is protected and amplified through these changes.

Beth gets to say two wonderful things to her brother and her brother-in-law: "You make a war" and "Like a woman-man." The first makes a point about what men do for and to women; the second, about what they could become with them. These central sayings are part of dialogues that did not exist in Shepard's "First Version." It was in Charleston, West Virginia, in early November 1984, that Shepard wrote the scene in which Beth confronts Mike and tells him that his "love" makes a war. And it was not until November of the next year that Shepard penciled these lines into the "Final Script": "With me. Gentle. Like a woman-man." He worked away on act 2, scene 3, even as the play went into production, as five pages of green-lined paper torn from a notebook attest. In the archaeology of Shepard's imagination the most radical material proves the most deeply buried, or difficult to retrieve. His discovery that the male avenger could become the androgynous lover was truly that, an emerging fiction he wrote his way toward over the eighteen months he worked on *A Lie of the Mind.* Shepard's growing willingness to revise suggests that self-editing may someday replace self-assertion in his work as the exemplary human performance.

* * *

Shepard's continual reimagining of *A Lie of the Mind* leads him into a complex of insights about the relations between performance and male power. And he locates these insights within the voice and experience of a woman. Everyone complains that up until Beth, his women characters aren't given much to do. They inhabit the stage as objects or audiences. Shepard has said that "the real mystery in American life lies between men, not between men and women." Shepard seems to be tiring not only of the mystery "between men"—*True West*'s struggle of the brothers—but also of the entire ethic of performance, of the desperate "vying" such a mystique expresses and entails. But to give up performing—to cease the lie of the mind—is also to risk being unmanned. This is the dangerous territory into which he has now strayed, as he evolves from the poet into the critic of American manhood.

David Leverenz has written that if "women writers portray manhood as patriarchy, male writers from Melville to Sam Shepard, David Mamet, and David

Rabe portray manhood as a rivalry for dominance." A woman's experience of men differs from a man's experience of being a man, and while the latter certainly carries its cultural privileges, it is not without its pains and burdens. Why recent American theater has been centered around these men and their preoccupation with being male is a question perhaps worth exploring. It is a theater dominated by hurt or angry sons. Try as we will to incorporate Beckett, we seem to end up recapitulating O'Neill.

Shepard's stance toward experience is an openly "male" one, confrontational, aggressive, penetrating. Entering "into" something is a recurrent figure of his speech. "So rather than avoid the issue, why not take a dive into it?" He asks this in response to a question about his supposed "macho" image:

> Just because machismo exists, doesn't mean that it shouldn't exist. There's this attitude today that certain antagonistic forces have to be ignored or completely shut out rather than entered into in order to explore and get to the heart of them. All you have to do is enter one rodeo event to find out what that's all about . . . and you find out fast—in about eight seconds! So rather than avoid the issue, why not take a dive into it? I'm not saying whether it's good or bad—I think that the moralistic approach to these notions is stupid. It's not a "moral" issue, it's an issue of existence. Machismo may be an evil force . . . but what in fact is it?

The imagery of ordeal may be no more persuasive here than the work done by prepositions like "in" and verbs like "enter." Shepard brilliantly begs the interviewer's question by answering in a language that presupposes that the world is a place requiring a certain kind of courage, one willing to get to the heart of things. It's a courage possessed by persons seasoned through many falls, persons—and here is the circularity of the argument—who usually happen to be men.

But there is another Shepard, one that antedates the uneasy machismo of *A Lie of the Mind,* one that even in his oldest surviving play longs for a different stance and style. This counterpressure issues in what I call the dream of liquidity.

The first image from the earliest play Shepard chooses to reprint is of spilled milk. "(*The GIRL drops her glass and spills the milk.*)" It is the same milk Gatsby's father spills from the glass he is handed at his son's funeral, the same "incomparable milk of wonder" Gatsby forsakes when he kisses Daisy and enters fallen time. The dream of the imperial self—of being an eternal suckling—tumbles out of the glass at the novel's end, and so marks an end. Shepard begins with this moment. From the start the self is spilled, scattered, lost to wholeness or a sense of origin. Yet spilling and being spilled also appeal in early Shepard: they afford escape from the hardness of identity, the need to "practice" and perform. The closing monologue of *The Rock Garden* captures Shepard's ambivalence about overflow:

(*A long pause*)

BOY:

> When I come it's like a river. It's all over the bed and the sheets and everything. You know? I mean a short vagina gives me security. I can't help it. I like to feel like I'm really turning a girl on. It's a much better screw is what it amounts to. I mean if a girl has a really small vagina it's really better to go in from behind. You know? I mean she can sit with her legs together and you can sit facing her. You know? But that's different. It's a different kind of thing. You can do it standing, you know? Just by backing her up, you know? You just stand and she goes down and down until she's almost sitting on your dick. You know what I mean? She'll come a hundred times and you just stand there holding on to it. That way you don't even have to undress. You know? I mean she may not want to undress is all. I like to undress myself but some girls just don't want to. I like going down on girls, too. You know what I mean? She gives me some head and then I give her some. Just sort of a give-and-take thing. You know? The thing with a big vagina is that there isn't as much contact. There isn't as much friction. I mean you can move around inside her. There's different ways of ejaculation. I mean the leading up to it can be different. You can rotate motions. Actually girls really like fingers almost as well as a penis. You know? If you move your fingers fast enough they'd rather have it that way almost. I learned to use my thumb, you know? You can get your thumb in much farther, actually. I mean the thumb can go almost eight inches whereas a finger goes only five or six. You know? I don't know. I really like to come almost out and then go all the way into the womb. You know, very slowly. Just come down to the end and all the way back and in and hold it. You know what I mean?

Here a Shepard speaker first steps into wild verbal space. The verbal transgression matches the sexual one; the boy's saying is above all a disturbance of speech, a protest against and relief from the talking past each other of the play. Shepard has said that *"The Rock Garden* is about leaving my mom and dad." Just as little in family life prepares us for the shocking discoveries in sex, so nothing in the play has signaled the boy's latent verbal power. The fantasy here is of control ("holding on") and the challenge, as ever in Shepard, is to "go in." But what arrests and amazes the boy is his own capacity for meltdown, the self "like a river." In the very act of proving his manhood he dissolves it, confounding the categories of loss and gain.

Men in early Shepard often turn to juice. "Juice" is a big word in *Hawk Moon* (1981), Shepard's most violent meditation on the liquification syndrome. *Chicago* (1965) imagines "a mound of greasy bodies rolling in sperm." *Icarus's Mother* (1965) turns upon a pee on the beach. In the unfinished *Machismo Sagas* (1978), Frankie fantasizes about being able to "vomit like a man." *Red Cross* (1967) ends with a white world stained red, the blood that streams down Jim's forehead. *La Turista* (1973) has Kent reduced to a "stream of fluid" by dysentery. Here Shepard goes beyond liquification to "abjection." This is Leonard Wilcox's judgment on *Red Cross*. He reads the suddenly bloodied face as a castration "upwardly displaced," the agony of a man caught between the maternal and patriarchal orders. If Jim is Shepard's sacrifice to such pressures, Kent seems to have passed beyond them. In the second act of *La Turista* his affliction gets refigured into a "thing of beauty" as he passes into a vision of a completely unsolid and unsullied self.

Shepard shows that for a straight man the experience of sex requires entrance into another and an alien body, and that achieved union with that body requires a transformation of his own. Solid flesh melts. Hamlet puns this into a kind of suicide, and frequently Shepard's meltdowns mingle ecstasy with extinction. *Hawk Moon* delivers up a catalog of exhausted males: "An orgasm would be nice but not all the love making preparation." This book poises stick shifts and guns and guitars against salt water, semen, blood, milk, urine, gasoline, sweat. The violence against women ("bleeding pussy") expresses the persistent fear of and desire for the loss of self in a woman's body: "I keep waking up in whoever's / Body I was with last." Shepard's anger at sex flows from the sheer fact of sex differences ("Boy or girl?" he asks), from a universe in which "The Sex of Fishes" could even be an issue. These unlike bodies compel some into an act of fusion as momentary as it is unforgettable. Sex risks the perpetual fulfillment and frustration of the human desire to be, as expressed in the last line of *Curse of the Starving Class* (1978), "like one whole thing." And on the insufficient dynamics of this act the culture has built an entire further set of expectations and demands. Better to be beyond desire and its consequences, the despairing *Hawk Moon* suggests, better to be a "Stone man."

Shepard's sexual material, like Hemingway's, expresses anxiety rather than bravado, a felt need for alternatives, not a smug posturing from within an embraced stance. They both see and see through early the imperative of performance. As the act that requires of the man the assertion and the loss of control, sex ought to provide a model for performance itself. But of course for Shepard's characters it does not. It is precisely the "give-and-take" of which the boy speaks in *The Rock Garden* (the 1970 *Operation Sidewinder* inverts the phrase: "[I]t's all about take and give") that is absent from these performances, especially the mutuality of verbal exchange.

Dialogue becomes like liquidity, then, a desired and feared thing in Shepard, a state which, if achieved, could signal a scary break-through to a new way of being. "You gotta talk or you'll die," Tilden says in *Buried Child*. No one fails to talk in these plays, or at least to make noise. They are "Dyin' for attention," in the words of *The Tooth of Crime* (1972). These characters speak like actors, bypassing the intimacy of conversation for the insistence of monologue. Speech is directed outward, forensic, not to be heard but overheard. Talking forces with little to say press for a piece of turf onstage. The most poignant of questions may be Salem's, in *La Turista*: "Are you listening?" The typography of the play's final pages gives an answer: two columns of print each assigned to one speaker. The lines are meant to be spoken simultaneously; here the "back" does not wait for the "forth."

These are style matches, and victory depends less on physical strength than the invention and mastery of a unique language. In *The Tooth of Crime* the duel unfolds between two visions of the status and power of words. For Hoss, language expresses; for Crow, it constitutes. Hoss displays a psyche; Crow inhabits a discourse. The values of sincerity and authenticity vie with those of arbitrariness and recombination. The price of victory is utter loneliness; Crow "wins" and becomes stellified, a star revolving in unpeopled space.

But these contesting plays—and *True West* is the other strong example—actually eschew victory for standoff. At the end one man has beaten or talked down another, but the real situation is parity, a kind of endless struggle of the brothers. *True West* gets divided into nine scenes, with each scene in turn divided into mood units by "pause." The lack of strong act or scene divisions or even of a simple rising action testifies to repetitive rather than climactic outcomes. The appearance of the mother near the end of *True West* confirms this. This may be the most astonishing entrance in Shepard's work. It is as if Lee and Austin have been fighting in order to grab a little of her notice, and this is what she cannot give. Her focus relentlessly elsewhere, she is the ever-present Shepard absent mother, the one for whom there is no here. Shepard's plays explore the uncanny continual return of the prodigal parent:

> (AUSTIN *makes more notes,* LEE *walks around, pours beer on his arms and rubs it over his chest feeling good about the new progress, as he does this* MOM *enters unobtrusively down left with her luggage, she stops and stares at the scene . . .*)

It will take five utterances from the sons before Mom finally speaks: "I'm back." If the moment of coming onstage is epiphanic for a Shepard character, none enter with a greater sense of diffidence than these perpetually missing persons, the women whose bland, insistent, unnoticing voices seem beyond the register of dramatic change or effect. "I don't recognize any of you": the voice is Shelly's, in **Buried Child,** but she speaks for most of Shepard's characters and virtually all of his parents, especially the female ones. These are anti-Oedipal dramas which deny that the self can be found—recognized—at home. So many of his plays dramatize the avoidance of love because for Shepard, as Joseph Chaiken has written, "the human experience of love" risks "the difficulty of expressing tenderness, and the dread of being replaced." People keep exiting and entering in the hope that they will be uniquely loved, but at the beginning of things stands a woman who refuses to be an audience for her child.

To forget; to be male; to be loved, or, at least, noticed: the drive toward performance is perhaps Shepard's most overdetermined, one pressed upon him by all the complexities of his being. And although this last incentive seems to me the most comprehensive, performance for Shepard is finally an excess, a gratuitous human impulse beyond explanation or the need for it. That we perform is his redundant truth; why we do so, he, this least analytical of dramatists, usually doesn't wonder. As Shepard says of Bob Dylan: "The point isn't to figure him out but to take him in."

\* \* \*

Increasingly, then, the interest in the career lies less in the will to perform than in its consequences. Shepard's reluctant celebrity is one of the more curious stances of our time. He dislikes interviews, and grants them. He prizes privacy and models for a photo spread in *Vanity Fair*. He has written brilliant plays but expends his time on mostly mediocre movies. Sam Shepard aspires to the very status his best work imagines to be death to the spirit. He wants to be a star.

In the small brown notebook where he sketched out ideas for **A Lie of the Mind** can be found an early draft of the song Shepard wrote with Dylan for *Knocked Out Loaded*. "Brownsville Girl" ends with a lament for a time "long before the stars were torn down." The song centers around Gregory Peck in *The Gunfighter*, a movie that images the price of celebrity as continual and failed vigilance against the murderous admiration of fans. After Peck gets ambushed by a rising young punk, the dying curse he passes on is that his murderer shall never escape the notice of those who will, in turn, try to supplant him. So Shepard teams up with the biggest star he can imagine in order to write about the cost of being one.

Is stardom simply one more cultural option that must be gone "into"? There seems more than a touch of bravado in Shepard's expense of spirit in a waste of fame. As he says, "So rather than avoid the issue, why not take a dive into it?" Anonymity is an anxiety for our time, one producing a craving for notice at once stimulated and resolvable through the media. As Frank Lentricchia has written about Don DeLillo's media-driven characters, especially Lee Harvey Oswald, "to be real in America is to be in the position of the 'I' who would be 'he' or 'she,'" to abandon our obscure first-person lives and to enter the realm of the "third-person singular," where we can speak of the self as an object of common attention, not the subject of our private fantasies. To make oneself something unique, to overcome the fury over likeness, to be irreplaceable—this dream drifts back over us as a collective wish, one Shepard has gone into with a reluctance almost self-sacrificing.

Between movies and drama Shepard now not only divides his time, but his imaginative needs. The pattern reveals an amazing fusion of talents; American life contains no precedent for an artist who is playwright, screenwriter, director—and actor. This more than double career allows Shepard to explore what it feels like—rather than means—to project an image.

It is as an actor that Shepard has become famous, and it was as an actor that he perhaps most dramatically confronted his ambivalence about performing. On 29 April 1971, Shepard's **Cowboy Mouth** had its American premiere. Shepard played the lead opposite Patti Smith. The next day Shepard disappeared, and Smith had to apologize to the audience for the no-show. "I attempted to play a part once," he explained a few years later. "Opening night was the only time I did it. I was in a state and ran off to New England, which wasn't very responsible. I like experimenting with acting, but I don't like the performance part of it. That's where it seems to get deadly." Since 1971, Shepard has performed in thirteen movies.

Things were tense the night he took off. **Cowboy Mouth** was presented as an afterpiece to **Back Bog Beast Bait.** *Bait* starred O-lan Johnson, Shepard's wife. Smith was his new girlfriend; he had been living with her at the Chelsea Hotel. The play rationalizes the predicament. Slim believes himself kidnapped away from his wife and child into a life of rock & roll stardom. "I ain't no star! Not me! Not me, boy! Not me!" These are Slim's words, spoken that one and only night by Shepard. Just what was he running from, as he fled to New England? Perhaps not so much the split between but the awesome fusion of art and life, the terrifying convergence of the twain. Who is the character, and who the author here? And what of the double compulsion acted out by both—to mount and renounce a performance? The one split Shepard cannot maintain is the one he seems most deeply to desire, the split between the on- and offstage worlds. It has proven even tougher to maintain the split between the on- and off-*screen* worlds.

The work in film Shepard has done since his first screenplay (nineteen movies from the 1967 **Me and My**

*Brother* to the 1991 *Defenseless*) can be read as a meditation on the difference between life on a stage and life on a screen. First and last, in America movies make you famous. Plays don't. When Shepard does his Gary Cooper imitation in *The Right Stuff* (1983) and rises phoenix-like from the burning plane, one of the ground crew sees a speck in the distance and asks, "Is that a man?" The other replies, "Yeah, you damn right it is." In this moment Shepard strides into focus and also into stardom, an actor who has earned, as the script acknowledges in these lines, his culture's most minimal and therefore highest term of praise. "Man." In a further twist of fame, he also insures through this performance Chuck Yeager's ability to finance his golden years by hawking engine lubricants on TV.

Since Shepard has been most successful in movies as an actor, his sense of the difference between movies and plays comes down to what it's like to be "in" them. The key variables are continuity and dimension. Movies lack much of either. They are made in lurches, short takes. The movie actor never acts, on one evening, his entire role. Moreover, while movies are acted in actual space, they are projected onto a two-dimensional plane, one the actor and audience cannot enter. The scale of a movie screen is inversely proportional to its accessibility, its vulnerability to intrusion or surprise. Shepard wrote the script for the brilliant *Paris, Texas* (1984). At the movie's end, a man in search of a woman finally finds her, and she is hidden behind a mirror. The climax in the movie reenacts the experience of a movie; when Harry Dean Stanton gets to Natassia Kinski, it is an encounter simply with a screen. Movies provide, for the audience, the illusion of space (dimension) and time (continuity) without affording for the actor the experience of either. Yet they continue to share with plays the emphasis on speaking bodies that are seen. They thus allow the actor—Shepard—to keep on projecting an image without having to risk the open-endedness of an actual historical occasion, or a performance in "three dimensions."

The 1982 *Motel Chronicles* contains Shepard's most extended inquiry into the ironies of working for the screen. The movie actor in Texas tries "to keep his mind on his business. What the scene they were shooting was about. Where it fit into the continuity." He can find no fit, and so drives away, out of the movie but into the character he was slated to play. Later a screenwriter remarks that "I've abandoned my film." "What happened?" a voice asks. "I lost the continuity." The continuity that a movie must evince proves shockingly fugitive in life, as the spliced-up structure of Shepard's book implies. One of its male voices simply intones, "The most intimate things were very broken off." There is a link here between formal structure and psychological concerns; one can see it in the typed manuscript versions of *Motel Chronicles*. Originally titled "Transfiction" or "Transfixion," the book was begun in 1978 and composed over some three years. By replacing the "c" with the "x," Shepard links fiction-making and suffering—writing becomes a kind of crucifixion. By finally abandoning both titles, he backs off from the melodrama in the claim. But he does not back off from the personal. *Motel Chronicles* begins and ends with memories of the mother; the speaker's birth; a mother's final illness. The last section on his mother-in-law's stroke was added late—on "9/29/80." The opening about Shepard's mother was added on the first day of that month. So the book moved toward the classic fictional openings and closings—birth and death, origins and ends. Yet these memories provide not continuity but merely arbitrary starting and stopping points. The most powerful impression of the mother comes in a fantasy of seeing her body after the speaker's birth: "I watched her body. I knew I'd come from her body but I wasn't sure how. I knew I was away from her body now. Separate." This is a discontinuity that cannot be edited into shape. Movies are not "as dumb as life," because they project a seamless continuity in which parts of the story are not broken off.

But the price of continuity is impotence, the powerlessness of an audience to share, enter, or alter the movie's space. Space is what plays provide. Kevin J. O'Connor says of Shepard that "most of his plays were meant to take place on a proscenium—he writes for that—or a space in front of you. He sees things coming on from the side or going off from the side—that's part of the world he's creating." Shepard's stage directions are detailed and architectural: he maps out the walls, doors, rooms. But despite his affection for the dimensional world, Shepard's plays also express a desire to escape its mortal limits. They thus advance a subtle rationalization for his own professional shift from stage to screen, outlining as they do so a pathology rather than a poetics of space.

The pathology is distinctively American. "I take SPACE to be the central fact to man born in America from Folsom cave to now." So Charles Olson begins his 1947 *Call Me Ishmael*. "I spell it large," he says, "because it comes large here. Large, and without mercy." (*Paris, Texas* opens with a "lone man" crossing a "fissured, empty, almost lunar landscape—seen from a bird's-eye view.") Large, Olson seems to be saying, like Moby-Dick. Olson's American stands toward space as Ahab does toward the whale. "We must go over space, or we wither." There is not a little phallic ambition in Olson's call for a continual westering, as if Manifest Destiny were a massive repression of castration anxiety. D. H. Lawrence would have agreed, and had already supplied the word "phallic." But he was less sanguine about the prospects for fulfillment in space, in America's "true west." As he says in *Studies in Classic American Literature*: "Absolutely the safest thing to get your emotional reactions over is NATURE." It is a big claim, like Olson's, and each writer capitalizes his key word. SPACE. NATURE. Like Mike in *A Lie of the Mind,* they "have a big idea." Big words. And today, Shepard seems to be telling us, nearly dead words.

Olson's book celebrates the discovery of a new American space: the Pacific. Lawrence's details the sentimentalization of a continent. We persist in both activities. America now lives in the era of the Pacific Rim, and there is no dearth of pieties about the renovating powers of the increasingly abused natural world. But to the immediate data of consciousness, the continuing colonization of space and valorization of nature are mere sideshows, distractions of history. To live in America as the century ends is to have withdrawn from the realm of the outside. We suffer from a greenhouse effect that owes more to the voracious will to enclosure imagined in Raymond Chandler's *The Big Sleep* than to excess carbon dioxide. We suffer, Shepard's work argues, from a sort of national agoraphobia—a fear of space.

In the southern California where Shepard grew up, the spaces inhabited had names like these: playground, downtown, driveway, front yard. The words imply a scene of relation and proportion between institutions in a built world of schools, roads, stores, and free-standing homes. Beyond all that lay the found world, what can be called the landscape. For many of us these words and spaces have become unrecognizable. We inhabit another order of terms focused on an interior world; in the True West of today, we can hear the sound of the crickets in the hills, but nobody leaves the house. If the primal American scene has heretofore been a body in a landscape—Wallace Stevens's "empty spirit / In vacant space"—then in the 1990s it has become a pair of eyes staring at a screen.

The new words are VCR, television, computer, FAX machine. People seem reluctant to leave them behind, to go outside, into space. I am married to a woman who owns a repertory movie theater. People have stopped coming; attendance was down in 1989 by seven thousand. Perhaps it's an aversion to going out at night into "cities under siege" in order to sit with strangers in a large, dark space. Our audience apparently prefers to stay at home and manage the screening of experience on a reduced scale. (In 1990 70 percent of American homes owned one VCR; 25 percent owned two.) The bunker mentality has triumphed, and we live less in space than in representations of space. What we increasingly have in common is not the physical landscape around our homes, but, in Michael Herr's words, a "glamour space" projected onto a screen. This is where we live, and move, and have our being.

Since *The Tooth of Crime,* Shepard's plays have argued that the price of the celebrity we most value—stardom on a screen—is *dis*location, the erasure of specific identity in local space. Because such stardom relieves us of an even greater anxiety—"Dying," as Tympani says in *Angel City*—it is a price we are perhaps willing to pay. The play in which Tympani appears gives this paradox its most elegant expression. The action of the 1976 *Angel City* follows a crazed Culver City production company as it tries to make a hit disaster movie. At one point, script-doctor Rabbit and musician Tympani enjoy this exchange. Rabbit asks, "What is the most terrifying thing in the world?" Tympani replies: "(*blankly*) A space." Space scares because it is the medium of vulnerability, even mortality:

RABBIT:

So now you're just taking up space?

TYMPANI:

I'm facing my death.

The human choice presents itself here as between facing death in space or achieving a dimensionless immortality on-screen. Rabbit states the case for the power of film:

> The vision of a celluloid tape with a series of moving images telling a story to millions. Millions anywhere. Millions seen and unseen. Millions seeing the same story without ever knowing each other. Without even having to be together. Effecting their dreams and actions. Replacing their books. Replacing religion, politics, art, conversation. Replacing their minds.

If Rabbit tries to control this process, and its effects, Miss Scoons is content simply to be its victim:

> I look at the screen and I am the screen. I'm not me. I don't know who I am. I look at the movie and I am the movie. I am the star. I am the star in the movie. For days I am the star and I'm not me. I'm me being the star. I look at my life when I come down. I look and I hate my life when I come down. I hate my life not being a movie. I hate my life not being a star. I hate being myself in my life which isn't a movie and never will be.

The recognition that Shepard's plays honestly refuse to provide is not even a promise of the movies. The self is lost while watching a movie, merged into the infinite "I am" of the star. The cycle of watching and coming down produces in the viewer an endlessly aroused and frustrated fantasy of imperial being.

*Angel City* sets out to show, despite its rhetoric to the contrary, that a screen is the most terrifying thing in the world. The play begins on a "*Basically bare stage. Upstage center is a large suspended blue neon rectangle with empty space in the middle. The rectangle is lit from time to time. . . . Upstage, directly behind the rectangle, is a narrow platform. . . . When the actors enter on this platform they have been framed by the rectangle.*" This framing rectangle is the play's key protagonist, a kind of ever-present movie screen that treats the characters, as they enter, to a momentary apotheosis as a star. There is the illusion of being "captured in celluloid." It is a pleasant illusion, until it becomes fully literalized in the play's action. The company has been trying to introduce something "totally new"—something "three-dimensional"—into the medium of film. But the reverse happens. At the end, producer Wheeler gets trapped in the movie of his own imagining; one of the most terrifying moments in Shepard is when Wheeler's staff becomes an audience that watches him but refuses to wave back. They know that people on the screen cannot see people watching it. The terror here is that everyone collaborates in treating the stage as if it were a screen, as if it were not three-dimensional, as if Wheeler had passed from the space of drama's struggle to the nonspace of projected form. But this is what Shepard's characters typically do. They refuse the option of action and dialogue in a fully dimensioned space and play their parts as if they were audiences to—at best actors in—a movie. If "the plays," as Shepard said in 1977, "were a kind of chronicle I was keeping on myself," then his movies are perhaps a fable he is composing about us. Movies are for Shepard in his plays and prose a metaphor for American life as so often it is lived, and it is this urge toward withdrawal into the amplified, the dimensionless, and the continuity-ridden that he has set out, from the beginning, to place before us on the stage.

The conflicts that drive Shepard's career are not resolved—they are staged. By stepping with such willing reluctance into the felt tensions of American life, he continues to perfect his role as one of his country's leading cultural agonists. He takes things on, goes into them, acts them out. Experience must be overcome. The decision to write has been, he says, "a process of overcoming a tremendous morning despair. It's been diminishing over the years. But I still feel a trace of this thing that I can't really track down." The best way out is always through, and the end is not understanding, or reconciliation. The end is to keep the forces that make the play *at play*. Shepard remains willingly conflicted, generously divided. As he says of the Old Man and his feeling for the lovers in **Fool for Love**: "From his point of view, there's a danger of wholeness. Once they become whole, it shatters his entire existence, which depends on being split. . . . But there are a lot of different ways of looking at it."

## Donald L. Carveth (essay date fall 1992)

SOURCE: Carveth, Donald L. "The Borderline Dilemma in *Paris, Texas*: Psychoanalytic Approaches to Sam Shepard." *Mosaic* 25, no. 4 (fall 1992): 99-120.

[*In the following essay, Carveth explores Shepard's examination of the human "self" in* Paris, Texas.]

As early as the 1950s, psychoanalysts began to report significant changes in the forms of psychopathology that appear to have emerged in response to a sociocultural situation characterized by Martin Buber as one of metaphysical "homelessness" and by Peter Berger and other sociological descendants of Emile Durkheim as one of an increasingly pervasive "anomie." In contrast to the intrapsychic or neurotic conflicts of the relatively structured personality of an earlier era, the variety of psychic suffering typical of our postmodern condition takes the form of the sense of fragmentation, estrangement and emptiness characteristic of what Christopher Lasch has called "the narcissistic personality of our time."

The preoccupation with the personal and interpersonal dilemmas of the contemporary disordered self that typifies the work of the American playwright, Sam Shepard, is clearly reflected in the central themes of **Paris, Texas,** a film directed by Wim Wenders (who collaborated with Shepard on the screenplay) and which was awarded the *Palme d'Or* for 1984 at Cannes. In the following essay, I wish to discuss the screenplay in the light of two contrasting psychoanalytic theories of the origins of pathological narcissism: one which, following Herbert Marcuse and Jacques Lacan, locates its roots in the breakdown of paternal authority in society and the family; and the other which, following post-Freudian object-relations theory and the psychology of the self, traces it to a wider failure of empathic responsiveness on the part of the early (maternal and paternal) "selfobject" environment of childhood.

\* \* \*

Just as some caretakers are more successful than others in enabling children to develop what Erik Erikson called "basic trust" and R. D. Laing referred to as "ontological security," and which is the necessary foundation for the "cohesive self" of Heinz Kohut's self psychology, so some societies are better able than others to provide their members with a coherent world-view, a sense of confidence and belonging, and an integrated system of meaning and value as the foundation of both personal identity and social order. Under conditions of rapid social change and resulting widespread sociocultural dislocation and "anomie," a society's capacity to integrate, socialize and provide its members with a meaningful identity (that is, its capacity to fulfill what Kohut called a "selfobject" function) is impaired; in such a situation numbers of individuals are forced to endure the condition Erikson called "identity diffusion," which is characterized by a sense of isolation, meaninglessness, fragmentation, diffuse anxiety and "emptiness" depression.

It is a commonplace of that stream of classical social theory summarized, for example, in Robert Nisbet's *The Sociological Tradition,* that since the rise of both capitalism and science caused the break-up of what David Riesman labeled the "tradition-directed" medieval agrarian social order, such large-scale social processes as rationalization of production, industrialization, urbanization and bureaucratization have inexorably undermined the social basis of the religious world-view (Berger's "sacred canopy") which had hitherto provided the foundation of both social integration and personal identity. In this view, despite continuing religious revivals which attempt to stem the wider tide of disbelief, the overall direction of modernization has entailed what Max Weber viewed as the increasing "disenchantment of the world" (307). Although a few visionary nineteenth-century artists and thinkers, such as Nietzsche, were able to anticipate "the coming of European nihilism," for most people in the West this recognition was long obscured by the apparent continued viability of Judeo-Christian values, albeit cut loose from their transcendent foundation, and by confidence in the capacity of human reason, science, industry and technology to fill the gap left by an apparently absent or nonexistent deity.

In the nineteenth and early twentieth centuries communities and families could continue to live, as it were, off the borrowed capital of a religious world-view increasingly regarded as outmoded. Despite increasing secularization, a degree of social integration was nevertheless maintained on the basis of common values (which appeared, at least for a time, to stand despite the loss of their transcendent foundation), on belief in the "Protestant ethic" of virtuous achievement, and on faith in the inevitability of both social progress and individual advancement through industry and science. Riesman's so-called "inner-directed" personality with its firmly internalized values and goals was the product of a normatively integrated family life sustained by a social order still confident in the virtue and viability of its essentially materialistic vision. According to Marcuse, it was in this social and psychological context that Freud created psychoanalysis as the psychology of the inner-directed bourgeois character, with its rationally calculating ego endeavoring to work out practical compromises between the pressures of external reality, the demands of its firmly internalized superego, and its energetic and unruly id.

As many observers of the Western "encounter with nothingness" have pointed out, in the course of the present century our secular substitute faith in progress through science and technology has been severely shaken, not only by the evidence of human irrationality provided by the spectacle of two world wars of unparalleled destructiveness and by growing doubt concerning our capacity to control our own inventions, but also by what William Barrett has described as "the encounter with finitude" arising from developments within the most advanced of Western sciences, physics and mathematics, which "have in our time become paradoxical: that is, they have arrived at the state where they breed paradoxes for reason itself" (37). Faced with these challenges to our surrogate faith, as well as by the continued socially disintegrating effects of secularization and modernization, the coherent identity, confidence and "inner-direction" of the bourgeois individual increasingly gives way to the identity diffusion and "other-direction" characteristic of the contemporary narcissistic or schizoid character and to what George Steiner perceives as a widespread "nostalgia for the absolute" (5). In this perspective, the central psychic difficulty of the postmodern personality is less that of containing the conflicting elements of a structured self than of maintaining any sense of a coherent or integrated identity at all.

In its focus upon conflict, repression and neurosis, classical psychoanalysis amounts to what Kohut described as a psychology of "Guilty Man" (*Restoration* 132-33). It accurately reflects the society in which it arose, a society with sufficient normative integration to sustain a family life with enough coherence and stability to permit its offspring to develop the relatively well-structured or cohesive self and the internalized superego, ego-ideal and ego-identity characteristic of the "inner-directed" personality of Freudian theory. Among those who perceive a relative decline of this type and the emergence of the unstructured personality, some seek to explain these changes in terms of the diminution of paternal authority in both the family and society at large; that is, they offer an explanation in terms of what Lacan would see as a relative failure of "the paternal function" (179-255) normatively to structure the personality in accordance with the social law.

Marcuse, for example, argues that due to sociohistorical changes in the structure of the nuclear family in post-industrial societies which have significantly undermined the authority of the father as an object of identification, "the 'individual' as the embodiment of id, ego, and superego has become obsolete in the social reality" (44) and a new personality type has emerged whose ego-identity is diffuse and shifting due to its lack of inner support from internalized values and ideals. In this situation, the "mediation between the self and the other gives way to immediate identification" while "the ego shrinks to such an extent that it seems no longer capable of sustaining itself, as a self, in distinction from id and superego" (47). In a society characterized by what Alexander Mitscherlich sees as a condition of fatherlessness, the "inner-directed" character formed in the struggle against and the identification with the father gives way to an "other-directed" personality; this character-type is oriented less by the "gyroscope" constituted by internalized values and goals than by a wish to achieve a positive self-image in the mirror constituted by significant others and by a radar-like sensitivity to their expectations and responses.

Whereas Marcuse locates the social roots of identity diffusion in a condition of fatherlessness, writers in the traditions of psychoanalytic object-relations theory and self psychology (such as Balint, Bowlby, Fairbairn, Guntrip, Kohut, Mahler, Suttie and Winnicott) offer an account which emphasizes not merely the father's emotional absence, but that of the mother as well. It is the empathic unavailability or unattunement of the early caretakers—that is, of the "selfobject" milieu in general—which constitutes the psychological basis of the disordered self, the "Tragic Man" of Kohut's self psychology. Kohut himself suggests that whereas the more extended and integrated family of the nineteenth and early twentieth century may have overstimulated children and promoted the structural conflicts that are the focus of the classical psychoanalytic understanding of neurosis, the modern nuclear family—isolated from wider kinship ties, subject to social and geographical mobility, pressed by the need for two incomes and by the desire of both parents for careers outside the home, and faced with the threat of separation and divorce—may well provide an environment in which children are understimulated and deprived of the emotional responsiveness essential for the formation of a cohesive self (*Restoration* 267-80).

\* \* \*

The themes of homelessness, anomie, interpersonal disconnection and personal disintegration, as well as of deprivation of fathering and mothering, are richly developed in **Paris, Texas.** The film opens upon a scene of Devil's Graveyard, Big Bend, Texas, "a fissured, empty, almost lunar" desert landscape through which Travis, a strange, derelict figure, trudges toward a settlement just over the Mexican border in Texas. Having regained consciousness after collapsing in a cantina, this broken and in some ways Christ-like character, who has emerged on bandaged feet from the desert wilderness, remains silent in the face of a physician's interrogation regarding his identity and the causes of his mysterious injuries. Travis's younger brother Walt, an average, middle-class businessman living in Los Angeles with his French wife Anne and their adopted son Hunter, is notified, but just before Walt arrives to fetch him, Travis wanders off into the desert again. Walt manages to catch up with him as he marches determinedly into the nothingness of the desert landscape and, despite his resistance to being touched, finally succeeds in getting him into the car and takes him to a motel. When Walt leaves briefly to buy him some new clothes, Travis prepares to have a shower but, catching a glimpse of himself in the bathroom mirror, he heads straight out the door and back into the desert. Once again, Walt catches up with him and persuades him to return.

For some time during the drive through the Mohave desert to Los Angeles, Travis continues to refuse to speak, but finally, in the face of Walt's impatience, he utters the word "Paris" from the back seat of the car. He asks Walt if he has ever been to Paris and could they go there now. Walt naturally thinks he means Paris, France, but Travis, smiling to himself, traces the location of Paris, Texas on a road map. Soon, having "returned to the land of the living" by resuming speaking and eating, but not yet sleeping, Travis is permitted to drive while Walt sleeps, but he turns off the main highway (in search of Paris, Texas?) and they wind up in the middle of nowhere.

It turns out that Travis has been missing for four years. His wife Jane had also disappeared around the same time. Their four-year-old son Hunter had been dropped at the door of Walt and Anne's who had cared for him as their own ever since. Every month Jane had been depositing varying amounts of money in a Houston bank account in the name of her son. Now four years later, Travis is introduced to Hunter as his real father, but he is initially unable to evoke any recognition or acceptance from his son. Partly as a result of a viewing of a home movie Walt had taken some five years earlier, depicting an ecstatically happy vacation by the sea in which Travis, Jane and Hunter seemed happily united, and partly as a result of Travis's efforts to master the father role, the father-son relationship is reestablished, much to the regret of the boy's surrogate mother Anne who fears her marriage to Walt may disintegrate if they lose Hunter.

Having set out together to contact Jane when she makes her monthly deposit in Houston, Travis has Hunter telephone Anne and then hang up on her, leaving her distraught. Spotting Jane at the bank, father and son follow her to her workplace, the Keyhole Club, where, downstairs, the customers are able to hold private conversations via one-way mirrors and intercoms with women of their choice in fantasy booths of various types ("Hotel," "Poolside," etc.). After talking to Jane and, without revealing his identity, attempting to establish whether or not she is willing to meet her customers outside the Club, Travis leaves and, with Hunter, drives to a bar where he proceeds to get drunk. Father and son wind up for the night in the sitting room of a laundromat. While his eight-year-old son sits behind him in a big leather chair, Travis reclines on a couch and proceeds to "freely associate" (in an ironic allusion to psychoanalysis?) about his shy and sensitive mother who was embarrassed by her husband's jokes about her being "a fancy woman" from Paris.

The next day, Travis returns to the Club, this time telling Jane the story of their life together in a way that gradually leads her to recognize him. It is not until the concluding monologues that we learn that Travis's paranoid jealousy and possessiveness had led him constantly to quit his jobs to be with his much younger wife; that Jane had felt trapped by the arrival of her child; and that by the end Travis had taken to tying a cow-bell to her ankle to prevent her from escaping from their trailer-home while he slept. One night she did manage to sneak away, but Travis caught her and dragged her back and tied her to a stove. Falling asleep despite her screams and those of their child, Travis later awakened to find the trailer on fire. Stumbling through the flames "toward the only two people he loved," Travis, finding them gone, ran into the wilderness "until every sign of man had disappeared" (92). At the film's conclusion, Travis arranges for a reunion of Hunter and Jane at the Meridien Hotel but, as he explains in a tape he leaves for Hunter, he cannot participate in this reunion and, instead, drives off alone into the night.

\* \* \*

From its opening scenes of desert wasteland, this film is pervaded by images of absence, anonymity, geographical and mental vacancy, interpersonal disconnection and personal isolation. As a speechless, identityless derelict trudging through a parched and barren landscape, Travis is the ultimate symbol of human brokenness in general and of the particular predicament of the postmodern individual who, in what Buber viewed as our current epoch of homelessness, "lives in the world as in an open field and at times does not even have four pegs with which to set up a tent" (157). A man without language, memory or identity, Travis is in search of his lost origin, the point at which he understands he might have been conceived, but having turned off the main highway somewhere that "didn't have a name," he ends up in a place where "the emptiness is broken only by some randomly dumped, rusty car wrecks" (28-29).

In marked contrast to the historical tradition and the rich cultural heritage of the "old world" (Paris, France), is the "new world" (Paris, Texas) created by modernization, a world symbolized here by a vacant lot in the middle of the desert, by miles of highway dotted with tacky motels and hamburger joints, and by rusted car wrecks signifying the dead-end of a materialistic, technological society. Reminiscent of Nietzsche's madman who enters the marketplace and proclaims the death of god, Travis encounters a psychotic on a bridge over a freeway shouting into the void below his prophetic warnings to the socially adjusted who have blinded themselves to the nothingness he sees at the center of being:

> You will all be caught with your diapers down. I promise you that. . . . They will invade you in your beds, they will snap you from your hot-tubs, they will pluck you right out from your fancy sports cars. There is nowhere, absolutely nowhere in this godforsaken valley. My voice is reaching you from here where I'm standing to clear out into the goddamn Mohave desert and through this Vale of Tears all the way to Arizona. . . . Not one square foot of that will still be a safety zone. There will be no more safety zone. I can guarantee you: the safety zone will be eliminated. Eradicated. You will all be extradited to the land of no return. You'll be flying blind to nowhere.
>
> (54-55)

As a number of the critical essays collected by Bonnie Marranca suggest, much of Sam Shepard's dramatic work can be read as an account of the failure of the American Dream. Certainly, *Paris, Texas* can be viewed as a critique of the alienation and anomie characterizing an uprooted and traditionless commercial technological society which falsifies experience through advertising and media images and reduces human relations to essentially anonymous encounters mediated by a cash nexus: Walt is a manufacturer of advertising billboards which cover the natural landscape; it is implied that the images of happy family life in the film within the film are about as real as those of Hollywood, since at the time the home movie was made relations between Travis and Jane had been severely strained for years; the father image is something one finds in a magazine and practices before a mirror; the mother-child contact is maintained through cash transfers and their reunion is initiated at a computerized drive-in bank; the mother is employed in a porno-palace catering to voyeuristic fantasies (the film industry?) in Houston, the point from which the technological society will launch its nothingness into the emptiness of space.

At the same time, as members of Riesman's "lonely crowd," Travis and Jane are representative of the growing numbers of those who, in the face of the disintegrating forces of contemporary social life, are able to sustain neither relationship nor identity, let alone a stable family life capable of adequately nurturing children. In Travis we see someone whose inner emptiness renders him unable to tolerate any separation from Jane. As the indispensable, albeit archaic, selfobject support for his disintegrating self, he attempts to keep her in a state of literal bondage, an act that ultimately results in the type of explosion and conflagration that not infrequently marks the desperate finale of such primitive, sadomasochistic relationships.

The attempt on the part of Travis and Jane to overcome their inner emptiness through what Margaret Mahler would regard as a pathological fusion or symbiosis would be viewed, in a Lacanian framework, as symptomatic of fixation in the narcissistic or Imaginary realm originating in "the mirror stage" (1-7) due to regression from, or "foreclosure" of accession to, the more differentiated order of the Symbolic. In the perspective of the early Kohut this would be seen as an "archaic merger" and in current selfobject theory as a primitive type of self-selfobject bond. Such longings are beautifully conveyed in the film in a shot which shows Travis's reflection super-imposed upon the image of Jane's face seen through the one-way mirror in such a way that "his features are reflected in hers" (93) and the two images fuse into one. In keeping with Lacanian ideas, it would seem that the only way they can sustain a symbolic space between them, a space in which they can remain separate enough to *speak* to one another, is by turning their backs to each other, as if the separation by the one-way mirror and intercom are not enough to resist the lure of a regressive merger. This longing for merger (or, more accurately, for mirroring and empathic selfobject responsiveness) is again expressed in the scene of reunion between Hunter and Jane at the Meridien Hotel: not only are their images mirrored in the floor to ceiling glass windows, but they appear as mirror-images of one another: as they turn, face to face, in one another's arms, recapitulating the scene of joyous dancing by the sea in the film within the film, their similarity in appearance, coloring and dress makes them seem almost indistinguishable.

At the root of the relational difficulties of characters such as Travis and Jane is what the British School of psychoanalysis (Klein, Fairbairn, Winnicott, Guntrip and Laing, among others) describes as a schizoid condition, one which Kohut conceives as a fundamental deficiency in the cohesion of the self, and Mahler attributes to impairment in the area of self and object constancy. Travis, for example, speaks of an inner gap that cannot be healed. As he explains in the tape he leaves for Hunter (communication, typically, occurring at one remove): "But I can't stay with you. I could never heal up what happened. That's just the way it is. I can't even hardly remember what happened. It's like a gap. But it left me alone in a way that I haven't gotten over" (86). Earlier in the film, while looking at the family photograph album together, Hunter asks Travis whether, after his father died, he could still feel him "walking around and talking some place" (49). In the next shot, the two examine a photograph of an arc of water issuing from a garden hose in which the ordinarily invisible gaps separating the intermittent streams of water are clearly visible (50). Similarly, Jane explains that she had to give Hunter up because "I didn't have what I knew he needed. And I didn't want to use him to fill up all my emptiness" (94). For a long period after their separation, Jane remained inwardly involved with Travis, until one day his image seemed to disappear from her psychological universe altogether:

> I . . . I used to make long speeches to you after you left. I used to talk to you all the time, even though I was alone. . . . I even imagined you talking back to me. We'd have long conversations, the two of us. It was almost like you were there. I could hear you, I could see you, smell you. I could hear your voice. Sometimes your voice would wake me up. It would wake me up in the middle of the night, just like you were in the room with me. Then . . . it slowly faded. I couldn't picture you any more. I tried to talk out loud to you like I used to, but there was nothing there. I couldn't hear you. Then . . . I just gave it up. Everything stopped. You just . . . disappeared. And now I'm working here. I hear your voice all the time. Every man has your voice.
>
> (95; Shepard's ellipses)

Due to her own inner emptiness, for Jane human contact must either assume the archaic, symbiotic form of the relationship she shared with Travis, or that of the impersonal pseudo-relationships she has with anonymous men safely distanced from her by the barrier of the one-way mirror of the Keyhole Club.

In Lacanian theory this haunting sense of inner emptiness and the regressive longings for merger to which it gives rise would signify a failure of oedipalization resulting in insufficient recognition and acceptance of the inevitable gap separating subject and object in normal mental functioning. In contrast to this view of the sense of inner absence as an intensification of the socialized individual's normal sense of "lack" arising from an inability to master *separation,* current object-relations theory and self psychology would regard it as evidence of a failure to establish the confident sense of inner *connection* that makes normal self-regulation possible (and, hence, separation tolerable) due to early environmental failure and the child's resulting inability to internalize what Howard Bacal describes as an "optimally responsive" selfobject. The film provides evidence supporting both theories: the former which locates the causes of identity diffusion in the decline of paternal authority (the condition of fatherlessness) and consequent failures in differentiation or oedipalization; and the latter which traces it to a more fundamental failure on the part of the early selfobjects (both fathers and mothers) to demonstrate the "response-ability" essential for the child's development of faith in the ultimate reliability or fidelity of the Other and of Being itself as the essential foundation for confidence in the integrity, value and viability of the self.

\* \* \*

Despite what many regard as the obvious structural weaknesses of his plays, which frequently seem fragmentary, unfinished and inconclusive, Sam Shepard is often considered one of the most significant American playwrights of his generation, a situation which leads us to try to account for the enormous appeal of his work. This appeal derives, at least in part, I believe, from the fact that, through his characters with their disintegrated selves and torturous relationships and even through the fragmentary structure of his drama itself,

Shepard has succeeded in representing the predominant forms in which the psychopathology of *our* time, as opposed to Freud's, finds its characteristic expression.

In his popular biography of Shepard, Don Shewey draws attention to the collaborative nature of this film. Wenders had been wanting to work with Shepard for some time and felt that the latter's **Motel Chronicles** could serve as the basis for a film, but instead of adapting this work, they decided to start the story from scratch and worked together on the screenplay: "Although the script was complete before Shepard left . . . Wenders started changing it almost as soon as shooting began. He brought in screenwriter Kit Carson to help with daily re-writing. . . . Toward the end Shepard started phoning in . . . with new scenes, including the crucial last scenes of the movie" (Shewey 182).

This type of collective production, which is rather the rule than the exception in film-making, causes difficulty for those who would apply to the analysis of film one of the major strategies of psychoanalytic literary criticism, namely the psychobiographic method of viewing the creative product as a reflection of its author's psyche, analogous to one of his dreams or symptoms, a view which justifies decoding the text in light of the author's personality, his typical conflicts, obsessions and the like. The trouble is that a film like **Paris, Texas** emanates from the interaction of several psyches (Shepard's, Wenders's and Carson's, among others) so that to see it exclusively in the context of Shepard's previous work or his personality is problematic. Despite these reservations, however, I think we can clearly detect in this film the major themes that have tended to characterize much of Shepard's work: the absent or defective father; the precarious, artificial, insubstantial and divided nature of the self; the problematic nature of language and communication; the obsessive exploration of symbiotic and sadomasochistically enmeshed relationships.

Like Shepard's play **Fool for Love, Paris, Texas** concerns a father who leaves. Around the time when he was working with Wenders on the film, Shepard also reestablished contact with his father through a visit to New Mexico that Shewey thinks probably formed the basis of a father-son encounter described in **Motel Chronicles**:

> He was sitting hunched over in a Maple rocker with stained pillows strapped to the seat and back. He was just sitting there in a barren cement room. . . . He hadn't been visited in quite a while. On the floor beside him was a bottle of Dickel's Sour Mash in a brown bag, a white plastic plate overflowing with cigarette butts and a small cardboard box with newspaper sticking out the top of it. . . . The father reached down and picked up the small cardboard box. He began pulling objects out of it wrapped in newspaper and revealed a black and white plastic horse with a rubber saddle. He handed it to his son. The father kept unwrapping more objects. A silver belt buckle with a star and the words State of Texas running around the star in a circle, a small green ceramic frog with somebody's initials carved into the bottom, a black rock from the High Desert. The son kept collecting all the objects in his lap and wished he'd brought something for the old man. He took off his straw Resistol cowboy hat, reached over and placed it on his father's head. It fit perfect.
>
> (91-92)

In **Motel Chronicles,** Shepard wrote: "My dad lives alone on the desert. He says he doesn't fit with people" (56). In **Paris, Texas,** Travis says: "I am looking for *the* father . . . just a father. Any father . . . I just need one" (45). According to Shewey:

> His father's death was devastating to Shepard. After fighting with the old man all through adolescence and keeping his distance throughout much of his adult life, he was just beginning to make peace with his father, to care for him as a person, to recognize in his father many aspects of himself. Especially now that he had an adolescent son of his own, especially now that he had left his son's mother to go live on the edge of the desert with another woman, Shepard found himself *becoming* his father in ways he'd never dreamed of, and he felt a new compassion for this wizened, helpless old man he'd judged so harshly for so long. And now he was gone.
>
> (156)

The theme of father-son reunion between Travis and Hunter in **Paris, Texas** would appear to echo these preoccupations of Shepard's, especially the scenes in which an emotionally wounded man struggles to assume the paternal role for his son, and those in which, in a reversal of roles, the son performs the paternal function for his drunken or disoriented father. Such themes are reminiscent of Marcuse's notion that the decline of paternal authority is at the root of the contemporary problem of identity, as well as of Lacan's idea that the paternal function performed by the symbolic father (*the* father) is essential to the formation of social identity and that the failure of this function leaves the subject enmeshed in a narcissistic state of fusional identification with the mother and with mirror images of the self.

The theme of the absent or defective father in Shepard's plays is closely associated with another of his major preoccupations: the elusive, shifting, contradictory and fabricated nature of personal identity.

Shepard was born on 5 November 1943, while his father was with the U.S. Army in Italy. Named Samuel Shepard Rogers III, he was called Steve. In **Motel Chronicles** Shepard wrote:

> My name came down through seven generations of men with the same name each naming the first son the same name as the father then the mothers nicknaming

the sons so as not to confuse them with the fathers when hearing their names called in the open air while working side by side in the waist-high wheat. The sons came to believe their names were the nicknames they heard floating across these fields and answered to these names building ideas of who they were around the sound never dreaming their real legal name was lying in wait for them written on some paper in Chicago and that name was the name they'd prefix with "Mr." and that name would be the name they'd die with.

(49)

But not Shepard. Having spent the first years of his life with his father absent, and after his return enduring a stormy relationship with him, Steve Rogers would later abandon the Name-of-the-Father (which, in Lacanian theory, as *le-nom-du-pere* is homophonic with *le-non-du-pere,* the No—i.e., the Law—of the father). Shewey quotes from an interview with Shepard: "I always thought Rogers was a corny name. . . . But Samuel Shepard Rogers was kind of a long handle. So, I just dropped the Rogers part of it. That had gone on for generations, that name, seven generations of it. It kind of shocked my grandparents more than anybody, I think, 'cause they kind of hoped I would carry it on. Then I called my kid Jesse, so that blew it entirely. Now in a way I kind of regret it. But it was, you know, one of those reactions to your background" (30-31). To the extent that the name we derive from our fathers (in our patriarchal and patrilineal culture) is central to personal identity, Shepard's rejection of the paternal name offers, beyond its obvious oedipal significance, a clue to his preoccupation with the elusive nature of personal identity.

"In Shepard's early plays," writes Shewey, "the characters change a lot, play different roles . . . and go through different moods. . . ." It has been suggested that from the Open Theatre, Shepard picked up the technique of "transformations" in which actors were asked to switch immediately to a new scene and therefore to wholly new characters. However, "Shepard carried the idea of transformations much farther . . . by actually writing them into his texts . . . [so that] characters became wholly different in abrupt movements within the course of the work . . ." (51). Shewey reports that in the 60s in New York, "Some found it disturbing the way Shepard could switch personalities from one moment to the next, and in fact he frequently popped tablets of niacin, a vitamin used to treat schizophrenics, saying 'This is my together drug'" (38). Regarding his play **True West,** Shewey quotes Shepard as follows: "I wanted to write a play about double nature . . . one that wouldn't be symbolic or metaphorical or any of that stuff. I just wanted to give a taste of what it feels like to be two-sided. It's a real thing, double nature. I think we're split in a much more devastating way than psychology can ever reveal. It's not so cute. Not some little thing we can get over. It's something we've got to live with." (141)

Perhaps of all Shepard's works, **Paris, Texas** most explicitly and dramatically represents the problem of identity. Initially without language, memory or a name, in the course of the film Travis recovers each of these, but in a way that dramatizes Shepard's sense of the artificial and socially constructed nature of human identity—the father, for example, being an image one takes from a magazine and a role one assumes before a mirror, coached in its proper performance by others, a matter of costume and bearing, a *persona* that, at the end of the film, Travis may be in the process of discarding as, I at least imagine, he heads back to the desert.

Both in his conviction regarding our "double-nature" or intrinsic two-sidedness and in his view of identity as a range of artificially and socially fabricated images, Shepard is in agreement with Lacan who viewed the split between the "subject" and the "ego" as an inevitable feature of the "decentred self," the "ego," or "specular image" itself being regarded as a product of the subject's misidentification with its mirror-image and the images of others in "the mirror stage" (1-7). From the standpoint of psychoanalytic object-relations theory and self psychology, however, the divided or contradictory quality of the self, as well as the sense of its imaginary, artificial or fabricated nature, would be seen as symptomatic of schizoid or self pathology. Although at times Lacan's "ego" and "subject" appear to resemble Winnicott's "false self" and "true self" respectively, whereas Winnicott regarded the splitting of the psyche entailed in false-self development as a sign of psychopathology (at least when it went beyond the necessary evolution of a socially functional *persona*), Lacan universalizes this splitting as an inevitable feature of the human condition. And while Lacan regarded mirroring as central to the development of the "ego" (Winnicott's "false self"), Kohut, like his British precursors Suttie, Fairbairn, Balint and Winnicott, drew attention to the importance of empathic mirroring and recognition by its significant others for the child's development of its "true self," just as they emphasized the splitting and fragmentation that result from significant empathic failure on the part of the early selfobjects.

The debate between those, in object-relations theory and self psychology, who regard the divided self as a manifestation of schizoid pathology relative to particular environmental failures and those, like Lacan (and Shepard himself), who regard our "double-nature" as a universal feature of our "broken" human condition, is a reflection in psychoanalytic theory of the wider philosophical disagreement between historical or sociological as opposed to ontological theories of the sources of human suffering and evil. Traditionally, those psychoanalysts, like Freud and Melanie Klein, who have opted for the ontological side of this debate (while admitting that the universal flaw is exacerbated by unfavorable environmental conditions) have done so on the basis of a questionable biological reductionism that finds the root of the corruption in human nature in somatically-based, anti-social instinctual drives of sex and aggression or Eros and Thanatos. In so doing, they diverge in a fundamentally gnostic or Manichean direction from the Judeo-Christian understanding of our "fallen" nature as arising not from the drives of our bodies which, as a part of the Creation, are good, but rather from our uniquely human capacity for self-centeredness—that is, from what in psychoanalysis is regarded as our narcissism. In the biblical view, the problem of human nature arises not in connection with our animal selves (the Freudian "id"), but rather from what Lacan called the specular "ego" or self-image which forms the basis of an idolatry of the self which estranges us from the Other. In bringing the psychoanalytic understanding of the human predicament into congruence with the biblical critique of the "original sin" of pride, Lacanian theory can meaningfully be read as the Catholicization of psychoanalysis in the process of its belated assimilation into the French intellectual milieu.

Aside from his personal decision to change his name, Shepard's drama also reflects his sense of the artificiality and inauthenticity of words. Shewey observes that Shepard speaks of language as "a veil hiding demons and angels which the characters are always out of touch with" (14). Especially in his early works, Shepard seems to struggle to find a direct, spontaneous and authentic mode of speech capable of capturing the immediacy of experience without falsifying it. This suspicion of words and language was characteristic of the antinomianism of the youth culture of the 1960s which shaped Shepard's sensibility; it was expressed in longings to break through the screen of language and of the personal selfhood constructed by it in order to reach some deeper and more authentic self somehow existing in a state of unity or harmony with the whole of nature. This suspicion of language went hand in hand with the longing to shed a separate identity in favor of ecstatic fusional experiences sought through meditation, drugs, orgiastic sex or frank psychosis. From a Lacanian perspective, such longings would be seen as symptomatic of a failure of oedipalization and a consequent narcissistic regression from the Symbolic to the preverbal or Imaginary level of experience. From the perspective of contemporary selfobject theory, however, such wishes would seem rather to be distorted expressions of the desperate hunger of a disordered and fragmenting self for recognition, holding and mirroring by an empathically responsive and harmoniously attuned selfobject.

In Lacanian theory, it is precisely through the child's entry into the Symbolic order, through the learning of language and the internalization of the Name-of-the-Father as the medium of the patriarchal law against incest, that the subject is liberated through the oedipalization process from its illusory fusion with its mirror-image and the images of others, as well as from the binary oppositions, envy and sado-masochism which characterize experience in the Imaginary. Hence, it is only to be expected that a preoccupation with fatherlessness, the elusiveness of personal identity, and fixation upon symbiotic relationships, would be accompanied by a sense of the problematic nature of language and communication. For Lacan, these themes reflect different elements of a single psychic complex in that the failure of oedipalization—that is, the failure to internalize the Name-of-the-Father—is at the same time a failure of symbolization resulting in the subject's inability to transcend both the identity confusion characteristic of the Imaginary ego and the extremities of the all-or-nothing thinking which underlies the symbiotic and sado-masochistically enmeshed relationship.

In his later work, Shepard's focus appears to shift from the problem of the domination of experience by language to "the very difficulty of finding a language of social communication and a means to express feeling" (Shewey 98). The problem now is not that language obscures communication, but rather that communication is distorted or blocked due to the absence of a common language. In *A Lie of the Mind,* for example, one of the central characters is aphasic, having suffered brain damage as a result of a beating by her husband, and she struggles, very like Travis, to remember the words for things and to make herself understood. People misunderstand and talk over, around or past one another. Whereas in ***Paris, Texas*** communication is at one remove, distanced by technological devices like telephones, tape recorders, walkie-talkies, intercoms and one-way mirrors, or interfered with by verbal ambiguity of various types (Paris, France or Paris, Texas?), in ***A Lie of the Mind*** the message often fails to get through altogether.

In play after play, Shepard returns to the theme of the symbiotic and sado-masochistically enmeshed relationship, the couple who can neither live with nor without one another, whose relationship embodies the need/fear dilemma or approach/avoidance conflict characteristic of the disordered self. In such "borderline" personalities, painful states of inner isolation, disintegration and emptiness drive the subject into a binding attachment to another who, as an archaic selfobject, supports its fragmenting self. Paradoxically, however, even while sustaining the self on the one hand, sooner or later (if not from the outset) this selfobject comes, on the other hand, to be experienced (due to transference distortion or actual repetition) as a representative of the original bad or persecutory object and, hence, appears to threaten re-traumatization and self-annihilation. Threatened with the fragmentation of the self—either through the absence of response or through the presence of the wrong responses—and being unable, owing to the repetition compulsion, to obtain the essential empathic attunement—or even, often enough, to recognize or make use of it when it is available—the disordered self is truly caught in a double-bind. Either the good (selfobject) is unavailable, or being available inevitably turns out to be bad: in no case, short of successful therapy, is a good self-selfobject relationship attainable.

Perhaps this pattern is most clearly delineated in *Fool for Love* where the incestuous pair seem fated endlessly to repeat their pattern of reunion and explosive separation, their pathological version of the *Fort! Da!* game of disappearance and return that Freud, in *Beyond the Pleasure Principle,* reported having observed in his little grandson, a version of the early Peek-a-Boo game enjoyed by mothers and their infants. Here, however, rather than a game lovingly and voluntarily engaged in, we witness a violent and compulsive repetition. On the one hand, Shepard's text supports a Lacanian reading: it is the repeated abandonment of both children and their mothers by the Old Man (that is, the failure of the paternal function) that appears to lie at the root of their incestuous entanglement. On the other hand, current self and object-relations theory would suggest that this failure on the part of the father (Kohut's "idealized selfobject") is insufficient to account for this level of psychopathology and would tend to view the paternal failure as exacerbating or failing to compensate for an earlier narcissistic injury in the relationship with the mother (the "mirroring selfobject"). In this perspective, a fundamental failure to internalize an empathically attuned and responsive primary caretaker as the basis for both secure attachment and a cohesive and positive sense of self has led to a hostile, sado-masochistic dependency upon external objects as sustainers of identity and self-esteem. Such objects are needed far too much to be genuinely loved, and because, in the transference repetition, they inevitably come to represent the original bad objects, they must be perpetually destroyed and then, in the face of intolerable separation and annihilation anxiety, brought to life again.

\* \* \*

This pattern of hostile dependency is clearly evident in *Paris, Texas* in the symbiotic or archaic self-selfobject relationship between Travis and Jane. At the outset, Travis, the archetypal borderline personality, wanders out of the desert, the land "without language or streets" (92), into a border town called *Terlingua,* the land of language, where, after asking him if he knows which side of the border he is on, a doctor searches in vain for any clue to his name or identity. In the course of the film, Travis experiences a type of resurrection, rebirth or resocialization, a re-entry into the Symbolic order after an existential or psychic catastrophe, a sort of crucifixion, has led to a profound regression to a pre-verbal level of experience tantamount to a kind of psychological or spiritual death. In accordance with Lacanian theory (and for that matter with Kohutian theory as well)—and at this point one begins to suspect that Wenders, if not Shepard, has been consciously influenced by Lacan—the initial phase of the development of identity involves the process of mirroring. It is his encounter with his mirror image in the bathroom of the first motel that sends Travis back into the desert, as if this reminder of the problem and burden of identity is simply too much for him to bear. Throughout the film, there is repetitive recourse to mirror images and images of mirrors: the mirror in the bathroom of the first motel; the one in the second motel room; the recurrent shots of Walt and Travis in the rear-view mirror of the car; the mirror held up to Walt, Anne, Travis and Hunter by the film within the film; the mirror before which Travis rehearses the father role; the one-way mirrors in the Keyhole Club; the mirrors constituted by the windows in the Meridien Hotel which mirror Hunter and Jane even as they mirror one another.

Once again, in keeping with Lacanian theory, Travis's reintegration into the Symbolic order involves the gradual relinquishment of his mutism and his initial use of words. Significantly, and in keeping with semiotic theories as well as with the nature of psychotic speech disturbances, Travis is fascinated by verbal ambiguity, puns and double meanings. Echoing his father's joke, Travis speaks of Paris and is amused by Walt's misunderstanding. There is further miscommunication regarding whether Travis had purchased a photograph of an empty lot or the land itself. While both enjoying and being frustrated by the polysemy of language, Travis is unable to accept that automobiles, like verbal signifiers, are substitutable for one another: as far as he is concerned, the car, like Winnicott's "transitional object," is unique and non-transferable: "We need the same car, Walt. How are we going to go in another car?" (24).

Whereas the automobile is a transitional object, the shoes and boots Travis collects, shines and arranges one morning, seem to have a phallic significance evident both in Travis's comparison of the size of his boots with Walt's, who at this moment represents more of a father than a younger brother, and in his desire to switch boots with him, representing the son's desire to fill his father's shoes, so to speak. At this point in the film, there is a redistribution of roles. Hunter now represents the son in an idealizing relation to Travis who struggles to represent a suitable father figure and an appropriate paternal ego-ideal. Travis's initial overture toward his son is rejected. This setback necessitates that he study up on the father role by looking in a magazine (that cultural reservoir) for suitable paternal imagery. In keeping with the Lacanian theory of *le-nom-du-pere,* or the paternal metaphor, it is evident that in order for a son to be successfully oedipalized a viable father-image, a symbolic father, must be internalized. Travis's own vulnerability to narcissistic regression might suggest, to a Lacanian at least, a relative failure of the oedipalization process in his case.

Travis rehearses the father role before a mirror. The maid informs him that there are only two kinds of fathers, rich ones and poor ones—that is, phallic fathers and castrated ones, those capable of performing the paternal function for their sons and those who are not. And what *is* the paternal function? Again, in keeping with Lacanian theory (179-255), the film makes clear that the (symbolic) father's mission is to break into and disrupt the symbiotic connection between mother and child. Anne senses this and reproaches Walt for encouraging "this father-and-son business between them," but in keeping with Shepard's valorization of biological paternity, Walt argues in favor of the inviolability of the natural tie between father and son: "It's no business! Travis IS his father! And Hunter IS his son!" (51). Anne's worst fears are soon realized. Having succeeded in attracting Hunter into a mirroring and idealizing relationship with him (witness their mutual imitation and mimicry on the walk home from school), and having introduced him to his patrilineage through the medium of the photograph album, Travis takes Hunter on a quest for his biological mother. In a scene heavy with symbolism, Travis has Hunter telephone Anne and when the message has been delivered instructs him to "Just . . . hang up!" on her (63; Shepard's ellipses), which he does, figuratively breaking the psychological umbilical cord connecting him to one mother, even as they set out to reestablish the link to another.

On the one hand, the film's depiction of the father's disruption of the mother-child symbiosis is congruent with the Lacanian theory of psychosis as arising from a failure of this (oedipalization) process and a consequent "foreclosure" (179-225) of the gap normally opened up between subject and object by the primal "castration" inscribed in the Name-of-the-Father. In addition, such themes as that of the quest to reestablish the connection between Hunter and Jane, Travis's intense archaic selfobject transference wishes, and his reminiscences of and displaced longings for *his* mother, are congruent with the Lacanian idea that the failure of oedipalization results in fixation upon the narcissistic quest to *be* the "phallus" for the mother—that is, to be the object of her desire, that which satisfies her "lack." On the other hand, *contra* Lacan, theorists working within a self and object-relations framework would tend to view such intense narcissistic longings, whether directed toward the father or the mother, as symptoms, not of any failure of differentiation *per se* (that is, failure of the paternal function), but rather of an inability to consolidate a separate self due to insufficient phase-appropriate empathic responsiveness on the part of the early mirroring and idealized selfobjects.

According to Kohut, the very intensity of the need for a paternal identification may be a symptom of the child's earlier failure to consolidate a cohesive self through empathic mirroring by the mother. In turning to an idealizing relationship with the father, the child may not primarily be attempting to escape what Lacan views as a universal, pre-oedipal narcissistic enmeshment with the mother but, rather, seeking to remedy the defects in the self arising from maternal selfobject failure. In seeming to suggest that the psychological basis of the relational difficulties of characters such as Travis and Jane lies in a failure in the area of self and object constancy, the film conveys an understanding of the borderline dilemma that, I believe, is superior to Lacan's; for the need/fear conflict arises as much from a failure to establish a confident inner sense of ongoing human connection as from any "foreclosure" of differentiation or separation—that is, from any lack of an inner sense of "lack."

In actuality, the profound longings for and rage toward the mother which characterize both borderline and narcissistic personalities (the latter merely employing a manic or grandiose defence against identical deficits and conflicts) do not simply reflect the normal pre-oedipal child's desire to be the object of the mother's desire, only pathologically retained due to failure of the paternal function. On the contrary, such longings represent the pathological intensification of the normal desire for "merger" or selfobject responsiveness arising precisely from the failure to establish in childhood the necessary confidence that one was, in fact, the "apple of the mother's eye."

Indications of a profound fixation on the mother are prevalent in the film. The theme of the quest for identity as a quest for one's origin, which is ultimately a quest for the mother, is clearly evident, supplementing the theme of identification with the father. Having been permitted to drive while Walt sleeps on their return home through the desert, Travis turns off the main highway, apparently in search of Paris, Texas ("where I began. Me, Travis Clay Henderson. They named me that" [30]); for Paris is where he was told his parents first made love and where, he supposes, he might have been conceived and, therefore, where he might somehow refind and reinscribe himself in the Symbolic order, the land of language and streets.

Yet again, in keeping with the idea of the family romance as a search for one's true identity through the discovery of one's authentic origins, Travis and Hunter set out in search of Jane, Hunter's mother, who at the same time symbolically represents that of Travis as well. Just prior to taking Hunter in quest of the mother,

Travis is seen standing on a scaffold adjacent to one of Walt's billboards depicting a reclining female figure with the mid-section missing creating a gap where the womb should be. Travis, whose middle name is Clay, is afraid to leave the ground, Mother Earth, in an airplane—just as, according to Shewey (13), Shepard is afraid of flying. As they drive toward Houston, the point from which man is launched away from earth into space, Hunter (who is hunting for his mother) lectures his father over a walkie-talkie from the back of their pick-up truck about the arcane mysteries of the origins of the universe. In the final scene at the Meridien Hotel, as Hunter and Jane recapitulate the oceanic scene of joyous dancing by the sea in the home movie, their similarity in appearance, coloring and dress makes them seem almost indistinguishable. It would seem that Travis has succeeded in reestablishing a blissful mother-child reunion mirroring that earlier scene of harmony which turns out to have been Imaginary. However, even as the film now portrays an ecstatic reunion, it simultaneously depicts its opposite: the exclusion and isolation of Travis as he drives into the night alone.

While I think it would be a mistake to view this mother-fixation in predominantly oedipal terms, certain classically oedipal themes are clearly evident in the film. For example, echoing the Freudian concept of the family romance, Hunter discovers that Walt and Anne are merely surrogate parents and, having reunited with his actual father, together they embark on a quest for the mother. They finally locate her in a quasi-brothel where she is initially confused with Nurse Bibs (a pregenital mother imago?) and where her sexual morality is, to say the least, in question: is she a madonna or a whore? Travis's oedipally-tinged anxieties regarding Jane's fidelity echo his father's jealous delusions regarding *his* wife who, despite her shyness, he accused of being "a fancy woman." Yet while the father only joked about marrying a woman from Paris, his son Walt enacts the fantasy: his French wife Anne is thus a transference representation of the mother. Far from suggesting that these oedipal themes outweigh narcissistic issues of identity or the self, I would argue that the former are themselves manifestations of the latter; the pseudo-sexual longing for instinctual gratification from the mother is frequently, if not always, profoundly infiltrated by a more fundamental longing for recognition, harmony, holding and empathic mirroring by the maternal selfobject.

Compounding the conflict reflected in the film regarding the paternal versus the maternal bond is a wider ambivalence regarding the respective value of apparently normalized or oedipalized relationships, such as that of Walt and Anne, as opposed to regressive, sado-masochistic bonds such as that which unites Travis and Jane. On one hand, in contrast to the biological parents, Walt and Anne are represented as realistic, protective and responsible caretakers; yet their marriage is depicted as both conventional and literally barren, tenuously held together as a triangle by the presence of Hunter as a third. On the other hand, the arrival of Hunter as the third who disrupts the dual union of Travis and Jane only adds to the latter's sense of entrapment and intensifies her need for escape. And what Travis and Jane possess in the way of intensity of involvement is offset by their irresponsibility and incapacity for realistic and mature modes of relatedness.

If any third alternative is represented in the film, it is only that of the nothingness of the land of no return, the void or gap allegedly existing at the center of being or of the self, figuratively represented by the desert from which Travis emerges at the outset and of which he and we are reminded by the psychotic on the freeway overpass who shouts his prophetic warnings to the socially adjusted passers-by who have, at least temporarily, managed to deny it. Whether ultimate reality truly amounts to a void (a "devil's graveyard"), or rather a plenitude mistaken for a void, or even in some mysterious way both plenitude and void, or something transcending these binary categories altogether—these are questions we may certainly wish to raise in response to Shepard's essentially nihilistic vision. In the world of *Paris, Texas,* however, the only alternatives to the nothingness of the desert or of space are, on the one hand, a socially adjusted but devitalized life characterized by what Joyce McDougall has called "pathological normalcy" (463-86) and, on the other, one of intense but destructive relationships lived on the margins of both society and sanity. Either one relates to no object at all; or one engages in conventional, but somewhat superficial and dispassionate object relations; or one experiences passionate but narcissistic and sado-masochistic pseudo-relations with bad objects. In no case is there an authentically good self-selfobject relationship.

On the social-historical plane, Buber observed that in epochs of homelessness in which the social order fails to function as a psychic container for its members, they are torn by a range of apparently insoluble existential conflicts and dilemmas (subject/object, mind/body, good/evil, masculine/feminine, etc). Likewise, the experience of the subject estranged from the empathic responsiveness of its selfobject milieu (interpersonal, communal and metaphysical) is fragmented or split into a range of opposing psychic and emotional states and enmeshed in a paralysing ambivalence. Perhaps the historical and ontological understandings of human suffering can be reconciled after all. If salvation from the crucifying contradictions of our nature requires a kind of containment or holding of the self by others (or by the Other)—a healing response through which we may be resurrected from deadening conflict to creative life—it is also true that such grace appears to be mediated by historically situated social institutions and conditions. If we are largely dependent upon the containing or selfobject function of the social surround for access to the "safety zone"—the middle ground or "transitional area," the "area of faith" or "field of Being" that exists between, beneath or beyond the polar opposites—then it is the significant failure of this function in contemporary culture that gives rise to the dilemmas of the fragmented self in a society in which the development of a cohesive personal identity and stable interpersonal relationships has become increasingly problematic.[1]

*Note*

1. Earlier versions of this essay, co-winner of the 1992 Miguel Prados Essay Prize of the Canadian Psychoanalytic Society, were presented at meetings of the Toronto Psychoanalytic Society and the Canadian Psychiatric Association. I wish to thank the many colleagues whose comments have informed its revision.

*Works Cited*

Bacal, Howard A. "Optimal Responsiveness and the Therapeutic Process." *Progress in Self Psychology*. Ed. A. Goldberg. New York: Guilford, 1985. 202-26.

Balint, Michael. *The Basic Fault: Therapeutic Aspects of Regression*. New York: Brunner/Mazel, 1968.

Barrett, William. *Irrational Man: A Study in Existential Philosophy*. New York: Doubleday, 1958.

Berger, Peter. *The Sacred Canopy: Elements of a Sociological Theory of Religion*. New York: Doubleday, 1969.

Bowlby, John. *Child Care and the Growth of Love*. Harmondsworth: Pelican, 1953.

———. *Attachment and Loss*. 3 vols. London: Hogarth, 1969-80.

Buber, Martin. *Between Man and Man*. Trans. R. G. Smith. London: Collins, 1961.

Durkheim, Emile. *Suicide: A Study in Sociology*. New York: Free, 1951.

Erikson, Erik. *Childhood and Society*. New York: Norton, 1950.

———. *Identity and the Life Cycle: Selected Papers*. Psychological Issues Monograph 1. New York: International UP, 1959.

Fairbairn, W. R. D. *Psychoanalytic Studies of the Personality*. London: Routledge, 1952.

Freud, Sigmund. *Beyond the Pleasure Principle* (1920). *The Standard Edition of the Complete Psychological Works of Sigmund Freud*. Vol. 18: 7-64. Ed. J. Strachey. London: Hogarth, 1955.

Guntrip, Harry. *Schizoid Phenomena, Object Relations and the Self*. New York: International UP, 1969.

Klein, Melanie. *The Selected Melanie Klein*. Ed. Juliet Mitchell. Middlesex: Penguin, 1986.

Kohut, Heinz. *The Analysis of the Self*. New York: International UP, 1971.

———. *The Restoration of the Self*. New York: International UP, 1977.

Lacan, Jacques. *Ecrits: A Selection*. Trans. Alan Sheridan. New York: Norton, 1977.

Laing, R. D. *The Divided Self: An Existential Study in Sanity and Madness*. Middlesex: Penguin, 1960.

Lasch, Christopher. *The Culture of Narcissism: American Life in an Age of Diminishing Expectations*. New York: Warner, 1979.

Mahler, Margaret S., Fred Pine, and Annie Bergman. *The Psychological Birth of the Human Infant*. New York: Basic, 1975.

Marcuse, Herbert. *Five Lectures: Psychoanalysis, Politics, and Utopia*. Trans. J. J. Shapiro and S. M. Weber. Boston: Beacon, 1970.

Marranca, Bonnie, ed. *American Dreams: The Imagination of Sam Shepard*. New York: Performing Arts, 1981.

McDougall, Joyce. *Plea for a Measure of Abnormality*. New York: International UP, 1980.

Mitscherlich, Alexander. *Society without the Father: A Contribution to Social Psychology*. Trans. E. Mosbacher. New York: Schocken, 1970.

Nietzsche, F. *The Joyful Wisdom*. Trans. T. Common. Introduction by Kurt Reinhardt. New York: Ungar, 1960.

Nisbet, Robert. *The Sociological Tradition*. New York: Basic, 1966.

Riesman, David, Nathan Glazer, and Raoul Denney. *The Lonely Crowd: A Study in the Changing American Character*. New Haven: Yale UP, 1961.

Shepard, Sam. *Angel City and Other Plays*. Introduction by Jack Gelber. New York: Urizen, 1976.

———. *Motel Chronicles*. San Francisco: City Lights, 1982.

———. *Fool for Love and Other Plays*. Introduction by Ross Wetzsteon. New York: Bantam, 1984.

———. *A Lie of the Mind*. New York: Dramatists Play Service, 1985.

———, and Wim Wenders. *Paris, Texas*. Screenplay edited by C. Sievernich. Berlin: Road Movies, 1984.

Shewey, Don. *Sam Shepard*. New York: Dell, 1985.

Steiner, George. *Nostalgia for the Absolute.* Massey Lectures, Fourteenth Series. Toronto: CBC, 1974.

Suttie, Ian. *The Origins of Love and Hate.* London: Free Association, 1988.

Weber, Max. *From Max Weber: Essays in Sociology.* Ed. H. H. Gerth and C. Wright Mills. New York: Oxford UP, 1953.

Winnicott, Donald. *The Maturational Processes and the Facilitating Environment.* London: Hogarth, 1976.

———. *Playing and Reality.* London: Tavistock, 1971.

## Robert B. Heilman (essay date fall 1992)

SOURCE: Heilman, Robert B. "Shepard's Plays: Stylistic and Thematic Ties." *Sewanee Review* 100, no. 4 (fall 1992): 630-44.

[*In the following essay, Heilman provides a thematic overview of Shepard's plays, highlighting his literary style in each play.*]

Any playwright with such a highly individualized manner as flashes out at us in the plays of Sam Shepard is likely to be called unique. There is of course no need to deny the uniqueness of Shepard's work. Even in his life, one can observe some shadow or flavor of uniqueness, or unusualness, or elected difference. Born Samuel Shepard Rogers, Jr., in 1943, he chose to be Sam Shepard. He began writing one-act plays, and having them produced, when he was twenty. By 1967, when he was twenty-four, he did his first full-length play, *La Turista,* and from then on he kept turning out numerous one-act-ers and full-length plays at the rate of almost one a year. In early years he went to a junior college, worked at a race track, and was drummer in a touring rock-pop band. One could imagine his turning toward the life of a professional outsider in the Kerouac manner.

Yet the overall Shepard career is hardly unique. It follows the lines of an American success story that is almost trite. He starts modestly and then makes it big in the manner of an American folk hero. The early career is small plays, small audiences, small off-off-Broadway productions. Then the later career is all success by the usual standards—production all over the country, wide critical discussion, and, when Shepard is thirty-five, the Pulitzer prize for *Buried Child* (1978). He is Dickensian in productivity (the only rival to Joyce Carol Oates, five years his senior), and in having energy for diverse activities—writing songs (words and music) for some plays, acting, making movies. And the once race-track handyman would later raise Appaloosa horses on a California ranch.

Again, if the plays often strike us as hallucinatory—discontinuous in action, mysterious in motivation, bizarre in humanity, incontinently dashing from puzzling shock to shocking puzzle, preferring madness to cliché—there are recurrences that suggest, if not positive coherence and even system, at least a recognizable sense of scene, movement, and human style. Since Shepard's career follows the design of the American success story, it is interesting that the materia dramatica often seem to critics to be quintessentially American. Of course Shepard does not use European or Asian or South American scenes, but American playwrights rarely do. Perhaps the idea is that he seldom uses metropolitan or cosmopolitan scenes. (The action of *Angel City* [1976] takes place in Hollywood, and of *True West* [1979] in a Los Angeles suburb; these are infrequent uses of an urban milieu.) He does not often use well-to-do, professional, or "successful" individuals as characters. What "American" apparently comes down to, then, is mostly rural scenes and characters who can be described variously as common people—marginal, dispossessed, wandering, lower middle class, and so on. The scenes are set repeatedly in the Southwest, Mexico, the desert, Louisiana bayou country, the beach. Shepard occasionally shows an interest in cowboy types, western singers, rock-and-roll musicians (he uses their kind of song in several plays; for the songs in one play he wrote both music and words), would-be writers, Indians, football players, farmers, racketeers. Often he specifies that a character is to wear blue jeans. He devotes one whole play to a phantasmagoria of hopes and yearnings in American events and characters that are now almost mythical: the Gold Rush, buried treasure, Paul Bunyan, Jesse James, Mae West, Marlena (*Mad Dog Blues,* 1979, an Americans-only version of Tennessee Williams's *Camino Real*). He can base a play on a common ailment of American travelers (*La Turista*) and include a madly fantastic satire of doctors, who appear as medicine men (or witch doctors) and as pretentious phonies.

Shepard is often described as a self-conscious critic of the American life that appears in his plays. It is a possible reading, but I am not sure that it gets to the heart of things. Shepard is too original to be simply another censorious observer of a highly organized, institutionalized, technological, commercialized credit-economy life. Such matters may appear, but they do not seem primary. When he deals with a rich old man, Henry Hackamore, in *Seduced* (1979)—a recluse who makes us think of Howard Hughes—Shepard presents him not only as a miserable medley of paranoia and delusions of power, but also as the possessor of a kind of mysterious hold on people. Shepard does not fall into the obvious romantic alternative of glorifying the primitive: while he may see in it an unsophisticated close-to-nature kind of goodness (as in the Indians in *Operation Sidewinder* [1970], and the cowboy rescuers in *Geogra-*

phy of a *Horse Dreamer* [1974]; he can also see in it a superstitiousness and a capacity for bestial violence [*Back Bog Beast Bait*, 1971]). One doesn't have to be rich to be wretched: misery of one kind or another is widespread in Shepard's cast of characters. If one looks at them sociologically, one can find plenty or evidence of a malaise often ascribed to American life: noncommunication, isolation, alienation. *Action* (1975) parodies a Christmas dinner: four participants seem to live wholly in private lives, talking to but almost unaware of each other. In various plays, including *Rock Garden* (1964) and *Buried Child* (1978), the characters sometimes talk at cross purposes, or as if no one else were there, or as if they did not hear or could not make sense of what others say. Such separateness may lead to total withdrawal or to hostility, and hence to the family infighting that is one staple of Shepard drama (and one that I will return to later). In this dramatic material Shepard gives a special flavor to a theme that Arthur Miller has dealt with in several plays beginning in 1949, and that two other playwrights had used brilliantly just a year or two before Shepard's first one-act-ers: Arthur Kopit's *Oh Dad, Poor Dad, Mamma's Hung You in the Closet and I'm Feelin' So Sad* (1962) and Edward Albee's *Who's Afraid of Virginia Woolf?* (1962) and *The American Dream* (1961). Many critics have, as it were, picked up Albee's title—*The American Dream*—to denote what they believe Shepard is poking full of holes. Maybe he is, but it is doubtful that this is a primary or principal objective of his, or even a side effect of his theatrical style.

For one thing various aspects of his plays, as other critics have noted, suggest affiliations that lie outside the narrow arena of national debunking. More than once what Shepard does reminds us of European writing. For instance *Operation Sidewinder* (1970), a fantasy in the sci-fi style, has resemblances to *R.U.R.* (1920) by Karel Capek, a Czech. In Capek's play, robots manufactured by men acquire "souls"; in *Operation Sidewinder* a new master computer in the form of a snake seems to be in tune with cosmic rhythms or transcendental forces, and thus can serve in a Hopi Indian snake ritual presaging a new vitality of nature immune to the hostility of organized society. The Indian as a natural being with special powers is a D. H. Lawrence conception. Likewise Lawrence is brought to mind by Shepard's *Geography of a Horse Dreamer* (1974), a play about the artist exploited by commercial interests, for Shepard's central situation is almost identical with that in Lawrence's short story, "The Rocking-Horse Winner": a character with a special intuition or extrasensory perception or clairvoyance can "see" which horses will win races, and so he is mercilessly or even destructively victimized by gamblers. The interpolation of songs, which Shepard uses in several plays, is a technique made familiar by Bertolt Brecht. While Shepard is justly credited with an unusual ear for speech rhythms, his frequent reliance on an apparently characterless dialogue that is made striking by flatness and repetitiousness is remarkably like that of Pinter and Beckett (*Waiting for Godot*). Like these two playwrights Shepard uses such dialogue as the unlikely context for extraordinary, puzzling, apparently nonrational events, a combination that also reminds some readers of the fiction of Franz Kafka. The use of a familiar everyday scene in which there is an air, occasional or persistent, of the ominous or sinister, is standard Pinter; such a scene as the background for flamboyantly out-of-the-ordinary actions is written in the manner of Jean Genet. It makes sense to think of *Buried Child* as T. S. Eliot's *Family Reunion* (1939) filtered through Pinter's *The Homecoming* (1965). The pattern is that of a son or grandson (one with a wife, one with a girlfriend) returning to a home where all is not serene, where past or present mysteries seize our attention, where a parent dies, and where one of the newcomers departs for a different life. In *Cowboy Mouth* (1971) characters quote W. B. Yeats and various innovative, antitraditional French poets, notably Gerard de Nerval (1808-55), a wandering, highly productive, periodically insane poet and prose writer who often wrote in a striking nonrealistic, even grotesque vein, re-creating fantasies and visions. Thus de Nerval—and a little later Jarry—was a precursor of such movements and fashions as surrealism, expressionism, dadaism, and automatic or hallucinatory writing. The simplest over-all term for this long succession of radical antirational modes is symbolism. Though Shepard does not like this term and its synonyms, it serves very well to describe what he does in many plays. At times he uses a realistic style (characters talk and act in ways that come logically out of personalities and situations), and at times a symbolic style (actions and events seem to have their source elsewhere than in the "normal" probabilities of character and situation, and we have to go outside our expectations in order to get their drift).

II

We can sense a connection between this effect and the writing process as Shepard describes it. For him, he insists, writing is an "unending mystery," based not on "ideas," but on an "inner visualizing," a "picture . . . moving in the mind and being allowed to move more and more freely as you follow it." He feels as if "something in me writes but it's not necessarily me." The result is an "open-ended structure where anything could happen," not a "carefully planned and regurgitated event." Behind this lies "the real quest of a writer," which is "to penetrate into another world." Thus we get, so to speak, a familiar "this world" and "another world" that may be surprising or puzzling. "Ideas emerge from plays . . . not the other way around" (*The Drama Review,* 21 [1971]).

We need not take too seriously Shepard's claim that his work is not "carefully planned." But it is probably right to think of him primarily as spontaneous producer of "pictures," images or "visions" of people in action. He is fertile and energetic in his productivity. In ***Buried Child*** the products of his rich imagination are generally clear enough: there is a troubled family with a dark event in its past, a great deal of dissatisfaction and quarrelsomeness in its present, and a reliance on different consolations—liquor, religion, and a "security blanket" that several adults quarrel over. These are shown in various fresh and unusual ways, although the situation is realistic in its basic outlines and indeed in most of the details. Insofar as the technique is symbolic, the symbolic drift is often a byproduct or implication of basic facts that are plain enough. When one son is dead, another an amputee, and a third apparently brain-damaged, they represent both a defect in the family life and a defeat of the hopes that parents attach to the next generation: the atmosphere in this house "cripples" the children. This situation and its meaning could be the work of Eugene O'Neill (the former football player as retarded or permanently immature appears both in Arthur Miller's *Death of a Salesman* and Tennessee Williams's *Cat on a Hot Tin Roof*, and in this connection we think also of Jason Miller's *That Championship Season*). But other Shepard "visualizations" lead to a free-wheeling, usually startling, symbolism that lies outside the realistic: often we cannot make literal interpretations but have to let the symbols soak into our imagination and work as best they may. In ***Buried Child*** we can usually sense the drift of the nonrealistic symbols. Bradley's hair-clipping is a resentful man's style of attack and triumph; his putting his hand into Shelly's mouth a kind of triumph-by-rape. Everyone's failure or unwillingness to recognize Vince and to pay attention to Shelly suggests the self-enclosure of the others, their shut-off-ness from their kind, the elusiveness of identities. When Halie goes out to lunch dressed in black, and comes back a day later dressed in yellow, we can, if we want to, speculate about what happened literally; but the main point is that she has undergone a striking change of mood. Vince's mad "war games" when he returns belong to a battle of moods which ends in his decision to stay. Finally Shepard takes the worn-out figure of speech, "skeleton in the closet" (compare Kopit's *Oh Dad, Poor Dad*), and revitalizes it as a literal skeleton in the back yard, and one that appears shockingly. But the point is not the detective-story surprise or the criminal charges that might follow in a literal account. Instead, the skeleton gives physical reality to a destructive family life, and at the same time, we assume, its being brought to light exorcises a dark past. (Here we remember a similar exorcism of the past—ironically the killing of a fantasy life—that may be conducive to peace in the present—the final scene of *Who's Afraid of Virginia Woolf?*.)

III

Symbols and myths are interconnected, as we know; one can think of myth as the extension of the symbolic element into a narrative structure in which the individualized tale reveals an archetypal pattern of experience. Shepard is drawn to myths, but, as we might expect, he pulls away from a feared triteness (in a sense his whole career is a campaign against triteness, though perhaps more instinctive than planned). By myth he means, he says, "a sense of mystery and not necessarily a traditional formula." He constantly achieves the "sense of mystery" through characters' actions that conform, not to our everyday expectations, but to hidden forces of personality or to meanings that the personality illustrates, often quite obscurely. Still, while Shepard naturally backs away from the stereotype, his "not necessarily" allows him some leeway to explore traditional patterns of action that may stimulate him. At least we can find him elaborating plots in which appears, however disguised, a "traditional formula"—i.e., a style of action that embodies some constant of human behavior. In one play he actually reworks an ancient mythic theme that he reveals in his title, ***Icarus's Mother*** (1965). Icarus's mother is of course the earth. Shepard's Icarus is an airplane pilot, and he seems to some young picnickers—some of the time on the beach—to be interested in them. And they in him, apparently through the clandestine smoke signals sent up by several men, and more unmistakably by two girls who, having taken down their panties to urinate on the beach, make sexy gestures in his direction. His plane finally roars into the sea with a tremendous luminous explosion that outdoes the formal fireworks display expected by the young people. Since "fireworks going off all around" is a standard idiom for experiencing orgasm, we can understand that the pilot is entering, or reentering, the mother in a climactic death (we can't help remember the older meaning of dying as sexual climax). Thus the action alludes to the best-known Greek story of mother-son incest, a subject to which we will return.

The Icarus myth is latent in another death of a high flier, Henry Hackamore, in *Seduced*. Likewise there are traces of *Everyman* in Henry's hanging on to his riches, and their supposed power, at death's door. Shot dead but apparently immortal, Henry, as it were, flies untouchable in the skies, so strong an embodiment of popular aspirations that even his murderer helplessly surrenders to the vision. Here Icarus flies on, a symbol of man's dreams of going up in, and having power over, the world. Immortality is conferred by popular imagination.

If in ***Seduced*** it is people in general who exercise the creative imagination, the traditional possessors of that gift, the artists, draw Shepard's attention more than once. The myth of the artist is a recurrent theme of his. In *Angel City* the artist is overcome by Hollywood values. In *Geography of a Horse Dreamer* he is exploited by money-making agencies but rescued by cowboy brothers (an American embodiment of the classical deus ex machina) and taken to safety in Wyoming (another American myth: safety and purity in the big-sky country). *The Tooth of Crime* (1972) embodies a much deeper vision: a young artist, a popular singer, defeats an old established one in personal combat. Though this battle seems wholly contemporary (and could indeed dramatize Shepard's own fantasy of rising to the top of the world of popular music and drama), it is especially interesting because it actually employs an ancient mythical pattern. The archetypal version occurs in the introductory story of Frazer's *Golden Bough*: an older order, represented by a priest or ruler, is upset by a new, more vigorous one as the young aspirant fights and kills the old incumbent. The very form of the battle between Shepard's two singers—they conduct a verbal duel technically known as the flyting—goes back to the practice of ancient epics in all cultures. For this flyting Shepard invents a strikingly weird language which reminds us a little of the gang "slanguage" in Anthony Burgess's *A Clockwork Orange*.

When he again takes up the problem of the artist four years later—in [*Suicide in B-Flat*] (1976)—Shepard turns to a more difficult problem than that of the struggle between rivals and generations: the integrity of the artist in the development of his own career, and in his relationship with a public and critics who are almost hostilely on his trail, trying to pin him down, come to grips with him, "detect" him, as it were. Shepard manages this theme with great originality. At the beginning he startlingly flings us into what looks like another version of the detective myth: Louis and Pablo, two detectives, are investigating the apparent death of a musician which may be a murder, a suicide, or a planned disappearance. Though they differ and even quarrel, they are full of the clichés of loyalty, justice, and a job to be stuck to until finished. Then, in a sort of play-within-the-play manner, the central figure Niles, the musician who may be killer or suicide or neither, is brought on to enact (as a sort of play for the temporarily blacked-out detective group) the prior events that led to the detectives' investigation. We see Niles, directed and aided by a young woman, undergoing several ritual "deaths" that signify his turning away from earlier phases of his career as a musician: the need to cut off the old, grow, try the new. The arrows that she shoots into him leave him unharmed but also strike and "kill" the detectives: the critics are done in by the changes that leave them unable to understand the changing and growing artist. But they recover and still seek to "arrest" him—i.e., stop and control him. The young woman—his "soul"?, his spirit of independence?—cries that he is in a "trap" and flees, and he is handcuffed to the detectives. This artist, we assume, is finally a "prisoner" of public and critics, or at least in some essential way not free of them. But this bald summary of the contents of the action hardly does justice to the extraordinarily original use of the detective myth in this new version of a recurrent theme of his—the myth of the artist.

Shepard is drawn both to a myth of decline and death and to the myth of recovery and survival. In *La Turista* and *Angel City* the movement is all downhill. In *The Curse of the Starving Class* (1977) the father is "reborn," but apparently too late. As in Chekhov's *Cherry Orchard*, to which Shepard's play has been compared, the farm is taken over by a new order, but Shepard's incoming regime is that of strange Pinter-esque racketeers rather than that of a hard working, upward-bound ex-serf. When we find the note of ring out the old, ring in the new in Shepard, we are always aware of the ambiguity. The troubling, weird, and shocking events that are Shepard's staples prevent any triteness in images of recovery, and they may even obscure his sense of cycles in human experience, of a kind of regeneration that may follow decay, or a peace that may follow conflict or disaster. In *Operation Sidewinder* the Indian ritual suggests a drawing upon the forces of nature for an enduring order in contrast with our technological one. In *Mad Dog Blues* (1971) and *The Unseen Hand* (1970) various characters settle into an apparently satisfying ordinary existence, the former after fantastic trials in a no-man's land, the latter after rebellion against an Orwellian "Nogoland."

Shepard's ability to imagine either downfall or rebirth appears very clearly in his attraction to the myth of the curse on the house. In this, as elsewhere, we see Shepard, for all of the exciting and disturbing uniqueness of his surfaces, drawn to recognizable themes with a long history: in the West the curse on the house appears, as we need hardly say, in the Greek myths of the House of Thebes and the House of Mycenae. In *The Curse of the Starving Class* the key word is in the title, and it occurs several times in the dialogue, once in reference to the sad state of the family. The physical messiness of the place is a dim reminder of Poe's "The Fall of the House of Usher," in which *house* means both family line and dwelling place. The skinning of the lamb is a parody of the crucifixion of the Lamb of God, but in this version of the myth of salvation, the death has no redemptive value, and the spiritual hunger is unsatisfied.

In *The Buried Child* the curse on the house is made concrete in the self-centeredness, in the various animosities, and especially in the distant murder that symbolize the human failure of the family. If the dead infant was, as one critic suggests, the product of an incestuous union, we have specific echoes of the Oedipus story: the same wrongdoing long ago, and the purgative effect of bringing it to light. A new spirit, however, appears to enter through a visitor from an outer world—a suggestion of another mythical pattern. Since the visitor is a member of the family, we tend to think of the return of the prodigal son. Over all these events there hangs Shepard's recurrent sense of the cyclical: the old order passes (the grandfather dies), and the new takes over. Perhaps Vince's future is an ironic illusion, but it is possible that the hope and promise are genuine. Surely regeneration is implied by the vegetable that Tilden brings in, by the new sunlight, and by the announcement that green goods are again growing like mad in the long-barren area. These events are of course symbolic rather than realistic: if we cannot explain them by literal cause and effect, we can understand them as signs of a new vitality and of available sustenance. The fertility myth may not completely possess Shepard's imagination, but it has a hold on it.

## IV

When we say "house," we think of generational continuities, the influence of the past, the presence of forebears and their actions in the living. But if you can't have a house without a family, you can have a family without a house, that is, a domestic drama conceived only in terms of the present. In an early one-act play, *Fourteen Hundred Thousand* (1967), Shepard dealt with some limited husband-wife tensions. Then in the 70s there were two plays we have just looked at—*The Curse of the Starving Class* and *Buried Child*: Shepard was, as it were, discovering a theme in which he found growing congeniality. For in the 80s three major plays are rooted in intense intrafamily conflicts and passions—*True West* (1980), *A Fool for Love* (1983) and *A Lie of the Mind* (1986).

While one of these plays, *True West,* uses raw materials that are specifically American (the idea of the West and Hollywood's use of it), they are primarily addressing, not specifically regional or American matters, but an ancient universal theme—the modes of conflict between spouses, parents and children, and others in the realm of kinship. In this Shepard is being Aristotelian. Aristotle specifies that the best tragic plots are those that occur within families: "But when the tragic incident occurs between those who are near or dear to one another—if, for example, a brother kills, or intends to kill, a brother, a son his father, a mother her son, or any other deed of the kind is done—those are the situations to be looked for by the poet" (*Poetics*, XIV, 4, trans. S. H. Butcher). We should not overlook the double significance of Shepard's choice of such materials. For one thing it underscores a Shepard direction easily overlooked: away from local color, regional themes and styles, and national problems and toward basic human realities that transcend geographical boundaries and present times. Further the surface uniqueness of Shepard's theatrical method—disconcerting shifts, psychic shocks, baffling symbolism, nonrealistic plunges, and characters like those of D. H. Lawrence, of whom it has been said that they represent not traditional portraits of identifiable whole personalities but novel outbursts of unpatternable instinctive passions and drives—should not blind us to the recognizable centrality of the human modes and interactions that are his true business. If his people are strange in visible behavior and audible speech, they are central in psychological reality. To put it another way, he avoids clichés, but he hits upon traditional patterns of human conduct (or, in other words, archetypes without stereotypes).

*A Fool for Love* (1983) does happen to involve two generations: a love in the second in some sense duplicates a love in the first, or carries it on in a new dimension. But the stress is on the present rather than on influence or recurrency (as in plays about the house). In the past a married man had a long affair with another woman. On a visit to the second household, he once took along a young son, who thus met the daughter of the other woman. Half-brother and half-sister fell in love then, and the main burden of the play is the dramatization of the intense and enduring feeling between them—a feeling that survives long absences by the man, his other affairs, and much jealous quarreling and recriminating and even physical blows when the pair are periodically together (for the meeting that provides the action of the play, the man claims to have driven 2840 miles). They could be a common-life Romeo and Juliet who, without external bafflements to face, have lived on into young adulthood. But the big difference is that the affair is technically incestuous or close to it. Shepard is not only working in a traditional domain of intense passion, but he successfully creates a sense of mysterious bonding that, though it is not explicitly defined, makes the stormy but apparently unbreakable relationship seem inevitable. Unlike John Ford in his *'Tis Pity She's a Whore* Shepard is not setting up rival moralities and exploring an issue, and neither character is case-making. There is no theoretical issue at all. Shepard is simply dramatizing the powerful feelings that are the central determinants of two lives. In dealing with an ancient theme, Shepard once again finds a fresh and original staging: the ghost of the father is present throughout, occasionally making interpretative comments: and the inner human tempests are weirdly set off by flashing headlights from without the building, shots, broken glass, and other disturbing effects.

Oddly enough the Romeo-and-Juliet analogy that one thinks of vaguely in reading *A Fool for Love* is also suggested by *A Lie of the Mind* (1986), which centers on a young couple and hostile families. On each side, however, we also see the intrafamilial conflicts and animosities that give the play an exceptional complexity of plot. But the more fundamental Shakespeare analogy is with *Othello*: Jake unjustifiably jealous of Beth (the Cassio is Jake's innocent brother Frankie; there is no Iago), so badly beats Beth up that he thinks he has killed her. He does not know the truth, since both stay with their families in different communities, isolated in the sense that no one seems to think of ordinary communication (mythical wastelands, as it were, where vagueness of outer identity perhaps intensifies inner realities). Othello's primitive action leads to his death; Jake's to a morose, testy withdrawal that is close to moral or spiritual death. Beth recovers from the beating but seems a strange inhabitant of another world—her form of mental death. The fabric of the play is woven of three strands of action: the life in Jake's family, the life in Beth's family, and the interplay of these two households, side by side on the stage, but mysteriously distant in the reality represented. Each family exists in a mode of disorder generated by Jake's wife-battering—a cohesion without coherence as they stick together in constant indeterminate disharmonies. Jake, moody, edgy, combative, in effect a cripple/invalid, is quarreled over by his mother Lorraine and his sister Sally; they really compete for the role of nurse, caretaker, baby-sitter, and intimate. There is a strong suggestion of incestuous feeling, such as ***A Fool for Love*** centered in; and since one of the female rivals is the man's mother, we feel the presence of the Oedipus story. In the other family Beth's brother Mike is so tirelessly and violently vengeful against Jake that it is difficult not to sense an incestuous feeling for his sister. Again we have ancient patterns of human behavior in modern dress.

The action takes a new turn when Jake's younger brother Frankie, determined to find out the truth about Beth, sets out on a mythic action, the quest, and actually reaches Beth's family home. But he is accidentally shot in the leg by Beth's father Baylor, and he mysteriously becomes a permanent patient-inmate in Beth's house, untreated, the infected wound making him constantly weaker and sicker. Beth is attracted to him, but he resists valiantly and pleads the cause of her husband, whom Beth seems not to remember. Then Jake follows Frankie in the quest for Beth, finds the place, apparently worn out, is captured by Beth's brother Mike, and is so beaten up physically and mentally by Mike that he becomes virtually a beast on all fours. Mike lets him into the house only to give a Mike-dictated apology to Beth. She does not recognize him and turns again to ailing Frankie. Thus the life-in-death termini of jealous Othello and sweet Desdemona. And Beth's parents and Jake's mother and sister drift off into striking irrelevancies for which Shepard has an extraordinary flair. They are, as it were, checking out of the myth and perhaps achieving a peace, all passion spent.

The intrafamilial tensions that turn partly on semiunderground psychological attractions have one other manifestation. We have seen Jake's mother wanting virtually to move in with him as nurse and caretaker and thus to achieve an intimacy perhaps beyond her own understanding of it. The Oedipus outline is filled in a little more with a flashback in which Sally describes to her mother Lorraine the death of their husband-and-father down in Mexico years ago. Jake and his father had got into a mad relentless competition of drinking in bars and racing from one to another on public streets. The father had staggered, fallen, been run over by a truck, and killed. Sally says outright that her brother had "killed" her father. Since this happened on a public highway, we have a literal replay, with variations in detail, of the Oedipus-Laius confrontation in which Oedipus murdered Laius. And later Oedipus-Jake is desired by Jocasta-Lorraine. While portraying family strife, Shepard virtually reenacts a great myth of forbidden, but persisting, relationships.

We cannot help wondering whether ***A Lie of the Mind*** (where *lie* could mean both *set* and *falsehood*) is a more overt treatment of a theme that had been lingering in Shepard's imagination. In one action the later play reminds us of a much earlier one—***The Holy Ghostly*** (1970)—in which a father and son meet in a desert. The son is supposed to be helping his father against ghosts, but they quarrel, in a manner a little reminiscent of Goneril/Regan against Lear. The son shoots the father, but the singular thing is that the father is already dead. It could be a soft-pedaled version of the patricide that occurs, albeit only in a later report, in ***A Lie of the Mind***.

V

Though ***True West*** preceded ***A Fool for Love*** and ***A Lie of the Mind***, I deal with it last because it is very rich in traditional and mythic materials and uniquely combines these with some uproarious farcical effects. Shepard remarkably brings together the family theme, the myth of the artist that has attracted him periodically, and some rollicking fun.

The recurrent family theme takes a special form: the rivalry and antagonism of two brothers. Holed up temporarily in his mother's home in southern California, Austin is trying to complete a film script that has been tentatively accepted by a cliché-bound Hollywood mogul, Saul Kimmer. Austin's brother Lee drops in from his desert hangout and abrasively and contentiously asserts himself as a rival film-concocter, a connoisseur of the "true West." He brazenly takes over Saul Kimmer, sells Saul his plot idea, and thus gets Austin's offering rejected. The pattern becomes clear: Shepard is doing the Cain-vs.-Abel myth, with Saul Kimmer as a wonderfully vulgar version of the God who evaluates the brothers' offerings. Things take an unbiblical turn when the brothers get drunk and trash their mother's house (she is a delightful ironic observer who, instead of going to pieces in the mêlée, quietly opts for a motel). Shepard innovates by merging or at least alternating the Cain and Abel types. Lee's nasty truculence suggests Cain, and Austin's mild self-possession, Abel. But drink turns the apparently unflappable Austin into an agile aggressor; he wraps some telephone wire around Lee's neck and extorts various promises from him. Lee, the winner with God Saul, is not killed, but we do not know what will happen in the hostilities that appear to lie ahead. Nothing is prefabricated.

Shepard extraordinarily unites the Cain-Abel myth with his recurrent subject, the myth of the artist; and in this fourth treatment of it he really approaches it from three directions. There is some reminiscence of the *Angel City* formulation: the corruption of the artist by Hollywood, personified in Saul's mechanical money-making formulae of judgment. When Lee first boasts about his original "true West" ideas for a script, he seems to be, perhaps, a speaker for Shepard's own originality. But Saul's approval of Lee's ideas tells us that they are only the conventional in another key. The war is not between disinterested and profitable art, but between two money-making competitors, with different formulae.

Then Shepard explores the myth of the artist from a wholly different point of view. Lee has an idea, not a script, and he wants to pay the technician Austin to turn his rough plot into usable studio form. Austin refuses, Lee takes on the task himself, and what he really wrestles with is this: the relation between raw materials and artistic form, between the true West as he has seen or imagined it, and the representation of it in the verbal and dramatic medium. In part the problem is his own ineptness and impatience, but the underlying issue is the larger one dramatized in Pirandello's *Six Characters in Search of an Author*: the disjunction between reality as experienced or perceived, and the transfiguration of it by the artistic medium that has its own conventions: the resistance of history to poetic incarnation. Lee is so frustrated by this problem that he bashes his typewriter—a splendid farcical expression of revenge for his defeat by an intractable problem of art.

The third phase of Shepard's myth of the artist has to do with the romantic sense of the artist as outsider, a Rimbaud in at least petty matters. Thus Lee prefers stealing to buying things, and he arrives at his mother's home with a stolen radio. He derides Austin for not achieving such symbolic proofs of creative independence. Nettled, Austin rambles through the neighborhood and returns with ten stolen toasters—a charming stage send-up of Genet anti-society-ism, especially when the toasters go into action and spray toast all over the place (a masterly scene in the Ayckbourn idiom).

Finally *True West* makes two allusions to a social myth—the myth of the rustic paradise, an innocent Arcadian refuge from the corruptions of the world. As the brothers get drunker, Austin begins to feel that he would like to join Lee in the desert for a simpler and better life. Lee argues that it simply wouldn't do for Austin: the out-of-town world is only for those who know it, not a never-never land for disillusioned urbanites. And finally Lee, anticipating his own return to the desert, makes a gesture at assembling supplies. As for dishes, he wants china, not plastic. Walden is best when you have the best from home. These are neat puncturings of an aspect of the romantic primitivism that emerged in the latter eighteenth century: the dream of the pure golden life in unspoiled nature.

Shepard not only employs a wide range of mythic materials in this play and does it with great originality, but he also innovates by treating traditional materials with rich comic and indeed farcical devices. To have certain recurrent issues and ideas bandied about by a pair of drunks is a beguiling way of avoiding scholastic solemnity without denying the significance of the issues.

Its range of theme and tone makes *True West* a good closer to this survey. I have been trying to place an original artist on some ground that will neither make his uniqueness solipsistic nor ascribe to him a style that too much narrows the broad range of his raw materials. His surfaces, strange events on stage, his surprises and apparent inconsecutiveness, his mysteries, his upsettings of standard theatrical expectations—all these are individual enough. But they are not singular: in them we can see a theatrical tradition—antirealist, symbolic, absurdist—that in one form or another has had almost a century of life. Still Shepard goes on to add some novelty to familiar new rules, the rules that deny traditional rules. So, in seeking to place him, we sometimes identify him as a wholly American voice, one that harps on specifically American frailties. This cuts him back too much. Of course he uses American scenes and ways, notably those of the West, as his foreground materials. In this he does only what every writer does—speaks through the ways of life that he himself knows best. But they are not what the plays are "about," any more than southern novelists, using southern scenes and characters, are simply making statements about the South. The regional materials are agencies of a vision of realities not bound by geography. I have tried to identify the beyond-the-regional, beyond-the-national substance of Shepard's work by showing how his plots repeatedly embody materials of a mythic order—literally in the Icarus play, all but literally in the plays that present or imply oedipal relationships; and recognizably in the plot that turns on the troubles of the house, the war within the bonds of kinship, especially in the Cain-and-Abel rivalry, and in the various plays that present the ways and ideals of the artist—his relations with the economic world, with the raw materials to be transformed into art, with other artists, with himself. Such matters were once called "timeless" or "universal," terms now too sonorous for an age deep in various skepticisms. But, call them what we will, they are realities beyond ordinary boundaries of space and time, and Shepard is drawn to them, deny them though he may seem to do by a singularly vivacious unexpectedness of the dramatic medium.

### Sam Shepard and Carol Rosen (interview date March 1993)

SOURCE: Shepard, Sam, and Carol Rosen. "Emotional Territory: An Interview with Sam Shepard." *Modern Drama* 36, no. 1 (March 1993): 1-11.

[*In the following interview—which is excerpted from Rosen's book* Sam Shepard: A Poetic Rodeo—*Shepard discusses his theatrical style and stage imagery as well as his concepts of rhythm, myth, voice, and character.*]

Sam Shepard is, of course, a conundrum. He is undoubtedly one of the most intuitive practitioners of what Cocteau called "poetry of the theatre," creating a personal, concrete, physical language of the stage to be apprehended sensually. This encoder of American signs onstage is also an actor's playwright, among the most subtle and sympathetic chroniclers of characters' emotional states since O'Neill. Yet although he occasionally still produces a new play, most recently **States of Shock** in 1991, Sam Shepard now works primarily in prose and films. He has just completed filming **Silent Tongue,** a "truly different Western" about an 1870s Indian Medicine Show, which he both scripted and directed.

Shepard feels incredibly "lucky." He often says so, and he often laughs. His gift for writing is one he accepts; he never expects to run dry and will easily discard work that strikes him as gone awry; this gift has delivered him from his demons. His demons—"actual demons" he used to feel in the air and in his life—have mercifully left him in peace. Like one of his own characters who crashes through a rear wall of the stage, leaving a jagged silhouette in his place, he has escaped.

Trying to maintain some degree of privacy, Shepard consistently turns down requests for interviews. For my book on his work, *Sam Shepard: A Poetic Rodeo,* forthcoming from Macmillan, however, Shepard graciously talked at length about myth, character, music, food and women in his plays; his influences in the theater and his method of writing and revising; his work as a film director and prose writer; the Gulf War; broken pacts and emotional territory. Apologetic whenever he hears himself sounding "esoteric" or "intellectual," he is, of course, both. With Shepard, famous for "burning bridges" and "escaping" to "new territory," every conversation is a discovery. He is, after all, the most original and vital playwright of our age.

Here, in the following abbreviated "soundbites" from our interview (which was previewed in the *Village Voice* [August 4, 1992]), are excerpts pertaining to Shepard's theatrical style, use of stage imagery, concepts of rhythm, myth, voice, and transformations, and his continuing sense of character as fluid, among other topics of interest to *Modern Drama* readers. The full-length interview will be included in my book on Shepard's work. It is the first interview of substance Shepard has granted in over a decade.

#### On Directing

[*Rosen*]: *Have you as a director developed your own particular way to communicate with actors? Is there a Shepardesque actor?*

[Shepard]: When I started, with the first play I ever directed in London, I was terrified of the situation because I'd never done it before. So I immediately conferred with two people who I thought were the best directors in the world. One was Peter Brook and the other was Joe [Chaikin].

I sort of talked to them at length about the process and all that kind of stuff. When I went in, I found myself sort of trying to imitate certain things from their points of view, but discovered that it was futile, that you have to deal with the actors that you've got right in front of you and find out what the experience is like: directing. You can't use a formula to approach it, so I never developed a formula for it. . . .

I like actors who are incredibly courageous and enthusiastic. I think [John] Malkovich is a good example: extremely intelligent, fearless and enthusiastic. Just does not give a shit about how this fits into somebody else's idea of what it should be, just goes for ideas that are completely off the wall. They may be wrong but he'll go for them.

#### Stage vs. Film: Methods of Exploring Emotional Territory

*But it's very clear, there are certain things you can do on film that you can't do on stage or in a novel. There are several images in* **Far North,** *for example the loon, the shot of an eagle flying with a horse, the shot of the* horse's profile turning into Katie's profile—certain images that are filmic, certain visual techniques that can't be achieved onstage or in a novel.

One thing that's great about film, I think, if you actually are lucky enough to get to make one, is the thing of parallel time, which is very difficult onstage. I tried it in *A Lie of the Mind* to a certain extent, but it's very cumbersome. It works, but with film it's immediate. You go: here's a story, and then you cut and here's another story.

And you can follow these two stories parallel. You can follow three or four stories in parallel time, because film allows you to do that. It's like music; you just move into time. Or you can go to the past or the future or wherever you want. Whereas onstage, it's much more awkward to do that kind of instantaneous time shift.

*On stage, flashbacks have to emerge from language.*

Or from some sort of standard shadow of the character in the background Back lighting, whatever.

*You know all the tricks, right?*

Well, I've been doing it for twenty-five years.

*Yes. That's why it seems so interesting that critics second-guess your work and your choices onstage. I would assume you know what you're doing, and that if you choose to structure a play a certain way, you have made a conscious choice. It's not that you haven't figured out any other technique. Are you aiming for different effects?*

Not effect so much, it's territory, emotional territory. I'm interested in effects only to the extent that they serve some purpose, some purpose of emotional terrain. Developing a new style of theater is not something I'm interested in.

*You've used that term "emotional territory" in the past to suggest the destination of your plays. Which of your plays do you think go there? To emotional territory.*

Oh, they all do.

*All of them.*

Yes, but some of them do it better than the others.

*Which ones "do it better"? That's always the destination, right?*

Yes, hopefully, when you start out, when you begin, your great hope is that it moves into something that is true. Sometimes that happens, sometimes it doesn't happen. Like with *Fool for Love,* it began to move into a certain kind of territory. I don't think it eventually succeeded at it. It became too formal toward the end. But it attempted to move into a certain kind of emotional terrain that was true to itself. It depicted itself. That's what I'm looking for: something that is its own feature.

*So it's not imitating something else?*

Right. Or it's not trying to represent something else. It becomes its own animal.

### Imagery

*Much has been made about that eagle and tomcat story in the monologue [that ends* **Curse of the Starving Class***].*

Probably, yeah.

*So, what do you make of it?*

I didn't intend it as a metaphor. It was just an image, which actually happened. I remember that happening, not exactly as it was written, but I remember that was the case. When you castrated ram lambs, there would always be a hawk or something around.

And then I think later I came across a story similar to that in an old western magazine, about an eagle. But I think it was with calf testes. I just kind of adapted it. But I didn't mean it as a-metaphor. It can be taken that way, if you want. . . .

*It's not about masculinity or anything like that. Unless you want it to be.*

*I'd like to ask you about all your imagery of food.*

(Shepard laughs.)

*I can't think of a single play of yours where characters haven't been having breakfast, or boiling artichokes, or burning toast, or spilling cream of broccoli soup all over the bed or—*

Well, it was an interesting thing, because I don't think I really discovered the meaning of it, if you want to put it that way, until I worked with Joe [Chaikin] on *Tongues.* In *Tongues* we have a little monologue about hunger, where he gets into: do you want to eat, why do you want to eat now? You know, I have a hunger. And it builds into this momentum.

When we got into that, Joe started to talk about it in a way that suddenly revealed what it really was to me, I think. Because I don't think I'd really understood it before. But his sense of it was that a person's profound emptiness, the profound sense of emptiness in a person's life is answered by eating in many ways. Somehow, when you eat, food fills some kind of void that's not only physical but emotional. And I think that there's something to that. People who have the hunger for anything—the hunger for drugs, the hunger for sex—this hunger is a direct response to a profound sense of emptiness and aloneness, maybe, or disconnectedness. And I think that there's some truth to that.

*Yes, but you dealt with food long before you wrote* **Tongues.**

Yes, I know it. But I think there's something connected there, maybe unconsciously.

### ACTING: CONTROLLED ANARCHY

*There's a lot of slapstick in* **True West.** *When Malkovich played Lee, he seemed just crazy. It was as if he was going to destroy the stage.*

Yes, with the golf club.

*With the golf club. And then there was slapstick when the toast was hurled everywhere. Do you aim for that kind of anarchy in production?*

It's a controlled anarchy. It's not: everybody go crazy and have fun; it's really controlled. Like for instance, when Malkovich hit his partner, Gary Sinise [who played Austin in the Steppenwolf production of **True West**], Sinise had glasses on, and Malkovich tapped his glasses with the golf club. That's controlled; that's absolute control. The character is freaking out, and the actor has the ability to be able to draw that stroke with the golf club so that he can tap his glasses like that and not hurt somebody. That's what we're looking for.

### MYTH

*I want to ask you about myth*

You've never seen that word in one of my plays. It comes up after the fact.

*After the fact. You once said a myth is a lie of the mind.*

Yes, but our language has been so laundered that we don't—we can say the same word to each other and not know what we mean.

*That's why I ask you what you mean.*

There's myth in the sense of a lie. There's myth in the sense of fantasy. There's myth in all those senses. But the traditional meaning of myth, the ancient meaning of myth is that it served a purpose in our life. The purpose had to do with being able to trace ourselves back through time and follow our emotional self.

Myth served as a story in which people could connect themselves in time to the past. And thereby connect themselves to the present and the future. Because they were hooked up with the lineage of myth. It was so powerful and so strong that it acted as a thread in culture. And that's been destroyed.

Myth in its truest form has now been demolished. It doesn't exist any more. All we have is fantasies about it. Or ideas that don't speak to our inner self at all, they just speak to some lame notions about the past. But they don't connect with anything. We've lost touch with the essence of myth.

*A lot of the characters in your plays try to connect with that essence, don't they?*

Fruitlessly, yes.

*In* **Buried Child** *Vince has that speech about the face reflected in the windshield. And in* **Far North** *Katie has a very similar speech as she drives, tracing her lineage.*

Well, those instances are more in terms of just immediate hereditary things, having to do with family. But see, myth not only connects you and me to our personal families, but it connects us to the family of generations and generations of races of people, tribes, the mythology of the ancient people.

The same with the American Indian: they were connected to the ancestors, people they never knew but are connected to through myth, through prayer, through ritual, through—dance, music, all of those forms that lead people into a river of myth. And there was a connecting river, not a fragmented river.

*And that's gone.*

It's gone, yes.

*Does Wesley attempt to create a ritual that will lead into a river of myth in* **Curse of the Starving Class***? He fails.*

Yes, but all contemporary efforts will fail. They have to be connected to ancient stuff. They can't be just contemporary or else it will come apart. It will become a fashion show, like rap music.

### ENDINGS AND MUSICAL STRUCTURE

*In terms of musical structure, do your plays end the way music ends?*

I hate endings. You have to end it somehow. I like beginnings. Middles are tough, but endings are just a pain in the ass. It's very hard to end stuff.

*I thought* **Lie of the Mind** *ended perfectly.*

Yeah, I found a good ending for that. I liked the ending of **True West**.

*Yes, but* **True West** *doesn't end.*

No, but that's why I like it.

**A Lie of the Mind** *ends with a silhouette, one of those images that Peter Brook talks about in* The Empty Space.

Yes, I finally discovered an ending for that. Endings are so hard. Because the temptation always is a sense that you're supposed to wrap it up somehow. You're supposed to culminate it in something fruitful. And it always feels so phony, when you try to wrap it all up.

*That's why it seems more like music, because music is not supposed to wrap it up at the end. It's supposed to keep going in your mind.*

Yes, I think that's the right kind of ending. That it leaves you on the next note. See, what interested me is the seven-note scale. That the first and the seventh are the same note, just an octave higher, so things are cycled. So that you go through something that you are really returning to: the place you began.

But then you get into scales from other countries, like China or Japan, and they go on—what are they, thirteen-note scales or twenty-one sometimes?

### Feminisms

*Do you ever think about* **Far North** *or* **A Lie of the Mind** *as feminist pieces?*

What does that mean? What is a feminist piece? Following the feminist cause or something?

*That they perceive the world from the point of view of women as opposed to superimposing a male view on history.*

To a certain extent, yes. But what became curious for me was—there was that certain period of time, and now I think it's actually over, or it's changed into something else—but there was a period of time when there was a kind of awareness happening about the female side of things. Not necessarily women but just the female force in nature becoming interesting to people.

And it became more and more interesting to me because of how that female thing relates to being a man. You know, in yourself, that the female part of one's self as a man is, for the most part, battered and beaten up and kicked to shit just like some women in relationships. That men themselves batter their own female part to their own detriment. And it became interesting from that angle: as a man what is it like to embrace the female part of yourself that you historically damaged for one reason or another?

So from that point of view, it was interesting to me. But not from the cultural feminist point of view because I don't really understand that. I would never try to be a spokesman for it.

*Starting with Emma in* **Curse of the Starving Class,** *you create some really vibrant women characters. And in* **A Lie of the Mind** *and in* **Far North,** *you explore the female side of character, even in the men.*

I felt that, too. That was one of the big changes for me in those few pieces, that the women suddenly took on a different light than they had before. Because before it felt so sort of overwhelmed by the confusion about masculinity, about the confusion about how these men identify themselves. That sort of overwhelmed the female. There wasn't even any room to consider the female, because the men were so fucked up. You spent the whole play trying to figure out what these men were about, who had no idea themselves. But then, when the women characters began to emerge, then something began to make more sense for the men, too.

*To explore the "female side of things" did you ever think of doing* **True West,** *for example, with women? Two sisters?*

No. People get funny ideas about writers, like for instance, Beckett stopped a production of *Endgame* that was a black production. Now, he didn't stop it because he's a racist, he stopped it because he wrote it with a certain inclination. And to cast it black, regardless of how good the actors are, is going to completely throw something else into it. . . . He's just protecting his play.

I wouldn't want to see **True West** done by women because it's a scam on the play; it's not the play. Not that—I don't have anything against women. I'm just telling you it would distort the play.

### Transformations and Characters

*The way characters shift and change in your plays suggests the idea of "transformation" in performance. Do you remember that Open Theater exercise in transformation?*

Yes, it influenced it to a certain extent but then, see a lot of the things that they used in the Open Theater were actually techniques that you can't really transpose to a play without it looking like a technique. You know what I mean? (snaps his fingers) That an actor suddenly jumps from one thing to another. As a technique in an actor, in the Open Theater, working with pieces of writing, it looked great.

But I can't just turn around and say I'm going to write a play—going to appropriate its transformation. Because then it looks like a play exercise.

There are notions inside that of instantaneous change that I think are legitimate. Like can a character suddenly speak in a totally different way? Or move into a whole other world?

*In* **Angel City** *and in other plays, you sometimes leave characters, as you've put it, "marooned with language," isolated with long reveries of transformation.*

Yes, that was—it was that whole severe break with so-called naturalism that happened back there. And I think it was a healthy thing. Why should we be anchored to these notions of Eugene O'Neill and all this burden of having your character be believable from the outside in terms of the artist saying well, he really is in a living room serving tea to his mother. And he's really talking the way he would be talking in real life.

What the hell is that? Where is that going to take us? (laughs) Why doesn't he pour the tea on her head and start screaming and carrying on, climbing walls and then come back and sit down and—you know what I mean?

*Why not just jump through the wall?*

Yes, or whatever. And I think that a lot of those breaks back then had to do with incredible frustration, the straitjacket of that kind of theater that we had been told was great theater.

*Dead theater.*

Dead theater, yes. Living room theater.

*Is character larger than personality?*

Well see, I don't think character really has anything to do with personality. I think character and personality are two entirely different animals. Really. When you get right down to it.

See, I think character is something that can't be helped, it's like destiny. It's something that's essential. And maybe it includes personality, but personality is something so frivolous compared to character they're not even in the same ball park. Personality is putting on a different hat.

*But character is permanent?*

Yes, I think character is an essential tendency that can't be—it can be covered up, it can be messed with, it can be screwed around with, but it can't be ultimately changed. It's like the structure of our bones, the blood that runs through our veins.

*Is character also the same for a whole family?*

I think, yes, there is a character, characteristics, if you want to call them that, that run through families that are undeniable. So many people get screwed up because they try to deny them, try to say I'm not like my father, I'm not like my mother, I'm not going to be this way. I'm not going to be that way. When, in fact, there's nothing you can do about it. (laughs)

*So many of your plays revolve around the hopelessness of ever getting out of that bind. Unless a character embraces that family character or accepts it he's doomed.*

Yes, I think so. I think that there is no escape, that the wholehearted acceptance of it leads to another possibility. But the possibility of somehow miraculously making myself into a different person is a hoax, a futile game. And it leads to insanity, actually. (laughs)

*In the plays?*

No, in people. People go insane trying to deny what they really are.

### The Artist as American Hero

*There are other plays and films around that recall* **Angel City**, *plays about the artist/hero, exploited and devoured by movies.*

Yes, but they've been singing that song forever. What was the great—*Day of the Locust*? It was such a brilliant book. There's no reason—I mean, that says it all right there. That book says the whole thing about Hollywood and dealing with Hollywood and dealing with the machinery of it. And the thing of it is, Hollywood is impervious to criticism. You cannot puncture the skin of that mechanism. Even more so today. It's like steel armor. You can't even get next to it, because it's so completely locked up, guarded by the mechanism.

*I thought you got around that with* **Paris, Texas** *by working with Wim Wenders, a German filmmaker who sees America the way you do. You don't see America the way an American does. You step away from it and look at it from a distance.*

(laughs) Right. It's true. Europeans, particularly Germans, have a very critical eye—not a critical eye but it's an eye that *embraces* a certain thing about America that I don't think Americans have. For the most part, I think Americans have lost the compassion for their own country.

### States of Shock

*What brought about* **States of Shock**? *Where did that come from?*

I was in Kentucky when the war opened. I was in a bar . . . and it was stone silence. The TV was on, and these planes were coming in, and I had the sense that—it just seemed like doomsday to me. I could not believe the systematic kind of insensitivity of it. That there was this punitive attitude: we're going to just knock these people off the face of the earth.

And then it's devastating. Not only that, but they've convinced the American public that this was a good deed. . . . the notion of this being a heroic event is just outrageous. I couldn't believe it. I still can't believe it. I can't believe that, having come out of the sixties and the incredible reaction to Vietnam, [that voice] has all but disappeared. Vanished. There's no voice any more.

*But* **States of Shock** *doesn't only respond to the Gulf War.*

No. I wanted to create a character of such outrageous, repulsive, military, fascist demonism that the audience would recognize it, and say, "Oh, this is the essence of this thing."

I thought Malkovich came pretty close to it. Just creating this monster fascist.

### Reality and Danger

*Should theater be real, and dangerous in the same way as the rodeo, for example?*

Well, to a certain extent. You don't want to hurt anybody. I don't believe in theater that hurts people physically at all. I don't think that's what Artaud meant by "the theater of cruelty." And I don't like to see people maim themselves or do anything ridiculous.

But on the emotional level, there can be a comparable experience without hurting anyone. I don't think you should hurt anyone. What's the point in that?

*On the emotional level, are you aiming towards Artaud's idea of theater exteriorizing latent cruelty? Your plays do put the audience in touch with things they don't think about when they think about themselves as civilized.*

Yes, hopefully, although it sounds high faluting when you couch it with Artaud, because Artaud has become so misused, I think, over the years. He's become an excuse for a whole kind of theater that he probably wouldn't endorse if he was alive today. He'd laugh at it. Or maybe he wouldn't, I don't know because I never met the man.

### Early Plays

*Are you still fond of any of your early plays?*

Yes, I like **Action**.

And I like **Rock Garden** all right. The funny thing about **Rock Garden** is, if you look at that play—it's surprising to me even because when I look at it, I see the germ right in that little play of a whole lot of different things. The germ [is] in that play of many, many to come, much more so than **Cowboys**, for instance, or a lot of those other plays.

**Rock Garden** was sort of the beginning of something that reverberated from there, which I didn't realize at the time.

*There's a recipe in* **Rock Garden** *for* Angels on Horseback, *which would be a very nice subtitle for* **Far North**.

Angels on horseback, yeah, it would be.

*And why are you fond of* **Action**?

Because it was such a complete breakaway from anything I'd done before. It's completely in another domain. The play itself surprised me, the way it moved and the idiosyncrasy of it and the way it shifted.

I thought it was a satisfying combination of slapstick and something more serious. I don't know what you call it, realism or something like that.

**Action** *has that haunting speech about the moths.*

The moths and the breaking of the chair and the clothes on the clothesline and things like that. And I think it's an interesting play.

And in fact, **States of Shock** is probably an outcome of that play, in form, in structure, in its quirkiness, its instant changes. Things like that.

*And do you have any fondness for* **Tooth of Crime**?

To some extent. But I think it's dated now. A lot of that early stuff I couldn't really say was dated. But it [**Tooth of Crime**] seems too topical. Underlying it, the combat thing is interesting, the clash of forces, but then the whole thing about pop culture kind of turns me off. There's this pretense of being a commentary on pop culture.

### Writing

*I've read that you've wished you would never have to write another play.*

That was a little period I was going through.

*But not any more? You no longer feel that it's some kind of curse, that you have to write and you would like to be free of it?*

No, not necessarily, no. Because see, the thing that's interesting about writing is if it really is something that you get in your blood, it keeps opening and opening and opening. It doesn't shut down. I think to a certain extent the play thing has narrowed. But then there's other writing, there's other kinds of writing that have opened up as a result of that narrowing down.

And you get involved in that and then maybe, who knows, the playwriting all comes back up again. You can't really predict that stuff.

*You can't turn your back on a gift like that.*

It's not only a gift, it's a kind of way of life. I feel lucky that I have something like that where experience can be shuffled back into another form, as opposed to not having a form or structure to put an expression into. I suppose you do that with anything but with writing—it's really lucky to be a writer, I think.

**Susanne Willadt (essay date March 1993)**

SOURCE: Willadt, Susanne. "States of War in Sam Shepard's *States of Shock*." *Modern Drama* 36, no. 1 (March 1993): 147-66.

[*In the following essay, Willadt analyzes the structure of* States of Shock, *emphasizing Shepard's sense of machismo and his portrayal of relationships between men.*]

I

After a six-year silence, Sam Shepard, formerly one of the most prolific and most produced American playwrights, finally returned to the American theater with *States of Shock*. The play was first presented by The American Place Theatre in New York City on April 30, 1991, for a very limited run.[1] As has been the case for so many other Shepard plays before, *States of Shock* was eagerly anticipated by New York, theater critics as an opportunity to fight another critical war about Shepard. Shepard has always had what Walter Kerr, the "high priest" of the New York theater critics, once named his "cult audience." However, the surprising fact is that the Shepard cult is split in two: he is either loved or hated, and both with equal passion.[2] (Kerr, needless to say, hates him!) Consequently, much Shepard criticism can hardly be called objective. It seems that Shepard, who once said that he is not interested in an intellectual but only in an emotional response to his plays, has reached his goal, at least in view of the emotionally charged reactions of the critics. With *States of Shock,* Shepard's supporters, i.e., Frank Rich, Jack Kroll and Michael Feingold, at first reacted with relief to the simple fact that he had at least written a new play. Above all, they saw the play as proof that Shepard's productive phase, against all speculations, has not yet come to an end, much to the regret of Shepard's harshest critics. John Simon, for example, who renamed the play "States of Schlock," finds it wholly pointless "except for adding to the Shepard myth"; Mimi Kramer, still "in search of the good Shepard," finds the play is simply "an index of the bankruptcy" of Shepard's theatrical vocabulary.[3] Even Shepard's defenders, though, have to admit that something was not quite right with the play, that in the end, in keeping with the war imagery in it, "it blows itself up," "like a defective grenade" (Kroll). Never before was the general critical response to a new Shepard play as negative as in the case of *States of Shock*. Shepard is conscious of this fact. He tries to explain it away as the result of frustrated expectations, since *States of Shock* is, according to Shepard, "so radically different from *A Lie of the Mind,*" and of the difficulty that most critics have in categorizing the play: "They couldn't find a place to put it. They couldn't put it . . . Some of them called it absurdism or . . . They couldn't fit it into anything" (Rosen, 34).

However, *States of Shock* does make one wonder if Shepard's once extraordinary theatrical talent has not actually imploded. By looking closely at the structure of the play, the *states of war* dramatized, and Shepard's intentions, the following analysis will try to show that Shepard has finally become a victim of his most prominent personal and artistic obsession: his fascination with machismo and with the "mystery" he finds solely in relationships between men.[4]

II

Shepard once said that he was not interested in the "American social scene at all"[5] and that he doesn't have "any political theories."[6] *States of Shock,* which was first staged right after the end of the Gulf War, is his first overtly political play, a play "on war and machismo," in Frank Rich's words. Shepard does not consider it "unfair" to read a political or social meaning into his plays but finds it "an incomplete, a partial way of looking at the play" if it is reduced to only one of these meanings (Lippman, 9). He wants to reach what he once called a "much wider dimension,"[7] one that goes beyond a mere political or social meaning and reaches "emotional territory" (an expression he just recently used in an interview with Carol Rosen, [34]). Some of Shepard's early plays, i.e., *Icarus's Mother* (1965), *Forensic and the Navigators* (1967), *The Unseen Hand* (1970), or *Action* (1975),[8] as well as his later plays dealing with the disintegration of the American family, can nevertheless be called political plays. But, even in his more overtly political work Shepard's attitude is both critical and nostalgic; his condemnation of civilization and modern technology in contemporary America is always connected with some nostalgic longing for its pastoral past. Moreover, even in these plays Shepard is mainly concerned with psychological, moral and personal obsessions, obsessions which dominate most of his work and which, underneath its political surface, can also be found in *States of Shock.*

The crux of *States of Shock* is that Shepard seems to have lost track of the "much wider dimension" he is searching for. Before completing this play, he had obviously gone through a dry spell in his writing career, not having produced a new play in six years or published one in seven.[9] One gets the impression that *States of Shock* was put together in haste right after the end of the gulf War because Shepard somehow felt obliged to give a personal comment on the present *state* of the American nation. For the first time he took an actual event as the starting point for a play, reversing his former artistic credo that "Ideas emerge from plays—not the other way around."[10] The effort, to write a play on the Gulf War at a time when this war was interpreted as a kind of successful replay of the Vietnam War, is in itself laudable. Shepard says he cannot but feel outraged by the general reaction to the Gulf War in America:

> The notion of this being a heroic event is just outrageous. I couldn't believe it. I still can't believe it. I can't believe that, having come out of the '60s and the incredible reaction to Vietnam, that voice has all but disappeared. Vanished. There's no voice anymore. This is supposed to be what America is about?
>
> (Rosen, 39)

Shepard willingly lends his own voice to help examine from a different angle what America is about. But, for a writer who has always been praised for his visionary and poetic qualities, he is trying very hard and sometimes with very obvious means to fulfill his mission. Never before has he come so close to narrow preaching, bringing to mind Bertolt Brecht's didactic rigidity or Arthur Miller's moral finger, and giving the play an outdated, even "isolated," quality, as if it had been written "at a reclusive distance from the ongoing torments of life," as Michael Feingold observes.

For all its (intended) relation to the current situation, however, the play could have almost been written in the sixties, at a time when it still seemed possible to change the course of politics in America and to change society itself. Although seeming somewhat old-fashioned, *States of Shock* actually does show what Jack Kroll calls "a political passion badly needed in American theater," and it truly is "written with the earnest . . . conviction that the stage is still an effective platform for political dissent and mobilizing public opinion" (Rich, C1). Shepard, after all, did begin his career in the sixties and is one of the creators of the American drama of that decade. His early plays overturned theatrical conventions and brought a poetic voice to the American theater, who were either connected with Joseph Papp's Public Theatre or, like Shepard himself, with Joseph Chaikin's Open Theatre, whose transformation theory probably had the most profound influence on Shepard's (early) writing. Shepard has always wanted to give the impression that he existed *sui generis,* without any artistic roots, debts, or relations to any theatrical tradition, but *States of Shock* seems to investigate his theatrical origins in the sixties.

In one of his rare theoretical essays, **"American Experimental Theatre—Then and Now,"** Shepard defines what he regards as the most profound influence of the sixties on the theater in general and on his own writing in particular:

> To me the influence of the sixties [. . .] was a combination of hallucinogenic drugs, the effect of those drugs on the perceptions of those I came in contact with, the effect of those drugs on my own perceptions, the Viet Nam war, and all the rest of it which is now all gone.[11]

Drugs were a part of Shepard's life-style in the sixties and, from the beginning, a part of his free-form writing habit. (In 1965, he escaped the draft by pretending to be a heroin addict.) Many of his early plays deal with hallucinatory states, drug-induced or not. In their own way these plays are expressions of the general atmosphere of the time. They all have apocalyptic overtones and end with catastrophes, but none of these plays deals explicitly with the Vietnam War. *States of Shock,* however, almost immediately recalls American anti-war plays of the sixties (and the seventies) dealing with that event.[12] Shepard's portrayal of a mutilated and mentally disturbed war veteran sitting in a wheelchair also brings to mind what seems to be the prevalent image of the homecoming veteran depicted in so many American films.[13]

As another reminiscence of the sixties, *States of Shock* sometimes comes close to a musical or multi-media show through the use of video, music, dancing and sound effects.[14] It also often works more as performance art than theater, as, for example, in the final tableau where Stubbs threatens to decapitate Colonel while the other characters sing "Goodnight Irene," or when Glory Bee repeatedly walks across the stage in slow motion.[15] Some of these elements and other aspects of the play clearly also fall into the range of Absurd theater.

*States of Shock* is a strange conglomerate of different reminiscences and analogies. Nothing that happens in this play is exactly predictable, but everything is recognizable in a way, not only from the analogies mentioned above but also from prior Shepard plays. It might actually be the beginning of a third period in Shepard's writing, a combination of his early plays and his family plays, a period that Michael Feingold is hesitant to call "late Shepard." The experimental atmosphere of the play, with its shifting realities and absurd, though mostly apocalyptic, overtones and Shepard's use of sometimes bizarre visual and verbal imagery, has much in common with his early writing. Shepard himself sees a connection to *Action*; he thinks that *States of Shock* is "probably an outcome of that play, in form, in structure, in its quirkiness, its instant changes" (Rosen, 41). But, its subject matter also recalls Shepard's more recent naturalistic family plays, dealing only superficially with war in the political sense of the word. Underneath its surface hovers Shepard's most pronounced obsession. *States of Shock* is a dramatization of a ritualized war between two men and, as in so many other Shepard plays, it is a war between a father and his son.

### III

*States of Shock* takes place in a coffee-shop, a "family restaurant," as is repeatedly emphasized in the play (e.g., 8), presumably somewhere in the South of the United States. The play dramatizes a conflict between a man simply called Colonel, a choleric character, whose explosive personality dominates the whole play, and a younger man called Stubbs, a veteran of an unidentified war who is bound to a wheelchair decorated with small American flags. Stubbs may or may not be Colonel's son. Colonel insists that his son died heroically in combat. Stubbs, he says, is his son's best friend who was severely wounded by "friendly" artillery fire while unsuccessfully trying to save the life of his son (27). Colonel has apparently kidnapped Stubbs from a hospital and brought him to the restaurant to "celebrate" the anniversary of his son's death. The conflict between Colonel and Stubbs intensifies when Colonel wants to go through what seems to be an old ritual for the two men (Colonel says, "I know we've done this before," [12]). He asks Stubbs to reenact the battle scene in which his son was killed and Stubbs himself was wounded, by means of toy soldiers, tanks, airplanes, cutlery (shore lines) and a sugar dispenser (a mountain). Stubbs, at first, plays Colonel's game. But, his frustration builds, and he then accuses Colonel repeatedly of having "invented my death" (e.g., 33). Stubbs (rightly) suspects that Colonel cannot accept him as his son because he returned from the war severely wounded and, what is more, impotent. He does not embody Colonel's picture of a war hero and a real American man. To prove that he *is* a man and worthy to be Colonel's son, Stubbs starts to flirt with the waitress, Glory Bee, and finally feels his "thing" coming back, which is to say his long lost and yearned-for manhood (36). His "thing" also brings back his memory and finally gives him a stronger position in his conflict with Colonel. Colonel feels he is losing control over the situation and, most of all, over Stubbs. At the end, Colonel still does not want to admit that Stubbs is his son, but he admits that they could be "somehow remotely related" (35). To escape the danger of losing his power over Stubbs he promises to take him back and even to "make it official," but Stubbs seems to be determined finally to free himself from Colonel (39).

During the course of the play, the two men fight a duel-by-language that ends in a physically violent showdown typical of almost every Shepard play—to the sheer amazement and total lack of understanding of the two other customers in the restaurant, an older middle-class couple called the White Man and the White Woman, who are appropriately dressed all in white. Their main problem is that they have trouble getting service from the waitress, presumably because they didn't order the "Express" (11). The White Man and Woman appear to be in a "deep state of catharsis" (Shepard's stage direction); they are like "cadavers" (5). Their presence hardly adds anything to the principal action, barely even connects with it. They merely act as some kind of commentary to it. This negative portrayal of the emissaries of the middle class, the representatives of the establishment for whom Shepard only has contempt, recalls similar middle-class Shepard characters, such as the priest in *Buried Child,* the lawyer in *Curse of the Starving Class,* or the film producer in *True West,* characters whose main function is to embody Shepard's condemnation of modern civilization. Glory Bee, the waitress, repeatedly walks across the stage in slow motion in her hapless efforts to serve coffee, banana splits and clam chowder to her customers. She adds a lot of entertainment to the play with her choreographic interludes, her crawling back and forth on the stage, her dancing with Colonel, her rolling around on the floor with Stubbs and her musical numbers (at one point she starts to sing). She cannot be called a rounded character; but, contrary to the White Man and Woman, she serves a real function in the play. She is another one of Shepard's female messengers of eroticism; her sexual function is her most important one and in this respect, it does not matter that she is working as a waitress, even though she has been inept at carrying things "since I was very little!" (9).

Like so many other Shepard plays, *States of Shock* has no real ending, no solution. Apart from the fact that Shepard admits that he has difficulty finding endings for his plays—"endings are just a pain in the ass," he says (Rosen, 36)—he also thinks "it's a cheap trick to resolve things. It's totally a complete lie to make resolutions" (Lippman, 11). For him, a solution at the end of a play is not an ending but a "strangulation" (Lippman, 11). *States of Shock,* like *True West,* almost ends with a literal strangulation topped by the threat of a decapitation. Like Lee and Austin in *True West,* the two male protagonists in *States of Shock* stand frozen in a position of eternal confrontation and hostility—it is not clear whether one of them (Stubbs) will kill the other (Colonel), and even at the end it is not absolutely clear if Stubbs is or is not Colonel's son. Given Shepard's work, he most probably is, but Shepard never gives one the satisfaction of being sure.

## IV

***States of Shock*** deals with "states of war" on several levels, the political as well as the personal and individual. The play's initial metaphor is no doubt taken from the Gulf War. But, the real war that is going on in this play takes place on battlefields known from former Shepard plays: in the family (between male family members), and between the sexes.

The war in which Stubbs was injured is never specifically identified. It could be any war. The timing of the production of ***States of Shock*** and a few features of the play—references to a war taking place on land and sea that everybody thought "would all be done in a day" (16) and to soldiers who are killed or wounded by friendly artillery fire, and the presence of a big cyclorama showing pictures of a war recalling coverage on CNN—indicate that Shepard was thinking of the Gulf War. At the same time, Shepard has also emphasized that he was searching for the "essence" of what is happening in and through a war in general (Rosen 39). Accordingly, Colonel is dressed up in a "strange ensemble of military uniforms and paraphernalia" (5) taken from America's war-making past, from the Civil War, the Second World War and the Vietnam War. Images of war are ever-present, on both the visual and the verbal level. The cyclorama upstage, covering the entire wall, brings the war home to an all-American family restaurant. It repeatedly shows pictures of an unidentified war, tracer fire, rockets, explosions, a whole "war panorama," (5). Sounds of explosions alternate with the driving rhythms of two live percussionists, situated extreme right and left behind the cyclorama, attacking the audience's ears and probably meant to give a taste of what war sounds like.[16] At first, the war scenes shown on the back wall seem like somebody's dream or memory, but the war is actually much closer to the restaurant than one first believes. The family restaurant itself is under siege: we learn from Glory Bee that the manager has died (19) and that the cook has been wounded (22). The White Woman, who is angry about Glory Bee's service, insists that "She ought to be shot" (15), and Glory Bee keeps a supply of candles for "the black-outs" (18). Glory Bee at one point says that she misses the "'quiet times' just before the sirens[.] Way back when it first started" (33). "It" obviously stands for a war during which the restaurant was invaded and "the first wave of missiles hit us" (34). All the characters on stage seem to have learned to live in a "state of war" and accept it as something quite normal. Towards the end of the play a wagon loaded with gas masks is rolled on stage. Thinking nothing of it, the characters put on the gas masks and the White Woman says, "Shouldn't we be getting under the table by now? Shouldn't we be tucking our heads between our knees?" (35).

Stubbs is living proof of the reality and the effects of war, though in his case one that did not take place on American territory (he remembers the sea that "didn't smell American to me. It smelled like a foreign sea" [17]). Stubbs sits in a wheelchair, his legs covered by an old army blanket. He was severely wounded in the war and repeatedly shows his red chest wound to the other characters on stage or directly to the audience. He says that he is "eighty per cent mutilated" (e.g., 13), not only physically, it seems, but also mentally. He acts and talks as if he still is in a "state of shock" because of some horrible experience in the past. One gets the impression that he has either lost his mind or been brainwashed. Stubbs, at first, is unable to communicate. To make his presence acknowledged he either blows his whistle relentlessly or keeps repeating the same, mostly senseless, phrases. At the beginning, his recollections of the war and of his own past are more or less reduced to one simple statement (also his very first words in the play), which he keeps repeating in slight variations throughout the course of the play: "When I was hit—It went straight through me. Out the other side. Someone was killed. But, it wasn't me. I'm not the one. I'm the lucky one" (8). With the sad picture of Stubbs in mind, it is hard to believe that he thinks he is "the lucky one." He could only be called lucky in one respect: he lives in an absolute "state of oblivion" that has even made him forget what he had to endure in and after the war. Only Colonel's wish to re-enact the battle scene in which Stubbs got wounded slowly brings back his memory. In short glimpses he then remembers the fear he felt at the moment when he stood in the middle of the cross-fire that finally hit him (30-31) or the other dead and wounded people around him, friends and enemies alike (24).

But, contrary to the homecoming war heroes of other plays (and films), there are no indications that Stubbs is haunted or brought to an existential or moral crisis by what he did and experienced in the war, friends he lost, people he might have killed, etc. Strangely enough, or maybe not for Shepard, the horrors of war are reduced to the single fact that the war has made Stubbs impotent, the only fact that he is really conscious of even at the very beginning of the play. There is one phrase in ***States of Shock*** that runs through it like a *leitmotif* and gives it a totally different drift from what one would expect from an anti-war play. It is Stubb's outcry "MY THING HANGS LIKE DEAD MEAT!!!" (11), which is repeated in several variations either by Stubbs himself or by Colonel, and which makes ***States of Shock*** another Shepard play on what it takes to be, or rather to become, a "real man," namely, a "thing" that "grows straight and strong and tall" (29).

Stubbs survived one war just to come home and fight another, and this one really is existential for him. He has to fight his worst enemy: his father. For both men this fight is a matter of life and death. In the beginning, Stubbs seems to have no chance against Colonel, who has used "all those horrible long days without the enemy" to prepare himself for his return (33). Now, Stubbs is back and Colonel knows that "the enemy has the same hunger for me as I have for him" (34). Both men repeatedly agree to the fact that "WITHOUT THE ENEMY WE'RE NOTHING!" (e.g., 13). For them, only male competition and aggressiveness lead to a truly male identity, and this is what both men are aiming at. For Stubbs, Colonel even seems to have power over life and death: Stubbs believes that Colonel has "invented my death" (e.g., 20). Colonel's inability to understand and, what is more important, accept his son for what he is, has "killed" Stubbs. Thus, according to Shepard, Colonel is following an archetypal male tradition that goes back to the Bible: "Abraham, maybe. Maybe Abraham. Judas," says Stubbs (37-38), who is searching for the "original moment" that triggered the everlasting war between fathers and sons (37).[17] Because Stubbs thinks that there is "No way of knowing for sure" why fathers kill their sons, he is full of resignation:

> Best way is to kill all the sons. Wipe them off the face of the earth. Bleed them of all their blood. Let it pour down into the soil. Let it fill every river. Every hole in this earth. Let it pour through every valley. Flood every town. Let us drown in the blood of our own. Let us drown and drink it. Let us go down screaming in the blood of our sons.
>
> (38)

Shepard may be drawing a direct parallel to another anti-war play, Arthur Miller's *All My Sons* (1947), which, like **States of Shock,** deals with the subject of war through a dramatization of a father-son conflict. In *All My Sons,* the father Joe Keller, sold cracked cylinder heads to the American Air Force, an act that caused twenty-one airplanes to crash and twenty-one pilots, among them maybe even one of his own sons, to be killed. Stubbs, like the second surviving son in *All My Sons,* yearns to understand why his father has forsaken him (33). It is not the bullet that hit him and left a hole in his chest, but rather his father's betrayal that has put him into a complete "state of shock:" "When you left me it went straight through me and out the other side. It left a hole I can never fill" (20). Like Abraham, who was willing to sacrifice his son Isaac to God, Colonel is willing to sacrifice his son Stubbs to the God of War. It is a sacrifice for a violent concept of manhood, for the belief that fighting in a war is a manly and heroic deed. The son, however, cannot measure up to this concept because he himself has become a victim of it. On a metaphoric level, Shepard is saying that America is the father willing to sacrifice all the sons for what he considers to be a "hoax" (Rosen, 39). According to Shepard, "the betrayal is definitely on the side of the father" (Rosen, 36).

Colonel is a man of war through and through. His military rank has even replaced his real name. Shepard said that with him he wanted to create a "monster fascist," "a character of such outrageous, repulsive, military, fascist demonism that the audience would recognize it and say, 'Oh, this is the essence of this thing'" (Rosen, 39). For Colonel it is an "American virtue" to fight willingly for one's country. His battle cry is "A soldier for his nation!" (21). If one dies for his country, one has "not died in vain" but followed a great American tradition: "We can't forget that we were generated from the bravest stock. The Pioneer. The Mountain Man. The Plainsman. The Texas Ranger. The Lone Ranger." For Colonel, American men have "a legacy to continue" (21), which is to prove that one is a "real man" because "This country wasn't founded on spineless, spur-of-the-moment whimsy" (17). Colonel is confident that he himself plays a worthy part in this legacy. He understands his "purpose in the grand scheme of things" and is convinced that he is "a God among men" (28).

By personifying this male American legacy, Colonel clearly dominates the play with his explosive and violent actions.[18] Like all of Shepard's father figures, he lives in his own fantasy world, has a taste for alcohol and prefers to eat alone ("I've loved to eat alone. I've gone out of my way to eat alone. I've walked miles in search of empty restaurants" [20-21]) and, above all, to live alone: "I was born in isolation. If I can't have companionship it won't kill me" (33). The only thing he really needs is the enemy, somebody to measure his strength against. Colonel's most characteristic feature, however, is his penchant for violent outbursts. For Colonel, "aggression is the only answer," and for him, as for most of Shepard's male characters, violence is the preferred method to prove his manliness (33). In an interview Shepard once admitted that violence is "the source of a lot of intrigue" for him:

> I think there's something about American violence that to me is very touching. [. . .] In full force it's very ugly, but there's also something very moving about it, because it has to do with humiliation. There's some hidden, deeply rooted thing in the Anglo male American that has to do with inferiority, that has to do with not being a man, and always, continually having to act out some idea of manhood that invariably is violent.[19]

With the exception of one incident where Colonel even threatens Glory Bee with "a good beating," his acts of violence are directed against Stubbs (28). Every time Stubbs does not function the way Colonel expects him to, he threatens to punish him. Colonel asks for "total, absolute, unconditional submission" (36). He treats

Stubbs like a little boy who needs a "good solid thrashing" or a "good spanking" (23), if he doesn't do what father tells him. At first, Colonel is only verbally violent, but later on he does not hesitate to whip Stubbs savagely with a belt, spank him or slap him in the face (24-25). Every time, Colonel's violent outbursts are accompanied by the sounds of explosions and/or by pictures of war shown on the cyclorama. Shepard makes the connection between male violence and war obvious, but he also makes it clear that, for him, the real war rages on a personal, interhuman level.

In *States of Shock,* as in all of his plays that dramatize a father-son conflict, Shepard's sympathies lie solely on the side of the son. Stubbs is one of his typical questers for identity and *States of Shock* dramatizes his initiation journey. At the beginning of the play he has no idea who he really is. He is a *tabula rasa,* a white sheet of paper ready for Colonel's inscriptions. (The color white is associated with Stubbs several times in the play.)[20] His identity and memory are totally dependent on what Colonel has told him about himself. "Stubbs," it seems, is not even his real name (Stubbs says to Colonel: "You had my name changed!" [37]). He must have received this name from Colonel because the war has turned his limbs into stubs. Like *Fool for Love, States of Shock* is a story-telling-duel. The character telling the most convincing story is the one supposedly telling the truth. Since Stubbs, most of the time, either is speechless or speaks words that do not make sense, Colonel's story seems to be the real one, especially since Colonel insists, "That's the truth of it. Pretending is not for us. What we're after is the hard facts. The bare bones" (14).[21] Each of Stubbs's attempts to defend his own point of view is dismissed by Colonel as hallucination (36) or imagination ("Your imagination has done you in, Stubbs" [33]). For a long time Stubbs, too, believes Colonel's story, since he has no memory of his own. This brings him into a difficult position. If he is not Colonel's son, as Colonel says, he has no role model to follow. For Stubbs, as for so many Shepard "heroes" before him, the only way to find an identity is to follow the role model of the father and finally be accepted by the father as a worthy successor. Colonel knows this, for he asks Stubbs to "Imitate my every move. I'm your only chance now" (35).

Stubbs fights two wars at the same time: one against his father, and one against a fantasy brother. In many Shepard plays, two brothers fight out a war over inheritance and the rightful succession to their father.[22] The archetypal fight between two hostile brothers is most convincingly dramatized in one of Shepard's best plays, *True West* (1980), where Lee and Austin embody complete opposites. Their fight is a modern version of the fight between Cain and Abel. In *True West,* Shepard intended "to write a play about double nature,"[23] so that Lee and Austin can also be seen to represent two complementary sides of one and the same person, the two sides of a "divided self."[24] Stubbs's adversary in *States of Shock* is not, however, a real brother. Like the female characters in Shepard's gender-conflict plays, *Fool for Love* (1983), *A Lie of the Mind* (1985), and *Paris, Texas* (1983; the screenplay for Wim Wenders's film), Stubbs has to fight against an imaginary opposite. The female characters in these plays are victims of the male characters' inability to distinguish between reality and fantasy. The men confuse their real wives or lovers with the fantasy creatures they have created out of them.[25] Stubbs in *States of Shock* suffers from the same circumstances. He has to compete with Colonel's fantasy son. To maintain the illusion that his real son was a courageous war hero and a real man (just as he sees himself), unlike the mutilated and impotent Stubbs, Colonel has "invented" Stubbs's death. Stubbs knows that he can never measure up to Colonel's illusion. Consequently, he is afraid that Colonel will "wipe" him out, or "erase" him (30), the same fear that haunts May in *Fool for Love,* who uses exactly the same words to express this fear: "You're gonna' erase me. [. . .] You're either gonna' erase me or have me erased" (22). To defend or rather to find his own identity Stubbs has to kill Colonel's fantasy of his heroic dead son by telling him his recollections of what happened on the battlefield. The following passage, where Stubbs speaks about himself as if he were divided into two different persons, shows the profound split in his identity:

> Your son. *Your* son. I remember him running. Crazy. Running toward the beach. Throwing his rifle in the green sea. Throwing his arms to the sky. Running to the mountain. Back to the beach. Screaming. I remember his eyes. . . . I remember him falling. Picking him up. Dragging him down the beach. Screaming his head off. Carrying him on my back.
>
> (31-32)

Stubbs's revelation threatens Colonel's fantasy world. In the last third of the play, it is Stubbs who, after having regained his memory, tells the more convincing version of the story. He overturns Colonel's concept of manhood and the principles that he thought were "enduring" (17). In order to emphasize that the power has shifted from one man to the other, Shepard created one of his typical role changes. Suddenly, it is Stubbs who is back up on his feet staggering around the stage (31) and Colonel who sits in the wheelchair (33). As a last way to prove that he is the only man in charge and that Stubbs could not possibly be his son, Colonel plays on his own virility and Stubbs's impotence: Stubbs cannot be his son because "No son of mine has a 'thing' like that. It's not possible" (29). At this point both men try to prove their manhood with the help (or, rather, use) of a woman.

The principal action of *States of Shock* takes place solely between Colonel and Stubbs. The two female characters in the play, the White Woman and Glory Bee (and for that matter also the White Man), are present mainly for decorative purposes. In the presentation of the female characters, *States of Shock* clearly falls into the range of what Felicia Londré once called Shepard's "mindless macho period."[26] Women characters in Shepard's plays, as in *States of Shock,* very often are marginalized and portrayed mainly by negative stereotypes. They have no part in the men's search for identity, except that they represent everything that the male characters want to avoid. *States of Shock* is about "men's business." However, in plays by other authors dealing with the homecoming from a war, there is not only a father but also a mother or wife to come home to. In *States of Shock,* there is a (would-be) father but not the slightest indication of a mother (or wife) at all.

However, the White Woman actually recalls Shepard's former mother figures in her total lack of interest in and understanding of the existential crises of the men around her. She is interested only in worldly things like shopping, and she repeatedly complains about the service or tells on Colonel when he drinks alcohol in a family restaurant. One of the few times she seems to notice what is going on around her is when Colonel slaps Stubbs across the face. She seems to enjoy this, because she says, "Give it to him! You should have done that when he was just a little boy. All of this could have been avoided" (25). Later on she even follows Colonel's example when she yells at her husband and finally "whacks [him] across the head with her purse" (34). Like Colonel's outbursts, this act of violence is also accompanied by the sound of "An explosion in the distance" (34). The White Man does not react; he is obviously used to his wife's sadistic spells. He is in an even deeper state of "catharsis" (Shepard's word) than she is and gives the impression that he is completely under her control. (Michael Feingold calls him a "passive nitwit.") If the two represent what Shepard thinks is the average middle-aged, middle-class American couple, they give a sorry picture indeed, one that could definitely not be seen as an alternative to Colonel's preferred isolation. When Stubbs once directs his speech to the White Couple to explain why he suffers so much from his impotence, his words sound like pure irony:

> The middle of me is all dead. The core. I'm eighty per cent mutilated, The part of me that goes on living has no memory of the parts that are all dead. They've been separated for all time. They'll never have a partner. You're lucky to have a partner.
>
> (13)

The second woman in the play, Glory Bee, follows the Shepard stereotype of the sexy, dumb woman. The way in which Glory Bee is presented can only lead to the conclusion that she is too dumb to have anything to say about the principal action taking place between Colonel and Stubbs. In fact, she has hardly anything at all to say, except for the usual phrases of a waitress (e.g., "Do you have a smoking preference?" [6], or "Have you decided on something, sir?" [10]). Female characters in Shepard's plays, apart from mother figures, have to catch the interest of the male characters with the help of their erotic appeal. Only this can make them part of the plays' action. The Costume Plot (43) signifies Glory Bee's sexual function for the male characters by her "White pettipants" under her "Yellow and white cotton waitress uniform." As a waitress, Glory Bee symbolically offers her female sexuality on a tray to Stubbs and Colonel. She passively waits for the orders of the two men and shows her willingness to serve her sexuality to them at any time. Glory Bee's scope of action is reduced to what Shepard presents as typically female activities: domestic chores and the readiness to be used sexually whenever the male characters are in need.[27]

For quite some time, Glory Bee has nothing to do but to take orders, serve drinks and food to her (male) customers, or clean up the mess they make. In this she resembles many of Shepard's former female characters, e.g., the secretary, Miss Scoons, in *Angel City* (1976), who prepares coffee for her boss or scrubs the floor on her hands and knees (dressed in a nun's costume), or Liza and Lupe in *Action* (1975), who prepare a turkey dinner, wash dishes and hang up laundry on a clothesline. Unlike these female characters, Glory Bee is not even able to perform her simple duties satisfactorily. As a waitress she is a complete failure. She serves her customers in slow motion and sometimes, for whatever reasons, does not serve them at all, as in the case of the White Couple. She either ignores the White Couple completely or gives them insolent answers. Consequently, all the comments made about Glory Bee are derogatory. Apart from the White Woman thinking that she ought to be shot for her service, the White Man also says that "She realizes nothing" (19), while the White Woman says "She understands nothing" (21). Colonel repeatedly tries to show her how to balance a tray, but Glory Bee is incapable of doing it right. Once, Colonel loses his temper and yells at her, "Can't you remember the simplest thing!" (27). Later on he even threatens to hit her if she does not follow his orders: "You don't want a beating do you?" (28). Yet, Glory Bee is quite eager to wait on Colonel and Stubbs. Evidently she recognizes a "real man" immediately when she sees one. She all too willingly does everything Colonel and, later on, Stubbs expect her to do.

Glory Bee lives in her own dream world and appears not to understand what is going on around her. She comes alive only when she suddenly starts to sing, something she has wanted to do for quite some time. Only then does she carry her tray "quickly and freely with no concern about spilling" (25). She also seems to enjoy her dancing with Colonel. The two of them "move like a dance team with Glory Bee falling right into the rhythm" (28). In the production at The American Place Theatre, Glory Bee was played by the black actress Erica Gimpel. Since Shepard regularly attended the rehearsals in New York, one may assume that he intended the role to be played by a black actress, although he never makes this explicit in the text. The race factor throws an even more ambiguous light on Glory Bee. She then is a woman who has all the characteristics associated with derogatory, simplistic stereotypes of black women: she is all too obviously left to serve white men and clean up their mess, she is too dumb (or lazy) to perform the simplest work duties, she is at her best when she can sing and dance (since she has the "rhythm"), and white men can use her sexually for their own purposes at any time.

Not surprisingly, considering Glory Bee's sexual appeal, Stubbs talks for the first time about his "thing," his main obsession, when he notices Glory Bee. Twice, he tells her, even screams at her, "When I was hit I could no longer get my 'thing' up. It just hangs there now. Like dead meat. Like road kill" and, once more, "MY THING HANGS LIKE DEAD MEAT!!!" (11). Glory Bee only stares at him and shows no further reaction. Instantly, the presence of this willing, subservient and presumably young woman reminds Stubbs of his impotence. That sexual potency is an essential part of masculinity is literally proved to Stubbs when Glory Bee dumps a bowl of clam chowder into the White Man's lap. The White Man takes a napkin to clean from his lap the white, semen-like mess and the cleaning slowly turns into masturbation. At this point Colonel tells Stubbs that he has "to learn to pay for [his] actions. Become a man" (23). Stubbs picks up the last sentence: "Become a man" is repeated five times in a row, like an incantation or even a revelation. The White Man continues masturbating, while his wife continues eating, totally oblivious of what is going on. Colonel, to keep up with the White Man, then fools around with his Civil War sword. The crude symbolism of the masturbation scene must have provoked Frank Rich to say that "Surely Mae West made the analogy between machismo and weaponry with rather more wit" (C7).

Glory Bee now becomes an object of competition and blackmail for Colonel and Stubbs. She also becomes the catalyst in their conflict. The two men fight for glory, which is the most important thing to win in a war. Glory Bee's name alludes to "Glory be to God," and it is "Glory be" to the one who will finally win the war. Since Colonel believes that he is "a God among men" he is sure that "Glory" will be to himself.[28] He waltzes around the stage with Glory Bee, tells Stubbs that he is in love with her and spins romantic dreams of running away to Mexico with her. (Mexico is one of the favorite hideouts for Shepard's heroes when the situation gets difficult!) With her, he wants to "begin to spawn children. All boys! Each of them physically perfect in their own way. Each of them beyond reproach" (30). Whether Glory Bee wants to conceive his sons is no matter of interest for Colonel. The point for him is to make clear that he can use her sexually and that Stubbs cannot because he is, as Colonel now emphasizes, "maimed" (29) and a "cripple" (31). Colonel shows Stubbs that he can easily find a replacement for him and does not have to listen to his accusations.

At first, Colonel seems to succeed: Stubbs is afraid that he will "abandon" him (31). In his despair, he tries to get up from his wheelchair and nearly falls over, but Glory Bee rushes to his side to support him. Instantly, Colonel reminds Stubbs not to forget about his "thing": "What're you going to do when she finds out about your 'thing,' Stubbs? How're you going to explain that one?" (32). (A little later he reminds him of this again [35]). Since Stubbs shows no reaction, Colonel tries to discredit Glory Bee: "She's playing you for a sucker, Stubbs. You can see right through it" (35). But Colonel has no more influence on the situation. After Glory Bee strokes Stubbs's back "softly but mechanically," Stubbs "rolls over on his back and embraces Glory Bee, pulling her on top of him" (35). The two start to roll around on the floor, and miraculously Stubbs feels his "thing is coming back!" Glory Bee thinks that this is "great," and after that she has nothing else to say (36). Finally, she has fulfilled her function and for the rest of the play her presence is no longer necessary. Only at the very end does she join in the final song, after she has put a gas mask on Stubbs and one on herself. She also "curls into fetal position" to symbolize that Stubbs, like Colonel, now is also able to spawn children (38).

Shepard's female characters are almost without exception symbols of the male fear and rejection of female sexuality. They are usually made responsible for the sexual impotence almost all of Shepard's male characters suffer from. It is a novelty in Shepard's plays that a woman restores sexual potency to a man. Yet, the restoration of Stubbs's potency with Glory Bee's help has the single function to bring the combat between Stubbs and Colonel to its climax. Glory Bee symbolizes the connection of Eros and Thanatos in the play.[29] She restores sexual potency to a man who in turn unloads it in a symbolic climactic killing (which is like an orgasm). The implication is that female sexuality is the origin of war. Stubbs once brings up this question in his own search for the origin: "Eve. Maybe her" (38). Glory Bee's sexuality not only has the effect of restoring Stubbs's potency, it also brings back his male aggressiveness and lust for blood. When Glory Bee at the end puts a gas mask on Stubbs she can be interpreted as the one who sends him into war and consequently as the one who is to blame for the existence of war.

Stubbs's sexual potency is invariably linked to his aggressiveness and his memory. His "thing" has brought everything else back ("It's all coming back to me now" [36]). When Colonel, who now is afraid that Stubbs will leave him, speaks his last words in the play, Stubbs stands behind him and holds him in a stranglehold. He then releases his hold and grabs Colonel's sword (again a rather obvious phallic symbol). With the sword in both hands he indicates that he is going to decapitate Colonel, but then freezes in that posture. He finally proves that he has become a man by an act of violence. Stubbs has been regenerated through violence and reborn a real man. His initiation journey has come to an end. His last words are "GOD BLESS THE ENEMY!!!!!!!" spoken through a gas mask (39). Stubbs blesses his enemy, which includes Colonel, because he needs him to prove that he has finally found his male identity. As a celebration of this "happy circumstance" all the characters on stage, except Stubbs, again start singing "Goodnight Irene."

Colonel and Stubbs in *States of Shock* are left in the same situation as Lee and Austin in *True West*. However, *True West* would have lost some of its impact without its ambiguous, unresolved ending. *States of Shock* leaves only frustration. It literally puts the reader/audience in a "state of shock" by its utter pessimism and lack of solution. Shepard leaves his male protagonists in "various states of insanity and self-abuse" (21). To achieve a male identity, and this is what the play is primarily about, Shepard still sees no other way than to continue the ancient male tradition of competitiveness, machismo and violence which finally leads to war. In this case, it is the son who is about to kill the father and with the use of violence he follows the role model of the father. In Shepard's plays, blood relations hover like a curse over the sons' search for a true male identity. The sons have to surrender to the mysterious and inescapable power of blood relations in order to find their own identity. They invariably have to become like their fathers, even when they are "monster fascists" like Colonel in *States of Shock*. For Shepard, everything is connected with the family, particularly male family members:

> What doesn't have to do with the family? There isn't anything, you know what I mean? Even a love story has to do with family. Crime has to do with family. We all come out of each other—everyone is born out of a mother and father, and then you go on to be a father. It is an endless cycle.[30]

Stubbs is caught up in the "endless cycle" of male family relations which forces him to repeat the old patterns of typically male behavior. Violence and machismo are essential parts of this male self. They both lead to war: on the home front, that is in the family, and on the political front. Since these patterns of behavior are passed on from one generation to the next there is absolutely no escape. War repeats itself in an endless, unbreakable cycle.

In *States of Shock*, Shepard has dramatized the motivations, failures and results of macho behavior. However, at the same time the play shows that he is personally caught up in it; he derides it and yet is unable to release himself totally from the pure physicality of violence, masturbation and the possession of a sex object. According to Shepard, machismo is not "a moral issue, it's an issue of existence." He says:

> I know what this thing [machismo] is about because I was a victim of it, it was part of my life, my old man tried to force on me a notion of what it was to be a "man." And it destroyed my dad. But you can't avoid facing it.[31]

Shepard faces this issue, and one can assume that he agrees when Colonel comments on Stubbs's wailings about his "thing": "Your 'thing' is not the issue, Your 'thing' is beside the point. It has little consequence. It's a selfish, stupid, little tiny concern" (36). The major failure of *States of Shock* is, however, that in the end Shepard merely comes up with another version of "what it takes to be a man," even though he knows the futility and exaggeration of the male "thing." This outcome seems inadequate, considering the starting point of his mission. The plot of the play and especially its ending can only be seen as a "strangulation" of a more universal discussion of the origins and "the essence" of war. The play leaves too many questions unanswered, among them the most important one: "How could we be so victorious and still suffer this terrible loss?" (25)

### Notes

1. *States of Shock* played at The American Place Theatre from April 30, 1991, for a two-week run. The production was directed by Bill Hart; in the cast were Michael Wincott as Stubbs, Erica Gimpel as Glory Bee (she formerly had a part in the musical *Fame*), Steve Nelson as White Man, Isa Thomas as White Woman, and, hardly a surprise, John Malkovich as Colonel. Malkovich came to prominence in his 1982 Steppenwolf Theater-production of Shepard's *True West,* where he played the role of Lee; and since then has been considered to be a born Shepard outlaw. Even Shepard agrees that he is "a good example" of what Rosen termed a "Shepardesque actor." Carol Rosen, "Silent Tongues: Sam Shepard's Explorations of Emotional Territory," *Village Voice* 4 August 1992, 34. (Subsequent references to Rosen will appear in parentheses in the text.) Surprisingly, Shepard, although his own productions of his last two plays, *Fool for Love* (1983) and *A Lie of the Mind* (1985), were critical successes (he even won an Obie Award for the direction of *Fool for Love*), did not direct the new play himself this time. However, he regularly attended the rehearsals in New York. *States of Shock* was published in

1992, almost exactly one year after its premiere, through Dramatists Play Service, New York. All citations are taken from this edition, with page numbers indicated in parentheses at the end of the citation.

2. Walter Kerr, "Where Has Sam Shepard Led His Audience?" *New York Times,* 5 June 1983, sec. 2; 3.

3. The reviews I referred to are: Michael Feingold, "Savage Tongues," *Village Voice,* 28 May 1991, 99; Mimi Kramer, "Toxic Shock," *New Yorker,* 3 June 1991, 78-79; Jack Kroll, "Sam Shepard Tosses a Grenade," *Newsweek,* 27 May 1991, 57; Frank Rich, "Sam Shepard Returns: On War and Machismo," *New York Times,* 17 May 1991, C1, C7; John Simon, "States of Schlock," *New York,* 27 May 1991, 71. Subsequent references to these reviews will appear in the text.

4. Shepard in an interview with Michiko Kakutani, "Myths, Dreams, Realities—Sam Shepard's America," *New York Times,* 29 January 1984, Section 2, 26.

5. Amy Lippman, "Rhythm and Truths: An Interview with Playwright Sam Shepard," *American Theatre,* 1 (April 1984), 9. Further quotations from this interview will be indicated in parentheses.

6. Kenneth Chubb and the editors of *Theatre Quarterly,* "Metaphors, Mad Dogs and Old Time Cowboys: An Interview with Sam Shepard," in Bonnie Marranca, ed., *American Dreams: The Imagination of Sam Shepard* (New York, 1981), 195. Shepard's anti-political attitude became very obvious in his failed collaboration with Italian film director Michelangelo Antonioni on his film *Zabriskie Point* (1969). Shepard finally fled the scene because "Antonioni wanted to make a political statement about contemporary youth, write in a lot of Marxist jargon and Black Power speeches. I couldn't do it. I just wasn't interested." (Michael White, "Underground Landscape," *Guardian,* 20 February 1974, 8).

7. Jonathan Cott, "The *Rolling Stone* Interview: Sam Shepard," *Rolling Stone,* 18 December 1986-1 January 1987, 172.

8. In *Icarus's Mother* the airplane represents an ominous outer (political) threat; *Forensic and the Navigators* is set in a revolutionary hideout and shows radical overtones; *The Unseen Hand* confronts the nostalgia and conservatism of the Cowboy era with a modern and sinister technology; the people are held in thrall by the oppressors with "the unseen hand"; in *Action,* the four characters in the play could be interpreted to be the only survivors of a holocaust.

9. Since the publication and production of Shepard's last full-length play, *A Lie of the Mind,* in 1985, he only had one play published: *True Dylan,* a conversation between Sam Shepard and Bob Dylan, "a one-act play as it really happened one afternoon in California" (*Esquire Magazine,* July 1987, 59-68). In addition he also wrote and directed his first film, *Far North* (1988), in theme and atmosphere similar to his family plays.

10. Sam Shepard, "Language, Visualization, and the Inner Library," *Drama Review,* 21 (December 1977), 49-58; repr. in Marranca, 215. In this essay Shepard describes his creative process.

11. Sam Shepard, "American Experimental Theatre—Then and Now," *Performing Arts Journal,* 2:2 (Fall 1977), 13-14; repr. in Marranca, 212.

12. It recalls such diverse plays as Megan Terry's rock musical *Viet Rock* (1966), a collaborative effort by Joseph Chaikin's Open Theater and the very first protest play about the Vietnam War, or the plays by Vietnam veteran David Rabe, one of the few dramatists to write about it with conviction and success, as, for example, in *The Basic Training of Pavlo Hummel* (1971), *Sticks and Bones* (1971) (where a mutilated war veteran brings the war home to an all-American family), and *Streamers* (1976), as well as Terrence McNally's four one-act plays—*Tour* (1967), *Botticelli* (1968), *Next* (1968), and *Bringing It All Back Home* (1969)—which either focus upon the Vietnam War directly by representing soldiers or indirectly by dramatizing the schism between those who remained at home and those who were subjected to being drafted and killed.

13. As, for example, in Hal Ashby's *Coming Home* (1978), Michael Cimino's *The Deer Hunter* (1978), and most recently, in *Born on the Fourth of July* (1989), written and directed by Vietnam veterans Ron Kovic and Oliver Stone.

14. The music for *States of Shock* was composed by Shepard and J. A. Deane. Shepard had already worked together with Deane in San Francisco, when he was playwright-in-residence at the Magic Theatre. In the interview with Carol Rosen, Shepard says that he thinks *States of Shock,* like *A Lie of the Mind* or *The Tooth of Crime,* is a musical: "It's got a lot of music in it. You don't have to have actors standing around singing to each other for it to be a musical" (36).

15. The use of slow motion is also a characteristic element of many productions of another of Shepard's contemporaries—the director Robert Wilson. Reminiscent in tone of Japanese Noh-Theater, most of his pieces take place in slow motion, alter-

ing the audience's sense of time. A simple action like crossing the stage sometimes can take more than an hour. When Rosen asked Shepard about the "business of balancing," in *States of Shock,* Shepard said that it had no purpose: it was "just a way to get the waitress across the stage" (39).

16. Shepard's use of sound effects as a structural element was very prominent in his own production of his family play *Fool for Love,* where he amplified the sounds of slamming doors and booming walls with the help of microphones. Shepard gives a list of sound effects used in *States of Shock*: "Distant explosion, Explosion at close range, War sounds, and Crash of dishes" (2).

17. Colonel utters many exclamations that refer to the Bible, as: "Thank God! Thank Christ! Thank the Holy Ghost!" (26). Once, he even asks Stubbs to "swear on a stack of bibles to submit!" (36).

18. Unlike most of Shepard's former father figures, Colonel is actually present in the play. In *True West* and *A Lie of the Mind* the father figures are absent; in *Curse of the Starving Class, Buried Child,* and *Fool for Love* the fathers actually are present on stage but either flee to the desert at one point or totally withdraw into their own fantasy worlds.

19. Kakutani, "Myths, Dreams, Realities," 26.

20. For example, when Stubbs talks to the "white" couple for the second time he says, "When I was hit . . . the sky went white" (9); or when Stubbs and Colonel are trying to re-enact the battle scene with toy soldiers and Stubbs first is meant to be the red soldiers but then suddenly is the white one, Colonel says, "White is you!" (15). The color white, seen in a military context, also means a sign of surrender or even capitulation.

21. "Bare bones," again, like Stubbs's "thing" that hangs like "dead meat," are a result of war.

22. Most obviously Lee and Austin in *True West,* but also Jake and Frankie in *A Lie of the Mind,* Walt and Travis in *Paris, Texas,* and the whole ensemble of warring male family members, grandfather, father and his brothers, and grandson, in *Buried Child.*

23. Robert Coe, "Saga of Sam Shepard," *New York Times Magazine,* 23 November 1980, 122.

24. For William Kleb, *True West* is a dramatization of the thesis of *The Divided Self* of the British psychiatrist and psychoanalyst R. D. Laing (see Kleb, "Sam Shepard's *True West,*" *Theater,* 12 [Fall-Winter 1980], 65-71). Tucker Orbison sees Jungian aspects in Shepard's portrayal of the two brothers. For him, Lee is the shadow figure of Austin (see Orbison, "Mythic Levels in Sam Shepard's *True West,*" *Modern Drama,* 27 [1984], 506-19).

25. May in *Fool for Love* reacts to her brother/lover Eddie's fantasy of her with the words: "You get me confused with somebody else." Sam Shepard, *Fool for Love and Other Plays* (New York, 1984), 25.

26. Felicia Londré, "Sam Shepard Works Out: The Masculinization of America," *Studies in American Drama, 1945-Present,* 2 (1987), 20.

27. For Florence Falk, the female characters in Shepard's plays are "the domestic caretakers of the plays, their responsibilities ranging from cooking to fucking on command." See "Men without Women: The Shepard Landscape," in Marranca, 96.

28. In Emily Mann's Vietnam play *Still, Life* (1980), which was also produced at The American Place Theatre, a wife explains her husband's definition of glory: "I mean men would not be going on fighting like this / for centuries if there wasn't something besides / having to do it for their country. / It has to be something like Mark says. / I mean he said it was like orgasm. / He said it was the best sex he ever had. / You know where he can take that remark. / But what better explanation can you want? / And believe me, that is Mark's definition of glory. / Orgasm is GLORY to Mark." See *Coming to Terms: American Plays and the Vietnam War* (New York, 1985), 232.

29. Glory Bee's fetal position at the end of the play can also be understood as a fatal position: she is preparing herself for her death in the threat of a coming war.

30. Shepard in an interview with Jennifer Allen, "The Man on the High Horse: On the Trail of Sam Shepard," *Esquire Magazine* (November 1988), 143.

31. Cott, "The *Rolling Stone* Interview," 172.

## Robert Brustein (review date 2 January 1995)

SOURCE: Brustein, Robert. "Plays for the Parch." *New Republic* 212, no. 1 (2 January 1995): 28.

[*In the following excerpt, Brustein offers a mixed assessment of* Simpatico, *faulting the play for its "manipulated suspense."*]

Sam Shepard's new play, *Simpatico,* which he also directed (at the New York Public Theater), has taken as many critical lumps as his last play, *States of Shock.*

Viewed as an overarching dramatic work, *Simpatico* probably deserves a few knocks, but I found it an absorbing evening nevertheless, Shepard's best since *Buried Child*—not because of the cryptic writing, which is strong in individual scenes but ultimately too swamped by its own mysteries. I admired it largely for its acting values. Shepard's directorial technique has advanced considerably in confidence and precision since he last staged *A Lie of the Mind*. He's a whiz now with scene work: there isn't a slack moment in the play. But, as in *Lie of the Mind*, the director is too reluctant to edit the playwright; some fat could have been profitably cut. At three hours, *Simpatico* is simply too long for its subject matter. Even supplied with ample detail to distract you from the thin dramatic purpose, you tend to leave the theater feeling a little unsatisfied. Still, the evening is wonderfully conceived and performed, and riveting moment by moment. *Simpatico* is a sustained piece of virtuosity that makes you happy Sam Shepard has returned to the stage.

At some point in the proceedings, a character says, "Who is it decided to do away with all the plots?" Well, whoever it was, all the plots ended up in *Simpatico*, which has enough for a dozen such plays. It is true that Shepard has already written some of these plots, and has often written them better. He has looted *True West* for the symbiotic tension between his once "simpatico" central male characters. *Geography of a Horse Dreamer* for reflections on the corruptions of the racetrack and *A Fool for Love* for a sultry love scene. He has also borrowed some sexual teasing from Tennessee Williams's *Baby Doll*, some film noir atmosphere from James M. Cain's *The Postman Always Rings Twice* and *Double Indemnity*, and a whole character (a drifter masquerading as a detective) from the movie *Miami Blues*. This is larceny on a grand creative scale, but *Simpatico* still bears the characteristic stamp of its author. Like Brecht, Shepard knows how to convert others' private property into his own idiosyncratic real estate.

The trouble is that a coherent dramatic purpose tends to get lost in the underbrush. *Simpatico* is tantalizing enough in its narrative twists and turns to hold your interest, but what it finally delivers is not sufficient substance to reward your patience. As the action drifts from Cucamonga, California, to bluegrass Kentucky and back again, *Simpatico* begins to revolve around a racetrack scam that is now causing Carter, the central character, to come apart at the seams. Fifteen years before the action begins, Carter switched a couple of thoroughbreds in order to make a quick bundle and, when the racing commissioner detected the swindle, arranged to have him discredited. In the manner of a private eye collecting evidence for a divorce, he had photos taken of the commissioner in a motel encounter with a young woman, and blackmailed him into silence.

The commissioner (Simms) agreed to hold his tongue and go to another town under an assumed name. But Vinnie Webb, the accomplice who took the photographs (his ex-wife, Rosie, was the woman in the motel room), now wants to expose the truth, partly to come out from under his long exile, partly to pay Carter back for stealing Rosie and his '58 Buick. As in most Shepard plays, the sibling rivalry between these longtime companions is the nub of the action. The playwright draws a familiar contrast between a slick successful achiever (Carter) who is nevertheless riddled with guilt, and a disheveled, disreputable loner (Vinnie) who maintains the moral high ground.

Carter and Vinnie are played by Ed Harris and Fred Ward, both of them (along with Shepard) alumni of *The Right Stuff*, so the casting is like a class reunion. Harris, wearing a tan double-breasted suit in danger of being shredded by his muscles, does a subtle take on a rigid man without a center, an ex-ex-alcoholic with quivering shoulders, an eggshell in the process of being fragmented. Ward, sporting a two-day growth of beard and a mischievous glint as Vinnie, fully inhabits the role of a derelict masquerading as a private dick and only dicking himself.

Vinnie takes a tour of Kentucky, carrying a shoebox full of the incriminating photographs, eager to find "the man who fell from grace," the mysterious Simms. Simms (another strong, raspy performance by James Gammon), while denying his identity, nevertheless admits that he once heard of a man who had been vilified and railroaded out of town, at the loss of his entire family (though, Simms adds, "loss can be a powerful elixir"). When Simms spurns the photos, Vinnie goes to Lexington to offer them to Rosie, his ex-wife (Beverly D'Angelo in a steamy, gin-soaked performance). First she refuses to recognize him, then also refuses the negatives.

In the meantime, Carter has been making time with Vinnie's girlfriend, Cecilia (Marcia Gay Harden). He eventually persuades her to visit Simms by telling her hypnotic sagas of the Kentucky Derby. She believes Simms has bought Vinnie's negatives and now wants to buy them back for Carter. But Simms's ironic manner, his insinuating stories of great thoroughbreds such as Secretariat, work on her like an aphrodisiac, making her short of breath. Simms tells her he was betrayed by two snakes: "Some of us get caught with our pants down and some of us don't—I was one of the lucky ones."

When Vinnie rejoins Carter, who is holed up in Vinnie's bed, he finds a shivering wreck of man who can't put on his own pants and believes his number is up. Carter now wants to swap lives, just as he once swapped horses. He offers Vinnie his fortune, his estate and Rosie in return for Vinnie's purity of conscience. Vinnie, "working on a new case," ignores him and leaves. Cecilia returns to pour Carter's money over him on the bed, just as Tilden in **Buried Child** once poured vegetables over his father's sleeping body. The phone rings. Carter is too paralyzed to answer it.

Aside from its impressionist portrait of treachery, betrayal and failed redemption, this doesn't add up to much more than manipulated suspense, but it is a wonder how Shepard can keep us traveling with him on this long day's journey into blight. **Simpatico** is a treasure hunt that never yields much treasure, except as a demonstration of fine ensemble acting and powerful directing (along with sharp minimalist designing by Loy Arcenas, who can even make a dirty kitchen sink look like a sinister symbol). If it doesn't entirely deliver as a play, **Simpatico** certainly satisfies as a rich theatrical effluvium, and that's no small thing in a time of drought.

## Robert Brustein (essay date 15-22 July 1996)

SOURCE: Brustein, Robert. "Shepard's Choice." *New Republic* 215, nos. 3/4 (15-22 July 1996): 27-9.

[*In the following essay, Brustein offers a mixed assessment of Shepard's works, particularly* Buried Child *and* Cruising Paradise, *within the context of Shepard's attitudes towards being a celebrity.*]

Challenging the camera over a period of thirty years, Sam Shepard's face appears in sepia and black-and-white on the jackets of three newly issued books. The chiseled bones, the two deep furrows in his forehead, the uncombed mane and dimpled chin are physical constants. What the camera also reveals is how the acid of years and circumstance have etched radical mutations in Shepard's appearance. Something more than passing time is responsible for his transformation from the youthful hipster depicted in Bruce Weber's unposed photo for **The Unseen Hand and Other Plays,** to the engaging, rather shy young man of Weber's cover shot for **Simpatico,** to the unshaven, haggard, vaguely anguished figure in Brigitte Lacombe's portrait for **Cruising Paradise,** to the harrowing, glowering desperado in Richard Avedon's recent celebrity mug shot for *The New Yorker.* Avedon's black-bordered photograph shows the face and neck of its now middle-aged subject weathered by outdoor and indoor experience, his brow threatening, his mouth drooping at the edges with surly contempt. You can almost sense him tapping his foot, an unwilling subject, impatient to return to his horses and the open air, who doesn't know what in hell he's doing in a New York studio.

Why, he might be asking, is a man who prided himself on being a private, even reclusive writer now willing to cooperate with this cosmopolitan world of hype and fashion? Once a mysterious presence behind a wealth of cryptic plays, today he finds himself a highly publicized celebrity, not through his theater work, which never managed to draw a mainstream public, but largely as a result of screen appearances, beginning with *The Right Stuff,* which brought him momentary fame as the new Gary Cooper. It is true that Shepard's movie roles have been occasional, even desultory lately, and that the once-prolific dramatist has only produced three plays in more than a decade. Yet, we are told, this will be Shepard's jubilee year. He has just enjoyed his first Broadway premiere—a revised version of the 1979 Pulitzer Prize-winning play **Buried Child** in the splendid Steppenwolf production (which will soon be closing). The Signature Theatre will stage a series of Shepard works next year off-Broadway, some old, some revised, some newly written. And Knopf and Vintage are issuing a series of Shepard volumes, the latest among them a collection of "tales" called **Cruising Paradise.**

Reading **Cruising Paradise** after seeing **Buried Child** (Brooks Atkinson Theatre) reinforces the impression that Shepard's writing is becoming increasingly autobiographical, if not self-absorbed. By common consent his masterpiece, **Buried Child** was the beginning of a relatively new phase in Shepard's work. Not long before he was discovered by Hollywood, he turned away from the rock-and-rolling hallucinogenics of **Tooth of Crime** and **The Unseen Hand** ("impulsive chronicles," as he now calls them, "representing a chaotic, subjective world") to compose domestic plays in a relatively realistic style. It was around the same time that this itinerant road warrior settled into domesticity with Jessica Lange and permitted the studios to replace his broken front tooth. What was jagged and chaotic and parentless in the Shepard persona was now turning familiar and familial.

Indeed, **Cruising Paradise** suggests that the characters depicted in **Buried Child** (and other plays of the period: **Curse of the Starving Class, A Lie of the Mind, Simpatico**) bear a family resemblance to Shepard's own ancestors. As a matter of fact, a few **Buried Child** character names—Dodge, Vinnie, Ansel—are mentioned (though in different guises) in these brief stories, along with the weird names of some recurrent Shepard locales (Azusa, Cucamonga).

The name of Dodge, a cantankerous drunkard in **Buried Child,** reappears in the stories as his great-great-great-grandfather, Lemuel Dodge, who lost an ear fighting for the North and an arm fighting for the South. (These amputated parts may have inspired Bradley's prosthetic leg in **Buried Child.**) But Dodge, the dramatic character, is probably much closer to Shepard's own father, whose bourbon-soaked presence dominates the first half of **Cruising Paradise.** In **"The Self-Made Man,"** Shepard remembers his father as a World War II fighter pilot in a silk scarf, who mournfully concluded that "aloneness was a fact of nature." In **"The Real Gabby Hayes,"** he recalls him as man who loved the open desert and loaded guns, two passions inherited by his son. In **"A Small Circle of Friends,"** he describes the way his father gradually estranged all his close companions as a result of his drinking bouts and temper tantrums. At one point, he attacked a man he suspected of having an affair with his wife, smashing his face on his raised knee and splitting his nose. And in **"See You in My Dreams,"** Shepard recounts (in an episode recapitulated in *A Lie of the Mind*) how his father was run over by a car in Bernalillo after a three-day binge of fighting, fishing and drinking with a Mexican woman. His son buried his ashes in a plain pine box in Santa Fe's National Cemetery, feeling "a terrible knotted grief that couldn't find expression."

Most of these stories, like many of his plays, take place in motor courts—Shepard may be the most inveterate chronicler of motel culture since Nabokov made Humbert Humbert chase Lolita through the back lots of America. (Both writers recognize that nothing better suggests the bleak rootlessness of American life than a rented room.) In one of the stories—**"Hail from Nowhere"**—a man (the author?) is looking for his wife in a motel room, and discovers that she has abandoned him. He can't remember what they fought about, but in a companion piece, **"Just Space,"** the woman describes him to her mother as someone who "carries guns" and tried to shoot her. I was reminded of a time when Shepard, having driven to Boston with a brace of shotguns in his trunk, threatened to use them on a *Herald* photographer who was stalking him and Jessica Lange through the streets of Beacon Hill. Rage, alcohol and a profound respect and awe for trackless nature—these constitute the basic Shepard inheritances.

They also constitute the essence of **Buried Child.** Set in central Illinois in 1978, the play is about an alcoholic couch potato (Dodge), his hectoring unfaithful wife (Halie), two dysfunctional sons (the half-wit Tilden and the sadistic amputee Bradley), a grandson (Vince) and his girlfriend (Shelly). Some past nastiness is afflicting this family, a secret that is gradually exhumed (along with the child) in Ibsenite fashion: Halie has borne a baby out of wedlock by her own son, Tilden.

Shepard monitors this story through strong and violent metaphors. At the end of the first act, Bradley cuts his father's hair until his scalp bleeds, and, at the close of the second, thrusts his fingers into Shelly's mouth in a gesture equivalent to rape. When Vince returns to the family, no one recognizes him. He responds by drinking himself into a stupor with his grandfather's whiskey. By the end of the play, Dodge has quietly expired, Vince has inherited his house, and Tilden—who earlier carried corn and carrots to dump them into Dodge's lap in some vague vegetative rite—enters with the decaying remains of the child who was buried in the garden. It is a remarkable moment, contrasting fertility and drought, invoking the lost innocence and failed expectations not just of a family but of an entire nation. **Buried Child** reverberates with echoes of *The Waste Land*, *Tobacco Road*, *Of Mice and Men*, even *Long Day's Journey into Night*, but it is at the same time an entirely original Shepard concoction.

And the production that director Gary Sinise has fashioned with his Chicago company is a corker—easily the finest staging of a Shepard work I have ever seen. Robert Brill's vast set is composed of an endless staircase ascending to nowhere and wooden slatted walls decorated with the head of a lopsided moose that seems to be as drunk as the owner. The accomplished cast fills this space entirely, investing this dark gothic concerto of a play with elaborate comic cadenzas. James Gammon, a quintessential Shepard actor, is especially powerful as Dodge, rasping his part as if he were swallowing razor blades. Leo Burmester as Bradley drags his leg along the floor like Walter Slezak stalking John Garfield in *The Fallen Sparrow*. Terry Kinney plays the lobotomized Tilden in filthy boots and trousers, as if he had just been plucked from the earth himself. And Lois Smith is an eerie, frenzied, nattering Halie.

While **Buried Child** uses the family as a commentary on an entire nation, **Cruising Paradise** is oddly insulated from anything but Shepard memories. In most of these stories, this is not a pressing problem. Whether told in first or third person, they are drenched in a powerful nostalgia. "I found myself lost in the past more often than not," Shepard writes in **"The Devouring Lion,"** which may explain why he has chosen the reflectiveness of narrative rather than the immediacy of drama for evoking his family history: the short tale is the perfect medium for reminiscing about yourself and your ancestors.

It is not, however, an ideal medium for talking about your experiences as a movie star. And what weakens and finally enfeebles **Cruising Paradise** is the self-regarding, oddly conflicted nature of the final stories. Here, in a series of twelve impressionistic vignettes, mostly written on location in 1990 for a film he was shooting at the time, presumably Volker Schlondorff's *Voyager*, Shepard goes by train to California for an initial meeting with the German director, then by car to Mexico for the filming. "I'm an actor now," he writes. "I confess, I don't fly. I've been having some trouble landing jobs lately because of this not wanting to fly; plus, I refuse to live in L.A." He also doesn't own a fax machine or a word processor, and he won't do "press junkets."

During appointments with costume and makeup, he realizes that he is going to be thrown together with perfect strangers on a long shoot. This makes him want to "either run or puke." He gets in a hassle with an assistant to the director who, because of Shepard's fear of flying, is required to make arrangements for a special limo. These arrangements are complicated by Mexican border regulations and Shepard's taste in cars. "I don't need a limo. Just get me a Chevy," he remarks. The L.A. weather reminds him of murder, "the perfect weather to kill someone in." Passing some "very chic people" in the hotel, "sinking into paisley, overstuffed sofas, reaching for silver trays full of cashews and almonds," he again thinks of murder. He remembers what Céline said in his very last interview: "I just want to be left alone."

Since he won't fly, or use technology, or engage himself socially, Shepard manages to create as much trouble for the studio as the most demanding star. He harasses his Austrian driver because he insists on wearing a tux while driving through the desert. He feels alienated from the director when, sick with "la turista," he cries over a lost love ("I barely know the man"). In short, he behaves like a royal pain in the ass.

He arrives in Mexico finally after a series of harrowing adventures. The limo is stopped and stripped by some narcs looking for drugs. Shepard can only get a work permit by lying to a female bureaucrat, telling her he's Spencer Tracy. "I'm not an actor. I'm a criminal," he muses. "Maybe there is some inherent crime attached to pretending." These last stories contain some finely observed paragraphs about the Mexican landscape, the local villages and the Indian extras, but the very act of writing them while acting in a movie suggests the effort to maintain a literary identity.

Shepard knows that there is something inherently contradictory about his twin careers. It is a little jarring to find a man noted for his reserve and taciturnity talking about "this scene I'm playing now," about having "no idea whatsoever how to play this character." He has elected to follow the career of a public personality without sacrificing his privacy as an artist. This is not an easy choice. The face in the Avedon portrait suggests it's a choice that is tearing him apart.

## Sam Shepard and Stephanie Coen (interview date September 1996)

SOURCE: Shepard, Sam, and Stephanie Coen. "Things at Stake Here." *American Theatre* 13, no. 7 (September 1996): 28.

[*In the following interview, Shepard discusses* Buried Child *and his likes and dislikes among his various other works.*]

[*Coen*]: *In a 1983 interview, you called* **Buried Child** *"verbose and overblown" and "unnecessarily complicated." Is it still something of a problem play for you?*

[Shepard]: No, not any more. I think I solved it. (*Laughter.*) But it was due to this production being able to cast a new light on it—and I guess, too, the amount of time between when it was originally written and the current production. It gives you a different perspective.

*What changed the most for you?*

There were a lot of things that were hanging, particularly with the character of Vince and his lostness and dismay at not being recognized. His predicament became clearer in retrospect. My emphasis was on the old man, on Dodge.

*It's interesting that your focus went from the older character to the younger.*

It's because of the structure of the play. You see the weaknesses, and one of the weaknesses is that Vince hadn't been fully explored. For one thing, the old man was a lot more fun. I could really go with him, but the kid wasn't so much fun. Now the kid is starting to become more and more apparent to me.

*The revised text makes it clear from very early on that Tilden is the father of the buried child, something that is much more mysterious in the original play.*

It was always implicated that he was, even in the original. I didn't want anything in the play to be gratuitously mysterious. And I felt that certain questions that were ignited in the play should find—not resolution, they shouldn't be resolved—but they should be at least followed through. One of them was this insinuation that Tilden was the father. And I thought, yes, of course he is, go with that.

*Were you surprised that the Steppenwolf production was hailed as so funny?*

I geared the play towards this humor, because I felt that the play in our first production was too heavy. There's a lot of humor in it—based mainly on Dodge's kind of out-of-the-side-of-the-mouth humor, his sarcasm, that strange World War II humor—that I wanted to emphasize. I think the play works because the audience is allowed into this kind of strange humor in spite of themselves. They have to laugh at this character, even though he's killed a child. Otherwise, it's deadly.

*For this year's Signature Theatre Company season, you're rewriting your 1972 play* **The Tooth of Crime.** *What is the impulse for revisiting that play?*

Well, I felt again that there was something incomplete about it. There's a strength to the play, and it doesn't go where I hoped it would go.

These are not easy plays. **Buried Child** and **Tooth of Crime** were tough plays to write. Other plays are easy to write, like **Curse of the Starving Class, True West**—they just kind of happened. But these plays were struggles. Not to say that I didn't have fun with them, but they were not the same breed of animal.

*Which of your plays wouldn't you touch?*

(*Laughter.*) I don't think any of them are perfect, but there are certain ones I wouldn't mess around with, because I think they are what they are, like **Action,** for instance. Probably **True West.** But again, nothing is perfect, it's just I have no desire to elaborate on them. They work.

*Is it fair to say that your work suggests that the past is something you can deny, but you can't escape from?*

I suppose you could say that. (*Laughter.*) It's not the main deal. The past is a memory. I mean, what is the past? Of course, as you grow older, the past looms a lot larger—you don't have as much future. (*Laughter.*)

*As you grow older, are you more conscious of writing for history?*

No, but I am aware of this chain of being, which takes on a different value than when I was 19, for instance, when you're trying to deny the chain of being—whatever came before me doesn't matter. That's cool for a while, but now it becomes important to me to understand the way my stuff is interconnected, the way it's a result of the past. I'm beginning to understand that I'm the direct product of something that's wild and woolly. They probably never even really had a notion about where they were going back then. Nobody could foresee this disaster.

*Vince says in* **Buried Child,** *"His face became his father's face." Do you see that speech as a signature, of sorts?*

This problem of identity has always interested me. Who in fact are we? Nobody will say we don't know who we are, because that seems like an adolescent question—we've passed beyond existentialism, let's talk about really important things, like the fucking budget! (*Laughter.*) Give me a break! There are things at stake here—things of the soul and of the heart—and we talk about the budget! Sorry to get excited. I'm sure that won't appear in *Esquire.*

*In what?*

What is this, *Esquire?*

American Theatre.

Sorry.

*So do you think we'll just crash and burn?*

Something good always comes out of it. I'm not a doomsday person. No matter what, the creative forces are powerful. Publicity is on the side of negativity, but it doesn't mean it's more powerful.

*Is there anything about popular culture that's interesting you now?*

Rodeo. There's some good music going on. The commercial aspect of what's going on deadens everything. It's very hard to get to something that has heart anymore, because everything's for sale, and it's for sale real cheap. You end up with a lot of what my Granddad used to call poppycock.

## Francis King (review date 16 November 1996)

SOURCE: King, Francis. "Splinters and Doodles." *Spectator* 277, no. 8783 (16 November 1996): 51.

[*In the following review, King compares Shepard's fiction in* Cruising Paradise *with his dramas, faulting the stories as the "literary equivalent of doodles."*]

A few writers—Chekhov, Pirandello and Maugham at once come to mind—have achieved equal distinction in fiction and drama. But on the evidence of this collection of 'tales' (as the dust-jacket terms them), fiction is no more than a subsidiary occupation for the brilliant American dramatist Sam Shepard, along with his other subsidiary occupations, acting, the directing of films and the playing of rock music.

Shepard has always been obsessed with barren lives in barren places. Out of the emotional desert in which his characters subsist, a geyser of violent feeling suddenly erupts, in most cases not to irrigate their existences but to obliterate them with its scalding force. The most memorable story [in *Cruising Paradise*], a model of terseness and audacity, about such a life is **'The Package Man',** in which a cattle hand finds himself sitting at a bar next to a stranger who at once subjects him to a relentlessly rambling monologue. The cattle hand barely responds. The story ends with the sound of a shot from the lavatory of the bar. Unable to communicate with anyone and therefore alone in his private hell, the stranger has killed himself.

There are three or four other stories almost as good as this, among them a dazzling account of a terminal row between a man and his wife in a South Dakota hotel, and a brief, haunting anecdote about a man who unwittingly fathers a son for a lesbian couple. Most of the other tales, however, read as though they were sharp, glittering splinters from works either still to be completed or abandoned.

One guesses that there is a strong element of autobiography in the first-person accounts of a childhood and adolescence spent in the baleful shadow of an alcoholic father, a former wartime pilot, who is given to smashing up whole rooms during his drunken fugues. For Shepard, as for Hemingway and many other American writers, drunkenness is all too often an indication of manliness, even heroism. European writers tend to see it as an indication of social or emotional inadequacy.

Fiction and reality all but converge in the vivid accounts, at the end of the volume, of filming in Mexico—where location scenes were shot for *Thunderheart,* in which Shepard gave a memorable performance. The show-business diary, mordantly successful in the hands of someone like Simon Gray, and messily unsuccessful in the hands of someone like Madonna, has become a commonplace in recent years. These Mexican pieces might well be worked-up jottings of the same kind.

A page or two long, sometimes no more than an overheard snatch of stage dialogue between two unidentified participants, all too many of these tales give the impression of being the literary equivalent of doodles executed by a highly regarded painter while awaiting his next sitter or his next social engagement. Of course one values Shepard's doodles, just as one would value doodles by Hockney or Freud. But a doodle is not really an adequate substitute for a true work of art.

### Don Shewey (essay date July/August 1997)

SOURCE: Shewey, Don. "Sam Shepard's Identity Dance." *American Theatre* 14, no. 6 (July/August 1997): 12-17.

[*In the following essay, Shewey debates Shepard's midlife quandaries, discussing the all-Shepard season at the Signature Theatre in New York, Shepard's collaborations with Joseph Chaikin, and his recent revisions to some of his best known works.*]

Since 1991, the Signature Theatre Company in New York has been devoting its entire season to reconsidering a single playwright's body of work. In the past, artistic director James Houghton's choice of playwrights to honor has been undeniably worthy, yet the seasons Signature produced didn't so much alter as confirm the way we think about these writers. Edward Albee? Good playwright, an American master. Horton Foote? Solid craftsman. Adrienne Kennedy? Fascinating and formally challenging.

This year Signature turned its attention to Sam Shepard; and the results have been erratic, unpredictable, perverse, surprising, unnerving—which is to say, a very interesting season indeed.

For one thing, the gems of the season have been terrific stagings of three tiny and extravagantly disparate one-act plays: *Chicago,* which Shepard wrote in one day and which earned him his first Obie award in 1965; *The Sad Lament of Pecos Bill on the Eve of Killing His Wife,* a wacky 20-minute musical he wrote for the Bicentennial; and *Killer's Head,* a 10-minute monologue/conceptual-art piece. The newest work on hand was also the slightest: *When the World Was Green (A Chef's Fable),* a collaboration between Shepard and Joseph Chaikin commissioned for the Olympic Arts Festival last summer in Atlanta.

When the season lineup was first announced, conspicuously absent were any of the semi-autobiographical family plays for which Shepard is best known. This bold and brave strategy fell by the wayside, however, when Shepard failed to deliver the new play he'd promised as season finale, forcing Signature to schedule in its place *Curse of the Starving Class*—an excellent but hardly neglected Shepard triumph. *Action,* the minor masterpiece that I secretly hoped would be the discovery of the season, wasn't, thanks to a misconceived production. And the show everybody hoped would be a long-running Off-Broadway hit, a revised version of *The Tooth of Crime* (subtitled "Second Dance"), was an unmitigated disaster—yet Shepard's rewrite contained ideas I'm still thinking about, and it had the most to say about the state of the art of Sam Shepard.

"Something's been coming to me lately about this whole question of being lost," Shepard wrote to Chaikin in 1983 from Iowa, where he was shooting the film *Country* with Jessica Lange. "It only makes sense to me in relation to an idea of one's identity being shattered under severe personal circumstances—in a state of crisis where everything that I've previously identified with in myself suddenly falls away. A shock state, I guess you might call it. I don't think it makes much difference what the shock itself is—whether it's a trauma to do with a loved one or a physical accident or whatever—the resulting emptiness or aloneness is what interests me. Particularly to do with questions like home? family? the identification of others over time? people I've known who are now lost to me even though still alive?"

At the time, Shepard was simply staking out the territory he and Chaikin would explore in their third collaboration, *The War in Heaven.* Yet that one letter alone contains seeds—especially the brooding about identity—that would eventually bear fruit in his subsequent plays *A Lie of the Mind, States of Shock, Simpatico,* the overhauled *Tooth of Crime* and *When the World Was Green.*

The two characters in *Green* are an old man on death row for murder and a young woman who comes to interview him for a newspaper story. "How did this all begin?" she asks. "There was an insult 200 years ago," he says. Because of this insult seven generations back, the Old Man's father pointed out to him when he was five years old the cousin it was his duty to kill. The Old Man tracked his cousin Carl for many years, became head chef of his favorite restaurant in New Orleans and finally poisoned his potatoes. According to the Interviewer, however, it was a case of mistaken identity: Instead of his cousin, the Old Man killed someone who may or may not have been the Interviewer's long-lost father.

Much about the play is left purposely mysterious and open-ended. Where does this story take place? Some references are clearly American and some are not. The word "Bosnia" is never spoken, but a viewer in 1996 couldn't help thinking about the genocidal "ethnic cleansing" in the former Yugoslavia when watching a play about a generations-old conflict whose roots can only be described as mythological. The Beckett-like setting (a simple prison cell, a gray slate wall, a single high window) and the interrogatory format are recognizable trademarks from Chaikin's theatre background. Meanwhile, the themes and imagery—that ancient curse, the male-female standoff, the search for the father, the echo of old folk ballads—seem like pure Shepard.

**When the World Was Green** is the first of the Shepard-Chaikin collaborations that Chaikin did not perform himself, which was too bad. Alvin Epstein, a veteran actor whose credits include the American premieres of *Waiting for Godot* and *Endgame,* gave an overemphatic, disconnected performance that made this brief play seem tedious and overlong. I couldn't help pining for the light touch and poetic reverie Chaikin might have summoned, before a series of strokes made performing all but impossible for him.

Fortunately, the double-bill evening finished with Chaikin's delightful staging of *Chicago* as a tour-de-force for Wayne Maugans as Stu. Bare-chested in an empty bathtub, he paddled through a stream-of-consciousness monologue as the world (his girlfriend Joy and her friends) paraded by with their telephones, dark glasses and rollaway luggage. It felt like a tribute to the free-spirited innocence of '60s pop culture (Chaikin placed Stu's bathtub at the center of a huge Jasper Johns—like target painted on the floor) and to the theatrical vitality of the improvisational scripts Shepard spewed in his youth. It was also a reminder of Chaikin's gift for weightless comedy, no less valuable than his penchant for soul-searching poetic theatre.

The best thing about Darrell Larson's triple bill of *Pecos Bill, Killer's Head* and *Action* is that it simultaneously represented the breadth of Shepard's writing for the theatre and almost demonically defied any attempt to confine him to any category. *Pecos Bill* was originally commissioned by Robert Woodruff for the Bay Area Playwrights Festival. It later showed up in New York on a double bill with *Superstitions* (adapted from Shepard's prose anthology *Motel Chronicles*), an evening most memorable for the earthy presence of Shepard's then-wife O-Lan as Slue-Foot Sue, who rides in on a giant catfish to warble her cowboy cantata with Pecos Bill. The Signature production replaced Catherine Stone's somewhat pedestrian three-chord country-folk music with a more ambitious score by resident composer Loren Toolajian and featured two fine singers, Romain Fruge and Julie Christensen. In this brief surreal musicale, they managed to peel back the surface of deadpan comedy. Underneath, we glimpsed Shepard's yearning for the mind-and-soul-expanding aspects of Wild West mythology, heroes who can harness cyclones and heroines who can shoot the moon. "Why is we both dyin' on this land?" they lamented. "Why is we forgotten in the memories of man?"

Although *Pecos Bill* is a curiosity in the Shepard canon, this kind of quirky musical is a specialte de la maison of Overtone Industries, the production company originally founded in San Francisco by O-Lan Shepard, who took it with her when she relocated to Los Angeles. She continues to subsidize Overtone's work with her acting jobs—under the name O-Lan Jones—in movies like Tim Burton's *Edward Scissorhands* and *Mars Attacks!* The most ambitious Overtone project in recent years was a quartet of myth-based musicals called *String of Pearls,* whose cast included Julie Christensen and which was produced at the Met Theatre, a frequent venue for Darrell Larson as both actor and director. It was Larson's production of *Action* and *Killer's Head* at the Met that inspired Shepard to recommend him to Signature Theatre's James Houghton.

**Killer's Head** is an almost fail-safe theatre piece. Blindfolded and strapped to an electric chair, the nameless character chatters about buying a new pickup and breeding race horses—the kind of talk that's music to Shepard's ears—until the lights dim and the switch gets flipped. It's also a tailor-made showpiece for actors, an attribute which Larson and Signature exploited for maximum publicity value by casting a variety of studly stage and screen actors to alternate in the role, including Jamey Sheridan, Treat Williams, Arliss Howard, Scott Glenn. Dermot Mulroney and Ethan Hawke. The performance I saw featured Bill Pullman, whose recent film appearances include *Independence Day* and David Lynch's *Lost Highway.* Pullman blustered his way through the monologue with a kind of heedless bravado, for all the world as if he were ordering another round at the saloon. Slowly, almost imperceptibly, though, his confidence started to drain away before the final blackout.

*Pecos Bill* and *Killer's Head* are both imagistic theatre pieces. The central images—that giant mythical catfish, the electric chair—give the audience an experience that goes beyond anything the play dramatizes or the text verbalizes. They are essentially and existentially theatrical. None of Shepard's plays is more so than *Action*, whose title is almost comically ambiguous. Nothing happens in terms of a plot. Two men and two women gather for a turkey dinner with a Christmas tree blinking in the background. The sense is that of a secluded cabin in the dead of winter, perhaps an experiment in communal living that has outlived its usefulness. Yet the play is full of strong actions that have a particularly theatrical power because they are performed in front of the audience in real time with no faking.

Jeep picks up his chair and smashes it to pieces three times; each time Liza brings in a new one and sweeps up the old one. Shooter pulls his overcoat over his head and imitates a dancing bear; Lupe does a soft-shoe sitting down. They carve and eat the turkey. Jeep stands for a long time dipping his cup into a bucket of water and pouring it back until he suddenly pulls a dead fish out of the bucket, cuts it open, and disembowels it on the dinner table. The women hang wet laundry on a clothesline that crosses the stage. There's no motivation and often no consequence for these actions. "Why?" yields no satisfactory answers. Action becomes identity; it replaces character development and shifts mercurially. Instead of explaining something about these characters, Shepard wants to bypass the thinking brain and go right for the senses: smell the fish! hear the water pouring! feel the shock waves of smashing chairs! As the actions and interactions accumulate, the play becomes a metaphor for itself, a virtuosically self-enclosed theatrical event like *Waiting for Godot* or *Endgame*—and equally bleak philosophically. In each of these plays, four people struggling for community, fumbling to find their place in *The Book of Life,* represent the human soul making its way through the world. In the brief flash between darkness and darkness, "you act yourself out."

Curiously, the Signature production ignored the play's existentialism. Right off the bat, director Larson made the mistake of treating the play as if it were a naturalistic drama. In the play's very first line, Jeep looks out at the audience and announces, "I'm looking forward to my life. I'm looking forward to uh—me. The way I picture me." Shooter says, "Who're you talking to?" which is Shepard's sly way of shattering the fourth wall, of having the characters acknowledge that they're onstage using certain theatrical conventions. In Larson's production, Jeep earnestly aimed his opening salvo at the women sitting at the table with him, which not only made Shooter's line incomprehensible but turned the audience into voyeurs rather than breathing partners. The set sprawled across an enormous amount of space, conveying neither the claustrophobia of communal living nor the external pressure of a raging winter storm or the oppressive isolation of self-exile. Meanwhile, the play and the characters seemed to have no inner life. Reducing their actions to behavior, Larson turned *Action* into Acting: the performers did so much yelling and strenuous over-emoting that I felt like I was watching a bad parody of a Steppenwolf show.

To be fair, *Action* is a tricky play to pull off. The actions are absolutely down-to-earth and concrete, not "symbolic" or airy-fairy. Yet they must unfold within a context that recognizes the impact of everything unseen and unspoken in the play: the catastrophe that has already taken place. *Action* is a Shepard play that I would love to see directed by Chaikin, both because of his history with Beckett and because I suspect that the "inside/outside" exercises he developed for the Open Theatre had something to do with the strange metaphysical quality of this opus.

*The Tooth of Crime* has always been the most dazzling and well-regarded of Shepard's pre-family plays. A lethal showdown between two killer rock stars, it is an unconventional hybrid of play and musical, and its dense patches of invented pop-culture neo-lingo (part computerspeak, part hipster jive, part sci-fi comic book) make it both challenging and fun to undertake. Carole Rothman, artistic director of New York's Second Stage Theatre, had been after Shepard for years to get permission to revive *The Tooth of Crime*; as Richard Schechner's assistant director on the New York premiere in 1973 (which featured Spalding Gray in the lead), she practically knew the play by heart. Shepard put her off because he felt it needed a new musical score and he couldn't decide who should do it. Suddenly, in 1995, he called Rothman and (as they say in Hollywood) greenlighted the project with T-Bone Burnett, a former member of Bob Dylan's band, as composer. (Shepard met Burnett while traveling with Dylan's Rolling Thunder Revue in 1976, an adventure he chronicled in *Rolling Thunder Logbook.*) When the Signature season came about, it made sense for the Second Stage to co-produce *Tooth.* One indication of the great expectations surrounding the production was that, while the rest of the Signature season took place at the Public Theater, the revival of *The Tooth of Crime* was slated for the Lucille Lortel, one of Off-Broadway's prime commercial houses.

Just before he went to work revising and updating *The Tooth of Crime* for the Signature season, Shepard had revised *Buried Child* for the Steppenwolf Theatre production in Chicago that transferred to Broadway in the spring of 1996. Despite the machinations that resulted in its being considered a new play for Tony award considerations, the version of *Buried Child* that appeared on Broadway (and was published in the Sept. '96 issue of *American Theatre*) was not substantially different from the one that won the Pulitzer Prize in 1979. By contrast, Shepard's new version of *The Tooth of Crime* differed so drastically from the original that he gave it a new name: *Tooth of Crime (Second Dance)*. To use an automotive metaphor, if *Buried Child* got a tune-up, *Tooth of Crime* got a new transmission.

For one thing, Shepard had ruthlessly cut anything that made the play seem dated, including almost all references to sports cars and rock music idols (Dylan, Jagger, Townshend) as well as two of the most memorable set-pieces from the original play, Hoss's reminiscence of a high-school rumble as class warfare and Becky's rape-scene soliloquy. He'd stripped the text of most curse words and renamed several of the characters. Hoss's sidekick Cheyenne had become Chaser, the jive DJ Galactic Jack was called Ruido Ran, and Star-Man was now Meera (a reference, perhaps, to the Indian-born spiritual teacher Mother Meera). In a hundred large and small ways, he'd made the play "leaner and meaner," as Houghton put it. "The focus of the play has shifted," Rothman elaborated. "There was always a fine line between whether it was really about rock-and-roll or really about killing. Now it's gone over the line toward killing."

Ultimately, the new *Tooth of Crime* became more about dying than killing. The play originally wielded its peculiar babel of pop-culture jargons as an attack on the contemporary fixation on style and media image. Shepard's rewrite pushed farther into the metaphysical realm. It became about the death of the Self, about transcending identity altogether. The climax of the play is still the second-act showdown between Hoss, the reigning star "Marker" (whatever mixture of rocker and killer Shepard means that to be), and Crow, his upstart challenger. But in this version, the referee bails after the first round, unable to make heads or tails of the strange moves he's witnessing. After the referee's exit, the duel suddenly shifts into almost mystical territory. It conjures up all the alter-ego conflicts that inhabit Shepard's plays (Austin and Lee circling each other at the end of *True West*, for instance). Crow hypnotizes Hoss into a kind of shamanic trance. Instead of viewing Crow as the enemy to be slaughtered, Hoss suddenly sees him as a mirror. He recognizes in Crow a younger version of himself, consumed with jockeying for status, blazing new fashion trails, and trashing the past—overgrown adolescent antics that seem empty now to Hoss. He realizes that smashing the mirror won't kill the image. If he wants to get rid of the thing he hates, he has to turn the knife on himself (his self?).

In the original version, Hoss's suicide was a defiant act, even noble, but undeniably an admission of defeat. His former colleagues rallied around Crow as the new champion and prepared to play the game all over again. In *Tooth of Crime (Second Dance)*, Hoss dies from his own knife rather than a gunshot. And like the Samurai warrior's hara-kiri, it comes across as a spiritual triumph. It's a relief to leave behind the exhausting game of images. Hoss is liberated in the way that Buddhist philosophy defines liberation: recognition that nothing is permanent, that human experience leads to suffering and that there is no individual self. Escaping from the cycle of death and rebirth, ignorance and illusion—what the Buddhists call *samsara*—leads to nirvana. Hoss collapses on the floor in the same outline that shows up on the floor in Shepard's 1976 play *Suicide in B-Flat*, where it represents the last earthly trace of Niles, who wanders through that play unseen, like a soul after death.

These elements may have lurked somewhere under the surface of the original *Tooth of Crime*. In his 1996 revision, Shepard succeeded in drawing out these philosophical concerns with identity and self-transcendence that place the play on a continuum with his other work rather than off in its own rock-musical corner. However, the new version acquired some literary depth at the expense of its theatricality. Without the topical references to hook the audience and make the world of the play seem fun or at least dazzling to encounter, *Tooth of Crime* became heavier, more somber, certainly less of a crowd-pleaser. The production, directed by Bill Hart, bombed with critics and audiences. Many nights, more than half the audience streamed out of the theatre at intermission, never to return.

The best thing about the production was T-Bone Burnett's score, a vast improvement over Shepard's original music. Burnett's witty, spring-loaded lyrics meshed well with Shepard's made-up argot. "Somebody's got to monitor all this darkness darkness darkness," Hoss sings. "Somebody's got to locate the bomb—dot com." And two lyrical numbers in the first act eerily captured the clock-stopping quality of a drug-induced reverie, especially "Kill Zone" (co-written with Roy Orbison), beautifully sung by Jesse Lenat as Chaser. During early previews, the show knocked the audience back in their seats with a blast of grunge-rock that seemed to link Hoss to Eddie Vedder and Kurt Cobain, charismatic icons of '90s rock. By opening night, the opening number had been transformed into a cool blues delivered like beatnik poetry—theatrically more inviting though oddly anachronistic.

This kind of confusion typified Hart's undercooked direction, which didn't help the audience's appreciation of *Tooth of Crime*. He was partly hampered by less-than-ideal casting. Although names like Christopher Walken and Tim Roth had been bruited about, the role of Hoss ended up being played by Vincent D'Onofrio, who came across as too lightweight to convincingly play a burned-out character whose first lines are "People tell me I look like hell / Well, I am hell." But Hart's production crucially lacked an overall vision of the play. The director seemed to have staged the play as if it were the 1973 *Tooth of Crime* without bothering to account for Shepard's rethinking. Only after seeing the show twice and reading the text, with its veiled references to the *Tibetan Book of the Dead,* did I begin to understand what was at stake in the showdown between Hoss and Crow. Perhaps the set was not just the throne room of a rock star's castle but some version of a bardo, one of the stages between death and rebirth in Tibetan teachings. Of course, I may be reading into the play a more specifically Buddhist interpretation than Shepard meant for it to have. Nonetheless, it seems clear to me that the play addresses identity-shift as a profoundly spiritual crisis in a way that Hart's production for Signature Theatre failed even to suggest.

As a longtime student and fan of Shepard's work, I've always been intrigued by the hints of mysticism in his plays. Beneath their surface reality, Shepard often uses the elements of theatre to explore (if obliquely) the life of the soul that escapes intellectual perception or material representation. And I'm repeatedly frustrated at the slack, flat, slavishly naturalistic productions his plays get, even when Shepard himself is directing. Admittedly, it's difficult to communicate a spiritual perspective in the theatre without getting too pious or pretentious. But the greatest theatremakers of our time achieve nothing less in their best work—whether it's Peter Brook or Elizabeth LeCompte or JoAnne Akalaitis or Robert Lepage. With the exception of Joe Chaikin, none of them, and no directors like them, seem to take any interest in Shepard.

At least in this country. European directors seem less invested in handcuffing Shepard to naturalistic theatre. Imaginative design choices are always a simple way of churning up submerged, less-than-obvious resonances in a strong text. At a 1993 conference on Shepard in Brussels, the German director-dramaturg team of Hartmut Wickert and Alfred Nordmann gave a fascinating paper about their production of *States of Shock* at Stadttheater Konstanz. Intrigued by Shepard's account in the *Village Voice* of the play's genesis as a response to the Persian Gulf War, they decided that this interpretation was too narrow to interest a European audience. Taking inspiration from Jack Gelber's 1976 essay on Shepard called "The Playwright as Shaman," Wickert and Nordmann conceived *States of Shock*—ostensibly an absurdist one-act about a retired military man and a wheelchair-bound Vietnam vet terrorizing an elderly couple and an inept waitress in a roadside diner—as a shamanic session in which urgently needed healing energy arrives not as the gentle, beneficent "white light" of New Age visualizations but in the raging, disruptive form of a "monster-fascist."

Judging from the scene they showed on videotape, their production was extraordinary to look at. The director had gotten permission to incorporate into the set replicas of sculptures by two prominent contemporary American artists—Edward Kienholz's *The Portable War Memorial* and Bruce Naumann's take-off on roadside diner signage, a neon sign that alternately flashes "EAT" and "DEATH." The show also included lots of music in addition to two live drummers, stylized choreography and meticulous lighting à la Robert Wilson. It seemed like the most exciting directorial approach to staging Shepard that I'd ever seen. When I raved about it to Nordmann (who teaches philosophy at the University of North Carolina), he cautioned me to remember that the long European rehearsal periods militate against the thing that's best about American productions of Shepard: fresh, spontaneous acting.

It's true that Shepard's plays are ideal opportunities for the kind of woolly, uninhibited acting Americans are known for. Gary Sinise's productions of *True West* (which launched John Malkovich's career) and *Buried Child* were completely actor-driven, as were Shepard's own productions of *Fool for Love* and *A Lie of the Mind.* Still, I want it all. I long for productions that feature not just sizzling performances but also a bolder theatricality that taps into the poetic soul of the plays. I'd love to see Des McAnuff or Scott Elliott take on *Tooth of Crime (Second Dance)*—those are directors who know how to marshal stylized visual design and to plug into the kinetic energy of rock music without leaving actors high and dry—or Robert Woodruff, who first earned his stripes directing Shepard plays, give it the kind of intellectually challenging treatment he's applied to his recent productions of *A Man's a Man, The Dutchess of Malfi* and *The Changeling.*

When Shepard created the original *Tooth of Crime,* he was experiencing the second big identity shift of his life. The first happened when he left his family home in California as Steve Rogers and arrived in New York calling himself Sam Shepard. Then after eight years of intense creative discovery, fame, glory, social entree and consumption of pharmaceuticals, he pulled up stakes and moved to London, to begin a new life as a husband and father. *The Tooth of Crime* is in some ways a "look back in horror" at the excesses of his life in New York. You could say it's about realizing that the things you wanted so desperately when you were 22 seem unimportant, if not tacky, by the time you turn 30. In a larger sense, the play penetrates an essential truth about the increasingly celebrity-fixated media-culture that America has foisted on the world. Hoss thinks he got to the top through sheer talent; his encounter with Crow reveals the sickening reality that a "Star" is just another consumer commodity, a role American culture always wants someone to play, and it scarcely matters who.

Twenty-some years and a few identity shifts later, Shepard's rewrite of *Tooth of Crime* rings some new variations on this theme whose implications are both more personal and more universal. He's less interested in love-hating the notion of media stardom and more curious about identity shift as psychic suicide. In fact, you could say he's obsessed with this theme. His latest new play, *Simpatico* (Written in 1993), seems rather dull and cryptic on the most literal level. It re-enacts the kind of identity exchange between a successful guy and his lowlife alter-ego that occurrs in *True West,* only this time in the milieu of horse racing rather than moviemaking. But there is something mysterious going on under-neath the surface. In a *New York Times* interview, Shepard hinted as much when he said, "Identity is a question for everybody in the play. Some of them are more firmly aligned with who they are, or who they think they are. To me, a strong sense of self isn't believing in a lot." At the end of the play, the slippery character Vinnie seems to thrive specifically because he doesn't cling to a set identity, and despite his Rolex and cell phone, Carter seems to be dying because he does.

In *Tooth of Crime (Second Dance),* Shepard comes closer to saying that out loud. As Hoss approaches his moment of transcendence and starts to see things no one else onstage can, he says:

> No, look! Right here it comes! Emergence. I see him now. A true killer. True to his heart. True to his voice. Whole. Unshakable. There! See? He's coming out! Right toward me now. There! Stepping out! A body as sure as you or me. See? Identity!

When Hoss kills himself, is he shuffling off one identity for another, or is he abandoning altogether the notion of identity as a solid state? Is "the idea of one's identity being shattered" a tragedy or a cause for celebration or both? I guess this is the essential mystery of the play, and like all mysteries meant to be witnessed rather than explained.

It's not surprising that Shepard should dwell on the dance of identity in his plays. His life history pushes those buttons. He's both Steve Rogers and Sam Shepard, he's achieved fame and fortune as both a playwright and movie actor, he's fathered children by two different women. How do these complex realities intertwine for him, or any of us? These are typical burning questions of midlife as well. Shepard's recent plays seem to leap off from the famous opening lines of Dante's *Divine Comedy*: "In the middle of the road of my life I awoke in a dark wood where the true way was wholly lost."

And questions of identity inevitably inspire meditations on mortality. "Who am I after I die?" is no more or less mysterious than "Who am I before I die?"

In the Signature Theatre season devoted to Sam Shepard, these psycho-spiritual intimations remained submerged. The best thing about the season was that it inspired Shepard's exciting re-examination of *The Tooth of Crime.* Now it's up to somebody else to stir the deep waters and see what rises from the murk.

### Susan Harris Smith (essay date 1998)

SOURCE: Smith, Susan Harris. "Trying to Like Sam Shepard: Or, the Emperor's New Dungarees." *Contemporary Theatre Review* 8, no. 3 (1998): 31-40.

[*In the following essay, Smith assesses Shepard's current problematic critical reception, accounting for his early acclaim and his subsequently diminished reputation.*]

When Eric Bentley tackled the problem of Eugene O'Neill's prominence, popularity and decline in his testy essay, "Trying to Like O'Neill", in 1952, he began with a curse: "It would be nice to like O'Neill. He is the leading American playwright; damn him, damn all; and in damning all is a big responsibility. It is tempting to damn all the rest and make of O'Neill an exception. He *is* an exception in so many ways". Commending O'Neill for his reticence, self-respect and independence from commercial pressure, Bentley wrote, "In a theatre, which chiefly attracts idiots and crooks he was a model of good sense and honor" (331).

Bentley attributed O'Neill's fall from grace, first, to press puffery, which had made him a popular, national celebrity and, second, to O'Neill's own vaulting ambition to take on the big question of America. Celebrity, Bentley argued, altered O'Neill's focus as a playwright and resulted in a diminution of his talent. Of O'Neill's celebrity, Bentley complained that "in 1946, he was raised to the American peerage: his picture was on the cover of *Time* magazine. The national playwright was interviewed by the national press. It was his chance to talk rot and be liked for it" (1952: 331).

Bentley was even harsher about O'Neill's ambition, his desire to be eloquent, to be profound, to create a Big Work, to make America into Athens. O'Neill suffered, as Bentley so sharply put it, from "cultural gas" (342). For Bentley, as O'Neill moved away from "the humbler forms of American life" and a realistic and melodramatic mode to the "rotten fruit of unreality", "obvious and unimaginative symbolism" and "grandiloquent lugubriousness" (334), he was heralded by what Bentley termed "the Broadway intelligentsia", the "subintelligentsia in the theatre world", "the realm of false culture". According to Bentley, the willingly gullible public, brow-beaten by "propaganda and publicity", acclaimed O'Neill "for strengthening the pavement of hell". Author and audience needed each other to be mutually convinced that they were both concerned with "the crying questions of our time [. . .] a writer like O'Neill does not give them the optimism of an 'American century', but he provides profundities galore, and technical innovations, and (as he himself says) Mystery" (341).

In conclusion, Bentley absolved O'Neill of his complicity with the odd rationale that O'Neill was "seduced" (341). "If one does not like O'Neill", Bentley suggested, "it is not really he that one dislikes: it is our age—of which like the rest of us he is more the victim than the master" (345). So, to recapitulate, as Bentley saw it, O'Neill's decline could be attributed to four factors: the celebrity factor, the Big American topic factor, the move away from realism to unreality and victimization by the age.

We have been convened to look at Sam Shepard's current problematic situation and, because I come not as a specialist in Sam Shepard, but as a historian of modern American drama, I want to take the long view, that is from a historical perspective stretching back to the late nineteenth century and offer some reasons, first, for Shepard's early acclaim and, second, for his repositioning which, as I suggest in my title, may be deserved. I should note that I am not the first to compare Eugene O'Neill and Sam Shepard: Henry Schvey recently analysed the two as being nationally prominent and as sharing thematic concerns, but I make different uses of the comparison. I will argue that just as O'Neill's reputation mutated, so, too, Sam Shepard now is caught in the convergence of a number of factors, no one of which could account for his diminished reputation but which, taken together, contextualize him differently than he was in previous decades and which, I contend, actually are part of the historical patterning of American drama about which I want to make three points.

First, American drama, of course, does not exist. What has been called "American" drama is a narrow body of English language texts marked by a perpetually shifting conflation of American essentialism, amplified by Frederick Jackson Turner's "frontier thesis", fixed on moral, progressive and didactic purposes, concerned with domestic and nativist subjects, focused on masculine protagonists, and dependent on largely realistic dramaturgy. With the exception of the realistic dramaturgy (which I will get to later), most of Sam Shepard's work places him precisely in this realm of "American" drama.

Doris Auerbach is typical of the majority of critics when she identifies Sam Shepard as a writer whose patronymic is "mythmaker," because his subject is America, the dream betrayed, even though she also locates him in Off and Off-Off Broadway, that is, in an unrestrained, non-commercial theatre. Of his commitment to language, she says that "he came into the foreground of the American theatre scene when the written aspects of drama were being downplayed in favor of ritual, performance, and the non-verbal. He brought the word back into the theatre. [. . .] The heart of the theatrical experience for Shepard is language" (1982: 5). Expansive and experimental though Shepard's language practices are, I would contend that his thematic concerns are narrow. I do agree with Auerbach who characterizes Shepard's subject matter as "simply this—America" (1). "He portrays a man's world—brutal and cold, where adversaries struggle endlessly for domination and power over each other. The female characters are of no help to the protagonists, for they are mere macho fantasies of familiar female stereotypes, castrating mothers, and devouring sex goddesses, who offer no hope for transcendence" (6).

Sam Shepard's plays, for all their experimental novelty, still fit tidily into the thematic mainstream of American literature. The topic of the estranged intellectual's return to a rural home is a common trope for many writers over the past century, from Willa Cather to Thomas Wolfe. Take, for instance, a Hamlin Garland short story, in *Main-Travelled Roads* (1891), a collection of stories about the harsh life of the American farmer in Wisconsin and Iowa. In "Up the Coulé" a successful actor and playwright returns to the threatened family farm and his angry brother for whom the farm is a prison. Shades of **Buried Child**!

Second, not only does Shepard write within the received autochthonic American literary tradition, he also fills drama's need for a figurehead. The historical narratives of American drama show it to have been in a metaphorically bi-polar and self-contradictory state of either perpetual emergence and adolescence or infancy and death needing either resuscitation or salvation. The infantile and morbid states have been common tropes for critics from the beginning of the large-scale institutionalizing, anthologizing, and professionalizing of drama as an academic discipline, which began around 1886. A few examples must suffice to demonstrate the pervasiveness of this metaphorical approach. In 1886, drama was dead and ought to stay that way as far as William Dean Howells was concerned but for Brander Matthews in 1888, the drama was only on the verge of dying. The drama was dawning for John Corbin in 1907, in infancy for Walter Eaton in 1908, insurgent for Thomas Dickinson in 1917, in adolescence for Edward Goodman in 1910, just developing for William Archer in 1920, in decline for George Jean Nathan in 1921, moribund for Virgil Geddes in 1931, on the brink of death for Louis Kronenberger in 1935, dying for Samuel Barron in 1935, dying for Paul Green in 1943, at ebb for Eric Bentley in *The Kenyon Review* in the spring of 1945 but fully dead for Eric Bentley in *Partisan Review* in the same spring. The critics, sensitive to the shortcomings of the contemporary playwrights who were always being compared unflatteringly to their European counterparts, anxiously scanned the horizon for the saviour who must be emerging to redeem American drama from its provincialism, crudeness and lack of poetry.

For Barrett Clark, as for most modern critics, December 20, 1920, marked the moment at which a respectable American drama was born. On that day, Eugene O'Neill's *Beyond the Horizon,* which would win the Pulitzer Prize the following year, opened at a special matinee at the Morosco Theatre. Travis Bogard, O'Neill's chronicler, observes that "it was a signal, the first important view of the American drama" (1972: 117). So great was the impact of O'Neill on the American theatre and so anxious were the critics to locate one purely American playwright of whom they could be proud, that the waters parted for O'Neill almost from the start of his career. In 1924, Arthur Hobson Quinn, dizzy with relief, wrote of O'Neill that "he is too great a dramatist to be classified or to be placed in a school of playwrights. He, like Napoleon, is himself an ancestor" (7). Given that this judgment was made on the basis of *The Emperor Jones* and *The Hairy Ape,* expressionist plays heavily indebted to the European movement about which O'Neill learned through Kenneth Macgowan, and on *Beyond the Horizon* and *Anna Christie,* domestic dramas which owe much to O'Neill's extensive interest in Ibsen, Quinn's isolating claim is an index of the critics' urgent desire to identify a native and nativist playwright.

As America had by 1946 made of O'Neill the "banshee Shakespeare" in Bernard Shaw's apt phrasing, so Sam Shepard, the junk yard dog of motel parking lots, became himself a cultural commodity when, in 1985, he was placed on the long-vacant throne, the cover of *Newsweek* (Nov. 11, 1985). Only a few months after his coronation as figurehead, Shepard, in an article in *Vogue* magazine, disingenuously shrugged off the attention, if not the acclaim, noting that "I just look on those as publicity gimmicks. Journalism is so hard-up for heroes that it has to create them. It's an American tradition. We invent heroes all the time" (qtd. in Fay, 1985: 216).

My third point is that in his self-conscious public statements as well as in his plays not only does Shepard dramatize the American males' "angst", he also clearly genders playwriting as a masculine enterprise. Literary history shows that those who created the idea of American drama, that is a nativist and indigenous body of plays, have needed not only figureheads, but also specifically *male* figureheads; hence William Dunlap was called the "Father" of American drama and Howard Bronson was named the "Dean". If O'Neill was the saviour for modern American drama, Shepard has been the second coming.

The history of American drama reveals it to have been shadowed by explicit fears of being feminized. For instance, in 1915 Brander Matthews and others were energetically authorizing the writing of drama as masculine, scientific, vital and dynamic. At that moment, for the men who were creating the disciplinary field and the canon, the history of the drama in America necessitated this forceful strategy. As Herbert Brown detailed in a survey of the didactic sensibility in eighteenth-century American drama, "sentimentality reigned triumphant on the English stage from 1760 to 1800, the period of the beginnings of our native professional drama" (Brown, 1932: 47). That sentiment and moralizing were understood to "gratify feminine fancy" increased the sense of urgency for academics, such as Matthews who wanted to legitimate the writing of American drama as a masculine profession.

Matthews asserted that not only could women not handle "largeness in topic," but also they were incapable of "strictness in treatment. [. . .] And here we come close to the most obvious explanation for the dearth of female dramatists—in the relative incapacity of women to build a plan, to make a single whole compounded of many parts, and yet dominated in every detail by but one purpose" (1916: 120). After subordinating women to the ranks of "decorators" and elevating men to the scientific realm of "architects", Matthews concluded that "women are likely to have only a definitely limited knowledge of life" and are also "deficient in the faculty of construction" (1916: 124).

George Pierce Baker was also active in gendering American playwriting as a masculine activity. Even though his most promising students were women, according to his biographer, Wisner Payne Kinne, about 1910 Baker "became impatient that the preponderant interest in what he cared so much about was feminine" (1968: 154). Most of his audience when he spoke publicly was female, specifically club women. In fact, Baker turned to a women's club, the MacDowell Club of New York, to fund a fellowship in playwriting at Harvard (Kinne, 1968: 155). That John Frederick Ballard, one of the first masters of arts, won the Craig Prize and had a Broadway success with *Believe Me, Xantippe!,* proved to Baker that he would be instrumental in producing male playwrights for the American theatre.

This historical context for the nativist gendering of American playwriting makes it clear why, given that ever since O'Neill's death the press had been sniffing about for his successor, those who needed a man at the helm of American drama embraced Sam Shepard with unrestrained eagerness. Consider the other potential candidates and their qualifications. Tennessee Williams's regionalism and homosexuality excluded him from consideration, Arthur Miller was a Jewish leftist, and neither were as prolific as Shepard, who, like Mozart who said that he wrote music as freely as he urinated, has stretched credibility with his volume of plays. I also should observe that though Megan Terry can match Sam Shepard for both volume and experimental inventiveness, she is discounted automatically because she is a woman.

When Shepard won the Pulitzer Prize in 1979 for **Buried Child**, he safely could be embraced and sanctified by the middle-class and middle-brow audience he vilified in his plays. Now, the "tall, dark stranger", trumpeted by Jack Kroll in *Newsweek* in 1985 as "an American fantasy", "America's cowboy laureate" with "million-dollar movie bankability", the "fascinating, complex, even explosive" once-unwashed phenomenon who had burst onto the popular culture scene trailing clouds of prairie dust all the way from Paris appeared to be wearing O'Neill's neglected crown (Kroll: 68).

Like giddy guests hurling rice at a wedding, the profligate critics showered Shepard with superlatives: "the new American hero" (Pete Hamill), "the most exciting talent in the movie world" (Marsha Norman), "the most talented of his generation" (Stanley Kauffmann), and "the quintessential American playwright" (Bonnie Marranca). The *Partisan Review* described him as one of the two greatest dramatists of the American theatre (the other being O'Neill). Robert Brustein called Shepard "America's leading playwright" (1983: 25). Perhaps even more noteworthy is the fact that *The New York Review of Books,* which rarely deigns to consider drama, let alone American drama, has published two articles on Shepard, one by Elizabeth Hardwick in 1968 and the other by Robert Mazzocco in 1985. More than merely a talented playwright who pleases drama and theatre critics, therefore, Sam Shepard is a cultural phenomenon who fulfills national expectations and roles that have a high place in our desiderata: he is a figure who seems to embody the emergent opposition to commercial theatre and bourgeois hegemony and yet is attractively packaged as a movie star.

Of Sam Shepard's complicity in the celebrity game, David Wyatt, in a recent issue of *The South Atlantic Quarterly,* notes that Shepard "wants to be a star" (1992: 352) and, as a consequence, has participated in a "bifurcation" of himself: the actor who has become a media-driven, common commodity and the writer who "continues to perfect his role as one of the country's leading cultural antagonists" (359). Though Wyatt does not make of Shepard the cultural victim that Bentley made of O'Neill, nonetheless, he describes Shepard as a "reluctant celebrity", as if celebrity could be avoided in a post-Warholian world.

Not all critics have been adulatory and several would no doubt suggest that if Shepard's star seems to have dimmed it is because to begin with it was not very bright. For instance, Harold Clurman, in a consideration of the state of American theatre in 1978, worried that it was threatened by a star system, which was promoting "talented amateurs" like Shepard and Mamet who had not worked at their craft (20). Mimi Kramer, in the characteristically conservative *The New Criterion,* cast a cold eye on the "mysticism" surrounding Shepard: "Sam Shepard is not as good a playwright as everyone says". However, even she admits that "on the other hand, he is a far better playwright than one might be led to suppose from the quality of his followers' thought" (53). Given that the title of this paper dresses Shepard in "the emperor's new dungarees", I must confess to sharply conflicted responses to Shepard's work; on the one hand, I am repelled by the repetitious sexual violence and bored by the narrow thematics but, on the other, I am intrigued by his inventive dramaturgical strategies and richly poetic polyphony.

In the light of what I have just suggested about the gendered nativism of American drama, I offer four possible reasons for Shepard's current status. First, August Wilson's success notwithstanding, American drama continues to be predominantly white though it is no longer predominantly the province of men. The "where are the women playwrights?" question has been answered with the sharp and welcome rise of both feminist and pseudofeminist writers and, though none of these has displaced Shepard, the dominance of a single masculine voice as the voice of America perhaps has been modified. As well, feminist criticism strenuously has resisted and reassessed the Shepardian mystique and message (Bank, 1989; Hart, 1989; Schuler, 1990).

Second, though less forceful to date, are the contiguous, but growing moves to pluralism and multiculturalism in American drama which, with feminism, point to a paradigm shift away from the loner male in a state of angst on the existential prairie. This state of being, repeatedly associated with Sam Shepard, is no longer the quintessential American experience. The masculinist mythic approach characteristic of Shepard is now regarded by cultural critics as ideologically faulty essentializing in a multicultural nation increasingly absorbed in wide social issues, such as immigration, AIDS and urban violence.

Third, the academic shift from literary criticism to postmodern literary theory, in which intentionality has been removed from the creative process and in which an aesthetic appreciation of formal qualities is politically incorrect, has effected a critical and cultural repositioning of Shepard despite the fact that, through his notebooks and interviews, Shepard has proven himself to be a self-consciously creative and highly-intentioned writer. Obviously, this critical shift has altered the course of all critical analyses of drama. For instance, the cultural studies approach, increasingly advocated by theatre historians, if not yet by critics of drama, is devaluing reductionist, theme-driven readings of plays and such readings continue to dominate the Shepard industry.

Fourth, at this moment Shepard's claim on popular attention has been displaced by David Mamet whose ear is tuned to the street, to a closely monitored, if severely limited and xenophobic realism. In his early work, Sam Shepard's dialogue revealed how effectively he listened to his musical imagination; he was a poet to Mamet's tape recorder. Recently, however, Shepard's experimental dramaturgy and exploratory language practices have crept from the cradle of the anti-illusionistic avant-garde to the grave's edge of realism. Given that Bentley deplored O'Neill's move away from realism to the "rotten fruit of unreality", it is ironic that Shepard's own shift to increasingly realistic playwriting has not been welcomed by the critics. For instance, in his review of *A Lie of the Mind* for *The New Republic,* Robert Brustein, noting that Shepard's "most ambitious play to date" is also "the closest he has come to entering the mainstream of American drama", regards this change as a narrowing of his talent and as reductively and repetitiously autobiographical (1986: 25). Complaining about the "bloated text" and the "domestic style", Brustein remarks that "Shepard is moving inexorably toward the heart of American realism" and, unfortunately, opening the way for biographical speculation. In short, as far as Brustein is concerned, Shepard the public figure has revealed too much about himself to journalists and lost the "fantastic" and "demonic" power of eruptive and subversive subterraneanisms that were the compelling characteristics of Shepard the destabilizing playwright (26). Though not as harshly, Gerald Weales expressed doubts about *A Lie of the Mind* because of "the play's extended length and a sense of amorphousness that suggests authorial indifference rather than a desirable ambiguity" (1986: 522). Set against Shepard's early dazzlers, **Buried Child, True West, Red Cross** and *The Tooth of Crime, A Lie of the Mind* is, for Weales, "tepid by comparison" (523).

I would add that a related factor in the decline of Shepard's reputation is the increase in popularity of performance art, in which the primacy of visual modes displaces verbal ones. This revitalized theatrical mode has had consequences for Shepard's reputation because his imagistic disruptions or distortions of reality have been largely psychological and have been depicted more through language than by physical stagings.

Shepard's situation is unique and it is so because he is not a realist playwright. Narrow realism, the narcissistic solipsism of dramaturgy, has dominated modern American drama. Despite periodic, brief flirtations with experimental drama which exposes contradictions and the illusion of hegemony, American theatergoers more often pay their admission to return to the reassuring womb of realism. As an expression of assimilation and accommodation, contemporary dramatic realism is a hangover from American Progressivist notions of conciliatory communities and from dramatic practices, which promoted the illusion of a world that could be made workable.

Traditionally, there has been a privileging of realism in the American canon for two reasons: first, the "organic" approach to changes in drama as "progressive", moving from weakness and simplicity to strength and sophistication, as in the move from melodrama to realism, which most literary critics herald as an "advance". Second, since the early decades of this century, there was resistance to and suspicion of unrealistic drama as "un-American," because unrealistic drama was associated with nihilism, Europeanism, Jewish intellectualism, radicalism and leftism. The disturbing and revelatory powers of new dramaturgical perspectives such as expressionism, symbolism, absurdism, which moved beyond a narrow empiricism and which portrayed both the internal and external worlds, truly exposed contradictions and at their best, as they are in some of Shepard's plays, moved beyond a monologistic reality to a dream discourse of poetic polyphony.

So, despite what the critics have seen as his drift towards realism, I would contend that Sam Shepard remains an experimentalist and that, though he fulfills the traditional American literary need for a masculine and autochthonic mythologizer, he continues to remain well outside the dominating discourse of realism. Unlike Bentley, I am not inclined to curse my subject for embracing celebrity and attempting profundities about America nor am I willing to cast him as a victim of the age and exonerate him of complicity in the cultural commodity game. I find it deeply ironic that whereas O'Neill was faulted for his move away from realism, Shepard is being targeted for his move to realism. In the end, I think the real issue here, as I have suggested, is not Sam Shepard, but the larger historical problem of generic tyranny.

*Works Cited*

Archer, William. "The Development of American Drama". *Harper's* 142 (1920): 75-86.

Auerbach, Doris. *Sam Shepard, Arthur Kopit, and Off Broadway Theater.* Boston: Twayne, 1982.

Bank, Rosemarie. "Self as Other: Sam Shepard's *Fool for Love* and *A Lie of the Mind*". *Feminist Rereadings of Modern American Drama.* Rutherford: Fairleigh Dickinson UP, 1989. 227-40.

Barron, Samuel. "The Dying Theater". *Harper's* 172 (1935): 108-17.

Bentley, Eric. "Drama Now". *Partisan Review* 12 (1945a): 244-51.

———. "The Drama at Ebb". *The Kenyon Review* 7 (1945b): 169-84.

———. *In Search of Theatre.* New York: Knopf, 1952.

Bogard, Travis. *Contour in Time: The Plays of Eugene O'Neill.* New York: Oxford UP, 1972.

Brown, Herbert R. "Sensibility in Eighteenth-Century American Drama". *American Literature* 4 (1932): 47-61.

Brustein, Robert. "Love from Two Sides of the Ocean". *New Republic* 27 June 1983: 24-25.

———. "The Shepard Enigma". *New Republic* Jan. 27 1986: 25-28.

Clark, Barrett. "American Drama in Its Second Decade". *The English Journal* 21 (1932): 1-11.

Clurman, Harold, and Stanley Kauffmann. "Dialogue: Theatre in America". *Performing Arts Journal* 3.1 (1978): 20-34.

Corbin, John. "The Dawn of the American Drama". *The Atlantic Monthly* 99 (1907): 637-44.

Dickinson, Thomas H. *The Insurgent Theatre.* New York: B. W. Huebsch, 1917.

Eaton, Walter Prichard. "Our Infant Industry". *The American Stage Today.* Boston: Small, Maynard and Company, 1908. 6-26.

Fay, Stephen. "The Silent Type". *Vogue* Feb. 1985: 213-18.

Geddes, Virgil. "The Rebirth of Drama". *The Drama* March 1931: 7.

Goodman, Edward. "The American Dramatic Problem". *The Forum* 43 (1910): 182-91.

Hardwick, Elizabeth. "Notes on the New Theatre". *New York Review of Books* June 20 1968: 5.

Hart, Lynda. "Sam Shepard's Spectacle of Impossible Heterosexuality: *Fool for Love*". *Feminist Rereadings of Modern American Drama.* Ed. June Schlueter. Rutherford: Fairleigh Dickinson UP, 1989. 227-40.

Howells, William Dean. *Editor's Study.* Ed. James W. Simpson. January 1886 to March 1892. Troy, NY: The Whitson Publishing Company, 1983.

Kinne, Wisner Payne. *George Pierce Baker and the American Theatre.* New York: Greenwood, 1968.

Kramer, Mimi. "In Search of the Good Shepard". *The New Criterion* Oct. 1983: 51-57.

Kroll, Jack, Constance Guthrie, and Janet Huck. "Who's That Tall, Dark Stranger?" *Newsweek* Nov. 11 1985: 68-74.

Kronenberger, Louis. "The Decline of the Theater". *Commentary* 1 (1935): 47-51.

Matthews, Brander. *A Book about the Theatre.* New York: Charles Scribners' Sons, 1916.

———. *Studies of the Stage.* New York: Harper and Brothers, 1894.

Mazzocco, Robert. "Heading for the Last Roundup". *The New York Review of Books* May 9 1985: 21-27.

Nathan, George Jean. *The Theatre, the Drama, the Girls.* New York: Knopf, 1921.

Quinn, Arthur Hobson. "Modern American Drama". *The English Journal* 13 (1924): 1-10.

Schuler, Catherine A. "Gender Perspective and Violence in the Plays of Marie Irene Fornes and Sam Shepard". *Modern American Drama: The Female Canon.* Ed. June Schlueter. Rutherford: Farleigh Dickinson UP, 1990. 218-28.

Schvey, Henry I. "The Master and His Double: Eugene O'Neill and Sam Shepard". *Journal of Dramatic Theory and Criticism* 5.2 (1991): 49-60.

Weales, Gerald. "American Theater Watch, 1985-1986". *The Georgia Review* 40.2 (1986): 520-31.

Wyatt, David. "Shepard's Split". *The South Atlantic Quarterly* 91.2 (1992): 333-60.

## Sam Shepard and Michael Phillips (interview date 8 November 2000)

SOURCE: Shepard, Sam, and Michael Phillips. "Sam Shepard's Family Values." *Los Angeles Times* (8 November 2000): F1.

[*In the following interview, Shepard discusses his casting decisions for and the inspirations behind* The Late Henry Moss.]

Halloween Day 2000. Outside Theatre on the Square on Post Street, a woman sporting a French maid outfit trots up the sidewalk with a couple of Draculas and a faux homeless man. Nearby a genuine homeless man looks up from his fragment of bagel, muttering.

Inside, away from the sun, Sam Shepard and company are wading deep into rehearsals for **The Late Henry Moss** which opens Nov. 14. The wood-paneled hallway near the tiny, second-story box office is dark and shadowy and, Halloween-wise, a little more like it.

Lunch break. Nick Nolte, with the voice that launched a thousand gargles, eases through the door on crutches and makes his way toward the elevator. A minute later, Sean Penn, who plays Nolte's brother, whips the doors open and bounds down the stairs as if staring down invisible track hurdles. A few other rehearsal denizens file out, and then comes the playwright, who is also the director.

Five minutes later at a nearby diner, the waitress makes herself at home, plopping down on Shepard's side of the booth.

She has two questions. "You decided what you want? Who is that guy?"

"Which guy?" Shepard asks.

"The one over there."

"Jim Gammon, you mean? With the hat?" It's Shepard's longtime cohort James Gammon, a regular on the San Francisco-based television show *Nash Bridges,* as is Cheech Marin. Both Marin and Gammon are in *The Late Henry Moss,* along with Penn and Nolte, Woody Harrelson and Sheila Tousey.

"Very famous actor," Shepard says, smiling. "Go get his autograph."

For Shepard, who turned 57 over the weekend, *The Late Henry Moss* represents his highest-profile theatrical venture since *A Lie of the Mind* 15 years ago.

The project has brought the Illinois-born military brat back to one of his formative artistic homes. Shepard's association with the Magic Theatre launched many a Shepard premiere, from the wilds of *Angel City* (1976) and *Inacoma* (1977) to the more straightforward and widely traveled *Buried Child* (1978), *True West* (1980) and *Fool for Love* (1983).

The geography of these works ranges from urban Los Angeles to a coma state (no jokes, now) to a Southwestern roadside motel to the farmland of Illinois. But they're all part of the same lie of the mind, the same comically desolate and bruising terrain.

"At first it was kind of shocking to be back here," Shepard says of his Magic return. "But now I feel better about it. Twenty-five years later, you know? Very strange. A lot of history. In a way it feels like you never left, and in another way it feels like you were never there." As he wrote in *True West*: Time stands still when you're having fun.

### Into the Past to Probe Characters' 'Father Issues'

Earlier this year in New York, a revived *True West* proved a phenomenon, with John C. Reilly and Philip Seymour Hoffman alternating in the roles of Mojave Desert rat Lee and fledging Hollywood screenwriter Austin—brothers waging mortal combat in mom's suburban Los Angeles kitchen.

Shepard once described L.A. as a "sprawling, demented snake . . . its fanged mouth wide open, eyes blazing, paralyzed in a lunge of pure paranoia." His latest work, *The Late Henry Moss,* takes place farther east, but the atmosphere's no less paranoid. In the New Mexico desert adobe home where Henry Moss (Gammon) has died, a reunion of his sons Earl (Nolte) and Ray (Penn) takes place.

Shepard's latest set of uneasy siblings is dealing with what might be called "father issues," here augmented by a neighbor (Marin), a cabby (Woody Harrelson) who saw Moss just before he died, and Moss' lover (Tousey, who appeared in the Public Theatre workshop before this full production). The old man's story, and that of his boys, unfolds by way of flashbacks, the first extensive use thereof in Shepard's career.

By contrast, this isn't Shepard's first father figure named Moss. While living in New York, Shepard wrote a 1969 one-act called *The Holy Ghostly,* a standoff between a murderous "bohemian" son and his mewling, scraggly father. Years ago Shepard knew a rodeo guy "who had a cattle dog named Moss. I guess I always loved that name."

When Shepard laughs, it's surprising because his easy, well-worn, tough-guy presence seems at odds with the staccato chuckle. It's a character actor's laugh stuck inside a leading man.

Not for nothing did Shepard write a story (in the *Cruising Paradise* collection) called **"The Real Gabby Hayes,"** which obliquely but tellingly deals with Shepard's relationship with his father.

*The Late Henry Moss* is a three-act exploration of family secrets, blood rivalry and other classic themes favored by Shepard. "It more or less directly comes from the death of my father, which was in 1983," he says. "The first peripheral stab at it was with *A Lie of the Mind,* with the father's ashes and the folded flag." (The late father didn't actually appear.) Only now, Shepard says, was he "willing to put the corpse on stage, to actually put the corpse up there with the brothers."

He began *The Late Henry Moss* in 1989 and got an act and a half into it. "Then I just threw up my hands and said, 'I don't wanna do this.' Ran from it, in a way. Made up all kinds of excuses: that it was another rehash of *True West,* who's gonna care? I actually sent the play to the [Shepard] archives at the University of Texas and forgot about it."

But an unfinished Shepard play tends to attract attention. Jim Houghton of New York's Signature Theatre, which devoted an entire season to Shepard's works a few years ago, got hold of it. Then others, including Shepard's friend and mentor Joe Chaikin, encouraged its completion.

"The second act," he says of the original version, "went off into all kinds of weird, tangential stuff about the Spanish conquistadors and blood and Christ, and the Sangre de Cristo mountains. It got goofy. That was part of the reason I abandoned it."

All that went in the rewrites. Shepard acknowledges the inspiration of Frank O'Connor's short story "The Late Henry Conran" regarding a narrative device used in the play.

Credit for assembling such a formidable cast must go, Shepard says, to Penn, a Marin County resident who wanted to do the play close to home. "I always wanted Sean in it," he says, "and Sean actually suggested Nick. Cheech [Marin] kinds came through through Jim [Gammon], because of *Nash Bridges*.

"Because these actors are so extraordinary, you learn a lot about intention. You very clearly see the places the material wants to go, places you've forced it to go or pretended it should go.

"A good actor always sets you straight. If you've written a false moment and thought it was probably pretty great, the actor's gonna show you when he gets to that moment. They're the great test of the validity of the material.

"At first, I didn't want to believe that," Shepard says, with a quick chuckle. "When you're 19 and writing plays, you think every actor is full of it. They just can't handle your brilliant material."

Penn and Nolte bring nicely complementary sensibilities to a rehearsal room, Shepard says. "Sean tends to work at a slower pace; he's continually absorbing stuff but not necessarily acting on it. He likes to let it drizzle on him awhile, let it all accrue. Nick'll take leaps out there and then come back and then take another leap. Woody Harrelson's like that too.

"Cheech is absolutely incredible. Here's a man who has never done a play, but with his long career in stand-up comedy with Cheech and Chong, he's obviously learned a lot about showmanship. He's an extraordinary character actor. They say TV has a tendency to diminish actors, and I think that's probably true in the long run—it wears on 'em like bad dental work—but Cheech doesn't show any of the signs of being damaged that way. And as a man, he's fantastic."

The sold-out run of **The Late Henry Moss** is scheduled to end Dec. 17. No one has committed to a second production as yet, though New York and regional interest clearly is running high.

A CERTAIN PERIOD OF GRIEF HAS TO GO BY

His ham and cheese gone, Shepard wants to stress one thing: This isn't his life or his father he's dealing with, strictly speaking. It's no more directly autobiographical, he says, than J. M. Synge writing about an unruly man and his thorny father in *The Playboy of the Western World*, a raucous Irish classic Shepard loves.

Nonetheless, he says, this one needed a few years' distance.

"A certain period of time has to pass, with a death that's devastating like the death of a father. A certain period of grief has to go by before you can make this other leap. And when you make that leap—not necessarily writing about it but using the event as a catalyst for something else—it's no longer strictly personal. It's no longer strictly about your own father.

"Grief is bizarre territory because there's no predicting how long it'll take to get over certain things. You just don't know how long it's going to resound in your life. Or, after it's apparently stopped resounding, when it'll come up again. It's extremely personal. That's why I could never understand this thing of grief 'counseling' or grieving 'clinics.' That doesn't make any sense to me at all. Why would you wanna be counseled in your grief? It's too private."

Emotional truth is one thing, but Shepard is just as interested these days in matters of craft. "That other stuff is always gonna be with you, the emotional earthquakes and volcanoes and all that. They're a given; they're a part of who you are. But the craftsmanship is what separates the men from the boys, the wheat from the chaff.

"The emotional [material] is there, always. But it has to have a house, a place to rattle around in. And it's not a question of neatness; it's a question of integrity. You can have the neatest house in the world, but the structural integrity has to be there, and it has to be dictated by the emotional content.

"It's not a question of building an empty house and then living in it," he says, about to venture back into rehearsals. "You have to live in it while you're building it."

## Michael Phillips (review date 17 November 2000)

SOURCE: Phillips, Michael. "A Man's Life Passes before His Bleary Eyes." *Los Angeles Times* (17 November 2000): F1.

[*In the following review, Phillips offers a mixed assessment of* The Late Henry Moss, *noting that the play has "nuggets of gold."*]

In 1986, Robert De Niro returned to the New York stage for a play called *Cuba and His Teddy Bear*. Two years later, Steve Martin and Robin Williams decided to wait for Samuel Beckett's *Godot* at Lincoln Center, provoking a similarly noisy stampede for tickets.

You'd have to go back that far, arguably, for the last time such attention-getting film actors caused such a theatrical stir, anywhere in this country.

Nick Nolte and Sean Penn, two of America's best when it comes to cinematic tough-guy poetics, have returned to the boards for the world premiere of Sam Shepard's **The Late Henry Moss**. The play is being staged by Shepard under the auspices of the Magic Theatre—home to many Shepard premieres of yore, before he started doing all that infernal acting.

At this early stage, all too apt for a work about identity, **The Late Henry Moss** is still searching for itself. It's a boozy, meandering affair. Even if Shepard were to cut 30 or 45 minutes tomorrow, he'd have larger matters awaiting him. For a play about uneasily reunited brothers—comparisons to **True West,** among others, are inevitable—one of those brothers, the malignant, hurting Ray portrayed by Penn, remains more a functionary and instigator of flashbacks than a fully stage-worthy creation.

Yet in flashes, mostly in Act 3, Shepard finds gold. It's there, sweetly and painfully, in one of the evening's rare moments of calm: An unexpected dreamlike truce between Earl Moss (Nolte) and his New Mexico desert rat of a father, Henry (James Gammon).

Their hot-asphalt voices almost hilariously well-matched, Nolte and Gammon slowly stagger toward each other, looking in each other's eyes. "Are you seeing me right now?" Henry asks. Searching for signs of life and tenderness in the old man's eyes, Earl says yes, he recognizes a voice, a smell, a few other things.

Ever since being pronounced "dead" by his lover, Conchalla (Sheila Tousey), Henry has felt the way Willy Loman felt: temporary about himself. Yet this rageful alcoholic has been haunted for decades by a particularly nasty incident of domestic violence, one that battered his wife, sent Earl flying out of the house and left Earl's brother Ray behind, betrayed and alone.

Henry's slow death, Shepard's play suggests, began that night. Here and there, with tantalizing unevenness, **The Late Henry Moss** captures that creeping sense of past misdeeds shadowing the present.

It's set up like a mystery, albeit of the three-hour, beating-around-the-bush variety. At the start, Henry's dead body lies under a sheet in his sparse adobe house.

Earl tells the newly arrived Ray that he was summoned a few days ago by a call from Henry's neighbor, Esteban (Cheech Marin). Ray doesn't believe Earl's account, so he tracks down the taxi driver (Woody Harrelson) who took Henry and Conchalla fishing just before Henry died.

Shepard eventually reveals what went down in Henry's final hours. The character of Conchalla is deployed as a symbolic angel of mercy. Esteban is amiable servitude incarnate. (There's a lovely comic moment in which Tousey picks up Esteban, an indistinct role wonderfully played by Marin, promises him a good "bounce" and flops him around like a rag doll.) With these peripheral characters, Shepard isn't so much flirting with cliche here as diving in head first.

More problematically, Shepard hasn't yet fleshed out Henry. He is pretty much what Earl says he is: a "breathing and yelling" machine. It's a conundrum for any playwright: How do you enliven characters who alternately bore and exasperate each other? Shepard can answer that one better than just about anyone else, but he's still a rewrite away.

And like many a first-rank playwright, Shepard probably shouldn't direct his own stuff. The production flattens out the pacing and the dynamics. It's mostly a text issue—many of the play's explosive moments come out of nowhere, and not in a good way—but sharper staging would help.

It's fascinating watching this starry cast wrestle with an unwieldy work. Nolte and Penn take full advantage of the Theatre on the Square's miked stage, which is another way of saying they need to watch their volume. Penn has it toughest: Ray seems a pale holdover from any number of previous Shepard works. The character's decision to claim the family home recalls the climax of **Buried Child.** Yet the decision lacks heft in this context; we just don't know enough about the guy, and not just in some hackneyed back-story fashion.

As a result, Penn mostly hangs back. In his own way, so does Nolte. Theirs are anything but grandstanding performances. Both actors clearly are trying to find their way inside characters not easy to activate. Nolte, having more to play (while smoking pretty much constantly), has the advantage of that memorable encounter with Gammon.

Harrelson's cabby acts as best supporting hambone. He doesn't know when to quit—at one point during Penn's interrogation of Harrelson, you could sense the impatience in Penn's eyes—but he has stage chops to spare. As does Marin, brand-new to the theater but fully at home.

In the end, a loosely tied mixed bag. But that bag has its nuggets of gold.

## Katherine Duncan-Jones (review date 23 July 2001)

SOURCE: Duncan-Jones, Katherine. "A Little Legend about Love." *New Statesman* 130, no. 4547 (23 July 2001): 45.

[*In the following review, Duncan-Jones praises a London production of* A Lie of the Mind, *calling the play a "triumph."*]

To label Sam Shepard's modern family melodrama *A Lie of the Mind* as "Greek", "Shakespearean" or "Chekhovian" would be reductive, even though it has elements of all three. It is, above all, thoroughly American, right up to the symbolic climax in which a crumpled and bloodied Stars and Stripes is first unfurled, then carefully folded, and the choric old man Baylor (Keith Bartlett), seeming scarcely to notice the visible collapse of his entire family, staggers up to bed saying: "I don't wanna get woke up in the middle of a good dream." For this stubborn pioneer alone, the American dream lives on and still has value, almost like a memory of Troy or Camelot.

Tom Piper's clever set clearly locates this play about two abusive families in a western wilderness stretching from southern California to Montana. Its alien landscape is scarred with anonymous highways and pocked with undifferentiated human settlements. Yet it is not these towns or highways that we see, but the small, bleak nests of human habitation that are characteristic of Shepard's plays: a motel room on the edge of a desert: a side room in a hospital: a lightweight cabin in the snowy woods of Montana, far too fragile to withstand the shouting and shooting that take place inside. In such remote places, each of the eight characters struggles for self-definition through escape from the past, and especially from the oppressive personal history embodied in parents, spouses and siblings. These people inhabit a cultural wilderness, as well as a physical one.

In a more naturalistic play, one might protest at the unlikelihood of any kind of theatricals being performed there. But Beth, a battered wife, has provoked her husband's murderous jealousy by going out each evening to rehearse a play. This well-constructed tragedy, with its subtle symmetries, carries off even its most stagey or meta-theatrical conceits with assurance. It becomes clear that Beth truly is an actress in the brief scene that I cannot refrain from calling "Shakespearean", in which, wearing her father's huge shirt, she plays Rosalind to her Orlando, the wounded Frankie. Beth's "brain damage", which causes her staccato speech, matches the even deeper "damage" endured in different ways by all the characters, each of them hurt in their minds, none of them able to escape from the lies that fester within.

First performed in New York in 1985, *A Lie of the Mind* has its own past. Shepard described it as "a love ballad . . . a little legend about love". But that is not at all how it comes across in Wilson Milam's superb production. It seems, rather, to be an intricately patterned study of madness and the family, madness in the family, and the extraordinary ways in which families, especially mothers, when they try to offer solace, make things worse. Some of the best black humour in the play stems from this theme.

As in Shepard's *Fool for Love* (1982), the abusively violent "hero", Jake (Andy Serkis), continues to "love", or at least be obsessed by, the woman he has injured, but this is hardly the play's most compelling theme. What consistently grip the audience are the diverse performances of pain—of both mind and body. Even Jake's brother, the gentle Frankie (Peter McDonald), is shaking in septicaemic agony by the end, though only the audience seems to notice. Serkis is wholly convincing in his rage and despair, as is Catherine McCormack as the histrionic and radiantly beautiful Beth. *A Lie of the Mind* is altogether a triumph for the Donmar.

## Ann Wilson (essay date 2001)

SOURCE: Wilson, Ann. "Great Expectations: Language and the Problem of Presence in Sam Shepard's Writing." In *Modern Dramatists: A Casebook of Major British, Irish, and American Playwrights,* edited by Kimball King, pp. 257-72. New York and London: Routledge, 2001.

[*In the following essay, Wilson examines the issue of linguistic "presence" in Shepard's plays, exploring the theological dimension of Shepard's dramatic language.*]

> Walt Whitman was a great man. He expected something from America. He had this great expectation.
>
> —Sam Shepard, *Action*

Sam Shepard is the pre-eminent playwright of the contemporary American theatre. His work has received numerous awards including the Pulitzer Prize in 1979 for *Buried Child.* Despite his success, Shepard has not always felt comfortable identifying himself as a writer. In the program note to *Cowboy Mouth,* the play which he co-wrote with Patti Smith, he announced, "I don't want to be a playwright, I want to be a rock and roll star" (Shewey 81). Later in the same note, he claims that "writing is neat because you do it on a physical level. Just like rock and roll" (Shewey 81). As glib as these two remarks may seem at first, they do suggest reasons for Shepard's ambivalence about writing.

The writer's medium is language which Shepard believes "has become so corrupt, laundered, stripped of meaning. We often don't know what we mean anymore" (Wren 90). In forging the link between writing and music, particularly jazz and rock-and-roll—two modes of music which often involve improvisation, Shepard expresses his yearning for a pure language which does not mediate experience but acts as a transparent medium which reveals fully the signified. He wants to discover a language in which the signifier does not *re*present the signified but makes it present. It is this sense of language which allows Michael Earley to suggest that Shepard is heir to the transcendentalist tradition of American writing because he "brings to the drama a liberating interplay of word, theme and image that has always been the hallmark of romantic writing" (127). While I agree with Earley that there is a strain in Shepard's writing which relates his work to that of the transcendentalist poets (especially Whitman), it is misleading to suggest that this is a strictly literary influence. The desire to discover a language or mode of representation which makes fully present the signifier is evident in a number of American cultural projects including the work of Shepard's friend and sometime collaborator, Joseph Chaikin and music (particularly jazz and rock and roll).

In an essay called **"Language, Visualization and the Inner Library,"** he writes,

> From time to time I've practiced Jack Kerouac's discovery of jazz-sketching with words. Following the exact same principles as a musician does when he's jamming. After periods of this kind of practice, I begin to get the haunting sense that something in me writes but it's not necessarily me. At least it's not the "me" that takes credit for it. This identical experience happened to me once when I was playing drums with the Holy Modal Rounders, and it scared the shit out of me. Peter Stampfel, the fiddle player, explained it as being visited by the Holy Ghost, which sounded reasonable enough at the time.
>
> (205)

Shepard's remarks suggest that he constructs writing as a mysterious process which requires inspiration and which, when truly executed, has the power to reveal the unknown. He said, "I feel a lot of reluctance in attempting to describe any part of a process which, by its truest nature, holds unending mystery" (214). In answer to Amy Lippman's question about why he writes, Shepard responded, "I try to go into parts of myself that are unknown. And I think that those parts are related to everybody. They are not unique to me. They're not my personal domain" (21). From such a perspective the writer records his privileged vision; yet, necessarily, the rendering of the vision is always distorted and imperfect. "Words, at best, can only give a partial glimpse into the total world of sensate experience" (Shepard, 216). Despite his recognition of the limitations of language, Shepard still believes in the unrealized ideal of a language which can represent fully.

Although his remark about the inspiration of the Holy Ghost seems off-hand, it indicates his sense of the essential mystery of writing. If we remember that "inspiration" is from the Latin words *in* and *spirare,* then the writer who has been inspired (or "visited") by the Holy Ghost is one into whom the Holy Ghost has breathed. The entry of the Holy Ghost into the body of the writer is a moment of unity when the spirit and body are one and utterance is pure because the signifier (spirit) and the signified (the sign) are one. Within a religious context, the unification of thought and expression which is said to create a pure, unmediated language, is called glossolalia. This is not to suggest that Shepard's theatre is evangelical but rather that his sense of language gives it a theological impulse. He admires Shakespeare because his language authentically represents the human condition. He "traveled very far in himself to find it. The language didn't come out of the air, it came from a tremendous search, a religious experience" (Wren 81).

Shepard seeks to discover within himself the language which will make the signified fully present by overcoming loss which attends the separation of the signifier and the signified. Jacques Derrida in his essay "Theater of Cruelty" calls this language "glossopoeia."

> Glossopoeia, which is neither an imitative language nor a creation of names, takes us back to the borderline of the moment when the word has not yet been born, when articulation is no longer a shout but not yet discourse, when repetition is *almost* impossible, and along with it language in general: the separation of concept and sound, of the signified from signifier, of the pneumatical and the grammatical, the freedom of translation and tradition, the movement of interpretation, the difference between the soul and the body, the master and the slave, God and man, author and actor.
>
> (240)

Derrida suggests that the failure of the project is inscribed at the moment of inception when he writes "repetition is *almost* impossible." As indicated, emphasis falls on "almost" because if glossopoeia is a language, albeit one which is liminal, then there must be the possibility of its repetition because this is the defining characteristic of language. Thus, the originary moment of language when the signified is made fully present by the signifier is always elusive, approached but never reached.

This sense of the failure of language to reveal fully that which it signifies marks the particularly American quality of Shepard's writing. Harold Bloom suggests, "Emerson wanted Freedom, reconciled himself to Fate, but loved only Power, from first to last and I believe this to be true also of the central line of American poets coming after him" (*Poems* 8). He explains that Emerson defines the terms "Freedom," "Fate," and "Power" as follows:

> Freedom or "the free spirit" makes form into *potentia*, into strength that Emerson defines as eloquence. . . . Fate, as a word, comes from a root meaning "speech," but by one of Emerson's characteristic dialectical reversals Power takes on meaning as eloquent speech while Fate is a script or writing opposed to speech.
>
> (*Poems* 7)

Bloom argues that the Emersonian triad of Fate-Freedom-Power appears in Whitman's work as "*my soul-myself-the real me or me myself*" (*Poems* 7). This triad is found in Shepard's work, too, although Freedom, the impulse or spirit which informs writing, is subsumed by Power: Freedom (eloquence) can be expressed only in Power (speech) thereby reducing the Emersonian triad to a pair, Fate and Power. This reduction is important because now the two elements are seen clearly as oppositional: Fate is the antithesis of Power. In this duality, speech is privileged over writing and so is attributed primacy. It is represented as an inchoate, less mediated mode of expression than writing, as having greater capacity to reveal the authentic self. Writing—merely a supplement to the privileged mode of expression, speech—is always secondary.[1]

This tension, although not addressed directly by Shepard, is implied by several remarks he has made. Speaking to the participants in a seminar on playwriting which he taught as part of the Bay Area Playwrights Festival III (1980), Shepard warned, "There is the tendency to trade experience itself for language which never really captures it and ultimately cheats experience" (Wren 81). He suggests that experience is pure but becomes sullied when expressed. Implied by his remark is the position that the plenitude of experience can never be spoken fully. This raises the question: how do we recognize experience except through language?

In **"Language, Visualization and the Inner Library,"** Shepard writes,

> The picture is moving in the mind and being allowed to move more and more freely as you follow it. The following of it is the writing part. In other words, I'm taking notes in as much detail as possible on an event that's happening somewhere inside me. The extent to which I can actually follow the picture and intervene with my own two-cents worth is where inspiration and crafts-manship hold their meaning. If I find myself pushing a character in a certain direction, it's almost a sure sign that I've fallen back on technique and lost the real thread of the thing.
>
> (215)

That the writer records the action as it unfolds in his imagination without intervening and shaping it, implies that this action exists independent of and prior to language.

Shepard, while he is reluctant to admit that experience is inseparable from language, is not successful in suppressing the interpretative function of the writer. One of the participants in Shepard's seminar on playwriting, Scott Christopher Wren recalls, "Shepard comments that there is a real sense of following the action from the inside . . ." (85). Again, he insists that experience and language are separate and that language is secondary to experience or, as he says, that it "follows." Subtly, almost imperceptibly, he amends his initial statement of the writer's role:

> . . . There is a real sense of following the action from the inside, such that the accidental gesture has purpose. It's no longer accidental because it's witnessed, followed very carefully moment to moment.
>
> (85)

The repetition of "follow" obscures the important shift of ideas in the remark. Initially the writer "follows" the action which implies that action occurs independently and he merely records. What interests me is the ascription of purpose to the gesture because it is the writer who assigns it. The writer no longer follows the scene but witnesses the action and, in so doing, actively enters the scene because in witnessing the action, he reads it. It is the writer who interprets the gesture as significant. Despite his professed belief that action is distinct from language, the ascription of purpose by the writer suggests that Shepard, to some degree, understands them as inseparable. Recognizing action is predicated on our ability to differentiate one action from another which can only be done through categories which are created within language. Shepard's suggestion that the imagination operates independent of language is a bit fanciful; yet, as fanciful as is this idealization of imagination, it is this which informs both Shepard's writing and Whitman's.

Both Whitman and Shepard yearn to discover a language which will make fully present the signified. Necessarily, this language is corporeal, the union of the body (signifier) and spirit (signified) celebrated by the sound of the voice. Wren recalls that Shepard taught "that developing characters is a process of coming in touch with *voice*" (81). He recalls Shepard saying "Voice is the nut of it. Character is an expression of voice, the emotional tone underneath. If a writer is totally connected with the voice, it will be in the words" (76). Shepard's remark implies a sense of character as an essence which is realized only through voice. The breath (spirit) translates this essence from its pure state of interiority to the exteriority of the sign (the actor's body or words).

For Shepard, the crux of the problem of identity is this process of translation. We can only constitute identity through language; but language is debased and so inevitably we lose sight of our "true" or "real" selves. In an interview with Michiko Kakutani, he explained the effect of debased language on identity:

> Personality is everything that is false in a human being. It is everything that's been added on to him and contrived. It seems to me that the struggle all the time is between this sense of falseness and the other haunting sense of what is true—an essential thing that we're born with and tend to lose track of. This naturally sets up a great contradiction in everybody between what they represent and what they know to be themselves.
>
> (26)

This nostalgic yearning for an authentic self is perhaps the single most striking feature common both to Shepard's writing and to Whitman's. We need only to think of the title of one of Whitman's poems, "Song of Myself," to recognize the importance of voice to his project of self-representation. The poem is a song which attempts to celebrate masturbation both as an image and inscription of *jouissance* of self-discovery. Here I use "*jouissance*" in Kristeva's sense:

> . . . "Jouissance" is total joy or ecstasy (without any mystical connotation; also, through the working of the signifier, this implies the presence of meaning (jouissance = j'ouis sens = I heard meaning), requiring it by going beyond it.
>
> (Roudiez, 16)

"Song of Myself" suggests that the ecstatic moment of orgasm is the moment when the true or essential self is realized fully:

> I merely stir, press, feel with my fingers, and am happy,
> To touch my person to some else's is about as much as I can stand.
> Is then a touch? . . . quivering me to a new identity,
> Flames and ether making a rush for my veins,
>
> (616-20)

---

> I am given up by traitor:
> I talk wildly. . . . I have lost my wits. . . . I and nobody else am the greatest traitor,
> I went myself first to the headland . . . my own hands carried me there.
>
> You villain touch! what are you doing?. . . . my breath is tight in its throat;
> unclench your floodgates! you are too much for me.
>
> (636-41)

Two aspects of "Song of Myself" are relevant to a discussion of the relationship between Whitman's writing and Shepard's. First, although the poem clearly celebrates masturbation, orgasm is marked by ellipses, by the absence of words. We are given only a description—that the poet talks wildly—but no transcription of what he says. If orgasm is indeed the moment when the true self is realized, then the true self is beyond language. We are reminded of Derrida's contention that the originary moment is beyond knowledge, is always already lost. Secondly, there is the sense of the poet's guilt suggested by the words "traitor" and "villain touch." On the simplest level, it is the expression of self-reproach for daring to acknowledge masturbation. It is the guilt of someone who feels that he is a traitor to himself because he engages in a practice which has been taught, and to some degree believes, is wrong. The expression of guilt divides the self into the traitor and betrayed which, ironically, replicates the onanistic gesture which divides the self into the toucher and the touched thereby recognizing the binary opposition of interiority/exteriority. ". . . The outside, the exposed surface of the body signifies and marks forever the division that shapes auto-affection" (*Grammatology* 165). That the touched surface of the body is exterior insinuates the existence of the interior which remains hidden by the surface. This structure, which recognizes the duality of interior/exterior, is the structure of the sign which is divided into the significd and signifier thus allowing Derrida to claim that "auto affection is a universal structure of experience" (*Grammatology* 165).

For our purposes, what is important about this duality is that knowledge of the interior is possible only through exteriority. The signified is known only through the agency of signifier so that it is never itself present but is always represented. The signified is idealized as that which cannot itself be known. From such a perspective the "real-Me" is beyond knowledge because it cannot be made present. The poet is betrayed by onanism but not simply in the sense of sexual activity. The masturbatory gesture becomes a paradigm for signification because the poet is betrayed by his medium, language, which cannot realize the presence of the "real-Me" that it signifies. Yet, paradoxically, the "real-Me" is idealized only because of the structure of signification which admits the notion of the ideal. The project of making fully present the signified, which is common to Whitman and Shepard, is marked by failure from the outset because the structure of the sign protects the signified as the ideal beyond knowledge. Put simply, once the signified is known, it ceases to be the signified because it is now the signifier.

Chaikin's work never alludes to the influence of American literary figures;[2] however, accounts of his work (particularly in *The Presence of the Actor*) suggest the interest common to his work, Whitman's and Shepard's. The title of Chaikin's book points to his preoccupation with the notion of "presence"; yet, despite its importance to his work, he never offers an exact definition of the term. Eileen Blumenthal interprets presence as "the quality of being here right now, with an awareness of the actual space and the actual moment of the vital meeting of lives in that space and moment" (113). In contrast, Chaikin's own description of "presence" is noteworthy for its refusal to define the term with any degree of precision. He writes:

> This "presence" on the stage is a quality given to some and absent from others. All of the history of the theater refers to actors who possess this presence.
>
> It's quality that makes you feel as though you're sitting in the theatre. . . . There may be nothing of this quality off stage or in any other circumstance in the life of such an actor. It's a deep libidinal surrender which the performer reserves for his anonymous audience.
>
> (20)

Later in *The Presence of the Actor* Chaikin writes, "Just before a performance, the actor usually has additional energy like an electrical field" (21). The image of currents of energy recurs:

> . . . The actor must find an empty place where the living current moves through him uninformed. A clear place. Let's say the place from where the breath is drawn . . . not the breath . . . but from where the inhalation starts. . . .
>
> There are streams of human experience which are deep and constant moving through us on a level below sound. As we become occupied with our own noises, we're unable to be in the stream. The more an actor boasts of his feeling as he feels it, the farther he is from the current.
>
> First, the actor must be present in his body, present in his voice . . . The voice originates inside the body and comes to exist in the room.
>
> (66)

These passages illustrate Chaikin's insistence on a lexis of "presence," a lexis which is reminiscent of that developed by Whitman to write the "real Me." "Presence" is a kind of "deep libidinal surrender" which Chaikin renders metaphorically as "the living current." Like Chaikin, Whitman and Shepard use the image of energy to suggest the dynamic, ever-changing and mysterious nature of reality. Whitman, in *Leaves of Grass*, titles a poem "I Sing the Body Electric"; Shepard writes of "Words as tools of imagery in motion" (216) and of a work as having a "life-stream" (Wren 90). For Shepard, the sense of language in motion is particularly important because reality is inconstant. If it is to be made present, it must be done in a flash. "In these lightning-like eruptions words are not thought, they're felt. They cut through space and make perfect sense without having to hesitate for the 'meaning'" (Shepard 217).

In the writings of all three, the image of energy suggests the dynamic, ever-changing nature of reality, constituted as mysterious and unknowable, which relates this reality to identity: in Whitman's poetry, the "real Me" is the originary site of his identity; Shepard claims that through his writing he tries "to go into parts of myself that are unknown" (Lippman 21); Chaikin suggests that the actor attempts to reach an empty place where "the living current moves through him uninformed." Expressed in the work of all three is a nostalgic yearning for a moment of signification when the sign is inseparable from that which it signifies, the condition of language before it has fallen.

The romantic nature of this impulse is suggested by Shepard's remark "that the real quest of a writer is to penetrate into another world" (Shepard 217). Chaikin, too, uses the motif of the quest to describe his work:

> Julian Beck said that an actor has to be like Columbus: he has to go out and discover something, and come back and report on what he discovers. Voyages have to be taken, but there has to be a place to come back to, and this place has to be different from the established theatre. It is not likely to be a business place.
>
> (34)

Indeed, in Chaikin's work the quixotic sentiment is so pronounced that it is manifest as a theme. In 1968, the Open Theater performed their collaborative piece, *The Serpent*, which is based on the account of creation in Genesis. "None of us," wrote Chaikin "believe there is or ever was a real Garden of Eden, but it lives in the mind as certain as memory" (67). For Chaikin, the Garden of Eden is not a geographic location now lost but a lost place within each person. Because of the post-lapsarian condition of language, this place cannot be recuperated in language; instead it can only be constituted through the allegoric resonances of myth.

Chaikin's desire to know the Edenic within man replicates Whitman's desire for the "real Me" which Bloom has suggested is a desire for the presexual:

> Whitman's "real Me" is what is best and oldest in him, and like the faculty Emerson called "Spontaneity" it is both nature's creation and Whitman's verbal cosmos. It is like a surviving fragment of the original Abyss preceding nature, not Adamic but pre-Adamic. The "real Me" is thus also presexual.
>
> ("The Real Me" 6)

The erotic in Whitman's poetry, the longing to express the "real Me" which is presexual, marks the failure of his poetic project. He can never satisfy his desire to retrieve his ideal, presexual self because of the relation between desire and language. Desire is the recognition of absence which is experienced as yearning. Because recognition is possible only through language, desire can only be recognized through language. But, language is itself an expression of desire because the signifier represents, and thus marks the absence of, the signified.

That desire should be experienced only through that which is the product of desire is an unresolvable paradox which determines that Whitman can never retrieve his ideal presexual self because language cannot represent that which is presexual.

This problem, which faces Shepard as a writer, is reflected in the characters which he creates. Shepard comments, "Writing is born from a need. A deep burn. If there's no need, there is no desire" (218). He told Michiko Kakutani,

> People are starved for the truth and when something comes along that even looks like the truth, people will latch on to it because everything's so false. People are starved for a way of life—they're hunting for a way to be or act toward the world.
>
> (26)

Shepard's characters are often so hungry that they speak of themselves as starving. Think, for example, of Shooter in *Action* who says, "I'm starving. Did we eat already?" (139); or, in *Curse of the Starving Class,* of Ella's emphatic declaration to her daughter, "WE'RE HUNGRY, AND THAT'S STARVING ENOUGH FOR ME!" (142); or of the Speaker in *Tongues* who says, "This hunger knows no bounds. This hunger is eating me alive it's so hungry!" (311) and concludes, "Nothing left but the hunger eating itself. Nothing left but the hunger" (312).

The "Hunger Dialogue" is a paradigm for Shepard's use of hunger or appetite throughout his plays. In this piece, hunger is at first the physiological desire for food but, as the dialogue develops, it is clear that the food will not satisfy the speaker's hunger. Indeed, there is nothing which will sate his appetite because he is conscious only of his appetite and cannot identify what it is that he wants. Whether their appetites are for food, for the erotic (as in *Fool for Love* or *A Lie of the Mind,* for example) or the simple desire to tell the true story (for example, in *Buried Child* or *Curse of the Starving Class*), many of Shepard's characters are desirous, their appetites impelling their actions. Yet their desires rarely are satisfied completely, as if the objects of their desire are impossible, which necessarily they are, because the structure of desire is such that desire can never be fully sated. As discussed, desire is recognized only through language which is itself the product of desire. This paradox marks the impossibility of desire being satisfied because the recognition of desire is predicated on language which marks the loss of the full presence of signified.

Invariably the impossible object of the characters' desire is themselves, whom they seek to realize through modes of performance which Florence Falk categorizes as role-playing, story-telling and music-making (188, 189). Shepard comments

> The stories my characters tell are stories that are always unfinished, always imagistic—having to do with recalling experiences through a certain kind of vision. They're always fractured and fragmented and broken.
>
> (Kakutani 26)

Given that identity is the story each of us tells about ourselves, the fact that Shepard's characters tell fractured, incomplete stories signals that none of them has a coherent sense of self. In a sense, each tries to call himself into being by performing himself.

As Richard Gilman notes, Shepard's sense of character as ever changing is influenced by Chaikin's work with actors in the Open Theater, particularly the transformation exercises (xv).

> Briefly, a transformation exercise was an improvised scene—a birthday party, survivors in a lifeboat, etc.—in which after a while, and suddenly, the actors were asked to switch immediately to a new scene and therefore wholly new characters. . . .
>
> Shepard carried the idea of transformations much farther than the group had by actually writing them into his texts, in plays like *Angel City, Back Bog Beast Bait* and *The Tooth of Crime* where the characters become wholly different in abrupt movements within the course of the work, or speak suddenly as someone else, while the scene may remain the same.
>
> (Gilman xv)

The purpose of the transformation exercise is to strip away the actors' contrived sense of how characters behave so that their performances do not rely on theatrical clichés. In theory, this sort of improvisational work encourages the actors to discover different aspects of themselves. As Shepard explains, "The voices of a lot of external-world characters are inside you. For example, when you write about a nun, it's not your 'idea' of a nun, it's the nun inside of you" (Wren 80). Chaikin suggests that each of us has a myriad of characters inside us because within everyone is "a stream of human experiences which are deep and constant" (66). His remark echoes Shepard's answer to Amy Lippman, cited earlier, that the reason he writes is to go into parts of himself which are unknown but are related to everyone (21). In order to reach this place, Chaikin claims that the actor must first "be present in his body, in his own voice" (67); speaking about writing, Shepard corroborates Chaikin's remarks emphasizing "that writers have to begin with what they know and one of the best places is the body because the body is relating to everything and is grounded in experience rather than ideas" (Wren 86). Like Whitman who attempts to inscribe the "real Me" in "Song of Myself," Chaikin and Shepard use the analogy of music, in their case jazz, to explain how an actor will realize character. Chaikin suggests jamming a structure for improvisational work:

> The term comes from jazz, from the jam session. One actor comes in and moves in contemplation of a theme, traveling within rhythms, going through and out of the phrasing, sometimes using just the gesture, sometimes reducing the whole thing to pure sound. . . . During the jamming, if the performers let it, the theme moves into associations, a combination of free and structured form.
>
> (116)

In *Angel City,* jamming became Shepard's structural principle for the creation character. He instructs,

> The term "character" could be thought of in a different way when working on this play. Instead of the idea of a "whole character" with logical motives behind this behaviour which the actor submerges himself into, he should consider instead a fractured whole with bits and pieces of character flying off the central theme. In other words, more in terms of collage construction or jazz improvisation.
>
> (6)

As Florence Falk explains, "jazz in its very structure is improvisational—that is an alert, spontaneous, and dynamic creation" (190). It operates, as Shepard noted about rock music in the program note to *Cowboy Mouth,* on a physical level which allows (or at any rate gives the illusion of allowing) the union of impulse and expression: the signified is one with the signifier. Writing techniques based on jazz inhibit the mediation imposed by intellectualizing the process of writing. "When you're writing inside of a character like this, you aren't pausing every ten seconds to figure out what it all means," explains Shepard (217). We are returned to Shepard's sense of the writer following and recording the action.

Shepard's quest for an ideal language which will make fully present the signified clearly situates his project within the larger frame of American culture. "Presence" is not simply an attitude towards language but indicates no ideology which informs many aspects of this culture. It is manifest thematically as popular images of the frontier which is the borderline between civilization and wilderness. The frontier is a myth of eternal presence because when the frontier is encroached upon either by wilderness or civilization, it is not transformed but moves and is reconstituted in a new location. A frontier is always the same, is always the borderline. There may be a history of frontiers, but the frontier is itself a place without history because it is unchanging. In this sense the myth of the frontier enacts spatially the transcendentalist poetics to which Shepard is heir because the writer's desire is the discovery of a language which is pure, at the borderline when utterance is first made, "no longer a shout but not yet discourse."

Shepard's celebrated language is realized through his recurring interest in the West of popular culture (as, for example, in *Angel City, The Tooth of Crime, The Unseen Hand*). This thematic preoccupation exposes the ideological implications of presence in his work. First, the frontier is the domain of the cowboy who, as he is popularly represented, affirms the pre-adolescent values of a white, American boy. The sensibility is "usually anti-intellectual and anti-school" and so physical prowess is counted upon to resolve any conflict or problem (Davis 94-95). His strongest emotional tie (other than to his horse) is to

> a group of buddies, playing poker, chasing horse thieves, riding in masculine company. He is contemptuous of farmers, has no interest in children, and considers men who have lived among women as effete. Usually he left his own family at a tender age and rebelled against the restrictions of mothers and older sisters.
>
> (Davis 89)

Bonnie Marranca notes that the determination of the frontier myth is evident in Shepard's characterization of women:

> One of the most problematic aspects of the plays is Shepard's consistent refusal or inability, whichever the case may be, to create female characters whose imaginative range matches that of the males. . . . For a young man Shepard's portrayal of women is as outdated as the frontier ethic he celebrates: men have their showdowns or face the proverbial abyss while the women are absorbed in simple activities and simplistic thoughts.
>
> (30)

The pre-pubescent impulse of the myth casts women as dominating figures (mothers and sisters who are rebelled against) who want to rob men of their masculinity. In reaction to this fear of woman, the myth contains her by casting her as the complement to men. A woman, in westerns, is simply the site for a man to express tenderness. She "brings out qualities in him which we could not see otherwise. Without her, he would be too much the brute for a real folk hero, at least in the modern age" (Davis 89; Marranca 31).

In a broader political context, the myth of the frontier has important implications for Shepard's work. Although cowboys belong to gangs, these fraternal groups are devoid of any political (as distinct from moral) consciousness. The fact that the frontier is a borderline informs all aspects of life there. The social structures are informal, neither wilderness which has no social order nor civilization which is highly ordered but the liminality of emerging social organization. The structure of this paradigm replicates that of the transcendentalist's language which is seen as the threshold, "no longer a shout but not yet discourse." What is paradoxical is that the ideology of "present"—as it is articulated in the myth of the frontier and in the poetics of the transcendentalism—inscribes a politic which is both radical and conservative. It is radical because the individual is allowed to realize himself fully, unencumbered by social restraint; yet, the project is predicated on the existence of ideals which are accepted uncritically: the "true" self which can be realized; the triumph of good as the moral imperative of the frontier where the cowboy in the white hat always wins.

Shepard's romantic belief in the "true" self which is betrayed by language tends toward, if not conservatism, at least an apolitical perspective. The individual turns inward to discover himself rather than outward to the world in which he lives. Shepard's characters almost never indicate any sense of themselves as socially constructed beings. Perhaps by simple virtue of some concern for issues related to "class" as indicated by the title, **Curse of the Starving Class** comes closest to exploring the social determination of character. Yet even in that play, political concerns are transformed into concerns about performance. Faced with losing their land, the characters deny their situation by retreating into the world of fiction and memory as they tell the story of the eagle and the cat, even as the word around them literally and metaphorically blows up.

The concern with performance over politics characterizes all Shepard's work and is particularly important given his thematic preoccupation with the West. Shepard is critical of aspects of the West, for example, the new West represented by the film industry of Hollywood which manufactures images that delude people, thereby denying their realization of their identities. He does not examine, however, the relation of the new West to the old. The Old West, in which Shepard so delights, was generated by Hollywood and bears little relation to the historical reality.[3] This mythical West where men are men and women are their complements (and everybody is white) is surely not the place where the "true" self can be realized. Or perhaps this is the final paradox: the "true" self can be realized through fiction.

## Notes

1. For a fuller discussion of the notion of the supplement see: Jacques Derrida, "The Supplement of Copula: Philosophy *before* Linguistics," *Textual Strategies*, ed. Josue Harari (Ithaca: Cornell University Press, 1979). 82-121.

2. In *Presence of the Actor*, Chaikin cites theatre practitioners as having the greatest influence on his work. These include: Nola Chilton, Mira Roshiva, Judith Malina and Julian Beck, members of the Open Theater (45).

3. Historically, the age of the cowboy is brief: from the period just after the American Civil War until just after 1874 when barbed wire was invented. With the invention of barbed wire, ranches were fenced in and the work of the cowboy became redundant. "The early cowboys were Texans—white, Negro, and Mexican, but outsiders of almost every nationality were also represented." Philip Durham, "The Cowboy and the Myth Makers," *Journal of Popular Culture* 1, No. 1 (Summer 1967): 58.

## Works Cited

Bloom, Harold. *Poems of Our Climate*. Ithaca: Cornell University Press, 1976.

———. "The Real Me." Review of *Walt Whitman: The Making of the Poet* by Paul Zweig, *The New York Review of Books* 31, no. 7 (April 26, 1984).

Blumenthal, Eileen. "Joseph Chaikin: An Open Theory of Acting," *Yale/Theater* 8, nos. 2 and 3 (Spring 1977): 112-33.

Chaikin, Joseph. *The Presence of the Actor*. New York: Atheneum, 1972.

Davis, David Brion. "Ten Gallon Hero." *Myth and the American Experience*. Vol. 2. Ed. Nicholas Gage and Patrick Gerster. New York: Glencoe Press, 1973.

Derrida, Jacques. *Of Grammatology*. Trans. Gayatri Chakravorty Spivak. Baltimore: Johns Hopkins University, 1976.

———. "The Supplement to Copula: Philosophy *before* Linguistics." *Textual Strategies*. Ed. Josue Harari. Ithaca: Cornell University Press, 1979.

———. "The Theater of Cruelty." *Writing and Difference*. Trans. Alan Bass. Chicago: University of Chicago Press, 1980.

Durham, Philip. "The Cowboy and the Myth Makers," *Journal of Popular Culture* 1, no. 1 (Summer 1967): 58-62.

Earley, Michael. "Of Life Immense in Passion, Pulse and Power." *American Dreams: The Imagination of Sam Shepard*. Ed. Bonnie Marranca. New York: Performing Arts Journal Publications, 1981, pp. 126-33.

Falk, Florence. "The Role of Performance in Sam Shepard's Plays," *Theatre Journal* 33, no. 2 (May 1981): 182-98.

Gilman, Richard. Introduction. *Seven Plays* by Sam Shepard. New York: Bantam Books, 1981.

Kakutani, Michiko. "Myths, Dreams, Realities—Sam Shepard's America," *The New York Times*, 29 January 1984, Section 2.

Lippman, Amy. "A Conversation with Sam Shepard," *The Harvard Advocate* (March 1983). Reprinted *Gamut* 5 (January 1984): 10-28.

Marranca, Bonnie. "Alphabetical Shepard: The Play of Words." *American Dreams: The Imagination of Sam Shepard.* Ed. Bonnie Marranca. New York: Performing Arts Journal Publications, 1981, pp. 13-34.

Roudiez, Leon S. Introduction. *Desire in Language: A Semiotic Approach to Literature and Art.* Ed. Leon S. Roudiez. Trans. Thomas Gora, Alice Jardine and Leon S. Roudiez. New York: Columbia University Press, 1980.

Shewey, Don. *Sam Shepard.* New York: Dell, 1985.

——. *Curse of the Starving Class. Seven Plays* by Sam Shepard. New York: Bantam Books, 1981.

——. "Language, Visualization and the Inner Library." *The Drama Review* 21, no. 4 (December 1977): 49-58. Reprinted in *American Dreams: The Imagination of Sam Shepard.* Ed. Bonnie Marranca. New York: Performing Arts Journal Publications, 1981.

——, and Joseph Chaikin. *Tongues. Seven Plays.* By Sam Shepard. New York: Performing Arts Journal Publications, 1981.

Whitman, Walt. *Leaves of Grass.* Harmondsworth: Penguin Books, 1981. Fp. in Brooklyn, 1855.

Wren, Scott Christopher. "Camp Shepard: Exploring the Geography of Character." *West Coast Plays* 7 (1980): 71-106.

---

# FURTHER READING

## Criticism

Brater, Enoch. "American Clocks: Sam Shepard's Time Plays." *Modern Drama* 37, no. 4 (winter 1994): 603-12.
　　Enoch examines issues of time in Shepard's plays, focusing on *A Lie of the Mind* and *Fool for Love.*

DeRose, David J. "A Kind of Cavorting: Superpresence and Shepard's Family Dramas." In *Rereading Shepard: Contemporary Critical Essays on the Plays of Sam Shepard,* edited by Leonard Wilcox, pp. 131-49. New York: St. Martin, 1993.
　　DeRose explores how Shepard's plays incorporate contradictory definitions of postmodernism, tracing his artistic development toward conventional dramatic forms and themes in his family dramas.

——. "Indian Country: Sam Shepard and the Cultural Other." *Contemporary Theatre Review* 8, no. 4 (1998): 55-73.
　　DeRose utilizes *Silent Tongue* as a starting and ending point to look back over thirty years of Shepard's writing, examining his evolving treatment of various racial minorities, particularly Native Americans, as cultural "Others."

Garner, Stanton B., Jr. "Staging 'Things': Realism and the Theatrical Object in Shepard's Theatre." *Contemporary Theatre Review* 8, no. 4 (1998): 55-66.
　　Garner suggests a different valuation of theatrical realism in light of Shepard's attention to the stage's dimension.

Grant, Gary. "Shifting the Paradigm: Shepard, Myth and the Transformation of Consciousness." *Modern Drama* 36, no. 1 (March 1993): 120-29.
　　Grant focuses on Shepard's efforts in creating a paradigm shift for the theatre, including examples from several of his works.

Kamine, Mark. "Small Shifts in Loving." *Times Literary Supplement,* no. 5198 (15 November 2002): 23.
　　Kamine praises *Great Dream of Heaven: Stories,* commenting that "the pleasant surprise in [Shepard's] prose is his easy way with narrative voice."

Lanier, Gregory W. "The Killer's Ancient Mask: Unity and Dualism in Shepard's *The Tooth of Crime.*" *Modern Drama* 36, no. 1 (March 1993): 48-60.
　　Lanier offers an in-depth analysis of *The Tooth of Crime,* including a discussion of the proverbial mask of the killer.

Londré, Felicia Hardison. "A Motel of the Mind: *Fool for Love* and *A Lie of the Mind.*" In *Rereading Shepard: Contemporary Critical Essays on the Plays of Sam Shepard,* edited by Leonard Wilcox, pp. 215-24. New York: St. Martin, 1993.
　　Londré examines the correlation between the stage props and the character's mental states in *Fool for Love* and *A Lie of the Mind.*

Orbison, Tucker. "Authorization and Subversion of Myth in Shepard's *Buried Child.*" *Modern Drama* 37, no. 4 (fall 1994): 509-20.
　　Orbison focuses on Shepard's use of myth in *Buried Child.*

Shewey, Don. "Hidden in Plain Sight: 25 Notes on Shepard's Stage Silence and Screen Presence, 1984-1993." *Contemporary Theatre Review* 8, no. 4 (1998): 75-89.
　　Shewey presents a descriptive overview of Shepard's work in theatre and film during the third decade of his career.

Williams, Megan. "Nowhere Man and the Twentieth-Century Cowboy: Images of Identity and American History in Sam Shepard's *True West.*" *Modern Drama* 40, no. 1 (spring 1997): 57-73.

Williams discusses the themes of character and identity in *True West*.

---

**Additional coverage of Shepard's life and career is contained in the following sources published by the Gale Group:** *American Writers Supplement,* Vol. 3; *Authors and Artists for Young Adults,* Vol. 1; *Contemporary American Dramatists; Contemporary Authors,* Vols. 69-72; *Contemporary Authors Bibliographical Series,* Vol. 3; *Contemporary Authors New Revision Series,* Vol. 22; *Contemporary Dramatists,* Ed. 5; *Contemporary Literary Criticism,* Vols. 4, 6, 17, 34, 41, 44; *Dictionary of Literary Biography,* Vols. 7, 212; *DISCovering Authors Modules: Dramatists; DISCovering Authors 3.0; Drama Criticism,* Vol. 5; *Drama for Students,* Vols. 3, 6, 7, 14; *International Dictionary of Films and Filmmakers: Writers and Production Artists,* Eds. 3, 4; *Literature Resource Center; Major 20th-Century Writers,* Eds. 1, 2; and *Reference Guide to American Literature,* Ed. 4.

# Elaine Showalter
## 1941-

American critic, nonfiction writer, essayist, and editor.

The following entry presents an overview of Showalter's career through 2003.

## INTRODUCTION

One of America's foremost academic literary scholars, Showalter is renowned for her pioneering feminist studies of nineteenth- and twentieth-century female authors and her provocative cultural analysis of women's oppression in the history of psychiatry. In her influential book *A Literature of Their Own: British Women Novelists from Brontë to Lessing* (1977), Showalter advanced a new form of feminist literary theory under the term "gynocriticism," offering an alternative framework for the interpretation of women's literary history. Likewise, in works such as *The Female Malady: Women, Madness, and English Culture, 1830-1980* (1985) and *Hystories: Hysterical Epidemics and Modern Culture* (1997), Showalter forged the branch of feminist criticism known as "hystory," an attempt to reinterpret and redefine the pejorative notion of women's hysteria as embodied in literary and social history. Showalter's contributions to feminist criticism and women's studies have helped influence the canon of British and American literature, bringing new visibility and legitimacy to often forgotten or under-appreciated female authors.

## BIOGRAPHICAL INFORMATION

Showalter was born in Cambridge, Massachusetts, in 1941 to parents Paul Cottler and Violet Rottenberg Cottler. Though he never finished grammar school, Showalter's immigrant father was a successful wool merchant. Showalter's mother completed high school but remained at home in the role of housewife. Showalter chose to attend Bryn Mawr College against the wishes of her parents who both disapproved of their daughter's intellectual leanings and educational ambitions. Nonetheless, Showalter completed her bachelor's degree in English at Bryn Mawr in 1962 and subsequently pursued graduate studies in English at Brandeis University. Her parents also objected to her engagement to English Showalter, a French scholar, who was not Jewish. When Showalter began her graduate work at Brandeis, her parents stopped supporting her financially,

and after she married Showalter in 1963, they disowned her. Showalter completed her master's degree in English at Brandeis in 1964 and embarked upon her doctoral studies at the University of California at Davis, where her husband had taken a teaching appointment in the French department. In 1970, after starting a family and moving to Princeton University, where her husband had accepted a faculty position, Showalter received her doctorate in English from UC Davis and was hired as an assistant professor at Douglass College of Rutgers University in New Jersey. In the late 1960s, she became active in the new women's movement and served as president of the Princeton chapter of the National Organization for Women (NOW) in 1969. Her involvement in NOW brought her into contact with other emerging feminist leaders, most notably feminist literary scholar Kate Millett and feminist art historian Linda Nochlin. During this early period of activism, Showalter edited *Women's Liberation and Literature* (1971) and published *A Literature of Their Own,* her first major work of literary scholarship. While at Douglass, she moved from assistant professor to associate professor in 1974, and became a full professor of English in 1983. She also served as a visiting professor of English and women's studies at the University of Delaware between 1976 and 1977. During this period, she received several important fellowships, including a Guggenheim fellowship in 1977 and a Rockefeller humanities fellowship in 1981. In 1984 Showalter left Douglass for Princeton University, where she accepted a position as a professor of English and was later named the Avalon Professor of Humanities. She has worked as an editor for several feminist scholarly journals and publishers, including *Women's Studies, Signs,* the Feminist Press, and Virago Press. A member of the Modern Language Association (MLA), Showalter served on its Commission on the Status of Women in the Profession from 1971 to 1972 and as the organization's president from 1998 to 1999. Showalter has also worked as a freelance journalist in both the print and broadcast media.

## MAJOR WORKS

Among the founding scholars of feminist literary criticism and women's studies in America, Showalter broke new ground in the 1970s by creating a progressive literary theory known as "gynocriticism." Unlike traditional literary criticism, gynocriticism focused on the "history, themes, genres, and structures of literature by women," seeking to create a method of analyzing literature written by women and to develop models of interpretation based on female experience, rather than adapting male interpretive theories and models. Putting her theory into practice, Showalter edited the anthology *Women's Liberation and Literature,* consisting of excerpts from works considered essential to feminist literary study, such as Mary Wollstonecraft's *A Vindication of the Rights of Women* and Henrik Ibsen's *A Doll's House.* In *A Literature of Their Own,* a revision and elaboration of her doctoral dissertation, Showalter rebukes the unfair critical standards applied to the work of English women writers in the nineteenth century and contends that, as a result, female artists paid a terrible price for their creative work in terms of guilt, self-loathing, and frustrated effort. Showalter divides the evolution of women's writing into three phases—"feminine," from 1840 to the death of George Eliot in 1880; "feminist," from 1880 to 1920, the date of female suffrage in America; and "female," from 1920 to the present. Between 1975 and 1981, Showalter published three essays in academic journals that, taken together with *A Literature of Their Own,* form the foundation of her literary critical outlook and have become major tenets of American feminist literary criticism. The first, "Literary Criticism" (1975), published in the journal *Signs,* discusses two approaches to feminist criticism—feminist critique, which examines the anti-female biases of traditional readings and literary canons; and feminist reevaluation of women writers considered to be minor figures, as they represent the idea of a historical female subculture. Showalter's next seminal essay, "Toward a Feminist Poetics," was originally published in Mary Jacobus's anthology *Women Writing and Writing about Women* (1979). In this piece, Showalter introduced the term "gynocritics" and demonstrated its efficacy with a feminist critique of Thomas Hardy's *The Mayor of Casterbridge* and its male-centered critical interpretations. In the third essay, "Feminist Criticism in the Wilderness" (1981), originally published in the journal *Critical Inquiry,* Showalter used the female cultural analysis developed by Oxford anthropologists Shirley and Edwin Ardner to argue that women form a muted group within the dominant male culture, a group whose reality and culture overlap with those of the dominant culture, but is not contained within it. She further maintained that women's writing constitutes a "double-voiced discourse that always embodies the social, literary, and cultural heritages of both the muted and the dominant."

As editor of *The New Feminist Criticism: Essays on Women, Literature, and Theory* (1985), Showalter brought together one of the most comprehensive collections of feminist literary theory and criticism to date, including examples of French feminism, gynocriticism, and African-American and lesbian feminist criticism. Showalter subsequently published *Sister's Choice: Tradition and Change in American Women's Writing* (1991), a critical counterpart to *A Literature of Their Own,* in which she traces the development of American women's writing through a wide-ranging literary survey and close studies of Margaret Fuller and Louisa May Alcott, Kate Chopin's *The Awakening,* Edith Wharton's *The House of Mirth,* and various gothic forms of women's writing from the 1960s. In the mid-1980s, Showalter extended her critical outlook from literary criticism to cultural history, focusing on embedded conceptions of mental health and the expression of sexual issues in terms of gender. In *The Female Malady,* a study of the sexual politics of British psychiatric history, Showalter argued that a feminization of madness occurred in the nineteenth century, and that women became the primary recipients of psychiatric treatment, serving as the cultural exemplars of insanity. She further maintained that until the late 1970s, psychiatry treated women in the confining context of "femininity," which was largely responsible for their psychological demoralization. *Sexual Anarchy: Gender and Culture at the Fin-de-Siècle* (1990) presents a literary and cultural analysis of the corresponding millennial crises of the 1890s and the 1990s, particularly as evident in the anxiety wrought by female sexual liberation and the corresponding scourges of syphilis and AIDS, and expressed in homoerotic elements of male adventure fiction by Robert Louis Stevenson and Rider Haggard, and late-twentieth-century films. Showalter returned to the subject of mental health in *Hystories,* in which she examines a variety of mysterious afflictions that emerged during the 1980s and 1990s, including chronic fatigue syndrome, Gulf War syndrome, alien abductions, and recovered memories of sexual abuse. Turning a skeptical eye to these ambiguous epidemics, Showalter asserts that all are psychosomatic conditions that reflect a proliferation of mass hysteria, amplified by widespread communication media and millennial anxiety. *Inventing Herself: Claiming a Feminist Intellectual Heritage* (2000) presents a survey of various "feminist icons," a broad label that Showalter affixes to intellectuals such as Wollstonecraft, Fuller, Eleanor Marx, and Simone de Beauvoir as well as contemporary celebrity figures such as Oprah Winfrey and Diana, Princess of Wales. Showalter has also edited *Daughters of Decadence: Women Writers of the Fin-de-Siècle* (1993), an anthology of women's writings from the late-nineteenth century, and *Scribbling Women: Short Stories by Nineteenth-Century American Women* (1997), a collection of short stories by nineteenth-century American women, both of which seek to introduce readers to the work of previously obscure or underrated female authors.

## CRITICAL RECEPTION

Showalter has been widely appreciated by critics for her prodigious knowledge, insightful analysis, and accessible prose. Most feminist literary scholars have lauded her achievement in helping to legitimize and further develop feminist critique, particularly by reevaluating the social and historical context within which women's writing is studied. However, some critics have contended that Showalter's reach often exceeds her grasp, faulting her for raising provocative questions and presenting a wealth of material without analyzing it, or trying unsuccessfully to force-fit her usually expansive subject matter into a rigid critical context. Others have criticized Showalter for omitting or glossing over women writers who do not fit neatly into her thesis or analytical construct. In addition, some reviewers have objected to Showalter's literary biases, especially in regards to the Victorian era, and her dubious psychoanalytic assumptions. Showalter's works of cultural history, particularly *The Female Malady* and *Sexual Anarchy,* have received mixed reviews, but have been generally praised for their broad, interdisciplinary approach to literary, cultural, and social trends. Showalter's feminist history of psychiatry in *The Female Malady* has been commended for raising disturbing and important questions about the politics of interpretation and the power of gender as a determining factor in psychiatric treatment. Her focus on the psychiatric patient—rather than the history of the psychiatric profession—has also been viewed as a valuable contribution to the subject. However, some reviewers have faulted Showalter for her selective use of data and statistics, and her imprecise use of key terms, such as "hysteria." In later works such as *Hystories* and *Inventing Herself,* critics have hailed Showalter's impressive synthesis of evidence, though some have found her arguments less substantial and convincing than in previous works. Despite such shortcomings, Showalter has been highly regarded for calling attention to complex issues surrounding gender and sexual politics. Many of her works, most notably *A Literature of Their Own* and *The Female Malady,* have endured as staples of feminist literary criticism in university curricula.

## PRINCIPAL WORKS

*Women's Liberation and Literature* [editor] (criticism) 1971
*A Literature of Their Own: British Women Novelists from Brontë to Lessing* (nonfiction) 1977
*These Modern Women: Autobiographical Essays from the Twenties* [editor] (essays) 1978
*The Female Malady: Women, Madness, and English Culture, 1830-1980* (criticism) 1985
*The New Feminist Criticism: Essays on Women, Literature, and Theory* [editor] (criticism) 1985
*Alternative Alcott* [editor] (criticism) 1988
*Speaking of Gender* [editor] (criticism) 1989
*Sexual Anarchy: Gender and Culture at the Fin-de-Siècle* (criticism) 1990
*Modern American Women Writers* [editor; with Lea Baechler and A. Walton Litz] (nonfiction) 1991
*Sister's Choice: Tradition and Change in American Women's Writing* (criticism) 1991
*Daughters of Decadence: Women Writers of the Fin-de-Siècle* [editor] (criticism) 1993
*Hystories: Hysterical Epidemics and Modern Culture* (criticism) 1997
*Scribbling Women: Short Stories by Nineteenth-Century American Women* [editor] (short stories) 1997
*Inventing Herself: Claiming a Feminist Intellectual Heritage* (criticism) 2000
*Teaching Literature* (nonfiction) 2003

## CRITICISM

### Marcia Landy (review date winter 1977-1978)

SOURCE: Landy, Marcia. Review of *A Literature of Their Own: British Women Novelists from Brontë to Lessing,* by Elaine Showalter. *Modern Fiction Studies* 23, no. 4 (winter 1977-1978): 637-45.

[*In the following excerpt, Landy praises Showalter's broad historical analysis of female authors in* A

Literature of Their Own, *but criticizes her tendency to offer unsympathetic, overly negative judgments of individual writers.*]

Two of the four books reviewed here are distinguished by new and challenging critical methodologies, and two are not. Gabriel Josipovici's edited collection of essays on the modern novel reveals a primarily structuralist and linguistic orientation and Elaine Showalter's work, **A Literature of Their Own,** presents an exploration in feminist criticism. The third book, Lisa Ruddick's essay, is a reading of Woolf's *To the Lighthouse,* and the fourth, Ronald Hayman's British Council pamphlet, while raising some critical issues, makes little pretense to critical analysis. The latter is restricted to a discussion of fifty English and Commonwealth novelists and their works....

The second book, Elaine Showalter's **A Literature of Their Own** has a more overt concern for the immediate social context of the writers she discusses than do the essays in *The Modern English Novel* [by Josipovici]. Showalter attempts to provide the reader with critical categories for understanding and evaluating women's writing. She shares with *The Modern English Novel* the desire to identify a literary tradition, in this case a woman's literary history. Showalter describes her project thus: "This book is an effort to describe the female literary tradition in the English novel from the generation of the Brontës to the present day, and to show how the development of this tradition is similar to the development of any literary subculture" (p. 11). Showalter charts three phases in this tradition which she identifies as feminine, feminist, and female. These stages reflect similar movements in other literary subcultures such as black, Jewish, Anglo-Indian (often described as imitation, protest and advocacy, and self-discovery).

The book sets itself a large and comprehensive task: to chart history, to discuss representative writers and their work from the three literary phases, to reconstruct a sense for the reader of the literary context, and to utilize both major and minor writers: Jane Austen, Charlotte Brontë, George Eliot—but Sarah Grand and Diana Craik, too. The book also tests generalizations about women writers. For example, Showalter affirms the high percentage of women writers drawn from the middle class, though she explodes the idea, propounded by male writers like Wilkie Collins, that women were invading and overwhelming the literary market in the nineteenth century. Not every woman undertook writing novels, even less found her way into print. Women writers, in short, were in a minority. Because of inferior education or little formal schooling, women like George Eliot and Charlotte Brontë sought to overcompensate and set very high standards for themselves. Furthermore, women writers were more dependent on writing for income than men, because so few professions were available to them. Women had to grapple also with guilt over the "sinfulness" of taking time away from the family to indulge in writing.

Showalter balances her observations and generalizations: she does not merely detail negative instances of women's role and failures of the woman writer; she also cites instances where women succeed. For example, while noting the role father-daughter conflicts play from Elizabeth Barrett Browning to Virginia Woolf, she also notes that identification with the father can be linked to high achievement. Furthermore, "the subordination of self to filial duty gave these women confidence in their own abilities to love" (p. 64).

Showalter describes the prevailing double standard for women's fiction; she also describes how from the 1840's to the 1870's there was some serious criticism of women's contribution to the novel. Women's novels were considered inferior to men's. Because reproduction and motherhood were thought to affect brain size and intelligence, women's artistic abilities were considered inferior. Women's limited experiences were also considered to create circumscribed and lesser artistic productions. Women were believed to excel in emotion rather than in the recreation of actual experiences. This criticism was dealt with sympathetically by George Eliot and by Mrs. Oliphant who, though they "criticized the overemphasis on love and passion in feminine fiction, . . . understood that lack of education, isolation, and boredom had distorted women's values and channeled creative energy into romantic fantasy and emotional self-dramatization" (p. 80).

Breaking down these literary stereotypes was not easy. A common game of the period was deciphering the sex of the author behind the pseudonym. For example, Blackmore was thought in *Clara Vaughan* to be a female author because he utilized a female narrator. George Eliot was considered to be a man because of the superiority of her work. When it became known that the author of *Adam Bede* was a woman, criticism changed markedly to a negative and stereotypical attack. Eliot herself had directed her attention to the question of women's contribution to the novel. She was impatient with most feminine fiction, but she did anticipate that women's "maternal affections would lead to 'distinctive forms and combinations' in the novel" (p. 97).

The mid-nineteenth century was characterized by a quest for heroines as "both professional role-models and fictional ideals" (p. 100). By 1860, the dominant role-models were Jane Austen and George Sand, on the one hand, George Eliot and Charlotte Brontë, on the other. These writers exerted a tremendous influence on other women writers. Eliot and Brontë myths continued even into the twentieth century to influence styles of writing and attitudes toward the woman writer's role. Virginia Woolf, Doris Lessing, and Muriel Spark were touched by that "tradition." Showalter compares *Jane Eyre* and *The Mill on the Floss*. Both are "classic feminine novels" and present "powerful descriptions of growing up a female in Victorian England" (p. 112), but Jane Eyre is fulfilled, while Maggie Tulliver is not. Both novels explore female sexuality and utilize folklore to convey negative myths about sexuality. Both heroines experience the conflict between passion and duty, but Jane escapes toward independence while Maggie chooses self-sacrifice. Both "solutions" are representative of women's novels.

Another outlet for women writers' fantasies, struggles, and imagination was the "woman's man," a common phenomenon in fiction: "It is customary for critics of the Victorian novel to see women's heroes as fantasy lovers, daydreams of romantic suitors. Critics have been rather slow to perceive that much of the wish-fulfillment in the feminine novel comes from women wishing they were men with the greater freedom and range masculinity confers" (p. 136). Showalter catalogues and describes some of the characteristics of the woman's man. He is master of guilt (Guy Morville in *The Heir of Radclyff*, 1853). Self-sacrifice and masochism are common, too. Another type of woman's man is the brute, the heir to Byron's Corsair and Brontës Rochester. Such men are rough, mysterious, and impulsive. The clergyman hero was yet another common figure. Of intermediate or neutral sex, he was considered by critics of the time to be the male figure most appropriate for the woman writer to use. In many of these novels, men are wounded or they experience illness which reflects the woman writer's sense that men must be initiated into dependency through coercion.

In the late 1860's, changes in women's novels became obvious. New opportunities for women writers appeared through the growth of women's presses. Reviews and serialization also became possible outlets for creativity. One begins to see women in fiction in different and more daring roles. The sensation novel was a genre which was compatible with these new roles; it was also a vehicle for articulating discontent. One finds a new kind of heroine who "expressed female anger, frustration, and sexual energy more directly than had been done previously" (p. 160). The themes were more social than sexual and often reversed traditional stereotypes as in the novels of Mary Braddon. In *Lady Audley's Secret*, the "frail blond angel" is the threat. The novel explores bigamy, violence, and madness. The "real secret" is that "Lady Audley . . . is *sane* and, moreover, representative" (p. 167). The sensation novels tackled divorce, domestic discontent, and sexual conflict. Yet Showalter finds these novels "limited explorations of women's consciousness" (p. 180), for they did not pursue a genuine examination and radical critique of women's social roles.

The 80's and 90's saw the rise of the feminist novelists who "had a highly developed sense of belonging to a sisterhood of women writers" (p. 182). These writers maintained the Victorian ideal of the sacred influence of women, but they transferred the feminine ideal into politics. They attacked male violence, male sexuality, and even syphilis. They envisioned worlds without men. Showalter reveals writers like Olive Schreiner as presenting in their lives and in their writing the painful and problematic situation of women. Schreiner's ambivalent attitudes toward women, her psychological struggles, are reflected in her meager output. Sarah Grand and George Egerton represent "a turning point in the female tradition, and they turn inward" (p. 215). They begin with high hopes for women and end in their own private experiences. Indulging in what seems to be a judgment, Showalter says that "it is a pity that the feminists, showing the limits of their world in their writing, also elevated their restricted view into a sacred vision" (p. 215). Showalter finds the consequences of the suffrage movement equally disappointing, though she does note Elizabeth Robins' and Cecily Hamilton's critical explorations of the future for women's literature and criticism. Many opposed the feminists. Mrs. Humphrey Ward, who was a supporter of women's roles as philanthropists and moral uplifters and was an advocate of education for women, was not a supporter of feminism. The suffragists were also opposed by socialists who were against separatism and saw women's liberation in broad sexual, psychological, and social terms. In general, Showalter does not find the suffrage movement a "happy stimulus to women writers" (p. 236), and she credits the movement with many women's retreat from active social involvement into the cultivation of sensibility.

The pre-World War I and war-generation of women writers developed a "female aesthetic" which was characterized by the abandonment of realism, the cultivation of spirituality, and a rejection of "objectivity" as too representative of the dominant male culture. The heroines of this fiction find themselves trapped and exploited by both marriage and free love, and by self-consciousness. For example, self-awareness in Katherine Mansfield is self-betrayal. The literature reflects negative attitudes toward men. The novels of Dorothy Richardson exemplify the "female aesthetic." Though often compared to Proust, Richardson is best understood as belonging to the female tradition in literature. Her life reveals familial conflict and instability culminating in the suicide of her mother. Her personal struggles and her struggles with feminism are reflected in her commitment to the novel of consciousness. Her idea that women's language differs from men's and her use of stream-of-consciousness, of fragmented language, and of loose formal structures also reveal her feelings of estrangement, her turning away from traditional forms of literature and from dominant values. Showalter ends her chapter on the "female aesthetic" with the wish that Richardson and other female writers of the period could have "forgiven themselves . . . could have faced the anger instead of denying it . . . could have translated the consciousness of their own darkness into confrontation instead of struggling to transcend it" (p. 262).

Showalter's examination of Virginia Woolf is, above all, a critique of Woolf as an androgynous writer. "I think it is important to demystify the legend of Virginia Woolf," she says (p. 265). Instead of androgyny, Showalter sees sexual polarity. She prods the reader to examine Woolf' relationship to her parents and to Leonard Woolf. She raises questions about Woolf's suicide in the context of her relationship to her husband, her history of depression, her childlessness, and to her experience of menopause. Woolf's advocacy of a room of one's own is "a symbol of psychic withdrawal," which Showalter interprets as "an escape from the demands of other people" (p. 286). Identifying Woolf with the tradition of female aestheticism, she sees "Woolf's vision of womanhood . . . as deadly as it is disembodied. The ultimate room of one's own is the grave" (p. 297). In this evaluation of Woolf, as in the evaluation of the writers of the sensation novel, the suffragists, and Dorothy Richardson, Showalter reveals an inability to empathize with and identify the heroic and positive dimensions of the struggles of these writers. In her quest for demystification, she falls, perhaps unwittingly, into a one-sided analysis.

The final chapter, **"Beyond the Female Aesthetic: Contemporary Women Novelists,"** explores the phase of self-discovery in women's novels. Showalter finds a new frankness, a greater flexibility of boundaries between men's and women's roles. These writers—Doris Lessing, Jean Rhys, Margaret Drabble, Muriel Spark—confront class issues, the relationship between tradition and change, and the meaning of personal and cultural liberation. According to Showalter, their attitudes represent the significant distance between the tomb, a room of one's own, and acting and creating in the world.

The strengths of Showalter's study are obvious. She provides the reader with an historical and social context, a tradition, from which to examine the writings of women novelists. She creates a methodology which critics must now debate and test. She treats major and minor writers and places different modes of writing into a comprehensible framework. But the strengths of the book also reveal certain weaknesses. In her desire for coherence, pattern, and meaning, Showalter minimizes the struggles and the positive contributions of writers like Richardson and Woolf. At times, she also simplifies the forces which have molded these writers. For example, Richardson's indebtedness to modernism can be interpreted also as a response to complex social and historical conditions of which the woman's question is only one important factor.

### Daniel J. Cahill (review date winter 1978)

SOURCE: Cahill, Daniel J. Review of *A Literature of Their Own: British Women Novelists from Brontë to Lessing,* by Elaine Showalter. *World Literature Today* 52, no. 1 (winter 1978): 114-15.

[*In the following review, Cahill praises the range and the scope of material in* A Literature of Their Own, *noting that the work "change the content and perspective of literary history as it is currently taught in our colleges and universities."*]

The truly significant accomplishment of *A Literature of Their Own* is the creation of a new perceptual framework, an accurate and systematic literary history for women writers in the British tradition. In the most comprehensive and convincing study to date, Showalter has extended a radically new awareness of the evolution of a female literary tradition. In 1869 John Stuart Mill argued that if women lived in a different country from men and had never read any of their writings, they would have a literature of their own. To many observers—past and present—it seemed that the besetting sin of women was to write as men write. In contradiction to Mill, Showalter argues that many readers of the novel over the past two centuries have had the indistinct but persistent impression of a unifying voice in women's literature. This distinctive female identity in art has been obscured by a "residual Great Traditionalism," which has reduced and condensed the extraordinary range and diversity of English women writers to a tiny band of the "great": Jane Austen, the Brontës, George Eliot and Virginia Woolf. Through the focus upon these happy few, the links in the chain that bound one generation to the next have been lost.

The purpose of *A Literature of Their Own* is an effort to describe the female literary tradition in the English novel from the generation of the Brontës to the present day and to show how the development of this tradition is similar to the development of any literary subculture. In constructing the thesis, Showalter views the process of the female subculture as evolving in three phases: imitation, protest and self-discovery—a final turning inward freed from some of the dependency of opposition, a search for identity. Showalter calls her stages Feminine, Feminist and Female. These categories are not rigid periods with distinct shifts in values, and the author is respectful of the many overlapping elements. Feminine, feminist or female, the woman's novel has always had to struggle against the cultural and historical forces that relegated women's experience to the second rank; but despite prejudice, despite guilt, despite inhibition, women began to write. Through the power of accurate scholarship and detail Showalter gives the reader a new and informed sense of the strength of purpose which possessed the female writer. She has dramatically rendered the sense of continuity which sustained a unique tradition and which produced a powerful segment of literary awareness.

In the most original chapters of the book—"The Female Aesthetic" and "Flight into Androgyny"—Showalter explores the distinction between consciousness and experience, an important determinant of the direction of modernist women's writing. In this analysis her critical judgment of Virginia Woolf may be severely contested, since she ultimately sees Woolf as elevating passivity into a creed: "Refined to its essences, abstracted from its physicality and anger, denied any action, Woolf's vision of womanhood is as deadly as it is disembodied."

Obviously, no brief review can be just to the complexity and significance of this excellent study of the female tradition. One of its immediate effects will be to change the content and perspective of literary history as it is currently taught in our colleges and universities. *A Literature of Their Own* begins to record new choices in a new literary history.

### Agate Nesaule Krouse (review date spring 1978)

SOURCE: Krouse, Agate Nesaule. Review of *A Literature of Their Own: British Women Novelists from Brontë to Lessing*, by Elaine Showalter. *Criticism* 20, no. 2 (spring 1978): 216-18.

[*In the following excerpt, Krouse compliments Showalter's examination of "the female literary tradition" in* A Literature of Their Own, *but finds fault with Showalter's treatment of twentieth-century writers, including Virginia Woolf.*]

Only recently have critics become fully aware that knowledge about women writers and therefore literary history itself is fragmentary and biased. Innumerable articles and some books from a feminist perspective have reinterpreted the achievements of well known women writers, reassessed the work of neglected ones, exposed the shortcomings of "phallic" criticism, and developed concepts useful for the theory and practice of feminist criticism. Meanwhile extensive and diverse new research about women in other disciplines has contributed to the need for intelligent synthesis of information about the work and experience of women writers.

Professor Showalter's *A Literature of Their Own: British Women Novelists from Brontë to Lessing* provides such a synthesis and more. Unlike Ellen Moers's *Literary Women* (Doubleday, 1976), the earlier widely discussed study which took the implications of the gender of writers seriously, Showalter's book is an orderly, balanced, and highly readable account unmarred by awkward coinage (e.g., Moers's "Heroinism"), impressionistic organization, contradictions, and inadequate distinctions. Showalter's book can thus serve as a model for critics examining the work of women in other genres and historical periods. In addition, *A Literature of Their Own* is informative enough to be useful as a reference work, yet imaginative enough to invite continued reexamination and considerable controversy.

Professor Showalter rejects the notion of "a sense of collective identity of women writers" which might have produced a literary movement; she also dismisses the concept of a specifically female sensibility or imagination. Instead, she chooses "to describe a female literary tradition in the English novel and to show how the development of this tradition is similar to the development of any literary subculture."

Showalter identifies three distinct stages in "the female literary tradition [which] comes from the still-evolving relationships between women writers and their society." Imitation and internalization of the dominant male traditions produced the Feminine stage (1840-80); protest and advocacy of women's rights resulted in the Feminist phase (1880-1920); the search for and discovery of self is evident in the Female phase (1920-present).

One of the major strengths of this study is the order Showalter brings to a vast and complex body of material without oversimplification or contradiction. She provides informative discussion of innumerable writers besides Brontë, Eliot, Woolf, and Lessing. She makes further distinctions within the three major stages, so that neither common elements nor differences between writers and generations are slighted. She shows that the easy generalizations (e.g., women writers suffered from sexism; women writers opposing the suffrage were unsympathetic to women) can be considerably refined by research and analysis to yield more complex yet more vividly convincing conclusions. Thus, for example, the chapters on **"The Feminine Novelists and the Will to Write"** and **"The Double Critical Standard and the Feminine Novel"** indirectly create sympathy and respect for those women who wrote for publication in spite of the critical standards used by both male and female reviewers, by both attackers and defenders. Even trends seemingly contrary to prevailing literary and social conventions are acknowledged and explicated as in the chapter on **"Subverting the Feminine Novel: Sensationalism and Feminine Protest."** In addition, Showalter often notes revealing continuities in the fiction of women: her striking comments on the function of the forcibly confined mad wife in *Jane Eyre* versus that of the mad wife who helps the protagonist gain essential knowledge in *The Four-Gated City* are just one example. The perceptive and tactful use Showalter makes of research from other disciplines to explicate the fiction and lives of writers constitutes another major strength.

Although *A Literature of Their Own* is clearly the best of recent studies dealing with several women writers, it is by no means the last word. Novels published in the first half of the roughly one-hundred and thirty years encompassed by the study receive proportionately fuller and more sympathetic treatment. Twentieth century novelists are dealt with in less than a hundred pages; of these about one-fifth are devoted to the writing from the suffrage movement which Showalter accurately evaluates as being historically interesting but aesthetically undistinguished. Many contemporary novelists whose achievements deserve more detailed examination (e.g., Rhys, Spark, O'Brien, Murdock) are passed over in a sentence or omitted altogether. Lessing and Drabble are rightfully treated at greater length, though even here one does not have the comfortable sense that Professor Showalter is as thoroughly familiar with the canon of modern women writers or as perceptive about their relationships to each other, to modern critical standards, or to current concepts of femininity as she is with the literature and society of nineteenth century.

The chapter **"Virginia Woolf and the Flight into Androgyny"** is likely to be the most controversial. It is undeniably appropriate to reexamine stringently the work and influence of a writer elevated to near-sainthood by feminists and feminist critics. Harriet Rosenstein similarly questioned the irrational admiration accorded to Plath, another suicide, by exposing the shortcomings of *The Bell Jar* and reaffirming the achievements of the poetry ("Reconsidering Sylvia Plath," *Ms.* 1, September, 1972, pp. 44-51). Her essay did much to begin more balanced discussion by feminists of Plath's work. Showalter's refusal to see Woolf's "suicide as a beautiful act of faith, or a philosophical gesture toward androgyny" is a healthy corrective. Less convincing, however, is the ascription of Woolf's major breakdowns to "crises in female identity": menstruation, frigidity, childlessness, and menopause. While Professor Showalter says she has "no wish to substitute one magical explanation of her [Woolf's] anguish for another," she nevertheless does so implicitly by the full discussion of these crises and the reliance on Helen Deutsch's highly questionable analysis of female psychology.

While it is refreshing to see *Orlando* characterized by a particularly apt phrase ("tedious high camp"), it is more difficult to accept Showalter's argument that Woolf's "vision of womanhood is as deadly as it is disembodied." This is especially true since *A Room of One's Own* and *Three Guineas* rather than the fiction are used as evidence more extensively. Even in these Showalter finds an unacceptable suppression of anger and withdrawal from life—"the ultimate room of one's own is the grave"—rather than a vision of the privacy and economic freedom essential to the woman writer. Woolf's work is thus too quickly once again dismissed as politically uninvolved, a label feminist critics have only recently begun to remove.

Even the suicidal, destructive, deadly influence Professor Showalter isolates needs further discussion. For example, the suicidal young man is by no means restricted to *Mrs. Dalloway.* As a contrast to the female protagonist he appears in other major modern novels: e.g., Lessing's *The Golden Notebook* and Drabble's *The Realms of Gold.* It can be argued that these novels echo an entirely different positive pattern evident in Woolf's work: an affirmation of life and triumphant survival by women rather than the attractiveness of death.

*A Literature of Their Own* is an impressive work that fully engages the attention of the reader. Any disagreements or reservations attest to its vitality and importance. . . .

Hopefully the continued interest in women writers will encourage additional analyses of Lessing's art and thought. Singleton and Showalter are absolutely right in seeing Lessing as a major contemporary writer.

### Tom Paulin (review date 21 July 1978)

SOURCE: Paulin, Tom. "Fugitive Spirits." *New Statesman* 96, no. 2470 (21 July 1978): 94.

[*In the following excerpt, Paulin offers a negative assessment of* A Literature of Their Own, *arguing that the work makes a "snobbish mockery of Women's Liberation."*]

Those Victorian photographs of bearded patriarchs flanked by their unsmiling families may seem merely quaint to us nowadays, but it's important to remember how they were once the agents of hideously formidable cultural tyranny. As Gloria Fromm shows in her long, loving biography of Dorothy Richardson, the effort to escape the domination of 'masculine culture' involved an intense struggle against a series of possessive father-figures. Dorothy Richardson's father was a cultivated, eventually bankrupt despot who made her mother feel both damned and stupid, and finally drove her to commit suicide. Stricken by guilt, Dorothy left home to become a dentist's receptionist in London. She wrote reviews, attended Fabian meetings and had an affair with H. G. Wells. She came to realise that Wells was a tyrant who preached freedom, and throughout her life she remained a shrewdly critical friend of the man who appears as 'Hypo Wilson' in her now neglected novel-sequence *Pilgrimage*. Wells put her in his novel *The Passionate Friends* as a minor character called Stella Summersby Satchel, who is 'blonde, erect, huffy-mannered'. . . .

Unfortunately, Dorothy Richardson is dismissed by Elaine Showalter [in *A Literature of Their Own*], who complains that she 'risked self-destruction through psychic overload, ego death from that state of pure receptivity that George Eliot had described as the roar on the other side of silence'. This modish piece of jargon distorts what George Eliot meant in that famous passage in *Middlemarch,* and it wrongly attributes the passivity of Richardson's impressionism to the fact that she lived 'at the perilous borders of egolessness, in the female country of multiple receptivity'. What this simply means is that she wrote in the way she did because she was a woman—a bit of critical melodrama which is sexist in its implications.

So, too, is this remark about Olive Schreiner's supposedly 'nagging' narrative voice: 'that voice, soft, heavy, continuous, is a genuine accent of womanhood, one of the chorus of secret voices speaking out of our bones, dreadful and irritating but instantly recognisable'. Change the 'our' to 'their' and this sentence could have been written by any old buffer who wanted to put Olive Schreiner down with a convenient stereotype. Similarly, when Ms Showalter comments that a passage in *A Room of One's Own* 'certainly sounds like a feline swipe at Cantabridgian impotence' we are meant to notice that because Virginia Woolf was a woman her wit must be 'feline'.

Ms Showalter believes that there is such a thing as 'feminised language'—it is 'delicate' and 'fastidious'—and she supports her belief by quoting one Ernest Baker, who stated that 'the woman of letters has peculiarities that mark her off from the other sex as distinctly as peculiarities of race or of ancestral tradition'. She is very willing to be patronised by this racial analogy because she believes that 'British women novelists have always, in a sense, lived in a different country from men—and have a literature of their own'. This assumption is literally chauvinist, and not only is it defensive and exclusive but it also merges over 200 very varying talents into a mute sorority where George Eliot and Charlotte Brontë are treated on the same level as Lady Georgiana Chatterton, Julia Pardoe and others now forgotten.

The trouble with these novelists, she suggests, is that they didn't 'band together' and insist that their vocation 'made them superior to the ordinary woman, and perhaps happier'. By this argument, all women ought to aspire to be women novelists, and if they don't then they are merely 'ordinary'. This makes a snobbish mockery of Women's Liberation, which is concerned with equality, not superiority. And because of its central assumption that women writers inhabit an imaginary sub-culture 'within the frame-work of a larger society', *A Literature of Their Own* has very little to do with feminism.

This emerges most noticeably in the remark that 'the tender and adoring friendship of women for women' in one of Mrs Humphry Ward's novels reflects 'the intense bonds of the female subculture'. What this essentially represents is a wish to secede from the territory we all live in. Women must seek solidarity in order to cultivate tender relationships with each other, and not for the sake of challenging sexual injustice and exploitation. As a message this is clearly defeatist, and it's very much to be hoped that no one listens to it.

**Vineta Colby (review date February 1980)**

SOURCE: Colby, Vineta. Review of *A Literature of Their Own: British Women Novelists from Brontë to Lessing,* by Elaine Showalter. *Modern Philology* 77, no. 3 (February 1980): 357-60.

[*In the following review, Colby praises the range of material covered in* A Literature of Their Own, *but criticizes Showalter's assertions about Victorian feminism and her analysis of Charlotte Brontë and George Eliot.*]

*A Literature of Their Own* is by far the best account yet published of the emergence of the feminine sensibility in the English novel. It documents with sound research and reasoned, if sometimes controversial, theory a subject that too many writers in recent years have exploited irresponsibly, with too little reading and too much hasty prejudgment. Elaine Showalter rides no hobbyhorses after fashionable trends in psychology or sociology, and it is refreshing to find in her index no entry for Herbert Marcuse or Norman O. Brown, and only passing references to Karen Horney, Erik Erikson, and R. D. Laing. This is not to suggest that she is anything but aware of and sensitive to studies in feminine psychology and sexuality. Her reading in these areas is extensive, ranging from too often neglected contemporary Victorian sources—journals, memoirs and periodicals—to the latest (1976) scholarly books and articles. Her bibliography and biographical appendix, which lists 213 prominent English literary women, will be invaluable to every student in the field. But mainly and most impressively, Professor Showalter has read the novels themselves, a staggering number of them, good, bad, and indifferent. She has assembled the results of her reading in a coherent and cogent book that has a fair chance of being the definitive work on the subject.

In tracing the emergence of this literary "subculture," Showalter identifies three stages and looks toward the emergence of a fourth. These are the Feminine, roughly from 1840 to 1880 (with the death of George Eliot), defined by imitation of the traditional forms of the novel and acceptance of the prevailing social and moral values of the period, but also reflecting implicit protest against these; the Feminist, from 1880 to the winning of the suffrage in 1920, expressing outright protest and advocacy of minority rights; and the Female, from the 1920s to about 1970, when the woman writer's search for self-identification produced an aesthetic if not a real autonomy. In all three stages, Showalter detects an ultimate internalization, a withdrawal in one form or another that constitutes "at heart evasions of reality" (p. 318). Only, and she is cautiously optimistic here, in the increasing openness of the contemporary English woman novelist, in writers like A. S. Byatt, Margaret Drabble, and Doris Lessing, is the female voice beginning to speak for itself, without guilt or self-consciousness.

As a framework for literary history, Showalter's categories are useful. They are not rigidly applied. Indeed, in showing the interrelationships and the continuity of influence, especially as these are reflected in the minor fiction of each period, she enriches our appreciation not only of the "liberation" of women writers but of the novel itself as a mirror of its total culture and context. As a framework for literary criticism, however, they become constricting. They fail to recognize, for example, that in struggling to identify themselves as novelists (as the subtitle of this book reminds us, the range of the study is the novel, not other art forms) these women were fighting much the same battle as men, though granted under additional handicaps of prejudice and patronizing tolerance. There was, and there lingers, a critical double standard for men and women writers: "To their contemporaries," she writers of the Victorians, "women writers were women first, artists second" (p. 73). But also among the Victorians there was a double standard for the novel. The problem was not simply to establish the respectability and worth of novels by women but of the novel itself. The struggle was aesthetic primarily and sexist only secondarily. Dickens and Trollope, for all their enormous popularity, fought a losing battle to be received as more than entertainers, conveyors of "useful" social and moral truths delivered in the palatable form of fiction. Only Thackeray and, significantly, George Eliot achieved the stature of serious artists that was so readily granted to poets. *A Literature of Their Own* therefore has more bearing on the history of the novel than on the history of women's literature. When, for example, Showalter writes that at the close of the Feminine phase, around 1880, "a kind of richness was lost; a sense of intimacy and shared understanding between novelists and readers disappeared" (p. 181), she is making an important observation on the history of the popular novel. With the demise of the three-decker, monthly part serialization, and family reading (traced by Richard Altick, Guinevere Griest, and others) that intimacy and its rewarding richness did in fact disappear—a phenomenon of technology and sociology rather than a retreat on the part of the women novelists of the period.

Similarly, Showalter's fascinating survey of the sensation novel of the 1860s and 1870s, identifying women's remarkable contribution to this genre as an expression of Feminine protest (her chapter is called **"Subverting the Feminine Novel"**), shifts the balances arbitrarily. To be sure, the female characters of these "sexually provocative" novels show extraordinary capacity for evil and are strikingly different from the passive victim-heroines of the earlier Gothic novels (many of these also written by women). But are they, as she suggests, deliberate feminist challenges to traditional Victorian sex roles? The stereotypes of feminine docility and submissiveness were indeed coming under serious challenge, not in the conventional calculated violence of the sensation novel but in the growing realism of much mid- and late-Victorian fiction. The bold and "shocking" Jane Eyre fostered a generation of independent-spirited women in the work of men as well as women novelists—Meredith, Gissing, Moore. I am not convinced, even by Showalter's penetrating analysis of *Lady Audley's Secret,* that clever, industrious, but hardly subtle M. E. Braddon was subliminally undermining Victorian sexism. That she and Mrs. Henry Wood had "a large and desperate audience" (p. 173) of trapped, unhappily married women is probable (though not provable), but it was much the same audience that Dickens addressed with Louisa Bounderby and Edith Dombey; Thackeray with Clara, Barnes Newcome's wretched wife; Hardy with Eustacia Vye, or even, more lightly, Meredith with Clara Middleton running away from arranged marriage to the insufferable Willoughby Patterne. Nor were all the women characters in sensation novels by men "conventional in terms of their social and sexual attitudes" (p. 162). True, Collins made brave, gallant Marian Halcombe unfeminine and ugly and Laura Fairlie sweet and blonde, but he also created the glamorous and lethal Miss Gwilt of *Armadale* and the beautiful but unscrupulous Magdalene Vanstone of

*No Name.* And to stretch the point a bit, Thackeray's actually murderous Catherine and potentially murderous Becky Sharp are striking departures from Victorian stereotypes. The genre, I suspect, not the author's sex, dictated the terms.

The real value of *A Literature of Their Own* is its broad survey of the achievements of the neglected, so-called minor women novelists of the nineteenth and early twentieth centuries—M. E. Braddon, Sarah Grand, George Egerton, May Sinclair, Olive Schreiner, Dorothy Richardson. Showalter's recognition of their seriousness and importance, without undue inflation of their talents, is a real contribution to a critical history of the English novel. She is far less sound, however, with major figures like Charlotte Brontë and George Eliot. Her reading of *Jane Eyre* as a courageous but in the end compromising novel, with Jane achieving "as full and healthy a womanhood as the feminine novelists could have imagined" (p. 112), emphasizes "female sexual fantasy and eroticism" (p. 115), reducing Jane's stature from spiritual heroine to physiological woman. At ten, little rebel Jane is undergoing "emotional menarche" (p. 113) and flagellation. In her young womanhood, she is a divided soul, one half of her the submissive feminine spirit of Helen Burns, the other the bestial madwoman Bertha Mason. At best Jane can only make do with marriage to a mutilated and chastened Rochester because "in feminine fiction men and women become equals by submitting to mutual limitation, not by allowing each other mutual growth" (p. 124). Such a reading ignores the profound discoveries Jane makes in the course of the novel about herself and her relationship to her God, in her renunciation of Rochester ("I care for myself . . . I will keep the law given by God . . . I will hold to the principles received by me. . . ."), producing perhaps the most stirring affirmation of female autonomy in all literature. It also ignores Brontë's later *Villette* in which a man and woman fall in love precisely because they respect and cultivate each other's mutual growth.

Even more questionable is her dismissal of *The Mill on the Floss* as a novel that "elevates suffering into a female career" (p. 125). To read Maggie as a neurotic perversely returning home in search of punishment for her impulsive flight is to ignore the major theme of the novel—the powerful human instinct to return to the family. As weak Mrs. Tulliver, out of biological-maternal instinct, and narrow-minded Aunt Glegg, driven by a sense of family loyalty, rise to Maggie's defense when society (mainly male, including her own brother) repudiates her, George Eliot affirms a feminine solidarity that transcends sexism.

Psychology serves Showalter better when she turns from art to life. Her assessment of Virginia Woolf is original and convincing because it is based on the twentieth-century candor and self-exposure of the letters and memoirs of Woolf and her circle. She makes a strong case that Woolf's idealized conception of female aestheticism and androgyny was "a rationalization of her own fears" (p. 289) and sexual repression that produced, in her work, an enervated prose and an unreal vision. Woolf's "flight into androgyny," in Showalter's opinion, was a retreat: "The ultimate room of one's own is the grave" (p. 297).

In identifying woman's literature as a subculture, Elaine Showalter has cast much light on the shared experiences of their sex to which women writers necessarily respond differently from men, and some light on that literature itself. Women are only now beginning to realize their potential as novelists—not as crusaders, polemicists, literary breadwinners or self-conscious aesthetes. Yet the woman novelist today is at loose ends. Having defined a feminist sensibility in literature, she finds herself beyond protest and radical experiment. She is now a novelist and confronts problems imposed not by her sex but by the form itself. It is no longer a question of the survival of a feminine literary subculture, now that it has been identified and its status affirmed, but of the survival of the culture itself.

## Catherine Belsey (review date 28 March 1986)

SOURCE: Belsey, Catherine. "The Work of Womankind." *New Statesman* 111, no. 2870 (28 March 1986): 24-5.

[*In the following review of* The New Feminist Criticism: Essays on Women, Literature, and Theory, *Belsey examines the differences between American and British feminist criticism and asserts that more attention should be paid to the social construction of women's reality rather than to promoting a gender-inclusive "populist" canon.*]

Feminist criticism has come of age. Eighteen years on from Mary Ellman's *Thinking about Women,* these two collections of essays are elegant, accomplished and quite free from the (tomboyish?) high spirits that antagonised some women and electrified others in the early years. Feminist criticism is now ready to assume adult responsibilities. Confidently, fluently, readably, both *Making a Difference* [edited by Gayle Greene and Coppelia Kahn] and ***The New Feminist Criticism*** [edited by Showalter] reiterate the case for reading as a woman, point to the work that has already been done and define a series of projects for the future.

Both these volumes are predominantly American. Taken together, they give the impression that before the advent of feminism literary criticism was even more misogynistic there than it was here. Elaine Showalter reprints Nina Baym's witty analysis of the American literary canon as a series of 'melodramas of beset manhood'. In the Great American Novel man (and the sexist term is the appropriate one) seeks the freedom that comes from escaping the constraints of the social. In the end real men always light out, like Huckleberry Finn, for the Territory. Women, as agents of domestication and socialisation, try to hold them back. Meanwhile, however, the Territory too is identified as feminine—but this time in the right way. The wilderness invites conquest and once subdued it becomes compliant, nurturing, supportive.

Repeatedly these feminist critics insist that the American equivalent of the Great Tradition does not include a single woman author. British values have not been quite so overtly virile. Since the Thirties at least Jane Austen, the Brontës and George Eliot have been taken seriously. Of F. R. Leavis's four great English novelists two were women.

And yet courses on women's writing and feminist criticism are now much more common, more acceptable in the United States than they are here. Perhaps in the Home of Human Rights things were easier for the feminists? It was not hard to demonstrate that women writers had been systematically excluded from equal access to the pursuit of happiness. Harriet Beecher Stowe was not taken seriously; Kate Chopin was reviled; lesbians and black women had no voice at all. Among the feminist critics of the Seventies Showalter herself was one of the pioneers in giving back to women a literature of their own. Both these new volumes reaffirm and develop that project.

Was there, however, a price to pay for the success of feminist criticism in the States? The emphasis has been on reinstating writing by women, broadening the canon to include what has been repressed. Women's writing, varying with race, class and sexual orientation, is held to emanate from women's culture and is seen as expressive of women's experience. But, as Lilian Robinson points out in the Showalter collection, this project of inclusive pluralism doesn't go much beyond a new kind of populism and in a programme for the reorganisation of social relations populism doesn't go very far at all.

In this instance it leaves in place what seem to me some very dubious assumptions about literary criticism. One of these is the belief that fiction is a transcription of the author's experience of real life. Another is that the purpose of criticism is to evaluate the fiction and thus the experience. And yet another is that readers will in some not very clearly specified way derive benefit from the works of fiction prescribed by critics. These commonplaces have not proved very progressive in the past.

British feminist criticism, developing in a different cultural context, has tended to move in another direction. In Britain the sexist assumptions of conventional criticism, though no less powerful, have been at first glance less glaring. Women were included in the Great Tradition. But this was always on the unspoken condition that they were not treated as women. Similarly, the fact that Elizabeth Bennet, Jane Eyre and Dorothea Brooke were women also conventionally went unmentioned and their struggles for identity and independence in a patriarchal society were represented as the necessary process of learning to bring their unruly dispositions under moral control.

Obviously the sexism of the reading process was not to be transformed simply by putting more women authors on the syllabus and British feminism consequently took a rather different turn. The only one of these essays which I know to be British is Rosalind Coward's 'Are Women's Novels Feminist Novels?' in the Showalter collection. As the title indicates, Coward raises questions about the difference between being a female and being a feminist (between anatomy and politics) and between telling it (like it is, or otherwise) and intervening in it in order to change things. An essay about the politics of form, Coward's stands out from most of the others in its attention to writing itself, to the ways in which fiction addresses readers.

Ann Rosalind Jones, who writes in both volumes about French feminism, also displays the kind of political edge more familiar to feminists on this side of the Atlantic. 'We need,' she argues in the Showalter collection, 'to know how women have come to be who they are through history . . . and only then will we discover what women are or can be.'

And that perhaps is the point for a feminism which wants to move beyond populism towards a politics of change. In this context what women can be matters as much as what they have experienced. But what we take to be possible depends on how we understand both what we are and what history has made us.

Women's experience, at least as far back as it is documented, has been experience of or within patriarchal societies. To that extent it needs to be analysed as an effect of culture, not its origin. If women are better at personal relationships (and we are), if women are more caring and more compassionate (and we may be), we are so not only in the context of a patriarchal culture but also as a consequence of it. In the liberal West the place that has been allotted to women is precisely private, emotional, supportive and nurturing.

What more we can be is to some extent conjectural, but we can best discuss it on the basis of an analysis which firmly frees both women and men from the determinism of the natural. It is because experience is culturally produced that experience itself can change.

Feminism needs to recover women's writing. But it also needs to produce a historical and cultural analysis of the system of differences which has held women in place. Nelly Furman in the Greene and Kahn volume draws on new developments in critical theory to move in this direction. She argues that the institution of marriage, which depends on the affirmation of a polarity between men and women, serves as an analogy for a feminist criticism which finally reaffirms the position of women as the *opposite* sex. 'Women's writing' is always what is *not* men's writing, is always the transcription of an experience which is identified as inevitably other. This is not just 'making a difference': it's freezing it into place. Neither marriage nor the reinstatement of women's writing quite makes the break that will release us from the constraints of the stereotype.

**Patricia Meyer Spacks (review date 28 April 1986)**

SOURCE: Spacks, Patricia Meyer. "Crazy Ladies?" *New Republic* 194, no. 17 (28 April 1986): 34-6.

[*In the following review, Spacks commends Showalter's extensive knowledge and detailed accounts of psychiatric abuses in* The Female Malady: Women, Madness, and English Culture, 1830-1980, *but finds shortcomings in Showalter's myopic thesis and oversimplified interpretations.*]

Uncovering the sexual politics of British psychiatric history, Elaine Showalter tells an often lurid, sometimes blackly comic, usually surprising story [in *The Female Malady: Women, Madness, and English Culture, 1830-1980,*] that raises disturbing questions. England has a distinctive association with madness. In the early 18th century, Showalter reports, George Cheyne, a medical doctor, lent official sanction to popular belief by writing a book on insanity called *The English Malady.* Because of their climate (according to many Europeans) or their natural sensitivity (as Cheyne argued) the English were considered especially susceptible to mental disorders. The most vulnerable portion of this vulnerable population allegedly consisted of women, whose physical and psychic makeup presumably increased the likelihood of their descending into madness. From Ophelia to Sir Walter Scott's Lucy of Lammermoor (who murdered her bridegroom on their wedding night) to Doris Lessing's Lynda Coldridge (in *The Four-Gated City*), literary embodiments of female mania helped to solidify a mythology that both records and elucidates cultural attitudes toward Freud's "Dark Continent" of womanhood.

Showalter sets out to write "both a feminist history of psychiatry and a cultural history of madness as a female malady." A simple but plausible classification scheme allows her to organize a mass of social data into a coherent record of what might somewhat dubiously be called psychiatric progress. She sets this account of changing medical treatment in a context of literary and pictorial renditions of madness over a century and a half. Her story speaks to the well-nigh universal human fascination with those mysterious forms of otherness we have defined as madness; it also sheds light on a persistent pattern of unconscious abuse of women.

The last 150 years of psychiatric history, in Showalter's view, divide into three stages: psychiatric Victorianism, psychiatric Darwinism, and psychiatric modernism. The "Victorian" period in psychiatry (1830-1870) brought a new emphasis on possibilities of curing psychic illness by a kind of pseudo-domestic confinement: asylums aimed to "manage" madness, which was understood to originate in moral defect, by providing moral instruction. More obviously rigid in approach, the practitioners of "Darwinism" (1870-1920) saw lunacy as degeneracy stemming from "organic defect, poor heredity, and an evil environment." They offered stern prescriptions to protect society and to dictate proper behavior; women were their principal targets. The "modernist" phase arrived not immediately with Freud but with the First World War and its thousands of "shell-shocked" soldiers: male hysterics manifesting behavior often perceived as "feminine." Schizophrenia succeeded hysteria as the most frequent form of female disturbance, and the talking treatments sometimes seen as appropriate for soldiers yielded to more strictly medical remedies: psychosurgery, shock therapy, and drugs, all used heavily on women.

Showalter focuses her accounts of the three periods on individual medical practitioners of powerful influence, "*symptoms of the times,*" as R. D. Laing described himself. John Conolly, who presided over the superficially benign manifestations of Victorian psychiatry, attempted to make the madhouse a place of harmony. He eliminated the use of physical restraints in favor of moral suasion. Under his governance, such phenomena as the "lunatic's ball," during which inmates danced under the gaze of many spectators, flourished. Only slowly did the coercive aspects of Conolly's methods become apparent, as he himself increasingly revealed his reliance on "paternal authority."

The Victorian ideological setting encouraged paternalism. Women were thought delicate creatures, particularly susceptible at puberty and after child-birth, but always at emotional risk, endangered by biology and by their weak wills and dangerous impulses. Florence Nightingale's *Cassandra,* an account of Victorian women's confinement in "the prison which is called a family," indicates the high cost for women of their social deprivation as a result of society's assumptions about their natures; psychic disturbance, Nightingale suggests, was among those costs. "The rise of the Victorian madwoman," Showalter concludes, "was one of history's self-fulfilling prophecies."

With the advent of "Darwinism," psychiatrists sought to apply strict scientific method to the diagnosis and treatment of insanity. Henry Maudsley, Conolly's son-in-law (who explicitly and rather brutally repudiated his precursor), exemplifies the new way, harsh in its distinctions and fixed in its certainties. Showalter cites many instances of the new scientism, with its stress on physical signs of moral weakness. Certain women, one commentator concluded, "had the unfortunate hereditary combination of delicate skin, thin eyebrows, convex spine, and sharp tongue that made men unable to resist hitting them." Should the reader giggle or shudder? For a Victorian woman, shudders would be appropriate: this extreme example accurately suggests the misuses of allegedly objective research at the end of the 19th century. Meanwhile, "nervous women" proliferated: seeking education or political rights, unaccountably starving themselves, manifesting hysteria. Some doctors recommended enforced rest and milk drinking. (Charlotte Perkins Gilman's famous story "The Yellow Wallpaper" belongs to this period.) Others advocated ridicule, threats, and personal chastisement. Showalter, citing testimony by Virginia Woolf and Alice James as well as Gilman, concludes that "The nervous women of the *fin de siècle* were ravenous for a fuller life than their society offered them, famished for the freedom to act and to make real choices." The repressive tactics of physicians could not silence the voices of a generation of unhappy women.

Male hysteria became a social problem in the aftermath of the Great War. Officers and enlisted men alike suffered the psychic effects of combat. Psychiatric diagnosis, however, differentiated between them, finding that the hysterical soldier ("simple, emotional, unthinking, passive, suggestible, dependent, and weak") resembled his female counterpart, whereas the more complex officer better conformed to a heroic ideal. (Showalter accounts for the differentiation by suggesting that the enlisted man's actual situation of oppression corresponded to that of women.) Diverse methods of treatment developed. Dr. Lewis Yealland epitomized the punitive approach. **The Female Malady** provides a detailed and horrifying account of his procedures. Superficially far more benevolent was Dr. W. H. R. Rivers, who treated Siegfried Sassoon. Showalter demonstrates that he too "reprogrammed" his patients, using less obviously sinister methods.

The final section of this study dwells on the 20th-century situation of the female schizophrenic, whom Showalter sees as the symbolic figure of her age. R. D. Laing—whose career, personality, and ideology Showalter presents in considerable detail—emerges as the representative of a mid-20th-century therapy that proclaimed itself concerned with the dignity and rights of its recipients. Laing seems a benign successor to those who treated female mania with electric shocks, insulin shock, and lobotomies, but Showalter demonstrates the persistence in his language and his proceedings of a powerful "male mythology," potentially damaging to female psyches. Not until women speak for themselves, she believes, will psychiatric therapies truly answer women's needs. The vagueness of this formulation belongs to Showalter herself. She does not define the form women's "speaking" might take, although she alludes to new feminist theories based on the mother-daughter relationship. The book ends by insisting that

> the best hope for the future is the feminist therapy movement. . . . Until women break them for themselves, the chains that connect madness with the feminine, like Blake's "mind-forg'd manacles," will simply forge themselves anew.

This work lives most vividly in its specific detail; not even elaborate summary can convey the energy of its accumulated descriptive evidence. A full sense of Laing's "male mythology" requires his actual "metaphors of heroic adventure and conquest," his actual routine of presiding "sacerdotally" over dinner and dancing at his therapeutic community, Kingsley Hall. Showalter tells us exactly how women protesters were force-fed (and provides a photograph), how much weight women gained from insulin treatments, what biological results Victorian conservatives anticipated as a consequence of female demands for higher education. She writes with the authority of both conviction and knowledge. Her study profits by its multiplicity of data and by its singleness of thesis: the same message, about the endless, protean, inescapable social oppression of women, repeatedly and ingeniously hammered home.

Yet, like many single-minded works, it perhaps raises more questions than it answers. The monolithic thesis of persecution does not adequately account for the data. To say that "schizophrenic symptoms of passivity, depersonalization, disembodiment, and fragmentation have parallels in the social situation of women" in fact says little: one might observe with equal cogency that these symptoms have parallels in the social situation of factory workers. To observe that "the schizophrenic woman has become as central a cultural figure for the twentieth century as the hysteric was for the nineteenth" blurs together phenomena of very different sorts. If, as Showalter goes on to say, "psychotic women [in the 20th century] . . . speak for a revolutionary potential repressed in the society at large," the female psychotic as symbol might be seen as empowering for women instead of as one more vague emblem of appropriation and mistreatment.

To conclude that the feminist therapy movement offers hope for solving the problems of female madness is to ignore both physiological components and the possibility of causality relatively unrelated to a woman's social situation. The etiologies of madness that Showalter provides are simplistic in the extreme—less shocking to modern sensibilities than the Victorian physician's diagnosis of insanity for a woman who wished to leave her husband, but equally blinkered. Women go mad, this writer believes, because society leaves them so little room. But surely one must acknowledge other— *many* other—possibilities.

One of the most striking of the many remarkable photographs Showalter prints depicts a Victorian woman from the West Riding Asylum whom the medical director (also, in this instance, the photographer) characterizes as suffering from "Intense Vanity." Bedecked with flowers, ruffles, and a locket, she gazes fiercely at a point above the lens, her mouth compressed into a grimace of what looks like desperate rage. Showalter comments on her inappropriate garb, but not on the ferocity of her expression, which makes the frivolity of her costume and curls seem a futile attempt to disguise impermissibly violent feeling. The complex implications of her appearance suggest a range of interpretations unsanctioned and unacknowledged by the text; and the same may be said about others among the photographs. At least Showalter makes her readers aware of a politics of interpretation—and hence, perhaps inevitably, of the interpretive limitations of her own political commitment.

### Nancy Scheper-Hughes (review date 1987)

SOURCE: Scheper-Hughes, Nancy. Review of *The Female Malady: Women, Madness, and English Culture, 1830-1980*, by Elaine Showalter. *Women's Studies* 13, no. 4 (1987): 390-96.

[*In the following review, Scheper-Hughes praises the "original and exciting" subject material in* The Female Malady, *despite citing flaws in Showalter's analysis of schizophrenia.*]

Foucault's brilliant social history of western madness [*Madness and Civilization*, 1967] opens with a compelling image, Sebastian Brant's *Das Narrenschiff*, the "ship of fools", in order to fix in the reader's mind a picture of madness as it was prior to the "Enlightenment" when the insane still circulated freely through society on land and sea, their incessant babbling forming the backdrop of everyday language and experience. Similarly, Elaine Showalter opens her daring account of the recent history of English madness [*The Female Malady: Women, Madness, and English Culture, 1830-1980*] with Tony Robert-Fleury's painting of Philippe Pinel's freeing the insane at the Bicêtre and the Salpêtrière. The historical moment that Showalter wishes to fix in the minds of her readers is the late 18th century (the Age of Reason) when, she argues, the cultural representation of madness is transformed from a violently *male* to a sickly *female* condition.

Prior to the 19th century the dominant cultural image of lunacy is male—raving, violent, bestial, dangerous, something to be fettered and punished. Following the revolutionary ethos of the late 18th century and in the wake of the great mental health reformers like Philippe Pinel in France and John Connolly in England, the madman becomes viewed as less a criminal to be punished than as a pityful, wayward, and *sick* individual to be disciplined and treated. Correspondingly the prototypical mad*man* became the prototypical mad*woman*. Hence the famous painting in which Pinel and his associates, all sober, rational gentleman, dain to liberate the mournful, disheveled, but also lovely and seductive female lunatics of Bicêtre, turning them at one stroke from common criminals dangerous to the State into common mental patients dangerous mostly to themselves. In short, Professor Showalter gives us a history of the origins of modern psychiatry as a variety of discursive theories and practices with a single unifying theme: the medicalization of human misery, the suppression of one form of human resistance, and the negative representation of one sex: the female.

Although the social history of madness has been told many times, Showalter retells it through a feminist lens as a history of internal colonization in which the object of subjugation is women, both in cultural representation and in actual practice. This is not the first such account—a more passionate account appears earlier in Phyllis Chesler's *Women and Madness* (1972) and in Sandra Gilbert and Susan Gubar's more purely literary treatment of the subject in *The Madwoman in the Attic* (1979). The particular value of this book lies in the author's skillful blending of cultural history, literary criticism, and social science into a book that makes for absorbing, fascinating, very good reading indeed. My criticisms should not detract from the overall importance of this highly original, beautifully illustrated, and elegantly written work.

Showalter divides the history of modern psychiatry into three somewhat arbitrary and overlapping phases: "Psychiatric Victorianism" (1830-1870), roughly the period of "moral treatment" when "benevolent" forms of asylum confinement and work therapies predominated as treatment models; "Psychiatric Darwinism" (1870-1920), the period when organicist and bio-evolutionary theories and treatment models achieved pre-eminence in England and the United States; "Psychiatric Modernism" (1920-1980), the period corresponding to the rise (and fall) of Freudian psychoanalysis up through R. D. Laing's anti-psychiatry revolution. Unfortunately the author leaves out the return to organicist models and treatment with the discovery of psychotropic drugs in the 1950s and the consequent deinstitutionalization and community psychiatry movements beginning in the 1960s up through the present.

Showalter's argument concerning the "feminization" of madness in the 19th and 20th centuries is perhaps strongest and her evidence (statistical and iconographic) most compelling in her treatment of the first period. The public asylums of Victorian England indeed housed an excess of female patients, and the prevailing theories and treatment of madness evidenced a strongly patriarchal and androcentric bias. Model institutions were designed to instill in the hearts of unruly women female virtue and in their bodies a docile industriousness. "Moral Treatment" as it was practiced in the Victorian asylums became exemplary of the values and behaviors expected of women in the society at large. Hence, we readily see the origins of modern psychiatry as an institution of social control, and of psychiatrists as willing agents of the social consensus in the service of male hegemony.

With the spread of social Darwinism at the turn of the 19th century madness was recast as a problem in biological (rather than social) control requiring preventive measures (such as selective breeding) on the one hand, and social policing (such as the containment of physical and moral "degenerates" from the rest of society) on the other. Showalter argues that immigrants of tainted, lowly or uncertain stock, the disorderly lower classes, common criminals, *and women* were the primary targets of Psychiatric Darwinism. The inclusion of women in this context is rather forced and unconvincing. Certainly psychiatric hospital censuses from the United States, England, and Italy during this period would indicate that while the poor, disruptive, and disreputable social classes do crowd the back wards of public mental hospitals, these are in roughly equal distribution by sex, and in some instances male patients are in great "excess". As for the dominant cultural representation of madness under the organicist models of psychiatric Darwinism, it is most certainly *male*. The model of organic psychiatry during the period was the male tertiary syphilitic whose delirium, ataxia, and dementia were finally linked to a demonstrable, "true", organic cause. It is really only with respect to the psychiatric "treatment" of suffragette women during the first feminist revolution that we can see any link between psychiatric Darwinism and gender. While the psychiatric treatment of these angry female dissidents is an important case, the actual numbers of women affected by psychiatry in this way were, of course, rather small.

At the turn of the century the female malady *par excellence* was hysteria around which Freud developed his psychoanalytic psychiatry and his career. Showalter is on sure (if somewhat well-tred) ground here in asserting that for psychoanalysis at least the malady in question (i.e. the neurosis) was decidedly female, a response to the pathogenic physical and social circumstances of women's lives. However, it is unclear why the Freudian revolution is chronologically placed under the heading of "psychiatric Darwinism" rather than at the forefront of psychiatric Modernism (unless it was to bolster the argument for that earlier period for which the data are otherwise very weak in support of the "female malady" thesis).

By far the most original and exciting discussion in this book is to be found in the chapter on male hysteria with which the author opens the treatment of "Psychiatric Modernism". Showalter argues that Freud's discovery of the psychogenic origins of female hysteria was insufficient to reverse the tide of organicist thinking in psychiatry. To do so it would take World War I and the appearance of a new psychiatric phenomenon when tens of thousands of previously healthy and able-bodied soldiers were stricken with a neurotic malady that was first labeled "shell shock". When the search for an organic etiology failed, military psychiatrists were forced to conclude that what they had on their hands was more than 80,000 cases of a male neurosis that looked suspiciously similar to the more classic forms of *female* hysteria. The theories and treatments that followed demonstrated the great dismay that the medical profession experienced upon discovering that males were as prone as females to neurotic forms of mental breakdown. Insofar as their illness emasculated them, shell shock victims were treated by their psychiatrists as discredited men, as moral invalids and as latent homosexuals. Undoubtedly, contact with male hysteria brought out latent anxieties in some psychiatrists who, like Lewis Yelland tried to forceably inject the germ of masculinity back into their shell shock patients with the aid of electro-convulsive therapy. Perhaps this "treatment" was a remnant of an earlier homeopathic medical logic—shocks for the shell shocked! More "civilized" but equally compromising was the psychoanalytically-informed brainwashing engaged in by Dr. W. H. R. Rivers [incidentally a hero and founding father of my own sub-discipline of medical anthropology!] who sought to reprograme war resistors and conscientious objectors by convincing them, first of all, of their unstable mental condition. This chapter demonstrates, above all perhaps, the crucial significance of gender in psychiatric definitions of the normative. What is continuous throughout the history of modern psychiatry is an obsession with sexual and gender outlaws, *whether male or female.*

During the postwar years psychiatric interest turns away from female hysterics and male war neurotics toward the advancing problem of public mental health enemy #1: schizophrenia. Here Showalter's argument for a female representation of the disorder is weakest. Although stating that most epidemiological studies indicate a roughly equal incidence of the malady by sex, she nonetheless maintains that "schizophrenia offers a remarkable example of the cultural conflation of femininity and insanity" (p. 204) and she further asserts that "schizophrenia does carry gender-specific meanings" (*ibid.*) The author supports her assertions by reference to the "feminizing" treatments of schizophrenia: shock treatments, insulin coma therapy, lobotomy, all of them designed to render the disorderly, irrational schizophrenic quiet, docile, passive, in short, safely "female", as it were. Then, drawing on highly selective examples from modern literature, art and film (much of it American) Showalter argues that *female* insanity is the modern metaphor of all female experiences of claustrophobia, confinement, passivity, and control and of modern women's growing resistance to the conditions of, and constraints on, their lives.

The case for the "femaleness" of schizophrenia—indeed a master illness of our times—falters on several grounds. Statistically speaking there are pockets of western Europe and the British Isles (rural Ireland, for example) where male schizophrenics outnumber female schizophrenics in hospital two to one, and where consequently the popular cultural image of the malady is tied up with that of the inadequate *male* (*see* Scheper-Hughes, 1982). Moreover, the classic profile of the schizophrenic patient in the postwar psychiatric literature is that of the harried, dominated, or "double-binded" *son* persecuted by his "schizophrenogenic" *mother*. It is the men (or the boys) who *get* schizophrenia, and the females (especially the mothers) who *give* it according to this particular psychiatric morality tale. It is too bad that Dr. Showalter did not focus her astute and penetrating analytic skills on *this* gender-linked psychiatric and cultural myth of our times.

Moving to the representations of schizophrenia in the popular media one need only think, for example, of "Indian" in *One Flew over the Cuckoo's Nest* or the beleaguered paranoid schizophrenic son in Alfred Hitchcock's film, *Psycho,* to recall that male images of the malady have been as potent in the media as female images. And, in today's media reporting on the problem of the homeless mentally ill the plight of "grate gentleman" is as commonly portrayed as that of the proverbial "shopping bag lady". In all, Dr. Showalter's argument for the particularly female character of modern schizophrenia is less convincing and less intuitively true than R. D. Laing's argument for schizophrenia as metaphor of the "divided self" (male or female) in the post-modern, ego-dystonic, and nihilistic nuclear age.

Finally, I would also take issue with the author's brief epilogue in which she suggests that "the best hope for the future is the feminist therapy movement" (p. 249). Here Showalter falls prey to the very problem that she so compellingly describes at the start of her book—the "medicalization" of social distress *and* of resistance to that same distress. If the "female malady" is anything at all in the late 20th century it is most certainly that devil, depression which so many epidemiological studies indicate fills a particular female space—that of the young, poor or working class woman, without a job and confined at home with pre-school aged children and saddled to an emotionally immature and inadequate husband. The social and economic origins of the female malady—whether we are referring to Freud's upper middle class hysterics or to the 20th century female depressives—cannot be resolved by chemotherapy or by psychotherapy, feminist or otherwise. Only when private troubles are recognized for what they often are—social and historical ills—can appropriate, collective action be taken to remedy them.

*The Female Malady* is, nonetheless, an extraordinary *tour de force* of trans-disciplinary scholarship, a model of the great insights that literary criticism can bring to bear on the understanding and cultural analysis of a most vexing social problem.

ACKNOWLEDGEMENTS

The writing of this review followed fast on the heels of a lively evening study group discussion of the book in question with my colleagues Aihwa Ong, Judith Stacey, Debbi Rosenfelt and Estelle Freedman to whom I am indebted for pricking my conscience and stimulating these thoughts.

*References*

Chesler, Phyllis, *Women and Madness* (Garden City, New York; Doubleday, 1972).

Foucault, Michel, *Madness and Civilization* (New York: American Library, 1967).

Gilbert, Sandra and Susan Gubar, *The Madwoman in the Attic: The Woman Writer and the Nineteenth-Century Literary Imagination* (New Haven: Yale University Press, 1979).

Scheper-Hughes, Nancy, *Saints, Scholars and Schizophrenics: Mental Illness in Rural Ireland* (Berkeley: University of California Press, 1982).

### Linda Kauffman (review date winter 1987)

SOURCE: Kauffman, Linda. Review of *The New Feminist Criticism: Essays on Women, Literature, and Theory,* by Elaine Showalter. Signs 12, no. 2 (winter 1987): 405-09.

[*In the following excerpt, Kauffman offers a positive assessment of* The New Feminist Criticism, *but notes that the collection lacks any substantial analysis of film and French feminism.*]

> The great danger to avoid is the self-isolating nature of critical discourse.
>
> [Jean Starobinski]

> "Literature" is what gets taught.
>
> [Roland Barthes]

These four collections evoke distinct stages in the recent history of feminism: *Women's Personal Narratives* recalls the remarkable efficacy of grass-roots consciousness-raising in the early 1970s, and Elaine Showalter's introduction to *The New Feminist Criticism* reminds us that a female literary tradition was one of the hallmarks of feminist criticism in the late 1970s. Showalter argues that literary theory has always been a "zealously guarded bastion of male intellectual endeavor," whereas "the success of feminist criticism has opened a space for the authority of the woman critic" (3). In the 1980s, however, that approach has come to seem as insular as New Criticism was in its day. But, to Showalter's credit, some of the essays she selects reveal the enormous influence of theories of linguistics, semiotics, poststructuralism, psychoanalysis, and reader response. It is not a matter of merely appending feminism to an already existing body of theory. Rather the opposite: deconstruction and reader-response criticism have often been criticized for ignoring the historical and material aspects of lived existence, for a too-consuming preoccupation with language and signification at the expense of political change. Feminist theory, conversely, has long been praised for offering ways to combine analyses of language *and* politics, signifiers *and* referents. As Patrocinio P. Schweickart explains in *Gender and Reading*: "Reader-response criticism . . . overlook[s] the issues of race, class, and sex, and give[s] no hint of the conflict, sufferings, and passions that attend these realities. . . . To put the matter plainly, reader-response criticism needs feminist criticism. The two have yet to engage each other in a sustained and serious way, but if the promise of the former is to be fulfilled, such an encounter must soon occur" (35-36).

Thus, in the mid-1980s, dialogic and dialectical theoretical models are flourishing in feminist literary criticism, and a number of surprising encounters occur in these collections. *Rewriting English,* for instance, is thoroughly grounded in the British tradition of socialism and Marxist criticism, but it criticizes socialism's traditional exclusion of women and Marxist literary criticism's unexamined assumptions about the relation of literature to life. *Women's Personal Narratives* could analyze those assumptions more vigorously than it does, but it nevertheless includes some interesting exercises in demystifying literature and the writing process and in giving the silent, the powerless, the disenfranchised a voice.

All four collections, indeed, share a common commitment to empowering through discourse: we hear the voices of freshmen, graduate men and women, older women in adult education, and modern teenage schoolgirls in England. They all tell us much about the struggle for and the power that comes from discourse. What emerges is a remarkable polyphony: far from pluralistic, yet committed to certain shared political goals of feminism.

Two dominant issues unite the four books. The first is dismantling the objectivist illusion. By this I mean that distinctions between "high" literature and "low" literature have (mercifully) disappeared. The pedestal for Literature was never as suffocating or as inaccessible as the one that used to confine Woman, but it was still a sterile, isolated place. In *Women's Personal Narratives,* Leonore Hoffman notes, "As texts become more than objects of aesthetic interest, the forms of discourse appropriate for study become more various" (2). In all four of these collections, that infinite variety is everywhere apparent: in the actual letters, diaries, and journals, as well as the oral testimonies, of everyday women who are the subjects and authors of personal narratives; in the analyses of childhood reading, gothic romances, and recent women's bestsellers in *Gender and Reading*; in the analyses of male as well as female romances in *Rewriting English*; and in the analyses of black women's literature, lesbian fiction, and nineteenth- and twentieth-century American bestsellers in *The New Feminist Criticism.* The aesthetic object is no longer a fetish; verbal icons have been shattered and Literature must now be studied as one among many discursive practices worthy of sustained intellectual analysis: that is the first result of dismantling the objectivist illusion.

Another result concerns interpretation: academic criticism traditionally claimed to transcend ideology, to be disinterested, apolitical, rationally objective. Feminist theory put the nails in the coffin; with poststructuralism, with the fusion in France of linguistics and psychoanalysis, and with reader-response criticism, the corpse began to stink. We now recognize that the most dangerous ideologues are those who refuse to recognize their own ideological biases.

The second issue uniting these four collections is reading as a political act. All four texts discuss how reading, rather than transcending ideology, is in fact a major weapon in its dissemination. *Rewriting English* offers the most comprehensive (and the most theoretical) historical overview of this phenomenon. The interrelations between the growth of literacy and the rise of empire reveal that "'English literature' was born, as a school and college subject, not in England but in the mission schools and training colleges of Africa and India" (23). From the eighteenth century onward, Literature—not history, not science, not technical training, but a proper explication of English literary classics—was the tool of indoctrination into "culture," the only way to stave off the inevitable "anarchy" of interests based on class, race, or sex.

Is the canon a pragmatic instrument or an abstract concept? All four of these texts demonstrate that it is both: such powerful abstractions as "universality" and "humanism"—as well as "femininity"—are the foundations upon which pragmatic strategies of oppression are built. *The New Feminist Criticism* is particularly valuable for its multivalent response to such issues. Many of the essays are now classics in their own right, and it is a pleasure to have them collected in one volume: Sandra M. Gilbert's "What Do Feminist Critics Want? A Postcard from the Volcano"; Nina Baym's "Melodramas of Beset Manhood"; Jane P. Tompkins's "Sentimental Power: Uncle Tom's Cabin and the Politics of Literary History"; and Lillian S. Robinson's "Treason Our Text" all challenge the contingencies of value upon which the canon rested and the academy slumbered. Part 2, on "Feminist Criticisms and Women's Cultures," includes Deborah E. McDowell's essay on black feminist criticism and Bonnie Zimmerman's overview of lesbian feminist criticism. Rosalind Coward's superb theoretical essay on women's bestsellers makes one yearn for an essay that would incorporate her research interests on language, materialism, and visual communication. (The absence of any work on feminist film studies is a pity.) Part 3, on "Women's Writing and Feminist Critical Theories," includes work by Susan Gubar, Nancy K. Miller, and Alicia Ostriker. French feminisms, however, are underrepresented; Ann Rosalind Jones's essay on "Writing the Body" could have been supplemented by a post-structuralist analysis of the canon and the academy, such as Peggy Kamuf's "Replacing Feminist Criticism" (*Diacritics* 12 [Summer 1982]: 42-47). . . .

Who speaks, and by what authority? The dialogic and dialectical models of feminist theory in the 1980s confront these complex questions. Strategies to empower numerous speaking subjects, to instill a "powerful literacy," are outlined in these four texts. The capacity for self-critique (for which feminist criticism is justly renowned) is as vital as ever in these four volumes. Dismantling the objectivist illusion, reconstructing literary history, and rereading and rewriting English all ensure that neither the canon nor the academy will ever rest again.

## Nancy Tomes (review date February 1987)

SOURCE: Tomes, Nancy. Review of *The Female Malady: Women, Madness, and English Culture, 1830-1980,* by Elaine Showalter. *American Historical Review* 92, no. 1 (February 1987): 131-32.

[*In the following review of* The Female Malady, *Tomes commends Showalter's provocative cultural analysis, but finds shortcomings in her exaggerated premise and flawed historical interpretation of women's psychiatric treatment.*]

[In *The Female Malady: Women, Madness, and English Culture, 1830-1980,*] Elaine Showalter, a feminist literary critic, has set out to write a "feminist history of psychiatry and a cultural history of madness as a female malady" (p. 5). Analyzing medical and literary texts as well as photographs and paintings, she traces the conception and treatment of women's insanity through three phases of English psychiatry: psychiatric Victorianism (1830-70), psychiatric Darwinism (1870-1920), and psychiatric modernism (1920-80). Showalter's central premise is that a "feminization" of madness took place in the nineteenth century; women not only became the primary recipients of psychiatric treatment but also served as the cultural exemplars of madness. She also argues that, until very recently, psychiatrists treated female patients within the context of a restrictive femininity that was itself the origin of their psychological demoralization. Showalter concludes that women have begun to break "the chains that make madness a female malady" only in the past few decades, with the rise of a feminist therapy movement (p. 350).

The book makes a powerful case for the influence of gender on psychiatric conceptions and treatment of female patients. But Showalter pushes her argument too far in according the madwoman such an exclusive hold on the psychiatric imagination. Her perspective greatly exaggerates the extent to which psychiatrists have viewed insanity as a peculiarly female complaint or regarded women as their primary clientele. (One suspects she is projecting backward the relatively recent tendency for women to seek psychotherapy in far greater numbers than men.) Given the numerical predominance of women over men in the general population and the tendency of women to live longer, the slight majority of women in nineteenth-century English asylums—54 percent in 1872, according to her own data—hardly seems to constitute a "feminization" of the asylum. Further, nineteenth-century psychiatrists differed considerably more over the relative liability of the sexes to insanity than Showalter's analysis implies.

Ironically, in a book about women and madness, the best chapter focuses on male "shell-shock" victims in World War I and the female novelists who appropriated the soldiers' experience as a symbol of their own psychic helplessness and repression. But Showalter's assertion that "the Great War was the first, and, so far, the last time in the twentieth century that men and the wrongs of men occupied a central position in the history of madness" suggests a highly selective and ultimately inaccurate reading of the sources (p. 194).

Showalter's considerable skills as a literary critic are simply unequal to the complexity of her topic. She is at her best when treating the cultural representations of female madness, such as the Ophelia convention in psychiatric literature, Hugh Diamond's highly stylized photographs of female asylum inmates, and women's fictional accounts of madness. When she moves from cultural representations to the reality of psychiatric institutions, her analysis falters. Still, Showalter's work raises valuable questions about the power of gender as a determinant of psychiatric treatment. However much one may disagree with some of her conclusions, Showalter's book should provoke a fresh examination of this significant but neglected topic.

**Dierdre Bair (review date 2 September 1990)**

SOURCE: Bair, Dierdre. "End-of-the-Century Birth Throes." *Los Angeles Times Book Review* (2 September 1990): 12.

[*In the following review, Bair praises Showalter's amusing and informative discussions in* Sexual Anarchy: Gender and Culture at the Fin-de-Siècle.]

Elaine Showalter is a distinguished feminist critic whose new book, **Sexual Anarchy,** is a provocative comparison of the last years of the 19th Century (the *fin de siècle*) with the final decade of our own. Her view is optimistic, as she chooses to view the 1990s as "the embryonic stirrings of a new order, a future that is utopian rather than apocalyptic." She soundly rejects the idea that our century's "terminal decade" is in "the death throes of a diseased society and the winding down of an exhausted culture."

In effect, she is agreeing that history is indeed doomed to repeat itself, and even though we have begun the 1990s describing the decade with words like exhaustion, malaise, epidemic and violence, (pretty much the same terms as were used in the 1890s), we can cheer ourselves up if only by thinking back to the early years of this century and the renewal and change inspired by *modernism* and all that the term has come to mean.

Showalter, chairperson of the department of English at Princeton and a specialist in Victorian literature, has written what might well be called a "crossover" book; that is, one that is solidly grounded in a vast range of scholarship but also informative and appealing to a general audience. She describes the book she has written as being about the "myths, metaphors and images of sexual crises and apocalypse that marked both the late 19th Century and our own . . . and its representations in English and American literature, art and film."

Her book is primarily a study of the great writers of the 19th Century (and this is where it most satisfies), but her stated aim is to treat the "images rather than issues" and to show how fiction reflects the historical development of sexuality through comparisons with contemporary novels and films. A quick glance at some of her chapters will give an idea of how she goes about this.

To discuss women's options, for example, she uses George Gissing's *The Odd Women* (published in 1891) to represent those who for whatever reason could not or would not marry, who "undermined the comfortable binary system of Victorian sexuality and gender roles." Comparing this to Gail Godwin's *The Odd Woman* (1975), she makes the point that "representations of the single woman do not seem to have changed much since the *fin de siècle*."

Showalter reinforces her view by contrasting Henry James' 1886 novel about the condition of women, *The Bostonians,* with the 1984 Merchant & Ivory film version that starred Vanessa Redgrave and Christopher Reeve. Although she finds James' view of unmarried women harsh, she views the film as "even less optimistic about the prospects of the modern odd woman," and from that she glides gracefully into a discussion ranging from articles in the *New York Times Magazine* ("Why Wed? The Ambivalent American Bachelor") to serious feminist studies such as Andrea Dworkin's *Intercourse,* which states flatly that "sexual intercourse is the basis and symbol of women's oppression." Throughout this chapter, Showalter roams authoritatively through British, American and even Continental history and culture, citing examples from Punch to Havelock Ellis and Freud to sustain her views.

Showalter both amuses and informs in her discussion of how the realism of "Queen George" (Eliot) led naturally to the great male "King Romance" writers: Kipling, H. Rider Haggard, Robert Louis Stevenson. Again, she makes some nice ironic points by contrasting Kipling's *The Man Who Would Be King* with John Huston's 1975 film of the same name starring Michael Caine and Sean Connery.

This allows her to glide into an explication of one of the most important novels of the turn of the century, Joseph Conrad's *Heart of Darkness,* which she rightly sees as "an exposé of imperialism and an allegory of male bonding and the flight from women." Then she contrasts Conrad's novel with Francis Ford Coppola's film version, *Apocalypse Now,* much of which is filtered through the perceptions of Eleanor Coppola's journal about how the film was made on location in the Philippines.

Showalter also buttresses her literary musings with examples from her own experience. She relates the fussing, fuming and foibles of academic conferences with a light, ironic touch, and her account of participating in a New York City "porn tour" with the group Women

Against Pornography is harrowing simply because much of what she saw is on the one hand so ordinary and banal, on the other so upsetting.

She makes serious comparisons of the great fear syphilis inspired in the 19th Century and the terror that AIDS has produced in our own, but she ends her discussion with a fine note of optimism. If we consider the history of syphilis, she argues, we can be confident that some medical miracle will come along to end the AIDS epidemic as well. Showalter shares the British feminist critic Lynn Segal's belief that fighting this disease (and by extension, all other social injustices and afflictions) will do away with "evasion and hypocrisy around sex," and thus will lead naturally to "more equal sexual relations between women and men and the recognition of sexual diversity." Then and then only, Showalter agrees, can "the sexual revolution begin in earnest."

She begins and ends her book with a paragraph about the Génitron, the huge time machine that hangs above the entrance to the Musée Beaubourg in Paris, counting down the final years, minutes and seconds of our century. To stand in front of the Génitron is both awe-inspiring and frightening. Most viewers describe themselves as being almost paralyzed in the face of time's swift and relentless ticking away, but Showalter, as she does throughout the book, chooses to regard the inexorable passage of time positively.

Just as time cannot be stopped or turned back, neither in her analogy should we "legislate or intimidate men and women into the shame and repression of the past." Fear, she argues, should not "push us into a cruel homophobia, make us abandon our commitment to women's sexual autonomy."

Although some may view our present-day society as a kind of "frightening sexual anarchy," for her, it is "the birth throes of a new sexual democracy."

## Julie Wheelwright (review date 29 March 1991)

SOURCE: Wheelwright, Julie. "Odd Women." *New Statesman and Society* 4, no. 144 (29 March 1991): 29-30.

[*In the following review, Wheelwright lauds the "fundamental questions" raised by* Sexual Anarchy: Gender and Culture at the Fin-de-Siècle, *but notes that the work focuses too heavily on the Victorian era.*]

The final decades of a century often spawn apocalyptic fantasies, doom-sayers and outlandish prophets. Like the anti-nuclear scientists' vision of the world at "two minutes to mid-night", we fear that time, for our species, is not only finite, but rapidly running out. If death by chemical warfare or terrorist sabotage during the Gulf war wasn't enough to worry about, mad cow disease, burning oil wells, the greenhouse effect and homelessness continue to haunt us. As Angela Carter recently noted, "the *fin* is coming a little early this *siècle*."

For many social critics, sexual anxieties are masked as end-of-the-century worries. Tory party pundits decry the breakdown of the family, laying the blame for falling education standards and rising Aids statistics on the permissive society. The American right condemns the women's movement and gay rights, drug epidemics, satanism and the decline of religion for causing the nation's ills.

None of this future-fear is new. George Gissing once described the 1880s and 1890s as decades of "sexual anarchy", when the laws governing sexual identity and behaviour were in tatters. "In periods of cultural insecurity, when there are fears of regression and degeneration," writes Princeton literary critic Elaine Showalter in **Sexual Anarchy,** "the longing for strict border controls around the definition of gender, as well as race, class and nationality, becomes especially intense."

Tackling the neuroses of two generations across continents is a dauntingly ambitious project. But Showalter has produced a triumph; a highly readable volume on the myths, metaphors, and images of sexual crises and apocalypse that shaped both the late 19th-century, and our own, nightmares. The book gleams with wit and wry insight as Showalter unravels the constructs of late-Victorian and late-Thatcherian morality.

Drawing on literary sources, she reveals how the metaphors of death and rebirth are projected onto a century's final decades. In revolutionary periods, argues Showalter, the fear of social and political equality between the sexes generates opponents bent on establishing scientific proof for the absolute mental and physical differences between the sexes. To the Victorians, sexual anarchy began with the Odd Woman who disrupted the neat binary system of Victorian sexuality and gender roles by refusing to marry.

These maligned women (*Punch* cartoonists revelled in portraits of po-faced spinsters in trousers and tie) were constructed as a new political and social group. Emerging definitions of female sexuality revealed that women had desires equal to men; abstinence would result in the "evil" of masturbation or, worse, lesbianism. Victorian women, raised to believe in spiritual and physical passivity, found these scientific and social views difficult to reconcile. Newly publicised traumas of sexual abuse furthered feminists' view that sex was not just male-defined, but *male,* prompting women to claim the high moral ground as asexual crusaders.

The mannish female orator, whose repressed sexuality finds devious outlets in manipulating a younger, passionate disciple, became a popular satiric figure in novels. According to Showalter, Gissing's *The Odd Women* (1891) was typical in its exploration of feminist celibacy, "womanliness" and sexual repression, while submerging a male agenda about competition with women for power and speech. His archly named character Rhoda Nunn, a self-proclaimed Odd Woman, fiercely opposes marriage as an institution and believes her celibacy gives her power.

Rhoda, however, succumbed to the charms of a cynical ex-radical Everad Barfoot, allowing Gissing to hint that sexuality and loss were necessary for a compassionate social movement. Showalter's insistence that the gender crisis affected both men and women, resulting not in a battle *between* the sexes but a battle *within* the sexes, allows for a sophisticated reading of the period. Even social writers such as Gissing embodied the contradictions of a "woman-worshipping misogynist with an interest in female emancipation".

The New Woman, who insisted on sexual independence and rejected marriage, was threatening even to the Victorian radicals. To the world, she was "an anarchic figure who threatened to turn the world upside down and to be on top in a wild carnival of social and sexual misrule". In reality, the New Women such as Eleanor Marx and the South African Oliver Schreiner were cruelly disappointed in attempts to live out their ideals for a more equal relationship.

Eleanor Marx, daughter of Karl, established her own sexual rules with her lover Edward Aveling, with whom she wrote *The Woman Question* (1886). Their union was to be the model for a future of free men and women, but when Marx discovered Aveling's secret marriage to a younger woman, she killed herself. She was only 43. Oliver Schreiner, the South African writer and close friend of Marx, fared little better. After a series of self-destructive relationships with radical men, including Havelock Ellis and Karl Pearson, she concluded that, until New Man was educated to appreciate the love of free women, she was doomed to celibacy and loneliness.

While women of all political persuasions were left to fight their battles without much support, men could escape to Clubland. Showalter skillfully analyses 19th-century male romance writers whose fiction, like their clubs, offered a haven from bourgeois domestic life. While clubland supported respectable bachelorhood, perpetuating endless boyhood for some, the novels embraced the hearty male bonding that thinly distinguished "manly misogyny from disgusting homoeroticism".

Rudyard Kipling, G H Henty, Rider Haggard and Robert Louis Stevenson created adventures that enabled Victorian gentlemen safely to explore homoeroticism. These writers quickly occupied the vacuum George Eliot left for women novelists, who had dominated the literary scene until her death in 1880. Symbolically, the boys got their own back at Queen/Mother/George. "One defence against the mother's reign is to appropriate her power by repressing the maternal role in procreation and creation," writes Showalter, "and replacing it with a fantasy of self-fathering."

So doubling, cloning, reproduction and self-replication provided a focus for best-selling male romances. Rider Haggard's sensational success *She,* which sold more than 300,000 copies, featured a mysterious African kingdom ruled by an immortal white queen, Ayesha. Holly, a Cambridge don whose hatred of women endows him with intellectual prestige, raises his widowed friend's son, Leo (hence the theme of male reproduction). When Leo reaches adulthood, they venture to Kor, the heart of Africa, in search of his real mother, the reincarnated priest of Isis or She.

Written in 1881, the year that women were first admitted to Cambridge exams, the story is a quest for the mythical Mother who holds the secret of life, with the goal of appropriating her power. Tricked into entering a pillar of fire, Ayesha ages 2,000 years in two minutes. Leo and Holly make their escape to experience their "joint life" somewhere in Tibet, where no women will find them.

Showalter often compares such loaded literary figures with their Hollywood counterparts. Although the film analysis is intriguing, the 19th-century novelists' replacement by (mostly male) film producers raises fundamental questions about how popular culture is packaged and received. The book also seems lop-sided at times, with the Victorians given the lion's share of analysis.

The final chapter returns neatly to the image of the Genitron at the Pompidou Centre in Paris, ticking away our—final—hours. Showalter ends on a powerful, optimistic note; a reminder that psychologically imposed endings are merely part of a mutable reality. But will our *fin-de-siècle,* wracked with pain, blossom onto Showalter's vision of a new sexual equality?

Stay tuned.

## Sara Maitland (review date 6 April 1991)

SOURCE: Maitland, Sara. "The Way They Were Then, Too." *Spectator* 266, no. 8491 (6 April 1991): 28.

[*In the following review of* Sexual Anarchy: Gender and Culture at the Fin-de-Siècle, *Maitland finds shortcomings in Showalter's emphasis on popular male, rather than female, writers and her premature effort to draw parallels between the 1890s and the 1990s.*]

I am a fan of Elaine Showalter's, and have been since *A Literature of Their Own*—a study of women writers, particularly novelists, through the 19th century up until the creation of the present phase of the Women's Liberation Movement. I am a fan because she seems to have read everything and her readings are solid responses to actual novels based within feminist theory and within a historical social reality. Moreover, she writes about books so that you want to read them too.

In all these senses **Sexual Anarchy** does not disappoint. Showalter suggests a neatly packaged set of parallels between the 1880s and 1980s and the 1990s and . . . well that is a problem. We have not had a lot of the 1990s yet; and though we doubtless will, the book has an awkward shift to make between reportage and prophesy. Nonetheless, given that inevitable constriction, the parallels are there—'feminism' and 'homosexuality,' as words, were invented in the 1880s. They were created to meet a social need: a radical attempt to redefine the concepts of masculinity and femininity, of which women's suffrage and Oscar Wilde's trial were memorable moments. Then, as now, challenges to these quite abstract concepts were seen as a dangerous threat to 'the family'. Syphilis, like Aids now, was seen as both punishment for vice, and a danger to the nation. The 'art for art's sake', or 'decadent' movement has close connections with post-modernist practice, and establishment responses show remarkably little change.

What Showalter does best is place really very careful analyses of individual texts within an accessible historical narrative. Her reading of Rider Haggard's *She*, for example, is not radically different from other feminist readings (e.g. Gilbert and Gubar), but the book and the author are so well located within the literary and social history of their time that the analysis (briefly, that the male *Boy's Own* adventure stories of the time recount homophile desires to escape from the threat of the female) actually makes much better sense.

This sort of handling works particularly impressively with middle-brow popular books: *Dr Jekyll and Mr Hyde, Dracula,* and *She,* where some nerve of common feeling is touched and there is continuing evidence of a mass response—in imitations, repetitions, films, etc. And this may explain why, despite Showalter's best efforts, her book often seems to deal more with male writers and the male responses to the challenges of gender meaning than it does with women and their work. After the death of George Eliot—as Showalter is at pains to point out—male writers were liberated but many women seem to have lost their way. Earlier in the 19th century, novel writing was deemed to offer chances of equality for women in terms of prestige and readership, and long-term influence (*Frankenstein,* for example, very much a woman's fantasy, has created a sub-literature as strong as *Dracula*). But in this period—although we are offered many glimpses of serious and engaged women novelists, there seems no enduring female equivalents to Stevenson, Haggard, Kipling, and Wilde. (Male manipulation or female deficiency?) And, of course, when looking at contemporary work, it is difficult to tell yet which novelists of the last ten years will have that sort of effect on cultural production.

Perhaps Showalter might have strengthened her case by delving lower down the scale of popular culture. Surely there are interesting parallels to be found in the rise of the female music-hall comedienne in the 1880s and 90s, (many of whom, like Marie Lloyd and Vesta Tilley, either attacked or satirised gender roles and expectations in complex and subtle ways), and the popular women TV comics of today—Roseanne Barr, Victoria Wood, and Bette Midler. Comparative studies of male uses of performance in drag and camp, outside the gay community, would also seem worth exploring. On the other side, religious revival in the form of millennialist sects and puritan Christianity, also suggest cultural similarities between the 1890s and 1990s.

It is never quite fair to criticise a book for not being about what it isn't about, but there is an ethical sub-text to this volume which is interesting. Showalter, despite being open about the profound conflict between New Women and what might be called new men during the last *fin de siècle,* nonetheless wants to suggest that this time, this *siècle,* we might get it right, forge a new alliance, break the boundaries of past failure. She ends her book on a high rhetorical note:

> What seem today like apocalyptic warnings of a frightening sexual anarchy may be really the birth throes of a new sexual equality.

Indeed, I hope she may be right. But I fear we are going to need to move beyond the confines of the middle-class novel if we want either to prove it is happening, or (given that we have nine-and-a-half years) to make it happen.

### Pamela Young (review date 20 May 1991)

SOURCE: Young, Pamela. "A New Sexual Order." *Maclean's* 104, no. 20 (20 May 1991): 68.

[*In the following review, Young praises Showalter's central arguments in* Sexual Anarchy: Gender and Culture at the Fin-de-Siècle, *calling the work "provocative" and "eloquent."*]

The twilight of the 20th century is deepening beneath an overcast sky. In the current era of AIDS, economic decline and environmental decay, it is perhaps natural to wonder whether the world is plunging into unending night. In an intriguing new book, Elaine Showalter, head of English at Princeton University, points out that the same dire speculation shadowed the last two decades of the 19th century—for some of the same reasons. In *Sexual Anarchy: Gender and Culture at the Fin-de-Siècle,* the feminist author focuses on late-19th- and late-20th-century responses to such issues as women's rights, homosexuality and sexually transmitted diseases. And she concludes that, on the sex-and-gender front at least, there is room for cautious optimism. "What seems today like the apocalyptic warnings of a frightening sexual anarchy," she writes, "may be really the birth throes of a new sexual equality."

Showalter argues that *fin-de-siècle* periods seem especially portentous because societies tend to graft metaphors of death and rebirth onto the years at the end of centuries. She notes that, like the present, the last 20 years of the 19th century struck many observers as a time when "all the laws that governed sexual identity and behavior seemed to be breaking down." The period saw the rise of educated, sexually independent females known as New Women, and of the so-called Decadents, homosexual writers and artists who included Oscar Wilde and Aubrey Beardsley. Syphilis, meanwhile, was the sexual scourge of the day, spreading death and fear. Then, as now, Showalter writes, there was a backlash of "social purity campaigns" and "demands, often successful, for restrictive legislation and censorship."

*Sexual Anarchy* is a wide-ranging book, one that interweaves social history and the portrayal of the sexes in literature and other art forms. Early chapters deal with the public unease generated by the emergence of feminists and New Women. Showalter quotes the British journalist William R. Greg, who was alarmed by the increasing number of unmarried women in the early 1870s. Writing in the *Westminster Review,* Greg observed that the statistics were "indicative of an unwholesome social state." In the late 20th century, Showalter observes, single women have gained greater acceptance—but, in all sorts of subtle and not-so-subtle ways, they are still being warned against competing with men. She cites as an example the 1987 film *Fatal Attraction,* a cautionary tale that "makes its psychotic villain an elegant woman editor, while the 'good' woman is a nonworking wife and mother in jeans."

Showalter's book is as much about relations *within* the sexes as between the sexes. Some of its most provocative ideas pertain to relationships among men in the late 19th century. In Victorian times, a network of men's clubs provided husbands, fathers and bachelors from various social classes with alternatives to domestic life. "*Fin-de-siècle* Clubland," Showalter writes, "existed on the fragile borderline that separated male bonding from homosexuality."

The author makes a fascinating case for interpreting Robert Louis Stevenson's *The Strange Case of Dr. Jekyll and Mr. Hyde* (1886) as "a fable of *fin-de-siècle* homosexual panic, the discovery and resistance of the homosexual self." Unable to form a romantic attachment with a woman or another man, Henry Jekyll "divides himself, and finds his only mate in his double, Edward Hyde." Jekyll's eventual suicide, Showalter argues, was "the only form of narrative closure thought appropriate to the Gay Gothic, where the protagonist's death is both martyrdom and retribution."

Above all else, *Sexual Anarchy* is an eloquent plea to respond to the sexual crises of the late 20th century with clear-headedness rather than panic, and with tolerance rather than repression. Showalter points out that while mainstream 19th-century society feared both New Women and the homosexual Decadents, the two minorities also tended to fear and mistrust each other. Even in the late 20th century, she adds, relations between feminists and lesbians on one hand and gay men on the other have often been strained. But with the advent of the AIDS epidemic, the groups appear to be learning how to "fight against the disease and not each other."

Showalter's book has its faults. In particular, she occasionally falls prey to the academic's vice of reading excessively elaborate symbolism into literary passages. But on the whole, *Sexual Anarchy* is a fine piece of work—and even an uplifting one. "If we can learn something from the fears and myths of the past," she writes, "it is that they are so often exaggerated and unreal, that what looks like sexual anarchy in the context of *fin-de-siècle* anxieties may be the embryonic stirrings of a new order." In other words, centuries end, life goes on, and change *can* actually be for the better.

## Helen Carr (review date 27 September 1991)

SOURCE: Carr, Helen. "Patchwork Quilt." *New Statesman and Society* 4, no. 170 (27 September 1991): 54.

[*In the following review, Carr compliments Showalter's research and analysis in* Sister's Choice: Tradition and Change in American Women's Writing, *but faults Showalter's romanticized notion of female community and virtue.*]

*Sister's Choice* is, so to speak, the American sister of Elaine Showalter's first book, *A Literature of Their Own,* which traced a distinctive literary tradition through British women writers of the 19th and 20th centuries. Her argument then was that women formed a subculture, and their writing had to be interpreted like that of other literary subcultures. It was not the story of the classics alone: the rediscovery of forgotten and disparaged female writing was an essential part of drawing the historical line.

*A Literature of Their Own* was a landmark of feminist criticism. Yet, as Showalter says at the beginning of *Sister's Choice,* although critics took issue with her feminist arguments, nobody commented on the oddity of an American writing about British women novelists as if she shared *their* culture. Now, 14 years later, she has turned to her native land, but it has not been "an easy reclamation". She wants to extend the practice of what she has since named "gynocriticism"—the study of women's writing—to American literature. Yet terms that would have seemed simple unities 14 years ago—like "women" and "American"—have broken into fragments before her eyes.

The earlier book had a clear historical outline. Women's writing, Showalter argued, followed the three stages of other subliteratures: imitation of the dominant culture, protest against it, and self-discovery—which she named feminine, feminist, and female.

The structure of this new book is very different. A postmodernist gale has played havoc with the terrain. But postmodernism is not a concept Showalter invokes: the book perhaps is best described through the metaphor she uses for American women's writing, that of the patchwork quilt, to which *Sister's Choice,* a quilt pattern, refers. In her first chapter she lays out the ripped up pieces and scraps that she must work with. In those following, she tries out different patterns in which these hybrid pieces can be sewn together.

Showalter doesn't abandon her idea of the subculture, but knows it must become a much more complex one. Issues of race and class have splintered the notion of "woman" and of "the American": the writing of history has become a deeply problematic kind of fiction. She describes Americans as the possessors of the first postcolonial literature, following that same trajectory of imitation, protest, and self-discovery. Further sub-groups (women, black women) within America infinitely repeat the process. In some chapters, using Homi Bhabha's description of cultures as "symbol-forming" practices, she explores recurring symbols in women's writing—Miranda, the quilt, Gothic horror: in others, she traces out a more tentative but specifically American history of women's writing, from the celebration of the "women's sphere" in the pre-Civil War years to the contemporary international influence of writers like Alice Walker.

Once again she has uncovered an extraordinary range of little-known writing, and little-known shades to those better known. Louisa May Alcott takes on a new light when you discover she could write to a reader, "Though I do not enjoy writing moral tales for the young . . . I do it because it pays well."

Perhaps necessarily at this moment, this book suggests ideas rather than developing them, or, as in the chapter on quilting, produces a dazzling, virtuoso cornucopia of examples that finally just lie side by side. Metaphors can be traps as well as maps, and the images of quilt-making tempts Showalter into an over-romantic evocation of the sharing and communal nature of women's creativity. Certainly she is no essentialist, as she wryly complains some poststructuralist feminists have stigmatised her. Women's culture, for her, is always the product of specific historical and local circumstances. But perhaps she has too rosy a notion of the moral virtues of the culture those circumstances have produced. Yet in that she shows her links with those early American celebrants of the women's sphere.

### Florence Boos (review date November 1991)

SOURCE: Boos, Florence. "The Anatomy of Culture." *Women's Review of Books* 9, no. 2 (November 1991): 26-7.

[*In the following excerpt, Boos lauds Showalter's "eclectic virtuosity" in* Sexual Anarchy: Gender and Culture at the Fin-de-Siècle *but finds shortcomings in her ambiguous use of the term "anarchy" and her treatment of class issues and AIDS.*]

Each of these three books treats late nineteenth- and early twentieth-century attitudes towards women's sexuality, health and physical capacities. All three focus on men's more than women's actions and beliefs, document repellent forms of sexist and gynophobic regimentation with horrific examples and note ways in which the constrictive patterns they describe remain with us Patricia Vertinsky and Ornella Moscucci modulate and focus their outrage with the aid of careful historical method, Elaine Showalter with irrepressibly eclectic virtuosity of arrangement and presentation. . . .

The style of Elaine Showalter's *Sexual Anarchy: Gender and Culture at the Fin-de-Siècle* contrasts markedly with Vertinsky and Moscucci's scrupulously anatomized world of medical control over women's bodies. Showalter surveys the literary, cinematographic and cultural effect of debates about gender and sexuality in two societies—Great Britain of the 1890s and late twentieth-century United States—in an impressive 240 page tour de force.

New-historicist protocol dictates that one alternate discussions of a period's texts with free-associated interpretation of contemporary or later writings or films, and Showalter's chapters follow this pattern. In the chapter on **"Odd Women,"** for example, she Juxtaposes an account of late Victorian attitudes toward single women with a description of the constraints imposed on single professional women in late twentieth-century North America. In another, neutrally entitled **"The**

Woman's Case," she assimilates nineteenth-century physicians' clitoridectomies to late twentieth-century acts of criminal mutilation. In still another, she segues from Rider Haggard's *She* and Conrad's *Heart of Darkness* to an analysis of several versions of Coppola's 1979 film *Apocalypse Now.*

The *fin de siècle* cultural world tolerates such leaps rather well, for it was a period of great variety and ferment, in which women debated and fought repressive restrictions in every area of their lives, a few men allied with them, and most mounted counteroffensives of fictional and editorial backlash. Showalter has a marked gift for dissection of Victorian plots, as her capsule interpretations of *She,* Olive Schreiner's "Dreams," Robert Louis Stevenson's *Dr. Jekyll and Mr. Hyde* and Bram Stoker's *Dracula* make clear.

At her best, she applies the methodology of recent academic gender studies in a vigorous, jargon-free manner, and deftly interprets an impressive range of recondite and intriguing facts in her discussions of 1890s sexual debates. She also moves freely across the current spectrum of gender studies in her discussions of late nineteenth-century feminism, male phobias and sexual violence directed against women, male homosexuality and homoerotic subcultures, and recent literary responses to AIDS. Showalter's tacit claim is that all the phenomena she observes are related, as she fast-forwards from sexual debates in 1890s culture to their 1990s counterparts, and shakes in her kaleidoscope hundreds of fragmented and crystallized *mentalités.*

But why the "anarchy" in her title? Within the book, the word has ambiguous connotations. Attempts at reform seem "anarchic" to their enemies, for example, but fantasies of violence and repression are also "anarchic." Such dialectical ambiguities reflect something of the work's method and tone; unfortunately, Showalter's treatment of 1890s culture and "anarchy" gives little or no attention to the anarchist movement's significant political history and feminist associations. Nineteenth-century political anarchism was noted for its prominent women activists, among them Louise Michel and Charlotte Wilson, and these women and other writers and speakers such as Emma Goldman and Crystal Eastman contributed radical critiques of the family and sexual coercion.

The book's subtitle is "Gender and Culture at the Fin de Siècle." Everything is now "culture," of course; but Showalter's "culture" is that of literature, polemic, film and performance, not art, music, history, or folk legend. Her implicit assumptions about "gender" categories also seem more pervasively psychological than economic or political. She makes no systematic attempt, for example, to apply her ideas of "sexual anarchy" to members of the turn-of-the-century working class, or consider what the writings of poor women might have revealed about their conformity to and rebellion against sexual norms. A brief discussion of *fin de siècle* prostitution (largely a poor woman's occupation), for example, might have balanced well the book's account of the prevalence of male syphilis. Are there also no late twentieth-century forms of women's economic or political activism which Showalter might have used to balance the work's grimly extended accounts of the *mentalités* of the radical right?

Anyone looking for a sympathetic brief introduction to British *fin de siècle* literature and social issues might well begin with this book. I am somewhat less certain whether Showalter has points of comparable insight and authority to make about contemporary gay literature, or about AIDS, now a catastrophic Third World pandemic. The author and editor of four important books of feminist criticism may have decided to turn her attention briefly but resolutely to one form of "the Other," and registers sincere horror at the destruction this disease has wrought, but her tone in these sections is pontificatory, at once grieving and helplessly detached.

In fairness, Showalter's decision to end her book with a discussion of the Anglo-American literature associated with AIDS does give **Sexual Anarchy** a sense of open-ended mordant discomfort—a quasi-postmodern reality-check and source of (literal) malaise which is balanced in part by her final reminder of familiar hopes and ideals: "What seems today like the apocalyptic warnings of a frightening sexual anarchy ['frightening' to whom?] may be really the birth throes of a new sexual equality."

All three of these books—historicist and new-historicist—present some of the somber and obsessive realities of a continuing history of male control, lightened by impressive acts of judgment and resistance. Vertinsky's and Moscucci's scrupulous reconstruction of the heavy burdens of an evolving patriarchal past seem animated, in part at least, by an implicit conviction that we may yet overcome the *diktat* of male control over women's lives and bodies. Showalter's virtuoso leaps seem in the end markedly less hopeful and meliorist, for their achronological cross-cuts suggest a grim vision of a sexually troubled world, one in which the competing forms of struggle have partially neutralized each other.

Despite her many humanist calls for enlightened tolerance ("If we can learn something from the fears and myths of the past, it is that they are so often exaggerated and unreal, that what looks like sexual anarchy in the context of *fin-de-siècle* anxieties may be the embryonic stirrings of a new order"), I put down her book with a sense of lingering anxiety that the "new order" she invokes may be indefinitely postponed. Only the finest of spectral lines may separate breadth of vision from the "helpless detachment" I spoke of above;

Showalter's eloquent but cautious overview of sexual malaise suggests that this is a line we have not yet learned to cross.

## Hermione Lee (review date 15 November 1991)

SOURCE: Lee, Hermione. "Separate Spheres and Common Threads." *Times Literary Supplement,* no. 4624 (15 November 1991): 8.

[*In the following review, Lee offers a negative assessment of* Sister's Choice: Tradition and Change in American Women's Writing.]

This is a friendly title, [*Sister's Choice,*] and it comes in a positive red colour, with a bold quilt-pattern design, because "Sister's Choice" is the name of the quilt made by Celie and Shug in *The Color Purple* by Alice Walker, and the quilt is an emblem, Elaine Showalter says, of "a universalist, interracial, and intertextual tradition". In deliberately selecting a title from a non-literary and non-white context, Showalter makes her main point: that American women's writing does not, or "must" no longer, belong to a "separate sphere", but belongs, or "must" belong, to a common, pluralistic heritage of races, genders and cultures. These are rousing sentiments, and this short book (based on her Clarendon Lectures of 1989) is lavishly bolstered with a utopian rhetoric which makes "sister's choice" into a bravely hopeful prescription for "a new map of a changing America". But one sister's choice may be another sister's anathema.

Showalter is no newcomer to anathematizing: she has been "dancing in the minefield" (in Annette Kolodny's famously perilous phrase) of feminist literary criticism for a long time. The controversy over her treatment of *A Room of One's Own* provides a good example. In her important book on the emergence of a "female tradition" in English fiction, ***A Literature of Their Own*** (1977), Showalter reproached Virginia Woolf for evasiveness and denial of feeling. She read androgyny as an unsatisfactorily impersonal retreat from women's problems, and the room of one's own as, ultimately, a tomb. By contrast with the phrase which inspired her title, Showalter suggested that "a literature of their own" for women should not, as Woolf recommended, transcend sexual identity, but should derive strength from confrontation and interaction, from "an understanding of what it means, in every respect, to be a woman". The central belief, here as in Showalter's later work, is that writing by women constitutes a direct record of their experience and that what she calls "gynocriticism" can make a feminist analysis of such writing by paying attention to it *as* a record of experience.

The word "experience" is a red rag to a critic such as Toril Moi, whose feminist readings, derived from Derrida and Kristeva, are made via psychology and linguistics and not "bourgeois realism" or "traditional humanism". (This kind of opposition is often used to sum up the standard split between French and Anglo-American feminist schools, though in ***Sister's Choice*** Showalter is impatient with this sort of monolithic and undifferentiated account of "American feminist criticism"). Woolf's inauthenticity for Showalter comes, says Moi (in *Sexual/Textual Politics,* 1985), from her assumption that "feminist writers should want to use realist fictional forms in the first place". But this, according to Moi, is just an inheritance from that patriarchal ideology which had the humanist creator as the author in control of "his" text. A feminist reading of Woolf should rather attend to the scepticism and playfulness of her literary strategies, the endless deferral of meaning in her text, her refusal to commit herself to "a so-called rational or logical form of writing". By this reading, evasiveness becomes, not a retreat from, but an essential of, feminist writing.

The trouble with this is that it makes it sound as if *A Room of One's Own* could be about anything at all: political content, whether truthful or not, gets the boot. But Moi isn't alone in her impatience with Showalter's imperviousness to irony and play of language. The point is made, very differently, by Edmund White, writing recently in these pages on the clodhopping Freudianism, "brutal rejection of authorial intention" and insensitivity to nuance, of Showalter's book on *fin de siècle* fiction, ***Sexual Anarchy.*** Wildly different though they are, both White and Moi have it in for Showalter for what they perceive as an inability to *read*: "What's puzzling", says White, with his devastating levity, "is why literature should play a role at all in this book. . . . fiction is notoriously a poor vehicle for ideas". These are serious challenges to a critic whose whole work is based on the belief that fiction is a fine vehicle for ideas, and that historical and cultural developments can be deduced from it.

Showalter is aware that in applying her belief, this time, to American rather than British women writers, she is facing more complicated difficulties than accusations of naivety or unsubtlety. Her first essay, **"American Questions"**, describes the perils of trying to write an American feminist literary history at a time of "dissensus", when the acceptance of an established, traditional American literary canon is bursting apart, in reading lists and anthologies and faculty appointments and publishers' investments, into "diversity, division and discord". In this context, a feminist literary history

> must be critical of any single paradigm of American women's history or culture; attentive to the articulation of gender, race and class; and aware that women's writing is produced within a complex intertextual network. It cannot be defined by biological essences, stereotypes of femininity, or nationalist myths. It must avoid both over-feminization, the insistence that everything in

women's writing can be explained by gender; and under-feminization, or the neglect of gender inscriptions in women's texts.

Well, that should please everybody, you can feel her thinking. There is a careful political correctness about all this which made my heart sink. But what follows, as she takes the opportunity to suggest one possible tradition of American women's writing, is often interesting.

She starts well, in the fathers' libraries, where many of the great American women writers (and others too, of course, from Woolf to de Beauvoir) began their literary journeys. Margaret Fuller was kept from novels, plays and poetry and drilled in Latin and logic. Like Miranda (whose appropriation in American literature Showalter describes in useful detail), Fuller was in thrall to her father's "language and power", and could never escape the magic dominion of Emerson-as-Prospero. Others broke out of the library more successfully. Louisa Alcott, whose transcendentalist-philosopher father, Bronson, used to leave forbidden apples around the house to test his children's obedience, always used to eat the apple ("Me *must* have it!"). She tried out forbidden fruit in her secret, pseudonymous sensation writing, and found her own voice, domestic, colloquial and direct, in *Little Women* (even if she did later give in to her male publishers' bowdlerizing demands). Charlotte Perkins Gilman (more famous now for her Gothic fantasy of female incarceration than for her rational feminist Utopias), whose father was a distinguished librarian, couldn't bear to look at an index after her breakdown. A brilliant quotation from Alice James expresses one daughter's "waves of violent inclination" in the library, imagining "throwing myself out of the window, or knocking off the head of the benignant pater as he sat with his silver locks, writing at his table".

Showalter makes a trajectory from the thwarted resistance of the daughters to the open community of the sisters. Just as in *A Literature of Their Own,* where she described the evolutionary stages of women's writing from the nineteenth to the twentieth century as "feminine", "feminist" and "female", so now she traces a progression from Fuller's and Alcott's struggle with patriarchy, via Kate Chopin's and Edith Wharton's painfully transitional tragedies of solitary women, through the anxieties of modernism and the challenges to American feminism in the 1920s and 30s, and on towards "the honest exploration of female experience and female lives". She concludes with the post-1960s process of reclamation (of silenced authors, uncanonized texts, neglected domestic arts) as crucial to the making of an American feminist aesthetic. That this aesthetic is no longer confined to "separate spheres" is demonstrated by her account of the AIDS quilt (a giant memorial to those who have died of the disease, made of over 11,000 pieces and exhibited in the late 1980s in twenty-five American cities), which shows the transition for "traditions of women's culture" from private to public symbols, from "separate spheres" to "common threads".

Though this historical survey is always readable and informative, I found its relentlessly progressive view of literary history—whereby Joyce Carol Oates and Alice Walker are bound to be more fulfilled and liberated writers than Edith Wharton or Kate Chopin—sentimental and tyrannical. I noticed that Showalter bypassed those awkward American women writers who cannot easily be read as "precursors of a literary history of female mastery and growth": so Willa Cather's distaste for Kate Chopin's emotional "Bovaryisme", so alien to her own more impersonal and tougher aims, is passed over with some bewilderment, and Flannery O'Connor is put where she most hated to be put, along with Carson McCullers under "American Gothic", with no room here for her savagely ironic metaphysics, which have nothing at all to do with sisterhood.

The word I most distrusted in this book was "must", and it is often used. "We must make its myths together or not at all"; the AIDS quilt "must be read in its own new terms"; "the work of exploration must be carried on". This orthodoxy of sisterhood can be as domineering as the old rule of the fathers. Showalter recommends plurality, interconnectedness, true democracy: no more rooms of one's own. But books go on being written alone, and read alone, as well as together, by writers who may want to say "Me *must* have it!" in quite other ways to those recommended here. Novels, after all, are not the same things as giant memorial quilts.

### Elizabeth Shannon (review date 6 December 1991)

SOURCE: Shannon, Elizabeth. Review of *Sexual Anarchy: Gender and Culture at the Fin-de-Siècle,* by Elaine Showalter. *Commonweal* 118, no. 21 (6 December 1991): 728.

[*In the following review, Shannon offers high praise for Showalter's scholarly examination of "social, sexual, and political attitudes" in* Sexual Anarchy.]

There is one book I especially want to recommend this year, Elaine Showalter's **Sexual Anarchy: Gender and Culture at the Fin-de-Siècle.** Showalter is both engaging and scholarly in comparing social, sexual, and political attitudes prevalent at the end of the nineteenth century to our own *fin de siècle*. The parallels she discusses are fascinating in their similarities, but depressing in their recurrence.

She discusses literature, art, and film, both American and English, and finds that the *fin de siècle* brings with it an earthquake of social and sexual upheavals, and that this occurs cyclically, perhaps caused by a "sense of an ending." She quotes Frank Kermode, who suggests that "we project our existential anxieties onto history; there is a real correlation between the ends of centuries and the peculiarity of our imagination, that it [increased anxiety] chooses always to be at the end of an era."

Public dialogue at the end of the nineteenth century created the use of the words "feminism" and "homosexuality." Attempts to redefine gender, to explore sexual and psychological borders, and to understand the meaning of feminine liberation filled the art and literature of the day. Reaction to this "sexual anarchy" was typically reactionary: worries about sexually transmitted disease (particularly syphilis, which had reached epidemic proportions by 1900), concern that the liberation of women would erode family life, and efforts to impose codes of Victorian morality on the whole population.

Late nineteenth-century concern with the horrors of an imminent feminist takeover were fed by fantasy, not fact, and yet "the nineteenth century had cherished a belief in the separate spheres of femininity and masculinity that amounted almost to religious faith . . . post-Darwinian 'sexual science' offered . . . testimony on the evolutionary differences between men and women," finding, of course, that "women's nurturant domestic capabilities fitted them for home and hearth . . . while men's aggressive, competitive abilities fitted them for public life."

While women looked for a new feminist order at the turn of the last century, men too searched for new definitions of masculinity. In the world of male "Clubland," and in the literature of "quest romances," written especially for boys ("little boys who read will become big boys who rule"), the need for male superiority and exclusiveness became a virulent theme. Gerard Manley Hopkins wrote in 1886 that "the begetting of one's thoughts on paper . . . is a kind of male gift," and writers of the period fantasized about alternate forms of male reproduction, such as "splitting or cloning, as in *Dr. Jekyll and Mr. Hyde*; reincarnation, as in Rider Haggard's *She*; transfusion, as in *Dracula*; aesthetic duplication, as in *The Picture of Dorian Gray*. . . ."

All have a familiar echo as the last decade of our century draws to a close. AIDS has taken the place of syphilis, the right-wing movement in America still tries to impose cultural and artistic censorship on our population, the senators who sought to degrade Anita Hill could have quoted Teddy Roosevelt at the turn of the century: "There is no place in the world for nations who have . . . lost their fiber of vigorous hardness and masculinity."

The parallels in Ms. Showalter's book are not only in the sexual arena; the last two decades of the nineteenth century in England were a time of severe economic depression, and the expression "unemployment" was coined, an expression used with frightening and relentless repetition in America today. The homeless population of America's cities, camped out on hot air vents, must be reminiscent of London in the 1890s, where hordes of people made a home in Trafalgar Square and the city's parks.

Ms. Showalter's writing is crisp, full of verve, anecdotes, and wit; though well-researched, the book avoids the pitfalls of academic dryness. She has no ax to grind; her book is not a political statement nor a sociological scaremonger. She detaches herself by her humor and scholarship. Most of her facts are annotated and the view-points provided in quotations from acknowledged and usually witty sources.

Her picture of the dreary past makes a return to it impossible, and she is optimistic about the future. As she describes the Genitron, an electric clock above the Pompidou Center in Paris, flashing the remaining seconds and minutes of the decade, time cannot be stopped or turned back . . . "nor can we legislate or intimidate men and women into shame and repression of the past. We must not allow fear to push us into cruel homophobia, make us abandon our commitment to women's sexual autonomy, or lead us to repudiate the *fin-de-siècle* vision of a future in which sexuality is a source of pleasure, comfort, and joy. . . . What seems today like the apocalyptic warnings of a frightening sexual anarchy may be really the birth throes of a new sexual equality."

I wish I could give copies of her book as Christmas presents to members of the United States Senate.

### Nina Baym (review date spring 1992)

SOURCE: Baym, Nina. Review of *Sister's Choice: Tradition and Change in American Women's Writing*, by Elaine Showalter. *American Literature* 64, no. 3 (spring 1992): 629-30.

[*In the following review, Baym compliments the structure and subject material of* Sister's Choice.]

From its dust jacket illustration of a quilt block to a final chapter on quilting, this book takes "piecing"—women's creation of patterned art from snips of available fabric—as the metaphor for American women's writing. The book itself is artfully pieced, inserting four previously published essays between two each of four Clarendon Lectures delivered in 1989. This elegant congruence of content and form forestalls (though it cannot entirely eliminate) concern about completeness;

the book presents itself not as master narrative but as scrap-bag assemblage. The first chapter uses postcolonialist theory to deny the aptness of master narratives for histories of muted or minority discourses; piecing becomes, implicitly, the most responsible way to generalize about women's writing.

As readers familiar with Showalter's influential work in feminist theory and English literature might expect, her overview is immensely perceptive and wonderfully accomplished. Oscillating between close reading and survey, merging biography with textual analysis, and enacting the sisterliness of its title in generous footnotes and quotations of other feminists' scholarship, *Sister's Choice* moves chronologically from Margaret Fuller and Louisa May Alcott (chapters 2 and 3), to turn-of-the-century writing represented by Kate Chopin's *Awakening* and Edith Wharton's *House of Mirth* (chapters 4 and 5), to surveys of women's interwar writings and of contemporary female Gothic (chapters 6 and 7). Showalter shows how texts in each era register historically specific conflicts between women's creativity and their relationship to literary traditions, as well as between their fantasies and cultural reality. In Showalter's view, antebellum female culture, dominated by a homosocial woman's sphere, gave way in the 1880s to the semi-independent New Women, followed by a heterosexual modernist synthesis (73, 86)—a surprising assertion in view of the significant lesbian component in female modernism—a synthesis which has now given way to postmodernity. She finds that in every era social conditions have frustrated literary women's fantasies of "lives that successfully balanced love and work" (107).

The essays are eminently readable and jargon-free, studded with quotable insights. The significance of Fuller's Miranda image and the trajectory of that image in later women's writing; Alcott's preference, in *Little Women*, for the "dearly cherished sister of us all" over the "unattainable genius, Shakespeare's American sister" (64); Chopin's mapping of her heroine's imaginative failings; Wharton's implicit rejection, in Lily Bart, of the debilitating constraints on "lady" writers; women's struggles in the 1920s and 1930s to celebrate women in an antifeminist era; the recent resurgence of female Gothic in response to ubiquitous physical violence against women—"Female Gothic looks more and more like a realist mode" (144)—are the main topics in this remarkably efficient study.

The index names approximately 72 American women writers, a huge number for a book of under 200 pages. Still, thousands are missing, guaranteeing that *Sister's Choice* by no means exhausts its subject. Indeed, whereas quilting originated as the art of using every scrap, the accumulated scraps of American women's writing far exceed the capacity of any quilter, even one so inspired and dedicated as Showalter, to contain them.

## Brenda Foglio Lyons (review date October 1992)

SOURCE: Lyons, Brenda Foglio. "American Patchwork." *Essays in Criticism* 42, no. 4 (October 1992): 338-44.

[*In the following review, Lyons argues that* Sister's Choice: Tradition and Change in American Women's Writing *is an inconsistent and incomplete, though entertaining, literary history of American women's writing.*]

The notion of being simultaneously inside and outside patriarchy and its institutional processes is a feminist ideological construct that has achieved the status of mainstream cliché. Titles by French writers have surfaced which name this borderline as a discursive subject: *Inside* by Hélène Cixous, which won the *Prix Medicis* in 1969, is a fictive elaboration of *l'écriture féminine*; *Outside: Selected Writings* (1984) by Marguerite Duras, released in an English translation by Carol Barko in 1986, is a diverse collection of short pieces that comment on social and political injustices. Elaine Showalter's book, *Sister's Choice,* asks questions that concern boundary disputes on a remapped topography of English studies—for example, how and where to position a literary history of American women's writing: is it inside or outside British or masculine traditions, an American canon, national borders, European influences? The terrain has been complicated, readers are informed in the first chapter, **'American Questions',** by the difficulties of defining 'American'. How do the politics of language and literature interconnect with those of race, class, and gender to determine canon and curriculum selections? To what extent does a national(ist) literature covertly reinforce its own politics?

Showalter's texts have become a tradition in Anglo-American feminist discourse; she has produced seven volumes of literary/cultural criticism, two of which are now included on most contemporary English reading lists. It is not surprising that the patterns of tradition and change are of recurring interest in her work, as they identify links between her position within a new tradition of American women's writing and the problem of locating a female literary history in relation to a 'feminist' and 'American' ethos. *The New Feminist Criticism* (1985, Virago 1986) was a pluralist landmark, which she introduced as part of a 'critical revolution' emerging from the changed assumptions of the Sixties, but distanced from structuralism, Freudian/Lacanian psychoanalysis, Marxism, and deconstructive approaches. An earlier anthology by Mary Jacobus, *Women Writing and Writing about Women* (1979) had, however, included Showalter's own essay, **'Towards a Feminist Poetics'**.

Her work has often traced metaphorical patterns in search of continuities; she forms orderly narratives out of the gaps and chaos of female and, more recently, African American works of nineteenth- and twentieth-century English fiction, historically and culturally contextualised. Louisa May Alcott's ambidexterity was identified as a metaphor of creativity in *Alternative Alcott,* keyed to doubling efficiency as a 'writing machine'. In *Sexual Anarchy* 'civilisation' is a racial metaphor for colonial oppression, demonstrated by Dan's imposition of imperialism in the coronation episode of John Huston's film of the Kipling tale, *The Man Who Would Be King* (1888); and the veil is a mysterious metaphorical link to 'feminine' definition and difference. Her critique of Virginia Woolf's 'room of one's own' as an isolationist tomb continues more than a decade later to spark Anglo-European controversy over whether or not women's writing may be interpreted as directly recorded experience. The infamous chapter in *A Literature of Their Own,* **'Virginia Woolf and the Flight into Androgyny',** was mentioned by Hermione Lee in the *Times Literary Supplement* (November 15, 1991) as engendering a debate that represents the standard split between Anglo-American and French feminisms—between, that is, Toril Moi's defence of Woolf's concept of androgyny, based on psycholinguistic readings, and Showalter's bourgeois, traditional-humanist accusations of Woolf's purported insensitivity and withdrawal.

Most critics would probably agree at least that Showalter has imbued a once-diminished body of women's writings with renewed significance. Her reputation rests on *A Literature of Their Own: From Charlotte Brontë to Doris Lessing,* sensitive to metaphors of landscape, temporal and spatial; it set the scene of the English novel in a trans-Atlantic context distinguished by Austen peaks, Brontë cliffs, the Eliot range, and Woolf hills. She clarified a teleology of 'the female tradition', catalogued monumental and briefly momentary texts of more than two hundred women writers, and traced a pattern from 'feminine' subcultural ideology to a female aesthetic that applied an evolved 'feminist ideology' to language.

In *Sister's Choice* the metaphor of another country as the ground of literary critical differences is fertile soil from which Showalter embarks on her personal tale of the difficulties of travel and homecoming. She begins with a first person narrative of her return to America and its literature after experiencing English Culture, an uncomfortable arrival after adventurous wanderings, albeit on well-trodden public footpaths, through Yorkshire and bibliophile temptations of London and Southeast England. A provocatively distanced interest in male classicism is piqued with the quotation from William Carlos Williams's letter to Robert Lowell that called Europe a Circe, wishing him well on the occasion of his homecoming to Penelope/America. *Sister's Choice* is also a return to the primary metaphor of *A Literature of Their Own,* in which women's writing becomes a different, subcultural country within English fiction and the basis of a cultural opposition; America is England's 'other'. She emphasises the inverted way in which American women's writing now influences its historically dominant cultural readership and that of an international audience; a self-consciousness is suggested, and the sensibility of self-critical consciousness.

*Sister's Choice* entertains anecdotally, as befits an American tradition of story-telling. Eight chapters are purposefully patched together and unified by the metaphor of quilting, which Showalter explicates as quintessentially female and American. The title is from a passage in Alice Walker's *The Color Purple,* which transforms the metaphor into an icon of black liberalism. Celie and Sophia fashion a quilt called 'sister's choice' from torn curtains and a yellow dress; the choice is either to remain in their local black Southern community or to enter a multicoloured international world. For Showalter this is a 'womanist novel' because it exercises a 'sister's choice'. In her final chapter, she returns to the metaphor of the patchwork quilt to describe populist American heterogeneity. Having replaced the 'melting pot' in twentieth-century ideological iconography, American quilting for Showalter represents an ingenious woman's art of conservation: it crosses boundaries of race, region, and class; is historically central to women's writing in America; and corresponds to the actual process of writing seen in a variety of fictional texts. Its multi-textured fabric suggests associations with radical, conservative, and middle-of-the-road sexual politics; aesthetically, it has been revered for anti-establishment originality and beauty, reviled as feminine and trivial; a double-sided product is also the historical in-process artefact that lends significance to its representational value in American storytelling.

The metaphors of piecing and patchwork as threads common to a female aesthetic for sisterhood and for a politics of feminist survival are offered in the hope of cultural cohesion. In the first chapter a density of interconnected questions may unsettle a reader ill prepared for complications by an engagingly straightforward title. There is no central question, but rather many contextually related ones, which overlap in an intricate enquiry into the cultural, geographical, ethnological, and gendered texture of female literary Americana. Showalter declares the project another exercise of 'gynocriticism', her neologism for identifying what is 'female' or 'feminine' by reading women's texts, in this case also seeking a uniquely American tradition in two vicissitudinous centuries of women's writings in the United States. Inspiringly appropriate though the metaphor appears, it dramatically covers its own questions: instead of digging into the theoretical materials, Showalter skirts most of the 'American questions', leaving readers to ponder such interesting asides as Sacvan

Berkovich's notion of exceptionalism as a critical ideology that may alter what 'American' means in 'a time of dissensus'. Many introductory questions end up as digressions. Denying her status as 'American feminist critic', Showalter asks what these terms mean, but then shies away from theory, returning instead to a less rigorous form of gynocritical activity. But the questions are well worth repeating. Does a muted culture have a literature of its own? *Can* there be an 'authentic' language in a heterogeneous culture? What is the relationship between literary theory and non-canonised literatures?

The book is designed as a patchwork of nineteenth- and twentieth-century pieces of literature about and by women, mostly plot summaries and biographical sketches, but the scope and weight of the subject are too vast for such selectivity. The structure does not hold its subject; it wavers between the attempt to represent an incomplete female American literary history, and a clever patching together of cultural parts as a postcolonial response to male, European intellectual oppression. There are missing patches, and loose threads, when pulled, unravel to destroy the design, which operates by an association of pieces. More than a third of the book comprises readings of only three novels—*Little Women* by Louisa May Alcott, *The Awakening* by Kate Chopin, and *The House of Mirth* by Edith Wharton—the stuff of which has more to do with the authors' creative practices than either 'American questions' or quilts. The patches hang together by a few 'common threads', while more significant issues that Virginia Woolf raised— economic and sexual independence and theories of language that are not exclusive of European intrication—are more relevant to all these than quilting is to any of them.

What Showalter calls **'Miranda's Story'** in Chapter Two is an intriguing transposition of father/daughter relations in *The Tempest* to a series of revisionary texts by American women. Margaret Fuller, Susan Sontag's predecessor as Manhattan Dark Lady, a privileged position to which Showalter had aspired, called herself Miranda, metaphorical Daughter of Prospero, archetypal Literary Father. In the wake of a failed 'Prospero-Caliban trope' of the Eighties, inadequate because of its exclusion of women, Showalter gives accounts of Miranda as a woman artist or intellectual in fiction by Harriet Beecher Stowe, Louisa May Alcott, Katherine Ann Porter, Sylvia Plath, and Gloria Naylor. Miranda's changed forms in American fiction begin with Fuller's autobiographical self-identification, embodying a 'feminist ideal' fraught with external and internalized contradictions peculiar to cross-gendered hybrids. South of the Canadian border, the 'Miranda story' is that of revolutionary women's replays of knowledge, while to the north a conservative tale of political power has cast Miranda as 'dutiful daughter' to her national father.

This archaeological projection of a Shakespearean metaphor merits attention for exposing differing cultural strata in the politics of language, but Showalter's story would benefit from leaving it at that. An enquiry into questions raised by the dramatic closure of her 'Miranda story', its oppositional syntagm of American and Canadian Miranda's, would have usefully gone beyond figurative appropriations to a developed argument. Gloria Naylor's novel *Mama Day* has transformed the figure of the Republican Miranda's sedate, white Northern sister to the matriarchal, androgynous Mama Day of Willow Springs, who prospers from her father's knowledge and enacts his magic. Here the metaphor is alive with contemporary struggles for the survival of American island cultures. In the relations of female cultures and writings and in swatches of questions and tropes, Showalter reveals knottily visible seams that may enhance our understanding of American female literature, but the study becomes trapped in its own metaphors, sewing up American literature, regardless of gender, into a single monolithic quilted image.

A feminist/modernist sixth chapter, **'The Other Lost Generation',** details the bleak underside of a male preserve of Twenties and Thirties radicalism. Female modernism was marked by confinement, reticence, and silence; there was a crisis in the divided female consciousness; women poets suffered relegation to minority status; and the New Woman was systematically silenced by exclusion and poverty. Chapter Seven marks a shift from negation and poverty to the Sixties renaissance of hermeneutical innovation, and emphasizes the notion of an 'American female gothic'. A few missed stitches from the nineteenth century are picked up here, to include Charlotte Perkins Gilman, and at least a mention of Alice James; there is a nod to Native American and immigrant cultures as part of the American patchwork. However, much is left out, from Abigail Adams's letters to the fiction, diaries, and other writings of, for example, Gwendolyn Brooks, Djuna Barnes, Maxine Kumin, Anais Nin, Mary Oliver, Carolyn Kizer, Pearl Buck, May Sarton, Maxine Hong Kingston, and Maya Angelou.

The nature of American literature, female or male, is much more ambiguous and dynamic than any single metaphor can imaginatively contain; if *Sister's Choice* is approached as a decorative Gestalt, rather than the literary historical account of American women's fiction it ambitiously and interrogatively attempts, the reader may enjoy a good read. The complexities raised in Chapter One are only superficially attached to an expanse of layered materials, which are more violently tattered than *Sister's Choice* presents: too many pieces have disintegrated with time, in witch hunts, censorship battles, wars, Native American genocide. In Showalter's rewritten catalogue, a poetics of American women's writing has been sacrificed to metaphorical rhetoric.

Theoretical rigour is lacking, and female literary history, uneasily balanced between aesthetics and political history, ends up as inconsistent critical practice.

**Susan Fraiman (review date spring 1993)**

SOURCE: Fraiman, Susan. Review of *Sexual Anarchy: Gender and Culture at the Fin-de-Siècle,* by Elaine Showalter. *Tulsa Studies in Women's Literature* 12, no. 1 (spring 1993): 119-22.

[*In the following excerpt, Fraiman praises* Sexual Anarchy *for its "gripping" examination of such works as Robert Louis Stevenson's* The Strange Case of Dr. Jekyll and Mr. Hyde *and Ann Ardis's* New Women, New Novels.]

At the center of Elaine Showalter's gripping study of the *fin de siècle* is a reading of *The Strange Case of Dr. Jekyll and Mr. Hyde.* I cannot help appropriating this duo to figure the relation between Ann Ardis's upbeat, brightly lit *New Women, New Novels* and Showalter's own darker and more disconcerting work. True that, in their attention to proto-modern texts by men as well as women and in their historicizing ways, both books represent a second phase of American feminist criticism, beyond its earliest thematic readings of nineteenth-century women's fiction; indeed *Sexual Anarchy,* treating books and plays alongside films and crimes, actresses and autopsies, is an exhilarating example of the newest, thickest kind of cultural description. Nevertheless, in their different emotional emphases these two works remind me of the old, axiomatic distinction (worded most famously by Showalter herself) between one feminist approach that celebrates writings by women and another that exposes the bias in writings by men. Whereas Ardis typically travels the utopian terrain of Jane Hume Clapperton's *Margaret Dunmore; or, A Socialist Home* (1888) and Florence Dixie's *Gloriana; or, The Revolution of 1900* (1890), Showalter takes us to the misogynist heart of darkness in Rider Haggard's *She* (1886) and Bram Stoker's *Dracula* (1897). Like Dr. Jekyll and Mr. Hyde, *New Women, New Novels* and *Sexual Anarchy* are in some schematic sense doubles, and reading them in tandem suggests that the *fin de siècle* was itself a divided personality. . . .

Though Showalter opens with chapters on **"Odd Women"** and **"New Women"** (the former's plight elected by the latter as a badge of independence), its general movement is away from women toward the disordered masculine imagination. In this Mr. Hyde-version of the *fin de siècle,* Ardis's innovative women writers are few and far between. They are represented most prominently by Olive Schreiner and Eleanor Marx, whose lives are offered as examples of paralyzed creativity and personal tragedy. Caird, Grand, and Cholmondeley are discussed as daughters of George Eliot, rewriting her for feminism; but Showalter concludes that "on the whole . . . both the novels and the careers of the novelists ended in defeat and despair" (p. 66). So while each scholar notes the demise in this period of the three-volume form, what Ardis views as an opportunity for women writers—"the democratization/feminization of the literary marketplace" (p. 41)—Showalter regards as a shift "away from subjects, themes, and forms associated with femininity and maternity" (p. 17). Invoking Patricia Stubbs and Terry Lovell, Showalter argues that the century closed with "the striking, although temporary, eclipse of women writers" (p. 16).

This said, *Sexual Anarchy* proceeds along more or less Sedgwickian lines to unveil the violence against women and denied desire for men in, for example, Rudyard Kipling's "The Man Who Would Be King" (1888), Oscar Wilde's *Salomé* (1893), Joseph Conrad's *Heart of Darkness* (1899), and the many spin-offs generated by these texts. Showalter's genealogies of figures such as Salomé and narratives such as Conrad's, ending with filmic variations by Ken Russell and Francis Ford Coppola in our own *fin de siècle,* stand out among the many fascinations of her study. *Sexual Anarchy*'s dramatic sweep—taking in everything from clitoridectomies to Courbet—along with the brilliant readings we have come to expect from this author, makes for a rich and readable cultural history indeed. I have associated its mode of interrogating masculinity with what Showalter once called "feminist critique"; in fact, retooled by scholars in gay and cultural studies, this approach has been geared up to a power and sophistication only intimated by Kate Millett. *Sexual Anarchy* places Showalter at the forefront of the new "gender studies," completing a turn away from *A Literature of Their Own* (1977), implicit in *The Female Malady* (1985), and announced by *Speaking of Gender* (1989). For feminists the risks as well as rewards of her venture are, I suggest, those intrinsic to the rubric itself.

There are obvious advantages to making masculinity the object of a feminist anatomy. As Showalter demonstrates in her chapter **"The Woman's Case,"** men from Jack the Ripper to Freud have opened up and peered into the female body with a serial vengeance. To analyze and, in doing so, reverse this gendered pattern of penetration and witnessing is no small triumph. Moreover to explore the closet of same-sex love—which hovers, for instance, between a gaunt Robert Louis Stevenson and his spectral wife in a portrait by John Singer Sargent (pp. 107-08)—is to further a project of major critical and political import. What concerns me, however, is that this project threatens at times to privilege the *same sex* (men), leaving women once again the *second sex*. Thus even such a strongly feminist work as Showalter's, while taking every opportunity to ask "Can there be a woman in Dr. Jekyll's closet?" (p. 118), ends up with "lesbianism" as a *see also*, subordinate to a "homosexuality" defined as male. Nor can the marginal status of women writers as well as lesbianism in **Sexual Anarchy** be attributed solely to the failure of the one and discursive vagueness of the other during the period under consideration; Ardis demonstrates too thoroughly that such an account has been biased by high modernist assumptions.

I return, then, to the usefulness of placing Ardis and Showalter in dialogue with one another, both for cultural historians in search of the *fin de siècle* and for feminist critics seeking a methodology. It is a point I would make, finally, by juxtaposing the cover illustrations of their books. *New Women, New Novels* features two women reading, side by side on a bench, and perhaps their tranquil sisterhood understates the sexual turmoil of the early modern era. **Sexual Anarchy** needs these two women, however, to comment on its own Beardsleyesque cover, whose figures, however breasted and winged, slip in the direction of the phallic—angels of a sexual order less promisingly anarchic after all.

## Andrea Stuart (review date 18 June 1993)

SOURCE: Stuart, Andrea. "Missing Links." *New Statesman and Society* 6, no. 257 (18 June 1993): 38.

[*In the following review, Stuart offers a generally positive assessment of* Daughters of Decadence: Women Writers of the Fin-de-Siècle.]

Elaine Showalter has made something of a literary cottage industry out of the angst and alienation of the *fin-de-siècle*. In her book **The Female Malady**, she turned the tables on the men of knowledge who spent so long dissecting "the woman problem" in lieu of confronting their own anxieties. And in **Sexual Anarchy,** she explored the fears that stalked the psyches of those nervy Wildean decadents and their brittle female counterparts, the "New Women", as they made their uneasy journey into the 20th century.

So it was no great surprise to see her edit this collection of short stories by women writers of the period [**Daughters of Decadence**]. But as spin-off books go, this is quite a creditable offering. In the introduction, for example, Showalter, steers clear of the gratuitous hermeticism that plagues most academic writers and manages to be both informative and pithy. And she really *works* her choice of stories, making them reveal as much about the present as about the past.

"Endism", the fear of the end of the century, seems to have gripped our collective consciousnesses in much the same way then as now. In the twilight of the last century—just as on the pages of today's *Cosmo*—miscommunication and romantic disillusion shadow these characters' lives. A careless young man discovers only after a farewell kiss that it is his best friend, a "far too" independent woman, he really loves; another that the woman he wants cannot be his because she is simply too desirable.

It is the original battle of the sexes and the combatants are bemused and battered. Men are lost in a haze of frustration or narcissism; women suffer in silence, suppressing, as one puts it, "a restless craving for sun and love and motion". Their aspirations to be creative, sexually ambiguous or even active fester beneath their virtue.

Some of the stories are whimsical, like Kate Chopin's "An Egyptian Cigarette", in which a woman transforms herself into androgyny via an opium-induced fantasy. Others are simply terrifying, like Charlotte Perkins Gilman's "The Yellow Wallpaper", in which a woman is pushed to the edges of insanity by the stifling inertia of marriage.

In many ways, this enormously varied collection of female writers, whose names are now largely forgotten, is an old-fashioned job of feminist reclaiming. And certainly reading these women is like finding the lost piece of a cultural jigsaw. They are the bridge, the "missing link" between the Victorian giants such as George Eliot and the modernist brigade led by Woolf and Stein.

But did they deserve to be forgotten? The answer is yes and no. Showalter certainly presents these women writers as an unequivocal antidote to the male literary dominance of the period, and some are undoubtedly rare excavations. But the truth is that the short story is a notoriously difficult route to literary immortality; and some of these feel as transitional and amorphous as the nervy and restless "New Women" who penned them.

## Chris Baldick (review date 3 September 1993)

SOURCE: Baldick, Chris. "Secular Variations." *Times Literary Supplement*, no. 4718 (3 September 1993): 20-1.

[*In the following excerpt, Baldick praises Showalter's exploration of the* fin-de-siècle *in* Daughters of Decadence: Women Writers of the Fin-de-Siècle.]

Like the widow in Wilde's play whose hair has turned gold with grief, the study of the last century's Nineties sports an unseemly glow of prosperity. Nothing flourishes quite like decadence, and productivity is booming in the languor industry. The shiny new conference centre at Warwick University accommodates symposia on world-weariness, while publishers look forward to issuing fresh volumes on cultural exhaustion. The calendar has, of course, something to do with it, but unlike the Nineties of Mary Wollstonecraft or of Christopher Marlowe, no less deserving of resurrection by rote, the Yellow Nineties or Naughty Nineties seem to address us with the additional sinister allure of the hypochondriac, superstitiously mesmerized by his self-assigned curse of decadence, degeneracy and the knelling phrase *fin de siècle*.

Our unfinished business with this *fin* has much to do with its confounding of ends with beginnings, under the presidency of Janus Bifrons. Blink again at this twilit decade of pessimism—or simply substitute Shaw and Morris for Beardsley and Dowson—and it transforms itself into the dawn of Utopian promise, preoccupied with the New Woman, the New Drama, the New Fiction and the New Journalism, not to mention the Golden Dawn of the Theosophists. For this self-consciously paradoxical decade, in which materialists by day became spiritualists by night, terminus appears as threshold, or, more bewildering still, the boundary itself evaporates into a haze of uncertainties. Rebecca Stott, who has a keen eye for the telling quotation, cites the English version of the notorious work *Degeneration* (1895) by the quack cultural analyst Max Nordau:

> Over the earth the shadows creep with deepening gloom", wrapping all objects in a mysterious dimness, in which all certainty is destroyed and any guess seems plausible. Forms lose their outlines and are dissolved in floating mist.

Alongside this impression of the contemporary mood, she produces, in *The Fabrication of the Late-Victorian Femme Fatale*, a letter from Joseph Conrad, writing in 1899 about the irresolutions of writing: "Every image floats vaguely in a sea of doubt—and the doubt itself is lost in an unexplored universe of incertitudes."

The modern writer who sets out to explore the cultural contradictions of the *fin de siècle* moment has a choice of two possible strategies by which to resolve the incertitudes into some kind of narrative order: the first is to emphasize the recurring pattern of anxiety or dread in the cultural products of the period, yoking them under the dominant myth of degeneration; the second is to repudiate all the talk of decline and to reconstruct the grave of Victorian confidence as the cradle of modernist innovation. If you take the first path, you will speak of the period in terms of decadence and the *fin de siècle*, and tend to conjure up a Phobic Nineties, a decade if not yellow then at least running scared from the otherness of women, "inverts", slum-dwellers and foreigners. If you take the second, you will prefer to speak of Symbolism instead of decadence, and to present Shaw, Wilde, Symons and their associates less as late Victorians than as pioneers of twentieth-century artistic liberty, engaged in a dress rehearsal for the modern movements. Each of these lines of approach brings with it its own selective omissions and its risks of condescension or of anachronism, along with certain rewards.

The phobic model of the *fin de siècle* is adopted, although by no means unthinkingly, in Stott's study of *femmes fatales*, and in several contributions to John Stokes's collection, *Fin de Siècle/Fin du Globe*, a gathering of conference papers given at Warwick in 1990. The subtitle of Stokes's volume—*Fears and Fantasies of the Late Nineteenth Century*—is itself indicative of the currently favoured resort to dread as the key to the period's culture. The collection is substantially better than one usually expects from the proceedings of academic conferences, carrying contributions from several of the period's foremost interpreters. Some of the essays are detailed analyses of particular works (John Lucas on the urban poor in poems by Hopkins and Symons, Chris Snodgrass on the sexual mischief of Beardsley's illustrations), others range more widely across the intellectual currents of the time (William Greenslade on social Darwinism and degeneration theories, J. E. Chamberlin on aesthetics and science), but in either case fears come to the fore: Elaine Showalter writes on gynophobia in Wells, while Patrick Parrinder sifts through accounts of African devil-worship and cannibalism. The most adventurous essay here is Chamberlin's "Whose Spirit Is This?", which swerves back from Ramon Fernandez (the "pale Ramon" curiously immortalized by Wallace Stevens) through Crocean aesthetics and Machian physics to the problems of *fin de siècle* mathematics; even here, though, the invocation of anxiety runs the risk of becoming self-parodic:

> The number "e", which is the base of the natural system of logarithms (or, expressed differently, the limit of (1 + 1/n) to the nth power as n increases without limit) was confirmed as an irrational in 1873; and *pi* in 1882. Both were also proved to be transcendentals. This was disturbing stuff.

Other commentators, like Showalter in her recent book, ***Sexual Anarchy*** (1990), have held to the safer claim that the most disturbing stuff of late Victorian culture (at least for innumerates) was clustered around notions of sexuality and gender. This line of investigation has already yielded a number of valuable works, among them Bram Dijkstra's startling *Idols of Perversity* (1986), a lavishly illustrated compendium of *femmes fatales* and other productions of decadent misogyny in the visual arts. Stott's *Fabrication of the Late-Victorian Femme Fatale* does not attempt to match the range of Dijkstra's or Showalter's work, but settles instead to the detailed investigation of a small group of prose fictions: Stoker's *Dracula,* Haggard's *She,* Hardy's *Tess of the D'Urbervilles,* and the early novels of Conrad. Drawing on the work of Michel Foucault, Edward Said and contemporary feminist critics for their theories of the cultural "Other", she shows how the figure of the fatal woman in these works is compounded from overlapping fearsome associations of foreignness, darkness, degeneracy and atavism; and she establishes some valuable connections between her adopted texts, tracing, for instance, the recurring pattern in which teams of male vigilantes surround and contain the threatening female monster in both *She* and *Dracula,* forcing her back into the shadow-world of which she is the imagined agent. Moving on to Conrad and Hardy, Stott sets herself a harder test, made more intriguing by her choice of Tess Durbeyfield rather than the more obvious Sue Bridehead as the *femme fatale* figure; this Stott passes convincingly, scanning the novels not just for evidences of the misogynist "framing" of women characters, but for the complications and ironies of these subtler narratives, in which the framing process itself is called into question. This is an impressively intelligent work of investigation, which makes good use of late Victorian imperial history and criminology. . . .

Introducing her anthology, **Daughters of Decadence,** Elaine Showalter also invokes the Nineties as the gateway to modernism, presenting the authors of her chosen short stories as "the missing links between the great women writers of the Victorian novel and the modern fiction of Mansfield, Woolf, and Stein". There are, of course, other links between these generations, which, for better or for worse, involve the influence of male writers like James and Chekhov; but the stories Showalter selects can in any case justify their reappearance without resort to genealogies. The anthology provides, at the very least, a welcome corrective to the varieties of male narcissism that dominate our picture of the age. Despite its title, it is actually a gathering of feminist or otherwise "advanced" fiction, whether "decadent" or not. (As Ruth Robbins observes in her essay on Vernon Lee in Stokes's collection, there are problems in attaching the label "decadent" to women writers, since the pejorative use of the term was designed for men who lapsed from a masculine standard deemed unattainable to their sisters.) Two of the best stories collected here—"The Yellow Wallpaper" by Charlotte Perkins Gilman and "The Muse's Tragedy" by Edith Wharton—are easily available elsewhere, but there are forgotten treasures exhumed, too, notably Charlotte Mew's controlled and sinister tale, "A White Night", and Vernon Lee's mischievous novella, "Lady Tal", which infuriated Henry James by using him as a character. Alongside these, are less sophisticated parables and sketches by Ada Leverson, "George Fleming", Mabel E. Wotton, Olive Schreiner and others, most of which add something to our sense of the New Woman and her times.

## Elaine Hedges (review date winter 1994)

SOURCE: Hedges, Elaine. Review of *Sister's Choice: Tradition and Change in American Women's Writing,* by Elaine Showalter. *Signs* 19, no. 2 (winter 1994): 507-11.

[*In the following excerpt, Hedges criticizes* Sister's Choice, *drawing attention to Showalter's historically inaccurate understanding of quiltmaking.*]

Of the three authors whose books are reviewed here, Cheryl Walker and Elaine Showalter bring to their material familiar feminist critical approaches. Lev Raphael, in contrast, offers a new critical methodology—one, he argues, that will provide "revolutionary insights into human motivation" (322), but that feminists concerned with issues of gender may find questionable. Although Showalter's book also raises serious questions—of fact and historical accuracy—the problems with Raphael's are more apparent. . . .

In *Sister's Choice,* Showalter also sees Walker's poets as "casualties" of their time (108). The tenor of her book, however, is better represented by her interpretation of Wharton, whom she views, unlike Raphael, as overcoming her emotional conflicts to become a precursor of a literature of "female mastery and growth" (103). *Sister's Choice* reads American women's literary history expansively: once comprising a separate tradition, its texts, genres, and metaphors now have entered the literary and cultural mainstream.

A loosely connected set of essays, *Sister's Choice* includes chapters on three novels (Alcott's *Little Women,* Chopin's *The Awakening,* and Wharton's *The House of Mirth*) and on the use of Shakespeare's Miranda figure by writers from Margaret Fuller to Gloria Naylor, on the genre of the female gothic, and on women writers of the 1920s and 1930s. Many of the essays cover familiar material, but they deftly synthesize current scholarship while often adding fresh insights, as in the discussion of music in *The Awakening.* The essays on the female gothic and the Miranda figure provide informative overviews while also advancing Showalter's argument that women's writings today no longer comprise a separate tradition but are part of broad national, and even international, contexts.

Tying these assorted items together is the metaphor of the quilt, addressed in the book's title (taken from a quilt pattern in Alice Walker's *The Color Purple*) and in a final essay, **"Common Threads."** The quilt is Showalter's controlling metaphor for her interpretation of American women's literary history, first advanced in her 1986 essay **"Piecing and Writing,"** to explain the themes, structures, and genres of nineteenth-century women's fiction.[1] In **"Common Threads,"** Showalter discusses the AIDS quilt and recent uses of the quilt as a metaphor to explore the current broad cultural appropriation of women's quilt tradition, arguing that the quilt has become the "central metaphor of American cultural identity" (169). She also again presents her earlier argument for the quilt as a paradigm for nineteenth-century women's writing.

That paradigm, however, needs to be seriously questioned. Given research (including my own) into the relationship of quilts to women's writing that has appeared since 1986, Showalter has modified part of her earlier argument.[2] Nevertheless, what remains is still crucially—even irretrievably—flawed. Briefly put, Showalter posits a trajectory for nineteenth-century women's writing that (to select only a few of its key points) moves from Harriet Beecher Stowe's use of "the most popular" midcentury quilt pattern, the log cabin (153), as structuring principle for *Uncle Tom's Cabin,* to an Ann Stephens story about a quilting party that is used to demonstrate "women's culture at its ripest and most romantic," to an 1887 story by Marietta Holley that, Showalter argues, registers the decline of that culture through a quilting bee where slander has replaced sisterhood. Unfortunately, each proposition in this argument is invalidated by the historical and factual inaccuracies on which it is based. The earliest evidence we have of log cabin quilts dates from ten years after Stowe's novel was published; Stephens's full story (Showalter has carelessly relied on an excerpt with a different title and date) is actually a debunking of "women's culture"; and satires of quilting bees such as Holley's (whose story was first published in 1868) are part of a literary tradition dating back at least to the 1840s—and to which Stephens's story also belongs.

These are not Showalter's only errors. Her account of the history of quiltmaking contains other mistakes that further invalidate the narrative she constructs. Meanwhile, those cited should serve as caveats. The unprecedented valorization of quilts, by feminists and others, since their rediscovery in the 1960s has too often relied on long-prevalent myths and misinformation that current quilt scholarship is correcting. Any use of the quilt as explanatory model for women's literary history—if indeed it can be so used—must take this scholarship more carefully into account, just as it must more scrupulously research the quilt-related texts that women actually wrote.

### Notes

1. Elaine Showalter, "Piecing and Writing," in *The Poetics of Gender,* ed. Nancy K. Miller (New York: Columbia University Press, 1986).
2. Elaine Hedges, "The Needle or the Pen: The Literary Rediscovery of Women's Needlework," in *Tradition and the Talents of Women,* ed. Florence Howe (Bloomington: Indiana University Press, 1991).

## Navina Krishna Hooker (review date May 1994)

SOURCE: Hooker, Navina Krishna. Review of *Sister's Choice: Tradition and Change in American Women's Writing,* by Elaine Showalter. *Review of English Studies* 45, no. 178 (May 1994): 288-90.

[*In the following review, Hooker commends the variety of questions that Showalter raises in* Sister's Choice, *but notes minor flaws in Showalter's "untimely polemics."*]

Elaine Showalter's **Sister's Choice** grapples with the problem of first identifying and then adequately describing a philosophical and aesthetic framework that links the work of major American women writers from Fuller onwards. The question is an important and challenging one, for it addresses a key problem of feminist literary theory, and has rightly attracted much recent critical attention. As Showalter states on the first page of her book, 'Could women . . . ever hope to have a criticism of their own?', given that the linguistic tools at their disposal are the same ones handed down to them by their male literary predecessors. Showalter correctly, although as she herself admits unoriginally, ties the female plight to discover a voice and vocabulary with which to express itself to that of third-world writers such as the novelist Raja Rao who remarks, 'The telling has not been easy. One has to convey in a language that is not one's own the spirit that is one's own' (p. 7). The call for an authentic, pure, and original language is, however, balanced against other concerns of feminist criticism—the impulse towards integration and union with other artistic models. Showalter asserts:

> The stories, genres, and symbols that once came out of a separate American literary sisterhood are no longer, however, either uniquely American or uniquely a sister's choice . . . as it becomes part of the common heritage of American men as well as women, as through translation and dissemination it influences readers far from the United States, American women's writing ceases to be a 'literature of our own'.
>
> (p. 21)

From this point of departure Showalter sets out to provide an account of American female literary history with a view to uncovering latent parallels between such disparate writers as Louisa May Alcott and Margaret Fuller. Unfortunately, these parallels are frequently negative and take the form of shared grievances against patriarchal authority. While Showalter justifiably maintains here and elsewhere, such as in **The New Feminist Criticism,** that feminist writing is by its nature 'political and polemical', making a case for a distinct tradition in women's literature based on the male influence in the shaping of the female artistic identity is not wholly satisfying. For example, in her chapter on Alcott, **'*Little Women*: The American Female Myth'**,

Showalter presents two common approaches to *Little Women*: the first posits Alcott's self-characterization as the 'dutiful daughter' as a 'capitulation to the dominant culture's image of feminine propriety' and thus 'a serious flaw' (p. 43); the second stance regards 'the tension between feminine identity and artistic freedom, and even more important, between patriarchal models of the literary career and those more relevant to women's lives' inherent in Alcott's text as a potent defence of the work's artistic and historical significance. And in Chapter 5, **'The Death of the Lady (Novelist): Wharton's *House of Mirth*',** Showalter remarks that 'Wharton refuses to sentimentalize Lily's (the heroine's) class position but rather, through associating it with her own limitations as the Perfect Lady Novelist, makes us aware of the cramped possibilities of the lady whose creative roles are defined and controlled by men' (p. 87).

Chapter 2, **'Miranda's Story',** also focuses on the power of the Miranda figure for many women novelists and poets as a metaphor for the female artist's relationship to patriarchal language, authority, and creativity. Showalter explains:

> Miranda has learned all her language, the father tongue, from Prospero; and it is a language full of sexual slurs on women. Moreover, she has been educated within the world of Prospero's great library. She has learned to adore her father's magic, to be subject to his spells, and to believe that she has no magic of her own.
>
> (p. 29)

Showalter is too good a critic, however, to overlook the fundamental problem of employing this type of self-defeating constant referral to Shakespeare, male canonical authorship itself. She quotes Henry Louis Gates's salient remarks on this strategy: 'We must resist the description of the works of women and the works of persons of colour as . . . shadowy fragments of a Master Text that we, somehow, have been unable to imitate precisely, or to recite correctly, or to ventriloquize eloquently enough' (p. 41).

When Showalter actively utilizes this wisdom, as she does in her chapter on the American Female Gothic, she is brilliant. In fact, the chapters most powerfully argued are, for the most part, the ones derived from the Clarendon Lectures delivered in 1989, in which she presents such feminine conventions as the Gothic as evidence for a unique and significant tradition in women's thought and art, and one that doesn't rest on female responses to male dictates. The book's best offerings are found in its concluding chapter, **'Common Threads',** which gathers her many insightful comments on American female literary history into the single powerful metaphor of American quilt-making. The aptness of the metaphor is embedded both in the formal structure of quilts and in the values that quilting represents. Quilting, the process of piecing or joining bits of spare fabric, 'is an art of making do and eking out, an art of ingenuity, and conservation. It reflects the fragmentation of women's time, the scrappiness and uncertainty of women's creative or solitary moments' (p. 149). Furthermore, Showalter suggestively relates the structure of quilts, many discreet units that join others to form a whole, to the form of female writing itself: 'In feminist literary theories of a Female Aesthetic, piecing became the metaphor for the decentered structure of a women's text' (p. 161). Stowe's *Uncle Tom's Cabin,* for instance, 'does not obey the rules which dictate a unity of action leading to a denouement, but rather operates through the cumulative effect of block of event structured on a parallel design' (p. 155).

Showalter's ultimate response to the question that begins her book is a resounding yes. The path to that conclusion is an enriching and gratifying one, which is only slightly marred by what here is untimely polemics.

### Todd Gitlin (review date 27 April 1997)

SOURCE: Gitlin, Todd. "Millennial Mumbo Jumbo." *Los Angeles Times Book Review* (27 April 1997): 8.

[*In the following excerpt, Gitlin commends Showalter's cultural analysis of texts and fads in* Hystories: Hysterical Epidemics and Modern Culture, *but finds shortcomings in her selective approach and tendency toward "ultra-Freudian logic."*]

Headlong passion was always said to be female, while men, even as they lost their heads, were supposed to be cool. Throughout history, men have been the accusers, diagnosticians and judges, women the witches, patients and victims. Today, allegations of satanic abuse, extraterrestrial abduction, multiple personality and chronic fatigue tend to come from women too. What is new is that, curiously, many of these charges come from feminists apparently more committed to unearthing evidence of their own frailty than to claiming their human powers.

Elaine Showalter, Avalon Foundation professor of the humanities and a professor of English at Princeton University, a historian of medicine and one of America's distinguished feminist literary critics, will have none of what she calls today's "psychological plagues." "As we approach our own millennium," she writes [in ***Hystories***], "the epidemic of hysterical disorders, imaginary illnesses, and hypnotically induced pseudo-memories that have flooded the media seem to be reaching a high-water mark."

Such delusions merge with the conspiracy theories, religious revivals and mass paranoia traditional in America, especially at century's close, when Heaven's

Gate swings open for many of the credulous. As the mass suicide in Rancho Santa Fe shows, such fads are not harmless: "The hysterical epidemics of the 1990s," Showalter writes, ". . . do damage: in distracting us from the real problems and crises of modern society, in undermining a respect for evidence and truth, and in helping support an atmosphere of conspiracy and suspicion. They prevent us from claiming our full humanity as free and responsible beings."

For criticizing the literature of recovered memory to an audience of other feminists, Showalter writes that she has been accused of washing "our dirty linen, so to speak, in front of men." Just so, the feminist psychologist Carol Tavris, who has written comparable criticism, was accused in three full pages in the *New York Times* of joining "the side of the molesters, rapists, pedophiles and other misogynists." Such love-it-or-leave-it Manichaeism of cultivators of victimhood is a sign of shoddy thinking and panic, not of clearheadedness and confidence. Showalter writes boldly and valuably when she points out that to believe in women's equality, you are required to believe that huge proportions of women have been routinely and systematically subjected to sexual abuse.

Showalter displays both the strengths and the weaknesses of her profession. She is adept at scrutinizing texts, "cultural narratives of hysteria," which, with academia's penchant for labored puns and neologisms, she calls "hystories." Drawing on philosopher Ian Hacking's critique of multiple personality and on various journalists' critiques of Gulf War syndrome, chronic fatigue and other "hystories," she amasses many good reasons to cast a skeptical eye on them.

She is less thorough, though, in accounting for them or tracing their origins. She does not systematically compare American paranoias with French, Italian or Latin American. She writes interestingly on the case histories of Charcot, Freud and Lacan and the dramas of Ibsen and others, but these anatomies are only loosely connected to an analysis of social trends.

As for the dating of these uproars, is it as clear as she suggests that the final decades in various centuries (the 1690s and Salem witches, the 1890s and the original hysteria diagnosis and the 1990s and Satanism, recovered memory, chronic fatigue, multiple personality and Gulf War syndrome) are peculiarly prone to binges of wild paranoia? This conclusion is warranted only if we compare those decades with others. But then what of the 1750s' anti-Indian panic, the 1850s' anti-immigrant nativism and the 1950s' McCarthyism and alarms over fluoridation and horror comics? If hysteria is "a cultural symptom of anxiety and stress," when would it ever be out of fashion?

Showalter is also prone at times to a sort of ultra-Freudian logic, in which the eruption of a symptom is taken to be evidence that its preconditions were present or is explained by the previous nonexistence of its symptoms. The British are unflappable, but "the furor over mad cow disease in 1996 owed some of its intensity to British fear and denial of anything mad." Heads you're nuts; tails you're really nuts.

Showalter is on stronger ground when she draws on a considerable body of refutations in dissecting today's fads. She points out that between 1922 and 1972, according to the standard psychological literature, only 50 cases of multiple personality disorder were diagnosed in America; between 1973 and 1990, about 20,000 were diagnosed. What might be going on? Waves of hysteria—or the circulation of unwarranted "hystories," to use Showalter's ungainly neologism—reflect the return of the repressed. But why in the United States? Today's cults involve "the projection of sexual fantasy and real or imagined guilt." Puritan heritage lives! Abstractly, she hopes feminism can "resist regression into victimization, infantilization or revenge." Most of all, and rightly, she regards with favor the much-scorned Enlightenment, knowing that to cede reason to those who reason badly is always mistaken.

### Frederick Crews (review date 12 May 1997)

SOURCE: Crews, Frederick. "Keeping Us In Hysterics." *New Republic* 216, no. 19 (12 May 1997): 35-8, 40-3.

[*In the following review, Crews argues that Showalter "builds no conceptual bridge" between her topics in* Hystories: Hysterical Epidemics and Modern Culture, *noting that Showalter's arguments are weak and poorly supported.*]

For over a decade now, the object of keenest interest within American interdisciplinary scholarship has been a disease, and a possibly nonexistent one. As Elaine Showalter, Avalon Foundation Professor of the Humanities at Princeton University, puts it near the outset of her own latest contribution to the field [***Hystories: Hysterical Epidemics and Modern Culture***]:

> While physicians and psychiatrists have long been writing obituaries for hysteria, scholars in the humanities and social sciences have given it new life. Social historians, philosophers, anthropologists, literary critics, and art historians have taken up the subject of hysteria because it cuts across historical periods and national boundaries, poses fundamental questions about gender and culture, and offers insights into language, narrative, and representation.

This statement is certainly right about the disillusionment of the medical authorities. By now it is reasonably clear that hysteria, which was once thought to cause nervous women and some men to experience paralyses, seizures, tics, linguistic impediments and hallucinations, is not a stable disorder with characteristics that occur independently of social expectations. As a relatively fixed cluster of symptoms, it evaporated after the Victorian heyday of its chief theoreticians, Jean-Martin Charcot, Pierre Janet, Josef Breuer and the early Sigmund Freud—a likely sign that the syndrome was not only psychogenic but artifactual, coaxed into approved forms largely by the therapeutic interventions that were meant to cure it. Hysteria was probably an umbrella term that described a diverse phenomenon; it included symptoms of organic disorders, some outright malingering, and psychogenic suffering of a kind that suited the temper of the age.

Strictly speaking, of course, an ailment cannot "pose questions about gender and culture" and "offer insights into language, narrative, and representation." That is the work of the academics, who would have graced us with their thoughts on those matters with or without hysteria as a pretext. But their enthusiasm for this particular syndrome is understandable. In the nineteenth century, hysteria served as a magnet for masculinist and racialist notions that are now often assumed to have occupied the inmost layer of the smug Victorian mind. Indeed, one common way of regarding the disease, amply developed in Showalter's influential study *The Female Malady: Women, Madness, and English Culture, 1830-1980,* which appeared in 1985, is to say that its diagnosis and its treatment were a medicalization of misogyny itself.

As we recently learned from *Approaching Hysteria,* Marc Micale's comprehensive survey of hysteria studies, that idea of Showalter's has been variously assessed as fertile and regrettably one-dimensional. But Showalter herself is sure that she occupies the cutting edge of research in this field. She, Micale and a few others, she declares in *Hystories,* constitute "the New Hysterians," who understand that hysteria has always been "a body language for people who otherwise might not be able to speak or even to admit what they feel." And her group is in touch with findings in all of the disciplines that matter. The New Hysterians have established themselves, she proudly reports, "at the busy crossroad [sic] where psychoanalytic theory, narratology, feminist criticism, and the history of medicine intersect. . . ."

In the academy as it is currently constituted, that methodological lineup appears thoroughly unproblematic. Showalter sees nothing here requiring further explanation. Yet it may not be immediately obvious to an outsider why two fields of study, medical history and the structure of narrative, are being matched with two vortexes of controversy, psychoanalysis and feminism. Is this intellectual-ideological hybrid really the best available equipment for making sense of hysteria? And don't rival allegiances within the contentious Freudian and feminist traditions dictate very different apprehensions of the social past?

This latter point is especially pertinent to "hysterical" women, whom Freud either cured or persecuted, depending on one's perspective. If, like Showalter, one is inclined to settle for "equity feminism" as opposed to the "gender feminism" that feeds on rage against men, one will be sympathetic to misdiagnosed "hysterics" but wary of glamorizing their helplessness and histrionics. And that tendency will be reinforced if, again like Showalter, one feels more comfortable with classical Freudian notions than with the radical view (common among gender feminists) that psychoanalysis needs to be purged of its oppressive patriarchal features. Showalter's theoretical affinities, never cogently defended, thus press her continually toward a middle-of-the-road outlook that could pass for sheer reasonableness. But it is, I am afraid, more a matter of dodging trouble and taking refuge in received ideas.

Until now, the clearest instance of this weakness has been Showalter's inability to be consistent about whether she regards hysteria as an authentic malady. She has supported both sides without appearing to notice that she is contradicting herself. Her usual view is that hysteria was less an affliction than a somatic idiom for otherwise silenced people—an attractive hypothesis that is somewhat incommoded by the managerial style of such wealthy and manipulative hysterics as Breuer's "Anna O." (Bertha Pappenheim) and Freud's "Frau Cäcilie M." (Anna von Lieben). Yet in *The Female Malady* Showalter also upheld Charcot's opposite judgment—it was briefly influential but fiercely contested—that hysteria was a true disease whose manifestations were visited upon, not suggested to or invented by, the sufferer. "Through careful observation, physical examination, and the use of hypnosis," she wrote, "Charcot was able to prove that hysterical symptoms, while produced by emotions rather than by physical injury, were genuine, and not under the conscious control of the patient."

That last claim was already out of step with informed opinion when it appeared in 1985. To be sure, Charcot did regard hypnosis as crucial to an understanding of hysteria, whose symptoms, he believed, were produced when a trauma sent the organism into a quasi-hypnotic state. By "rehypnotizing" his resident hysterics and putting them through their symptomatic paces, supposedly without their conscious awareness of obeying an instruction, Charcot imagined that he was demonstrating the integrity of hysteria and its isolation from conscious will. But in truth he had proved little more than his own gullibility. His critics and later students were able to show that coaching and suggestibility, not to mention dissimulation, amply account for all of Charcot's hypnotic results.

Why does this matter? The point is, in fact, momentous. For the young Freud sat reverently at Charcot's feet in 1885-86, enthralled by what he would eventually regard as hypnotic evidence of "split consciousness." It was on that basis that he would begin his fateful quest for unconscious mental causes of neuroses. In 1888, in the preface to his translation of Hippolyte Bernheim's book *Suggestion,* he explicitly rejected the idea that Charcot could have obtained his findings through suggestion, since otherwise "[w]e should not learn from the study of major hypnotism what alterations in excitability succeed one another in the nervous system of hysterical patients . . . ; we should merely learn what intentions Charcot suggested (in a manner of which he himself was unconscious) to the subjects of his experiments—a thing entirely irrelevant to our understanding alike of hypnosis and of hysteria." Here is Freud as Quixote, taking the measure of his first windmill.

The more clearly we realize that Showalter in 1985 was quite justified in regarding hysteria as jointly "constructed" by doctors and patients, the more ludicrous it seems that Freud could have dismissed the threat of suggestion not just in Charcot's case but throughout his own career. The joke, however, was lost on Showalter, who has always displayed a novitiate's piety toward the founding legend of psychoanalysis. Like Breuer, whose Anna O. case she badly misrepresented in **The Female Malady,** Charcot is an indispensable "precursor" in that legend, and Showalter was therefore unable to adopt a sufficiently critical view of his mistakes.

In **Hystories,** Showalter finally takes a harder line toward Charcot and hysteria. But now she is able to keep the hysterical ball in play by deliberately blurring the line between hysteria as a mental illness of individuals and the popular notion of "mass hysteria," or waves of fear, morbidity, and physical unease that ripple through collectivities in the grip of shared delusions. Her central claim is that hysteria recurs in more or less regular cycles—and that we today, like the Victorians, are living through a peak phase of the phenomenon. The chief hysterias of our time, for Showalter, are chronic fatigue syndrome, Gulf War syndrome, recovered memory of childhood sexual abuse, multiple personality disorder, satanic ritual abuse and alien abduction, all of them resulting from a contagion of erroneous ideas.

Showalter does a creditable journalistic job of marshaling informed opinion about each of her six American "hysterias." Even so, misgivings arise from the outset. For one thing, she builds no conceptual bridge from individual pathology to the social dynamics of rumor-formation. Is it hysterical to pick up a faddish idea about UFOs, or about one's feeling of listlessness? Do we gain anything by labeling as hysterical the serene self-cancelers of Heaven's Gate? The desired linkage of such instances with hysteria à la Charcot, Janet, Breuer and Freud is little more than semantic. And even within her modern instances, Showalter has yoked together vastly disparate phenomena. She sees no significant difference, for her analysis, between mistaken, correctable beliefs on the part of normal people and paranoid phantasms and lasting physical debility. She is even willing to count as hysterical the panic of Japanese subway riders in the wake of a poison gas attack, as if there were no distinction to be drawn between well-founded fear and pure delusion.

There is something peremptory about Showalter's list of recent hysterias. She has married two items on which the medical jury is still out—chronic fatigue syndrome and Gulf War syndrome—to four others whose iatrogenic (doctor-induced) and hallucinatory basis is by now evident to most observers. Malingerers and copycats are always with us, but it seems especially early, while investigations into possible toxic exposure are still underway, for Showalter to be asserting so categorically that Gulf War syndrome "does not exist."

By casting the hysterical net as widely as possible, Showalter is apparently seeking to gain certain tactical advantages. She wants us to believe, for example, that our hysteria-plagued society urgently needs the ministrations of literary critics, without whom the "story" of hysteria would be indecipherable or vulnerable to ingenuous literal interpretation. We must turn to fiction, she maintains, if we are to fortify ourselves against present and future hysterical outbreaks, for novels "can tell us a lot more about the causes and cures of hysteria than most of the self-help books on the market." And it is critics, naturally, with their keen attunement to genre conventions, who can save us from the fallacy of thinking that similarities among "hystories" (reports of abduction, etc.) are a warrant of their truth.

Showalter is right to emphasize that popular narratives in our time have transmitted destructive misapprehensions about the mind. Think of *Sybil, Michelle Remembers* and *The Three Faces of Eve,* which have variously primed Americans to believe in satanism, multiple personality, and repressed memories of sexual abuse. Understanding the conventions and the structure of those books, however, is of negligible utility. What we chiefly need to know about them is that their stories are false. These texts call not for formal analysis, but for research into their suspect origins. A literary critic could conduct such research as well as the next person, but Showalter has not even perceived its value, so bent is she upon commentary of a more usual but irrelevant kind.

On its face, *Hystories* seems to be saying that we Americans are living through one of the most perilous junctures of our history. Showalter points out that we are approaching the year 2000, a perfect witching hour for mass hysteria. Millennial panic is drawing us inexorably toward an Armageddon in which "traumatists and ufologists, experiencers and abductees, survivors and survivalists" will all join forces against public sanity. This "coming hysterical plague" may yet be averted, but only if we mobilize all our resources of prevention. As a sample of such preparedness, Showalter walks us through the hysterical and paranoid themes of *Batman Forever*, one of many cultural products that are allegedly laying the groundwork for a new Salem on a nationwide scale.

The reader who finds all this hard to swallow needn't feel apologetic. Showalter doesn't really believe it herself. On the penultimate page of her book, she admits that

> [t]he hysterical witch-hunts of our own time may be waning. . . . People accused of abuse on the basis of recovered memory are being acquitted. Convictions have been overturned. Retractors are taking back their accusations of satanic ritual or childhood abuse. Journalists in Britain and the United States have taken up the cause of those falsely accused. Books and TV documentaries have helped turn the tide of credibility. . . .

Thus Showalter's own attempt to whip up a little hysteria, if only to lend urgency to her discourse, eventually comes to naught.

Watching Showalter's argument self-destruct, one has to wonder whether she doesn't have some other end in view. There are grounds for inferring that *Hystories* was conceived in mindfulness not of millennial frenzy but of something quite opposite: the turning of the tide against recovered memory, acknowledged here as a seeming afterthought. Showalter has perceived that the therapeutic craze of the late 1980s and early 1990s, whereby patients have been encouraged to concoct images of early sexual violation and then to suppose that those images must be memories, is rapidly becoming a liability, both intellectually and ethically. Sensing the movement's imminent collapse, Showalter wants to assure us that she never meant to endorse it.

I single out recovered memory as the core "hysteria" in Showalter's list for two reasons. The first is that recovered memory is the common denominator of all four of her syndromes that involve delusions and not just physical symptoms. Belatedly "recalled" childhood sexual abuse, multiple personality, satanic ritual abuse and interplanetary abduction all tend to blossom on the same branch, namely, suggestive prompting by therapists who use hypnosis and/or related techniques to bring the client's perceived history into alignment with a favorite diagnosis. Indeed, the "memory" of satanic rites and the emergence of "dissociated alters" are simply later stages of the search for more and more grisly instances of sexual abuse. And it is only in therapy, typically, that the lost souls who suspect that they may have been wafted into hovering spaceships succeed in "remembering" for certain that it was so.

Second, Showalter tells us, in a commendable act of self-criticism, that she must now reconsider her declaration at the end of *The Female Malady* that "the best hope for the future is the feminist therapy movement," including "women's self-help groups." She now recognizes that just such groups, at the very time that she was exalting them, were crucially responsible for launching the recovered memory movement; and she sees that even today they remain a breeding ground of false sexual accusations. *Hystories* is Showalter's vehicle not only for correcting her mistake, but also for challenging the whole conception of "women's ways of knowing"—a conception that, for many radical feminists and distraught women under their influence, has turned the suspicion of early sexual violation into a foregone conclusion.

This is a worthwhile purpose on Showalter's part, but it immediately comes up against a delicate point of diplomacy. Just how much recantation can she afford without jeopardizing her stature within the fiercely politicized field of women's studies? Feminists, she asserts, owe a primary obligation to the truth. Yet she also knows that the very concept of truth has taken a pummeling from some of her sisters as an oppressive phallocentric ideal. Showalter is not about to walk the plank on behalf of truth-for-its-own-sake. Instead, she adopts a politic stance of more feminist than thou. Feminism itself, she points out, possesses its own "strong enlightenment, rationalist tradition," and so she will "ask feminist questions" about the conspiratorial illusions of our time. And with less fanfare, she will backpedal and equivocate whenever her challenge to radical feminism threatens to become a permanent estrangement.

Note, for example, how Showalter professes to be scandalized that Lynne Cheney

> draws a sinister analogy between women's studies discussions and therapeutic coercion: "Indeed, there are many parallels between the recovered memory movement and feminism as it has come to be practiced on campuses. The encouragement—even the requirement—in feminist classrooms to confess personal views and traumas establishes an environment very much like the one that exists in victim recovery groups." Feminist activists are understandably angry about these attacks. . . .

Now, Showalter knows perfectly well that the "recovery group" approach to pedagogy is practiced and openly advocated by some feminist academics, and she also knows that many women students, with little or no assistance from therapists, have disastrously acquired "memories" of sexual abuse when their seminar leaders and classmates effectively demanded that they do so. For Showalter to make that charge, however, would be a virtual declaration of academic civil war. Instead, she rounds up the usual suspect, the impenitently conservative Cheney, and offers her as a hostage to the militants.

Showalter's distaste for factional strife may also account for the emphasis that she now places on male hysteria. As she uneasily remarks, hysteria is "a term that particularly enrages some feminists because for centuries it has been used to ridicule and trivialize women's medical and political complaints." But if the recovered memory movement is hysterical, and Showalter insists that it is, then she herself is bestowing the h-word on the feminist mainstays of that movement. Only by stipulating that men, too, fall victim to hysteria—including "our war veterans" who "had to deal with frightening gossip" in the Persian Gulf—can Showalter acquire some insurance against the accusation of having betrayed her sex.

Once that insurance has been purchased, Showalter feels confident enough to dissent not only from recovered memory theory but also from a peculiarly defeatist, victim-minded style of feminist thought that fed into it. This is the 1970s modified-Lacanian doctrine of Hélène Cixous, Julia Kristeva, Catherine Clément and Luce Irigaray, according to which the whole realm of rational knowledge was ceded to men while "absence" and "lack" were celebrated as innately feminine. Those voluble champions of muteness elevated the hysterical woman of the nineteenth century to heroic status. They proclaimed that "the discourse of the hysteric" was the true speech of womankind, to be cherished in defiance of such patriarchal straitjackets as grammar and syntax. Not so, objects Showalter, joining what has by now become a chorus of protest against "essentialist" stereotyping of the incoherent female mind.

Again, however, the thinness of Showalter's critique becomes painfully apparent. In her view, it was only a lapse of prudence for Parisian feminists to chant, in 1972, "Nous sommes toutes des hystériques!" In doing so, "they came dangerously close to acting like hysterical divas," and those among them who were psychoanalysts accordingly found themselves penalized by their Freudian or Lacanian establishments. For Showalter, playing Dear Abby for the moment, the lesson is clear: "Claiming hysteria is not the wisest strategy for professional success." But what about the Freudian/Lacanian premises of French feminism? Shouldn't they be reviewed and judged?

If Showalter were to undertake such an inquiry, however, it could lead to awkward questions about her own unexamined psychoanalytic assumptions. Discretion is therefore preferable. Thus, when she relates that Cixous and company located the origin of hysterical female discourse in "the pre-Oedipal phase of feminine development, when the baby daughter takes the mother as her primary object of desire," Showalter observes only that the idea possessed "tremendous intellectual and emotional appeal." Evidently, her professed allegiance to Enlightenment standards does not extend to a concern for the empirical basis of theories about the mind.

Here we return to a source of confusion in Showalter's work that is even more consequential than her bending to every feminist breeze. I mean her unreflective loyalty to the broad outlines of the psychoanalytic revelation. That loyalty appears to be tested at various moments in her book, partly in response to cited objections that I myself have posed. But the Freudian unconscious remains Showalter's master key not just to psychological sophistication, but to the alleviation of mental woe everywhere. As she puts it, "Freud's message never got through to millions of people, who still distrust and fear the unconscious and its power over us. As a result, they suffer needlessly."

I would like to say that Showalter and I disagree about psychoanalysis and leave it at that, but something more symptomatic of "humanistic" complacency is on display here: a bland refusal to think consecutively. Remarkably, Showalter concedes the truth of nearly every negative observation about Freud and psychoanalysis that comes to her notice. Yet those concessions leave her argument completely unaffected, as if she were just going through the motions of acknowledging a distant, boring debate. Her faith in Freud has about it a dreaminess that cannot be penetrated by mundane considerations of evidence and logic.

Showalter grants that Freud was a self-publicizing "showman" who was less interested in curing his patients than in turning them into exhibits of his pet notions. More significantly, he was a "stubborn, bullying interrogator" who "pressured his patients to produce narratives congruent with his theories." And she further admits that, when Freud adopted his Oedipal explanation of the psychoneuroses, his system of thought became (in Richard Webster's quoted words) "almost completely freed from the constraints of empirical reality." Does it not follow that we should hesitate to adopt that system as our own lens upon reality? But the issue is never raised.

In this respect Showalter proves to be typical of her fellow New Hysterians, who are uniformly partial to psychoanalysis though often stern toward its creator. Take Sander L. Gilman, an eminent cultural historian and a recent president of the Modern Language Association, whose blurb for *Hystories* calls it "the standard for all future studies of mental illness and culture." In learned and provocative books such as *Freud, Race, and Gender* and *The Case of Sigmund Freud,* Gilman goes further than any accused Freud-basher toward reducing psychoanalysis to a manifestation of one madcap improviser's eccentricity. In Gilman's account, Freud's universal castration complex was his attempt to pin on the human race what Germanic anti-Semites were saying about the circumcised Jews; and again, his psychology of women is presented as yet another deflection of racist slanders. These charges saddle Freud with a craven furtiveness that sits ill with the Promethean legend he took such pains to promote. Yet Gilman's startling indictment never causes him to reconsider his own Freudianism. Some commitments, I suppose, are just too deep for thought.

Showalter herself is far more protective of Freud the man. Indeed, when she has to decide which movements to approve and which to shun, she applies a simple litmus test: Do these people show sufficient respect for the discoverer of the unconscious? Thus the French feminists, despite their "appealing" manipulation of Freudian developmental notions, placed themselves beyond the reach of her forgiveness when they depicted Freud as the male oppressor par excellence and characterized his female patients as martyrs to a sexist institutional practice.

Preeminent among those rehabilitated "stars" and "supermodels," as Showalter scornfully calls them, stands the teenage "Dora" (Ida Bauer), whose brief treatment at Freud's hands ended rancorously when she refused to accede to his view of her as an Oedipally fixated bisexual whose symptoms had been prompted not by her gruesome family predicament, but by early masturbation and a desire to suck her father's penis. Showalter is uncomfortable with that diagnosis, but her outrage is reserved for those feminists who have called Freud, not Dora, the real hysteric in the case. "They made Freud the fall guy, pinning the blame for Dora's symptoms onto him. . . ." And again: "Dramatizing the psychoanalyst's hysteria, reducing his theories to performance or farce, is another way of fending off the specter of the unconscious." It is time, decrees Showalter, to forsake the perverse outlook that prizes "women's stories" over "doctors' studies," the latter presumably being trustworthy because doctors know best, especially if their name is Freud.

Yet the doctor in Dora's case was not just wrong, he was also relentlessly cruel, and his cruelty was fed by the theory of mental conflict that Showalter sentimentally misconstrues. Freud's harrying of Dora rested on his Charcot-inspired conviction that hysteria was as regular in its laws of operation as epilepsy or syphilis, and on his utterly mechanical view of its causation. That is why he could write to Wilhelm Fliess, soon after beginning his attempt to break Dora's will, that the case had "smoothly opened to the existing collection of picklocks." Freud was sure that he could force to the surface an admission of a specific early practice, event, or fantasy (masturbation, the primal scene, an incest-wish) to match each symptom. The contrast with Showalter's empathetic, socially aware, symptom-as-protest conception of hysteria could hardly be greater— but she draws no conclusion from that fact.

On the crucial topic of recovered memory, finally, Showalter's psychoanalytic partisanship once again requires her to don blinders and give out useless advice. She is eager to believe that the alleged link between Freudianism and recovered memory is merely a defamation by "one-sided" and "vitriolic" extremists such as myself. As she mentions in passing, however, therapeutic epidemics can only get going if they possess a theoretical superstructure. And though Showalter won't come near to admitting it, nothing could be more obvious than that the theory behind recovered memory was drawn almost entirely from the Freudian picture of the mind.

It was Freud who gave us the idea of repression, and of the vivid, accurate retrieval of derepressed material after a lapse of decades. It was Freud who arbitrarily singled out sexual trauma as uniquely pathogenic and refused to allow for normal infantile amnesia, instead invoking the repression of sexual vicissitudes. And it was Freud who taught us that symptoms are really disguised memories, that the interpretation of dreams can lead to accurate knowledge of the distant past, that permanent psychological relief can come only from revisiting that past, and that a patient's agitated behavior during therapy can be safely ascribed to torment by the repressed. Where would recovered memory therapy be without all those unsubstantiated tenets?

For Showalter, predictably, the key to halting outbreaks such as the recovered memory madness is to "defend Freud's insights and try to restore confidence in serious psychotherapy," mainly psychoanalysis. But psychoanalysis evolved from a recovered memory inquisition—Freud's "seduction theory" of the mid-1890s—and it contains a built-in potential to revert to that state. When disheartened analysts, sensing public resistance, tire of ascribing murderous and incestuous designs to small children and of telling real victims of early molestation that they are suffering only from illusory "screen memories," the hunt for Oedipal fantasies can get swiftly replaced by a hunt for repressed sexual abuse and its "perpetrators."

Just such a turn was taken around 1930, when Freud's anguished disciple Sándor Ferenczi, chafing against the master's icy and controlling ways, decided that his women patients deserved sympathy as probable survivors of early molestation. And, since about 1990, it has been happening again. As C. Brooks Brenneis documents in a new book, *Recovered Memories of Trauma: Transferring the Present to the Past* (International Universities Press), considerable numbers of certified analysts, many of them radical feminists, have themselves been adapting psychoanalytic technique to recovered memory practice.

When Showalter at last awakens to this appalling phenomenon, she will doubtless say that the analysts in question have not chosen the best style of feminism or Freudianism and are behaving badly—in fact, just like a pack of hysterics. A more effective response might be to call into question the whole unproven idea that colloquy between a therapist and a patient can reliably unlock repressed secrets from the patient's early childhood. And to that end, a truly skeptical history of "dynamic" psychotherapy and its favorite diseases might be an important source of illumination. Unfortunately, it isn't likely to be forthcoming from any of Showalter's New Hysterians.

## Mark S. Micale (review date 16 May 1997)

SOURCE: Micale, Mark S. "Strange Signs of the Times." *Times Literary Supplement,* no. 4911 (16 May 1997): 6-7.

[*In the following review, Micale praises Showalter's examination of feminine hysteria in* Hysteries: Hysterical Epidemics and Modern Culture.]

The ritualized self-immolation of thirty-nine members of the Heaven's Gate sect near San Diego, California, late last March could almost be seen as a promotional event for **Hystories: Hysterical Epidemics and Modern Culture,** Elaine Showalter's provocative and immensely readable new book. Showalter examines a series of large-scale functional psychopathologies, originating in the United States but now metastasizing, that she reads as the pandemic hysterias, or "psychological plagues", of the late twentieth century. That emotional distress can emerge through bodily symptoms, and that styles of psychosomatic suffering vary among cultures and periods, is an accepted insight of modern medicine. On the eve of the millennium, Showalter's book suggests, the dominant psychogenic sicknesses have taken especially florid and dramatic forms.

Hysteria has had many past meanings. In Hippocratic times, physicians believed that the uterus, or *hystera,* moved mischievously through the female body cavity, causing dizziness, loss of sensation and laboured breathing (including the sensation of a ball lodged in the throat, or *globus hysterious*) as well as extravagant emotional behaviours. During the later Middle Ages and Renaissance, hysteria was viewed as a sign of possession by the devil; witch-hysterias developed anaesthetic spots and patches, or *stigmata diaboli,* on their bodies. In Enlightenment Europe, "vaporous" Salon women swooned from noxious uterine emanations to the heart and head. And in *fin-de-siècle* Paris and Vienna, the disorder achieved its golden age; Jean-Martin Charcot, the "Napoleon of the Neuroses", observed rampant motor paralyses and stylized, epileptiform attacks in his hospital patients. Freud confronted the complex and idiosyncratic neurotica of his affluent clientele, which he interpreted as the symbolically coded manifestations of repressed sexual desires, anxieties and fantasies. A generation later, the great neurosis metamorphosed again: confronted with the intolerable realities of trench warfare, masses of British, French, German and Italian infantry soldiers broke down with hysterical tremors, blindness and stuttering.

Strikingly, present-day Western medicine is rapidly abandoning the concept of hysteria. Over the past several decades, the major textbooks and diagnostic manuals of psychiatry have replaced hysteria with a more scientific-sounding vocabulary of "undifferentiated somatoform disorder", "psychogenic pain disorder", "histrionic personality type" and "factitious illness disorder". In addition to this repackaging, some observers say that the liberalization of social and sexual norms has permitted greater self-expression for women and, therefore, led to the decline of a classically Victorian neurotic disorder. Others maintain that, as the psychodynamics of repression became widely understood, hysterical symptom-formation was unconsciously discarded in favour of more inward-looking neuroses, like depression and narcissism. Equally, hysteria's associations with Freud, who used it as the founding neurosis of psychoanalysis, have become a liability; in an age of ascendant bio-psychiatry, the categories of classic psycho-analysis are out of favour. Whatever the causes, hysteria as a single, unified diagnosis is becoming increasingly obsolete in medical theory and practice. Our own *fin de siècle,* it appears, has brought the *fin d'hystérie.*

Ironically, the very period that has witnessed the progressive clinical dismantling of hysteria within Anglo-American psychiatry has brought a burst of interest among scholars in social and cultural history, literary theory and criticism, the history of science, women's and gender studies, art history and film studies. Several factors explain the new academic interest in hysteria. At a time when the ideology of the avant-garde has penetrated the university, the study of hysteria, with its mixture of science, sexuality and sensationalism, is irresistible. Likewise, hysteria occupies a prominent position in the mythology of women. Studying its past, when it often provided theoretical ammunition for female sub-ordination, is part of the great metacritique of gender that will doubtless be judged one of the defining features of late twentieth-century society. In addition, the very disappearance of hysteria from the medical field seems to have freed the concept for appropriation by other disciplines.

There's a reason, too, I suspect, why literary critics in particular are drawn to the topic as the metaphor of choice for behaviour deemed extreme, emotional, or irrational. In modern medicine, hysteria is a "neuromimetic" affliction. It is the illness that has no essence, but rather emerges, chameleon-like, by aping the symptomatological form of other, organic, usually neurological, pathologies. This makes it perfect for literary academics in a relativist climate pre-occupied with crises of representation. Hysteria is the postmodernist malady *par excellence,* a signifier without a signified which represents the limits of representation within the medical sciences and which therefore has been quietly abandoned as an object of positivist investigation.

Whatever the causes, no author has contributed more importantly to the new literature in this area than Elaine Showalter. Arguably the leading Anglo-American feminist historian of psychiatry, Showalter has, in the past decade, given us a series of sensitive and probing studies of gender, medicine and culture (beginning with *The Female Malady: Women, Madness and English Culture, 1830-1980* in 1985). Showalter's gift is for lively, literate and interpretative synthesis of specialized academic scholarship, in language that bridges the popular and scholarly worlds.

So what are the major transmutations of hysteria today? According to Showalter, the rolling eyes, arched backs and writhing convulsions of earlier times have given way to a set of individual hysterias connected with modern social movements and amplified by technological communications to produce full-scale psychological epidemics. She calls the public, cultural narratives these movements produce "hystories". The provocative part of her book gives examples of what she considers to be contemporary psychogenic diseases, placed in order of increasing irrationality: chronic fatigue syndrome, Gulf War Syndrome (GWS), recovered memory, multiple personality syndrome, satanic ritual abuse and alien abduction. The mere sequential listing of these items in a single table of contents is likely to infuriate those who have experienced any of these—or believe they have.

CFS, dubbed "the yuppie flu" during the 1980s, is a mishmash of symptoms, including a mysterious and debilitating *malaise,* that affects primarily white middle-class men and women, and that many sufferers believe is caused by an unidentified environmental pathogene.

The subject of intensive media coverage, GWS now allegedly affects thousands of veterans who have developed a rush of crippling symptoms, from insomnia and impotence to cancer and birth defects. In the recovered memory movement, survivors of rape, domestic battery and incest dredge up previously repressed recollections of past traumas under the hypnotic inducement of specially trained therapists. Linked to this is multiple personality syndrome, in which a portion of an individual's psyche splits off and develops a separate identity as a coping strategy in the face of severely painful experience—often childhood sexual abuse. Believers in satanic ritual abuse hold that secret groups of devil-worshippers seize people to perform ghoulish and sadistic rituals on them. And adherents to the idea of alien abduction believe that extra-terrestrial beings regularly visit the earth, where they have slowly infiltrated the human population and are conducting experiments, including invasive sexual procedures, on inhabitants.

Showalter demonstrates in alarming detail that tens, even hundreds, of thousands of people, many educated and informed, share such beliefs and participate in these well-organized movements. Her notes brim with references to book-length studies of each category, many published by well known presses. Sixty thousand veterans have reported post-Gulf War symptoms. The United States Government now makes disability payments to many claimants, and huge institutional resources are being deployed in its investigation. Similarly, by 1994 over 300 court cases involving recovered memory testimony had been heard in the USA; many proceedings led to prosecution and internment, some of which have since been overturned. In the past two decades, the FBI has investigated hundreds of instances of alleged satanic abuse. Not only the victims, but lawyers, academics, the media, pharmaceutical companies and mental-health professionals of all stripes are increasingly endorsing these beliefs. Furthermore, respectable journals, institutions and authorities—indeed, sometimes prestigious academics—support each of these movements. The most visible American proponent of extra-terrestrial visitation is John E. Mack, author of *Abduction: Human Encounters with Aliens* (1994). Mack, whose 1977 biography of Lawrence of Arabia received a Pulitzer Prize, teaches at Harvard Medical School and founded the psychiatry department at Cambridge Hospital. (Efforts by the Harvard administration to muzzle Mack have thus far failed.)

Showalter, it should clearly be stated, responsibly qualifies her critique. She does not consider these behaviours fake or fraudulent. She accepts the reality of the symptoms and acknowledges that many cases involve intense suffering. She also grants that individual cases designated as chronic fatigue, GWS and multiple personality may well include an organic component of some sort. What is more, she repeatedly cites widespread sexualized violence against women. "The sexual, physical, and emotional abuse of children", she adds, "is a terrible reality." It is less the individual cases, then, that Showalter objects to than the retrospective constructions of these experiences—the illness ideologies, therapy cults and patient campaigns of the 1980s and 1990s, with their vested social, political and economic interests.

Overwhelmingly, Showalter reads these movements as expressions of personal stress and cultural anxiety in late twentieth-century life. In men and women alike, psychogenic symptoms should entail no stigma. On the contrary, in the author's analysis, hysteria is part of the human condition; it is a universal capacity for the conversion of emotional pain and conflict into the camouflaged but culturally acceptable language of body illness. The current equation of psychogenesis with weakness, especially in adult men, effectively forbids the direct expression of these anxieties. Consequently,

> culture forces people to deny the psychological and emotional sources of their symptoms and to insist that they must be biological and beyond their control in order for them to view themselves as legitimately ill and entitled to the privileges of the sick role.

Members of these movements will be enraged by Showalter's book. Despite her credentials in the field, some academic feminists may also feel betrayed by her presentation of recovered memory and multiple personality syndrome, which draw on recent feminist thought. Similarly, clinicians will most likely have trouble with Showalter's elastic usage of the term "hysteria", alternately a disease, a reaction, a metaphor and a description. Historians of medicine may find the scholarship in the opening historical chapters thin. And I was irritated by the author's integration of widely incongruous sources, ranging from the fiction of Flaubert, Conrad and James, to the neurological case histories of Charcot, to contemporary films such as *The Piano* and *Batman Forever,* all of which contain characters breezily pronounced hysterical. The power and importance of the book, however, lie in its cultural-critical analysis. Showalter has brought together a series of the more *outré* socio-scientific phenomena of our time that may very profitably be considered together. She provides, moreover, a shrewd and unrelenting analysis of the structural elements these movements share.

Typically, individuals who are unhappy or unfulfilled in their lives develop diffuse and evolving nervous complaints and eventually seek help. A physician, or some other scientific authority figure, concocts "a unified field theory providing a clear and coherent explanation for the confusing symptoms", as well as a new and memorable name for the syndrome. This explanation draws on contemporary disease theory, usually viral and immunological ideas. An individual case or two, often involving a well-known public personality, provides a popular paradigm for the new synthesis of symptoms. A best-selling novel (*Three Faces of Eve, Sybil, Rosemary's Baby, Communion,* for instance), soon to become a major motion picture, first advertises the syndrome to a large audience. Magazine stories and television documentaries further publicize the symptoms. High-profile books for persons seeking information appear, as do patients' autobiographies. Most recently, daily talk-shows, those agencies of mass pop psychotherapy, unite sufferers and therapists in order to dramatize their life stories and to explain the meaning of their disorder for millions; in the process, participants cite enormous projected numbers of the afflicted and encourage others to come forward.

These are acutely communicable diseases. As a result, vulnerable and impressionable viewers exposed to the illness model engage in a kind of psychogenic self-fashioning. The mental-health establishment, responding to what it sees as a new psychopathology (and an emerging patient population), adds the diagnosis to its list of official diagnoses, which lends further credence to the idea and makes health insurance coverage easier to obtain. In the mean time, the original diagnostician has earned widespread recognition, and a new psychotherapeutic subspeciality, sometimes with specialized clinics, emerges. Journals, newsletters and international societies crop up. Eventually, patients themselves join together to hold seminars and workshops and form, "survivors sessions" and self-help groups. The Internet instantaneously disseminates information across the world. (The World Wide Web lists dozens of on-line publications and organizations for survivors of psychological traumata.) In this way, Showalter's six phenomena have gone from virtual non-existence a generation ago to epidemic proportions with large patient-therapist movements in the late 1990s.

What, then, lies behind today's proliferating hysterias? Showalter emphasizes a cluster of causes: unrealistic expectations of fulfilment, happiness and productivity in life; a series of recent disease scares (AIDS, foremost); religious fundamentalism; the medical market-place; the pervasive presence of the media and their immense powers of popularization; alarmist and sensationalist medical journalism; the gratification of believing that vague emotional and physical complaints express a (nonfatal) bodily disorder; and the companionship of like-minded sufferers. To these factors she adds the role of "American millenarian paranoia". She notes, too, that a suspicious number of scenarios in each category include a sexual component, which is often displaced on to some external source.

Combined with this concatenation are assuredly deeper cultural preconditions: with secularization comes the inevitable search for alternative messages of meaning and sources of hope, solace and confession. Furthermore, ages of high scientism have typically spawned counter-cultures: mesmerism during the late Enlightenment, faith-healing and hypnosis at the turn of the last century, our own New Age psychologies and alternative medicines. Along similar lines, improvements in public hygiene and the lengthening of life expectancy have had the odd effect of making health a universal, all-consuming concern.

In all of this, modern science, and particularly the sciences of the mind, occupy an ambiguous position. According to standard historical accounts, scientific naturalism and experimental rationalism progressively supplant superstition and irrationality in the professional and popular mind. Yet, these six syndromes are cast precisely in the languages of contemporary science. CFS, GWS and multiple personality disorder are medical representations of human distress. Their victims have read deeply in the technical writings about their condition. Members of the mental health professions fuel the multiple-personality and recovered-memory movements. The prestige of psychiatry today issues partly from advances in understanding the physiology and chemistry of the brain. The most recent technologies of communication spread these pseudo-pathologies. Even the brouhaha about alien abduction is spurred by the latest scientific search for extraterrestrial intelligence.

The interface between scientific research and the life of the individual is formed, of course, by psychotherapy. For better or worse, we turn today to the psychosciences to improve our moods, raise our children, try our criminals, interpret our works of art and energize our sex lives. But, in this case, is more better? In Showalter's exposition, there is good psychotherapy and bad psychotherapy. We need an enlightened psychology (including Freud) to understand these new syndromes, especially to elucidate the interconnection between mind and body, and the operations of emotional anxiety, physical somatization and sexual suppression. It is psychological illiteracy that underlays these subcultures of sickness in the first place. And serious, responsible psychotherapy, she argues, can do much to alleviate the anxieties and discontents of many of their adherents.

Fair enough. Yet surely these pages also establish that the place of psychotherapy in Western society has become exceedingly complex and qualified and that, to adapt Karl Kraus's formulation, psychotherapy has to a degree become the illness it purports to cure. In the 1990s, psychological medicine provides the very intellectual technologies that create and sustain these epidemics. With the secularization of suffering and the subsequent spread of psychiatry into our everyday emotional lives, a disorder, a diagnosis, a therapist and a support group become sources of existential identity. In our advanced psychiatric society, as the French critic Robert Castel called it, to get a life is to get an illness.

One response to the new acronymic illnesses of the age is to dismiss them as pathologies of self and society peculiar to America. Victorian medics, after all, believed that male hysteria in particular was un-English, limited by and large to the volatile Latin races on the Continent. But there is a good deal of evidence that these contemporary hysterias are now dispersing globally, and that includes Britain. Showalter's opening cases of chronic fatigue hail from England and Scotland. Medical Britons contribute mightily to the debate about CFS, here styled "ME", or myalgic encephalomyelitis, so as to sound somatic. Hundreds of sympathetic reports of GWS have appeared in the British press. Courses in the dissociative disorders are increasing. British feminist theorists have taken up the issue of satanic abuse more energetically than their counterparts elsewhere, and the most effective proponent of its reality is a child psychotherapist at London's Tavistock Clinic. In the past decade, the British Isles have been second only to the US in the number of reported UFO sightings. Public media discourse in the UK and US becomes more uniform by the day, and the causes outlined above are spreading widely.

I should acknowledge that on first reading I felt by turns informed, entertained and astounded by Showalter's story, while dismissing most of it as the antics of obscure and minuscule minorities. However, the day after I finished the book, in Boston, I picked up the *New York Times* to read about the San Diego suicides. (Apparently the world-view of sect members was a blend of Christian utopianism, sci-fi mythology and astrological divination, popularized through cyberspace. Their immediate motive was the belief that they were about to be saved by alien beings travelling in spacecraft in the wake of the Hale-Bopp comet.) Later that day, *The X-Files,* an award-winning television show with a huge and obsessive following, about aliens, cults and cover-ups, was broadcast. And the following evening, an hour-long, prime-time television documentary reported with equanimity on both sides of the alien abduction issue. The following week, in the lead story of the evening network news, jury selection began for the trial of Timothy McVeigh, indicted in the Oklahoma City bombing that killed 136 people. The "hystory" of McVeigh's paramilitary movement, with its ideas of governmental conspiracies to destroy civil liberties, shares many of the features discussed by Showalter.

Strange signs—or, rather, symptoms of the times. There may be hope, however. A number of these scourges are now generating counter-literatures. Also, uncovering the *modus operandi* of past psychological plagues has often contributed to their remission. In a good Enlightenment topos, knowledge is cure. Moreover, earlier contagions have tended to spread during the terminal years of centuries (and millennia) and then quickly to pass. If we can endure for three more years, we may survive, although, in light of the recent news, I fear things will worsen before they improve. In the mean time, we can be thankful for a commentator as sane, courageous and clear-headed as Elaine Showalter.

**Melissa Benn (review date 13 June 1997)**

SOURCE: Benn, Melissa. "Out of Control?" *New Statesman* 126, no. 4338 (13 June 1997): 48.

[*In the following review of* Hystories: Hysterical Epidemics and Modern Culture, *Benn commends the "impressive clarity" of Showalter's discussion, but finds flaws in her presumptuous assertions about the nature of mysterious new afflictions.*]

It is rare for a book of cultural criticism to make so much real world trouble. But Elaine Showalter, professor of English at Princeton University and a television critic, has provoked outraged reactions in the US with [**Hystories: Hysterical Epidemics and Modern Culture,**] even to the point of death threats. A male friend and I bickered for hours over its central thesis. So why this hysteria about hysteria?

The problem is, in part, etymological. In common usage hysteria means making a fuss over nothing. Showalter returns it to its 19th-century meaning: the bodily expression of unspeakable distress. There is even a group of academics called the New Hysterians who are rediscovering its many manifestations, as Peter Melville Logan's rather opaque book [*Nerves and Narrative*] on hysteria and the early 19th century British novel demonstrates. Logan argues that this period was not only the point where hysteria passed from being the province of the aristocracy to the new middle class but that "nervous narratives", such as De Quincey's *Confessions of an English Opium Eater,* became a useful, if complex, tool for the criticism of wider social conditions.

Showalter picks up the story from the late 19th century, with Charcot's famous experiments on female hysterics that so impressed and influenced Freud, and, later, shell-shock in the first world war, a clear example of male hysteria. Far from disappearing, hysteria has, says Showalter, returned with a vengeance in the mass psychogenic epidemics of the 1990s, such as chronic fatigue, Gulf war syndrome, recovered memory of sexual abuse and alien abduction.

What characterises modern hysteria, however, is the making of "hystories", the role not only of medicine but of the media in constructing and distorting symptoms and stories. In her account of chronic fatigue Showalter shows that reports of isolated outbreaks in the mid-1980s snowballed until millions of people claimed similar clusters of symptoms. The same has happened with recovered memory, which might explain why so many families find themselves trapped in such bizarrely similar narratives.

Showalter marshals her argument with impressive clarity but she is, in places, too sure of herself. Yes, there have been press distortions and misinformation about aspects of Gulf war syndrome, but can she really be so certain that it is entirely psychosomatic? The use of chemicals, drugs and vaccinations provides an organic basis, at least, for depressive illness. No single virus has been found for ME sufferers, but the syndrome is often triggered by identifiable conditions such as labyrinthitis (a disorder of the inner ear). Is Showalter not contributing to a false duality in insisting there is no organic element in these diseases? And are the manifestly ridiculous stories of alien abduction really on par with either Gulf war syndrome or recovered memory claims?

True hysteria is aphasia, wrote Hélène Cixous. Yet what's so striking about these modern manifestations of "hysteria" is not the muteness of the sufferers, but their militance, their loud presence in the public sphere. Recovered memory has spawned dozens of books and meetings and workshops; so has ME. These are quasi-political movements, demanding their right to be heard about their claim that they are *not* being heard. And yet, if Showalter is right, their grounds for complaint are more diffuse, more difficult to pin down than even they know.

For instance, it is striking how many middle-class young-ish women are struck by ME or make accusations of long-ago abuse by fathers or babysitters. Whatever the justice of their terrible claims, it suggests that something has gone particularly wrong in women's lives. It would be too simple to read off disappointment from illness; but I do wonder if these women are "acting out" something both individually and for the culture as a whole. Like the mad ugly sister or the mad woman in the attic, their bitter, out-of-control and yet oddly passive stories offer a perverse mirror image to those of contemporary female high achievement.

I have lost count of the magazines and newspapers that have listed the "top" 50 women, in terms of beauty or business acumen, brain or bosom power. With their Alpha personalities and high expectations, many ME sufferers seem to share with "top" women an allergy to ordinary life. Except that, in their case, the allergy expresses itself as disabling distress or illness rather than high-fevered success. And does our "culture of feelings" (the rise of therapy, talk shows) allow them to express distress and yet, at the same time, somehow bury themselves in it?

This is also, still, a strangely non-political time. The American writer Louise Armstrong (whom Showalter quotes approvingly) has written about how the politics of incest—analysing and organising against male power—was transformed into a politics of personal victimisation. Gulf war syndrome reconfigured horror at war into the personal suffering of victorious combatants. Discussion of mysterious sores and sick babies has taken the place of discussion of what even Showalter uncritically calls a "just war". Iraq was a despotic state, but the killing of thousands of civilians is another story. Where is *that* horror expressed?

At the end of Arthur Miller's play *The Crucible,* fury and righteousness drain away from the once-possessed participants. Showalter wants fury and righteousness to drain away from those who choose "hystories" as their personal crucible for unconscious fears and fantasies. It may be too late: last month it was reported that ME is the biggest single reason given by parents for children's long-term absence from school. Showalter wants people to have the courage of their own afflictions. Why, in our supposed culture of feelings, that remains so difficult is a Hystery to me.

**Steve Sailer (review date 1 September 1997)**

SOURCE: Sailer, Steve. "Hysteria, His and Hers." *National Review* 45, no. 16 (1 September 1997): 48-50.

[*In the following review, Sailer contends that* Hystories: Hysterical Epidemics and Modern Culture *is a "sensible but limited book" as a result of Showalter's rationalist feminist perspective.*]

Sometimes you get what you ask for. Back in 1985 Elaine Showalter, a Princeton English professor specializing in the social history of mental health, concluded her critique of the traditional psychotherapy profession by proclaiming: "The best hope for the future is the feminist therapy movement." By 1997, the mental-health industry has become thoroughly feminized, but Professor Showalter has had second thoughts: "The therapist's role is more and more to affirm, support, and endorse the patient's narrative, . . . and not to challenge the truth or historical reality of the patient's assertions." This credulous atmosphere, she believes, has helped unleash "hysterical epidemics," such as the disgraceful witchhunts for satanic cults running daycare centers. Mrs. Showalter cites five other "hysterical" outbreaks: the booms in recovered memory of incestuous abuse, multiple-personality disorders, alien abductions, Chronic Fatigue Syndrome, and Gulf War Syndrome. For an academic treatise with a first printing of only 7,500 copies, **Hystories** has already generated quite a backlash. In hounding the author, Chronic Fatigue sufferers have proved especially energetic.

Mrs. Showalter's strongest chapters are on epidemics like the satanic-abuse and alien-abduction scares, whose alleged causes are wholly imaginary; and on Gulf War Syndrome, whose primary cause is real but not specific to that conflict: "war makes people sick." While it may turn out that chemical weapons or sand fleas really did afflict some minority of the sufferers, on the whole GWS appears to be the latest version of what other eras labeled "shell shock," "battle fatigue," or "post-traumatic stress disorder." America must realize that one of the costs of going to war is later paying fully for treatment and disability leaves for a substantial number of psychologically injured soldiers, although treating mental traumas as honorable wounds will no doubt let some hypochondriacs and malingerers slip through.

Unfortunately, Miss Showalter's literary world view is too black-and-white for those epidemics where some but not all of the patients' stories are true, e.g., incestuous abuse. The acrimony of these debates stems in part from both sides' thinking about all patients as Platonic abstractions ("incest victims" *v.* "hysterics"). In reality, mental health is more like an unsettlingly random pachinko game. The classic case study of how psychological debates tend toward dogmatism has been running for a full century since Sigmund Freud analyzed 18 unhappy young women. After much bullying by Freud, they all produced stories of childhood sexual abuse. First announcing an epidemic of incest, Freud then publicly changed his mind and blamed all the women for repressing Oedipal fantasies. Millions of words have since been written about this controversy. Most feminists contend that all 18 really were incest victims. In contrast, after a decade of listening to the nonsensical narratives that present-day therapists can elicit, Professor Showalter thinks Freud was right to recant.

Few, however, seem to have remarked how unlikely it is that any single diagnosis was right for all 18. In truth, some of the troubled women probably *were* child-abuse victims, while some others may have been repressing guilty fantasies. Probably a large proportion were suffering from other root problems that weren't understood back then, such as chemical imbalances in the brain that strike largely at random. Serotonin, for instance, acts rather like motor oil for your emotional engine, keeping your mental gears from grinding. It can run low—often, it appears, just from wear and tear. Since the cause of the emotional illnesses stemming from serotonin shortages is commonly not apparent, victims are susceptible to whatever tall tales (a/k/a hysterical epidemics) their therapists or the media happen to be spreading at the moment. Thankfully, we now have drugs like Prozac, and a new, more pragmatic school of psychiatrists who no longer set out on ideologically motivated searches for the root causes of your unhappiness, but instead concentrate on rebalancing your brain chemistry.

A beneficial side effect of a more realistic conception of hysterical epidemics allows this useful concept to be profitably applied to other current brouhahas where facts and feelings get hopelessly entangled, e.g., date rape and sexual harassment.

This sensible but limited book illustrates the strengths and weaknesses of what has recently become a lonely rump of feminism: "equity" or "rationalist" feminism. Appalled by the flapdoodle peddled by most feminists today, Mrs. Showalter wearily protests, "Feminism has a strong Enlightenment, rationalist tradition of debate and skepticism, whose memory I attempt to recover and reassert." She bravely points out that the great majority of these epidemics' self-proclaimed victims are women, even the alien abductees. (Gulf War Syndrome, of course, is the exception, but the number of soldiers' wives who have also come down with GWS is striking.)

Unfortunately, rationalist feminism is itself founded on a death-defying leap of faith: the assumption that there are no biological bases for differences in behavior between the sexes. Thus, equity feminism was much to blame for the imprisoning of so many young women day-care workers on absurd charges of raping children and eating babies. If we know anything about sex abuse, we know it's a solitary male crime, not something women do, especially not in groups. But equity feminism has made such stereotypes unacceptable, so all those young women, whose only crime was that they loved little kids so much they'd work with them for $5 an hour, had to go to jail.

Further, rationalist feminism's fundamental dogma of sexual uniformity prevents Miss Showalter from grasping why feminist movements are so vulnerable to the irrationalism she despises. It's not because women aren't as smart as men. Although the sexes do differ on average in mathematical skills, women may well be superior in verbal logic. (Try eavesdropping on two teenage girls analyzing the endless possibilities of what some boy really meant when he said, "Maybe, like, I'll see you around sometime, you know?") So why, in practice, are the terms "feminist theory" and "scientific theory" mutually exclusive?

The particular form of rationality that originated in the Enlightenment requires more than just the ability to construct castles of logical conjecture in the air. Galileo wasn't any more ingenious at conceiving interlocking celestial spheres than his ancient rival Ptolemy. What distinguished Galileo, and the Enlightenment in general, was that masculine competitive delight in risking the destruction of your own hypotheses in order to smash the other guy's beautiful celestial spheres of theory. The Enlightenment turned reason into a contact sport. Feminist movements careen into gullibility because women, especially when talking mostly to other women, find it more emotionally difficult than men to treat intellectual debate as a game. Women tend to take it much more personally, closing their minds to opponents and pulling their punches with friends.

**Taner Edis and Amy Sue Bix (review date September-October 1997)**

SOURCE: Edis, Taner, and Amy Sue Bix. "Tales of Hysteria." *Skeptical Inquirer* 21, no. 5 (September-October 1997): 52-3.

[*In the following review, Edis and Bix offer a positive assessment of* Hystories: Hysterical Epidemics and Modern Culture, *but note flaws in Showalter's exaggeration of medieval millennial panic, her defense of psychoanalysis, and her premature dismissal of chronic fatigue and Gulf War syndrome.*]

We skeptics do more these days than shake our heads at psychics or roll our eyes at UFO-abduction tales. Because postmodern humanities scholars seem out to drag science down, the *Skeptical Inquirer* keeps tabs on relativist philosophers, literary critics, Freudian psychoanalysts, and feminist critics of science, as well as the usual suspects. So when a feminist literary critic with a soft spot for psychoanalysis writes a book about topics like alien abduction and satanic ritual abuse, we might expect some gobbledygook about validating the experiences of those people dismissed by the scientific elite and so on. Elaine Showalter—president-elect of the Modern Language Association, no less—would make us think again. **Hystories** is not only a skeptical book, but an important book many skeptics can benefit from.

Showalter is not interested in defending the truth of recovered memories or alien-abduction tales; in fact, she thinks they're obviously false. She does, however, want to explain why such beliefs are so common. Her central idea is that these beliefs are part of *hysterical epidemics*. She describes America as "a hot zone of psychogenic diseases, new and mutating forms of hysteria amplified by modern communications and *fin de siècle* anxiety." Modern media and rapid electronic communications make it possible for "microtales of individual affliction" to explode into "panics fueled by rumors about medical, familial, community, or governmental conspiracy." Our culture creates plenty of opportunity for psychological trouble and then provides fantastic tales for people to grasp at to make sense of their condition. Especially when troubled people connect to support networks and authority figures like therapists, stories with no basis in reality take on a life of their own.

No surprises so far. In an alien-abduction report, for example, we can easily see a stereotyped, media-spread tale that helps people make sense of sexual conflicts and strange experiences like sleep paralysis. We also notice therapists who collaborate not so much in revealing what happened as in creating the story in the first place. Showalter, however, uses her background as an English professor to explore the *stories* and the cultural and political landscape in which these stories come to life. She also looks at the history of psychology and contagious delusions and puts it in a context of gender politics, cultural anxieties, even literary inspiration. The result is a portrait of hysteria that gives no quarter to false beliefs yet is also aware of how the label "hysteria" has long been employed "to ridicule and trivialize women's medical and political complaints." Showalter leads us to see hysteria as a way, sometimes the only way, suffering people can express themselves.

What, then, are the hysterical epidemics of our day? Showalter talks about recovered memories, multiple personalities, satanic ritual abuse, and alien abduction. More controversially, she adds chronic fatigue illness and Gulf War syndrome. These, she argues, are all troubles for which no convincing medical or external explanation can be found, and all follow the typical pattern of a hysterical epidemic. Showalter's treatment of subjects like recovered memories, ritual abuse, and alien abductions reflects sources and themes from the skeptical literature, and her direct and sympathetic style of writing makes her account attractive. Humor also helps, as when she skewers Harvard psychiatrist John Mack for his support of UFO abductions by coining "Showalter's Law: As the hystories get more bizarre, the experts get more impressive."

*Hystories* is a good book, but it also has its dubious points. For example, Showalter overemphasizes end-of-century panics. She treats claims of extraordinary apocalyptic fears around the year 1000 as fact, while most historians think no unusual panic occurred at the time. Skeptics are not likely to share Showalter's favorable view of psychoanalysis either. She mostly agrees with recent critics of Freud, such as Frederick Crews, but believes we have no alternative as yet to modern psychoanalysis as a way of thinking about ourselves and our stories.

Showalter is also overly hasty in calling chronic fatigue and Gulf War syndrome hysterias. New information is still emerging about operations in the Gulf War, and researchers have just begun exploring how different medicines, chemicals, and environmental exposure may interact in complex, unanticipated ways. Certainly, veterans' affairs have become politicized, and psychological factors and communication of rumors have spread questionable beliefs. But Showalter should also have underlined more explicitly the uncertainty, incompleteness, and mistakes in emerging science. A physical ailment with unconventional, complex causes is not as outlandish a hypothesis as an alien abduction. Showalter should also have done more to acknowledge the non-paranoid reasons some women can be suspicious of our medical system. Medical science has produced real disasters like the Dalkon Shield and DES, and it has a history of neglecting women as research subjects. This is no excuse to support hysterias or alternative medicine, but skeptics should be more aware of the problematic historical relationship between women and medical science.

Though not without flaws, **Hystories** is especially important for showing how skeptics can build bridges to communities that seem indifferent and sometimes even hostile to skepticism. For example, skeptics have an ambiguous relationship with feminism. Hysteria is largely a female affliction, and too many feminists have supported movements like recovered memory and satanic ritual abuse. Showalter describes hysteria as a desperate expression of pains and fears that cannot find any other socially acceptable voice, and she challenges us to find ways to meet our genuine emotional and sexual needs without endorsing hysterical stories. She declares, "Feminists have an ethical as well as an intellectual responsibility to ask tough questions about the current narratives of illness, trauma, accusation, and conspiracy," adding that, "[T]oday's feminists need models rather than martyrs . . . courage to think as well as the courage to heal." Those people to whose stories Showalter denies truth will not see her as a sympathetic critic, but she is unapologetic about her skepticism: "Feminism has a strong enlightenment, rationalist tradition of debate and skepticism. . . . Our primary obligation must always be to the truth." On the flip side, skeptics who are tempted to think of feminism only as a shrill political movement out to corrupt science have much to learn from Showalter as well. **Hystories** raises important questions for skeptics, feminists, and those who consider themselves members of both communities.

Showalter also shows us that skepticism has roots in the humanities as well as in natural science. UFOlogists like to argue that the similarity among alien-abduction narratives indicates their truth; skeptics explain these by common psychological and social factors and stories spread by the media. A literary critic like Showalter also tends to explain such similarities as resulting from a common background story-template. Indeed, postmodern relativists are, in a sense, extreme skeptics: they claim even the theories of natural science are but stories with social and psychological roots. It is perhaps obvious to us that science is not just a story. But literary critics can help skeptics sort out when we can *appropriately* say common narrative features are not good evidence for the truth of a story. To be properly skeptical, we need to strike a balance, and the humanities, as well as science, can help us achieve this balance.

*Hystories* gets us thinking: about how skeptics might understand real emotional problems without making believers into demented loonies, about how much attention we should pay to our culture when trying to explain false beliefs, and, not the least, about how we can find allies in unexpected places.

**Virginia T. Bemis (review date spring 1998)**

SOURCE: Bemis, Virginia T. Review of *Hystories: Hysterical Epidemics and Modern Culture,* by Elaine Showalter. *NWSA Journal* 10, no. 1 (spring 1998): 172-73.

[*In the following review of* Hystories, *Bemis commends Showalter's historical overview of psychoanalytic theory, but objects to her "Eurocentric" view of millennial panic and her generalized, dismissive treatment of chronic fatigue and Gulf War syndrome.*]

Controversial books relating to Women's Studies reach the shelves fairly regularly. Some are picked up by the mass media, land their authors on the talk-show circuit, and occasion much debate outside the standard academic circles. In the past few years, we have seen Camille Paglia, Katie Roiphe and Christina Hoff Sommers follow this path, and their work has been used as ammunition by a wide variety of pundits. The latest book to follow along this road is *Hystories,* Elaine Showalter's study of hysterical epidemics.

Showalter has a distinguished record of literary scholarship from a feminist perspective, including such standards as *A Literature of Their Own* (1977), *The Female Malady* (1986) and *Sexual Anarchy* (1990). In *Hystories,* she seems to take up where she left off in *The Female Malady,* with a discussion of labeling, how mental illness has been defined and its "rules" set by the medical profession, and that women's mental illness is a protest against a system which silences women.

Starting from her discussion of Charcot and Freud in the earlier book, Showalter here focuses on hysteria, its prevalence in the past, and its recurrence in various forms in the present day. Part One of *Hystories* forms a useful recapitulation of Charcot and Freud, adding in the theoretical insights Lacan provides. Here her documentation is convincing, and her portrayal of how Charcot, in particular, manipulated his patients and constructed their illnesses is truly horrifying.

In Part Two, Showalter uses her background as a Victorianist and her regular studies at Britain's Wellcome Institute for the History of Medicine to examine hysteria as a literary subject and as a narrative mode. The hysterical narrative, or "Hystory," becomes a way of communicating fears and anger in nonverbal ways, "saying" what cannot be said, and at the same time removing responsibility from the patient. These culturally fashionable narratives interact with the culture until they reach epidemic proportions, particularly at the end of a century or millennium.

This Eurocentric insistence on the approaching millennium and its encouragement of such hysterical phenomena as alien abductions, multiple personality disorder, satanic ritual abuse and recovered memory syndrome is perplexing, since hysterical epidemics happen in a variety of times and places, and in cultures that care little or nothing about common era dating or the possible Second Coming of Christ.

More problematic still is the content of Part Three, and it is this content that has sparked the most controversy. Here she takes her theory of the "hysterical narrative," constructed by patients, doctors, and a sympathetic culture, and applies it to the contemporary phenomena above, to argue that they have no concrete existence, and are but psychological constructs. So far, many would agree with at least parts of her analysis. Having seen a "Satanic Panic," in which false accusations of abuse tore a community apart, it is possible for me to appreciate the showing of how such things grow and take on a life of their own.

Where one cannot follow wholeheartedly along her Freudo-literary analytical path is in the chapters on Gulf War Syndrome (GWS) and Chronic Fatigue Syndrome (CFS), where the jury is very much still out. Here, her theory becomes a bed of Procrustes, as she stretches parts and lops off others, to make the facts fit the frame. Ignoring or dismissing medical evidence of concrete conditions, often in a flip and abrasive tone, she argues that both GWS and CFS are simply stress-reactions, ways of dealing with uncomfortable reality. Her tendency to overgeneralize leads to arguing that because some cases are hysterical, all are hysterical.

Further, one wonders whether narrative theory is the best way of looking at disability. And if a disability is a story, does that mean that all the stories are the same? Sociologists and scholars of disability dispute her assigning of narrative categories. So does the larger disability community, where the disabled insist on having their experience recognized as part of the story.

Showalter's admirable insistence that hysteria is real, to be respected and treated, is marred by her less laudable insistence that everything is hysteria.

### Deirdre English (review date 11 June 2001)

SOURCE: English, Deirdre. "Wollstonecraft to Lady Di." *Nation* 272, no. 23 (11 June 2001): 44-9.

[*In the following review, English lauds the central themes of* Inventing Herself: Claiming a Feminist Intellectual Heritage, *complimenting the unlikely parallels that Showalter creates between the lives of Mary Wollstonecraft and Diana, Princess of Wales.*]

Here we go, starting on what promises to be a pleasantly engrossing tour of the landmarks of three centuries of Anglo-American intellectual feminism, guided by a seriously impressive scholar, Elaine Showalter of Princeton University. Showalter is the erudite author of some classic feminist literary texts and a founder of women's studies, yet she has a light and deft hand on the wheel. It's only that—there aren't a lot of signposts that tell us where we're going as we start out, and Showalter breezily informs us that whether women participated in the organized women's movements of their day or thought of themselves as intellectuals or not, "I am most interested in the risk-takers and adventurers" of the past.

She illustrates what she means with the book's [*Inventing Herself: Claiming a Feminist Intellectual Heritage*] very first paragraph, in a way that seems perplexing—by equating Mary Wollstonecraft, the eighteenth-century author of *A Vindication of the Rights of Woman*, with Princess Diana, of all people, as examples of the sort of feminists—or "icons," she calls them—she is looking for.

A bit of a further worry is her flippant reassurance, "Life stories retain their power when theories fade." This comes off as defiant, or defensive. Feminist literary theory, which she helped initiate, has been producing a lot of heat in the English departments for some twenty or thirty years now, and some women outside academia, including myself, have wondered if the whole theory thing was going to produce any light to guide the women's movement by. Otherwise, what are all those feminist professors doing in there?

We can guess that Showalter hasn't lived immersed in literature and theory without picking up a few tricks about how to spin a story, so her deflection seems to be a broad hint that she will be expressing her opinions indirectly, speaking through the biographies she picks. Because if she says she's staking a claim to the feminist intellectual heritage, she must have an argument to make about what's important, and who's in and who's out. That means it will be up to us, as readers, to absorb the moral of her stories, or to play the literary critic ourselves, and try to pry the meanings out.

The book is pitched away from potential critics, though. It's a book most ordinary readers will love—I loved it myself the first time through, as a popularly written ode to great women in history, sort of an *Intellectual Feminists for Dummies*. Showalter is a good writer, very Modern Language Association (of which she is a past president) meets *People* magazine (where she took a yearlong joy ride as a media critic). Her central theme, as it emerges in the telling, is as delicious and guiltily indulgent as a box of Godiva chocolates: the educated woman's timeless quest for identity, especially the reconciliation of love and ambition. It could be an alumni seminar at Reunion Week.

"Biography, as a genre," writes Carol Brightman, in "Character in Biography," "has undergone a fundamental shift in recent decades . . . to what the market in its infinite wisdom calls 'Advice, How-To and Miscellaneous.' Especially among women writing about women for women." Showalter proposes that we see ourselves, today, in the courageous lives of heroines who refused to "accept limits . . . on the basis of sex" and so were "ahead of [their] time." They are a mirror of us.

A perhaps unsettling mirror. Settling down with the book, one is amazed to read how many of our feminist foremothers had unhappy love affairs, with some real bounders, too, and how many died tragically! Look at Mary Wollstonecraft, first on the "in" list. Her brief biography reveals the themes that Showalter is interested in. We read little about Wollstonecraft's breakthrough feminist political philosophy. What she calls our attention to is Wollstonecraft's life—and her struggle to be both a thinker, when that was forbidden, and a woman.

Wollstonecraft spun from rejecting romance, intellectually, to being romantically rejected by a man with whom, against her principles, she had fallen passionately in love and had an out-of-wedlock baby, and over whom she tried to commit suicide. Her story almost had a happy ending: She found harmony at last in a marriage to the philosopher William Godwin and gave birth to their daughter, who became the writer Mary Shelley. But Wollstonecraft died in that childbirth.

Wollstonecraft's story sets the goal of the inquiry—can a woman ever find satisfaction in both work and love? Men face this problem, but not as a self-negating paradox. Traditionally, a man who has the drive to be successful will be loved for it, but a woman who is ambitious for success may be deprived of love for that very reason. She is asked to choose, or suffer the consequences.

The daisy chain of brief biographies that follow are all variations on this theme, set out as interconnected parables from which feminist instruction may be deduced. Here is Margaret Fuller, the great transcendentalist writer, who pined, "a man's ambition with a woman's heart—'tis an accursed lot." Abandoning the cold Yankees who had rejected her sexually, she overthrew her own Puritan ideas and embraced love in Italy, emerging as her "radiant sovereign self" at last. But Fuller died tragically in a shipwreck.

The powerful South African figure Olive Schreiner, was one of the *fin de siècle* New Women who, Showalter writes, "came to see themselves as a tragic generation, compelled to sacrifice love or motherhood or both in the interests of women's future freedom."

Eleanor Marx, Karl's daughter and Schreiner's friend and a committed socialist activist, committed suicide in despair over her husband's betrayal. According to Showalter, the New Women of the nineteenth century never found happiness because they were unable to "suppress guilt for behaving in 'unfeminine' ways."

But with the twentieth century, Showalter promises, newer women would imagine a fuller life. The American author of *Women and Economics,* Charlotte Perkins Gilman ("Work first—love next"), was a member of Heterodoxy, a feminist women's club that flourished in New York from 1912 to 1920. We meet the wonderful tribe of feminist anthropologists: Elsie Clews Parsons; the incredible Ruth Benedict, who was the mentor of Margaret Mead; and Zora Neale Hurston, who had to surmount the tribulations of race as well as sex, and whose "presence at Columbia was almost miraculous."

There is a section on Mary McCarthy, never a feminist but rather the first twentieth-century "dark lady" of letters, selected to be one of the boys by the New York intellectuals at *Partisan Review*. McCarthy had a long correspondence with her friend, the German Jewish refugee Hannah Arendt, who came to this country imbued with the ideas of Martin Heidegger, her philosopher ideal, lover and, in very real ways, her enemy. We meet again the incomparable Simone de Beauvoir, and hear about her love affair with the tough-guy Chicagoan Nelson Algren, and her lifelong sexual-intellectual relationship with her philosopher-lover, Sartre. Then on to Susan Sontag, who first read Beauvoir when she was 18 and pregnant, vowed to live the life of an independent woman and, according to the rites of the male intellectual tribe of her day, was initiated as the successor "dark lady," picked to replace the aging McCarthy. One declining diva to the upcoming one,

McCarthy is said to have hissed, on meeting Sontag, "Oh, you're the imitation me." As Sontag displaced McCarthy in the iconography of the intellectuals, so Camille Paglia tried desperately to replace Sontag (and Showalter ruefully admits that she at one time tried, too, to succeed Sontag as America's singular woman of letters). Paglia is skewered as a brilliant madwoman and fool, and on the jacket copy are the words of Showalter's friend Joyce Carol Oates: Paglia's comical pursuit of Susan Sontag . . . is worth the price of the book alone." It's true, and there are tons of similarly gossipy tales of women's sexual peccadilloes and the embarrassments of ambition. But we have lost the thread of feminism.

Instead, one gets the feeling of a picaresque tale of trial and error, with plenty of tragic pitfalls in the past yielding to more humorous pratfalls as women continued their epic struggle with their two *bête-noires*: intellectual and sexual frustration, and the confounding connection between them. Showalter's decision to focus on the psychobiographies of female intellectuals, then, while hardly constituting an intellectual history of feminism, is illuminating in its own right—but more depressing than she wants to acknowledge.

Showalter yearns for more upbeat spin in a tale of progress and success for women who choose both love and freedom. Perhaps not finding any other, she portrays her own story, uniquely, as one that has reconciled love, marriage, feminism, ambition and success. Her autobiography is interwoven with the emergence of the second wave of feminism, represented primarily as an "I was there" memoir of Showalter and her own close friends and colleagues in women's studies and literature, especially at Douglass College, set against the background of the distant outbursts of radical women all over the country.

"I have tried to write about my heroines of the past as if they were my friends and contemporaries, and to write about my friends and contemporaries as if they were historical figures," she explains, which seems just the tiniest bit narcissistic, especially at the expense of influential feminist figures representing such disparate streams as Gloria Steinem, Florynce Kennedy, Alice Paul, Eleanor Smeal, Toni Morrison, Adrienne Rich, Alice Walker, Kate Millett, Maxine Hong Kingston, Betty Friedan or Ruth Bader Ginsburg.

Since Showalter does not portray herself as a romantic adventurer, she substitutes food imagery for sexual escapades as metaphors for risk. Thus we hear of her first cheeseburger, the intimidations of brie and camembert served at Bryn Mawr, heaping platters of food passed at a black church, dysentery on a honeymoon in Mexico. Mostly, though, she looks back nostalgically at the 1970s as a golden age of solidarity among women that we may not see again.

When Showalter finally leaves the 1970s and zooms in on the present day, we're in for a shock, though it was foreshadowed from the very first paragraph. We might have expected that the problems that educated women have always had reconciling love and work might now, after the successes of the second wave, be re-examined as the more widespread and familiar problems of most educated women. To do so would have required that Showalter expand her discussion of love from romance to the questions of combining work with motherhood, family and childcare. She might have had to ask, as Arlie Hochschild and many other imaginative feminists are doing, whether the ethics of love and care can migrate from being women's sole, private and familial responsibility to a place more shared with men and also closer to the center of society. But, incredibly, the question of children and their welfare never comes up for discussion in this book. Only romantic love matters to intellectuals?

Veering away from the modern woman's dilemmas, Showalter praises celebrities—Oprah Winfrey, Hillary Clinton and Princess Diana, as the three prime role models for "the way we live now." Turns out that Showalter has a wicked case of Dianamania, and here in the book's triumphalist finale, she is really driving us straight to the Princess's shrine, which she describes in loving detail, complete with women on the grounds weeping.

"I realized that Diana Spencer, like Mary Wollstonecraft, had become a role model of her time. She too had evolved an ideal of the fullest, most meaningful life she might dare to live as a woman in her historical circumstances, and then courageously tried to live it." This comparison is bizarre, but by this point Showalter has completely lost control of her own vehicle, declaring, "By the time of her death, she had achieved independence against enormous odds and seemed to be on the brink of realizing Freud's formula for adult psychological health: love and work."

Love? With an immature, though aging, rich man's heir, unremarked for any achievement but notorious for his playboy lifestyle and compulsive infidelities? Work—what work? Independence? Was her death, in a car chase fueled even more by multiple testosterone sources than by alcohol and gasoline, really the last act of a woman in charge of her life—or even trying to be?

Elaine Showalter couldn't really mean it, could she, putting this forth as the trajectory of feminism, intellectual feminism no less! From thinker to celebrity, from social outcast to star, from iconoclast to icon? Could she?

This was the mystery I found myself confronting as I reeled from the sight of the smoking, intellectual wreck that is the conclusion of what is sure to be Elaine Showalter's most marketable crossover book to date. What would lead a self-respecting academic intellectual to an unabashed celebration of celebrity? Was Showalter shamelessly mercenary, academically suicidal . . . or, the victim of a deadly theoretical error?

To get some perspective on Showalter I had to go back—way back—to 1985, the year she received a famous shellacking at the hands of postmodern feminist critical literary theory's elite wing, personified by one bright, blonde Norwegian dame named Toril Moi. My impression that Showalter was fending off an unspecified critique had not been wrong.

It seems that there is still no better book to read against *Inventing Herself* than Moi's *Sexual/Textual Politics*—the book that started these particular culture wars by first applying critical theory to Showalter's 1970s feminist classic *A Literature of Their Own* and attacking Anglo-American literary feminism in general as dull-witted and un-revolutionary. Although Showalter has published several books and many other writings since then, her new book is her clearest, and in some ways cleverest, riposte to Moi. I found a used copy of Moi in a Berkeley bookstore, black covered and thin as a stiletto to slip between an aging mother's ribs. And sure enough, there is a story here, too—of Showalter, a pioneer of feminist theory, and of the next generation of critical theory stepdaughters who deny that there can ever be an unsuspicious "woman's point of view" and so, it was sometimes feared by the jargon-phobic feminists, were going to "deconstruct" the feminist baby in its crib.

For her part, Moi had predicted back then that Showalter would come to no good end if she did not mend her ways. Moi complained, "Showalter's aim, in effect, is to create a separate canon of women's writing, not to abolish all canons."

Showalter had argued that women's literature could be divided into three phases, which she labeled the feminine, followed by the feminist and finally the female. In the first, prefeminist stage, women imitated the dominant tradition to win acceptance. The second was a phase of protest against these standards and values, and advocacy of minority rights and values, including a demand for autonomy. Finally, after enough protest, followed presumably by a goodly measure of vindication and success, there is a phase of self-discovery, a turning inward freed from some of the dependency of opposition, a search for identity.

Moi had a lot of problems with phase three, and its notions of a woman's singular "autonomy" and searching inward for identity. How could she not, informed as she was by poststructuralist theories that meaning is contextual and historical, and that identity is socially, and linguistically, constructed? If the European avant-garde that Moi was speaking for got it right, then the last place feminists would find a road map to liberation would be from a bunch of educated women searching within themselves. A woman might be a woman, and she might be an intellectual, but the meaning of these "situations" could never be her autonomous creation. She would have to contend with the construction of meanings that she had not agreed to. The friction encountered there (and embedded in language, and internalized in the psyche) is where the pressures of patriarchal power come into play.

Moi's critique, and her introduction of French feminist thinking to the US cultural studies scene, hit a big nerve. In ultra-serious circles in the humanities, the perpetuation of an "essentialist" conception of woman (where there was some un compromised inner female to discover and give freedom to, a la Showalter) received a giant thumbs-down (in the biological sciences, it was a different story, but not one we have room for here). What is a woman? Philosophically speaking, no one can be sure.

Showalter's essentialist theorizing, and the search for a "woman's literature" with special characteristics, put her in bed with the wrong people. According to Moi,

> [there is a] fundamental complicity between this empiricist and humanist variety of feminist criticism and the male academic hierarchy it rightly resists. . . . The humanist believes in literature as an excellent instrument of education: by reading "great works" the student will become a finer human being. . . . The literary canon of "great literature" ensures that it is this "representative experience" (one selected by male bourgeois critics) that is transmitted to future generations, rather than those deviant, unrepresentative experiences discoverable in much female, ethnic and working class writing. Anglo-American feminist criticism has waged war on this self-sufficient canonization of middle-class male values. But they have rarely challenged the very notion of such a canon. . . . But a new canon would not be intrinsically less oppressive than the old.

As the poststructuralist critique of identity politics took hold over the following decade and more, it became unfashionable, in ideas and in dress, it seemed, for the avant-garde of the female professoriate to identify with either men or women, which must have made it harder than ever to figure out what to wear to teach a class (unless, luckily, you were a public cross-dresser or male to female gender-bender, armed with queer theory—the only ones allowed, in a sort of campy way, to have fun with frippery). Basic black might be the obvious answer, but some confident women rejected that straitjacket and had the chutzpah to break the taboos.

Elaine Showalter was one of them, enjoying fashion and even flaunting her "political incorrectness" in Vogue in 1997, when she was president of the MLA. In a feature for Lingua Franca ("Who's Afraid of Elaine Showalter?") Emily Eakin wrote,

> few colleagues were taken in by the piece's lighthearted, gamely self-mocking tone. Here, masquerading as a paean to lipstick and Loehman's, was nothing less than a political manifesto. "From Mary Wollstonecraft to Naomi Wolf, feminism has often taken a hard line on fashion, shopping, and the whole beauty Monty," Showalter wrote [in Vogue]. "But for those of us sisters hiding Welcome to Your Facelift inside The Second Sex, a passion for fashion can sometimes seem a shameful secret life. . . . I think it's time I came out of the closet."

That took some admirable nerve, and Eakin's article (which first led me back to Moi) reports that the backlash was fierce in academic circles. "What did it mean for a leading academic feminist to come out in favor of . . . symbols . . . of consumer capitalism and traditional femininity?" Eakin says that at Cornell University, feminists raged for a month in online debates.

Incisive as Moi's critique was at the time, one has to have sympathy, too, with what Showalter was rebelling against later, especially to the degree that it became another form of timid conformity. Moi and Showalter could each accuse the other of political correctness of different kinds. A feminism that is insufficiently self-critical and requires a reverent attitude toward women, without even being able to give an adequate definition of "women," must be shallow and doctrinaire, and that is the charge against Showalter. Moi had predicted that her lack of critical thinking would put Showalter in the "painful position" of colluding with the "patriarchal elite" she thought she was resisting. This would mean that Showalter privileged a "pro-woman" perspective at the cost of excluding other points of view, and remained willfully ignorant of the flaws in her theory.

On the other hand, a feminism that loses sight of real women who come to it with a sense of their needs and desires, and occupies itself instead with nervous philosophical hairsplitting, could be a charge leveled against the postmoderns. Moi, with her egalitarian Norwegian background, could probably not appreciate what it was like for American feminists to take on the educational establishment. Showalter scolds her critics: "We needn't fall into postmodern apocalyptic despair about the futility of political action or the impossibility of theoretical correctness as a pre-condition for action." (It's good to remember, as these feminists face off, that in the current climate, a conservative antifeminist like Lynne Cheney would lash them together and toss them both overboard.)

Still, this book leaves us at the scene of the shrine where Showalter intones her eulogy to Princess Diana: "Her elegance, taste and style were truly exceptional even in a beauty-conscious age," writes Showalter. "She was a feminist who championed feminine values." The question for us is, has Showalter's frustration with the (say it slow) po-mo-fem/lit/crit hellhounds on her trail driven her around the bend? Or, had Toril Moi's old prediction proved true? Moi had predicted that, as the reader also produces the text, eventually feminist critics would give "irreverent scrutiny" to the work of women writers, and cast doubt on Showalter's essentialist biases. Curious thought—could it be that I, a feminist critic, with my unflattering opinion that Showalter's veneration of Princess Di represents an intellectual crack-up, am partially the author of that crackup and hence an unwitting agent helping to make Moi's 1985 prediction come true? Such are the headachy ideas that wandering among lit/cit texts can give you.

Perhaps it would be foolish to dwell too long in that arcane world of academic feminism which, in the words of Katha Pollitt, "absorbs vast amounts of female brain power and probably does less to liberate real women than Brandi Chastain's picture on a cereal box."

The skepticism of a woman in search of common sense comes as welcome relief. Unimpressed by all sides of the canon wars, in an essay called "Canon to the Right of Me . . ." Pollitt went so far as to defend (gasp) even the dead white males of the conservatives—meaning Homer, Shakespeare, etc. Yet Pollitt admits, just like a feminist, that finding poetry written by women (even very bad poetry) had been vitally important to inspiring her when she was a girl, and she goes on to argue, like a postmodernist, for a much broader and more inclusive syllabus when it comes to our reading. And right she was, in all these perspectives, too, and her undogmatic freedom to pick and choose among them.

So what, if anything, do these pomo critiques of feminist canons, shrines, lists, essentialist ideas or concepts of gender-identity mean from the point of view—dear to readers of *The Nation*—of politically engaged, activist feminism? What is that called these days, anyway? Liberal, or bourgeois, feminism are the terms one used to have for people with the politics of Elaine Showalter—where the goal is empowering women while somehow keeping their identity as women intact. In this posture, they are expected to enter the professional and intellectual classes without disarranging the furniture too much, or bringing in too much of a cool breeze relating to other aspects of the status quo. To such a woman, the conventional terms of success—making money, being beautiful, strong, a celebrity—are all seen as identical with the markers of feminist success. Today, with the disappearance of the left and the dismantling of liberalism, this is garden variety feminism, and it is this paralyzing expectation of individual achievement that young women have inherited and bravely but foolishly accepted as their mission. What were once socialist feminists, radical feminists, cultural feminists or women's liberationists had different points of view, but shared ideas of more sweeping social changes, to put it mildly. The vitality of feminism came not merely from women's integrationist demands but from this insistent and radical questioning of everything about the way the world was structured.

If the liberal, assimilationist idea of feminism has really won the day, and claims, as in this book's subtitle, the "intellectual heritage" of feminism, one still wishes that Showalter would have a more inclusive concept of what made up feminism in the first place. As Pollitt writes in the introduction to her recent book of columns from *The Nation*, "feminism is not a single, independent, all-powerful force, but is connected in complicated and even contradictory ways with other historical forces—egalitarianism and individualism, hedonism and puritanism, capitalism and the critique of capitalism." Showalter has the individualist, hedonist and capitalist parts down, but shows little interest in the other dimensions.

If this is her perspective, it's fair enough for her to uphold it. But it's hard to believe that Mary Wollstonecraft, Margaret Fuller, Margaret Mead, Simone de Beauvoir, Hannah Arendt and others in her pantheon would feel comfortable being force-marched down a path that leads to such a worldview, especially once they catch sight of Diana coming down the pike.

Woman's struggles with her splintered psyche, her often-failing attempts to live fully, are only one part of the story. The other part of feminism is woman's struggles to reimagine and to change society, her political fight (also often failing) not just for herself but for all the generations to come—and that is a transcendent and romantic quest, too. If Showalter thought so, she would have included such heroines as Elizabeth Cady Stanton, Susan B. Anthony, Emma Goldman, Margaret Sanger, Eleanor Roosevelt and others who were more socially minded thinkers than some of her pure intellectuals. In this light, Moi's critical theory descends from past radical critics of society, feminists and others, and its contribution serves to reinvigorate the arguments of a less established feminism, without a doctrinaire heroizing of women.

In contrast, Showalter's film criticism in *The American Prospect* proves what a confused place you can land in following the I-Am-Woman-Hear-Me-Roar line. In her recent column, "The Film Critic," Showalter liked *Charlie's Angels,* though it is "lite, or low" feminism, because "I think it would have made a real impact on me if I had seen this on-screen when I was a girl, in addition to my trusty *Wonder Woman* comics." OK, fine, this is like the updraft from Pollitt's very bad women poets. But she bashes the plump and plucky Bridget

Jones, chastising her as "incompetent in every area of her life—work, cooking, dating, drinking," and sternly states that the film, though it was made by a woman writer and woman director, has "no feminist consciousness whatsoever." *Bridget Jones's Diary* may be lite feminism too, but it's sad that Showalter doesn't appreciate a story about a woman who does stand for up herself (she tells off the rotter who is her boss and bedmate in front of cheering female office workers—that would have done a lot for me as a girl!), who can laugh at her own sorry messes and who, by the way, walks off at the end with a good looking, politically conscious barrister who loves her "just as she is." Like *Charlie's Angels,* the apotheosis of Princess Di may serve as escapist fare, but today's younger American scene seems full of complicated, doubting, ironic Bridget Joneses who can't be—and as their feminist consciousness continuously grows, don't want to try to be—anybody's perfectionist fantasy.

## Kathryn Hughes (review date 18 June 2001)

SOURCE: Hughes, Kathryn. "Holding the Middle Ground." *New Statesman* 130, no. 4542 (18 June 2001): 52-3.

[*In the following review of* Inventing Herself: Claiming a Feminist Intellectual Heritage, *Hughes praises Showalter's accessible writing style, but criticizes her methodology and diluted analysis.*]

When Elaine Showalter published *A Literature of Their Own* in 1977, it was a revelation and a celebration all in one. In her characteristically fluent prose, she suggested that British women's writing in the 19th and 20th centuries (her bookends were the Brontës and Doris Lessing) had been systematically sidelined, obscured and trivialised. Now here was Showalter, an American academic at the forefront of the new wave of "women's studies", showing us not only why those muffled voices mattered, but how they connected to one another to create, if not exactly a lineage, certainly a web of influence and sympathy.

It was perhaps inevitable that Showalter's work would lose some of its glamour after that high point. In the 1980s, the intellectual beacon in women's studies passed from the Americans with their biographical bias to the intricate linguistic and psychoanalytical teasings of French feminists such as Julia Kristeva.

Increasingly, the work of Anglo-American academic feminists seemed naive, dull and slightly beside the point. In *The Female Malady* (1985), for instance, Showalter was more interested in showing how historical circumstances had consistently conspired to label intelligent or independent women as mad than she was in trying to understand how Lacan was once again making Freud respectable.

*Inventing Herself* continues in what has now become recognisably the Showalter way of writing about women: low on theory, high on history. Her aim is to recover and realign the life and works of those women writers who have proved an inspiration during her 40-year career as a feminist academic. In this sense, she is offering a necessary corrective to the pervasive effects off F R Leavis's *The Great Tradition* (1948), which was responsible for so many good women dropping out of sight. Thus *Inventing Herself* starts with the mother of all feminists, Mary Wollstonecraft; works its way through Margaret Fuller and Charlotte Perkins Gilman; swerves back to the UK for Vera Brittain and Germaine Greer; and then nips over to France for Simone de Beauvoir.

Why Showalter has decided to choose some women and leave out others is never quite clear. She suggests in her introduction, in a phrase that would not sound out of place in *Cosmopolitan* magazine, that this is a book "about women with a passionate attitude to living"; she then lists a whole range of people, including Mother Teresa and Margaret Thatcher, who are automatically disqualified. Confusingly, however, Hillary Clinton, Oprah Winfrey and Princess Diana are all judged to demonstrate the right degree of passion, and are rewarded with a place in the "feminist intellectual heritage" of the book's subtitle.

*Inventing Herself* is constructed as a series of mini-biographies. Some subjects, such as Margaret Fuller, get a whole chapter to themselves. Others, such as Naomi Wolf, are given only three pages. But the themes stay the same. What comes up again and again is the old problem that stymies women still: how to live an autonomous creative and intellectual life without giving up the satisfactions of sexual love and motherhood. The outcomes that emerge are quirky and sometimes full of pain. There is Charlotte Perkins Gilman's proposal of the kitchenless flat (apartments would he built around a central restaurant in order to spare women the chore of cooking, an idea that has recently taken off in New York City). And then there is Eleanor Marx, who killed herself in 1898 because, despite all the progressive talk at the Men's and Women's Club, she never found a way of having an equal relationship with her husband, the appalling Edward Aveling.

Showalter has necessarily depended on secondary sources, biographies mostly, to put this book together. Her method is to take what she wants from a life—the emblematic conflicts, the occasional happy solutions—and to make them repeat or amplify the experience of her other subjects (she is, after all, trying to build up a "heritage"). As a result, the whole enterprise has a synthetic feel, as if the grit and gumption of all those different lives had been thrown away, leaving homogenised pap of the lowest common order. Despite Showalter insisting in her introduction that she was not going to include Marie Curie, *Inventing Herself* none the less reads like one of those "Heroines of History" books that used to be given out as prizes to serious-minded little girls.

This is a shame, because Showalter continues to write with a fluency that puts virtually every other American academic to shame. And her prose style is not merely a matter of incidental pleasure. For nearly 25 years, she has provided a pathway between the dense discourses of academic feminist studies and the commercial market, which supplies the reading needs of Everywoman. During the 1980s and 1990s, these two markets became increasingly separated, with the result that writing by and about women has been either parochially intense or journalistically banal. Showalter's example shows that it is still possible to hold a middle, and higher, ground.

### Sara Maitland (review date 30 June 2001)

SOURCE: Maitland, Sara. "Oprah Winfrey Joins Diana, Princess of Wales." *Spectator* 286, no. 9021 (30 June 2001): 44.

[*In the following review, Maitland argues that* Inventing Herself: Claiming a Feminist Intellectual Heritage *suffers from a lack of thematic focus and overall "trivial" subject material.*]

Something has gone wildly awry with [*Inventing Herself: Claiming a Feminist Intellectual Heritage*]. I am bemused. I am especially bemused because I am an Elaine Showalter fan. Over many years and generous books she has opened up aspects of feminist 'critical theory' (both literary and cultural) to a wider audience by the elegance and readability of her writing and the good sense of her opinions. But in the first place the book cannot decide what it is *about*.

From the subtitle you might anticipate a history of feminist ideas, but more probably, knowing Showalter, a history of women who had intellectual ideas. We might be encouraged to explore the way these ideas shaped the experiences of the women who held them. And indeed there is quite a lot of that here—although, however much one may admire her, it is difficult to pin down the exact part in my 'intellectual heritage' that I have gained from Oprah Winfrey.

Even with women whose claim on our attention is genuinely intellectual, Showalter offers only 'gossip'. Hannah Arendt, for example, is little known in the UK. I know virtually nothing about her life, except that she was the student and mistress of Heidegger, and nothing at all about her philosophy. I can hardly claim her for my 'intellectual heritage' just because I now know that, in addition to this, she smoked a lot, was a close friend of Mary McCarthy's and wore brown dresses at Heidegger's behest. What her contribution to Western philosophy or to women's intellectual development may have been is not revealed.

Yes, the living out of ideas is important and particularly important for feminist intellectuals because so many of their ideas were about how to live the 'good' life, against the grain of convention and expectation. But the expressed ideas that inform their choices are precisely what distinguish these women from all the rest of us who would also like to find 'good enough lives'.

Not that this matters too much, because Showalter actually abandons this aspect of the book, apparently without noticing, and goes shambling off on a completely different trip. Instead of the feminist intellectual heritage of the subtitle we are now in pursuit of the 'feminist icon'. Showalter defines an 'icon' as a 'revered symbol', but I cannot escape the historical knowledge that an icon is necessarily a 'representation'. An icon is not a role model and it is, I suspect, not helpful to the development of feminist thought to elide the two.

Even within these dodgy definitions Showalter's choices of such 'icons' feels odd. This may be because a US tradition will be different from a British one, but some acknowledgment of that would be encouraging. A list which has no socialists other than Eleanor Marx, no suffragists, no psychoanalysts, and Rebecca West as the only British novelist feels a little eccentric, to put it mildly. Josephine Butler? Sylvia Pankhurst? George Eliot? Virginia Woolf? The three latter, at least, provide material for the speculative gossip about their sex lives that Showalter seems so concerned with.

The whole thing feels rather trivial. At one point Showalter makes the interesting suggestion that British feminists around the beginning of the 20th century were not buttressed intellectually, as their US sisters were, by an engagement with anthropology. She does not, however, note that in the UK socialist thought may have provided an alternative. This might explain the rather different feminisms that emerged in Europe and in the US in the 1960s and 1970s. (Feminism beyond Europe and the US is not even touched on.) It is from such differences and histories that feminists must reclaim our intellectual heritage if the continuing global gender inequalities are to be challenged.

One of the problems, perhaps, is that nearly a third of Showalter's subjects are still alive. I do not see how anyone can be a living 'icon'. I certainly do not see how such women can—as the blurb assures us—'have been rediscovered and reinvented by successive generations . . . of daughters'. The book leaps suddenly into describing the dress sense of certain of the more flamboyant contemporary feminist academics, some of whom (e.g. Paglia) Showalter makes clear she does not even like much, let alone 'revere'.

And finally the only individual woman in the book who could possibly be said to have 'iconic' status, the late Princess of Wales, does not and cannot form part of my feminist *intellectual* heritage. Frankly most of us would do better to stick with the Virgin Mary (redefined family structures, wrote a great poem, had an unusual sex life, and has attracted the veneration of 'successive generations' of daughters).

## Brenda Wineapple (review date July 2001)

SOURCE: Wineapple, Brenda. "Unparalleled Lives." *Women's Review of Books* 18, nos. 10-11 (July 2001): 34-5.

[*In the following review, Wineapple offers a generally favorable assessment of* Inventing Herself: Claiming a Feminist Intellectual Heritage.]

Everybody's doing it: in the fourteenth century Boccaccio did it in tales of 106 famous women that extol their dominion and inventiveness—as well as some more predictable virtues, like long-suffering patience. (They've just been freshly translated by Virginia Brown and republished by Harvard.) More recently Phyllis Rose did it in her slim collection, *Writing of Women* (1985), and Susan Ware did it in her ambitious *Letter to the World* (1997), celebrating seven women who, as she put it, shaped the American century. Sylvia Brownrigg did it too, though in her *Ten Women Who Shook the World* (1997), the women, though not their ability to shake, are fictional. And just last year, Claudia Roth Pierpont's women did it in a best-selling volume of essays, *Passionate Minds,* a trenchant exploration of twelve female pioneers, unlikely bedfellows who include Gertrude Stein, Mae West, Ayn Rand, Marina Tsvetaeva and Margaret Mitchell.

Now Elaine Showalter's new book chronologically sketches the lives of a motley collection of writers, thinkers, politicians, celebrities and superstars "who would not accept limits to a woman's life on the basis of sex." Of course, Showalter is no stranger to eclectic, inclusive compendia of women's lives and work. Her excellent first book, the ground-breaking ***A Literature of Their Own: British Women Novelists from Brontë to Lessing*** (1977), implicitly called for a reconsideration—really, the development—of a female literary tradition in the English novel through a consideration of Katherine Mansfield, George Eliot and many a lesser known—read: many an obscure—writer, like Mary Braddon and Mary Chavelita Dunne.

In ***Inventing Herself,*** Showalter is still concerned with iconoclastic canon-making, or to use her current phrase, "feminist icons," women from whom we do not demand perfection because "their fallibility and humanity make them real to us and even their tragedies are instructive and inspiring for women today who try to combine independence, adventure, and love." True, Showalter rounds up many of the usual suspects—Mary Wollstonecraft, Charlotte Perkins Gilman, Olive Schreiner, Simone de Beauvoir, Margaret Mead, Zora Neale Hurston, Mary McCarthy, Hannah Arendt—all of whom have been anatomized by critics and biographers (including Susan Ware and Claudia Pierpont). Regardless, according to Showalter "we still lack a sense of a feminist past." Though their faces may decorate postage stamps, "women have no national holidays, no days of celebration for their births or deaths," Showalter reminds us, and only a handful of monuments commemorate their existence.

In writing about women who have "a passionate attitude toward living," Showalter (with implicit reference to Pierpont) includes in her roster several less predictable, more controversial names: Eleanor Marx, Susan Sontag, Germaine Greer, Oprah Winfrey, Camille Paglia—and Elaine Showalter. Her intent is to write an energetic, upbeat and popular history of "the risk-takers and adventurers" who have intersected with her life, whether in fantasy, in a coffee shop or at a feminist symposium, because, she says, "as I've studied the lives of my heroines, of course I've also asked whether these patterns describe and help explain phases in my own life."

Eschewing neat formulations, Showalter prefers instead to outline some of the coincidences she has discovered in the lives of all her subjects. Armed with the work of critic Lorna Sage, she finds a tendency among feminist icons to rebel against their mothers, to form romantic or life-long friendships with other women and, in their relationships with men, develop some kind of "eroticotheoretical transference relations" with their male lovers. What's more, as a literary critic in step with the autobiographical, critical and pop-cultural penchant of today's academy, Showalter feels free to draw from her own personal experience, relishing cavalier comparisons that are doubtless intended to startle: Margaret Fuller's shipwreck off the coast of Fire Island is the nineteenth-century equivalent of John Kennedy, Jr.'s befogged flight to Martha's Vineyard, and poor Frida Kirchwey (past owner, editor and publisher of *The Nation*) is the Tina Brown of her day.

Showalter begins *Inventing Herself* with an exuberant prank. In the summer of '97, a famous young Englishwoman, a mother of two who some years before had tried to commit suicide but who had, more recently, seemed to find a measure of stability and happiness in her life, dies suddenly despite heroic attempts to save her. The joke is that the woman is Mary Wollstonecraft, not Diana Spencer, even though Showalter considers both of them iconic—the latter because of her gritty determination to lead an independent, meaningful existence not typical of her class or kind. To Showalter, critics of the Princess—as well as those of us who find her finally uninteresting—display the kind of snobbishness once reserved for the academic elite. Academics today, to the contrary, are busily "placing Diana in context," Showalter cheerfully reports, offering lectures, monographs and conferences on her life and death.

The changing state of academe is actually one of the subtexts of *Inventing Herself.* Showalter has spent her adulthood within its sacred grove, where, as the last third of the book documents, she and her friends have nudged, irritated, defied and often capsized the male academic establishment since the 1970s. But because Showalter has devoted her life to upending the academic status quo, her discussion of contemporary women generally takes place, if not exactly under the scholar's lamp, at least never too far from its ivory light. We learn, for example, that Juliet Mitchell read *The Second Sex* at Oxford (and Showalter read it in high school); that before *Sexual Politics,* Kate Millett was brought to Douglass College in 1970 (by Showalter) to help launch a feminist, non-coeducational experiment; that Showalter delivered her first professional paper, **"Women and the Literary Curriculum,"** at the Women's Caucus of the Modern Language Association in 1970, alongside Adrienne Rich and Tillie Olsen; and that in America, "feminists were more active in academia than in the counterculture."

Perhaps so; perhaps not. In either case, after ten chapters on the lives of a number of nineteenth- and twentieth-century women, *Inventing Herself* metamorphoses into a history of academic feminism. Many readers are likely to find Showalter's own memoir here far more appealing than the thumbnail portraits of what she calls the "divas" (Jane Gallop, Eve Sedgwick) and the "young, streetwise, glamorous women writers outside of academia" (Naomi Wolf, Katie Roiphe, Susan Faludi). When Showalter documents her own coming-of-feminist-age less in terms of academic accomplishments (B.A. from Bryn Mawr, Ph.D. from the University of California-Davis, up the ranks at Rutgers, job offer from Princeton, where her husband teaches) than in terms of foods forbidden and coveted, her story takes on a real warmth. Isaac Asimov bought Showalter her first cheeseburger; at the formal teas of Bryn Mawr, she tasted Camembert and panettone; the Father Divine community served chocolate ice cream piled in petals; and in Paris, while she was married, raising a daughter and trying to finish a dissertation, she learned to cook for the hordes of friends dropping in and out of her family's Left Bank apartment. Nuggets of real experience save the Showalter story from dry triumphalism.

So does her persistent, outspoken and unswerving commitment to women. Even though she says that in 1989 she stopped writing essays in feminist criticism—"they outlived their usefulness, like the cat we got for the children, who hung on, hungry, demanding, and querulous, long after the children had grown up and left home. The stage was being cleared for the next act"—*Inventing Herself* is a kind of feminist criticism of an earlier or gentler sort: anecdotal stories about our sisters, intended to console and inspire. "Life stories retain their power when theories fade," Showalter declares at the outset of her book, as if to say she's grown bit weary of the academy she loves. As a good sister, Showalter refuses to cannibalize the work of other toilers in the field. She generously credits her sources, which include Elizabeth Hardwick, Victoria Glendinning, Susan Sontag and Carolyn Heilbrun. And though the life of, say, Mary Wollstonecraft has been told many times before (most perceptively by Claire Tomalin, whom Showalter quotes to excellent effect), Showalter's portraits make one want to turn both to Wollstonecraft and her biographer.

Not so with the charismatic Margaret Fuller. Showalter considers her major work, *Woman in the Nineteenth Century,* muddy and long-winded. However, she isn't concerned much with Fuller's ideas, or those of any of her subjects, so we learn less about Fuller's politics, her newspaper journalism and the revolutions of 1848 to which she was fiercely committed than about her being "swept away" by one man and only putatively married to another, who happened to be the father of her child. Showalter admits that she is less concerned with the women "frequently prescribed to us as role models" than with independent-minded women who lived boldly and loved bravely, who dared and defied and suffered consequences.

Margaret Fuller is a touchstone in *Inventing Herself.* Friend of Giuseppe Mazzini and Adam Mickiewicz, she was cast as the exotic feminist Zenobia in Nathaniel Hawthorne's *The Blithedale Romance.* In a chapter called **"Zenobia on the Hudson,"** Showalter recapitulates the arguments of Philip Rahv's "The Dark Lady of Salem," transforming Zenobia into Mary McCarthy, the sexy intellectual woman of the 1930s and 1940s whom men, particularly the *Partisan Review* crowd, wished to destroy. In the chapter **"Talkin' 'Bout My Generation: The 1970s,"** Showalter includes a subsection called "Fullerites," arguing that "women breaking the academic rules and flying too close to the sun in the 1970s risked crashing and burning." She cites Gail Parker, former president of Bennington, and critic Ann Douglas, not just because her *Feminization of American Culture* contains an excellent chapter on Fuller, but because Douglas is somehow "Fuller reincarnated, only beautiful as well."

Beauty, ambition, adventure, academia, good clothes and a dash of celebrity, if only of the fifteen-minute variety: such qualities mainly fill the bill for Showalter's feminist icons. As she says, they faced difficult choices with guts and defined, or redefined, themselves with panache. Evidently, it is women like them who will tread the boards of feminism's next stage.

### Hermione Lee (review date 10 August 2001)

SOURCE: Lee, Hermione. "Rule-breakers Rule." *Times Literary Supplement,* no. 5132 (10 August 2001): 22.

[*In the following review, Lee commends Showalter's "energetic and opinionated" arguments in* Inventing Herself: Claiming a Feminist Intellectual Heritage.]

"Life stories retain their power when theories fade." So Elaine Showalter claims at the start of her book of energetic and opinionated "claiming", [*Inventing Herself: Claiming a Feminist Intellectual Heritage,*] turning her back on feminist literary criticism and social history in favour of a collection of potted biographies of notable women. These are not, as she explains, the standard high-achieving, exemplary success stories (her examples of that would be Marie Curie, Eleanor Roosevelt, Margaret Thatcher). Nor are they necessarily women who defined themselves as feminists. The intention is to broaden the definition of feminism, to claim for it (whatever "it" is, under this rubric) a much more inclusive membership. These are women who, as Showalter puts it, have refused to be constrained in their ambitions by the fact of being female. They are "risk takers and adventurers", "trouble makers and rule breakers". They struggle to combine independence with personal happiness, often to no avail. Their lives are flawed, even tragic. Such lives, she says, have been unduly neglected.

Yet the argument about neglect includes, in its pantheon of preponderantly white, Anglo-American names, some extremely high-profile women. She starts with Mary Wollstonecraft, Margaret Fuller, Olive Schreiner, Eleanor Marx and Charlotte Perkins Gilman, and then goes on to Zora Neale Hurston, Margaret Mead, Rebecca West, Vera Brittain and Simone de Beauvoir. Mary McCarthy and Hannah Arendt lead on to Susan Sontag, Germaine Greer, Camille Paglia and an assortment of late twentieth-century feminists. She ends with Hillary Clinton, Oprah Winfrey and Diana Spencer, Princess of Wales, as examples of women who "succeeded in an epic life of resonant action". So a book which sets out to widen the claims to fame of neglected heroines ends by claiming feminist status for celebrities. This blurring of distinctions is deliberate Showalter's aim is to be inclusive, encouraging and life-enhancing. But by broadening the definition of feminism to the point where it seems to apply to any famous, ambitious or notorious woman whose life story arouses public interest, it risks throwing away the whole concept. By the end of *Inventing Herself* Showalter's subtitle looks very strange.

Along the way, there are some good stories of eccentricity, audacity and determination. Some of these are well known, and read like résumés filleted from the available biographies. Here's the painful tale of Olive Schreiner's attempts to combine feminist writing with love and marriage, or of Eleanor Marx's hopeless relationship and her suicide, or the story, so moving and rational, of Mary Wollstonecraft's arrangement with William Godwin in the last two years of her life, in 1796 and 97, to live in separate houses, write all day and meet in the evening. But there are some less well-known stories, too, like the admiring accounts of Margaret Fuller teaching adult-education classes in Boston in 1839. Or of the anthropologist Elsie Parsons, in the 1900s, determined not to behave in the expected ways, wearing tennis shoes with evening gowns, refusing honours and full-time jobs and never saying hello, goodbye, or Merry Christmas.

There is a tremendous amount of anecdotal gossip. So we learn that Mary McCarthy didn't shave her legs, that Hélène Cixous was an "eyeliner queen" and that Hannah Arendt chain-smoked. When we get to Simone de Beauvoir, we hear quite as much about her "trademark" turban (the only time she was ever seen with it coming undone was at Sartre's burial) and her affairs (in 1947 de Beauvoir "fell passionately in love with a sexually competent man . . . who looked like a young Sylvester Stallone") as we do about the argument of *The Second Sex.*

One of the life stories is that of Elaine Showalter who puts herself in here in order to explain how these heroines affected or intersected with her own career. So at the heart of the book is the story of a Jewish American academic feminist coming into her own in the 1950s and 60s, an interesting story which I would have preferred, as the main subject, to this second-hand procession of iconic names. Describing herself reading everything she could lay her hands on in the Brookline Public Library in the Boston suburbs in the 1940s, eating her first Gentile cheeseburger at sixteen while doing an interview with Isaac Asimov, getting away to Bryn Mawr and finding nothing but snobbery and puritanism, breaking off a youthful engagement for a graduate place at intellectual Brandeis, becoming politicized (and getting married to a Southern Episcopalian) in the early 1960s, working on what would become *A Literature of Their Own* in Paris in 1968, surrounded by English anarchists and French revolutionary students, turning herself into a feminist teacher and activist through the 1960s and 70s, and setting up the new discipline of women's studies (first at Douglas College, then at Rutgers and at Princeton), she is always candid, vigorous and full of enjoyment at having "made up her life as she went along".

Showalter is generous, too, to all the women (dead and alive, on paper and in person) who helped her shape this life: Kate Millett, Ann Douglas, Adrienne Rich, Tillie Olsen, among many others. One of the book's main narratives is of a chain of female influences, friendships and working relationships. The audacious Elsie Parsons taught a course on "Sex in Ethnology" to a young American anthropologist, Ruth Benedict, who started work in 1914 on a book on Mary Wollstonecraft, Margaret Fuller and Oliver Schreiner—"new women of three centuries"—as a way of investigating the perpetual "restlessness and groping inherent in the nature of women". Benedict in turn was a great influence on Margaret Mead. Such links are everywhere, in the anti-apartheid activist Ruth First's writing on Olive Schreiner, in Sontag's debt to de Beauvois, who turned her into a feminist, in the friendship between Winifred Holtby and Vera Brittain, or between Hannah Arendt and Mary McCarthy, or in McCarthy's galvanizing effect on a whole generation of American women. Elizabeth Hardwick praised her difficult subversive career of "candour and dissent"; Alison Lurie said that she invented herself as a "totally new type of woman who stood for both sense and sensibility". This is all very encouraging, even if Showalter is content to celebrate these lines of connection rather than investigate them in any critical depth, and even if she conflates the past with the present rather too easily. So Mary Wollstonecraft is described as feeling "comfortable" with motherhood; Freda Kirchway, the socialist Editor of the *Nation* in the 1920s, is called the "Tina Brown" of her day (since when was Tina Brown a radical feminist?), and it is said of the 1890s feminist lecturer and writer Charlotte Perkins Gilman that "having a daughter intensified her desire to become a role model". A cosy likeness with the past, not a sense of otherness, strangeness, or difference, is what is sought for here: these are "our heroines, our sisters, our contemporaries".

But not all these connections are supportive. Some of the most virulent opposition to the women's movement came, "of course," from other women. Many of the outstanding "feminist heroines", such as Arendt, disliked the feminist movement, and thought that women should not write like women, but should "adapt to masculine standards of intellectual style". There are many stories of rivalry, some told with an energy that suggests the settling of scores. "Oh, you're the imitation me", McCarthy said to Sontag when she first met her in the late 1960s. When Camille Paglia, in turn, invited Sontag to give a guest reading at Bennington in 1973, and was rebuffed by her ("Sontag asked: 'What is it you *want* from me?', to which Paglia wanted to reply, 'I'm your successor, dammit, and you don't have the wit to realize it'"), Paglia's torching of all possible "female mentors", and of every feminist American academic in her path (including Showalter), was under way.

There is a great deal of vigour and enthusiasm in this book. All the same, it is depressing. For those women readers and teachers who derived so much from *A Literature of Their Own* (1977), and who have admired Showalter's analysis of the gendered attitudes to mental illness in *The Female Malady* (1987) and of the *fin-de-siècle* in *Sexual Anarchy* (1990), it is disheartening to hear her saying that she stopped writing feminist essays in 1989 because they had "outlived their usefulness". And her description of the lives of these women almost entirely in terms of their personal relationships, and, at least in the last part of this book, in terms of media attention and celebrity status, makes for a dubious redefinition of feminism.

Surely there is a difference between women who have changed the way we think and live by their imaginations, their mental rigour, their knowledge and intellect—as well as or in spite of their "life stories"—and women who have achieved celebrity by other means—political ambition, marriage, glamour and wealth, the confessional culture of television? Showalter doesn't think so, placing Wollstonecraft and Arendt alongside "Celebrity First Ladies" such as Hillary Clinton, Oprah Winfrey or Diana Spencer. There will be some support for Clinton and Winfrey as feminist icons, but less, I would have thought, for Diana. Showalter has complained that her last few (extremely emotional) pages about the dead princess have overshadowed the rest of her book, especially in Britain. But to argue that narcissism, self-promotion, deep personal confusion played out for media attention, exploitation of looks and social position, a battle for revenge against an unpleasant husband, and a struggle for survival in an institution that remained entirely unchallenged, constitute the exemplary life story of a "courageous activist", is questionable. It is as if Showalter, at this point in her book, has decided to unhook the word feminism from any kind of political agenda, or from any idea of working for, or with, other women.

This is disappointing, because, before it gets on to divas and prima donnas, *Inventing Herself* invokes a long history of feminist polemics, key manifestos that have developed or altered the perception of women's lives, from Wollstonecraft's *Vindication of the Rights of Women* to de Beauvoir's *The Second Sex*. One writer of feminist polemics who is conspicuously passed over, however, is Virginia Woolf. In *A Literature of Their Own,* Showalter was critical of *A Room of One's Own,* for what she saw as its private, isolationist argument, withdrawing from political commitment into the idea of androgyny. "If a room of one's own becomes the destination, a feminine secession from the political world . . . it is a tomb, like Clarissa Dalloway's attic bedroom." Yet Woolf's argument in *A Room of One's Own* is somewhat echoed here. Woolf says that women can move and have moved forward, but must also always keep their mothers' pasts—of oppression, silencing, exclusion, poverty—in mind. Showalter too presents a progressive model of women's self-invention: "In the next wave of rule-breakers [after the New Women], newer women would imagine a fuller life." Her insistence on influence and "heritage" calls to mind Woolf's famous example of Shakespeare's sister, the woman of genius destroyed by the fact of her sex, whom the women of the future have to bring back to life through their work. Though she gives little space to Woolf, Showalter echoes her when she says "we need a sense of our feminist past".

But there is another argument raised by Woolf, in *Three Guineas,* which might also be set alongside Showalter's book. In the late 1930s, writing in the shadow of the impending war and of fascism, Woolf says that now that women have much greater educational and professional opportunities, they should think hard about how they are going to enter the male-dominated world, and should form what she calls a "Society of Outsiders", taking a critical, adversarial stance. This tricky, utopian idea is essentially a communal one, and it is also rather quiet: her Society of Outsiders might even be a secret society. Showalter's American celebration of glitzy feminist icons—individualist, glamorous, egocentric—is the opposite of that obscure English concept of outsiders, which she utterly repudiates. Her book argues that feminism must take the form of celebrity in order to have any life at all. And perhaps she is right; when we debated this recently in public, the strong reactions of the audience (who mostly wanted to talk admiringly about Oprah Winfrey) proved her point. But I miss the Elaine Showalter who wrote, not so long ago, in *Hystories,* that "feminism has a strong enlightenment, rationalist tradition of debate and skepticism. . . . We betray our tradition if we succumb to easy answers. Our primary obligation must always be to the truth."

## David Nokes (review date 25 January 2003)

SOURCE: Nokes, David. "Classics in the Classroom." *Spectator* 291, no. 9103 (25 January 2003): 48-9.

[*In the following review, Nokes criticizes* Teaching Literature, *arguing that Showalter fails to present "any serious or settled argument about the nature of teaching English."*]

There comes a time when all professors of literature think of writing a book like this [*Teaching Literature*]. Elaine Showalter has been professing it for 40 years, and after such a long and varied career what could be more apposite or timely than to share the wisdom of such experience with her younger colleagues? The answer, I fear, is much. She should have been gently dissuaded from writing a book which ranges from the tendentious ('methods can be overrated') to the banal ("the main difference between lectures and seminars was that in seminars the tutor sat down.'). One says 'writing', but the word is misapplied; 'compiling' would be a better term to register the very many practices which are commented upon, both by the teachers and the taught, throughout this book. There are about three citations per page, thrown in without discernible order, to give the book the appearance of variety; but pretty soon that appearance breaks down into a welter of frantic asides ('it does not have to be original to be good') or fussy advice ('wear a different suit every day of the week').

It hardly seems to matter that some of these references are meant ironically; for example the last, given to Norman Maclean when 'he couldn't afford that many suits' so wore 'a different necktie every day instead'. This scattergun technique has the effect of weakening any serious or settled argument about the nature of teaching English. There is a tendency to go uncomplainingly along with Isobel Armstrong when she states that 'students don't have the time to go deeply into any one author' and to sympathise with Peter V. Conroy on his 'struggle' though the 'discouraging' early weeks of term when his students, informed that they 'must read' *Pamela,* suggested to him that it 'somehow be made shorter'. Steven Axelrod confesses that 'one class memorably hissed me' when he announced, on the first day of a course on *Moby-Dick,* 'that they would have to read the whole book'. Jeff Nunowka bewails 'the sheer length of Victorian novels' and Showalter (I believe it's the author, but can't swear to it) much applauds the 'recent shift of academic interest' to the shorter fiction of the 1880s and 1890s. 'It is much easier,' she writes, to plan a course on Stoker, Stevenson and Wilde than to tackle the 'loose baggy monsters' of the mid-Victorians. One looks in vain for some definition of 'academic' or 'interest' or both.

This is not a book to engage in such debates; it far prefers or feels the need to impart such helpful hints as, 'The classroom offers the rudiments of a stage' or 'I compare lecturing to narration in the novel.' This last remark stands out because of the personal pronoun that introduces it. Just occasionally Showalter allows herself a paragraph or two of personal didactic commentary and the result, if not electrifying, is at least interesting. More of these observations, lengthened to make an argument, might have been quite readable; but they are set aside in favour of endless anecdotes. Towards the end of this book there is a section entitled 'Suicide' of which the first sentence is, 'The most dangerous of the dangerous subjects is suicide.' Lest anyone should become interested in the topic and concerned at how to tackle it, they should be immediately warned off. The section is less than two pages long and, without the handout Professor Showalter offers when tackling Plath's *The Bell Jar*, there is the danger of turning theory into practice. The other topic mentioned in this extremely brief chapter on **'Teaching Dangerous Subjects'** is 'Explicit Sexual Language' which, apart from sniggering at the *Literary Review*'s Bad Sex Prize, backs away from mentioning anything tendentious. Faced with a difficult issue such as rape, it advises, if the topic cannot be ducked, maintaining a 'sensitive atmosphere in the classroom' and not feeling 'like wimps' for doing so. I was hoping for some advice on tackling the issue in Clarissa, but Showalter is silent on the subject and anyway that novel (twice the length of *Pamela* or *Moby-Dick*) is far too long to be included.

# FURTHER READING

## Criticism

Cohen, David. "Gullibility Is Catching." *New Scientist* 154, no. 2086 (14 June 1997): 45.

>   Cohen offers a positive assessment of *Hystories: Hysterical Epidemics and Modern Culture.*

Cott, Nancy F. "A Canon of One's Own." *American Prospect* 12, no. 10 (4 June 2001): 46-7.

>   Cott offers a mixed assessment of *Inventing Herself: Claiming a Feminist Intellectual Heritage,* concluding that Showalter's "idiosyncratic book" may appeal to the general reader but not to scholars.

Harris, Ruth. Review of *The Female Malady: Women, Madness, and English Culture, 1830-1980,* by Elaine Showalter. *Signs* 15, no. 2 (winter 1990): 408-10.

>   Harris praises *The Female Malady,* but argues that Showalter's discussion of "Darwinist psychiatry" and the medical rationale behind the practice of lobotomies is incomplete and flawed.

Heller, Scott. "Scholar Sees Hysteria behind Many Modern Maladies." *Chronicle of Higher Education* 43, no. 32 (18 April 1997): A15-A16.

>   Heller discusses Showalter's controversial assertions about hysteria, presented in *The Female Malady: Women, Madness, and English Culture, 1830-1980* and *Hystories: Hysterical Epidemics and Modern Culture.*

Ignatieff, Michael. "Sergeant Jones's Sleeping-Bag." *London Review of Books* 19, no. 14 (17 July 1997): 20-1.

>   Ignatieff lauds Showalter's investigation in *Hystories: Hysterical Epidemics and Modern Culture,* but finds shortcomings in her tendency toward exaggeration and excessive psychologizing.

Lystra, Karen. Review of *Sexual Anarchy: Gender and Culture at the Fin-de-Siècle,* by Elaine Showalter. *Archives of Sexual Behavior* 22, no. 6 (December 1993): 647-50.

>   Lystra offers a positive assessment of *Sexual Anarchy.*

Moglen, Helene. "Studies of Women." *Yale Review* 67, no. 1 (October 1977): 150-57.

>   Moglen compliments Showalter's scholarship and erudition in *A Literature of Their Own,* but criticizes her capricious and overly harsh assessments of women authors, such as Virginia Woolf, who failed to live up to Showalter's own feminist standards.

Myslobodsky, Michael S. "Grande Hystérie as the Grand Mentor." *American Journal of Psychology* 112, no. 1 (spring 1999): 158-66.

>   Myslobodsky commends Showalter's challenge to medical psychiatry in *Hystories: Women, Madness, and English Culture, 1830-1980,* but finds flaws in her misunderstanding of hysteria and epidemics and her selection of fundamentally unrelated syndromes as the basis of her study.

Scull, Andrew. "Dazeland." *London Review of Books* 9, no. 19 (29 October 1987): 14-15.

>   Scull praises *The Female Malady,* but notes that Showalter's analysis is occasionally exaggerated and tainted by a romanticized view of madness.

Showalter, Elaine, and Pryde Brown. "Syndrome Syndrome." *Reason* 29, no. 3 (July 1997): 21.

>   Showalter discusses her examination of the concept of hysteria and the media creation of modern psychosomatic illnesses in *Hystories: Women, Madness, and English Culture, 1830-1980.*

Showalter, Elaine, and Clarence Bard Cole. "Anarchist in Academia." *Christopher Street* 14, no. 12 (23 December 1991): 22-5.

Showalter discusses her analysis of *fin-de-siècle* culture and sexuality in *Sexual Anarchy: Gender and Culture at the Fin-de-Siècle*.

Sutherland, Stuart. "Tales of Memory and Imagination." *Nature* 388, no. 6639 (17 July 1997): 239.

    Sutherland criticizes Showalter's central argument in *Hystories: Women, Madness, and English Culture, 1830-1980*.

Tippett, Maria. "Seven Veils and Umpteen Versions." *London Review of Books* 14, no. 2 (30 January 1992): 19-20.

    Tippett offers a positive assessment of *Sexual Anarchy: Gender and Culture at the Fin-de-Siècle*.

White, Edmund. "When the Genders Got Confused." *Times Literary Supplement*, no. 4593 (12 April 1991): 5-6.

    White praises Showalter's comparative study of *fin-de-siècle* gender politics in *Sexual Anarchy: Gender and Culture at the Fin-de-Siècle*, but strongly objects to her use of literary criticism, especially sex-obsessed psychoanalytic interpretations, to advance her sociological argument.

---

**Additional coverage of Showalter's life and career is contained in the following sources published by the Gale Group:** *Contemporary Authors,* **Vols. 57-60;** *Contemporary Authors New Revision Series,* **Vols. 58, 106;** *Dictionary of Literary Biography,* **Vol. 67;** *Feminist Writers; Gay and Lesbian Literature,* **Ed. 2; and** *Literature Resource Center.*

# How to Use This Index

**The main references**

> **Calvino, Italo**
> 1923-1985 ....... CLC 5, 8, 11, 22, 33, 39, 73; SSC 3, 48

list all author entries in the following Gale Literary Criticism series:

*AAL* = *Asian American Literature*
*BLC* = *Black Literature Criticism*
*BLCS* = *Black Literature Criticism Supplement*
*CLC* = *Contemporary Literary Criticism*
*CLR* = *Children's Literature Review*
*CMLC* = *Classical and Medieval Literature Criticism*
*DC* = *Drama Criticism*
*HLC* = *Hispanic Literature Criticism*
*HLCS* = *Hispanic Literature Criticism Supplement*
*LC* = *Literature Criticism from 1400 to 1800*
*NCLC* = *Nineteenth-Century Literature Criticism*
*NNAL* = *Native North American Literature*
*PC* = *Poetry Criticism*
*SSC* = *Short Story Criticism*
*TCLC* = *Twentieth-Century Literary Criticism*
*WLC* = *World Literature Criticism, 1500 to the Present*
*WLCS* = *World Literature Criticism Supplement*

**The cross-references**

> See also CA 85-88, 116; CANR 23, 61;
> DAM NOV; DLB 196; EW 13; MTCW 1, 2;
> RGSF 2; RGWL 2; SFW 4; SSFS 12

list all author entries in the following Gale biographical and literary sources:

*AAYA* = *Authors & Artists for Young Adults*
*AFAW* = *African American Writers*
*AFW* = *African Writers*
*AITN* = *Authors in the News*
*AMW* = *American Writers*
*AMWR* = *American Writers Retrospective Supplement*
*AMWS* = *American Writers Supplement*
*ANW* = *American Nature Writers*
*AW* = *Ancient Writers*
*BEST* = *Bestsellers*
*BPFB* = *Beacham's Encyclopedia of Popular Fiction: Biography and Resources*
*BRW* = *British Writers*
*BRWS* = *British Writers Supplement*
*BW* = *Black Writers*
*BYA* = *Beacham's Guide to Literature for Young Adults*
*CA* = *Contemporary Authors*
*CAAS* = *Contemporary Authors Autobiography Series*
*CABS* = *Contemporary Authors Bibliographical Series*
*CAD* = *Contemporary American Dramatists*
*CANR* = *Contemporary Authors New Revision Series*
*CAP* = *Contemporary Authors Permanent Series*
*CBD* = *Contemporary British Dramatists*
*CCA* = *Contemporary Canadian Authors*
*CD* = *Contemporary Dramatists*
*CDALB* = *Concise Dictionary of American Literary Biography*
*CDALBS* = *Concise Dictionary of American Literary Biography Supplement*
*CDBLB* = *Concise Dictionary of British Literary Biography*
*CMW* = *St. James Guide to Crime & Mystery Writers*
*CN* = *Contemporary Novelists*

*CP* = *Contemporary Poets*
*CPW* = *Contemporary Popular Writers*
*CSW* = *Contemporary Southern Writers*
*CWD* = *Contemporary Women Dramatists*
*CWP* = *Contemporary Women Poets*
*CWRI* = *St. James Guide to Children's Writers*
*CWW* = *Contemporary World Writers*
*DA* = *DISCovering Authors*
*DA3* = *DISCovering Authors 3.0*
*DAB* = *DISCovering Authors: British Edition*
*DAC* = *DISCovering Authors: Canadian Edition*
*DAM* = *DISCovering Authors: Modules*
   **DRAM:** *Dramatists Module;* **MST:** *Most-studied Authors Module;*
   **MULT:** *Multicultural Authors Module;* **NOV:** *Novelists Module;*
   **POET:** *Poets Module;* **POP:** *Popular Fiction and Genre Authors Module*
*DFS* = *Drama for Students*
*DLB* = *Dictionary of Literary Biography*
*DLBD* = *Dictionary of Literary Biography Documentary Series*
*DLBY* = *Dictionary of Literary Biography Yearbook*
*DNFS* = *Literature of Developing Nations for Students*
*EFS* = *Epics for Students*
*EXPN* = *Exploring Novels*
*EXPP* = *Exploring Poetry*
*EXPS* = *Exploring Short Stories*
*EW* = *European Writers*
*FANT* = *St. James Guide to Fantasy Writers*
*FW* = *Feminist Writers*
*GFL* = *Guide to French Literature,* Beginnings to 1789, 1798 to the Present
*GLL* = *Gay and Lesbian Literature*
*HGG* = *St. James Guide to Horror, Ghost & Gothic Writers*
*HW* = *Hispanic Writers*
*IDFW* = *International Dictionary of Films and Filmmakers: Writers and Production Artists*
*IDTP* = *International Dictionary of Theatre: Playwrights*
*LAIT* = *Literature and Its Times*
*LAW* = *Latin American Writers*
*JRDA* = *Junior DISCovering Authors*
*MAICYA* = *Major Authors and Illustrators for Children and Young Adults*
*MAICYAS* = *Major Authors and Illustrators for Children and Young Adults Supplement*
*MAWW* = *Modern American Women Writers*
*MJW* = *Modern Japanese Writers*
*MTCW* = *Major 20th-Century Writers*
*NCFS* = *Nonfiction Classics for Students*
*NFS* = *Novels for Students*
*PAB* = *Poets: American and British*
*PFS* = *Poetry for Students*
*RGAL* = *Reference Guide to American Literature*
*RGEL* = *Reference Guide to English Literature*
*RGSF* = *Reference Guide to Short Fiction*
*RGWL* = *Reference Guide to World Literature*
*RHW* = *Twentieth-Century Romance and Historical Writers*
*SAAS* = *Something about the Author Autobiography Series*
*SATA* = *Something about the Author*
*SFW* = *St. James Guide to Science Fiction Writers*
*SSFS* = *Short Stories for Students*
*TCWW* = *Twentieth-Century Western Writers*
*WLIT* = *World Literature and Its Times*
*WP* = *World Poets*
*YABC* = *Yesterday's Authors of Books for Children*
*YAW* = *St. James Guide to Young Adult Writers*

# Literary Criticism Series
# Cumulative Author Index

**20/1631**
  See Upward, Allen
**A/C Cross**
  See Lawrence, T(homas) E(dward)
**Abasiyanik, Sait Faik** 1906-1954
  See Sait Faik
**Abbey, Edward** 1927-1989 .......... **CLC 36, 59**
  See also ANW; CA 45-48; CANR 2, 41; DLB 256, 275; MTCW 2; TCWW 2
**Abbott, Lee K(ittredge)** 1947- .......... **CLC 48**
  See also CA 124; CANR 51, 101; DLB 130
**Abe, Kobo** 1924-1993 ...... **CLC 8, 22, 53, 81; TCLC 131**
  See also CA 65-68; CANR 24, 60; DAM NOV; DFS 14; DLB 182; MJW; MTCW 1, 2; RGWL 3; SFW 4
**Abe Kobo**
  See Abe, Kobo
**Abelard, Peter** c. 1079-c. 1142 ...... **CMLC 11**
  See also DLB 115, 208
**Abell, Kjeld** 1901-1961 ...... **CLC 15**
  See also CA 191; DLB 214
**Abish, Walter** 1931- ............. **CLC 22; SSC 44**
  See also CA 101; CANR 37, 114; CN 7; DLB 130, 227
**Abrahams, Peter (Henry)** 1919- .......... **CLC 4**
  See also AFW; BW 1; CA 57-60; CANR 26; CDWLB 3; CN 7; DLB 117, 225; MTCW 1, 2; RGEL 2; WLIT 2
**Abrams, M(eyer) H(oward)** 1912- ... **CLC 24**
  See also CA 57-60; CANR 13, 33; DLB 67
**Abse, Dannie** 1923- .......... **CLC 7, 29; PC 41**
  See also CA 53-56; CAAS 1; CANR 4, 46, 74; CBD; CP 7; DAB; DAM POET; DLB 27, 245; MTCW 1
**Abutsu** 1222(?)-1283 ...... **CMLC 46**
  See Abutsu-ni
**Abutsu-ni**
  See Abutsu
  See also DLB 203
**Achebe, (Albert) Chinua(lumogu)**
  1930- ..... **BLC 1; CLC 1, 3, 5, 7, 11, 26, 51, 75, 127, 152; WLC**
  See also AAYA 15; AFW; BPFB 1; BW 2, 3; CA 1-4R; CANR 6, 26, 47; CDWLB 3; CLR 20; CN 7; CP 7; CWRI 5; DA; DAB; DAC; DAM MST, MULT, NOV; DLB 117; DNFS 1; EXPN; EXPS; LAIT 2; MAICYA 1, 2; MTCW 1, 2; NFS 2; RGEL 2; RGSF 2; SATA 38, 40; SATA-Brief 38; SSFS 3, 13; TWA; WLIT 2
**Acker, Kathy** 1948-1997 ........... **CLC 45, 111**
  See also AMWS 12; CA 122; CANR 55; CN 7
**Ackroyd, Peter** 1949- .......... **CLC 34, 52, 140**
  See also BRWS 6; CA 127; CANR 51, 74, 99; CN 7; DLB 155, 231; HGG; INT 127; MTCW 1; RHW; SUFW 2

**Acorn, Milton** 1923-1986 ................... **CLC 15**
  See also CA 103; CCA 1; DAC; DLB 53; INT 103
**Adamov, Arthur** 1908-1970 ......... **CLC 4, 25**
  See also CA 17-18; CAP 2; DAM DRAM; GFL 1789 to the Present; MTCW 1; RGWL 2, 3
**Adams, Alice (Boyd)** 1926-1999 .. **CLC 6, 13, 46; SSC 24**
  See also CA 81-84; CANR 26, 53, 75, 88; CN 7; CSW; DLB 234; DLBY 1986; INT CANR-26; MTCW 1, 2; SSFS 14
**Adams, Andy** 1859-1935 ................. **TCLC 56**
  See also TCWW 2; YABC 1
**Adams, Brooks** 1848-1927 ............. **TCLC 80**
  See also DLB 47
**Adams, Douglas (Noel)** 1952-2001 .. **CLC 27, 60**
  See also AAYA 4, 33; BEST 89:3; BYA 14; CA 106; CANR 34, 64; CPW; DAM POP; DLB 261; DLBY 1983; JRDA; MTCW 1; NFS 7; SATA 116; SATA-Obit 128; SFW 4
**Adams, Francis** 1862-1893 ............. **NCLC 33**
**Adams, Henry (Brooks)**
  1838-1918 ............................ **TCLC 4, 52**
  See also AMW; CA 133; CANR 77; DA; DAB; DAC; DAM MST; DLB 12, 47, 189; MTCW 1; NCFS 1; RGAL 4; TUS
**Adams, John** 1735-1826 ............... **NCLC 106**
  See also DLB 31, 183
**Adams, Richard (George)** 1920- ... **CLC 4, 5, 18**
  See also AAYA 16; AITN 1, 2; BPFB 1; BYA 5; CA 49-52; CANR 3, 35; CLR 20; CN 7; DAM NOV; DLB 261; FANT; JRDA; LAIT 5; MAICYA 1, 2; MTCW 1, 2; NFS 11; SATA 7, 69; YAW
**Adamson, Joy(-Friederike Victoria)**
  1910-1980 ................................ **CLC 17**
  See also CA 69-72; CANR 22; MTCW 1; SATA 11; SATA-Obit 22
**Adcock, Fleur** 1934- ............................ **CLC 41**
  See also CA 25-28R, 182; CAAE 182; CAAS 23; CANR 11, 34, 69, 101; CP 7; CWP; DLB 40; FW
**Addams, Charles (Samuel)**
  1912-1988 ................................ **CLC 30**
  See also CA 61-64; CANR 12, 79
**Addams, Jane** 1860-1935 ................. **TCLC 76**
  See also AMWS 1; FW
**Addams, (Laura) Jane** 1860-1935 . **TCLC 76**
  See also AMWS 1; CA 194; FW
**Addison, Joseph** 1672-1719 ................. **LC 18**
  See also BRW 3; CDBLB 1660-1789; DLB 101; RGEL 2; WLIT 3
**Adler, Alfred (F.)** 1870-1937 ........... **TCLC 61**
  See also CA 159

**Adler, C(arole) S(chwerdtfeger)**
  1932- ........................................... **CLC 35**
  See also AAYA 4, 41; CA 89-92; CANR 19, 40, 101; CLR 78; JRDA; MAICYA 1, 2; SAAS 15; SATA 26, 63, 102, 126; YAW
**Adler, Renata** 1938- ..................... **CLC 8, 31**
  See also CA 49-52; CANR 95; CN 7; MTCW 1
**Adorno, Theodor W(iesengrund)**
  1903-1969 .............................. **TCLC 111**
  See also CA 89-92; CANR 89; DLB 242
**Ady, Endre** 1877-1919 .................... **TCLC 11**
  See also CDWLB 4; DLB 215; EW 9
**A.E.** ........................................... **TCLC 3, 10**
  See Russell, George William
  See also DLB 19
**Aelfric** c. 955-c. 1010 .................. **CMLC 46**
  See also DLB 146
**Aeschines** c. 390B.C.-c. 320B.C. ..... **CMLC 47**
  See also DLB 176
**Aeschylus** 525(?)B.C.-456(?)B.C. .. **CMLC 11, 51; DC 8; WLCS**
  See also AW 1; CDWLB 1; DA; DAB; DAC; DAM DRAM, MST; DFS 5, 10; DLB 176; RGWL 2, 3; TWA
**Aesop** 620(?)B.C.-560(?)B.C. .......... **CMLC 24**
  See also CLR 14; MAICYA 1, 2; SATA 64
**Affable Hawk**
  See MacCarthy, Sir (Charles Otto) Desmond
**Africa, Ben**
  See Bosman, Herman Charles
**Afton, Effie**
  See Harper, Frances Ellen Watkins
**Agapida, Fray Antonio**
  See Irving, Washington
**Agee, James (Rufus)** 1909-1955 ...... **TCLC 1, 19**
  See also AAYA 44; AITN 1; AMW; CA 148; CDALB 1941-1968; DAM NOV; DLB 2, 26, 152; DLBY 1989; LAIT 3; MTCW 1; RGAL 4; TUS
**Aghill, Gordon**
  See Silverberg, Robert
**Agnon, S(hmuel) Y(osef Halevi)**
  1888-1970 ........... **CLC 4, 8, 14; SSC 30**
  See also CA 17-18; CANR 60, 102; CAP 2; MTCW 1, 2; RGSF 2; RGWL 2, 3
**Agrippa von Nettesheim, Henry Cornelius**
  1486-1535 ...................... **LC 27**
**Aguilera Malta, Demetrio**
  1909-1981 ................................ **HLCS 1**
  See also CA 124; CANR 87; DAM MULT, NOV; DLB 145; HW 1; RGWL 3
**Agustini, Delmira** 1886-1914 ........... **HLCS 1**
  See also CA 166; HW 1, 2; LAW
**Aherne, Owen**
  See Cassill, R(onald) V(erlin)

381

**Ai** 1947- .................................. **CLC 4, 14, 69**
See also CA 85-88; CAAS 13; CANR 70; DLB 120; PFS 16

**Aickman, Robert (Fordyce)**
1914-1981 .................................. **CLC 57**
See also CA 5-8R; CANR 3, 72, 100; DLB 261; HGG; SUFW 1, 2

**Aiken, Conrad (Potter)** 1889-1973 .... **CLC 1, 3, 5, 10, 52; PC 26; SSC 9**
See also AMW; CA 5-8R; CANR 4, 60; CDALB 1929-1941; DAM NOV, POET; DLB 9, 45, 102; EXPS; HGG; MTCW 1, 2; RGAL 4; RGSF 2; SATA 3, 30; SSFS 8; TUS

**Aiken, Joan (Delano)** 1924- ............... **CLC 35**
See also AAYA 1, 25; CA 9-12R, 182; CAAE 182; CANR 4, 23, 34, 64; CLR 1, 19; DLB 161; FANT; HGG; JRDA; MAICYA 1, 2; MTCW 1; RHW; SAAS 1; SATA 2, 30, 73; SATA-Essay 109; SUFW 2; WYA; YAW

**Ainsworth, William Harrison**
1805-1882 .................................. **NCLC 13**
See also DLB 21; HGG; RGEL 2; SATA 24; SUFW 1

**Aitmatov, Chingiz (Torekulovich)**
1928- ........................................ **CLC 71**
See also CA 103; CANR 38; MTCW 1; RGSF 2; SATA 56

**Akers, Floyd**
See Baum, L(yman) Frank

**Akhmadulina, Bella Akhatovna**
1937- .......................... **CLC 53; PC 43**
See also CA 65-68; CWP; CWW 2; DAM POET

**Akhmatova, Anna** 1888-1966 ..... **CLC 11, 25, 64, 126; PC 2**
See also CA 19-20; CANR 35; CAP 1; DAM POET; EW 10; MTCW 1, 2; RGWL 2, 3

**Aksakov, Sergei Timofeyvich**
1791-1859 .................................. **NCLC 2**
See also DLB 198

**Aksenov, Vassily**
See Aksyonov, Vassily (Pavlovich)

**Akst, Daniel** 1956- ........................... **CLC 109**
See also CA 161; CANR 110

**Aksyonov, Vassily (Pavlovich)**
1932- ........................... **CLC 22, 37, 101**
See also CA 53-56; CANR 12, 48, 77; CWW 2

**Akutagawa Ryunosuke** 1892-1927 ... **SSC 44; TCLC 16**
See also CA 154; DLB 180; MJW; RGSF 2; RGWL 2, 3

**Alain** 1868-1951 .............................. **TCLC 41**
See also CA 163; GFL 1789 to the Present

**Alain de Lille** c. 1116-c. 1203 ........ **CMLC 53**
See also DLB 208

**Alain-Fournier** ................................ **TCLC 6**
See Fournier, Henri Alban
See also DLB 65; GFL 1789 to the Present; RGWL 2, 3

**Alanus de Insluis**
See Alain de Lille

**Alarcon, Pedro Antonio de**
1833-1891 ................................. **NCLC 1**

**Alas (y Urena), Leopoldo (Enrique Garcia)**
1852-1901 ................................. **TCLC 29**
See also CA 131; HW 1; RGSF 2

**Albee, Edward (Franklin III)** 1928- . **CLC 1, 2, 3, 5, 9, 11, 13, 25, 53, 86, 113; DC 11; WLC**
See also AITN 1; AMW; CA 5-8R; CABS 3; CAD; CANR 8, 54, 74; CD 5; CDALB 1941-1968; DA; DAB; DAC; DAM DRAM, MST; DFS 2, 3, 8, 10, 13, 14; DLB 7, 266; INT CANR-8; LAIT 4; MTCW 1, 2; RGAL 4; TUS

**Alberti, Rafael** 1902-1999 .................. **CLC 7**
See also CA 85-88; CANR 81; DLB 108; HW 2; RGWL 2, 3

**Albert the Great** 1193(?)-1280 ...... **CMLC 16**
See also DLB 115

**Alcala-Galiano, Juan Valera y**
See Valera y Alcala-Galiano, Juan

**Alcayaga, Lucila Godoy**
See Godoy Alcayaga, Lucila

**Alcott, Amos Bronson** 1799-1888 .... **NCLC 1**
See also DLB 1, 223

**Alcott, Louisa May** 1832-1888 . **NCLC 6, 58, 83; SSC 27; WLC**
See also AAYA 20; AMWS 1; BPFB 1; BYA 2; CDALB 1865-1917; CLR 1, 38; DA; DAB; DAC; DAM MST, NOV; DLB 1, 42, 79, 223, 239, 242; DLBD 14; FW; JRDA; LAIT 2; MAICYA 1, 2; NFS 12; RGAL 4; SATA 100; TUS; WCH; WYA; YABC 1; YAW

**Aldanov, M. A.**
See Aldanov, Mark (Alexandrovich)

**Aldanov, Mark (Alexandrovich)**
1886(?)-1957 ............................. **TCLC 23**
See also CA 181

**Aldington, Richard** 1892-1962 .......... **CLC 49**
See also CA 85-88; CANR 45; DLB 20, 36, 100, 149; RGEL 2

**Aldiss, Brian W(ilson)** 1925- . **CLC 5, 14, 40; SSC 36**
See also AAYA 42; CA 5-8R; CAAE 190; CAAS 2; CANR 5, 28, 64; CN 7; DAM NOV; DLB 14, 261, 271; MTCW 1, 2; SATA 34; SFW 4

**Aldrich, Bess Streeter**
1881-1954 ................................. **TCLC 125**
See also CLR 70

**Alegria, Claribel** 1924- .... **CLC 75; HLCS 1; PC 26**
See also CA 131; CAAS 15; CANR 66, 94; CWW 2; DAM MULT; DLB 145; HW 1; MTCW 1

**Alegria, Fernando** 1918- ................... **CLC 57**
See also CA 9-12R; CANR 5, 32, 72; HW 1, 2

**Aleichem, Sholom** ....... **SSC 33; TCLC 1, 35**
See Rabinovitch, Sholem
See also TWA

**Aleixandre, Vicente** 1898-1984 ....... **HLCS 1; TCLC 113**
See also CANR 81; DLB 108; HW 2; RGWL 2, 3

**Aleman, Mateo** 1547-1615(?) ............... **LC 81**

**Alencon, Marguerite d'**
See de Navarre, Marguerite

**Alepoudelis, Odysseus**
See Elytis, Odysseus
See also CWW 2

**Aleshkovsky, Joseph** 1929-
See Aleshkovsky, Yuz
See also CA 128

**Aleshkovsky, Yuz** ............................ **CLC 44**
See Aleshkovsky, Joseph

**Alexander, Lloyd (Chudley)** 1924- ... **CLC 35**
See also AAYA 1, 27; BPFB 1; BYA 5, 6, 7, 9, 10, 11; CA 1-4R; CANR 1, 24, 38, 55, 113; CLR 1, 5, 48; CWRI 5; DLB 52; FANT; JRDA; MAICYA 1, 2; MAICYAS 1; MTCW 1; SAAS 19; SATA 3, 49, 81, 129, 135; SUFW; TUS; WYA; YAW

**Alexander, Meena** 1951- ................... **CLC 121**
See also CA 115; CANR 38, 70; CP 7; CWP; FW

**Alexander, Samuel** 1859-1938 ........ **TCLC 77**

**Alexie, Sherman (Joseph, Jr.)**
1966- ..................... **CLC 96, 154; NNAL**
See also AAYA 28; CA 138; CANR 95; DAM MULT; DLB 175, 206; MTCW 1

**Alfau, Felipe** 1902-1999 ..................... **CLC 66**
See also CA 137

**Alfieri, Vittorio** 1749-1803 ............ **NCLC 101**
See also EW 4; RGWL 2, 3

**Alfred, Jean Gaston**
See Ponge, Francis

**Alger, Horatio, Jr.** 1832-1899 .... **NCLC 8, 83**
See also DLB 42; LAIT 2; RGAL 4; SATA 16; TUS

**Al-Ghazali, Muhammad ibn Muhammad**
1058-1111 ............................. **CMLC 50**
See also DLB 115

**Algren, Nelson** 1909-1981 ..... **CLC 4, 10, 33; SSC 33**
See also AMWS 9; BPFB 1; CA 13-16R; CANR 20, 61; CDALB 1941-1968; DLB 9; DLBY 1981, 1982, 2000; MTCW 1, 2; RGAL 4; RGSF 2

**Ali, Ahmed** 1908-1998 ....................... **CLC 69**
See also CA 25-28R; CANR 15, 34

**Alighieri, Dante**
See Dante

**Allan, John B.**
See Westlake, Donald E(dwin)

**Allan, Sidney**
See Hartmann, Sadakichi

**Allan, Sydney**
See Hartmann, Sadakichi

**Allard, Janet** ..................................... **CLC 59**

**Allen, Edward** 1948- ......................... **CLC 59**

**Allen, Fred** 1894-1956 ....................... **TCLC 87**

**Allen, Paula Gunn** 1939- ..... **CLC 84; NNAL**
See also AMWS 4; CA 143; CANR 63; CWP; DAM MULT; DLB 175; FW; MTCW 1; RGAL 4

**Allen, Roland**
See Ayckbourn, Alan

**Allen, Sarah A.**
See Hopkins, Pauline Elizabeth

**Allen, Sidney H.**
See Hartmann, Sadakichi

**Allen, Woody** 1935- ..................... **CLC 16, 52**
See also AAYA 10; CA 33-36R; CANR 27, 38, 63; DAM POP; DLB 44; MTCW 1

**Allende, Isabel** 1942- . **CLC 39, 57, 97; HLC 1; WLCS**
See also AAYA 18; CA 130; CANR 51, 74; CDWLB 3; CWW 2; DAM MULT, NOV; DLB 145; DNFS 1; FW; HW 1, 2; INT CA-130; LAIT 5; LAWS 1; MTCW 1, 2; NCFS 1; NFS 6; RGSF 2; RGWL 3; SSFS 11, 16; WLIT 1

**Alleyn, Ellen**
See Rossetti, Christina (Georgina)

**Alleyne, Carla D.** ............................. **CLC 65**

**Allingham, Margery (Louise)**
1904-1966 .................................. **CLC 19**
See also CA 5-8R; CANR 4, 58; CMW 4; DLB 77; MSW; MTCW 1, 2

**Allingham, William** 1824-1889 ....... **NCLC 25**
See also DLB 35; RGEL 2

**Allison, Dorothy E.** 1949- ......... **CLC 78, 153**
See also CA 140; CANR 66, 107; CSW; FW; MTCW 1; NFS 11; RGAL 4

**Alloula, Malek** ................................. **CLC 65**

**Allston, Washington** 1779-1843 ....... **NCLC 2**
See also DLB 1, 235

**Almedingen, E. M.** ........................... **CLC 12**
See Almedingen, Martha Edith von
See also SATA 3

**Almedingen, Martha Edith von** 1898-1971
See Almedingen, E. M.
See also CA 1-4R; CANR 1

**Almodovar, Pedro** 1949(?)- ............. **CLC 114; HLCS 1**
See also CA 133; CANR 72; HW 2

**Almqvist, Carl Jonas Love**
1793-1866 .................................. **NCLC 42**
**Alonso, Damaso** 1898-1990 .............. **CLC 14**
See also CA 131; CANR 72; DLB 108; HW 1, 2
**Alov**
See Gogol, Nikolai (Vasilyevich)
**Alta** 1942- ............................................ **CLC 19**
See also CA 57-60
**Alter, Robert B(ernard)** 1935- ......... **CLC 34**
See also CA 49-52; CANR 1, 47, 100
**Alther, Lisa** 1944- ......................... **CLC 7, 41**
See also BPFB 1; CA 65-68; CAAS 30; CANR 12, 30, 51; CN 7; CSW; GLL 2; MTCW 1
**Althusser, L.**
See Althusser, Louis
**Althusser, Louis** 1918-1990 ............. **CLC 106**
See also CA 131; CANR 102; DLB 242
**Altman, Robert** 1925- ................. **CLC 16, 116**
See also CA 73-76; CANR 43
**Alurista** ................................................ **HLCS 1**
See Urista, Alberto H.
See also DLB 82
**Alvarez, A(lfred)** 1929- .................. **CLC 5, 13**
See also CA 1-4R; CANR 3, 33, 63, 101; CN 7; CP 7; DLB 14, 40
**Alvarez, Alejandro Rodriguez** 1903-1965
See Casona, Alejandro
See also CA 131; HW 1
**Alvarez, Julia** 1950- .......... **CLC 93; HLCS 1**
See also AAYA 25; AMWS 7; CA 147; CANR 69, 101; MTCW 1; NFS 5, 9; SATA 129; WLIT 1
**Alvaro, Corrado** 1896-1956 ............ **TCLC 60**
See also CA 163; DLB 264
**Amado, Jorge** 1912-2001 ... **CLC 13, 40, 106; HLC 1**
See also CA 77-80; CANR 35, 74; DAM MULT, NOV; DLB 113; HW 2; LAW; LAWS 1; MTCW 1, 2; RGWL 2, 3; TWA; WLIT 1
**Ambler, Eric** 1909-1998 .............. **CLC 4, 6, 9**
See also BRWS 4; CA 9-12R; CANR 7, 38, 74; CMW 4; CN 7; DLB 77; MSW; MTCW 1, 2; TEA
**Ambrose, Stephen E(dward)**
1936-2002 .................................. **CLC 145**
See also AAYA 44; CA 1-4R; CANR 3, 43, 57, 83, 105; NCFS 2; SATA 40
**Amichai, Yehuda** 1924-2000 .. **CLC 9, 22, 57, 116; PC 38**
See also CA 85-88; CANR 46, 60, 99; CWW 2; MTCW 1
**Amichai, Yehudah**
See Amichai, Yehuda
**Amiel, Henri Frederic** 1821-1881 .... **NCLC 4**
See also DLB 217
**Amis, Kingsley (William)**
1922-1995 ...... **CLC 1, 2, 3, 5, 8, 13, 40, 44, 129**
See also AITN 2; BPFB 1; BRWS 2; CA 9-12R; CANR 8, 28, 54; CDBLB 1945-1960; CN 7; CP 7; DA; DAB; DAC; DAM MST, NOV; DLB 15, 27, 100, 139; DLBY 1996; HGG; INT CANR-8; MTCW 1, 2; RGEL 2; RGSF 2; SFW 4
**Amis, Martin (Louis)** 1949- .... **CLC 4, 9, 38, 62, 101**
See also BEST 90:3; BRWS 4; CA 65-68; CANR 8, 27, 54, 73, 95; CN 7; DLB 14, 194; INT CANR-27; MTCW 1
**Ammons, A(rchie) R(andolph)**
1926-2001 ...... **CLC 2, 3, 5, 8, 9, 25, 57, 108; PC 16**
See also AITN 1; AMWS 7; CA 9-12R; CANR 6, 36, 51, 73, 107; CP 7; CSW; DAM POET; DLB 5, 165; MTCW 1, 2; RGAL 4

**Amo, Tauraatua i**
See Adams, Henry (Brooks)
**Amory, Thomas** 1691(?)-1788 .............. **LC 48**
See also DLB 39
**Anand, Mulk Raj** 1905- ............... **CLC 23, 93**
See also CA 65-68; CANR 32, 64; CN 7; DAM NOV; MTCW 1, 2; RGSF 2
**Anatol**
See Schnitzler, Arthur
**Anaximander** c. 611B.C.-c. 546B.C. .................................... **CMLC 22**
**Anaya, Rudolfo A(lfonso)** 1937- ...... **CLC 23, 148; HLC 1**
See also AAYA 20; BYA 13; CA 45-48; CAAS 4; CANR 1, 32, 51; CN 7; DAM MULT, NOV; DLB 82, 206; HW 1; LAIT 4; MTCW 1, 2; NFS 12; RGAL 4; RGSF 2; WLIT 1
**Andersen, Hans Christian**
1805-1875 ....... **NCLC 7, 79; SSC 6, 56; WLC**
See also CLR 6; DA; DAB; DAC; DAM MST, POP; EW 6; MAICYA 1, 2; RGSF 2; RGWL 2, 3; SATA 100; TWA; WCH; YABC 1
**Anderson, C. Farley**
See Mencken, H(enry) L(ouis); Nathan, George Jean
**Anderson, Jessica (Margaret) Queale**
1916- ....................................... **CLC 37**
See also CA 9-12R; CANR 4, 62; CN 7
**Anderson, Jon (Victor)** 1940- ............. **CLC 9**
See also CA 25-28R; CANR 20; DAM POET
**Anderson, Lindsay (Gordon)**
1923-1994 .................................. **CLC 20**
See also CA 128; CANR 77
**Anderson, Maxwell** 1888-1959 ......... **TCLC 2**
See also CA 152; DAM DRAM; DFS 16; DLB 7, 228; MTCW 2; RGAL 4
**Anderson, Poul (William)**
1926-2001 ................................... **CLC 15**
See also AAYA 5, 34; BPFB 1; BYA 6, 8, 9; CA 1-4R, 181; CAAE 181; CAAS 2; CANR 2, 15, 34, 64, 110; CLR 58; DLB 8; FANT; INT CANR-15; MTCW 1, 2; SATA 90; SATA-Brief 39; SATA-Essay 106; SCFW 2; SFW 4; SUFW 1, 2
**Anderson, Robert (Woodruff)**
1917- ........................................... **CLC 23**
See also AITN 1; CA 21-24R; CANR 32; DAM DRAM; DLB 7; LAIT 5
**Anderson, Roberta Joan**
See Mitchell, Joni
**Anderson, Sherwood** 1876-1941 .. **SSC 1, 46; TCLC 1, 10, 24, 123; WLC**
See also AAYA 30; AMW; BPFB 1; CA 121; CANR 61; CDALB 1917-1929; DA; DAB; DAC; DAM MST, NOV; DLB 4, 9, 86; DLBD 1; EXPS; GLL 2; MTCW 1, 2; NFS 4; RGAL 4; RGSF 2; SSFS 4, 10, 11; TUS
**Andier, Pierre**
See Desnos, Robert
**Andouard**
See Giraudoux, Jean(-Hippolyte)
**Andrade, Carlos Drummond de** ..... **CLC 18**
See Drummond de Andrade, Carlos
See also RGWL 2, 3
**Andrade, Mario de** ........................ **TCLC 43**
See de Andrade, Mario
See also LAW; RGWL 2, 3; WLIT 1
**Andreae, Johann V(alentin)**
1586-1654 ..................................... **LC 32**
See also DLB 164
**Andreas Capellanus** fl. c. 1185- .... **CMLC 45**
See also DLB 208
**Andreas-Salome, Lou** 1861-1937 ... **TCLC 56**
See also CA 178; DLB 66

**Andress, Lesley**
See Sanders, Lawrence
**Andrewes, Lancelot** 1555-1626 ............. **LC 5**
See also DLB 151, 172
**Andrews, Cicily Fairfield**
See West, Rebecca
**Andrews, Elton V.**
See Pohl, Frederik
**Andreyev, Leonid (Nikolaevich)**
1871-1919 ................................ **TCLC 3**
See also CA 185
**Andric, Ivo** 1892-1975 .......... **CLC 8; SSC 36**
See also CA 81-84; CANR 43, 60; CDWLB 4; DLB 147; EW 11; MTCW 1; RGSF 2; RGWL 2, 3
**Androvar**
See Prado (Calvo), Pedro
**Angelique, Pierre**
See Bataille, Georges
**Angell, Roger** 1920- .......................... **CLC 26**
See also CA 57-60; CANR 13, 44, 70; DLB 171, 185
**Angelou, Maya** 1928- ... **BLC 1; CLC 12, 35, 64, 77, 155; PC 32; WLCS**
See also AAYA 7, 20; AMWS 4; BPFB 1; BW 2, 3; BYA 2; CA 65-68; CANR 19, 42, 65, 111; CDALBS; CLR 53; CP 7; CPW; CSW; CWP; DA; DAB; DAC; DAM MST, MULT, POET, POP; DLB 38; EXPN; EXPP; LAIT 4; MAICYA 2; MAICYAS 1; MAWW; MTCW 1, 2; NCFS 2; NFS 2; PFS 2, 3; RGAL 4; SATA 49, 136; WYA; YAW
**Angouleme, Marguerite d'**
See de Navarre, Marguerite
**Anna Comnena** 1083-1153 ............ **CMLC 25**
**Annensky, Innokenty (Fyodorovich)**
1856-1909 .................................. **TCLC 14**
See also CA 155
**Annunzio, Gabriele d'**
See D'Annunzio, Gabriele
**Anodos**
See Coleridge, Mary E(lizabeth)
**Anon, Charles Robert**
See Pessoa, Fernando (Antonio Nogueira)
**Anouilh, Jean (Marie Lucien Pierre)**
1910-1987 . **CLC 1, 3, 8, 13, 40, 50; DC 8**
See also CA 17-20R; CANR 32; DAM DRAM; DFS 9, 10; EW 13; GFL 1789 to the Present; MTCW 1, 2; RGWL 2, 3; TWA
**Anthony, Florence**
See Ai
**Anthony, John**
See Ciardi, John (Anthony)
**Anthony, Peter**
See Shaffer, Anthony (Joshua); Shaffer, Peter (Levin)
**Anthony, Piers** 1934- ......................... **CLC 35**
See also AAYA 11; BYA 7; CA 21-24R; CAAE 200; CANR 28, 56, 73, 102; CPW; DAM POP; DLB 8; FANT; MAICYA 2; MAICYAS 1; MTCW 1, 2; SAAS 22; SATA 84; SATA-Essay 129; SFW 4; SUFW 1, 2; YAW
**Anthony, Susan B(rownell)**
1820-1906 .................................. **TCLC 84**
See also FW
**Antiphon** c. 480B.C.-c. 411B.C. ..... **CMLC 55**
**Antoine, Marc**
See Proust, (Valentin-Louis-George-Eugene-)Marcel
**Antoninus, Brother**
See Everson, William (Oliver)
**Antonioni, Michelangelo** 1912- ........ **CLC 20, 144**
See also CA 73-76; CANR 45, 77

**Antschel, Paul** 1920-1970
See Celan, Paul
See also CA 85-88; CANR 33, 61; MTCW 1

**Anwar, Chairil** 1922-1949 .............. **TCLC 22**
See also RGWL 3

**Anzaldua, Gloria (Evanjelina)**
1942- ........................................... **HLCS 1**
See also CA 175; CSW; CWP; DLB 122; FW; RGAL 4

**Apess, William** 1798-1839(?) ........ **NCLC 73; NNAL**
See also DAM MULT; DLB 175, 243

**Apollinaire, Guillaume** 1880-1918 ....... **PC 7; TCLC 3, 8, 51**
See Kostrowitzki, Wilhelm Apollinaris de
See also CA 152; DAM POET; DLB 258; EW 9; GFL 1789 to the Present; MTCW 1; RGWL 2, 3; TWA; WP

**Apollonius of Rhodes**
See Apollonius Rhodius
See also AW 1; RGWL 2, 3

**Apollonius Rhodius** c. 300B.C.-c. 220B.C. ................................... **CMLC 28**
See Apollonius of Rhodes
See also DLB 176

**Appelfeld, Aharon** 1932- ... **CLC 23, 47; SSC 42**
See also CA 133; CANR 86; CWW 2; RGSF 2

**Apple, Max (Isaac)** 1941- .... **CLC 9, 33; SSC 50**
See also CA 81-84; CANR 19, 54; DLB 130

**Appleman, Philip (Dean)** 1926- ........ **CLC 51**
See also CA 13-16R; CAAS 18; CANR 6, 29, 56

**Appleton, Lawrence**
See Lovecraft, H(oward) P(hillips)

**Apteryx**
See Eliot, T(homas) S(tearns)

**Apuleius, (Lucius Madaurensis)**
125(?)-175(?) ............................ **CMLC 1**
See also AW 2; CDWLB 1; DLB 211; RGWL 2, 3; SUFW

**Aquin, Hubert** 1929-1977 .................. **CLC 15**
See also CA 105; DLB 53

**Aquinas, Thomas** 1224(?)-1274 ..... **CMLC 33**
See also DLB 115; EW 1; TWA

**Aragon, Louis** 1897-1982 ............. **CLC 3, 22; TCLC 123**
See also CA 69-72; CANR 28, 71; DAM NOV, POET; DLB 72, 258; EW 11; GFL 1789 to the Present; GLL 2; MTCW 1, 2; RGWL 2, 3

**Arany, Janos** 1817-1882 ................. **NCLC 34**

**Aranyos, Kakay** 1847-1910
See Mikszath, Kalman

**Arbuthnot, John** 1667-1735 ................... **LC 1**
See also DLB 101

**Archer, Herbert Winslow**
See Mencken, H(enry) L(ouis)

**Archer, Jeffrey (Howard)** 1940- ........ **CLC 28**
See also AAYA 16; BEST 89:3; BPFB 1; CA 77-80; CANR 22, 52, 95; CPW; DAM POP; INT CANR-22

**Archer, Jules** 1915- ............................ **CLC 12**
See also CA 9-12R; CANR 6, 69; SAAS 5; SATA 4, 85

**Archer, Lee**
See Ellison, Harlan (Jay)

**Archilochus** c. 7th cent. B.C.- ........ **CMLC 44**
See also DLB 176

**Arden, John** 1930- ................. **CLC 6, 13, 15**
See also BRWS 2; CA 13-16R; CAAS 4; CANR 31, 65, 67; CBD; CD 5; DAM DRAM; DFS 9; DLB 13, 245; MTCW 1

**Arenas, Reinaldo** 1943-1990 .. **CLC 41; HLC 1**
See also CA 128; CANR 73, 106; DAM MULT; DLB 145; GLL 2; HW 1; LAW; LAWS 1; MTCW 1; RGSF 2; RGWL 3; WLIT 1

**Arendt, Hannah** 1906-1975 ........ **CLC 66, 98**
See also CA 17-20R; CANR 26, 60; DLB 242; MTCW 1, 2

**Aretino, Pietro** 1492-1556 .................... **LC 12**
See also RGWL 2, 3

**Arghezi, Tudor** -1967 ........................ **CLC 80**
See Theodorescu, Ion N.
See also CA 167; CDWLB 4; DLB 220

**Arguedas, Jose Maria** 1911-1969 .... **CLC 10, 18; HLCS 1**
See also CA 89-92; CANR 73; DLB 113; HW 1; LAW; RGWL 2, 3; WLIT 1

**Argueta, Manlio** 1936- ....................... **CLC 31**
See also CA 131; CANR 73; CWW 2; DLB 145; HW 1; RGWL 3

**Arias, Ron(ald Francis)** 1941- ............ **HLC 1**
See also CA 131; CANR 81; DAM MULT; DLB 82; HW 1, 2; MTCW 2

**Ariosto, Ludovico** 1474-1533 .... **LC 6; PC 42**
See also EW 2; RGWL 2, 3

**Aristides**
See Epstein, Joseph

**Aristophanes** 450B.C.-385B.C. ........ **CMLC 4, 51; DC 2; WLCS**
See also AW 1; CDWLB 1; DA; DAB; DAC; DAM DRAM, MST; DFS 10; DLB 176; RGWL 2, 3; TWA

**Aristotle** 384B.C.-322B.C. ............. **CMLC 31; WLCS**
See also AW 1; CDWLB 1; DA; DAB; DAC; DAM MST; DLB 176; RGEL 2, 3; TWA

**Arlt, Roberto (Godofredo Christophersen)**
1900-1942 .................. **HLC 1; TCLC 29**
See also CA 131; CANR 67; DAM MULT; HW 1, 2; LAW

**Armah, Ayi Kwei** 1939- . **BLC 1; CLC 5, 33, 136**
See also AFW; BW 1; CA 61-64; CANR 21, 64; CDWLB 3; CN 7; DAM MULT, POET; DLB 117; MTCW 1; WLIT 2

**Armatrading, Joan** 1950- .................. **CLC 17**
See also CA 186

**Armitage, Frank**
See Carpenter, John (Howard)

**Arnette, Robert**
See Silverberg, Robert

**Arnim, Achim von (Ludwig Joachim von Arnim)** 1781-1831 ..... **NCLC 5; SSC 29**
See also DLB 90

**Arnim, Bettina von** 1785-1859 ....... **NCLC 38**
See also DLB 90; RGWL 2, 3

**Arnold, Matthew** 1822-1888 ..... **NCLC 6, 29, 89; PC 5; WLC**
See also BRW 5; CDBLB 1832-1890; DA; DAB; DAC; DAM MST, POET; DLB 32, 57; EXPP; PAB; PFS 2; TEA; WP

**Arnold, Thomas** 1795-1842 ............ **NCLC 18**
See also DLB 55

**Arnow, Harriette (Louisa) Simpson**
1908-1986 ............................ **CLC 2, 7, 18**
See also BPFB 1; CA 9-12R; CANR 14; DLB 6; FW; MTCW 1, 2; RHW; SATA 42; SATA-Obit 47

**Arouet, Francois-Marie**
See Voltaire

**Arp, Hans**
See Arp, Jean

**Arp, Jean** 1887-1966 ....... **CLC 5; TCLC 115**
See also CA 81-84; CANR 42, 77; EW 10

**Arrabal**
See Arrabal, Fernando

**Arrabal, Fernando** 1932- ... **CLC 2, 9, 18, 58**
See also CA 9-12R; CANR 15

**Arreola, Juan Jose** 1918-2001 ....... **CLC 147; HLC 1; SSC 38**
See also CA 131; CANR 81; DAM MULT; DLB 113; DNFS 2; HW 1, 2; LAW; RGSF 2

**Arrian** c. 89(?)-c. 155(?) ................ **CMLC 43**
See also DLB 176

**Arrick, Fran** ....................................... **CLC 30**
See Gaberman, Judie Angell
See also BYA 6

**Arriey, Richmond**
See Delany, Samuel R(ay), Jr.

**Artaud, Antonin (Marie Joseph)**
1896-1948 ................. **DC 14; TCLC 3, 36**
See also CA 149; DAM DRAM; DLB 258; EW 11; GFL 1789 to the Present; MTCW 1; RGWL 2, 3

**Arthur, Ruth M(abel)** 1905-1979 ..... **CLC 12**
See also CA 9-12R; CANR 4; CWRI 5; SATA 7, 26

**Artsybashev, Mikhail (Petrovich)**
1878-1927 ................................ **TCLC 31**
See also CA 170

**Arundel, Honor (Morfydd)**
1919-1973 ................................ **CLC 17**
See also CA 21-22; CAP 2; CLR 35; CWRI 5; SATA 4; SATA-Obit 24

**Arzner, Dorothy** 1900-1979 ............... **CLC 98**

**Asch, Sholem** 1880-1957 ................... **TCLC 3**
See also GLL 2

**Ash, Shalom**
See Asch, Sholem

**Ashbery, John (Lawrence)** 1927- .. **CLC 2, 3, 4, 6, 9, 13, 15, 25, 41, 77, 125; PC 26**
See Berry, Jonas
See also AMWS 3; CA 5-8R; CANR 9, 37, 66, 102; CP 7; DAM POET; DLB 5, 165; DLBY 1981; INT CANR-9; MTCW 1, 2; PAB; PFS 11; RGAL 4; WP

**Ashdown, Clifford**
See Freeman, R(ichard) Austin

**Ashe, Gordon**
See Creasey, John

**Ashton-Warner, Sylvia (Constance)**
1908-1984 ................................ **CLC 19**
See also CA 69-72; CANR 29; MTCW 1, 2

**Asimov, Isaac** 1920-1992 ..... **CLC 1, 3, 9, 19, 26, 76, 92**
See also AAYA 13; BEST 90:2; BPFB 1; BYA 4, 6, 7, 9; CA 1-4R; CANR 2, 19, 36, 60; CLR 12, 79; CMW 4; CPW; DAM POP; DLB 8; DLBY 1992; INT CANR-19; JRDA; LAIT 5; MAICYA 1, 2; MTCW 1, 2; RGAL 4; SATA 1, 26, 74; SCFW 2; SFW 4; TUS; YAW

**Askew, Anne** 1521(?)-1546 ................... **LC 81**
See also DLB 136

**Assis, Joaquim Maria Machado de**
See Machado de Assis, Joaquim Maria

**Astell, Mary** 1666-1731 ....................... **LC 68**
See also DLB 252; FW

**Astley, Thea (Beatrice May)** 1925- .. **CLC 41**
See also CA 65-68; CANR 11, 43, 78; CN 7

**Astley, William** 1855-1911
See Warung, Price

**Aston, James**
See White, T(erence) H(anbury)

**Asturias, Miguel Angel** 1899-1974 .... **CLC 3, 8, 13; HLC 1**
See also CA 25-28; CANR 32; CAP 2; CDWLB 3; DAM MULT, NOV; DLB 113; HW 1; LAW; MTCW 1, 2; RGWL 2, 3; WLIT 1

**Atares, Carlos Saura**
See Saura (Atares), Carlos

**Athanasius** c. 295-c. 373 ................ **CMLC 48**
**Atheling, William**
　See Pound, Ezra (Weston Loomis)
**Atheling, William, Jr.**
　See Blish, James (Benjamin)
**Atherton, Gertrude (Franklin Horn)**
　1857-1948 ..................... **TCLC 2**
　See also CA 155; DLB 9, 78, 186; HGG; RGAL 4; SUFW 1; TCWW 2
**Atherton, Lucius**
　See Masters, Edgar Lee
**Atkins, Jack**
　See Harris, Mark
**Atkinson, Kate** 1951- .......................... **CLC 99**
　See also CA 166; CANR 101; DLB 267
**Attaway, William (Alexander)**
　1911-1986 ..................... **BLC 1; CLC 92**
　See also BW 2, 3; CA 143; CANR 82; DAM MULT; DLB 76
**Atticus**
　See Fleming, Ian (Lancaster); Wilson, (Thomas) Woodrow
**Atwood, Margaret (Eleanor)** 1939- ... **CLC 2, 3, 4, 8, 13, 15, 25, 44, 84, 135; PC 8; SSC 2, 46; WLC**
　See also AAYA 12, 47; BEST 89:2; BPFB 1; CA 49-52; CANR 3, 24, 33, 59, 95; CN 7; CP 7; CPW; CWP; DA; DAB; DAC; DAM MST, NOV, POET; DLB 53, 251; EXPN; FW; INT CANR-24; LAIT 5; MTCW 1, 2; NFS 4, 12, 13, 14; PFS 7; RGSF 2; SATA 50; SSFS 3, 13; TWA; YAW
**Aubigny, Pierre d'**
　See Mencken, H(enry) L(ouis)
**Aubin, Penelope** 1685-1731(?) ............... **LC 9**
　See also DLB 39
**Auchincloss, Louis (Stanton)** 1917- .. **CLC 4, 6, 9, 18, 45; SSC 22**
　See also AMWS 4; CA 1-4R; CANR 6, 29, 55, 87; CN 7; DAM NOV; DLB 2, 244; DLBY 1980; INT CANR-29; MTCW 1; RGAL 4
**Auden, W(ystan) H(ugh)** 1907-1973 . **CLC 1, 2, 3, 4, 6, 9, 11, 14, 43, 123; PC 1; WLC**
　See also AAYA 18; AMWS 2; BRW 7; BRWR 1; CA 9-12R; CANR 5, 61, 105; CDBLB 1914-1945; DA; DAB; DAC; DAM DRAM, MST, POET; DLB 10, 20; EXPP; MTCW 1, 2; PAB; PFS 1, 3, 4, 10; TUS; WP
**Audiberti, Jacques** 1900-1965 ........... **CLC 38**
　See also DAM DRAM
**Audubon, John James** 1785-1851 . **NCLC 47**
　See also ANW; DLB 248
**Auel, Jean M(arie)** 1936- ........... **CLC 31, 107**
　See also AAYA 7; BEST 90:4; BPFB 1; CA 103; CANR 21, 64; CPW; DAM POP; INT CANR-21; NFS 11; RHW; SATA 91
**Auerbach, Erich** 1892-1957 ........... **TCLC 43**
　See also CA 155
**Augier, Emile** 1820-1889 ................ **NCLC 31**
　See also DLB 192; GFL 1789 to the Present
**August, John**
　See De Voto, Bernard (Augustine)
**Augustine, St.** 354-430 ....... **CMLC 6; WLCS**
　See also DA; DAB; DAC; DAM MST; DLB 115; EW 1; RGWL 2, 3
**Aunt Belinda**
　See Braddon, Mary Elizabeth
**Aunt Weedy**
　See Alcott, Louisa May
**Aurelius**
　See Bourne, Randolph S(illiman)
**Aurelius, Marcus** 121-180 ............. **CMLC 45**
　See Marcus Aurelius
　See also RGWL 2, 3

**Aurobindo, Sri**
　See Ghose, Aurabinda
**Austen, Jane** 1775-1817 ...... **NCLC 1, 13, 19, 33, 51, 81, 95, 119; WLC**
　See also AAYA 19; BRW 4; BRWR 2; BYA 3; CDBLB 1789-1832; DA; DAB; DAC; DAM MST, NOV; DLB 116; EXPN; LAIT 2; NFS 1, 14; TEA; WLIT 3; WYAS 1
**Auster, Paul** 1947- ..................... **CLC 47, 131**
　See also AMWS 12; CA 69-72; CANR 23, 52, 75; CMW 4; CN 7; DLB 227; MTCW 1; SUFW 2
**Austin, Frank**
　See Faust, Frederick (Schiller)
　See also TCWW 2
**Austin, Mary (Hunter)** 1868-1934 . **TCLC 25**
　See Stairs, Gordon
　See also ANW; CA 178; DLB 9, 78, 206, 221, 275; FW; TCWW 2
**Averroes** 1126-1198 ......................... **CMLC 7**
　See also DLB 115
**Avicenna** 980-1037 ......................... **CMLC 16**
　See also DLB 115
**Avison, Margaret** 1918- ............. **CLC 2, 4, 97**
　See also CA 17-20R; CP 7; DAC; DAM POET; DLB 53; MTCW 1
**Axton, David**
　See Koontz, Dean R(ay)
**Ayckbourn, Alan** 1939- ...... **CLC 5, 8, 18, 33, 74; DC 13**
　See also BRWS 5; CA 21-24R; CANR 31, 59; CBD; CD 5; DAB; DAM DRAM; DFS 7; DLB 13, 245; MTCW 1, 2
**Aydy, Catherine**
　See Tennant, Emma (Christina)
**Ayme, Marcel (Andre)** 1902-1967 ... **CLC 11; SSC 41**
　See also CA 89-92; CANR 67; CLR 25; DLB 72; EW 12; GFL 1789 to the Present; RGSF 2; RGWL 2, 3; SATA 91
**Ayrton, Michael** 1921-1975 ............... **CLC 7**
　See also CA 5-8R; CANR 9, 21
**Azorin** ................................................. **CLC 11**
　See Martinez Ruiz, Jose
　See also EW 9
**Azuela, Mariano** 1873-1952 .. **HLC 1; TCLC 3**
　See also CA 131; CANR 81; DAM MULT; HW 1, 2; LAW; MTCW 1, 2
**Baastad, Babbis Friis**
　See Friis-Baastad, Babbis Ellinor
**Bab**
　See Gilbert, W(illiam) S(chwenck)
**Babbis, Eleanor**
　See Friis-Baastad, Babbis Ellinor
**Babel, Isaac**
　See Babel, Isaak (Emmanuilovich)
　See also EW 11; SSFS 10
**Babel, Isaak (Emmanuilovich)**
　1894-1941(?) ......... **SSC 16; TCLC 2, 13**
　See Babel, Isaac
　See also CA 155; CANR 113; DLB 272; MTCW 1; RGSF 2; RGWL 2, 3; TWA
**Babits, Mihaly** 1883-1941 .............. **TCLC 14**
　See also CDWLB 4; DLB 215
**Babur** 1483-1530 .................................. **LC 18**
**Babylas** 1898-1962
　See Ghelderode, Michel de
**Baca, Jimmy Santiago** 1952- . **HLC 1; PC 41**
　See also CA 131; CANR 81, 90; CP 7; DAM MULT; DLB 122; HW 1, 2
**Baca, Jose Santiago**
　See Baca, Jimmy Santiago
**Bacchelli, Riccardo** 1891-1985 .......... **CLC 19**
　See also CA 29-32R; DLB 264

**Bach, Richard (David)** 1936- ............. **CLC 14**
　See also AITN 1; BEST 89:2; BPFB 1; BYA 5; CA 9-12R; CANR 18, 93; CPW; DAM NOV, POP; FANT; MTCW 1; SATA 13
**Bache, Benjamin Franklin**
　1769-1798 .................................... **LC 74**
　See also DLB 43
**Bachelard, Gaston** 1884-1962 ...... **TCLC 128**
　See also CA 97-100; GFL 1789 to the Present
**Bachman, Richard**
　See King, Stephen (Edwin)
**Bachmann, Ingeborg** 1926-1973 ....... **CLC 69**
　See also CA 93-96; CANR 69; DLB 85; RGWL 2, 3
**Bacon, Francis** 1561-1626 .............. **LC 18, 32**
　See also BRW 1; CDBLB Before 1660; DLB 151, 236, 252; RGEL 2; TEA
**Bacon, Roger** 1214(?)-1294 ........... **CMLC 14**
　See also DLB 115
**Bacovia, George** 1881-1957 ............ **TCLC 24**
　See Vasiliu, Gheorghe
　See also CDWLB 4; DLB 220
**Badanes, Jerome** 1937- ..................... **CLC 59**
**Bagehot, Walter** 1826-1877 ............ **NCLC 10**
　See also DLB 55
**Bagnold, Enid** 1889-1981 ................. **CLC 25**
　See also BYA 2; CA 5-8R; CANR 5, 40; CBD; CWD; CWRI 5; DAM DRAM; DLB 13, 160, 191, 245; FW; MAICYA 1, 2; RGEL 2; SATA 1, 25
**Bagritsky, Eduard** 1895-1934 ......... **TCLC 60**
**Bagrjana, Elisaveta**
　See Belcheva, Elisaveta Lyubomirova
**Bagryana, Elisaveta** -1991 ................. **CLC 10**
　See Belcheva, Elisaveta Lyubomirova
　See also CA 178; CDWLB 4; DLB 147
**Bailey, Paul** 1937- ............................. **CLC 45**
　See also CA 21-24R; CANR 16, 62; CN 7; DLB 14, 271; GLL 2
**Baillie, Joanna** 1762-1851 ................ **NCLC 71**
　See also DLB 93; RGEL 2
**Bainbridge, Beryl (Margaret)** 1934- . **CLC 4, 5, 8, 10, 14, 18, 22, 62, 130**
　See also BRWS 6; CA 21-24R; CANR 24, 55, 75, 88; CN 7; DAM NOV; DLB 14, 231; MTCW 1, 2
**Baker, Carlos (Heard)**
　1909-1987 ................................. **TCLC 119**
　See also CA 5-8R; CANR 3, 63; DLB 103
**Baker, Elliott** 1922- ............................ **CLC 8**
　See also CA 45-48; CANR 2, 63; CN 7
**Baker, Jean H.** .............................. **TCLC 3, 10**
　See Russell, George William
**Baker, Nicholson** 1957- ............. **CLC 61, 165**
　See also CA 135; CANR 63; CN 7; CPW; DAM POP; DLB 227
**Baker, Ray Stannard** 1870-1946 .... **TCLC 47**
**Baker, Russell (Wayne)** 1925- ........... **CLC 31**
　See also BEST 89:4; CA 57-60; CANR 11, 41, 59; MTCW 1, 2
**Bakhtin, M.**
　See Bakhtin, Mikhail Mikhailovich
**Bakhtin, M. M.**
　See Bakhtin, Mikhail Mikhailovich
**Bakhtin, Mikhail**
　See Bakhtin, Mikhail Mikhailovich
**Bakhtin, Mikhail Mikhailovich**
　1895-1975 .................................... **CLC 83**
　See also CA 128; DLB 242
**Bakshi, Ralph** 1938(?)- ...................... **CLC 26**
　See also CA 138; IDFW 3
**Bakunin, Mikhail (Alexandrovich)**
　1814-1876 ........................... **NCLC 25, 58**
**Baldwin, James (Arthur)** 1924-1987 .. **BLC 1; CLC 1, 2, 3, 4, 5, 8, 13, 15, 17, 42, 50, 67, 90, 127; DC 1; SSC 10, 33; WLC**
　See also AAYA 4, 34; AFAW 1, 2; AMWR 2; AMWS 1; BPFB 1; BW 1; CA 1-4R;

CABS 1; CAD; CANR 3, 24; CDALB 1941-1968; CPW; DA; DAB; DAC; DAM MST, MULT, NOV, POP; DFS 15; DLB 2, 7, 33, 249; DLBY 1987; EXPS; LAIT 5; MTCW 1, 2; NCFS 4; NFS 4; RGAL 4; RGSF 2; SATA 9; SATA-Obit 54; SSFS 2; TUS

**Bale, John** 1495-1563 .......................... **LC 62**
See also DLB 132; RGEL 2; TEA

**Ball, Hugo** 1886-1927 .................... **TCLC 104**

**Ballard, J(ames) G(raham)** 1930- . **CLC 3, 6, 14, 36, 137; SSC 1, 53**
See also AAYA 3; BRWS 5; CA 5-8R; CANR 15, 39, 65, 107; CN 7; DAM NOV, POP; DLB 14, 207, 261; HGG; MTCW 1, 2; NFS 8; RGEL 2; RGSF 2; SATA 93; SFW 4

**Balmont, Konstantin (Dmitriyevich)** 1867-1943 ............................... **TCLC 11**
See also CA 155

**Baltausis, Vincas** 1847-1910
See Mikszath, Kalman

**Balzac, Honore de** 1799-1850 ... **NCLC 5, 35, 53; SSC 5; WLC**
See also DA; DAB; DAC; DAM MST, NOV; DLB 119; EW 5; GFL 1789 to the Present; RGSF 2; RGWL 2, 3; SSFS 10; SUFW; TWA

**Bambara, Toni Cade** 1939-1995 ........ **BLC 1; CLC 19, 88; SSC 35; TCLC 116; WLCS**
See also AAYA 5; AFAW 2; AMWS 11; BW 2, 3; BYA 12, 14; CA 29-32R; CANR 24, 49, 81; CDALBS; DA; DAC; DAM MST, MULT; DLB 38, 218; EXPS; MTCW 1, 2; RGAL 4; RGSF 2; SATA 112; SSFS 4, 7, 12

**Bamdad, A.**
See Shamlu, Ahmad

**Banat, D. R.**
See Bradbury, Ray (Douglas)

**Bancroft, Laura**
See Baum, L(yman) Frank

**Banim, John** 1798-1842 .................. **NCLC 13**
See also DLB 116, 158, 159; RGEL 2

**Banim, Michael** 1796-1874 ............. **NCLC 13**
See also DLB 158, 159

**Banjo, The**
See Paterson, A(ndrew) B(arton)

**Banks, Iain**
See Banks, Iain M(enzies)

**Banks, Iain M(enzies)** 1954- .............. **CLC 34**
See also CA 128; CANR 61, 106; DLB 194, 261; HGG; INT 128; SFW 4

**Banks, Lynne Reid** .......................... **CLC 23**
See Reid Banks, Lynne
See also AAYA 6; BYA 7

**Banks, Russell** 1940- ..... **CLC 37, 72; SSC 42**
See also AAYA 45; AMWS 5; CA 65-68; CAAS 15; CANR 19, 52, 73; CN 7; DLB 130; NFS 13

**Banville, John** 1945- .................. **CLC 46, 118**
See also CA 128; CANR 104; CN 7; DLB 14, 271; INT 128

**Banville, Theodore (Faullain) de** 1832-1891 ................................. **NCLC 9**
See also DLB 217; GFL 1789 to the Present

**Baraka, Amiri** 1934- ..... **BLC 1; CLC 1, 2, 3, 5, 10, 14, 33, 115; DC 6; PC 4; WLCS**
See Jones, LeRoi
See also AFAW 1, 2; AMWS 2; BW 2, 3; CA 21-24R; CABS 3; CAD; CANR 27, 38, 61; CDALB 1941-1968; CP 7; CPW; DA; DAC; DAM MST, MULT, POET, POP; DFS 3, 11, 16; DLB 5, 7, 16, 38; DLBD 8; MTCW 1, 2; PFS 9; RGAL 4; TUS; WP

**Baratynsky, Evgenii Abramovich** 1800-1844 ............................... **NCLC 103**
See also DLB 205

**Barbauld, Anna Laetitia** 1743-1825 ............................... **NCLC 50**
See also DLB 107, 109, 142, 158; RGEL 2

**Barbellion, W. N. P.** .......................... **TCLC 24**
See Cummings, Bruce F(rederick)

**Barber, Benjamin R.** 1939- ............ **CLC 141**
See also CA 29-32R; CANR 12, 32, 64

**Barbera, Jack (Vincent)** 1945- ......... **CLC 44**
See also CA 110; CANR 45

**Barbey d'Aurevilly, Jules-Amedee** 1808-1889 .................... **NCLC 1; SSC 17**
See also DLB 119; GFL 1789 to the Present

**Barbour, John** c. 1316-1395 .......... **CMLC 33**
See also DLB 146

**Barbusse, Henri** 1873-1935 .............. **TCLC 5**
See also CA 154; DLB 65; RGWL 2, 3

**Barclay, Bill**
See Moorcock, Michael (John)

**Barclay, William Ewert**
See Moorcock, Michael (John)

**Barea, Arturo** 1897-1957 ................ **TCLC 14**
See also CA 201

**Barfoot, Joan** 1946- ........................ **CLC 18**
See also CA 105

**Barham, Richard Harris** 1788-1845 ............................... **NCLC 77**
See also DLB 159

**Baring, Maurice** 1874-1945 ............... **TCLC 8**
See also CA 168; DLB 34; HGG

**Baring-Gould, Sabine** 1834-1924 ... **TCLC 88**
See also DLB 156, 190

**Barker, Clive** 1952- ............. **CLC 52; SSC 53**
See also AAYA 10; BEST 90:3; BPFB 1; CA 129; CANR 71, 111; CPW; DAM POP; DLB 261; HGG; INT 129; MTCW 1, 2; SUFW 2

**Barker, George Granville** 1913-1991 ............................... **CLC 8, 48**
See also CA 9-12R; CANR 7, 38; DAM POET; DLB 20; MTCW 1

**Barker, Harley Granville**
See Granville-Barker, Harley
See also DLB 10

**Barker, Howard** 1946- ...................... **CLC 37**
See also CA 102; CBD; CD 5; DLB 13, 233

**Barker, Jane** 1652-1732 .............. **LC 42, 82**
See also DLB 39, 131

**Barker, Pat(ricia)** 1943- ...... **CLC 32, 94, 146**
See also BRWS 4; CA 122; CANR 50, 101; CN 7; DLB 271; INT 122

**Barlach, Ernst (Heinrich)** 1870-1938 ............................... **TCLC 84**
See also CA 178; DLB 56, 118

**Barlow, Joel** 1754-1812 .................. **NCLC 23**
See also AMWS 2; DLB 37; RGAL 4

**Barnard, Mary (Ethel)** 1909- ........... **CLC 48**
See also CA 21-22; CAP 2

**Barnes, Djuna** 1892-1982 .... **CLC 3, 4, 8, 11, 29, 127; SSC 3**
See Steptoe, Lydia
See also AMWS 3; CA 9-12R; CAD; CANR 16, 55; CWD; DLB 4, 9, 45; GLL 1; MTCW 1, 2; RGAL 4; TUS

**Barnes, Julian (Patrick)** 1946- . **CLC 42, 141**
See also BRWS 4; CA 102; CANR 19, 54; CN 7; DAB; DLB 194; DLBY 1993; MTCW 1

**Barnes, Peter** 1931- ...................... **CLC 5, 56**
See also CA 65-68; CAAS 12; CANR 33, 34, 64, 113; CBD; CD 5; DFS 6; DLB 13, 233; MTCW 1

**Barnes, William** 1801-1886 ............ **NCLC 75**
See also DLB 32

**Baroja (y Nessi), Pio** 1872-1956 ........ **HLC 1; TCLC 8**
See also EW 9

**Baron, David**
See Pinter, Harold

**Baron Corvo**
See Rolfe, Frederick (William Serafino Austin Lewis Mary)

**Barondess, Sue K(aufman)** 1926-1977 ............................... **CLC 8**
See Kaufman, Sue
See also CA 1-4R; CANR 1

**Baron de Teive**
See Pessoa, Fernando (Antonio Nogueira)

**Baroness Von S.**
See Zangwill, Israel

**Barres, (Auguste-)Maurice** 1862-1923 ............................... **TCLC 47**
See also CA 164; DLB 123; GFL 1789 to the Present

**Barreto, Afonso Henrique de Lima**
See Lima Barreto, Afonso Henrique de

**Barrett, Andrea** 1954- ..................... **CLC 150**
See also CA 156; CANR 92

**Barrett, Michele** .............................. **CLC 65**

**Barrett, (Roger) Syd** 1946- ............... **CLC 35**

**Barrett, William (Christopher)** 1913-1992 ............................... **CLC 27**
See also CA 13-16R; CANR 11, 67; INT CANR-11

**Barrie, J(ames) M(atthew)** 1860-1937 ............................... **TCLC 2**
See also BRWS 3; BYA 4, 5; CA 136; CANR 77; CDBLB 1890-1914; CLR 16; CWRI 5; DAB; DAM DRAM; DFS 7; DLB 10, 141, 156; FANT; MAICYA 1, 2; MTCW 1; SATA 100; SUFW; WCH; WLIT 4; YABC 1

**Barrington, Michael**
See Moorcock, Michael (John)

**Barrol, Grady**
See Bograd, Larry

**Barry, Mike**
See Malzberg, Barry N(athaniel)

**Barry, Philip** 1896-1949 .................. **TCLC 11**
See also CA 199; DFS 9; DLB 7, 228; RGAL 4

**Bart, Andre Schwarz**
See Schwarz-Bart, Andre

**Barth, John (Simmons)** 1930- ... **CLC 1, 2, 3, 5, 7, 9, 10, 14, 27, 51, 89; SSC 10**
See also AITN 1, 2; AMW; BPFB 1; CA 1-4R; CABS 1; CANR 5, 23, 49, 64, 113; CN 7; DAM NOV; DLB 2, 227; FANT; MTCW 1; RGAL 4; RGSF 2; RHW; SSFS 6; TUS

**Barthelme, Donald** 1931-1989 ... **CLC 1, 2, 3, 5, 6, 8, 13, 23, 46, 59, 115; SSC 2, 55**
See also AMWS 4; BPFB 1; CA 21-24R; CANR 20, 58; DAM NOV; DLB 2, 234; DLBY 1980, 1989; FANT; MTCW 1, 2; RGAL 4; RGSF 2; SATA 7; SATA-Obit 62; SSFS 3

**Barthelme, Frederick** 1943- ...... **CLC 36, 117**
See also AMWS 11; CA 122; CANR 77; CN 7; CSW; DLB 244; DLBY 1985; INT CA-122

**Barthes, Roland (Gerard)** 1915-1980 ............................... **CLC 24, 83**
See also CA 130; CANR 66; EW 13; GFL 1789 to the Present; MTCW 1, 2; TWA

**Barzun, Jacques (Martin)** 1907- ...... **CLC 51, 145**
See also CA 61-64; CANR 22, 95

**Bashevis, Isaac**
See Singer, Isaac Bashevis

**Bashkirtseff, Marie** 1859-1884 ....... **NCLC 27**

**Basho, Matsuo**
See Matsuo Basho
See also RGWL 2, 3; WP

**Basil of Caesaria** c. 330-379 .......... **CMLC 35**

**Bass, Kingsley B., Jr.**
See Bullins, Ed

**Bass, Rick** 1958- ......................... **CLC 79, 143**
See also ANW; CA 126; CANR 53, 93; CSW; DLB 212, 275

**Bassani, Giorgio** 1916-2000 ................ **CLC 9**
See also CA 65-68; CANR 33; CWW 2; DLB 128, 177; MTCW 1; RGWL 2, 3

**Bastian, Ann** ..................................... **CLC 70**

**Bastos, Augusto (Antonio) Roa**
See Roa Bastos, Augusto (Antonio)

**Bataille, Georges** 1897-1962 ............... **CLC 29**
See also CA 101

**Bates, H(erbert) E(rnest)**
1905-1974 ..................... **CLC 46; SSC 10**
See also CA 93-96; CANR 34; DAB; DAM POP; DLB 162, 191; EXPS; MTCW 1, 2; RGSF 2; SSFS 7

**Bauchart**
See Camus, Albert

**Baudelaire, Charles** 1821-1867 . **NCLC 6, 29, 55; PC 1; SSC 18; WLC**
See also DA; DAB; DAC; DAM MST, POET; DLB 217; EW 7; GFL 1789 to the Present; RGWL 2, 3; TWA

**Baudouin, Marcel**
See Peguy, Charles (Pierre)

**Baudouin, Pierre**
See Peguy, Charles (Pierre)

**Baudrillard, Jean** 1929- ....................... **CLC 60**

**Baum, L(yman) Frank** 1856-1919 ... **TCLC 7**
See also AAYA 46; CA 133; CLR 15; CWRI 5; DLB 22; FANT; JRDA; MAICYA 1, 2; MTCW 1, 2; NFS 13; RGAL 4; SATA 18, 100; WCH

**Baum, Louis F.**
See Baum, L(yman) Frank

**Baumbach, Jonathan** 1933- .......... **CLC 6, 23**
See also CA 13-16R; CAAS 5; CANR 12, 66; CN 7; DLBY 1980; INT CANR-12; MTCW 1

**Bausch, Richard (Carl)** 1945- ........... **CLC 51**
See also AMWS 7; CA 101; CAAS 14; CANR 43, 61, 87; CSW; DLB 130

**Baxter, Charles (Morley)** 1947- . **CLC 45, 78**
See also CA 57-60; CANR 40, 64, 104; CPW; DAM POP; DLB 130; MTCW 2

**Baxter, George Owen**
See Faust, Frederick (Schiller)

**Baxter, James K(eir)** 1926-1972 ....... **CLC 14**
See also CA 77-80

**Baxter, John**
See Hunt, E(verette) Howard, (Jr.)

**Bayer, Sylvia**
See Glassco, John

**Baynton, Barbara** 1857-1929 .......... **TCLC 57**
See also DLB 230; RGSF 2

**Beagle, Peter S(oyer)** 1939- ......... **CLC 7, 104**
See also AAYA 47; BPFB 1; BYA 9, 10; CA 9-12R; CANR 4, 51, 73, 110; DLBY 1980; FANT; INT CANR-4; MTCW 1; SATA 60, 130; SUFW 1, 2; YAW

**Bean, Normal**
See Burroughs, Edgar Rice

**Beard, Charles A(ustin)**
1874-1948 ................... **TCLC 15**
See also CA 189; DLB 17; SATA 18

**Beardsley, Aubrey** 1872-1898 .......... **NCLC 6**

**Beattie, Ann** 1947- ..... **CLC 8, 13, 18, 40, 63, 146; SSC 11**
See also AMWS 5; BEST 90:2; BPFB 1; CA 81-84; CANR 53, 73; CN 7; CPW; DAM NOV, POP; DLB 218; DLBY 1982; MTCW 1, 2; RGAL 4; RGSF 2; SSFS 9; TUS

**Beattie, James** 1735-1803 ............... **NCLC 25**
See also DLB 109

**Beauchamp, Kathleen Mansfield** 1888-1923
See Mansfield, Katherine
See also CA 134; DA; DAC; DAM MST; MTCW 2; TEA

**Beaumarchais, Pierre-Augustin Caron de**
1732-1799 ............................ **DC 4; LC 61**
See also DAM DRAM; DFS 14, 16; EW 4; GFL Beginnings to 1789; RGWL 2, 3

**Beaumont, Francis** 1584(?)-1616 .. **DC 6; LC 33**
See also BRW 2; CDBLB Before 1660; DLB 58; TEA

**Beauvoir, Simone (Lucie Ernestine Marie Bertrand) de** 1908-1986 .... **CLC 1, 2, 4, 8, 14, 31, 44, 50, 71, 124; SSC 35; WLC**
See also BPFB 1; CA 9-12R; CANR 28, 61; DA; DAB; DAC; DAM MST, NOV; DLB 72; DLBY 1986; EW 12; FW; GFL 1789 to the Present; MTCW 1, 2; RGSF 2; RGWL 2, 3; TWA

**Becker, Carl (Lotus)** 1873-1945 ..... **TCLC 63**
See also CA 157; DLB 17

**Becker, Jurek** 1937-1997 ............... **CLC 7, 19**
See also CA 85-88; CANR 60; CWW 2; DLB 75

**Becker, Walter** 1950- ......................... **CLC 26**

**Beckett, Samuel (Barclay)**
1906-1989 .. **CLC 1, 2, 3, 4, 6, 9, 10, 11, 14, 18, 29, 57, 59, 83; SSC 16; WLC**
See also BRWR 1; BRWS 1; CA 5-8R; CANR 33, 61; CBD; CDBLB 1945-1960; DA; DAB; DAC; DAM DRAM, MST, NOV; DFS 2, 7; DLB 13, 15, 233; DLBY 1990; GFL 1789 to the Present; MTCW 1, 2; RGSF 2; RGWL 2, 3; SSFS 15; TEA; WLIT 4

**Beckford, William** 1760-1844 ......... **NCLC 16**
See also BRW 3; DLB 39, 213; HGG; SUFW

**Beckman, Gunnel** 1910- ..................... **CLC 26**
See also CA 33-36R; CANR 15, 114; CLR 25; MAICYA 1, 2; SAAS 9; SATA 6

**Becque, Henri** 1837-1899 .................. **NCLC 3**
See also DLB 192; GFL 1789 to the Present

**Becquer, Gustavo Adolfo**
1836-1870 .............. **HLCS 1; NCLC 106**
See also DAM MULT

**Beddoes, Thomas Lovell** 1803-1849 .. **DC 15; NCLC 3**
See also DLB 96

**Bede** c. 673-735 ................................ **CMLC 20**
See also DLB 146; TEA

**Bedford, Donald F.**
See Fearing, Kenneth (Flexner)

**Beecher, Catharine Esther**
1800-1878 ................................ **NCLC 30**
See also DLB 1, 243

**Beecher, John** 1904-1980 .................... **CLC 6**
See also AITN 1; CA 5-8R; CANR 8

**Beer, Johann** 1655-1700 ...................... **LC 5**
See also DLB 168

**Beer, Patricia** 1924- ........................... **CLC 58**
See also CA 61-64; CANR 13, 46; CP 7; CWP; DLB 40; FW

**Beerbohm, Max**
See Beerbohm, (Henry) Max(imilian)

**Beerbohm, (Henry) Max(imilian)**
1872-1956 ............................. **TCLC 1, 24**
See also BRWS 2; CA 154; CANR 79; DLB 34, 100; FANT

**Beer-Hofmann, Richard**
1866-1945 ............................. **TCLC 60**
See also CA 160; DLB 81

**Beg, Shemus**
See Stephens, James

**Begiebing, Robert J(ohn)** 1946- ....... **CLC 70**
See also CA 122; CANR 40, 88

**Behan, Brendan** 1923-1964 ...... **CLC 1, 8, 11, 15, 79**
See also BRWS 2; CA 73-76; CANR 33; CBD; CDBLB 1945-1960; DAM DRAM; DFS 7; DLB 13, 233; MTCW 1, 2

**Behn, Aphra** 1640(?)-1689 .. **DC 4; LC 1, 30, 42; PC 13; WLC**
See also BRWS 3; DA; DAB; DAC; DAM DRAM, MST, NOV, POET; DFS 16; DLB 39, 80, 131; FW; TEA; WLIT 3

**Behrman, S(amuel) N(athaniel)**
1893-1973 ................................ **CLC 40**
See also CA 13-16; CAD; CAP 1; DLB 7, 44; IDFW 3; RGAL 4

**Belasco, David** 1853-1931 ................ **TCLC 3**
See also CA 168; DLB 7; RGAL 4

**Belcheva, Elisaveta Lyubomirova**
1893-1991 ................................ **CLC 10**
See Bagryana, Elisaveta

**Beldone, Phil "Cheech"**
See Ellison, Harlan (Jay)

**Beleno**
See Azuela, Mariano

**Belinski, Vissarion Grigoryevich**
1811-1848 ................................. **NCLC 5**
See also DLB 198

**Belitt, Ben** 1911- .............................. **CLC 22**
See also CA 13-16R; CAAS 4; CANR 7, 77; CP 7; DLB 5

**Bell, Gertrude (Margaret Lowthian)**
1868-1926 ............................... **TCLC 67**
See also CA 167; CANR 110; DLB 174

**Bell, J. Freeman**
See Zangwill, Israel

**Bell, James Madison** 1826-1902 ........ **BLC 1; TCLC 43**
See also BW 1; CA 124; DAM MULT; DLB 50

**Bell, Madison Smartt** 1957- ....... **CLC 41, 102**
See also AMWS 10; BPFB 1; CA 111, 183; CAAE 183; CANR 28, 54, 73; CN 7; CSW; DLB 218; MTCW 1

**Bell, Marvin (Hartley)** 1937- ........ **CLC 8, 31**
See also CA 21-24R; CAAS 14; CANR 59, 102; CP 7; DAM POET; DLB 5; MTCW 1

**Bell, W. L. D.**
See Mencken, H(enry) L(ouis)

**Bellamy, Atwood C.**
See Mencken, H(enry) L(ouis)

**Bellamy, Edward** 1850-1898 ....... **NCLC 4, 86**
See also DLB 12; NFS 15; RGAL 4; SFW 4

**Belli, Gioconda** 1949- ........................ **HLCS 1**
See also CA 152; CWW 2; RGWL 3

**Bellin, Edward J.**
See Kuttner, Henry

**Belloc, (Joseph) Hilaire (Pierre Sebastien Rene Swanton)** 1870-1953 .......... **PC 24; TCLC 7, 18**
See also CA 152; CWRI 5; DAM POET; DLB 19, 100, 141, 174; MTCW 1; SATA 112; WCH; YABC 1

**Belloc, Joseph Peter Rene Hilaire**
See Belloc, (Joseph) Hilaire (Pierre Sebastien Rene Swanton)

**Belloc, Joseph Pierre Hilaire**
See Belloc, (Joseph) Hilaire (Pierre Sebastien Rene Swanton)

**Belloc, M. A.**
See Lowndes, Marie Adelaide (Belloc)

**Belloc-Lowndes, Mrs.**
See Lowndes, Marie Adelaide (Belloc)

**Bellow, Saul** 1915- . **CLC 1, 2, 3, 6, 8, 10, 13, 15, 25, 33, 34, 63, 79; SSC 14; WLC**
See also AITN 2; AMW; AMWR 2; BEST 89:3; BPFB 1; CA 5-8R; CABS 1; CANR 29, 53, 95; CDALB 1941-1968; CN 7; DA; DAB; DAC; DAM MST, NOV, POP; DLB 2, 28; DLBD 3; DLBY 1982; MTCW 1, 2; NFS 4, 14; RGAL 4; RGSF 2; SSFS 12; TUS

**Belser, Reimond Karel Maria de** 1929-
See Ruyslinck, Ward
See also CA 152

**Bely, Andrey** .................. **PC 11; TCLC 7**
See Bugayev, Boris Nikolayevich
See also EW 9; MTCW 1

**Belyi, Andrei**
See Bugayev, Boris Nikolayevich
See also RGWL 2, 3

**Bembo, Pietro** 1470-1547 .......... **LC 79**
See also RGWL 2, 3

**Benary, Margot**
See Benary-Isbert, Margot

**Benary-Isbert, Margot** 1889-1979 .... **CLC 12**
See also CA 5-8R; CANR 4, 72; CLR 12; MAICYA 1, 2; SATA 2; SATA-Obit 21

**Benavente (y Martinez), Jacinto** 1866-1954 .................. **HLCS 1; TCLC 3**
See also CA 131; CANR 81; DAM DRAM, MULT; GLL 2; HW 1, 2; MTCW 1, 2

**Benchley, Peter (Bradford)** 1940- .. **CLC 4, 8**
See also AAYA 14; AITN 2; BPFB 1; CA 17-20R; CANR 12, 35, 66; CPW; DAM NOV, POP; HGG; MTCW 1, 2; SATA 3, 89

**Benchley, Robert (Charles)** 1889-1945 ................... **TCLC 1, 55**
See also CA 153; DLB 11; RGAL 4

**Benda, Julien** 1867-1956 ............. **TCLC 60**
See also CA 154; GFL 1789 to the Present

**Benedict, Ruth (Fulton)** 1887-1948 ................... **TCLC 60**
See also CA 158; DLB 246

**Benedikt, Michael** 1935- ............. **CLC 4, 14**
See also CA 13-16R; CANR 7; CP 7; DLB 5

**Benet, Juan** 1927-1993 ............... **CLC 28**
See also CA 143

**Benet, Stephen Vincent** 1898-1943 ... **SSC 10; TCLC 7**
See also AMWS 11; CA 152; DAM POET; DLB 4, 48, 102, 249; DLBY 1997; HGG; MTCW 1; RGAL 4; RGSF 2; SUFW; WP; YABC 1

**Benet, William Rose** 1886-1950 ..... **TCLC 28**
See also CA 152; DAM POET; DLB 45; RGAL 4

**Benford, Gregory (Albert)** 1941- ..... **CLC 52**
See also BPFB 1; CA 69-72; CAAE 175; CAAS 27; CANR 12, 24, 49, 95; CSW; DLBY 1982; SCFW 2; SFW 4

**Bengtsson, Frans (Gunnar)** 1894-1954 .................... **TCLC 48**
See also CA 170

**Benjamin, David**
See Slavitt, David R(ytman)

**Benjamin, Lois**
See Gould, Lois

**Benjamin, Walter** 1892-1940 ......... **TCLC 39**
See also CA 164; DLB 242; EW 11

**Benn, Gottfried** 1886-1956 .. **PC 35; TCLC 3**
See also CA 153; DLB 56; RGWL 2, 3

**Bennett, Alan** 1934- ..................... **CLC 45, 77**
See also BRWS 8; CA 103; CANR 35, 55, 106; CBD; CD 5; DAB; DAM MST; MTCW 1, 2

**Bennett, (Enoch) Arnold** 1867-1931 .................... **TCLC 5, 20**
See also BRW 6; CA 155; CDBLB 1890-1914; DLB 10, 34, 98, 135; MTCW 2

**Bennett, Elizabeth**
See Mitchell, Margaret (Munnerlyn)

**Bennett, George Harold** 1930-
See Bennett, Hal
See also BW 1; CA 97-100; CANR 87

**Bennett, Hal** ......................... **CLC 5**
See Bennett, George Harold
See also DLB 33

**Bennett, Jay** 1912- ..................... **CLC 35**
See also AAYA 10; CA 69-72; CANR 11, 42, 79; JRDA; SAAS 4; SATA 41, 87; SATA-Brief 27; WYA; YAW

**Bennett, Louise (Simone)** 1919- ........ **BLC 1; CLC 28**
See also BW 2, 3; CA 151; CDWLB 3; CP 7; DAM MULT; DLB 117

**Benson, A. C.** 1862-1925 ............... **TCLC 123**
See also DLB 98

**Benson, E(dward) F(rederic)** 1867-1940 .................. **TCLC 27**
See also CA 157; DLB 135, 153; HGG; SUFW 1

**Benson, Jackson J.** 1930- .................. **CLC 34**
See also CA 25-28R; DLB 111

**Benson, Sally** 1900-1972 .................. **CLC 17**
See also CA 19-20; CAP 1; SATA 1, 35; SATA-Obit 27

**Benson, Stella** 1892-1933 ............. **TCLC 17**
See also CA 154, 155; DLB 36, 162; FANT; TEA

**Bentham, Jeremy** 1748-1832 .......... **NCLC 38**
See also DLB 107, 158, 252

**Bentley, E(dmund) C(lerihew)** 1875-1956 .................... **TCLC 12**
See also DLB 70; MSW

**Bentley, Eric (Russell)** 1916- ............. **CLC 24**
See also CA 5-8R; CAD; CANR 6, 67; CBD; CD 5; INT CANR-6

**Beranger, Pierre Jean de** 1780-1857 .................. **NCLC 34**

**Berdyaev, Nicolas**
See Berdyaev, Nikolai (Aleksandrovich)

**Berdyaev, Nikolai (Aleksandrovich)** 1874-1948 .................. **TCLC 67**
See also CA 157

**Berdyayev, Nikolai (Aleksandrovich)**
See Berdyaev, Nikolai (Aleksandrovich)

**Berendt, John (Lawrence)** 1939- ...... **CLC 86**
See also CA 146; CANR 75, 93; MTCW 1

**Beresford, J(ohn) D(avys)** 1873-1947 .................... **TCLC 81**
See also CA 155; DLB 162, 178, 197; SFW 4; SUFW 1

**Bergelson, David** 1884-1952 ........... **TCLC 81**

**Berger, Colonel**
See Malraux, (Georges-)Andre

**Berger, John (Peter)** 1926- ............. **CLC 2, 19**
See also BRWS 4; CA 81-84; CANR 51, 78; CN 7; DLB 14, 207

**Berger, Melvin H.** 1927- ..................... **CLC 12**
See also CA 5-8R; CANR 4; CLR 32; SAAS 2; SATA 5, 88; SATA-Essay 124

**Berger, Thomas (Louis)** 1924- .. **CLC 3, 5, 8, 11, 18, 38**
See also BPFB 1; CA 1-4R; CANR 5, 28, 51; CN 7; DAM NOV; DLB 2; DLBY 1980; FANT; INT CANR-28; MTCW 1, 2; RHW; TCWW 2

**Bergman, (Ernst) Ingmar** 1918- ...... **CLC 16, 72**
See also CA 81-84; CANR 33, 70; DLB 257; MTCW 2

**Bergson, Henri(-Louis)** 1859-1941 . **TCLC 32**
See also CA 164; EW 8; GFL 1789 to the Present

**Bergstein, Eleanor** 1938- ..................... **CLC 4**
See also CA 53-56; CANR 5

**Berkeley, George** 1685-1753 ................. **LC 65**
See also DLB 31, 101, 252

**Berkoff, Steven** 1937- ........................ **CLC 56**
See also CA 104; CANR 72; CBD; CD 5

**Berlin, Isaiah** 1909-1997 ............... **TCLC 105**
See also CA 85-88

**Bermant, Chaim (Icyk)** 1929-1998 ... **CLC 40**
See also CA 57-60; CANR 6, 31, 57, 105; CN 7

**Bern, Victoria**
See Fisher, M(ary) F(rances) K(ennedy)

**Bernanos, (Paul Louis) Georges** 1888-1948 ................... **TCLC 3**
See also CA 130; CANR 94; DLB 72; GFL 1789 to the Present; RGWL 2, 3

**Bernard, April** 1956- ......................... **CLC 59**
See also CA 131

**Berne, Victoria**
See Fisher, M(ary) F(rances) K(ennedy)

**Bernhard, Thomas** 1931-1989 ..... **CLC 3, 32, 61; DC 14**
See also CA 85-88; CANR 32, 57; CDWLB 2; DLB 85, 124; MTCW 1; RGWL 2, 3

**Bernhardt, Sarah (Henriette Rosine)** 1844-1923 ................... **TCLC 75**
See also CA 157

**Bernstein, Charles** 1950- ................. **CLC 142**
See also CA 129; CAAS 24; CANR 90; CP 7; DLB 169

**Berriault, Gina** 1926-1999 ....... **CLC 54, 109; SSC 30**
See also CA 129; CANR 66; DLB 130; SSFS 7,11

**Berrigan, Daniel** 1921- ..................... **CLC 4**
See also CA 33-36R; CAAE 187; CAAS 1; CANR 11, 43, 78; CP 7; DLB 5

**Berrigan, Edmund Joseph Michael, Jr.** 1934-1983
See Berrigan, Ted
See also CA 61-64; CANR 14, 102

**Berrigan, Ted** ..................... **CLC 37**
See Berrigan, Edmund Joseph Michael, Jr.
See also DLB 5, 169; WP

**Berry, Charles Edward Anderson** 1931-
See Berry, Chuck
See also CA 115

**Berry, Chuck** ............................. **CLC 17**
See Berry, Charles Edward Anderson

**Berry, Jonas**
See Ashbery, John (Lawrence)
See also GLL 1

**Berry, Wendell (Erdman)** 1934- ... **CLC 4, 6, 8, 27, 46; PC 28**
See also AITN 1; AMWS 10; ANW; CA 73-76; CANR 50, 73, 101; CP 7; CSW; DAM POET; DLB 5, 6, 234, 275; MTCW 1

**Berryman, John** 1914-1972 ... **CLC 1, 2, 3, 4, 6, 8, 10, 13, 25, 62**
See also AMW; CA 13-16; CABS 2; CANR 35; CAP 1; CDALB 1941-1968; DAM POET; DLB 48; MTCW 1, 2; PAB; RGAL 4; WP

**Bertolucci, Bernardo** 1940- ...... **CLC 16, 157**
See also CA 106

**Berton, Pierre (Francis Demarigny)** 1920- ................................. **CLC 104**
See also CA 1-4R; CANR 2, 56; CPW; DLB 68; SATA 99

**Bertrand, Aloysius** 1807-1841 ........ **NCLC 31**
See Bertrand, Louis oAloysiusc

**Bertrand, Louis oAloysiusc**
See Bertrand, Aloysius
See also DLB 217

**Bertran de Born** c. 1140-1215 ........ **CMLC 5**

**Besant, Annie (Wood)** 1847-1933 ..... **TCLC 9**
See also CA 185

**Bessie, Alvah** 1904-1985 .................. **CLC 23**
See also CA 5-8R; CANR 2, 80; DLB 26

**Bethlen, T. D.**
See Silverberg, Robert

**Beti, Mongo** .................. **BLC 1; CLC 27**
See Biyidi, Alexandre
See also AFW; CANR 79; DAM MULT; WLIT 2

**Betjeman, John** 1906-1984 ...... **CLC 2, 6, 10, 34, 43**
See also BRW 7; CA 9-12R; CANR 33, 56; CDBLB 1945-1960; DAB; DAM MST, POET; DLB 20; DLBY 1984; MTCW 1, 2

**Bettelheim, Bruno** 1903-1990 ........... **CLC 79**
See also CA 81-84; CANR 23, 61; MTCW 1, 2

**Betti, Ugo** 1892-1953 ........................ **TCLC 5**
See also CA 155; RGWL 2, 3

**Betts, Doris (Waugh)** 1932- ..... **CLC 3, 6, 28; SSC 45**
See also CA 13-16R; CANR 9, 66, 77; CN 7; CSW; DLB 218; DLBY 1982; INT CANR-9; RGAL 4

**Bevan, Alistair**
See Roberts, Keith (John Kingston)

**Bey, Pilaff**
See Douglas, (George) Norman

**Bialik, Chaim Nachman** 1873-1934 ................ **TCLC 25**
See also CA 170

**Bickerstaff, Isaac**
See Swift, Jonathan

**Bidart, Frank** 1939- .......................... **CLC 33**
See also CA 140; CANR 106; CP 7

**Bienek, Horst** 1930- .................... **CLC 7, 11**
See also CA 73-76; DLB 75

**Bierce, Ambrose (Gwinett)** 1842-1914(?) ..... **SSC 9; TCLC 1, 7, 44; WLC**
See also AMW; BYA 11; CA 139; CANR 78; CDALB 1865-1917; DA; DAC; DAM MST; DLB 11, 12, 23, 71, 74, 186; EXPS; HGG; LAIT 2; RGAL 4; RGSF 2; SSFS 9; SUFW 1

**Biggers, Earl Derr** 1884-1933 ........ **TCLC 65**
See also CA 153

**Billiken, Bud**
See Motley, Willard (Francis)

**Billings, Josh**
See Shaw, Henry Wheeler

**Billington, (Lady) Rachel (Mary)** 1942- .......................... **CLC 43**
See also AITN 2; CA 33-36R; CANR 44; CN 7

**Binchy, Maeve** 1940- ....................... **CLC 153**
See also BEST 90:1; BPFB 1; CA 134; CANR 50, 96; CN 7; CPW; DAM POP; INT CA-134; MTCW 1; RHW

**Binyon, T(imothy) J(ohn)** 1936- ....... **CLC 34**
See also CA 111; CANR 28

**Bion** 335B.C.-245B.C. ....................... **CMLC 39**

**Bioy Casares, Adolfo** 1914-1999 ... **CLC 4, 8, 13, 88; HLC 1; SSC 17**
See Casares, Adolfo Bioy; Miranda, Javier; Sacastru, Martin
See also CA 29-32R; CANR 19, 43, 66; DAM MULT; DLB 113; HW 1, 2; LAW; MTCW 1

**Birch, Allison** ..................... **CLC 65**

**Bird, Cordwainer**
See Ellison, Harlan (Jay)

**Bird, Robert Montgomery** 1806-1854 ............................. **NCLC 1**
See also DLB 202; RGAL 4

**Birkerts, Sven** 1951- .......................... **CLC 116**
See also CA 133, 176; CAAE 176; CAAS 29; INT 133

**Birney, (Alfred) Earle** 1904-1995 .. **CLC 1, 4, 6, 11**
See also CA 1-4R; CANR 5, 20; CP 7; DAC; DAM MST, POET; DLB 88; MTCW 1; PFS 8; RGEL 2

**Biruni, al** 973-1048(?) .................... **CMLC 28**

**Bishop, Elizabeth** 1911-1979 ..... **CLC 1, 4, 9, 13, 15, 32; PC 3, 34; TCLC 121**
See also AMWR 2; AMWS 1; CA 5-8R; CABS 2; CANR 26, 61, 108; CDALB 1968-1988; DA; DAC; DAM MST, POET; DLB 5, 169; EXPP; MAWW; MTCW 1, 2; PAB; PFS 6, 12; SATA-Obit 24; TUS; WP

**Bishop, John** 1935- ............................ **CLC 10**
See also CA 105

**Bishop, John Peale** 1892-1944 ..... **TCLC 103**
See also CA 155; DLB 4, 9, 45; RGAL 4

**Bissett, Bill** 1939- ................. **CLC 18; PC 14**
See also CA 69-72; CAAS 19; CANR 15; CCA 1; CP 7; DLB 53; MTCW 1

**Bissoondath, Neil (Devindra)** 1955- ...................................... **CLC 120**
See also CA 136; CN 7; DAC

**Bitov, Andrei (Georgievich)** 1937- ... **CLC 57**
See also CA 142

**Biyidi, Alexandre** 1932-
See Beti, Mongo
See also BW 1, 3; CA 124; CANR 81; MTCW 1, 2

**Bjarme, Brynjolf**
See Ibsen, Henrik (Johan)

**Bjoernson, Bjoernstjerne (Martinius)** 1832-1910 ............................ **TCLC 7, 37**

**Black, Robert**
See Holdstock, Robert P.

**Blackburn, Paul** 1926-1971 .......... **CLC 9, 43**
See also BG 2; CA 81-84; CANR 34; DLB 16; DLBY 1981

**Black Elk** 1863-1950 ......... **NNAL; TCLC 33**
See also CA 144; DAM MULT; MTCW 1; WP

**Black Hobart**
See Sanders, (James) Ed(ward)

**Blacklin, Malcolm**
See Chambers, Aidan

**Blackmore, R(ichard) D(oddridge)** 1825-1900 ................................ **TCLC 27**
See also DLB 18; RGEL 2

**Blackmur, R(ichard) P(almer)** 1904-1965 ............................ **CLC 2, 24**
See also AMWS 2; CA 11-12; CANR 71; CAP 1; DLB 63

**Black Tarantula**
See Acker, Kathy

**Blackwood, Algernon (Henry)** 1869-1951 ................................ **TCLC 5**
See also CA 150; DLB 153, 156, 178; HGG; SUFW 1

**Blackwood, Caroline** 1931-1996 .... **CLC 6, 9, 100**
See also CA 85-88; CANR 32, 61, 65; CN 7; DLB 14, 207; HGG; MTCW 1

**Blade, Alexander**
See Hamilton, Edmond; Silverberg, Robert

**Blaga, Lucian** 1895-1961 ................... **CLC 75**
See also CA 157; DLB 220

**Blair, Eric (Arthur)** 1903-1950 .... **TCLC 123**
See Orwell, George
See also CA 132; DA; DAB; DAC; DAM MST, NOV; MTCW 1, 2; SATA 29

**Blair, Hugh** 1718-1800 ................... **NCLC 75**

**Blais, Marie-Claire** 1939- .... **CLC 2, 4, 6, 13, 22**
See also CA 21-24R; CAAS 4; CANR 38, 75, 93; DAC; DAM MST; DLB 53; FW; MTCW 1, 2; TWA

**Blaise, Clark** 1940- ........................... **CLC 29**
See also AITN 2; CA 53-56; CAAS 3; CANR 5, 66, 106; CN 7; DLB 53; RGSF 2

**Blake, Fairley**
See De Voto, Bernard (Augustine)

**Blake, Nicholas**
See Day Lewis, C(ecil)
See also DLB 77; MSW

**Blake, Sterling**
See Benford, Gregory (Albert)

**Blake, William** 1757-1827 ....... **NCLC 13, 37, 57; PC 12; WLC**
See also AAYA 47; BRW 3; BRWR 1; CDBLB 1789-1832; CLR 52; DA; DAB; DAC; DAM MST, POET; DLB 93, 163; EXPP; MAICYA 1, 2; PAB; PFS 2, 12; SATA 30; TEA; WCH; WLIT 3; WP

**Blanchot, Maurice** 1907- ................. **CLC 135**
See also CA 144; DLB 72

**Blasco Ibanez, Vicente** 1867-1928 . **TCLC 12**
See also BPFB 1; CA 131; CANR 81; DAM NOV; EW 8; HW 1, 2; MTCW 1

**Blatty, William Peter** 1928- ................. **CLC 2**
See also CA 5-8R; CANR 9; DAM POP; HGG

**Bleeck, Oliver**
See Thomas, Ross (Elmore)

**Blessing, Lee** 1949- ........................... **CLC 54**
See also CAD; CD 5

**Blight, Rose**
See Greer, Germaine

**Blish, James (Benjamin)** 1921-1975 . **CLC 14**
See also BPFB 1; CA 1-4R; CANR 3; DLB 8; MTCW 1; SATA 66; SCFW 2; SFW 4

**Bliss, Reginald**
See Wells, H(erbert) G(eorge)

**Blixen, Karen (Christentze Dinesen)** 1885-1962
See Dinesen, Isak
See also CA 25-28; CANR 22, 50; CAP 2; DLB 214; MTCW 1, 2; SATA 44

**Bloch, Robert (Albert)** 1917-1994 ..... **CLC 33**
See also AAYA 29; CA 5-8R, 179; CAAE 179; CAAS 20; CANR 5, 78; DLB 44; HGG; INT CANR-5; MTCW 1; SATA 12; SATA-Obit 82; SFW 4; SUFW 1, 2

**Blok, Alexander (Alexandrovich)** 1880-1921 ...................... **PC 21; TCLC 5**
See also CA 183; EW 9; RGWL 2, 3

**Blom, Jan**
See Breytenbach, Breyten

**Bloom, Harold** 1930- .................. **CLC 24, 103**
See also CA 13-16R; CANR 39, 75, 92; DLB 67; MTCW 1; RGAL 4

**Bloomfield, Aurelius**
See Bourne, Randolph S(illiman)

**Blount, Roy (Alton), Jr.** 1941- .......... **CLC 38**
See also CA 53-56; CANR 10, 28, 61; CSW; INT CANR-28; MTCW 1, 2

**Bloy, Leon** 1846-1917 ....................... **TCLC 22**
See also CA 183; DLB 123; GFL 1789 to the Present

**Bluggage, Oranthy**
See Alcott, Louisa May

**Blume, Judy (Sussman)** 1938- .... **CLC 12, 30**
See also AAYA 3, 26; BYA 1, 8, 12; CA 29-32R; CANR 13, 37, 66; CLR 2, 15, 69; CPW; DAM NOV, POP; DLB 52; JRDA; MAICYA 1, 2; MAICYAS 1; MTCW 1, 2; SATA 2, 31, 79; WYA; YAW

**Blunden, Edmund (Charles)** 1896-1974 ............................... **CLC 2, 56**
See also BRW 6; CA 17-18; CANR 54; CAP 2; DLB 20, 100, 155; MTCW 1; PAB

**Bly, Robert (Elwood)** 1926- ........ **CLC 1, 2, 5, 10, 15, 38, 128; PC 39**
See also AMWS 4; CA 5-8R; CANR 41, 73; CP 7; DAM POET; DLB 5; MTCW 1, 2; PFS 17; RGAL 4

**Boas, Franz** 1858-1942 ..................... **TCLC 56**
See also CA 181

**Bobette**
See Simenon, Georges (Jacques Christian)

**Boccaccio, Giovanni** 1313-1375 ... **CMLC 13, 57; SSC 10**
See also EW 2; RGSF 2; RGWL 2, 3; TWA

**Bochco, Steven** 1943- ......................... **CLC 35**
See also AAYA 11; CA 138

**Bode, Sigmund**
See O'Doherty, Brian

**Bodel, Jean** 1167(?)-1210 ............... **CMLC 28**

**Bodenheim, Maxwell** 1892-1954 .... **TCLC 44**
See also CA 187; DLB 9, 45; RGAL 4

**Bodenheimer, Maxwell**
See Bodenheim, Maxwell

**Bodker, Cecil** 1927- .......................... **CLC 21**
See also CA 73-76; CANR 13, 44, 111; CLR 23; MAICYA 1, 2; SATA 14, 133

**Bødker, Cecil** 1927-
See Bodker, Cecil

**Boell, Heinrich (Theodor)** 1917-1985 ..... **CLC 2, 3, 6, 9, 11, 15, 27, 32, 72; SSC 23; WLC**
See Boll, Heinrich
See also CA 21-24R; CANR 24; DA; DAB; DAC; DAM MST, NOV; DLB 69; DLBY 1985; MTCW 1, 2; TWA

**Boerne, Alfred**
See Doeblin, Alfred

**Boethius** c. 480-c. 524 ..................... **CMLC 15**
See also DLB 115; RGWL 2, 3

**Boff, Leonardo (Genezio Darci)** 1938- ............................. **CLC 70; HLC 1**
See also CA 150; DAM MULT; HW 2

**Bogan, Louise** 1897-1970 ....... **CLC 4, 39, 46, 93; PC 12**
See also AMWS 3; CA 73-76; CANR 33, 82; DAM POET; DLB 45, 169; MAWW; MTCW 1, 2; RGAL 4

**Bogarde, Dirk**
See Van Den Bogarde, Derek Jules Gaspard Ulric Niven
See also DLB 14

**Bogosian, Eric** 1953- ................. **CLC 45, 141**
See also CA 138; CAD; CANR 102; CD 5

**Bograd, Larry** 1953- ......................... **CLC 35**
See also CA 93-96; CANR 57; SAAS 21; SATA 33, 89; WYA

**Boiardo, Matteo Maria** 1441-1494 ........ **LC 6**

**Boileau-Despreaux, Nicolas** 1636-1711 . **LC 3**
See also DLB 268; EW 3; GFL Beginnings to 1789; RGWL 2, 3

**Boissard, Maurice**
See Leautaud, Paul

**Bojer, Johan** 1872-1959 ................. **TCLC 64**
See also CA 189

**Bok, Edward W.** 1863-1930 .......... **TCLC 101**
See also DLB 91; DLBD 16

**Boland, Eavan (Aisling)** 1944- .. **CLC 40, 67, 113**
See also BRWS 5; CA 143; CANR 61; CP 7; CWP; DAM POET; DLB 40; FW; MTCW 2; PFS 12

**Boll, Heinrich**
See Boell, Heinrich (Theodor)
See also BPFB 1; CDWLB 2; EW 13; RGSF 2; RGWL 2, 3

**Bolt, Lee**
See Faust, Frederick (Schiller)

**Bolt, Robert (Oxton)** 1924-1995 ....... **CLC 14**
See also CA 17-20R; CANR 35, 67; CBD; DAM DRAM; DFS 2; DLB 13, 233; LAIT 1; MTCW 1

**Bombal, Maria Luisa** 1910-1980 .... **HLCS 1; SSC 37**
See also CA 127; CANR 72; HW 1; LAW; RGSF 2

**Bombet, Louis-Alexandre-Cesar**
See Stendhal

**Bomkauf**
See Kaufman, Bob (Garnell)

**Bonaventura** .................................. **NCLC 35**
See also DLB 90

**Bond, Edward** 1934- ............. **CLC 4, 6, 13, 23**
See also BRWS 1; CA 25-28R; CANR 38, 67, 106; CBD; CD 5; DAM DRAM; DFS 3,8; DLB 13; MTCW 1

**Bonham, Frank** 1914-1989 ................ **CLC 12**
See also AAYA 1; BYA 1, 3; CA 9-12R; CANR 4, 36; JRDA; MAICYA 1, 2; SAAS 3; SATA 1, 49; SATA-Obit 62; TCWW 2; YAW

**Bonnefoy, Yves** 1923- ............ **CLC 9, 15, 58**
See also CA 85-88; CANR 33, 75, 97; CWW 2; DAM MST, POET; DLB 258; GFL 1789 to the Present; MTCW 1, 2

**Bontemps, Arna(ud Wendell)** 1902-1973 ..... **BLC 1; CLC 1, 18; HR 2**
See also BW 1; CA 1-4R; CANR 4, 35; CLR 6; CWRI 5; DAM MULT, NOV, POET; DLB 48, 51; JRDA; MAICYA 1, 2; MTCW 1, 2; SATA 2, 44; SATA-Obit 24; WCH; WP

**Booth, Martin** 1944- ......................... **CLC 13**
See also CA 93-96; CAAE 188; CAAS 2; CANR 92

**Booth, Philip** 1925- ............................ **CLC 23**
See also CA 5-8R; CANR 5, 88; CP 7; DLBY 1982

**Booth, Wayne C(layson)** 1921- ......... **CLC 24**
See also CA 1-4R; CAAS 5; CANR 3, 43; DLB 67

**Borchert, Wolfgang** 1921-1947 ........ **TCLC 5**
See also CA 188; DLB 69, 124

**Borel, Petrus** 1809-1859 ................. **NCLC 41**
See also DLB 119; GFL 1789 to the Present

**Borges, Jorge Luis** 1899-1986 ... **CLC 1, 2, 3, 4, 6, 8, 9, 10, 13, 19, 44, 48, 83; HLC 1; PC 22, 32; SSC 4, 41; TCLC 109; WLC**
See also AAYA 26; BPFB 1; CA 21-24R; CANR 19, 33, 75, 105; CDWLB 3; DA; DAB; DAC; DAM MST, MULT; DLB 113; DLBY 1986; DNFS 1, 2; HW 1, 2; LAW; MSW; MTCW 1, 2; RGSF 2; RGWL 2, 3; SFW 4; SSFS 4, 9; TWA; WLIT 1

**Borowski, Tadeusz** 1922-1951 ........... **SSC 48; TCLC 9**
See also CA 154; CDWLB 4, 4; DLB 215; RGSF 2; RGWL 3; SSFS 13

**Borrow, George (Henry)** 1803-1881 ................................. **NCLC 9**
See also DLB 21, 55, 166

**Bosch (Gavino), Juan** 1909-2001 ..... **HLCS 1**
See also CA 151; DAM MST, MULT; DLB 145; HW 1, 2

**Bosman, Herman Charles** 1905-1951 ................................. **TCLC 49**
See Malan, Herman
See also CA 160; DLB 225; RGSF 2

**Bosschere, Jean de** 1878(?)-1953 ... **TCLC 19**
See also CA 186

**Boswell, James** 1740-1795 ... **LC 4, 50; WLC**
See also BRW 3; CDBLB 1660-1789; DA; DAB; DAC; DAM MST; DLB 104, 142; TEA; WLIT 3

**Bottomley, Gordon** 1874-1948 ..... **TCLC 107**
See also CA 107; DLB 10

**Bottoms, David** 1949- ....................... **CLC 53**
See also CA 105; CANR 22; CSW; DLB 120; DLBY 1983

**Boucicault, Dion** 1820-1890 ........... **NCLC 41**

**Boucolon, Maryse**
See Conde, Maryse

**Bourget, Paul (Charles Joseph)** 1852-1935 ............................. **TCLC 12**
See also CA 196; DLB 123; GFL 1789 to the Present

**Bourjaily, Vance (Nye)** 1922- ........ **CLC 8, 62**
See also CA 1-4R; CAAS 1; CANR 2, 72; CN 7; DLB 2, 143

**Bourne, Randolph S(illiman)** 1886-1918 ................................. **TCLC 16**
See also AMW; CA 155; DLB 63

**Bova, Ben(jamin William)** 1932- ........ **CLC 45**
See also AAYA 16; CA 5-8R; CAAS 18; CANR 11, 56, 94, 111; CLR 3; DLBY 1981; INT CANR-11; MAICYA 1, 2; MTCW 1; SATA 6, 68, 133; SFW 4

**Bowen, Elizabeth (Dorothea Cole)** 1899-1973 . **CLC 1, 3, 6, 11, 15, 22, 118; SSC 3, 28**
See also BRWS 2; CA 17-18; CANR 35, 105; CAP 2; CDBLB 1945-1960; DAM NOV; DLB 15, 162; EXPS; FW; HGG; MTCW 1, 2; NFS 13; RGSF 2; SSFS 5; SUFW 1; TEA; WLIT 4

**Bowering, George** 1935- .............. **CLC 15, 47**
See also CA 21-24R; CAAS 16; CANR 10; CP 7; DLB 53

**Bowering, Marilyn R(uthe)** 1949- .... **CLC 32**
See also CA 101; CANR 49; CP 7; CWP

**Bowers, Edgar** 1924-2000 ................... **CLC 9**
See also CA 5-8R; CANR 24; CP 7; CSW; DLB 5

**Bowers, Mrs. J. Milton** 1842-1914
See Bierce, Ambrose (Gwinett)

**Bowie, David** .................................... **CLC 17**
See Jones, David Robert

**Bowles, Jane (Sydney)** 1917-1973 ..... **CLC 3, 68**
See also CA 19-20; CAP 2

**Bowles, Paul (Frederick)** 1910-1999 . **CLC 1, 2, 19, 53; SSC 3**
See also AMWS 4; CA 1-4R; CAAS 1; CANR 1, 19, 50, 75; CN 7; DLB 5, 6, 218; MTCW 1, 2; RGAL 4

**Bowles, William Lisle** 1762-1850 . **NCLC 103**
See also DLB 93

**Box, Edgar**
See Vidal, Gore
See also GLL 1

**Boyd, James** 1888-1944 ................. **TCLC 115**
See also CA 186; DLB 9; DLBD 16; RGAL 4; RHW

**Boyd, Nancy**
See Millay, Edna St. Vincent
See also GLL 1

**Boyd, Thomas (Alexander)** 1898-1935 ................................. **TCLC 111**
See also CA 183; DLB 9; DLBD 16

**Boyd, William** 1952- .............. **CLC 28, 53, 70**
See also CA 120; CANR 51, 71; CN 7; DLB 231

**Boyle, Kay** 1902-1992 ........ **CLC 1, 5, 19, 58, 121; SSC 5**
See also CA 13-16R; CAAS 1; CANR 29, 61, 110; DLB 4, 9, 48, 86; DLBY 1993; MTCW 1, 2; RGAL 4; RGSF 2; SSFS 10, 13, 14

**Boyle, Mark**
See Kienzle, William X(avier)

**Boyle, Patrick** 1905-1982 ................... **CLC 19**
See also CA 127

**Boyle, T. C.**
See Boyle, T(homas) Coraghessan
See also AMWS 8

**Boyle, T(homas) Coraghessan** 1948- ................ **CLC 36, 55, 90; SSC 16**
See Boyle, T. C.
See also AAYA 47; BEST 90:4; BPFB 1; CA 120; CANR 44, 76, 89; CN 7; CPW; DAM POP; DLB 218; DLBY 1986; MTCW 2; SSFS 13

**Boz**
See Dickens, Charles (John Huffam)

**Brackenridge, Hugh Henry**
1748-1816 .................................. **NCLC 7**
See also DLB 11, 37; RGAL 4

**Bradbury, Edward P.**
See Moorcock, Michael (John)
See also MTCW 2

**Bradbury, Malcolm (Stanley)**
1932-2000 .......................... **CLC 32, 61**
See also CA 1-4R; CANR 1, 33, 91, 98; CN 7; DAM NOV; DLB 14, 207; MTCW 1, 2

**Bradbury, Ray (Douglas)** 1920- .... **CLC 1, 3, 10, 15, 42, 98; SSC 29, 53; WLC**
See also AAYA 15; AITN 1, 2; AMWS 4; BPFB 1; BYA 4, 5, 11; CA 1-4R; CANR 2, 30, 75; CDALB 1968-1988; CN 7; CPW; DA; DAB; DAC; DAM MST, NOV, POP; DLB 2, 8; EXPN; EXPS; HGG; LAIT 3, 5; MTCW 1, 2; NFS 1; RGAL 4; RGSF 2; SATA 11, 64, 123; SCFW 2; SFW 4; SSFS 1; SUFW 1, 2; TUS; YAW

**Braddon, Mary Elizabeth**
1837-1915 .................................. **TCLC 111**
See also BRWS 8; CA 179; CMW 4; DLB 18, 70, 156; HGG

**Bradford, Gamaliel** 1863-1932 ....... **TCLC 36**
See also CA 160; DLB 17

**Bradford, William** 1590-1657 .............. **LC 64**
See also DLB 24, 30; RGAL 4

**Bradley, David (Henry), Jr.** 1950- .... **BLC 1; CLC 23, 118**
See also BW 1, 3; CA 104; CANR 26, 81; CN 7; DAM MULT; DLB 33

**Bradley, John Ed(mund, Jr.)** 1958- . **CLC 55**
See also CA 139; CANR 99; CN 7; CSW

**Bradley, Marion Zimmer**
1930-1999 ........................... **CLC 30**
See Chapman, Lee; Dexter, John; Gardner, Miriam; Ives, Morgan; Rivers, Elfrida
See also AAYA 40; BPFB 1; CA 57-60; CAAS 10; CANR 7, 31, 51, 75, 107; CPW; DAM POP; DLB 8; FANT; FW; MTCW 1, 2; SATA 90; SATA-Obit 116; SFW 4; SUFW 2; YAW

**Bradshaw, John** 1933- ........................... **CLC 70**
See also CA 138; CANR 61

**Bradstreet, Anne** 1612(?)-1672 ....... **LC 4, 30; PC 10**
See also AMWS 1; CDALB 1640-1865; DA; DAC; DAM MST, POET; DLB 24; EXPP; FW; PFS 6; RGAL 4; TUS; WP

**Brady, Joan** 1939- .................................. **CLC 86**
See also CA 141

**Bragg, Melvyn** 1939- ........................... **CLC 10**
See also BEST 89:3; CA 57-60; CANR 10, 48, 89; CN 7; DLB 14, 271; RHW

**Brahe, Tycho** 1546-1601 ......................... **LC 45**

**Braine, John (Gerard)** 1922-1986 . **CLC 1, 3, 41**
See also CA 1-4R; CANR 1, 33; CDBLB 1945-1960; DLB 15; DLBY 1986; MTCW 1

**Bramah, Ernest** 1868-1942 .............. **TCLC 72**
See also CA 156; CMW 4; DLB 70; FANT

**Brammer, William** 1930(?)-1978 ...... **CLC 31**

**Brancati, Vitaliano** 1907-1954 ........ **TCLC 12**
See also DLB 264

**Brancato, Robin F(idler)** 1936- ......... **CLC 35**
See also AAYA 9; BYA 6; CA 69-72; CANR 11, 45; CLR 32; JRDA; MAICYA 2; MAICYAS 1; SAAS 9; SATA 97; WYA; YAW

**Brand, Max**
See Faust, Frederick (Schiller)
See also BPFB 1; TCWW 2

**Brand, Millen** 1906-1980 ...................... **CLC 7**
See also CA 21-24R; CANR 72

**Branden, Barbara** .............................. **CLC 44**
See also CA 148

**Brandes, Georg (Morris Cohen)**
1842-1927 .................................. **TCLC 10**
See also CA 189

**Brandys, Kazimierz** 1916-2000 ......... **CLC 62**

**Branley, Franklyn M(ansfield)**
1915-2002 ........................... **CLC 21**
See also CA 33-36R; CANR 14, 39; CLR 13; MAICYA 1, 2; SAAS 16; SATA 4, 68, 136

**Brathwaite, Edward Kamau**
1930- .................................. **BLCS; CLC 11**
See also BW 2, 3; CA 25-28R; CANR 11, 26, 47, 107; CDWLB 3; CP 7; DAM POET; DLB 125

**Brathwaite, Kamau**
See Brathwaite, Edward Kamau

**Brautigan, Richard (Gary)**
1935-1984 ..... **CLC 1, 3, 5, 9, 12, 34, 42**
See also BPFB 1; CA 53-56; CANR 34; DAM NOV; DLB 2, 5, 206; DLBY 1980, 1984; FANT; MTCW 1; RGAL 4; SATA 56

**Brave Bird, Mary** .............................. **NNAL**
See Crow Dog, Mary (Ellen)

**Braverman, Kate** 1950- .................... **CLC 67**
See also CA 89-92

**Brecht, (Eugen) Bertolt (Friedrich)**
1898-1956 ..... **DC 3; TCLC 1, 6, 13, 35; WLC**
See also CA 133; CANR 62; CDWLB 2; DA; DAB; DAC; DAM DRAM, MST; DFS 4, 5, 9; DLB 56, 124; EW 11; IDTP; MTCW 1, 2; RGWL 2, 3; TWA

**Brecht, Eugen Berthold Friedrich**
See Brecht, (Eugen) Bertolt (Friedrich)

**Bremer, Fredrika** 1801-1865 .......... **NCLC 11**
See also DLB 254

**Brennan, Christopher John**
1870-1932 .................................. **TCLC 17**
See also CA 188; DLB 230

**Brennan, Maeve** 1917-1993 ... **CLC 5; TCLC 124**
See also CA 81-84; CANR 72, 100

**Brent, Linda**
See Jacobs, Harriet A(nn)

**Brentano, Clemens (Maria)**
1778-1842 .................................. **NCLC 1**
See also DLB 90; RGWL 2, 3

**Brent of Bin Bin**
See Franklin, (Stella Maria Sarah) Miles (Lampe)

**Brenton, Howard** 1942- .................... **CLC 31**
See also CA 69-72; CANR 33, 67; CBD; CD 5; DLB 13; MTCW 1

**Breslin, James** 1930-
See Breslin, Jimmy
See also CA 73-76; CANR 31, 75; DAM NOV; MTCW 1, 2

**Breslin, Jimmy** .............................. **CLC 4, 43**
See Breslin, James
See also AITN 1; DLB 185; MTCW 2

**Bresson, Robert** 1901(?)-1999 ........... **CLC 16**
See also CA 110; CANR 49

**Breton, Andre** 1896-1966 .. **CLC 2, 9, 15, 54; PC 15**
See also CA 19-20; CANR 40, 60; CAP 2; DLB 65, 258; EW 11; GFL 1789 to the Present; MTCW 1, 2; RGWL 2, 3; TWA; WP

**Breytenbach, Breyten** 1939(?)- .. **CLC 23, 37, 126**
See also CA 129; CANR 61; CWW 2; DAM POET; DLB 225

**Bridgers, Sue Ellen** 1942- .................. **CLC 26**
See also AAYA 8; BYA 7, 8; CA 65-68; CANR 11, 36; CLR 18; DLB 52; JRDA; MAICYA 1, 2; SAAS 1; SATA 22, 90; SATA-Essay 109; WYA; YAW

**Bridges, Robert (Seymour)**
1844-1930 .................... **PC 28; TCLC 1**
See also BRW 6; CA 152; CDBLB 1890-1914; DAM POET; DLB 19, 98

**Bridie, James** .................................. **TCLC 3**
See Mavor, Osborne Henry
See also DLB 10

**Brin, David** 1950- .................................. **CLC 34**
See also AAYA 21; CA 102; CANR 24, 70; INT CANR-24; SATA 65; SCFW 2; SFW 4

**Brink, Andre (Philippus)** 1935- . **CLC 18, 36, 106**
See also AFW; BRWS 6; CA 104; CANR 39, 62, 109; CN 7; DLB 225; INT CA-103; MTCW 1, 2; WLIT 2

**Brinsmead, H. F.**
See Brinsmead, H(esba) F(ay)

**Brinsmead, H. F(ay)**
See Brinsmead, H(esba) F(ay)

**Brinsmead, H(esba) F(ay)** 1922- ...... **CLC 21**
See also CA 21-24R; CANR 10; CLR 47; CWRI 5; MAICYA 1, 2; SAAS 5; SATA 18, 78

**Brittain, Vera (Mary)** 1893(?)-1970 . **CLC 23**
See also CA 13-16; CANR 58; CAP 1; DLB 191; FW; MTCW 1, 2

**Broch, Hermann** 1886-1951 ............ **TCLC 20**
See also CDWLB 2; DLB 85, 124; EW 10; RGWL 2, 3

**Brock, Rose**
See Hansen, Joseph
See also GLL 1

**Brod, Max** 1884-1968 .................... **TCLC 115**
See also CA 5-8R; CANR 7; DLB 81

**Brodkey, Harold (Roy)** 1930-1996 .. **CLC 56; TCLC 123**
See also CA 111; CANR 71; CN 7; DLB 130

**Brodskii, Iosif**
See Brodsky, Joseph

**Brodsky, Iosif Alexandrovich** 1940-1996
See Brodsky, Joseph
See also AITN 1; CA 41-44R; CANR 37, 106; DAM POET; MTCW 1, 2; RGWL 2, 3

**Brodsky, Joseph** . **CLC 4, 6, 13, 36, 100; PC 9**
See Brodsky, Iosif Alexandrovich
See also AMWS 8; CWW 2; MTCW 1

**Brodsky, Michael (Mark)** 1948- ........ **CLC 19**
See also CA 102; CANR 18, 41, 58; DLB 244

**Brodzki, Bella ed.** .............................. **CLC 65**

**Brome, Richard** 1590(?)-1652 .............. **LC 61**
See also DLB 58

**Bromell, Henry** 1947- ........................... **CLC 5**
See also CA 53-56; CANR 9

**Bromfield, Louis (Brucker)**
1896-1956 .................................. **TCLC 11**
See also CA 155; DLB 4, 9, 86; RGAL 4; RHW

**Broner, E(sther) M(asserman)**
1930- .................................. **CLC 19**
See also CA 17-20R; CANR 8, 25, 72; CN 7; DLB 28

**Bronk, William (M.)** 1918-1999 ........ **CLC 10**
See also CA 89-92; CANR 23; CP 7; DLB 165

**Bronstein, Lev Davidovich**
See Trotsky, Leon

**Bronte, Anne** 1820-1849 ..... **NCLC 4, 71, 102**
See also BRW 5; BRWR 1; DLB 21, 199; TEA

**Bronte, (Patrick) Branwell**
1817-1848 .................................... **NCLC 109**

**Bronte, Charlotte** 1816-1855 ...... **NCLC 3, 8, 33, 58, 105; WLC**
See also AAYA 17; BRW 5; BRWR 1; BYA 2; CDBLB 1832-1890; DA; DAB; DAC; DAM MST, NOV; DLB 21, 159, 199; EXPN; LAIT 2; NFS 4; TEA; WLIT 4

**Bronte, Emily (Jane)** 1818-1848 ... **NCLC 16, 35; PC 8; WLC**
See also AAYA 17; BPFB 1; BRW 5; BRWR 1; BYA 3; CDBLB 1832-1890; DA; DAB; DAC; DAM MST, NOV, POET; DLB 21, 32, 199; EXPN; LAIT 1; TEA; WLIT 3

**Brontes**
See Bronte, Anne; Bronte, Charlotte; Bronte, Emily (Jane)

**Brooke, Frances** 1724-1789 .............. **LC 6, 48**
See also DLB 39, 99

**Brooke, Henry** 1703(?)-1783 ................... **LC 1**
See also DLB 39

**Brooke, Rupert (Chawner)**
1887-1915 ...... **PC 24; TCLC 2, 7; WLC**
See also BRWS 3; CA 132; CANR 61; CDBLB 1914-1945; DA; DAB; DAC; DAM MST, POET; DLB 19, 216; EXPP; GLL 2; MTCW 1, 2; PFS 7; TEA

**Brooke-Haven, P.**
See Wodehouse, P(elham) G(renville)

**Brooke-Rose, Christine** 1926(?)- ...... **CLC 40**
See also BRWS 4; CA 13-16R; CANR 58; CN 7; DLB 14, 231; SFW 4

**Brookner, Anita** 1928- .. **CLC 32, 34, 51, 136**
See also BRWS 4; CA 120; CANR 37, 56, 87; CN 7; CPW; DAB; DAM POP; DLB 194; DLBY 1987; MTCW 1, 2; TEA

**Brooks, Cleanth** 1906-1994 . **CLC 24, 86, 110**
See also CA 17-20R; CANR 33, 35; CSW; DLB 63; DLBY 1994; INT CANR-35; MTCW 1, 2

**Brooks, George**
See Baum, L(yman) Frank

**Brooks, Gwendolyn (Elizabeth)**
1917-2000 ... **BLC 1; CLC 1, 2, 4, 5, 15, 49, 125; PC 7; WLC**
See also AAYA 20; AFAW 1, 2; AITN 1; AMWS 3; BW 2, 3; CA 1-4R; CANR 1, 27, 52, 75; CDALB 1941-1968; CLR 27; CP 7; CWP; DA; DAC; DAM MST, MULT, POET; DLB 5, 76, 165; EXPP; MAWW; MTCW 1, 2; PFS 1, 2, 4, 6; RGAL 4; SATA 6; SATA-Obit 123; TUS; WP

**Brooks, Mel** ............................................. **CLC 12**
See Kaminsky, Melvin
See also AAYA 13; DLB 26

**Brooks, Peter (Preston)** 1938- ........... **CLC 34**
See also CA 45-48; CANR 1, 107

**Brooks, Van Wyck** 1886-1963 ............ **CLC 29**
See also AMW; CA 1-4R; CANR 6; DLB 45, 63, 103; TUS

**Brophy, Brigid (Antonia)**
1929-1995 .................. **CLC 6, 11, 29, 105**
See also CA 5-8R; CAAS 4; CANR 25, 53; CBD; CN 7; CWD; DLB 14, 271; MTCW 1, 2

**Brosman, Catharine Savage** 1934- ...... **CLC 9**
See also CA 61-64; CANR 21, 46

**Brossard, Nicole** 1943- ............. **CLC 115, 169**
See also CA 122; CAAS 16; CCA 1; CWP; CWW 2; DLB 53; FW; GLL 2; RGWL 3

**Brother Antoninus**
See Everson, William (Oliver)

**The Brothers Quay**
See Quay, Stephen; Quay, Timothy

**Broughton, T(homas) Alan** 1936- ...... **CLC 19**
See also CA 45-48; CANR 2, 23, 48, 111

**Broumas, Olga** 1949- .................... **CLC 10, 73**
See also CA 85-88; CANR 20, 69, 110; CP 7; CWP; GLL 2

**Broun, Heywood** 1888-1939 ......... **TCLC 104**
See also DLB 29, 171

**Brown, Alan** 1950- ............................. **CLC 99**
See also CA 156

**Brown, Charles Brockden**
1771-1810 .................. **NCLC 22, 74, 122**
See also AMWS 1; CDALB 1640-1865; DLB 37, 59, 73; FW; HGG; RGAL 4; TUS

**Brown, Christy** 1932-1981 ................. **CLC 63**
See also BYA 13; CA 105; CANR 72; DLB 14

**Brown, Claude** 1937-2002 ... **BLC 1; CLC 30**
See also AAYA 7; BW 1, 3; CA 73-76; CANR 81; DAM MULT

**Brown, Dee (Alexander)** 1908- ... **CLC 18, 47**
See also AAYA 30; CA 13-16R; CAAS 6; CANR 11, 45, 60; CPW; CSW; DAM POP; DLBY 1980; LAIT 2; MTCW 1, 2; SATA 5, 110; TCWW 2

**Brown, George**
See Wertmueller, Lina

**Brown, George Douglas**
1869-1902 .......................................... **TCLC 28**
See Douglas, George
See also CA 162

**Brown, George Mackay** 1921-1996 ... **CLC 5, 48, 100**
See also BRWS 6; CA 21-24R; CAAS 6; CANR 12, 37, 67; CN 7; CP 7; DLB 14, 27, 139, 271; MTCW 1; RGSF 2; SATA 35

**Brown, (William) Larry** 1951- ......... **CLC 73**
See also CA 134; CSW; DLB 234; INT 133

**Brown, Moses**
See Barrett, William (Christopher)

**Brown, Rita Mae** 1944- ........ **CLC 18, 43, 79**
See also BPFB 1; CA 45-48; CANR 2, 11, 35, 62, 95; CN 7; CPW; CSW; DAM NOV, POP; FW; INT CANR-11; MTCW 1, 2; NFS 9; RGAL 4; TUS

**Brown, Roderick (Langmere) Haig-**
See Haig-Brown, Roderick (Langmere)

**Brown, Rosellen** 1939- ....................... **CLC 32**
See also CA 77-80; CAAS 10; CANR 14, 44, 98; CN 7

**Brown, Sterling Allen** 1901-1989 ...... **BLC 1; CLC 1, 23, 59; HR 2**
See also AFAW 1, 2; BW 1, 3; CA 85-88; CANR 26; DAM MULT, POET; DLB 48, 51, 63; MTCW 1, 2; RGAL 4; WP

**Brown, Will**
See Ainsworth, William Harrison

**Brown, William Wells** 1815-1884 ...... **BLC 1; DC 1; NCLC 2, 89**
See also DAM MULT; DLB 3, 50, 183, 248; RGAL 4

**Browne, (Clyde) Jackson** 1948(?)- ... **CLC 21**
See also CA 120

**Browning, Elizabeth Barrett**
1806-1861 ... **NCLC 1, 16, 61, 66; PC 6; WLC**
See also BRW 4; CDBLB 1832-1890; DA; DAB; DAC; DAM MST, POET; DLB 32, 199; EXPP; PAB; PFS 2, 16; TEA; WLIT 4; WP

**Browning, Robert** 1812-1889 . **NCLC 19, 79; PC 2; WLCS**
See also BRW 4; BRWR 2; CDBLB 1832-1890; DA; DAB; DAC; DAM MST, POET; DLB 32, 163; EXPP; PAB; PFS 1, 15; RGEL 2; TEA; WLIT 4; WP; YABC 1

**Browning, Tod** 1882-1962 ................. **CLC 16**
See also CA 141

**Brownmiller, Susan** 1935- ................ **CLC 159**
See also CA 103; CANR 35, 75; DAM NOV; FW; MTCW 1, 2

**Brownson, Orestes Augustus**
1803-1876 ......................................... **NCLC 50**
See also DLB 1, 59, 73, 243

**Bruccoli, Matthew J(oseph)** 1931- ... **CLC 34**
See also CA 9-12R; CANR 7, 87; DLB 103

**Bruce, Lenny** ........................................... **CLC 21**
See Schneider, Leonard Alfred

**Bruin, John**
See Brutus, Dennis

**Brulard, Henri**
See Stendhal

**Brulls, Christian**
See Simenon, Georges (Jacques Christian)

**Brunner, John (Kilian Houston)**
1934-1995 ................................ **CLC 8, 10**
See also CA 1-4R; CAAS 8; CANR 2, 37; CPW; DAM POP; DLB 261; MTCW 1, 2; SCFW 2; SFW 4

**Bruno, Giordano** 1548-1600 ................ **LC 27**
See also RGWL 2, 3

**Brutus, Dennis** 1924- ... **BLC 1; CLC 43; PC 24**
See also AFW; BW 2, 3; CA 49-52; CAAS 14; CANR 2, 27, 42, 81; CDWLB 3; CP 7; DAM MULT, POET; DLB 117, 225

**Bryan, C(ourtlandt) D(ixon) B(arnes)**
1936- .................................................. **CLC 29**
See also CA 73-76; CANR 13, 68; DLB 185; INT CANR-13

**Bryan, Michael**
See Moore, Brian
See also CCA 1

**Bryan, William Jennings**
1860-1925 ......................................... **TCLC 99**

**Bryant, William Cullen** 1794-1878 . **NCLC 6, 46; PC 20**
See also AMWS 1; CDALB 1640-1865; DA; DAB; DAC; DAM MST, POET; DLB 3, 43, 59, 189, 250; EXPP; PAB; RGAL 4; TUS

**Bryusov, Valery Yakovlevich**
1873-1924 ......................................... **TCLC 10**
See also CA 155; SFW 4

**Buchan, John** 1875-1940 .................... **TCLC 41**
See also CA 145; CMW 4; DAB; DAM POP; DLB 34, 70, 156; HGG; MSW; MTCW 1; RGEL 2; RHW; YABC 2

**Buchanan, George** 1506-1582 ................ **LC 4**
See also DLB 132

**Buchanan, Robert** 1841-1901 ....... **TCLC 107**
See also CA 179; DLB 18, 35

**Buchheim, Lothar-Guenther** 1918- .... **CLC 6**
See also CA 85-88

**Buchner, (Karl) Georg** 1813-1837 . **NCLC 26**
See also CDWLB 2; DLB 133; EW 6; RGSF 2; RGWL 2, 3; TWA

**Buchwald, Art(hur)** 1925- ................. **CLC 33**
See also AITN 1; CA 5-8R; CANR 21, 67, 107; MTCW 1, 2; SATA 10

**Buck, Pearl S(ydenstricker)**
1892-1973 ................ **CLC 7, 11, 18, 127**
See also AAYA 42; AITN 1; AMWS 2; BPFB 1; CA 1-4R; CANR 1, 34; CDALBS; DA; DAB; DAC; DAM MST, NOV; DLB 9, 102; LAIT 3; MTCW 1, 2; RGAL 4; RHW; SATA 1, 25; TUS

**Buckler, Ernest** 1908-1984 ................. **CLC 13**
See also CA 11-12; CAP 1; CCA 1; DAC; DAM MST; DLB 68; SATA 47

**Buckley, Christopher (Taylor)**
1952- ................................................ **CLC 165**
See also CA 139

**Buckley, Vincent (Thomas)**
1925-1988 .......................................... **CLC 57**
See also CA 101

**Buckley, William F(rank), Jr.** 1925- . **CLC 7, 18, 37**
See also AITN 1; BPFB 1; CA 1-4R; CANR 1, 24, 53, 93; CMW 4; CPW; DAM POP; DLB 137; DLBY 1980; INT CANR-24; MTCW 1, 2; TUS

**Buechner, (Carl) Frederick** 1926- . **CLC 2, 4, 6, 9**
See also AMWS 12; BPFB 1; CA 13-16R; CANR 11, 39, 64, 114; CN 7; DAM NOV; DLBY 1980; INT CANR-11; MTCW 1, 2

**Buell, John (Edward)** 1927- .............. **CLC 10**
See also CA 1-4R; CANR 71; DLB 53

**Buero Vallejo, Antonio** 1916-2000 ... **CLC 15, 46, 139; DC 18**
See also CA 106; CANR 24, 49, 75; DFS 11; HW 1; MTCW 1, 2

**Bufalino, Gesualdo** 1920(?)-1990 ...... **CLC 74**
See also CWW 2; DLB 196

**Bugayev, Boris Nikolayevich** 1880-1934 ...................... **PC 11; TCLC 7**
See Bely, Andrey; Belyi, Andrei
See also CA 165; MTCW 1

**Bukowski, Charles** 1920-1994 ... **CLC 2, 5, 9, 41, 82, 108; PC 18; SSC 45**
See also CA 17-20R; CANR 40, 62, 105; CPW; DAM NOV, POET; DLB 5, 130, 169; MTCW 1, 2

**Bulgakov, Mikhail (Afanas'evich)** 1891-1940 ............. **SSC 18; TCLC 2, 16**
See also BPFB 1; CA 152; DAM DRAM, NOV; DLB 272; NFS 8; RGSF 2; RGWL 2, 3; SFW 4; TWA

**Bulgya, Alexander Alexandrovich** 1901-1956 ..................... **TCLC 53**
See Fadeev, Aleksandr Aleksandrovich; Fadeyev, Alexander
See also CA 181

**Bullins, Ed** 1935- ... **BLC 1; CLC 1, 5, 7; DC 6**
See also BW 2, 3; CA 49-52; CAAS 16; CAD; CANR 24, 46, 73; CD 5; DAM DRAM, MULT; DLB 7, 38, 249; MTCW 1, 2; RGAL 4

**Bulwer-Lytton, Edward (George Earle Lytton)** 1803-1873 .............. **NCLC 1, 45**
See also DLB 21; RGEL 2; SFW 4; SUFW 1; TEA

**Bunin, Ivan Alexeyevich** 1870-1953 ... **SSC 5; TCLC 6**
See also RGSF 2; RGWL 2, 3; TWA

**Bunting, Basil** 1900-1985 ...... **CLC 10, 39, 47**
See also BRWS 7; CA 53-56; CANR 7; DAM POET; DLB 20; RGEL 2

**Bunuel, Luis** 1900-1983 ... **CLC 16, 80; HLC 1**
See also CA 101; CANR 32, 77; DAM MULT; HW 1

**Bunyan, John** 1628-1688 ..... **LC 4, 69; WLC**
See also BRW 2; BYA 5; CDBLB 1660-1789; DA; DAB; DAC; DAM MST; DLB 39; RGEL 2; TEA; WCH; WLIT 3

**Buravsky, Alexandr** ......................... **CLC 59**

**Burckhardt, Jacob (Christoph)** 1818-1897 ............... **NCLC 49**
See also EW 6

**Burford, Eleanor**
See Hibbert, Eleanor Alice Burford

**Burgess, Anthony** . **CLC 1, 2, 4, 5, 8, 10, 13, 15, 22, 40, 62, 81, 94**
See Wilson, John (Anthony) Burgess
See also AAYA 25; AITN 1; BRWS 1; CD-BLB 1960 to Present; DAB; DLB 14, 194, 261; DLBY 1998; MTCW 1; RGEL 2; RHW; SFW 4; YAW

**Burke, Edmund** 1729(?)-1797 ........ **LC 7, 36; WLC**
See also BRW 3; DA; DAB; DAC; DAM MST; DLB 104, 252; RGEL 2; TEA

**Burke, Kenneth (Duva)** 1897-1993 ... **CLC 2, 24**
See also AMW; CA 5-8R; CANR 39, 74; DLB 45, 63; MTCW 1, 2; RGAL 4

**Burke, Leda**
See Garnett, David

**Burke, Ralph**
See Silverberg, Robert

**Burke, Thomas** 1886-1945 .............. **TCLC 63**
See also CA 155; CMW 4; DLB 197

**Burney, Fanny** 1752-1840 ....... **NCLC 12, 54, 107**
See also BRWS 3; DLB 39; NFS 16; RGEL 2; TEA

**Burney, Frances**
See Burney, Fanny

**Burns, Robert** 1759-1796 ... **LC 3, 29, 40; PC 6; WLC**
See also BRW 3; CDBLB 1789-1832; DA; DAB; DAC; DAM MST, POET; DLB 109; EXPP; PAB; RGEL 2; TEA; WP

**Burns, Tex**
See L'Amour, Louis (Dearborn)
See also TCWW 2

**Burnshaw, Stanley** 1906- ........ **CLC 3, 13, 44**
See also CA 9-12R; CP 7; DLB 48; DLBY 1997

**Burr, Anne** 1937- ................................. **CLC 6**
See also CA 25-28R

**Burroughs, Edgar Rice** 1875-1950 . **TCLC 2, 32**
See also AAYA 11; BPFB 1; BYA 4, 9; CA 132; DAM NOV; DLB 8; FANT; MTCW 1, 2; RGAL 4; SATA 41; SCFW 2; SFW 4; TUS; YAW

**Burroughs, William S(eward)** 1914-1997 .. **CLC 1, 2, 5, 15, 22, 42, 75, 109; TCLC 121; WLC**
See Lee, William; Lee, Willy
See also AITN 2; AMWS 3; BG 2; BPFB 1; CA 9-12R; CANR 20, 52, 104; CN 7; CPW; DA; DAB; DAC; DAM MST, NOV, POP; DLB 2, 8, 16, 152, 237; DLBY 1981, 1997; HGG; MTCW 1, 2; RGAL 4; SFW 4

**Burton, Sir Richard F(rancis)** 1821-1890 ................................. **NCLC 42**
See also DLB 55, 166, 184

**Burton, Robert** 1577-1640 ................... **LC 74**
See also DLB 151; RGEL 2

**Buruma, Ian** 1951- .............................. **CLC 163**
See also CA 128; CANR 65

**Busch, Frederick** 1941- ... **CLC 7, 10, 18, 47, 166**
See also CA 33-36R; CAAS 1; CANR 45, 73, 92; CN 7; DLB 6, 218

**Bush, Ronald** 1946- ............................ **CLC 34**
See also CA 136

**Bustos, F(rancisco)**
See Borges, Jorge Luis

**Bustos Domecq, H(onorio)**
See Bioy Casares, Adolfo; Borges, Jorge Luis

**Butler, Octavia E(stelle)** 1947- .. **BLCS; CLC 38, 121**
See also AAYA 18; AFAW 2; BPFB 1; BW 2, 3; CA 73-76; CANR 12, 24, 38, 73; CLR 65; CPW; DAM MULT, POP; DLB 33; MTCW 1, 2; NFS 8; SATA 84; SCFW 2; SFW 4; SSFS 6; YAW

**Butler, Robert Olen, (Jr.)** 1945- ....... **CLC 81, 162**
See also AMWS 12; BPFB 1; CA 112; CANR 66; CSW; DAM POP; DLB 173; INT CA-112; MTCW 1; SSFS 11

**Butler, Samuel** 1612-1680 .............. **LC 16, 43**
See also DLB 101, 126; RGEL 2

**Butler, Samuel** 1835-1902 ......... **TCLC 1, 33; WLC**
See also BRWS 2; CA 143; CDBLB 1890-1914; DA; DAB; DAC; DAM MST, NOV; DLB 18, 57, 174; RGEL 2; SFW 4; TEA

**Butler, Walter C.**
See Faust, Frederick (Schiller)

**Butor, Michel (Marie Francois)** 1926- ................ **CLC 1, 3, 8, 11, 15, 161**
See also CA 9-12R; CANR 33, 66; DLB 83; EW 13; GFL 1789 to the Present; MTCW 1, 2

**Butts, Mary** 1890(?)-1937 ............... **TCLC 77**
See also CA 148; DLB 240

**Buxton, Ralph**
See Silverstein, Alvin; Silverstein, Virginia B(arbara Opshelor)

**Buzo, Alexander (John)** 1944- .......... **CLC 61**
See also CA 97-100; CANR 17, 39, 69; CD 5

**Buzzati, Dino** 1906-1972 .................... **CLC 36**
See also CA 160; DLB 177; RGWL 2, 3; SFW 4

**Byars, Betsy (Cromer)** 1928- ............ **CLC 35**
See also AAYA 19; BYA 3; CA 33-36R, 183; CAAE 183; CANR 18, 36, 57, 102; CLR 1, 16, 72; DLB 52; INT CANR-18; JRDA; MAICYA 1, 2; MAICYAS 1; MTCW 1; SAAS 1; SATA 4, 46, 80; SATA-Essay 108; WYA; YAW

**Byatt, A(ntonia) S(usan Drabble)** 1936- ................................ **CLC 19, 65, 136**
See also BPFB 1; BRWS 4; CA 13-16R; CANR 13, 33, 50, 75, 96; DAM NOV, POP; DLB 14, 194; MTCW 1, 2; RGSF 2; RHW; TEA

**Byrne, David** 1952- ........................... **CLC 26**
See also CA 127

**Byrne, John Keyes** 1926-
See Leonard, Hugh
See also CA 102; CANR 78; INT CA-102

**Byron, George Gordon (Noel)** 1788-1824 ...... **NCLC 2, 12, 109; PC 16; WLC**
See also BRW 4; CDBLB 1789-1832; DA; DAB; DAC; DAM MST, POET; DLB 96, 110; EXPP; PAB; PFS 1, 14; RGEL 2; TEA; WLIT 3; WP

**Byron, Robert** 1905-1941 ............... **TCLC 67**
See also CA 160; DLB 195

**C. 3. 3.**
See Wilde, Oscar (Fingal O'Flahertie Wills)

**C. 3. 3.,**
See Wilde, Oscar (Fingal O'Flahertie Wills)

**Caballero, Fernan** 1796-1877 ......... **NCLC 10**

**Cabell, Branch**
See Cabell, James Branch

**Cabell, James Branch** 1879-1958 .... **TCLC 6**
See also CA 152; DLB 9, 78; FANT; MTCW 1; RGAL 4; SUFW 1

**Cabeza de Vaca, Alvar Nunez** 1490-1557(?) ................................. **LC 61**

**Cable, George Washington** 1844-1925 .................... **SSC 4; TCLC 4**
See also CA 155; DLB 12, 74; DLBD 13; RGAL 4; TUS

**Cabral de Melo Neto, Joao** 1920-1999 ............................. **CLC 76**
See also CA 151; DAM MULT; LAW; LAWS 1

**Cabrera Infante, G(uillermo)** 1929- . **CLC 5, 25, 45, 120; HLC 1; SSC 39**
See also CA 85-88; CANR 29, 65, 110; CD-WLB 3; DAM MULT; DLB 113; HW 1, 2; LAW; LAWS 1; MTCW 1, 2; RGSF 2; WLIT 1

**Cade, Toni**
See Bambara, Toni Cade

**Cadmus and Harmonia**
See Buchan, John
**Caedmon** fl. 658-680 .................. **CMLC 7**
See also DLB 146
**Caeiro, Alberto**
See Pessoa, Fernando (Antonio Nogueira)
**Caesar, Julius** ............................ **CMLC 47**
See Julius Caesar
See also AW 1; RGWL 2, 3
**Cage, John (Milton, Jr.)** 1912-1992 . **CLC 41**
See also CA 13-16R; CANR 9, 78; DLB 193; INT CANR-9
**Cahan, Abraham** 1860-1951 ........... **TCLC 71**
See also CA 154; DLB 9, 25, 28; RGAL 4
**Cain, G.**
See Cabrera Infante, G(uillermo)
**Cain, Guillermo**
See Cabrera Infante, G(uillermo)
**Cain, James M(allahan)** 1892-1977 .. **CLC 3, 11, 28**
See also AITN 1; BPFB 1; CA 17-20R; CANR 8, 34, 61; CMW 4; DLB 226; MSW; MTCW 1; RGAL 4
**Caine, Hall** 1853-1931 .................. **TCLC 97**
See also RHW
**Caine, Mark**
See Raphael, Frederic (Michael)
**Calasso, Roberto** 1941- ...................... **CLC 81**
See also CA 143; CANR 89
**Calderon de la Barca, Pedro**
1600-1681 .......... **DC 3; HLCS 1; LC 23**
See also EW 2; RGWL 2, 3; TWA
**Caldwell, Erskine (Preston)**
1903-1987 .... **CLC 1, 8, 14, 50, 60; SSC 19; TCLC 117**
See also AITN 1; AMW; BPFB 1; CA 1-4R; CAAS 1; CANR 2, 33; DAM NOV; DLB 9, 86; MTCW 1, 2; RGAL 4; RGSF 2; TUS
**Caldwell, (Janet Miriam) Taylor (Holland)**
1900-1985 ............ **CLC 2, 28, 39**
See also BPFB 1; CA 5-8R; CANR 5; DAM NOV, POP; DLBD 17; RHW
**Calhoun, John Caldwell**
1782-1850 ................................. **NCLC 15**
See also DLB 3, 248
**Calisher, Hortense** 1911- ..... **CLC 2, 4, 8, 38, 134; SSC 15**
See also CA 1-4R; CANR 1, 22; CN 7; DAM NOV; DLB 2, 218; INT CANR-22; MTCW 1, 2; RGAL 4; RGSF 2
**Callaghan, Morley Edward**
1903-1990 .................. **CLC 3, 14, 41, 65**
See also CA 9-12R; CANR 33, 73; DAC; DAM MST; DLB 68; MTCW 1, 2; RGEL 2; RGSF 2
**Callimachus** c. 305B.C.-c. 240B.C. ................................. **CMLC 18**
See also AW 1; DLB 176; RGWL 2, 3
**Calvin, Jean**
See Calvin, John
See also GFL Beginnings to 1789
**Calvin, John** 1509-1564 ...................... **LC 37**
See Calvin, Jean
**Calvino, Italo** 1923-1985 .... **CLC 5, 8, 11, 22, 33, 39, 73; SSC 3, 48**
See also CA 85-88; CANR 23, 61; DAM NOV; DLB 196; EW 13; MTCW 1, 2; RGSF 2; RGWL 2, 3; SFW 4; SSFS 12
**Camden, William** 1551-1623 ............... **LC 77**
See also DLB 172
**Cameron, Carey** 1952- ........................ **CLC 59**
See also CA 135
**Cameron, Peter** 1959- .......................... **CLC 44**
See also AMWS 12; CA 125; CANR 50; DLB 234; GLL 2
**Camoens, Luis Vaz de** 1524(?)-1580
See Camoes, Luis de
See also EW 2

**Camoes, Luis de** 1524(?)-1580 . **HLCS 1; LC 62; PC 31**
See Camoens, Luis Vaz de
See also RGWL 2, 3
**Campana, Dino** 1885-1932 ............. **TCLC 20**
See also DLB 114
**Campanella, Tommaso** 1568-1639 ....... **LC 32**
See also RGWL 2, 3
**Campbell, John W(ood, Jr.)**
1910-1971 .................................. **CLC 32**
See also CA 21-22; CANR 34; CAP 2; DLB 8; MTCW 1; SCFW; SFW 4
**Campbell, Joseph** 1904-1987 ............ **CLC 69**
See also AAYA 3; BEST 89:2; CA 1-4R; CANR 3, 28, 61, 107; MTCW 1, 2
**Campbell, Maria** 1940- ....... **CLC 85; NNAL**
See also CA 102; CANR 54; CCA 1; DAC
**Campbell, Paul N.** 1923-
See hooks, bell
See also CA 21-24R
**Campbell, (John) Ramsey** 1946- ..... **CLC 42; SSC 19**
See also CA 57-60; CANR 7, 102; DLB 261; HGG; INT CANR-7; SUFW 1, 2
**Campbell, (Ignatius) Roy (Dunnachie)**
1901-1957 ................................... **TCLC 5**
See also AFW; CA 155; DLB 20, 225; MTCW 2; RGEL 2
**Campbell, Thomas** 1777-1844 ....... **NCLC 19**
See also DLB 93, 144; RGEL 2
**Campbell, Wilfred** ........................... **TCLC 9**
See Campbell, William
**Campbell, William** 1858(?)-1918
See Campbell, Wilfred
See also DLB 92
**Campion, Jane** .................................. **CLC 95**
See also AAYA 33; CA 138; CANR 87
**Campion, Thomas** 1567-1620 .............. **LC 78**
See also CDBLB Before 1660; DAM POET; DLB 58, 172; RGEL 2
**Camus, Albert** 1913-1960 ....... **CLC 1, 2, 4, 9, 11, 14, 32, 63, 69, 124; DC 2; SSC 9; WLC**
See also AAYA 36; AFW; BPFB 1; CA 89-92; DA; DAB; DAC; DAM DRAM, MST, NOV; DLB 72; EW 13; EXPN; EXPS; GFL 1789 to the Present; MTCW 1, 2; NFS 6, 16; RGSF 2; RGWL 2, 3; SSFS 4; TWA
**Canby, Vincent** 1924-2000 .................. **CLC 13**
See also CA 81-84
**Cancale**
See Desnos, Robert
**Canetti, Elias** 1905-1994 .. **CLC 3, 14, 25, 75, 86**
See also CA 21-24R; CANR 23, 61, 79; CDWLB 2; CWW 2; DLB 85, 124; EW 12; MTCW 1, 2; RGWL 2, 3; TWA
**Canfield, Dorothea F.**
See Fisher, Dorothy (Frances) Canfield
**Canfield, Dorothea Frances**
See Fisher, Dorothy (Frances) Canfield
**Canfield, Dorothy**
See Fisher, Dorothy (Frances) Canfield
**Canin, Ethan** 1960- ............................ **CLC 55**
See also CA 135
**Cankar, Ivan** 1876-1918 ................. **TCLC 105**
See also CDWLB 4; DLB 147
**Cannon, Curt**
See Hunter, Evan
**Cao, Lan** 1961- .................................. **CLC 109**
See also CA 165
**Cape, Judith**
See Page, P(atricia) K(athleen)
See also CCA 1
**Capek, Karel** 1890-1938 ........ **DC 1; SSC 36; TCLC 6, 37; WLC**
See also CA 140; CDWLB 4; DA; DAB; DAC; DAM DRAM, MST, NOV; DFS 7, 11; DLB 215; EW 10; MTCW 1; RGSF 2; RGWL 2, 3; SCFW 2; SFW 4

**Capote, Truman** 1924-1984 . **CLC 1, 3, 8, 13, 19, 34, 38, 58; SSC 2, 47; WLC**
See also AMWS 3; BPFB 1; CA 5-8R; CANR 18, 62; CDALB 1941-1968; CPW; DA; DAB; DAC; DAM MST, NOV, POP; DLB 2, 185, 227; DLBY 1980, 1984; EXPS; GLL 1; LAIT 3; MTCW 1, 2; NCFS 2; RGAL 4; RGSF 2; SATA 91; SSFS 2; TUS
**Capra, Frank** 1897-1991 .................. **CLC 16**
See also CA 61-64
**Caputo, Philip** 1941- ......................... **CLC 32**
See also CA 73-76; CANR 40; YAW
**Caragiale, Ion Luca** 1852-1912 ...... **TCLC 76**
See also CA 157
**Card, Orson Scott** 1951- ...... **CLC 44, 47, 50**
See also AAYA 11, 42; BPFB 1; BYA 5, 8; CA 102; CANR 27, 47, 73, 102, 106; CPW; DAM POP; FANT; INT CANR-27; MTCW 1, 2; NFS 5; SATA 83, 127; SCFW 2; SFW 4; SUFW 2; YAW
**Cardenal, Ernesto** 1925- .......... **CLC 31, 161; HLC 1; PC 22**
See also CA 49-52; CANR 2, 32, 66; CWW 2; DAM MULT, POET; HW 1, 2; LAWS 1; MTCW 1, 2; RGWL 2, 3
**Cardozo, Benjamin N(athan)**
1870-1938 ................................. **TCLC 65**
See also CA 164
**Carducci, Giosue (Alessandro Giuseppe)**
1835-1907 ................................. **TCLC 32**
See also CA 163; EW 7; RGWL 2, 3
**Carew, Thomas** 1595(?)-1640 . **LC 13; PC 29**
See also BRW 2; DLB 126; PAB; RGEL 2
**Carey, Ernestine Gilbreth** 1908- ....... **CLC 17**
See also CA 5-8R; CANR 71; SATA 2
**Carey, Peter** 1943- .................. **CLC 40, 55, 96**
See also CA 127; CANR 53, 76; CN 7; INT CA-127; MTCW 1, 2; RGSF 2; SATA 94
**Carleton, William** 1794-1869 ............ **NCLC 3**
See also DLB 159; RGEL 2; RGSF 2
**Carlisle, Henry (Coffin)** 1926- .......... **CLC 33**
See also CA 13-16R; CANR 15, 85
**Carlsen, Chris**
See Holdstock, Robert P.
**Carlson, Ron(ald F.)** 1947- ................ **CLC 54**
See also CA 105; CAAE 189; CANR 27; DLB 244
**Carlyle, Thomas** 1795-1881 ...... **NCLC 22, 70**
See also BRW 4; CDBLB 1789-1832; DA; DAB; DAC; DAM MST; DLB 55, 144, 254; RGEL 2; TEA
**Carman, (William) Bliss** 1861-1929 ... **PC 34; TCLC 7**
See also CA 152; DAC; DLB 92; RGEL 2
**Carnegie, Dale** 1888-1955 ............... **TCLC 53**
**Carossa, Hans** 1878-1956 ............... **TCLC 48**
See also CA 170; DLB 66
**Carpenter, Don(ald Richard)**
1931-1995 ................................... **CLC 41**
See also CA 45-48; CANR 1, 71
**Carpenter, Edward** 1844-1929 ....... **TCLC 88**
See also CA 163; GLL 1
**Carpenter, John (Howard)** 1948- ... **CLC 161**
See also AAYA 2; CA 134; SATA 58
**Carpenter, Johnny**
See Carpenter, John (Howard)
**Carpentier (y Valmont), Alejo**
1904-1980 . **CLC 8, 11, 38, 110; HLC 1; SSC 35**
See also CA 65-68; CANR 11, 70; CDWLB 3; DAM MULT; DLB 113; HW 1, 2; LAW; RGSF 2; RGWL 2, 3; WLIT 1
**Carr, Caleb** 1955(?)- ........................... **CLC 86**
See also CA 147; CANR 73
**Carr, Emily** 1871-1945 .................... **TCLC 32**
See also CA 159; DLB 68; FW; GLL 2

**Carr, John Dickson** 1906-1977 .......... **CLC 3**
See Fairbairn, Roger
See also CA 49-52; CANR 3, 33, 60; CMW 4; MSW; MTCW 1, 2

**Carr, Philippa**
See Hibbert, Eleanor Alice Burford

**Carr, Virginia Spencer** 1929- ............ **CLC 34**
See also CA 61-64; DLB 111

**Carrere, Emmanuel** 1957- ................ **CLC 89**
See also CA 200

**Carrier, Roch** 1937- ..................... **CLC 13, 78**
See also CA 130; CANR 61; CCA 1; DAC; DAM MST; DLB 53; SATA 105

**Carroll, James Dennis**
See Carroll, Jim

**Carroll, James P.** 1943(?)- ................ **CLC 38**
See also CA 81-84; CANR 73; MTCW 1

**Carroll, Jim** 1951- ..................... **CLC 35, 143**
See Carroll, James Dennis
See also AAYA 17; CA 45-48; CANR 42

**Carroll, Lewis** ... **NCLC 2, 53; PC 18; WLC**
See Dodgson, Charles L(utwidge)
See also AAYA 39; BRW 5; BYA 5, 13; CDBLB 1832-1890; CLR 2, 18; DLB 18, 163, 178; DLBY 1998; EXPN; EXPP; FANT; JRDA; LAIT 1; NFS 7; PFS 11; RGEL 2; SUFW 1; TEA; WCH

**Carroll, Paul Vincent** 1900-1968 ...... **CLC 10**
See also CA 9-12R; DLB 10; RGEL 2

**Carruth, Hayden** 1921- ..... **CLC 4, 7, 10, 18, 84; PC 10**
See also CA 9-12R; CANR 4, 38, 59, 110; CP 7; DLB 5, 165; INT CANR-4; MTCW 1, 2; SATA 47

**Carson, Rachel**
See Carson, Rachel Louise
See also DLB 275

**Carson, Rachel Louise** 1907-1964 .... **CLC 71**
See Carson, Rachel
See also AMWS 9; ANW; CA 77-80; CANR 35; DAM POP; FW; LAIT 4; MTCW 1, 2; NCFS 1; SATA 23

**Carter, Angela (Olive)** 1940-1992 ...... **CLC 5, 41, 76; SSC 13**
See also BRWS 3; CA 53-56; CANR 12, 36, 61, 106; DLB 14, 207, 261; EXPS; FANT; FW; MTCW 1, 2; RGSF 2; SATA 66; SATA-Obit 70; SFW 4; SSFS 4, 12; SUFW 2; WLIT 4

**Carter, Nick**
See Smith, Martin Cruz

**Carver, Raymond** 1938-1988 ..... **CLC 22, 36, 53, 55, 126; SSC 8, 51**
See also AAYA 44; AMWS 3; BPFB 1; CA 33-36R; CANR 17, 34, 61, 103; CPW; DAM NOV; DLB 130; DLBY 1984, 1988; MTCW 1, 2; PFS 17; RGAL 4; RGSF 2; SSFS 3, 6, 12, 13; TCWW 2; TUS

**Cary, Elizabeth, Lady Falkland** 1585-1639 ...................... **LC 30**

**Cary, (Arthur) Joyce (Lunel)** 1888-1957 ....................... **TCLC 1, 29**
See also BRW 7; CA 164; CDBLB 1914-1945; DLB 15, 100; MTCW 2; RGEL 2; TEA

**Casanova de Seingalt, Giovanni Jacopo** 1725-1798 ................... **LC 13**

**Casares, Adolfo Bioy**
See Bioy Casares, Adolfo
See also RGSF 2

**Casas, Bartolome de las** 1474-1566
See Las Casas, Bartolome de
See also WLIT 1

**Casely-Hayford, J(oseph) E(phraim)** 1866-1903 ................ **BLC 1; TCLC 24**
See also BW 2; CA 152; DAM MULT

**Casey, John (Dudley)** 1939- .............. **CLC 59**
See also BEST 90:2; CA 69-72; CANR 23, 100

**Casey, Michael** 1947- .......................... **CLC 2**
See also CA 65-68; CANR 109; DLB 5

**Casey, Patrick**
See Thurman, Wallace (Henry)

**Casey, Warren (Peter)** 1935-1988 .... **CLC 12**
See also CA 101; INT 101

**Casona, Alejandro** .......................... **CLC 49**
See Alvarez, Alejandro Rodriguez

**Cassavetes, John** 1929-1989 .............. **CLC 20**
See also CA 85-88; CANR 82

**Cassian, Nina** 1924- .......................... **PC 17**
See also CWP; CWW 2

**Cassill, R(onald) V(erlin)** 1919- ... **CLC 4, 23**
See also CA 9-12R; CAAS 1; CANR 7, 45; CN 7; DLB 6, 218

**Cassiodorus, Flavius Magnus** c. 490(?)-c. 583(?) ........................................ **CMLC 43**

**Cassirer, Ernst** 1874-1945 ............... **TCLC 61**
See also CA 157

**Cassity, (Allen) Turner** 1929- ........ **CLC 6, 42**
See also CA 17-20R; CAAS 8; CANR 11; CSW; DLB 105

**Castaneda, Carlos (Cesar Aranha)** 1931(?)-1998 ..................... **CLC 12, 119**
See also CA 25-28R; CANR 32, 66, 105; DNFS 1; HW 1; MTCW 1

**Castedo, Elena** 1937- ......................... **CLC 65**
See also CA 132

**Castedo-Ellerman, Elena**
See Castedo, Elena

**Castellanos, Rosario** 1925-1974 ....... **CLC 66; HLC 1; SSC 39**
See also CA 131; CANR 58; CDWLB 3; DAM MULT; DLB 113; FW; HW 1; LAW; MTCW 1; RGSF 2; RGWL 2, 3

**Castelvetro, Lodovico** 1505-1571 ........ **LC 12**

**Castiglione, Baldassare** 1478-1529 ...... **LC 12**
See Castiglione, Baldesar
See also RGWL 2, 3

**Castiglione, Baldesar**
See Castiglione, Baldassare
See also EW 2

**Castillo, Ana (Hernandez Del)** 1953- .................................... **CLC 151**
See also AAYA 42; CA 131; CANR 51, 86; CWP; DLB 122, 227; DNFS 2; FW; HW 1

**Castle, Robert**
See Hamilton, Edmond

**Castro (Ruz), Fidel** 1926(?)- ............... **HLC 1**
See also CA 129; CANR 81; DAM MULT; HW 2

**Castro, Guillen de** 1569-1631 .............. **LC 19**

**Castro, Rosalia de** 1837-1885 ... **NCLC 3, 78; PC 41**
See also DAM MULT

**Cather, Willa (Sibert)** 1873-1947 . **SSC 2, 50; TCLC 1, 11, 31, 99, 125; WLC**
See also AAYA 24; AMW; AMWC 1; AMWR 1; BPFB 1; CA 128; CDALB 1865-1917; DA; DAB; DAC; DAM MST, NOV; DLB 9, 54, 78, 256; DLBD 1; EXPN; EXPS; LAIT 3; MAWW; MTCW 1, 2; NFS 2; RGAL 4; RGSF 2; RHW; SATA 30; SSFS 2, 7, 16; TCWW 2; TUS

**Catherine II**
See Catherine the Great
See also DLB 150

**Catherine the Great** 1729-1796 ........... **LC 69**
See Catherine II

**Cato, Marcus Porcius** 234B.C.-149B.C. ..................... **CMLC 21**
See Cato the Elder

**Cato, Marcus Porcius, the Elder**
See Cato, Marcus Porcius

**Cato the Elder**
See Cato, Marcus Porcius
See also DLB 211

**Catton, (Charles) Bruce** 1899-1978 . **CLC 35**
See also AITN 1; CA 5-8R; CANR 7, 74; DLB 17; SATA 2; SATA-Obit 24

**Catullus** c. 84B.C.-54B.C. ............... **CMLC 18**
See also AW 2; CDWLB 1; DLB 211; RGWL 2, 3

**Cauldwell, Frank**
See King, Francis (Henry)

**Caunitz, William J.** 1933-1996 ......... **CLC 34**
See also BEST 89:3; CA 130; CANR 73; INT 130

**Causley, Charles (Stanley)** 1917- ....... **CLC 7**
See also CA 9-12R; CANR 5, 35, 94; CLR 30; CWRI 5; DLB 27; MTCW 1; SATA 3, 66

**Caute, (John) David** 1936- ................ **CLC 29**
See also CA 1-4R; CAAS 4; CANR 1, 33, 64; CBD; CD 5; CN 7; DAM NOV; DLB 14, 231

**Cavafy, C(onstantine) P(eter)** .......... **PC 36; TCLC 2, 7**
See Kavafis, Konstantinos Petrou
See also CA 148; DAM POET; EW 8; MTCW 1; RGWL 2, 3; WP

**Cavalcanti, Guido** c. 1250-c. 1300 ........................................ **CMLC 54**

**Cavallo, Evelyn**
See Spark, Muriel (Sarah)

**Cavanna, Betty** ................................ **CLC 12**
See Harrison, Elizabeth (Allen) Cavanna
See also JRDA; MAICYA 1; SAAS 4; SATA 1, 30

**Cavendish, Margaret Lucas** 1623-1673 ................................ **LC 30**
See also DLB 131, 252; RGEL 2

**Caxton, William** 1421(?)-1491(?) ......... **LC 17**
See also DLB 170

**Cayer, D. M.**
See Duffy, Maureen

**Cayrol, Jean** 1911- ............................ **CLC 11**
See also CA 89-92; DLB 83

**Cela, Camilo Jose** 1916-2002 ....... **CLC 4, 13, 59, 122; HLC 1**
See also BEST 90:2; CA 21-24R; CAAS 10; CANR 21, 32, 76; DAM MULT; DLBY 1989; EW 13; HW 1; MTCW 1, 2; RGSF 2; RGWL 2, 3

**Celan, Paul** -1970 .... **CLC 10, 19, 53, 82; PC 10**
See Antschel, Paul
See also CDWLB 2; DLB 69; RGWL 2, 3

**Celine, Louis-Ferdinand** .. **CLC 1, 3, 4, 7, 9, 15, 47, 124**
See Destouches, Louis-Ferdinand
See also DLB 72; EW 11; GFL 1789 to the Present; RGWL 2, 3

**Cellini, Benvenuto** 1500-1571 ................ **LC 7**

**Cendrars, Blaise** ......................... **CLC 18, 106**
See Sauser-Hall, Frederic
See also DLB 258; GFL 1789 to the Present; RGWL 2, 3; WP

**Centlivre, Susanna** 1669(?)-1723 ......... **LC 65**
See also DLB 84; RGEL 2

**Cernuda (y Bidon), Luis** 1902-1963 . **CLC 54**
See also CA 131; DAM POET; DLB 134; GLL 1; HW 1; RGWL 2, 3

**Cervantes, Lorna Dee** 1954- ..... **HLCS 1; PC 35**
See also CA 131; CANR 80; CWP; DLB 82; EXPP; HW 1

**Cervantes (Saavedra), Miguel de** 1547-1616 .... **HLCS; LC 6, 23; SSC 12; WLC**
See also BYA 1, 14; DA; DAB; DAC; DAM MST, NOV; EW 2; LAIT 1; NFS 8; RGSF 2; RGWL 2, 3; TWA

**Cesaire, Aime (Fernand)** 1913- ......... **BLC 1; CLC 19, 32, 112; PC 25**
See also BW 2, 3; CA 65-68; CANR 24, 43, 81; DAM MULT, POET; GFL 1789 to the Present; MTCW 1, 2; WP

**Chabon, Michael** 1963- ............. **CLC 55, 149**
See also AAYA 45; AMWS 11; CA 139; CANR 57, 96

**Chabrol, Claude** 1930- ...................... **CLC 16**
See also CA 110

**Challans, Mary** 1905-1983
See Renault, Mary
See also CA 81-84; CANR 74; MTCW 2; SATA 23; SATA-Obit 36; TEA

**Challis, George**
See Faust, Frederick (Schiller)
See also TCWW 2

**Chambers, Aidan** 1934- ...................... **CLC 35**
See also AAYA 27; CA 25-28R; CANR 12, 31, 58; JRDA; MAICYA 1, 2; SAAS 12; SATA 1, 69, 108; WYA; YAW

**Chambers, James** 1948-
See Cliff, Jimmy

**Chambers, Jessie**
See Lawrence, D(avid) H(erbert Richards)
See also GLL 1

**Chambers, Robert W(illiam)** 1865-1933 ................ **TCLC 41**
See also CA 165; DLB 202; HGG; SATA 107; SUFW 1

**Chambers, (David) Whittaker** 1901-1961 ................ **TCLC 129**

**Chamisso, Adelbert von** 1781-1838 ................ **NCLC 82**
See also DLB 90; RGWL 2, 3; SUFW 1

**Chance, James T.**
See Carpenter, John (Howard)

**Chance, John T.**
See Carpenter, John (Howard)

**Chandler, Raymond (Thornton)** 1888-1959 .............. **SSC 23; TCLC 1, 7**
See also AAYA 25; AMWS 4; BPFB 1; CA 129; CANR 60, 107; CDALB 1929-1941; CMW 4; DLB 226, 253; DLBD 6; MSW; MTCW 1, 2; RGAL 4; TUS

**Chang, Eileen** 1921-1995 ................ **SSC 28**
See also CA 166; CWW 2

**Chang, Jung** 1952- .............. **CLC 71**
See also CA 142

**Chang Ai-Ling**
See Chang, Eileen

**Channing, William Ellery** 1780-1842 .............. **NCLC 17**
See also DLB 1, 59, 235; RGAL 4

**Chao, Patricia** 1955- ...................... **CLC 119**
See also CA 163

**Chaplin, Charles Spencer** 1889-1977 ...................... **CLC 16**
See Chaplin, Charlie
See also CA 81-84

**Chaplin, Charlie**
See Chaplin, Charles Spencer
See also DLB 44

**Chapman, George** 1559(?)-1634 . **DC 19; LC 22**
See also BRW 1; DAM DRAM; DLB 62, 121; RGEL 2

**Chapman, Graham** 1941-1989 ......... **CLC 21**
See Monty Python
See also CA 116; CANR 35, 95

**Chapman, John Jay** 1862-1933 ....... **TCLC 7**
See also CA 191

**Chapman, Lee**
See Bradley, Marion Zimmer
See also GLL 1

**Chapman, Walker**
See Silverberg, Robert

**Chappell, Fred (Davis)** 1936- .... **CLC 40, 78, 162**
See also CA 5-8R; CAAE 198; CAAS 4; CANR 8, 33, 67, 110; CN 7; CP 7; CSW; DLB 6, 105; HGG

**Char, Rene(-Emile)** 1907-1988 .... **CLC 9, 11, 14, 55**
See also CA 13-16R; CANR 32; DAM POET; DLB 258; GFL 1789 to the Present; MTCW 1, 2; RGWL 2, 3

**Charby, Jay**
See Ellison, Harlan (Jay)

**Chardin, Pierre Teilhard de**
See Teilhard de Chardin, (Marie Joseph) Pierre

**Chariton** fl. 1st cent. (?)- ................ **CMLC 49**

**Charlemagne** 742-814 ................... **CMLC 37**

**Charles I** 1600-1649 ............................ **LC 13**

**Charriere, Isabelle de** 1740-1805 .. **NCLC 66**

**Chartier, Emile-Auguste**
See Alain

**Charyn, Jerome** 1937- ............... **CLC 5, 8, 18**
See also CA 5-8R; CAAS 1; CANR 7, 61, 101; CMW 4; CN 7; DLBY 1983; MTCW 1

**Chase, Adam**
See Marlowe, Stephen

**Chase, Mary (Coyle)** 1907-1981 ............ **DC 1**
See also CA 77-80; CAD; CWD; DFS 11; DLB 228; SATA 17; SATA-Obit 29

**Chase, Mary Ellen** 1887-1973 ........... **CLC 2; TCLC 124**
See also CA 13-16; CAP 1; SATA 10

**Chase, Nicholas**
See Hyde, Anthony
See also CCA 1

**Chateaubriand, Francois Rene de** 1768-1848 ................ **NCLC 3**
See also DLB 119; EW 5; GFL 1789 to the Present; RGWL 2, 3; TWA

**Chatterje, Sarat Chandra** 1876-1936(?)
See Chatterji, Saratchandra

**Chatterji, Bankim Chandra** 1838-1894 ................ **NCLC 19**

**Chatterji, Saratchandra** ................ **TCLC 13**
See Chatterje, Sarat Chandra
See also CA 186

**Chatterton, Thomas** 1752-1770 ....... **LC 3, 54**
See also DAM POET; DLB 109; RGEL 2

**Chatwin, (Charles) Bruce** 1940-1989 ..................... **CLC 28, 57, 59**
See also AAYA 4; BEST 90:1; BRWS 4; CA 85-88; CPW; DAM POP; DLB 194, 204

**Chaucer, Daniel**
See Ford, Ford Madox
See also RHW

**Chaucer, Geoffrey** 1340(?)-1400 .. **LC 17, 56; PC 19; WLCS**
See also BRW 1; BRWR 2; CDBLB Before 1660; DA; DAB; DAC; DAM MST, POET; DLB 146; LAIT 1; PAB; PFS 14; RGEL 2; TEA; WLIT 3; WP

**Chavez, Denise (Elia)** 1948- ................ **HLC 1**
See also CA 131; CANR 56, 81; DAM MULT; DLB 122; FW; HW 1, 2; MTCW 2

**Chaviaras, Strates** 1935-
See Haviaras, Stratis
See also CA 105

**Chayefsky, Paddy** ............................ **CLC 23**
See Chayefsky, Sidney
See also CAD; DLB 7, 44; DLBY 1981; RGAL 4

**Chayefsky, Sidney** 1923-1981
See Chayefsky, Paddy
See also CA 9-12R; CANR 18; DAM DRAM

**Chedid, Andree** 1920- ...................... **CLC 47**
See also CA 145; CANR 95

**Cheever, John** 1912-1982 ...... **CLC 3, 7, 8, 11, 15, 25, 64; SSC 1, 38, 57; WLC**
See also AMWS 1; BPFB 1; CA 5-8R; CABS 1; CANR 5, 27, 76; CDALB 1941-1968; CPW; DA; DAB; DAC; DAM MST, NOV, POP; DLB 2, 102, 227; DLBY 1980, 1982; EXPS; INT CANR-5; MTCW 1, 2; RGAL 4; RGSF 2; SSFS 2, 14; TUS

**Cheever, Susan** 1943- ................ **CLC 18, 48**
See also CA 103; CANR 27, 51, 92; DLBY 1982; INT CANR-27

**Chekhonte, Antosha**
See Chekhov, Anton (Pavlovich)

**Chekhov, Anton (Pavlovich)** 1860-1904 ...... **DC 9; SSC 2, 28, 41, 51; TCLC 3, 10, 31, 55, 96; WLC**
See also BYA 14; CA 124; DA; DAB; DAC; DAM DRAM, MST; DFS 1, 5, 10, 12; EW 7; EXPS; LAIT 3; RGSF 2; RGWL 2, 3; SATA 90; SSFS 5, 13, 14; TWA

**Cheney, Lynne V.** 1941- ...................... **CLC 70**
See also CA 89-92; CANR 58

**Chernyshevsky, Nikolai Gavrilovich**
See Chernyshevsky, Nikolay Gavrilovich
See also DLB 238

**Chernyshevsky, Nikolay Gavrilovich** 1828-1889 ................ **NCLC 1**
See Chernyshevsky, Nikolai Gavrilovich

**Cherry, Carolyn Janice** 1942-
See Cherryh, C. J.
See also CA 65-68; CANR 10

**Cherryh, C. J.** ................ **CLC 35**
See Cherry, Carolyn Janice
See also AAYA 24; BPFB 1; DLBY 1980; FANT; SATA 93; SCFW 2; SFW 4; YAW

**Chesnutt, Charles W(addell)** 1858-1932 .... **BLC 1; SSC 7, 54; TCLC 5, 39**
See also AFAW 1, 2; BW 1, 3; CA 125; CANR 76; DAM MULT; DLB 12, 50, 78; MTCW 1, 2; RGAL 4; RGSF 2; SSFS 11

**Chester, Alfred** 1929(?)-1971 ............. **CLC 49**
See also CA 196; DLB 130

**Chesterton, G(ilbert) K(eith)** 1874-1936 . **PC 28; SSC 1, 46; TCLC 1, 6, 64**
See also BRW 6; CA 132; CANR 73; CD-BLB 1914-1945; CMW 4; DAM NOV, POET; DLB 10, 19, 34, 70, 98, 149, 178; FANT; MSW; MTCW 1, 2; RGEL 2; RGSF 2; SATA 27; SUFW 1

**Chiang, Pin-chin** 1904-1986
See Ding Ling

**Ch'ien, Chung-shu** 1910-1998 .......... **CLC 22**
See also CA 130; CANR 73; MTCW 1, 2

**Chikamatsu Monzaemon** 1653-1724 ... **LC 66**
See also RGWL 2, 3

**Child, L. Maria**
See Child, Lydia Maria

**Child, Lydia Maria** 1802-1880 .. **NCLC 6, 73**
See also DLB 1, 74, 243; RGAL 4; SATA 67

**Child, Mrs.**
See Child, Lydia Maria

**Child, Philip** 1898-1978 ............... **CLC 19, 68**
See also CA 13-14; CAP 1; DLB 68; RHW; SATA 47

**Childers, (Robert) Erskine** 1870-1922 ................... **TCLC 65**
See also CA 153; DLB 70

**Childress, Alice** 1920-1994 . **BLC 1; CLC 12, 15, 86, 96; DC 4; TCLC 116**
See also AAYA 8; BW 2, 3; BYA 2; CA 45-48; CAD; CANR 3, 27, 50, 74; CLR 14; CWD; DAM DRAM, MULT, NOV; DFS

2, 8, 14; DLB 7, 38, 249; JRDA; LAIT 5; MAICYA 1, 2; MAICYAS 1; MTCW 1, 2; RGAL 4; SATA 7, 48, 81; TUS; WYA; YAW

**Chin, Frank (Chew, Jr.)** 1940- ...... **CLC 135; DC 7**
See also CA 33-36R; CANR 71; CD 5; DAM MULT; DLB 206; LAIT 5; RGAL 4

**Chin, Marilyn (Mei Ling)** 1955- ......... **PC 40**
See also CA 129; CANR 70, 113; CWP

**Chislett, (Margaret) Anne** 1943- ...... **CLC 34**
See also CA 151

**Chitty, Thomas Willes** 1926- ............. **CLC 11**
See Hinde, Thomas
See also CA 5-8R; CN 7

**Chivers, Thomas Holley** 1809-1858 ................. **NCLC 49**
See also DLB 3, 248; RGAL 4

**Choi, Susan** ....................... **CLC 119**

**Chomette, Rene Lucien** 1898-1981
See Clair, Rene

**Chomsky, (Avram) Noam** 1928- ..... **CLC 132**
See also CA 17-20R; CANR 28, 62, 110; DLB 246; MTCW 1, 2

**Chopin, Kate** ..... **SSC 8; TCLC 127; WLCS**
See Chopin, Katherine
See also AAYA 33; AMWR 2; AMWS 1; CDALB 1865-1917; DA; DAB; DLB 12, 78; EXPN; EXPS; FW; LAIT 3; MAWW; NFS 3; RGAL 4; RGSF 2; SSFS 2, 13; TUS

**Chopin, Katherine** 1851-1904
See Chopin, Kate
See also CA 122; DAC; DAM MST, NOV

**Chretien de Troyes** c. 12th cent. - . **CMLC 10**
See also DLB 208; EW 1; RGWL 2, 3; TWA

**Christie**
See Ichikawa, Kon

**Christie, Agatha (Mary Clarissa)** 1890-1976 .. **CLC 1, 6, 8, 12, 39, 48, 110**
See also AAYA 9; AITN 1, 2; BPFB 1; BRWS 2; CA 17-20R; CANR 10, 37, 108; CBD; CDBLB 1914-1945; CMW 4; CPW; CWD; DAB; DAC; DAM NOV; DFS 2; DLB 13, 77, 245; MSW; MTCW 1, 2; NFS 8; RGEL 2; RHW; SATA 36; TEA; YAW

**Christie, Philippa** ............................. **CLC 21**
See Pearce, Philippa
See also BYA 5; CANR 109; CLR 9; DLB 161; MAICYA 1; SATA 1, 67, 129

**Christine de Pizan** 1365(?)-1431(?) ....... **LC 9**
See also DLB 208; RGWL 2, 3

**Chuang Tzu** c. 369B.C.-c. 286B.C. .................. **CMLC 57**

**Chubb, Elmer**
See Masters, Edgar Lee

**Chulkov, Mikhail Dmitrievich** 1743-1792 ..................................... **LC 2**
See also DLB 150

**Churchill, Caryl** 1938- ....... **CLC 31, 55, 157; DC 5**
See also BRWS 4; CA 102; CANR 22, 46, 108; CBD; CWD; DFS 12, 16; DLB 13; FW; MTCW 1; RGEL 2

**Churchill, Charles** 1731-1764 ................. **LC 3**
See also DLB 109; RGEL 2

**Churchill, Sir Winston (Leonard Spencer)** 1874-1965 ............... **TCLC 113**
See also BRW 6; CA 97-100; CDBLB 1890-1914; DLB 100; DLBD 16; LAIT 4; MTCW 1, 2

**Chute, Carolyn** 1947- ........................ **CLC 39**
See also CA 123

**Ciardi, John (Anthony)** 1916-1986 . **CLC 10, 40, 44, 129**
See also CA 5-8R; CAAS 2; CANR 5, 33; CLR 19; CWRI 5; DAM POET; DLB 5; DLBY 1986; INT CANR-5; MAICYA 1, 2; MTCW 1, 2; RGAL 4; SAAS 26; SATA 1, 65; SATA-Obit 46

**Cibber, Colley** 1671-1757 ..................... **LC 66**
See also DLB 84; RGEL 2

**Cicero, Marcus Tullius** 106B.C.-43B.C. ........................ **CMLC 3**
See also AW 1; CDWLB 1; DLB 211; RGWL 2, 3

**Cimino, Michael** 1943- ...................... **CLC 16**
See also CA 105

**Cioran, E(mil) M.** 1911-1995 ............ **CLC 64**
See also CA 25-28R; CANR 91; DLB 220

**Cisneros, Sandra** 1954- .. **CLC 69, 118; HLC 1; SSC 32**
See also AAYA 9; AMWS 7; CA 131; CANR 64; CWP; DAM MULT; DLB 122, 152; EXPN; FW; HW 1, 2; LAIT 5; MAICYA 1, 2; MTCW 2; NFS 2; RGAL 4; RGSF 2; SSFS 3, 13; WLIT 1; YAW

**Cixous, Helene** 1937- ........................ **CLC 92**
See also CA 126; CANR 55; CWW 2; DLB 83, 242; FW; GLL 2; MTCW 1, 2; TWA

**Clair, Rene** ........................ **CLC 20**
See Chomette, Rene Lucien

**Clampitt, Amy** 1920-1994 .... **CLC 32; PC 19**
See also AMWS 9; CA 110; CANR 29, 79; DLB 105

**Clancy, Thomas L., Jr.** 1947-
See Clancy, Tom
See also CA 131; CANR 62, 105; INT CA-131; MTCW 1, 2

**Clancy, Tom** ........................ **CLC 45, 112**
See Clancy, Thomas L., Jr.
See also AAYA 9; BEST 89:1, 90:1; BPFB 1; BYA 10, 11; CMW 4; CPW; DAM NOV, POP; DLB 227

**Clare, John** 1793-1864 ..... **NCLC 9, 86; PC 23**
See also DAB; DAM POET; DLB 55, 96; RGEL 2

**Clarin**
See Alas (y Urena), Leopoldo (Enrique Garcia)

**Clark, Al C.**
See Goines, Donald

**Clark, (Robert) Brian** 1932- ............. **CLC 29**
See also CA 41-44R; CANR 67; CBD; CD 5

**Clark, Curt**
See Westlake, Donald E(dwin)

**Clark, Eleanor** 1913-1996 ............. **CLC 5, 19**
See also CA 9-12R; CANR 41; CN 7; DLB 6

**Clark, J. P.**
See Clark Bekederemo, J(ohnson) P(epper)
See also CDWLB 3; DLB 117

**Clark, John Pepper**
See Clark Bekederemo, J(ohnson) P(epper)
See also AFW; CD 5; CP 7; RGEL 2

**Clark, M. R.**
See Clark, Mavis Thorpe

**Clark, Mavis Thorpe** 1909-1999 ...... **CLC 12**
See also CA 57-60; CANR 8, 37, 107; CLR 30; CWRI 5; MAICYA 1, 2; SAAS 5; SATA 8, 74

**Clark, Walter Van Tilburg** 1909-1971 ........................ **CLC 28**
See also CA 9-12R; CANR 63, 113; DLB 9, 206; LAIT 2; RGAL 4; SATA 8

**Clark Bekederemo, J(ohnson) P(epper)** 1935- ................. **BLC 1; CLC 38; DC 5**
See Clark, J. P.; Clark, John Pepper
See also BW 1; CA 65-68; CANR 16, 72; DAM DRAM, MULT; DFS 13; MTCW 1

**Clarke, Arthur C(harles)** 1917- .... **CLC 1, 4, 13, 18, 35, 136; SSC 3**
See also AAYA 4, 33; BPFB 1; BYA 13; CA 1-4R; CANR 2, 28, 55, 74; CN 7; CPW; DAM POP; DLB 261; JRDA; LAIT 5; MAICYA 1, 2; MTCW 1, 2; SATA 13, 70, 115; SCFW; SFW 4; SSFS 4; YAW

**Clarke, Austin** 1896-1974 ................ **CLC 6, 9**
See also CA 29-32; CAP 2; DAM POET; DLB 10, 20; RGEL 2

**Clarke, Austin C(hesterfield)** 1934- .. **BLC 1; CLC 8, 53; SSC 45**
See also BW 1; CA 25-28R; CAAS 16; CANR 14, 32, 68; CN 7; DAC; DAM MULT; DLB 53, 125; DNFS 2; RGSF 2

**Clarke, Gillian** 1937- ........................ **CLC 61**
See also CA 106; CP 7; CWP; DLB 40

**Clarke, Marcus (Andrew Hislop)** 1846-1881 ............................. **NCLC 19**
See also DLB 230; RGEL 2; RGSF 2

**Clarke, Shirley** 1925-1997 ................ **CLC 16**
See also CA 189

**Clash, The**
See Headon, (Nicky) Topper; Jones, Mick; Simonon, Paul; Strummer, Joe

**Claudel, Paul (Louis Charles Marie)** 1868-1955 ........................ **TCLC 2, 10**
See also CA 165; DLB 192, 258; EW 8; GFL 1789 to the Present; RGWL 2, 3; TWA

**Claudian** 370(?)-404(?) .................. **CMLC 46**
See also RGWL 2, 3

**Claudius, Matthias** 1740-1815 ....... **NCLC 75**
See also DLB 97

**Clavell, James (duMaresq)** 1925-1994 ........................ **CLC 6, 25, 87**
See also BPFB 1; CA 25-28R; CANR 26, 48; CPW; DAM NOV, POP; MTCW 1, 2; NFS 10; RHW

**Clayman, Gregory** ........................ **CLC 65**

**Cleaver, (Leroy) Eldridge** 1935-1998 ............... **BLC 1; CLC 30, 119**
See also BW 1, 3; CA 21-24R; CANR 16, 75; DAM MULT; MTCW 2; YAW

**Cleese, John (Marwood)** 1939- ......... **CLC 21**
See Monty Python
See also CA 116; CANR 35; MTCW 1

**Cleishbotham, Jebediah**
See Scott, Sir Walter

**Cleland, John** 1710-1789 .................. **LC 2, 48**
See also DLB 39; RGEL 2

**Clemens, Samuel Langhorne** 1835-1910
See Twain, Mark
See also CA 135; CDALB 1865-1917; DA; DAB; DAC; DAM MST, NOV; DLB 12, 23, 64, 74, 186, 189; JRDA; MAICYA 1, 2; NCFS 4; SATA 100; SSFS 16; YABC 2

**Clement of Alexandria** 150(?)-215(?) .......................... **CMLC 41**

**Cleophil**
See Congreve, William

**Clerihew, E.**
See Bentley, E(dmund) C(lerihew)

**Clerk, N. W.**
See Lewis, C(live) S(taples)

**Cliff, Jimmy** ....................... **CLC 21**
See Chambers, James
See also CA 193

**Cliff, Michelle** 1946- ........... **BLCS; CLC 120**
See also BW 2; CA 116; CANR 39, 72; CDWLB 3; DLB 157; FW; GLL 2

**Clifford, Lady Anne** 1590-1676 ........... **LC 76**
See also DLB 151

**Clifton, (Thelma) Lucille** 1936- ......... **BLC 1; CLC 19, 66, 162; PC 17**
See also AFAW 2; BW 2, 3; CA 49-52; CANR 2, 24, 42, 76, 97; CLR 5; CP 7; CSW; CWP; CWRI 5; DAM MULT,

POET; DLB 5, 41; EXPP; MAICYA 1, 2; MTCW 1, 2; PFS 1, 14; SATA 20, 69, 128; WP

**Clinton, Dirk**
See Silverberg, Robert

**Clough, Arthur Hugh** 1819-1861 ... **NCLC 27**
See also BRW 5; DLB 32; RGEL 2

**Clutha, Janet Paterson Frame** 1924-
See Frame, Janet
See also CA 1-4R; CANR 2, 36, 76; MTCW 1, 2; SATA 119

**Clyne, Terence**
See Blatty, William Peter

**Cobalt, Martin**
See Mayne, William (James Carter)

**Cobb, Irvin S(hrewsbury)**
1876-1944 .................................. **TCLC 77**
See also CA 175; DLB 11, 25, 86

**Cobbett, William** 1763-1835 .......... **NCLC 49**
See also DLB 43, 107, 158; RGEL 2

**Coburn, D(onald) L(ee)** 1938- ......... **CLC 10**
See also CA 89-92

**Cocteau, Jean (Maurice Eugene Clement)**
1889-1963 ...... **CLC 1, 8, 15, 16, 43; DC 17; TCLC 119; WLC**
See also CA 25-28; CANR 40; CAP 2; DA; DAB; DAC; DAM DRAM, MST, NOV; DLB 65, 258; EW 10; GFL 1789 to the Present; MTCW 1, 2; RGWL 2, 3; TWA

**Codrescu, Andrei** 1946- ............. **CLC 46, 121**
See also CA 33-36R; CAAS 19; CANR 13, 34, 53, 76; DAM POET; MTCW 2

**Coe, Max**
See Bourne, Randolph S(illiman)

**Coe, Tucker**
See Westlake, Donald E(dwin)

**Coen, Ethan** 1958- ......................... **CLC 108**
See also CA 126; CANR 85

**Coen, Joel** 1955- ............................... **CLC 108**
See also CA 126

**The Coen Brothers**
See Coen, Ethan; Coen, Joel

**Coetzee, J(ohn) M(ichael)** 1940- ...... **CLC 23, 33, 66, 117, 161, 162**
See also AAYA 37; AFW; BRWS 6; CA 77-80; CANR 41, 54, 74, 114; CN 7; DAM NOV; DLB 225; MTCW 1, 2; WLIT 2

**Coffey, Brian**
See Koontz, Dean R(ay)

**Coffin, Robert P(eter) Tristram**
1892-1955 .................................. **TCLC 95**
See also CA 169; DLB 45

**Cohan, George M(ichael)**
1878-1942 .................................. **TCLC 60**
See also CA 157; DLB 249; RGAL 4

**Cohen, Arthur A(llen)** 1928-1986 ...... **CLC 7, 31**
See also CA 1-4R; CANR 1, 17, 42; DLB 28

**Cohen, Leonard (Norman)** 1934- ...... **CLC 3, 38**
See also CA 21-24R; CANR 14, 69; CN 7; CP 7; DAC; DAM MST; DLB 53; MTCW 1

**Cohen, Matt(hew)** 1942-1999 ............ **CLC 19**
See also CA 61-64; CAAS 18; CANR 40; CN 7; DAC; DLB 53

**Cohen-Solal, Annie** 19(?)- ............... **CLC 50**

**Colegate, Isabel** 1931- ..................... **CLC 36**
See also CA 17-20R; CANR 8, 22, 74; CN 7; DLB 14, 231; INT CANR-22; MTCW 1

**Coleman, Emmett**
See Reed, Ishmael

**Coleridge, Hartley** 1796-1849 ......... **NCLC 90**
See also DLB 96

**Coleridge, M. E.**
See Coleridge, Mary E(lizabeth)

**Coleridge, Mary E(lizabeth)**
1861-1907 .................................. **TCLC 73**
See also CA 166; DLB 19, 98

**Coleridge, Samuel Taylor**
1772-1834 ...... **NCLC 9, 54, 99, 111; PC 11, 39; WLC**
See also BRW 4; BRWR 2; BYA 4; CDBLB 1789-1832; DA; DAB; DAC; DAM MST, POET; DLB 93, 107; EXPP; PAB; PFS 4, 5; RGEL 2; TEA; WLIT 3; WP

**Coleridge, Sara** 1802-1852 ............. **NCLC 31**
See also DLB 199

**Coles, Don** 1928- ............................. **CLC 46**
See also CA 115; CANR 38; CP 7

**Coles, Robert (Martin)** 1929- ......... **CLC 108**
See also CA 45-48; CANR 3, 32, 66, 70; INT CANR-32; SATA 23

**Colette, (Sidonie-Gabrielle)**
1873-1954 ......... **SSC 10; TCLC 1, 5, 16**
See Willy, Colette
See also CA 131; DAM NOV; DLB 65; EW 9; GFL 1789 to the Present; MTCW 1, 2; RGWL 2, 3; TWA

**Collett, (Jacobine) Camilla (Wergeland)**
1813-1895 .................................. **NCLC 22**

**Collier, Christopher** 1930- ................. **CLC 30**
See also AAYA 13; BYA 2; CA 33-36R; CANR 13, 33, 102; JRDA; MAICYA 1, 2; SATA 16, 70; WYA; YAW 1

**Collier, James Lincoln** 1928- ........... **CLC 30**
See also AAYA 13; BYA 2; CA 9-12R; CANR 4, 33, 60, 102; CLR 3; DAM POP; JRDA; MAICYA 1, 2; SAAS 21; SATA 8, 70; WYA; YAW 1

**Collier, Jeremy** 1650-1726 ................. **LC 6**

**Collier, John** 1901-1980 . **SSC 19; TCLC 127**
See also CA 65-68; CANR 10; DLB 77, 255; FANT; SUFW 1

**Collier, Mary** 1690-1762 ..................... **LC 86**
See also DLB 95

**Collingwood, R(obin) G(eorge)**
1889(?)-1943 ............................... **TCLC 67**
See also CA 155; DLB 262

**Collins, Hunt**
See Hunter, Evan

**Collins, Linda** 1931- ........................... **CLC 44**
See also CA 125

**Collins, (William) Wilkie**
1824-1889 .................... **NCLC 1, 18, 93**
See also BRWS 6; CDBLB 1832-1890; CMW 4; DLB 18, 70, 159; MSW; RGEL 2; RGSF 2; SUFW 1; WLIT 4

**Collins, William** 1721-1759 ........... **LC 4, 40**
See also BRW 3; DAM POET; DLB 109; RGEL 2

**Collodi, Carlo** ............................. **NCLC 54**
See Lorenzini, Carlo
See also CLR 5; WCH

**Colman, George**
See Glassco, John

**Colonna, Vittoria** 1492-1547 ............... **LC 71**
See also RGWL 2, 3

**Colt, Winchester Remington**
See Hubbard, L(afayette) Ron(ald)

**Colter, Cyrus J.** 1910-2002 ................. **CLC 58**
See also BW 1; CA 65-68; CANR 10, 66; CN 7; DLB 33

**Colton, James**
See Hansen, Joseph
See also GLL 1

**Colum, Padraic** 1881-1972 ................. **CLC 28**
See also BYA 4; CA 73-76; CANR 35; CLR 36; CWRI 5; DLB 19; MAICYA 1, 2; MTCW 1; RGEL 2; SATA 15; WCH

**Colvin, James**
See Moorcock, Michael (John)

**Colwin, Laurie (E.)** 1944-1992 .... **CLC 5, 13, 23, 84**
See also CA 89-92; CANR 20, 46; DLB 218; DLBY 1980; MTCW 1

**Comfort, Alex(ander)** 1920-2000 ........ **CLC 7**
See also CA 1-4R; CANR 1, 45; CP 7; DAM POP; MTCW 1

**Comfort, Montgomery**
See Campbell, (John) Ramsey

**Compton-Burnett, I(vy)**
1892(?)-1969 .......... **CLC 1, 3, 10, 15, 34**
See also BRW 7; CA 1-4R; CANR 4; DAM NOV; DLB 36; MTCW 1; RGEL 2

**Comstock, Anthony** 1844-1915 ...... **TCLC 13**
See also CA 169

**Comte, Auguste** 1798-1857 ............. **NCLC 54**

**Conan Doyle, Arthur**
See Doyle, Sir Arthur Conan
See also BPFB 1; BYA 4, 5, 11

**Conde (Abellan), Carmen**
1901-1996 ..................................... **HLCS 1**
See also CA 177; DLB 108; HW 2

**Conde, Maryse** 1937- ...... **BLCS; CLC 52, 92**
See also BW 2, 3; CA 110; CAAE 190; CANR 30, 53, 76; CWW 2; DAM MULT; MTCW 1

**Condillac, Etienne Bonnot de**
1714-1780 ...................................... **LC 26**

**Condon, Richard (Thomas)**
1915-1996 ........ **CLC 4, 6, 8, 10, 45, 100**
See also BEST 90:3; BPFB 1; CA 1-4R; CAAS 1; CANR 2, 23; CMW 4; CN 7; DAM NOV; INT CANR-23; MTCW 1, 2

**Confucius** 551B.C.-479B.C. ............ **CMLC 19; WLCS**
See also DA; DAB; DAC; DAM MST

**Congreve, William** 1670-1729 ... **DC 2; LC 5, 21; WLC**
See also BRW 2; CDBLB 1660-1789; DA; DAB; DAC; DAM DRAM, MST, POET; DFS 15; DLB 39, 84; RGEL 2; WLIT 3

**Connell, Evan S(helby), Jr.** 1924- . **CLC 4, 6, 45**
See also AAYA 7; CA 1-4R; CAAS 2; CANR 2, 39, 76, 97; CN 7; DAM NOV; DLB 2; DLBY 1981; MTCW 1, 2

**Connelly, Marc(us Cook)** 1890-1980 . **CLC 7**
See also CA 85-88; CANR 30; DFS 12; DLB 7; DLBY 1980; RGAL 4; SATA-Obit 25

**Connor, Ralph** ............................. **TCLC 31**
See Gordon, Charles William
See also DLB 92; TCWW 2

**Conrad, Joseph** 1857-1924 . **SSC 9; TCLC 1, 6, 13, 25, 43, 57; WLC**
See also AAYA 26; BPFB 1; BRW 6; BRWR 2; BYA 2; CA 131; CANR 60; CDBLB 1890-1914; DA; DAB; DAC; DAM MST, NOV; DLB 10, 34, 98, 156; EXPN; EXPS; LAIT 2; MTCW 1, 2; NFS 2, 16; RGEL 2; RGSF 2; SATA 27; SSFS 1, 12; TEA; WLIT 4

**Conrad, Robert Arnold**
See Hart, Moss

**Conroy, (Donald) Pat(rick)** 1945- ... **CLC 30, 74**
See also AAYA 8; AITN 1; BPFB 1; CA 85-88; CANR 24, 53; CPW; CSW; DAM NOV, POP; DLB 6; LAIT 5; MTCW 1, 2

**Constant (de Rebecque), (Henri) Benjamin**
1767-1830 .................................... **NCLC 6**
See also DLB 119; EW 4; GFL 1789 to the Present

**Conway, Jill K(er)** 1934- ................. **CLC 152**
See also CA 130; CANR 94

**Conybeare, Charles Augustus**
See Eliot, T(homas) S(tearns)

**Cook, Michael** 1933-1994 ................. **CLC 58**
See also CA 93-96; CANR 68; DLB 53

**Cook, Robin** 1940- .................................. **CLC 14**
See also AAYA 32; BEST 90:2; BPFB 1; CA 111; CANR 41, 90, 109; CPW; DAM POP; HGG; INT CA-111

**Cook, Roy**
See Silverberg, Robert

**Cooke, Elizabeth** 1948- ......................... **CLC 55**
See also CA 129

**Cooke, John Esten** 1830-1886 .......... **NCLC 5**
See also DLB 3, 248; RGAL 4

**Cooke, John Estes**
See Baum, L(yman) Frank

**Cooke, M. E.**
See Creasey, John

**Cooke, Margaret**
See Creasey, John

**Cooke, Rose Terry** 1827-1892 ...... **NCLC 110**
See also DLB 12, 74

**Cook-Lynn, Elizabeth** 1930- ............ **CLC 93; NNAL**
See also CA 133; DAM MULT; DLB 175

**Cooney, Ray** ........................................ **CLC 62**
See also CBD

**Cooper, Douglas** 1960- ........................ **CLC 86**

**Cooper, Henry St. John**
See Creasey, John

**Cooper, J(oan) California** (?)- ........... **CLC 56**
See also AAYA 12; BW 1; CA 125; CANR 55; DAM MULT; DLB 212

**Cooper, James Fenimore**
1789-1851 ....................... **NCLC 1, 27, 54**
See also AAYA 22; AMW; BPFB 1; CDALB 1640-1865; DLB 3, 183, 250, 254; LAIT 1; NFS 9; RGAL 4; SATA 19; TUS; WCH

**Coover, Robert (Lowell)** 1932- ...... **CLC 3, 7, 15, 32, 46, 87, 161; SSC 15**
See also AMWS 5; BPFB 1; CA 45-48; CANR 3, 37, 58; CN 7; DAM NOV; DLB 2, 227; DLBY 1981; MTCW 1, 2; RGAL 4; RGSF 2

**Copeland, Stewart (Armstrong)**
1952- ................................................. **CLC 26**

**Copernicus, Nicolaus** 1473-1543 ......... **LC 45**

**Coppard, A(lfred) E(dgar)**
1878-1957 ................... **SSC 21; TCLC 5**
See also BRWS 8; CA 167; DLB 162; HGG; RGEL 2; RGSF 2; SUFW 1; YABC 1

**Coppee, Francois** 1842-1908 .......... **TCLC 25**
See also CA 170; DLB 217

**Coppola, Francis Ford** 1939- ... **CLC 16, 126**
See also AAYA 39; CA 77-80; CANR 40, 78; DLB 44

**Corbiere, Tristan** 1845-1875 .......... **NCLC 43**
See also DLB 217; GFL 1789 to the Present

**Corcoran, Barbara (Asenath)**
1911- ................................................. **CLC 17**
See also AAYA 14; CA 21-24R; CAAE 191; CAAS 2; CANR 11, 28, 48; CLR 50; DLB 52; JRDA; MAICYA 2; MAICYAS 1; RHW; SAAS 20; SATA 3, 77, 125

**Cordelier, Maurice**
See Giraudoux, Jean(-Hippolyte)

**Corelli, Marie** ................................... **TCLC 51**
See Mackay, Mary
See also DLB 34, 156; RGEL 2; SUFW 1

**Corman, Cid** ........................................... **CLC 9**
See Corman, Sidney
See also CAAS 2; DLB 5, 193

**Corman, Sidney** 1924-
See Corman, Cid
See also CA 85-88; CANR 44; CP 7; DAM POET

**Cormier, Robert (Edmund)**
1925-2000 ................................... **CLC 12, 30**
See also AAYA 3, 19; BYA 1, 2, 6, 8, 9; CA 1-4R; CANR 5, 23, 76, 93; CDALB 1968-1988; CLR 12, 55; DA; DAB; DAC; DAM MST, NOV; DLB 52; EXPN; INT CANR-23; JRDA; LAIT 5; MAICYA 1, 2; MTCW 1, 2; NFS 2; SATA 10, 45, 83; SATA-Obit 122; WYA; YAW

**Corn, Alfred (DeWitt III)** 1943- ....... **CLC 33**
See also CA 179; CAAE 179; CAAS 25; CANR 44; CP 7; CSW; DLB 120; DLBY 1980

**Corneille, Pierre** 1606-1684 ................. **LC 28**
See also DAB; DAM MST; DLB 268; EW 3; GFL Beginnings to 1789; RGWL 2, 3; TWA

**Cornwell, David (John Moore)**
1931- ........................................... **CLC 9, 15**
See le Carre, John
See also CA 5-8R; CANR 13, 33, 59, 107; DAM POP; MTCW 1, 2

**Cornwell, Patricia (Daniels)** 1956- . **CLC 155**
See also AAYA 16; BPFB 1; CA 134; CANR 53; CMW 4; CPW; CSW; DAM POP; MSW; MTCW 1

**Corso, (Nunzio) Gregory** 1930-2001 . **CLC 1, 11; PC 33**
See also AMWS 12; BG 2; CA 5-8R; CANR 41, 76; CP 7; DLB 5, 16, 237; MTCW 1, 2; WP

**Cortazar, Julio** 1914-1984 ... **CLC 2, 3, 5, 10, 13, 15, 33, 34, 92; HLC 1; SSC 7**
See also BPFB 1; CA 21-24R; CANR 12, 32, 81; CDWLB 3; DAM MULT, NOV; DLB 113; EXPS; HW 1, 2; LAW; MTCW 1, 2; RGSF 2; RGWL 2, 3; SSFS 3; TWA; WLIT 1

**Cortes, Hernan** 1485-1547 .................... **LC 31**

**Corvinus, Jakob**
See Raabe, Wilhelm (Karl)

**Corvo, Baron**
See Rolfe, Frederick (William Serafino Austin Lewis Mary)
See also GLL 1; RGEL 2

**Corwin, Cecil**
See Kornbluth, C(yril) M.

**Cosic, Dobrica** 1921- ........................ **CLC 14**
See also CA 138; CDWLB 4; CWW 2; DLB 181

**Costain, Thomas B(ertram)**
1885-1965 ........................................ **CLC 30**
See also BYA 3; CA 5-8R; DLB 9; RHW

**Costantini, Humberto** 1924(?)-1987 . **CLC 49**
See also CA 131; HW 1

**Costello, Elvis** 1954- .......................... **CLC 21**
See also CA 204

**Costenoble, Philostene**
See Ghelderode, Michel de

**Cotes, Cecil V.**
See Duncan, Sara Jeannette

**Cotter, Joseph Seamon Sr.**
1861-1949 ................... **BLC 1; TCLC 28**
See also BW 1; CA 124; DAM MULT; DLB 50

**Couch, Arthur Thomas Quiller**
See Quiller-Couch, Sir Arthur (Thomas)

**Coulton, James**
See Hansen, Joseph

**Couperus, Louis (Marie Anne)**
1863-1923 ...................................... **TCLC 15**
See also RGWL 2, 3

**Coupland, Douglas** 1961- .......... **CLC 85, 133**
See also AAYA 34; CA 142; CANR 57, 90; CCA 1; CPW; DAC; DAM POP

**Court, Wesli**
See Turco, Lewis (Putnam)

**Courtenay, Bryce** 1933- ....................... **CLC 59**
See also CA 138; CPW

**Courtney, Robert**
See Ellison, Harlan (Jay)

**Cousteau, Jacques-Yves** 1910-1997 .. **CLC 30**
See also CA 65-68; CANR 15, 67; MTCW 1; SATA 38, 98

**Coventry, Francis** 1725-1754 ............... **LC 46**

**Coverdale, Miles** c. 1487-1569 ............. **LC 77**
See also DLB 167

**Cowan, Peter (Walkinshaw)** 1914- .... **SSC 28**
See also CA 21-24R; CANR 9, 25, 50, 83; CN 7; DLB 260; RGSF 2

**Coward, Noel (Peirce)** 1899-1973 . **CLC 1, 9, 29, 51**
See also AITN 1; BRWS 2; CA 17-18; CANR 35; CAP 2; CDBLB 1914-1945; DAM DRAM; DFS 3, 6; DLB 10, 245; IDFW 3, 4; MTCW 1, 2; RGEL 2; TEA

**Cowley, Abraham** 1618-1667 ............... **LC 43**
See also BRW 2; DLB 131, 151; PAB; RGEL 2

**Cowley, Malcolm** 1898-1989 ............. **CLC 39**
See also AMWS 2; CA 5-8R; CANR 3, 55; DLB 4, 48; DLBY 1981, 1989; MTCW 1, 2

**Cowper, William** 1731-1800 ..... **NCLC 8, 94; PC 40**
See also BRW 3; DAM POET; DLB 104, 109; RGEL 2

**Cox, William Trevor** 1928-
See Trevor, William
See also CA 9-12R; CANR 4, 37, 55, 76, 102; DAM NOV; INT CANR-37; MTCW 1, 2; TEA

**Coyne, P. J.**
See Masters, Hilary

**Cozzens, James Gould** 1903-1978 . **CLC 1, 4, 11, 92**
See also AMW; BPFB 1; CA 9-12R; CANR 19; CDALB 1941-1968; DLB 9; DLBD 2; DLBY 1984, 1997; MTCW 1, 2; RGAL 4

**Crabbe, George** 1754-1832 .... **NCLC 26, 121**
See also BRW 3; DLB 93; RGEL 2

**Crace, Jim** 1946- ................................ **CLC 157**
See also CA 135; CANR 55, 70; CN 7; DLB 231; INT CA-135

**Craddock, Charles Egbert**
See Murfree, Mary Noailles

**Craig, A. A.**
See Anderson, Poul (William)

**Craik, Mrs.**
See Craik, Dinah Maria (Mulock)
See also RGEL 2

**Craik, Dinah Maria (Mulock)**
1826-1887 ..................................... **NCLC 38**
See Craik, Mrs.; Mulock, Dinah Maria
See also DLB 35, 163; MAICYA 1, 2; SATA 34

**Cram, Ralph Adams** 1863-1942 ..... **TCLC 45**
See also CA 160

**Cranch, Christopher Pearse**
1813-1892 ................................... **NCLC 115**
See also DLB 1, 42, 243

**Crane, (Harold) Hart** 1899-1932 ......... **PC 3; TCLC 2, 5, 80; WLC**
See also AMW; AMWR 2; CA 127; CDALB 1917-1929; DA; DAB; DAC; DAM MST, POET; DLB 4, 48; MTCW 1, 2; RGAL 4; TUS

**Crane, R(onald) S(almon)**
1886-1967 ......................................... **CLC 27**
See also CA 85-88; DLB 63

**Crane, Stephen (Townley)**
1871-1900 ...... **SSC 7, 56; TCLC 11, 17, 32; WLC**
See also AAYA 21; AMW; AMWC 1; BPFB 1; BYA 3; CA 140; CANR 84; CDALB 1865-1917; DA; DAB; DAC; DAM MST, NOV, POET; DLB 12, 54, 78; EXPN; EXPS; LAIT 2; NFS 4; PFS 9; RGAL 4; RGSF 2; SSFS 4; TUS; WYA; YABC 2

**Cranshaw, Stanley**
See Fisher, Dorothy (Frances) Canfield

**Crase, Douglas** 1944- .................... **CLC 58**
See also CA 106
**Crashaw, Richard** 1612(?)-1649 .......... **LC 24**
See also BRW 2; DLB 126; PAB; RGEL 2
**Cratinus** c. 519B.C.-c. 422B.C. ..... **CMLC 54**
**Craven, Margaret** 1901-1980 ............ **CLC 17**
See also BYA 2; CA 103; CCA 1; DAC; LAIT 5
**Crawford, F(rancis) Marion**
1854-1909 ......................... **TCLC 10**
See also CA 168; DLB 71; HGG; RGAL 4; SUFW 1
**Crawford, Isabella Valancy**
1850-1887 ......................... **NCLC 12**
See also DLB 92; RGEL 2
**Crayon, Geoffrey**
See Irving, Washington
**Creasey, John** 1908-1973 ................... **CLC 11**
See Marric, J. J.
See also CA 5-8R; CANR 8, 59; CMW 4; DLB 77; MTCW 1
**Crebillon, Claude Prosper Jolyot de (fils)**
1707-1777 ........................... **LC 1, 28**
See also GFL Beginnings to 1789
**Credo**
See Creasey, John
**Credo, Alvaro J. de**
See Prado (Calvo), Pedro
**Creeley, Robert (White)** 1926- .. **CLC 1, 2, 4, 8, 11, 15, 36, 78**
See also AMWS 4; CA 1-4R; CAAS 10; CANR 23, 43, 89; CP 7; DAM POET; DLB 5, 16, 169; DLBD 17; MTCW 1, 2; RGAL 4; WP
**Crevecoeur, Hector St. John de**
See Crevecoeur, Michel Guillaume Jean de
See also ANW
**Crevecoeur, Michel Guillaume Jean de**
1735-1813 ......................... **NCLC 105**
See Crevecoeur, Hector St. John de
See also AMWS 1; DLB 37
**Crevel, Rene** 1900-1935 ................. **TCLC 112**
See also GLL 2
**Crews, Harry (Eugene)** 1935- ..... **CLC 6, 23, 49**
See also AITN 1; AMWS 11; BPFB 1; CA 25-28R; CANR 20, 57; CN 7; CSW; DLB 6, 143, 185; MTCW 1, 2; RGAL 4
**Crichton, (John) Michael** 1942- .... **CLC 2, 6, 54, 90**
See also AAYA 10; AITN 2; BPFB 1; CA 25-28R; CANR 13, 40, 54, 76; CMW 4; CN 7; CPW; DAM NOV, POP; DLBY 1981; INT CANR-13; JRDA; MTCW 1, 2; SATA 9, 88; SFW 4; YAW
**Crispin, Edmund** ............................. **CLC 22**
See Montgomery, (Robert) Bruce
See also DLB 87; MSW
**Cristofer, Michael** 1945(?)- ................ **CLC 28**
See also CA 152; CAD; CD 5; DAM DRAM; DFS 15; DLB 7
**Croce, Benedetto** 1866-1952 ........... **TCLC 37**
See also CA 155; EW 8
**Crockett, David** 1786-1836 ............... **NCLC 8**
See also DLB 3, 11, 183, 248
**Crockett, Davy**
See Crockett, David
**Crofts, Freeman Wills** 1879-1957 .. **TCLC 55**
See also CA 195; CMW 4; DLB 77; MSW
**Croker, John Wilson** 1780-1857 .... **NCLC 10**
See also DLB 110
**Crommelynck, Fernand** 1885-1970 .. **CLC 75**
See also CA 189
**Cromwell, Oliver** 1599-1658 ............ **LC 43**
**Cronenberg, David** 1943- ................ **CLC 143**
See also CA 138; CCA 1

**Cronin, A(rchibald) J(oseph)**
1896-1981 ......................... **CLC 32**
See also BPFB 1; CA 1-4R; CANR 5; DLB 191; SATA 47; SATA-Obit 25
**Cross, Amanda**
See Heilbrun, Carolyn G(old)
See also BPFB 1; CMW; CPW; MSW
**Crothers, Rachel** 1878-1958 ............ **TCLC 19**
See also CA 194; CAD; CWD; DLB 7, 266; RGAL 4
**Croves, Hal**
See Traven, B.
**Crow Dog, Mary (Ellen)** (?)- ............. **CLC 93**
See Brave Bird, Mary
See also CA 154
**Crowfield, Christopher**
See Stowe, Harriet (Elizabeth) Beecher
**Crowley, Aleister** ............................. **TCLC 7**
See Crowley, Edward Alexander
See also GLL 1
**Crowley, Edward Alexander** 1875-1947
See Crowley, Aleister
See also HGG
**Crowley, John** 1942- .......................... **CLC 57**
See also BPFB 1; CA 61-64; CANR 43, 98; DLBY 1982; SATA 65; SFW 4; SUFW 2
**Crud**
See Crumb, R(obert)
**Crumarums**
See Crumb, R(obert)
**Crumb, R(obert)** 1943- ...................... **CLC 17**
See also CA 106; CANR 107
**Crumbum**
See Crumb, R(obert)
**Crumski**
See Crumb, R(obert)
**Crum the Bum**
See Crumb, R(obert)
**Crunk**
See Crumb, R(obert)
**Crustt**
See Crumb, R(obert)
**Crutchfield, Les**
See Trumbo, Dalton
**Cruz, Victor Hernandez** 1949- ... **HLC 1; PC 37**
See also BW 2; CA 65-68; CAAS 17; CANR 14, 32, 74; CP 7; DAM MULT, POET; DLB 41; DNFS 1; EXPP; HW 1, 2; MTCW 1; PFS 16; WP
**Cryer, Gretchen (Kiger)** 1935- ......... **CLC 21**
See also CA 123
**Csath, Geza** 1887-1919 ................... **TCLC 13**
**Cudlip, David R(ockwell)** 1933- ....... **CLC 34**
See also CA 177
**Cullen, Countee** 1903-1946 .... **BLC 1; HR 2; PC 20; TCLC 4, 37; WLCS**
See also AFAW 2; AMWS 4; BW 1; CA 124; CDALB 1917-1929; DA; DAC; DAM MST, MULT, POET; DLB 4, 48, 51; EXPP; MTCW 1, 2; PFS 3; RGAL 4; SATA 18; WP
**Cum, R.**
See Crumb, R(obert)
**Cummings, Bruce F(rederick)** 1889-1919
See Barbellion, W. N. P.
**Cummings, E(dward) E(stlin)**
1894-1962 .. **CLC 1, 3, 8, 12, 15, 68; PC 5; WLC**
See also AAYA 41; AMW; CA 73-76; CANR 31; CDALB 1929-1941; DA; DAB; DAC; DAM MST, POET; DLB 4, 48; EXPP; MTCW 1, 2; PAB; PFS 1, 3, 12, 13; RGAL 4; TUS; WP
**Cunha, Euclides (Rodrigues Pimenta) da**
1866-1909 ......................... **TCLC 24**
See also LAW; WLIT 1
**Cunningham, E. V.**
See Fast, Howard (Melvin)

**Cunningham, J(ames) V(incent)**
1911-1985 ......................... **CLC 3, 31**
See also CA 1-4R; CANR 1, 72; DLB 5
**Cunningham, Julia (Woolfolk)**
1916- ................................. **CLC 12**
See also CA 9-12R; CANR 4, 19, 36; CWRI 5; JRDA; MAICYA 1, 2; SAAS 2; SATA 1, 26, 132
**Cunningham, Michael** 1952- ............. **CLC 34**
See also CA 136; CANR 96; GLL 2
**Cunninghame Graham, R. B.**
See Cunninghame Graham, Robert (Gallnigad) Bontine
**Cunninghame Graham, Robert (Gallnigad) Bontine** 1852-1936 ................. **TCLC 19**
See Graham, R(obert) B(ontine) Cunninghame
See also CA 184
**Currie, Ellen** 19(?)- ........................... **CLC 44**
**Curtin, Philip**
See Lowndes, Marie Adelaide (Belloc)
**Curtin, Phillip**
See Lowndes, Marie Adelaide (Belloc)
**Curtis, Price**
See Ellison, Harlan (Jay)
**Cusanus, Nicolaus** 1401-1464 ............ **LC 80**
See Nicholas of Cusa
**Cutrate, Joe**
See Spiegelman, Art
**Cynewulf** c. 770- ............................. **CMLC 23**
See also DLB 146; RGEL 2
**Cyrano de Bergerac, Savinien de**
1619-1655 ............................. **LC 65**
See also DLB 268; GFL Beginnings to 1789; RGWL 2, 3
**Czaczkes, Shmuel Yosef Halevi**
See Agnon, S(hmuel) Y(osef Halevi)
**Dabrowska, Maria (Szumska)**
1889-1965 ........................... **CLC 15**
See also CA 106; CDWLB 4; DLB 215
**Dabydeen, David** 1955- ..................... **CLC 34**
See also BW 1; CA 125; CANR 56, 92; CN 7; CP 7
**Dacey, Philip** 1939- ......................... **CLC 51**
See also CA 37-40R; CAAS 17; CANR 14, 32, 64; CP 7; DLB 105
**Dagerman, Stig (Halvard)**
1923-1954 ........................... **TCLC 17**
See also CA 155; DLB 259
**D'Aguiar, Fred** 1960- ....................... **CLC 145**
See also CA 148; CANR 83, 101; CP 7; DLB 157
**Dahl, Roald** 1916-1990 ....... **CLC 1, 6, 18, 79**
See also AAYA 15; BPFB 1; BRWS 4; BYA 5; CA 1-4R; CANR 6, 32, 37, 62; CLR 1, 7, 41; CPW; DAB; DAC; DAM MST, NOV, POP; DLB 139, 255; HGG; JRDA; MAICYA 1, 2; MTCW 1, 2; RGSF 2; SATA 1, 26, 73; SATA-Obit 65; SSFS 4; TEA; YAW
**Dahlberg, Edward** 1900-1977 .. **CLC 1, 7, 14**
See also CA 9-12R; CANR 31, 62; DLB 48; MTCW 1; RGAL 4
**Daitch, Susan** 1954- ....................... **CLC 103**
See also CA 161
**Dale, Colin** .................................... **TCLC 18**
See Lawrence, T(homas) E(dward)
**Dale, George E.**
See Asimov, Isaac
**Dalton, Roque** 1935-1975(?) ..... **HLCS 1; PC 36**
See also CA 176; HW 2
**Daly, Elizabeth** 1878-1967 ................ **CLC 52**
See also CA 23-24; CANR 60; CAP 2; CMW 4
**Daly, Maureen** 1921- ....................... **CLC 17**
See also AAYA 5; BYA 6; CANR 37, 83, 108; JRDA; MAICYA 1, 2; SAAS 1; SATA 2, 129; WYA; YAW

**Damas, Leon-Gontran** 1912-1978 .... **CLC 84**
See also BW 1; CA 125
**Dana, Richard Henry Sr.**
1787-1879 .................................. **NCLC 53**
**Daniel, Samuel** 1562(?)-1619 ............... **LC 24**
See also DLB 62; RGEL 2
**Daniels, Brett**
See Adler, Renata
**Dannay, Frederic** 1905-1982 ............. **CLC 11**
See Queen, Ellery
See also CA 1-4R; CANR 1, 39; CMW 4; DAM POP; DLB 137; MTCW 1
**D'Annunzio, Gabriele** 1863-1938 ... **TCLC 6, 40**
See also CA 155; EW 8; RGWL 2, 3; TWA
**Danois, N. le**
See Gourmont, Remy(-Marie-Charles) de
**Dante** 1265-1321 .... **CMLC 3, 18, 39; PC 21; WLCS**
See also DA; DAB; DAC; DAM MST, POET; EFS 1; EW 1; LAIT 1; RGWL 2, 3; TWA; WP
**d'Antibes, Germain**
See Simenon, Georges (Jacques Christian)
**Danticat, Edwidge** 1969- ........... **CLC 94, 139**
See also AAYA 29; CA 152; CAAE 192; CANR 73; DNFS 1; EXPS; MTCW 1; SSFS 1; YAW
**Danvers, Dennis** 1947- ...................... **CLC 70**
**Danziger, Paula** 1944- ....................... **CLC 21**
See also AAYA 4, 36; BYA 6, 7, 14; CA 115; CANR 37; CLR 20; JRDA; MAICYA 1, 2; SATA 36, 63, 102; SATA-Brief 30; WYA; YAW
**Da Ponte, Lorenzo** 1749-1838 ........ **NCLC 50**
**Dario, Ruben** 1867-1916 ....... **HLC 1; PC 15; TCLC 4**
See also CA 131; CANR 81; DAM MULT; HW 1, 2; LAW; MTCW 1, 2; RGWL 2, 3
**Darley, George** 1795-1846 ................ **NCLC 2**
See also DLB 96; RGEL 2
**Darrow, Clarence (Seward)**
1857-1938 ................................ **TCLC 81**
See also CA 164
**Darwin, Charles** 1809-1882 ............ **NCLC 57**
See also BRWS 7; DLB 57, 166; RGEL 2; TEA; WLIT 4
**Darwin, Erasmus** 1731-1802 ........ **NCLC 106**
See also DLB 93; RGEL 2
**Daryush, Elizabeth** 1887-1977 ....... **CLC 6, 19**
See also CA 49-52; CANR 3, 81; DLB 20
**Das, Kamala** 1934- ................................. **PC 43**
See also CA 101; CANR 27, 59; CP 7; CWP; FW
**Dasgupta, Surendranath**
1887-1952 ................................ **TCLC 81**
See also CA 157
**Dashwood, Edmee Elizabeth Monica de la Pasture** 1890-1943
See Delafield, E. M.
See also CA 154
**da Silva, Antonio Jose**
1705-1739 .................................. **NCLC 114**
See Silva, Jose Asuncion
**Daudet, (Louis Marie) Alphonse**
1840-1897 ................................. **NCLC 1**
See also DLB 123; GFL 1789 to the Present; RGSF 2
**Daumal, Rene** 1908-1944 ................ **TCLC 14**
**Davenant, William** 1606-1668 ............. **LC 13**
See also DLB 58, 126; RGEL 2
**Davenport, Guy (Mattison, Jr.)**
1927- .............. **CLC 6, 14, 38; SSC 16**
See also CA 33-36R; CANR 23, 73; CN 7; CSW; DLB 130
**David, Robert**
See Nezval, Vitezslav

**Davidson, Avram (James)** 1923-1993
See Queen, Ellery
See also CA 101; CANR 26; DLB 8; FANT; SFW 4; SUFW 1, 2
**Davidson, Donald (Grady)**
1893-1968 ........................... **CLC 2, 13, 19**
See also CA 5-8R; CANR 4, 84; DLB 45
**Davidson, Hugh**
See Hamilton, Edmond
**Davidson, John** 1857-1909 .............. **TCLC 24**
See also DLB 19; RGEL 2
**Davidson, Sara** 1943- ......................... **CLC 9**
See also CA 81-84; CANR 44, 68; DLB 185
**Davie, Donald (Alfred)** 1922-1995 .... **CLC 5, 8, 10, 31; PC 29**
See also BRWS 6; CA 1-4R; CAAS 3; CANR 1, 44; CP 7; DLB 27; MTCW 1; RGEL 2
**Davie, Elspeth** 1919-1995 ................... **SSC 52**
See also CA 126; DLB 139
**Davies, Ray(mond Douglas)** 1944- ... **CLC 21**
See also CA 146; CANR 92
**Davies, Rhys** 1901-1978 ..................... **CLC 23**
See also CA 9-12R; CANR 4; DLB 139, 191
**Davies, (William) Robertson**
1913-1995 ....... **CLC 2, 7, 13, 25, 42, 75, 91; WLC**
See Marchbanks, Samuel
See also BEST 89:2; BPFB 1; CA 33-36R; CANR 17, 42, 103; CN 7; CPW; DA; DAB; DAC; DAM MST, NOV, POP; DLB 68; HGG; INT CANR-17; MTCW 1, 2; RGEL 2; TWA
**Davies, Sir John** 1569-1626 ................. **LC 85**
See also DLB 172
**Davies, Walter C.**
See Kornbluth, C(yril) M.
**Davies, William Henry** 1871-1940 ... **TCLC 5**
See also CA 179; DLB 19, 174; RGEL 2
**Da Vinci, Leonardo** 1452-1519 ..... **LC 12, 57, 60**
See also AAYA 40
**Davis, Angela (Yvonne)** 1944- ........... **CLC 77**
See also BW 2, 3; CA 57-60; CANR 10, 81; CSW; DAM MULT; FW
**Davis, B. Lynch**
See Bioy Casares, Adolfo; Borges, Jorge Luis
**Davis, Gordon**
See Hunt, E(verette) Howard, (Jr.)
**Davis, H(arold) L(enoir)** 1896-1960 . **CLC 49**
See also ANW; CA 178; DLB 9, 206; SATA 114
**Davis, Rebecca (Blaine) Harding**
1831-1910 ..................... **SSC 38; TCLC 6**
See also CA 179; DLB 74, 239; FW; NFS 14; RGAL 4; TUS
**Davis, Richard Harding**
1864-1916 ................................ **TCLC 24**
See also CA 179; DLB 12, 23, 78, 79, 189; DLBD 13; RGAL 4
**Davison, Frank Dalby** 1893-1970 ..... **CLC 15**
See also DLB 260
**Davison, Lawrence H.**
See Lawrence, D(avid) H(erbert Richards)
**Davison, Peter (Hubert)** 1928- ......... **CLC 28**
See also CA 9-12R; CAAS 4; CANR 3, 43, 84; CP 7; DLB 5
**Davys, Mary** 1674-1732 .................. **LC 1, 46**
See also DLB 39
**Dawson, (Guy) Fielding (Lewis)**
1930-2002 ............................... **CLC 6**
See also CA 85-88; CANR 108; DLB 130
**Dawson, Peter**
See Faust, Frederick (Schiller)
See also TCWW 2, 2

**Day, Clarence (Shepard, Jr.)**
1874-1935 .................................. **TCLC 25**
See also DLB 11
**Day, John** 1574(?)-1640(?) .................. **LC 70**
See also DLB 62, 170; RGEL 2
**Day, Thomas** 1748-1789 ........................ **LC 1**
See also DLB 39; YABC 1
**Day Lewis, C(ecil)** 1904-1972 . **CLC 1, 6, 10; PC 11**
See Blake, Nicholas
See also BRWS 3; CA 13-16; CANR 34; CAP 1; CWRI 5; DAM POET; DLB 15, 20; MTCW 1, 2; RGEL 2
**Dazai Osamu** .................. **SSC 41; TCLC 11**
See Tsushima, Shuji
See also CA 164; DLB 182; MJW; RGSF 2; RGWL 2, 3; TWA
**de Andrade, Carlos Drummond**
See Drummond de Andrade, Carlos
**de Andrade, Mario** 1892-1945
See Andrade, Mario de
See also CA 178; HW 2
**Deane, Norman**
See Creasey, John
**Deane, Seamus (Francis)** 1940- ...... **CLC 122**
See also CA 118; CANR 42
**de Beauvoir, Simone (Lucie Ernestine Marie Bertrand)**
See Beauvoir, Simone (Lucie Ernestine Marie Bertrand) de
**de Beer, P.**
See Bosman, Herman Charles
**de Brissac, Malcolm**
See Dickinson, Peter (Malcolm)
**de Campos, Alvaro**
See Pessoa, Fernando (Antonio Nogueira)
**de Chardin, Pierre Teilhard**
See Teilhard de Chardin, (Marie Joseph) Pierre
**Dee, John** 1527-1608 ............................ **LC 20**
See also DLB 136, 213
**Deer, Sandra** 1940- ............................. **CLC 45**
See also CA 186
**De Ferrari, Gabriella** 1941- ............... **CLC 65**
See also CA 146
**de Filippo, Eduardo** 1900-1984 ... **TCLC 127**
See also CA 132; MTCW 1; RGWL 2, 3
**Defoe, Daniel** 1660(?)-1731 .. **LC 1, 42; WLC**
See also AAYA 27; BRW 3; BRWR 1; BYA 4; CDBLB 1660-1789; CLR 61; DA; DAB; DAC; DAM MST, NOV; DLB 39, 95, 101; JRDA; LAIT 1; MAICYA 1, 2; NFS 9, 13; RGEL 2; SATA 22; TEA; WCH; WLIT 3
**de Gourmont, Remy(-Marie-Charles)**
See Gourmont, Remy(-Marie-Charles) de
**de Hartog, Jan** 1914- ........................ **CLC 19**
See also CA 1-4R; CANR 1; DFS 12
**de Hostos, E. M.**
See Hostos (y Bonilla), Eugenio Maria de
**de Hostos, Eugenio M.**
See Hostos (y Bonilla), Eugenio Maria de
**Deighton, Len** ................... **CLC 4, 7, 22, 46**
See Deighton, Leonard Cyril
See also AAYA 6; BEST 89:2; BPFB 1; CDBLB 1960 to Present; CMW 4; CN 7; CPW; DLB 87
**Deighton, Leonard Cyril** 1929-
See Deighton, Len
See also CA 9-12R; CANR 19, 33, 68; DAM NOV, POP; MTCW 1, 2
**Dekker, Thomas** 1572(?)-1632 ...... **DC 12; LC 22**
See also CDBLB Before 1660; DAM DRAM; DLB 62, 172; RGEL 2
**de Laclos, Pierre Ambroise Franois**
See Laclos, Pierre Ambroise Francois

**Delafield, E. M.** .............................. **TCLC 61**
See Dashwood, Edmee Elizabeth Monica de la Pasture
See also DLB 34; RHW

**de la Mare, Walter (John)**
1873-1956 . **SSC 14; TCLC 4, 53; WLC**
See also CA 163; CDBLB 1914-1945; CLR 23; CWRI 5; DAB; DAC; DAM MST, POET; DLB 19, 153, 162, 255; EXPP; HGG; MAICYA 1, 2; MTCW 1; RGEL 2; RGSF 2; SATA 16; SUFW 1; TEA; WCH

**de Lamartine, Alphonse (Marie Louis Prat)**
See Lamartine, Alphonse (Marie Louis Prat) de

**Delaney, Franey**
See O'Hara, John (Henry)

**Delaney, Shelagh** 1939- ....................... **CLC 29**
See also CA 17-20R; CANR 30, 67; CBD; CD 5; CDBLB 1960 to Present; CWD; DAM DRAM; DFS 7; DLB 13; MTCW 1

**Delany, Martin Robison**
1812-1885 .................................. **NCLC 93**
See also DLB 50; RGAL 4

**Delany, Mary (Granville Pendarves)**
1700-1788 ........................................ **LC 12**

**Delany, Samuel R(ay), Jr.** 1942- ........ **BLC 1; CLC 8, 14, 38, 141**
See also AAYA 24; AFAW 2; BPFB 1; BW 2, 3; CA 81-84; CANR 27, 43; CN 7; DAM MULT; DLB 8, 33; FANT; MTCW 1, 2; RGAL 4; SATA 92; SCFW; SFW 4; SUFW 2

**De la Ramee, Marie Louise (Ouida)**
1839-1908
See Ouida
See also CA 204; SATA 20

**de la Roche, Mazo** 1879-1961 ........... **CLC 14**
See also CA 85-88; CANR 30; DLB 68; RGEL 2; RHW; SATA 64

**De La Salle, Innocent**
See Hartmann, Sadakichi

**de Laureamont, Comte**
See Lautreamont

**Delbanco, Nicholas (Franklin)**
1942- ................................. **CLC 6, 13, 167**
See also CA 17-20R; CAAE 189; CAAS 2; CANR 29, 55; DLB 6, 234

**del Castillo, Michel** 1933- ................... **CLC 38**
See also CA 109; CANR 77

**Deledda, Grazia (Cosima)**
1875(?)-1936 ............................. **TCLC 23**
See also DLB 264; RGWL 2, 3

**Deleuze, Gilles** 1925-1995 ................ **TCLC 116**

**Delgado, Abelardo (Lalo) B(arrientos)**
1930- ................................................... **HLC 1**
See also CA 131; CAAS 15; CANR 90; DAM MST, MULT; DLB 82; HW 1, 2

**Delibes, Miguel** ............................ **CLC 8, 18**
See Delibes Setien, Miguel

**Delibes Setien, Miguel** 1920-
See Delibes, Miguel
See also CA 45-48; CANR 1, 32; HW 1; MTCW 1

**DeLillo, Don** 1936- ..... **CLC 8, 10, 13, 27, 39, 54, 76, 143**
See also AMWS 6; BEST 89:1; BPFB 1; CA 81-84; CANR 21, 76, 92; CN 7; CPW; DAM NOV, POP; DLB 6, 173; MTCW 1, 2; RGAL 4; TUS

**de Lisser, H. G.**
See De Lisser, H(erbert) G(eorge)
See also DLB 117

**De Lisser, H(erbert) G(eorge)**
1878-1944 ................................... **TCLC 12**
See de Lisser, H. G.
See also BW 2; CA 152

**Deloire, Pierre**
See Peguy, Charles (Pierre)

**Deloney, Thomas** 1543(?)-1600 ............ **LC 41**
See also DLB 167; RGEL 2

**Deloria, Vine (Victor), Jr.** 1933- ...... **CLC 21, 122; NNAL**
See also CA 53-56; CANR 5, 20, 48, 98; DAM MULT; DLB 175; MTCW 1; SATA 21

**del Valle-Inclan, Ramon (Maria)**
See Valle-Inclan, Ramon (Maria) del

**Del Vecchio, John M(ichael)** 1947- .. **CLC 29**
See also CA 110; DLBD 9

**de Man, Paul (Adolph Michel)**
1919-1983 ................................... **CLC 55**
See also CA 128; CANR 61; DLB 67; MTCW 1, 2

**DeMarinis, Rick** 1934- ....................... **CLC 54**
See also CA 57-60, 184; CAAE 184; CAAS 24; CANR 9, 25, 50; DLB 218

**de Maupassant, (Henri Rene Albert) Guy**
See Maupassant, (Henri Rene Albert) Guy de

**Dembry, R. Emmet**
See Murfree, Mary Noailles

**Demby, William** 1922- ......... **BLC 1; CLC 53**
See also BW 1, 3; CA 81-84; CANR 81; DAM MULT; DLB 33

**de Menton, Francisco**
See Chin, Frank (Chew, Jr.)

**Demetrius of Phalerum** c. 307B.C.- ......................... **CMLC 34**

**Demijohn, Thom**
See Disch, Thomas M(ichael)

**Deming, Richard** 1915-1983
See Queen, Ellery
See also CA 9-12R; CANR 3, 94; SATA 24

**Democritus** c. 460B.C.-c. 370B.C. . **CMLC 47**

**de Montaigne, Michel (Eyquem)**
See Montaigne, Michel (Eyquem) de

**de Montherlant, Henry (Milon)**
See Montherlant, Henry (Milon) de

**Demosthenes** 384B.C.-322B.C. ...... **CMLC 13**
See also AW 1; DLB 176; RGWL 2, 3

**de Musset, (Louis Charles) Alfred**
See Musset, (Louis Charles) Alfred de

**de Natale, Francine**
See Malzberg, Barry N(athaniel)

**de Navarre, Marguerite** 1492-1549 ..... **LC 61**
See Marguerite d'Angouleme; Marguerite de Navarre

**Denby, Edwin (Orr)** 1903-1983 ........ **CLC 48**
See also CA 138

**de Nerval, Gerard**
See Nerval, Gerard de

**Denham, John** 1615-1669 ................... **LC 73**
See also DLB 58, 126; RGEL 2

**Denis, Julio**
See Cortazar, Julio

**Denmark, Harrison**
See Zelazny, Roger (Joseph)

**Dennis, John** 1658-1734 ....................... **LC 11**
See also DLB 101; RGEL 2

**Dennis, Nigel (Forbes)** 1912-1989 ....... **CLC 8**
See also CA 25-28R; DLB 13, 15, 233; MTCW 1

**Dent, Lester** 1904(?)-1959 ............... **TCLC 72**
See also CA 161; CMW 4; SFW 4

**De Palma, Brian (Russell)** 1940- ...... **CLC 20**
See also CA 109

**De Quincey, Thomas** 1785-1859 ..... **NCLC 4, 87**
See also BRW 4; CDBLB 1789-1832; DLB 110, 144; RGEL 2

**Deren, Eleanora** 1908(?)-1961
See Deren, Maya
See also CA 192

**Deren, Maya** ............................ **CLC 16, 102**
See Deren, Eleanora

**Derleth, August (William)**
1909-1971 ................................... **CLC 31**
See also BPFB 1; BYA 9, 10; CA 1-4R; CANR 4; CMW 4; DLB 9; DLBD 17; HGG; SATA 5; SUFW 1

**Der Nister** 1884-1950 ...................... **TCLC 56**

**de Routisie, Albert**
See Aragon, Louis

**Derrida, Jacques** 1930- ............... **CLC 24, 87**
See also CA 127; CANR 76, 98; DLB 242; MTCW 1; TWA

**Derry Down Derry**
See Lear, Edward

**Dersonnes, Jacques**
See Simenon, Georges (Jacques Christian)

**Desai, Anita** 1937- ................ **CLC 19, 37, 97**
See also BRWS 5; CA 81-84; CANR 33, 53, 95; CN 7; CWRI 5; DAB; DAM NOV; DLB 271; DNFS 2; FW; MTCW 1, 2; SATA 63, 126

**Desai, Kiran** 1971- ........................... **CLC 119**
See also CA 171

**de Saint-Luc, Jean**
See Glassco, John

**de Saint Roman, Arnaud**
See Aragon, Louis

**Desbordes-Valmore, Marceline**
1786-1859 .................................. **NCLC 97**
See also DLB 217

**Descartes, Rene** 1596-1650 ........... **LC 20, 35**
See also DLB 268; EW 3; GFL Beginnings to 1789

**De Sica, Vittorio** 1901(?)-1974 .......... **CLC 20**

**Desnos, Robert** 1900-1945 ............... **TCLC 22**
See also CA 151; CANR 107; DLB 258

**Destouches, Louis-Ferdinand**
1894-1961 ................................ **CLC 9, 15**
See Celine, Louis-Ferdinand
See also CA 85-88; CANR 28; MTCW 1

**de Tolignac, Gaston**
See Griffith, D(avid Lewelyn) W(ark)

**Deutsch, Babette** 1895-1982 ............. **CLC 18**
See also BYA 3; CA 1-4R; CANR 4, 79; DLB 45; SATA 1; SATA-Obit 33

**Devenant, William** 1606-1649 ............ **LC 13**

**Devkota, Laxmiprasad** 1909-1959 . **TCLC 23**

**De Voto, Bernard (Augustine)**
1897-1955 ................................... **TCLC 29**
See also CA 160; DLB 9, 256

**De Vries, Peter** 1910-1993 ..... **CLC 1, 2, 3, 7, 10, 28, 46**
See also CA 17-20R; CANR 41; DAM NOV; DLB 6; DLBY 1982; MTCW 1, 2

**Dewey, John** 1859-1952 .................. **TCLC 95**
See also CA 170; DLB 246, 270; RGAL 4

**Dexter, John**
See Bradley, Marion Zimmer
See also GLL 1

**Dexter, Martin**
See Faust, Frederick (Schiller)
See also TCWW 2

**Dexter, Pete** 1943- ........................ **CLC 34, 55**
See also BEST 89:2; CA 131; CPW; DAM POP; INT 131; MTCW 1

**Diamano, Silmang**
See Senghor, Leopold Sedar

**Diamond, Neil** 1941- ........................... **CLC 30**
See also CA 108

**Diaz del Castillo, Bernal**
1496-1584 ........................ **HLCS 1; LC 31**
See also LAW

**di Bassetto, Corno**
See Shaw, George Bernard

**Dick, Philip K(indred)** 1928-1982 ... **CLC 10, 30, 72; SSC 57**
See also AAYA 24; BPFB 1; BYA 11; CA 49-52; CANR 2, 16; CPW; DAM NOV, POP; DLB 8; MTCW 1, 2; NFS 5; SCFW; SFW 4

**Dickens, Charles (John Huffam)** 1812-1870 .... **NCLC 3, 8, 18, 26, 37, 50, 86, 105, 113; SSC 17, 49; WLC**
See also AAYA 23; BRW 5; BYA 1, 2, 3, 13, 14; CDBLB 1832-1890; CMW 4; DA; DAB; DAC; DAM MST, NOV; DLB 21, 55, 70, 159, 166; EXPN; HGG; JRDA; LAIT 1, 2; MAICYA 1, 2; NFS 4, 5, 10, 14; RGEL 2; RGSF 2; SATA 15; SUFW 1; TEA; WCH; WLIT 4; WYA

**Dickey, James (Lafayette)** 1923-1997 .... **CLC 1, 2, 4, 7, 10, 15, 47, 109; PC 40**
See also AITN 1, 2; AMWS 4; BPFB 1; CA 9-12R; CABS 2; CANR 10, 48, 61, 105; CDALB 1968-1988; CP 7; CPW; CSW; DAM NOV, POET, POP; DLB 5, 193; DLBD 7; DLBY 1982, 1993, 1996, 1997, 1998; INT CANR-10; MTCW 1, 2; NFS 9; PFS 6, 11; RGAL 4; TUS

**Dickey, William** 1928-1994 .......... **CLC 3, 28**
See also CA 9-12R; CANR 24, 79; DLB 5

**Dickinson, Charles** 1951- ................ **CLC 49**
See also CA 128

**Dickinson, Emily (Elizabeth)** 1830-1886 ... **NCLC 21, 77; PC 1; WLC**
See also AAYA 22; AMW; AMWR 1; CDALB 1865-1917; DA; DAB; DAC; DAM MST, POET; DLB 1, 243; EXPP; MAWW; PAB; PFS 1, 2, 3, 4, 5, 6, 8, 10, 11, 13, 16; RGAL 4; SATA 29; TUS; WP; WYA

**Dickinson, Mrs. Herbert Ward**
See Phelps, Elizabeth Stuart

**Dickinson, Peter (Malcolm)** 1927- .. **CLC 12, 35**
See also AAYA 9; BYA 5; CA 41-44R; CANR 31, 58, 88; CLR 29; CMW 4; DLB 87, 161; JRDA; MAICYA 1, 2; SATA 5, 62, 95; SFW 4; WYA; YAW

**Dickson, Carr**
See Carr, John Dickson

**Dickson, Carter**
See Carr, John Dickson

**Diderot, Denis** 1713-1784 ..................... **LC 26**
See also EW 4; GFL Beginnings to 1789; RGWL 2, 3

**Didion, Joan** 1934- . **CLC 1, 3, 8, 14, 32, 129**
See also AITN 1; AMWS 4; CA 5-8R; CANR 14, 52, 76; CDALB 1968-1988; CN 7; DAM NOV; DLB 2, 173, 185; DLBY 1981, 1986; MAWW; MTCW 1, 2; NFS 3; RGAL 4; TCWW 2; TUS

**Dietrich, Robert**
See Hunt, E(verette) Howard, (Jr.)

**Difusa, Pati**
See Almodovar, Pedro

**Dillard, Annie** 1945- .............. **CLC 9, 60, 115**
See also AAYA 6, 43; AMWS 6; ANW; CA 49-52; CANR 3, 43, 62, 90; DAM NOV; DLB 275; DLBY 1980; LAIT 4, 5; MTCW 1; NCFS 1; RGAL 4; SATA 10; TUS

**Dillard, R(ichard) H(enry) W(ilde)** 1937- ............................................. **CLC 5**
See also CA 21-24R; CAAS 7; CANR 10; CP 7; CSW; DLB 5, 244

**Dillon, Eilis** 1920-1994 ....................... **CLC 17**
See also CA 9-12R, 182; CAAE 182; CAAS 3; CANR 4, 38, 78; CLR 26; MAICYA 1, 2; MAICYAS 1; SATA 2, 74; SATA-Essay 105; SATA-Obit 83; YAW

**Dimont, Penelope**
See Mortimer, Penelope (Ruth)

**Dinesen, Isak** .......... **CLC 10, 29, 95; SSC 7**
See Blixen, Karen (Christentze Dinesen)
See also EW 10; EXPS; FW; HGG; LAIT 3; MTCW 1; NCFS 2; NFS 9; RGSF 2; RGWL 2, 3; SSFS 3, 6, 13; WLIT 2

**Ding Ling** ........................................ **CLC 68**
See Chiang, Pin-chin
See also RGWL 3

**Diphusa, Patty**
See Almodovar, Pedro

**Disch, Thomas M(ichael)** 1940- ... **CLC 7, 36**
See also AAYA 17; BPFB 1; CA 21-24R; CAAS 4; CANR 17, 36, 54, 89; CLR 18; CP 7; DLB 8; HGG; MAICYA 1, 2; MTCW 1, 2; SAAS 15; SATA 92; SCFW; SFW 4; SUFW 2

**Disch, Tom**
See Disch, Thomas M(ichael)

**d'Isly, Georges**
See Simenon, Georges (Jacques Christian)

**Disraeli, Benjamin** 1804-1881 ... **NCLC 2, 39, 79**
See also BRW 4; DLB 21, 55; RGEL 2

**Ditcum, Steve**
See Crumb, R(obert)

**Dixon, Paige**
See Corcoran, Barbara (Asenath)

**Dixon, Stephen** 1936- ......... **CLC 52; SSC 16**
See also AMWS 12; CA 89-92; CANR 17, 40, 54, 91; CN 7; DLB 130

**Doak, Annie**
See Dillard, Annie

**Dobell, Sydney Thompson** 1824-1874 .................................. **NCLC 43**
See also DLB 32; RGEL 2

**Doblin, Alfred** ................................ **TCLC 13**
See Doeblin, Alfred
See also CDWLB 2; RGWL 2, 3

**Dobrolyubov, Nikolai Alexandrovich** 1836-1861 ................................... **NCLC 5**

**Dobson, Austin** 1840-1921 .............. **TCLC 79**
See also DLB 35, 144

**Dobyns, Stephen** 1941- ...................... **CLC 37**
See also CA 45-48; CANR 2, 18, 99; CMW 4; CP 7

**Doctorow, E(dgar) L(aurence)** 1931- ....... **CLC 6, 11, 15, 18, 37, 44, 65, 113**
See also AAYA 22; AITN 2; AMWS 4; BEST 89:3; BPFB 1; CA 45-48; CANR 2, 33, 51, 76, 97; CDALB 1968-1988; CN 7; CPW; DAM NOV, POP; DLB 2, 28, 173; DLBY 1980; LAIT 3; MTCW 1, 2; NFS 6; RGAL 4; RHW; TUS

**Dodgson, Charles L(utwidge)** 1832-1898
See Carroll, Lewis
See also CLR 2; DA; DAB; DAC; DAM MST, NOV, POET; MAICYA 1, 2; SATA 100; YABC 2

**Dodson, Owen (Vincent)** 1914-1983 .. **BLC 1; CLC 79**
See also BW 1; CA 65-68; CANR 24; DAM MULT; DLB 76

**Doeblin, Alfred** 1878-1957 .............. **TCLC 13**
See Doblin, Alfred
See also CA 141; DLB 66

**Doerr, Harriet** 1910- ......................... **CLC 34**
See also CA 122; CANR 47; INT 122

**Domecq, H(onorio Bustos)**
See Bioy Casares, Adolfo

**Domecq, H(onorio) Bustos**
See Bioy Casares, Adolfo; Borges, Jorge Luis

**Domini, Rey**
See Lorde, Audre (Geraldine)
See also GLL 1

**Dominique**
See Proust, (Valentin-Louis-George-Eugene-)Marcel

**Don, A**
See Stephen, Sir Leslie

**Donaldson, Stephen R(eeder)** 1947- ....................................... **CLC 46, 138**
See also AAYA 36; BPFB 1; CA 89-92; CANR 13, 55, 99; CPW; DAM POP; FANT; INT CANR-13; SATA 121; SFW 4; SUFW 1, 2

**Donleavy, J(ames) P(atrick)** 1926- .... **CLC 1, 4, 6, 10, 45**
See also AITN 2; BPFB 1; CA 9-12R; CANR 24, 49, 62, 80; CBD; CD 5; CN 7; DLB 6, 173; INT CANR-24; MTCW 1, 2; RGAL 4

**Donne, John** 1572-1631 ..... **LC 10, 24; PC 1, 43; WLC**
See also BRW 1; BRWR 2; CDBLB Before 1660; DA; DAB; DAC; DAM MST, POET; DLB 121, 151; EXPP; PAB; PFS 2, 11; RGEL 2; TEA; WLIT 3; WP

**Donnell, David** 1939(?)- ...................... **CLC 34**
See also CA 197

**Donoghue, P. S.**
See Hunt, E(verette) Howard, (Jr.)

**Donoso (Yanez), Jose** 1924-1996 ... **CLC 4, 8, 11, 32, 99; HLC 1; SSC 34**
See also CA 81-84; CANR 32, 73; CDWLB 3; DAM MULT; DLB 113; HW 1, 2; LAW; LAWS 1; MTCW 1, 2; RGSF 2; WLIT 1

**Donovan, John** 1928-1992 ................. **CLC 35**
See also AAYA 20; CA 97-100; CLR 3; MAICYA 1, 2; SATA 72; SATA-Brief 29; YAW

**Don Roberto**
See Cunninghame Graham, Robert (Gallnigad) Bontine

**Doolittle, Hilda** 1886-1961 . **CLC 3, 8, 14, 31, 34, 73; PC 5; WLC**
See H. D.
See also AMWS 1; CA 97-100; CANR 35; DA; DAC; DAM MST, POET; DLB 4, 45; FW; GLL 1; MAWW; MTCW 1, 2; PFS 6; RGAL 4

**Doppo, Kunikida** ............................. **TCLC 99**
See Kunikida Doppo

**Dorfman, Ariel** 1942- .... **CLC 48, 77; HLC 1**
See also CA 130; CANR 67, 70; CWW 2; DAM MULT; DFS 4; HW 1, 2; INT CA-130; WLIT 1

**Dorn, Edward (Merton)** 1929-1999 ............................................. **CLC 10, 18**
See also CA 93-96; CANR 42, 79; CP 7; DLB 5; INT 93-96; WP

**Dor-Ner, Zvi** ...................................... **CLC 70**

**Dorris, Michael (Anthony)** 1945-1997 .................... **CLC 109; NNAL**
See also AAYA 20; BEST 90:1; BYA 12; CA 102; CANR 19, 46, 75; CLR 58; DAM MULT, NOV; DLB 175; LAIT 5; MTCW 2; NFS 3; RGAL 4; SATA 75; SATA-Obit 94; TCWW 2; YAW

**Dorris, Michael A.**
See Dorris, Michael (Anthony)

**Dorsan, Luc**
See Simenon, Georges (Jacques Christian)

**Dorsange, Jean**
See Simenon, Georges (Jacques Christian)

**Dos Passos, John (Roderigo)** 1896-1970 ... **CLC 1, 4, 8, 11, 15, 25, 34, 82; WLC**
See also AMW; BPFB 1; CA 1-4R; CANR 3; CDALB 1929-1941; DA; DAB; DAC; DAM MST, NOV; DLB 4, 9; DLBD 1, 15; DLBY 1996; MTCW 1, 2; NFS 14; RGAL 4; TUS

**Dossage, Jean**
See Simenon, Georges (Jacques Christian)

**Dostoevsky, Fedor Mikhailovich**
1821-1881 .. **NCLC 2, 7, 21, 33, 43, 119; SSC 2, 33, 44; WLC**
See Dostoevsky, Fyodor
See also AAYA 40; DA; DAB; DAC; DAM MST, NOV; EW 7; EXPN; NFS 3, 8; RGSF 2; RGWL 2, 3; SSFS 8; TWA

**Dostoevsky, Fyodor**
See Dostoevsky, Fedor Mikhailovich
See also DLB 238

**Doughty, Charles M(ontagu)**
1843-1926 ................................. **TCLC 27**
See also CA 178; DLB 19, 57, 174

**Douglas, Ellen** ................................. **CLC 73**
See Haxton, Josephine Ayres; Williamson, Ellen Douglas
See also CN 7; CSW

**Douglas, Gavin** 1475(?)-1522 ............... **LC 20**
See also DLB 132; RGEL 2

**Douglas, George**
See Brown, George Douglas
See also RGEL 2

**Douglas, Keith (Castellain)**
1920-1944 ................................. **TCLC 40**
See also BRW 7; CA 160; DLB 27; PAB; RGEL 2

**Douglas, Leonard**
See Bradbury, Ray (Douglas)

**Douglas, Michael**
See Crichton, (John) Michael

**Douglas, (George) Norman**
1868-1952 ................................. **TCLC 68**
See also BRW 6; CA 157; DLB 34, 195; RGEL 2

**Douglas, William**
See Brown, George Douglas

**Douglass, Frederick** 1817(?)-1895 ..... **BLC 1; NCLC 7, 55; WLC**
See also AFAW 1, 2; AMWC 1; AMWS 3; CDALB 1640-1865; DA; DAC; DAM MST, MULT; DLB 1, 43, 50, 79, 243; FW; LAIT 2; NCFS 2; RGAL 4; SATA 29

**Dourado, (Waldomiro Freitas) Autran**
1926- ................................. **CLC 23, 60**
See also CA 25-28R, 179; CANR 34, 81; DLB 145; HW 2

**Dourado, Waldomiro Autran**
See Dourado, (Waldomiro Freitas) Autran
See also CA 179

**Dove, Rita (Frances)** 1952- . **BLCS; CLC 50, 81; PC 6**
See also AAYA 46; AMWS 4; BW 2; CA 109; CAAS 19; CANR 27, 42, 68, 76, 97; CDALBS; CP 7; CSW; CWP; DAM MULT, POET; DLB 120; EXPP; MTCW 1; PFS 1, 15; RGAL 4

**Doveglion**
See Villa, Jose Garcia

**Dowell, Coleman** 1925-1985 .............. **CLC 60**
See also CA 25-28R; CANR 10; DLB 130; GLL 2

**Dowson, Ernest (Christopher)**
1867-1900 ................................. **TCLC 4**
See also CA 150; DLB 19, 135; RGEL 2

**Doyle, A. Conan**
See Doyle, Sir Arthur Conan

**Doyle, Sir Arthur Conan**
1859-1930 ....... **SSC 12; TCLC 7; WLC**
See Conan Doyle, Arthur
See also AAYA 14; BRWS 2; CA 122; CDBLB 1890-1914; CMW 4; DA; DAB; DAC; DAM MST, NOV; DLB 18, 70, 156, 178; EXPS; HGG; LAIT 2; MSW; MTCW 1, 2; RGEL 2; RGSF 2; RHW; SATA 24; SCFW 2; SFW 4; SSFS 2; TEA; WCH; WLIT 4; WYA; YAW

**Doyle, Conan**
See Doyle, Sir Arthur Conan

**Doyle, John**
See Graves, Robert (von Ranke)

**Doyle, Roddy** 1958(?)- ....................... **CLC 81**
See also AAYA 14; BRWS 5; CA 143; CANR 73; CN 7; DLB 194

**Doyle, Sir A. Conan**
See Doyle, Sir Arthur Conan

**Dr. A**
See Asimov, Isaac; Silverstein, Alvin; Silverstein, Virginia B(arbara Opshelor)

**Drabble, Margaret** 1939- ...... **CLC 2, 3, 5, 8, 10, 22, 53, 129**
See also BRWS 4; CA 13-16R; CANR 18, 35, 63, 112; CDBLB 1960 to Present; CN 7; CPW; DAB; DAC; DAM MST, NOV, POP; DLB 14, 155, 231; FW; MTCW 1, 2; RGEL 2; SATA 48; TEA

**Drapier, M. B.**
See Swift, Jonathan

**Drayham, James**
See Mencken, H(enry) L(ouis)

**Drayton, Michael** 1563-1631 .................. **LC 8**
See also DAM POET; DLB 121; RGEL 2

**Dreadstone, Carl**
See Campbell, (John) Ramsey

**Dreiser, Theodore (Herman Albert)**
1871-1945 .... **SSC 30; TCLC 10, 18, 35, 83; WLC**
See also AMW; AMWR 2; CA 132; CDALB 1865-1917; DA; DAC; DAM MST, NOV; DLB 9, 12, 102, 137; DLBD 1; LAIT 2; MTCW 1, 2; NFS 8; RGAL 4; TUS

**Drexler, Rosalyn** 1926- ...................... **CLC 2, 6**
See also CA 81-84; CAD; CANR 68; CD 5; CWD

**Dreyer, Carl Theodor** 1889-1968 ...... **CLC 16**

**Drieu la Rochelle, Pierre(-Eugene)**
1893-1945 ................................. **TCLC 21**
See also DLB 72; GFL 1789 to the Present

**Drinkwater, John** 1882-1937 .......... **TCLC 57**
See also CA 149; DLB 10, 19, 149; RGEL 2

**Drop Shot**
See Cable, George Washington

**Droste-Hulshoff, Annette Freiin von**
1797-1848 ................................. **NCLC 3**
See also CDWLB 2; DLB 133; RGSF 2; RGWL 2, 3

**Drummond, Walter**
See Silverberg, Robert

**Drummond, William Henry**
1854-1907 ................................. **TCLC 25**
See also CA 160; DLB 92

**Drummond de Andrade, Carlos**
1902-1987 ................................. **CLC 18**
See Andrade, Carlos Drummond de
See also CA 132; LAW

**Drummond of Hawthornden, William**
1585-1649 ................................. **LC 83**
See also DLB 121, 213; RGEL 2

**Drury, Allen (Stuart)** 1918-1998 ....... **CLC 37**
See also CA 57-60; CANR 18, 52; CN 7; INT CANR-18

**Dryden, John** 1631-1700 ..... **DC 3; LC 3, 21; PC 25; WLC**
See also BRW 2; CDBLB 1660-1789; DA; DAB; DAC; DAM DRAM, MST, POET; DLB 80, 101, 131; EXPP; IDTP; RGEL 2; TEA; WLIT 3

**Duberman, Martin (Bauml)** 1930- ..... **CLC 8**
See also CA 1-4R; CAD; CANR 2, 63; CD 5

**Dubie, Norman (Evans)** 1945- .......... **CLC 36**
See also CA 69-72; CANR 12; CP 7; DLB 120; PFS 12

**Du Bois, W(illiam) E(dward) B(urghardt)**
1868-1963 ..... **BLC 1; CLC 1, 2, 13, 64, 96; HR 2; WLC**
See also AAYA 40; AFAW 1, 2; AMWC 1; AMWS 2; BW 1, 3; CA 85-88; CANR 34, 82; CDALB 1865-1917; DA; DAC; DAM MST, MULT, NOV; DLB 47, 50, 91, 246; EXPP; LAIT 2; MTCW 1, 2; NCFS 1; PFS 13; RGAL 4; SATA 42

**Dubus, Andre** 1936-1999 ..... **CLC 13, 36, 97; SSC 15**
See also AMWS 7; CA 21-24R; CANR 17; CN 7; CSW; DLB 130; INT CANR-17; RGAL 4; SSFS 10

**Duca Minimo**
See D'Annunzio, Gabriele

**Ducharme, Rejean** 1941- ................... **CLC 74**
See also DLB 60

**Duchen, Claire** ................................. **CLC 65**

**Duclos, Charles Pinot-** 1704-1772 ......... **LC 1**
See also GFL Beginnings to 1789

**Dudek, Louis** 1918- ....................... **CLC 11, 19**
See also CA 45-48; CAAS 14; CANR 1; CP 7; DLB 88

**Duerrenmatt, Friedrich** 1921-1990 ... **CLC 1, 4, 8, 11, 15, 43, 102**
See Durrenmatt, Friedrich
See also CA 17-20R; CANR 33; CMW 4; DAM DRAM; DLB 69, 124; MTCW 1, 2

**Duffy, Bruce** 1953(?)- ......................... **CLC 50**
See also CA 172

**Duffy, Maureen** 1933- ....................... **CLC 37**
See also CA 25-28R; CANR 33, 68; CBD; CN 7; CP 7; CWD; CWP; DFS 15; DLB 14; FW; MTCW 1

**Du Fu**
See Tu Fu
See also RGWL 2, 3

**Dugan, Alan** 1923- ........................... **CLC 2, 6**
See also CA 81-84; CP 7; DLB 5; PFS 10

**du Gard, Roger Martin**
See Martin du Gard, Roger

**Duhamel, Georges** 1884-1966 ............. **CLC 8**
See also CA 81-84; CANR 35; DLB 65; GFL 1789 to the Present; MTCW 1

**Dujardin, Edouard (Emile Louis)**
1861-1949 ................................. **TCLC 13**
See also DLB 123

**Duke, Raoul**
See Thompson, Hunter S(tockton)

**Dulles, John Foster** 1888-1959 ....... **TCLC 72**
See also CA 149

**Dumas, Alexandre (pere)**
1802-1870 ............... **NCLC 11, 71; WLC**
See also AAYA 22; BYA 3; DA; DAB; DAC; DAM MST, NOV; DLB 119, 192; EW 6; GFL 1789 to the Present; LAIT 1, 2; NFS 14; RGWL 2, 3; SATA 18; TWA; WCH

**Dumas, Alexandre (fils)** 1824-1895 ....... **DC 1; NCLC 9**
See also DLB 192; GFL 1789 to the Present; RGWL 2, 3

**Dumas, Claudine**
See Malzberg, Barry N(athaniel)

**Dumas, Henry L.** 1934-1968 ......... **CLC 6, 62**
See also BW 1; CA 85-88; DLB 41; RGAL 4

**du Maurier, Daphne** 1907-1989 .. **CLC 6, 11, 59; SSC 18**
See also AAYA 37; BPFB 1; BRWS 3; CA 5-8R; CANR 6, 55; CMW 4; CPW; DAB; DAC; DAM MST, POP; DLB 191; HGG; LAIT 3; MSW; MTCW 1, 2; NFS 12; RGEL 2; RGSF 2; RHW; SATA 27; SATA-Obit 60; SSFS 14, 16; TEA

**Du Maurier, George** 1834-1896 ..... **NCLC 86**
See also DLB 153, 178; RGEL 2

**Dunbar, Paul Laurence** 1872-1906 ... **BLC 1; PC 5; SSC 8; TCLC 2, 12; WLC**
See also AFAW 1, 2; AMWS 2; BW 1, 3; CA 124; CANR 79; CDALB 1865-1917; DA; DAC; DAM MST, MULT, POET; DLB 50, 54, 78; EXPP; RGAL 4; SATA 34

**Dunbar, William** 1460(?)-1520(?) ........ **LC 20**
See also BRWS 8; DLB 132, 146; RGEL 2

**Duncan, Dora Angela**
See Duncan, Isadora

**Duncan, Isadora** 1877(?)-1927 ....... **TCLC 68**
See also CA 149

**Duncan, Lois** 1934- ............................. **CLC 26**
See also AAYA 4, 34; BYA 6, 8; CA 1-4R; CANR 2, 23, 36, 111; CLR 29; JRDA; MAICYA 1, 2; MAICYAS 1; SAAS 2; SATA 1, 36, 75, 133; WYA; YAW

**Duncan, Robert (Edward)**
1919-1988 .... **CLC 1, 2, 4, 7, 15, 41, 55; PC 2**
See also BG 2; CA 9-12R; CANR 28, 62; DAM POET; DLB 5, 16, 193; MTCW 1, 2; PFS 13; RGAL 4; WP

**Duncan, Sara Jeannette**
1861-1922 .................................. **TCLC 60**
See also CA 157; DLB 92

**Dunlap, William** 1766-1839 .............. **NCLC 2**
See also DLB 30, 37, 59; RGAL 4

**Dunn, Douglas (Eaglesham)** 1942- .... **CLC 6, 40**
See also CA 45-48; CANR 2, 33; CP 7; DLB 40; MTCW 1

**Dunn, Katherine (Karen)** 1945- ....... **CLC 71**
See also CA 33-36R; CANR 72; HGG; MTCW 1

**Dunn, Stephen (Elliott)** 1939- ........... **CLC 36**
See also AMWS 11; CA 33-36R; CANR 12, 48, 53, 105; CP 7; DLB 105

**Dunne, Finley Peter** 1867-1936 ...... **TCLC 28**
See also CA 178; DLB 11, 23; RGAL 4

**Dunne, John Gregory** 1932- ............. **CLC 28**
See also CA 25-28R; CANR 14, 50; CN 7; DLBY 1980

**Dunsany, Lord** ......................... **TCLC 2, 59**
See Dunsany, Edward John Moreton Drax Plunkett
See also DLB 77, 153, 156, 255; FANT; IDTP; RGEL 2; SFW 4; SUFW 1

**Dunsany, Edward John Moreton Drax Plunkett** 1878-1957
See Dunsany, Lord
See also CA 148; DLB 10; MTCW 1

**du Perry, Jean**
See Simenon, Georges (Jacques Christian)

**Durang, Christopher (Ferdinand)**
1949- .................................... **CLC 27, 38**
See also CA 105; CAD; CANR 50, 76; CD 5; MTCW 1

**Duras, Marguerite** 1914-1996 . **CLC 3, 6, 11, 20, 34, 40, 68, 100; SSC 40**
See also BPFB 1; CA 25-28R; CANR 50; CWW 2; DLB 83; GFL 1789 to the Present; IDFW 4; MTCW 1, 2; RGWL 2, 3; TWA

**Durban, (Rosa) Pam** 1947- ............... **CLC 39**
See also CA 123; CANR 98; CSW

**Durcan, Paul** 1944- ...................... **CLC 43, 70**
See also CA 134; CP 7; DAM POET

**Durkheim, Emile** 1858-1917 ........... **TCLC 55**

**Durrell, Lawrence (George)**
1912-1990 ..... **CLC 1, 4, 6, 8, 13, 27, 41**
See also BPFB 1; BRWS 1; CA 9-12R; CANR 40, 77; CDBLB 1945-1960; DAM NOV; DLB 15, 27, 204; DLBY 1990; MTCW 1, 2; RGEL 2; SFW 4; TEA

**Durrenmatt, Friedrich**
See Duerrenmatt, Friedrich
See also CDWLB 2; EW 13; RGWL 2, 3

**Dutt, Michael Madhusudan**
1824-1873 ................................ **NCLC 118**

**Dutt, Toru** 1856-1877 ...................... **NCLC 29**
See also DLB 240

**Dwight, Timothy** 1752-1817 .......... **NCLC 13**
See also DLB 37; RGAL 4

**Dworkin, Andrea** 1946- ............... **CLC 43, 123**
See also CA 77-80; CAAS 21; CANR 16, 39, 76, 96; FW; GLL 1; INT CANR-16; MTCW 1, 2

**Dwyer, Deanna**
See Koontz, Dean R(ay)

**Dwyer, K. R.**
See Koontz, Dean R(ay)

**Dwyer, Thomas A.** 1923- ................. **CLC 114**
See also CA 115

**Dybek, Stuart** 1942- .......... **CLC 114; SSC 55**
See also CA 97-100; CANR 39; DLB 130

**Dye, Richard**
See De Voto, Bernard (Augustine)

**Dyer, Geoff** 1958- ............................. **CLC 149**
See also CA 125; CANR 88

**Dylan, Bob** 1941- .... **CLC 3, 4, 6, 12, 77; PC 37**
See also CA 41-44R; CANR 108; CP 7; DLB 16

**Dyson, John** 1943- ............................. **CLC 70**
See also CA 144

**E. V. L.**
See Lucas, E(dward) V(errall)

**Eagleton, Terence (Francis)** 1943- .. **CLC 63, 132**
See also CA 57-60; CANR 7, 23, 68; DLB 242; MTCW 1, 2

**Eagleton, Terry**
See Eagleton, Terence (Francis)

**Early, Jack**
See Scoppettone, Sandra
See also GLL 1

**East, Michael**
See West, Morris L(anglo)

**Eastaway, Edward**
See Thomas, (Philip) Edward

**Eastlake, William (Derry)**
1917-1997 .................................... **CLC 8**
See also CA 5-8R; CAAS 1; CANR 5, 63; CN 7; DLB 6, 206; INT CANR-5; TCWW 2

**Eastman, Charles A(lexander)**
1858-1939 .................... **NNAL; TCLC 55**
See also CA 179; CANR 91; DAM MULT; DLB 175; YABC 1

**Eberhart, Richard (Ghormley)**
1904- ........................... **CLC 3, 11, 19, 56**
See also AMW; CA 1-4R; CANR 2; CDALB 1941-1968; CP 7; DAM POET; DLB 48; MTCW 1; RGAL 4

**Eberstadt, Fernanda** 1960- ............... **CLC 39**
See also CA 136; CANR 69

**Echegaray (y Eizaguirre), Jose (Maria Waldo)** 1832-1916 .... **HLCS 1; TCLC 4**
See also CANR 32; HW 1; MTCW 1

**Echeverria, (Jose) Esteban (Antonino)**
1805-1851 .................................. **NCLC 18**
See also LAW

**Echo**
See Proust, (Valentin-Louis-George-Eugene-)Marcel

**Eckert, Allan W.** 1931- ..................... **CLC 17**
See also AAYA 18; BYA 2; CA 13-16R; CANR 14, 45; INT CANR-14; MAICYA 2; MAICYAS 1; SAAS 21; SATA 29, 91; SATA-Brief 27

**Eckhart, Meister** 1260(?)-1327(?) ... **CMLC 9**
See also DLB 115

**Eckmar, F. R.**
See de Hartog, Jan

**Eco, Umberto** 1932- ............ **CLC 28, 60, 142**
See also BEST 90:1; BPFB 1; CA 77-80; CANR 12, 33, 55, 110; CPW; CWW 2; DAM NOV, POP; DLB 196, 242; MSW; MTCW 1, 2; RGWL 3

**Eddison, E(ric) R(ucker)**
1882-1945 .................................. **TCLC 15**
See also CA 156; DLB 255; FANT; SFW 4; SUFW 1

**Eddy, Mary (Ann Morse) Baker**
1821-1910 .................................. **TCLC 71**
See also CA 174

**Edel, (Joseph) Leon** 1907-1997 .. **CLC 29, 34**
See also CA 1-4R; CANR 1, 22, 112; DLB 103; INT CANR-22

**Eden, Emily** 1797-1869 .................... **NCLC 10**

**Edgar, David** 1948- ............................. **CLC 42**
See also CA 57-60; CANR 12, 61, 112; CBD; CD 5; DAM DRAM; DFS 15; DLB 13, 233; MTCW 1

**Edgerton, Clyde (Carlyle)** 1944- ...... **CLC 39**
See also AAYA 17; CA 134; CANR 64; CSW; INT 134; YAW

**Edgeworth, Maria** 1768-1849 .... **NCLC 1, 51**
See also BRWS 3; DLB 116, 159, 163; FW; RGEL 2; SATA 21; TEA; WLIT 3

**Edmonds, Paul**
See Kuttner, Henry

**Edmonds, Walter D(umaux)**
1903-1998 .................................. **CLC 35**
See also BYA 2; CA 5-8R; CANR 2; CWRI 5; DLB 9; LAIT 1; MAICYA 1; RHW; SAAS 4; SATA 1, 27; SATA-Obit 99

**Edmondson, Wallace**
See Ellison, Harlan (Jay)

**Edson, Russell** 1935- ......................... **CLC 13**
See also CA 33-36R; DLB 244; WP

**Edwards, Bronwen Elizabeth**
See Rose, Wendy

**Edwards, G(erald) B(asil)**
1899-1976 .................................. **CLC 25**
See also CA 201

**Edwards, Gus** 1939- ........................... **CLC 43**
See also CA 108; INT 108

**Edwards, Jonathan** 1703-1758 ........ **LC 7, 54**
See also AMW; DA; DAC; DAM MST; DLB 24, 270; RGAL 4; TUS

**Efron, Marina Ivanovna Tsvetaeva**
See Tsvetaeva (Efron), Marina (Ivanovna)

**Egoyan, Atom** 1960- ......................... **CLC 151**
See also CA 157

**Ehle, John (Marsden, Jr.)** 1925- ...... **CLC 27**
See also CA 9-12R; CSW

**Ehrenbourg, Ilya (Grigoryevich)**
See Ehrenburg, Ilya (Grigoryevich)

**Ehrenburg, Ilya (Grigoryevich)**
1891-1967 ....................... **CLC 18, 34, 62**
See Erenburg, Il'ia Grigor'evich
See also CA 102

**Ehrenburg, Ilyo (Grigoryevich)**
See Ehrenburg, Ilya (Grigoryevich)

**Ehrenreich, Barbara** 1941- ............... **CLC 110**
See also BEST 90:4; CA 73-76; CANR 16, 37, 62; DLB 246; FW; MTCW 1, 2

**Eich, Gunter**
See Eich, Gunter
See also RGWL 2, 3

**Eich, Gunter** 1907-1972 ..................... **CLC 15**
See Eich, Gunter
See also CA 111; DLB 69, 124

**Eichendorff, Joseph** 1788-1857 ........ **NCLC 8**
See also DLB 90; RGWL 2, 3

**Eigner, Larry** ....................................... **CLC 9**
See Eigner, Laurence (Joel)
See also CAAS 23; DLB 5; WP

**Eigner, Laurence (Joel)** 1927-1996
See Eigner, Larry
See also CA 9-12R; CANR 6, 84; CP 7; DLB 193

**Einhard** c. 770-840 ............... **CMLC 50**
See also DLB 148

**Einstein, Albert** 1879-1955 ............ **TCLC 65**
See also CA 133; MTCW 1, 2

**Eiseley, Loren**
See Eiseley, Loren Corey
See also DLB 275

**Eiseley, Loren Corey** 1907-1977 ......... **CLC 7**
See Eiseley, Loren
See also AAYA 5; ANW; CA 1-4R; CANR 6; DLBD 17

**Eisenstadt, Jill** 1963- ........................ **CLC 50**
See also CA 140

**Eisenstein, Sergei (Mikhailovich)**
1898-1948 ............................... **TCLC 57**
See also CA 149

**Eisner, Simon**
See Kornbluth, C(yril) M.

**Ekeloef, (Bengt) Gunnar**
1907-1968 ...................... **CLC 27; PC 23**
See Ekelof, (Bengt) Gunnar
See also CA 123; DAM POET

**Ekelof, (Bengt) Gunnar** 1907-1968
See Ekeloef, (Bengt) Gunnar
See also DLB 259; EW 12

**Ekelund, Vilhelm** 1880-1949 ......... **TCLC 75**
See also CA 189

**Ekwensi, C. O. D.**
See Ekwensi, Cyprian (Odiatu Duaka)

**Ekwensi, Cyprian (Odiatu Duaka)**
1921- .............................. **BLC 1; CLC 4**
See also AFW; BW 2, 3; CA 29-32R; CANR 18, 42, 74; CDWLB 3; CN 7; CWRI 5; DAM MULT; DLB 117; MTCW 1, 2; RGEL 2; SATA 66; WLIT 2

**Elaine** ............................................ **TCLC 18**
See Leverson, Ada Esther

**El Crummo**
See Crumb, R(obert)

**Elder, Lonne III** 1931-1996 ..... **BLC 1; DC 8**
See also BW 1, 3; CA 81-84; CAD; CANR 25; DAM MULT; DLB 7, 38, 44

**Eleanor of Aquitaine** 1122-1204 ... **CMLC 39**

**Elia**
See Lamb, Charles

**Eliade, Mircea** 1907-1986 ................... **CLC 19**
See also CA 65-68; CANR 30, 62; CDWLB 4; DLB 220; MTCW 1; RGWL 3; SFW 4

**Eliot, A. D.**
See Jewett, (Theodora) Sarah Orne

**Eliot, Alice**
See Jewett, (Theodora) Sarah Orne

**Eliot, Dan**
See Silverberg, Robert

**Eliot, George** 1819-1880 ...... **NCLC 4, 13, 23, 41, 49, 89, 118; PC 20; WLC**
See also BRW 5; BRWR 2; CDBLB 1832-1890; CN 7; CPW; DA; DAB; DAC; DAM MST, NOV; DLB 21, 35, 55; RGEL 2; RGSF 2; SSFS 8; TEA; WLIT 3

**Eliot, John** 1604-1690 ........................... **LC 5**
See also DLB 24

**Eliot, T(homas) S(tearns)**
1888-1965 ...... **CLC 1, 2, 3, 6, 9, 10, 13, 15, 24, 34, 41, 55, 57, 113; PC 5, 31; WLC**
See also AAYA 28; AMW; AMWC 1; AMWR 1; BRW 7; BRWR 2; CA 5-8R; CANR 41; CDALB 1929-1941; DA; DAB; DAC; DAM DRAM, MST, POET; DFS 4, 13; DLB 7, 10, 45, 63, 245; DLBY 1988; EXPP; LAIT 3; MTCW 1, 2; PAB; PFS 1, 7; RGAL 4; RGEL 2; TUS; WLIT 4; WP

**Elizabeth** 1866-1941 ........................ **TCLC 41**

**Elkin, Stanley L(awrence)**
1930-1995 .. **CLC 4, 6, 9, 14, 27, 51, 91; SSC 12**
See also AMWS 6; BPFB 1; CA 9-12R; CANR 8, 46; CN 7; CPW; DAM NOV, POP; DLB 2, 28, 218; DLBY 1980; INT CANR-8; MTCW 1, 2; RGAL 4

**Elledge, Scott** ..................................... **CLC 34**

**Elliot, Don**
See Silverberg, Robert

**Elliott, Don**
See Silverberg, Robert

**Elliott, George P(aul)** 1918-1980 ........ **CLC 2**
See also CA 1-4R; CANR 2; DLB 244

**Elliott, Janice** 1931-1995 ................... **CLC 47**
See also CA 13-16R; CANR 8, 29, 84; CN 7; DLB 14; SATA 119

**Elliott, Sumner Locke** 1917-1991 ..... **CLC 38**
See also CA 5-8R; CANR 2, 21

**Elliott, William**
See Bradbury, Ray (Douglas)

**Ellis, A. E.** ........................................... **CLC 7**

**Ellis, Alice Thomas** ......................... **CLC 40**
See Haycraft, Anna (Margaret)
See also DLB 194; MTCW 1

**Ellis, Bret Easton** 1964- ...... **CLC 39, 71, 117**
See also AAYA 2, 43; CA 123; CANR 51, 74; CN 7; CPW; DAM POP; HGG; INT CA-123; MTCW 1; NFS 11

**Ellis, (Henry) Havelock**
1859-1939 ................................ **TCLC 14**
See also CA 169; DLB 190

**Ellis, Landon**
See Ellison, Harlan (Jay)

**Ellis, Trey** 1962- ................................ **CLC 55**
See also CA 146; CANR 92

**Ellison, Harlan (Jay)** 1934- ... **CLC 1, 13, 42, 139; SSC 14**
See also AAYA 29; BPFB 1; BYA 14; CA 5-8R; CANR 5, 46; CPW; DAM POP; DLB 8; HGG; INT CANR-5; MTCW 1, 2; SCFW 2; SFW 4; SSFS 13, 14, 15; SUFW 1, 2

**Ellison, Ralph (Waldo)** 1914-1994 .... **BLC 1; CLC 1, 3, 11, 54, 86, 114; SSC 26; WLC**
See also AAYA 19; AFAW 1, 2; AMWR 2; AMWS 2; BPFB 1; BW 1, 3; BYA 2; CA 9-12R; CANR 24, 53; CDALB 1941-1968; CSW; DA; DAB; DAC; DAM MST, MULT, NOV; DLB 2, 76, 227; DLBY 1994; EXPN; EXPS; LAIT 4; MTCW 1, 2; NCFS 3; NFS 2; RGAL 4; RGSF 2; SSFS 1, 11; YAW

**Ellmann, Lucy (Elizabeth)** 1956- ..... **CLC 61**
See also CA 128

**Ellmann, Richard (David)**
1918-1987 ................................. **CLC 50**
See also BEST 89:2; CA 1-4R; CANR 2, 28, 61; DLB 103; DLBY 1987; MTCW 1, 2

**Elman, Richard (Martin)**
1934-1997 .................................. **CLC 19**
See also CA 17-20R; CAAS 3; CANR 47

**Elron**
See Hubbard, L(afayette) Ron(ald)

**Eluard, Paul** ................. **PC 38; TCLC 7, 41**
See Grindel, Eugene
See also GFL 1789 to the Present; RGWL 2, 3

**Elyot, Thomas** 1490(?)-1546 ................ **LC 11**
See also DLB 136; RGEL 2

**Elytis, Odysseus** 1911-1996 ........ **CLC 15, 49, 100; PC 21**
See Alepoudelis, Odysseus
See also CA 102; CANR 94; CWW 2; DAM POET; EW 13; MTCW 1, 2; RGWL 2, 3

**Emecheta, (Florence Onye) Buchi**
1944- ............... **BLC 2; CLC 14, 48, 128**
See also AFW; BW 2, 3; CA 81-84; CANR 27, 81; CDWLB 3; CN 7; CWRI 5; DAM MULT; DLB 117; FW; MTCW 1, 2; NFS 12, 14; SATA 66; WLIT 2

**Emerson, Mary Moody**
1774-1863 ................................ **NCLC 66**

**Emerson, Ralph Waldo** 1803-1882 . **NCLC 1, 38, 98; PC 18; WLC**
See also AMW; ANW; CDALB 1640-1865; DA; DAB; DAC; DAM MST, POET; DLB 1, 59, 73, 183, 223, 270; EXPP; LAIT 2; NCFS 3; PFS 4, 17; RGAL 4; TUS; WP

**Eminescu, Mihail** 1850-1889 .......... **NCLC 33**

**Empedocles** 5th cent. B.C.- ............. **CMLC 50**
See also DLB 176

**Empson, William** 1906-1984 ... **CLC 3, 8, 19, 33, 34**
See also BRWS 2; CA 17-20R; CANR 31, 61; DLB 20; MTCW 1, 2; RGEL 2

**Enchi, Fumiko (Ueda)** 1905-1986 ..... **CLC 31**
See Enchi Fumiko
See also CA 129; FW; MJW

**Enchi Fumiko**
See Enchi, Fumiko (Ueda)
See also DLB 182

**Ende, Michael (Andreas Helmuth)**
1929-1995 .................................. **CLC 31**
See also BYA 5; CA 124; CANR 36, 110; CLR 14; DLB 75; MAICYA 1, 2; MAICYAS 1; SATA 61, 130; SATA-Brief 42; SATA-Obit 86

**Endo, Shusaku** 1923-1996 ..... **CLC 7, 14, 19, 54, 99; SSC 48**
See Endo Shusaku
See also CA 29-32R; CANR 21, 54; DAM NOV; MTCW 1, 2; RGSF 2; RGWL 2, 3

**Endo Shusaku**
See Endo, Shusaku
See also DLB 182

**Engel, Marian** 1933-1985 ................... **CLC 36**
See also CA 25-28R; CANR 12; DLB 53; FW; INT CANR-12

**Engelhardt, Frederick**
See Hubbard, L(afayette) Ron(ald)

**Engels, Friedrich** 1820-1895 .. **NCLC 85, 114**
See also DLB 129

**Enright, D(ennis) J(oseph)** 1920- .. **CLC 4, 8, 31**
See also CA 1-4R; CANR 1, 42, 83; CP 7; DLB 27; SATA 25

**Enzensberger, Hans Magnus**
1929- ............................... **CLC 43; PC 28**
See also CA 119; CANR 103

**Ephron, Nora** 1941- ..................... **CLC 17, 31**
See also AAYA 35; AITN 2; CA 65-68; CANR 12, 39, 83

**Epicurus** 341B.C.-270B.C. ............. **CMLC 21**
See also DLB 176

**Epsilon**
See Betjeman, John

**Epstein, Daniel Mark** 1948- ................. **CLC 7**
See also CA 49-52; CANR 2, 53, 90

**Epstein, Jacob** 1956- ........................... **CLC 19**
See also CA 114

**Epstein, Jean** 1897-1953 ................. **TCLC 92**

**Epstein, Joseph** 1937- ........................ **CLC 39**
See also CA 119; CANR 50, 65

**Epstein, Leslie** 1938- .......................... **CLC 27**
See also AMWS 12; CA 73-76; CAAS 12; CANR 23, 69

**Equiano, Olaudah** 1745(?)-1797 . **BLC 2; LC 16**
See also AFAW 1, 2; CDWLB 3; DAM MULT; DLB 37, 50; WLIT 2

**Erasmus, Desiderius** 1469(?)-1536 ...... **LC 16**
See also DLB 136; EW 2; RGWL 2, 3; TWA
**Erdman, Paul E(mil)** 1932- ................ **CLC 25**
See also AITN 1; CA 61-64; CANR 13, 43, 84
**Erdrich, Louise** 1954- ........ **CLC 39, 54, 120; NNAL**
See also AAYA 10, 47; AMWS 4; BEST 89:1; BPFB 1; CA 114; CANR 41, 62; CDALBS; CN 7; CP 7; CPW; CWP; DAM MULT, NOV, POP; DLB 152, 175, 206; EXPP; LAIT 5; MTCW 1; NFS 5; PFS 14; RGAL 4; SATA 94; SSFS 14; TCWW 2
**Erenburg, Ilya (Grigoryevich)**
See Ehrenburg, Ilya (Grigoryevich)
**Erickson, Stephen Michael** 1950-
See Erickson, Steve
See also CA 129; SFW 4
**Erickson, Steve** ................................. **CLC 64**
See Erickson, Stephen Michael
See also CANR 60, 68; SUFW 2
**Ericson, Walter**
See Fast, Howard (Melvin)
**Eriksson, Buntel**
See Bergman, (Ernst) Ingmar
**Ernaux, Annie** 1940- ......................... **CLC 88**
See also CA 147; CANR 93; NCFS 3
**Erskine, John** 1879-1951 ................ **TCLC 84**
See also CA 159; DLB 9, 102; FANT
**Eschenbach, Wolfram von**
See Wolfram von Eschenbach
See also RGWL 3
**Eseki, Bruno**
See Mphahlele, Ezekiel
**Esenin, Sergei (Alexandrovich)**
1895-1925 ......................................... **TCLC 4**
See also RGWL 2, 3
**Eshleman, Clayton** 1935- ................... **CLC 7**
See also CA 33-36R; CAAS 6; CANR 93; CP 7; DLB 5
**Espriella, Don Manuel Alvarez**
See Southey, Robert
**Espriu, Salvador** 1913-1985 ................ **CLC 9**
See also CA 154; DLB 134
**Espronceda, Jose de** 1808-1842 ..... **NCLC 39**
**Esquivel, Laura** 1951(?)- ... **CLC 141; HLCS 1**
See also AAYA 29; CA 143; CANR 68, 113; DNFS 2; LAIT 3; MTCW 1; NFS 5; WLIT 1
**Esse, James**
See Stephens, James
**Esterbrook, Tom**
See Hubbard, L(afayette) Ron(ald)
**Estleman, Loren D.** 1952- ................. **CLC 48**
See also AAYA 27; CA 85-88; CANR 27, 74; CMW 4; CPW; DAM NOV, POP; DLB 226; INT CANR-27; MTCW 1, 2
**Etherege, Sir George** 1636-1692 .......... **LC 78**
See also BRW 2; DAM DRAM; DLB 80; PAB; RGEL 2
**Euclid** 306B.C.-283B.C. ................... **CMLC 25**
**Eugenides, Jeffrey** 1960(?)- ................ **CLC 81**
See also CA 144
**Euripides** c. 484B.C.-406B.C. ....... **CMLC 23, 51; DC 4; WLCS**
See also AW 1; CDWLB 1; DA; DAB; DAC; DAM DRAM, MST; DFS 1, 4, 6; DLB 176; LAIT 1; RGWL 2, 3
**Evan, Evin**
See Faust, Frederick (Schiller)
**Evans, Caradoc** 1878-1945 ... **SSC 43; TCLC 85**
See also DLB 162
**Evans, Evan**
See Faust, Frederick (Schiller)
See also TCWW 2

**Evans, Marian**
See Eliot, George
**Evans, Mary Ann**
See Eliot, George
**Evarts, Esther**
See Benson, Sally
**Everett, Percival**
See Everett, Percival L.
See also CSW
**Everett, Percival L.** 1956- ................. **CLC 57**
See Everett, Percival
See also BW 2; CA 129; CANR 94
**Everson, R(onald) G(ilmour)**
1903-1992 ......................................... **CLC 27**
See also CA 17-20R; DLB 88
**Everson, William (Oliver)**
1912-1994 ............................ **CLC 1, 5, 14**
See also BG 2; CA 9-12R; CANR 20; DLB 5, 16, 212; MTCW 1
**Evtushenko, Evgenii Aleksandrovich**
See Yevtushenko, Yevgeny (Alexandrovich)
See also RGWL 2, 3
**Ewart, Gavin (Buchanan)**
1916-1995 ........................... **CLC 13, 46**
See also BRWS 7; CA 89-92; CANR 17, 46; CP 7; DLB 40; MTCW 1
**Ewers, Hanns Heinz** 1871-1943 ..... **TCLC 12**
See also CA 149
**Ewing, Frederick R.**
See Sturgeon, Theodore (Hamilton)
**Exley, Frederick (Earl)** 1929-1992 .... **CLC 6, 11**
See also AITN 2; BPFB 1; CA 81-84; DLB 143; DLBY 1981
**Eynhardt, Guillermo**
See Quiroga, Horacio (Sylvestre)
**Ezekiel, Nissim** 1924- ....................... **CLC 61**
See also CA 61-64; CP 7
**Ezekiel, Tish O'Dowd** 1943- ............. **CLC 34**
See also CA 129
**Fadeev, Aleksandr Aleksandrovich**
See Bulgya, Alexander Alexandrovich
See also DLB 272
**Fadeyev, A.**
See Bulgya, Alexander Alexandrovich
**Fadeyev, Alexander** ......................... **TCLC 53**
See Bulgya, Alexander Alexandrovich
**Fagen, Donald** 1948- ......................... **CLC 26**
**Fainzilberg, Ilya Arnoldovich** 1897-1937
See Ilf, Ilya
See also CA 165
**Fair, Ronald L.** 1932- ......................... **CLC 18**
See also BW 1; CA 69-72; CANR 25; DLB 33
**Fairbairn, Roger**
See Carr, John Dickson
**Fairbairns, Zoe (Ann)** 1948- ............. **CLC 32**
See also CA 103; CANR 21, 85; CN 7
**Fairfield, Flora**
See Alcott, Louisa May
**Fairman, Paul W.** 1916-1977
See Queen, Ellery
See also SFW 4
**Falco, Gian**
See Papini, Giovanni
**Falconer, James**
See Kirkup, James
**Falconer, Kenneth**
See Kornbluth, C(yril) M.
**Falkland, Samuel**
See Heijermans, Herman
**Fallaci, Oriana** 1930- ................. **CLC 11, 110**
See also CA 77-80; CANR 15, 58; FW; MTCW 1
**Faludi, Susan** 1959- ......................... **CLC 140**
See also CA 138; FW; MTCW 1; NCFS 3
**Faludy, George** 1913- ......................... **CLC 42**
See also CA 21-24R

**Faludy, Gyoergy**
See Faludy, George
**Fanon, Frantz** 1925-1961 .... **BLC 2; CLC 74**
See also BW 1; CA 116; DAM MULT; WLIT 2
**Fanshawe, Ann** 1625-1680 ................... **LC 11**
**Fante, John (Thomas)** 1911-1983 ..... **CLC 60**
See also AMWS 11; CA 69-72; CANR 23, 104; DLB 130; DLBY 1983
**Farah, Nuruddin** 1945- ...... **BLC 2; CLC 53, 137**
See also AFW; BW 2, 3; CA 106; CANR 81; CDWLB 3; CN 7; DAM MULT; DLB 125; WLIT 2
**Fargue, Leon-Paul** 1876(?)-1947 .... **TCLC 11**
See also CANR 107; DLB 258
**Farigoule, Louis**
See Romains, Jules
**Farina, Richard** 1936(?)-1966 ............. **CLC 9**
See also CA 81-84
**Farley, Walter (Lorimer)**
1915-1989 .................................. **CLC 17**
See also BYA 14; CA 17-20R; CANR 8, 29, 84; DLB 22; JRDA; MAICYA 1, 2; SATA 2, 43, 132; YAW
**Farmer, Philip Jose** 1918- ............. **CLC 1, 19**
See also AAYA 28; BPFB 1; CA 1-4R; CANR 4, 35, 111; DLB 8; MTCW 1; SATA 93; SCFW 2; SFW 4
**Farquhar, George** 1677-1707 ............. **LC 21**
See also BRW 2; DAM DRAM; DLB 84; RGEL 2
**Farrell, J(ames) G(ordon)**
1935-1979 .................................. **CLC 6**
See also CA 73-76; CANR 36; DLB 14, 271; MTCW 1; RGEL 2; RHW; WLIT 4
**Farrell, James T(homas)** 1904-1979 . **CLC 1, 4, 8, 11, 66; SSC 28**
See also AMW; BPFB 1; CA 5-8R; CANR 9, 61; DLB 4, 9, 86; DLBD 2; MTCW 1, 2; RGAL 4
**Farrell, Warren (Thomas)** 1943- ...... **CLC 70**
See also CA 146
**Farren, Richard J.**
See Betjeman, John
**Farren, Richard M.**
See Betjeman, John
**Fassbinder, Rainer Werner**
1946-1982 .................................. **CLC 20**
See also CA 93-96; CANR 31
**Fast, Howard (Melvin)** 1914- ... **CLC 23, 131**
See also AAYA 16; BPFB 1; CA 1-4R, 181; CAAE 181; CAAS 18; CANR 1, 33, 54, 75, 98; CMW 4; CN 7; CPW; DAM NOV; DLB 9; INT CANR-33; MTCW 1; RHW; SATA 7; SATA-Essay 107; TCWW 2; YAW
**Faulcon, Robert**
See Holdstock, Robert P.
**Faulkner, William (Cuthbert)**
1897-1962 ........ **CLC 1, 3, 6, 8, 9, 11, 14, 18, 28, 52, 68; SSC 1, 35, 42; WLC**
See also AAYA 7; AMW; AMWR 1; BPFB 1; BYA 5; CA 81-84; CANR 33; CDALB 1929-1941; DA; DAB; DAC; DAM MST, NOV; DLB 9, 11, 44, 102; DLBD 2; DLBY 1986, 1997; EXPN; EXPS; LAIT 2; MTCW 1, 2; NFS 4, 8, 13; RGAL 4; RGSF 2; SSFS 2, 5, 6, 12; TUS
**Fauset, Jessie Redmon**
1882(?)-1961 .. **BLC 2; CLC 19, 54; HR 2**
See also AFAW 2; BW 1; CA 109; CANR 83; DAM MULT; DLB 51; FW; MAWW
**Faust, Frederick (Schiller)**
1892-1944(?) ................................. **TCLC 49**
See Austin, Frank; Brand, Max; Challis, George; Dawson, Peter; Dexter, Martin;

Evans, Evan; Frederick, John; Frost, Frederick; Manning, David; Silver, Nicholas
See also CA 152; DAM POP; DLB 256; TUS

**Faust, Irvin** 1924- .................... **CLC 8**
See also CA 33-36R; CANR 28, 67; CN 7; DLB 2, 28, 218; DLBY 1980

**Fawkes, Guy**
See Benchley, Robert (Charles)

**Fearing, Kenneth (Flexner)**
1902-1961 ..................... **CLC 51**
See also CA 93-96; CANR 59; CMW 4; DLB 9; RGAL 4

**Fecamps, Elise**
See Creasey, John

**Federman, Raymond** 1928- ......... **CLC 6, 47**
See also CA 17-20R; CAAS 8; CANR 10, 43, 83, 108; CN 7; DLBY 1980

**Federspiel, J(uerg) F.** 1931- ............. **CLC 42**
See also CA 146

**Feiffer, Jules (Ralph)** 1929- ...... **CLC 2, 8, 64**
See also AAYA 3; CA 17-20R; CAD; CANR 30, 59; CD 5; DAM DRAM; DLB 7, 44; INT CANR-30; MTCW 1; SATA 8, 61, 111

**Feige, Hermann Albert Otto Maximilian**
See Traven, B.

**Feinberg, David B.** 1956-1994 .......... **CLC 59**
See also CA 135

**Feinstein, Elaine** 1930- ..................... **CLC 36**
See also CA 69-72; CAAS 1; CANR 31, 68; CN 7; CP 7; CWP; DLB 14, 40; MTCW 1

**Feke, Gilbert David** ......................... **CLC 65**

**Feldman, Irving (Mordecai)** 1928- ..... **CLC 7**
See also CA 1-4R; CANR 1; CP 7; DLB 169

**Felix-Tchicaya, Gerald**
See Tchicaya, Gerald Felix

**Fellini, Federico** 1920-1993 ......... **CLC 16, 85**
See also CA 65-68; CANR 33

**Felsen, Henry Gregor** 1916-1995 ..... **CLC 17**
See also CA 1-4R; CANR 1; SAAS 2; SATA 1

**Felski, Rita** ................................... **CLC 65**

**Fenno, Jack**
See Calisher, Hortense

**Fenollosa, Ernest (Francisco)**
1853-1908 ......................... **TCLC 91**

**Fenton, James Martin** 1949- ............. **CLC 32**
See also CA 102; CANR 108; CP 7; DLB 40; PFS 11

**Ferber, Edna** 1887-1968 ............... **CLC 18, 93**
See also AITN 1; CA 5-8R; CANR 68, 105; DLB 9, 28, 86, 266; MTCW 1, 2; RGAL 4; RHW; SATA 7; TCWW 2

**Ferdowsi, Abu'l Qasem** 940-1020 . **CMLC 43**
See also RGWL 2, 3

**Ferguson, Helen**
See Kavan, Anna

**Ferguson, Niall** 1964- ..................... **CLC 134**
See also CA 190

**Ferguson, Samuel** 1810-1886 ......... **NCLC 33**
See also DLB 32; RGEL 2

**Fergusson, Robert** 1750-1774 ............. **LC 29**
See also DLB 109; RGEL 2

**Ferling, Lawrence**
See Ferlinghetti, Lawrence (Monsanto)

**Ferlinghetti, Lawrence (Monsanto)**
1919(?)- ...... **CLC 2, 6, 10, 27, 111; PC 1**
See also CA 5-8R; CANR 3, 41, 73; CDALB 1941-1968; CP 7; DAM POET; DLB 5, 16; MTCW 1, 2; RGAL 4; WP

**Fern, Fanny**
See Parton, Sara Payson Willis

**Fernandez, Vicente Garcia Huidobro**
See Huidobro Fernandez, Vicente Garcia

**Fernandez-Armesto, Felipe** ............. **CLC 70**

**Fernandez de Lizardi, Jose Joaquin**
See Lizardi, Jose Joaquin Fernandez de

**Ferre, Rosario** 1942- ...... **CLC 139; HLCS 1; SSC 36**
See also CA 131; CANR 55, 81; CWW 2; DLB 145; HW 1, 2; LAWS 1; MTCW 1; WLIT 1

**Ferrer, Gabriel (Francisco Victor) Miro**
See Miro (Ferrer), Gabriel (Francisco Victor)

**Ferrier, Susan (Edmonstone)**
1782-1854 ......................... **NCLC 8**
See also DLB 116; RGEL 2

**Ferrigno, Robert** 1948(?)- ................. **CLC 65**
See also CA 140

**Ferron, Jacques** 1921-1985 ............... **CLC 94**
See also CA 129; CCA 1; DAC; DLB 60

**Feuchtwanger, Lion** 1884-1958 ........ **TCLC 3**
See also CA 187; DLB 66

**Feuillet, Octave** 1821-1890 ............. **NCLC 45**
See also DLB 192

**Feydeau, Georges (Leon Jules Marie)**
1862-1921 ......................... **TCLC 22**
See also CA 152; CANR 84; DAM DRAM; DLB 192; GFL 1789 to the Present; RGWL 2, 3

**Fichte, Johann Gottlieb**
1762-1814 ......................... **NCLC 62**
See also DLB 90

**Ficino, Marsilio** 1433-1499 ................ **LC 12**

**Fiedeler, Hans**
See Doeblin, Alfred

**Fiedler, Leslie A(aron)** 1917-2003 ..... **CLC 4, 13, 24**
See also CA 9-12R; CANR 7, 63; CN 7; DLB 28, 67; MTCW 1, 2; RGAL 4; TUS

**Field, Andrew** 1938- ......................... **CLC 44**
See also CA 97-100; CANR 25

**Field, Eugene** 1850-1895 .................. **NCLC 3**
See also DLB 23, 42, 140; DLBD 13; MAICYA 1, 2; RGAL 4; SATA 16

**Field, Gans T.**
See Wellman, Manly Wade

**Field, Michael** 1915-1971 ................ **TCLC 43**

**Field, Peter**
See Hobson, Laura Z(ametkin)
See also TCWW 2

**Fielding, Helen** 1959(?)- .................. **CLC 146**
See also CA 172; DLB 231

**Fielding, Henry** 1707-1754 ....... **LC 1, 46, 85; WLC**
See also BRW 3; BRWR 1; CDBLB 1660-1789; DA; DAB; DAC; DAM DRAM, MST, NOV; DLB 39, 84, 101; RGEL 2; TEA; WLIT 3

**Fielding, Sarah** 1710-1768 ............... **LC 1, 44**
See also DLB 39; RGEL 2; TEA

**Fields, W. C.** 1880-1946 .................. **TCLC 80**
See also DLB 44

**Fierstein, Harvey (Forbes)** 1954- ..... **CLC 33**
See also CA 129; CAD; CD 5; CPW; DAM DRAM, POP; DFS 6; DLB 266; GLL

**Figes, Eva** 1932- ............................... **CLC 31**
See also CA 53-56; CANR 4, 44, 83; CN 7; DLB 14, 271; FW

**Filippo, Eduardo de**
See de Filippo, Eduardo

**Finch, Anne** 1661-1720 .............. **LC 3; PC 21**
See also DLB 95

**Finch, Robert (Duer Claydon)**
1900-1995 ......................... **CLC 18**
See also CA 57-60; CANR 9, 24, 49; CP 7; DLB 88

**Findley, Timothy** 1930- ............. **CLC 27, 102**
See also CA 25-28R; CANR 12, 42, 69, 109; CCA 1; CN 7; DAC; DAM MST; DLB 53; FANT; RHW

**Fink, William**
See Mencken, H(enry) L(ouis)

**Firbank, Louis** 1942-
See Reed, Lou

**Firbank, (Arthur Annesley) Ronald**
1886-1926 ......................... **TCLC 1**
See also BRWS 2; CA 177; DLB 36; RGEL 2

**Fish, Stanley**
See Fish, Stanley Eugene

**Fish, Stanley E.**
See Fish, Stanley Eugene

**Fish, Stanley Eugene** 1938- ............. **CLC 142**
See also CA 132; CANR 90; DLB 67

**Fisher, Dorothy (Frances) Canfield**
1879-1958 ......................... **TCLC 87**
See also CA 136; CANR 80; CLR 71,; CWRI 5; DLB 9, 102; MAICYA 1, 2; YABC 1

**Fisher, M(ary) F(rances) K(ennedy)**
1908-1992 ......................... **CLC 76, 87**
See also CA 77-80; CANR 44; MTCW 1

**Fisher, Roy** 1930- ........................... **CLC 25**
See also CA 81-84; CAAS 10; CANR 16; CP 7; DLB 40

**Fisher, Rudolph** 1897-1934 .... **BLC 2; HR 2; SSC 25; TCLC 11**
See also BW 1, 3; CA 124; CANR 80; DAM MULT; DLB 51, 102

**Fisher, Vardis (Alvero)** 1895-1968 ...... **CLC 7**
See also CA 5-8R; CANR 68; DLB 9, 206; RGAL 4; TCWW 2

**Fiske, Tarleton**
See Bloch, Robert (Albert)

**Fitch, Clarke**
See Sinclair, Upton (Beall)

**Fitch, John IV**
See Cormier, Robert (Edmund)

**Fitzgerald, Captain Hugh**
See Baum, L(yman) Frank

**FitzGerald, Edward** 1809-1883 ....... **NCLC 9**
See also BRW 4; DLB 32; RGEL 2

**Fitzgerald, F(rancis) Scott (Key)**
1896-1940 ... **SSC 6, 31; TCLC 1, 6, 14, 28, 55; WLC**
See also AAYA 24; AITN 1; AMW; AMWR 1; BPFB 1; CA 123; CDALB 1917-1929; DA; DAB; DAC; DAM MST, NOV; DLB 4, 9, 86, 219; DLBD 1, 15, 16; DLBY 1981, 1996; EXPN; EXPS; LAIT 3; MTCW 1, 2; NFS 2; RGAL 4; RGSF 2; SSFS 4, 15; TUS

**Fitzgerald, Penelope** 1916-2000 . **CLC 19, 51, 61, 143**
See also BRWS 5; CA 85-88; CAAS 10; CANR 56, 86; CN 7; DLB 14, 194; MTCW 2

**Fitzgerald, Robert (Stuart)**
1910-1985 ......................... **CLC 39**
See also CA 1-4R; CANR 1; DLBY 1980

**FitzGerald, Robert D(avid)**
1902-1987 ......................... **CLC 19**
See also CA 17-20R; DLB 260; RGEL 2

**Fitzgerald, Zelda (Sayre)**
1900-1948 ......................... **TCLC 52**
See also AMWS 9; CA 126; DLBY 1984

**Flanagan, Thomas (James Bonner)**
1923- ..................... **CLC 25, 52**
See also CA 108; CANR 55; CN 7; DLBY 1980; INT 108; MTCW 1; RHW

**Flaubert, Gustave** 1821-1880 .... **NCLC 2, 10, 19, 62, 66; SSC 11; WLC**
See also DA; DAB; DAC; DAM MST, NOV; DLB 119; EW 7; EXPS; GFL 1789 to the Present; LAIT 2; NFS 14; RGSF 2; RGWL 2, 3; SSFS 6; TWA

**Flavius Josephus**
See Josephus, Flavius

**Flecker, Herman Elroy**
See Flecker, (Herman) James Elroy

**Flecker, (Herman) James Elroy**
1884-1915 .................................... **TCLC 43**
See also CA 150; DLB 10, 19; RGEL 2

**Fleming, Ian (Lancaster)** 1908-1964 . **CLC 3, 30**
See also AAYA 26; BPFB 1; CA 5-8R; CANR 59; CDBLB 1945-1960; CMW 4; CPW; DAM POP; DLB 87, 201; MSW; MTCW 1, 2; RGEL 2; SATA 9; TEA; YAW

**Fleming, Thomas (James)** 1927- ...... **CLC 37**
See also CA 5-8R; CANR 10, 102; INT CANR-10; SATA 8

**Fletcher, John** 1579-1625 .......... **DC 6; LC 33**
See also BRW 7; CDBLB Before 1660; DLB 58; RGEL 2; TEA

**Fletcher, John Gould** 1886-1950 .... **TCLC 35**
See also CA 167; DLB 4, 45; RGAL 4

**Fleur, Paul**
See Pohl, Frederik

**Floogleburkle, Al**
See Spiegelman, Art

**Flora, Fletcher** 1914-1969
See Queen, Ellery
See also CA 1-4R; CANR 3, 85

**Flying Officer X**
See Bates, H(erbert) E(rnest)

**Fo, Dario** 1926- ............. **CLC 32, 109; DC 10**
See also CA 128; CANR 68, 114; CWW 2; DAM DRAM; DLBY 1997; MTCW 1, 2

**Fogarty, Jonathan Titulescu Esq.**
See Farrell, James T(homas)

**Follett, Ken(neth Martin)** 1949- ....... **CLC 18**
See also AAYA 6; BEST 89:4; BPFB 1; CA 81-84; CANR 13, 33, 54, 102; CMW 4; CPW; DAM NOV, POP; DLB 87; DLBY 1981; INT CANR-33; MTCW 1

**Fontane, Theodor** 1819-1898 ......... **NCLC 26**
See also CDWLB 2; DLB 129; EW 6; RGWL 2, 3; TWA

**Fontenot, Chester** ............................ **CLC 65**

**Fonvizin, Denis Ivanovich**
1744(?)-1792 ................. **LC 81**
See also DLB 150; RGWL 2, 3

**Foote, Horton** 1916- ..................... **CLC 51, 91**
See also CA 73-76; CAD; CANR 34, 51, 110; CD 5; CSW; DAM DRAM; DLB 26, 266; INT CANR-34

**Foote, Mary Hallock** 1847-1938 .. **TCLC 108**
See also DLB 186, 188, 202, 221

**Foote, Shelby** 1916- ............................. **CLC 75**
See also AAYA 40; CA 5-8R; CANR 3, 45, 74; CN 7; CPW; CSW; DAM NOV, POP; DLB 2, 17; MTCW 2; RHW

**Forbes, Cosmo**
See Lewton, Val

**Forbes, Esther** 1891-1967 .................. **CLC 12**
See also AAYA 17; BYA 2; CA 13-14; CAP 1; CLR 27; DLB 22; JRDA; MAICYA 1, 2; RHW; SATA 2, 100; YAW

**Forche, Carolyn (Louise)** 1950- ....... **CLC 25, 83, 86; PC 10**
See also CA 117; CANR 50, 74; CP 7; CWP; DAM POET; DLB 5, 193; INT CA-117; MTCW 1; RGAL 4

**Ford, Elbur**
See Hibbert, Eleanor Alice Burford

**Ford, Ford Madox** 1873-1939 ... **TCLC 1, 15, 39, 57**
See Chaucer, Daniel
See also BRW 6; CA 132; CANR 74; CDBLB 1914-1945; DAM NOV; DLB 34, 98, 162; MTCW 1, 2; RGEL 2; TEA

**Ford, Henry** 1863-1947 .................... **TCLC 73**
See also CA 148

**Ford, Jack**
See Ford, John

**Ford, John** 1586-1639 ............... **DC 8; LC 68**
See also BRW 2; CDBLB Before 1660; DAM DRAM; DFS 7; DLB 58; IDTP; RGEL 2

**Ford, John** 1895-1973 ....................... **CLC 16**
See also CA 187

**Ford, Richard** 1944- ..................... **CLC 46, 99**
See also AMWS 5; CA 69-72; CANR 11, 47, 86; CN 7; CSW; DLB 227; MTCW 1; RGAL 4; RGSF 2

**Ford, Webster**
See Masters, Edgar Lee

**Foreman, Richard** 1937- .................... **CLC 50**
See also CA 65-68; CAD; CANR 32, 63; CD 5

**Forester, C(ecil) S(cott)** 1899-1966 ... **CLC 35**
See also CA 73-76; CANR 83; DLB 191; RGEL 2; RHW; SATA 13

**Forez**
See Mauriac, Francois (Charles)

**Forman, James**
See Forman, James D(ouglas)

**Forman, James D(ouglas)** 1932- ....... **CLC 21**
See also AAYA 17; CA 9-12R; CANR 4, 19, 42; JRDA; MAICYA 1, 2; SATA 8, 70; YAW

**Forman, Milos** 1932- ....................... **CLC 164**
See also CA 109

**Fornes, Maria Irene** 1930- . **CLC 39, 61; DC 10; HLCS 1**
See also CA 25-28R; CAD; CANR 28, 81; CD 5; CWD; DLB 7; HW 1, 2; INT CANR-28; MTCW 1; RGAL 4

**Forrest, Leon (Richard)**
1937-1997 ........................ **BLCS; CLC 4**
See also AFAW 2; BW 2; CA 89-92; CAAS 7; CANR 25, 52, 87; CN 7; DLB 33

**Forster, E(dward) M(organ)**
1879-1970 ...... **CLC 1, 2, 3, 4, 9, 10, 13, 15, 22, 45, 77; SSC 27; TCLC 125; WLC**
See also AAYA 2, 37; BRW 6; BRWR 2; CA 13-14; CANR 45; CAP 1; CDBLB 1914-1945; DA; DAB; DAC; DAM MST, NOV; DLB 34, 98, 162, 178, 195; DLBD 10; EXPN; LAIT 3; MTCW 1, 2; NCFS 1; NFS 3, 10, 11; RGEL 2; RGSF 2; SATA 57; SUFW 1; TEA; WLIT 4

**Forster, John** 1812-1876 ................. **NCLC 11**
See also DLB 144, 184

**Forster, Margaret** 1938- ................... **CLC 149**
See also CA 133; CANR 62; CN 7; DLB 155, 271

**Forsyth, Frederick** 1938- .......... **CLC 2, 5, 36**
See also BEST 89:4; CA 85-88; CANR 38, 62; CMW 4; CN 7; CPW; DAM NOV, POP; DLB 87; MTCW 1, 2

**Forten, Charlotte L.** 1837-1914 ........ **BLC 2; TCLC 16**
See Grimke, Charlotte L(ottie) Forten
See also DLB 50, 239

**Fortinbras**
See Grieg, (Johan) Nordahl (Brun)

**Foscolo, Ugo** 1778-1827 ............. **NCLC 8, 97**
See also EW 5

**Fosse, Bob** ......................................... **CLC 20**
See Fosse, Robert Louis

**Fosse, Robert Louis** 1927-1987
See Fosse, Bob

**Foster, Hannah Webster**
1758-1840 .......................... **NCLC 99**
See also DLB 37, 200; RGAL 4

**Foster, Stephen Collins**
1826-1864 ................... **NCLC 26**
See also RGAL 4

**Foucault, Michel** 1926-1984 . **CLC 31, 34, 69**
See also CA 105; CANR 34; DLB 242; EW 13; GFL 1789 to the Present; GLL 1; MTCW 1, 2; TWA

**Fouque, Friedrich (Heinrich Karl) de la Motte** 1777-1843 ...................... **NCLC 2**
See also DLB 90; RGWL 2, 3; SUFW 1

**Fourier, Charles** 1772-1837 ............ **NCLC 51**

**Fournier, Henri Alban** 1886-1914
See Alain-Fournier
See also CA 179

**Fournier, Pierre** 1916- ....................... **CLC 11**
See Gascar, Pierre
See also CA 89-92; CANR 16, 40

**Fowles, John (Robert)** 1926- . **CLC 1, 2, 3, 4, 6, 9, 10, 15, 33, 87; SSC 33**
See also BPFB 1; BRWS 1; CA 5-8R; CANR 25, 71, 103; CDBLB 1960 to Present; CN 7; DAB; DAC; DAM MST; DLB 14, 139, 207; HGG; MTCW 1, 2; RGEL 2; RHW; SATA 22; TEA; WLIT 4

**Fox, Paula** 1923- ..................... **CLC 2, 8, 121**
See also AAYA 3, 37; BYA 3, 8; CA 73-76; CANR 20, 36, 62, 105; CLR 1, 44; DLB 52; JRDA; MAICYA 1, 2; MTCW 1; NFS 12; SATA 17, 60, 120; WYA; YAW

**Fox, William Price (Jr.)** 1926- ........... **CLC 22**
See also CA 17-20R; CAAS 19; CANR 11; CSW; DLB 2; DLBY 1981

**Foxe, John** 1517(?)-1587 ...................... **LC 14**
See also DLB 132

**Frame, Janet** .. **CLC 2, 3, 6, 22, 66, 96; SSC 29**
See Clutha, Janet Paterson Frame
See also CN 7; CWP; RGEL 2; RGSF 2; TWA

**France, Anatole** ............................... **TCLC 9**
See Thibault, Jacques Anatole Francois
See also DLB 123; GFL 1789 to the Present; MTCW 1; RGWL 2, 3; SUFW 1

**Francis, Claude** ................................. **CLC 50**
See also CA 192

**Francis, Dick** 1920- .......... **CLC 2, 22, 42, 102**
See also AAYA 5, 21; BEST 89:3; BPFB 1; CA 5-8R; CANR 9, 42, 68, 100; CDBLB 1960 to Present; CMW 4; CN 7; DAM POP; DLB 87; INT CANR-9; MSW; MTCW 1, 2

**Francis, Robert (Churchill)**
1901-1987 ...................... **CLC 15; PC 34**
See also AMWS 9; CA 1-4R; CANR 1; EXPP; PFS 12

**Francis, Lord Jeffrey**
See Jeffrey, Francis
See also DLB 107

**Frank, Anne(lies Marie)**
1929-1945 ..................... **TCLC 17; WLC**
See also AAYA 12; BYA 1; CA 133; CANR 68; DA; DAB; DAC; DAM MST; LAIT 4; MAICYA 2; MAICYAS 1; MTCW 1, 2; NCFS 2; SATA 87; SATA-Brief 42; WYA; YAW

**Frank, Bruno** 1887-1945 .................... **TCLC 81**
See also CA 189; DLB 118

**Frank, Elizabeth** 1945- ....................... **CLC 39**
See also CA 126; CANR 78; INT 126

**Frankl, Viktor E(mil)** 1905-1997 ...... **CLC 93**
See also CA 65-68

**Franklin, Benjamin**
See Hasek, Jaroslav (Matej Frantisek)

**Franklin, Benjamin** 1706-1790 ........... **LC 25; WLCS**
See also AMW; CDALB 1640-1865; DA; DAB; DAC; DAM MST; DLB 24, 43, 73, 183; LAIT 1; RGAL 4; TUS

**Franklin, (Stella Maria Sarah) Miles (Lampe)** 1879-1954 ................... **TCLC 7**
See also CA 164; DLB 230; FW; MTCW 2; RGEL 2; TWA

**Fraser, (Lady) Antonia (Pakenham)**
1932- ................................. **CLC 32, 107**
See also CA 85-88; CANR 44, 65; CMW; MTCW 1, 2; SATA-Brief 32

**Fraser, George MacDonald** 1925- ...... **CLC 7**
See also CA 45-48, 180; CAAE 180; CANR 2, 48, 74; MTCW 1; RHW

**Fraser, Sylvia** 1935- .................................. **CLC 64**
See also CA 45-48; CANR 1, 16, 60; CCA 1

**Frayn, Michael** 1933- .......... **CLC 3, 7, 31, 47**
See also BRWS 7; CA 5-8R; CANR 30, 69, 114; CBD; CD 5; CN 7; DAM DRAM, NOV; DLB 13, 14, 194, 245; FANT; MTCW 1, 2; SFW 4

**Fraze, Candida (Merrill)** 1945- ........ **CLC 50**
See also CA 126

**Frazer, Andrew**
See Marlowe, Stephen

**Frazer, J(ames) G(eorge)**
1854-1941 ................................ **TCLC 32**
See also BRWS 3

**Frazer, Robert Caine**
See Creasey, John

**Frazer, Sir James George**
See Frazer, J(ames) G(eorge)

**Frazier, Charles** 1950- ..................... **CLC 109**
See also AAYA 34; CA 161; CSW

**Frazier, Ian** 1951- ............................... **CLC 46**
See also CA 130; CANR 54, 93

**Frederic, Harold** 1856-1898 ........... **NCLC 10**
See also AMW; DLB 12, 23; DLBD 13; RGAL 4

**Frederick, John**
See Faust, Frederick (Schiller)
See also TCWW 2

**Frederick the Great** 1712-1786 ........... **LC 14**

**Fredro, Aleksander** 1793-1876 ......... **NCLC 8**

**Freeling, Nicolas** 1927- ....................... **CLC 38**
See also CA 49-52; CAAS 12; CANR 1, 17, 50, 84; CMW 4; CN 7; DLB 87

**Freeman, Douglas Southall**
1886-1953 ................................ **TCLC 11**
See also CA 195; DLB 17; DLBD 17

**Freeman, Judith** 1946- ....................... **CLC 55**
See also CA 148; DLB 256

**Freeman, Mary E(leanor) Wilkins**
1852-1930 ............... **SSC 1, 47; TCLC 9**
See also CA 177; DLB 12, 78, 221; EXPS; FW; HGG; MAWW; RGAL 4; RGSF 2; SSFS 4, 8; SUFW 1; TUS

**Freeman, R(ichard) Austin**
1862-1943 ................................ **TCLC 21**
See also CANR 84; CMW 4; DLB 70

**French, Albert** 1943- .......................... **CLC 86**
See also BW 3; CA 167

**French, Antonia**
See Kureishi, Hanif

**French, Marilyn** 1929- .......... **CLC 10, 18, 60**
See also BPFB 1; CA 69-72; CANR 3, 31; CN 7; CPW; DAM DRAM, NOV, POP; FW; INT CANR-31; MTCW 1, 2

**French, Paul**
See Asimov, Isaac

**Freneau, Philip Morin** 1752-1832 .. **NCLC 1, 111**
See also AMWS 2; DLB 37, 43; RGAL 4

**Freud, Sigmund** 1856-1939 ............. **TCLC 52**
See also CA 133; CANR 69; EW 8; MTCW 1, 2; NCFS 3; TWA

**Freytag, Gustav** 1816-1895 .......... **NCLC 109**
See also DLB 129

**Friedan, Betty (Naomi)** 1921- ........... **CLC 74**
See also CA 65-68; CANR 18, 45, 74; DLB 246; FW; MTCW 1, 2

**Friedlander, Saul** 1932- ...................... **CLC 90**
See also CA 130; CANR 72

**Friedman, B(ernard) H(arper)**
1926- ....................................... **CLC 7**
See also CA 1-4R; CANR 3, 48

**Friedman, Bruce Jay** 1930- ...... **CLC 3, 5, 56**
See also CA 9-12R; CAD; CANR 25, 52, 101; CD 5; CN 7; DLB 2, 28, 244; INT CANR-25

**Friel, Brian** 1929- .... **CLC 5, 42, 59, 115; DC 8**
See also BRWS 5; CA 21-24R; CANR 33, 69; CBD; CD 5; DFS 11; DLB 13; MTCW 1; RGEL 2; TEA

**Friis-Baastad, Babbis Ellinor**
1921-1970 ................................. **CLC 12**
See also CA 17-20R; SATA 7

**Frisch, Max (Rudolf)** 1911-1991 ... **CLC 3, 9, 14, 18, 32, 44; TCLC 121**
See also CA 85-88; CANR 32, 74; CDWLB 2; DAM DRAM, NOV; DLB 69, 124; EW 13; MTCW 1, 2; RGWL 2, 3

**Fromentin, Eugene (Samuel Auguste)**
1820-1876 ................................. **NCLC 10**
See also DLB 123; GFL 1789 to the Present

**Frost, Frederick**
See Faust, Frederick (Schiller)
See also TCWW 2

**Frost, Robert (Lee)** 1874-1963 .. **CLC 1, 3, 4, 9, 10, 13, 15, 26, 34, 44; PC 1, 39; WLC**
See also AAYA 21; AMW; AMWR 1; CA 89-92; CANR 33; CDALB 1917-1929; CLR 67; DA; DAB; DAC; DAM MST, POET; DLB 54; DLBD 7; EXPP; MTCW 1, 2; PAB; PFS 1, 2, 3, 4, 5, 6, 7, 10, 13; RGAL 4; SATA 14; TUS; WP; WYA

**Froude, James Anthony**
1818-1894 ................................. **NCLC 43**
See also DLB 18, 57, 144

**Froy, Herald**
See Waterhouse, Keith (Spencer)

**Fry, Christopher** 1907- ............. **CLC 2, 10, 14**
See also BRWS 3; CA 17-20R; CAAS 23; CANR 9, 30, 74; CBD; CD 5; CP 7; DAM DRAM; DLB 13; MTCW 1, 2; RGEL 2; SATA 66; TEA

**Frye, (Herman) Northrop**
1912-1991 ................................. **CLC 24, 70**
See also CA 5-8R; CANR 8, 37; DLB 67, 68, 246; MTCW 1, 2; RGAL 4; TWA

**Fuchs, Daniel** 1909-1993 ............... **CLC 8, 22**
See also CA 81-84; CAAS 5; CANR 40; DLB 9, 26, 28; DLBY 1993

**Fuchs, Daniel** 1934- ........................... **CLC 34**
See also CA 37-40R; CANR 14, 48

**Fuentes, Carlos** 1928- .. **CLC 3, 8, 10, 13, 22, 41, 60, 113; HLC 1; SSC 24; WLC**
See also AAYA 4, 45; AITN 2; BPFB 1; CA 69-72; CANR 10, 32, 68, 104; CDWLB 3; CWW 2; DA; DAB; DAC; DAM MST, MULT, NOV; DLB 113; DNFS 2; HW 1, 2; LAIT 3; LAW; LAWS 1; MTCW 1, 2; NFS 8; RGSF 2; RGWL 2, 3; TWA; WLIT 1

**Fuentes, Gregorio Lopez y**
See Lopez y Fuentes, Gregorio

**Fuertes, Gloria** 1918-1998 .................... **PC 27**
See also CA 178, 180; DLB 108; HW 2; SATA 115

**Fugard, (Harold) Athol** 1932- . **CLC 5, 9, 14, 25, 40, 80; DC 3**
See also AAYA 17; AFW; CA 85-88; CANR 32, 54; CD 5; DAM DRAM; DFS 3, 6, 10; DLB 225; DNFS 1, 2; MTCW 1; RGEL 2; WLIT 2

**Fugard, Sheila** 1932- ........................... **CLC 48**
See also CA 125

**Fukuyama, Francis** 1952- ................. **CLC 131**
See also CA 140; CANR 72

**Fuller, Charles (H., Jr.)** 1939- .. **BLC 2; CLC 25; DC 1**
See also BW 2; CA 112; CAD; CANR 87; CD 5; DAM DRAM, MULT; DFS 8; DLB 38, 266; INT CA-112; MTCW 1

**Fuller, Henry Blake** 1857-1929 .... **TCLC 103**
See also CA 177; DLB 12; RGAL 4

**Fuller, John (Leopold)** 1937- ............. **CLC 62**
See also CA 21-24R; CANR 9, 44; CP 7; DLB 40

**Fuller, Margaret**
See Ossoli, Sarah Margaret (Fuller)
See also AMWS 2; DLB 183, 223, 239

**Fuller, Roy (Broadbent)** 1912-1991 ... **CLC 4, 28**
See also BRWS 7; CA 5-8R; CAAS 10; CANR 53, 83; CWRI 5; DLB 15, 20; RGEL 2; SATA 87

**Fuller, Sarah Margaret**
See Ossoli, Sarah Margaret (Fuller)

**Fuller, Sarah Margaret**
See Ossoli, Sarah Margaret (Fuller)
See also DLB 1, 59, 73

**Fulton, Alice** 1952- ............................. **CLC 52**
See also CA 116; CANR 57, 88; CP 7; CWP; DLB 193

**Furphy, Joseph** 1843-1912 ............... **TCLC 25**
See also CA 163; DLB 230; RGEL 2

**Fuson, Robert H(enderson)** 1927- .... **CLC 70**
See also CA 89-92; CANR 103

**Fussell, Paul** 1924- ............................. **CLC 74**
See also BEST 90:1; CA 17-20R; CANR 8, 21, 35, 69; INT CANR-21; MTCW 1, 2

**Futabatei, Shimei** 1864-1909 .......... **TCLC 44**
See Futabatei Shimei
See also CA 162; MJW

**Futabatei Shimei**
See Futabatei, Shimei
See also DLB 180

**Futrelle, Jacques** 1875-1912 ............. **TCLC 19**
See also CA 155; CMW 4

**Gaboriau, Emile** 1835-1873 ........... **NCLC 14**
See also CMW 4; MSW

**Gadda, Carlo Emilio** 1893-1973 ....... **CLC 11**
See also CA 89-92; DLB 177

**Gaddis, William** 1922-1998 ... **CLC 1, 3, 6, 8, 10, 19, 43, 86**
See also AMWS 4; BPFB 1; CA 17-20R; CANR 21, 48; CN 7; DLB 2; MTCW 1, 2; RGAL 4

**Gaelique, Moruen le**
See Jacob, (Cyprien-)Max

**Gage, Walter**
See Inge, William (Motter)

**Gaines, Ernest J(ames)** 1933- .. **BLC 2; CLC 3, 11, 18, 86**
See also AAYA 18; AFAW 1, 2; AITN 1; BPFB 2; BW 2, 3; BYA 6; CA 9-12R; CANR 6, 24, 42, 75; CDALB 1968-1988; CLR 62; CN 7; CSW; DAM MULT; DLB 2, 33, 152; DLBY 1980; EXPN; LAIT 5; MTCW 1, 2; NFS 5, 7, 16; RGAL 4; RGSF 2; RHW; SATA 86; SSFS 5; YAW

**Gaitskill, Mary** 1954- ......................... **CLC 69**
See also CA 128; CANR 61; DLB 244

**Galdos, Benito Perez**
See Perez Galdos, Benito
See also EW 7

**Gale, Zona** 1874-1938 ...................... **TCLC 7**
See also CA 153; CANR 84; DAM DRAM; DLB 9, 78, 228; RGAL 4

**Galeano, Eduardo (Hughes)** 1940- . **CLC 72; HLCS 1**
See also CA 29-32R; CANR 13, 32, 100; HW 1

**Galiano, Juan Valera y Alcala**
See Valera y Alcala-Galiano, Juan

**Galilei, Galileo** 1564-1642 ................... **LC 45**

**Gallagher, Tess** 1943- ........ **CLC 18, 63; PC 9**
See also CA 106; CP 7; CWP; DAM POET; DLB 120, 212, 244; PFS 16

**Gallant, Mavis** 1922- . **CLC 7, 18, 38; SSC 5**
See also CA 69-72; CANR 29, 69; CCA 1; CN 7; DAC; DAM MST; DLB 53; MTCW 1, 2; RGEL 2; RGSF 2

**Gallant, Roy A(rthur)** 1924- ............. **CLC 17**
See also CA 5-8R; CANR 4, 29, 54; CLR 30; MAICYA 1, 2; SATA 4, 68, 110

**Gallico, Paul (William)** 1897-1976 ...... **CLC 2**
See also AITN 1; CA 5-8R; CANR 23; DLB 9, 171; FANT; MAICYA 1, 2; SATA 13

**Gallo, Max Louis** 1932- ..................... **CLC 95**
See also CA 85-88

**Gallois, Lucien**
See Desnos, Robert

**Gallup, Ralph**
See Whitemore, Hugh (John)

**Galsworthy, John** 1867-1933 ............ **SSC 22; TCLC 1, 45; WLC**
See also BRW 6; CA 141; CANR 75; CDBLB 1890-1914; DA; DAB; DAC; DAM DRAM, MST, NOV; DLB 10, 34, 98, 162; DLBD 16; MTCW 1; RGEL 2; SSFS 3; TEA

**Galt, John** 1779-1839 ................ **NCLC 1, 110**
See also DLB 99, 116, 159; RGEL 2; RGSF 2

**Galvin, James** 1951- .......................... **CLC 38**
See also CA 108; CANR 26

**Gamboa, Federico** 1864-1939 ......... **TCLC 36**
See also CA 167; HW 2; LAW

**Gandhi, M. K.**
See Gandhi, Mohandas Karamchand

**Gandhi, Mahatma**
See Gandhi, Mohandas Karamchand

**Gandhi, Mohandas Karamchand**
1869-1948 ..................... **TCLC 59**
See also CA 132; DAM MULT; MTCW 1, 2

**Gann, Ernest Kellogg** 1910-1991 ..... **CLC 23**
See also AITN 1; BPFB 2; CA 1-4R; CANR 1, 83; RHW

**Garber, Eric** 1943(?)-
See Holleran, Andrew
See also CANR 89

**Garcia, Cristina** 1958- ....................... **CLC 76**
See also AMWS 11; CA 141; CANR 73; DNFS 1; HW 2

**Garcia Lorca, Federico** 1898-1936 ...... **DC 2; HLC 2; PC 3; TCLC 1, 7, 49; WLC**
See Lorca, Federico Garcia
See also AAYA 46; CA 131; CANR 81; DA; DAB; DAC; DAM DRAM, MST, MULT, POET; DFS 10; DLB 108; HW 1, 2; MTCW 1, 2; TWA

**Garcia Marquez, Gabriel (Jose)**
1928- ..... **CLC 2, 3, 8, 10, 15, 27, 47, 55, 68; HLC 1; SSC 8; WLC**
See also AAYA 3, 33; BEST 89:1, 90:4; BPFB 2; BYA 12; CA 33-36R; CANR 10, 28, 50, 75, 82; CDWLB 3; CPW; DA; DAB; DAC; DAM MST, MULT, NOV, POP; DLB 113; DNFS 1, 2; EXPN; EXPS; HW 1, 2; LAIT 2; LAW; LAWS 1; MTCW 1, 2; NCFS 3; NFS 1, 5, 10; RGSF 2; RGWL 2, 3; SSFS 1, 6, 16; TWA; WLIT 1

**Garcilaso de la Vega, El Inca**
1503-1536 ...................... **HLCS 1**
See also LAW

**Gard, Janice**
See Latham, Jean Lee

**Gard, Roger Martin du**
See Martin du Gard, Roger

**Gardam, Jane (Mary)** 1928- ............. **CLC 43**
See also CA 49-52; CANR 2, 18, 33, 54, 106; CLR 12; DLB 14, 161, 231; MAICYA 1, 2; MTCW 1; SAAS 9; SATA 39, 76, 130; SATA-Brief 28; YAW

**Gardner, Herb(ert)** 1934- ................. **CLC 44**
See also CA 149; CAD; CD 5

**Gardner, John (Champlin), Jr.**
1933-1982 ...... **CLC 2, 3, 5, 7, 8, 10, 18, 28, 34; SSC 7**
See also AAYA 45; AITN 1; AMWS 6; BPFB 2; CA 65-68; CANR 33, 73; CDALBS; CPW; DAM NOV, POP; DLB 2; DLBY 1982; FANT; MTCW 1; NFS 3; RGAL 4; RGSF 2; SATA 40; SATA-Obit 31; SSFS 8

**Gardner, John (Edmund)** 1926- ....... **CLC 30**
See also CA 103; CANR 15, 69; CMW 4; CPW; DAM POP; MTCW 1

**Gardner, Miriam**
See Bradley, Marion Zimmer
See also GLL 1

**Gardner, Noel**
See Kuttner, Henry

**Gardons, S. S.**
See Snodgrass, W(illiam) D(e Witt)

**Garfield, Leon** 1921-1996 .................. **CLC 12**
See also AAYA 8; BYA 1, 3; CA 17-20R; CANR 38, 41, 78; CLR 21; DLB 161; JRDA; MAICYA 1, 2; MAICYAS 1; SATA 1, 32, 76; SATA-Obit 90; TEA; WYA; YAW

**Garland, (Hannibal) Hamlin**
1860-1940 ................... **SSC 18; TCLC 3**
See also DLB 12, 71, 78, 186; RGAL 4; RGSF 2; TCWW 2

**Garneau, (Hector de) Saint-Denys**
1912-1943 ......................... **TCLC 13**
See also DLB 88

**Garner, Alan** 1934- ........................... **CLC 17**
See also AAYA 18; BYA 3, 5; CA 73-76, 178; CAAE 178; CANR 15, 64; CLR 20; CPW; DAB; DAM POP; DLB 161, 261; FANT; MAICYA 1, 2; MTCW 1, 2; SATA 18, 69; SATA-Essay 108; SUFW 1, 2; YAW

**Garner, Hugh** 1913-1979 ................... **CLC 13**
See Warwick, Jarvis
See also CA 69-72; CANR 31; CCA 1; DLB 68

**Garnett, David** 1892-1981 .................. **CLC 3**
See also CA 5-8R; CANR 17, 79; DLB 34; FANT; MTCW 2; RGEL 2; SFW 4; SUFW 1

**Garos, Stephanie**
See Katz, Steve

**Garrett, George (Palmer)** 1929- .. **CLC 3, 11, 51; SSC 30**
See also AMWS 7; BPFB 2; CA 1-4R; CAAE 202; CAAS 5; CANR 1, 42, 67, 109; CN 7; CP 7; CSW; DLB 2, 5, 130, 152; DLBY 1983

**Garrick, David** 1717-1779 ................... **LC 15**
See also DAM DRAM; DLB 84, 213; RGEL 2

**Garrigue, Jean** 1914-1972 ............... **CLC 2, 8**
See also CA 5-8R; CANR 20

**Garrison, Frederick**
See Sinclair, Upton (Beall)

**Garro, Elena** 1920(?)-1998 ............... **HLCS 1**
See also CA 131; CWW 2; DLB 145; HW 1; LAWS 1; WLIT 1

**Garth, Will**
See Hamilton, Edmond; Kuttner, Henry

**Garvey, Marcus (Moziah, Jr.)**
1887-1940 ....... **BLC 2; HR 2; TCLC 41**
See also BW 1; CA 124; CANR 79; DAM MULT

**Gary, Romain** ..................................... **CLC 25**
See Kacew, Romain
See also DLB 83

**Gascar, Pierre** ..................................... **CLC 11**
See Fournier, Pierre

**Gascoyne, David (Emery)**
1916-2001 ................................. **CLC 45**
See also CA 65-68; CANR 10, 28, 54; CP 7; DLB 20; MTCW 1; RGEL 2

**Gaskell, Elizabeth Cleghorn**
1810-1865 ....... **NCLC 5, 70, 97; SSC 25**
See also BRW 5; CDBLB 1832-1890; DAB; DAM MST; DLB 21, 144, 159; RGEL 2; RGSF 2; TEA

**Gass, William H(oward)** 1924- . **CLC 1, 2, 8, 11, 15, 39, 132; SSC 12**
See also AMWS 6; CA 17-20R; CANR 30, 71, 100; CN 7; DLB 2, 227; MTCW 1, 2; RGAL 4

**Gassendi, Pierre** 1592-1655 ................. **LC 54**
See also GFL Beginnings to 1789

**Gasset, Jose Ortega y**
See Ortega y Gasset, Jose

**Gates, Henry Louis, Jr.** 1950- ... **BLCS; CLC 65**
See also BW 2, 3; CA 109; CANR 25, 53, 75; CSW; DAM MULT; DLB 67; MTCW 1; RGAL 4

**Gautier, Theophile** 1811-1872 .. **NCLC 1, 59; PC 18; SSC 20**
See also DAM POET; DLB 119; EW 6; GFL 1789 to the Present; RGWL 2, 3; SUFW; TWA

**Gawsworth, John**
See Bates, H(erbert) E(rnest)

**Gay, John** 1685-1732 ........................... **LC 49**
See also BRW 3; DAM DRAM; DLB 84, 95; RGEL 2; WLIT 3

**Gay, Oliver**
See Gogarty, Oliver St. John

**Gay, Peter (Jack)** 1923- ................... **CLC 158**
See also CA 13-16R; CANR 18, 41, 77; INT CANR-18

**Gaye, Marvin (Pentz, Jr.)**
1939-1984 ................................. **CLC 26**
See also CA 195

**Gebler, Carlo (Ernest)** 1954- ............. **CLC 39**
See also CA 133; CANR 96; DLB 271

**Gee, Maggie (Mary)** 1948- ................ **CLC 57**
See also CA 130; CN 7; DLB 207

**Gee, Maurice (Gough)** 1931- ............ **CLC 29**
See also AAYA 42; CA 97-100; CANR 67; CLR 56; CN 7; CWRI 5; MAICYA 2; RGSF 2; SATA 46, 101

**Gelbart, Larry (Simon)** 1928- .... **CLC 21, 61**
See Gelbart, Larry
See also CA 73-76; CANR 45, 94

**Gelbart, Larry** 1928-
See Gelbart, Larry (Simon)
See also CAD; CD 5

**Gelber, Jack** 1932- .............. **CLC 1, 6, 14, 79**
See also CA 1-4R; CAD; CANR 2; DLB 7, 228

**Gellhorn, Martha (Ellis)**
1908-1998 ............................. **CLC 14, 60**
See also CA 77-80; CANR 44; CN 7; DLBY 1982, 1998

**Genet, Jean** 1910-1986 .. **CLC 1, 2, 5, 10, 14, 44, 46; TCLC 128**
See also CA 13-16R; CANR 18; DAM DRAM; DFS 10; DLB 72; DLBY 1986; EW 13; GFL 1789 to the Present; GLL 1; MTCW 1, 2; RGWL 2, 3; TWA

**Gent, Peter** 1942- ............................... **CLC 29**
See also AITN 1; CA 89-92; DLBY 1982

**Gentile, Giovanni** 1875-1944 .......... **TCLC 96**

**Gentlewoman in New England, A**
See Bradstreet, Anne

**Gentlewoman in Those Parts, A**
See Bradstreet, Anne

**Geoffrey of Monmouth** c.
1100-1155 ................. **CMLC 44**
See also DLB 146; TEA

**George, Jean**
See George, Jean Craighead
**George, Jean Craighead** 1919- ......... **CLC 35**
See also AAYA 8; BYA 2, 4; CA 5-8R; CANR 25; CLR 1; 80; DLB 52; JRDA; MAICYA 1, 2; SATA 2, 68, 124; WYA; YAW
**George, Stefan (Anton)** 1868-1933 . **TCLC 2, 14**
See also CA 193; EW 8
**Georges, Georges Martin**
See Simenon, Georges (Jacques Christian)
**Gerhardi, William Alexander**
See Gerhardie, William Alexander
**Gerhardie, William Alexander**
1895-1977 ...................................... **CLC 5**
See also CA 25-28R; CANR 18; DLB 36; RGEL 2
**Gerson, Jean** 1363-1429 ...................... **LC 77**
See also DLB 208
**Gersonides** 1288-1344 .................... **CMLC 49**
See also DLB 115
**Gerstler, Amy** 1956- ........................... **CLC 70**
See also CA 146; CANR 99
**Gertler, T.** ......................................... **CLC 134**
See also CA 121
**Ghalib** ....................................... **NCLC 39, 78**
See also Ghalib, Asadullah Khan
**Ghalib, Asadullah Khan** 1797-1869
See Ghalib
See also DAM POET; RGWL 2, 3
**Ghelderode, Michel de** 1898-1962 ..... **CLC 6, 11; DC 15**
See also CA 85-88; CANR 40, 77; DAM DRAM; EW 11; TWA
**Ghiselin, Brewster** 1903-2001 ........... **CLC 23**
See also CA 13-16R; CAAS 10; CANR 13; CP 7
**Ghose, Aurabinda** 1872-1950 ......... **TCLC 63**
See also CA 163
**Ghose, Zulfikar** 1935- ...................... **CLC 42**
See also CA 65-68; CANR 67; CN 7; CP 7
**Ghosh, Amitav** 1956- ................. **CLC 44, 153**
See also CA 147; CANR 80; CN 7
**Giacosa, Giuseppe** 1847-1906 ........... **TCLC 7**
**Gibb, Lee**
See Waterhouse, Keith (Spencer)
**Gibbon, Lewis Grassic** ...................... **TCLC 4**
See Mitchell, James Leslie
See also RGEL 2
**Gibbons, Kaye** 1960- ........... **CLC 50, 88, 145**
See also AAYA 34; AMWS 10; CA 151; CANR 75; CSW; DAM POP; MTCW 1; NFS 3; RGAL 4; SATA 117
**Gibran, Kahlil** 1883-1931 . **PC 9; TCLC 1, 9**
See also CA 150; DAM POET, POP; MTCW 2
**Gibran, Khalil**
See Gibran, Kahlil
**Gibson, William** 1914- ....................... **CLC 23**
See also CA 9-12R; CAD 2; CANR 9, 42, 75; CD 5; DA; DAB; DAC; DAM DRAM, MST; DFS 2; DLB 7; LAIT 2; MTCW 2; SATA 66; YAW
**Gibson, William (Ford)** 1948- ... **CLC 39, 63; SSC 52**
See also AAYA 12; BPFB 2; CA 133; CANR 52, 90, 106; CN 7; CPW; DAM POP; DLB 251; MTCW 2; SCFW 2; SFW 4
**Gide, Andre (Paul Guillaume)**
1869-1951 ..... **SSC 13; TCLC 5, 12, 36; WLC**
See also CA 124; DA; DAB; DAC; DAM MST, NOV; DLB 65; EW 8; GFL 1789 to the Present; MTCW 1, 2; RGSF 2; RGWL 2, 3; TWA
**Gifford, Barry (Colby)** 1946- ........... **CLC 34**
See also CA 65-68; CANR 9, 30, 40, 90

**Gilbert, Frank**
See De Voto, Bernard (Augustine)
**Gilbert, W(illiam) S(chwenck)**
1836-1911 .................................... **TCLC 3**
See also CA 173; DAM DRAM, POET; RGEL 2; SATA 36
**Gilbreth, Frank B(unker), Jr.**
1911-2001 .................................. **CLC 17**
See also CA 9-12R; SATA 2
**Gilchrist, Ellen (Louise)** 1935- .. **CLC 34, 48, 143; SSC 14**
See also BPFB 2; CA 116; CANR 41, 61, 104; CN 7; CPW; CSW; DAM POP; DLB 130; EXPS; MTCW 1, 2; RGAL 4; RGSF 2; SSFS 9
**Giles, Molly** 1942- ............................ **CLC 39**
See also CA 126; CANR 98
**Gill, Eric** 1882-1940 ....................... **TCLC 85**
**Gill, Patrick**
See Creasey, John
**Gillette, Douglas** ............................. **CLC 70**
**Gilliam, Terry (Vance)** 1940- .... **CLC 21, 141**
See Monty Python
See also AAYA 19; CA 113; CANR 35; INT 113
**Gillian, Jerry**
See Gilliam, Terry (Vance)
**Gilliatt, Penelope (Ann Douglass)**
1932-1993 .................. **CLC 2, 10, 13, 53**
See also AITN 2; CA 13-16R; CANR 49; DLB 14
**Gilman, Charlotte (Anna) Perkins (Stetson)**
1860-1935 ..... **SSC 13; TCLC 9, 37, 117**
See also AMWS 11; BYA 11; CA 150; DLB 221; EXPS; FW; HGG; LAIT 2; MAWW; MTCW 1; RGAL 4; RGSF 2; SFW 4; SSFS 1
**Gilmour, David** 1946- ......................... **CLC 35**
**Gilpin, William** 1724-1804 ............. **NCLC 30**
**Gilray, J. D.**
See Mencken, H(enry) L(ouis)
**Gilroy, Frank D(aniel)** 1925- ............. **CLC 2**
See also CA 81-84; CAD; CANR 32, 64, 86; CD 5; DLB 7
**Gilstrap, John** 1957(?)- ....................... **CLC 99**
See also CA 160; CANR 101
**Ginsberg, Allen** 1926-1997 .... **CLC 1, 2, 3, 4, 6, 13, 36, 69, 109; PC 4; TCLC 120; WLC**
See also AAYA 33; AITN 1; AMWC 1; AMWS 2; BG 2; CA 1-4R; CANR 2, 41, 63, 95; CDALB 1941-1968; CP 7; DA; DAB; DAC; DAM MST, POET; DLB 5, 16, 169, 237; GLL 1; MTCW 1, 2; PAB; PFS 5; RGAL 4; TUS; WP
**Ginzburg, Eugenia** ............................... **CLC 59**
**Ginzburg, Natalia** 1916-1991 ....... **CLC 5, 11, 54, 70**
See also CA 85-88; CANR 33; DFS 14; DLB 177; EW 13; MTCW 1, 2; RGWL 2, 3
**Giono, Jean** 1895-1970 .... **CLC 4, 11; TCLC 124**
See also CA 45-48; CANR 2, 35; DLB 72; GFL 1789 to the Present; MTCW 1; RGWL 2, 3
**Giovanni, Nikki** 1943- ...... **BLC 2; CLC 2, 4, 19, 64, 117; PC 19; WLCS**
See also AAYA 22; AITN 1; BW 2, 3; CA 29-32R; CAAS 6; CANR 18, 41, 60, 91; CDALBS; CLR 6, 73; CP 7; CSW; CWP; CWRI 5; DA; DAB; DAC; DAM MST, MULT, POET; DLB 5, 41; EXPP; INT CANR-18; MAICYA 1, 2; MTCW 1, 2; PFS 17; RGAL 4; SATA 24, 107; TUS; YAW
**Giovene, Andrea** 1904-1998 ................. **CLC 7**
See also CA 85-88

**Gippius, Zinaida (Nikolayevna)** 1869-1945
See Hippius, Zinaida
**Giraudoux, Jean(-Hippolyte)**
1882-1944 ................................. **TCLC 2, 7**
See also CA 196; DAM DRAM; DLB 65; EW 9; GFL 1789 to the Present; RGWL 2, 3; TWA
**Gironella, Jose Maria** 1917-1991 ..... **CLC 11**
See also CA 101; RGWL 2, 3
**Gissing, George (Robert)**
1857-1903 ....... **SSC 37; TCLC 3, 24, 47**
See also BRW 5; CA 167; DLB 18, 135, 184; RGEL 2; TEA
**Giurlani, Aldo**
See Palazzeschi, Aldo
**Gladkov, Fedor Vasil'evich**
See Gladkov, Fyodor (Vasilyevich)
See also DLB 272
**Gladkov, Fyodor (Vasilyevich)**
1883-1958 ................................ **TCLC 27**
See Gladkov, Fedor Vasil'evich
See also CA 170
**Glanville, Brian (Lester)** 1931- ........... **CLC 6**
See also CA 5-8R; CAAS 9; CANR 3, 70; CN 7; DLB 15, 139; SATA 42
**Glasgow, Ellen (Anderson Gholson)**
1873-1945 ............... **SSC 34; TCLC 2, 7**
See also AMW; CA 164; DLB 9, 12; MAWW; MTCW 2; RGAL 4; RHW; SSFS 9; TUS
**Glaspell, Susan** 1882(?)-1948 ..... **DC 10; SSC 41; TCLC 55**
See also AMWS 3; CA 154; DFS 8; DLB 7, 9, 78, 228; MAWW; RGAL 4; SSFS 3; TCWW 2; TUS; YABC 2
**Glassco, John** 1909-1981 ..................... **CLC 9**
See also CA 13-16R; CANR 15; DLB 68
**Glasscock, Amnesia**
See Steinbeck, John (Ernst)
**Glasser, Ronald J.** 1940(?)- ............... **CLC 37**
**Glassman, Joyce**
See Johnson, Joyce
**Gleick, James (W.)** 1954- .................. **CLC 147**
See also CA 137; CANR 97; INT CA-137
**Glendinning, Victoria** 1937- .............. **CLC 50**
See also CA 127; CANR 59, 89; DLB 155
**Glissant, Edouard (Mathieu)**
1928- ........................................ **CLC 10, 68**
See also CA 153; CANR 111; CWW 2; DAM MULT; RGWL 3
**Gloag, Julian** 1930- ........................... **CLC 40**
See also AITN 1; CA 65-68; CANR 10, 70; CN 7
**Glowacki, Aleksander**
See Prus, Boleslaw
**Gluck, Louise (Elisabeth)** 1943- .. **CLC 7, 22, 44, 81, 160; PC 16**
See also AMWS 5; CA 33-36R; CANR 40, 69, 108; CP 7; CWP; DAM POET; DLB 5; MTCW 2; PFS 5, 15; RGAL 4
**Glyn, Elinor** 1864-1943 ................... **TCLC 72**
See also DLB 153; RHW
**Gobineau, Joseph-Arthur**
1816-1882 ................................. **NCLC 17**
See also DLB 123; GFL 1789 to the Present
**Godard, Jean-Luc** 1930- .................... **CLC 20**
See also CA 93-96
**Godden, (Margaret) Rumer**
1907-1998 .................................. **CLC 53**
See also AAYA 6; BPFB 2; BYA 2, 5; CA 5-8R; CANR 4, 27, 36, 55, 80; CLR 20; CN 7; CWRI 5; DLB 161; MAICYA 1, 2; RHW; SAAS 12; SATA 3, 36; SATA-Obit 109; TEA
**Godoy Alcayaga, Lucila** 1899-1957 .. **HLC 2; PC 2; TCLC 2**
See Mistral, Gabriela
See also BW 2; CA 131; CANR 81; DAM MULT; DNFS 1, 2; HW 1, 2; MTCW 1, 2

**Godwin, Gail (Kathleen)** 1937- ..... **CLC 5, 8, 22, 31, 69, 125**
See also BPFB 2; CA 29-32R; CANR 15, 43, 69; CN 7; CPW; CSW; DAM POP; DLB 6, 234; INT CANR-15; MTCW 1, 2

**Godwin, William** 1756-1836 ........... **NCLC 14**
See also CDBLB 1789-1832; CMW 4; DLB 39, 104, 142, 158, 163, 262; HGG; RGEL 2

**Goebbels, Josef**
See Goebbels, (Paul) Joseph

**Goebbels, (Paul) Joseph**
1897-1945 ................................. **TCLC 68**
See also CA 148

**Goebbels, Joseph Paul**
See Goebbels, (Paul) Joseph

**Goethe, Johann Wolfgang von**
1749-1832 ... **NCLC 4, 22, 34, 90; PC 5; SSC 38; WLC**
See also CDBLB 2; DA; DAB; DAC; DAM DRAM, MST, POET; DLB 94; EW 5; RGWL 2, 3; TWA

**Gogarty, Oliver St. John**
1878-1957 ................................. **TCLC 15**
See also CA 150; DLB 15, 19; RGEL 2

**Gogol, Nikolai (Vasilyevich)**
1809-1852 .............. **DC 1; NCLC 5, 15, 31; SSC 4, 29, 52; WLC**
See also DA; DAB; DAC; DAM DRAM, MST; DFS 12; DLB 198; EW 6; EXPS; RGSF 2; RGWL 2, 3; SSFS 7; TWA

**Goines, Donald** 1937(?)-1974 ... **BLC 2; CLC 80**
See also AITN 1; BW 1, 3; CA 124; CANR 82; CMW 4; DAM MULT, POP; DLB 33

**Gold, Herbert** 1924- ... **CLC 4, 7, 14, 42, 152**
See also CA 9-12R; CANR 17, 45; CN 7; DLB 2; DLBY 1981

**Goldbarth, Albert** 1948- ................ **CLC 5, 38**
See also AMWS 12; CA 53-56; CANR 6, 40; CP 7; DLB 120

**Goldberg, Anatol** 1910-1982 ............ **CLC 34**
See also CA 131

**Goldemberg, Isaac** 1945- ................ **CLC 52**
See also CA 69-72; CAAS 12; CANR 11, 32; HW 1; WLIT 1

**Golding, William (Gerald)**
1911-1993 ..... **CLC 1, 2, 3, 8, 10, 17, 27, 58, 81; WLC**
See also AAYA 5, 44; BPFB 2; BRWR 1; BRWS 1; BYA 2; CA 5-8R; CANR 13, 33, 54; CDBLB 1945-1960; DA; DAB; DAC; DAM MST, NOV; DLB 15, 100, 255; EXPN; HGG; LAIT 4; MTCW 1, 2; NFS 2; RGEL 2; RHW; SFW 4; TEA; WLIT 4; YAW

**Goldman, Emma** 1869-1940 .......... **TCLC 13**
See also CA 150; DLB 221; FW; RGAL 4; TUS

**Goldman, Francisco** 1954- ............... **CLC 76**
See also CA 162

**Goldman, William (W.)** 1931- ...... **CLC 1, 48**
See also BPFB 2; CA 9-12R; CANR 29, 69, 106; CN 7; DLB 44; FANT; IDFW 3, 4

**Goldmann, Lucien** 1913-1970 ........... **CLC 24**
See also CA 25-28; CAP 2

**Goldoni, Carlo** 1707-1793 ..................... **LC 4**
See also DAM DRAM; EW 4; RGWL 2, 3

**Goldsberry, Steven** 1949- ................. **CLC 34**
See also CA 131

**Goldsmith, Oliver** 1730-1774 .... **DC 8; LC 2, 48; WLC**
See also BRW 3; CDBLB 1660-1789; DA; DAB; DAC; DAM DRAM, MST, NOV, POET; DFS 1; DLB 39, 89, 104, 109, 142; IDTP; RGEL 2; SATA 26; TEA; WLIT 3

**Goldsmith, Peter**
See Priestley, J(ohn) B(oynton)

**Gombrowicz, Witold** 1904-1969 .... **CLC 4, 7, 11, 49**
See also CA 19-20; CANR 105; CAP 2; CDWLB 4; DAM DRAM; DLB 215; EW 12; RGWL 2, 3; TWA

**Gomez de Avellaneda, Gertrudis**
1814-1873 ................................ **NCLC 111**
See also LAW

**Gomez de la Serna, Ramon**
1888-1963 ................................... **CLC 9**
See also CA 153; CANR 79; HW 1, 2

**Goncharov, Ivan Alexandrovich**
1812-1891 ............................. **NCLC 1, 63**
See also DLB 238; EW 6; RGWL 2, 3

**Goncourt, Edmond (Louis Antoine Huot) de**
1822-1896 .................................. **NCLC 7**
See also DLB 123; EW 7; GFL 1789 to the Present; RGWL 2, 3

**Goncourt, Jules (Alfred Huot) de**
1830-1870 .................................. **NCLC 7**
See also DLB 123; EW 7; GFL 1789 to the Present; RGWL 2, 3

**Gongora (y Argote), Luis de**
1561-1627 ...................................... **LC 72**
See also RGWL 2, 3

**Gontier, Fernande** 19(?)- ................... **CLC 50**

**Gonzalez Martinez, Enrique**
1871-1952 ................................... **TCLC 72**
See also CA 166; CANR 81; HW 1, 2

**Goodison, Lorna** 1947- .......................... **PC 36**
See also CA 142; CANR 88; CP 7; CWP; DLB 157

**Goodman, Paul** 1911-1972 ..... **CLC 1, 2, 4, 7**
See also CA 19-20; CAD; CANR 34; CAP 2; DLB 130, 246; MTCW 1; RGAL 4

**Gordimer, Nadine** 1923- ...... **CLC 3, 5, 7, 10, 18, 33, 51, 70, 123, 160, 161; SSC 17; WLCS**
See also AAYA 39; AFW; BRWS 2; CA 5-8R; CANR 3, 28, 56, 88; CN 7; DA; DAB; DAC; DAM MST, NOV; DLB 225; EXPS; INT CANR-28; MTCW 1, 2; NFS 4; RGEL 2; RGSF 2; SSFS 2, 14; TWA; WLIT 2; YAW

**Gordon, Adam Lindsay**
1833-1870 ................................. **NCLC 21**
See also DLB 230

**Gordon, Caroline** 1895-1981 . **CLC 6, 13, 29, 83; SSC 15**
See also AMW; CA 11-12; CANR 36; CAP 1; DLB 4, 9, 102; DLBD 17; DLBY 1981; MTCW 1, 2; RGAL 4; RGSF 2

**Gordon, Charles William** 1860-1937
See Connor, Ralph

**Gordon, Mary (Catherine)** 1949- .... **CLC 13, 22, 128**
See also AMWS 4; BPFB 2; CA 102; CANR 44, 92; CN 7; DLB 6; DLBY 1981; FW; INT CA-102; MTCW 1

**Gordon, N. J.**
See Bosman, Herman Charles

**Gordon, Sol** 1923- ............................. **CLC 26**
See also CA 53-56; CANR 4; SATA 11

**Gordone, Charles** 1925-1995 .. **CLC 1, 4; DC 8**
See also BW 1, 3; CA 93-96, 180; CAAE 180; CAD; CANR 55; DAM DRAM; DLB 7; INT 93-96; MTCW 1

**Gore, Catherine** 1800-1861 ............ **NCLC 65**
See also DLB 116; RGEL 2

**Gorenko, Anna Andreevna**
See Akhmatova, Anna

**Gorky, Maxim** ....... **SSC 28; TCLC 8; WLC**
See Peshkov, Alexei Maximovich
See also DAB; DFS 9; EW 8; MTCW 2; TWA

**Goryan, Sirak**
See Saroyan, William

**Gosse, Edmund (William)**
1849-1928 ................................. **TCLC 28**
See also DLB 57, 144, 184; RGEL 2

**Gotlieb, Phyllis Fay (Bloom)** 1926- .. **CLC 18**
See also CA 13-16R; CANR 7; DLB 88, 251; SFW 4

**Gottesman, S. D.**
See Kornbluth, C(yril) M.; Pohl, Frederik

**Gottfried von Strassburg** fl. c.
1170-1215 ................................ **CMLC 10**
See also CDWLB 2; DLB 138; EW 1; RGWL 2, 3

**Gotthelf, Jeremias** 1797-1854 ....... **NCLC 117**
See also DLB 133; RGWL 2, 3

**Gottschalk, Laura Riding**
See Jackson, Laura (Riding)

**Gould, Lois** 1932(?)-2002 ............. **CLC 4, 10**
See also CA 77-80; CANR 29; MTCW 1

**Gould, Stephen Jay** 1941-2002 ........ **CLC 163**
See also AAYA 26; BEST 90:2; CA 77-80; CANR 10, 27, 56, 75; CPW; INT CANR-27; MTCW 1, 2

**Gourmont, Remy(-Marie-Charles) de**
1858-1915 ................................. **TCLC 17**
See also CA 150; GFL 1789 to the Present; MTCW 2

**Govier, Katherine** 1948- ..................... **CLC 51**
See also CA 101; CANR 18, 40; CCA 1

**Gower, John** c. 1330-1408 ..................... **LC 76**
See also BRW 1; DLB 146; RGEL 2

**Goyen, (Charles) William**
1915-1983 ...................... **CLC 5, 8, 14, 40**
See also AITN 2; CA 5-8R; CANR 6, 71; DLB 2, 218; DLBY 1983; INT CANR-6

**Goytisolo, Juan** 1931- .... **CLC 5, 10, 23, 133; HLC 1**
See also CA 85-88; CANR 32, 61; CWW 2; DAM MULT; GLL 1; HW 1, 2; MTCW 1, 2

**Gozzano, Guido** 1883-1916 .................. **PC 10**
See also CA 154; DLB 114

**Gozzi, (Conte) Carlo** 1720-1806 .... **NCLC 23**

**Grabbe, Christian Dietrich**
1801-1836 ................................... **NCLC 2**
See also DLB 133; RGWL 2, 3

**Grace, Patricia Frances** 1937- .......... **CLC 56**
See also CA 176; CN 7; RGSF 2

**Gracian y Morales, Baltasar**
1601-1658 ...................................... **LC 15**

**Gracq, Julien** ............................ **CLC 11, 48**
See Poirier, Louis
See also CWW 2; DLB 83; GFL 1789 to the Present

**Grade, Chaim** 1910-1982 .................. **CLC 10**
See also CA 93-96

**Graduate of Oxford, A**
See Ruskin, John

**Grafton, Garth**
See Duncan, Sara Jeannette

**Grafton, Sue** 1940- ........................... **CLC 163**
See also AAYA 11; BEST 90:3; CA 108; CANR 31, 55, 111; CMW 4; CPW; CSW; DAM POP; DLB 226; FW; MSW

**Graham, John**
See Phillips, David Graham

**Graham, Jorie** 1951- ..................... **CLC 48, 118**
See also CA 111; CANR 63; CP 7; CWP; DLB 120; PFS 10, 17

**Graham, R(obert) B(ontine) Cunninghame**
See Cunninghame Graham, Robert (Gallnigad) Bontine
See also DLB 98, 135, 174; RGEL 2; RGSF 2

**Graham, Robert**
See Haldeman, Joe (William)

**Graham, Tom**
See Lewis, (Harry) Sinclair

**Graham, W(illiam) S(idney)**
1918-1986 .................................. **CLC 29**
See also BRWS 7; CA 73-76; DLB 20; RGEL 2

**Graham, Winston (Mawdsley)**
1910- ........................................ **CLC 23**
See also CA 49-52; CANR 2, 22, 45, 66; CMW 4; CN 7; DLB 77; RHW

**Grahame, Kenneth** 1859-1932 ....... **TCLC 64**
See also BYA 5; CA 136; CANR 80; CLR 5; CWRI 5; DAB; DLB 34, 141, 178; FANT; MAICYA 1, 2; MTCW 2; RGEL 2; SATA 100; TEA; WCH; YABC 1

**Granger, Darius John**
See Marlowe, Stephen

**Granin, Daniil** .................................. **CLC 59**

**Granovsky, Timofei Nikolaevich**
1813-1855 .................................. **NCLC 75**
See also DLB 198

**Grant, Skeeter**
See Spiegelman, Art

**Granville-Barker, Harley**
1877-1946 ...................................... **TCLC 2**
See Barker, Harley Granville
See also CA 204; DAM DRAM; RGEL 2

**Granzotto, Gianni**
See Granzotto, Giovanni Battista

**Granzotto, Giovanni Battista**
1914-1985 .................................... **CLC 70**
See also CA 166

**Grass, Guenter (Wilhelm)** 1927- ... **CLC 1, 2, 4, 6, 11, 15, 22, 32, 49, 88; WLC**
See also BPFB 2; CA 13-16R; CANR 20, 75, 93; CDWLB 2; DA; DAB; DAC; DAM MST, NOV; DLB 75, 124; EW 13; MTCW 1, 2; RGWL 2, 3; TWA

**Gratton, Thomas**
See Hulme, T(homas) E(rnest)

**Grau, Shirley Ann** 1929- ....... **CLC 4, 9, 146; SSC 15**
See also CA 89-92; CANR 22, 69; CN 7; CSW; DLB 2, 218; INT CA-89-92, CANR-22; MTCW 1

**Gravel, Fern**
See Hall, James Norman

**Graver, Elizabeth** 1964- ..................... **CLC 70**
See also CA 135; CANR 71

**Graves, Richard Perceval**
1895-1985 ...................................... **CLC 44**
See also CA 65-68; CANR 9, 26, 51

**Graves, Robert (von Ranke)**
1895-1985 .. **CLC 1, 2, 6, 11, 39, 44, 45; PC 6**
See also BPFB 2; BRW 7; BYA 4; CA 5-8R; CANR 5, 36; CDBLB 1914-1945; DAB; DAC; DAM MST, POET; DLB 20, 100, 191; DLBD 18; DLBY 1985; MTCW 1, 2; NCFS 2; RGEL 2; RHW; SATA 45; TEA

**Graves, Valerie**
See Bradley, Marion Zimmer

**Gray, Alasdair (James)** 1934- ........... **CLC 41**
See also CA 126; CANR 47, 69, 106; CN 7; DLB 194, 261; HGG; INT CA-126; MTCW 1, 2; RGSF 2; SUFW 2

**Gray, Amlin** 1946- ............................ **CLC 29**
See also CA 138

**Gray, Francine du Plessix** 1930- ..... **CLC 22, 153**
See also BEST 90:3; CA 61-64; CAAS 2; CANR 11, 33, 75, 81; DAM NOV; INT CANR-11; MTCW 1, 2

**Gray, John (Henry)** 1866-1934 ....... **TCLC 19**
See also CA 162; RGEL 2

**Gray, Simon (James Holliday)**
1936- ............................ **CLC 9, 14, 36**
See also AITN 1; CA 21-24R; CAAS 3; CANR 32, 69; CD 5; DLB 13; MTCW 1; RGEL 2

**Gray, Spalding** 1941- ..... **CLC 49, 112; DC 7**
See also CA 128; CAD; CANR 74; CD 5; CPW; DAM POP; MTCW 2

**Gray, Thomas** 1716-1771 .... **LC 4, 40; PC 2; WLC**
See also BRW 3; CDBLB 1660-1789; DA; DAB; DAC; DAM MST; DLB 109; EXPP; PAB; PFS 9; RGEL 2; TEA; WP

**Grayson, David**
See Baker, Ray Stannard

**Grayson, Richard (A.)** 1951- ............ **CLC 38**
See also CA 85-88; CANR 14, 31, 57; DLB 234

**Greeley, Andrew M(oran)** 1928- ....... **CLC 28**
See also BPFB 2; CA 5-8R; CAAS 7; CANR 7, 43, 69, 104; CMW 4; CPW; DAM POP; MTCW 1, 2

**Green, Anna Katharine**
1846-1935 ................................ **TCLC 63**
See also CA 159; CMW 4; DLB 202, 221; MSW

**Green, Brian**
See Card, Orson Scott

**Green, Hannah**
See Greenberg, Joanne (Goldenberg)

**Green, Hannah** 1927(?)-1996 ............. **CLC 3**
See also CA 73-76; CANR 59, 93; NFS 10

**Green, Henry** ......................... **CLC 2, 13, 97**
See Yorke, Henry Vincent
See also BRWS 2; CA 175; DLB 15; RGEL 2

**Green, Julian (Hartridge)** 1900-1998
See Green, Julien
See also CA 21-24R; CANR 33, 87; DLB 4, 72; MTCW 1

**Green, Julien** ........................... **CLC 3, 11, 77**
See Green, Julian (Hartridge)
See also GFL 1789 to the Present; MTCW 2

**Green, Paul (Eliot)** 1894-1981 .......... **CLC 25**
See also AITN 1; CA 5-8R; CANR 3; DAM DRAM; DLB 7, 9, 249; DLBY 1981; RGAL 4

**Greenaway, Peter** 1942- .................. **CLC 159**
See also CA 127

**Greenberg, Ivan** 1908-1973
See Rahv, Philip
See also CA 85-88

**Greenberg, Joanne (Goldenberg)**
1932- ...................................... **CLC 7, 30**
See also AAYA 12; CA 5-8R; CANR 14, 32, 69; CN 7; SATA 25; YAW

**Greenberg, Richard** 1959(?)- ............ **CLC 57**
See also CA 138; CAD; CD 5

**Greenblatt, Stephen J(ay)** 1943- ....... **CLC 70**
See also CA 49-52

**Greene, Bette** 1934- ......................... **CLC 30**
See also AAYA 7; BYA 3; CA 53-56; CANR 4; CLR 2; CWRI 5; JRDA; LAIT 4; MAICYA 1; NFS 10; SAAS 16; SATA 8, 102; WYA; YAW

**Greene, Gael** ......................................... **CLC 8**
See also CA 13-16R; CANR 10

**Greene, Graham (Henry)**
1904-1991 .... **CLC 1, 3, 6, 9, 14, 18, 27, 37, 70, 72, 125; SSC 29; WLC**
See also AITN 2; BPFB 2; BRWR 2; BRWS 1; BYA 3; CA 13-16R; CANR 35, 61; CBD; CDBLB 1945-1960; CMW 4; DA; DAB; DAC; DAM MST, NOV; DLB 13, 15, 77, 100, 162, 201, 204; DLBY 1991; MSW; MTCW 1, 2; NFS 16; RGEL 2; SATA 20; SSFS 14; TEA; WLIT 4

**Greene, Robert** 1558-1592 .................. **LC 41**
See also BRWS 8; DLB 62, 167; IDTP; RGEL 2; TEA

**Greer, Germaine** 1939- .................... **CLC 131**
See also AITN 1; CA 81-84; CANR 33, 70; FW; MTCW 1, 2

**Greer, Richard**
See Silverberg, Robert

**Gregor, Arthur** 1923- ......................... **CLC 9**
See also CA 25-28R; CAAS 10; CANR 11; CP 7; SATA 36

**Gregor, Lee**
See Pohl, Frederik

**Gregory, Lady Isabella Augusta (Persse)**
1852-1932 ................................. **TCLC 1**
See also BRW 6; CA 184; DLB 10; IDTP; RGEL 2

**Gregory, J. Dennis**
See Williams, John A(lfred)

**Grekova, I.** ......................................... **CLC 59**

**Grendon, Stephen**
See Derleth, August (William)

**Grenville, Kate** 1950- ........................ **CLC 61**
See also CA 118; CANR 53, 93

**Grenville, Pelham**
See Wodehouse, P(elham) G(renville)

**Greve, Felix Paul (Berthold Friedrich)**
1879-1948
See Grove, Frederick Philip
See also CA 141, 175; CANR 79; DAC; DAM MST

**Greville, Fulke** 1554-1628 ..................... **LC 79**
See also DLB 62, 172; RGEL 2

**Grey, Zane** 1872-1939 ....................... **TCLC 6**
See also BPFB 2; CA 132; DAM POP; DLB 9, 212; MTCW 1, 2; RGAL 4; TCWW 2; TUS

**Grieg, (Johan) Nordahl (Brun)**
1902-1943 ................................ **TCLC 10**
See also CA 189

**Grieve, C(hristopher) M(urray)**
1892-1978 ........................... **CLC 11, 19**
See MacDiarmid, Hugh; Pteleon
See also CA 5-8R; CANR 33, 107; DAM POET; MTCW 1; RGEL 2

**Griffin, Gerald** 1803-1840 ................... **NCLC 7**
See also DLB 159; RGEL 2

**Griffin, John Howard** 1920-1980 ..... **CLC 68**
See also AITN 1; CA 1-4R; CANR 2

**Griffin, Peter** 1942- ........................... **CLC 39**
See also CA 136

**Griffith, D(avid) W(ark)**
1875(?)-1948 ............................ **TCLC 68**
See also CA 150; CANR 80

**Griffith, Lawrence**
See Griffith, D(avid) Lewelyn) W(ark)

**Griffiths, Trevor** 1935- ................. **CLC 13, 52**
See also CA 97-100; CANR 45; CBD; CD 5; DLB 13, 245

**Griggs, Sutton (Elbert)**
1872-1930 ................................ **TCLC 77**
See also CA 186; DLB 50

**Grigson, Geoffrey (Edward Harvey)**
1905-1985 ............................. **CLC 7, 39**
See also CA 25-28R; CANR 20, 33; DLB 27; MTCW 1, 2

**Grile, Dod**
See Bierce, Ambrose (Gwinett)

**Grillparzer, Franz** 1791-1872 ............ **DC 14; NCLC 1, 102; SSC 37**
See also CDWLB 2; DLB 133; EW 5; RGWL 2, 3; TWA

**Grimble, Reverend Charles James**
See Eliot, T(homas) S(tearns)

**Grimke, Charlotte L(ottie) Forten**
1837(?)-1914
See Forten, Charlotte L.
See also BW 1; CA 124; DAM MULT, POET

**Grimm, Jacob Ludwig Karl**
1785-1863 ............. **NCLC 3, 77; SSC 36**
See also DLB 90; MAICYA 1, 2; RGSF 2; RGWL 2, 3; SATA 22; WCH

**Grimm, Wilhelm Karl** 1786-1859 .. **NCLC 3, 77; SSC 36**
See also CDWLB 2; DLB 90; MAICYA 1, 2; RGSF 2; RGWL 2, 3; SATA 22; WCH

**Grimmelshausen, Hans Jakob Christoffel von**
See Grimmelshausen, Johann Jakob Christoffel von
See also RGWL 2, 3

**Grimmelshausen, Johann Jakob Christoffel von** 1621-1676 .................. **LC 6**
See Grimmelshausen, Hans Jakob Christoffel von
See also CDWLB 2; DLB 168

**Grindel, Eugene** 1895-1952
See Eluard, Paul
See also CA 193

**Grisham, John** 1955- ...................... **CLC 84**
See also AAYA 14, 47; BPFB 2; CA 138; CANR 47, 69, 114; CMW 4; CN 7; CPW; CSW; DAM POP; MSW; MTCW 2

**Grossman, David** 1954- ................... **CLC 67**
See also CA 138; CANR 114; CWW 2

**Grossman, Vasilii Semenovich**
See Grossman, Vasily (Semenovich)
See also DLB 272

**Grossman, Vasily (Semenovich)** 1905-1964 ..................... **CLC 41**
See Grossman, Vasilii Semenovich
See also CA 130; MTCW 1

**Grove, Frederick Philip** ................. **TCLC 4**
See Greve, Felix Paul (Berthold Friedrich)
See also DLB 92; RGEL 2

**Grubb**
See Crumb, R(obert)

**Grumbach, Doris (Isaac)** 1918- . **CLC 13, 22, 64**
See also CA 5-8R; CAAS 2; CANR 9, 42, 70; CN 7; INT CANR-9; MTCW 2

**Grundtvig, Nicolai Frederik Severin** 1783-1872 ................... **NCLC 1**

**Grunge**
See Crumb, R(obert)

**Grunwald, Lisa** 1959- ..................... **CLC 44**
See also CA 120

**Guare, John** 1938- ............. **CLC 8, 14, 29, 67**
See also CA 73-76; CAD; CANR 21, 69; CD 5; DAM DRAM; DFS 8, 13; DLB 7, 249; MTCW 1, 2; RGAL 4

**Gubar, Susan (David)** 1944- .......... **CLC 145**
See also CA 108; CANR 45, 70; FW; MTCW 1; RGAL 4

**Gudjonsson, Halldor Kiljan** 1902-1998
See Laxness, Halldor
See also CA 103; CWW 2

**Guenter, Erich**
See Eich, Gunter

**Guest, Barbara** 1920- ...................... **CLC 34**
See also BG 2; CA 25-28R; CANR 11, 44, 84; CP 7; CWP; DLB 5, 193

**Guest, Edgar A(lbert)** 1881-1959 ... **TCLC 95**
See also CA 168

**Guest, Judith (Ann)** 1936- ............ **CLC 8, 30**
See also AAYA 7; CA 77-80; CANR 15, 75; DAM NOV, POP; EXPN; INT CANR-15; LAIT 5; MTCW 1, 2; NFS 1

**Guevara, Che** .................... **CLC 87; HLC 1**
See Guevara (Serna), Ernesto

**Guevara (Serna), Ernesto** 1928-1967 ................ **CLC 87; HLC 1**
See Guevara, Che
See also CA 127; CANR 56; DAM MULT; HW 1

**Guicciardini, Francesco** 1483-1540 ..... **LC 49**

**Guild, Nicholas M.** 1944- ................... **CLC 33**
See also CA 93-96

**Guillemin, Jacques**
See Sartre, Jean-Paul

**Guillen, Jorge** 1893-1984 . **CLC 11; HLCS 1; PC 35**
See also CA 89-92; DAM MULT, POET; DLB 108; HW 1; RGWL 2, 3

**Guillen, Nicolas (Cristobal)** 1902-1989 .... **BLC 2; CLC 48, 79; HLC 1; PC 23**
See also BW 2; CA 125; CANR 84; DAM MST, MULT, POET; HW 1; LAW; RGWL 2, 3; WP

**Guillen y Alvarez, Jorge**
See Guillen, Jorge

**Guillevic, (Eugene)** 1907-1997 .......... **CLC 33**
See also CA 93-96; CWW 2

**Guillois**
See Desnos, Robert

**Guillois, Valentin**
See Desnos, Robert

**Guimaraes Rosa, Joao** 1908-1967 .... **HLCS 2**
See also CA 175; LAW; RGSF 2; RGWL 2, 3

**Guiney, Louise Imogen** 1861-1920 ................. **TCLC 41**
See also CA 160; DLB 54; RGAL 4

**Guinizelli, Guido** c. 1230-1276 ...... **CMLC 49**

**Guiraldes, Ricardo (Guillermo)** 1886-1927 ................. **TCLC 39**
See also CA 131; HW 1; LAW; MTCW 1

**Gumilev, Nikolai (Stepanovich)** 1886-1921 ................. **TCLC 60**
See also CA 165

**Gunesekera, Romesh** 1954- .............. **CLC 91**
See also CA 159; CN 7; DLB 267

**Gunn, Bill** ........................................ **CLC 5**
See Gunn, William Harrison
See also DLB 38

**Gunn, Thom(son William)** 1929- .. **CLC 3, 6, 18, 32, 81; PC 26**
See also BRWS 4; CA 17-20R; CANR 9, 33; CDBLB 1960 to Present; CP 7; DAM POET; DLB 27; INT CANR-33; MTCW 1; PFS 9; RGEL 2

**Gunn, William Harrison** 1934(?)-1989
See Gunn, Bill
See also AITN 1; BW 1, 3; CA 13-16R; CANR 12, 25, 76

**Gunn Allen, Paula**
See Allen, Paula Gunn

**Gunnars, Kristjana** 1948- ................. **CLC 69**
See also CA 113; CCA 1; CP 7; CWP; DLB 60

**Gunter, Erich**
See Eich, Gunter

**Gurdjieff, G(eorgei) I(vanovich)** 1877(?)-1949 ........................... **TCLC 71**
See also CA 157

**Gurganus, Allan** 1947- ...................... **CLC 70**
See also BEST 90:1; CA 135; CANR 114; CN 7; CPW; CSW; DAM POP; GLL 1

**Gurney, A. R.**
See Gurney, A(lbert) R(amsdell), Jr.
See also DLB 266

**Gurney, A(lbert) R(amsdell), Jr.** 1930- ............................ **CLC 32, 50, 54**
See Gurney, A. R.
See also AMWS 5; CA 77-80; CAD; CANR 32, 64; CD 5; DAM DRAM

**Gurney, Ivor (Bertie)** 1890-1937 ... **TCLC 33**
See also BRW 6; CA 167; PAB; RGEL 2

**Gurney, Peter**
See Gurney, A(lbert) R(amsdell), Jr.

**Guro, Elena** 1877-1913 ................... **TCLC 56**

**Gustafson, James M(oody)** 1925- ... **CLC 100**
See also CA 25-28R; CANR 37

**Gustafson, Ralph (Barker)** 1909-1995 ..................... **CLC 36**
See also CA 21-24R; CANR 8, 45, 84; CP 7; DLB 88; RGEL 2

**Gut, Gom**
See Simenon, Georges (Jacques Christian)

**Guterson, David** 1956- ...................... **CLC 91**
See also CA 132; CANR 73; MTCW 2; NFS 13

**Guthrie, A(lfred) B(ertram), Jr.** 1901-1991 ................. **CLC 23**
See also CA 57-60; CANR 24; DLB 6, 212; SATA 62; SATA-Obit 67

**Guthrie, Isobel**
See Grieve, C(hristopher) M(urray)

**Guthrie, Woodrow Wilson** 1912-1967
See Guthrie, Woody
See also CA 113

**Guthrie, Woody** ................................ **CLC 35**
See Guthrie, Woodrow Wilson
See also LAIT 3

**Gutierrez Najera, Manuel** 1859-1895 ................... **HLCS 2**
See also LAW

**Guy, Rosa (Cuthbert)** 1925- ............. **CLC 26**
See also AAYA 4, 37; BW 2; CA 17-20R; CANR 14, 34, 83; CLR 13; DLB 33; DNFS 1; JRDA; MAICYA 1, 2; SATA 14, 62, 122; YAW

**Gwendolyn**
See Bennett, (Enoch) Arnold

**H. D.** ............ **CLC 3, 8, 14, 31, 34, 73; PC 5**
See Doolittle, Hilda

**H. de V.**
See Buchan, John

**Haavikko, Paavo Juhani** 1931- .. **CLC 18, 34**
See also CA 106

**Habbema, Koos**
See Heijermans, Herman

**Habermas, Juergen** 1929- ................. **CLC 104**
See also CA 109; CANR 85; DLB 242

**Habermas, Jurgen**
See Habermas, Juergen

**Hacker, Marilyn** 1942- . **CLC 5, 9, 23, 72, 91**
See also CA 77-80; CANR 68; CP 7; CWP; DAM POET; DLB 120; FW; GLL 2

**Hadrian** 76-138 ............................... **CMLC 52**

**Haeckel, Ernst Heinrich (Philipp August)** 1834-1919 ................... **TCLC 83**
See also CA 157

**Hafiz** c. 1326-1389(?) ...................... **CMLC 34**
See also RGWL 2, 3

**Haggard, H(enry) Rider** 1856-1925 ................... **TCLC 11**
See also BRWS 3; BYA 4, 5; CA 148; CANR 112; DLB 70, 156, 174, 178; FANT; MTCW 2; RGEL 2; RHW; SATA 16; SCFW; SFW 4; SUFW 1; WLIT 4

**Hagiosy, L.**
See Larbaud, Valery (Nicolas)

**Hagiwara, Sakutaro** 1886-1942 .......... **PC 18; TCLC 60**
See also CA 154; RGWL 3

**Haig, Fenil**
See Ford, Ford Madox

**Haig-Brown, Roderick (Langmere)** 1908-1976 ................... **CLC 21**
See also CA 5-8R; CANR 4, 38, 83; CLR 31; CWRI 5; DLB 88; MAICYA 1, 2; SATA 12

**Haight, Rip**
See Carpenter, John (Howard)

**Hailey, Arthur** 1920- ........................... **CLC 5**
See also AITN 2; BEST 90:3; BPFB 2; CA 1-4R; CANR 2, 36, 75; CCA 1; CN 7; CPW; DAM NOV, POP; DLB 88; DLBY 1982; MTCW 1, 2

**Hailey, Elizabeth Forsythe** 1938- ..... **CLC 40**
See also CA 93-96; CAAE 188; CAAS 1; CANR 15, 48; INT CANR-15

**Haines, John (Meade)** 1924- ............. **CLC 58**
See also AMWS 12; CA 17-20R; CANR 13, 34; CSW; DLB 5, 212

**Hakluyt, Richard** 1552-1616 .................. **LC 31**
See also DLB 136; RGEL 2
**Haldeman, Joe (William)** 1943- ........ **CLC 61**
See Graham, Robert
See also AAYA 38; CA 53-56, 179; CAAE 179; CAAS 25; CANR 6, 70, 72; DLB 8; INT CANR-6; SCFW 2; SFW 4
**Hale, Sarah Josepha (Buell)**
1788-1879 ................................. **NCLC 75**
See also DLB 1, 42, 73, 243
**Halevy, Elie** 1870-1937 .................. **TCLC 104**
**Haley, Alex(ander Murray Palmer)**
1921-1992 ........... **BLC 2; CLC 8, 12, 76**
See also AAYA 26; BPFB 2; BW 2, 3; CA 77-80; CANR 61; CDALBS; CPW; CSW; DA; DAB; DAC; DAM MST, MULT, POP; DLB 38; LAIT 5; MTCW 1, 2; NFS 9
**Haliburton, Thomas Chandler**
1796-1865 ................................. **NCLC 15**
See also DLB 11, 99; RGEL 2; RGSF 2
**Hall, Donald (Andrew, Jr.)** 1928- ...... **CLC 1, 13, 37, 59, 151**
See also CA 5-8R; CAAS 7; CANR 2, 44, 64, 106; CP 7; DAM POET; DLB 5; MTCW 1; RGAL 4; SATA 23, 97
**Hall, Frederic Sauser**
See Sauser-Hall, Frederic
**Hall, James**
See Kuttner, Henry
**Hall, James Norman** 1887-1951 ..... **TCLC 23**
See also CA 173; LAIT 1; RHW 1; SATA 21
**Hall, (Marguerite) Radclyffe**
1880-1943 ................................. **TCLC 12**
See also BRWS 6; CA 150; CANR 83; DLB 191; MTCW 2; RGEL 2; RHW
**Hall, Rodney** 1935- ........................ **CLC 51**
See also CA 109; CANR 69; CN 7; CP 7
**Hallam, Arthur Henry**
1811-1833 ................................. **NCLC 110**
See also DLB 32
**Halleck, Fitz-Greene** 1790-1867 .... **NCLC 47**
See also DLB 3, 250; RGAL 4
**Halliday, Michael**
See Creasey, John
**Halpern, Daniel** 1945- ..................... **CLC 14**
See also CA 33-36R; CANR 93; CP 7
**Hamburger, Michael (Peter Leopold)**
1924- .................................. **CLC 5, 14**
See also CA 5-8R; CAAE 196; CAAS 4; CANR 2, 47; CP 7; DLB 27
**Hamill, Pete** 1935- .......................... **CLC 10**
See also CA 25-28R; CANR 18, 71
**Hamilton, Alexander**
1755(?)-1804 ........................... **NCLC 49**
See also DLB 37
**Hamilton, Clive**
See Lewis, C(live) S(taples)
**Hamilton, Edmond** 1904-1977 ............ **CLC 1**
See also CA 1-4R; CANR 3, 84; DLB 8; SATA 118; SFW 4
**Hamilton, Eugene (Jacob) Lee**
See Lee-Hamilton, Eugene (Jacob)
**Hamilton, Franklin**
See Silverberg, Robert
**Hamilton, Gail**
See Corcoran, Barbara (Asenath)
**Hamilton, Mollie**
See Kaye, M(ary) M(argaret)
**Hamilton, (Anthony Walter) Patrick**
1904-1962 ................................. **CLC 51**
See also CA 176; DLB 10, 191
**Hamilton, Virginia (Esther)**
1936-2002 ................................. **CLC 26**
See also AAYA 2, 21; BW 2, 3; BYA 1, 2, 8; CA 25-28R; CANR 20, 37, 73; CLR 1, 11, 40; DAM MULT; DLB 33, 52; DLBY 01; INT CANR-20; JRDA; LAIT 5; MAI-CYA 1, 2; MAICYAS 1; MTCW 1, 2; SATA 4, 56, 79, 123; SATA-Obit 132; WYA; YAW
**Hammett, (Samuel) Dashiell**
1894-1961 .... **CLC 3, 5, 10, 19, 47; SSC 17**
See also AITN 1; AMWS 4; BPFB 2; CA 81-84; CANR 42; CDALB 1929-1941; CMW 4; DLB 226; DLBD 6; DLBY 1996; LAIT 3; MSW; MTCW 1, 2; RGAL 4; RGSF 2; TUS
**Hammon, Jupiter** 1720(?)-1800(?) .... **BLC 2; NCLC 5; PC 16**
See also DAM MULT, POET; DLB 31, 50
**Hammond, Keith**
See Kuttner, Henry
**Hamner, Earl (Henry), Jr.** 1923- ....... **CLC 12**
See also AITN 2; CA 73-76; DLB 6
**Hampton, Christopher (James)**
1946- ........................................ **CLC 4**
See also CA 25-28R; CD 5; DLB 13; MTCW 1
**Hamsun, Knut** ..................... **TCLC 2, 14, 49**
See Pedersen, Knut
See also EW 8; RGWL 2, 3
**Handke, Peter** 1942- .... **CLC 5, 8, 10, 15, 38, 134; DC 17**
See also CA 77-80; CANR 33, 75, 104; CWW 2; DAM DRAM, NOV; DLB 85, 124; MTCW 1, 2; TWA
**Handy, W(illiam) C(hristopher)**
1873-1958 ................................. **TCLC 97**
See also BW 3; CA 167
**Hanley, James** 1901-1985 ..... **CLC 3, 5, 8, 13**
See also CA 73-76; CANR 36; CBD; DLB 191; MTCW 1; RGEL 2
**Hannah, Barry** 1942- ............. **CLC 23, 38, 90**
See also BPFB 2; CA 110; CANR 43, 68, 113; CN 7; CSW; DLB 6, 234; INT CA-110; MTCW 1; RGSF 2
**Hannon, Ezra**
See Hunter, Evan
**Hansberry, Lorraine (Vivian)**
1930-1965 ... **BLC 2; CLC 17, 62; DC 2**
See also AAYA 25; AFAW 1, 2; AMWS 4; BW 1, 3; CA 109; CABS 3; CANR 58; CDALB 1941-1968; DA; DAB; DAC; DAM DRAM, MST, MULT; DFS 2; DLB 7, 38; FW; LAIT 4; MTCW 1, 2; RGAL 4; TUS
**Hansen, Joseph** 1923- ........................ **CLC 38**
See Brock, Rose; Colton, James
See also BPFB 2; CA 29-32R; CAAS 17; CANR 16, 44, 66; CMW 4; DLB 226; GLL 1; INT CANR-16
**Hansen, Martin A(lfred)**
1909-1955 ................................. **TCLC 32**
See also CA 167; DLB 214
**Hansen and Philipson eds.** .............. **CLC 65**
**Hanson, Kenneth O(stlin)** 1922- ....... **CLC 13**
See also CA 53-56; CANR 7
**Hardwick, Elizabeth (Bruce)** 1916- . **CLC 13**
See also AMWS 3; CA 5-8R; CANR 3, 32, 70, 100; CN 7; CSW; DAM NOV; DLB 6; MAWW; MTCW 1, 2
**Hardy, Thomas** 1840-1928 ....... **PC 8; SSC 2; TCLC 4, 10, 18, 32, 48, 53, 72; WLC**
See also BRW 6; BRWR 1; CA 123; CD-BLB 1890-1914; DA; DAB; DAC; DAM MST, NOV, POET; DLB 18, 19, 135; EXPN; EXPP; LAIT 2; MTCW 1, 2; NFS 3, 11, 15; PFS 3, 4; RGEL 2; RGSF 2; TEA; WLIT 4
**Hare, David** 1947- .............. **CLC 29, 58, 136**
See also BRWS 4; CA 97-100; CANR 39, 91; CBD; CD 5; DFS 4, 7, 16; DLB 13; MTCW 1; TEA
**Harewood, John**
See Van Druten, John (William)
**Harford, Henry**
See Hudson, W(illiam) H(enry)
**Hargrave, Leonie**
See Disch, Thomas M(ichael)
**Harjo, Joy** 1951- ..... **CLC 83; NNAL; PC 27**
See also AMWS 12; CA 114; CANR 35, 67, 91; CP 7; CWP; DAM MULT; DLB 120, 175; MTCW 2; PFS 15; RGAL 4
**Harlan, Louis R(udolph)** 1922- ........ **CLC 34**
See also CA 21-24R; CANR 25, 55, 80
**Harling, Robert** 1951(?)- .................. **CLC 53**
See also CA 147
**Harmon, William (Ruth)** 1938- ........ **CLC 38**
See also CA 33-36R; CANR 14, 32, 35; SATA 65
**Harper, F. E. W.**
See Harper, Frances Ellen Watkins
**Harper, Frances E. W.**
See Harper, Frances Ellen Watkins
**Harper, Frances E. Watkins**
See Harper, Frances Ellen Watkins
**Harper, Frances Ellen**
See Harper, Frances Ellen Watkins
**Harper, Frances Ellen Watkins**
1825-1911 ...... **BLC 2; PC 21; TCLC 14**
See also AFAW 1, 2; BW 1, 3; CA 125; CANR 79; DAM MULT, POET; DLB 50, 221; MAWW; RGAL 4
**Harper, Michael S(teven)** 1938- ... **CLC 7, 22**
See also AFAW 2; BW 1; CA 33-36R; CANR 24, 108; CP 7; DLB 41; RGAL 4
**Harper, Mrs. F. E. W.**
See Harper, Frances Ellen Watkins
**Harpur, Charles** 1813-1868 .......... **NCLC 114**
See also DLB 230; RGEL 2
**Harris, Christie** 1907-
See Harris, Christie (Lucy) Irwin
**Harris, Christie (Lucy) Irwin**
1907-2002 ................................. **CLC 12**
See also CA 5-8R; CANR 6, 83; CLR 47; DLB 88; JRDA; MAICYA 1, 2; SAAS 10; SATA 6, 74; SATA-Essay 116
**Harris, Frank** 1856-1931 .................. **TCLC 24**
See also CA 150; CANR 80; DLB 156, 197; RGEL 2
**Harris, George Washington**
1814-1869 ................................. **NCLC 23**
See also DLB 3, 11, 248; RGAL 4
**Harris, Joel Chandler** 1848-1908 ..... **SSC 19; TCLC 2**
See also CA 137; CANR 80; CLR 49; DLB 11, 23, 42, 78, 91; LAIT 2; MAICYA 1, 2; RGSF 2; SATA 100; WCH; YABC 1
**Harris, John (Wyndham Parkes Lucas) Beynon** 1903-1969
See Wyndham, John
See also CA 102; CANR 84; SATA 118; SFW 4
**Harris, MacDonald** ........................... **CLC 9**
See Heiney, Donald (William)
**Harris, Mark** 1922- ........................... **CLC 19**
See also CA 5-8R; CAAS 3; CANR 2, 55, 83; CN 7; DLB 2; DLBY 1980
**Harris, Norman** ............................... **CLC 65**
**Harris, (Theodore) Wilson** 1921- .... **CLC 25, 159**
See also BRWS 5; BW 2, 3; CA 65-68; CAAS 16; CANR 11, 27, 69, 114; CD-WLB 3; CN 7; CP 7; DLB 117; MTCW 1; RGEL 2
**Harrison, Barbara Grizzuti**
1934-2002 ................................. **CLC 144**
See also CA 77-80; CANR 15, 48; INT CANR-15
**Harrison, Elizabeth (Allen) Cavanna**
1909-2001
See Cavanna, Betty
See also CA 9-12R; CANR 6, 27, 85, 104; MAICYA 2; YAW

**Harrison, Harry (Max)** 1925- ............ **CLC 42**
See also CA 1-4R; CANR 5, 21, 84; DLB 8; SATA 4; SCFW 2; SFW 4

**Harrison, James (Thomas)** 1937- ...... **CLC 6, 14, 33, 66, 143; SSC 19**
See Harrison, Jim
See also CA 13-16R; CANR 8, 51, 79; CN 7; CP 7; DLBY 1982; INT CANR-8

**Harrison, Jim**
See Harrison, James (Thomas)
See also AMWS 8; RGAL 4; TCWW 2; TUS

**Harrison, Kathryn** 1961- ........... **CLC 70, 151**
See also CA 144; CANR 68

**Harrison, Tony** 1937- ................. **CLC 43, 129**
See also BRWS 5; CA 65-68; CANR 44, 98; CBD; CD 5; CP 7; DLB 40, 245; MTCW 1; RGEL 2

**Harriss, Will(ard Irvin)** 1922- .......... **CLC 34**
See also CA 111

**Hart, Ellis**
See Ellison, Harlan (Jay)

**Hart, Josephine** 1942(?)- .................... **CLC 70**
See also CA 138; CANR 70; CPW; DAM POP

**Hart, Moss** 1904-1961 ....................... **CLC 66**
See also CA 109; CANR 84; DAM DRAM; DFS 1; DLB 7, 266; RGAL 4

**Harte, (Francis) Bret(t)** 1836(?)-1902 ......... **SSC 8; TCLC 1, 25; WLC**
See also AMWS 2; CA 140; CANR 80; CDALB 1865-1917; DA; DAC; DAM MST; DLB 12, 64, 74, 79, 186; EXPS; LAIT 2; RGAL 4; RGSF 2; SATA 26; SSFS 3; TUS

**Hartley, L(eslie) P(oles)** 1895-1972 ... **CLC 2, 22**
See also BRWS 7; CA 45-48; CANR 33; DLB 15, 139; HGG; MTCW 1, 2; RGEL 2; RGSF 2; SUFW 1

**Hartman, Geoffrey H.** 1929- .............. **CLC 27**
See also CA 125; CANR 79; DLB 67

**Hartmann, Sadakichi** 1869-1944 ... **TCLC 73**
See also CA 157; DLB 54

**Hartmann von Aue** c. 1170-c. 1210 ......................................... **CMLC 15**
See also CDWLB 2; DLB 138; RGWL 2, 3

**Hartog, Jan de**
See de Hartog, Jan

**Haruf, Kent** 1943- ................................ **CLC 34**
See also AAYA 44; CA 149; CANR 91

**Harwood, Ronald** 1934- ..................... **CLC 32**
See also CA 1-4R; CANR 4, 55; CBD; CD 5; DAM DRAM, MST; DLB 13

**Hasegawa Tatsunosuke**
See Futabatei, Shimei

**Hasek, Jaroslav (Matej Frantisek)** 1883-1923 ..................................... **TCLC 4**
See also CA 129; CDWLB 4; DLB 215; EW 9; MTCW 1, 2; RGSF 2; RGWL 2, 3

**Hass, Robert** 1941- ... **CLC 18, 39, 99; PC 16**
See also AMWS 6; CA 111; CANR 30, 50, 71; CP 7; DLB 105, 206; RGAL 4; SATA 94

**Hastings, Hudson**
See Kuttner, Henry

**Hastings, Selina** ................................ **CLC 44**

**Hathorne, John** 1641-1717 ................... **LC 38**

**Hatteras, Amelia**
See Mencken, H(enry) L(ouis)

**Hatteras, Owen** .................................. **TCLC 18**
See Mencken, H(enry) L(ouis); Nathan, George Jean

**Hauptmann, Gerhart (Johann Robert)** 1862-1946 .................... **SSC 37; TCLC 4**
See also CA 153; CDWLB 2; DAM DRAM; DLB 66, 118; EW 8; RGSF 2; RGWL 2, 3; TWA

**Havel, Vaclav** 1936- ..... **CLC 25, 58, 65, 123; DC 6**
See also CA 104; CANR 36, 63; CDWLB 4; CWW 2; DAM DRAM; DFS 10; DLB 232; MTCW 1, 2; RGWL 3

**Haviaras, Stratis** ................................ **CLC 33**
See Chaviaras, Strates

**Hawes, Stephen** 1475(?)-1529(?) .......... **LC 17**
See also DLB 132; RGEL 2

**Hawkes, John (Clendennin Burne, Jr.)** 1925-1998 .. **CLC 1, 2, 3, 4, 7, 9, 14, 15, 27, 49**
See also BPFB 2; CA 1-4R; CANR 2, 47, 64; CN 7; DLB 2, 7, 227; DLBY 1980, 1998; MTCW 1, 2; RGAL 4

**Hawking, S. W.**
See Hawking, Stephen W(illiam)

**Hawking, Stephen W(illiam)** 1942- . **CLC 63, 105**
See also AAYA 13; BEST 89:1; CA 129; CANR 48; CPW; MTCW 2

**Hawkins, Anthony Hope**
See Hope, Anthony

**Hawthorne, Julian** 1846-1934 ........ **TCLC 25**
See also CA 165; HGG

**Hawthorne, Nathaniel** 1804-1864 ... **NCLC 2, 10, 17, 23, 39, 79, 95; SSC 3, 29, 39; WLC**
See also AAYA 18; AMW; AMWC 1; AMWR 1; BPFB 2; BYA 3; CDALB 1640-1865; DA; DAB; DAC; DAM MST, NOV; DLB 1, 74, 183, 223, 269; EXPN; EXPS; HGG; LAIT 1; NFS 1; RGAL 4; RGSF 2; SSFS 1, 7, 11, 15; SUFW 1; TUS; WCH; YABC 2

**Haxton, Josephine Ayres** 1921-
See Douglas, Ellen
See also CA 115; CANR 41, 83

**Hayaseca y Eizaguirre, Jorge**
See Echegaray (y Eizaguirre), Jose (Maria Waldo)

**Hayashi, Fumiko** 1904-1951 ........... **TCLC 27**
See Hayashi Fumiko
See also CA 161

**Hayashi Fumiko**
See Hayashi, Fumiko
See also DLB 180

**Haycraft, Anna (Margaret)** 1932-
See Ellis, Alice Thomas
See also CA 122; CANR 85, 90; MTCW 2

**Hayden, Robert E(arl)** 1913-1980 ..... **BLC 2; CLC 5, 9, 14, 37; PC 6**
See also AFAW 1, 2; AMWS 2; BW 1, 3; CA 69-72; CABS 2; CANR 24, 75, 82; CDALB 1941-1968; DA; DAC; DAM MST, MULT, POET; DLB 5, 76; EXPP; MTCW 1, 2; PFS 1; RGAL 4; SATA 19; SATA-Obit 26; WP

**Hayek, F(riedrich) A(ugust von)** 1899-1992 ..................... **TCLC 109**
See also CA 93-96; CANR 20; MTCW 1, 2

**Hayford, J(oseph) E(phraim) Casely**
See Casely-Hayford, J(oseph) E(phraim)

**Hayman, Ronald** 1932- ....................... **CLC 44**
See also CA 25-28R; CANR 18, 50, 88; CD 5; DLB 155

**Hayne, Paul Hamilton** 1830-1886 . **NCLC 94**
See also DLB 3, 64, 79, 248; RGAL 4

**Hays, Mary** 1760-1843 .................. **NCLC 114**
See also DLB 142, 158; RGEL 2

**Haywood, Eliza (Fowler)** 1693(?)-1756 ...................... **LC 1, 44**
See also DLB 39; RGEL 2

**Hazlitt, William** 1778-1830 ...... **NCLC 29, 82**
See also BRW 4; DLB 110, 158; RGEL 2; TEA

**Hazzard, Shirley** 1931- ...................... **CLC 18**
See also CA 9-12R; CANR 4, 70; CN 7; DLBY 1982; MTCW 1

**Head, Bessie** 1937-1986 ...... **BLC 2; CLC 25, 67; SSC 52**
See also AFW; BW 2, 3; CA 29-32R; CANR 25, 82; CDWLB 3; DAM MULT; DLB 117, 225; EXPS; FW; MTCW 1, 2; RGSF 2; SSFS 5, 13; WLIT 2

**Headon, (Nicky) Topper** 1956(?)- ..... **CLC 30**

**Heaney, Seamus (Justin)** 1939- ...... **CLC 5, 7, 14, 25, 37, 74, 91; PC 18; WLCS**
See also BRWR 1; BRWS 2; CA 85-88; CANR 25, 48, 75, 91; CDBLB 1960 to Present; CP 7; DAB; DAM POET; DLB 40; DLBY 1995; EXPP; MTCW 1, 2; PAB; PFS 2, 5, 8, 17; RGEL 2; TEA; WLIT 4

**Hearn, (Patricio) Lafcadio (Tessima Carlos)** 1850-1904 ................................. **TCLC 9**
See also CA 166; DLB 12, 78, 189; HGG; RGAL 4

**Hearne, Vicki** 1946-2001 .................. **CLC 56**
See also CA 139

**Hearon, Shelby** 1931- .......................... **CLC 63**
See also AITN 2; AMWS 8; CA 25-28R; CANR 18, 48, 103; CSW

**Heat-Moon, William Least** .............. **CLC 29**
See Trogdon, William (Lewis)
See also AAYA 9

**Hebbel, Friedrich** 1813-1863 ......... **NCLC 43**
See also CDWLB 2; DAM DRAM; DLB 129; EW 6; RGWL 2, 3

**Hebert, Anne** 1916-2000 ........... **CLC 4, 13, 29**
See also CA 85-88; CANR 69; CCA 1; CWP; CWW 2; DAC; DAM MST, POET; DLB 68; GFL 1789 to the Present; MTCW 1, 2

**Hecht, Anthony (Evan)** 1923- ...... **CLC 8, 13, 19**
See also AMWS 10; CA 9-12R; CANR 6, 108; CP 7; DAM POET; DLB 5, 169; PFS 6; WP

**Hecht, Ben** 1894-1964 ..... **CLC 8; TCLC 101**
See also CA 85-88; DFS 9; DLB 7, 9, 25, 26, 28, 86; FANT; IDFW 3, 4; RGAL 4

**Hedayat, Sadeq** 1903-1951 ............. **TCLC 21**
See also RGSF 2

**Hegel, Georg Wilhelm Friedrich** 1770-1831 ................................ **NCLC 46**
See also DLB 90; TWA

**Heidegger, Martin** 1889-1976 ........... **CLC 24**
See also CA 81-84; CANR 34; MTCW 1, 2

**Heidenstam, (Carl Gustaf) Verner von** 1859-1940 ........................................ **TCLC 5**

**Heifner, Jack** 1946- ............................ **CLC 11**
See also CA 105; CANR 47

**Heijermans, Herman** 1864-1924 .... **TCLC 24**

**Heilbrun, Carolyn G(old)** 1926- ........ **CLC 25**
See Cross, Amanda
See also CA 45-48; CANR 1, 28, 58, 94; FW

**Hein, Christoph** 1944- ...................... **CLC 154**
See also CA 158; CANR 108; CDWLB 2; CWW 2; DLB 124

**Heine, Heinrich** 1797-1856 ....... **NCLC 4, 54; PC 25**
See also CDWLB 2; DLB 90; EW 5; RGWL 2, 3; TWA

**Heinemann, Larry (Curtiss)** 1944- .. **CLC 50**
See also CA 110; CAAS 21; CANR 31, 81; DLBD 9; INT CANR-31

**Heiney, Donald (William)** 1921-1993
See Harris, MacDonald
See also CA 1-4R; CANR 3, 58; FANT

**Heinlein, Robert A(nson)** 1907-1988 . **CLC 1, 3, 8, 14, 26, 55; SSC 55**
See also AAYA 17; BPFB 2; BYA 4, 13; CA 1-4R; CANR 1, 20, 53; CLR 75; CPW; DAM POP; DLB 8; EXPS; JRDA; LAIT 5; MAICYA 1, 2; MTCW 1, 2;

RGAL 4; SATA 9, 69; SATA-Obit 56; SCFW; SFW 4; SSFS 7; YAW
**Helforth, John**
See Doolittle, Hilda
**Heliodorus** fl. 3rd cent. - ................ **CMLC 52**
**Hellenhofferu, Vojtech Kapristian z**
See Hasek, Jaroslav (Matej Frantisek)
**Heller, Joseph** 1923-1999 . **CLC 1, 3, 5, 8, 11, 36, 63; TCLC 131; WLC**
See also AAYA 24; AITN 1; AMWS 4; BPFB 2; BYA 1; CA 5-8R; CABS 1; CANR 8, 42, 66; CN 7; CPW; DA; DAB; DAC; DAM MST, NOV, POP; DLB 2, 28, 227; DLBY 1980; EXPN; INT CANR-8; LAIT 4; MTCW 1, 2; NFS 1; RGAL 4; TUS; YAW
**Hellman, Lillian (Florence)** 1906-1984 .. **CLC 2, 4, 8, 14, 18, 34, 44, 52; DC 1; TCLC 119**
See also AAYA 47; AITN 1, 2; AMWS 1; CA 13-16R; CAD; CANR 33; CWD; DAM DRAM; DFS 1, 3, 14; DLB 7, 228; DLBY 1984; FW; LAIT 3; MAWW; MTCW 1, 2; RGAL 4; TUS
**Helprin, Mark** 1947- ......... **CLC 7, 10, 22, 32**
See also CA 81-84; CANR 47, 64; CDALBS; CPW; DAM NOV, POP; DLBY 1985; FANT; MTCW 1, 2; SUFW 2
**Helvetius, Claude-Adrien** 1715-1771 .. **LC 26**
**Helyar, Jane Penelope Josephine** 1933-
See Poole, Josephine
See also CA 21-24R; CANR 10, 26; CWRI 5; SATA 82
**Hemans, Felicia** 1793-1835 ...... **NCLC 29, 71**
See also DLB 96; RGEL 2
**Hemingway, Ernest (Miller)** 1899-1961 .... **CLC 1, 3, 6, 8, 10, 13, 19, 30, 34, 39, 41, 44, 50, 61, 80; SSC 1, 25, 36, 40; TCLC 115; WLC**
See also AAYA 19; AMW; AMWC 1; AMWR 1; BPFB 2; BYA 2, 3, 13; CA 77-80; CANR 34; CDALB 1917-1929; DA; DAB; DAC; DAM MST, NOV; DLB 4, 9, 102, 210; DLBD 1, 15, 16; DLBY 1981, 1987, 1996, 1998; EXPN; EXPS; LAIT 3, 4; MTCW 1, 2; NFS 1, 5, 6, 14; RGAL 4; RGSF 2; SSFS 1, 6, 8, 9, 11; TUS; WYA
**Hempel, Amy** 1951- .......................... **CLC 39**
See also CA 137; CANR 70; DLB 218; EXPS; MTCW 2; SSFS 2
**Henderson, F. C.**
See Mencken, H(enry) L(ouis)
**Henderson, Sylvia**
See Ashton-Warner, Sylvia (Constance)
**Henderson, Zenna (Chlarson)** 1917-1983 ....................................... **SSC 29**
See also CA 1-4R; CANR 1, 84; DLB 8; SATA 5; SFW 4
**Henkin, Joshua** ............................... **CLC 119**
See also CA 161
**Henley, Beth** ..................... **CLC 23; DC 6, 14**
See Henley, Elizabeth Becker
See also CABS 3; CAD; CD 5; CSW; CWD; DFS 2; DLBY 1986; FW
**Henley, Elizabeth Becker** 1952-
See Henley, Beth
See also CA 107; CANR 32, 73; DAM DRAM, MST; MTCW 1, 2
**Henley, William Ernest** 1849-1903 .. **TCLC 8**
See also DLB 19; RGEL 2
**Hennissart, Martha**
See Lathen, Emma
See also CA 85-88; CANR 64
**Henry VIII** 1491-1547 ......................... **LC 10**
See also DLB 132

**Henry, O.** ..... **SSC 5, 49; TCLC 1, 19; WLC**
See Porter, William Sydney
See also AAYA 41; AMWS 2; EXPS; RGAL 4; RGSF 2; SSFS 2
**Henry, Patrick** 1736-1799 .................... **LC 25**
See also LAIT 1
**Henryson, Robert** 1430(?)-1506(?) ...... **LC 20**
See also BRWS 7; DLB 146; RGEL 2
**Henschke, Alfred**
See Klabund
**Hentoff, Nat(han Irving)** 1925- ......... **CLC 26**
See also AAYA 4, 42; BYA 6; CA 1-4R; CAAS 6; CANR 5, 25, 77, 114; CLR 1, 52; INT CANR-25; JRDA; MAICYA 1, 2; SATA 42, 69, 133; SATA-Brief 27; WYA; YAW
**Heppenstall, (John) Rayner** 1911-1981 ................................... **CLC 10**
See also CA 1-4R; CANR 29
**Heraclitus** c. 540B.C.-c. 450B.C. ... **CMLC 22**
See also DLB 176
**Herbert, Frank (Patrick)** 1920-1986 .......... **CLC 12, 23, 35, 44, 85**
See also AAYA 21; BPFB 2; BYA 4, 14; CA 53-56; CANR 5, 43; CDALBS; CPW; DAM POP; DLB 8; INT CANR-5; LAIT 5; MTCW 1, 2; SATA 9, 37; SATA-Obit 47; SCFW 2; SFW 4; YAW
**Herbert, George** 1593-1633 ....... **LC 24; PC 4**
See also BRW 2; BRWR 2; CDBLB Before 1660; DAB; DAM POET; DLB 126; EXPP; RGEL 2; TEA; WP
**Herbert, Zbigniew** 1924-1998 ....... **CLC 9, 43**
See also CA 89-92; CANR 36, 74; CDWLB 4; CWW 2; DAM POET; DLB 232; MTCW 1
**Herbst, Josephine (Frey)** 1897-1969 .................................... **CLC 34**
See also CA 5-8R; DLB 9
**Herder, Johann Gottfried von** 1744-1803 ................................ **NCLC 8**
See also DLB 97; EW 4; TWA
**Heredia, Jose Maria** 1803-1839 ....... **HLCS 2**
See also LAW
**Hergesheimer, Joseph** 1880-1954 ... **TCLC 11**
See also CA 194; DLB 102, 9; RGAL 4
**Herlihy, James Leo** 1927-1993 ........... **CLC 6**
See also CA 1-4R; CAD; CANR 2
**Herman, William**
See Bierce, Ambrose (Gwinett)
**Hermogenes** fl. c. 175- ...................... **CMLC 6**
**Hernandez, Jose** 1834-1886 ............ **NCLC 17**
See also LAW; RGWL 2, 3; WLIT 1
**Herodotus** c. 484B.C.-c. 420B.C. .. **CMLC 17**
See also AW 1; CDWLB 1; DLB 176; RGWL 2, 3; TWA
**Herrick, Robert** 1591-1674 ....... **LC 13; PC 9**
See also BRW 2; DA; DAB; DAC; DAM MST, POP; DLB 126; EXPP; PFS 13; RGAL 4; RGEL 2; TEA; WP
**Herring, Guilles**
See Somerville, Edith Oenone
**Herriot, James** 1916-1995 ................. **CLC 12**
See Wight, James Alfred
See also AAYA 1; BPFB 2; CANR 40; CLR 80; CPW; DAM POP; LAIT 3; MAICYA 2; MAICYAS 1; MTCW 2; SATA 86, 135; TEA; YAW
**Herris, Violet**
See Hunt, Violet
**Herrmann, Dorothy** 1941- ................. **CLC 44**
See also CA 107
**Herrmann, Taffy**
See Herrmann, Dorothy

**Hersey, John (Richard)** 1914-1993 .... **CLC 1, 2, 7, 9, 40, 81, 97**
See also AAYA 29; BPFB 2; CA 17-20R; CANR 33; CDALBS; CPW; DAM POP; DLB 6, 185; MTCW 1, 2; SATA 25; SATA-Obit 76; TUS
**Herzen, Aleksandr Ivanovich** 1812-1870 ............................. **NCLC 10, 61**
**Herzl, Theodor** 1860-1904 ............. **TCLC 36**
See also CA 168
**Herzog, Werner** 1942- ..................... **CLC 16**
See also CA 89-92
**Hesiod** c. 8th cent. B.C.- ................... **CMLC 5**
See also AW 1; DLB 176; RGWL 2, 3
**Hesse, Hermann** 1877-1962 ... **CLC 1, 2, 3, 6, 11, 17, 25, 69; SSC 9, 49; WLC**
See also AAYA 43; BPFB 2; CA 17-18; CAP 2; CDWLB 2; DA; DAB; DAC; DAM MST, NOV; DLB 66; EW 9; EXPN; LAIT 1; MTCW 1, 2; NFS 6, 15; RGWL 2, 3; SATA 50; TWA
**Hewes, Cady**
See De Voto, Bernard (Augustine)
**Heyen, William** 1940- ................. **CLC 13, 18**
See also CA 33-36R; CAAS 9; CANR 98; CP 7; DLB 5
**Heyerdahl, Thor** 1914-2002 ............. **CLC 26**
See also CA 5-8R; CANR 5, 22, 66, 73; LAIT 4; MTCW 1, 2; SATA 2, 52
**Heym, Georg (Theodor Franz Arthur)** 1887-1912 ................................. **TCLC 9**
See also CA 181
**Heym, Stefan** 1913-2001 ................... **CLC 41**
See also CA 9-12R; CANR 4; CWW 2; DLB 69
**Heyse, Paul (Johann Ludwig von)** 1830-1914 ................................. **TCLC 8**
See also DLB 129
**Heyward, (Edwin) DuBose** 1885-1940 ...................... **HR 2; TCLC 59**
See also CA 157; DLB 7, 9, 45, 249; SATA 21
**Heywood, John** 1497(?)-1580(?) .......... **LC 65**
See also DLB 136; RGEL 2
**Hibbert, Eleanor Alice Burford** 1906-1993 ................................. **CLC 7**
See Holt, Victoria
See also BEST 90:4; CA 17-20R; CANR 9, 28, 59; CMW 4; CPW; DAM POP; MTCW 2; RHW; SATA 2; SATA-Obit 74
**Hichens, Robert (Smythe)** 1864-1950 ............................... **TCLC 64**
See also CA 162; DLB 153; HGG; RHW; SUFW
**Higgins, George V(incent)** 1939-1999 ................ **CLC 4, 7, 10, 18**
See also BPFB 2; CA 77-80; CAAS 5; CANR 17, 51, 89, 96; CMW 4; CN 7; DLB 2; DLBY 1981, 1998; INT CANR-17; MSW; MTCW 1
**Higginson, Thomas Wentworth** 1823-1911 ............................. **TCLC 36**
See also CA 162; DLB 1, 64, 243
**Higgonet, Margaret** ed. ..................... **CLC 65**
**Highet, Helen**
See MacInnes, Helen (Clark)
**Highsmith, (Mary) Patricia** 1921-1995 ............ **CLC 2, 4, 14, 42, 102**
See Morgan, Claire
See also BRWS 5; CA 1-4R; CANR 1, 20, 48, 62, 108; CMW 4; CPW; DAM NOV, POP; MSW; MTCW 1, 2
**Highwater, Jamake (Mamake)** 1942(?)-2001 ............................. **CLC 12**
See also AAYA 7; BPFB 2; BYA 4; CA 65-68; CAAS 7; CANR 10, 34, 84; CLR 17; CWRI 5; DLB 52; DLBY 1985; JRDA; MAICYA 1, 2; SATA 32, 69; SATA-Brief 30

**Highway, Tomson** 1951- ...... **CLC 92; NNAL**
See also CA 151; CANR 75; CCA 1; CD 5; DAC; DAM MULT; DFS 2; MTCW 2

**Hijuelos, Oscar** 1951- .......... **CLC 65; HLC 1**
See also AAYA 25; AMWS 8; BEST 90:1; CA 123; CANR 50, 75; CPW; DAM MULT, POP; DLB 145; HW 1, 2; MTCW 2; RGAL 4; WLIT 1

**Hikmet, Nazim** 1902(?)-1963 ............ **CLC 40**
See also CA 141

**Hildegard von Bingen** 1098-1179 . **CMLC 20**
See also DLB 148

**Hildesheimer, Wolfgang** 1916-1991 .. **CLC 49**
See also CA 101; DLB 69, 124

**Hill, Geoffrey (William)** 1932- ...... **CLC 5, 8, 18, 45**
See also BRWS 5; CA 81-84; CANR 21, 89; CDBLB 1960 to Present; CP 7; DAM POET; DLB 40; MTCW 1; RGEL 2

**Hill, George Roy** 1921- ....................... **CLC 26**
See also CA 122

**Hill, John**
See Koontz, Dean R(ay)

**Hill, Susan (Elizabeth)** 1942- ...... **CLC 4, 113**
See also CA 33-36R; CANR 29, 69; CN 7; DAB; DAM MST, NOV; DLB 14, 139; HGG; MTCW 1; RHW

**Hillard, Asa G. III** ............................ **CLC 70**

**Hillerman, Tony** 1925- ........................ **CLC 62**
See also AAYA 40; BEST 89:1; BPFB 2; CA 29-32R; CANR 21, 42, 65, 97; CMW 4; CPW; DAM POP; DLB 206; MSW; RGAL 4; SATA 6; TCWW 2; YAW

**Hillesum, Etty** 1914-1943 ............... **TCLC 49**
See also CA 137

**Hilliard, Noel (Harvey)** 1929-1996 ... **CLC 15**
See also CA 9-12R; CANR 7, 69; CN 7

**Hillis, Rick** 1956- ............................... **CLC 66**
See also CA 134

**Hilton, James** 1900-1954 ................ **TCLC 21**
See also CA 169; DLB 34, 77; FANT; SATA 34

**Himes, Chester (Bomar)** 1909-1984 .. **BLC 2; CLC 2, 4, 7, 18, 58, 108**
See also AFAW 2; BPFB 2; BW 2; CA 25-28R; CANR 22, 89; CMW 4; DAM MULT; DLB 2, 76, 143, 226; MSW; MTCW 1, 2; RGAL 4

**Hinde, Thomas** ........................... **CLC 6, 11**
See Chitty, Thomas Willes

**Hine, (William) Daryl** 1936- ............. **CLC 15**
See also CA 1-4R; CAAS 15; CANR 1, 20; CP 7; DLB 60

**Hinkson, Katharine Tynan**
See Tynan, Katharine

**Hinojosa(-Smith), Rolando (R.)** 1929- .............................................. **HLC 1**
See also CA 131; CAAS 16; CANR 62; DAM MULT; DLB 82; HW 1, 2; MTCW 2; RGAL 4

**Hinton, S(usan) E(loise)** 1950- .. **CLC 30, 111**
See also AAYA 2, 33; BPFB 2; BYA 2, 3; CA 81-84; CANR 32, 62, 92; CDALBS; CLR 3, 23; CPW; DA; DAB; DAC; DAM MST, NOV; JRDA; LAIT 5; MAICYA 1, 2; MTCW 1, 2; NFS 5, 9, 15, 16; SATA 19, 58, 115; WYA; YAW

**Hippius, Zinaida** ................................ **TCLC 9**
See Gippius, Zinaida (Nikolayevna)

**Hiraoka, Kimitake** 1925-1970
See Mishima, Yukio
See also CA 97-100; DAM DRAM; GLL 1; MTCW 1, 2

**Hirsch, E(ric) D(onald), Jr.** 1928- .... **CLC 79**
See also CA 25-28R; CANR 27, 51; DLB 67; INT CANR-27; MTCW 1

**Hirsch, Edward** 1950- ................. **CLC 31, 50**
See also CA 104; CANR 20, 42, 102; CP 7; DLB 120

**Hitchcock, Alfred (Joseph)** 1899-1980 ................................. **CLC 16**
See also AAYA 22; CA 159; SATA 27; SATA-Obit 24

**Hitchens, Christopher (Eric)** 1949- ............................................. **CLC 157**
See also CA 152; CANR 89

**Hitler, Adolf** 1889-1945 ................... **TCLC 53**
See also CA 147

**Hoagland, Edward** 1932- ................... **CLC 28**
See also ANW; CA 1-4R; CANR 2, 31, 57, 107; CN 7; DLB 6; SATA 51; TCWW 2

**Hoban, Russell (Conwell)** 1925- ... **CLC 7, 25**
See also BPFB 2; CA 5-8R; CANR 23, 37, 66, 114; CLR 3, 69; CN 7; CWRI 5; DAM NOV; DLB 52; FANT; MAICYA 1, 2; MTCW 1, 2; SATA 1, 40, 78, 136; SFW 4; SUFW 2

**Hobbes, Thomas** 1588-1679 ................. **LC 36**
See also DLB 151, 252; RGEL 2

**Hobbs, Perry**
See Blackmur, R(ichard) P(almer)

**Hobson, Laura Z(ametkin)** 1900-1986 ................................... **CLC 7, 25**
See Field, Peter
See also BPFB 2; CA 17-20R; CANR 55; DLB 28; SATA 52

**Hoccleve, Thomas** c. 1368-c. 1437 ...... **LC 75**
See also DLB 146; RGEL 2

**Hoch, Edward D(entinger)** 1930-
See Queen, Ellery
See also CA 29-32R; CANR 11, 27, 51, 97; CMW 4; SFW 4

**Hochhuth, Rolf** 1931- ............... **CLC 4, 11, 18**
See also CA 5-8R; CANR 33, 75; CWW 2; DAM DRAM; DLB 124; MTCW 1, 2

**Hochman, Sandra** 1936- ................. **CLC 3, 8**
See also CA 5-8R; DLB 5

**Hochwaelder, Fritz** 1911-1986 .......... **CLC 36**
See Hochwalder, Fritz
See also CA 29-32R; CANR 42; DAM DRAM; MTCW 1; RGWL 3

**Hochwalder, Fritz**
See Hochwaelder, Fritz
See also RGWL 2

**Hocking, Mary (Eunice)** 1921- ......... **CLC 13**
See also CA 101; CANR 18, 40

**Hodgins, Jack** 1938- ........................... **CLC 23**
See also CA 93-96; CN 7; DLB 60

**Hodgson, William Hope** 1877(?)-1918 ........................... **TCLC 13**
See also CA 164; CMW 4; DLB 70, 153, 156, 178; HGG; MTCW 2; SFW 4; SUFW 1

**Hoeg, Peter** 1957- ....................... **CLC 95, 156**
See also CA 151; CANR 75; CMW 4; DLB 214; MTCW 2; RGWL 3

**Hoffman, Alice** 1952- ........................ **CLC 51**
See also AAYA 37; AMWS 10; CA 77-80; CANR 34, 66, 100; CN 7; CPW; DAM NOV; MTCW 1, 2

**Hoffman, Daniel (Gerard)** 1923- . **CLC 6, 13, 23**
See also CA 1-4R; CANR 4; CP 7; DLB 5

**Hoffman, Stanley** 1944- ....................... **CLC 5**
See also CA 77-80

**Hoffman, William** 1925- .................. **CLC 141**
See also CA 21-24R; CANR 9, 103; CSW; DLB 234

**Hoffman, William M(oses)** 1939- ..... **CLC 40**
See Hoffman, William M.
See also CA 57-60; CANR 11, 71

**Hoffmann, E(rnst) T(heodor) A(madeus)** 1776-1822 ................... **NCLC 2; SSC 13**
See also CDWLB 2; DLB 90; EW 5; RGSF 2; RGWL 2, 3; SATA 27; SUFW 1; WCH

**Hofmann, Gert** 1931- ......................... **CLC 54**
See also CA 128

**Hofmannsthal, Hugo von** 1874-1929 ... **DC 4; TCLC 11**
See also CA 153; CDWLB 2; DAM DRAM; DFS 12; DLB 81, 118; EW 9; RGWL 2, 3

**Hogan, Linda** 1947- ...... **CLC 73; NNAL; PC 35**
See also AMWS 4; ANW; BYA 12; CA 120; CANR 45, 73; CWP; DAM MULT; DLB 175; SATA 132; TCWW 2

**Hogarth, Charles**
See Creasey, John

**Hogarth, Emmett**
See Polonsky, Abraham (Lincoln)

**Hogg, James** 1770-1835 ............ **NCLC 4, 109**
See also DLB 93, 116, 159; HGG; RGEL 2; SUFW 1

**Holbach, Paul Henri Thiry Baron** 1723-1789 ...................................... **LC 14**

**Holberg, Ludvig** 1684-1754 .................. **LC 6**
See also RGWL 2, 3

**Holcroft, Thomas** 1745-1809 .......... **NCLC 85**
See also DLB 39, 89, 158; RGEL 2

**Holden, Ursula** 1921- ......................... **CLC 18**
See also CA 101; CAAS 8; CANR 22

**Holderlin, (Johann Christian) Friedrich** 1770-1843 ........................ **NCLC 16; PC 4**
See also CDWLB 2; DLB 90; EW 5; RGWL 2, 3

**Holdstock, Robert**
See Holdstock, Robert P.

**Holdstock, Robert P.** 1948- ................ **CLC 39**
See also CA 131; CANR 81; DLB 261; FANT; HGG; SFW 4; SUFW 2

**Holinshed, Raphael** fl. 1580- ................ **LC 69**
See also DLB 167; RGEL 2

**Holland, Isabelle (Christian)** 1920-2002 ............................... **CLC 21**
See also AAYA 11; CA 21-24R, 181; CAAE 181; CANR 10, 25, 47; CLR 57; CWRI 5; JRDA; LAIT 4; MAICYA 1, 2; SATA 8, 70; SATA-Essay 103; SATA-Obit 132; WYA

**Holland, Marcus**
See Caldwell, (Janet Miriam) Taylor (Holland)

**Hollander, John** 1929- .......... **CLC 2, 5, 8, 14**
See also CA 1-4R; CANR 1, 52; CP 7; DLB 5; SATA 13

**Hollander, Paul**
See Silverberg, Robert

**Holleran, Andrew** 1943(?)- ................ **CLC 38**
See Garber, Eric
See also CA 144; GLL 1

**Holley, Marietta** 1836(?)-1926 ........ **TCLC 99**
See also DLB 11

**Hollinghurst, Alan** 1954- ............. **CLC 55, 91**
See also CA 114; CN 7; DLB 207; GLL 1

**Hollis, Jim**
See Summers, Hollis (Spurgeon, Jr.)

**Holly, Buddy** 1936-1959 ................. **TCLC 65**

**Holmes, Gordon**
See Shiel, M(atthew) P(hipps)

**Holmes, John**
See Souster, (Holmes) Raymond

**Holmes, John Clellon** 1926-1988 ...... **CLC 56**
See also BG 2; CA 9-12R; CANR 4; DLB 16, 237

**Holmes, Oliver Wendell, Jr.** 1841-1935 ...................................... **TCLC 77**
See also CA 186

**Holmes, Oliver Wendell** 1809-1894 .......................... **NCLC 14, 81**
See also AMWS 1; CDALB 1640-1865; DLB 1, 189, 235; EXPP; RGAL 4; SATA 34

**Holmes, Raymond**
See Souster, (Holmes) Raymond

**Holt, Victoria**
See Hibbert, Eleanor Alice Burford
See also BPFB 2

**Holub, Miroslav** 1923-1998 ............... **CLC 4**
See also CA 21-24R; CANR 10; CDWLB 4; CWW 2; DLB 232; RGWL 3

**Homer** c. 8th cent. B.C.- .... **CMLC 1, 16; PC 23; WLCS**
See also AW 1; CDWLB 1; DA; DAB; DAC; DAM MST, POET; DLB 176; EFS 1; LAIT 1; RGWL 2, 3; TWA; WP

**Hongo, Garrett Kaoru** 1951- .............. **PC 23**
See also CA 133; CAAS 22; CP 7; DLB 120; EXPP; RGAL 4

**Honig, Edwin** 1919- ........................ **CLC 33**
See also CA 5-8R; CAAS 8; CANR 4, 45; CP 7; DLB 5

**Hood, Hugh (John Blagdon)** 1928- . **CLC 15, 28; SSC 42**
See also CA 49-52; CAAS 17; CANR 1, 33, 87; CN 7; DLB 53; RGSF 2

**Hood, Thomas** 1799-1845 .................. **NCLC 16**
See also BRW 4; DLB 96; RGEL 2

**Hooker, (Peter) Jeremy** 1941- ........... **CLC 43**
See also CA 77-80; CANR 22; CP 7; DLB 40

**hooks, bell** ................................... **CLC 94**
See Watkins, Gloria Jean
See also DLB 246

**Hope, A(lec) D(erwent)** 1907-2000 .... **CLC 3, 51**
See also BRWS 7; CA 21-24R; CANR 33, 74; MTCW 1, 2; PFS 8; RGEL 2

**Hope, Anthony** 1863-1933 ............... **TCLC 83**
See also CA 157; DLB 153, 156; RGEL 2; RHW

**Hope, Brian**
See Creasey, John

**Hope, Christopher (David Tully)**
1944- ............................................. **CLC 52**
See also AFW; CA 106; CANR 47, 101; CN 7; DLB 225; SATA 62

**Hopkins, Gerard Manley**
1844-1889 ....... **NCLC 17; PC 15; WLC**
See also BRW 5; BRWR 2; CDBLB 1890-1914; DA; DAB; DAC; DAM MST, POET; DLB 35, 57; EXPP; PAB; RGEL 2; TEA; WP

**Hopkins, John (Richard)** 1931-1998 .. **CLC 4**
See also CA 85-88; CBD; CD 5

**Hopkins, Pauline Elizabeth**
1859-1930 .................. **BLC 2; TCLC 28**
See also AFAW 2; BW 2, 3; CA 141; CANR 82; DAM MULT; DLB 50

**Hopkinson, Francis** 1737-1791 ............ **LC 25**
See also DLB 31; RGAL 4

**Hopley-Woolrich, Cornell George** 1903-1968
See Woolrich, Cornell
See also CA 13-14; CANR 58; CAP 1; CMW 4; DLB 226; MTCW 2

**Horace** 65B.C.-8B.C. ...................... **CMLC 39**
See also AW 2; CDWLB 1; DLB 211; RGWL 2, 3

**Horatio**
See Proust, (Valentin-Louis-George-Eugene-)Marcel

**Horgan, Paul (George Vincent O'Shaughnessy)** 1903-1995 .. **CLC 9, 53**
See also BPFB 2; CA 13-16R; CANR 9, 35; DAM NOV; DLB 102, 212; DLBY 1985; INT CANR-9; MTCW 1, 2; SATA 13; SATA-Obit 84; TCWW 2

**Horn, Peter**
See Kuttner, Henry

**Hornem, Horace Esq.**
See Byron, George Gordon (Noel)

**Horney, Karen (Clementine Theodore Danielsen)** 1885-1952 ............. **TCLC 71**
See also CA 165; DLB 246; FW

**Hornung, E(rnest) W(illiam)**
1866-1921 ................................ **TCLC 59**
See also CA 160; CMW 4; DLB 70

**Horovitz, Israel (Arthur)** 1939- ........ **CLC 56**
See also CA 33-36R; CAD; CANR 46, 59; CD 5; DAM DRAM; DLB 7

**Horton, George Moses**
1797(?)-1883(?) ........................ **NCLC 87**
See also DLB 50

**Horvath, odon von** 1901-1938
See von Horvath, Odon

**Horvath, Oedoen von** -1938
See von Horvath, Odon

**Horwitz, Julius** 1920-1986 ................ **CLC 14**
See also CA 9-12R; CANR 12

**Hospital, Janette Turner** 1942- ........ **CLC 42, 145**
See also CA 108; CANR 48; CN 7; RGSF 2

**Hostos, E. M. de**
See Hostos (y Bonilla), Eugenio Maria de

**Hostos, Eugenio M. de**
See Hostos (y Bonilla), Eugenio Maria de

**Hostos, Eugenio Maria**
See Hostos (y Bonilla), Eugenio Maria de

**Hostos (y Bonilla), Eugenio Maria de**
1839-1903 ................................ **TCLC 24**
See also CA 131; HW 1

**Houdini**
See Lovecraft, H(oward) P(hillips)

**Hougan, Carolyn** 1943- ..................... **CLC 34**
See also CA 139

**Household, Geoffrey (Edward West)**
1900-1988 ................................... **CLC 11**
See also CA 77-80; CANR 58; CMW 4; DLB 87; SATA 14; SATA-Obit 59

**Housman, A(lfred) E(dward)**
1859-1936 ......... **PC 2, 43; TCLC 1, 10; WLCS**
See also BRW 6; CA 125; DA; DAB; DAC; DAM MST, POET; DLB 19; EXPP; MTCW 1, 2; PAB; PFS 4, 7; RGEL 2; TEA; WP

**Housman, Laurence** 1865-1959 ....... **TCLC 7**
See also CA 155; DLB 10; FANT; RGEL 2; SATA 25

**Howard, Elizabeth Jane** 1923- ..... **CLC 7, 29**
See also CA 5-8R; CANR 8, 62; CN 7

**Howard, Maureen** 1930- ........ **CLC 5, 14, 46, 151**
See also CA 53-56; CANR 31, 75; CN 7; DLBY 1983; INT CANR-31; MTCW 1, 2

**Howard, Richard** 1929- .......... **CLC 7, 10, 47**
See also AITN 1; CA 85-88; CANR 25, 80; CP 7; DLB 5; INT CANR-25

**Howard, Robert E(rvin)**
1906-1936 .................................... **TCLC 8**
See also BPFB 2; BYA 5; CA 157; FANT; SUFW 1

**Howard, Warren F.**
See Pohl, Frederik

**Howe, Fanny (Quincy)** 1940- ............. **CLC 47**
See also CA 117; CAAE 187; CAAS 27; CANR 70; CP 7; CWP; SATA-Brief 52

**Howe, Irving** 1920-1993 ................... **CLC 85**
See also AMWS 6; CA 9-12R; CANR 21, 50; DLB 67; MTCW 1, 2

**Howe, Julia Ward** 1819-1910 ......... **TCLC 21**
See also CA 191; DLB 1, 189, 235; FW

**Howe, Susan** 1937- .................... **CLC 72, 152**
See also AMWS 4; CA 160; CP 7; CWP; DLB 120; FW; RGAL 4

**Howe, Tina** 1937- .............................. **CLC 48**
See also CA 109; CAD; CD 5; CWD

**Howell, James** 1594(?)-1666 ................ **LC 13**
See also DLB 151

**Howells, W. D.**
See Howells, William Dean

**Howells, William D.**
See Howells, William Dean

**Howells, William Dean** 1837-1920 ... **SSC 36; TCLC 7, 17, 41**
See also AMW; CA 134; CDALB 1865-1917; DLB 12, 64, 74, 79, 189; MTCW 2; RGAL 4; TUS

**Howes, Barbara** 1914-1996 .............. **CLC 15**
See also CA 9-12R; CAAS 3; CANR 53; CP 7; SATA 5

**Hrabal, Bohumil** 1914-1997 ........ **CLC 13, 67**
See also CA 106; CAAS 12; CANR 57; CWW 2; DLB 232; RGSF 2

**Hrotsvit of Gandersheim** c. 935-c. 1000 ............................................. **CMLC 29**
See also DLB 148

**Hsi, Chu** 1130-1200 ....................... **CMLC 42**

**Hsun, Lu**
See Lu Hsun

**Hubbard, L(afayette) Ron(ald)**
1911-1986 ................................... **CLC 43**
See also CA 77-80; CANR 52; CPW; DAM POP; FANT; MTCW 2; SFW 4

**Huch, Ricarda (Octavia)**
1864-1947 ................................. **TCLC 13**
See also CA 189; DLB 66

**Huddle, David** 1942- ......................... **CLC 49**
See also CA 57-60; CAAS 20; CANR 89; DLB 130

**Hudson, Jeffrey**
See Crichton, (John) Michael

**Hudson, W(illiam) H(enry)**
1841-1922 ................................. **TCLC 29**
See also CA 190; DLB 98, 153, 174; RGEL 2; SATA 35

**Hueffer, Ford Madox**
See Ford, Ford Madox

**Hughart, Barry** 1934- ....................... **CLC 39**
See also CA 137; FANT; SFW 4; SUFW 2

**Hughes, Colin**
See Creasey, John

**Hughes, David (John)** 1930- ............. **CLC 48**
See also CA 129; CN 7; DLB 14

**Hughes, Edward James**
See Hughes, Ted
See also DAM MST, POET

**Hughes, (James Mercer) Langston**
1902-1967 ..... **BLC 2; CLC 1, 5, 10, 15, 35, 44, 108; DC 3; HR 2; PC 1; SSC 6; WLC**
See also AAYA 12; AFAW 1, 2; AMWR 1; AMWS 1; BW 1, 3; CA 1-4R; CANR 1, 34, 82; CDALB 1929-1941; CLR 17; DA; DAB; DAC; DAM DRAM, MST, MULT, POET; DLB 4, 7, 48, 51, 86, 228; EXPP; EXPS; JRDA; LAIT 3; MAICYA 1, 2; MTCW 1, 2; PAB; PFS 1, 3, 6, 10, 15; RGAL 4; RGSF 2; SATA 4, 33; SSFS 4, 7; TUS; WCH; WP; YAW

**Hughes, Richard (Arthur Warren)**
1900-1976 ................................. **CLC 1, 11**
See also CA 5-8R; CANR 4; DAM NOV; DLB 15, 161; MTCW 1; RGEL 2; SATA 8; SATA-Obit 25

**Hughes, Ted** 1930-1998 . **CLC 2, 4, 9, 14, 37, 119; PC 7**
See Hughes, Edward James
See also BRWR 2; BRWS 1; CA 1-4R; CANR 1, 33, 66, 108; CLR 3; CP 7; DAB; DAC; DLB 40, 161; EXPP; MAICYA 1, 2; MTCW 1, 2; PAB; PFS 4; RGEL 2; SATA 49; SATA-Brief 27; SATA-Obit 107; TEA; YAW

**Hugo, Richard**
See Huch, Ricarda (Octavia)

**Hugo, Richard F(ranklin)**
1923-1982 .......................... **CLC 6, 18, 32**
See also AMWS 6; CA 49-52; CANR 3; DAM POET; DLB 5, 206; PFS 17; RGAL 4

**Hugo, Victor (Marie)** 1802-1885 .... **NCLC 3, 10, 21; PC 17; WLC**
See also AAYA 28; DA; DAB; DAC; DAM DRAM, MST, NOV, POET; DLB 119, 192, 217; EFS 2; EW 6; EXPN; GFL 1789 to the Present; LAIT 1, 2; NFS 5; RGWL 2, 3; SATA 47; TWA

**Huidobro, Vicente**
See Huidobro Fernandez, Vicente Garcia
See also LAW

**Huidobro Fernandez, Vicente Garcia**
1893-1948 ........................ **TCLC 31**
See Huidobro, Vicente
See also CA 131; HW 1

**Hulme, Keri** 1947- ..................... **CLC 39, 130**
See also CA 125; CANR 69; CN 7; CP 7; CWP; FW; INT 125

**Hulme, T(homas) E(rnest)**
1883-1917 .............................. **TCLC 21**
See also BRWS 6; CA 203; DLB 19

**Hume, David** 1711-1776 ................ **LC 7, 56**
See also BRWS 3; DLB 104, 252; TEA

**Humphrey, William** 1924-1997 ......... **CLC 45**
See also AMWS 9; CA 77-80; CANR 68; CN 7; CSW; DLB 6, 212, 234; TCWW 2

**Humphreys, Emyr Owen** 1919- ....... **CLC 47**
See also CA 5-8R; CANR 3, 24; CN 7; DLB 15

**Humphreys, Josephine** 1945- ..... **CLC 34, 57**
See also CA 127; CANR 97; CSW; INT 127

**Huneker, James Gibbons**
1860-1921 .............................. **TCLC 65**
See also CA 193; DLB 71; RGAL 4

**Hungerford, Hesba Fay**
See Brinsmead, H(esba) F(ay)

**Hungerford, Pixie**
See Brinsmead, H(esba) F(ay)

**Hunt, E(verette) Howard, (Jr.)**
1918- ........................................ **CLC 3**
See also AITN 1; CA 45-48; CANR 2, 47, 103; CMW 4

**Hunt, Francesca**
See Holland, Isabelle (Christian)

**Hunt, Howard**
See Hunt, E(verette) Howard, (Jr.)

**Hunt, Kyle**
See Creasey, John

**Hunt, (James Henry) Leigh**
1784-1859 ........................... **NCLC 1, 70**
See also DAM POET; DLB 96, 110, 144; RGEL 2; TEA

**Hunt, Marsha** 1946- ........................ **CLC 70**
See also BW 2, 3; CA 143; CANR 79

**Hunt, Violet** 1866(?)-1942 ............... **TCLC 53**
See also CA 184; DLB 162, 197

**Hunter, E. Waldo**
See Sturgeon, Theodore (Hamilton)

**Hunter, Evan** 1926- ..................... **CLC 11, 31**
See McBain, Ed
See also AAYA 39; BPFB 2; CA 5-8R; CANR 5, 38, 62, 97; CMW 4; CN 7; CPW; DAM POP; DLBY 1982; INT CANR-5; MSW; MTCW 1; SATA 25; SFW 4

**Hunter, Kristin** 1931-
See Lattany, Kristin (Elaine Eggleston) Hunter

**Hunter, Mary**
See Austin, Mary (Hunter)

**Hunter, Mollie** 1922- ......................... **CLC 21**
See McIlwraith, Maureen Mollie Hunter
See also AAYA 13; BYA 6; CANR 37, 78; CLR 25; DLB 161; JRDA; MAICYA 1, 2; SAAS 7; SATA 54, 106; WYA; YAW

**Hunter, Robert** (?)-1734 ........................ **LC 7**

**Hurston, Zora Neale** 1891-1960 ........ **BLC 2; CLC 7, 30, 61; DC 12; HR 2; SSC 4; TCLC 121, 131; WLCS**
See also AAYA 15; AFAW 1, 2; AMWS 6; BW 1, 3; BYA 12; CA 85-88; CANR 61; CDALBS; DA; DAC; DAM MST, MULT, NOV; DFS 6; DLB 51, 86; EXPN; EXPS; FW; LAIT 3; MAWW; MTCW 1, 2; NFS 3; RGAL 4; RGSF 2; SSFS 1, 6, 11; TUS; YAW

**Husserl, E. G.**
See Husserl, Edmund (Gustav Albrecht)

**Husserl, Edmund (Gustav Albrecht)**
1859-1938 .............................. **TCLC 100**
See also CA 133

**Huston, John (Marcellus)**
1906-1987 ............................ **CLC 20**
See also CA 73-76; CANR 34; DLB 26

**Hustvedt, Siri** 1955- .......................... **CLC 76**
See also CA 137

**Hutten, Ulrich von** 1488-1523 ............ **LC 16**
See also DLB 179

**Huxley, Aldous (Leonard)**
1894-1963 ........ **CLC 1, 3, 4, 5, 8, 11, 18, 35, 79; SSC 39; WLC**
See also AAYA 11; BPFB 2; BRW 7; CA 85-88; CANR 44, 99; CDBLB 1914-1945; DA; DAB; DAC; DAM MST, NOV; DLB 36, 100, 162, 195, 255; EXPN; LAIT 5; MTCW 1, 2; NFS 6; RGEL 2; SATA 63; SCFW 2; SFW 4; TEA; YAW

**Huxley, T(homas) H(enry)**
1825-1895 .............................. **NCLC 67**
See also DLB 57; TEA

**Huysmans, Joris-Karl** 1848-1907 ... **TCLC 7, 69**
See also CA 165; DLB 123; EW 7; GFL 1789 to the Present; RGWL 2, 3

**Hwang, David Henry** 1957- .. **CLC 55; DC 4**
See also CA 132; CAD; CANR 76; CD 5; DAM DRAM; DFS 11; DLB 212, 228; INT CA-132; MTCW 2; RGAL 4

**Hyde, Anthony** 1946- ......................... **CLC 42**
See Chase, Nicholas
See also CA 136; CCA 1

**Hyde, Margaret O(ldroyd)** 1917- ..... **CLC 21**
See also CA 1-4R; CANR 1, 36; CLR 23; JRDA; MAICYA 1, 2; SAAS 8; SATA 1, 42, 76

**Hynes, James** 1956(?)- ....................... **CLC 65**
See also CA 164; CANR 105

**Hypatia** c. 370-415 ........................... **CMLC 35**

**Ian, Janis** 1951- ................................. **CLC 21**
See also CA 187

**Ibanez, Vicente Blasco**
See Blasco Ibanez, Vicente

**Ibarbourou, Juana de** 1895-1979 ..... **HLCS 2**
See also HW 1; LAW

**Ibarguengoitia, Jorge** 1928-1983 ....... **CLC 37**
See also CA 124; HW 1

**Ibn Battuta, Abu Abdalla**
1304-1368(?) .......................... **CMLC 57**
See also WLIT 2

**Ibsen, Henrik (Johan)** 1828-1906 ........ **DC 2; TCLC 2, 8, 16, 37, 52; WLC**
See also AAYA 46; CA 141; DA; DAB; DAC; DAM DRAM, MST; DFS 15; EW 7; LAIT 2; RGWL 2, 3

**Ibuse, Masuji** 1898-1993 ................... **CLC 22**
See Ibuse Masuji
See also CA 127; MJW; RGWL 3

**Ibuse Masuji**
See Ibuse, Masuji
See also DLB 180

**Ichikawa, Kon** 1915- ......................... **CLC 20**
See also CA 121

**Ichiyo, Higuchi** 1872-1896 ............. **NCLC 49**
See also MJW

**Idle, Eric** 1943-2000 ........................... **CLC 21**
See Monty Python
See also CA 116; CANR 35, 91

**Ignatow, David** 1914-1997 ....... **CLC 4, 7, 14, 40; PC 34**
See also CA 9-12R; CAAS 3; CANR 31, 57, 96; CP 7; DLB 5

**Ignotus**
See Strachey, (Giles) Lytton

**Ihimaera, Witi** 1944- ......................... **CLC 46**
See also CA 77-80; CN 7; RGSF 2

**Ilf, Ilya** ................................................. **TCLC 21**
See Fainzilberg, Ilya Arnoldovich

**Illyes, Gyula** 1902-1983 ....................... **PC 16**
See also CA 114; CDWLB 4; DLB 215; RGWL 2, 3

**Immermann, Karl (Lebrecht)**
1796-1840 .......................... **NCLC 4, 49**
See also DLB 133

**Ince, Thomas H.** 1882-1924 ............. **TCLC 89**
See also IDFW 3, 4

**Inchbald, Elizabeth** 1753-1821 ....... **NCLC 62**
See also DLB 39, 89; RGEL 2

**Inclan, Ramon (Maria) del Valle**
See Valle-Inclan, Ramon (Maria) del

**Infante, G(uillermo) Cabrera**
See Cabrera Infante, G(uillermo)

**Ingalls, Rachel (Holmes)** 1940- ......... **CLC 42**
See also CA 127

**Ingamells, Reginald Charles**
See Ingamells, Rex

**Ingamells, Rex** 1913-1955 ............... **TCLC 35**
See also CA 167; DLB 260

**Inge, William (Motter)** 1913-1973 ..... **CLC 1, 8, 19**
See also CA 9-12R; CDALB 1941-1968; DAM DRAM; DFS 1, 5, 8; DLB 7, 249; MTCW 1, 2; RGAL 4; TUS

**Ingelow, Jean** 1820-1897 ............... **NCLC 39, 107**
See also DLB 35, 163; FANT; SATA 33

**Ingram, Willis J.**
See Harris, Mark

**Innaurato, Albert (F.)** 1948(?)- ... **CLC 21, 60**
See also CA 122; CAD; CANR 78; CD 5; INT CA-122

**Innes, Michael**
See Stewart, J(ohn) I(nnes) M(ackintosh)
See also MSW

**Innis, Harold Adams** 1894-1952 .... **TCLC 77**
See also CA 181; DLB 88

**Insluis, Alanus de**
See Alain de Lille

**Iola**
See Wells-Barnett, Ida B(ell)

**Ionesco, Eugene** 1912-1994 ... **CLC 1, 4, 6, 9, 11, 15, 41, 86; DC 12; WLC**
See also CA 9-12R; CANR 55; CWW 2; DA; DAB; DAC; DAM DRAM, MST; DFS 4, 9; EW 13; GFL 1789 to the Present; MTCW 1, 2; RGWL 2, 3; SATA 7; SATA-Obit 79; TWA

**Iqbal, Muhammad** 1877-1938 ........ **TCLC 28**

**Ireland, Patrick**
See O'Doherty, Brian

**Irenaeus St.** 130- ............................. **CMLC 42**

**Irigaray, Luce** 1930- ......................... **CLC 164**
See also CA 154; FW

**Iron, Ralph**
See Schreiner, Olive (Emilie Albertina)

**Irving, John (Winslow)** 1942- ... **CLC 13, 23, 38, 112**
See also AAYA 8; AMWS 6; BEST 89:3; BPFB 2; CA 25-28R; CANR 28, 73, 112; CN 7; CPW; DAM NOV, POP; DLB 6; DLBY 1982; MTCW 1, 2; NFS 12, 14; RGAL 4; TUS

**Irving, Washington** 1783-1859 . **NCLC 2, 19, 95; SSC 2, 37; WLC**
See also AMW; CDALB 1640-1865; DA; DAB; DAC; DAM MST; DLB 3, 11, 30, 59, 73, 74, 183, 186, 250, 254; EXPS; LAIT 1; RGAL 4; RGSF 2; SSFS 1, 8, 16; SUFW 1; TUS; WCH; YABC 2

**Irwin, P. K.**
See Page, P(atricia) K(athleen)

**Isaacs, Jorge Ricardo** 1837-1895 ... **NCLC 70**
See also LAW

**Isaacs, Susan** 1943- ............................. **CLC 32**
See also BEST 89:1; BPFB 2; CA 89-92; CANR 20, 41, 65, 112; CPW; DAM POP; INT CANR-20; MTCW 1, 2

**Isherwood, Christopher (William Bradshaw)** 1904-1986 .... **CLC 1, 9, 11, 14, 44; SSC 56**
See also BRW 7; CA 13-16R; CANR 35, 97; DAM DRAM, NOV; DLB 15, 195; DLBY 1986; IDTP; MTCW 1, 2; RGAL 4; RGEL 2; TUS; WLIT 4

**Ishiguro, Kazuo** 1954- .. **CLC 27, 56, 59, 110**
See also BEST 90:2; BPFB 2; BRWS 4; CA 120; CANR 49, 95; CN 7; DAM NOV; DLB 194; MTCW 1, 2; NFS 13; WLIT 4

**Ishikawa, Hakuhin**
See Ishikawa, Takuboku

**Ishikawa, Takuboku** 1886(?)-1912 ..... **PC 10; TCLC 15**
See also CA 153; DAM POET

**Iskander, Fazil** 1929- .......................... **CLC 47**
See also CA 102

**Isler, Alan (David)** 1934- ................... **CLC 91**
See also CA 156; CANR 105

**Ivan IV** 1530-1584 ............................... **LC 17**

**Ivanov, Vyacheslav Ivanovich** 1866-1949 ................................ **TCLC 33**

**Ivask, Ivar Vidrik** 1927-1992 ............. **CLC 14**
See also CA 37-40R; CANR 24

**Ives, Morgan**
See Bradley, Marion Zimmer
See also GLL 1

**Izumi Shikibu** c. 973-c. 1034 ........ **CMLC 33**

**J. R. S.**
See Gogarty, Oliver St. John

**Jabran, Kahlil**
See Gibran, Kahlil

**Jabran, Khalil**
See Gibran, Kahlil

**Jackson, Daniel**
See Wingrove, David (John)

**Jackson, Helen Hunt** 1830-1885 ..... **NCLC 90**
See also DLB 42, 47, 186, 189; RGAL 4

**Jackson, Jesse** 1908-1983 .................. **CLC 12**
See also BW 1; CA 25-28R; CANR 27; CLR 28; CWRI 5; MAICYA 1, 2; SATA 2, 29; SATA-Obit 48

**Jackson, Laura (Riding)** 1901-1991 ..... **PC 44**
See Riding, Laura
See also CA 65-68; CANR 28, 89; DLB 48

**Jackson, Sam**
See Trumbo, Dalton

**Jackson, Sara**
See Wingrove, David (John)

**Jackson, Shirley** 1919-1965 . **CLC 11, 60, 87; SSC 9, 39; WLC**
See also AAYA 9; AMWS 9; BPFB 2; CA 1-4R; CANR 4, 52; CDALB 1941-1968; DA; DAC; DAM MST; DLB 6, 234; EXPS; HGG; LAIT 4; MTCW 2; RGAL 4; RGSF 2; SATA 2; SSFS 1; SUFW 1, 2

**Jacob, (Cyprien-)Max** 1876-1944 .... **TCLC 6**
See also CA 193; DLB 258; GFL 1789 to the Present; GLL 2; RGWL 2, 3

**Jacobs, Harriet A(nn)** 1813(?)-1897 ............................. **NCLC 67**
See also AFAW 1, 2; DLB 239; FW; LAIT 2; RGAL 4

**Jacobs, Jim** 1942- ................................. **CLC 12**
See also CA 97-100; INT 97-100

**Jacobs, W(illiam) W(ymark)** 1863-1943 ................................ **TCLC 22**
See also CA 167; DLB 135; EXPS; HGG; RGEL 2; RGSF 2; SSFS 2; SUFW 1

**Jacobsen, Jens Peter** 1847-1885 .... **NCLC 34**

**Jacobsen, Josephine** 1908- .......... **CLC 48, 102**
See also CA 33-36R; CAAS 18; CANR 23, 48; CCA 1; CP 7; DLB 244

**Jacobson, Dan** 1929- ...................... **CLC 4, 14**
See also AFW; CA 1-4R; CANR 2, 25, 66; CN 7; DLB 14, 207, 225; MTCW 1; RGSF 2

**Jacqueline**
See Carpentier (y Valmont), Alejo

**Jagger, Mick** 1944- ............................. **CLC 17**

**Jahiz, al-** c. 780-c. 869 ................... **CMLC 25**

**Jakes, John (William)** 1932- ............. **CLC 29**
See also AAYA 32; BEST 89:4; BPFB 2; CA 57-60; CANR 10, 43, 66, 111; CPW; CSW; DAM NOV, POP; DLBY 1983; FANT; INT CANR-10; MTCW 1, 2; RHW; SATA 62; SFW 4; TCWW 2

**James I** 1394-1437 ............................. **LC 20**
See also RGEL 2

**James, Andrew**
See Kirkup, James

**James, C(yril) L(ionel) R(obert)** 1901-1989 ...................... **BLCS; CLC 33**
See also BW 2; CA 125; CANR 62; DLB 125; MTCW 1

**James, Daniel (Lewis)** 1911-1988
See Santiago, Danny
See also CA 174

**James, Dynely**
See Mayne, William (James Carter)

**James, Henry Sr.** 1811-1882 .......... **NCLC 53**

**James, Henry** 1843-1916 ........ **SSC 8, 32, 47; TCLC 2, 11, 24, 40, 47, 64; WLC**
See also AMW; AMWC 1; AMWR 1; BPFB 2; BRW 6; CA 132; CDALB 1865-1917; DA; DAB; DAC; DAM MST, NOV; DLB 12, 71, 74, 189; DLBD 13; EXPS; HGG; LAIT 2; MTCW 1, 2; NFS 12, 16; RGAL 4; RGEL 2; RGSF 2; SSFS 9; SUFW 1; TUS

**James, M. R.**
See James, Montague (Rhodes)
See also DLB 156, 201

**James, Montague (Rhodes)** 1862-1936 .................. **SSC 16; TCLC 6**
See James, M. R.
See also HGG; RGEL 2; RGSF 2; SUFW 1

**James, P. D.** ......................... **CLC 18, 46, 122**
See White, Phyllis Dorothy James
See also BEST 90:2; BPFB 2; BRWS 4; CDBLB 1960 to Present; DLB 87; DLBD 17; MSW

**James, Philip**
See Moorcock, Michael (John)

**James, Samuel**
See Stephens, James

**James, Seumas**
See Stephens, James

**James, Stephen**
See Stephens, James

**James, William** 1842-1910 ....... **TCLC 15, 32**
See also AMW; CA 193; DLB 270; RGAL 4

**Jameson, Anna** 1794-1860 ............. **NCLC 43**
See also DLB 99, 166

**Jameson, Fredric (R.)** 1934- ........... **CLC 142**
See also CA 196; DLB 67

**Jami, Nur al-Din 'Abd al-Rahman** 1414-1492 ...................................... **LC 9**

**Jammes, Francis** 1868-1938 .......... **TCLC 75**
See also CA 198; GFL 1789 to the Present

**Jandl, Ernst** 1925-2000 ..................... **CLC 34**
See also CA 200

**Janowitz, Tama** 1957- ................ **CLC 43, 145**
See also CA 106; CANR 52, 89; CN 7; CPW; DAM POP

**Japrisot, Sebastien** 1931- .................. **CLC 90**
See Rossi, Jean Baptiste
See also CMW 4

**Jarrell, Randall** 1914-1965 .... **CLC 1, 2, 6, 9, 13, 49; PC 41**
See also AMW; BYA 5; CA 5-8R; CABS 2; CANR 6, 34; CDALB 1941-1968; CLR 6; CWRI 5; DAM POET; DLB 48, 52; EXPP; MAICYA 1, 2; MTCW 1, 2; PAB; PFS 2; RGAL 4; SATA 7

**Jarry, Alfred** 1873-1907 .... **SSC 20; TCLC 2, 14**
See also CA 153; DAM DRAM; DFS 8; DLB 192, 258; EW 9; GFL 1789 to the Present; RGWL 2, 3; TWA

**Jawien, Andrzej**
See John Paul II, Pope

**Jaynes, Roderick**
See Coen, Ethan

**Jeake, Samuel, Jr.**
See Aiken, Conrad (Potter)

**Jean Paul** 1763-1825 ......................... **NCLC 7**

**Jefferies, (John) Richard** 1848-1887 ................................ **NCLC 47**
See also DLB 98, 141; RGEL 2; SATA 16; SFW 4

**Jeffers, (John) Robinson** 1887-1962 .. **CLC 2, 3, 11, 15, 54; PC 17; WLC**
See also AMWS 2; CA 85-88; CANR 35; CDALB 1917-1929; DA; DAC; DAM MST, POET; DLB 45, 212; MTCW 1, 2; PAB; PFS 3, 4; RGAL 4

**Jefferson, Janet**
See Mencken, H(enry) L(ouis)

**Jefferson, Thomas** 1743-1826 . **NCLC 11, 103**
See also ANW; CDALB 1640-1865; DLB 31, 183; LAIT 1; RGAL 4

**Jeffrey, Francis** 1773-1850 .............. **NCLC 33**
See Francis, Lord Jeffrey

**Jelakowitch, Ivan**
See Heijermans, Herman

**Jelinek, Elfriede** 1946- ..................... **CLC 169**
See also CA 154; DLB 85; FW

**Jellicoe, (Patricia) Ann** 1927- ........... **CLC 27**
See also CA 85-88; CBD; CD 5; CWD; CWRI 5; DLB 13, 233; FW

**Jemyma**
See Holley, Marietta

**Jen, Gish** ............................................ **CLC 70**
See Jen, Lillian

**Jen, Lillian** 1956(?)-
See Jen, Gish
See also CA 135; CANR 89

**Jenkins, (John) Robin** 1912- ............. **CLC 52**
See also CA 1-4R; CANR 1; CN 7; DLB 14, 271

**Jennings, Elizabeth (Joan)** 1926-2001 ...................... **CLC 5, 14, 131**
See also BRWS 5; CA 61-64; CAAS 5; CANR 8, 39, 66; CP 7; CWP; DLB 27; MTCW 1; SATA 66

**Jennings, Waylon** 1937- ................... **CLC 21**

**Jensen, Johannes V.** 1873-1950 ...... **TCLC 41**
See also CA 170; DLB 214; RGWL 3

**Jensen, Laura (Linnea)** 1948- .......... **CLC 37**
See also CA 103

**Jerome, Saint** 345-420 .................. **CMLC 30**
See also RGWL 3

**Jerome, Jerome K(lapka)**
1859-1927 .................................. **TCLC 23**
See also CA 177; DLB 10, 34, 135; RGEL 2

**Jerrold, Douglas William**
1803-1857 ..................................... **NCLC 2**
See also DLB 158, 159; RGEL 2

**Jewett, (Theodora) Sarah Orne**
1849-1909 ......... **SSC 6, 44; TCLC 1, 22**
See also AMW; AMWR 2; CA 127; CANR 71; DLB 12, 74, 221; EXPS; FW; MAWW; NFS 15; RGAL 4; RGSF 2; SATA 15; SSFS 4

**Jewsbury, Geraldine (Endsor)**
1812-1880 .................................. **NCLC 22**
See also DLB 21

**Jhabvala, Ruth Prawer** 1927- . **CLC 4, 8, 29, 94, 138**
See also BRWS 5; CA 1-4R; CANR 2, 29, 51, 74, 91; CN 7; DAB; DAM NOV; DLB 139, 194; IDFW 3, 4; INT CANR-29; MTCW 1, 2; RGSF 2; RGWL 2; RHW; TEA

**Jibran, Kahlil**
See Gibran, Kahlil

**Jibran, Khalil**
See Gibran, Kahlil

**Jiles, Paulette** 1943- ..................... **CLC 13, 58**
See also CA 101; CANR 70; CWP

**Jimenez (Mantecon), Juan Ramon**
1881-1958 ......... **HLC 1; PC 7; TCLC 4**
See also CA 131; CANR 74; DAM MULT, POET; DLB 134; EW 9; HW 1; MTCW 1, 2; RGWL 2, 3

**Jimenez, Ramon**
See Jimenez (Mantecon), Juan Ramon

**Jimenez Mantecon, Juan**
See Jimenez (Mantecon), Juan Ramon

**Jin, Ha** ................................................ **CLC 109**
See Jin, Xuefei
See also CA 152; DLB 244

**Jin, Xuefei** 1956-
See Jin, Ha
See also CANR 91

**Joel, Billy** ........................................... **CLC 26**
See Joel, William Martin

**Joel, William Martin** 1949-
See Joel, Billy
See also CA 108

**John, Saint** 107th cent. -100 .......... **CMLC 27**

**John of the Cross, St.** 1542-1591 ........ **LC 18**
See also RGWL 2, 3

**John Paul II, Pope** 1920- ................ **CLC 128**
See also CA 133

**Johnson, B(ryan) S(tanley William)**
1933-1973 ...................................... **CLC 6, 9**
See also CA 9-12R; CANR 9; DLB 14, 40; RGEL 2

**Johnson, Benjamin F., of Boone**
See Riley, James Whitcomb

**Johnson, Charles (Richard)** 1948- .... **BLC 2; CLC 7, 51, 65, 163**
See also AFAW 2; AMWS 6; BW 2, 3; CA 116; CAAS 18; CANR 42, 66, 82; CN 7; DAM MULT; DLB 33; MTCW 2; RGAL 4; SSFS 16

**Johnson, Denis** 1949- . **CLC 52, 160; SSC 56**
See also CA 121; CANR 71, 99; CN 7; DLB 120

**Johnson, Diane** 1934- ................ **CLC 5, 13, 48**
See also BPFB 2; CA 41-44R; CANR 17, 40, 62, 95; CN 7; DLBY 1980; INT CANR-17; MTCW 1

**Johnson, Eyvind (Olof Verner)**
1900-1976 ...................................... **CLC 14**
See also CA 73-76; CANR 34, 101; DLB 259; EW 12

**Johnson, J. R.**
See James, C(yril) L(ionel) R(obert)

**Johnson, James Weldon** 1871-1938 .. **BLC 2; HR 3; PC 24; TCLC 3, 19**
See also AFAW 1, 2; BW 1, 3; CA 125; CANR 82; CDALB 1917-1929; CLR 32; DAM MULT, POET; DLB 51; EXPP; MTCW 1, 2; PFS 1; RGAL 4; SATA 31; TUS

**Johnson, Joyce** 1935- ........................ **CLC 58**
See also BG 3; CA 129; CANR 102

**Johnson, Judith (Emlyn)** 1936- .... **CLC 7, 15**
See Sherwin, Judith Johnson
See also CA 25-28R, 153; CANR 34

**Johnson, Lionel (Pigot)**
1867-1902 .................................... **TCLC 19**
See also DLB 19; RGEL 2

**Johnson, Marguerite Annie**
See Angelou, Maya

**Johnson, Mel**
See Malzberg, Barry N(athaniel)

**Johnson, Pamela Hansford**
1912-1981 .............................. **CLC 1, 7, 27**
See also CA 1-4R; CANR 2, 28; DLB 15; MTCW 1, 2; RGEL 2

**Johnson, Paul (Bede)** 1928- ............ **CLC 147**
See also BEST 89:4; CA 17-20R; CANR 34, 62, 100

**Johnson, Robert** ................................. **CLC 70**

**Johnson, Robert** 1911(?)-1938 ........ **TCLC 69**
See also BW 3; CA 174

**Johnson, Samuel** 1709-1784 ......... **LC 15, 52; WLC**
See also BRW 3; BRWR 1; CDBLB 1660-1789; DA; DAB; DAC; DAM MST; DLB 39, 95, 104, 142, 213; RGEL 2; TEA

**Johnson, Uwe** 1934-1984 .. **CLC 5, 10, 15, 40**
See also CA 1-4R; CANR 1, 39; CDWLB 2; DLB 75; MTCW 1; RGWL 2, 3

**Johnston, George (Benson)** 1913- .... **CLC 51**
See also CA 1-4R; CANR 5, 20; CP 7; DLB 88

**Johnston, Jennifer (Prudence)**
1930- .......................................... **CLC 7, 150**
See also CA 85-88; CANR 92; CN 7; DLB 14

**Joinville, Jean de** 1224(?)-1317 ..... **CMLC 38**

**Jolley, (Monica) Elizabeth** 1923- ...... **CLC 46; SSC 19**
See also CA 127; CAAS 13; CANR 59; CN 7; RGSF 2

**Jones, Arthur Llewellyn** 1863-1947
See Machen, Arthur
See also CA 179; HGG

**Jones, D(ouglas) G(ordon)** 1929- ...... **CLC 10**
See also CA 29-32R; CANR 13, 90; CP 7; DLB 53

**Jones, David (Michael)** 1895-1974 .... **CLC 2, 4, 7, 13, 42**
See also BRW 6; BRWS 7; CA 9-12R; CANR 28; CDBLB 1945-1960; DLB 20, 100; MTCW 1; PAB; RGEL 2

**Jones, David Robert** 1947-
See Bowie, David
See also CA 103; CANR 104

**Jones, Diana Wynne** 1934- ................ **CLC 26**
See also AAYA 12; BYA 6, 7, 9, 11, 13; CA 49-52; CANR 4, 26, 56; CLR 23; DLB 161; FANT; JRDA; MAICYA 1, 2; SAAS 7; SATA 9, 70, 108; SFW 4; SUFW 2; YAW

**Jones, Edward P.** 1950- ........................ **CLC 76**
See also BW 2, 3; CA 142; CANR 79; CSW

**Jones, Gayl** 1949- ...... **BLC 2; CLC 6, 9, 131**
See also AFAW 1, 2; BW 2, 3; CA 77-80; CANR 27, 66; CN 7; CSW; DAM MULT; DLB 33; MTCW 1, 2; RGAL 4

**Jones, James** 1921-1977 ...... **CLC 1, 3, 10, 39**
See also AITN 1, 2; AMWS 11; BPFB 2; CA 1-4R; CANR 6; DLB 2, 143; DLBD 17; DLBY 1998; MTCW 1; RGAL 4

**Jones, John J.**
See Lovecraft, H(oward) P(hillips)

**Jones, LeRoi** ............. **CLC 1, 2, 3, 5, 10, 14**
See Baraka, Amiri
See also MTCW 2

**Jones, Louis B.** 1953- .......................... **CLC 65**
See also CA 141; CANR 73

**Jones, Madison (Percy, Jr.)** 1925- ...... **CLC 4**
See also CA 13-16R; CAAS 11; CANR 7, 54, 83; CN 7; CSW; DLB 152

**Jones, Mervyn** 1922- .................... **CLC 10, 52**
See also CA 45-48; CAAS 5; CANR 1, 91; CN 7; MTCW 1

**Jones, Mick** 1956(?)- ........................... **CLC 30**

**Jones, Nettie (Pearl)** 1941- ................ **CLC 34**
See also BW 2; CA 137; CAAS 20; CANR 88

**Jones, Preston** 1936-1979 .................. **CLC 10**
See also CA 73-76; DLB 7

**Jones, Robert F(rancis)** 1934- ............ **CLC 7**
See also CA 49-52; CANR 2, 61

**Jones, Rod** 1953- ................................ **CLC 50**
See also CA 128

**Jones, Terence Graham Parry**
1942- ............................................ **CLC 21**
See Jones, Terry; Monty Python
See also CA 116; CANR 35, 93; INT 116; SATA 127

**Jones, Terry**
See Jones, Terence Graham Parry
See also SATA 67; SATA-Brief 51

**Jones, Thom (Douglas)** 1945(?)- ...... **CLC 81; SSC 56**
See also CA 157; CANR 88; DLB 244

**Jong, Erica** 1942- ............ **CLC 4, 6, 8, 18, 83**
See also AITN 1; AMWS 5; BEST 90:2; BPFB 2; CA 73-76; CANR 26, 52, 75; CN 7; CP 7; CPW; DAM NOV, POP; DLB 2, 5, 28, 152; FW; INT CANR-26; MTCW 1, 2

**Jonson, Ben(jamin)** 1572(?)-1637 . **DC 4; LC 6, 33; PC 17; WLC**
See also BRW 1; BRWR 1; CDBLB Before 1660; DA; DAB; DAC; DAM DRAM, MST, POET; DFS 4, 10; DLB 62, 121; RGEL 2; TEA; WLIT 3

**Jordan, June (Meyer)**
1936-2002 .. **BLCS; CLC 5, 11, 23, 114; PC 38**
See also AAYA 2; AFAW 1, 2; BW 2, 3; CA 33-36R; CANR 25, 70, 114; CLR 10; CP 7; CWP; DAM MULT, POET; DLB 38; GLL 2; LAIT 5; MAICYA 1, 2; MTCW 1; SATA 4, 136; YAW

**Jordan, Neil (Patrick)** 1950- .............. **CLC 110**
See also CA 130; CANR 54; CN 7; GLL 2; INT 130

**Jordan, Pat(rick M.)** 1941- ................ **CLC 37**
See also CA 33-36R

**Jorgensen, Ivar**
See Ellison, Harlan (Jay)

**Jorgenson, Ivar**
See Silverberg, Robert

**Joseph, George Ghevarughese** ........ **CLC 70**

**Josephson, Mary**
See O'Doherty, Brian

**Josephus, Flavius** c. 37-100 ........... **CMLC 13**
See also AW 2; DLB 176

**Josiah Allen's Wife**
See Holley, Marietta

**Josipovici, Gabriel (David)** 1940- ...... **CLC 6, 43, 153**
See also CA 37-40R; CAAS 8; CANR 47, 84; CN 7; DLB 14

**Joubert, Joseph** 1754-1824 ................ **NCLC 9**

**Jouve, Pierre Jean** 1887-1976 ........... **CLC 47**
See also DLB 258

**Jovine, Francesco** 1902-1950 .......... **TCLC 79**
See also DLB 264

**Joyce, James (Augustine Aloysius)**
1882-1941 .... **DC 16; PC 22; SSC 3, 26, 44; TCLC 3, 8, 16, 35, 52; WLC**
See also AAYA 42; BRW 7; BRWR 1; BYA 11, 13; CA 126; CDBLB 1914-1945; DA; DAB; DAC; DAM MST, NOV, POET; DLB 10, 19, 36, 162, 247; EXPN; EXPS; LAIT 3; MTCW 1, 2; NFS 7; RGSF 2; SSFS 1; TEA; WLIT 4

**Jozsef, Attila** 1905-1937 ................. **TCLC 22**
See also CDWLB 4; DLB 215

**Juana Ines de la Cruz, Sor**
1651(?)-1695 ...... **HLCS 1; LC 5; PC 24**
See also FW; LAW; RGWL 2, 3; WLIT 1

**Juana Inez de La Cruz, Sor**
See Juana Ines de la Cruz, Sor

**Judd, Cyril**
See Kornbluth, C(yril) M.; Pohl, Frederik

**Juenger, Ernst** 1895-1998 ................. **CLC 125**
See Junger, Ernst
See also CA 101; CANR 21, 47, 106; DLB 56

**Julian of Norwich** 1342(?)-1416(?) . **LC 6, 52**
See also DLB 146

**Julius Caesar** 100B.C.-44B.C.
See Caesar, Julius
See also CDWLB 1; DLB 211

**Junger, Ernst**
See Juenger, Ernst
See also CDWLB 2; RGWL 2, 3

**Junger, Sebastian** 1962- ................... **CLC 109**
See also AAYA 28; CA 165

**Juniper, Alex**
See Hospital, Janette Turner

**Junius**
See Luxemburg, Rosa

**Just, Ward (Swift)** 1935- ................. **CLC 4, 27**
See also CA 25-28R; CANR 32, 87; CN 7; INT CANR-32

**Justice, Donald (Rodney)** 1925- .. **CLC 6, 19, 102**
See also AMWS 7; CA 5-8R; CANR 26, 54, 74; CP 7; CSW; DAM POET; DLBY 1983; INT CANR-26; MTCW 2; PFS 14

**Juvenal** c. 60-c. 130 ........................ **CMLC 8**
See also AW 2; CDWLB 1; DLB 211; RGWL 2, 3

**Juvenis**
See Bourne, Randolph S(illiman)

**Kabakov, Sasha** ................................. **CLC 59**

**Kacew, Romain** 1914-1980
See Gary, Romain
See also CA 108

**Kadare, Ismail** 1936- ......................... **CLC 52**
See also CA 161; RGWL 3

**Kadohata, Cynthia** .................... **CLC 59, 122**
See also CA 140

**Kafka, Franz** 1883-1924 ......... **SSC 5, 29, 35; TCLC 2, 6, 13, 29, 47, 53, 112; WLC**
See also AAYA 31; BPFB 2; CA 126; CDWLB 2; DA; DAB; DAC; DAM MST, NOV; DLB 81; EW 9; EXPS; MTCW 1, 2; NFS 7; RGSF 2; RGWL 2, 3; SFW 4; SSFS 3, 7, 12; TWA

**Kahanovitsch, Pinkhes**
See Der Nister

**Kahn, Roger** 1927- ............................. **CLC 30**
See also CA 25-28R; CANR 44, 69; DLB 171; SATA 37

**Kain, Saul**
See Sassoon, Siegfried (Lorraine)

**Kaiser, Georg** 1878-1945 ................... **TCLC 9**
See also CA 190; CDWLB 2; DLB 124; RGWL 2, 3

**Kaledin, Sergei** .................................. **CLC 59**

**Kaletski, Alexander** 1946- ................. **CLC 39**
See also CA 143

**Kalidasa** fl. c. 400-455 ........ **CMLC 9; PC 22**
See also RGWL 2, 3

**Kallman, Chester (Simon)**
1921-1975 ....................................... **CLC 2**
See also CA 45-48; CANR 3

**Kaminsky, Melvin** 1926-
See Brooks, Mel
See also CA 65-68; CANR 16

**Kaminsky, Stuart M(elvin)** 1934- ..... **CLC 59**
See also CA 73-76; CANR 29, 53, 89; CMW 4

**Kandinsky, Wassily** 1866-1944 ....... **TCLC 92**
See also CA 155

**Kane, Francis**
See Robbins, Harold

**Kane, Henry** 1918-
See Queen, Ellery
See also CA 156; CMW 4

**Kane, Paul**
See Simon, Paul (Frederick)

**Kanin, Garson** 1912-1999 .................. **CLC 22**
See also AITN 1; CA 5-8R; CAD; CANR 7, 78; DLB 7; IDFW 3, 4

**Kaniuk, Yoram** 1930- ........................ **CLC 19**
See also CA 134

**Kant, Immanuel** 1724-1804 ..... **NCLC 27, 67**
See also DLB 94

**Kantor, MacKinlay** 1904-1977 ........... **CLC 7**
See also CA 61-64; CANR 60, 63; DLB 9, 102; MTCW 2; RHW; TCWW 2

**Kanze Motokiyo**
See Zeami

**Kaplan, David Michael** 1946- ........... **CLC 50**
See also CA 187

**Kaplan, James** 1951- ......................... **CLC 59**
See also CA 135

**Karadzic, Vuk Stefanovic**
1787-1864 ..................................... **NCLC 115**
See also CDWLB 4; DLB 147

**Karageorge, Michael**
See Anderson, Poul (William)

**Karamzin, Nikolai Mikhailovich**
1766-1826 ..................................... **NCLC 3**
See also DLB 150; RGSF 2

**Karapanou, Margarita** 1946- ........... **CLC 13**
See also CA 101

**Karinthy, Frigyes** 1887-1938 ........... **TCLC 47**
See also CA 170; DLB 215

**Karl, Frederick R(obert)** 1927- ........ **CLC 34**
See also CA 5-8R; CANR 3, 44

**Kastel, Warren**
See Silverberg, Robert

**Kataev, Evgeny Petrovich** 1903-1942
See Petrov, Evgeny

**Kataphusin**
See Ruskin, John

**Katz, Steve** 1935- ............................... **CLC 47**
See also CA 25-28R; CAAS 14, 64; CANR 12; CN 7; DLBY 1983

**Kauffman, Janet** 1945- ...................... **CLC 42**
See also CA 117; CANR 43, 84; DLB 218; DLBY 1986

**Kaufman, Bob (Garnell)** 1925-1986 . **CLC 49**
See also BG 3; BW 1; CA 41-44R; CANR 22; DLB 16, 41

**Kaufman, George S.** 1889-1961 ....... **CLC 38; DC 17**
See also CA 108; DAM DRAM; DFS 1, 10; DLB 7; INT CA-108; MTCW 2; RGAL 4; TUS

**Kaufman, Sue** ................................. **CLC 3, 8**
See Barondess, Sue K(aufman)

**Kavafis, Konstantinos Petrou** 1863-1933
See Cavafy, C(onstantine) P(eter)

**Kavan, Anna** 1901-1968 .......... **CLC 5, 13, 82**
See also BRWS 7; CA 5-8R; CANR 6, 57; DLB 255; MTCW 1; RGEL 2; SFW 4

**Kavanagh, Dan**
See Barnes, Julian (Patrick)

**Kavanagh, Julie** 1952- ..................... **CLC 119**
See also CA 163

**Kavanagh, Patrick (Joseph)**
1904-1967 ...................... **CLC 22; PC 33**
See also BRWS 7; CA 123; DLB 15, 20; MTCW 1; RGEL 2

**Kawabata, Yasunari** 1899-1972 ..... **CLC 2, 5, 9, 18, 107; SSC 17**
See Kawabata Yasunari
See also CA 93-96; CANR 88; DAM MULT; MJW; MTCW 2; RGSF 2; RGWL 2, 3

**Kawabata Yasunari**
See Kawabata, Yasunari
See also DLB 180

**Kaye, M(ary) M(argaret)** 1909- ........ **CLC 28**
See also CA 89-92; CANR 24, 60, 102; MTCW 1, 2; RHW; SATA 62

**Kaye, Mollie**
See Kaye, M(ary) M(argaret)

**Kaye-Smith, Sheila** 1887-1956 ........ **TCLC 20**
See also CA 203; DLB 36

**Kaymor, Patrice Maguilene**
See Senghor, Leopold Sedar

**Kazakov, Yuri Pavlovich** 1927-1982 . **SSC 43**
See also CA 5-8R; CANR 36; MTCW 1; RGSF 2

**Kazan, Elia** 1909- ..................... **CLC 6, 16, 63**
See also CA 21-24R; CANR 32, 78

**Kazantzakis, Nikos** 1883(?)-1957 .... **TCLC 2, 5, 33**
See also BPFB 2; CA 132; EW 9; MTCW 1, 2; RGWL 2, 3

**Kazin, Alfred** 1915-1998 ..... **CLC 34, 38, 119**
See also AMWS 8; CA 1-4R; CAAS 7; CANR 1, 45, 79; DLB 67

**Keane, Mary Nesta (Skrine)** 1904-1996
See Keane, Molly
See also CA 114; CN 7; RHW

**Keane, Molly** ..................................... **CLC 31**
See Keane, Mary Nesta (Skrine)
See also INT 114

**Keates, Jonathan** 1946(?)- ................ **CLC 34**
See also CA 163

**Keaton, Buster** 1895-1966 ................ **CLC 20**
See also CA 194

**Keats, John** 1795-1821 ...... **NCLC 8, 73, 121; PC 1; WLC**
See also BRW 4; BRWR 1; CDBLB 1789-1832; DA; DAB; DAC; DAM MST, POET; DLB 96, 110; EXPP; PAB; PFS 1, 2, 3, 9, 16; RGEL 2; TEA; WLIT 3; WP

**Keble, John** 1792-1866 ................... **NCLC 87**
See also DLB 32, 55; RGEL 2

**Keene, Donald** 1922- ........................ **CLC 34**
See also CA 1-4R; CANR 5

**Keillor, Garrison** ...................... **CLC 40, 115**
See Keillor, Gary (Edward)
See also AAYA 2; BEST 89:3; BPFB 2; DLBY 1987; SATA 58; TUS

**Keillor, Gary (Edward)** 1942-
See Keillor, Garrison
See also CA 117; CANR 36, 59; CPW; DAM POP; MTCW 1, 2

**Keith, Carlos**
See Lewton, Val

**Keith, Michael**
See Hubbard, L(afayette) Ron(ald)

**Keller, Gottfried** 1819-1890 .... **NCLC 2; SSC 26**
See also CDWLB 2; DLB 129; EW; RGSF 2; RGWL 2, 3

**Keller, Nora Okja** 1965- .................. **CLC 109**
See also CA 187

**Kellerman, Jonathan** 1949- ............... **CLC 44**
See also AAYA 35; BEST 90:1; CA 106; CANR 29, 51; CMW 4; CPW; DAM POP; INT CANR-29

**Kelley, William Melvin** 1937- ............ **CLC 22**
See also BW 1; CA 77-80; CANR 27, 83; CN 7; DLB 33

**Kellogg, Marjorie** 1922- ..................... **CLC 2**
See also CA 81-84

**Kellow, Kathleen**
See Hibbert, Eleanor Alice Burford

**Kelly, M(ilton) T(errence)** 1947- ...... **CLC 55**
See also CA 97-100; CAAS 22; CANR 19, 43, 84; CN 7

**Kelly, Robert** 1935- ............................ **SSC 50**
See also CA 17-20R; CAAS 19; CANR 47; CP 7; DLB 5, 130, 165

**Kelman, James** 1946- .................. **CLC 58, 86**
See also BRWS 5; CA 148; CANR 85; CN 7; DLB 194; RGSF 2; WLIT 4

**Kemal, Yashar** 1923- .................. **CLC 14, 29**
See also CA 89-92; CANR 44; CWW 2

**Kemble, Fanny** 1809-1893 .............. **NCLC 18**
See also DLB 32

**Kemelman, Harry** 1908-1996 ............ **CLC 2**
See also AITN 1; BPFB 2; CA 9-12R; CANR 6, 71; CMW 4; DLB 28

**Kempe, Margery** 1373(?)-1440(?) ... **LC 6, 56**
See also DLB 146; RGEL 2

**Kempis, Thomas a** 1380-1471 ............. **LC 11**

**Kendall, Henry** 1839-1882 ............ **NCLC 12**
See also DLB 230

**Keneally, Thomas (Michael)** 1935- ... **CLC 5, 8, 10, 14, 19, 27, 43, 117**
See also BRWS 4; CA 85-88; CANR 10, 50, 74; CN 7; CPW; DAM NOV; MTCW 1, 2; RGEL 2; RHW

**Kennedy, Adrienne (Lita)** 1931- ........ **BLC 2; CLC 66; DC 5**
See also AFAW 2; BW 2, 3; CA 103; CAAS 20; CABS 3; CANR 26, 53, 82; CD 5; DAM MULT; DFS 9; DLB 38; FW

**Kennedy, John Pendleton** 1795-1870 ..................... **NCLC 2**
See also DLB 3, 248, 254; RGAL 4

**Kennedy, Joseph Charles** 1929-
See Kennedy, X. J.
See also CA 1-4R; CAAE 201; CANR 4, 30, 40; CP 7; CWRI 5; MAICYA 2; MAICYAS 1; SATA 14, 86; SATA-Essay 130

**Kennedy, William** 1928- ... **CLC 6, 28, 34, 53**
See also AAYA 1; AMWS 7; BPFB 2; CA 85-88; CANR 14, 31, 76; CN 7; DAM NOV; DLB 143; DLBY 1985; INT CANR-31; MTCW 1, 2; SATA 57

**Kennedy, X. J.** ............................... **CLC 8, 42**
See Kennedy, Joseph Charles
See also CAAS 9; CLR 27; DLB 5; SAAS 22

**Kenny, Maurice (Francis)** 1929- ..... **CLC 87; NNAL**
See also CA 144; CAAS 22; DAM MULT; DLB 175

**Kent, Kelvin**
See Kuttner, Henry

**Kenton, Maxwell**
See Southern, Terry

**Kenyon, Robert O.**
See Kuttner, Henry

**Kepler, Johannes** 1571-1630 ................. **LC 45**

**Ker, Jill**
See Conway, Jill K(er)

**Kerkow, H. C.**
See Lewton, Val

**Kerouac, Jack** 1922-1969 ...... **CLC 1, 2, 3, 5, 14, 29, 61; TCLC 117; WLC**
See Kerouac, Jean-Louis Lebris de
See also AAYA 25; AMWC 1; AMWS 3; BG 3; BPFB 2; CDALB 1941-1968; CPW; DLB 2, 16, 237; DLBD 3; DLBY 1995; GLL 1; MTCW 2; NFS 8; RGAL 4; TUS; WP

**Kerouac, Jean-Louis Lebris de** 1922-1969
See Kerouac, Jack
See also AITN 1; CA 5-8R; CANR 26, 54, 95; DA; DAB; DAC; DAM MST, NOV, POET, POP; MTCW 1, 2

**Kerr, Jean** 1923- ................................. **CLC 22**
See also CA 5-8R; CANR 7; INT CANR-7

**Kerr, M. E.** ............................... **CLC 12, 35**
See Meaker, Marijane (Agnes)
See also AAYA 2, 23; BYA 1, 7, 8; CLR 29; SAAS 1; WYA

**Kerr, Robert** ....................................... **CLC 55**

**Kerrigan, (Thomas) Anthony** 1918- .. **CLC 4, 6**
See also CA 49-52; CAAS 11; CANR 4

**Kerry, Lois**
See Duncan, Lois

**Kesey, Ken (Elton)** 1935-2001 ... **CLC 1, 3, 6, 11, 46, 64; WLC**
See also AAYA 25; BG 3; BPFB 2; CA 1-4R; CANR 22, 38, 66; CDALB 1968-1988; CN 7; CPW; DA; DAB; DAC; DAM MST, NOV, POP; DLB 2, 16, 206; EXPN; LAIT 4; MTCW 1, 2; NFS 2; RGAL 4; SATA 66; SATA-Obit 131; TUS; YAW

**Kesselring, Joseph (Otto)** 1902-1967 ..................... **CLC 45**
See also CA 150; DAM DRAM, MST

**Kessler, Jascha (Frederick)** 1929- ...... **CLC 4**
See also CA 17-20R; CANR 8, 48, 111

**Kettelkamp, Larry (Dale)** 1933- ....... **CLC 12**
See also CA 29-32R; CANR 16; SAAS 3; SATA 2

**Key, Ellen (Karolina Sofia)** 1849-1926 ..................... **TCLC 65**
See also DLB 259

**Keyber, Conny**
See Fielding, Henry

**Keyes, Daniel** 1927- ........................ **CLC 80**
See also AAYA 23; BYA 11; CA 17-20R, 181; CAAE 181; CANR 10, 26, 54, 74; DA; DAC; DAM MST, NOV; EXPN; LAIT 4; MTCW 2; NFS 2; SATA 37; SFW 4

**Keynes, John Maynard** 1883-1946 ..................... **TCLC 64**
See also CA 162, 163; DLBD 10; MTCW 2

**Khanshendel, Chiron**
See Rose, Wendy

**Khayyam, Omar** 1048-1131 ... **CMLC 11; PC 8**
See Omar Khayyam
See also DAM POET

**Kherdian, David** 1931- ................... **CLC 6, 9**
See also AAYA 42; CA 21-24R; CAAE 192; CAAS 2; CANR 39, 78; CLR 24; JRDA; LAIT 3; MAICYA 1, 2; SATA 16, 74; SATA-Essay 125

**Khlebnikov, Velimir** ....................... **TCLC 20**
See Khlebnikov, Viktor Vladimirovich
See also EW 10; RGWL 2, 3

**Khlebnikov, Viktor Vladimirovich** 1885-1922
See Khlebnikov, Velimir

**Khodasevich, Vladislav (Felitsianovich)** 1886-1939 ..................... **TCLC 15**

**Kielland, Alexander Lange** 1849-1906 ..................... **TCLC 5**

**Kiely, Benedict** 1919- ... **CLC 23, 43; SSC 58**
See also CA 1-4R; CANR 2, 84; CN 7; DLB 15

**Kienzle, William X(avier)** 1928-2001 ..................... **CLC 25**
See also CA 93-96; CAAS 1; CANR 9, 31, 59, 111; CMW 4; DAM POP; INT CANR-31; MSW; MTCW 1, 2

**Kierkegaard, Soren** 1813-1855 ..... **NCLC 34, 78**
See also EW 6; RGWL 3; TWA

**Kieslowski, Krzysztof** 1941-1996 .... **CLC 120**
See also CA 147

**Killens, John Oliver** 1916-1987 ........ **CLC 10**
See also BW 2; CA 77-80; CAAS 2; CANR 26; DLB 33

**Killigrew, Anne** 1660-1685 ............... **LC 4, 73**
See also DLB 131

**Killigrew, Thomas** 1612-1683 ............. **LC 57**
See also DLB 58; RGEL 2

**Kim**
See Simenon, Georges (Jacques Christian)

**Kincaid, Jamaica** 1949- ...... **BLC 2; CLC 43, 68, 137**
See also AAYA 13; AFAW 2; AMWS 7; BRWS 7; BW 2, 3; CA 125; CANR 47, 59, 95; CDALBS; CDWLB 3; CLR 63; CN 7; DAM MULT, NOV; DLB 157, 227; DNFS 1; EXPS; FW; MTCW 2; NCFS 1; NFS 3; SSFS 5, 7; TUS; YAW

**King, Francis (Henry)** 1923- ....... **CLC 8, 53, 145**
See also CA 1-4R; CANR 1, 33, 86; CN 7; DAM NOV; DLB 15, 139; MTCW 1

**King, Kennedy**
See Brown, George Douglas

**King, Martin Luther, Jr.** 1929-1968 . **BLC 2; CLC 83; WLCS**
See also BW 2, 3; CA 25-28; CANR 27, 44; CAP 2; DA; DAB; DAC; DAM MST, MULT; LAIT 5; MTCW 1, 2; SATA 14

**King, Stephen (Edwin)** 1947- .... **CLC 12, 26, 37, 61, 113; SSC 17, 55**
See also AAYA 1, 17; AMWS 5; BEST 90:1; BPFB 2; CA 61-64; CANR 1, 30, 52, 76; CPW; DAM NOV, POP; DLB 143; DLBY 1980; HGG; JRDA; LAIT 5; MTCW 1, 2; RGAL 4; SATA 9, 55; SUFW 1, 2; WYAS 1; YAW

**King, Steve**
See King, Stephen (Edwin)

**King, Thomas** 1943- ............. **CLC 89; NNAL**
See also CA 144; CANR 95; CCA 1; CN 7; DAC; DAM MULT; DLB 175; SATA 96

**Kingman, Lee** ................................. **CLC 17**
See Natti, (Mary) Lee
See also CWRI 5; SAAS 3; SATA 1, 67

**Kingsley, Charles** 1819-1875 ......... **NCLC 35**
See also CLR 77; DLB 21, 32, 163, 178, 190; FANT; MAICYA 2; MAICYAS 1; RGEL 2; WCH; YABC 2

**Kingsley, Henry** 1830-1876 .......... **NCLC 107**
See also DLB 21, 230; RGEL 2

**Kingsley, Sidney** 1906-1995 ............. **CLC 44**
See also CA 85-88; CAD; DFS 14; DLB 7; RGAL 4

**Kingsolver, Barbara** 1955- . **CLC 55, 81, 130**
See also AAYA 15; AMWS 7; CA 134; CANR 60, 96; CDALBS; CPW; CSW; DAM POP; DLB 206; INT CA-134; LAIT 5; MTCW 2; NFS 5, 10, 12; RGAL 4

**Kingston, Maxine (Ting Ting) Hong** 1940- ........... **AAL; CLC 12, 19, 58, 121; WLCS**
See also AAYA 8; AMWS 5; BPFB 2; CA 69-72; CANR 13, 38, 74, 87; CDALBS; CN 7; DAM MULT, NOV; DLB 173, 212; DLBY 1980; FW; INT CANR-13; LAIT 5; MAWW; MTCW 1, 2; NFS 6; RGAL 4; SATA 53; SSFS 3

**Kinnell, Galway** 1927- ..... **CLC 1, 2, 3, 5, 13, 29, 129; PC 26**
See also AMWS 3; CA 9-12R; CANR 10, 34, 66; CP 7; DLB 5; DLBY 1987; INT CANR-34; MTCW 1, 2; PAB; PFS 9; RGAL 4; WP

**Kinsella, Thomas** 1928- ........ **CLC 4, 19, 138**
See also BRWS 5; CA 17-20R; CANR 15; CP 7; DLB 27; MTCW 1, 2; RGEL 2; TEA

**Kinsella, W(illiam) P(atrick)** 1935- . **CLC 27, 43, 166**
See also AAYA 7; BPFB 2; CA 97-100; CAAS 7; CANR 21, 35, 66, 75; CN 7; CPW; DAC; DAM NOV, POP; FANT; INT CANR-21; LAIT 5; MTCW 1, 2; NFS 15; RGSF 2

**Kinsey, Alfred C(harles)** 1894-1956 .................. **TCLC 91**
See also CA 170; MTCW 2

**Kipling, (Joseph) Rudyard** 1865-1936 . **PC 3; SSC 5, 54; TCLC 8, 17; WLC**
See also AAYA 32; BRW 6; BYA 4; CA 120; CANR 33; CDBLB 1890-1914; CLR 39, 65; CWRI 5; DA; DAB; DAC; DAM MST, POET; DLB 19, 34, 141, 156; EXPS; FANT; LAIT 3; MAICYA 1, 2; MTCW 1, 2; RGEL 2; RGSF 2; SATA 100; SFW 4; SSFS 8; SUFW 1; TEA; WCH; WLIT 4; YABC 2

**Kirk, Russell (Amos)** 1918-1994 .. **TCLC 119**
See also AITN 1; CA 1-4R; CAAS 9; CANR 1, 20, 60; HGG; INT CANR-20; MTCW 1, 2

**Kirkland, Caroline M.** 1801-1864 . **NCLC 85**
See also DLB 3, 73, 74, 250, 254; DLBD 13

**Kirkup, James** 1918- .......................... **CLC 1**
See also CA 1-4R; CAAS 4; CANR 2; CP 7; DLB 27; SATA 12

**Kirkwood, James** 1930(?)-1989 .......... **CLC 9**
See also AITN 2; CA 1-4R; CANR 6, 40; GLL 2

**Kirshner, Sidney**
See Kingsley, Sidney

**Kis, Danilo** 1935-1989 ......................... **CLC 57**
See also CA 118; CANR 61; CDWLB 4; DLB 181; MTCW 1; RGSF 2; RGWL 2, 3

**Kissinger, Henry A(lfred)** 1923- ..... **CLC 137**
See also CA 1-4R; CANR 2, 33, 66, 109; MTCW 1

**Kivi, Aleksis** 1834-1872 ................... **NCLC 30**

**Kizer, Carolyn (Ashley)** 1925- ... **CLC 15, 39, 80**
See also CA 65-68; CAAS 5; CANR 24, 70; CP 7; CWP; DAM POET; DLB 5, 169; MTCW 2

**Klabund** 1890-1928 ......................... **TCLC 44**
See also CA 162; DLB 66

**Klappert, Peter** 1942- ........................ **CLC 57**
See also CA 33-36R; CSW; DLB 5

**Klein, A(braham) M(oses)** 1909-1972 ........................................ **CLC 19**
See also CA 101; DAB; DAC; DAM MST; DLB 68; RGEL 2

**Klein, Joe**
See Klein, Joseph

**Klein, Joseph** 1946- .......................... **CLC 154**
See also CA 85-88; CANR 55

**Klein, Norma** 1938-1989 ................... **CLC 30**
See also AAYA 2, 35; BPFB 2; BYA 6, 7, 8; CA 41-44R; CANR 15, 37; CLR 2, 19; INT CANR-15; JRDA; MAICYA 1, 2; SAAS 1; SATA 7, 57; WYA; YAW

**Klein, T(heodore) E(ibon) D(onald)** 1947- ........................................... **CLC 34**
See also CA 119; CANR 44, 75; HGG

**Kleist, Heinrich von** 1777-1811 ...... **NCLC 2, 37; SSC 22**
See also CDWLB 2; DAM DRAM; DLB 90; EW 5; RGSF 2; RGWL 2, 3

**Klima, Ivan** 1931- .............................. **CLC 56**
See also CA 25-28R; CANR 17, 50, 91; CDWLB 4; CWW 2; DAM NOV; DLB 232; RGWL 3

**Klimentev, Andrei Platonovich**
See Klimentov, Andrei Platonovich

**Klimentov, Andrei Platonovich** 1899-1951 ................. **SSC 42; TCLC 14**
See Platonov, Andrei Platonovich

**Klinger, Friedrich Maximilian von** 1752-1831 ..................... **NCLC 1**
See also DLB 94

**Klingsor the Magician**
See Hartmann, Sadakichi

**Klopstock, Friedrich Gottlieb** 1724-1803 ........................ **NCLC 11**
See also DLB 97; EW 4; RGWL 2, 3

**Knapp, Caroline** 1959-2002 .............. **CLC 99**
See also CA 154

**Knebel, Fletcher** 1911-1993 ................ **CLC 14**
See also AITN 1; CA 1-4R; CAAS 3; CANR 1, 36; SATA 36; SATA-Obit 75

**Knickerbocker, Diedrich**
See Irving, Washington

**Knight, Etheridge** 1931-1991 ... **BLC 2; CLC 40; PC 14**
See also BW 1, 3; CA 21-24R; CANR 23, 82; DAM POET; DLB 41; MTCW 2; RGAL 4

**Knight, Sarah Kemble** 1666-1727 ......... **LC 7**
See also DLB 24, 200

**Knister, Raymond** 1899-1932 ......... **TCLC 56**
See also CA 186; DLB 68; RGEL 2

**Knowles, John** 1926-2001 ... **CLC 1, 4, 10, 26**
See also AAYA 10; AMWS 12; BPFB 2; BYA 3; CA 17-20R; CANR 40, 74, 76; CDALB 1968-1988; CN 7; DA; DAC; DAM MST, NOV; DLB 6; EXPN; MTCW 1, 2; NFS 2; RGAL 4; SATA 8, 89; SATA-Obit 134; YAW

**Knox, Calvin M.**
See Silverberg, Robert

**Knox, John** c. 1505-1572 ..................... **LC 37**
See also DLB 132

**Knye, Cassandra**
See Disch, Thomas M(ichael)

**Koch, C(hristopher) J(ohn)** 1932- .... **CLC 42**
See also CA 127; CANR 84; CN 7

**Koch, Christopher**
See Koch, C(hristopher) J(ohn)

**Koch, Kenneth** 1925-2002 ........ **CLC 5, 8, 44**
See also CA 1-4R; CAD; CANR 6, 36, 57, 97; CD 5; CP 7; DAM POET; DLB 5; INT CANR-36; MTCW 2; SATA 65; WP

**Kochanowski, Jan** 1530-1584 .............. **LC 10**
See also RGWL 2, 3

**Kock, Charles Paul de** 1794-1871 . **NCLC 16**

**Koda Rohan**
See Koda Shigeyuki

**Koda Rohan**
See Koda Shigeyuki
See also DLB 180

**Koda Shigeyuki** 1867-1947 ............. **TCLC 22**
See Koda Rohan
See also CA 183

**Koestler, Arthur** 1905-1983 ... **CLC 1, 3, 6, 8, 15, 33**
See also BRWS 1; CA 1-4R; CANR 1, 33; CDBLB 1945-1960; DLBY 1983; MTCW 1, 2; RGEL 2

**Kogawa, Joy Nozomi** 1935- ....... **CLC 78, 129**
See also AAYA 47; CA 101; CANR 19, 62; CN 7; CWP; DAC; DAM MST, MULT; FW; MTCW 2; NFS 3; SATA 99

**Kohout, Pavel** 1928- .......................... **CLC 13**
See also CA 45-48; CANR 3

**Koizumi, Yakumo**
See Hearn, (Patricio) Lafcadio (Tessima Carlos)

**Kolmar, Gertrud** 1894-1943 ........... **TCLC 40**
See also CA 167

**Komunyakaa, Yusef** 1947- .. **BLCS; CLC 86, 94**
See also AFAW 2; CA 147; CANR 83; CP 7; CSW; DLB 120; PFS 5; RGAL 4

**Konrad, George**
See Konrad, Gyorgy
See also CWW 2

**Konrad, Gyorgy** 1933- ............ **CLC 4, 10, 73**
See Konrad, George
See also CA 85-88; CANR 97; CDWLB 4; CWW 2; DLB 232

**Konwicki, Tadeusz** 1926- ....... **CLC 8, 28, 54, 117**
See also CA 101; CAAS 9; CANR 39, 59; CWW 2; DLB 232; IDFW 3; MTCW 1

**Koontz, Dean R(ay)** 1945- ................. **CLC 78**
See also AAYA 9, 31; BEST 89:3, 90:2; CA 108; CANR 19, 36, 52, 95; CMW 4; CPW; DAM NOV, POP; HGG; MTCW 1; SATA 92; SFW 4; SUFW 2; YAW

**Kopernik, Mikolaj**
See Copernicus, Nicolaus

**Kopit, Arthur (Lee)** 1937- ....... **CLC 1, 18, 33**
See also AITN 1; CA 81-84; CABS 3; CD 5; DAM DRAM; DFS 7, 14; DLB 7; MTCW 1; RGAL 4

**Kopitar, Jernej (Bartholomaus)** 1780-1844 ................. **NCLC 117**

**Kops, Bernard** 1926- ........................... **CLC 4**
See also CA 5-8R; CANR 84; CBD; CN 7; CP 7; DLB 13

**Kornbluth, C(yril) M.** 1923-1958 .... **TCLC 8**
See also CA 160; DLB 8; SFW 4

**Korolenko, V. G.**
See Korolenko, Vladimir Galaktionovich

**Korolenko, Vladimir**
See Korolenko, Vladimir Galaktionovich

**Korolenko, Vladimir G.**
See Korolenko, Vladimir Galaktionovich

**Korolenko, Vladimir Galaktionovich** 1853-1921 ............................ **TCLC 22**

**Korzybski, Alfred (Habdank Skarbek)** 1879-1950 .............................. **TCLC 61**
See also CA 160

**Kosinski, Jerzy (Nikodem)** 1933-1991 .... **CLC 1, 2, 3, 6, 10, 15, 53, 70**
See also AMWS 7; BPFB 2; CA 17-20R; CANR 9, 46; DAM NOV; DLB 2; DLBY 1982; HGG; MTCW 1, 2; NFS 12; RGAL 4; TUS

**Kostelanetz, Richard (Cory)** 1940- .. **CLC 28**
See also CA 13-16R; CAAS 8; CANR 38, 77; CN 7; CP 7

**Kostrowitzki, Wilhelm Apollinaris de** 1880-1918
See Apollinaire, Guillaume

**Kotlowitz, Robert** 1924- ...................... **CLC 4**
See also CA 33-36R; CANR 36

**Kotzebue, August (Friedrich Ferdinand) von** 1761-1819 .......................... **NCLC 25**
See also DLB 94

**Kotzwinkle, William** 1938- ...... **CLC 5, 14, 35**
See also BPFB 2; CA 45-48; CANR 3, 44, 84; CLR 6; DLB 173; FANT; MAICYA 1, 2; SATA 24, 70; SFW 4; SUFW 2; YAW

**Kowna, Stancy**
See Szymborska, Wislawa

**Kozol, Jonathan** 1936- ........................ **CLC 17**
See also AAYA 46; CA 61-64; CANR 16, 45, 96

**Kozoll, Michael** 1940(?)- .................... **CLC 35**

**Kramer, Kathryn** 19(?)- ..................... **CLC 34**

**Kramer, Larry** 1935- ............. **CLC 42; DC 8**
See also CA 126; CANR 60; DAM POP; DLB 249; GLL 1

**Krasicki, Ignacy** 1735-1801 ............. **NCLC 8**

**Krasinski, Zygmunt** 1812-1859 ....... **NCLC 4**
See also RGWL 2, 3

**Kraus, Karl** 1874-1936 ..................... **TCLC 5**
See also DLB 118

**Kreve (Mickevicius), Vincas**
1882-1954 .................. **TCLC 27**
See also CA 170; DLB 220

**Kristeva, Julia** 1941- .................. **CLC 77, 140**
See also CA 154; CANR 99; DLB 242; FW

**Kristofferson, Kris** 1936- .................. **CLC 26**
See also CA 104

**Krizanc, John** 1956- .................. **CLC 57**
See also CA 187

**Krleza, Miroslav** 1893-1981 ........ **CLC 8, 114**
See also CA 97-100; CANR 50; CDWLB 4; DLB 147; EW 11; RGWL 2, 3

**Kroetsch, Robert** 1927- .. **CLC 5, 23, 57, 132**
See also CA 17-20R; CANR 8, 38; CCA 1; CN 7; CP 7; DAC; DAM POET; DLB 53; MTCW 1

**Kroetz, Franz**
See Kroetz, Franz Xaver

**Kroetz, Franz Xaver** 1946- .................. **CLC 41**
See also CA 130

**Kroker, Arthur (W.)** 1945- .................. **CLC 77**
See also CA 161

**Kropotkin, Peter (Aleksieevich)**
1842-1921 .................. **TCLC 36**

**Krotkov, Yuri** 1917-1981 .................. **CLC 19**
See also CA 102

**Krumb**
See Crumb, R(obert)

**Krumgold, Joseph (Quincy)**
1908-1980 .................. **CLC 12**
See also BYA 1, 2; CA 9-12R; CANR 7; MAICYA 1, 2; SATA 1, 48; SATA-Obit 23; YAW

**Krumwitz**
See Crumb, R(obert)

**Krutch, Joseph Wood** 1893-1970 ..... **CLC 24**
See also ANW; CA 1-4R; CANR 4; DLB 63, 206, 275

**Krutzch, Gus**
See Eliot, T(homas) S(tearns)

**Krylov, Ivan Andreevich**
1768(?)-1844 .................. **NCLC 1**
See also DLB 150

**Kubin, Alfred (Leopold Isidor)**
1877-1959 .................. **TCLC 23**
See also CA 149; CANR 104; DLB 81

**Kubrick, Stanley** 1928-1999 .................. **CLC 16; TCLC 112**
See also AAYA 30; CA 81-84; CANR 33; DLB 26

**Kueng, Hans** 1928-
See Kung, Hans
See also CA 53-56; CANR 66; MTCW 1, 2

**Kumin, Maxine (Winokur)** 1925- ..... **CLC 5, 13, 28, 164; PC 15**
See also AITN 2; AMWS 4; ANW; CA 1-4R; CAAS 8; CANR 1, 21, 69; CP 7; CWP; DAM POET; DLB 5; EXPP; MTCW 1, 2; PAB; SATA 12

**Kundera, Milan** 1929- .. **CLC 4, 9, 19, 32, 68, 115, 135; SSC 24**
See also AAYA 2; BPFB 2; CA 85-88; CANR 19, 52, 74; CDWLB 4; CWW 2; DAM NOV; DLB 232; EW 13; MTCW 1, 2; RGSF 2; RGWL 3; SSFS 10

**Kunene, Mazisi (Raymond)** 1930- ... **CLC 85**
See also BW 1, 3; CA 125; CANR 81; CP 7; DLB 117

**Kung, Hans** .................. **CLC 130**
See Kueng, Hans

**Kunikida Doppo** 1869(?)-1908
See Doppo, Kunikida
See also DLB 180

**Kunitz, Stanley (Jasspon)** 1905- .. **CLC 6, 11, 14, 148; PC 19**
See also AMWS 3; CA 41-44R; CANR 26, 57, 98; CP 7; DLB 48; INT CANR-26; MTCW 1, 2; PFS 11; RGAL 4

**Kunze, Reiner** 1933- .................. **CLC 10**
See also CA 93-96; CWW 2; DLB 75

**Kuprin, Aleksandr Ivanovich**
1870-1938 .................. **TCLC 5**
See also CA 182

**Kureishi, Hanif** 1954(?)- .................. **CLC 64, 135**
See also CA 139; CANR 113; CBD; CD 5; CN 7; DLB 194, 245; GLL 2; IDFW 4; WLIT 4

**Kurosawa, Akira** 1910-1998 ..... **CLC 16, 119**
See also AAYA 11; CA 101; CANR 46; DAM MULT

**Kushner, Tony** 1957(?)- ........ **CLC 81; DC 10**
See also AMWS 9; CA 144; CAD; CANR 74; CD 5; DAM DRAM; DFS 5; DLB 228; GLL 1; LAIT 5; MTCW 2; RGAL 4

**Kuttner, Henry** 1915-1958 .................. **TCLC 10**
See also CA 157; DLB 8; FANT; SCFW 2; SFW 4

**Kutty, Madhavi**
See Das, Kamala

**Kuzma, Greg** 1944- .................. **CLC 7**
See also CA 33-36R; CANR 70

**Kuzmin, Mikhail** 1872(?)-1936 ...... **TCLC 40**
See also CA 170

**Kyd, Thomas** 1558-1594 .................. **DC 3; LC 22**
See also BRW 1; DAM DRAM; DLB 62; IDTP; RGEL 2; TEA; WLIT 3

**Kyprianos, Iossif**
See Samarakis, Antonis

**L. S.**
See Stephen, Sir Leslie

**Labrunie, Gerard**
See Nerval, Gerard de

**La Bruyere, Jean de** 1645-1696 .................. **LC 17**
See also DLB 268; EW 3; GFL Beginnings to 1789

**Lacan, Jacques (Marie Emile)**
1901-1981 .................. **CLC 75**
See also CA 121; TWA

**Laclos, Pierre Ambroise Francois**
1741-1803 .................. **NCLC 4, 87**
See also EW 4; GFL Beginnings to 1789; RGWL 2, 3

**La Colere, Francois**
See Aragon, Louis

**Lacolere, Francois**
See Aragon, Louis

**La Deshabilleuse**
See Simenon, Georges (Jacques Christian)

**Lady Gregory**
See Gregory, Lady Isabella Augusta (Persse)

**Lady of Quality, A**
See Bagnold, Enid

**La Fayette, Marie-(Madelaine Pioche de la Vergne)** 1634-1693 .................. **LC 2**
See Lafayette, Marie-Madeleine
See also GFL Beginnings to 1789; RGWL 2, 3

**Lafayette, Marie-Madeleine**
See La Fayette, Marie-(Madelaine Pioche de la Vergne)
See also DLB 268

**Lafayette, Rene**
See Hubbard, L(afayette) Ron(ald)

**La Fontaine, Jean de** 1621-1695 .................. **LC 50**
See also DLB 268; EW 3; GFL Beginnings to 1789; MAICYA 1, 2; RGWL 2, 3; SATA 18

**Laforgue, Jules** 1860-1887 . **NCLC 5, 53; PC 14; SSC 20**
See also DLB 217; EW 7; GFL 1789 to the Present; RGWL 2, 3

**Layamon**
See Layamon
See also DLB 146

**Lagerkvist, Paer (Fabian)**
1891-1974 .................. **CLC 7, 10, 13, 54**
See Lagerkvist, Par
See also CA 85-88; DAM DRAM, NOV; MTCW 1, 2; TWA

**Lagerkvist, Par** .................. **SSC 12**
See Lagerkvist, Paer (Fabian)
See also DLB 259; EW 10; MTCW 2; RGSF 2; RGWL 2, 3

**Lagerloef, Selma (Ottiliana Lovisa)**
1858-1940 .................. **TCLC 4, 36**
See Lagerlof, Selma (Ottiliana Lovisa)
See also MTCW 2; SATA 15

**Lagerlof, Selma (Ottiliana Lovisa)**
See Lagerloef, Selma (Ottiliana Lovisa)
See also CLR 7; SATA 15

**La Guma, (Justin) Alex(ander)**
1925-1985 .................. **BLCS; CLC 19**
See also AFW; BW 1, 3; CA 49-52; CANR 25, 81; CDWLB 3; DAM NOV; DLB 117, 225; MTCW 1, 2; WLIT 2

**Laidlaw, A. K.**
See Grieve, C(hristopher) M(urray)

**Lainez, Manuel Mujica**
See Mujica Lainez, Manuel
See also HW 1

**Laing, R(onald) D(avid)** 1927-1989 . **CLC 95**
See also CA 107; CANR 34; MTCW 1

**Lamartine, Alphonse (Marie Louis Prat) de**
1790-1869 .................. **NCLC 11; PC 16**
See also DAM POET; DLB 217; GFL 1789 to the Present; RGWL 2, 3

**Lamb, Charles** 1775-1834 ..... **NCLC 10, 113; WLC**
See also BRW 4; CDBLB 1789-1832; DA; DAB; DAC; DAM MST; DLB 93, 107, 163; RGEL 2; SATA 17; TEA

**Lamb, Lady Caroline** 1785-1828 ... **NCLC 38**
See also DLB 116

**Lamming, George (William)** 1927- ... **BLC 2; CLC 2, 4, 66, 144**
See also BW 2, 3; CA 85-88; CANR 26, 76; CDWLB 3; CN 7; DAM MULT; DLB 125; MTCW 1, 2; NFS 15; RGEL 2

**L'Amour, Louis (Dearborn)**
1908-1988 .................. **CLC 25, 55**
See Burns, Tex; Mayo, Jim
See also AAYA 16; AITN 2; BEST 89:2; BPFB 2; CA 1-4R; CANR 3, 25, 40; CPW; DAM NOV, POP; DLB 206; DLBY 1980; MTCW 1, 2; RGAL 4

**Lampedusa, Giuseppe (Tomasi) di**
.................. **TCLC 13**
See Tomasi di Lampedusa, Giuseppe
See also CA 164; EW 11; MTCW 2; RGWL 2, 3

**Lampman, Archibald** 1861-1899 ... **NCLC 25**
See also DLB 92; RGEL 2; TWA

**Lancaster, Bruce** 1896-1963 .................. **CLC 36**
See also CA 9-10; CANR 70; CAP 1; SATA 9

**Lanchester, John** 1962- .................. **CLC 99**
See also CA 194; DLB 267

**Landau, Mark Alexandrovich**
See Aldanov, Mark (Alexandrovich)

**Landau-Aldanov, Mark Alexandrovich**
See Aldanov, Mark (Alexandrovich)

**Landis, Jerry**
See Simon, Paul (Frederick)

**Landis, John** 1950- .................. **CLC 26**
See also CA 122

**Landolfi, Tommaso** 1908-1979 .... **CLC 11, 49**
See also CA 127; DLB 177

**Landon, Letitia Elizabeth**
1802-1838 .................. **NCLC 15**
See also DLB 96

**Landor, Walter Savage**
1775-1864 .................. **NCLC 14**
See also BRW 4; DLB 93, 107; RGEL 2

**Landwirth, Heinz** 1927-
See Lind, Jakov
See also CA 9-12R; CANR 7
**Lane, Patrick** 1939- .......................... **CLC 25**
See also CA 97-100; CANR 54; CP 7; DAM POET; DLB 53; INT 97-100
**Lang, Andrew** 1844-1912 ................ **TCLC 16**
See also CA 137; CANR 85; DLB 98, 141, 184; FANT; MAICYA 1, 2; RGEL 2; SATA 16; WCH
**Lang, Fritz** 1890-1976 ............... **CLC 20, 103**
See also CA 77-80; CANR 30
**Lange, John**
See Crichton, (John) Michael
**Langer, Elinor** 1939- .......................... **CLC 34**
See also CA 121
**Langland, William** 1332(?)-1400(?) ..... **LC 19**
See also BRW 1; DA; DAB; DAC; DAM MST, POET; DLB 146; RGEL 2; TEA; WLIT 3
**Langstaff, Launcelot**
See Irving, Washington
**Lanier, Sidney** 1842-1881 ......... **NCLC 6, 118**
See also AMWS 1; DAM POET; DLB 64; DLBD 13; EXPP; MAICYA 1; PFS 14; RGAL 4; SATA 18
**Lanyer, Aemilia** 1569-1645 ...... **LC 10, 30, 83**
See also DLB 121
**Lao-Tzu**
See Lao Tzu
**Lao Tzu** c. 6th cent. B.C.-3rd cent. B.C. ............................................. **CMLC 7**
**Lapine, James (Elliot)** 1949- ............. **CLC 39**
See also CA 130; CANR 54; INT 130
**Larbaud, Valery (Nicolas)** 1881-1957 ......................... **TCLC 9**
See also CA 152; GFL 1789 to the Present
**Lardner, Ring**
See Lardner, Ring(gold) W(ilmer)
See also BPFB 2; CDALB 1917-1929; DLB 11, 25, 86, 171; DLBD 16; RGAL 4; RGSF 2
**Lardner, Ring W., Jr.**
See Lardner, Ring(gold) W(ilmer)
**Lardner, Ring(gold) W(ilmer)** 1885-1933 ............. **SSC 32; TCLC 2, 14**
See Lardner, Ring
See also AMW; CA 131; MTCW 1, 2; TUS
**Laredo, Betty**
See Codrescu, Andrei
**Larkin, Maia**
See Wojciechowska, Maia (Teresa)
**Larkin, Philip (Arthur)** 1922-1985 ... **CLC 3, 5, 8, 9, 13, 18, 33, 39, 64; PC 21**
See also BRWS 1; CA 5-8R; CANR 24, 62; CDBLB 1960 to Present; DAB; DAM MST, POET; DLB 27; MTCW 1, 2; PFS 3, 4, 12; RGEL 2
**La Roche, Sophie von** 1730-1807 ............................... **NCLC 121**
See also DLB 94
**Larra (y Sanchez de Castro), Mariano Jose de** 1809-1837 ............................ **NCLC 17**
**Larsen, Eric** 1941- ............................. **CLC 55**
See also CA 132
**Larsen, Nella** 1893(?)-1963 ....... **BLC 2; CLC 37; HR 3**
See also AFAW 1, 2; BW 1; CA 125; CANR 83; DAM MULT; DLB 51; FW
**Larson, Charles R(aymond)** 1938- ... **CLC 31**
See also CA 53-56; CANR 4
**Larson, Jonathan** 1961-1996 ............. **CLC 99**
See also AAYA 28; CA 156
**Las Casas, Bartolome de** 1474-1566 ........................ **HLCS; LC 31**
See Casas, Bartolome de las
See also LAW

**Lasch, Christopher** 1932-1994 ........ **CLC 102**
See also CA 73-76; CANR 25; DLB 246; MTCW 1, 2
**Lasker-Schueler, Else** 1869-1945 ... **TCLC 57**
See also CA 183; DLB 66, 124
**Laski, Harold J(oseph)** 1893-1950 . **TCLC 79**
See also CA 188
**Latham, Jean Lee** 1902-1995 ............ **CLC 12**
See also AITN 1; BYA 1; CA 5-8R; CANR 7, 84; CLR 50; MAICYA 1, 2; SATA 2, 68; YAW
**Latham, Mavis**
See Clark, Mavis Thorpe
**Lathen, Emma** ................................... **CLC 2**
See Hennissart, Martha; Latsis, Mary J(ane)
See also BPFB 2; CMW 4
**Lathrop, Francis**
See Leiber, Fritz (Reuter, Jr.)
**Latsis, Mary J(ane)** 1927(?)-1997
See Lathen, Emma
See also CA 85-88; CMW 4
**Lattany, Kristin**
See Lattany, Kristin (Elaine Eggleston) Hunter
**Lattany, Kristin (Elaine Eggleston) Hunter** 1931- ............................................ **CLC 35**
See also AITN 1; BW 1; BYA 3; CA 13-16R; CANR 13, 108; CLR 3; CN 7; DLB 33; INT CANR-13; MAICYA 1, 2; SAAS 10; SATA 12, 132; YAW
**Lattimore, Richmond (Alexander)** 1906-1984 ............................................. **CLC 3**
See also CA 1-4R; CANR 1
**Laughlin, James** 1914-1997 ............... **CLC 49**
See also CA 21-24R; CAAS 22; CANR 9, 47; CP 7; DLB 48; DLBY 1996, 1997
**Laurence, (Jean) Margaret (Wemyss)** 1926-1987 . **CLC 3, 6, 13, 50, 62; SSC 7**
See also BYA 13; CA 5-8R; CANR 33; DAC; DAM MST; DLB 53; FW; MTCW 1, 2; NFS 11; RGEL 2; RGSF 2; SATA-Obit 50; TCWW 2
**Laurent, Antoine** 1952- ...................... **CLC 50**
**Lauscher, Hermann**
See Hesse, Hermann
**Lautreamont** 1846-1870 .. **NCLC 12; SSC 14**
See Lautreamont, Isidore Lucien Ducasse
See also GFL 1789 to the Present; RGWL 2, 3
**Lautreamont, Isidore Lucien Ducasse**
See Lautreamont
See also DLB 217
**Laverty, Donald**
See Blish, James (Benjamin)
**Lavin, Mary** 1912-1996 . **CLC 4, 18, 99; SSC 4**
See also CA 9-12R; CANR 33; CN 7; DLB 15; FW; MTCW 1; RGEL 2; RGSF 2
**Lavond, Paul Dennis**
See Kornbluth, C(yril) M.; Pohl, Frederik
**Lawler, Raymond Evenor** 1922- ........ **CLC 58**
See also CA 103; CD 5; RGEL 2
**Lawrence, D(avid) H(erbert Richards)** 1885-1930 ... **SSC 4, 19; TCLC 2, 9, 16, 33, 48, 61, 93; WLC**
See Chambers, Jessie
See also BPFB 2; BRW 7; BRWR 2; CA 121; CDBLB 1914-1945; DA; DAB; DAC; DAM MST, NOV, POET; DLB 10, 19, 36, 98, 162, 195; EXPP; EXPS; LAIT 2, 3; MTCW 1, 2; PFS 6; RGEL 2; RGSF 2; SSFS 2, 6; TEA; WLIT 4; WP
**Lawrence, T(homas) E(dward)** 1888-1935 ................................ **TCLC 18**
See Dale, Colin
See also BRWS 2; CA 167; DLB 195
**Lawrence of Arabia**
See Lawrence, T(homas) E(dward)

**Lawson, Henry (Archibald Hertzberg)** 1867-1922 ................ **SSC 18; TCLC 27**
See also CA 181; DLB 230; RGEL 2; RGSF 2
**Lawton, Dennis**
See Faust, Frederick (Schiller)
**Laxness, Halldor** .................................. **CLC 25**
See Gudjonsson, Halldor Kiljan
See also EW 12; RGWL 2, 3
**Layamon** fl. c. 1200- ...................... **CMLC 10**
See Layamon
See also RGEL 2
**Laye, Camara** 1928-1980 ..... **BLC 2; CLC 4, 38**
See also AFW; BW 1; CA 85-88; CANR 25; DAM MULT; MTCW 1, 2; WLIT 2
**Layton, Irving (Peter)** 1912- ....... **CLC 2, 15, 164**
See also CA 1-4R; CANR 2, 33, 43, 66; CP 7; DAC; DAM MST, POET; DLB 88; MTCW 1, 2; PFS 12; RGEL 2
**Lazarus, Emma** 1849-1887 ....... **NCLC 8, 109**
**Lazarus, Felix**
See Cable, George Washington
**Lazarus, Henry**
See Slavitt, David R(ytman)
**Lea, Joan**
See Neufeld, John (Arthur)
**Leacock, Stephen (Butler)** 1869-1944 ................... **SSC 39; TCLC 2**
See also CA 141; CANR 80; DAC; DAM MST; DLB 92; MTCW 2; RGEL 2; RGSF 2
**Lead, Jane Ward** 1623-1704 ................ **LC 72**
See also DLB 131
**Leapor, Mary** 1722-1746 ..................... **LC 80**
See also DLB 109
**Lear, Edward** 1812-1888 .................. **NCLC 3**
See also BRW 5; CLR 1, 75; DLB 32, 163, 166; MAICYA 1, 2; RGEL 2; SATA 18, 100; WCH; WP
**Lear, Norman (Milton)** 1922- ........... **CLC 12**
See also CA 73-76
**Leautaud, Paul** 1872-1956 ............. **TCLC 83**
See also CA 203; DLB 65; GFL 1789 to the Present
**Leavis, F(rank) R(aymond)** 1895-1978 ........................... **CLC 24**
See also BRW 7; CA 21-24R; CANR 44; DLB 242; MTCW 1, 2; RGEL 2
**Leavitt, David** 1961- ........................... **CLC 34**
See also CA 122; CANR 50, 62, 101; CPW; DAM POP; DLB 130; GLL 1; INT 122; MTCW 2
**Leblanc, Maurice (Marie Emile)** 1864-1941 ................................ **TCLC 49**
See also CMW 4
**Lebowitz, Fran(ces Ann)** 1951(?)- ... **CLC 11, 36**
See also CA 81-84; CANR 14, 60, 70; INT CANR-14; MTCW 1
**Lebrecht, Peter**
See Tieck, (Johann) Ludwig
**le Carre, John** ................ **CLC 3, 5, 9, 15, 28**
See Cornwell, David (John Moore)
See also AAYA 42; BEST 89:4; BPFB 2; BRWS 2; CDBLB 1960 to Present; CMW 4; CN 7; CPW; DLB 87; MSW; MTCW 2; RGEL 2; TEA
**Le Clezio, J(ean) M(arie) G(ustave)** 1940- ................................................ **CLC 31, 155**
See also CA 128; DLB 83; GFL 1789 to the Present; RGSF 2
**Leconte de Lisle, Charles-Marie-Rene** 1818-1894 ................................ **NCLC 29**
See also DLB 217; EW 6; GFL 1789 to the Present
**Le Coq, Monsieur**
See Simenon, Georges (Jacques Christian)

**Leduc, Violette** 1907-1972 .................. **CLC 22**
See also CA 13-14; CANR 69; CAP 1; GFL 1789 to the Present; GLL 1

**Ledwidge, Francis** 1887(?)-1917 .... **TCLC 23**
See also CA 203; DLB 20

**Lee, Andrea** 1953- ................. **BLC 2; CLC 36**
See also BW 1, 3; CA 125; CANR 82; DAM MULT

**Lee, Andrew**
See Auchincloss, Louis (Stanton)

**Lee, Chang-rae** 1965- ........................ **CLC 91**
See also CA 148; CANR 89

**Lee, Don L.** ............................................ **CLC 2**
See Madhubuti, Haki R.

**Lee, George W(ashington)**
1894-1976 ..................... **BLC 2; CLC 52**
See also BW 1; CA 125; CANR 83; DAM MULT; DLB 51

**Lee, (Nelle) Harper** 1926- .......... **CLC 12, 60; WLC**
See also AAYA 13; AMWS 8; BPFB 2; BYA 3; CA 13-16R; CANR 51; CDALB 1941-1968; CSW; DA; DAB; DAC; DAM MST, NOV; DLB 6; EXPN; LAIT 3; MTCW 1, 2; NFS 2; SATA 11; WYA; YAW

**Lee, Helen Elaine** 1959(?)- ................. **CLC 86**
See also CA 148

**Lee, John** ............................................ **CLC 70**

**Lee, Julian**
See Latham, Jean Lee

**Lee, Larry**
See Lee, Lawrence

**Lee, Laurie** 1914-1997 ....................... **CLC 90**
See also CA 77-80; CANR 33, 73; CP 7; CPW; DAB; DAM POP; DLB 27; MTCW 1; RGEL 2

**Lee, Lawrence** 1941-1990 .................. **CLC 34**
See also CANR 43

**Lee, Li-Young** 1957- ........... **CLC 164; PC 24**
See also CA 153; CP 7; DLB 165; PFS 11, 15, 17

**Lee, Manfred B(ennington)**
1905-1971 .................................... **CLC 11**
See Queen, Ellery
See also CA 1-4R; CANR 2; CMW 4; DLB 137

**Lee, Shelton Jackson** 1957(?)- .. **BLCS; CLC 105**
See Lee, Spike
See also BW 2, 3; CA 125; CANR 42; DAM MULT

**Lee, Spike**
See Lee, Shelton Jackson
See also AAYA 4, 29

**Lee, Stan** 1922- ................................. **CLC 17**
See also AAYA 5; CA 111; INT 111

**Lee, Tanith** 1947- .............................. **CLC 46**
See also AAYA 15; CA 37-40R; CANR 53, 102; DLB 261; FANT; SATA 8, 88, 134; SFW 4; SUFW 1, 2; YAW

**Lee, Vernon** ....................... **SSC 33; TCLC 5**
See Paget, Violet
See also DLB 57, 153, 156, 174, 178; GLL 1; SUFW 1

**Lee, William**
See Burroughs, William S(eward)
See also GLL 1

**Lee, Willy**
See Burroughs, William S(eward)
See also GLL 1

**Lee-Hamilton, Eugene (Jacob)**
1845-1907 ................................ **TCLC 22**

**Leet, Judith** 1935- .............................. **CLC 11**
See also CA 187

**Le Fanu, Joseph Sheridan**
1814-1873 ............. **NCLC 9, 58; SSC 14**
See also CMW 4; DAM POP; DLB 21, 70, 159, 178; HGG; RGEL 2; RGSF 2; SUFW 1

**Leffland, Ella** 1931- ............................ **CLC 19**
See also CA 29-32R; CANR 35, 78, 82; DLBY 1984; INT CANR-35; SATA 65

**Leger, Alexis**
See Leger, (Marie-Rene Auguste) Alexis Saint-Leger

**Leger, (Marie-Rene Auguste) Alexis Saint-Leger** 1887-1975 .. **CLC 4, 11, 46; PC 23**
See Perse, Saint-John; Saint-John Perse
See also CA 13-16R; CANR 43; DAM POET; MTCW 1

**Leger, Saintleger**
See Leger, (Marie-Rene Auguste) Alexis Saint-Leger

**Le Guin, Ursula K(roeber)** 1929- ...... **CLC 8, 13, 22, 45, 71, 136; SSC 12**
See also AAYA 9, 27; AITN 1; BPFB 2; BYA 5, 8, 11, 14; CA 21-24R; CANR 9, 32, 52, 74; CDALB 1968-1988; CLR 3, 28; CN 7; CPW; DAB; DAC; DAM MST, POP; DLB 8, 52, 256, 275; EXPS; FANT; FW; INT CANR-32; JRDA; LAIT 5; MAICYA 1, 2; MTCW 1, 2; NFS 6, 9; SATA 4, 52, 99; SCFW 4; SFW 4; SSFS 2; SUFW 1, 2; WYA; YAW

**Lehmann, Rosamond (Nina)**
1901-1990 ..................................... **CLC 5**
See also CA 77-80; CANR 8, 73; DLB 15; MTCW 2; RGEL 2; RHW

**Leiber, Fritz (Reuter, Jr.)**
1910-1992 .................................... **CLC 25**
See also BPFB 2; CA 45-48; CANR 2, 40, 86; DLB 8; FANT; HGG; MTCW 1, 2; SATA 45; SATA-Obit 73; SCFW 2; SFW 4; SUFW 1, 2

**Leibniz, Gottfried Wilhelm von**
1646-1716 .................................... **LC 35**
See also DLB 168

**Leimbach, Martha** 1963-
See Leimbach, Marti
See also CA 130

**Leimbach, Marti** ............................... **CLC 65**
See Leimbach, Martha

**Leino, Eino** ...................................... **TCLC 24**
See Loennbohm, Armas Eino Leopold

**Leiris, Michel (Julien)** 1901-1990 ..... **CLC 61**
See also CA 128; GFL 1789 to the Present

**Leithauser, Brad** 1953- ........................ **CLC 27**
See also CA 107; CANR 27, 81; CP 7; DLB 120

**Lelchuk, Alan** 1938- ............................. **CLC 5**
See also CA 45-48; CAAS 20; CANR 1, 70; CN 7

**Lem, Stanislaw** 1921- ...... **CLC 8, 15, 40, 149**
See also CA 105; CAAS 1; CANR 32; CWW 2; MTCW 1; SCFW 2; SFW 4

**Lemann, Nancy** 1956- ......................... **CLC 39**
See also CA 136

**Lemonnier, (Antoine Louis) Camille**
1844-1913 .................................. **TCLC 22**

**Lenau, Nikolaus** 1802-1850 ............ **NCLC 16**

**L'Engle, Madeleine (Camp Franklin)**
1918- .......................................... **CLC 12**
See also AAYA 28; AITN 2; BPFB 2; BYA 2, 4, 5, 7; CA 1-4R; CANR 3, 21, 39, 66, 107; CLR 1, 14, 57; CPW; CWRI 5; DAM POP; DLB 52; JRDA; MAICYA 1, 2; MTCW 1, 2; RGAL 4; SAAS 15; SATA 1, 27, 75, 128; SFW 4; WYA; YAW

**Lengyel, Jozsef** 1896-1975 .................... **CLC 7**
See also CA 85-88; CANR 71; RGSF 2

**Lenin** 1870-1924
See Lenin, V. I.
See also CA 168

**Lenin, V. I.** ...................................... **TCLC 67**
See Lenin

**Lennon, John (Ono)** 1940-1980 .. **CLC 12, 35**
See also CA 102; SATA 114

**Lennox, Charlotte Ramsay**
1729(?)-1804 ............................. **NCLC 23**
See also DLB 39; RGEL 2

**Lentricchia, Frank, (Jr.)** 1940- ......... **CLC 34**
See also CA 25-28R; CANR 19, 106; DLB 246

**Lenz, Gunter** ...................................... **CLC 65**

**Lenz, Siegfried** 1926- ............. **CLC 27; SSC 33**
See also CA 89-92; CANR 80; CWW 2; DLB 75; RGSF 2; RGWL 2, 3

**Leon, David**
See Jacob, (Cyprien-)Max

**Leonard, Elmore (John, Jr.)** 1925- . **CLC 28, 34, 71, 120**
See also AAYA 22; AITN 1; BEST 89:1, 90:4; BPFB 2; CA 81-84; CANR 12, 28, 53, 76, 96; CMW 4; CN 7; CPW; DAM POP; DLB 173, 226; INT CANR-28; MSW; MTCW 1, 2; RGAL 4; TCWW 2

**Leonard, Hugh** ................................. **CLC 19**
See Byrne, John Keyes
See also CBD; CD 5; DFS 13; DLB 13

**Leonov, Leonid (Maximovich)**
1899-1994 ................................... **CLC 92**
See Leonov, Leonid Maksimovich
See also CA 129; CANR 74, 76; DAM NOV; MTCW 1, 2

**Leonov, Leonid Maksimovich**
See Leonov, Leonid (Maximovich)
See also DLB 272

**Leopardi, (Conte) Giacomo**
1798-1837 ................... **NCLC 22; PC 37**
See also EW 5; RGWL 2, 3; WP

**Le Reveler**
See Artaud, Antonin (Marie Joseph)

**Lerman, Eleanor** 1952- ....................... **CLC 9**
See also CA 85-88; CANR 69

**Lerman, Rhoda** 1936- ........................ **CLC 56**
See also CA 49-52; CANR 70

**Lermontov, Mikhail**
See Lermontov, Mikhail Yuryevich

**Lermontov, Mikhail Iur'evich**
See Lermontov, Mikhail Yuryevich
See also DLB 205

**Lermontov, Mikhail Yuryevich**
1814-1841 ................ **NCLC 5, 47; PC 18**
See Lermontov, Mikhail Iur'evich
See also EW 6; RGWL 2, 3; TWA

**Leroux, Gaston** 1868-1927 ............. **TCLC 25**
See also CA 136; CANR 69; CMW 4; SATA 65

**Lesage, Alain-Rene** 1668-1747 ........ **LC 2, 28**
See also EW 3; GFL Beginnings to 1789; RGWL 2, 3

**Leskov, N(ikolai) S(emenovich)** 1831-1895
See Leskov, Nikolai (Semyonovich)

**Leskov, Nikolai (Semyonovich)**
1831-1895 ................. **NCLC 25; SSC 34**
See Leskov, Nikolai Semenovich

**Leskov, Nikolai Semenovich**
See Leskov, Nikolai (Semyonovich)
See also DLB 238

**Lesser, Milton**
See Marlowe, Stephen

**Lessing, Doris (May)** 1919- ... **CLC 1, 2, 3, 6, 10, 15, 22, 40, 94; SSC 6; WLCS**
See also AFW; BRWS 1; CA 9-12R; CAAS 14; CANR 33, 54, 76; CD 5; CDBLB 1960 to Present; CN 7; DA; DAB; DAC; DAM MST, NOV; DLB 15, 139; DLBY

1985; EXPS; FW; LAIT 4; MTCW 1, 2; RGEL 2; RGSF 2; SFW 4; SSFS 1, 12; TEA; WLIT 2, 4

**Lessing, Gotthold Ephraim** 1729-1781 . **LC 8**
See also CDWLB 2; DLB 97; EW 4; RGWL 2, 3

**Lester, Richard** 1932- .................... **CLC 20**

**Levenson, Jay** ..................... **CLC 70**

**Lever, Charles (James)**
1806-1872 .................... **NCLC 23**
See also DLB 21; RGEL 2

**Leverson, Ada Esther**
1862(?)-1933(?) ..................... **TCLC 18**
See Elaine
See also CA 202; DLB 153; RGEL 2

**Levertov, Denise** 1923-1997 .. **CLC 1, 2, 3, 5, 8, 15, 28, 66; PC 11**
See also AMWS 3; CA 1-4R, 178; CAAE 178; CAAS 19; CANR 3, 29, 50, 108; CDALBS; CP 7; CWP; DAM POET; DLB 5, 165; EXPP; FW; INT CANR-29; MTCW 1, 2; PAB; PFS 7, 16; RGAL 4; TUS; WP

**Levi, Carlo** 1902-1975 .................... **TCLC 125**
See also CA 65-68; CANR 10; RGWL 2, 3

**Levi, Jonathan** ..................... **CLC 76**
See also CA 197

**Levi, Peter (Chad Tigar)**
1931-2000 ..................... **CLC 41**
See also CA 5-8R; CANR 34, 80; CP 7; DLB 40

**Levi, Primo** 1919-1987 ...... **CLC 37, 50; SSC 12; TCLC 109**
See also CA 13-16R; CANR 12, 33, 61, 70; DLB 177; MTCW 1, 2; RGWL 2, 3

**Levin, Ira** 1929- ..................... **CLC 3, 6**
See also CA 21-24R; CANR 17, 44, 74; CMW 4; CN 7; CPW; DAM POP; HGG; MTCW 1, 2; SATA 66; SFW 4

**Levin, Meyer** 1905-1981 ..................... **CLC 7**
See also AITN 1; CA 9-12R; CANR 15; DAM POP; DLB 9, 28; DLBY 1981; SATA 21; SATA-Obit 27

**Levine, Norman** 1924- ..................... **CLC 54**
See also CA 73-76; CAAS 23; CANR 14, 70; DLB 88

**Levine, Philip** 1928- .. **CLC 2, 4, 5, 9, 14, 33, 118; PC 22**
See also AMWS 5; CA 9-12R; CANR 9, 37, 52; CP 7; DAM POET; DLB 5; PFS 8

**Levinson, Deirdre** 1931- ..................... **CLC 49**
See also CA 73-76; CANR 70

**Levi-Strauss, Claude** 1908- ..................... **CLC 38**
See also CA 1-4R; CANR 6, 32, 57; DLB 242; GFL 1789 to the Present; MTCW 1, 2; TWA

**Levitin, Sonia (Wolff)** 1934- ..................... **CLC 17**
See also AAYA 13; CA 29-32R; CANR 14, 32, 79; CLR 53; JRDA; MAICYA 1, 2; SAAS 2; SATA 4, 68, 119; SATA-Essay 131; YAW

**Levon, O. U.**
See Kesey, Ken (Elton)

**Levy, Amy** 1861-1889 ..................... **NCLC 59**
See also DLB 156, 240

**Lewes, George Henry** 1817-1878 ... **NCLC 25**
See also DLB 55, 144

**Lewis, Alun** 1915-1944 ........ **SSC 40; TCLC 3**
See also BRW 7; CA 188; DLB 20, 162; PAB; RGEL 2

**Lewis, C. Day**
See Day Lewis, C(ecil)

**Lewis, C(live) S(taples)** 1898-1963 .... **CLC 1, 3, 6, 14, 27, 124; WLC**
See also AAYA 3, 39; BPFB 2; BRWS 3; CA 81-84; CANR 33, 71; CDBLB 1945-1960; CLR 3, 27; CWRI 5; DA; DAB; DAC; DAM MST, NOV, POP; DLB 15, 100, 160, 255; FANT; JRDA; MAICYA 1, 2; MTCW 1, 2; RGEL 2; SATA 13, 100; SCFW; SFW 4; SUFW 1; TEA; WCH; WYA; YAW

**Lewis, Cecil Day**
See Day Lewis, C(ecil)

**Lewis, Janet** 1899-1998 ..................... **CLC 41**
See Winters, Janet Lewis
See also CA 9-12R; CANR 29, 63; CAP 1; CN 7; DLBY 1987; RHW; TCWW 2

**Lewis, Matthew Gregory**
1775-1818 .................... **NCLC 11, 62**
See also DLB 39, 158, 178; HGG; RGEL 2; SUFW

**Lewis, (Harry) Sinclair** 1885-1951 . **TCLC 4, 13, 23, 39; WLC**
See also AMW; AMWC 1; BPFB 2; CA 133; CDALB 1917-1929; DA; DAB; DAC; DAM MST, NOV; DLB 9, 102; DLBD 1; LAIT 3; MTCW 1, 2; NFS 15; RGAL 4; TUS

**Lewis, (Percy) Wyndham**
1884(?)-1957 .. **SSC 34; TCLC 2, 9, 104**
See also BRW 7; CA 157; DLB 15; FANT; MTCW 2; RGEL 2

**Lewisohn, Ludwig** 1883-1955 ......... **TCLC 19**
See also DLB 4, 9, 28, 102

**Lewton, Val** 1904-1951 ..................... **TCLC 76**
See also CA 199; IDFW 3, 4

**Leyner, Mark** 1956- ..................... **CLC 92**
See also CA 110; CANR 28, 53; MTCW 2

**Lezama Lima, Jose** 1910-1976 .... **CLC 4, 10, 101; HLCS 2**
See also CA 77-80; CANR 71; DAM MULT; DLB 113; HW 1, 2; LAW; RGWL 2, 3

**L'Heureux, John (Clarke)** 1934- ...... **CLC 52**
See also CA 13-16R; CANR 23, 45, 88; DLB 244

**Liddell, C. H.**
See Kuttner, Henry

**Lie, Jonas (Lauritz Idemil)**
1833-1908(?) .................... **TCLC 5**

**Lieber, Joel** 1937-1971 ..................... **CLC 6**
See also CA 73-76

**Lieber, Stanley Martin**
See Lee, Stan

**Lieberman, Laurence (James)**
1935- ..................... **CLC 4, 36**
See also CA 17-20R; CANR 8, 36, 89; CP 7

**Lieh Tzu** fl. 7th cent. B.C.-5th cent. B.C. .................... **CMLC 27**

**Lieksman, Anders**
See Haavikko, Paavo Juhani

**Li Fei-kan** 1904-
See Pa Chin
See also CA 105; TWA

**Lifton, Robert Jay** 1926- ..................... **CLC 67**
See also CA 17-20R; CANR 27, 78; INT CANR-27; SATA 66

**Lightfoot, Gordon** 1938- ..................... **CLC 26**

**Lightman, Alan P(aige)** 1948- ..................... **CLC 81**
See also CA 141; CANR 63, 105

**Ligotti, Thomas (Robert)** 1953- ...... **CLC 44; SSC 16**
See also CA 123; CANR 49; HGG; SUFW 2

**Li Ho** 791-817 ..................... **PC 13**

**Liliencron, (Friedrich Adolf Axel) Detlev von** 1844-1909 .................... **TCLC 18**

**Lille, Alain de**
See Alain de Lille

**Lilly, William** 1602-1681 ..................... **LC 27**

**Lima, Jose Lezama**
See Lezama Lima, Jose

**Lima Barreto, Afonso Henrique de**
1881-1922 .................... **TCLC 23**
See also CA 181; LAW

**Lima Barreto, Afonso Henriques de**
See Lima Barreto, Afonso Henrique de

**Limonov, Edward** 1944- ..................... **CLC 67**
See also CA 137

**Lin, Frank**
See Atherton, Gertrude (Franklin Horn)

**Lincoln, Abraham** 1809-1865 ......... **NCLC 18**
See also LAIT 2

**Lind, Jakov** ..................... **CLC 1, 2, 4, 27, 82**
See Landwirth, Heinz
See also CAAS 4

**Lindbergh, Anne (Spencer) Morrow**
1906-2001 ..................... **CLC 82**
See also BPFB 2; CA 17-20R; CANR 16, 73; DAM NOV; MTCW 1, 2; SATA 33; SATA-Obit 125; TUS

**Lindsay, David** 1878(?)-1945 .......... **TCLC 15**
See also CA 187; DLB 255; FANT; SFW 4; SUFW 1

**Lindsay, (Nicholas) Vachel**
1879-1931 ........ **PC 23; TCLC 17; WLC**
See also AMWS 1; CA 135; CANR 79; CDALB 1865-1917; DA; DAC; DAM MST, POET; DLB 54; EXPP; RGAL 4; SATA 40; WP

**Linke-Poot**
See Doeblin, Alfred

**Linney, Romulus** 1930- ..................... **CLC 51**
See also CA 1-4R; CAD; CANR 40, 44, 79; CD 5; CSW; RGAL 4

**Linton, Eliza Lynn** 1822-1898 ......... **NCLC 41**
See also DLB 18

**Li Po** 701-763 ..................... **CMLC 2; PC 29**
See also WP

**Lipsius, Justus** 1547-1606 ..................... **LC 16**

**Lipsyte, Robert (Michael)** 1938- ....... **CLC 21**
See also AAYA 7, 45; CA 17-20R; CANR 8, 57; CLR 23, 76; DA; DAC; DAM MST, NOV; JRDA; LAIT 5; MAICYA 1, 2; SATA 5, 68, 113; WYA; YAW

**Lish, Gordon (Jay)** 1934- ... **CLC 45; SSC 18**
See also CA 117; CANR 79; DLB 130; INT 117

**Lispector, Clarice** 1925(?)-1977 ....... **CLC 43; HLCS 2; SSC 34**
See also CA 139; CANR 71; CDWLB 3; DLB 113; DNFS 1; FW; HW 2; LAW; RGSF 2; RGWL 2, 3; WLIT 1

**Littell, Robert** 1935(?)- ..................... **CLC 42**
See also CA 112; CANR 64; CMW 4

**Little, Malcolm** 1925-1965
See Malcolm X
See also BW 1, 3; CA 125; CANR 82; DA; DAB; DAC; DAM MST, MULT; MTCW 1, 2; NCFS 3

**Littlewit, Humphrey Gent.**
See Lovecraft, H(oward) P(hillips)

**Litwos**
See Sienkiewicz, Henryk (Adam Alexander Pius)

**Liu, E.** 1857-1909 ..................... **TCLC 15**
See also CA 190

**Lively, Penelope (Margaret)** 1933- .. **CLC 32, 50**
See also BPFB 2; CA 41-44R; CANR 29, 67, 79; CLR 7; CN 7; CWRI 5; DAM NOV; DLB 14, 161, 207; FANT; JRDA; MAICYA 1, 2; MTCW 1, 2; SATA 7, 60, 101; TEA

**Livesay, Dorothy (Kathleen)**
1909-1996 .................... **CLC 4, 15, 79**
See also AITN 2; CA 25-28R; CAAS 8; CANR 36, 67; DAC; DAM MST, POET; DLB 68; FW; MTCW 1; RGEL 2; TWA

**Livy** c. 59B.C.-c. 12 ..................... **CMLC 11**
See also AW 2; CDWLB 1; DLB 211; RGWL 2, 3

**Lizardi, Jose Joaquin Fernandez de**
1776-1827 .................. **NCLC 30**
See also LAW

**Llewellyn, Richard**
See Llewellyn Lloyd, Richard Dafydd Vivian
See also DLB 15

**Llewellyn Lloyd, Richard Dafydd Vivian**
1906-1983 ..................... **CLC 7, 80**
See Llewellyn, Richard
See also CA 53-56; CANR 7, 71; SATA 11; SATA-Obit 37

**Llosa, (Jorge) Mario (Pedro) Vargas**
See Vargas Llosa, (Jorge) Mario (Pedro)
See also RGWL 3

**Lloyd, Manda**
See Mander, (Mary) Jane

**Lloyd Webber, Andrew** 1948-
See Webber, Andrew Lloyd
See also AAYA 1, 38; CA 149; DAM DRAM; SATA 56

**Llull, Ramon** c. 1235-c. 1316 ........ **CMLC 12**

**Lobb, Ebenezer**
See Upward, Allen

**Locke, Alain (Le Roy)**
1886-1954 ........ **BLCS; HR 3; TCLC 43**
See also BW 1, 3; CA 124; CANR 79; DLB 51; RGAL 4

**Locke, John** 1632-1704 ..................... **LC 7, 35**
See also DLB 31, 101, 213, 252; RGEL 2; WLIT 3

**Locke-Elliott, Sumner**
See Elliott, Sumner Locke

**Lockhart, John Gibson** 1794-1854 .. **NCLC 6**
See also DLB 110, 116, 144

**Lockridge, Ross (Franklin), Jr.**
1914-1948 ..................... **TCLC 111**
See also CA 145; CANR 79; DLB 143; DLBY 1980; RGAL 4; RHW

**Lockwood, Robert**
See Johnson, Robert

**Lodge, David (John)** 1935- ........ **CLC 36, 141**
See also BEST 90:1; BRWS 4; CA 17-20R; CANR 19, 53, 92; CN 7; CPW; DAM POP; DLB 14, 194; INT CANR-19; MTCW 1, 2

**Lodge, Thomas** 1558-1625 ................. **LC 41**
See also DLB 172; RGEL 2

**Loewinsohn, Ron(ald William)**
1937- .................................. **CLC 52**
See also CA 25-28R; CANR 71

**Logan, Jake**
See Smith, Martin Cruz

**Logan, John (Burton)** 1923-1987 ....... **CLC 5**
See also CA 77-80; CANR 45; DLB 5

**Lo Kuan-chung** 1330(?)-1400(?) .......... **LC 12**

**Lombard, Nap**
See Johnson, Pamela Hansford

**Lomotey (editor), Kofi** ................... **CLC 70**

**London, Jack** 1876-1916 .. **SSC 4, 49; TCLC 9, 15, 39; WLC**
See London, John Griffith
See also AAYA 13; AITN 2; AMW; BPFB 2; BYA 4, 13; CDALB 1865-1917; DLB 8, 12, 78, 212; EXPS; LAIT 3; NFS 8; RGAL 4; RGSF 2; SATA 18; SFW 4; SSFS 7; TCWW 2; TUS; WYA; YAW

**London, John Griffith** 1876-1916
See London, Jack
See also CA 119; CANR 73; DA; DAB; DAC; DAM MST, NOV; JRDA; MAICYA 1, 2; MTCW 1, 2

**Long, Emmett**
See Leonard, Elmore (John, Jr.)

**Longbaugh, Harry**
See Goldman, William (W.)

**Longfellow, Henry Wadsworth**
1807-1882 .... **NCLC 2, 45, 101, 103; PC 30; WLCS**
See also AMW; AMWR 2; CDALB 1640-1865; DA; DAB; DAC; DAM MST, POET; DLB 1, 59, 235; EXPP; PAB; PFS 2, 7, 17; RGAL 4; SATA 19; TUS; WP

**Longinus** c. 1st cent. - ..................... **CMLC 27**
See also AW 2; DLB 176

**Longley, Michael** 1939- ..................... **CLC 29**
See also BRWS 8; CA 102; CP 7; DLB 40

**Longus** fl. c. 2nd cent. - ..................... **CMLC 7**

**Longway, A. Hugh**
See Lang, Andrew

**Lonnrot, Elias** 1802-1884 ............... **NCLC 53**
See also EFS 1

**Lonsdale, Roger ed.** .......................... **CLC 65**

**Lopate, Phillip** 1943- ......................... **CLC 29**
See also CA 97-100; CANR 88; DLBY 1980; INT 97-100

**Lopez, Barry (Holstun)** 1945- ........... **CLC 70**
See also AAYA 9; ANW; CA 65-68; CANR 7, 23, 47, 68, 92; DLB 256, 275; INT CANR-7, -23; MTCW 1; RGAL 4; SATA 67

**Lopez Portillo (y Pacheco), Jose**
1920- .................................. **CLC 46**
See also CA 129; HW 1

**Lopez y Fuentes, Gregorio**
1897(?)-1966 ............................. **CLC 32**
See also CA 131; HW 1

**Lorca, Federico Garcia**
See Garcia Lorca, Federico
See also DFS 4; EW 11; RGWL 2, 3; WP

**Lord, Bette Bao** 1938- ............. **AAL; CLC 23**
See also BEST 90:3; BPFB 2; CA 107; CANR 41, 79; INT CA-107; SATA 58

**Lord Auch**
See Bataille, Georges

**Lord Brooke**
See Greville, Fulke

**Lord Byron**
See Byron, George Gordon (Noel)

**Lorde, Audre (Geraldine)**
1934-1992 .. **BLC 2; CLC 18, 71; PC 12**
See Domini, Rey
See also AFAW 1, 2; BW 1, 3; CA 25-28R; CANR 16, 26, 46, 82; DAM MULT, POET; DLB 41; FW; MTCW 1, 2; PFS 16; RGAL 4

**Lord Houghton**
See Milnes, Richard Monckton

**Lord Jeffrey**
See Jeffrey, Francis

**Loreaux, Nichol** ................. **CLC 65**

**Lorenzini, Carlo** 1826-1890
See Collodi, Carlo
See also MAICYA 1, 2; SATA 29, 100

**Lorenzo, Heberto Padilla**
See Padilla (Lorenzo), Heberto

**Loris**
See Hofmannsthal, Hugo von

**Loti, Pierre** ..................................... **TCLC 11**
See Viaud, (Louis Marie) Julien
See also DLB 123; GFL 1789 to the Present

**Lou, Henri**
See Andreas-Salome, Lou

**Louie, David Wong** 1954- ................. **CLC 70**
See also CA 139

**Louis, Father M.**
See Merton, Thomas (James)

**Lovecraft, H(oward) P(hillips)**
1890-1937 ......... **SSC 3, 52; TCLC 4, 22**
See also AAYA 14; BPFB 2; CA 133; CANR 106; DAM POP; HGG; MTCW 1, 2; RGAL 4; SCFW; SFW 4; SUFW

**Lovelace, Earl** 1935- ......................... **CLC 51**
See also BW 2; CA 77-80; CANR 41, 72, 114; CD 5; CDWLB 3; CN 7; DLB 125; MTCW 1

**Lovelace, Richard** 1618-1657 ............... **LC 24**
See also BRW 2; DLB 131; EXPP; PAB; RGEL 2

**Lowell, Amy** 1874-1925 ... **PC 13; TCLC 1, 8**
See also AMW; CA 151; DAM POET; DLB 54, 140; EXPP; MAWW; MTCW 2; RGAL 4; TUS

**Lowell, James Russell** 1819-1891 ... **NCLC 2, 90**
See also AMWS 1; CDALB 1640-1865; DLB 1, 11, 64, 79, 189, 235; RGAL 4

**Lowell, Robert (Traill Spence, Jr.)**
1917-1977 .... **CLC 1, 2, 3, 4, 5, 8, 9, 11, 15, 37, 124; PC 3; WLC**
See also AMW; AMWR 2; CA 9-12R; CABS 2; CANR 26, 60; CDALBS; DA; DAB; DAC; DAM MST, NOV; DLB 5, 169; MTCW 1, 2; PAB; PFS 6, 7; RGAL 4; WP

**Lowenthal, Michael (Francis)**
1969- ........................................ **CLC 119**
See also CA 150

**Lowndes, Marie Adelaide (Belloc)**
1868-1947 ................................. **TCLC 12**
See also CMW 4; DLB 70; RHW

**Lowry, (Clarence) Malcolm**
1909-1957 ............. **SSC 31; TCLC 6, 40**
See also BPFB 2; BRWS 3; CA 131; CANR 62, 105; CDBLB 1945-1960; DLB 15; MTCW 1, 2; RGEL 2

**Lowry, Mina Gertrude** 1882-1966
See Loy, Mina
See also CA 113

**Loxsmith, John**
See Brunner, John (Kilian Houston)

**Loy, Mina** ............................. **CLC 28; PC 16**
See Lowry, Mina Gertrude
See also DAM POET; DLB 4, 54

**Loyson-Bridet**
See Schwob, Marcel (Mayer Andre)

**Lucan** 39-65 ............................. **CMLC 33**
See also AW 2; DLB 211; EFS 2; RGWL 2, 3

**Lucas, Craig** 1951- ............................. **CLC 64**
See also CA 137; CAD; CANR 71, 109; CD 5; GLL 2

**Lucas, E(dward) V(errall)**
1868-1938 ................................. **TCLC 73**
See also CA 176; DLB 98, 149, 153; SATA 20

**Lucas, George** 1944- ......................... **CLC 16**
See also AAYA 1, 23; CA 77-80; CANR 30; SATA 56

**Lucas, Hans**
See Godard, Jean-Luc

**Lucas, Victoria**
See Plath, Sylvia

**Lucian** c. 125-c. 180 ..................... **CMLC 32**
See also AW 2; DLB 176; RGWL 2, 3

**Lucretius** c. 94B.C.-c. 49B.C. ........ **CMLC 48**
See also AW 2; CDWLB 1; DLB 211; EFS 2; RGWL 2, 3

**Ludlam, Charles** 1943-1987 ........ **CLC 46, 50**
See also CA 85-88; CAD; CANR 72, 86; DLB 266

**Ludlum, Robert** 1927-2001 ......... **CLC 22, 43**
See also AAYA 10; BEST 89:1, 90:3; BPFB 2; CA 33-36R; CANR 25, 41, 68, 105; CMW 4; CPW; DAM NOV, POP; DLBY 1982; MSW; MTCW 1, 2

**Ludwig, Ken** ........................................ **CLC 60**
See also CA 195; CAD

**Ludwig, Otto** 1813-1865 ................... **NCLC 4**
See also DLB 129

**Lugones, Leopoldo** 1874-1938 ......... **HLCS 2; TCLC 15**
See also CA 131; CANR 104; HW 1; LAW

**Lu Hsun** .............................. **SSC 20; TCLC 3**
See Shu-Jen, Chou

**Lukacs, George** .............................. **CLC 24**
See Lukacs, Gyorgy (Szegeny von)

**Lukacs, Gyorgy (Szegeny von)** 1885-1971
See Lukacs, George
See also CA 101; CANR 62; CDWLB 4; DLB 215, 242; EW 10; MTCW 2

**Luke, Peter (Ambrose Cyprian)**
1919-1995 ..................................... **CLC 38**
See also CA 81-84; CANR 72; CBD; CD 5; DLB 13

**Lunar, Dennis**
See Mungo, Raymond

**Lurie, Alison** 1926- .............. **CLC 4, 5, 18, 39**
See also BPFB 2; CA 1-4R; CANR 2, 17, 50, 88; CN 7; DLB 2; MTCW 1; SATA 46, 112

**Lustig, Arnost** 1926- ........................ **CLC 56**
See also AAYA 3; CA 69-72; CANR 47, 102; CWW 2; DLB 232; SATA 56

**Luther, Martin** 1483-1546 ............... **LC 9, 37**
See also CDWLB 2; DLB 179; EW 2; RGWL 2, 3

**Luxemburg, Rosa** 1870(?)-1919 ..... **TCLC 63**

**Luzi, Mario** 1914- ............................ **CLC 13**
See also CA 61-64; CANR 9, 70; CWW 2; DLB 128

**L'vov, Arkady** .................................. **CLC 59**

**Lydgate, John** c. 1370-1450(?) ............... **LC 81**
See also BRW 1; DLB 146; RGEL 2

**Lyly, John** 1554(?)-1606 ............ **DC 7; LC 41**
See also BRW 1; DAM DRAM; DLB 62, 167; RGEL 2

**L'Ymagier**
See Gourmont, Remy(-Marie-Charles) de

**Lynch, B. Suarez**
See Borges, Jorge Luis

**Lynch, David (Keith)** 1946- ...... **CLC 66, 162**
See also CA 129; CANR 111

**Lynch, James**
See Andreyev, Leonid (Nikolaevich)

**Lyndsay, Sir David** 1485-1555 ............ **LC 20**
See also RGEL 2

**Lynn, Kenneth S(chuyler)**
1923-2001 ..................................... **CLC 50**
See also CA 1-4R; CANR 3, 27, 65

**Lynx**
See West, Rebecca

**Lyons, Marcus**
See Blish, James (Benjamin)

**Lyotard, Jean-Francois**
1924-1998 .................................. **TCLC 103**
See also DLB 242

**Lyre, Pinchbeck**
See Sassoon, Siegfried (Lorraine)

**Lytle, Andrew (Nelson)** 1902-1995 ... **CLC 22**
See also CA 9-12R; CANR 70; CN 7; CSW; DLB 6; DLBY 1995; RGAL 4; RHW

**Lyttelton, George** 1709-1773 ................ **LC 10**
See also RGEL 2

**Lytton of Knebworth, Baron**
See Bulwer-Lytton, Edward (George Earle Lytton)

**Maas, Peter** 1929-2001 ....................... **CLC 29**
See also CA 93-96; INT CA-93-96; MTCW 2

**Macaulay, Catherine** 1731-1791 .......... **LC 64**
See also DLB 104

**Macaulay, (Emilie) Rose**
1881(?)-1958 ........................ **TCLC 7, 44**
See also DLB 36; RGEL 2; RHW

**Macaulay, Thomas Babington**
1800-1859 ..................................... **NCLC 42**
See also BRW 4; CDBLB 1832-1890; DLB 32, 55; RGEL 2

**MacBeth, George (Mann)**
1932-1992 ............................. **CLC 2, 5, 9**
See also CA 25-28R; CANR 61, 66; DLB 40; MTCW 1; PFS 8; SATA 4; SATA-Obit 70

**MacCaig, Norman (Alexander)**
1910-1996 ..................................... **CLC 36**
See also BRWS 6; CA 9-12R; CANR 3, 34; CP 7; DAB; DAM POET; DLB 27; RGEL 2

**MacCarthy, Sir (Charles Otto) Desmond**
1877-1952 ..................................... **TCLC 36**
See also CA 167

**MacDiarmid, Hugh** .... **CLC 2, 4, 11, 19, 63; PC 9**
See Grieve, C(hristopher) M(urray)
See also CDBLB 1945-1960; DLB 20; RGEL 2

**MacDonald, Anson**
See Heinlein, Robert A(nson)

**Macdonald, Cynthia** 1928- ......... **CLC 13, 19**
See also CA 49-52; CANR 4, 44; DLB 105

**MacDonald, George** 1824-1905 ....... **TCLC 9, 113**
See also BYA 5; CA 137; CANR 80; CLR 67; DLB 18, 163, 178; FANT; MAICYA 1, 2; RGEL 2; SATA 33, 100; SFW 4; SUFW; WCH

**Macdonald, John**
See Millar, Kenneth

**MacDonald, John D(ann)**
1916-1986 .............................. **CLC 3, 27, 44**
See also BPFB 2; CA 1-4R; CANR 1, 19, 60; CMW 4; CPW; DAM NOV, POP; DLB 8; DLBY 1986; MSW; MTCW 1, 2; SFW 4

**Macdonald, John Ross**
See Millar, Kenneth

**Macdonald, Ross** ..... **CLC 1, 2, 3, 14, 34, 41**
See Millar, Kenneth
See also AMWS 4; BPFB 2; DLBD 6; MSW; RGAL 4

**MacDougal, John**
See Blish, James (Benjamin)

**MacDougal, John**
See Blish, James (Benjamin)

**MacDowell, John**
See Parks, Tim(othy Harold)

**MacEwen, Gwendolyn (Margaret)**
1941-1987 ............................... **CLC 13, 55**
See also CA 9-12R; CANR 7, 22; DLB 53, 251; SATA 50; SATA-Obit 55

**Macha, Karel Hynek** 1810-1846 .... **NCLC 46**

**Machado (y Ruiz), Antonio**
1875-1939 ....................................... **TCLC 3**
See also CA 174; DLB 108; EW 9; HW 2; RGWL 2, 3

**Machado de Assis, Joaquim Maria**
1839-1908 .... **BLC 2; HLCS 2; SSC 24; TCLC 10**
See also CA 153; CANR 91; LAW; RGSF 2; RGWL 2, 3; TWA; WLIT 1

**Machen, Arthur** ................ **SSC 20; TCLC 4**
See Jones, Arthur Llewellyn
See also DLB 179; DLB 156, 178; RGEL 2; SUFW 1

**Machiavelli, Niccolo** 1469-1527 ... **DC 16; LC 8, 36; WLCS**
See also DA; DAB; DAC; DAM MST; EW 2; LAIT 1; NFS 9; RGWL 2, 3; TWA

**MacInnes, Colin** 1914-1976 .......... **CLC 4, 23**
See also CA 69-72; CANR 21; DLB 14; MTCW 1, 2; RGEL 2; RHW

**MacInnes, Helen (Clark)**
1907-1985 ............................. **CLC 27, 39**
See also BPFB 2; CA 1-4R; CANR 1, 28, 58; CMW 4; CPW; DAM POP; DLB 87; MSW; MTCW 1, 2; SATA 22; SATA-Obit 44

**Mackay, Mary** 1855-1924
See Corelli, Marie
See also CA 177; FANT; RHW

**Mackenzie, Compton (Edward Montague)**
1883-1972 ............... **CLC 18; TCLC 116**
See also CA 21-22; CAP 2; DLB 34, 100; RGEL 2

**Mackenzie, Henry** 1745-1831 ......... **NCLC 41**
See also DLB 39; RGEL 2

**Mackintosh, Elizabeth** 1896(?)-1952
See Tey, Josephine
See also CMW 4

**MacLaren, James**
See Grieve, C(hristopher) M(urray)

**Mac Laverty, Bernard** 1942- ............ **CLC 31**
See also CA 118; CANR 43, 88; CN 7; DLB 267; INT CA-118; RGSF 2

**MacLean, Alistair (Stuart)**
1922(?)-1987 ............... **CLC 3, 13, 50, 63**
See also CA 57-60; CANR 28, 61; CMW 4; CPW; DAM POP; MTCW 1; SATA 23; SATA-Obit 50; TCWW 2

**Maclean, Norman (Fitzroy)**
1902-1990 .................... **CLC 78; SSC 13**
See also CA 102; CANR 49; CPW; DAM POP; DLB 206; TCWW 2

**MacLeish, Archibald** 1892-1982 ... **CLC 3, 8, 14, 68**
See also AMW; CA 9-12R; CAD; CANR 33, 63; CDALBS; DAM POET; DFS 15; DLB 4, 7, 45; DLBY 1982; EXPP; MTCW 1, 2; PAB; PFS 5; RGAL 4; TUS

**MacLennan, (John) Hugh**
1907-1990 ........................ **CLC 2, 14, 92**
See also CA 5-8R; CANR 33; DAC; DAM MST; DLB 68; MTCW 1, 2; RGEL 2; TWA

**MacLeod, Alistair** 1936- ............. **CLC 56, 165**
See also CA 123; CCA 1; DAC; DAM MST; DLB 60; MTCW 2; RGSF 2

**Macleod, Fiona**
See Sharp, William
See also RGEL 2; SUFW

**MacNeice, (Frederick) Louis**
1907-1963 .................... **CLC 1, 4, 10, 53**
See also BRW 7; CA 85-88; CANR 61; DAB; DAM POET; DLB 10, 20; MTCW 1, 2; RGEL 2

**MacNeill, Dand**
See Fraser, George MacDonald

**Macpherson, James** 1736-1796 ............ **LC 29**
See Ossian
See also BRWS 8; DLB 109; RGEL 2

**Macpherson, (Jean) Jay** 1931- ......... **CLC 14**
See also CA 5-8R; CANR 90; CP 7; CWP; DLB 53

**Macrobius** fl. 430- .......................... **CMLC 48**

**MacShane, Frank** 1927-1999 ............ **CLC 39**
See also CA 9-12R; CANR 3, 33; DLB 111

**Macumber, Mari**
See Sandoz, Mari(e Susette)

**Madach, Imre** 1823-1864 ............... **NCLC 19**

**Madden, (Jerry) David** 1933- ....... **CLC 5, 15**
See also CA 1-4R; CAAS 3; CANR 4, 45; CN 7; CSW; DLB 6; MTCW 1

**Maddern, Al(an)**
See Ellison, Harlan (Jay)

**Madhubuti, Haki R.** 1942- ... **BLC 2; CLC 6, 73; PC 5**
See Lee, Don L.
See also BW 2, 3; CA 73-76; CANR 24, 51, 73; CP 7; CSW; DAM MULT, POET; DLB 5, 41; DLBD 8; RGAL 4

**Maepenn, Hugh**
See Kuttner, Henry

**Maepenn, K. H.**
See Kuttner, Henry

**Maeterlinck, Maurice** 1862-1949 ..... **TCLC 3**
See also CA 136; CANR 80; DAM DRAM; DLB 192; EW 8; GFL 1789 to the Present; RGWL 2, 3; SATA 66; TWA

**Maginn, William** 1794-1842 ............. **NCLC 8**
See also DLB 110, 159

**Mahapatra, Jayanta** 1928- ................. **CLC 33**
See also CA 73-76; CAAS 9; CANR 15, 33, 66, 87; CP 7; DAM MULT

**Mahfouz, Naguib (Abdel Aziz Al-Sabilgi)**
1911(?)- ...................................... **CLC 153**
See Mahfuz, Najib (Abdel Aziz al-Sabilgi)
See also BEST 89:2; CA 128; CANR 55, 101; CWW 2; DAM NOV; MTCW 1, 2; RGWL 2, 3; SSFS 9

**Mahfuz, Najib (Abdel Aziz al-Sabilgi)**
............................................. **CLC 52, 55**
See Mahfouz, Naguib (Abdel Aziz Al-Sabilgi)
See also AFW; DLBY 1988; RGSF 2; WLIT 2

**Mahon, Derek** 1941- ......................... **CLC 27**
See also BRWS 6; CA 128; CANR 88; CP 7; DLB 40

**Maiakovskii, Vladimir**
See Mayakovski, Vladimir (Vladimirovich)
See also IDTP; RGWL 2, 3

**Mailer, Norman** 1923- ... **CLC 1, 2, 3, 4, 5, 8, 11, 14, 28, 39, 74, 111**
See also AAYA 31; AITN 2; AMW; AMWR 2; BPFB 2; CA 9-12R; CABS 1; CANR 28, 74, 77; CDALB 1968-1988; CN 7; CPW; DA; DAB; DAC; DAM MST, NOV, POP; DLB 2, 16, 28, 185; DLBD 3; DLBY 1980, 1983; MTCW 1, 2; NFS 10; RGAL 4; TUS

**Maillet, Antonine** 1929- ............. **CLC 54, 118**
See also CA 120; CANR 46, 74, 77; CCA 1; CWW 2; DAC; DLB 60; INT 120; MTCW 2

**Mais, Roger** 1905-1955 ...................... **TCLC 8**
See also BW 1, 3; CA 124; CANR 82; CDWLB 3; DLB 125; MTCW 1; RGEL 2

**Maistre, Joseph** 1753-1821 ............. **NCLC 37**
See also GFL 1789 to the Present

**Maitland, Frederic William**
1850-1906 ................................. **TCLC 65**

**Maitland, Sara (Louise)** 1950- .......... **CLC 49**
See also CA 69-72; CANR 13, 59; DLB 271; FW

**Major, Clarence** 1936- ... **BLC 2; CLC 3, 19, 48**
See also AFAW 2; BW 2, 3; CA 21-24R; CAAS 6; CANR 13, 25, 53, 82; CN 7; CP 7; CSW; DAM MULT; DLB 33; MSW

**Major, Kevin (Gerald)** 1949- .............. **CLC 26**
See also AAYA 16; CA 97-100; CANR 21, 38, 112; CLR 11; DAC; DLB 60; INT CANR-21; JRDA; MAICYA 1, 2; MAICYAS 1; SATA 32, 82, 134; WYA; YAW

**Maki, James**
See Ozu, Yasujiro

**Malabaila, Damiano**
See Levi, Primo

**Malamud, Bernard** 1914-1986 .. **CLC 1, 2, 3, 5, 8, 9, 11, 18, 27, 44, 78, 85; SSC 15; TCLC 129; WLC**
See also AAYA 16; AMWS 1; BPFB 2; CA 5-8R; CABS 1; CANR 28, 62, 114; CDALB 1941-1968; CPW; DA; DAB; DAC; DAM MST, NOV, POP; DLB 2, 28, 152; DLBY 1980, 1986; EXPS; LAIT 4; MTCW 1, 2; NFS 4, 9; RGAL 4; RGSF 2; SSFS 8, 13, 16; TUS

**Malan, Herman**
See Bosman, Herman Charles; Bosman, Herman Charles

**Malaparte, Curzio** 1898-1957 ........ **TCLC 52**
See also DLB 264

**Malcolm, Dan**
See Silverberg, Robert

**Malcolm X** .... **BLC 2; CLC 82, 117; WLCS**
See Little, Malcolm
See also LAIT 5

**Malherbe, Francois de** 1555-1628 ......... **LC 5**
See also GFL Beginnings to 1789

**Mallarme, Stephane** 1842-1898 ...... **NCLC 4, 41; PC 4**
See also DAM POET; DLB 217; EW 7; GFL 1789 to the Present; RGWL 2, 3; TWA

**Mallet-Joris, Francoise** 1930- ........... **CLC 11**
See also CA 65-68; CANR 17; DLB 83; GFL 1789 to the Present

**Malley, Ern**
See McAuley, James Phillip

**Mallowan, Agatha Christie**
See Christie, Agatha (Mary Clarissa)

**Maloff, Saul** 1922- ............................... **CLC 5**
See also CA 33-36R

**Malone, Louis**
See MacNeice, (Frederick) Louis

**Malone, Michael (Christopher)**
1942- ...................................... **CLC 43**
See also CA 77-80; CANR 14, 32, 57, 114

**Malory, Sir Thomas** 1410(?)-1471(?) . **LC 11; WLCS**
See also BRW 1; BRWR 2; CDBLB Before 1660; DA; DAB; DAC; DAM MST; DLB 146; EFS 2; RGEL 2; SATA 59; SATA-Brief 33; TEA; WLIT 3

**Malouf, (George Joseph) David**
1934- ...................................... **CLC 28, 86**
See also CA 124; CANR 50, 76; CN 7; CP 7; MTCW 2

**Malraux, (Georges-)Andre**
1901-1976 .......... **CLC 1, 4, 9, 13, 15, 57**
See also BPFB 2; CA 21-22; CANR 34, 58; CAP 2; DAM NOV; DLB 72; EW 12; GFL 1789 to the Present; MTCW 1, 2; RGWL 2, 3; TWA

**Malzberg, Barry N(athaniel)** 1939- ... **CLC 7**
See also CA 61-64; CAAS 4; CANR 16; CMW 4; DLB 8; SFW 4

**Mamet, David (Alan)** 1947- .. **CLC 9, 15, 34, 46, 91, 166; DC 4**
See also AAYA 3; CA 81-84; CABS 3; CANR 15, 41, 67, 72; CD 5; DAM DRAM; DFS 15; DLB 7; IDFW 4; MTCW 1, 2; RGAL 4

**Mamoulian, Rouben (Zachary)**
1897-1987 ................................. **CLC 16**
See also CA 25-28R; CANR 85

**Mandelshtam, Osip**
See Mandelstam, Osip (Emilievich)
See also EW 10; RGWL 2, 3

**Mandelstam, Osip (Emilievich)**
1891(?)-1943(?) ........ **PC 14; TCLC 2, 6**
See Mandelshtam, Osip
See also CA 150; MTCW 2; TWA

**Mander, (Mary) Jane** 1877-1949 ... **TCLC 31**
See also CA 162; RGEL 2

**Mandeville, Bernard** 1670-1733 .......... **LC 82**
See also DLB 101

**Mandeville, Sir John** fl. 1350- ...... **CMLC 19**
See also DLB 146

**Mandiargues, Andre Pieyre de** ........ **CLC 41**
See Pieyre de Mandiargues, Andre
See also DLB 83

**Mandrake, Ethel Belle**
See Thurman, Wallace (Henry)

**Mangan, James Clarence**
1803-1849 ................................. **NCLC 27**
See also RGEL 2

**Maniere, J.-E.**
See Giraudoux, Jean(-Hippolyte)

**Mankiewicz, Herman (Jacob)**
1897-1953 ................................. **TCLC 85**
See also CA 169; DLB 26; IDFW 3, 4

**Manley, (Mary) Delariviere**
1672(?)-1724 ............................. **LC 1, 42**
See also DLB 39, 80; RGEL 2

**Mann, Abel**
See Creasey, John

**Mann, Emily** 1952- ............................... **DC 7**
See also CA 130; CAD; CANR 55; CD 5; CWD; DLB 266

**Mann, (Luiz) Heinrich** 1871-1950 ... **TCLC 9**
See also CA 164, 181; DLB 66, 118; EW 8; RGWL 2, 3

**Mann, (Paul) Thomas** 1875-1955 ........ **SSC 5; TCLC 2, 8, 14, 21, 35, 44, 60; WLC**
See also BPFB 2; CA 128; CDWLB 2; DA; DAB; DAC; DAM MST, NOV; DLB 66; EW 9; GLL 1; MTCW 1, 2; RGSF 2; RGWL 2, 3; SSFS 4, 9; TWA

**Mannheim, Karl** 1893-1947 ........... **TCLC 65**
See also CA 204

**Manning, David**
See Faust, Frederick (Schiller)
See also TCWW 2

**Manning, Frederic** 1887(?)-1935 ... **TCLC 25**
See also DLB 260

**Manning, Olivia** 1915-1980 ........... **CLC 5, 19**
See also CA 5-8R; CANR 29; FW; MTCW 1; RGEL 2

**Mano, D. Keith** 1942- .................... **CLC 2, 10**
See also CA 25-28R; CAAS 6; CANR 26, 57; DLB 6

**Mansfield, Katherine** . **SSC 9, 23, 38; TCLC 2, 8, 39; WLC**
See Beauchamp, Kathleen Mansfield
See also BPFB 2; BRW 7; DAB; DLB 162; EXPS; FW; GLL 1; RGEL 2; RGSF 2; SSFS 2, 8, 10, 11

**Manso, Peter** 1940- ........................... **CLC 39**
See also CA 29-32R; CANR 44

**Mantecon, Juan Jimenez**
See Jimenez (Mantecon), Juan Ramon

**Mantel, Hilary (Mary)** 1952- .......... **CLC 144**
See also CA 125; CANR 54, 101; CN 7; DLB 271; RHW

**Manton, Peter**
See Creasey, John

**Man Without a Spleen, A**
See Chekhov, Anton (Pavlovich)

**Manzoni, Alessandro** 1785-1873 ... **NCLC 29, 98**
See also EW 5; RGWL 2, 3; TWA

**Map, Walter** 1140-1209 ................. **CMLC 32**

**Mapu, Abraham (ben Jekutiel)**
1808-1867 ................................. **NCLC 18**

**Mara, Sally**
See Queneau, Raymond

**Marat, Jean Paul** 1743-1793 ................ **LC 10**

**Marcel, Gabriel Honore** 1889-1973 . **CLC 15**
See also CA 102; MTCW 1, 2

**March, William** 1893-1954 ............. **TCLC 96**

**Marchbanks, Samuel**
See Davies, (William) Robertson
See also CCA 1

**Marchi, Giacomo**
See Bassani, Giorgio

**Marcus Aurelius**
See Aurelius, Marcus
See also AW 2

**Marguerite**
See de Navarre, Marguerite

**Marguerite d'Angouleme**
See de Navarre, Marguerite
See also GFL Beginnings to 1789
**Marguerite de Navarre**
See de Navarre, Marguerite
See also RGWL 2, 3
**Margulies, Donald** 1954- .................. **CLC 76**
See also CA 200; DFS 13; DLB 228
**Marie de France** c. 12th cent. - ...... **CMLC 8; PC 22**
See also DLB 208; FW; RGWL 2, 3
**Marie de l'Incarnation** 1599-1672 ...... **LC 10**
**Marier, Captain Victor**
See Griffith, D(avid Lewelyn) W(ark)
**Mariner, Scott**
See Pohl, Frederik
**Marinetti, Filippo Tommaso**
1876-1944 .................................. **TCLC 10**
See also DLB 114, 264; EW 9
**Marivaux, Pierre Carlet de Chamblain de**
1688-1763 ............................. **DC 7; LC 4**
See also GFL Beginnings to 1789; RGWL 2, 3; TWA
**Markandaya, Kamala** ................. **CLC 8, 38**
See Taylor, Kamala (Purnaiya)
See also BYA 13; CN 7
**Markfield, Wallace** 1926- .................. **CLC 8**
See also CA 69-72; CAAS 3; CN 7; DLB 2, 28
**Markham, Edwin** 1852-1940 .......... **TCLC 47**
See also CA 160; DLB 54, 186; RGAL 4
**Markham, Robert**
See Amis, Kingsley (William)
**Marks, J**
See Highwater, Jamake (Mamake)
**Marks, J.**
See Highwater, Jamake (Mamake)
**Marks-Highwater, J**
See Highwater, Jamake (Mamake)
**Marks-Highwater, J.**
See Highwater, Jamake (Mamake)
**Markson, David M(errill)** 1927- ........ **CLC 67**
See also CA 49-52; CANR 1, 91; CN 7
**Marlatt, Daphne (Buckle)** 1942- .... **CLC 168**
See also CA 25-28R; CANR 17, 39; CN 7; CP 7; CWP; DLB 60; FW
**Marley, Bob** ....................................... **CLC 17**
See Marley, Robert Nesta
**Marley, Robert Nesta** 1945-1981
See Marley, Bob
See also CA 107
**Marlowe, Christopher** 1564-1593 . **DC 1; LC 22, 47; WLC**
See also BRW 1; BRWR 1; CDBLB Before 1660; DA; DAB; DAC; DAM DRAM, MST; DFS 1, 5, 13; DLB 62; EXPP; RGEL 2; TEA; WLIT 3
**Marlowe, Stephen** 1928- .................. **CLC 70**
See Queen, Ellery
See also CA 13-16R; CANR 6, 55; CMW 4; SFW 4
**Marmontel, Jean-Francois** 1723-1799 .. **LC 2**
**Maron, Monika** 1941- ..................... **CLC 165**
See also CA 201
**Marquand, John P(hillips)**
1893-1960 .............................. **CLC 2, 10**
See also AMW; BPFB 2; CA 85-88; CANR 73; CMW 4; DLB 9, 102; MTCW 2; RGAL 4
**Marques, Rene** 1919-1979 .. **CLC 96; HLC 2**
See also CA 97-100; CANR 78; DAM MULT; DLB 113; HW 1, 2; LAW; RGSF 2
**Marquez, Gabriel (Jose) Garcia**
See Garcia Marquez, Gabriel (Jose)
**Marquis, Don(ald Robert Perry)**
1878-1937 ................................... **TCLC 7**
See also CA 166; DLB 11, 25; RGAL 4

**Marquis de Sade**
See Sade, Donatien Alphonse Francois
**Marric, J. J.**
See Creasey, John
See also MSW
**Marryat, Frederick** 1792-1848 ........ **NCLC 3**
See also DLB 21, 163; RGEL 2; WCH
**Marsden, James**
See Creasey, John
**Marsh, Edward** 1872-1953 ............. **TCLC 99**
**Marsh, (Edith) Ngaio** 1899-1982 .. **CLC 7, 53**
See also CA 9-12R; CANR 6, 58; CMW 4; CPW; DAM POP; DLB 77; MSW; MTCW 1, 2; RGEL 2; TEA
**Marshall, Garry** 1934- ....................... **CLC 17**
See also AAYA 3; CA 111; SATA 60
**Marshall, Paule** 1929- .. **BLC 3; CLC 27, 72; SSC 3**
See also AFAW 1, 2; AMWS 11; BPFB 2; BW 2, 3; CA 77-80; CANR 25, 73; CN 7; DAM MULT; DLB 33, 157, 227; MTCW 1, 2; RGAL 4; SSFS 15
**Marshallik**
See Zangwill, Israel
**Marsten, Richard**
See Hunter, Evan
**Marston, John** 1576-1634 ..................... **LC 33**
See also BRW 2; DAM DRAM; DLB 58, 172; RGEL 2
**Martha, Henry**
See Harris, Mark
**Marti (y Perez), Jose (Julian)**
1853-1895 .................. **HLC 2; NCLC 63**
See also DAM MULT; HW 2; LAW; RGWL 2, 3; WLIT 1
**Martial** c. 40-c. 104 ........... **CMLC 35; PC 10**
See also AW 2; CDWLB 1; DLB 211; RGWL 2, 3
**Martin, Ken**
See Hubbard, L(afayette) Ron(ald)
**Martin, Richard**
See Creasey, John
**Martin, Steve** 1945- ........................... **CLC 30**
See also CA 97-100; CANR 30, 100; MTCW 1
**Martin, Valerie** 1948- ........................ **CLC 89**
See also BEST 90:2; CA 85-88; CANR 49, 89
**Martin, Violet Florence** 1862-1915 .. **SSC 56; TCLC 51**
**Martin, Webber**
See Silverberg, Robert
**Martindale, Patrick Victor**
See White, Patrick (Victor Martindale)
**Martin du Gard, Roger**
1881-1958 ....................... **TCLC 24**
See also CANR 94; DLB 65; GFL 1789 to the Present; RGWL 2, 3
**Martineau, Harriet** 1802-1876 ...... **NCLC 26**
See also DLB 21, 55, 159, 163, 166, 190; FW; RGEL 2; YABC 2
**Martines, Julia**
See O'Faolain, Julia
**Martinez, Enrique Gonzalez**
See Gonzalez Martinez, Enrique
**Martinez, Jacinto Benavente y**
See Benavente (y Martinez), Jacinto
**Martinez de la Rosa, Francisco de Paula**
1787-1862 ............................. **NCLC 102**
See also TWA
**Martinez Ruiz, Jose** 1873-1967
See Azorin; Ruiz, Jose Martinez
See also CA 93-96; HW 1

**Martinez Sierra, Gregorio**
1881-1947 ................................... **TCLC 6**
**Martinez Sierra, Maria (de la O'LeJarraga)**
1874-1974 ................................... **TCLC 6**
**Martinsen, Martin**
See Follett, Ken(neth Martin)
**Martinson, Harry (Edmund)**
1904-1978 ................................. **CLC 14**
See also CA 77-80; CANR 34; DLB 259
**Martyn, Edward** 1859-1923 ......... **TCLC 131**
See also CA 179; DLB 10; RGEL 2
**Marut, Ret**
See Traven, B.
**Marut, Robert**
See Traven, B.
**Marvell, Andrew** 1621-1678 .... **LC 4, 43; PC 10; WLC**
See also BRW 2; BRWR 2; CDBLB 1660-1789; DA; DAB; DAC; DAM MST, POET; DLB 131; EXPP; PFS 5; RGEL 2; TEA; WP
**Marx, Karl (Heinrich)**
1818-1883 ............................ **NCLC 17, 114**
See also DLB 129; TWA
**Masaoka, Shiki** -1902 ..................... **TCLC 18**
See Masaoka, Tsunenori
See also RGWL 3
**Masaoka, Tsunenori** 1867-1902
See Masaoka, Shiki
See also CA 191; TWA
**Masefield, John (Edward)**
1878-1967 ............................. **CLC 11, 47**
See also CA 19-20; CANR 33; CAP 2; CDBLB 1890-1914; DAM POET; DLB 10, 19, 153, 160; EXPP; FANT; MTCW 1, 2; PFS 5; RGEL 2; SATA 19
**Maso, Carole** 19(?)- ............................ **CLC 44**
See also CA 170; GLL 2; RGAL 4
**Mason, Bobbie Ann** 1940- ... **CLC 28, 43, 82, 154; SSC 4**
See also AAYA 5, 42; AMWS 8; BPFB 2; CA 53-56; CANR 11, 31, 58, 83; CDALBS; CN 7; CSW; DLB 173; DLBY 1987; EXPS; INT CANR-31; MTCW 1, 2; NFS 4; RGAL 4; RGSF 2; SSFS 3,8; YAW
**Mason, Ernst**
See Pohl, Frederik
**Mason, Hunni B.**
See Sternheim, (William Adolf) Carl
**Mason, Lee W.**
See Malzberg, Barry N(athaniel)
**Mason, Nick** 1945- ............................ **CLC 35**
**Mason, Tally**
See Derleth, August (William)
**Mass, Anna** ......................................... **CLC 59**
**Mass, William**
See Gibson, William
**Massinger, Philip** 1583-1640 ............... **LC 70**
See also DLB 58; RGEL 2
**Master Lao**
See Lao Tzu
**Masters, Edgar Lee** 1868-1950 ...... **PC 1, 36; TCLC 2, 25; WLCS**
See also AMWS 1; CA 133; CDALB 1865-1917; DA; DAC; DAM MST, POET; DLB 54; EXPP; MTCW 1, 2; RGAL 4; TUS; WP
**Masters, Hilary** 1928- ........................ **CLC 48**
See also CA 25-28R; CANR 13, 47, 97; CN 7; DLB 244
**Mastrosimone, William** 19(?)- .......... **CLC 36**
See also CA 186; CAD; CD 5
**Mathe, Albert**
See Camus, Albert
**Mather, Cotton** 1663-1728 .................. **LC 38**
See also AMWS 2; CDALB 1640-1865; DLB 24, 30, 140; RGAL 4; TUS

**Mather, Increase** 1639-1723 .................. **LC 38**
See also DLB 24

**Matheson, Richard (Burton)** 1926- .. **CLC 37**
See also AAYA 31; CA 97-100; CANR 88, 99; DLB 8, 44; HGG; INT 97-100; SCFW 2; SFW 4; SUFW 2

**Mathews, Harry** 1930- .................. **CLC 6, 52**
See also CA 21-24R; CAAS 6; CANR 18, 40, 98; CN 7

**Mathews, John Joseph** 1894-1979 .. **CLC 84; NNAL**
See also CA 19-20; CANR 45; CAP 2; DAM MULT; DLB 175

**Mathias, Roland (Glyn)** 1915- .......... **CLC 45**
See also CA 97-100; CANR 19, 41; CP 7; DLB 27

**Matsuo Basho** 1644-1694 .......... **LC 62; PC 3**
See Basho, Matsuo
See also DAM POET; PFS 2, 7

**Mattheson, Rodney**
See Creasey, John

**Matthews, (James) Brander**
1852-1929 .................. **TCLC 95**
See also DLB 71, 78; DLBD 13

**Matthews, Greg** 1949- ...................... **CLC 45**
See also CA 135

**Matthews, William (Procter III)**
1942-1997 ............................ **CLC 40**
See also AMWS 9; CA 29-32R; CAAS 18; CANR 12, 57; CP 7; DLB 5

**Matthias, John (Edward)** 1941- ......... **CLC 9**
See also CA 33-36R; CANR 56; CP 7

**Matthiessen, F(rancis) O(tto)**
1902-1950 .................. **TCLC 100**
See also CA 185; DLB 63

**Matthiessen, Peter** 1927- ... **CLC 5, 7, 11, 32, 64**
See also AAYA 6, 40; AMWS 5; ANW; BEST 90:4; BPFB 2; CA 9-12R; CANR 21, 50, 73, 100; CN 7; DAM NOV; DLB 6, 173, 275; MTCW 1, 2; SATA 27

**Maturin, Charles Robert**
1780(?)-1824 .................. **NCLC 6**
See also BRWS 8; DLB 178; HGG; RGEL 2; SUFW

**Matute (Ausejo), Ana Maria** 1925- .. **CLC 11**
See also CA 89-92; MTCW 1; RGSF 2

**Maugham, W. S.**
See Maugham, W(illiam) Somerset

**Maugham, W(illiam) Somerset**
1874-1965 .. **CLC 1, 11, 15, 67, 93; SSC 8; WLC**
See also BPFB 2; BRW 6; CA 5-8R; CANR 40; CDBLB 1914-1945; CMW 4; DA; DAB; DAC; DAM DRAM, MST, NOV; DLB 10, 36, 77, 100, 162, 195; LAIT 3; MTCW 1, 2; RGEL 2; RGSF 2; SATA 54

**Maugham, William Somerset**
See Maugham, W(illiam) Somerset

**Maupassant, (Henri Rene Albert) Guy de**
1850-1893 ....... **NCLC 1, 42, 83; SSC 1; WLC**
See also BYA 14; DA; DAB; DAC; DAM MST; DLB 123; EW 7; EXPS; GFL 1789 to the Present; LAIT 2; RGSF 2; RGWL 2, 3; SSFS 4; SUFW; TWA

**Maupin, Armistead (Jones, Jr.)**
1944- ............................ **CLC 95**
See also CA 130; CANR 58, 101; CPW; DAM POP; GLL 1; INT 130; MTCW 2

**Maurhut, Richard**
See Traven, B.

**Mauriac, Claude** 1914-1996 ............ **CLC 9**
See also CA 89-92; CWW 2; DLB 83; GFL 1789 to the Present

**Mauriac, Francois (Charles)**
1885-1970 ........... **CLC 4, 9, 56; SSC 24**
See also CA 25-28; CAP 2; DLB 65; EW 10; GFL 1789 to the Present; MTCW 1, 2; RGWL 2, 3; TWA

**Mavor, Osborne Henry** 1888-1951
See Bridie, James

**Maxwell, William (Keepers, Jr.)**
1908-2000 .................. **CLC 19**
See also AMWS 8; CA 93-96; CANR 54, 95; CN 7; DLB 218; DLBY 1980; INT CA-93-96; SATA-Obit 128

**May, Elaine** 1932- ............................ **CLC 16**
See also CA 142; CAD; CWD; DLB 44

**Mayakovski, Vladimir (Vladimirovich)**
1893-1930 .................. **TCLC 4, 18**
See Maiakovskii, Vladimir; Mayakovsky, Vladimir
See also CA 158; MTCW 2; SFW 4; TWA

**Mayakovsky, Vladimir**
See Mayakovski, Vladimir (Vladimirovich)
See also EW 11; WP

**Mayhew, Henry** 1812-1887 ............. **NCLC 31**
See also DLB 18, 55, 190

**Mayle, Peter** 1939(?)- ...................... **CLC 89**
See also CA 139; CANR 64, 109

**Maynard, Joyce** 1953- ...................... **CLC 23**
See also CA 129; CANR 64

**Mayne, William (James Carter)**
1928- ............................ **CLC 12**
See also AAYA 20; CA 9-12R; CANR 37, 80, 100; CLR 25; FANT; JRDA; MAI-CYA 1, 2; MAICYAS 1; SAAS 11; SATA 6, 68, 122; SUFW 2; YAW

**Mayo, Jim**
See L'Amour, Louis (Dearborn)
See also TCWW 2

**Maysles, Albert** 1926- ...................... **CLC 16**
See also CA 29-32R

**Maysles, David** 1932-1987 .................. **CLC 16**
See also CA 191

**Mazer, Norma Fox** 1931- ...................... **CLC 26**
See also AAYA 5, 36; BYA 1, 8; CA 69-72; CANR 12, 32, 66; CLR 23; JRDA; MAI-CYA 1, 2; SAAS 1; SATA 24, 67, 105; WYA; YAW

**Mazzini, Guiseppe** 1805-1872 ........ **NCLC 34**

**McAlmon, Robert (Menzies)**
1895-1956 .................. **TCLC 97**
See also CA 168; DLB 4, 45; DLBD 15; GLL 1

**McAuley, James Phillip** 1917-1976 .. **CLC 45**
See also CA 97-100; DLB 260; RGEL 2

**McBain, Ed**
See Hunter, Evan
See also MSW

**McBrien, William (Augustine)**
1930- ............................ **CLC 44**
See also CA 107; CANR 90

**McCabe, Patrick** 1955- ...................... **CLC 133**
See also CA 130; CANR 50, 90; CN 7; DLB 194

**McCaffrey, Anne (Inez)** 1926- .......... **CLC 17**
See also AAYA 6, 34; AITN 2; BEST 89:2; BPFB 2; BYA 5; CA 25-28R; CANR 15, 35, 55, 96; CLR 49; CPW; DAM NOV, POP; DLB 8; JRDA; MAICYA 1, 2; MTCW 1, 2; SAAS 11; SATA 8, 70, 116; SFW 4; SUFW 2; WYA; YAW

**McCall, Nathan** 1955(?)- .................. **CLC 86**
See also BW 3; CA 146; CANR 88

**McCann, Arthur**
See Campbell, John W(ood, Jr.)

**McCann, Edson**
See Pohl, Frederik

**McCarthy, Charles, Jr.** 1933-
See McCarthy, Cormac
See also CANR 42, 69, 101; CN 7; CPW; CSW; DAM POP; MTCW 2

**McCarthy, Cormac** ........ **CLC 4, 57, 59, 101**
See McCarthy, Charles, Jr.
See also AAYA 41; AMWS 8; BPFB 2; CA 13-16R; CANR 10; DLB 6, 143, 256; TCWW 2

**McCarthy, Mary (Therese)**
1912-1989 .. **CLC 1, 3, 5, 14, 24, 39, 59; SSC 24**
See also AMW; BPFB 2; CA 5-8R; CANR 16, 50, 64; DLB 2; DLBY 1981; FW; INT CANR-16; MAWW; MTCW 1, 2; RGAL 4; TUS

**McCartney, (James) Paul** 1942- . **CLC 12, 35**
See also CA 146; CANR 111

**McCauley, Stephen (D.)** 1955- .......... **CLC 50**
See also CA 141

**McClaren, Peter** ............................ **CLC 70**

**McClure, Michael (Thomas)** 1932- ... **CLC 6, 10**
See also BG 3; CA 21-24R; CAD; CANR 17, 46, 77; CD 5; CP 7; DLB 16; WP

**McCorkle, Jill (Collins)** 1958- .......... **CLC 51**
See also CA 121; CANR 113; CSW; DLB 234; DLBY 1987

**McCourt, Frank** 1930- ...................... **CLC 109**
See also AMWS 12; CA 157; CANR 97; NCFS 1

**McCourt, James** 1941- ...................... **CLC 5**
See also CA 57-60; CANR 98

**McCourt, Malachy** 1931- .................. **CLC 119**
See also SATA 126

**McCoy, Horace (Stanley)**
1897-1955 .................. **TCLC 28**
See also CA 155; CMW 4; DLB 9

**McCrae, John** 1872-1918 ................. **TCLC 12**
See also DLB 92; PFS 5

**McCreigh, James**
See Pohl, Frederik

**McCullers, (Lula) Carson (Smith)**
1917-1967 .... **CLC 1, 4, 10, 12, 48, 100; SSC 9, 24; WLC**
See also AAYA 21; AMW; BPFB 2; CA 5-8R; CABS 1, 3; CANR 18; CDALB 1941-1968; DA; DAB; DAC; DAM MST, NOV; DFS 5; DLB 2, 7, 173, 228; EXPS; FW; GLL 1; LAIT 3, 4; MAWW; MTCW 1, 2; NFS 6, 13; RGAL 4; RGSF 2; SATA 27; SSFS 5; TUS; YAW

**McCulloch, John Tyler**
See Burroughs, Edgar Rice

**McCullough, Colleen** 1938(?)- .. **CLC 27, 107**
See also AAYA 36; BPFB 2; CA 81-84; CANR 17, 46, 67, 98; CPW; DAM NOV, POP; MTCW 1, 2; RHW

**McDermott, Alice** 1953- .................. **CLC 90**
See also CA 109; CANR 40, 90

**McElroy, Joseph** 1930- ...................... **CLC 5, 47**
See also CA 17-20R; CN 7

**McEwan, Ian (Russell)** 1948- .... **CLC 13, 66, 169**
See also BEST 90:4; BRWS 4; CA 61-64; CANR 14, 41, 69, 87; CN 7; DAM NOV; DLB 14, 194; HGG; MTCW 1, 2; RGSF 2; SUFW 2; TEA

**McFadden, David** 1940- ...................... **CLC 48**
See also CA 104; CP 7; DLB 60; INT 104

**McFarland, Dennis** 1950- .................. **CLC 65**
See also CA 165; CANR 110

**McGahern, John** 1934- ... **CLC 5, 9, 48, 156; SSC 17**
See also CA 17-20R; CANR 29, 68, 113; CN 7; DLB 14, 231; MTCW 1

**McGinley, Patrick (Anthony)** 1937- . **CLC 41**
See also CA 127; CANR 56; INT 127

**McGinley, Phyllis** 1905-1978 ............. **CLC 14**
See also CA 9-12R; CANR 19; CWRI 5; DLB 11, 48; PFS 9, 13; SATA 2, 44; SATA-Obit 24

**McGinniss, Joe** 1942- .......................... **CLC 32**
See also AITN 2; BEST 89:2; CA 25-28R; CANR 26, 70; CPW; DLB 185; INT CANR-26

**McGivern, Maureen Daly**
See Daly, Maureen

**McGrath, Patrick** 1950- ..................... **CLC 55**
See also CA 136; CANR 65; CN 7; DLB 231; HGG; SUFW 2

**McGrath, Thomas (Matthew)**
1916-1990 .............................. **CLC 28, 59**
See also AMWS 10; CA 9-12R; CANR 6, 33, 95; DAM POET; MTCW 1; SATA 41; SATA-Obit 66

**McGuane, Thomas (Francis III)**
1939- ..................... **CLC 3, 7, 18, 45, 127**
See also AITN 2; BPFB 2; CA 49-52; CANR 5, 24, 49, 94; CN 7; DLB 2, 212; DLBY 1980; INT CANR-24; MTCW 1; TCWW 2

**McGuckian, Medbh** 1950- ... **CLC 48; PC 27**
See also BRWS 5; CA 143; CP 7; CWP; DAM POET; DLB 40

**McHale, Tom** 1942(?)-1982 ............. **CLC 3, 5**
See also AITN 1; CA 77-80

**McIlvanney, William** 1936- ............... **CLC 42**
See also CA 25-28R; CANR 61; CMW 4; DLB 14, 207

**McIlwraith, Maureen Mollie Hunter**
See Hunter, Mollie
See also SATA 2

**McInerney, Jay** 1955- ................. **CLC 34, 112**
See also AAYA 18; BPFB 2; CA 123; CANR 45, 68; CN 7; CPW; DAM POP; INT 123; MTCW 2

**McIntyre, Vonda N(eel)** 1948- .......... **CLC 18**
See also CA 81-84; CANR 17, 34, 69; MTCW 1; SFW 4; YAW

**McKay, Claude** ...... **BLC 3; HR 3; PC 2; TCLC 7, 41; WLC**
See McKay, Festus Claudius
See also AFAW 1, 2; AMWS 10; DAB; DLB 4, 45, 51, 117; EXPP; GLL 2; LAIT 3; PAB; PFS 4; RGAL 4; WP

**McKay, Festus Claudius** 1889-1948
See McKay, Claude
See also BW 1, 3; CA 124; CANR 73; DA; DAC; DAM MST, MULT, NOV, POET; MTCW 1, 2; TUS

**McKuen, Rod** 1933- ........................ **CLC 1, 3**
See also AITN 1; CA 41-44R; CANR 40

**McLoughlin, R. B.**
See Mencken, H(enry) L(ouis)

**McLuhan, (Herbert) Marshall**
1911-1980 .............................. **CLC 37, 83**
See also CA 9-12R; CANR 12, 34, 61; DLB 88; INT CANR-12; MTCW 1, 2

**McManus, Declan Patrick Aloysius**
See Costello, Elvis

**McMillan, Terry (L.)** 1951- . **BLCS; CLC 50, 61, 112**
See also AAYA 21; BPFB 2; BW 2, 3; CA 140; CANR 60, 104; CPW; DAM MULT, NOV, POP; MTCW 2; RGAL 4; YAW

**McMurtry, Larry (Jeff)** 1936- .. **CLC 2, 3, 7, 11, 27, 44, 127**
See also AAYA 15; AITN 2; AMWS 5; BEST 89:2; BPFB 2; CA 5-8R; CANR 19, 43, 64, 103; CDALB 1968-1988; CN 7; CPW; CSW; DAM NOV, POP; DLB 2, 143, 256; DLBY 1980, 1987; MTCW 1, 2; RGAL 4; TCWW 2

**McNally, T. M.** 1961- ........................ **CLC 82**

**McNally, Terrence** 1939- .... **CLC 4, 7, 41, 91**
See also CA 45-48; CAD; CANR 2, 56; CD 5; DAM DRAM; DFS 16; DLB 7, 249; GLL 1; MTCW 2

**McNamer, Deirdre** 1950- ................... **CLC 70**

**McNeal, Tom** ................................... **CLC 119**

**McNeile, Herman Cyril** 1888-1937
See Sapper
See also CA 184; CMW 4; DLB 77

**McNickle, (William) D'Arcy**
1904-1977 ..................... **CLC 89; NNAL**
See also CA 9-12R; CANR 5, 45; DAM MULT; DLB 175, 212; RGAL 4; SATA-Obit 22

**McPhee, John (Angus)** 1931- ............ **CLC 36**
See also AMWS 3; ANW; BEST 90:1; CA 65-68; CANR 20, 46, 64, 69; CPW; DLB 185, 275; MTCW 1, 2; TUS

**McPherson, James Alan** 1943- . **BLCS; CLC 19, 77**
See also BW 1, 3; CA 25-28R; CAAS 17; CANR 24, 74; CN 7; CSW; DLB 38, 244; MTCW 1, 2; RGAL 4; RGSF 2

**McPherson, William (Alexander)**
1933- ............................................ **CLC 34**
See also CA 69-72; CANR 28; INT CANR-28

**McTaggart, J. McT. Ellis**
See McTaggart, John McTaggart Ellis

**McTaggart, John McTaggart Ellis**
1866-1925 ................................. **TCLC 105**
See also DLB 262

**Mead, George Herbert** 1863-1931 . **TCLC 89**
See also DLB 270

**Mead, Margaret** 1901-1978 ............... **CLC 37**
See also AITN 1; CA 1-4R; CANR 4; FW; MTCW 1, 2; SATA-Obit 20

**Meaker, Marijane (Agnes)** 1927-
See Kerr, M. E.
See also CA 107; CANR 37, 63; INT 107; JRDA; MAICYA 1, 2; MAICYAS 1; MTCW 1; SATA 20, 61, 99; SATA-Essay 111; YAW

**Medoff, Mark (Howard)** 1940- .... **CLC 6, 23**
See also AITN 1; CA 53-56; CAD; CANR 5; CD 5; DAM DRAM; DFS 4; DLB 7; INT CANR-5

**Medvedev, P. N.**
See Bakhtin, Mikhail Mikhailovich

**Meged, Aharon**
See Megged, Aharon

**Meged, Aron**
See Megged, Aharon

**Megged, Aharon** 1920- ........................ **CLC 9**
See also CA 49-52; CAAS 13; CANR 1

**Mehta, Ved (Parkash)** 1934- ............. **CLC 37**
See also CA 1-4R; CANR 2, 23, 69; MTCW 1

**Melanter**
See Blackmore, R(ichard) D(oddridge)

**Meleager** c. 140B.C.-c. 70B.C. ....... **CMLC 53**

**Melies, Georges** 1861-1938 ............. **TCLC 81**

**Melikow, Loris**
See Hofmannsthal, Hugo von

**Melmoth, Sebastian**
See Wilde, Oscar (Fingal O'Flahertie Wills)

**Meltzer, Milton** 1915- ........................ **CLC 26**
See also AAYA 8, 45; BYA 2, 6; CA 13-16R; CANR 38, 92, 107; CLR 13; DLB 61; JRDA; MAICYA 1, 2; SAAS 1; SATA 1, 50, 80, 128; SATA-Essay 124; WYA; YAW

**Melville, Herman** 1819-1891 ..... **NCLC 3, 12, 29, 45, 49, 91, 93; SSC 1, 17, 46; WLC**
See also AAYA 25; AMW; AMWR 1; CDALB 1640-1865; DA; DAB; DAC; DAM MST, NOV; DLB 3, 74, 250, 254; EXPN; EXPS; LAIT 1, 2; NFS 7, 9; RGAL 4; RGSF 2; SATA 59; SSFS 3; TUS

**Members, Mark**
See Powell, Anthony (Dymoke)

**Membreno, Alejandro** ..................... **CLC 59**

**Menander** c. 342B.C.-c. 293B.C. .... **CMLC 9, 51; DC 3**
See also AW 1; CDWLB 1; DAM DRAM; DLB 176; RGWL 2, 3

**Menchu, Rigoberta** 1959- .. **CLC 160; HLCS 2**
See also CA 175; DNFS 1; WLIT 1

**Mencken, H(enry) L(ouis)**
1880-1956 .................................. **TCLC 13**
See also AMW; CA 125; CDALB 1917-1929; DLB 11, 29, 63, 137, 222; MTCW 1, 2; NCFS 4; RGAL 4; TUS

**Mendelsohn, Jane** 1965- ..................... **CLC 99**
See also CA 154; CANR 94

**Menton, Francisco de**
See Chin, Frank (Chew, Jr.)

**Mercer, David** 1928-1980 ...................... **CLC 5**
See also CA 9-12R; CANR 23; CBD; DAM DRAM; DLB 13; MTCW 1; RGEL 2

**Merchant, Paul**
See Ellison, Harlan (Jay)

**Meredith, George** 1828-1909 ... **TCLC 17, 43**
See also CA 153; CANR 80; CDBLB 1832-1890; DAM POET; DLB 18, 35, 57, 159; RGEL 2; TEA

**Meredith, William (Morris)** 1919- .... **CLC 4, 13, 22, 55; PC 28**
See also CA 9-12R; CAAS 14; CANR 6, 40; CP 7; DAM POET; DLB 5

**Merezhkovsky, Dmitry Sergeyevich**
1865-1941 ................................. **TCLC 29**
See also CA 169

**Merimee, Prosper** 1803-1870 ... **NCLC 6, 65; SSC 7**
See also DLB 119, 192; EW 6; EXPS; GFL 1789 to the Present; RGSF 2; RGWL 2, 3; SSFS 8; SUFW

**Merkin, Daphne** 1954- ....................... **CLC 44**
See also CA 123

**Merlin, Arthur**
See Blish, James (Benjamin)

**Merrill, James (Ingram)** 1926-1995 .. **CLC 2, 3, 6, 8, 13, 18, 34, 91; PC 28**
See also AMWS 3; CA 13-16R; CANR 10, 49, 63, 108; DAM POET; DLB 5, 165; DLBY 1985; INT CANR-10; MTCW 1, 2; PAB; RGAL 4

**Merriman, Alex**
See Silverberg, Robert

**Merriman, Brian** 1747-1805 .......... **NCLC 70**

**Merritt, E. B.**
See Waddington, Miriam

**Merton, Thomas (James)**
1915-1968 . **CLC 1, 3, 11, 34, 83; PC 10**
See also AMWS 8; CA 5-8R; CANR 22, 53, 111; DLB 48; DLBY 1981; MTCW 1, 2

**Merwin, W(illiam) S(tanley)** 1927- ... **CLC 1, 2, 3, 5, 8, 13, 18, 45, 88; PC 45**
See also AMWS 3; CA 13-16R; CANR 15, 51, 112; CP 7; DAM POET; DLB 5, 169; INT CANR-15; MTCW 1, 2; PAB; PFS 5, 15; RGAL 4

**Metcalf, John** 1938- ............ **CLC 37; SSC 43**
See also CA 113; CN 7; DLB 60; RGSF 2; TWA

**Metcalf, Suzanne**
See Baum, L(yman) Frank

**Mew, Charlotte (Mary)** 1870-1928 .. **TCLC 8**
See also CA 189; DLB 19, 135; RGEL 2

**Mewshaw, Michael** 1943- ................... **CLC 9**
See also CA 53-56; CANR 7, 47; DLBY 1980

**Meyer, Conrad Ferdinand**
1825-1905 ................................. **NCLC 81**
See also DLB 129; EW; RGWL 2, 3

**Meyer, Gustav** 1868-1932
See Meyrink, Gustav
See also CA 190

**Meyer, June**
See Jordan, June (Meyer)

**Meyer, Lynn**
See Slavitt, David R(ytman)

**Meyers, Jeffrey** 1939- .................... **CLC 39**
See also CA 73-76; CAAE 186; CANR 54, 102; DLB 111

**Meynell, Alice (Christina Gertrude Thompson)** 1847-1922 .............. **TCLC 6**
See also CA 177; DLB 19, 98; RGEL 2

**Meyrink, Gustav** ........................ **TCLC 21**
See Meyer, Gustav
See also DLB 81

**Michaels, Leonard** 1933- .... **CLC 6, 25; SSC 16**
See also CA 61-64; CANR 21, 62; CN 7; DLB 130; MTCW 1

**Michaux, Henri** 1899-1984 ........... **CLC 8, 19**
See also CA 85-88; DLB 258; GFL 1789 to the Present; RGWL 2, 3

**Micheaux, Oscar (Devereaux)** 1884-1951 ............................... **TCLC 76**
See also BW 3; CA 174; DLB 50; TCWW 2

**Michelangelo** 1475-1564 ......... **LC 12**
See also AAYA 43

**Michelet, Jules** 1798-1874 .............. **NCLC 31**
See also EW 5; GFL 1789 to the Present

**Michels, Robert** 1876-1936 ........... **TCLC 88**

**Michener, James A(lbert)** 1907(?)-1997 .. **CLC 1, 5, 11, 29, 60, 109**
See also AAYA 27; AITN 1; BEST 90:1; BPFB 2; CA 5-8R; CANR 21, 45, 68; CN 7; CPW; DAM NOV, POP; DLB 6; MTCW 1, 2; RHW

**Mickiewicz, Adam** 1798-1855 . **NCLC 3, 101; PC 38**
See also EW 5; RGWL 2, 3

**Middleton, Christopher** 1926- ........... **CLC 13**
See also CA 13-16R; CANR 29, 54; CP 7; DLB 40

**Middleton, Richard (Barham)** 1882-1911 ............................... **TCLC 56**
See also CA 187; DLB 156; HGG

**Middleton, Stanley** 1919- .............. **CLC 7, 38**
See also CA 25-28R; CAAS 23; CANR 21, 46, 81; CN 7; DLB 14

**Middleton, Thomas** 1580-1627 ....... **DC 5; LC 33**
See also BRW 2; DAM DRAM, MST; DLB 58; RGEL 2

**Migueis, Jose Rodrigues** 1901- ......... **CLC 10**

**Mikszath, Kalman** 1847-1910 ........ **TCLC 31**
See also CA 170

**Miles, Jack** .................................. **CLC 100**
See also CA 200

**Miles, John Russiano**
See Miles, Jack

**Miles, Josephine (Louise)** 1911-1985 ............... **CLC 1, 2, 14, 34, 39**
See also CA 1-4R; CANR 2, 55; DAM POET; DLB 48

**Militant**
See Sandburg, Carl (August)

**Mill, Harriet (Hardy) Taylor** 1807-1858 ............................... **NCLC 102**
See also FW

**Mill, John Stuart** 1806-1873 .... **NCLC 11, 58**
See also CDBLB 1832-1890; DLB 55, 190, 262; FW 1; RGEL 2; TEA

**Millar, Kenneth** 1915-1983 ................ **CLC 14**
See Macdonald, Ross
See also CA 9-12R; CANR 16, 63, 107; CMW 4; CPW; DAM POP; DLB 2, 226; DLBD 6; DLBY 1983; MTCW 1, 2

**Millay, E. Vincent**
See Millay, Edna St. Vincent

**Millay, Edna St. Vincent** 1892-1950 .... **PC 6; TCLC 4, 49; WLCS**
See Boyd, Nancy
See also AMW; CA 130; CDALB 1917-1929; DA; DAB; DAC; DAM MST, POET; DLB 45, 249; EXPP; MAWW; MTCW 1, 2; PAB; PFS 3, 17; RGAL 4; TUS; WP

**Miller, Arthur** 1915- ...... **CLC 1, 2, 6, 10, 15, 26, 47, 78; DC 1; WLC**
See also AAYA 15; AITN 1; AMW; AMWC 1; CA 1-4R; CABS 3; CAD; CANR 2, 30, 54, 76; CD 5; CDALB 1941-1968; DA; DAB; DAC; DAM DRAM, MST; DFS 1, 3; DLB 7, 266; LAIT 1, 4; MTCW 1, 2; RGAL 4; TUS; WYAS 1

**Miller, Henry (Valentine)** 1891-1980 .... **CLC 1, 2, 4, 9, 14, 43, 84; WLC**
See also AMW; BPFB 2; CA 9-12R; CANR 33, 64; CDALB 1929-1941; DA; DAB; DAC; DAM MST, NOV; DLB 4, 9; DLBY 1980; MTCW 1, 2; RGAL 4; TUS

**Miller, Jason** 1939(?)-2001 .................. **CLC 2**
See also AITN 1; CA 73-76; CAD; DFS 12; DLB 7

**Miller, Sue** 1943- .............................. **CLC 44**
See also AMWS 12; BEST 90:3; CA 139; CANR 59, 91; DAM POP; DLB 143

**Miller, Walter M(ichael, Jr.)** 1923-1996 ................................. **CLC 4, 30**
See also BPFB 2; CA 85-88; CANR 108; DLB 8; SCFW; SFW 4

**Millett, Kate** 1934- ........................... **CLC 67**
See also AITN 1; CA 73-76; CANR 32, 53, 76, 110; DLB 246; FW; GLL 1; MTCW 1, 2

**Millhauser, Steven (Lewis)** 1943- .... **CLC 21, 54, 109; SSC 57**
See also CA 111; CANR 63, 114; CN 7; DLB 2; FANT; INT CA-111; MTCW 2

**Millin, Sarah Gertrude** 1889-1968 ... **CLC 49**
See also CA 102; DLB 225

**Milne, A(lan) A(lexander)** 1882-1956 ........................ **TCLC 6, 88**
See also BRWS 5; CA 133; CLR 1, 26; CMW 4; CWRI 5; DAB; DAC; DAM MST; DLB 10, 77, 100, 160; FANT; MAICYA 1, 2; MTCW 1, 2; RGEL 2; SATA 100; WCH; YABC 1

**Milner, Ron(ald)** 1938- ........ **BLC 3; CLC 56**
See also AITN 1; BW 1; CA 73-76; CAD; CANR 24, 81; CD 5; DAM MULT; DLB 38; MTCW 1

**Milnes, Richard Monckton** 1809-1885 ................................. **NCLC 61**
See also DLB 32, 184

**Milosz, Czeslaw** 1911- ....... **CLC 5, 11, 22, 31, 56, 82; PC 8; WLCS**
See also CA 81-84; CANR 23, 51, 91; CDWLB 4; CWW 2; DAM MST, POET; DLB 215; EW 13; MTCW 1, 2; PFS 16; RGWL 2, 3

**Milton, John** 1608-1674 ..... **LC 9, 43; PC 19, 29; WLC**
See also BRW 2; BRWR 2; CDBLB 1660-1789; DA; DAB; DAC; DAM MST, POET; DLB 131, 151; EFS 1; EXPP; LAIT 1; PAB; PFS 3, 17; RGEL 2; TEA; WLIT 3; WP

**Min, Anchee** 1957- ............................ **CLC 86**
See also CA 146; CANR 94

**Minehaha, Cornelius**
See Wedekind, (Benjamin) Frank(lin)

**Miner, Valerie** 1947- ......................... **CLC 40**
See also CA 97-100; CANR 59; FW; GLL 2

**Minimo, Duca**
See D'Annunzio, Gabriele

**Minot, Susan** 1956- .................... **CLC 44, 159**
See also AMWS 6; CA 134; CN 7

**Minus, Ed** 1938- ................................ **CLC 39**
See also CA 185

**Miranda, Javier**
See Bioy Casares, Adolfo
See also CWW 2

**Mirbeau, Octave** 1848-1917 ........... **TCLC 55**
See also DLB 123, 192; GFL 1789 to the Present

**Miro (Ferrer), Gabriel (Francisco Victor)** 1879-1930 ............................... **TCLC 5**
See also CA 185

**Misharin, Alexandr** ........................ **CLC 59**

**Mishima, Yukio** ... **CLC 2, 4, 6, 9, 27; DC 1; SSC 4**
See Hiraoka, Kimitake
See also BPFB 2; GLL 1; MJW; MTCW 2; RGSF 2; RGWL 2, 3; SSFS 5, 12

**Mistral, Frederic** 1830-1914 ........... **TCLC 51**
See also GFL 1789 to the Present

**Mistral, Gabriela**
See Godoy Alcayaga, Lucila
See also DNFS 1; LAW; RGWL 2, 3; WP

**Mistry, Rohinton** 1952- ..................... **CLC 71**
See also CA 141; CANR 86, 114; CCA 1; CN 7; DAC; SSFS 6

**Mitchell, James Leslie** 1901-1935
See Gibbon, Lewis Grassic
See also CA 188; DLB 15

**Mitchell, Joni** 1943- ........................ **CLC 12**
See also CA 112; CCA 1

**Mitchell, Joseph (Quincy)** 1908-1996 ................................. **CLC 98**
See also CA 77-80; CANR 69; CN 7; CSW; DLB 185; DLBY 1996

**Mitchell, Margaret (Munnerlyn)** 1900-1949 ............................... **TCLC 11**
See also AAYA 23; BPFB 2; BYA 1; CA 125; CANR 55, 94; CDALBS; DAM NOV, POP; DLB 9; LAIT 2; MTCW 1, 2; NFS 9; RGAL 4; RHW; TUS; WYAS 1; YAW

**Mitchell, Peggy**
See Mitchell, Margaret (Munnerlyn)

**Mitchell, S(ilas) Weir** 1829-1914 .... **TCLC 36**
See also CA 165; DLB 202; RGAL 4

**Mitchell, W(illiam) O(rmond)** 1914-1998 ................................. **CLC 25**
See also CA 77-80; CANR 15, 43; CN 7; DAC; DAM MST; DLB 88

**Mitchell, William** 1879-1936 .......... **TCLC 81**

**Mitford, Mary Russell** 1787-1855 ... **NCLC 4**
See also DLB 110, 116; RGEL 2

**Mitford, Nancy** 1904-1973 ................ **CLC 44**
See also CA 9-12R; DLB 191; RGEL 2

**Miyamoto, (Chujo) Yuriko** 1899-1951 ............................... **TCLC 37**
See Miyamoto Yuriko
See also CA 170, 174

**Miyamoto Yuriko**
See Miyamoto, (Chujo) Yuriko
See also DLB 180

**Miyazawa, Kenji** 1896-1933 ........... **TCLC 76**
See also CA 157; RGWL 3

**Mizoguchi, Kenji** 1898-1956 ........... **TCLC 72**
See also CA 167

**Mo, Timothy (Peter)** 1950(?)- ... **CLC 46, 134**
See also CA 117; CN 7; DLB 194; MTCW 1; WLIT 4

**Modarressi, Taghi (M.)** 1931-1997 ... **CLC 44**
See also CA 134; INT 134

**Modiano, Patrick (Jean)** 1945- ......... **CLC 18**
See also CA 85-88; CANR 17, 40; CWW 2; DLB 83

**Mofolo, Thomas (Mokopu)**
1875(?)-1948 .............. **BLC 3; TCLC 22**
See also AFW; CA 153; CANR 83; DAM MULT; DLB 225; MTCW 2; WLIT 2

**Mohr, Nicholasa** 1938- ........ **CLC 12; HLC 2**
See also AAYA 8, 46; CA 49-52; CANR 1, 32, 64; CLR 22; DAM MULT; DLB 145; HW 1, 2; JRDA; LAIT 5; MAICYA 2; MAICYAS 1; RGAL 4; SAAS 8; SATA 8, 97; SATA-Essay 113; WYA; YAW

**Mojtabai, A(nn) G(race)** 1938- ..... **CLC 5, 9, 15, 29**
See also CA 85-88; CANR 88

**Moliere** 1622-1673 ..... **DC 13; LC 10, 28, 64; WLC**
See also DA; DAB; DAC; DAM DRAM, MST; DFS 13; DLB 268; EW 3; GFL Beginnings to 1789; RGWL 2, 3; TWA

**Molin, Charles**
See Mayne, William (James Carter)

**Molnar, Ferenc** 1878-1952 .............. **TCLC 20**
See also CA 153; CANR 83; CDWLB 4; DAM DRAM; DLB 215; RGWL 2, 3

**Momaday, N(avarre) Scott** 1934- ...... **CLC 2, 19, 85, 95, 160; NNAL; PC 25; WLCS**
See also AAYA 11; AMWS 4; ANW; BPFB 2; CA 25-28R; CANR 14, 34, 68; CDALBS; CN 7; CPW; DA; DAB; DAC; DAM MST, MULT, NOV, POP; DLB 143, 175, 256; EXPP; INT CANR-14; LAIT 4; MTCW 1, 2; NFS 10; PFS 2, 11; RGAL 4; SATA 48; SATA-Brief 30; WP; YAW

**Monette, Paul** 1945-1995 ................... **CLC 82**
See also AMWS 10; CA 139; CN 7; GLL 1

**Monroe, Harriet** 1860-1936 ............ **TCLC 12**
See also CA 204; DLB 54, 91

**Monroe, Lyle**
See Heinlein, Robert A(nson)

**Montagu, Elizabeth** 1720-1800 ....... **NCLC 7, 117**
See also FW

**Montagu, Mary (Pierrepont) Wortley** 1689-1762 .................... **LC 9, 57; PC 16**
See also DLB 95, 101; RGEL 2

**Montagu, W. H.**
See Coleridge, Samuel Taylor

**Montague, John (Patrick)** 1929- ..... **CLC 13, 46**
See also CA 9-12R; CANR 9, 69; CP 7; DLB 40; MTCW 1; PFS 12; RGEL 2

**Montaigne, Michel (Eyquem) de** 1533-1592 ............................. **LC 8; WLC**
See also DA; DAB; DAC; DAM MST; EW 2; GFL Beginnings to 1789; RGWL 2, 3; TWA

**Montale, Eugenio** 1896-1981 ... **CLC 7, 9, 18; PC 13**
See also CA 17-20R; CANR 30; DLB 114; EW 11; MTCW 1; RGWL 2, 3; TWA

**Montesquieu, Charles-Louis de Secondat** 1689-1755 .................... **LC 7, 69**
See also EW 3; GFL Beginnings to 1789; TWA

**Montessori, Maria** 1870-1952 ...... **TCLC 103**
See also CA 147

**Montgomery, (Robert) Bruce** 1921(?)-1978
See Crispin, Edmund
See also CA 179; CMW 4

**Montgomery, L(ucy) M(aud)** 1874-1942 ................................. **TCLC 51**
See also AAYA 12; BYA 1; CA 137; CLR 8; DAC; DAM MST; DLB 92; DLBD 14; JRDA; MAICYA 1, 2; MTCW 2; RGEL 2; SATA 100; TWA; WCH; WYA; YABC 1

**Montgomery, Marion H., Jr.** 1925- .... **CLC 7**
See also AITN 1; CA 1-4R; CANR 3, 48; CSW; DLB 6

**Montgomery, Max**
See Davenport, Guy (Mattison, Jr.)

**Montherlant, Henry (Milon) de** 1896-1972 ................................. **CLC 8, 19**
See also CA 85-88; DAM DRAM; DLB 72; EW 11; GFL 1789 to the Present; MTCW 1

**Monty Python**
See Chapman, Graham; Cleese, John (Marwood); Gilliam, Terry (Vance); Idle, Eric; Jones, Terence Graham Parry; Palin, Michael (Edward)
See also AAYA 7

**Moodie, Susanna (Strickland)** 1803-1885 ........................ **NCLC 14, 113**
See also DLB 99

**Moody, Hiram (F. III)** 1961-
See Moody, Rick
See also CA 138; CANR 64, 112

**Moody, Minerva**
See Alcott, Louisa May

**Moody, Rick** ..................................... **CLC 147**
See Moody, Hiram (F. III)

**Moody, William Vaughan** 1869-1910 ................................... **TCLC 105**
See also CA 178; DLB 7, 54; RGAL 4

**Mooney, Edward** 1951-
See Mooney, Ted
See also CA 130

**Mooney, Ted** .................................... **CLC 25**
See Mooney, Edward

**Moorcock, Michael (John)** 1939- ...... **CLC 5, 27, 58**
See Bradbury, Edward P.
See also AAYA 26; CA 45-48; CAAS 5; CANR 2, 17, 38, 64; CN 7; DLB 14, 231, 261; FANT; MTCW 1, 2; SATA 93; SCFW 2; SFW 4; SUFW 1, 2

**Moore, Brian** 1921-1999 ... **CLC 1, 3, 5, 7, 8, 19, 32, 90**
See Bryan, Michael
See also CA 1-4R; CANR 1, 25, 42, 63; CCA 1; CN 7; DAB; DAC; DAM MST; DLB 251; FANT; MTCW 1, 2; RGEL 2

**Moore, Edward**
See Muir, Edwin
See also RGEL 2

**Moore, G. E.** 1873-1958 ................... **TCLC 89**
See also DLB 262

**Moore, George Augustus** 1852-1933 .................... **SSC 19; TCLC 7**
See also BRW 6; CA 177; DLB 10, 18, 57, 135; RGEL 2; RGSF 2

**Moore, Lorrie** ........................ **CLC 39, 45, 68**
See Moore, Marie Lorena
See also AMWS 10; DLB 234

**Moore, Marianne (Craig)** 1887-1972 ..... **CLC 1, 2, 4, 8, 10, 13, 19, 47; PC 4; WLCS**
See also AMW; CA 1-4R; CANR 3, 61; CDALB 1929-1941; DA; DAB; DAC; DAM MST, POET; DLB 45; DLBD 7; EXPP; MAWW; MTCW 1, 2; PAB; PFS 14, 17; RGAL 4; SATA 20; TUS; WP

**Moore, Marie Lorena** 1957- ........... **CLC 165**
See Moore, Lorrie
See also CA 116; CANR 39, 83; CN 7; DLB 234

**Moore, Thomas** 1779-1852 ....... **NCLC 6, 110**
See also DLB 96, 144; RGEL 2

**Moorhouse, Frank** 1938- .................... **SSC 40**
See also CA 118; CANR 92; CN 7; RGSF 2

**Mora, Pat(ricia)** 1942- ........................ **HLC 2**
See also CA 129; CANR 57, 81, 112; CLR 58; DAM MULT; DLB 209; HW 1, 2; MAICYA 2; SATA 92, 134

**Moraga, Cherrie** 1952- ..................... **CLC 126**
See also CA 131; CANR 66; DAM MULT; DLB 82, 249; FW; GLL 1; HW 1, 2

**Morand, Paul** 1888-1976 .... **CLC 41; SSC 22**
See also CA 184; DLB 65

**Morante, Elsa** 1918-1985 ................. **CLC 8, 47**
See also CA 85-88; CANR 35; DLB 177; MTCW 1, 2; RGWL 2, 3

**Moravia, Alberto** ........ **CLC 2, 7, 11, 27, 46; SSC 26**
See Pincherle, Alberto
See also DLB 177; EW 12; MTCW 2; RGSF 2; RGWL 2, 3

**More, Hannah** 1745-1833 ............... **NCLC 27**
See also DLB 107, 109, 116, 158; RGEL 2

**More, Henry** 1614-1687 ........................ **LC 9**
See also DLB 126, 252

**More, Sir Thomas** 1478(?)-1535 .... **LC 10, 32**
See also BRWS 7; DLB 136; RGEL 2; TEA

**Moreas, Jean** ................................... **TCLC 18**
See Papadiamantopoulos, Johannes
See also GFL 1789 to the Present

**Moreton, Andrew Esq.**
See Defoe, Daniel

**Morgan, Berry** 1919- .......................... **CLC 6**
See also CA 49-52; DLB 6

**Morgan, Claire**
See Highsmith, (Mary) Patricia
See also GLL 1

**Morgan, Edwin (George)** 1920- ........ **CLC 31**
See also CA 5-8R; CANR 3, 43, 90; CP 7; DLB 27

**Morgan, (George) Frederick** 1922- .. **CLC 23**
See also CA 17-20R; CANR 21; CP 7

**Morgan, Harriet**
See Mencken, H(enry) L(ouis)

**Morgan, Jane**
See Cooper, James Fenimore

**Morgan, Janet** 1945- .......................... **CLC 39**
See also CA 65-68

**Morgan, Lady** 1776(?)-1859 ........... **NCLC 29**
See also DLB 116, 158; RGEL 2

**Morgan, Robin (Evonne)** 1941- ........... **CLC 2**
See also CA 69-72; CANR 29, 68; FW; GLL 2; MTCW 1; SATA 80

**Morgan, Scott**
See Kuttner, Henry

**Morgan, Seth** 1949(?)-1990 ............... **CLC 65**
See also CA 185

**Morgenstern, Christian (Otto Josef Wolfgang)** 1871-1914 ................ **TCLC 8**
See also CA 191

**Morgenstern, S.**
See Goldman, William (W.)

**Mori, Rintaro**
See Mori Ogai

**Moricz, Zsigmond** 1879-1942 ......... **TCLC 33**
See also CA 165; DLB 215

**Morike, Eduard (Friedrich)** 1804-1875 ................................ **NCLC 10**
See also DLB 133; RGWL 2, 3

**Mori Ogai** 1862-1922 ...................... **TCLC 14**
See Ogai
See also CA 164; DLB 180; RGWL 3; TWA

**Moritz, Karl Philipp** 1756-1793 ........... **LC 2**
See also DLB 94

**Morland, Peter Henry**
See Faust, Frederick (Schiller)

**Morley, Christopher (Darlington)** 1890-1957 ................................ **TCLC 87**
See also DLB 9; RGAL 4

**Morren, Theophil**
See Hofmannsthal, Hugo von

**Morris, Bill** 1952- ................................ **CLC 76**

**Morris, Julian**
See West, Morris L(anglo)

**Morris, Steveland Judkins** 1950(?)-
See Wonder, Stevie

**Morris, William** 1834-1896 ............. **NCLC 4**
See also BRW 5; CDBLB 1832-1890; DLB 18, 35, 57, 156, 178, 184; FANT; RGEL 2; SFW 4; SUFW

**Morris, Wright** 1910-1998 .. **CLC 1, 3, 7, 18, 37; TCLC 107**
See also AMW; CA 9-12R; CANR 21, 81; CN 7; DLB 2, 206, 218; DLBY 1981; MTCW 1, 2; RGAL 4; TCWW 2

**Morrison, Arthur** 1863-1945 ............. **SSC 40; TCLC 72**
See also CA 157; CMW 4; DLB 70, 135, 197; RGEL 2

**Morrison, James Douglas** 1943-1971
See Morrison, Jim
See also CA 73-76; CANR 40

**Morrison, Jim** ................................. **CLC 17**
See Morrison, James Douglas

**Morrison, Toni** 1931- ..... **BLC 3; CLC 4, 10, 22, 55, 81, 87**
See also AAYA 1, 22; AFAW 1, 2; AMWC 1; AMWS 3; BPFB 2; BW 2, 3; CA 29-32R; CANR 27, 42, 67, 113; CDALB 1968-1988; CN 7; CPW; DA; DAB; DAC; DAM MST, MULT, NOV, POP; DLB 6, 33, 143; DLBY 1981; EXPN; FW; LAIT 2, 4; MAWW; MTCW 1, 2; NFS 1, 6, 8, 14; RGAL 4; RHW; SATA 57; SSFS 5; TUS; YAW

**Morrison, Van** 1945- ....................... **CLC 21**
See also CA 168

**Morrissy, Mary** 1957- ....................... **CLC 99**
See also CA 205; DLB 267

**Mortimer, John (Clifford)** 1923- ..... **CLC 28, 43**
See also CA 13-16R; CANR 21, 69, 109; CD 5; CDBLB 1960 to Present; CMW 4; CN 7; CPW; DAM DRAM, POP; DLB 13, 245, 271; INT CANR-21; MSW; MTCW 1, 2; RGEL 2

**Mortimer, Penelope (Ruth)**
1918-1999 ..................................... **CLC 5**
See also CA 57-60; CANR 45, 88; CN 7

**Mortimer, Sir John**
See Mortimer, John (Clifford)

**Morton, Anthony**
See Creasey, John

**Morton, Thomas** 1579(?)-1647(?) ........ **LC 72**
See also DLB 24; RGEL 2

**Mosca, Gaetano** 1858-1941 ............. **TCLC 75**

**Mosher, Howard Frank** 1943- .......... **CLC 62**
See also CA 139; CANR 65

**Mosley, Nicholas** 1923- ............... **CLC 43, 70**
See also CA 69-72; CANR 41, 60, 108; CN 7; DLB 14, 207

**Mosley, Walter** 1952- ............ **BLCS; CLC 97**
See also AAYA 17; BPFB 2; BW 2; CA 142; CANR 57, 92; CMW 4; CPW; DAM MULT, POP; MSW; MTCW 2

**Moss, Howard** 1922-1987 . **CLC 7, 14, 45, 50**
See also CA 1-4R; CANR 1, 44; DAM POET; DLB 5

**Mossgiel, Rab**
See Burns, Robert

**Motion, Andrew (Peter)** 1952- .......... **CLC 47**
See also BRWS 7; CA 146; CANR 90; CP 7; DLB 40

**Motley, Willard (Francis)**
1909-1965 ..................................... **CLC 18**
See also BW 1; CA 117; CANR 88; DLB 76, 143

**Motoori, Norinaga** 1730-1801 ......... **NCLC 45**

**Mott, Michael (Charles Alston)**
1930- ..................................... **CLC 15, 34**
See also CA 5-8R; CAAS 7; CANR 7, 29

**Mountain Wolf Woman** 1884-1960 . **CLC 92; NNAL**
See also CA 144; CANR 90

**Moure, Erin** 1955- ............................ **CLC 88**
See also CA 113; CP 7; CWP; DLB 60

**Mowat, Farley (McGill)** 1921- .......... **CLC 26**
See also AAYA 1; BYA 2; CA 1-4R; CANR 4, 24, 42, 68, 108; CLR 20; CPW; DAC; DAM MST; DLB 68; INT CANR-24; JRDA; MAICYA 1, 2; MTCW 1, 2; SATA 3, 55; YAW

**Mowatt, Anna Cora** 1819-1870 ..... **NCLC 74**
See also RGAL 4

**Moyers, Bill** 1934- ............................. **CLC 74**
See also AITN 2; CA 61-64; CANR 31, 52

**Mphahlele, Es'kia**
See Mphahlele, Ezekiel
See also AFW; CDWLB 3; DLB 125, 225; RGSF 2; SSFS 11

**Mphahlele, Ezekiel** 1919- ... **BLC 3; CLC 25, 133**
See Mphahlele, Es'kia
See also BW 2, 3; CA 81-84; CANR 26, 76; CN 7; DAM MULT; MTCW 2; SATA 119

**Mqhayi, S(amuel) E(dward) K(rune Loliwe)**
1875-1945 .................. **BLC 3; TCLC 25**
See also CA 153; CANR 87; DAM MULT

**Mrozek, Slawomir** 1930- ............... **CLC 3, 13**
See also CA 13-16R; CAAS 10; CANR 29; CDWLB 4; CWW 2; DLB 232; MTCW 1

**Mrs. Belloc-Lowndes**
See Lowndes, Marie Adelaide (Belloc)

**M'Taggart, John M'Taggart Ellis**
See McTaggart, John McTaggart Ellis

**Mtwa, Percy** (?)- ............................. **CLC 47**

**Mueller, Lisel** 1924- ........ **CLC 13, 51; PC 33**
See also CA 93-96; CP 7; DLB 105; PFS 9, 13

**Muggeridge, Malcolm (Thomas)**
1903-1990 ................................. **TCLC 120**
See also AITN 1; CA 101; CANR 33, 63; MTCW 1, 2

**Muir, Edwin** 1887-1959 ............. **TCLC 2, 87**
See Moore, Edward
See also BRWS 6; CA 193; DLB 20, 100, 191; RGEL 2

**Muir, John** 1838-1914 .................... **TCLC 28**
See also AMWS 9; ANW; CA 165; DLB 186, 275

**Mujica Lainez, Manuel** 1910-1984 ... **CLC 31**
See Lainez, Manuel Mujica
See also CA 81-84; CANR 32; HW 1

**Mukherjee, Bharati** 1940- ..... **AAL; CLC 53, 115; SSC 38**
See also AAYA 46; BEST 89:2; CA 107; CANR 45, 72; CN 7; DAM NOV; DLB 60, 218; DNFS 1, 2; FW; MTCW 1, 2; RGAL 4; RGSF 2; SSFS 7; TUS

**Muldoon, Paul** 1951- ............ **CLC 32, 72, 166**
See also BRWS 4; CA 129; CANR 52, 91; CP 7; DAM POET; DLB 40; INT 129; PFS 7

**Mulisch, Harry** 1927- ....................... **CLC 42**
See also CA 9-12R; CANR 6, 26, 56, 110

**Mull, Martin** 1943- ........................... **CLC 17**
See also CA 105

**Muller, Wilhelm** ............................. **NCLC 73**

**Mulock, Dinah Maria**
See Craik, Dinah Maria (Mulock)
See also RGEL 2

**Munford, Robert** 1737(?)-1783 .............. **LC 5**
See also DLB 31

**Mungo, Raymond** 1946- .................... **CLC 72**
See also CA 49-52; CANR 2

**Munro, Alice** 1931- .... **CLC 6, 10, 19, 50, 95; SSC 3; WLCS**
See also AITN 2; BPFB 2; CA 33-36R; CANR 33, 53, 75, 114; CCA 1; CN 7; DAC; DAM MST, NOV; DLB 53; MTCW 1, 2; RGEL 2; RGSF 2; SATA 29; SSFS 5, 13

**Munro, H(ector) H(ugh)** 1870-1916 .... **WLC**
See Saki
See also CA 130; CANR 104; CDBLB 1890-1914; DA; DAB; DAC; DAM MST, NOV; DLB 34, 162; EXPS; MTCW 1, 2; RGEL 2; SSFS 15

**Murakami, Haruki** 1949- ................. **CLC 150**
See Murakami Haruki
See also CA 165; CANR 102; MJW; RGWL 3; SFW 4

**Murakami Haruki**
See Murakami, Haruki
See also DLB 182

**Murasaki, Lady**
See Murasaki Shikibu

**Murasaki Shikibu** 978(?)-1026(?) ... **CMLC 1**
See also EFS 2; RGWL 2, 3

**Murdoch, (Jean) Iris** 1919-1999 ... **CLC 1, 2, 3, 4, 6, 8, 11, 15, 22, 31, 51**
See also BRWS 1; CA 13-16R; CANR 8, 43, 68, 103; CDBLB 1960 to Present; CN 7; DAB; DAC; DAM MST, NOV; DLB 14, 194, 233; INT CANR-8; MTCW 1, 2; RGEL 2; TEA; WLIT 4

**Murfree, Mary Noailles** 1850-1922 ... **SSC 22**
See also CA 176; DLB 12, 74; RGAL 4

**Murnau, Friedrich Wilhelm**
See Plumpe, Friedrich Wilhelm

**Murphy, Richard** 1927- .................... **CLC 41**
See also BRWS 5; CA 29-32R; CP 7; DLB 40

**Murphy, Sylvia** 1937- ....................... **CLC 34**
See also CA 121

**Murphy, Thomas (Bernard)** 1935- ... **CLC 51**
See also CA 101

**Murray, Albert L.** 1916- .................... **CLC 73**
See also BW 2; CA 49-52; CANR 26, 52, 78; CSW; DLB 38

**Murray, James Augustus Henry**
1837-1915 ................................. **TCLC 117**

**Murray, Judith Sargent**
1751-1820 .................................... **NCLC 63**
See also DLB 37, 200

**Murray, Les(lie Allan)** 1938- ............. **CLC 40**
See also BRWS 7; CA 21-24R; CANR 11, 27, 56, 103; CP 7; DAM POET; DLBY 01; RGEL 2

**Murry, J. Middleton**
See Murry, John Middleton

**Murry, John Middleton**
1889-1957 ................................. **TCLC 16**
See also DLB 149

**Musgrave, Susan** 1951- ............... **CLC 13, 54**
See also CA 69-72; CANR 45, 84; CCA 1; CP 7; CWP

**Musil, Robert (Edler von)**
1880-1942 .......... **SSC 18; TCLC 12, 68**
See also CANR 55, 84; CDWLB 2; DLB 81, 124; EW 9; MTCW 2; RGSF 2; RGWL 2, 3

**Muske, Carol** ................................... **CLC 90**
See Muske-Dukes, Carol (Anne)

**Muske-Dukes, Carol (Anne)** 1945-
See Muske, Carol
See also CA 65-68; CAAE 203; CANR 32, 70; CWP

**Musset, (Louis Charles) Alfred de**
1810-1857 ..................................... **NCLC 7**
See also DLB 192, 217; EW 6; GFL 1789 to the Present; RGWL 2, 3; TWA

**Mussolini, Benito (Amilcare Andrea)**
1883-1945 ................................... **TCLC 96**

**My Brother's Brother**
See Chekhov, Anton (Pavlovich)

**Myers, L(eopold) H(amilton)**
1881-1944 ................................... **TCLC 59**
See also CA 157; DLB 15; RGEL 2

**Myers, Walter Dean** 1937- .. **BLC 3; CLC 35**
See also AAYA 4, 23; BW 2; BYA 6, 8, 11; CA 33-36R; CANR 20, 42, 67, 108; CLR 4, 16, 35; DAM MULT, NOV; DLB 33; INT CANR-20; JRDA; LAIT 5; MAICYA 1, 2; MAICYAS 1; MTCW 2; SAAS 2; SATA 41, 71, 109; SATA-Brief 27; WYA; YAW

**Myers, Walter M.**
See Myers, Walter Dean

**Myles, Symon**
See Follett, Ken(neth Martin)

**Nabokov, Vladimir (Vladimirovich)** 1899-1977 ....... **CLC 1, 2, 3, 6, 8, 11, 15, 23, 44, 46, 64; SSC 11; TCLC 108; WLC**
See also AAYA 45; AMW; AMWC 1; AMWR 1; BPFB 2; CA 5-8R; CANR 20, 102; CDALB 1941-1968; DA; DAB; DAC; DAM MST, NOV; DLB 2, 244; DLBD 3; DLBY 1980, 1991; EXPS; MTCW 1, 2; NCFS 4; NFS 9; RGAL 4; RGSF 2; SSFS 6, 15; TUS

**Naevius** c. 265B.C.-201B.C. ........... **CMLC 37**
See also DLB 211

**Nagai, Kafu** ................................ **TCLC 51**
See Nagai, Sokichi
See also DLB 180

**Nagai, Sokichi** 1879-1959
See Nagai, Kafu

**Nagy, Laszlo** 1925-1978 ..................... **CLC 7**
See also CA 129

**Naidu, Sarojini** 1879-1949 ............... **TCLC 80**
See also RGEL 2

**Naipaul, Shiva(dhar Srinivasa)** 1945-1985 ............................ **CLC 32, 39**
See also CA 112; CANR 33; DAM NOV; DLB 157; DLBY 1985; MTCW 1, 2

**Naipaul, V(idiadhar) S(urajprasad)** 1932- ........ **CLC 4, 7, 9, 13, 18, 37, 105; SSC 38**
See also BPFB 2; BRWS 1; CA 1-4R; CANR 1, 33, 51, 91; CDBLB 1960 to Present; CDWLB 3; CN 7; DAB; DAC; DAM MST, NOV; DLB 125, 204, 207; DLBY 1985, 2001; MTCW 1, 2; RGEL 2; RGSF 2; TWA; WLIT 4

**Nakos, Lilika** 1899(?)- ....................... **CLC 29**

**Narayan, R(asipuram) K(rishnaswami)** 1906-2001 . **CLC 7, 28, 47, 121; SSC 25**
See also BPFB 2; CA 81-84; CANR 33, 61, 112; CN 7; DAM NOV; DNFS 1; MTCW 1, 2; RGEL 2; RGSF 2; SATA 62; SSFS 5

**Nash, (Frediric) Ogden** 1902-1971 . **CLC 23; PC 21; TCLC 109**
See also CA 13-14; CANR 34, 61; CAP 1; DAM POET; DLB 11; MAICYA 1, 2; MTCW 1, 2; RGAL 4; SATA 2, 46; WP

**Nashe, Thomas** 1567-1601(?) ............... **LC 41**
See also DLB 167; RGEL 2

**Nathan, Daniel**
See Dannay, Frederic

**Nathan, George Jean** 1882-1958 .... **TCLC 18**
See Hatteras, Owen
See also CA 169; DLB 137

**Natsume, Kinnosuke**
See Natsume, Soseki

**Natsume, Soseki** 1867-1916 ........ **TCLC 2, 10**
See Natsume Soseki; Soseki
See also CA 195; RGWL 2, 3; TWA

**Natsume Soseki**
See Natsume, Soseki
See also DLB 180

**Natti, (Mary) Lee** 1919-
See Kingman, Lee
See also CA 5-8R; CANR 2

**Navarre, Marguerite de**
See de Navarre, Marguerite

**Naylor, Gloria** 1950- ..... **BLC 3; CLC 28, 52, 156; WLCS**
See also AAYA 6, 39; AFAW 1, 2; AMWS 8; BW 2, 3; CA 107; CANR 27, 51, 74; CN 7; CPW; DA; DAC; DAM MST, MULT, NOV, POP; DLB 173; FW; MTCW 1, 2; NFS 4, 7; RGAL 4; TUS

**Neff, Debra** ........................................ **CLC 59**

**Neihardt, John Gneisenau** 1881-1973 .................................... **CLC 32**
See also CA 13-14; CANR 65; CAP 1; DLB 9, 54, 256; LAIT 2

**Nekrasov, Nikolai Alekseevich** 1821-1878 ..................................... **NCLC 11**

**Nelligan, Emile** 1879-1941 ............... **TCLC 14**
See also DLB 92

**Nelson, Willie** 1933- ............................ **CLC 17**
See also CA 107; CANR 114

**Nemerov, Howard (Stanley)** 1920-1991 ........ **CLC 2, 6, 9, 36; PC 24; TCLC 124**
See also AMW; CA 1-4R; CABS 2; CANR 1, 27, 53; DAM POET; DLB 5, 6; DLBY 1983; INT CANR-27; MTCW 1, 2; PFS 10, 14; RGAL 4

**Neruda, Pablo** 1904-1973 .. **CLC 1, 2, 5, 7, 9, 28, 62; HLC 2; PC 4; WLC**
See also CA 19-20; CAP 2; DA; DAB; DAC; DAM MST, MULT, POET; DNFS 2; HW 1; LAW; MTCW 1, 2; PFS 11; RGWL 2, 3; TWA; WLIT 1; WP

**Nerval, Gerard de** 1808-1855 ... **NCLC 1, 67; PC 13; SSC 18**
See also DLB 217; EW 6; GFL 1789 to the Present; RGSF 2; RGWL 2, 3

**Nervo, (Jose) Amado (Ruiz de)** 1870-1919 ................ **HLCS 2; TCLC 11**
See also CA 131; HW 1; LAW

**Nesbit, Malcolm**
See Chester, Alfred

**Nessi, Pio Baroja y**
See Baroja (y Nessi), Pio

**Nestroy, Johann** 1801-1862 ............ **NCLC 42**
See also DLB 133; RGWL 2, 3

**Netterville, Luke**
See O'Grady, Standish (James)

**Neufeld, John (Arthur)** 1938- ............ **CLC 17**
See also AAYA 11; CA 25-28R; CANR 11, 37, 56; CLR 52; MAICYA 1, 2; SAAS 3; SATA 6, 81; SATA-Essay 131; YAW

**Neumann, Alfred** 1895-1952 ......... **TCLC 100**
See also CA 183; DLB 56

**Neumann, Ferenc**
See Molnar, Ferenc

**Neville, Emily Cheney** 1919- .............. **CLC 12**
See also BYA 2; CA 5-8R; CANR 3, 37, 85; JRDA; MAICYA 1, 2; SAAS 2; SATA 1; YAW

**Newbound, Bernard Slade** 1930-
See Slade, Bernard
See also CA 81-84; CANR 49; CD 5; DAM DRAM

**Newby, P(ercy) H(oward)** 1918-1997 ............................. **CLC 2, 13**
See also CA 5-8R; CANR 32, 67; CN 7; DAM NOV; DLB 15; MTCW 1; RGEL 2

**Newcastle**
See Cavendish, Margaret Lucas

**Newlove, Donald** 1928- ........................ **CLC 6**
See also CA 29-32R; CANR 25

**Newlove, John (Herbert)** 1938- ......... **CLC 14**
See also CA 21-24R; CANR 9, 25; CP 7

**Newman, Charles** 1938- .................. **CLC 2, 8**
See also CA 21-24R; CANR 84; CN 7

**Newman, Edwin (Harold)** 1919- ....... **CLC 14**
See also AITN 1; CA 69-72; CANR 5

**Newman, John Henry** 1801-1890 . **NCLC 38, 99**
See also BRWS 7; DLB 18, 32, 55; RGEL 2

**Newton, (Sir) Isaac** 1642-1727 ...... **LC 35, 53**
See also DLB 252

**Newton, Suzanne** 1936- ..................... **CLC 35**
See also BYA 7; CA 41-44R; CANR 14; JRDA; SATA 5, 77

**New York Dept. of Ed.** ...................... **CLC 70**

**Nexo, Martin Andersen** 1869-1954 ................................. **TCLC 43**
See also CA 202; DLB 214

**Nezval, Vitezslav** 1900-1958 ........... **TCLC 44**
See also CDWLB 4; DLB 215

**Ng, Fae Myenne** 1957(?)- ................... **CLC 81**
See also CA 146

**Ngema, Mbongeni** 1955- ................... **CLC 57**
See also BW 2; CA 143; CANR 84; CD 5

**Ngugi, James T(hiong'o)** ......... **CLC 3, 7, 13**
See Ngugi wa Thiong'o

**Ngugi wa Thiong'o**
See Ngugi wa Thiong'o
See also DLB 125

**Ngugi wa Thiong'o** 1938- ..... **BLC 3; CLC 36**
See Ngugi, James T(hiong'o); Ngugi wa Thiong'o
See also AFW; BRWS 8; BW 2; CA 81-84; CANR 27, 58; CDWLB 3; DAM MULT, NOV; DNFS 2; MTCW 1, 2; RGEL 2

**Nichol, B(arrie) P(hillip)** 1944-1988 . **CLC 18**
See also CA 53-56; DLB 53; SATA 66

**Nicholas of Cusa** 1401-1464 ................. **LC 80**
See also DLB 115

**Nichols, John (Treadwell)** 1940- ....... **CLC 38**
See also CA 9-12R; CAAE 190; CAAS 2; CANR 6, 70; DLBY 1982; TCWW 2

**Nichols, Leigh**
See Koontz, Dean R(ay)

**Nichols, Peter (Richard)** 1927- .... **CLC 5, 36, 65**
See also CA 104; CANR 33, 86; CBD; CD 5; DLB 13, 245; MTCW 1

**Nicholson, Linda ed.** ....................... **CLC 65**

**Ni Chuilleanain, Eilean** 1942- .............. **PC 34**
See also CA 126; CANR 53, 83; CP 7; CWP; DLB 40

**Nicolas, F. R. E.**
See Freeling, Nicolas

**Niedecker, Lorine** 1903-1970 ..... **CLC 10, 42; PC 42**
See also CA 25-28; CAP 2; DAM POET; DLB 48

**Nietzsche, Friedrich (Wilhelm)** 1844-1900 ................... **TCLC 10, 18, 55**
See also CA 121; CDWLB 2; DLB 129; EW 7; RGWL 2, 3; TWA

**Nievo, Ippolito** 1831-1861 ............... **NCLC 22**

**Nightingale, Anne Redmon** 1943-
See Redmon, Anne
See also CA 103

**Nightingale, Florence** 1820-1910 ... **TCLC 85**
See also CA 188; DLB 166

**Nijo Yoshimoto** 1320-1388 ............ **CMLC 49**
See also DLB 203

**Nik. T. O.**
See Annensky, Innokenty (Fyodorovich)

**Nin, Anais** 1903-1977 ..... **CLC 1, 4, 8, 11, 14, 60, 127; SSC 10**
See also AITN 2; AMWS 10; BPFB 2; CA 13-16R; CANR 22, 53; DAM NOV, POP; DLB 2, 4, 152; GLL 2; MAWW; MTCW 1, 2; RGAL 4; RGSF 2

**Nisbet, Robert A(lexander)** 1913-1996 ................................ **TCLC 117**
See also CA 25-28R; CANR 17; INT CANR-17

**Nishida, Kitaro** 1870-1945 .............. **TCLC 83**
**Nishiwaki, Junzaburo**
   See Nishiwaki, Junzaburo
   See also CA 194
**Nishiwaki, Junzaburo** 1894-1982 ........ **PC 15**
   See Nishiwaki, Junzaburo
   See also CA 194; MJW; RGWL 3
**Nissenson, Hugh** 1933- .................... **CLC 4, 9**
   See also CA 17-20R; CANR 27, 108; CN 7; DLB 28
**Niven, Larry** ........................ **CLC 8**
   See Niven, Laurence Van Cott
   See also AAYA 27; BPFB 2; BYA 10; DLB 8; SCFW 2
**Niven, Laurence Van Cott** 1938-
   See Niven, Larry
   See also CA 21-24R; CAAS 12; CANR 14, 44, 66, 113; CPW; DAM POP; MTCW 1, 2; SATA 95; SFW 4
**Nixon, Agnes Eckhardt** 1927- ........... **CLC 21**
   See also CA 110
**Nizan, Paul** 1905-1940 .................... **TCLC 40**
   See also CA 161; DLB 72; GFL 1789 to the Present
**Nkosi, Lewis** 1936- ............... **BLC 3; CLC 45**
   See also BW 1, 3; CA 65-68; CANR 27, 81; CBD; CD 5; DAM MULT; DLB 157, 225
**Nodier, (Jean) Charles (Emmanuel)**
   1780-1844 ........................ **NCLC 19**
   See also DLB 119; GFL 1789 to the Present
**Noguchi, Yone** 1875-1947 ................ **TCLC 80**
**Nolan, Christopher** 1965- .................... **CLC 58**
   See also CA 111; CANR 88
**Noon, Jeff** 1957- ......................... **CLC 91**
   See also CA 148; CANR 83; DLB 267; SFW 4
**Norden, Charles**
   See Durrell, Lawrence (George)
**Nordhoff, Charles (Bernard)**
   1887-1947 ........................ **TCLC 23**
   See also DLB 9; LAIT 1; RHW 1; SATA 23
**Norfolk, Lawrence** 1963- .................... **CLC 76**
   See also CA 144; CANR 85; CN 7; DLB 267
**Norman, Marsha** 1947- ......... **CLC 28; DC 8**
   See also CA 105; CABS 3; CAD; CANR 41; CD 5; CSW; CWD; DAM DRAM; DFS 2; DLB 266; DLBY 1984; FW
**Normyx**
   See Douglas, (George) Norman
**Norris, (Benjamin) Frank(lin, Jr.)**
   1870-1902 ................ **SSC 28; TCLC 24**
   See also AMW; BPFB 2; CA 160; CDALB 1865-1917; DLB 12, 71, 186; NFS 12; RGAL 4; TCWW 2; TUS
**Norris, Leslie** 1921- ..................... **CLC 14**
   See also CA 11-12; CANR 14; CAP 1; CP 7; DLB 27, 256
**North, Andrew**
   See Norton, Andre
**North, Anthony**
   See Koontz, Dean R(ay)
**North, Captain George**
   See Stevenson, Robert Louis (Balfour)
**North, Captain George**
   See Stevenson, Robert Louis (Balfour)
**North, Milou**
   See Erdrich, Louise
**Northrup, B. A.**
   See Hubbard, L(afayette) Ron(ald)
**North Staffs**
   See Hulme, T(homas) E(rnest)
**Northup, Solomon** 1808-1863 ....... **NCLC 105**
**Norton, Alice Mary**
   See Norton, Andre
   See also MAICYA 1; SATA 1, 43

**Norton, Andre** 1912- ..................... **CLC 12**
   See Norton, Alice Mary
   See also AAYA 14; BPFB 2; BYA 4, 10, 12; CA 1-4R; CANR 68; CLR 50; DLB 8, 52; JRDA; MAICYA 2; MTCW 1; SATA 91; SUFW 1, 2; YAW
**Norton, Caroline** 1808-1877 ........... **NCLC 47**
   See also DLB 21, 159, 199
**Norway, Nevil Shute** 1899-1960
   See Shute, Nevil
   See also CA 102; CANR 85; MTCW 2
**Norwid, Cyprian Kamil**
   1821-1883 .................. **NCLC 17**
   See also RGWL 3
**Nosille, Nabrah**
   See Ellison, Harlan (Jay)
**Nossack, Hans Erich** 1901-1978 ......... **CLC 6**
   See also CA 93-96; DLB 69
**Nostradamus** 1503-1566 ...................... **LC 27**
**Nosu, Chuji**
   See Ozu, Yasujiro
**Notenburg, Eleanora (Genrikhovna) von**
   See Guro, Elena
**Nova, Craig** 1945- ..................... **CLC 7, 31**
   See also CA 45-48; CANR 2, 53
**Novak, Joseph**
   See Kosinski, Jerzy (Nikodem)
**Novalis** 1772-1801 ............................ **NCLC 13**
   See also CDWLB 2; DLB 90; EW 5; RGWL 2, 3
**Novick, Peter** 1934- .......................... **CLC 164**
   See also CA 188
**Novis, Emile**
   See Weil, Simone (Adolphine)
**Nowlan, Alden (Albert)** 1933-1983 ... **CLC 15**
   See also CA 9-12R; CANR 5; DAC; DAM MST; DLB 53; PFS 12
**Noyes, Alfred** 1880-1958 ...... **PC 27; TCLC 7**
   See also CA 188; DLB 20; EXPP; FANT; PFS 4; RGEL 2
**Nunn, Kem** ................................. **CLC 34**
   See also CA 159
**Nwapa, Flora** 1931-1993 .... **BLCS; CLC 133**
   See also BW 2; CA 143; CANR 83; CDWLB 3; CWRI 5; DLB 125; WLIT 2
**Nye, Robert** 1939- .................... **CLC 13, 42**
   See also CA 33-36R; CANR 29, 67, 107; CN 7; CP 7; CWRI 5; DAM NOV; DLB 14, 271; FANT; HGG; MTCW 1; RHW; SATA 6
**Nyro, Laura** 1947-1997 ..................... **CLC 17**
   See also CA 194
**Oates, Joyce Carol** 1938- .. **CLC 1, 2, 3, 6, 9, 11, 15, 19, 33, 52, 108, 134; SSC 6; WLC**
   See also AAYA 15; AITN 1; AMWS 2; BEST 89:2; BPFB 2; BYA 11; CA 5-8R; CANR 25, 45, 74, 113, 113; CDALB 1968-1988; CN 7; CP 7; CPW; CWP; DA; DAB; DAC; DAM MST, NOV, POP; DLB 2, 5, 130; DLBY 1981; EXPS; FW; HGG; INT CANR-25; LAIT 4; MAWW; MTCW 1, 2; NFS 8; RGAL 4; RGSF 2; SSFS 1, 8; SUFW 2; TUS
**O'Brian, E. G.**
   See Clarke, Arthur C(harles)
**O'Brian, Patrick** 1914-2000 ............ **CLC 152**
   See also CA 144; CANR 74; CPW; MTCW 2; RHW
**O'Brien, Darcy** 1939-1998 ................ **CLC 11**
   See also CA 21-24R; CANR 8, 59
**O'Brien, Edna** 1936- ..... **CLC 3, 5, 8, 13, 36, 65, 116; SSC 10**
   See also BRWS 5; CA 1-4R; CANR 6, 41, 65, 102; CDBLB 1960 to Present; CN 7; DAM NOV; DLB 14, 231; FW; MTCW 1, 2; RGSF 2; WLIT 4
**O'Brien, Fitz-James** 1828-1862 ..... **NCLC 21**
   See also DLB 74; RGAL 4; SUFW

**O'Brien, Flann** .......... **CLC 1, 4, 5, 7, 10, 47**
   See O Nuallain, Brian
   See also BRWS 2; DLB 231; RGEL 2
**O'Brien, Richard** 1942- ..................... **CLC 17**
   See also CA 124
**O'Brien, (William) Tim(othy)** 1946- . **CLC 7, 19, 40, 103**
   See also AAYA 16; AMWS 5; CA 85-88; CANR 40, 58; CDALBS; CN 7; CPW; DAM POP; DLB 152; DLBD 9; DLBY 1980; MTCW 2; RGAL 4; SSFS 5, 15
**Obstfelder, Sigbjoern** 1866-1900 .... **TCLC 23**
**O'Casey, Sean** 1880-1964 .... **CLC 1, 5, 9, 11, 15, 88; DC 12; WLCS**
   See also BRW 7; CA 89-92; CANR 62; CBD; CDBLB 1914-1945; DAB; DAC; DAM DRAM, MST; DLB 10; MTCW 1, 2; RGEL 2; TEA; WLIT 4
**O'Cathasaigh, Sean**
   See O'Casey, Sean
**Occom, Samson** 1723-1792 .... **LC 60; NNAL**
   See also DLB 175
**Ochs, Phil(ip David)** 1940-1976 ........ **CLC 17**
   See also CA 185
**O'Connor, Edwin (Greene)**
   1918-1968 .................... **CLC 14**
   See also CA 93-96
**O'Connor, (Mary) Flannery**
   1925-1964 .... **CLC 1, 2, 3, 6, 10, 13, 15, 21, 66, 104; SSC 1, 23; WLC**
   See also AAYA 7; AMW; AMWR 2; BPFB 3; CA 1-4R; CANR 3, 41; CDALB 1941-1968; DA; DAB; DAC; DAM MST, NOV; DLB 2, 152; DLBD 12; DLBY 1980; EXPS; LAIT 5; MAWW; MTCW 1, 2; NFS 3; RGAL 4; RGSF 2; SSFS 2, 7, 10; TUS
**O'Connor, Frank** ................. **CLC 23; SSC 5**
   See O'Donovan, Michael Francis
   See also DLB 162; RGSF 2; SSFS 5
**O'Dell, Scott** 1898-1989 .................... **CLC 30**
   See also AAYA 3, 44; BPFB 3; BYA 1, 2, 3, 5; CA 61-64; CANR 12, 30, 112; CLR 1, 16; DLB 52; JRDA; MAICYA 1, 2; SATA 12, 60, 134; WYA; YAW
**Odets, Clifford** 1906-1963 ...... **CLC 2, 28, 98; DC 6**
   See also AMWS 2; CA 85-88; CAD; CANR 62; DAM DRAM; DFS 3; DLB 7, 26; MTCW 1, 2; RGAL 4; TUS
**O'Doherty, Brian** 1928- ..................... **CLC 76**
   See also CA 105; CANR 108
**O'Donnell, K. M.**
   See Malzberg, Barry N(athaniel)
**O'Donnell, Lawrence**
   See Kuttner, Henry
**O'Donovan, Michael Francis**
   1903-1966 .................... **CLC 14**
   See O'Connor, Frank
   See also CA 93-96; CANR 84
**Oe, Kenzaburo** 1935- .. **CLC 10, 36, 86; SSC 20**
   See Oe Kenzaburo
   See also CA 97-100; CANR 36, 50, 74; DAM NOV; DLBY 1994; MTCW 1, 2; RGWL 3
**Oe Kenzaburo**
   See Oe, Kenzaburo
   See also CWW 2; DLB 182; EWL 3; MJW; RGSF 2; RGWL 2
**O'Faolain, Julia** 1932- ..... **CLC 6, 19, 47, 108**
   See also CA 81-84; CAAS 2; CANR 12, 61; CN 7; DLB 14, 231; FW; MTCW 1; RHW
**O'Faolain, Sean** 1900-1991 ...... **CLC 1, 7, 14, 32, 70; SSC 13**
   See also CA 61-64; CANR 12, 66; DLB 15, 162; MTCW 1, 2; RGEL 2; RGSF 2

**O'Flaherty, Liam** 1896-1984 ....... **CLC 5, 34; SSC 6**
See also CA 101; CANR 35; DLB 36, 162; DLBY 1984; MTCW 1, 2; RGEL 2; RGSF 2; SSFS 5

**Ogai**
See Mori Ogai
See also MJW

**Ogilvy, Gavin**
See Barrie, J(ames) M(atthew)

**O'Grady, Standish (James)** 1846-1928 .................... **TCLC 5**
See also CA 157

**O'Grady, Timothy** 1951- .................... **CLC 59**
See also CA 138

**O'Hara, Frank** 1926-1966 ....... **CLC 2, 5, 13, 78; PC 45**
See also CA 9-12R; CANR 33; DAM POET; DLB 5, 16, 193; MTCW 1, 2; PFS 8; 12; RGAL 4; WP

**O'Hara, John (Henry)** 1905-1970 . **CLC 1, 2, 3, 6, 11, 42; SSC 15**
See also AMW; BPFB 3; CA 5-8R; CANR 31, 60; CDALB 1929-1941; DAM NOV; DLB 9, 86; DLBD 2; MTCW 1, 2; NFS 11; RGAL 4; RGSF 2

**O Hehir, Diana** 1922- ......................... **CLC 41**
See also CA 93-96

**Ohiyesa**
See Eastman, Charles A(lexander)

**Okigbo, Christopher (Ifenayichukwu)** 1932-1967 .... **BLC 3; CLC 25, 84; PC 7**
See also AFW; BW 1, 3; CA 77-80; CANR 74; CDWLB 3; DAM MULT, POET; DLB 125; MTCW 1, 2; RGEL 2

**Okri, Ben** 1959- .................... **CLC 87**
See also AFW; BRWS 5; BW 2, 3; CA 138; CANR 65; CN 7; DLB 157, 231; INT CA-138; MTCW 2; RGSF 2; WLIT 2

**Olds, Sharon** 1942- .. **CLC 32, 39, 85; PC 22**
See also AMWS 10; CA 101; CANR 18, 41, 66, 98; CP 7; CPW; CWP; DAM POET; DLB 120; MTCW 2; PFS 17

**Oldstyle, Jonathan**
See Irving, Washington

**Olesha, Iurii**
See Olesha, Yuri (Karlovich)
See also RGWL 2

**Olesha, Iurii Karlovich**
See Olesha, Yuri (Karlovich)
See also DLB 272

**Olesha, Yuri (Karlovich)** 1899-1960 .. **CLC 8**
See Olesha, Iurii; Olesha, Iurii Karlovich
See also CA 85-88; EW 11; RGWL 3

**Oliphant, Mrs.**
See Oliphant, Margaret (Oliphant Wilson)
See also SUFW

**Oliphant, Laurence** 1829(?)-1888 .. **NCLC 47**
See also DLB 18, 166

**Oliphant, Margaret (Oliphant Wilson)** 1828-1897 ........... **NCLC 11, 61; SSC 25**
See Oliphant, Mrs.
See also DLB 18, 159, 190; HGG; RGEL 2; RGSF 2

**Oliver, Mary** 1935- ................. **CLC 19, 34, 98**
See also AMWS 7; CA 21-24R; CANR 9, 43, 84, 92; CP 7; CWP; DLB 5, 193; PFS 15

**Olivier, Laurence (Kerr)** 1907-1989 . **CLC 20**
See also CA 150

**Olsen, Tillie** 1912- ... **CLC 4, 13, 114; SSC 11**
See also BYA 11; CA 1-4R; CANR 1, 43, 74; CDALBS; CN 7; DA; DAB; DAC; DAM MST; DLB 28, 206; DLBY 1980; EXPS; FW; MTCW 1, 2; RGAL 4; RGSF 2; SSFS 1; TUS

**Olson, Charles (John)** 1910-1970 .. **CLC 1, 2, 5, 6, 9, 11, 29; PC 19**
See also AMWS 2; CA 13-16; CABS 2; CANR 35, 61; CAP 1; DAM POET; DLB 5, 16, 193; MTCW 1, 2; RGAL 4; WP

**Olson, Toby** 1937- ............................. **CLC 28**
See also CA 65-68; CANR 9, 31, 84; CP 7

**Olyesha, Yuri**
See Olesha, Yuri (Karlovich)

**Omar Khayyam**
See Khayyam, Omar
See also RGWL 2, 3

**Ondaatje, (Philip) Michael** 1943- .... **CLC 14, 29, 51, 76; PC 28**
See also CA 77-80; CANR 42, 74, 109; CN 7; CP 7; DAB; DAC; DAM MST; DLB 60; MTCW 2; PFS 8; TWA

**Oneal, Elizabeth** 1934-
See Oneal, Zibby
See also CA 106; CANR 28, 84; MAICYA 1, 2; SATA 30, 82; YAW

**Oneal, Zibby** .............................. **CLC 30**
See Oneal, Elizabeth
See also AAYA 5, 41; BYA 13; CLR 13; JRDA; WYA

**O'Neill, Eugene (Gladstone)** 1888-1953 ....... **TCLC 1, 6, 27, 49; WLC**
See also AITN 1; AMW; AMWC 1; CA 132; CAD; CDALB 1929-1941; DA; DAB; DAC; DAM DRAM, MST; DFS 9, 11, 12, 16; DLB 7; LAIT 3; MTCW 1, 2; RGAL 4; TUS

**Onetti, Juan Carlos** 1909-1994 ... **CLC 7, 10; HLCS 2; SSC 23; TCLC 131**
See also CA 85-88; CANR 32, 63; CDWLB 3; DAM MULT, NOV; DLB 113; HW 1, 2; LAW; MTCW 1, 2; RGSF 2

**O Nuallain, Brian** 1911-1966
See O'Brien, Flann
See also CA 21-22; CAP 2; DLB 231; FANT; TEA

**Ophuls, Max** 1902-1957 .................... **TCLC 79**

**Opie, Amelia** 1769-1853 .................. **NCLC 65**
See also DLB 116, 159; RGEL 2

**Oppen, George** 1908-1984 ..... **CLC 7, 13, 34; PC 35; TCLC 107**
See also CA 13-16R; CANR 8, 82; DLB 5, 165

**Oppenheim, E(dward) Phillips** 1866-1946 ............................... **TCLC 45**
See also CA 202; CMW 4; DLB 70

**Opuls, Max**
See Ophuls, Max

**Origen** c. 185-c. 254 ...................... **CMLC 19**

**Orlovitz, Gil** 1918-1973 .................... **CLC 22**
See also CA 77-80; DLB 2, 5

**Orris**
See Ingelow, Jean

**Ortega y Gasset, Jose** 1883-1955 ....... **HLC 2; TCLC 9**
See also CA 130; DAM MULT; EW 9; HW 1, 2; MTCW 1, 2

**Ortese, Anna Maria** 1914-1998 ........ **CLC 89**
See also DLB 177

**Ortiz, Simon J(oseph)** 1941- ............ **CLC 45; NNAL; PC 17**
See also AMWS 4; CA 134; CANR 69; CP 7; DAM MULT, POET; DLB 120, 175, 256; EXPP; PFS 4, 16; RGAL 4

**Orton, Joe** ................ **CLC 4, 13, 43; DC 3**
See Orton, John Kingsley
See also BRWS 5; CBD; CDBLB 1960 to Present; DFS 3, 6; DLB 13; GLL 1; MTCW 2; RGEL 2; TEA; WLIT 4

**Orton, John Kingsley** 1933-1967
See Orton, Joe
See also CA 85-88; CANR 35, 66; DAM DRAM; MTCW 1, 2

**Orwell, George** . **TCLC 2, 6, 15, 31, 51, 128, 129; WLC**
See Blair, Eric (Arthur)
See also BPFB 3; BRW 7; BYA 5; CDBLB 1945-1960; CLR 68; DAB; DLB 15, 98, 195, 255; EXPN; LAIT 4, 5; NFS 3, 7; RGEL 2; SCFW 2; SFW 4; SSFS 4; TEA; WLIT 4; YAW

**Osborne, David**
See Silverberg, Robert

**Osborne, George**
See Silverberg, Robert

**Osborne, John (James)** 1929-1994 .... **CLC 1, 2, 5, 11, 45; WLC**
See also BRWS 1; CA 13-16R; CANR 21, 56; CDBLB 1945-1960; DA; DAB; DAC; DAM DRAM, MST; DFS 4; DLB 13; MTCW 1, 2; RGEL 2

**Osborne, Lawrence** 1958- ................. **CLC 50**
See also CA 189

**Osbourne, Lloyd** 1868-1947 .......... **TCLC 93**

**Oshima, Nagisa** 1932- ...................... **CLC 20**
See also CA 121; CANR 78

**Oskison, John Milton** 1874-1947 .................... **NNAL; TCLC 35**
See also CA 144; CANR 84; DAM MULT; DLB 175

**Ossian** c. 3rd cent. - ......................... **CMLC 28**
See Macpherson, James

**Ossoli, Sarah Margaret (Fuller)** 1810-1850 .............................. **NCLC 5, 50**
See Fuller, Margaret; Fuller, Sarah Margaret
See also CDALB 1640-1865; FW; SATA 25

**Ostriker, Alicia (Suskin)** 1937- ........ **CLC 132**
See also CA 25-28R; CAAS 24; CANR 10, 30, 62, 99; CWP; DLB 120; EXPP

**Ostrovsky, Alexander** 1823-1886 .. **NCLC 30, 57**

**Otero, Blas de** 1916-1979 ................. **CLC 11**
See also CA 89-92; DLB 134

**Otto, Rudolf** 1869-1937 .................... **TCLC 85**

**Otto, Whitney** 1955- ........................... **CLC 70**
See also CA 140

**Ouida** .............................................. **TCLC 43**
See De la Ramee, Marie Louise (Ouida)
See also DLB 18, 156; RGEL 2

**Ouologuem, Yambo** 1940- ................. **CLC 146**
See also CA 176

**Ousmane, Sembene** 1923- ... **BLC 3; CLC 66**
See Sembene, Ousmane
See also BW 1, 3; CA 125; CANR 81; CWW 2; MTCW 1

**Ovid** 43B.C.-17 ....................... **CMLC 7; PC 2**
See also AW 2; CDWLB 1; DAM POET; DLB 211; RGWL 2, 3; WP

**Owen, Hugh**
See Faust, Frederick (Schiller)

**Owen, Wilfred (Edward Salter)** 1893-1918 ... **PC 19; TCLC 5, 27; WLC**
See also BRW 6; CA 141; CDBLB 1914-1945; DA; DAB; DAC; DAM MST, POET; DLB 20; EXPP; MTCW 2; PFS 10; RGEL 2; WLIT 4

**Owens, Rochelle** 1936- ........................... **CLC 8**
See also CA 17-20R; CAAS 2; CAD; CANR 39; CD 5; CP 7; CWD; CWP

**Oz, Amos** 1939- ........ **CLC 5, 8, 11, 27, 33, 54**
See also CA 53-56; CANR 27, 47, 65, 113; CWW 2; DAM NOV; MTCW 1, 2; RGSF 2; RGWL 3

**Ozick, Cynthia** 1928- ......... **CLC 3, 7, 28, 62, 155; SSC 15**
See also AMWS 5; BEST 90:1; CA 17-20R; CANR 23, 58; CN 7; CPW; DAM NOV, POP; DLB 28, 152; DLBY 1982; EXPS; INT CANR-23; MTCW 1, 2; RGAL 4; RGSF 2; SSFS 3, 12

**Ozu, Yasujiro** 1903-1963 .................. **CLC 16**
See also CA 112

**Pabst, G. W.** 1885-1967 .............. **TCLC 127**
**Pacheco, C.**
　See Pessoa, Fernando (Antonio Nogueira)
**Pacheco, Jose Emilio** 1939- .................. **HLC 2**
　See also CA 131; CANR 65; DAM MULT;
　HW 1, 2; RGSF 2
**Pa Chin** .................................................. **CLC 18**
　See Li Fei-kan
**Pack, Robert** 1929- ................................ **CLC 13**
　See also CA 1-4R; CANR 3, 44, 82; CP 7;
　DLB 5; SATA 118
**Padgett, Lewis**
　See Kuttner, Henry
**Padilla (Lorenzo), Heberto**
　1932-2000 ............................................. **CLC 38**
　See also AITN 1; CA 131; HW 1
**Page, James Patrick** 1944-
　See Page, Jimmy
　See also CA 204
**Page, Jimmy** 1944- .................................. **CLC 12**
　See Page, James Patrick
**Page, Louise** 1955- ................................ **CLC 40**
　See also CA 140; CANR 76; CBD; CD 5;
　CWD; DLB 233
**Page, P(atricia) K(athleen)** 1916- ...... **CLC 7,
　18; PC 12**
　See Cape, Judith
　See also CA 53-56; CANR 4, 22, 65; CP 7;
　DAC; DAM MST; DLB 68; MTCW 1;
　RGEL 2
**Page, Stanton**
　See Fuller, Henry Blake
**Page, Stanton**
　See Fuller, Henry Blake
**Page, Thomas Nelson** 1853-1922 ....... **SSC 23**
　See also CA 177; DLB 12, 78; DLBD 13;
　RGAL 4
**Pagels, Elaine Hiesey** 1943- ............. **CLC 104**
　See also CA 45-48; CANR 2, 24, 51; FW;
　NCFS 4
**Paget, Violet** 1856-1935
　See Lee, Vernon
　See also CA 166; GLL 1; HGG
**Paget-Lowe, Henry**
　See Lovecraft, H(oward) P(hillips)
**Paglia, Camille (Anna)** 1947- ............ **CLC 68**
　See also CA 140; CANR 72; CPW; FW;
　GLL 2; MTCW 2
**Paige, Richard**
　See Koontz, Dean R(ay)
**Paine, Thomas** 1737-1809 ................ **NCLC 62**
　See also AMWS 1; CDALB 1640-1865;
　DLB 31, 43, 73, 158; LAIT 1; RGAL 4;
　RGEL 2; TUS
**Pakenham, Antonia**
　See Fraser, (Lady) Antonia (Pakenham)
**Palamas, Costis**
　See Palamas, Kostes
**Palamas, Kostes** 1859-1943 ............... **TCLC 5**
　See also CA 190; RGWL 2, 3
**Palamas, Kostis**
　See Palamas, Kostes
**Palazzeschi, Aldo** 1885-1974 ............. **CLC 11**
　See also CA 89-92; DLB 114, 264
**Pales Matos, Luis** 1898-1959 ............ **HLCS 2**
　See Pales Matos, Luis
　See also HW 1; LAW
**Paley, Grace** 1922- .. **CLC 4, 6, 37, 140; SSC
　8**
　See also AMWS 6; CA 25-28R; CANR 13,
　46, 74; CN 7; CPW; DAM POP; DLB 28,
　218; EXPS; FW; INT CANR-13; MAWW;
　MTCW 1, 2; RGAL 4; RGSF 2; SSFS 3
**Palin, Michael (Edward)** 1943- ......... **CLC 21**
　See Monty Python
　See also CA 107; CANR 35, 109; SATA 67
**Palliser, Charles** 1947- ........................ **CLC 65**
　See also CA 136; CANR 76; CN 7

**Palma, Ricardo** 1833-1919 .............. **TCLC 29**
　See also CA 168; LAW
**Pancake, Breece Dexter** 1952-1979
　See Pancake, Breece D'J
　See also CA 123
**Pancake, Breece D'J** ......................... **CLC 29**
　See Pancake, Breece Dexter
　See also DLB 130
**Panchenko, Nikolai** ............................ **CLC 59**
**Pankhurst, Emmeline (Goulden)**
　1858-1928 ............................................ **TCLC 100**
　See also FW
**Panko, Rudy**
　See Gogol, Nikolai (Vasilyevich)
**Papadiamantis, Alexandros**
　1851-1911 ............................................. **TCLC 29**
　See also CA 168
**Papadiamantopoulos, Johannes** 1856-1910
　See Moreas, Jean
**Papini, Giovanni** 1881-1956 ........... **TCLC 22**
　See also CA 180; DLB 264
**Paracelsus** 1493-1541 ........................... **LC 14**
　See also DLB 179
**Parasol, Peter**
　See Stevens, Wallace
**Pardo Bazan, Emilia** 1851-1921 ........ **SSC 30**
　See also FW; RGSF 2; RGWL 2, 3
**Pareto, Vilfredo** 1848-1923 ............. **TCLC 69**
　See also CA 175
**Paretsky, Sara** 1947- ........................ **CLC 135**
　See also AAYA 30; BEST 90:3; CA 129;
　CANR 59, 95; CMW 4; CPW; DAM
　POP; INT CA-129; MSW; RGAL 4
**Parfenie, Maria**
　See Codrescu, Andrei
**Parini, Jay (Lee)** 1948- .............. **CLC 54, 133**
　See also CA 97-100; CAAS 16; CANR 32,
　87
**Park, Jordan**
　See Kornbluth, C(yril) M.; Pohl, Frederik
**Park, Robert E(zra)** 1864-1944 ..... **TCLC 73**
　See also CA 165
**Parker, Bert**
　See Ellison, Harlan (Jay)
**Parker, Dorothy (Rothschild)**
　1893-1967 .. **CLC 15, 68; PC 28; SSC 2**
　See also AMWS 9; CA 19-20; CAP 2; DAM
　POET; DLB 11, 45, 86; EXPP; FW;
　MAWW; MTCW 1, 2; RGAL 4; RGSF 2;
　TUS
**Parker, Robert B(rown)** 1932- .......... **CLC 27**
　See also AAYA 28; BEST 89:4; BPFB 3;
　CA 49-52; CANR 1, 26, 52, 89; CMW 4;
　CPW; DAM NOV, POP; INT CANR-26;
　MSW; MTCW 1
**Parkin, Frank** 1940- ............................ **CLC 43**
　See also CA 147
**Parkman, Francis, Jr.** 1823-1893 .. **NCLC 12**
　See also AMWS 2; DLB 1, 30, 183, 186,
　235; RGAL 4
**Parks, Gordon (Alexander Buchanan)**
　1912- .......................... **BLC 3; CLC 1, 16**
　See also AAYA 36; AITN 2; BW 2, 3; CA
　41-44R; CANR 26, 66; DAM MULT;
　DLB 33; MTCW 2; SATA 8, 108
**Parks, Tim(othy Harold)** 1954- ....... **CLC 147**
　See also CA 131; CANR 77; DLB 231; INT
　CA-131
**Parmenides** c. 515B.C.-c.
　450B.C. .................................... **CMLC 22**
　See also DLB 176
**Parnell, Thomas** 1679-1718 ................... **LC 3**
　See also DLB 95; RGEL 2
**Parr, Catherine** c. 1513(?)-1548 .......... **LC 86**
　See also DLB 136
**Parra, Nicanor** 1914- ... **CLC 2, 102; HLC 2;
　PC 39**
　See also CA 85-88; CANR 32; CWW 2;
　DAM MULT; HW 1; LAW; MTCW 1

**Parra Sanojo, Ana Teresa de la**
　1890-1936 .................................. **HLCS 2**
　See de la Parra, (Ana) Teresa (Sonojo)
　See also LAW
**Parrish, Mary Frances**
　See Fisher, M(ary) F(rances) K(ennedy)
**Parshchikov, Aleksei** ........................ **CLC 59**
**Parson, Professor**
　See Coleridge, Samuel Taylor
**Parson Lot**
　See Kingsley, Charles
**Parton, Sara Payson Willis**
　1811-1872 ................................. **NCLC 86**
　See also DLB 43, 74, 239
**Partridge, Anthony**
　See Oppenheim, E(dward) Phillips
**Pascal, Blaise** 1623-1662 ...................... **LC 35**
　See also DLB 268; EW 3; GFL Beginnings
　to 1789; RGWL 2, 3; TWA
**Pascoli, Giovanni** 1855-1912 .......... **TCLC 45**
　See also CA 170; EW 7
**Pasolini, Pier Paolo** 1922-1975 .. **CLC 20, 37,
　106; PC 17**
　See also CA 93-96; CANR 63; DLB 128,
　177; MTCW 1; RGWL 2, 3
**Pasquini**
　See Silone, Ignazio
**Pastan, Linda (Olenik)** 1932- ........... **CLC 27**
　See also CA 61-64; CANR 18, 40, 61, 113;
　CP 7; CSW; CWP; DAM POET; DLB 5;
　PFS 8
**Pasternak, Boris (Leonidovich)**
　1890-1960 ...... **CLC 7, 10, 18, 63; PC 6;
　SSC 31; WLC**
　See also BPFB 3; CA 127; DA; DAB;
　DAC; DAM MST, NOV, POET; EW 10;
　MTCW 1, 2; RGSF 2; RGWL 2, 3; TWA;
　WP
**Patchen, Kenneth** 1911-1972 .... **CLC 1, 2, 18**
　See also BG 3; CA 1-4R; CANR 3, 35;
　DAM POET; DLB 16, 48; MTCW 1;
　RGAL 4
**Pater, Walter (Horatio)** 1839-1894 . **NCLC 7,
　90**
　See also BRW 5; CDBLB 1832-1890; DLB
　57, 156; RGEL 2; TEA
**Paterson, A(ndrew) B(arton)**
　1864-1941 .............................. **TCLC 32**
　See also CA 155; DLB 230; RGEL 2; SATA
　97
**Paterson, Katherine (Womeldorf)**
　1932- ................................. **CLC 12, 30**
　See also AAYA 1, 31; BYA 1, 2, 7; CA 21-
　24R; CANR 28, 59, 111; CLR 7, 50;
　CWRI 5; DLB 52; JRDA; LAIT 4; MAI-
　CYA 1, 2; MAICYAS 1; MTCW 1; SATA
　13, 53, 92, 133; WYA; YAW
**Patmore, Coventry Kersey Dighton**
　1823-1896 .................................... **NCLC 9**
　See also DLB 35, 98; RGEL 2; TEA
**Paton, Alan (Stewart)** 1903-1988 ...... **CLC 4,
　10, 25, 55, 106; WLC**
　See also AAYA 26; AFW; BPFB 3; BRWS
　2; BYA 1; CA 13-16; CANR 22; CAP 1;
　DA; DAB; DAC; DAM MST, NOV; DLB
　225; DLBD 17; EXPN; LAIT 4; MTCW
　1, 2; NFS 3, 12; RGEL 2; SATA 11;
　SATA-Obit 56; TWA; WLIT 2
**Paton Walsh, Gillian** 1937- ............... **CLC 35**
　See Paton Walsh, Jill; Walsh, Jill Paton
　See also AAYA 11; CANR 38, 83; CLR 2,
　65; DLB 161; JRDA; MAICYA 1, 2;
　SAAS 3; SATA 4, 72, 109; YAW
**Paton Walsh, Jill**
　See Paton Walsh, Gillian
　See also AAYA 47; BYA 1, 8
**Patton, George S(mith), Jr.**
　1885-1945 ................................ **TCLC 79**
　See also CA 189

**Paulding, James Kirke** 1778-1860 ... **NCLC 2**
See also DLB 3, 59, 74, 250; RGAL 4

**Paulin, Thomas Neilson** 1949-
See Paulin, Tom
See also CA 128; CANR 98; CP 7

**Paulin, Tom** ........................................ **CLC 37**
See Paulin, Thomas Neilson
See also DLB 40

**Pausanias** c. 1st cent. - ................... **CMLC 36**

**Paustovsky, Konstantin (Georgievich)**
1892-1968 ................................. **CLC 40**
See also CA 93-96; DLB 272

**Pavese, Cesare** 1908-1950 .... **PC 13; SSC 19; TCLC 3**
See also CA 169; DLB 128, 177; EW 12; RGSF 2; RGWL 2, 3; TWA

**Pavic, Milorad** 1929- ........................ **CLC 60**
See also CA 136; CDWLB 4; CWW 2; DLB 181; RGWL 3

**Pavlov, Ivan Petrovich** 1849-1936 . **TCLC 91**
See also CA 180

**Payne, Alan**
See Jakes, John (William)

**Paz, Gil**
See Lugones, Leopoldo

**Paz, Octavio** 1914-1998 . **CLC 3, 4, 6, 10, 19, 51, 65, 119; HLC 2; PC 1; WLC**
See also CA 73-76; CANR 32, 65, 104; CWW 2; DA; DAB; DAC; DAM MST, MULT, POET; DLBY 1990, 1998; DNFS 1; HW 1; LAW; LAWS 1; MTCW 1, 2; RGWL 2, 3; SSFS 13; TWA; WLIT 1

**p'Bitek, Okot** 1931-1982 ..... **BLC 3; CLC 96**
See also AFW; BW 2, 3; CA 124; CANR 82; DAM MULT; DLB 125; MTCW 1, 2; RGEL 2; WLIT 2

**Peacock, Molly** 1947- ......................... **CLC 60**
See also CA 103; CAAS 21; CANR 52, 84; CP 7; CWP; DLB 120

**Peacock, Thomas Love**
1785-1866 ................................. **NCLC 22**
See also BRW 4; DLB 96, 116; RGEL 2; RGSF 2

**Peake, Mervyn** 1911-1968 ............. **CLC 7, 54**
See also CA 5-8R; CANR 3; DLB 15, 160, 255; FANT; MTCW 1; RGEL 2; SATA 23; SFW 4

**Pearce, Philippa**
See Christie, Philippa
See also CA 5-8R; CANR 4, 109; CWRI 5; FANT; MAICYA 2

**Pearl, Eric**
See Elman, Richard (Martin)

**Pearson, T(homas) R(eid)** 1956- ....... **CLC 39**
See also CA 130; CANR 97; CSW; INT 130

**Peck, Dale** 1967- ................................ **CLC 81**
See also CA 146; CANR 72; GLL 2

**Peck, John (Frederick)** 1941- ............. **CLC 3**
See also CA 49-52; CANR 3, 100; CP 7

**Peck, Richard (Wayne)** 1934- .......... **CLC 21**
See also AAYA 1, 24; BYA 1, 6, 8, 11; CA 85-88; CANR 19, 38; CLR 15; INT CANR-19; JRDA; MAICYA 1, 2; SAAS 2; SATA 18, 55, 97; SATA-Essay 110; WYA; YAW

**Peck, Robert Newton** 1928- ............... **CLC 17**
See also AAYA 3, 43; BYA 1, 6; CA 81-84, 182; CAAE 182; CANR 31, 63; CLR 45; DA; DAC; DAM MST; JRDA; LAIT 3; MAICYA 1, 2; SAAS 1; SATA 21, 62, 111; SATA-Essay 108; WYA; YAW

**Peckinpah, (David) Sam(uel)**
1925-1984 ................................. **CLC 20**
See also CA 109; CANR 82

**Pedersen, Knut** 1859-1952
See Hamsun, Knut
See also CA 119; CANR 63; MTCW 1, 2

**Peeslake, Gaffer**
See Durrell, Lawrence (George)

**Peguy, Charles (Pierre)**
1873-1914 ................................. **TCLC 10**
See also CA 193; DLB 258; GFL 1789 to the Present

**Peirce, Charles Sanders**
1839-1914 ................................. **TCLC 81**
See also CA 194; DLB 270

**Pellicer, Carlos** 1900(?)-1977 ............ **HLCS 2**
See also CA 153; HW 1

**Pena, Ramon del Valle y**
See Valle-Inclan, Ramon (Maria) del

**Pendennis, Arthur Esquir**
See Thackeray, William Makepeace

**Penn, William** 1644-1718 ..................... **LC 25**
See also DLB 24

**PEPECE**
See Prado (Calvo), Pedro

**Pepys, Samuel** 1633-1703 ... **LC 11, 58; WLC**
See also BRW 2; CDBLB 1660-1789; DA; DAB; DAC; DAM MST; DLB 101, 213; NCFS 4; RGEL 2; TEA; WLIT 3

**Percy, Thomas** 1729-1811 ............... **NCLC 95**
See also DLB 104

**Percy, Walker** 1916-1990 ....... **CLC 2, 3, 6, 8, 14, 18, 47, 65**
See also AMWS 3; BPFB 3; CA 1-4R; CANR 1, 23, 64; CPW; CSW; DAM NOV, POP; DLB 2; DLBY 1980, 1990; MTCW 1, 2; RGAL 4; TUS

**Percy, William Alexander**
1885-1942 ................................. **TCLC 84**
See also CA 163; MTCW 2

**Perec, Georges** 1936-1982 ......... **CLC 56, 116**
See also CA 141; DLB 83; GFL 1789 to the Present; RGWL 3

**Pereda (y Sanchez de Porrua), Jose Maria de** 1833-1906 ................. **TCLC 16**

**Pereda y Porrua, Jose Maria de**
See Pereda (y Sanchez de Porrua), Jose Maria de

**Peregoy, George Weems**
See Mencken, H(enry) L(ouis)

**Perelman, S(idney) J(oseph)**
1904-1979 .. **CLC 3, 5, 9, 15, 23, 44, 49; SSC 32**
See also AITN 1, 2; BPFB 3; CA 73-76; CANR 18; DAM DRAM; DLB 11, 44; MTCW 1, 2; RGAL 4

**Peret, Benjamin** 1899-1959 .... **PC 33; TCLC 20**
See also CA 186; GFL 1789 to the Present

**Peretz, Isaac Loeb** 1851(?)-1915 ....... **SSC 26; TCLC 16**

**Peretz, Yitzhok Leibush**
See Peretz, Isaac Loeb

**Perez Galdos, Benito** 1843-1920 ..... **HLCS 2; TCLC 27**
See Galdos, Benito Perez
See also CA 153; HW 1; RGWL 2, 3

**Peri Rossi, Cristina** 1941- .. **CLC 156; HLCS 2**
See also CA 131; CANR 59, 81; DLB 145; HW 1, 2

**Perlata**
See Peret, Benjamin

**Perloff, Marjorie G(abrielle)**
1931- ........................................ **CLC 137**
See also CA 57-60; CANR 7, 22, 49, 104

**Perrault, Charles** 1628-1703 ... **DC 12; LC 2, 56**
See also BYA 4; CLR 79; DLB 268; GFL Beginnings to 1789; MAICYA 1, 2; RGWL 2, 3; SATA 25; WCH

**Perry, Anne** 1938- ........................... **CLC 126**
See also CA 101; CANR 22, 50, 84; CMW 4; CN 7; CPW

**Perry, Brighton**
See Sherwood, Robert E(mmet)

**Perse, St.-John**
See Leger, (Marie-Rene Auguste) Alexis Saint-Leger

**Perse, Saint-John**
See Leger, (Marie-Rene Auguste) Alexis Saint-Leger
See also DLB 258; RGWL 3

**Perutz, Leo(pold)** 1882-1957 .......... **TCLC 60**
See also CA 147; DLB 81

**Peseenz, Tulio F.**
See Lopez y Fuentes, Gregorio

**Pesetsky, Bette** 1932- ........................ **CLC 28**
See also CA 133; DLB 130

**Peshkov, Alexei Maximovich** 1868-1936
See Gorky, Maxim
See also CA 141; CANR 83; DA; DAC; DAM DRAM, MST, NOV; MTCW 2

**Pessoa, Fernando (Antonio Nogueira)**
1898-1935 ..... **HLC 2; PC 20; TCLC 27**
See also CA 183; DAM MULT; EW 10; RGWL 2, 3; WP

**Peterkin, Julia Mood** 1880-1961 ...... **CLC 31**
See also CA 102; DLB 9

**Peters, Joan K(aren)** 1945- ................. **CLC 39**
See also CA 158; CANR 109

**Peters, Robert L(ouis)** 1924- ............... **CLC 7**
See also CA 13-16R; CAAS 8; CP 7; DLB 105

**Petofi, Sandor** 1823-1849 ................ **NCLC 21**
See also RGWL 2, 3

**Petrakis, Harry Mark** 1923- ................. **CLC 3**
See also CA 9-12R; CANR 4, 30, 85; CN 7

**Petrarch** 1304-1374 ............. **CMLC 20; PC 8**
See also DAM POET; EW 2; RGWL 2. 3

**Petronius** c. 20-66 ............................ **CMLC 34**
See also AW 2; CDWLB 1; DLB 211; RGWL 2, 3

**Petrov, Evgeny** ................................ **TCLC 21**
See Kataev, Evgeny Petrovich

**Petry, Ann (Lane)** 1908-1997 .. **CLC 1, 7, 18; TCLC 112**
See also AFAW 1, 2; BPFB 3; BW 1, 3; BYA 2; CA 5-8R; CAAS 6; CANR 4, 46; CLR 12; CN 7; DLB 76; JRDA; LAIT 1; MAICYA 1, 2; MAICYAS 1; MTCW 1; RGAL 4; SATA 5; SATA-Obit 94; TUS

**Petursson, Halligrimur** 1614-1674 ........ **LC 8**

**Peychinovich**
See Vazov, Ivan (Minchov)

**Phaedrus** c. 15B.C.-c. 50 ................ **CMLC 25**
See also DLB 211

**Phelps (Ward), Elizabeth Stuart**
See Phelps, Elizabeth Stuart
See also FW

**Phelps, Elizabeth Stuart**
1844-1911 ................................. **TCLC 113**
See Phelps (Ward), Elizabeth Stuart
See also DLB 74

**Philips, Katherine** 1632-1664 . **LC 30; PC 40**
See also DLB 131; RGEL 2

**Philipson, Morris H.** 1926- ............... **CLC 53**
See also CA 1-4R; CANR 4

**Phillips, Caryl** 1958- ............... **BLCS; CLC 96**
See also BRWS 5; BW 2; CA 141; CANR 63, 104; CBD; CD 5; CN 7; DAM MULT; DLB 157; MTCW 2; WLIT 4

**Phillips, David Graham**
1867-1911 ................................. **TCLC 44**
See also CA 176; DLB 9, 12; RGAL 4

**Phillips, Jack**
See Sandburg, Carl (August)

**Phillips, Jayne Anne** 1952- ........ **CLC 15, 33, 139; SSC 16**
See also BPFB 3; CA 101; CANR 24, 50, 96; CN 7; CSW; DLBY 1980; INT CANR-24; MTCW 1, 2; RGAL 4; RGSF 2; SSFS 4

**Phillips, Richard**
See Dick, Philip K(indred)

**Phillips, Robert (Schaeffer)** 1938- .... **CLC 28**
See also CA 17-20R; CAAS 13; CANR 8; DLB 105

**Phillips, Ward**
See Lovecraft, H(oward) P(hillips)

**Piccolo, Lucio** 1901-1969 ................... **CLC 13**
See also CA 97-100; DLB 114

**Pickthall, Marjorie L(owry) C(hristie)** 1883-1922 ............................. **TCLC 21**
See also DLB 92

**Pico della Mirandola, Giovanni** 1463-1494 ....................................... **LC 15**

**Piercy, Marge** 1936- .... **CLC 3, 6, 14, 18, 27, 62, 128; PC 29**
See also BPFB 3; CA 21-24R; CAAE 187; CAAS 1; CANR 13, 43, 66, 111; CN 7; CP 7; CWP; DLB 120, 227; EXPP; FW; MTCW 1, 2; PFS 9; SFW 4

**Piers, Robert**
See Anthony, Piers

**Pieyre de Mandiargues, Andre** 1909-1991
See Mandiargues, Andre Pieyre de
See also CA 103; CANR 22, 82; GFL 1789 to the Present

**Pilnyak, Boris** 1894-1938 . **SSC 48; TCLC 23**
See Vogau, Boris Andreyevich

**Pinchback, Eugene**
See Toomer, Jean

**Pincherle, Alberto** 1907-1990 ...... **CLC 11, 18**
See Moravia, Alberto
See also CA 25-28R; CANR 33, 63; DAM NOV; MTCW 1

**Pinckney, Darryl** 1953- ........................ **CLC 76**
See also BW 2, 3; CA 143; CANR 79

**Pindar** 518(?)B.C.-438(?)B.C. ....... **CMLC 12; PC 19**
See also AW 1; CDWLB 1; DLB 176; RGWL 2

**Pineda, Cecile** 1942- ............................. **CLC 39**
See also CA 118; DLB 209

**Pinero, Arthur Wing** 1855-1934 .... **TCLC 32**
See also CA 153; DAM DRAM; DLB 10; RGEL 2

**Pinero, Miguel (Antonio Gomez)** 1946-1988 ............................. **CLC 4, 55**
See also CA 61-64; CAD; CANR 29, 90; DLB 266; HW 1

**Pinget, Robert** 1919-1997 ....... **CLC 7, 13, 37**
See also CA 85-88; CWW 2; DLB 83; GFL 1789 to the Present

**Pink Floyd**
See Barrett, (Roger) Syd; Gilmour, David; Mason, Nick; Waters, Roger; Wright, Rick

**Pinkney, Edward** 1802-1828 .......... **NCLC 31**
See also DLB 248

**Pinkwater, Daniel**
See Pinkwater, Daniel Manus

**Pinkwater, Daniel Manus** 1941- ....... **CLC 35**
See also AAYA 1, 46; BYA 9; CA 29-32R; CANR 12, 38, 89; CLR 4; CSW; FANT; JRDA; MAICYA 1, 2; SAAS 3; SATA 8, 46, 76, 114; SFW 4; YAW

**Pinkwater, Manus**
See Pinkwater, Daniel Manus

**Pinsky, Robert** 1940- ....... **CLC 9, 19, 38, 94, 121; PC 27**
See also AMWS 6; CA 29-32R; CAAS 4; CANR 58, 97; CP 7; DAM POET; DLBY 1982, 1998; MTCW 2; RGAL 4

**Pinta, Harold**
See Pinter, Harold

**Pinter, Harold** 1930- .. **CLC 1, 3, 6, 9, 11, 15, 27, 58, 73; DC 15; WLC**
See also BRWR 1; BRWS 1; CA 5-8R; CANR 33, 65, 112; CBD; CD 5; CDBLB 1960 to Present; DA; DAB; DAC; DAM DRAM, MST; DFS 3, 5, 7, 14; DLB 13; IDFW 3, 4; MTCW 1, 2; RGEL 2; TEA

**Piozzi, Hester Lynch (Thrale)** 1741-1821 ............................. **NCLC 57**
See also DLB 104, 142

**Pirandello, Luigi** 1867-1936 .. **DC 5; SSC 22; TCLC 4, 29; WLC**
See also CA 153; CANR 103; DA; DAB; DAC; DAM DRAM, MST; DFS 4, 9; DLB 264; EW 8; MTCW 2; RGSF 2; RGWL 2, 3

**Pirsig, Robert M(aynard)** 1928- ... **CLC 4, 6, 73**
See also CA 53-56; CANR 42, 74; CPW 1; DAM POP; MTCW 1, 2; SATA 39

**Pisarev, Dmitry Ivanovich** 1840-1868 ............................. **NCLC 25**

**Pix, Mary (Griffith)** 1666-1709 ............. **LC 8**
See also DLB 80

**Pixerecourt, (Rene Charles) Guilbert de** 1773-1844 ............................. **NCLC 39**
See also DLB 192; GFL 1789 to the Present

**Plaatje, Sol(omon) T(shekisho)** 1878-1932 ................... **BLCS; TCLC 73**
See also BW 2, 3; CA 141; CANR 79; DLB 125, 225

**Plaidy, Jean**
See Hibbert, Eleanor Alice Burford

**Planche, James Robinson** 1796-1880 ............................. **NCLC 42**
See also RGEL 2

**Plant, Robert** 1948- ............................. **CLC 12**

**Plante, David (Robert)** 1940- . **CLC 7, 23, 38**
See also CA 37-40R; CANR 12, 36, 58, 82; CN 7; DAM NOV; DLBY 1983; INT CANR-12; MTCW 1

**Plath, Sylvia** 1932-1963 ..... **CLC 1, 2, 3, 5, 9, 11, 14, 17, 50, 51, 62, 111; PC 1, 37; WLC**
See also AAYA 13; AMWR 2; AMWS 1; BPFB 3; CA 19-20; CANR 34, 101; CAP 2; CDALB 1941-1968; DA; DAB; DAC; DAM MST, POET; DLB 5, 6, 152; EXPN; EXPP; FW; LAIT 4; MAWW; MTCW 1, 2; NFS 1; PAB; PFS 1, 15; RGAL 4; SATA 96; TUS; WP; YAW

**Plato** c. 428B.C.-347B.C. ... **CMLC 8; WLCS**
See also AW 1; CDWLB 1; DA; DAB; DAC; DAM MST; DLB 176; LAIT 1; RGWL 2, 3

**Platonov, Andrei**
See Klimentov, Andrei Platonovich

**Platonov, Andrei Platonovich**
See Klimentov, Andrei Platonovich
See also DLB 272

**Platt, Kin** 1911- ............................. **CLC 26**
See also AAYA 11; CA 17-20R; CANR 11; JRDA; SAAS 17; SATA 21, 86; WYA

**Plautus** c. 254B.C.-c. 184B.C. ...... **CMLC 24; DC 6**
See also AW 1; CDWLB 1; DLB 211; RGWL 2, 3

**Plick et Plock**
See Simenon, Georges (Jacques Christian)

**Plieksans, Janis**
See Rainis, Janis

**Plimpton, George (Ames)** 1927- ....... **CLC 36**
See also AITN 1; CA 21-24R; CANR 32, 70, 103; DLB 185, 241; MTCW 1, 2; SATA 10

**Pliny the Elder** c. 23-79 ................. **CMLC 23**
See also DLB 211

**Plomer, William Charles Franklin** 1903-1973 ............................. **CLC 4, 8**
See also AFW; CA 21-22; CANR 34; CAP 2; DLB 20, 162, 191, 225; MTCW 1; RGEL 2; RGSF 2; SATA 24

**Plotinus** 204-270 ............................. **CMLC 46**
See also CDWLB 1; DLB 176

**Plowman, Piers**
See Kavanagh, Patrick (Joseph)

**Plum, J.**
See Wodehouse, P(elham) G(renville)

**Plumly, Stanley (Ross)** 1939- ............. **CLC 33**
See also CA 110; CANR 97; CP 7; DLB 5, 193; INT 110

**Plumpe, Friedrich Wilhelm** 1888-1931 ............................. **TCLC 53**

**Po Chu-i** 772-846 ............................. **CMLC 24**

**Poe, Edgar Allan** 1809-1849 ..... **NCLC 1, 16, 55, 78, 94, 97, 117; PC 1; SSC 1, 22, 34, 35, 54; WLC**
See also AAYA 14; AMW; AMWC 1; AMWR 2; BPFB 3; BYA 5, 11; CDALB 1640-1865; CMW 4; DA; DAB; DAC; DAM MST, POET; DLB 3, 59, 73, 74, 248, 254; EXPP; EXPS; HGG; LAIT 2; MSW; PAB; PFS 1, 3, 9; RGAL 4; RGSF 2; SATA 23; SCFW 2; SFW 4; SSFS 2, 4, 7, 8, 16; SUFW; TUS; WP; WYA

**Poet of Titchfield Street, The**
See Pound, Ezra (Weston Loomis)

**Pohl, Frederik** 1919- ........... **CLC 18; SSC 25**
See also AAYA 24; CA 61-64; CAAE 188; CAAS 1; CANR 11, 37, 81; CN 7; DLB 8; INT CANR-11; MTCW 1, 2; SATA 24; SCFW 2; SFW 4

**Poirier, Louis** 1910-
See Gracq, Julien
See also CA 126; CWW 2

**Poitier, Sidney** 1927- ............................. **CLC 26**
See also BW 1; CA 117; CANR 94

**Polanski, Roman** 1933- ..................... **CLC 16**
See also CA 77-80

**Poliakoff, Stephen** 1952- .................... **CLC 38**
See also CA 106; CBD; CD 5; DLB 13

**Police, The**
See Copeland, Stewart (Armstrong); Summers, Andrew James; Sumner, Gordon Matthew

**Polidori, John William** 1795-1821 . **NCLC 51**
See also DLB 116; HGG

**Pollitt, Katha** 1949- ................... **CLC 28, 122**
See also CA 122; CANR 66, 108; MTCW 1, 2

**Pollock, (Mary) Sharon** 1936- .......... **CLC 50**
See also CA 141; CD 5; CWD; DAC; DAM DRAM, MST; DFS 3; DLB 60; FW

**Polo, Marco** 1254-1324 ................. **CMLC 15**

**Polonsky, Abraham (Lincoln)** 1910-1999 ............................. **CLC 92**
See also CA 104; DLB 26; INT 104

**Polybius** c. 200B.C.-c. 118B.C. ........ **CMLC 17**
See also AW 1; DLB 176; RGWL 2, 3

**Pomerance, Bernard** 1940- ................. **CLC 13**
See also CA 101; CAD; CANR 49; CD 5; DAM DRAM; DFS 9; LAIT 2

**Ponge, Francis** 1899-1988 ............. **CLC 6, 18**
See also CA 85-88; CANR 40, 86; DAM POET; GFL 1789 to the Present; RGWL 2, 3

**Poniatowska, Elena** 1933- . **CLC 140; HLC 2**
See also CA 101; CANR 32, 66, 107; CDWLB 3; DAM MULT; DLB 113; HW 1, 2; LAWS 1; WLIT 1

**Pontoppidan, Henrik** 1857-1943 .... **TCLC 29**
See also CA 170

**Poole, Josephine** ............................. **CLC 17**
See Helyar, Jane Penelope Josephine
See also SAAS 2; SATA 5

**Popa, Vasko** 1922-1991 ..................... **CLC 19**
See also CA 148; CDWLB 4; DLB 181; RGWL 2, 3

**Pope, Alexander** 1688-1744 ...... **LC 3, 58, 60, 64; PC 26; WLC**
See also BRW 3; BRWR 1; CDBLB 1660-1789; DA; DAB; DAC; DAM MST, POET; DLB 95, 101, 213; EXPP; PAB; PFS 12; RGEL 2; WLIT 3; WP

**Popov, Yevgeny** .................. **CLC 59**

**Poquelin, Jean-Baptiste**
See Moliere

**Porter, Connie (Rose)** 1959(?)- ......... **CLC 70**
See also BW 2, 3; CA 142; CANR 90, 109; SATA 81, 129

**Porter, Gene(va Grace) Stratton** .. **TCLC 21**
See Stratton-Porter, Gene(va Grace)
See also BPFB 3; CWRI 5; RHW

**Porter, Katherine Anne** 1890-1980 ... **CLC 1, 3, 7, 10, 13, 15, 27, 101; SSC 4, 31, 43**
See also AAYA 42; AITN 2; AMW; BPFB 3; CA 1-4R; CANR 1, 65; CDALBS; DA; DAB; DAC; DAM MST, NOV; DLB 4, 9, 102; DLBD 12; DLBY 1980; EXPS; LAIT 3; MAWW; MTCW 1, 2; NFS 14; RGAL 4; RGSF 2; SATA 39; SATA-Obit 23; SSFS 1, 8, 11, 16; TUS

**Porter, Peter (Neville Frederick)** 1929- .................. **CLC 5, 13, 33**
See also CA 85-88; CP 7; DLB 40

**Porter, William Sydney** 1862-1910
See Henry, O.
See also CA 131; CDALB 1865-1917; DA; DAB; DAC; DAM MST; DLB 12, 78, 79; MTCW 1, 2; TUS; YABC 2

**Portillo (y Pacheco), Jose Lopez**
See Lopez Portillo (y Pacheco), Jose

**Portillo Trambley, Estela** 1927-1998 .. **HLC 2**
See Trambley, Estela Portillo
See also CANR 32; DAM MULT; DLB 209; HW 1

**Posse, Abel** .................. **CLC 70**

**Post, Melville Davisson** 1869-1930 .................. **TCLC 39**
See also CA 202; CMW 4

**Potok, Chaim** 1929-2002 ... **CLC 2, 7, 14, 26, 112**
See also AAYA 15; AITN 1, 2; BPFB 3; BYA 1; CA 17-20R; CANR 19, 35, 64, 98; CN 7; DAM NOV; DLB 28, 152; EXPN; INT CANR-19; LAIT 4; MTCW 1, 2; NFS 4; SATA 33, 106; SATA-Obit 134; TUS; YAW

**Potter, Dennis (Christopher George)** 1935-1994 .................. **CLC 58, 86, 123**
See also CA 107; CANR 33, 61; CBD; DLB 233; MTCW 1

**Pound, Ezra (Weston Loomis)** 1885-1972 .. **CLC 1, 2, 3, 4, 5, 7, 10, 13, 18, 34, 48, 50, 112; PC 4; WLC**
See also AAYA 47; AMW; AMWR 1; CA 5-8R; CANR 40; CDALB 1917-1929; DA; DAB; DAC; DAM MST, POET; DLB 4, 45, 63; DLBD 15; EFS 2; EXPP; MTCW 1, 2; PAB; PFS 2, 8, 16; RGAL 4; TUS; WP

**Povod, Reinaldo** 1959-1994 .................. **CLC 44**
See also CA 136; CANR 83

**Powell, Adam Clayton, Jr.** 1908-1972 .................. **BLC 3; CLC 89**
See also BW 1, 3; CA 102; CANR 86; DAM MULT

**Powell, Anthony (Dymoke)** 1905-2000 .................. **CLC 1, 3, 7, 9, 10, 31**
See also BRW 7; CA 1-4R; CANR 1, 32, 62, 107; CDBLB 1945-1960; CN 7; DLB 15; MTCW 1, 2; RGEL 2; TEA

**Powell, Dawn** 1896(?)-1965 .................. **CLC 66**
See also CA 5-8R; DLBY 1997

**Powell, Padgett** 1952- .................. **CLC 34**
See also CA 126; CANR 63, 101; CSW; DLB 234; DLBY 01

**Powell, (Oval) Talmage** 1920-2000
See Queen, Ellery
See also CA 5-8R; CANR 2, 80

**Power, Susan** 1961- .................. **CLC 91**
See also BYA 14; CA 160; NFS 11

**Powers, J(ames) F(arl)** 1917-1999 ..... **CLC 1, 4, 8, 57; SSC 4**
See also CA 1-4R; CANR 2, 61; CN 7; DLB 130; MTCW 1; RGAL 4; RGSF 2

**Powers, John J(ames)** 1945-
See Powers, John R.
See also CA 69-72

**Powers, John R.** .................. **CLC 66**
See Powers, John J(ames)

**Powers, Richard (S.)** 1957- .................. **CLC 93**
See also AMWS 9; BPFB 3; CA 148; CANR 80; CN 7

**Pownall, David** 1938- .................. **CLC 10**
See also CA 89-92, 180; CAAS 18; CANR 49, 101; CBD; CD 5; CN 7; DLB 14

**Powys, John Cowper** 1872-1963 ... **CLC 7, 9, 15, 46, 125**
See also CA 85-88; CANR 106; DLB 15, 255; FANT; MTCW 1, 2; RGEL 2; SUFW

**Powys, T(heodore) F(rancis)** 1875-1953 .................. **TCLC 9**
See also BRWS 8; CA 189; DLB 36, 162; FANT; RGEL 2; SUFW

**Prado (Calvo), Pedro** 1886-1952 ... **TCLC 75**
See also CA 131; HW 1; LAW

**Prager, Emily** 1952- .................. **CLC 56**
See also CA 204

**Pratolini, Vasco** 1913-1991 .................. **TCLC 124**
See also DLB 177; RGWL 2, 3

**Pratt, E(dwin) J(ohn)** 1883(?)-1964 . **CLC 19**
See also CA 141; CANR 77; DAC; DAM POET; DLB 92; RGEL 2; TWA

**Premchand** .................. **TCLC 21**
See Srivastava, Dhanpat Rai

**Preussler, Otfried** 1923- .................. **CLC 17**
See also CA 77-80; SATA 24

**Prevert, Jacques (Henri Marie)** 1900-1977 .................. **CLC 15**
See also CA 77-80; CANR 29, 61; DLB 258; GFL 1789 to the Present; IDFW 3, 4; MTCW 1; RGWL 2, 3; SATA-Obit 30

**Prevost, (Antoine Francois)** 1697-1763 .................. **LC 1**
See also EW 4; GFL Beginnings to 1789; RGWL 2, 3

**Price, (Edward) Reynolds** 1933- ... **CLC 3, 6, 13, 43, 50, 63; SSC 22**
See also AMWS 6; CA 1-4R; CANR 1, 37, 57, 87; CN 7; CSW; DAM NOV; DLB 2, 218; INT CANR-37

**Price, Richard** 1949- .................. **CLC 6, 12**
See also CA 49-52; CANR 3; DLBY 1981

**Prichard, Katharine Susannah** 1883-1969 .................. **CLC 46**
See also CA 11-12; CANR 33; CAP 1; DLB 260; MTCW 1; RGEL 2; RGSF 2; SATA 66

**Priestley, J(ohn) B(oynton)** 1894-1984 .................. **CLC 2, 5, 9, 34**
See also BRW 7; CA 9-12R; CANR 33; CDBLB 1914-1945; DAM DRAM, NOV; DLB 10, 34, 77, 100, 139; DLBY 1984; MTCW 1, 2; RGEL 2; SFW 4

**Prince** 1958(?)- .................. **CLC 35**

**Prince, F(rank) T(empleton)** 1912- .. **CLC 22**
See also CA 101; CANR 43, 79; CP 7; DLB 20

**Prince Kropotkin**
See Kropotkin, Peter (Alekseevich)

**Prior, Matthew** 1664-1721 .................. **LC 4**
See also DLB 95; RGEL 2

**Prishvin, Mikhail** 1873-1954 .................. **TCLC 75**
See Prishvin, Mikhail Mikhailovich

**Prishvin, Mikhail Mikhailovich**
See Prishvin, Mikhail
See also DLB 272

**Pritchard, William H(arrison)** 1932- .................. **CLC 34**
See also CA 65-68; CANR 23, 95; DLB 111

**Pritchett, V(ictor) S(awdon)** 1900-1997 ... **CLC 5, 13, 15, 41; SSC 14**
See also BPFB 3; BRWS 3; CA 61-64; CANR 31, 63; CN 7; DAM NOV; DLB 15, 139; MTCW 1, 2; RGEL 2; RGSF 2; TEA

**Private 19022**
See Manning, Frederic

**Probst, Mark** 1925- .................. **CLC 59**
See also CA 130

**Prokosch, Frederic** 1908-1989 ....... **CLC 4, 48**
See also CA 73-76; CANR 82; DLB 48; MTCW 2

**Propertius, Sextus** c. 50B.C.-c. 16B.C. .................. **CMLC 32**
See also AW 2; CDWLB 1; DLB 211; RGWL 2, 3

**Prophet, The**
See Dreiser, Theodore (Herman Albert)

**Prose, Francine** 1947- .................. **CLC 45**
See also CA 112; CANR 46, 95; DLB 234; SATA 101

**Proudhon**
See Cunha, Euclides (Rodrigues Pimenta) da

**Proulx, Annie**
See Proulx, E(dna) Annie

**Proulx, E(dna) Annie** 1935- ....... **CLC 81, 158**
See also AMWS 7; BPFB 3; CA 145; CANR 65, 110; CN 7; CPW 1; DAM POP; MTCW 2

**Proust, (Valentin-Louis-George-Eugene-)Marcel** 1871-1922 .......... **TCLC 7, 13, 33; WLC**
See also BPFB 3; CA 120; CANR 110; DA; DAB; DAC; DAM MST, NOV; DLB 65; EW 8; GFL 1789 to the Present; MTCW 1, 2; RGWL 2, 3; TWA

**Prowler, Harley**
See Masters, Edgar Lee

**Prus, Boleslaw** 1845-1912 ............... **TCLC 48**
See also RGWL 2, 3

**Pryor, Richard (Franklin Lenox Thomas)** 1940- .................. **CLC 26**
See also CA 152

**Przybyszewski, Stanislaw** 1868-1927 .................. **TCLC 36**
See also CA 160; DLB 66

**Pteleon**
See Grieve, C(hristopher) M(urray)
See also DAM POET

**Puckett, Lute**
See Masters, Edgar Lee

**Puig, Manuel** 1932-1990 .... **CLC 3, 5, 10, 28, 65, 133; HLC 2**
See also BPFB 3; CA 45-48; CANR 2, 32, 63; CDWLB 3; DAM MULT; DLB 113; DNFS 1; GLL 1; HW 1, 2; LAW; MTCW 1, 2; RGWL 2, 3; TWA; WLIT 1

**Pulitzer, Joseph** 1847-1911 ............. **TCLC 76**
See also DLB 23

**Purchas, Samuel** 1577(?)-1626 ............ **LC 70**
See also DLB 151

**Purdy, A(lfred) W(ellington)** 1918-2000 .................. **CLC 3, 6, 14, 50**
See also CA 81-84; CAAS 17; CANR 42, 66; CP 7; DAC; DAM MST, POET; DLB 88; PFS 5; RGEL 2

**Purdy, James (Amos)** 1923- .... **CLC 2, 4, 10, 28, 52**
See also AMWS 7; CA 33-36R; CAAS 1; CANR 19, 51; CN 7; DLB 2, 218; INT CANR-19; MTCW 1; RGAL 4

**Pure, Simon**
See Swinnerton, Frank Arthur

**Pushkin, Aleksandr Sergeevich**
See Pushkin, Alexander (Sergeyevich)
See also DLB 205
**Pushkin, Alexander (Sergeyevich)**
1799-1837 ....... **NCLC 3, 27, 83; PC 10; SSC 27, 55; WLC**
See Pushkin, Aleksandr Sergeevich
See also DA; DAB; DAC; DAM DRAM, MST, POET; EW 5; EXPS; RGSF 2; RGWL 2, 3; SATA 61; SSFS 9; TWA
**P'u Sung-ling** 1640-1715 ....... **LC 49; SSC 31**
**Putnam, Arthur Lee**
See Alger, Horatio, Jr.
**Puzo, Mario** 1920-1999 ........ **CLC 1, 2, 6, 36, 107**
See also BPFB 3; CA 65-68; CANR 4, 42, 65, 99; CN 7; CPW; DAM NOV, POP; DLB 6; MTCW 1, 2; NFS 16; RGAL 4
**Pygge, Edward**
See Barnes, Julian (Patrick)
**Pyle, Ernest Taylor** 1900-1945
See Pyle, Ernie
See also CA 160
**Pyle, Ernie** ........................... **TCLC 75**
See Pyle, Ernest Taylor
See also DLB 29; MTCW 2
**Pyle, Howard** 1853-1911 ................. **TCLC 81**
See also BYA 2, 4; CA 137; CLR 22; DLB 42, 188; DLBD 13; LAIT 1; MAICYA 1, 2; SATA 16, 100; WCH; YAW
**Pym, Barbara (Mary Crampton)**
1913-1980 ............. **CLC 13, 19, 37, 111**
See also BPFB 3; BRWS 2; CA 13-14; CANR 13, 34; CAP 1; DLB 14, 207; DLBY 1987; MTCW 1, 2; RGEL 2; TEA
**Pynchon, Thomas (Ruggles, Jr.)**
1937- ....... **CLC 2, 3, 6, 9, 11, 18, 33, 62, 72, 123; SSC 14; WLC**
See also AMWS 2; BEST 90:2; BPFB 3; CA 17-20R; CANR 22, 46, 73; CN 7; CPW 1; DA; DAB; DAC; DAM MST, NOV, POP; DLB 2, 173; MTCW 1, 2; RGAL 4; SFW 4; TUS
**Pythagoras** c. 582B.C.-c. 507B.C. . **CMLC 22**
See also DLB 176
**Q**
See Quiller-Couch, Sir Arthur (Thomas)
**Qian, Chongzhu**
See Ch'ien, Chung-shu
**Qian Zhongshu**
See Ch'ien, Chung-shu
**Qroll**
See Dagerman, Stig (Halvard)
**Quarrington, Paul (Lewis)** 1953- ...... **CLC 65**
See also CA 129; CANR 62, 95
**Quasimodo, Salvatore** 1901-1968 ..... **CLC 10**
See also CA 13-16; CAP 1; DLB 114; EW 12; MTCW 1; RGWL 2, 3
**Quatermass, Martin**
See Carpenter, John (Howard)
**Quay, Stephen** 1947- .......... **CLC 95**
See also CA 189
**Quay, Timothy** 1947- ......... **CLC 95**
See also CA 189
**Queen, Ellery** ................................ **CLC 3, 11**
See Dannay, Frederic; Davidson, Avram (James); Deming, Richard; Fairman, Paul W.; Flora, Fletcher; Hoch, Edward D(entinger); Kane, Henry; Lee, Manfred B(ennington); Marlowe, Stephen; Powell, (Oval) Talmage; Sheldon, Walter J(ames); Sturgeon, Theodore (Hamilton); Tracy, Don(ald Fiske); Vance, John Holbrook
See also BPFB 3; CMW 4; MSW; RGAL 4
**Queen, Ellery, Jr.**
See Dannay, Frederic; Lee, Manfred B(ennington)

**Queneau, Raymond** 1903-1976 ..... **CLC 2, 5, 10, 42**
See also CA 77-80; CANR 32; DLB 72, 258; EW 12; GFL 1789 to the Present; MTCW 1, 2; RGWL 2, 3
**Quevedo, Francisco de** 1580-1645 ....... **LC 23**
**Quiller-Couch, Sir Arthur (Thomas)**
1863-1944 ................................ **TCLC 53**
See also CA 166; DLB 135, 153, 190; HGG; RGEL 2; SUFW 1
**Quin, Ann (Marie)** 1936-1973 ............. **CLC 6**
See also CA 9-12R; DLB 14, 231
**Quincey, Thomas de**
See De Quincey, Thomas
**Quinn, Martin**
See Smith, Martin Cruz
**Quinn, Peter** 1947- ............................. **CLC 91**
See also CA 197
**Quinn, Simon**
See Smith, Martin Cruz
**Quintana, Leroy V.** 1944- ...... **HLC 2; PC 36**
See also CA 131; CANR 65; DAM MULT; DLB 82; HW 1, 2
**Quiroga, Horacio (Sylvestre)**
1878-1937 .................. **HLC 2; TCLC 20**
See also CA 131; DAM MULT; HW 1; LAW; MTCW 1; RGSF 2; WLIT 1
**Quoirez, Francoise** 1935- ..................... **CLC 9**
See Sagan, Francoise
See also CA 49-52; CANR 6, 39, 73; CWW 2; MTCW 1, 2; TWA
**Raabe, Wilhelm (Karl)** 1831-1910 . **TCLC 45**
See also CA 167; DLB 129
**Rabe, David (William)** 1940- .. **CLC 4, 8, 33; DC 16**
See also CA 85-88; CABS 3; CAD; CANR 59; CD 5; DAM DRAM; DFS 3, 8, 13; DLB 7, 228
**Rabelais, Francois** 1494-1553 ........ **LC 5, 60; WLC**
See also DA; DAB; DAC; DAM MST; EW 2; GFL Beginnings to 1789; RGWL 2, 3; TWA
**Rabinovitch, Sholem** 1859-1916
See Aleichem, Sholom
**Rabinyan, Dorit** 1972- ..................... **CLC 119**
See also CA 170
**Rachilde**
See Vallette, Marguerite Eymery
**Racine, Jean** 1639-1699 ..................... **LC 28**
See also DAB; DAM MST; DLB 268; EW 3; GFL Beginnings to 1789; RGWL 2, 3; TWA
**Radcliffe, Ann (Ward)** 1764-1823 ... **NCLC 6, 55, 106**
See also DLB 39, 178; HGG; RGEL 2; SUFW; WLIT 3
**Radclyffe-Hall, Marguerite**
See Hall, (Marguerite) Radclyffe
**Radiguet, Raymond** 1903-1923 ....... **TCLC 29**
See also CA 162; DLB 65; GFL 1789 to the Present; RGWL 2, 3
**Radnoti, Miklos** 1909-1944 ............. **TCLC 16**
See also CDWLB 4; DLB 215; RGWL 2, 3
**Rado, James** 1939- ............................. **CLC 17**
See also CA 105
**Radvanyi, Netty** 1900-1983
See Seghers, Anna
See also CA 85-88; CANR 82
**Rae, Ben**
See Griffiths, Trevor
**Raeburn, John (Hay)** 1941- .............. **CLC 34**
See also CA 57-60
**Ragni, Gerome** 1942-1991 ................. **CLC 17**
See also CA 105
**Rahv, Philip** ........................................ **CLC 24**
See Greenberg, Ivan
See also DLB 137

**Raimund, Ferdinand Jakob**
1790-1836 ................................ **NCLC 69**
See also DLB 90
**Raine, Craig (Anthony)** 1944- .. **CLC 32, 103**
See also CA 108; CANR 29, 51, 103; CP 7; DLB 40; PFS 7
**Raine, Kathleen (Jessie)** 1908- ..... **CLC 7, 45**
See also CA 85-88; CANR 46, 109; CP 7; DLB 20; MTCW 1; RGEL 2
**Rainis, Janis** 1865-1929 .................. **TCLC 29**
See also CA 170; CDWLB 4; DLB 220
**Rakosi, Carl** ..................................... **CLC 47**
See Rawley, Callman
See also CAAS 5; CP 7; DLB 193
**Ralegh, Sir Walter**
See Raleigh, Sir Walter
See also BRW 1; RGEL 2; WP
**Raleigh, Richard**
See Lovecraft, H(oward) P(hillips)
**Raleigh, Sir Walter** 1554(?)-1618 ....... **LC 31, 39; PC 31**
See Ralegh, Sir Walter
See also CDBLB Before 1660; DLB 172; EXPP; PFS 14; TEA
**Rallentando, H. P.**
See Sayers, Dorothy L(eigh)
**Ramal, Walter**
See de la Mare, Walter (John)
**Ramana Maharshi** 1879-1950 ........ **TCLC 84**
**Ramoacn y Cajal, Santiago**
1852-1934 ................................ **TCLC 93**
**Ramon, Juan**
See Jimenez (Mantecon), Juan Ramon
**Ramos, Graciliano** 1892-1953 ........ **TCLC 32**
See also CA 167; HW 2; LAW; WLIT 1
**Rampersad, Arnold** 1941- ................. **CLC 44**
See also BW 2, 3; CA 133; CANR 81; DLB 111; INT 133
**Rampling, Anne**
See Rice, Anne
See also GLL 2
**Ramsay, Allan** 1686(?)-1758 ................. **LC 29**
See also DLB 95; RGEL 2
**Ramsay, Jay**
See Campbell, (John) Ramsey
**Ramuz, Charles-Ferdinand**
1878-1947 ................................ **TCLC 33**
See also CA 165
**Rand, Ayn** 1905-1982 ...... **CLC 3, 30, 44, 79; WLC**
See also AAYA 10; AMWS 4; BPFB 3; BYA 12; CA 13-16R; CANR 27, 73; CDALBS; CPW; DA; DAC; DAM MST, NOV, POP; DLB 227; MTCW 1, 2; NFS 10, 16; RGAL 4; SFW 4; TUS; YAW
**Randall, Dudley (Felker)** 1914-2000 . **BLC 3; CLC 1, 135**
See also BW 1, 3; CA 25-28R; CANR 23, 82; DAM MULT; DLB 41; PFS 5
**Randall, Robert**
See Silverberg, Robert
**Ranger, Ken**
See Creasey, John
**Rank, Otto** 1884-1939 .................. **TCLC 115**
**Ransom, John Crowe** 1888-1974 .. **CLC 2, 4, 5, 11, 24**
See also AMW; CA 5-8R; CANR 6, 34; CDALBS; DAM POET; DLB 45, 63; EXPP; MTCW 1, 2; RGAL 4; TUS
**Rao, Raja** 1909- ........................... **CLC 25, 56**
See also CA 73-76; CANR 51; CN 7; DAM NOV; MTCW 1, 2; RGEL 2; RGSF 2
**Raphael, Frederic (Michael)** 1931- ... **CLC 2, 14**
See also CA 1-4R; CANR 1, 86; CN 7; DLB 14
**Ratcliffe, James P.**
See Mencken, H(enry) L(ouis)

**Rathbone, Julian** 1935- .................... **CLC 41**
See also CA 101; CANR 34, 73

**Rattigan, Terence (Mervyn)**
1911-1977 ...................... **CLC 7; DC 18**
See also BRWS 7; CA 85-88; CBD; CD-BLB 1945-1960; DAM DRAM; DFS 8; DLB 13; IDFW 3, 4; MTCW 1, 2; RGEL 2

**Ratushinskaya, Irina** 1954- ............... **CLC 54**
See also CA 129; CANR 68; CWW 2

**Raven, Simon (Arthur Noel)**
1927-2001 ............................... **CLC 14**
See also CA 81-84; CANR 86; CN 7; DLB 271

**Ravenna, Michael**
See Welty, Eudora (Alice)

**Rawley, Callman** 1903-
See Rakosi, Carl
See also CA 21-24R; CANR 12, 32, 91

**Rawlings, Marjorie Kinnan**
1896-1953 ............................... **TCLC 4**
See also AAYA 20; AMWS 10; ANW; BPFB 3; BYA 3; CA 137; CANR 74; CLR 63; DLB 9, 22, 102; DLBD 17; JRDA; MAICYA 1, 2; MTCW 2; RGAL 4; SATA 100; WCH; YABC 1; YAW

**Ray, Satyajit** 1921-1992 ............. **CLC 16, 76**
See also CA 114; DAM MULT

**Read, Herbert Edward** 1893-1968 ..... **CLC 4**
See also BRW 6; CA 85-88; DLB 20, 149; PAB; RGEL 2

**Read, Piers Paul** 1941- ........... **CLC 4, 10, 25**
See also CA 21-24R; CANR 38, 86; CN 7; DLB 14; SATA 21

**Reade, Charles** 1814-1884 ......... **NCLC 2, 74**
See also DLB 21; RGEL 2

**Reade, Hamish**
See Gray, Simon (James Holliday)

**Reading, Peter** 1946- ......................... **CLC 47**
See also BRWS 8; CA 103; CANR 46, 96; CP 7; DLB 40

**Reaney, James** 1926- ......................... **CLC 13**
See also CA 41-44R; CAAS 15; CANR 42; CD 5; CP 7; DAC; DAM MST; DLB 68; RGEL 2; SATA 43

**Rebreanu, Liviu** 1885-1944 ............. **TCLC 28**
See also CA 165; DLB 220

**Rechy, John (Francisco)** 1934- ...... **CLC 1, 7, 14, 18, 107; HLC 2**
See also CA 5-8R; CAAE 195; CAAS 4; CANR 6, 32, 64; CN 7; DAM MULT; DLB 122; DLBY 1982; HW 1, 2; INT CANR-6; RGAL 4

**Redcam, Tom** 1870-1933 ................. **TCLC 25**

**Reddin, Keith** ................................. **CLC 67**
See also CAD

**Redgrove, Peter (William)** 1932- . **CLC 6, 41**
See also BRWS 6; CA 1-4R; CANR 3, 39, 77; CP 7; DLB 40

**Redmon, Anne** ............................... **CLC 22**
See Nightingale, Anne Redmon
See also DLBY 1986

**Reed, Eliot**
See Ambler, Eric

**Reed, Ishmael** 1938- ...... **BLC 3; CLC 2, 3, 5, 6, 13, 32, 60**
See also AFAW 1, 2; AMWS 10; BPFB 3; BW 2, 3; CA 21-24R; CANR 25, 48, 74; CN 7; CP 7; CSW; DAM MULT; DLB 2, 5, 33, 169, 227; DLBD 8; MSW; MTCW 1, 2; PFS 6; RGAL 4; TCWW 2

**Reed, John (Silas)** 1887-1920 ........... **TCLC 9**
See also CA 195; TUS

**Reed, Lou** ........................................ **CLC 21**
See Firbank, Louis

**Reese, Lizette Woodworth** 1856-1935 . **PC 29**
See also CA 180; DLB 54

**Reeve, Clara** 1729-1807 ................. **NCLC 19**
See also DLB 39; RGEL 2

**Reich, Wilhelm** 1897-1957 .............. **TCLC 57**
See also CA 199

**Reid, Christopher (John)** 1949- ....... **CLC 33**
See also CA 140; CANR 89; CP 7; DLB 40

**Reid, Desmond**
See Moorcock, Michael (John)

**Reid Banks, Lynne** 1929-
See Banks, Lynne Reid
See also CA 1-4R; CANR 6, 22, 38, 87; CLR 24; CN 7; JRDA; MAICYA 1, 2; SATA 22, 75, 111; YAW

**Reilly, William K.**
See Creasey, John

**Reiner, Max**
See Caldwell, (Janet Miriam) Taylor (Holland)

**Reis, Ricardo**
See Pessoa, Fernando (Antonio Nogueira)

**Remarque, Erich Maria** 1898-1970 . **CLC 21**
See also AAYA 27; BPFB 3; CA 77-80; CDWLB 2; DA; DAB; DAC; DAM MST, NOV; DLB 56; EXPN; LAIT 3; MTCW 1, 2; NFS 4; RGWL 2, 3

**Remington, Frederic** 1861-1909 ..... **TCLC 89**
See also CA 169; DLB 12, 186, 188; SATA 41

**Remizov, A.**
See Remizov, Aleksei (Mikhailovich)

**Remizov, A. M.**
See Remizov, Aleksei (Mikhailovich)

**Remizov, Aleksei (Mikhailovich)**
1877-1957 ................................. **TCLC 27**
See also CA 133

**Renan, Joseph Ernest** 1823-1892 .. **NCLC 26**
See also GFL 1789 to the Present

**Renard, Jules(-Pierre)** 1864-1910 .. **TCLC 17**
See also CA 202; GFL 1789 to the Present

**Renault, Mary** .................... **CLC 3, 11, 17**
See Challans, Mary
See also BPFB 3; BYA 2; DLBY 1983; GLL 1; LAIT 1; MTCW 2; RGEL 2; RHW

**Rendell, Ruth (Barbara)** 1930- .. **CLC 28, 48**
See Vine, Barbara
See also BPFB 3; CA 109; CANR 32, 52, 74; CN 7; CPW; DAM POP; DLB 87; INT CANR-32; MSW; MTCW 1, 2

**Renoir, Jean** 1894-1979 ..................... **CLC 20**
See also CA 129

**Resnais, Alain** 1922- .......................... **CLC 16**

**Reverdy, Pierre** 1889-1960 ................ **CLC 53**
See also CA 97-100; DLB 258; GFL 1789 to the Present

**Rexroth, Kenneth** 1905-1982 .... **CLC 1, 2, 6, 11, 22, 49, 112; PC 20**
See also BG 3; CA 5-8R; CANR 14, 34, 63; CDALB 1941-1968; DAM POET; DLB 16, 48, 165, 212; DLBY 1982; INT CANR-14; MTCW 1, 2; RGAL 4

**Reyes, Alfonso** 1889-1959 .... **HLCS 2; TCLC 33**
See also CA 131; HW 1; LAW

**Reyes y Basoalto, Ricardo Eliecer Neftali**
See Neruda, Pablo

**Reymont, Wladyslaw (Stanislaw)**
1868(?)-1925 ................................. **TCLC 5**

**Reynolds, Jonathan** 1942- ............. **CLC 6, 38**
See also CA 65-68; CANR 28

**Reynolds, Joshua** 1723-1792 ................. **LC 15**
See also DLB 104

**Reynolds, Michael S(hane)**
1937-2000 ................................... **CLC 44**
See also CA 65-68; CANR 9, 89, 97

**Reznikoff, Charles** 1894-1976 ............. **CLC 9**
See also CA 33-36; CAP 2; DLB 28, 45; WP

**Rezzori (d'Arezzo), Gregor von**
1914-1998 ................................... **CLC 25**
See also CA 136

**Rhine, Richard**
See Silverstein, Alvin; Silverstein, Virginia B(arbara Opshelor)

**Rhodes, Eugene Manlove**
1869-1934 ................................. **TCLC 53**
See also CA 198; DLB 256

**R'hoone, Lord**
See Balzac, Honore de

**Rhys, Jean** 1894(?)-1979 ...... **CLC 2, 4, 6, 14, 19, 51, 124; SSC 21**
See also BRWS 2; CA 25-28R; CANR 35, 62; CDBLB 1945-1960; CDWLB 3; DAM NOV; DLB 36, 117, 162; DNFS 2; MTCW 1, 2; RGEL 2; RGSF 2; RHW; TEA

**Ribeiro, Darcy** 1922-1997 .................. **CLC 34**
See also CA 33-36R

**Ribeiro, Joao Ubaldo (Osorio Pimentel)**
1941- ..................................... **CLC 10, 67**
See also CA 81-84

**Ribman, Ronald (Burt)** 1932- ............. **CLC 7**
See also CA 21-24R; CAD; CANR 46, 80; CD 5

**Ricci, Nino** 1959- ............................... **CLC 70**
See also CA 137; CCA 1

**Rice, Anne** 1941- ........................ **CLC 41, 128**
See Rampling, Anne
See also AAYA 9; AMWS 7; BEST 89:2; BPFB 3; CA 65-68; CANR 12, 36, 53, 74, 100; CN 7; CPW; CSW; DAM POP; GLL 2; HGG; MTCW 2; SUFW 2; YAW

**Rice, Elmer (Leopold)** 1892-1967 ...... **CLC 7, 49**
See also CA 21-22; CAP 2; DAM DRAM; DFS 12; DLB 4, 7; MTCW 1, 2; RGAL 4

**Rice, Tim(othy Miles Bindon)**
1944- ..................................... **CLC 21**
See also CA 103; CANR 46; DFS 7

**Rich, Adrienne (Cecile)** 1929- ... **CLC 3, 6, 7, 11, 18, 36, 73, 76, 125; PC 5**
See also AMWR 2; AMWS 1; CA 9-12R; CANR 20, 53, 74; CDALBS; CP 7; CSW; CWP; DAM POET; DLB 5, 67; EXPP; FW; MAWW; MTCW 1, 2; PAB; PFS 15; RGAL 4; WP

**Rich, Barbara**
See Graves, Robert (von Ranke)

**Rich, Robert**
See Trumbo, Dalton

**Richard, Keith** ................................. **CLC 17**
See Richards, Keith

**Richards, David Adams** 1950- .......... **CLC 59**
See also CA 93-96; CANR 60, 110; DAC; DLB 53

**Richards, I(vor) A(rmstrong)**
1893-1979 ............................. **CLC 14, 24**
See also BRWS 2; CA 41-44R; CANR 34, 74; DLB 27; MTCW 2; RGEL 2

**Richards, Keith** 1943-
See Richard, Keith
See also CA 107; CANR 77

**Richardson, Anne**
See Roiphe, Anne (Richardson)

**Richardson, Dorothy Miller**
1873-1957 ................................... **TCLC 3**
See also CA 192; DLB 36; FW; RGEL 2

**Richardson (Robertson), Ethel Florence Lindesay** 1870-1946
See Richardson, Henry Handel
See also CA 190; DLB 230; RHW

**Richardson, Henry Handel** ............. **TCLC 4**
See Richardson (Robertson), Ethel Florence Lindesay
See also DLB 197; RGEL 2; RGSF 2

**Richardson, John** 1796-1852 .......... **NCLC 55**
See also CCA 1; DAC; DLB 99

**Richardson, Samuel** 1689-1761 ...... **LC 1, 44; WLC**
See also BRW 3; CDBLB 1660-1789; DA; DAB; DAC; DAM MST, NOV; DLB 39; RGEL 2; TEA; WLIT 3

**Richler, Mordecai** 1931-2001 .... **CLC 3, 5, 9, 13, 18, 46, 70**
See also AITN 1; CA 65-68; CANR 31, 62, 111; CCA 1; CLR 17; CWRI 5; DAC; DAM MST, NOV; DLB 53; MAICYA 1, 2; MTCW 1, 2; RGEL 2; SATA 44, 98; SATA-Brief 27; TWA

**Richter, Conrad (Michael)** 1890-1968 ............................. **CLC 30**
See also AAYA 21; BYA 2; CA 5-8R; CANR 23; DLB 9, 212; LAIT 1; MTCW 1, 2; RGAL 4; SATA 3; TCWW 2; TUS; YAW

**Ricostranza, Tom**
See Ellis, Trey

**Riddell, Charlotte** 1832-1906 ......... **TCLC 40**
See Riddell, Mrs. J. H.
See also CA 165; DLB 156

**Riddell, Mrs. J. H.**
See Riddell, Charlotte
See also HGG; SUFW

**Ridge, John Rollin** 1827-1867 ...... **NCLC 82; NNAL**
See also CA 144; DAM MULT; DLB 175

**Ridgeway, Jason**
See Marlowe, Stephen

**Ridgway, Keith** 1965- ....................... **CLC 119**
See also CA 172

**Riding, Laura** ........................... **CLC 3, 7**
See Jackson, Laura (Riding)
See also RGAL 4

**Riefenstahl, Berta Helene Amalia** 1902-
See Riefenstahl, Leni
See also CA 108

**Riefenstahl, Leni** ......................... **CLC 16**
See Riefenstahl, Berta Helene Amalia

**Riffe, Ernest**
See Bergman, (Ernst) Ingmar

**Riggs, (Rolla) Lynn** 1899-1954 ................... **NNAL; TCLC 56**
See also CA 144; DAM MULT; DLB 175

**Riis, Jacob A(ugust)** 1849-1914 ..... **TCLC 80**
See also CA 168; DLB 23

**Riley, James Whitcomb** 1849-1916 ................................. **TCLC 51**
See also CA 137; DAM POET; MAICYA 1, 2; RGAL 4; SATA 17

**Riley, Tex**
See Creasey, John

**Rilke, Rainer Maria** 1875-1926 ............ **PC 2; TCLC 1, 6, 19**
See also CA 132; CANR 62, 99; CDWLB 2; DAM POET; DLB 81; EW 9; MTCW 1, 2; RGWL 2, 3; TWA; WP

**Rimbaud, (Jean Nicolas) Arthur** 1854-1891 ......... **NCLC 4, 35, 82; PC 3; WLC**
See also DA; DAB; DAC; DAM MST, POET; DLB 217; EW 7; GFL 1789 to the Present; RGWL 2, 3; TWA; WP

**Rinehart, Mary Roberts** 1876-1958 ................................. **TCLC 52**
See also BPFB 3; CA 166; RGAL 4; RHW

**Ringmaster, The**
See Mencken, H(enry) L(ouis)

**Ringwood, Gwen(dolyn Margaret) Pharis** 1910-1984 ..................... **CLC 48**
See also CA 148; DLB 88

**Rio, Michel** 1945(?)- ............................ **CLC 43**
See also CA 201

**Ritsos, Giannes**
See Ritsos, Yannis

**Ritsos, Yannis** 1909-1990 ........ **CLC 6, 13, 31**
See also CA 77-80; CANR 39, 61; EW 12; MTCW 1; RGWL 2, 3

**Ritter, Erika** 1948(?)- ........................ **CLC 52**
See also CD 5; CWD

**Rivera, Jose Eustasio** 1889-1928 ... **TCLC 35**
See also CA 162; HW 1, 2; LAW

**Rivera, Tomas** 1935-1984 .................. **HLCS 2**
See also CA 49-52; CANR 32; DLB 82; HW 1; RGAL 4; SSFS 15; TCWW 2; WLIT 1

**Rivers, Conrad Kent** 1933-1968 ......... **CLC 1**
See also BW 1; CA 85-88; DLB 41

**Rivers, Elfrida**
See Bradley, Marion Zimmer
See also GLL 1

**Riverside, John**
See Heinlein, Robert A(nson)

**Rizal, Jose** 1861-1896 ...................... **NCLC 27**

**Roa Bastos, Augusto (Antonio)** 1917- ............................. **CLC 45; HLC 2**
See also CA 131; DAM MULT; DLB 113; HW 1; LAW; RGSF 2; WLIT 1

**Robbe-Grillet, Alain** 1922- .... **CLC 1, 2, 4, 6, 8, 10, 14, 43, 128**
See also BPFB 3; CA 9-12R; CANR 33, 65; DLB 83; EW 13; GFL 1789 to the Present; IDFW 3, 4; MTCW 1, 2; RGWL 2, 3; SSFS 15

**Robbins, Harold** 1916-1997 ................. **CLC 5**
See also BPFB 3; CA 73-76; CANR 26, 54, 112; DAM NOV; MTCW 1, 2

**Robbins, Thomas Eugene** 1936-
See Robbins, Tom
See also CA 81-84; CANR 29, 59, 95; CN 7; CPW; CSW; DAM NOV, POP; MTCW 1, 2

**Robbins, Tom** ........................... **CLC 9, 32, 64**
See Robbins, Thomas Eugene
See also AAYA 32; AMWS 10; BEST 90:3; BPFB 3; DLBY 1980; MTCW 2

**Robbins, Trina** 1938- ......................... **CLC 21**
See also CA 128

**Roberts, Charles G(eorge) D(ouglas)** 1860-1943 ............................. **TCLC 8**
See also CA 188; CLR 33; CWRI 5; DLB 92; RGEL 2; RGSF 2; SATA 88; SATA-Brief 29

**Roberts, Elizabeth Madox** 1886-1941 ............................ **TCLC 68**
See also CA 166; CWRI 5; DLB 9, 54, 102; RGAL 4; RHW; SATA 33; SATA-Brief 27; WCH

**Roberts, Kate** 1891-1985 .................... **CLC 15**
See also CA 107

**Roberts, Keith (John Kingston)** 1935-2000 ................................. **CLC 14**
See also CA 25-28R; CANR 46; DLB 261; SFW 4

**Roberts, Kenneth (Lewis)** 1885-1957 ................................. **TCLC 23**
See also CA 199; DLB 9; RGAL 4; RHW

**Roberts, Michele (Brigitte)** 1949- ..... **CLC 48**
See also CA 115; CANR 58; CN 7; DLB 231; FW

**Robertson, Ellis**
See Ellison, Harlan (Jay); Silverberg, Robert

**Robertson, Thomas William** 1829-1871 ............................. **NCLC 35**
See Robertson, Tom
See also DAM DRAM

**Robertson, Tom**
See Robertson, Thomas William
See also RGEL 2

**Robeson, Kenneth**
See Dent, Lester

**Robinson, Edwin Arlington** 1869-1935 ......... **PC 1, 35; TCLC 5, 101**
See also AMW; CA 133; CDALB 1865-1917; DA; DAC; DAM MST, POET; DLB 54; EXPP; MTCW 1, 2; PAB; PFS 4; RGAL 4; WP

**Robinson, Henry Crabb** 1775-1867 ....................... **NCLC 15**
See also DLB 107

**Robinson, Jill** 1936- .......................... **CLC 10**
See also CA 102; INT 102

**Robinson, Kim Stanley** 1952- ........... **CLC 34**
See also AAYA 26; CA 126; CANR 113; CN 7; SATA 109; SCFW 2; SFW 4

**Robinson, Lloyd**
See Silverberg, Robert

**Robinson, Marilynne** 1944- ............... **CLC 25**
See also CA 116; CANR 80; CN 7; DLB 206

**Robinson, Smokey** ......................... **CLC 21**
See Robinson, William, Jr.

**Robinson, William, Jr.** 1940-
See Robinson, Smokey

**Robison, Mary** 1949- .................... **CLC 42, 98**
See also CA 116; CANR 87; CN 7; DLB 130; INT 116; RGSF 2

**Rochester**
See Wilmot, John
See also RGEL 2

**Rod, Edouard** 1857-1910 ................. **TCLC 52**

**Roddenberry, Eugene Wesley** 1921-1991
See Roddenberry, Gene
See also CA 110; CANR 37; SATA 45; SATA-Obit 69

**Roddenberry, Gene** ......................... **CLC 17**
See Roddenberry, Eugene Wesley
See also AAYA 5; SATA-Obit 69

**Rodgers, Mary** 1931- ......................... **CLC 12**
See also BYA 5; CA 49-52; CANR 8, 55, 90; CLR 20; CWRI 5; INT CANR-8; JRDA; MAICYA 1, 2; SATA 8, 130

**Rodgers, W(illiam) R(obert)** 1909-1969 ....................................... **CLC 7**
See also CA 85-88; DLB 20; RGEL 2

**Rodman, Eric**
See Silverberg, Robert

**Rodman, Howard** 1920(?)-1985 ........ **CLC 65**

**Rodman, Maia**
See Wojciechowska, Maia (Teresa)

**Rodo, Jose Enrique** 1871(?)-1917 .... **HLCS 2**
See also CA 178; HW 2; LAW

**Rodolph, Utto**
See Ouologuem, Yambo

**Rodriguez, Claudio** 1934-1999 ......... **CLC 10**
See also CA 188; DLB 134

**Rodriguez, Richard** 1944- .... **CLC 155; HLC 2**
See also CA 110; CANR 66; DAM MULT; DLB 82, 256; HW 1, 2; LAIT 5; NCFS 3; WLIT 1

**Roelvaag, O(le) E(dvart)** 1876-1931
See Rolvaag, O(le) E(dvart)
See also CA 171

**Roethke, Theodore (Huebner)** 1908-1963 ......... **CLC 1, 3, 8, 11, 19, 46, 101; PC 15**
See also AMW; CA 81-84; CABS 2; CDALB 1941-1968; DAM POET; DLB 5, 206; EXPP; MTCW 1, 2; PAB; PFS 3; RGAL 4; WP

**Rogers, Carl R(ansom)** 1902-1987 ................................. **TCLC 125**
See also CA 1-4R; CANR 1, 18; MTCW 1

**Rogers, Samuel** 1763-1855 ............. **NCLC 69**
See also DLB 93; RGEL 2

**Rogers, Thomas Hunton** 1927- ......... **CLC 57**
See also CA 89-92; INT 89-92

**Rogers, Will(iam Penn Adair)**
1879-1935 .............. **NNAL; TCLC 8, 71**
See also CA 144; DAM MULT; DLB 11; MTCW 2

**Rogin, Gilbert** 1929- ........................ **CLC 18**
See also CA 65-68; CANR 15

**Rohan, Koda**
See Koda Shigeyuki

**Rohlfs, Anna Katharine Green**
See Green, Anna Katharine

**Rohmer, Eric** ..................... **CLC 16**
See Scherer, Jean-Marie Maurice

**Rohmer, Sax** ..................... **TCLC 28**
See Ward, Arthur Henry Sarsfield
See also DLB 70; MSW; SUFW

**Roiphe, Anne (Richardson)** 1935- .. **CLC 3, 9**
See also CA 89-92; CANR 45, 73; DLBY 1980; INT 89-92

**Rojas, Fernando de** 1475-1541 ....... **HLCS 1; LC 23**
See also RGWL 2, 3

**Rojas, Gonzalo** 1917- ........................ **HLCS 2**
See also CA 178; HW 2; LAWS 1

**Rolfe, Frederick (William Serafino Austin Lewis Mary)** 1860-1913 ......... **TCLC 12**
See Corvo, Baron
See also DLB 34, 156; RGEL 2

**Rolland, Romain** 1866-1944 .......... **TCLC 23**
See also CA 197; DLB 65; GFL 1789 to the Present; RGWL 2, 3

**Rolle, Richard** c. 1300-c. 1349 ...... **CMLC 21**
See also DLB 146; RGEL 2

**Rolvaag, O(le) E(dvart)** ................ **TCLC 17**
See Roelvaag, O(le) E(dvart)
See also DLB 9, 212; NFS 5; RGAL 4

**Romain Arnaud, Saint**
See Aragon, Louis

**Romains, Jules** 1885-1972 .................... **CLC 7**
See also CA 85-88; CANR 34; DLB 65; GFL 1789 to the Present; MTCW 1

**Romero, Jose Ruben** 1890-1952 .... **TCLC 14**
See also CA 131; HW 1; LAW

**Ronsard, Pierre de** 1524-1585 . **LC 6, 54; PC 11**
See also EW 2; GFL Beginnings to 1789; RGWL 2, 3; TWA

**Rooke, Leon** 1934- ....................... **CLC 25, 34**
See also CA 25-28R; CANR 23, 53; CCA 1; CPW; DAM POP

**Roosevelt, Franklin Delano**
1882-1945 .................... **TCLC 93**
See also CA 173; LAIT 3

**Roosevelt, Theodore** 1858-1919 ..... **TCLC 69**
See also CA 170; DLB 47, 186, 275

**Roper, William** 1498-1578 .................. **LC 10**

**Roquelaure, A. N.**
See Rice, Anne

**Rosa, Joao Guimaraes** 1908-1967 ... **CLC 23; HLCS 1**
See also DLB 113; WLIT 1

**Rose, Wendy** 1948- . **CLC 85; NNAL; PC 13**
See also CA 53-56; CANR 5, 51; CWP; DAM MULT; DLB 175; PFS 13; RGAL 4; SATA 12

**Rosen, R. D.**
See Rosen, Richard (Dean)

**Rosen, Richard (Dean)** 1949- ........... **CLC 39**
See also CA 77-80; CANR 62; CMW 4; INT CANR-30

**Rosenberg, Isaac** 1890-1918 ........... **TCLC 12**
See also BRW 6; CA 188; DLB 20, 216; PAB; RGEL 2

**Rosenblatt, Joe** ..................... **CLC 15**
See Rosenblatt, Joseph

**Rosenblatt, Joseph** 1933-
See Rosenblatt, Joe
See also CA 89-92; CP 7; INT 89-92

**Rosenfeld, Samuel**
See Tzara, Tristan

**Rosenstock, Sami**
See Tzara, Tristan

**Rosenstock, Samuel**
See Tzara, Tristan

**Rosenthal, M(acha) L(ouis)**
1917-1996 ..................... **CLC 28**
See also CA 1-4R; CAAS 6; CANR 4, 51; CP 7; DLB 5; SATA 59

**Ross, Barnaby**
See Dannay, Frederic

**Ross, Bernard L.**
See Follett, Ken(neth Martin)

**Ross, J. H.**
See Lawrence, T(homas) E(dward)

**Ross, John Hume**
See Lawrence, T(homas) E(dward)

**Ross, Martin** 1862-1915
See Martin, Violet Florence
See also DLB 135; GLL 2; RGEL 2; RGSF 2

**Ross, (James) Sinclair** 1908-1996 ... **CLC 13; SSC 24**
See also CA 73-76; CANR 81; CN 7; DAC; DAM MST; DLB 88; RGEL 2; RGSF 2; TCWW 2

**Rossetti, Christina (Georgina)**
1830-1894 ......... **NCLC 2, 50, 66; PC 7; WLC**
See also BRW 5; BYA 4; DA; DAB; DAC; DAM MST, POET; DLB 35, 163, 240; EXPP; MAICYA 1, 2; PFS 10, 14; RGEL 2; SATA 20; TEA; WCH

**Rossetti, Dante Gabriel** 1828-1882 . **NCLC 4, 77; PC 44; WLC**
See also BRW 5; CDBLB 1832-1890; DA; DAB; DAC; DAM MST, POET; DLB 35; EXPP; RGEL 2; TEA

**Rossi, Cristina Peri**
See Peri Rossi, Cristina

**Rossi, Jean Baptiste** 1931-
See Japrisot, Sebastien
See also CA 201

**Rossner, Judith (Perelman)** 1935- . **CLC 6, 9, 29**
See also AITN 2; BEST 90:3; BPFB 3; CA 17-20R; CANR 18, 51, 73; CN 7; DLB 6; INT CANR-18; MTCW 1, 2

**Rostand, Edmond (Eugene Alexis)**
1868-1918 ............... **DC 10; TCLC 6, 37**
See also CA 126; DA; DAB; DAC; DAM DRAM, MST; DFS 1; DLB 192; LAIT 1; MTCW 1; RGWL 2, 3; TWA

**Roth, Henry** 1906-1995 ...... **CLC 2, 6, 11, 104**
See also AMWS 9; CA 11-12; CANR 38, 63; CAP 1; CN 7; DLB 28; MTCW 1, 2; RGAL 4

**Roth, (Moses) Joseph** 1894-1939 ... **TCLC 33**
See also CA 160; DLB 85; RGWL 2, 3

**Roth, Philip (Milton)** 1933- ... **CLC 1, 2, 3, 4, 6, 9, 15, 22, 31, 47, 66, 86, 119; SSC 26; WLC**
See also AMWR 2; AMWS 3; BEST 90:3; BPFB 3; CA 1-4R; CANR 1, 22, 36, 55, 89; CDALB 1968-1988; CN 7; CPW 1; DA; DAB; DAC; DAM MST, NOV, POP; DLB 2, 28, 173; DLBY 1982; MTCW 1, 2; RGAL 4; RGSF 2; SSFS 12; TUS

**Rothenberg, Jerome** 1931- ................ **CLC 6, 57**
See also CA 45-48; CANR 1, 106; CP 7; DLB 5, 193

**Rotter, Pat ed.** ..................... **CLC 65**

**Roumain, Jacques (Jean Baptiste)**
1907-1944 ..................... **BLC 3; TCLC 19**
See also BW 1; CA 125; DAM MULT

**Rourke, Constance Mayfield**
1885-1941 ..................... **TCLC 12**
See also CA 200; YABC 1

**Rousseau, Jean-Baptiste** 1671-1741 ...... **LC 9**

**Rousseau, Jean-Jacques** 1712-1778 .... **LC 14, 36; WLC**
See also DA; DAB; DAC; DAM MST; EW 4; GFL Beginnings to 1789; RGWL 2, 3; TWA

**Roussel, Raymond** 1877-1933 ........ **TCLC 20**
See also CA 201; GFL 1789 to the Present

**Rovit, Earl (Herbert)** 1927- ............. **CLC 7**
See also CA 5-8R; CANR 12

**Rowe, Elizabeth Singer** 1674-1737 ..... **LC 44**
See also DLB 39, 95

**Rowe, Nicholas** 1674-1718 ................ **LC 8**
See also DLB 84; RGEL 2

**Rowlandson, Mary** 1637(?)-1678 ......... **LC 66**
See also DLB 24, 200; RGAL 4

**Rowley, Ames Dorrance**
See Lovecraft, H(oward) P(hillips)

**Rowling, J(oanne) K(athleen)**
1965- ..................... **CLC 137**
See also AAYA 34; BYA 13, 14; CA 173; CLR 66, 80; MAICYA 2; SATA 109; SUFW 2

**Rowson, Susanna Haswell**
1762(?)-1824 ..................... **NCLC 5, 69**
See also DLB 37, 200; RGAL 4

**Roy, Arundhati** 1960(?)- ................. **CLC 109**
See also CA 163; CANR 90; DLBY 1997

**Roy, Gabrielle** 1909-1983 .............. **CLC 10, 14**
See also CA 53-56; CANR 5, 61; CCA 1; DAB; DAC; DAM MST; DLB 68; MTCW 1, 2; RGWL 2, 3; SATA 104

**Royko, Mike** 1932-1997 ................ **CLC 109**
See also CA 89-92; CANR 26, 111; CPW

**Rozanov, Vassili** 1856-1919 ........... **TCLC 104**

**Rozewicz, Tadeusz** 1921- ....... **CLC 9, 23, 139**
See also CA 108; CANR 36, 66; CWW 2; DAM POET; DLB 232; MTCW 1, 2; RGWL 3

**Ruark, Gibbons** 1941- ........................ **CLC 3**
See also CA 33-36R; CAAS 23; CANR 14, 31, 57; DLB 120

**Rubens, Bernice (Ruth)** 1923- ..... **CLC 19, 31**
See also CA 25-28R; CANR 33, 65; CN 7; DLB 14, 207; MTCW 1

**Rubin, Harold**
See Robbins, Harold

**Rudkin, (James) David** 1936- ........... **CLC 14**
See also CA 89-92; CBD; CD 5; DLB 13

**Rudnik, Raphael** 1933- ........................ **CLC 7**
See also CA 29-32R

**Ruffian, M.**
See Hasek, Jaroslav (Matej Frantisek)

**Ruiz, Jose Martinez** ..................... **CLC 11**
See Martinez Ruiz, Jose

**Rukeyser, Muriel** 1913-1980 . **CLC 6, 10, 15, 27; PC 12**
See also AMWS 6; CA 5-8R; CANR 26, 60; DAM POET; DLB 48; FW; GLL 2; MTCW 1, 2; PFS 10; RGAL 4; SATA-Obit 22

**Rule, Jane (Vance)** 1931- ................. **CLC 27**
See also CA 25-28R; CAAS 18; CANR 12, 87; CN 7; DLB 60; FW

**Rulfo, Juan** 1918-1986 .. **CLC 8, 80; HLC 2; SSC 25**
See also CA 85-88; CANR 26; CDWLB 3; DAM MULT; DLB 113; HW 1, 2; LAW; MTCW 1, 2; RGSF 2; RGWL 2, 3; WLIT 1

**Rumi, Jalal al-Din** 1207-1273 ...... **CMLC 20; PC 45**
See also RGWL 2, 3; WP

**Runeberg, Johan** 1804-1877 ........... **NCLC 41**

**Runyon, (Alfred) Damon**
1884(?)-1946 ..................... **TCLC 10**
See also CA 165; DLB 11, 86, 171; MTCW 2; RGAL 4

**Rush, Norman** 1933- ............................. **CLC 44**
See also CA 126; INT 126
**Rushdie, (Ahmed) Salman** 1947- .... **CLC 23, 31, 55, 100; WLCS**
See also BEST 89:3; BPFB 3; BRWS 4; CA 111; CANR 33, 56, 108; CN 7; CPW 1; DAB; DAC; DAM MST, NOV, POP; DLB 194; FANT; INT CA-111; MTCW 1, 2; RGEL 2; RGSF 2; TEA; WLIT 4
**Rushforth, Peter (Scott)** 1945- .......... **CLC 19**
See also CA 101
**Ruskin, John** 1819-1900 ................ **TCLC 63**
See also BRW 5; BYA 5; CA 129; CDBLB 1832-1890; DLB 55, 163, 190; RGEL 2; SATA 24; TEA; WCH
**Russ, Joanna** 1937- ............................. **CLC 15**
See also BPFB 3; CA 5-28R; CANR 11, 31, 65; CN 7; DLB 8; FW; GLL 1; MTCW 1; SCFW 2; SFW 4
**Russ, Richard Patrick**
See O'Brian, Patrick
**Russell, George William** 1867-1935
See A.E.; Baker, Jean H.
See also BRWS 8; CA 153; CDBLB 1890-1914; DAM POET; RGEL 2
**Russell, Jeffrey Burton** 1934- ........... **CLC 70**
See also CA 25-28R; CANR 11, 28, 52
**Russell, (Henry) Ken(neth Alfred)** 1927- ............................................ **CLC 16**
See also CA 105
**Russell, William Martin** 1947-
See Russell, Willy
See also CA 164; CANR 107
**Russell, Willy** ............................... **CLC 60**
See Russell, William Martin
See also CBD; CD 5; DLB 233
**Rutherford, Mark** ......................... **TCLC 25**
See White, William Hale
See also DLB 18; RGEL 2
**Ruyslinck, Ward** ............................. **CLC 14**
See Belser, Reimond Karel Maria de
**Ryan, Cornelius (John)** 1920-1974 ..... **CLC 7**
See also CA 69-72; CANR 38
**Ryan, Michael** 1946- ......................... **CLC 65**
See also CA 49-52; CANR 109; DLBY 1982
**Ryan, Tim**
See Dent, Lester
**Rybakov, Anatoli (Naumovich)** 1911-1998 ........................ **CLC 23, 53**
See also CA 135; SATA 79; SATA-Obit 108
**Ryder, Jonathan**
See Ludlum, Robert
**Ryga, George** 1932-1987 ................... **CLC 14**
See also CA 101; CANR 43, 90; CCA 1; DAC; DAM MST; DLB 60
**S. H.**
See Hartmann, Sadakichi
**S. S.**
See Sassoon, Siegfried (Lorraine)
**Saba, Umberto** 1883-1957 ............... **TCLC 33**
See also CA 144; CANR 79; DLB 114; RGWL 2, 3
**Sabatini, Rafael** 1875-1950 ............ **TCLC 47**
See also BPFB 3; CA 162; RHW
**Sabato, Ernesto (R.)** 1911- ........ **CLC 10, 23; HLC 2**
See also CA 97-100; CANR 32, 65; CDWLB 3; DAM MULT; DLB 145; HW 1, 2; LAW; MTCW 1, 2
**Sa-Carniero, Mario de** 1890-1916 . **TCLC 83**
**Sacastru, Martin**
See Bioy Casares, Adolfo
See also CWW 2

**Sacher-Masoch, Leopold von** 1836(?)-1895 ......................... **NCLC 31**
**Sachs, Marilyn (Stickle)** 1927- ......... **CLC 35**
See also AAYA 2; BYA 6; CA 17-20R; CANR 13, 47; CLR 2; JRDA; MAICYA 1, 2; SAAS 2; SATA 3, 68; SATA-Essay 110; WYA; YAW
**Sachs, Nelly** 1891-1970 ............... **CLC 14, 98**
See also CA 17-18; CANR 87; CAP 2; MTCW 2; RGWL 2, 3
**Sackler, Howard (Oliver)** 1929-1982 ............................. **CLC 14**
See also CA 61-64; CAD; CANR 30; DFS 15; DLB 7
**Sacks, Oliver (Wolf)** 1933- ............... **CLC 67**
See also CA 53-56; CANR 28, 50, 76; CPW; INT CANR-28; MTCW 1, 2
**Sadakichi**
See Hartmann, Sadakichi
**Sade, Donatien Alphonse Francois** 1740-1814 ............................ **NCLC 3, 47**
See also EW 4; GFL Beginnings to 1789; RGWL 2, 3
**Sade, Marquis de**
See Sade, Donatien Alphonse Francois
**Sadoff, Ira** 1945- ................................. **CLC 9**
See also CA 53-56; CANR 5, 21, 109; DLB 120
**Saetone**
See Camus, Albert
**Safire, William** 1929- ........................ **CLC 10**
See also CA 17-20R; CANR 31, 54, 91
**Sagan, Carl (Edward)** 1934-1996 .... **CLC 30, 112**
See also AAYA 2; CA 25-28R; CANR 11, 36, 74; CPW; MTCW 1, 2; SATA 58; SATA-Obit 94
**Sagan, Francoise** ............ **CLC 3, 6, 9, 17, 36**
See Quoirez, Francoise
See also CWW 2; DLB 83; GFL 1789 to the Present; MTCW 2
**Sahgal, Nayantara (Pandit)** 1927- .... **CLC 41**
See also CA 9-12R; CANR 11, 88; CN 7
**Said, Edward W.** 1935- ................... **CLC 123**
See also CA 21-24R; CANR 45, 74, 107; DLB 67; MTCW 2
**Saint, H(arry) F.** 1941- ...................... **CLC 50**
See also CA 127
**St. Aubin de Teran, Lisa** 1953-
See Teran, Lisa St. Aubin de
See also CA 126; CN 7; INT 126
**Saint Birgitta of Sweden** c. 1303-1373 ......................... **CMLC 24**
**Sainte-Beuve, Charles Augustin** 1804-1869 ................................ **NCLC 5**
See also DLB 217; EW 6; GFL 1789 to the Present
**Saint-Exupery, Antoine (Jean Baptiste Marie Roger) de** 1900-1944 .... **TCLC 2, 56; WLC**
See also BPFB 3; BYA 3; CA 132; CLR 10; DAM NOV; DLB 72; EW 12; GFL 1789 to the Present; LAIT 3; MAICYA 1, 2; MTCW 1, 2; RGWL 2, 3; SATA 20; TWA
**St. John, David**
See Hunt, E(verette) Howard, (Jr.)
**St. John, J. Hector**
See Crevecoeur, Michel Guillaume Jean de
**Saint-John Perse**
See Leger, (Marie-Rene Auguste) Alexis Saint-Leger
See also EW 10; GFL 1789 to the Present; RGWL 2
**Saintsbury, George (Edward Bateman)** 1845-1933 ........................... **TCLC 31**
See also CA 160; DLB 57, 149
**Sait Faik** ............................................ **TCLC 23**
See Abasiyanik, Sait Faik

**Saki** ................................ **SSC 12; TCLC 3**
See Munro, H(ector) H(ugh)
See also BRWS 6; LAIT 2; MTCW 2; RGEL 2; SSFS 1; SUFW
**Sakutaro, Hagiwara**
See Hagiwara, Sakutaro
**Sala, George Augustus** 1828-1895 . **NCLC 46**
**Saladin** 1138-1193 ......................... **CMLC 38**
**Salama, Hannu** 1936- ...................... **CLC 18**
**Salamanca, J(ack) R(ichard)** 1922- .. **CLC 4, 15**
See also CA 25-28R; CAAE 193
**Salas, Floyd Francis** 1931- ................. **HLC 2**
See also CA 119; CAAS 27; CANR 44, 75, 93; DAM MULT; DLB 82; HW 1, 2; MTCW 2
**Sale, J. Kirkpatrick**
See Sale, Kirkpatrick
**Sale, Kirkpatrick** 1937- ...................... **CLC 68**
See also CA 13-16R; CANR 10
**Salinas, Luis Omar** 1937- ... **CLC 90; HLC 2**
See also CA 131; CANR 81; DAM MULT; DLB 82; HW 1, 2
**Salinas (y Serrano), Pedro** 1891(?)-1951 ............................ **TCLC 17**
See also DLB 134
**Salinger, J(erome) D(avid)** 1919- .. **CLC 1, 3, 8, 12, 55, 56, 138; SSC 2, 28; WLC**
See also AAYA 2, 36; AMW; AMWC 1; BPFB 3; CA 5-8R; CANR 39; CDALB 1941-1968; CLR 18; CN 7; CPW 1; DA; DAB; DAC; DAM MST, NOV, POP; DLB 2, 102, 173; EXPN; LAIT 4; MAICYA 1, 2; MTCW 1, 2; NFS 1; RGAL 4; RGSF 2; SATA 67; TUS; WYA; YAW
**Salisbury, John**
See Caute, (John) David
**Salter, James** 1925- .. **CLC 7, 52, 59; SSC 58**
See also AMWS 9; CA 73-76; CANR 107; DLB 130
**Saltus, Edgar (Everton)** 1855-1921 . **TCLC 8**
See also DLB 202; RGAL 4
**Saltykov, Mikhail Evgrafovich** 1826-1889 ................................ **NCLC 16**
See also DLB 238:
**Saltykov-Shchedrin, N.**
See Saltykov, Mikhail Evgrafovich
**Samarakis, Antonis** 1919- ................... **CLC 5**
See also CA 25-28R; CAAS 16; CANR 36
**Sanchez, Florencio** 1875-1910 ........ **TCLC 37**
See also CA 153; HW 1; LAW
**Sanchez, Luis Rafael** 1936- ............... **CLC 23**
See also CA 128; DLB 145; HW 1; WLIT 1
**Sanchez, Sonia** 1934- .... **BLC 3; CLC 5, 116; PC 9**
See also BW 2, 3; CA 33-36R; CANR 24, 49, 74; CLR 18; CP 7; CSW; CWP; DAM MULT; DLB 41; DLBD 8; MAICYA 1, 2; MTCW 1, 2; SATA 22, 136; WP
**Sancho, Ignatius** 1729-1780 ................ **LC 84**
**Sand, George** 1804-1876 ..... **NCLC 2, 42, 57; WLC**
See also DA; DAB; DAC; DAM MST, NOV; DLB 119, 192; EW 6; FW; GFL 1789 to the Present; RGWL 2, 3; TWA
**Sandburg, Carl (August)** 1878-1967 . **CLC 1, 4, 10, 15, 35; PC 2, 41; WLC**
See also AAYA 24; AMW; BYA 1, 3; CA 5-8R; CANR 35; CDALB 1865-1917; CLR 67; DA; DAB; DAC; DAM MST, POET; DLB 17, 54; EXPP; LAIT 2; MAICYA 1, 2; MTCW 1, 2; PAB; PFS 3, 6, 12; RGAL 4; SATA 8; TUS; WCH; WP; WYA
**Sandburg, Charles**
See Sandburg, Carl (August)
**Sandburg, Charles A.**
See Sandburg, Carl (August)

**Sanders, (James) Ed(ward)** 1939- .... **CLC 53**
See Sanders, Edward
See also BG 3; CA 13-16R; CAAS 21; CANR 13, 44, 78; CP 7; DAM POET; DLB 16, 244

**Sanders, Edward**
See Sanders, (James) Ed(ward)
See also DLB 244

**Sanders, Lawrence** 1920-1998 .......... **CLC 41**
See also BEST 89:4; BPFB 3; CA 81-84; CANR 33, 62; CMW 4; CPW; DAM POP; MTCW 1

**Sanders, Noah**
See Blount, Roy (Alton), Jr.

**Sanders, Winston P.**
See Anderson, Poul (William)

**Sandoz, Mari(e Susette)** 1900-1966 .. **CLC 28**
See also CA 1-4R; CANR 17, 64; DLB 9, 212; LAIT 2; MTCW 1, 2; SATA 5; TCWW 2

**Sandys, George** 1578-1644 .................... **LC 80**
See also DLB 24, 121

**Saner, Reg(inald Anthony)** 1931- ....... **CLC 9**
See also CA 65-68; CP 7

**Sankara** 788-820 ............................ **CMLC 32**

**Sannazaro, Jacopo** 1456(?)-1530 ........... **LC 8**
See also RGWL 2, 3

**Sansom, William** 1912-1976 . **CLC 2, 6; SSC 21**
See also CA 5-8R; CANR 42; DAM NOV; DLB 139; MTCW 1; RGEL 2; RGSF 2

**Santayana, George** 1863-1952 ......... **TCLC 40**
See also AMW; CA 194; DLB 54, 71, 246, 270; DLBD 13; RGAL 4; TUS

**Santiago, Danny** ................................ **CLC 33**
See James, Daniel (Lewis)
See also DLB 122

**Santmyer, Helen Hooven** 1895-1986 ...................... **CLC 33**
See also CA 1-4R; CANR 15, 33; DLBY 1984; MTCW 1; RHW

**Santoka, Taneda** 1882-1940 ............ **TCLC 72**

**Santos, Bienvenido N(uqui)** 1911-1996 ...................... **CLC 22**
See also CA 101; CANR 19, 46; DAM MULT; RGAL 4

**Sapir, Edward** 1884-1939 ............. **TCLC 108**
See also DLB 92

**Sapper** ................................................. **TCLC 44**
See McNeile, Herman Cyril

**Sapphire**
See Sapphire, Brenda

**Sapphire, Brenda** 1950- ...................... **CLC 99**

**Sappho** fl. 6th cent. B.C.- ...... **CMLC 3; PC 5**
See also CDWLB 1; DAM POET; DLB 176; RGWL 2, 3; WP

**Saramago, Jose** 1922- ..... **CLC 119; HLCS 1**
See also CA 153; CANR 96

**Sarduy, Severo** 1937-1993 ........... **CLC 6, 97; HLCS 2**
See also CA 89-92; CANR 58, 81; CWW 2; DLB 113; HW 1, 2; LAW

**Sargeson, Frank** 1903-1982 ................ **CLC 31**
See also CA 25-28R; CANR 38, 79; GLL 2; RGEL 2; RGSF 2

**Sarmiento, Domingo Faustino** 1811-1888 ........................ **HLCS 2**
See also LAW; WLIT 1

**Sarmiento, Felix Ruben Garcia**
See Dario, Ruben

**Saro-Wiwa, Ken(ule Beeson)** 1941-1995 ............................ **CLC 114**
See also BW 2; CA 142; CANR 60; DLB 157

**Saroyan, William** 1908-1981 ... **CLC 1, 8, 10, 29, 34, 56; SSC 21; WLC**
See also CA 5-8R; CAD; CANR 30; CDALBS; DA; DAB; DAC; DAM DRAM, MST, NOV; DLB 7, 9, 86; DLBY 1981; LAIT 4; MTCW 1, 2; RGAL 4; RGSF 2; SATA 23; SATA-Obit 24; SSFS 14; TUS

**Sarraute, Nathalie** 1900-1999 .... **CLC 1, 2, 4, 8, 10, 31, 80**
See also BPFB 3; CA 9-12R; CANR 23, 66; CWW 2; DLB 83; EW 12; GFL 1789 to the Present; MTCW 1, 2; RGWL 2, 3

**Sarton, (Eleanor) May** 1912-1995 ...... **CLC 4, 14, 49, 91; PC 39; TCLC 120**
See also AMWS 8; CA 1-4R; CANR 1, 34, 55; CN 7; CP 7; DAM POET; DLB 48; DLBY 1981; FW; INT CANR-34; MTCW 1, 2; RGAL 4; SATA 36; SATA-Obit 86; TUS

**Sartre, Jean-Paul** 1905-1980 . **CLC 1, 4, 7, 9, 13, 18, 24, 44, 50, 52; DC 3; SSC 32; WLC**
See also CA 9-12R; CANR 21; DA; DAB; DAC; DAM DRAM, MST, NOV; DFS 5; DLB 72; EW 12; GFL 1789 to the Present; MTCW 1, 2; RGSF 2; RGWL 2, 3; SSFS 9; TWA

**Sassoon, Siegfried (Lorraine)** 1886-1967 .............. **CLC 36, 130; PC 12**
See also BRW 6; CA 104; CANR 36; DAB; DAM MST, NOV, POET; DLB 20, 191; DLBD 18; MTCW 1, 2; PAB; RGEL 2; TEA

**Satterfield, Charles**
See Pohl, Frederik

**Satyremont**
See Peret, Benjamin

**Saul, John (W. III)** 1942- ................... **CLC 46**
See also AAYA 10; BEST 90:4; CA 81-84; CANR 16, 40, 81; CPW; DAM NOV, POP; HGG; SATA 98

**Saunders, Caleb**
See Heinlein, Robert A(nson)

**Saura (Atares), Carlos** 1932-1998 .... **CLC 20**
See also CA 131; CANR 79; HW 1

**Sauser-Hall, Frederic** 1887-1961 ...... **CLC 18**
See Cendrars, Blaise
See also CA 102; CANR 36, 62; MTCW 1

**Saussure, Ferdinand de** 1857-1913 ............................. **TCLC 49**
See also DLB 242

**Savage, Catharine**
See Brosman, Catharine Savage

**Savage, Thomas** 1915- ....................... **CLC 40**
See also CA 132; CAAS 15; CN 7; INT 132; TCWW 2

**Savan, Glenn** (?)- ............................. **CLC 50**

**Sax, Robert**
See Johnson, Robert

**Saxton, Robert**
See Johnson, Robert

**Sayers, Dorothy L(eigh)** 1893-1957 ............................ **TCLC 2, 15**
See also BPFB 3; BRWS 3; CA 119; CANR 60; CDBLB 1914-1945; CMW 4; DAM POP; DLB 10, 36, 77, 100; MSW; MTCW 1, 2; RGEL 2; SSFS 12; TEA

**Sayers, Valerie** 1952- ...................... **CLC 50, 122**
See also CA 134; CANR 61; CSW

**Sayles, John (Thomas)** 1950- . **CLC 7, 10, 14**
See also CA 57-60; CANR 41, 84; DLB 44

**Scammell, Michael** 1935- ................... **CLC 34**
See also CA 156

**Scannell, Vernon** 1922- ...................... **CLC 49**
See also CA 5-8R; CANR 8, 24, 57; CP 7; CWRI 5; DLB 27; SATA 59

**Scarlett, Susan**
See Streatfeild, (Mary) Noel

**Scarron** 1847-1910
See Mikszath, Kalman

**Schaeffer, Susan Fromberg** 1941- ..... **CLC 6, 11, 22**
See also CA 49-52; CANR 18, 65; CN 7; DLB 28; MTCW 1, 2; SATA 22

**Schama, Simon (Michael)** 1945- ..... **CLC 150**
See also BEST 89:4; CA 105; CANR 39, 91

**Schary, Jill**
See Robinson, Jill

**Schell, Jonathan** 1943- ...................... **CLC 35**
See also CA 73-76; CANR 12

**Schelling, Friedrich Wilhelm Joseph von** 1775-1854 ............................... **NCLC 30**
See also DLB 90

**Scherer, Jean-Marie Maurice** 1920-
See Rohmer, Eric
See also CA 110

**Schevill, James (Erwin)** 1920- ............ **CLC 7**
See also CA 5-8R; CAAS 12; CAD; CD 5

**Schiller, Friedrich von** 1759-1805 ....... **DC 12; NCLC 39, 69**
See also CDWLB 2; DAM DRAM; DLB 94; EW 5; RGWL 2, 3; TWA

**Schisgal, Murray (Joseph)** 1926- ........ **CLC 6**
See also CA 21-24R; CAD; CANR 48, 86; CD 5

**Schlee, Ann** 1934- ............................. **CLC 35**
See also CA 101; CANR 29, 88; SATA 44; SATA-Brief 36

**Schlegel, August Wilhelm von** 1767-1845 ................................. **NCLC 15**
See also DLB 94; RGWL 2, 3

**Schlegel, Friedrich** 1772-1829 ......... **NCLC 45**
See also DLB 90; EW 5; RGWL 2, 3; TWA

**Schlegel, Johann Elias (von)** 1719(?)-1749 .................................. **LC 5**

**Schleiermacher, Friedrich** 1768-1834 ............................... **NCLC 107**
See also DLB 90

**Schlesinger, Arthur M(eier), Jr.** 1917- ........................................... **CLC 84**
See also AITN 1; CA 1-4R; CANR 1, 28, 58, 105; DLB 17; INT CANR-28; MTCW 1, 2; SATA 61

**Schmidt, Arno (Otto)** 1914-1979 ....... **CLC 56**
See also CA 128; DLB 69

**Schmitz, Aron Hector** 1861-1928
See Svevo, Italo
See also CA 122; MTCW 1

**Schnackenberg, Gjertrud (Cecelia)** 1953- ............................. **CLC 40; PC 45**
See also CANR 100; CP 7; CWP; DLB 120; PFS 13

**Schneider, Leonard Alfred** 1925-1966
See Bruce, Lenny
See also CA 89-92

**Schnitzler, Arthur** 1862-1931 ..... **DC 17; SSC 15; TCLC 4**
See also CDWLB 2; DLB 81, 118; EW 8; RGSF 2; RGWL 2, 3

**Schoenberg, Arnold Franz Walter** 1874-1951 ................................ **TCLC 75**
See also CA 188

**Schonberg, Arnold**
See Schoenberg, Arnold Franz Walter

**Schopenhauer, Arthur** 1788-1860 .. **NCLC 51**
See also DLB 90; EW 5

**Schor, Sandra (M.)** 1932(?)-1990 ..... **CLC 65**

**Schorer, Mark** 1908-1977 ..................... **CLC 9**
See also CA 5-8R; CANR 7; DLB 103

**Schrader, Paul (Joseph)** 1946- .......... **CLC 26**
See also CA 37-40R; CANR 41; DLB 44

**Schreber, Daniel** 1842-1911 .......... **TCLC 123**

**Schreiner, Olive (Emilie Albertina)** 1855-1920 ................................. **TCLC 9**
See also AFW; BRWS 2; CA 154; DLB 18, 156, 190, 225; FW; RGEL 2; TWA; WLIT 2

**Schulberg, Budd (Wilson)** 1914- .. **CLC 7, 48**
See also BPFB 3; CA 25-28R; CANR 19, 87; CN 7; DLB 6, 26, 28; DLBY 1981, 2001

**Schulman, Arnold**
See Trumbo, Dalton

**Schulz, Bruno** 1892-1942 .. **SSC 13; TCLC 5, 51**
See also CA 123; CANR 86; CDWLB 4; DLB 215; MTCW 2; RGSF 2; RGWL 2, 3

**Schulz, Charles M(onroe)** 1922-2000 ............................... **CLC 12**
See also AAYA 39; CA 9-12R; CANR 6; INT CANR-6; SATA 10; SATA-Obit 118

**Schumacher, E(rnst) F(riedrich)** 1911-1977 ........................... **CLC 80**
See also CA 81-84; CANR 34, 85

**Schuyler, James Marcus** 1923-1991 .. **CLC 5, 23**
See also CA 101; DAM POET; DLB 5, 169; INT 101; WP

**Schwartz, Delmore (David)** 1913-1966 ... **CLC 2, 4, 10, 45, 87; PC 8**
See also AMWS 2; CA 17-18; CANR 35; CAP 2; DLB 28, 48; MTCW 1, 2; PAB; RGAL 4; TUS

**Schwartz, Ernst**
See Ozu, Yasujiro

**Schwartz, John Burnham** 1965- ....... **CLC 59**
See also CA 132

**Schwartz, Lynne Sharon** 1939- ........ **CLC 31**
See also CA 103; CANR 44, 89; DLB 218; MTCW 2

**Schwartz, Muriel A.**
See Eliot, T(homas) S(tearns)

**Schwarz-Bart, Andre** 1928- ............ **CLC 2, 4**
See also CA 89-92; CANR 109

**Schwarz-Bart, Simone** 1938- . **BLCS; CLC 7**
See also BW 2; CA 97-100

**Schwerner, Armand** 1927-1999 ............ **PC 42**
See also CA 9-12R; CANR 50, 85; CP 7; DLB 165

**Schwitters, Kurt (Hermann Edward Karl Julius)** 1887-1948 .................... **TCLC 95**
See also CA 158

**Schwob, Marcel (Mayer Andre)** 1867-1905 ..................... **TCLC 20**
See also CA 168; DLB 123; GFL 1789 to the Present

**Sciascia, Leonardo** 1921-1989 .. **CLC 8, 9, 41**
See also CA 85-88; CANR 35; DLB 177; MTCW 1; RGWL 2, 3

**Scoppettone, Sandra** 1936- ............... **CLC 26**
See Early, Jack
See also AAYA 11; BYA 8; CA 5-8R; CANR 41, 73; GLL 1; MAICYA 2; MAICYAS 1; SATA 9, 92; WYA; YAW

**Scorsese, Martin** 1942- ................ **CLC 20, 89**
See also AAYA 38; CA 114; CANR 46, 85

**Scotland, Jay**
See Jakes, John (William)

**Scott, Duncan Campbell** 1862-1947 ........................ **TCLC 6**
See also CA 153; DAC; DLB 92; RGEL 2

**Scott, Evelyn** 1893-1963 ..................... **CLC 43**
See also CA 104; CANR 64; DLB 9, 48; RHW

**Scott, F(rancis) R(eginald)** 1899-1985 ............................ **CLC 22**
See also CA 101; CANR 87; DLB 88; INT CA-101; RGEL 2

**Scott, Frank**
See Scott, F(rancis) R(eginald)

**Scott, Joan** ............................... **CLC 65**

**Scott, Joanna** 1960- ......................... **CLC 50**
See also CA 126; CANR 53, 92

**Scott, Paul (Mark)** 1920-1978 ...... **CLC 9, 60**
See also BRWS 1; CA 81-84; CANR 33; DLB 14, 207; MTCW 1; RGEL 2; RHW

**Scott, Sarah** 1723-1795 ...................... **LC 44**
See also DLB 39

**Scott, Sir Walter** 1771-1832 .... **NCLC 15, 69, 110; PC 13; SSC 32; WLC**
See also AAYA 22; BRW 4; BYA 2; CDBLB 1789-1832; DA; DAB; DAC; DAM MST, NOV, POET; DLB 93, 107, 116, 144, 159; HGG; LAIT 1; RGEL 2; RGSF 2; SSFS 10; SUFW 1; TEA; WLIT 3; YABC 2

**Scribe, (Augustin) Eugene** 1791-1861 . **DC 5; NCLC 16**
See also DAM DRAM; DLB 192; GFL 1789 to the Present; RGWL 2, 3

**Scrum, R.**
See Crumb, R(obert)

**Scudery, Georges de** 1601-1667 ........... **LC 75**
See also GFL Beginnings to 1789

**Scudery, Madeleine de** 1607-1701 .. **LC 2, 58**
See also DLB 268; GFL Beginnings to 1789

**Scum**
See Crumb, R(obert)

**Scumbag, Little Bobby**
See Crumb, R(obert)

**Seabrook, John**
See Hubbard, L(afayette) Ron(ald)

**Sealy, I(rwin) Allan** 1951- ................. **CLC 55**
See also CA 136; CN 7

**Search, Alexander**
See Pessoa, Fernando (Antonio Nogueira)

**Sebastian, Lee**
See Silverberg, Robert

**Sebastian Owl**
See Thompson, Hunter S(tockton)

**Sebestyen, Igen**
See Sebestyen, Ouida

**Sebestyen, Ouida** 1924- ..................... **CLC 30**
See also AAYA 8; BYA 7; CA 107; CANR 40, 114; CLR 17; JRDA; MAICYA 1, 2; SAAS 10; SATA 39; WYA; YAW

**Secundus, H. Scriblerus**
See Fielding, Henry

**Sedges, John**
See Buck, Pearl S(ydenstricker)

**Sedgwick, Catharine Maria** 1789-1867 ......................... **NCLC 19, 98**
See also DLB 1, 74, 183, 239, 243, 254; RGAL 4

**Seelye, John (Douglas)** 1931- .............. **CLC 7**
See also CA 97-100; CANR 70; INT 97-100; TCWW 2

**Seferiades, Giorgos Stylianou** 1900-1971
See Seferis, George
See also CA 5-8R; CANR 5, 36; MTCW 1

**Seferis, George** ............................ **CLC 5, 11**
See Seferiades, Giorgos Stylianou
See also EW 12; RGWL 2, 3

**Segal, Erich (Wolf)** 1937- .............. **CLC 3, 10**
See also BEST 89:1; BPFB 3; CA 25-28R; CANR 20, 36, 65, 113; CPW; DAM POP; DLBY 1986; INT CANR-20; MTCW 1

**Seger, Bob** 1945- ................................ **CLC 35**

**Seghers, Anna** -1983 .......................... **CLC 7**
See Radvanyi, Netty
See also CDWLB 2; DLB 69

**Seidel, Frederick (Lewis)** 1936- ........ **CLC 18**
See also CA 13-16R; CANR 8, 99; CP 7; DLBY 1984

**Seifert, Jaroslav** 1901-1986 .. **CLC 34, 44, 93**
See also CA 127; CDWLB 4; DLB 215; MTCW 1, 2

**Sei Shonagon** c. 966-1017(?) ........... **CMLC 6**

**Sejour, Victor** 1817-1874 .................... **DC 10**
See also DLB 50

**Sejour Marcou et Ferrand, Juan Victor**
See Sejour, Victor

**Selby, Hubert, Jr.** 1928- ........ **CLC 1, 2, 4, 8; SSC 20**
See also CA 13-16R; CANR 33, 85; CN 7; DLB 2, 227

**Selzer, Richard** 1928- ........................ **CLC 74**
See also CA 65-68; CANR 14, 106

**Sembene, Ousmane**
See Ousmane, Sembene
See also AFW; CWW 2; WLIT 2

**Senancour, Etienne Pivert de** 1770-1846 ............................... **NCLC 16**
See also DLB 119; GFL 1789 to the Present

**Sender, Ramon (Jose)** 1902-1982 ...... **CLC 8; HLC 2**
See also CA 5-8R; CANR 8; DAM MULT; HW 1; MTCW 1; RGWL 2, 3

**Seneca, Lucius Annaeus** c. 4B.C.-c. 65 .................................. **CMLC 6; DC 5**
See also AW 2; CDWLB 1; DAM DRAM; DLB 211; RGWL 2, 3; TWA

**Senghor, Leopold Sedar** 1906-2001 ... **BLC 3; CLC 54, 130; PC 25**
See also AFW; BW 2; CA 125; CANR 47, 74; DAM MULT, POET; DNFS 2; GFL 1789 to the Present; MTCW 1, 2; TWA

**Senna, Danzy** 1970- ......................... **CLC 119**
See also CA 169

**Serling, (Edward) Rod(man)** 1924-1975 ................................. **CLC 30**
See also AAYA 14; AITN 1; CA 162; DLB 26; SFW 4

**Serna, Ramon Gomez de la**
See Gomez de la Serna, Ramon

**Serpieres**
See Guillevic, (Eugene)

**Service, Robert**
See Service, Robert W(illiam)
See also BYA 4; DAB; DLB 92

**Service, Robert W(illiam)** 1874(?)-1958 ................. **TCLC 15; WLC**
See Service, Robert
See also CA 140; CANR 84; DA; DAC; DAM MST, POET; PFS 10; RGEL 2; SATA 20

**Seth, Vikram** 1952- ....................... **CLC 43, 90**
See also CA 127; CANR 50, 74; CN 7; CP 7; DAM MULT; DLB 120, 271; INT 127; MTCW 2

**Seton, Cynthia Propper** 1926-1982 .. **CLC 27**
See also CA 5-8R; CANR 7

**Seton, Ernest (Evan) Thompson** 1860-1946 ........................ **TCLC 31**
See also ANW; BYA 3; CA 204; CLR 59; DLB 92; DLBD 13; JRDA; SATA 18

**Seton-Thompson, Ernest**
See Seton, Ernest (Evan) Thompson

**Settle, Mary Lee** 1918- ................ **CLC 19, 61**
See also BPFB 3; CA 89-92; CAAS 1; CANR 44, 87; CN 7; CSW; DLB 6; INT 89-92

**Seuphor, Michel**
See Arp, Jean

**Sevigne, Marie (de Rabutin-Chantal)** 1626-1696 ...................... **LC 11**
See Sevigne, Marie de Rabutin Chantal
See also GFL Beginnings to 1789; TWA

**Sevigne, Marie de Rabutin Chantal**
See Sevigne, Marie (de Rabutin-Chantal)
See also DLB 268

**Sewall, Samuel** 1652-1730 ................... **LC 38**
See also DLB 24; RGAL 4

**Sexton, Anne (Harvey)** 1928-1974 ..... **CLC 2, 4, 6, 8, 10, 15, 53, 123; PC 2; WLC**
See also AMWS 2; CA 1-4R; CABS 2; CANR 3, 36; CDALB 1941-1968; DA; DAB; DAC; DAM MST, POET; DLB 5,

169; EXPP; FW; MAWW; MTCW 1, 2; PAB; PFS 4, 14; RGAL 4; SATA 10; TUS
**Shaara, Jeff** 1952- .......................... **CLC 119**
See also CA 163; CANR 109
**Shaara, Michael (Joseph, Jr.)**
1929-1988 ................................. **CLC 15**
See also AITN 1; BPFB 3; CA 102; CANR 52, 85; DAM POP; DLBY 1983
**Shackleton, C. C.**
See Aldiss, Brian W(ilson)
**Shacochis, Bob** ............................ **CLC 39**
See Shacochis, Robert G.
**Shacochis, Robert G.** 1951-
See Shacochis, Bob
See also CA 124; CANR 100; INT 124
**Shaffer, Anthony (Joshua)**
1926-2001 ................................. **CLC 19**
See also CA 116; CBD; CD 5; DAM DRAM; DFS 13; DLB 13
**Shaffer, Peter (Levin)** 1926- .. **CLC 5, 14, 18, 37, 60; DC 7**
See also BRWS 1; CA 25-28R; CANR 25, 47, 74; CBD; CD 5; CDBLB 1960 to Present; DAB; DAM DRAM, MST; DFS 5, 13; DLB 13, 233; MTCW 1, 2; RGEL 2; TEA
**Shakey, Bernard**
See Young, Neil
**Shalamov, Varlam (Tikhonovich)**
1907(?)-1982 ........................... **CLC 18**
See also CA 129; RGSF 2
**Shamlu, Ahmad** 1925-2000 ............... **CLC 10**
See also CWW 2
**Shammas, Anton** 1951- ...................... **CLC 55**
See also CA 199
**Shandling, Arline**
See Berriault, Gina
**Shange, Ntozake** 1948- ... **BLC 3; CLC 8, 25, 38, 74, 126; DC 3**
See also AAYA 9; AFAW 1, 2; BW 2; CA 85-88; CABS 3; CAD; CANR 27, 48, 74; CD 5; CP 7; CWD; CWP; DAM DRAM, MULT; DFS 2, 11; DLB 38, 249; FW; LAIT 5; MTCW 1, 2; NFS 11; RGAL 4; YAW
**Shanley, John Patrick** 1950- ............. **CLC 75**
See also CA 133; CAD; CANR 83; CD 5
**Shapcott, Thomas W(illiam)** 1935- ... **CLC 38**
See also CA 69-72; CANR 49, 83, 103; CP 7
**Shapiro, Jane** 1942- .......................... **CLC 76**
See also CA 196
**Shapiro, Karl (Jay)** 1913-2000 ...... **CLC 4, 8, 15, 53; PC 25**
See also AMWS 2; CA 1-4R; CAAS 6; CANR 1, 36, 66; CP 7; DLB 48; EXPP; MTCW 1, 2; PFS 3; RGAL 4
**Sharp, William** 1855-1905 .............. **TCLC 39**
See Macleod, Fiona
See also CA 160; DLB 156; RGEL 2
**Sharpe, Thomas Ridley** 1928-
See Sharpe, Tom
See also CA 122; CANR 85; INT CA-122
**Sharpe, Tom** ................................ **CLC 36**
See Sharpe, Thomas Ridley
See also CN 7; DLB 14, 231
**Shatrov, Mikhail** ............................. **CLC 59**
**Shaw, Bernard**
See Shaw, George Bernard
See also DLB 190
**Shaw, G. Bernard**
See Shaw, George Bernard
**Shaw, George Bernard** 1856-1950 .. **TCLC 3, 9, 21, 45; WLC**
See Shaw, Bernard
See also BRW 6; BRWR 2; CA 128; CDBLB 1914-1945; DA; DAB; DAC; DAM DRAM, MST; DFS 1, 3, 6, 11; DLB 10, 57; LAIT 3; MTCW 1, 2; RGEL 2; TEA; WLIT 4
**Shaw, Henry Wheeler** 1818-1885 .. **NCLC 15**
See also DLB 11; RGAL 4
**Shaw, Irwin** 1913-1984 ........... **CLC 7, 23, 34**
See also AITN 1; BPFB 3; CA 13-16R; CANR 21; CDALB 1941-1968; CPW; DAM DRAM, POP; DLB 6, 102; DLBY 1984; MTCW 1, 21
**Shaw, Robert** 1927-1978 ..................... **CLC 5**
See also AITN 1; CA 1-4R; CANR 4; DLB 13, 14
**Shaw, T. E.**
See Lawrence, T(homas) E(dward)
**Shawn, Wallace** 1943- ........................ **CLC 41**
See also CA 112; CAD; CD 5; DLB 266
**Shchedrin, N.**
See Saltykov, Mikhail Evgrafovich
**Shea, Lisa** 1953- ................................. **CLC 86**
See also CA 147
**Sheed, Wilfrid (John Joseph)** 1930- . **CLC 2, 4, 10, 53**
See also CA 65-68; CANR 30, 66; CN 7; DLB 6; MTCW 1, 2
**Sheldon, Alice Hastings Bradley**
1915(?)-1987
See Tiptree, James, Jr.
See also CA 108; CANR 34; INT 108; MTCW 1
**Sheldon, John**
See Bloch, Robert (Albert)
**Sheldon, Walter J(ames)** 1917-1996
See Queen, Ellery
See also AITN 1; CA 25-28R; CANR 10
**Shelley, Mary Wollstonecraft (Godwin)**
1797-1851 ...... **NCLC 14, 59, 103; WLC**
See also AAYA 20; BPFB 3; BRW 3; BRWS 3; BYA 5; CDBLB 1789-1832; DA; DAB; DAC; DAM MST, NOV; DLB 110, 116, 159, 178; EXPN; HGG; LAIT 1; NFS 1; RGEL 2; SATA 29; SCFW; SFW 4; TEA; WLIT 3
**Shelley, Percy Bysshe** 1792-1822 .. **NCLC 18, 93; PC 14; WLC**
See also BRW 4; BRWR 1; CDBLB 1789-1832; DA; DAB; DAC; DAM MST, POET; DLB 96, 110, 158; EXPP; PAB; PFS 2; RGEL 2; TEA; WLIT 3; WP
**Shepard, Jim** 1956- .............................. **CLC 36**
See also CA 137; CANR 59, 104; SATA 90
**Shepard, Lucius** 1947- ......................... **CLC 34**
See also CA 141; CANR 81; HGG; SCFW 2; SFW 4; SUFW 2
**Shepard, Sam** 1943- .... **CLC 4, 6, 17, 34, 41, 44, 169; DC 5**
See also AAYA 1; AMWS 3; CA 69-72; CABS 3; CAD; CANR 22; CD 5; DAM DRAM; DFS 3, 6, 7, 14; DLB 7, 212; IDFW 3, 4; MTCW 1, 2; RGAL 4
**Shepherd, Michael**
See Ludlum, Robert
**Sherburne, Zoa (Lillian Morin)**
1912-1995 .................................. **CLC 30**
See also AAYA 13; CA 1-4R; CANR 3, 37; MAICYA 1, 2; SAAS 18; SATA 3; YAW
**Sheridan, Frances** 1724-1766 ................ **LC 7**
See also DLB 39, 84
**Sheridan, Richard Brinsley**
1751-1816 .... **DC 1; NCLC 5, 91; WLC**
See also BRW 3; CDBLB 1660-1789; DA; DAB; DAC; DAM DRAM, MST; DFS 15; DLB 89; WLIT 3
**Sherman, Jonathan Marc** ................ **CLC 55**
**Sherman, Martin** 1941(?)- ................. **CLC 19**
See also CA 123; CAD; CANR 86; CD 5; DLB 228; GLL 1; IDTP
**Sherwin, Judith Johnson**
See Johnson, Judith (Emlyn)
See also CANR 85; CP 7; CWP
**Sherwood, Frances** 1940- .................. **CLC 81**
See also CA 146
**Sherwood, Robert E(mmet)**
1896-1955 .................................. **TCLC 3**
See also CA 153; CANR 86; DAM DRAM; DFS 15; DLB 7, 26, 249; IDFW 3, 4; RGAL 4
**Shestov, Lev** 1866-1938 .................... **TCLC 56**
**Shevchenko, Taras** 1814-1861 ........ **NCLC 54**
**Shiel, M(atthew) P(hipps)**
1865-1947 .................................... **TCLC 8**
See Holmes, Gordon
See also CA 160; DLB 153; HGG; MTCW 2; SFW 4; SUFW
**Shields, Carol** 1935- .................... **CLC 91, 113**
See also AMWS 7; CA 81-84; CANR 51, 74, 98; CCA 1; CN 7; CPW; DAC; MTCW 2
**Shields, David** 1956- .......................... **CLC 97**
See also CA 124; CANR 48, 99, 112
**Shiga, Naoya** 1883-1971 ..... **CLC 33; SSC 23**
See Shiga Naoya
See also CA 101; MJW; RGWL 3
**Shiga Naoya**
See Shiga, Naoya
See also DLB 180; RGWL 3
**Shilts, Randy** 1951-1994 .................... **CLC 85**
See also AAYA 19; CA 127; CANR 45; GLL 1; INT 127; MTCW 2
**Shimazaki, Haruki** 1872-1943
See Shimazaki Toson
See also CA 134; CANR 84; RGWL 3
**Shimazaki Toson** ............................ **TCLC 5**
See Shimazaki, Haruki
See also DLB 180
**Sholokhov, Mikhail (Aleksandrovich)**
1905-1984 .............................. **CLC 7, 15**
See also CA 101; DLB 272; MTCW 1, 2; RGWL 2, 3; SATA-Obit 36
**Shone, Patric**
See Hanley, James
**Showalter, Elaine** 1941- .................. **CLC 169**
See also CA 57-60; CANR 58, 106; DLB 67; FW; GLL 2
**Shreve, Susan Richards** 1939- .......... **CLC 23**
See also CA 49-52; CAAS 5; CANR 5, 38, 69, 100; MAICYA 1, 2; SATA 46, 95; SATA-Brief 41
**Shue, Larry** 1946-1985 ...................... **CLC 52**
See also CA 145; DAM DRAM; DFS 7
**Shu-Jen, Chou** 1881-1936
See Lu Hsun
**Shulman, Alix Kates** 1932- ........... **CLC 2, 10**
See also CA 29-32R; CANR 43; FW; SATA 7
**Shusaku, Endo**
See Endo, Shusaku
**Shuster, Joe** 1914-1992 ...................... **CLC 21**
**Shute, Nevil** ..................................... **CLC 30**
See Norway, Nevil Shute
See also BPFB 3; DLB 255; NFS 9; RHW; SFW 4
**Shuttle, Penelope (Diane)** 1947- ......... **CLC 7**
See also CA 93-96; CANR 39, 84, 92, 108; CP 7; CWP; DLB 14, 40
**Sidhwa, Bapsy (N.)** 1938- ................ **CLC 168**
See also CA 108; CANR 25, 57; CN 7; FW
**Sidney, Mary** 1561-1621 .............. **LC 19, 39**
See Sidney Herbert, Mary
**Sidney, Sir Philip** 1554-1586 . **LC 19, 39; PC 32**
See also BRW 1; BRWR 2; CDBLB Before 1660; DA; DAB; DAC; DAM MST, POET; DLB 167; EXPP; PAB; RGEL 2; TEA; WP

**Sidney Herbert, Mary**
See Sidney, Mary
See also DLB 167

**Siegel, Jerome** 1914-1996 .................. CLC 21
See also CA 169

**Siegel, Jerry**
See Siegel, Jerome

**Sienkiewicz, Henryk (Adam Alexander Pius)**
1846-1916 ................................. TCLC 3
See also CA 134; CANR 84; RGSF 2; RGWL 2, 3

**Sierra, Gregorio Martinez**
See Martinez Sierra, Gregorio

**Sierra, Maria (de la O'LeJarraga) Martinez**
See Martinez Sierra, Maria (de la O'LeJarraga)

**Sigal, Clancy** 1926- ........................... CLC 7
See also CA 1-4R; CANR 85; CN 7

**Sigourney, Lydia H.**
See Sigourney, Lydia Howard (Huntley)
See also DLB 73, 183

**Sigourney, Lydia Howard (Huntley)**
1791-1865 ........................ NCLC 21, 87
See Sigourney, Lydia H.; Sigourney, Lydia Huntley
See also DLB 1

**Sigourney, Lydia Huntley**
See Sigourney, Lydia Howard (Huntley)
See also DLB 42, 239, 243

**Siguenza y Gongora, Carlos de**
1645-1700 ........................ HLCS 2; LC 8
See also LAW

**Sigurjonsson, Johann** 1880-1919 ... TCLC 27
See also CA 170

**Sikelianos, Angelos** 1884-1951 ........... PC 29; TCLC 39
See also RGWL 2, 3

**Silkin, Jon** 1930-1997 ................. CLC 2, 6, 43
See also CA 5-8R; CAAS 5; CANR 89; CP 7; DLB 27

**Silko, Leslie (Marmon)** 1948- ..... CLC 23, 74, 114; NNAL; SSC 37; WLCS
See also AAYA 14; AMWS 4; ANW; BYA 12; CA 122; CANR 45, 65; CN 7; CP 7; CPW 1; CWP; DA; DAC; DAM MST, MULT, POP; DLB 143, 175, 256, 275; EXPP; EXPS; LAIT 4; MTCW 2; NFS 4; PFS 9, 16; RGAL 4; RGSF 2; SSFS 4, 8, 10, 11

**Sillanpaa, Frans Eemil** 1888-1964 ... CLC 19
See also CA 129; MTCW 1

**Sillitoe, Alan** 1928- .. CLC 1, 3, 6, 10, 19, 57, 148
See also AITN 1; BRWS 5; CA 9-12R; CAAE 191; CAAS 2; CANR 8, 26, 55; CDBLB 1960 to Present; CN 7; DLB 14, 139; MTCW 1, 2; RGEL 2; RGSF 2; SATA 61

**Silone, Ignazio** 1900-1978 ..................... CLC 4
See also CA 25-28; CANR 34; CAP 2; DLB 264; EW 12; MTCW 1; RGSF 2; RGWL 2, 3

**Silone, Ignazione**
See Silone, Ignazio

**Silva, Jose Asuncion**
See da Silva, Antonio Jose
See also LAW

**Silver, Joan Micklin** 1935- ................. CLC 20
See also CA 121; INT 121

**Silver, Nicholas**
See Faust, Frederick (Schiller)
See also TCWW 2

**Silverberg, Robert** 1935- ............. CLC 7, 140
See also AAYA 24; BPFB 3; BYA 7, 9; CA 1-4R, 186; CAAE 186; CAAS 3; CANR 1, 20, 36, 85; CLR 59; CN 7; CPW; DAM POP; DLB 8; INT CANR-20; MAICYA 1, 2; MTCW 1, 2; SATA 13, 91; SATA-Essay 104; SCFW 2; SFW 4; SUFW 2

**Silverstein, Alvin** 1933- ..................... CLC 17
See also CA 49-52; CANR 2; CLR 25; JRDA; MAICYA 1, 2; SATA 8, 69, 124

**Silverstein, Virginia B(arbara Opshelor)**
1937- .......................................... CLC 17
See also CA 49-52; CANR 2; CLR 25; JRDA; MAICYA 1, 2; SATA 8, 69, 124

**Sim, Georges**
See Simenon, Georges (Jacques Christian)

**Simak, Clifford D(onald)** 1904-1988 . CLC 1, 55
See also CA 1-4R; CANR 1, 35; DLB 8; MTCW 1; SATA-Obit 56; SFW 4

**Simenon, Georges (Jacques Christian)**
1903-1989 ............ CLC 1, 2, 3, 8, 18, 47
See also BPFB 3; CA 85-88; CANR 35; CMW 4; DAM POP; DLB 72; DLBY 1989; EW 12; GFL 1789 to the Present; MSW; MTCW 1, 2; RGWL 2, 3

**Simic, Charles** 1938- .... CLC 6, 9, 22, 49, 68, 130
See also AMWS 8; CA 29-32R; CAAS 4; CANR 12, 33, 52, 61, 96; CP 7; DAM POET; DLB 105; MTCW 2; PFS 7; RGAL 4; WP

**Simmel, Georg** 1858-1918 ............... TCLC 64
See also CA 157

**Simmons, Charles (Paul)** 1924- ......... CLC 57
See also CA 89-92; INT 89-92

**Simmons, Dan** 1948- ......................... CLC 44
See also AAYA 16; CA 138; CANR 53, 81; CPW; DAM POP; HGG; SUFW 2

**Simmons, James (Stewart Alexander)**
1933- .......................................... CLC 43
See also CA 105; CAAS 21; CP 7; DLB 40

**Simms, William Gilmore**
1806-1870 ........................................ NCLC 3
See also DLB 3, 30, 59, 73, 248, 254; RGAL 4

**Simon, Carly** 1945- ............................. CLC 26
See also CA 105

**Simon, Claude** 1913-1984 ... CLC 4, 9, 15, 39
See also CA 89-92; CANR 33; DAM NOV; DLB 83; EW 13; GFL 1789 to the Present; MTCW 1

**Simon, Myles**
See Follett, Ken(neth Martin)

**Simon, (Marvin) Neil** 1927- ... CLC 6, 11, 31, 39, 70; DC 14
See also AAYA 32; AITN 1; AMWS 4; CA 21-24R; CANR 26, 54, 87; CD 5; DAM DRAM; DFS 2, 6, 12; DLB 7, 266; LAIT 4; MTCW 1, 2; RGAL 4; TUS

**Simon, Paul (Frederick)** 1941(?)- ...... CLC 17
See also CA 153

**Simonon, Paul** 1956(?)- ..................... CLC 30

**Simonson, Rick ed.** ............................. CLC 70

**Simpson, Harriette**
See Arnow, Harriette (Louisa) Simpson

**Simpson, Louis (Aston Marantz)**
1923- ............................ CLC 4, 7, 9, 32, 149
See also AMWS 9; CA 1-4R; CAAS 4; CANR 1, 61; CP 7; DAM POET; DLB 5; MTCW 1, 2; PFS 7, 11, 14; RGAL 4

**Simpson, Mona (Elizabeth)** 1957- ... CLC 44, 146
See also CA 135; CANR 68, 103; CN 7

**Simpson, N(orman) F(rederick)**
1919- ............................................ CLC 29
See also CA 13-16R; CBD; DLB 13; RGEL 2

**Sinclair, Andrew (Annandale)** 1935- . CLC 2, 14
See also CA 9-12R; CAAS 5; CANR 14, 38, 91; CN 7; DLB 14; FANT; MTCW 1

**Sinclair, Emil**
See Hesse, Hermann

**Sinclair, Iain** 1943- ............................ CLC 76
See also CA 132; CANR 81; CP 7; HGG

**Sinclair, Iain MacGregor**
See Sinclair, Iain

**Sinclair, Irene**
See Griffith, D(avid Lewelyn) W(ark)

**Sinclair, Mary Amelia St. Clair** 1865(?)-1946
See Sinclair, May
See also HGG; RHW

**Sinclair, May** .............................. TCLC 3, 11
See Sinclair, Mary Amelia St. Clair
See also CA 166; DLB 36, 135; RGEL 2; SUFW

**Sinclair, Roy**
See Griffith, D(avid Lewelyn) W(ark)

**Sinclair, Upton (Beall)** 1878-1968 ..... CLC 1, 11, 15, 63; WLC
See also AMWS 5; BPFB 3; BYA 2; CA 5-8R; CANR 7; CDALB 1929-1941; DA; DAB; DAC; DAM MST, NOV; DLB 9; INT CANR-7; LAIT 3; MTCW 1, 2; NFS 6; RGAL 4; SATA 9; TUS; YAW

**Singer, Isaac**
See Singer, Isaac Bashevis

**Singer, Isaac Bashevis** 1904-1991 .. CLC 1, 3, 6, 9, 11, 15, 23, 38, 69, 111; SSC 3, 53; WLC
See also AAYA 32; AITN 1, 2; AMW; AMWR 2; BPFB 3; BYA 1, 4; CA 1-4R; CANR 1, 39, 106; CDALB 1941-1968; CLR 1; CWRI 5; DA; DAB; DAC; DAM MST, NOV; DLB 6, 28, 52; DLBY 1991; EXPS; HGG; JRDA; LAIT 3; MAICYA 1, 2; MTCW 1, 2; RGAL 4; RGSF 2; SATA 3, 27; SATA-Obit 68; SSFS 2, 12, 16; TUS; TWA

**Singer, Israel Joshua** 1893-1944 .... TCLC 33
See also CA 169

**Singh, Khushwant** 1915- ................... CLC 11
See also CA 9-12R; CAAS 9; CANR 6, 84; CN 7; RGEL 2

**Singleton, Ann**
See Benedict, Ruth (Fulton)

**Singleton, John** 1968(?)- ................. CLC 156
See also BW 2, 3; CA 138; CANR 67, 82; DAM MULT

**Sinjohn, John**
See Galsworthy, John

**Sinyavsky, Andrei (Donatevich)**
1925-1997 ....................................... CLC 8
See Tertz, Abram
See also CA 85-88

**Sirin, V.**
See Nabokov, Vladimir (Vladimirovich)

**Sissman, L(ouis) E(dward)**
1928-1976 ................................. CLC 9, 18
See also CA 21-24R; CANR 13; DLB 5

**Sisson, C(harles) H(ubert)** 1914- ........ CLC 8
See also CA 1-4R; CAAS 3; CANR 3, 48, 84; CP 7; DLB 27

**Sitwell, Dame Edith** 1887-1964 ..... CLC 2, 9, 67; PC 3
See also BRW 7; CA 9-12R; CANR 35; CDBLB 1945-1960; DAM POET; DLB 20; MTCW 1, 2; RGEL 2; TEA

**Siwaarmill, H. P.**
See Sharp, William

**Sjoewall, Maj** 1935- ............................ CLC 7
See Sjowall, Maj
See also CA 65-68; CANR 73

**Sjowall, Maj**
See Sjoewall, Maj
See also BPFB 3; CMW 4; MSW

**Skelton, John** 1460(?)-1529 ...... LC 71; PC 25
See also BRW 1; DLB 136; RGEL 2

**Skelton, Robin** 1925-1997 ................ CLC 13
See Zuk, Georges
See also AITN 2; CA 5-8R; CAAS 5; CANR 28, 89; CCA 1; CP 7; DLB 27, 53

**Skolimowski, Jerzy** 1938- ................. CLC 20
See also CA 128

**Skram, Amalie (Bertha)**
1847-1905 .................................. TCLC 25
See also CA 165
**Skvorecky, Josef (Vaclav)** 1924- ...... CLC 15, 39, 69, 152
See also CA 61-64; CAAS 1; CANR 10, 34, 63, 108; CDWLB 4; DAC; DAM NOV; DLB 232; MTCW 1, 2
**Slade, Bernard** ............................ CLC 11, 46
See Newbound, Bernard Slade
See also CAAS 9; CCA 1; DLB 53
**Slaughter, Carolyn** 1946- ................ CLC 56
See also CA 85-88; CANR 85; CN 7
**Slaughter, Frank G(ill)** 1908-2001 ... CLC 29
See also AITN 2; CA 5-8R; CANR 5, 85; INT CANR-5; RHW
**Slavitt, David R(ytman)** 1935- ....... CLC 5, 14
See also CA 21-24R; CAAS 3; CANR 41, 83; CP 7; DLB 5, 6
**Slesinger, Tess** 1905-1945 ................ TCLC 10
See also CA 199; DLB 102
**Slessor, Kenneth** 1901-1971 ............... CLC 14
See also CA 102; DLB 260; RGEL 2
**Slowacki, Juliusz** 1809-1849 ........... NCLC 15
See also RGWL 3
**Smart, Christopher** 1722-1771 . LC 3; PC 13
See also DAM POET; DLB 109; RGEL 2
**Smart, Elizabeth** 1913-1986 ............... CLC 54
See also CA 81-84; DLB 88
**Smiley, Jane (Graves)** 1949- ...... CLC 53, 76, 144
See also AMWS 6; BPFB 3; CA 104; CANR 30, 50, 74, 96; CN 7; CPW 1; DAM POP; DLB 227, 234; INT CANR-30
**Smith, A(rthur) J(ames) M(arshall)**
1902-1980 ................................. CLC 15
See also CA 1-4R; CANR 4; DAC; DLB 88; RGEL 2
**Smith, Adam** 1723(?)-1790 ................ LC 36
See also DLB 104, 252; RGEL 2
**Smith, Alexander** 1829-1867 ........... NCLC 59
See also DLB 32, 55
**Smith, Anna Deavere** 1950- .............. CLC 86
See also CA 133; CANR 103; CD 5; DFS 2
**Smith, Betty (Wehner)** 1904-1972 .... CLC 19
See also BPFB 3; BYA 3; CA 5-8R; DLBY 1982; LAIT 3; RGAL 4; SATA 6
**Smith, Charlotte (Turner)**
1749-1806 ........................... NCLC 23, 115
See also DLB 39, 109; RGEL 2; TEA
**Smith, Clark Ashton** 1893-1961 ....... CLC 43
See also CA 143; CANR 81; FANT; HGG; MTCW 2; SCFW 2; SFW 4; SUFW
**Smith, Dave** ................................ CLC 22, 42
See Smith, David (Jeddie)
See also CAAS 7; DLB 5
**Smith, David (Jeddie)** 1942-
See Smith, Dave
See also CA 49-52; CANR 1, 59; CP 7; CSW; DAM POET
**Smith, Florence Margaret** 1902-1971
See Smith, Stevie
See also CA 17-18; CANR 35; CAP 2; DAM POET; MTCW 1, 2; TEA
**Smith, Iain Crichton** 1928-1998 ....... CLC 64
See also CA 21-24R; CN 7; CP 7; DLB 40, 139; RGSF 2
**Smith, John** 1580(?)-1631 ...................... LC 9
See also DLB 24, 30; TUS
**Smith, Johnston**
See Crane, Stephen (Townley)
**Smith, Joseph, Jr.** 1805-1844 ......... NCLC 53
**Smith, Lee** 1944- .......................... CLC 25, 73
See also CA 119; CANR 46; CSW; DLB 143; DLBY 1983; INT CA-119; RGAL 4
**Smith, Martin**
See Smith, Martin Cruz

**Smith, Martin Cruz** 1942- .. CLC 25; NNAL
See also BEST 89:4; BPFB 3; CA 85-88; CANR 6, 23, 43, 65; CMW 4; CPW; DAM MULT, POP; HGG; INT CANR-23; MTCW 2; RGAL 4
**Smith, Patti** 1946- ............................ CLC 12
See also CA 93-96; CANR 63
**Smith, Pauline (Urmson)**
1882-1959 ................................. TCLC 25
See also DLB 225
**Smith, Rosamond**
See Oates, Joyce Carol
**Smith, Sheila Kaye**
See Kaye-Smith, Sheila
**Smith, Stevie** ......... CLC 3, 8, 25, 44; PC 12
See Smith, Florence Margaret
See also BRWS 2; DLB 20; MTCW 2; PAB; PFS 3; RGEL 2
**Smith, Wilbur (Addison)** 1933- ........ CLC 33
See also CA 13-16R; CANR 7, 46, 66; CPW; MTCW 1, 2
**Smith, William Jay** 1918- ................ CLC 6
See also CA 5-8R; CANR 44, 106; CP 7; CSW; CWRI 5; DLB 5; MAICYA 1, 2; SAAS 22; SATA 2, 68
**Smith, Woodrow Wilson**
See Kuttner, Henry
**Smith, Zadie** 1976- .......................... CLC 158
See also CA 193
**Smolenskin, Peretz** 1842-1885 ........ NCLC 30
**Smollett, Tobias (George)** 1721-1771 ... LC 2, 46
See also BRW 3; CDBLB 1660-1789; DLB 39, 104; RGEL 2; TEA
**Snodgrass, W(illiam) D(e Witt)**
1926- ...................... CLC 2, 6, 10, 18, 68
See also AMWS 6; CA 1-4R; CANR 6, 36, 65, 85; CP 7; DAM POET; DLB 5; MTCW 1, 2; RGAL 4
**Snorri Sturluson** 1179-1241 .......... CMLC 56
See also RGWL 2, 3
**Snow, C(harles) P(ercy)** 1905-1980 ... CLC 1, 4, 6, 9, 13, 19
See also BRW 7; CA 5-8R; CANR 28; CDBLB 1945-1960; DAM NOV; DLB 15, 77; DLBD 17; MTCW 1, 2; RGEL 2; TEA
**Snow, Frances Compton**
See Adams, Henry (Brooks)
**Snyder, Gary (Sherman)** 1930- . CLC 1, 2, 5, 9, 32, 120; PC 21
See also AMWS 8; ANW; BG 3; CA 17-20R; CANR 30, 60; CP 7; DAM POET; DLB 5, 16, 165, 212, 237, 275; MTCW 2; PFS 9; RGAL 4; WP
**Snyder, Zilpha Keatley** 1927- ........... CLC 17
See also AAYA 15; BYA 1; CA 9-12R; CANR 38; CLR 31; JRDA; MAICYA 1, 2; SAAS 2; SATA 1, 28, 75, 110; SATA-Essay 112; YAW
**Soares, Bernardo**
See Pessoa, Fernando (Antonio Nogueira)
**Sobh, A.**
See Shamlu, Ahmad
**Sobol, Joshua** 1939- .......................... CLC 60
See Sobol, Yehoshua
See also CA 200; CWW 2
**Sobol, Yehoshua** 1939-
See Sobol, Joshua
See also CWW 2
**Socrates** 470B.C.-399B.C. ............... CMLC 27
**Soderberg, Hjalmar** 1869-1941 ...... TCLC 39
See also DLB 259; RGSF 2
**Soderbergh, Steven** 1963- ............... CLC 154
See also AAYA 43
**Sodergran, Edith (Irene)** 1892-1923
See Soedergran, Edith (Irene)
See also CA 202; DLB 259; EW 11; RGWL 2, 3

**Soedergran, Edith (Irene)**
1892-1923 .................................. TCLC 31
See Sodergran, Edith (Irene)
**Softly, Edgar**
See Lovecraft, H(oward) P(hillips)
**Softly, Edward**
See Lovecraft, H(oward) P(hillips)
**Sokolov, Raymond** 1941- ...................... CLC 7
See also CA 85-88
**Sokolov, Sasha** ............................... CLC 59
**Solo, Jay**
See Ellison, Harlan (Jay)
**Sologub, Fyodor** ............................. TCLC 9
See Teternikov, Fyodor Kuzmich
**Solomons, Ikey Esquir**
See Thackeray, William Makepeace
**Solomos, Dionysios** 1798-1857 ....... NCLC 15
**Solwoska, Mara**
See French, Marilyn
**Solzhenitsyn, Aleksandr I(sayevich)**
1918- .. CLC 1, 2, 4, 7, 9, 10, 18, 26, 34, 78, 134; SSC 32; WLC
See also AITN 1; BPFB 3; CA 69-72; CANR 40, 65; DA; DAB; DAC; DAM MST, NOV; EW 13; EXPS; LAIT 4; MTCW 1, 2; NFS 6; RGSF 2; RGWL 2, 3; SSFS 9; TWA
**Somers, Jane**
See Lessing, Doris (May)
**Somerville, Edith Oenone**
1858-1949 .................. SSC 56; TCLC 51
See also CA 196; DLB 135; RGEL 2; RGSF 2
**Somerville & Ross**
See Martin, Violet Florence; Somerville, Edith Oenone
**Sommer, Scott** 1951- ........................ CLC 25
See also CA 106
**Sondheim, Stephen (Joshua)** 1930- . CLC 30, 39, 147
See also AAYA 11; CA 103; CANR 47, 67; DAM DRAM; LAIT 4
**Song, Cathy** 1955- ..................... AAL; PC 21
See also CA 154; CWP; DLB 169; EXPP; FW; PFS 5
**Sontag, Susan** 1933- .... CLC 1, 2, 10, 13, 31, 105
See also AMWS 3; CA 17-20R; CANR 25, 51, 74, 97; CN 7; CPW; DAM POP; DLB 2, 67; MAWW; MTCW 1, 2; RGAL 4; RHW; SSFS 10
**Sophocles** 496(?)B.C.-406(?)B.C. ..... CMLC 2, 47, 51; DC 1; WLCS
See also AW 1; CDWLB 1; DA; DAB; DAC; DAM DRAM, MST; DFS 1, 4, 8; DLB 176; LAIT 1; RGWL 2, 3; TWA
**Sordello** 1189-1269 ......................... CMLC 15
**Sorel, Georges** 1847-1922 ............... TCLC 91
See also CA 188
**Sorel, Julia**
See Drexler, Rosalyn
**Sorokin, Vladimir** ............................ CLC 59
**Sorrentino, Gilbert** 1929- .. CLC 3, 7, 14, 22, 40
See also CA 77-80; CANR 14, 33; CN 7; CP 7; DLB 5, 173; DLBY 1980; INT CANR-14
**Soseki**
See Natsume, Soseki
See also MJW
**Soto, Gary** 1952- ... CLC 32, 80; HLC 2; PC 28
See also AAYA 10, 37; BYA 11; CA 125; CANR 50, 74, 107; CLR 38; CP 7; DAM MULT; DLB 82; EXPP; HW 1, 2; INT CA-125; JRDA; MAICYA 1; MAICYAS 1; MTCW 2; PFS 7; RGAL 4; SATA 80, 120; WYA; YAW

**Soupault, Philippe** 1897-1990 ........... **CLC 68**
See also CA 147; GFL 1789 to the Present

**Souster, (Holmes) Raymond** 1921- .... **CLC 5, 14**
See also CA 13-16R; CAAS 14; CANR 13, 29, 53; CP 7; DAC; DAM POET; DLB 88; RGEL 2; SATA 63

**Southern, Terry** 1924(?)-1995 ............. **CLC 7**
See also AMWS 11; BPFB 3; CA 1-4R; CANR 1, 55, 107; CN 7; DLB 2; IDFW 3, 4

**Southey, Robert** 1774-1843 ........ **NCLC 8, 97**
See also BRW 4; DLB 93, 107, 142; RGEL 2; SATA 54

**Southworth, Emma Dorothy Eliza Nevitte** 1819-1899 ..................... **NCLC 26**
See also DLB 239

**Souza, Ernest**
See Scott, Evelyn

**Soyinka, Wole** 1934- .. **BLC 3; CLC 3, 5, 14, 36, 44; DC 2; WLC**
See also AFW; BW 2, 3; CA 13-16R; CANR 27, 39, 82; CD 5; CDWLB 3; CN 7; CP 7; DA; DAB; DAC; DAM DRAM, MST, MULT; DFS 10; DLB 125; MTCW 1, 2; RGEL 2; TWA; WLIT 2

**Spackman, W(illiam) M(ode)** 1905-1990 ........................ **CLC 46**
See also CA 81-84

**Spacks, Barry (Bernard)** 1931- ........ **CLC 14**
See also CA 154; CANR 33, 109; CP 7; DLB 105

**Spanidou, Irini** 1946- ......................... **CLC 44**
See also CA 185

**Spark, Muriel (Sarah)** 1918- ..... **CLC 2, 3, 5, 8, 13, 18, 40, 94; SSC 10**
See also BRWS 1; CA 5-8R; CANR 12, 36, 76, 89; CDBLB 1945-1960; CN 7; CP 7; DAB; DAC; DAM MST, NOV; DLB 15, 139; FW; INT CANR-12; LAIT 4; MTCW 1, 2; RGEL 2; TEA; WLIT 4; YAW

**Spaulding, Douglas**
See Bradbury, Ray (Douglas)

**Spaulding, Leonard**
See Bradbury, Ray (Douglas)

**Spelman, Elizabeth** .......................... **CLC 65**

**Spence, J. A. D.**
See Eliot, T(homas) S(tearns)

**Spencer, Elizabeth** 1921- .... **CLC 22; SSC 57**
See also CA 13-16R; CANR 32, 65, 87; CN 7; CSW; DLB 6, 218; MTCW 1; RGAL 4; SATA 14

**Spencer, Leonard G.**
See Silverberg, Robert

**Spencer, Scott** 1945- ......................... **CLC 30**
See also CA 113; CANR 51; DLBY 1986

**Spender, Stephen (Harold)** 1909-1995 ......... **CLC 1, 2, 5, 10, 41, 91**
See also BRWS 2; CA 9-12R; CANR 31, 54; CDBLB 1945-1960; CP 7; DAM POET; DLB 20; MTCW 1; PAB; RGEL 2; TEA

**Spengler, Oswald (Arnold Gottfried)** 1880-1936 ................. **TCLC 25**
See also CA 189

**Spenser, Edmund** 1552(?)-1599 ..... **LC 5, 39; PC 8, 42; WLC**
See also BRW 1; CDBLB Before 1660; DA; DAB; DAC; DAM MST, POET; DLB 167; EFS 2; EXPP; PAB; RGEL 2; TEA; WLIT 3; WP

**Spicer, Jack** 1925-1965 ........... **CLC 8, 18, 72**
See also BG 3; CA 85-88; DAM POET; DLB 5, 16, 193; GLL 1; WP

**Spiegelman, Art** 1948- ...................... **CLC 76**
See also AAYA 10, 46; CA 125; CANR 41, 55, 74; MTCW 2; SATA 109; YAW

**Spielberg, Peter** 1929- ....................... **CLC 6**
See also CA 5-8R; CANR 4, 48; DLBY 1981

**Spielberg, Steven** 1947- .................... **CLC 20**
See also AAYA 8, 24; CA 77-80; CANR 32; SATA 32

**Spillane, Frank Morrison** 1918-
See Spillane, Mickey
See also CA 25-28R; CANR 28, 63; MTCW 1, 2; SATA 66

**Spillane, Mickey** .......................... **CLC 3, 13**
See Spillane, Frank Morrison
See also BPFB 3; CMW 4; DLB 226; MSW; MTCW 2

**Spinoza, Benedictus de** 1632-1677 .. **LC 9, 58**

**Spinrad, Norman (Richard)** 1940- ... **CLC 46**
See also BPFB 3; CA 37-40R; CAAS 19; CANR 20, 91; DLB 8; INT CANR-20; SFW 4

**Spitteler, Carl (Friedrich Georg)** 1845-1924 ................. **TCLC 12**
See also DLB 129

**Spivack, Kathleen (Romola Drucker)** 1938- ............................ **CLC 6**
See also CA 49-52

**Spoto, Donald** 1941- ......................... **CLC 39**
See also CA 65-68; CANR 11, 57, 93

**Springsteen, Bruce (F.)** 1949- ........... **CLC 17**
See also CA 111

**Spurling, Hilary** 1940- ...................... **CLC 34**
See also CA 104; CANR 25, 52, 94

**Spyker, John Howland**
See Elman, Richard (Martin)

**Squires, (James) Radcliffe** 1917-1993 ................................ **CLC 51**
See also CA 1-4R; CANR 6, 21

**Srivastava, Dhanpat Rai** 1880(?)-1936
See Premchand
See also CA 197

**Stacy, Donald**
See Pohl, Frederik

**Stael**
See Stael-Holstein, Anne Louise Germaine Necker
See also EW 5; RGWL 2, 3

**Stael, Germaine de**
See Stael-Holstein, Anne Louise Germaine Necker
See also DLB 119, 192; FW; GFL 1789 to the Present; TWA

**Stael-Holstein, Anne Louise Germaine Necker** 1766-1817 ............... **NCLC 3, 91**
See Stael; Stael, Germaine de

**Stafford, Jean** 1915-1979 .. **CLC 4, 7, 19, 68; SSC 26**
See also CA 1-4R; CANR 3, 65; DLB 2, 173; MTCW 1, 2; RGAL 4; RGSF 2; SATA-Obit 22; TCWW 2; TUS

**Stafford, William (Edgar)** 1914-1993 .......................... **CLC 4, 7, 29**
See also AMWS 11; CA 5-8R; CAAS 3; CANR 5, 22; DAM POET; DLB 5, 206; EXPP; INT CANR-22; PFS 2, 8, 16; RGAL 4; WP

**Stagnelius, Eric Johan** 1793-1823 . **NCLC 61**

**Staines, Trevor**
See Brunner, John (Kilian Houston)

**Stairs, Gordon**
See Austin, Mary (Hunter)
See also TCWW 2

**Stalin, Joseph** 1879-1953 ................ **TCLC 92**

**Stampa, Gaspara** c. 1524-1554 ........... **PC 43**
See also RGWL 2, 3

**Stancykowna**
See Szymborska, Wislawa

**Stannard, Martin** 1947- ..................... **CLC 44**
See also CA 142; DLB 155

**Stanton, Elizabeth Cady** 1815-1902 ..................... **TCLC 73**
See also CA 171; DLB 79; FW

**Stanton, Maura** 1946- ......................... **CLC 9**
See also CA 89-92; CANR 15; DLB 120

**Stanton, Schuyler**
See Baum, L(yman) Frank

**Stapledon, (William) Olaf** 1886-1950 ................. **TCLC 22**
See also CA 162; DLB 15, 255; SFW 4

**Starbuck, George (Edwin)** 1931-1996 ......................... **CLC 53**
See also CA 21-24R; CANR 23; DAM POET

**Stark, Richard**
See Westlake, Donald E(dwin)

**Staunton, Schuyler**
See Baum, L(yman) Frank

**Stead, Christina (Ellen)** 1902-1983 ... **CLC 2, 5, 8, 32, 80**
See also BRWS 4; CA 13-16R; CANR 33, 40; DLB 260; FW; MTCW 1, 2; RGEL 2; RGSF 2

**Stead, William Thomas** 1849-1912 ................. **TCLC 48**
See also CA 167

**Stebnitsky, M.**
See Leskov, Nikolai (Semyonovich)

**Steele, Sir Richard** 1672-1729 ............. **LC 18**
See also BRW 3; CDBLB 1660-1789; DLB 84, 101; RGEL 2; WLIT 3

**Steele, Timothy (Reid)** 1948- ............ **CLC 45**
See also CA 93-96; CANR 16, 50, 92; CP 7; DLB 120

**Steffens, (Joseph) Lincoln** 1866-1936 ................ **TCLC 20**

**Stegner, Wallace (Earle)** 1909-1993 .. **CLC 9, 49, 81; SSC 27**
See also AITN 1; AMWS 4; ANW; BEST 90:3; BPFB 3; CA 1-4R; CAAS 9; CANR 1, 21, 46; DAM NOV; DLB 9, 206, 275; DLBY 1993; MTCW 1, 2; RGAL 4; TCWW 2; TUS

**Stein, Gertrude** 1874-1946 ..... **DC 19; PC 18; SSC 42; TCLC 1, 6, 28, 48; WLC**
See also AMW; CA 132; CANR 108; CDALB 1917-1929; DA; DAB; DAC; DAM MST, NOV, POET; DLB 4, 54, 86, 228; DLBD 15; EXPS; GLL 1; MAWW; MTCW 1, 2; NCFS 4; RGAL 4; RGSF 2; SSFS 5; TUS; WP

**Steinbeck, John (Ernst)** 1902-1968 ... **CLC 1, 5, 9, 13, 21, 34, 45, 75, 124; SSC 11, 37; WLC**
See also AAYA 12; AMW; BPFB 3; BYA 2, 3, 13; CA 1-4R; CANR 1, 35; CDALB 1929-1941; DA; DAB; DAC; DAM DRAM, MST, NOV; DLB 7, 9, 212, 275; DLBD 2; EXPS; LAIT 3; MTCW 1, 2; NFS 1, 5, 7; RGAL 4; RGSF 2; RHW; SATA 9; SSFS 3, 6; TCWW 2; TUS; WYA; YAW

**Steinem, Gloria** 1934- ....................... **CLC 63**
See also CA 53-56; CANR 28, 51; DLB 246; FW; MTCW 1, 2

**Steiner, George** 1929- ......................... **CLC 24**
See also CA 73-76; CANR 31, 67, 108; DAM NOV; DLB 67; MTCW 1, 2; SATA 62

**Steiner, K. Leslie**
See Delany, Samuel R(ay), Jr.

**Steiner, Rudolf** 1861-1925 ............. **TCLC 13**

**Stendhal** 1783-1842 .. **NCLC 23, 46; SSC 27; WLC**
See also DA; DAB; DAC; DAM MST, NOV; DLB 119; EW 5; GFL 1789 to the Present; RGWL 2, 3; TWA

**Stephen, Adeline Virginia**
See Woolf, (Adeline) Virginia

**Stephen, Sir Leslie** 1832-1904 ........ **TCLC 23**
See also BRW 5; DLB 57, 144, 190
**Stephen, Sir Leslie**
See Stephen, Sir Leslie
**Stephen, Virginia**
See Woolf, (Adeline) Virginia
**Stephens, James** 1882(?)-1950 .......... **SSC 50; TCLC 4**
See also CA 192; DLB 19, 153, 162; FANT; RGEL 2; SUFW
**Stephens, Reed**
See Donaldson, Stephen R(eeder)
**Steptoe, Lydia**
See Barnes, Djuna
See also GLL 1
**Sterchi, Beat** 1949- ............................ **CLC 65**
See also CA 203
**Sterling, Brett**
See Bradbury, Ray (Douglas); Hamilton, Edmond
**Sterling, Bruce** 1954- ........................ **CLC 72**
See also CA 119; CANR 44; SCFW 2; SFW 4
**Sterling, George** 1869-1926 ............. **TCLC 20**
See also CA 165; DLB 54
**Stern, Gerald** 1925- ................... **CLC 40, 100**
See also AMWS 9; CA 81-84; CANR 28, 94; CP 7; DLB 105; RGAL 4
**Stern, Richard (Gustave)** 1928- .... **CLC 4, 39**
See also CA 1-4R; CANR 1, 25, 52; CN 7; DLB 218; DLBY 1987; INT CANR-25
**Sternberg, Josef von** 1894-1969 ....... **CLC 20**
See also CA 81-84
**Sterne, Laurence** 1713-1768 ........... **LC 2, 48; WLC**
See also BRW 3; CDBLB 1660-1789; DA; DAB; DAC; DAM MST, NOV; DLB 39; RGEL 2; TEA
**Sternheim, (William Adolf) Carl** 1878-1942 .................................. **TCLC 8**
See also CA 193; DLB 56, 118; RGWL 2, 3
**Stevens, Mark** 1951- .......................... **CLC 34**
See also CA 122
**Stevens, Wallace** 1879-1955 . **PC 6; TCLC 3, 12, 45; WLC**
See also AMW; AMWR 1; CA 124; CDALB 1929-1941; DA; DAB; DAC; DAM MST, POET; DLB 54; EXPP; MTCW 1, 2; PAB; PFS 13, 16; RGAL 4; TUS; WP
**Stevenson, Anne (Katharine)** 1933- ... **CLC 7, 33**
See also BRWS 6; CA 17-20R; CAAS 9; CANR 9, 33; CP 7; CWP; DLB 40; MTCW 1; RHW
**Stevenson, Robert Louis (Balfour)** 1850-1894 ...... **NCLC 5, 14, 63; SSC 11, 51; WLC**
See also AAYA 24; BPFB 3; BRW 5; BRWR 1; BYA 1, 2, 4, 13; CDBLB 1890-1914; CLR 10, 11; DA; DAB; DAC; DAM MST, NOV; DLB 18, 57, 141, 156, 174; DLBD 13; HGG; JRDA; LAIT 1, 3; MAICYA 1, 2; NFS 11; RGEL 2; RGSF 2; SATA 100; SUFW; TEA; WCH; WLIT 4; WYA; YABC 2; YAW
**Stewart, J(ohn) I(nnes) M(ackintosh)** 1906-1994 ......................... **CLC 7, 14, 32**
See Innes, Michael
See also CA 85-88; CAAS 3; CANR 47; CMW 4; MTCW 1, 2
**Stewart, Mary (Florence Elinor)** 1916- .................................. **CLC 7, 35, 117**
See also AAYA 29; BPFB 3; CA 1-4R; CANR 1, 59; CMW 4; CPW; DAB; FANT; RHW; SATA 12; YAW
**Stewart, Mary Rainbow**
See Stewart, Mary (Florence Elinor)

**Stifle, June**
See Campbell, Maria
**Stifter, Adalbert** 1805-1868 .. **NCLC 41; SSC 28**
See also CDWLB 2; DLB 133; RGSF 2; RGWL 2, 3
**Still, James** 1906-2001 ...................... **CLC 49**
See also CA 65-68; CAAS 17; CANR 10, 26; CSW; DLB 9; DLBY 01; SATA 29; SATA-Obit 127
**Sting** 1951-
See Sumner, Gordon Matthew
See also CA 167
**Stirling, Arthur**
See Sinclair, Upton (Beall)
**Stitt, Milan** 1941- ............................... **CLC 29**
See also CA 69-72
**Stockton, Francis Richard** 1834-1902
See Stockton, Frank R.
See also CA 137; MAICYA 1, 2; SATA 44; SFW 4
**Stockton, Frank R.** ........................ **TCLC 47**
See Stockton, Francis Richard
See also BYA 4, 13; DLB 42, 74; DLBD 13; EXPS; SATA-Brief 32; SSFS 3; SUFW; WCH
**Stoddard, Charles**
See Kuttner, Henry
**Stoker, Abraham** 1847-1912 ........ **SSC 55, 56**
See Stoker, Bram
See also CA 150; DA; DAC; DAM MST, NOV; HGG; SATA 29
**Stoker, Bram** ......................... **TCLC 8; WLC**
See Stoker, Abraham
See also AAYA 23; BPFB 3; BRWS 3; BYA 5; CDBLB 1890-1914; DAB; DLB 36, 70, 178; RGEL 2; SUFW; TEA; WLIT 4
**Stolz, Mary (Slattery)** 1920- ............. **CLC 12**
See also AAYA 8; AITN 1; CA 5-8R; CANR 13, 41, 112; JRDA; MAICYA 1, 2; SAAS 3; SATA 10, 71, 133; YAW
**Stone, Irving** 1903-1989 ..................... **CLC 7**
See also AITN 1; BPFB 3; CA 1-4R; CAAS 3; CANR 1, 23; CPW; DAM POP; INT CANR-23; MTCW 1, 2; RHW; SATA 3; SATA-Obit 64
**Stone, Oliver (William)** 1946 ........... **CLC 73**
See also AAYA 15; CA 110; CANR 55
**Stone, Robert (Anthony)** 1937- ... **CLC 5, 23, 42**
See also AMWS 5; BPFB 3; CA 85-88; CANR 23, 66, 95; CN 7; DLB 152; INT CANR-23; MTCW 1
**Stone, Zachary**
See Follett, Ken(neth Martin)
**Stoppard, Tom** 1937- ... **CLC 1, 3, 4, 5, 8, 15, 29, 34, 63, 91; DC 6; WLC**
See also BRWR 2; BRWS 1; CA 81-84; CANR 39, 67; CBD; CD 5; CDBLB 1960 to Present; DA; DAB; DAC; DAM DRAM, MST; DFS 2, 5, 8, 11, 13, 16; DLB 13, 233; DLBY 1985; MTCW 1, 2; RGEL 2; TEA; WLIT 4
**Storey, David (Malcolm)** 1933- . **CLC 2, 4, 5, 8**
See also BRWS 1; CA 81-84; CANR 36; CBD; CD 5; CN 7; DAM DRAM; DLB 13, 14, 207, 245; MTCW 1; RGEL 2
**Storm, Hyemeyohsts** 1935- ... **CLC 3; NNAL**
See also CA 81-84; CANR 45; DAM MULT
**Storm, Theodor** 1817-1888 ............... **SSC 27**
See also CDWLB 2; RGSF 2; RGWL 2
**Storm, (Hans) Theodor (Woldsen)** 1817-1888 .................. **NCLC 1; SSC 27**
See also DLB 129; EW; RGWL 3
**Storni, Alfonsina** 1892-1938 . **HLC 2; PC 33; TCLC 5**
See also CA 131; DAM MULT; HW 1; LAW

**Stoughton, William** 1631-1701 ............ **LC 38**
See also DLB 24
**Stout, Rex (Todhunter)** 1886-1975 ..... **CLC 3**
See also AITN 2; BPFB 3; CA 61-64; CANR 71; CMW 4; MSW; RGAL 4
**Stow, (Julian) Randolph** 1935- ... **CLC 23, 48**
See also CA 13-16R; CANR 33; CN 7; DLB 260; MTCW 1; RGEL 2
**Stowe, Harriet (Elizabeth) Beecher** 1811-1896 .............. **NCLC 3, 50; WLC**
See also AMWS 1; CDALB 1865-1917; DA; DAB; DAC; DAM MST, NOV; DLB 1, 12, 42, 74, 189, 239, 243; EXPN; JRDA; LAIT 2; MAICYA 1, 2; NFS 6; RGAL 4; TUS; YABC 1
**Strabo** c. 64B.C.-c. 25 .................... **CMLC 37**
See also DLB 176
**Strachey, (Giles) Lytton** 1880-1932 ....................... **TCLC 12**
See also BRWS 2; CA 178; DLB 149; DLBD 10; MTCW 2; NCFS 4
**Strand, Mark** 1934- .......... **CLC 6, 18, 41, 71**
See also AMWS 4; CA 21-24R; CANR 40, 65, 100; CP 7; DAM POET; DLB 5; PAB; PFS 9; RGAL 4; SATA 41
**Stratton-Porter, Gene(va Grace)** 1863-1924
See Porter, Gene(va Grace) Stratton
See also ANW; CA 137; DLB 221; DLBD 14; MAICYA 1, 2; SATA 15
**Straub, Peter (Francis)** 1943- ... **CLC 28, 107**
See also BEST 89:1; BPFB 3; CA 85-88; CANR 28, 65, 109; CPW; DAM POP; DLBY 1984; HGG; MTCW 1, 2; SUFW 2
**Strauss, Botho** 1944- ......................... **CLC 22**
See also CA 157; CWW 2; DLB 124
**Streatfeild, (Mary) Noel** 1897(?)-1986 ............................... **CLC 21**
See also CA 81-84; CANR 31; CLR 17, 83; CWRI 5; DLB 160; MAICYA 1, 2; SATA 20; SATA-Obit 48
**Stribling, T(homas) S(igismund)** 1881-1965 .................................. **CLC 23**
See also CA 189; CMW 4; DLB 9; RGAL 4
**Strindberg, (Johan) August** 1849-1912 ... **DC 18; TCLC 1, 8, 21, 47; WLC**
See also CA 135; DA; DAB; DAC; DAM DRAM, MST; DFS 4, 9; DLB 259; EW 7; IDTP; MTCW 2; RGWL 2, 3; TWA
**Stringer, Arthur** 1874-1950 ............. **TCLC 37**
See also CA 161; DLB 92
**Stringer, David**
See Roberts, Keith (John Kingston)
**Stroheim, Erich von** 1885-1957 ...... **TCLC 71**
**Strugatskii, Arkadii (Natanovich)** 1925-1991 .................................. **CLC 27**
See also CA 106; SFW 4
**Strugatskii, Boris (Natanovich)** 1933- .................................. **CLC 27**
See also CA 106; SFW 4
**Strummer, Joe** 1953(?)- ..................... **CLC 30**
**Strunk, William, Jr.** 1869-1946 ...... **TCLC 92**
See also CA 164
**Stryk, Lucien** 1924- ............................ **PC 27**
See also CA 13-16R; CANR 10, 28, 55, 110; CP 7
**Stuart, Don A.**
See Campbell, John W(ood, Jr.)
**Stuart, Ian**
See MacLean, Alistair (Stuart)
**Stuart, Jesse (Hilton)** 1906-1984 ... **CLC 1, 8, 11, 14, 34; SSC 31**
See also CA 5-8R; CANR 31; DLB 9, 48, 102; DLBY 1984; SATA 2; SATA-Obit 36
**Stubblefield, Sally**
See Trumbo, Dalton

**Sturgeon, Theodore (Hamilton)**
1918-1985 .............................. CLC 22, 39
See Queen, Ellery
See also BPFB 3; BYA 9, 10; CA 81-84; CANR 32, 103; DLB 8; DLBY 1985; HGG; MTCW 1, 2; SCFW; SFW 4; SUFW

**Sturges, Preston** 1898-1959 ............. TCLC 48
See also CA 149; DLB 26

**Styron, William** 1925- .... CLC 1, 3, 5, 11, 15, 60; SSC 25
See also AMW; BEST 90:4; BPFB 3; CA 5-8R; CANR 6, 33, 74; CDALB 1968-1988; CN 7; CPW; CSW; DAM NOV, POP; DLB 2, 143; DLBY 1980; INT CANR-6; LAIT 2; MTCW 1, 2; NCFS 1; RGAL 4; RHW; TUS

**Su, Chien** 1884-1918
See Su Man-shu

**Suarez Lynch, B.**
See Bioy Casares, Adolfo; Borges, Jorge Luis

**Suassuna, Ariano Vilar** 1927- ........... HLCS 1
See also CA 178; HW 2; LAW

**Suckert, Kurt Erich**
See Malaparte, Curzio

**Suckling, Sir John** 1609-1642. LC 75; PC 30
See also BRW 2; DAM POET; DLB 58, 126; EXPP; PAB; RGEL 2

**Suckow, Ruth** 1892-1960 ..................... SSC 18
See also CA 193; DLB 9, 102; RGAL 4; TCWW 2

**Sudermann, Hermann** 1857-1928 .. TCLC 15
See also CA 201; DLB 118

**Sue, Eugene** 1804-1857 ..................... NCLC 1
See also DLB 119

**Sueskind, Patrick** 1949- ..................... CLC 44
See Suskind, Patrick

**Sukenick, Ronald** 1932- ........ CLC 3, 4, 6, 48
See also CA 25-28R; CAAS 8; CANR 32, 89; CN 7; DLB 173; DLBY 1981

**Suknaski, Andrew** 1942- ..................... CLC 19
See also CA 101; CP 7; DLB 53

**Sullivan, Vernon**
See Vian, Boris

**Sully Prudhomme, Rene-Francois-Armand**
1839-1907 ..................................... TCLC 31
See also GFL 1789 to the Present

**Su Man-shu** ..................................... TCLC 24
See Su, Chien

**Summerforest, Ivy B.**
See Kirkup, James

**Summers, Andrew James** 1942- ....... CLC 26

**Summers, Andy**
See Summers, Andrew James

**Summers, Hollis (Spurgeon, Jr.)**
1916- .............................................. CLC 10
See also CA 5-8R; CANR 3; DLB 6

**Summers, (Alphonsus Joseph-Mary Augustus) Montague**
1880-1948 .................................... TCLC 16
See also CA 163

**Sumner, Gordon Matthew** ............... CLC 26
See Police, The; Sting

**Sun Tzu** c. 400B.C.-c. 320B.C. ...... CMLC 56

**Surtees, Robert Smith** 1805-1864 .. NCLC 14
See also DLB 21; RGEL 2

**Susann, Jacqueline** 1921-1974 ............ CLC 3
See also AITN 1; BPFB 3; CA 65-68; MTCW 1, 2

**Su Shi**
See Su Shih
See also RGWL 2, 3

**Su Shih** 1036-1101 .......................... CMLC 15
See Su Shi

**Suskind, Patrick**
See Sueskind, Patrick
See also BPFB 3; CA 145; CWW 2

**Sutcliff, Rosemary** 1920-1992 ........... CLC 26
See also AAYA 10; BYA 1, 4; CA 5-8R; CANR 37; CLR 1, 37; CPW; DAB; DAC; DAM MST, POP; JRDA; MAICYA 1, 2; MAICYAS 1; RHW; SATA 6, 44, 78; SATA-Obit 73; WYA; YAW

**Sutro, Alfred** 1863-1933 ..................... TCLC 6
See also CA 185; DLB 10; RGEL 2

**Sutton, Henry**
See Slavitt, David R(ytman)

**Suzuki, D. T.**
See Suzuki, Daisetz Teitaro

**Suzuki, Daisetz T.**
See Suzuki, Daisetz Teitaro

**Suzuki, Daisetz Teitaro**
1870-1966 .............................. TCLC 109
See also CA 121; MTCW 1, 2

**Suzuki, Teitaro**
See Suzuki, Daisetz Teitaro

**Svevo, Italo** ................. SSC 25; TCLC 2, 35
See Schmitz, Aron Hector
See also DLB 264; EW 8; RGWL 2, 3

**Swados, Elizabeth (A.)** 1951- ............. CLC 12
See also CA 97-100; CANR 49; INT 97-100

**Swados, Harvey** 1920-1972 ................. CLC 5
See also CA 5-8R; CANR 6; DLB 2

**Swan, Gladys** 1934- ........................... CLC 69
See also CA 101; CANR 17, 39

**Swanson, Logan**
See Matheson, Richard (Burton)

**Swarthout, Glendon (Fred)**
1918-1992 ..................................... CLC 35
See also CA 1-4R; CANR 1, 47; LAIT 5; SATA 26; TCWW 2; YAW

**Sweet, Sarah C.**
See Jewett, (Theodora) Sarah Orne

**Swenson, May** 1919-1989 ...... CLC 4, 14, 61, 106; PC 14
See also AMWS 4; CA 5-8R; CANR 36, 61; DA; DAB; DAC; DAM MST, POET; DLB 5; EXPP; GLL 2; MTCW 1, 2; PFS 16; SATA 15; WP

**Swift, Augustus**
See Lovecraft, H(oward) P(hillips)

**Swift, Graham (Colin)** 1949- ...... CLC 41, 88
See also BRWS 5; CA 122; CANR 46, 71; CN 7; DLB 194; MTCW 2; RGSF 2

**Swift, Jonathan** 1667-1745 .. LC 1, 42; PC 9; WLC
See also AAYA 41; BRW 3; BRWR 1; BYA 5, 14; CDBLB 1660-1789; CLR 53; DA; DAB; DAC; DAM MST, NOV, POET; DLB 39, 95, 101; EXPN; LAIT 1; NFS 6; RGEL 2; SATA 19; TEA; WCH; WLIT 3

**Swinburne, Algernon Charles**
1837-1909 ... PC 24; TCLC 8, 36; WLC
See also BRW 5; CA 140; CDBLB 1832-1890; DA; DAB; DAC; DAM MST, POET; DLB 35, 57; PAB; RGEL 2; TEA

**Swinfen, Ann** ..................................... CLC 34
See also CA 202

**Swinnerton, Frank Arthur**
1884-1982 ..................................... CLC 31
See also DLB 34

**Swithen, John**
See King, Stephen (Edwin)

**Sylvia**
See Ashton-Warner, Sylvia (Constance)

**Symmes, Robert Edward**
See Duncan, Robert (Edward)

**Symonds, John Addington**
1840-1893 .................................... NCLC 34
See also DLB 57, 144

**Symons, Arthur** 1865-1945 ............. TCLC 11
See also CA 189; DLB 19, 57, 149; RGEL 2

**Symons, Julian (Gustave)**
1912-1994 ...................... CLC 2, 14, 32
See also CA 49-52; CAAS 3; CANR 3, 33, 59; CMW 4; DLB 87, 155; DLBY 1992; MSW; MTCW 1

**Synge, (Edmund) J(ohn) M(illington)**
1871-1909 ................. DC 2; TCLC 6, 37
See also BRW 6; BRWR 1; CA 141; CD-BLB 1890-1914; DAM DRAM; DLB 10, 19; RGEL 2; TEA; WLIT 4

**Syruc, J.**
See Milosz, Czeslaw

**Szirtes, George** 1948- ........................ CLC 46
See also CA 109; CANR 27, 61; CP 7

**Szymborska, Wislawa** 1923- ...... CLC 99; PC 44
See also CA 154; CANR 91; CDWLB 4; CWP; CWW 2; DLB 232; DLBY 1996; MTCW 2; PFS 15; RGWL 3

**T. O., Nik**
See Annensky, Innokenty (Fyodorovich)

**Tabori, George** 1914- ........................ CLC 19
See also CA 49-52; CANR 4, 69; CBD; CD 5; DLB 245

**Tacitus** c. 55-c. 117 ........................ CMLC 56
See also AW 2; CDWLB 1; DLB 211; RGWL 2, 3

**Tagore, Rabindranath** 1861-1941 ......... PC 8; SSC 48; TCLC 3, 53
See also CA 120; DAM DRAM, POET; MTCW 1, 2; RGEL 2; RGSF 2; RGWL 2, 3; TWA

**Taine, Hippolyte Adolphe**
1828-1893 .................................... NCLC 15
See also EW 7; GFL 1789 to the Present

**Talese, Gay** 1932- ............................. CLC 37
See also AITN 1; CA 1-4R; CANR 9, 58; DLB 185; INT CANR-9; MTCW 1, 2

**Tallent, Elizabeth (Ann)** 1954- ......... CLC 45
See also CA 117; CANR 72; DLB 130

**Tally, Ted** 1952- ............................... CLC 42
See also CA 124; CAD; CD 5; INT 124

**Talvik, Heiti** 1904-1947 ................... TCLC 87

**Tamayo y Baus, Manuel**
1829-1898 .................................... NCLC 1

**Tammsaare, A(nton) H(ansen)**
1878-1940 .................................... TCLC 27
See also CA 164; CDWLB 4; DLB 220

**Tam'si, Tchicaya U**
See Tchicaya, Gerald Felix

**Tan, Amy (Ruth)** 1952- . AAL; CLC 59, 120, 151
See also AAYA 9; AMWS 10; BEST 89:3; BPFB 3; CA 136; CANR 54, 105; CDALBS; CN 7; CPW 1; DAM MULT, NOV, POP; DLB 173; EXPN; FW; LAIT 3, 5; MTCW 2; NFS 1, 13, 16; RGAL 4; SATA 75; SSFS 9; YAW

**Tandem, Felix**
See Spitteler, Carl (Friedrich Georg)

**Tanizaki, Jun'ichiro** 1886-1965 ... CLC 8, 14, 28; SSC 21
See Tanizaki Jun'ichiro
See also CA 93-96; MJW; MTCW 2; RGSF 2; RGWL 2

**Tanizaki Jun'ichiro**
See Tanizaki, Jun'ichiro
See also DLB 180

**Tanner, William**
See Amis, Kingsley (William)

**Tao Lao**
See Storni, Alfonsina

**Tarantino, Quentin (Jerome)**
1963- .......................................... CLC 125
See also CA 171

**Tarassoff, Lev**
See Troyat, Henri

**Tarbell, Ida M(inerva)** 1857-1944 . TCLC 40
See also CA 181; DLB 47

**Tarkington, (Newton) Booth**
 1869-1946 ................................... **TCLC 9**
 See also BPFB 3; BYA 3; CA 143; CWRI
 5; DLB 9, 102; MTCW 2; RGAL 4; SATA
 17

**Tarkovskii, Andrei Arsen'evich**
 See Tarkovsky, Andrei (Arsenyevich)

**Tarkovsky, Andrei (Arsenyevich)**
 1932-1986 ................................... **CLC 75**
 See also CA 127

**Tartt, Donna** 1964(?)- ......................... **CLC 76**
 See also CA 142

**Tasso, Torquato** 1544-1595 .................... **LC 5**
 See also EFS 2; EW 2; RGWL 2, 3

**Tate, (John Orley) Allen** 1899-1979 .. **CLC 2,
 4, 6, 9, 11, 14, 24**
 See also AMW; CA 5-8R; CANR 32, 108;
 DLB 4, 45, 63; DLBD 17; MTCW 1, 2;
 RGAL 4; RHW

**Tate, Ellalice**
 See Hibbert, Eleanor Alice Burford

**Tate, James (Vincent)** 1943- ..... **CLC 2, 6, 25**
 See also CA 21-24R; CANR 29, 57, 114;
 CP 7; DLB 5, 169; PFS 10, 15; RGAL 4;
 WP

**Tauler, Johannes** c. 1300-1361 ...... **CMLC 37**
 See also DLB 179

**Tavel, Ronald** 1940- ............................ **CLC 6**
 See also CA 21-24R; CAD; CANR 33; CD
 5

**Taviani, Paolo** 1931- .......................... **CLC 70**
 See also CA 153

**Taylor, Bayard** 1825-1878 ............... **NCLC 89**
 See also DLB 3, 189, 250, 254; RGAL 4

**Taylor, C(ecil) P(hilip)** 1929-1981 .... **CLC 27**
 See also CA 25-28R; CANR 47; CBD

**Taylor, Edward** 1642(?)-1729 ............... **LC 11**
 See also AMW; DA; DAB; DAC; DAM
 MST, POET; DLB 24; EXPP; RGAL 4;
 TUS

**Taylor, Eleanor Ross** 1920- ................. **CLC 5**
 See also CA 81-84; CANR 70

**Taylor, Elizabeth** 1932-1975 ..... **CLC 2, 4, 29**
 See also CA 13-16R; CANR 9, 70; DLB
 139; MTCW 1; RGEL 2; SATA 13

**Taylor, Frederick Winslow**
 1856-1915 ................................... **TCLC 76**
 See also CA 188

**Taylor, Henry (Splawn)** 1942- .......... **CLC 44**
 See also CA 33-36R; CAAS 7; CANR 31;
 CP 7; DLB 5; PFS 10

**Taylor, Kamala (Purnaiya)** 1924-
 See Markandaya, Kamala
 See also CA 77-80; NFS 13

**Taylor, Mildred D(elois)** 1943- .......... **CLC 21**
 See also AAYA 10, 47; BW 1; BYA 3, 8;
 CA 85-88; CANR 25; CLR 9, 59; CSW;
 DLB 52; JRDA; LAIT 3; MAICYA 1, 2;
 SAAS 5; SATA 135; WYA; YAW

**Taylor, Peter (Hillsman)** 1917-1994 .. **CLC 1,
 4, 18, 37, 44, 50, 71; SSC 10**
 See also AMWS 5; BPFB 3; CA 13-16R;
 CANR 9, 50; CSW; DLB 218; DLBY
 1981, 1994; EXPS; INT CANR-9; MTCW
 1, 2; RGSF 2; SSFS 9; TUS

**Taylor, Robert Lewis** 1912-1998 ....... **CLC 14**
 See also CA 1-4R; CANR 3, 64; SATA 10

**Tchekhov, Anton**
 See Chekhov, Anton (Pavlovich)

**Tchicaya, Gerald Felix** 1931-1988 .. **CLC 101**
 See also CA 129; CANR 81

**Tchicaya U Tam'si**
 See Tchicaya, Gerald Felix

**Teasdale, Sara** 1884-1933 .... **PC 31; TCLC 4**
 See also CA 163; DLB 45; GLL 1; PFS 14;
 RGAL 4; SATA 32; TUS

**Tegner, Esaias** 1782-1846 .................. **NCLC 2**

**Teilhard de Chardin, (Marie Joseph) Pierre**
 1881-1955 ................................... **TCLC 9**
 See also GFL 1789 to the Present

**Temple, Ann**
 See Mortimer, Penelope (Ruth)

**Tennant, Emma (Christina)** 1937- .. **CLC 13,
 52**
 See also CA 65-68; CAAS 9; CANR 10,
 38, 59, 88; CN 7; DLB 14; SFW 4

**Tenneshaw, S. M.**
 See Silverberg, Robert

**Tenney, Tabitha Gilman**
 1762-1837 .................................. **NCLC 122**
 See also DLB 37, 200

**Tennyson, Alfred** 1809-1892 ... **NCLC 30, 65,
 115; PC 6; WLC**
 See also BRW 4; CDBLB 1832-1890; DA;
 DAB; DAC; DAM MST, POET; DLB 32;
 EXPP; PAB; PFS 1, 2, 4, 11, 15; RGEL
 2; TEA; WLIT 4; WP

**Teran, Lisa St. Aubin de** ................... **CLC 36**
 See St. Aubin de Teran, Lisa

**Terence** c. 184B.C.-c. 159B.C. ...... **CMLC 14;
 DC 7**
 See also AW 1; CDWLB 1; DLB 211;
 RGWL 2, 3; TWA

**Teresa de Jesus, St.** 1515-1582 ............ **LC 18**

**Terkel, Louis** 1912-
 See Terkel, Studs
 See also CA 57-60; CANR 18, 45, 67;
 MTCW 1, 2

**Terkel, Studs** ..................................... **CLC 38**
 See Terkel, Louis
 See also AAYA 32; AITN 1; MTCW 2; TUS

**Terry, C. V.**
 See Slaughter, Frank G(ill)

**Terry, Megan** 1932- ................... **CLC 19; DC 13**
 See also CA 77-80; CABS 3; CAD; CANR
 43; CD 5; CWD; DLB 7, 249; GLL 2

**Tertullian** c. 155-c. 245 ................... **CMLC 29**

**Tertz, Abram**
 See Sinyavsky, Andrei (Donatevich)
 See also CWW 2; RGSF 2

**Tesich, Steve** 1943(?)-1996 .......... **CLC 40, 69**
 See also CA 105; CAD; DLBY 1983

**Tesla, Nikola** 1856-1943 .................. **TCLC 88**

**Teternikov, Fyodor Kuzmich** 1863-1927
 See Sologub, Fyodor

**Tevis, Walter** 1928-1984 ..................... **CLC 42**
 See also CA 113; SFW 4

**Tey, Josephine** ................................. **TCLC 14**
 See Mackintosh, Elizabeth
 See also DLB 77; MSW

**Thackeray, William Makepeace**
 1811-1863 .... **NCLC 5, 14, 22, 43; WLC**
 See also BRW 5; CDBLB 1832-1890; DA;
 DAB; DAC; DAM MST, NOV; DLB 21,
 55, 159, 163; NFS 13; RGEL 2; SATA
 23; TEA; WLIT 3

**Thakura, Ravindranatha**
 See Tagore, Rabindranath

**Thames, C. H.**
 See Marlowe, Stephen

**Tharoor, Shashi** 1956- ...................... **CLC 70**
 See also CA 141; CANR 91; CN 7

**Thelwell, Michael Miles** 1939- .......... **CLC 22**
 See also BW 2; CA 101

**Theobald, Lewis, Jr.**
 See Lovecraft, H(oward) P(hillips)

**Theocritus** c. 310B.C.- ................... **CMLC 45**
 See also AW 1; DLB 176; RGWL 2, 3

**Theodorescu, Ion N.** 1880-1967
 See Arghezi, Tudor

**Theriault, Yves** 1915-1983 ................. **CLC 79**
 See also CA 102; CCA 1; DAC; DAM
 MST; DLB 88

**Theroux, Alexander (Louis)** 1939- .... **CLC 2,
 25**
 See also CA 85-88; CANR 20, 63; CN 7

**Theroux, Paul (Edward)** 1941- ...... **CLC 5, 8,
 11, 15, 28, 46**
 See also AAYA 28; AMWS 8; BEST 89:4;
 BPFB 3; CA 33-36R; CANR 20, 45, 74;
 CDALBS; CN 7; CPW 1; DAM POP;
 DLB 2, 218; HGG; MTCW 1, 2; RGAL
 4; SATA 44, 109; TUS

**Thesen, Sharon** 1946- ........................ **CLC 56**
 See also CA 163; CP 7; CWP

**Thespis** fl. 6th cent. B.C.- ............... **CMLC 51**

**Thevenin, Denis**
 See Duhamel, Georges

**Thibault, Jacques Anatole Francois**
 1844-1924
 See France, Anatole
 See also CA 127; DAM NOV; MTCW 1, 2;
 TWA

**Thiele, Colin (Milton)** 1920- ............. **CLC 17**
 See also CA 29-32R; CANR 12, 28, 53,
 105; CLR 27; MAICYA 1, 2; SAAS 2;
 SATA 14, 72, 125; YAW

**Thistlethwaite, Bel**
 See Wetherald, Agnes Ethelwyn

**Thomas, Audrey (Callahan)** 1935- .... **CLC 7,
 13, 37, 107; SSC 20**
 See also AITN 2; CA 21-24R; CAAS 19;
 CANR 36, 58; CN 7; DLB 60; MTCW 1;
 RGSF 2

**Thomas, Augustus** 1857-1934 ......... **TCLC 97**

**Thomas, D(onald) M(ichael)** 1935- . **CLC 13,
 22, 31, 132**
 See also BPFB 3; BRWS 4; CA 61-64;
 CAAS 11; CANR 17, 45, 75; CDBLB
 1960 to Present; CN 7; CP 7; DLB 40,
 207; HGG; INT CANR-17; MTCW 1, 2;
 SFW 4

**Thomas, Dylan (Marlais)** 1914-1953 ... **PC 2;
 SSC 3, 44; TCLC 1, 8, 45, 105; WLC**
 See also AAYA 45; BRWS 1; CA 120;
 CANR 65; CDBLB 1945-1960; DA;
 DAB; DAC; DAM DRAM, MST, POET;
 DLB 13, 20, 139; EXPP; LAIT 3; MTCW
 1, 2; PAB; PFS 1, 3, 8; RGEL 2; RGSF 2;
 SATA 60; TEA; WLIT 4; WP

**Thomas, (Philip) Edward**
 1878-1917 ................................... **TCLC 10**
 See also BRW 6; BRWS 3; CA 153; DAM
 POET; DLB 19, 98, 156, 216; PAB;
 RGEL 2

**Thomas, Joyce Carol** 1938- ............... **CLC 35**
 See also AAYA 12; BW 2, 3; CA 116;
 CANR 48, 114; CLR 19; DLB 33; INT
 CA-116; JRDA; MAICYA 1, 2; MTCW
 1, 2; SAAS 7; SATA 40, 78, 123, 137;
 WYA; YAW

**Thomas, Lewis** 1913-1993 ................. **CLC 35**
 See also ANW; CA 85-88; CANR 38, 60;
 DLB 275; MTCW 1, 2

**Thomas, M. Carey** 1857-1935 ......... **TCLC 89**
 See also FW

**Thomas, Paul**
 See Mann, (Paul) Thomas

**Thomas, Piri** 1928- ............ **CLC 17; HLCS 2**
 See also CA 73-76; HW 1

**Thomas, R(onald) S(tuart)**
 1913-2000 .......................... **CLC 6, 13, 48**
 See also CA 89-92; CAAS 4; CANR 30;
 CDBLB 1960 to Present; CP 7; DAB;
 DAM POET; DLB 27; MTCW 1; RGEL
 2

**Thomas, Ross (Elmore)** 1926-1995 .. **CLC 39**
 See also CA 33-36R; CANR 22, 63; CMW
 4

**Thompson, Francis (Joseph)**
 1859-1907 ..................................... **TCLC 4**
 See also BRW 5; CA 189; CDBLB 1890-
 1914; DLB 19; RGEL 2; TEA

**Thompson, Francis Clegg**
See Mencken, H(enry) L(ouis)

**Thompson, Hunter S(tockton)**
1937(?)- ............... **CLC 9, 17, 40, 104**
See also AAYA 45; BEST 89:1; BPFB 3; CA 17-20R; CANR 23, 46, 74, 77, 111; CPW; CSW; DAM POP; DLB 185; MTCW 1, 2; TUS

**Thompson, James Myers**
See Thompson, Jim (Myers)

**Thompson, Jim (Myers)**
1906-1977(?) ............... **CLC 69**
See also BPFB 3; CA 140; CMW 4; CPW; DLB 226; MSW

**Thompson, Judith** ............... **CLC 39**
See also CWD

**Thomson, James** 1700-1748 .... **LC 16, 29, 40**
See also BRWS 3; DAM POET; DLB 95; RGEL 2

**Thomson, James** 1834-1882 ............ **NCLC 18**
See also DAM POET; DLB 35; RGEL 2

**Thoreau, Henry David** 1817-1862 .. **NCLC 7, 21, 61; PC 30; WLC**
See also AAYA 42; AMW; ANW; BYA 3; CDALB 1640-1865; DA; DAB; DAC; DAM MST; DLB 1, 183, 223, 270; LAIT 2; NCFS 3; RGAL 4; TUS

**Thorndike, E. L.**
See Thorndike, Edward L(ee)

**Thorndike, Edward L(ee)**
1874-1949 ............... **TCLC 107**

**Thornton, Hall**
See Silverberg, Robert

**Thubron, Colin (Gerald Dryden)**
1939- ............... **CLC 163**
See also CA 25-28R; CANR 12, 29, 59, 95; CN 7; DLB 204, 231

**Thucydides** c. 455B.C.-c. 395B.C. . **CMLC 17**
See also AW 1; DLB 176; RGWL 2, 3

**Thumboo, Edwin Nadason** 1933- ........ **PC 30**
See also CA 194

**Thurber, James (Grover)**
1894-1961 .. **CLC 5, 11, 25, 125; SSC 1, 47**
See also AMWS 1; BPFB 3; BYA 5; CA 73-76; CANR 17, 39; CDALB 1929-1941; CWRI 5; DA; DAB; DAC; DAM DRAM, MST, NOV; DLB 4, 11, 22, 102; EXPS; FANT; LAIT 3; MAICYA 1, 2; MTCW 1, 2; RGAL 4; RGSF 2; SATA 13; SSFS 1, 10; SUFW; TUS

**Thurman, Wallace (Henry)**
1902-1934 ......... **BLC 3; HR 3; TCLC 6**
See also BW 1, 3; CA 124; CANR 81; DAM MULT; DLB 51

**Tibullus** c. 54B.C.-c. 18B.C. ............ **CMLC 36**
See also AW 2; DLB 211; RGWL 2, 3

**Ticheburn, Cheviot**
See Ainsworth, William Harrison

**Tieck, (Johann) Ludwig**
1773-1853 ............... **NCLC 5, 46; SSC 31**
See also CDWLB 2; DLB 90; EW 5; IDTP; RGSF 2; RGWL 2, 3; SUFW

**Tiger, Derry**
See Ellison, Harlan (Jay)

**Tilghman, Christopher** 1948(?)- ........ **CLC 65**
See also CA 159; CSW; DLB 244

**Tillich, Paul (Johannes)**
1886-1965 ............... **CLC 131**
See also CA 5-8R; CANR 33; MTCW 1, 2

**Tillinghast, Richard (Williford)**
1940- ............... **CLC 29**
See also CA 29-32R; CAAS 23; CANR 26, 51, 96; CP 7; CSW

**Timrod, Henry** 1828-1867 ............... **NCLC 25**
See also DLB 3, 248; RGAL 4

**Tindall, Gillian (Elizabeth)** 1938- ....... **CLC 7**
See also CA 21-24R; CANR 11, 65, 107; CN 7

**Tiptree, James, Jr.** ....................... **CLC 48, 50**
See Sheldon, Alice Hastings Bradley
See also DLB 8; SCFW 2; SFW 4

**Tirone Smith, Mary-Ann** 1944- ........ **CLC 39**
See also CA 136; CANR 113

**Tirso de Molina** 1580(?)-1648 ............ **DC 13; HLCS 2; LC 73**
See also RGWL 2, 3

**Titmarsh, Michael Angelo**
See Thackeray, William Makepeace

**Tocqueville, Alexis (Charles Henri Maurice Clerel Comte) de** 1805-1859 .. **NCLC 7, 63**
See also EW 6; GFL 1789 to the Present; TWA

**Toffler, Alvin** 1928- ........................ **CLC 168**
See also CA 13-16R; CANR 15, 46, 67; CPW; DAM POP; MTCW 1, 2

**Toibin, Colm**
See Toibin, Colm
See also DLB 271

**Toibin, Colm** 1955- ........................ **CLC 162**
See Toibin, Colm
See also CA 142; CANR 81

**Tolkien, J(ohn) R(onald) R(euel)**
1892-1973 ............ **CLC 1, 2, 3, 8, 12, 38; WLC**
See also AAYA 10; AITN 1; BPFB 3; BRWS 2; CA 17-18; CANR 36; CAP 2; CDBLB 1914-1945; CLR 56; CPW 1; CWRI 5; DA; DAB; DAC; DAM MST, NOV, POP; DLB 15, 160, 255; EFS 2; FANT; JRDA; LAIT 1; MAICYA 1, 2; MTCW 1, 2; NFS 8; RGEL 2; SATA 2, 32, 100; SATA-Obit 24; SFW 4; SUFW; TEA; WCH; WYA; YAW

**Toller, Ernst** 1893-1939 ...................... **TCLC 10**
See also CA 186; DLB 124; RGWL 2, 3

**Tolson, M. B.**
See Tolson, Melvin B(eaunorus)

**Tolson, Melvin B(eaunorus)**
1898(?)-1966 ........ **BLC 3; CLC 36, 105**
See also AFAW 1, 2; BW 1, 3; CA 124; CANR 80; DAM MULT, POET; DLB 48, 76; RGAL 4

**Tolstoi, Aleksei Nikolaevich**
See Tolstoy, Alexey Nikolaevich

**Tolstoi, Lev**
See Tolstoy, Leo (Nikolaevich)
See also RGSF 2; RGWL 2, 3

**Tolstoy, Aleksei Nikolaevich**
See Tolstoy, Alexey Nikolaevich
See also DLB 272

**Tolstoy, Alexey Nikolaevich**
1882-1945 ............................ **TCLC 18**
See Tolstoi, Aleksei Nikolaevich
See also CA 158; SFW 4

**Tolstoy, Leo (Nikolaevich)**
1828-1910 . **SSC 9, 30, 45, 54; TCLC 4, 11, 17, 28, 44, 79; WLC**
See Tolstoi, Lev
See also CA 123; DA; DAB; DAC; DAM MST, NOV; DLB 238; EFS 2; EW 7; EXPS; IDTP; LAIT 2; NFS 10; SATA 26; SSFS 5; TWA

**Tolstoy, Count Leo**
See Tolstoy, Leo (Nikolaevich)

**Tomalin, Claire** 1933- ...................... **CLC 166**
See also CA 89-92; CANR 52, 88; DLB 155

**Tomasi di Lampedusa, Giuseppe** 1896-1957
See Lampedusa, Giuseppe (Tomasi) di
See also DLB 177

**Tomlin, Lily** ........................ **CLC 17**
See Tomlin, Mary Jean

**Tomlin, Mary Jean** 1939(?)-
See Tomlin, Lily

**Tomline, F. Latour**
See Gilbert, W(illiam) S(chwenck)

**Tomlinson, (Alfred) Charles** 1927- .... **CLC 2, 4, 6, 13, 45; PC 17**
See also CA 5-8R; CANR 33; CP 7; DAM POET; DLB 40

**Tomlinson, H(enry) M(ajor)**
1873-1958 ............... **TCLC 71**
See also CA 161; DLB 36, 100, 195

**Tonson, Jacob** fl. 1655(?)-1736 ............. **LC 86**
See also DLB 170

**Toole, John Kennedy** 1937-1969 ..... **CLC 19, 64**
See also BPFB 3; CA 104; DLBY 1981; MTCW 2

**Toomer, Eugene**
See Toomer, Jean

**Toomer, Eugene Pinchback**
See Toomer, Jean

**Toomer, Jean** 1892-1967 .. **BLC 3; CLC 1, 4, 13, 22; HR 3; PC 7; SSC 1, 45; WLCS**
See also AFAW 1, 2; AMWS 3, 9; BW 1; CA 85-88; CDALB 1917-1929; DAM MULT; DLB 45, 51; EXPP; EXPS; MTCW 1, 2; NFS 11; RGAL 4; RGSF 2; SSFS 5

**Toomer, Nathan Jean**
See Toomer, Jean

**Toomer, Nathan Pinchback**
See Toomer, Jean

**Torley, Luke**
See Blish, James (Benjamin)

**Tornimparte, Alessandra**
See Ginzburg, Natalia

**Torre, Raoul della**
See Mencken, H(enry) L(ouis)

**Torrence, Ridgely** 1874-1950 .......... **TCLC 97**
See also DLB 54, 249

**Torrey, E(dwin) Fuller** 1937- ............ **CLC 34**
See also CA 119; CANR 71

**Torsvan, Ben Traven**
See Traven, B.

**Torsvan, Benno Traven**
See Traven, B.

**Torsvan, Berick Traven**
See Traven, B.

**Torsvan, Berwick Traven**
See Traven, B.

**Torsvan, Bruno Traven**
See Traven, B.

**Torsvan, Traven**
See Traven, B.

**Tourneur, Cyril** 1575(?)-1626 ............. **LC 66**
See also BRW 2; DAM DRAM; DLB 58; RGEL 2

**Tournier, Michel (Edouard)** 1924- .... **CLC 6, 23, 36, 95**
See also CA 49-52; CANR 3, 36, 74; DLB 83; GFL 1789 to the Present; MTCW 1, 2; SATA 23

**Tournimparte, Alessandra**
See Ginzburg, Natalia

**Towers, Ivar**
See Kornbluth, C(yril) M.

**Towne, Robert (Burton)** 1936(?)- ...... **CLC 87**
See also CA 108; DLB 44; IDFW 3, 4

**Townsend, Sue** .................. **CLC 61**
See Townsend, Susan Lilian
See also AAYA 28; CA 127; CANR 65, 107; CBD; CD 5; CPW; CWD; DAB; DAC; DAM MST; DLB 271; INT 127; SATA 55, 93; SATA-Brief 48; YAW

**Townsend, Susan Lilian** 1946-
See Townsend, Sue

**Townshend, Pete**
See Townshend, Peter (Dennis Blandford)

**Townshend, Peter (Dennis Blandford)**
1945- ............... **CLC 17, 42**
See also CA 107

**Tozzi, Federigo** 1883-1920 .............. **TCLC 31**
See also CA 160; CANR 110; DLB 264

**Tracy, Don(ald Fiske)** 1905-1970(?)
See Queen, Ellery
See also CA 1-4R; CANR 2

**Trafford, F. G.**
See Riddell, Charlotte

**Traill, Catharine Parr** 1802-1899 .. **NCLC 31**
See also DLB 99

**Trakl, Georg** 1887-1914 ....... **PC 20; TCLC 5**
See also CA 165; EW 10; MTCW 2; RGWL 2, 3

**Tranquilli, Secondino**
See Silone, Ignazio

**Transtroemer, Tomas (Goesta)** 1931- ..................... **CLC 52, 65**
See Transtromer, Tomas
See also CA 129; CAAS 17; DAM POET

**Transtromer, Tomas**
See Transtroemer, Tomas (Goesta)
See also DLB 257

**Transtromer, Tomas Gosta**
See Transtroemer, Tomas (Goesta)

**Traven, B.** 1882(?)-1969 ................ **CLC 8, 11**
See also CA 19-20; CAP 2; DLB 9, 56; MTCW 1; RGAL 4

**Trediakovsky, Vasilii Kirillovich** 1703-1769 ...................... **LC 68**
See also DLB 150

**Treitel, Jonathan** 1959- ....................... **CLC 70**
See also DLB 267

**Trelawny, Edward John** 1792-1881 .................. **NCLC 85**
See also DLB 110, 116, 144

**Tremain, Rose** 1943- ........................... **CLC 42**
See also CA 97-100; CANR 44, 95; CN 7; DLB 14, 271; RGSF 2; RHW

**Tremblay, Michel** 1942- ............. **CLC 29, 102**
See also CA 128; CCA 1; CWW 2; DAC; DAM MST; DLB 60; GLL 1; MTCW 1, 2

**Trevanian** ............................. **CLC 29**
See Whitaker, Rod(ney)

**Trevor, Glen**
See Hilton, James

**Trevor, William** .. **CLC 7, 9, 14, 25, 71, 116; SSC 21, 58**
See Cox, William Trevor
See also BRWS 4; CBD; CD 5; CN 7; DLB 14, 139; MTCW 2; RGEL 2; RGSF 2; SSFS 10

**Trifonov, Iurii (Valentinovich)**
See Trifonov, Yuri (Valentinovich)
See also RGWL 2, 3

**Trifonov, Yuri (Valentinovich)** 1925-1981 .......................... **CLC 45**
See Trifonov, Iurii (Valentinovich)
See also CA 126; MTCW 1

**Trilling, Diana (Rubin)** 1905-1996 . **CLC 129**
See also CA 5-8R; CANR 10, 46; INT CANR-10; MTCW 1, 2

**Trilling, Lionel** 1905-1975 ....... **CLC 9, 11, 24**
See also AMWS 3; CA 9-12R; CANR 10, 105; DLB 28, 63; INT CANR-10; MTCW 1, 2; RGAL 4; TUS

**Trimball, W. H.**
See Mencken, H(enry) L(ouis)

**Tristan**
See Gomez de la Serna, Ramon

**Tristram**
See Housman, A(lfred) E(dward)

**Trogdon, William (Lewis)** 1939-
See Heat-Moon, William Least
See also CA 119; CANR 47, 89; CPW; INT CA-119

**Trollope, Anthony** 1815-1882 .... **NCLC 6, 33, 101; SSC 28; WLC**
See also BRW 5; CDBLB 1832-1890; DA; DAB; DAC; DAM MST, NOV; DLB 21, 57, 159; RGEL 2; RGSF 2; SATA 22

**Trollope, Frances** 1779-1863 .......... **NCLC 30**
See also DLB 21, 166

**Trotsky, Leon** 1879-1940 ................ **TCLC 22**
See also CA 167

**Trotter (Cockburn), Catharine** 1679-1749 ......................... **LC 8**
See also DLB 84, 252

**Trotter, Wilfred** 1872-1939 ............. **TCLC 97**

**Trout, Kilgore**
See Farmer, Philip Jose

**Trow, George W. S.** 1943- .................. **CLC 52**
See also CA 126; CANR 91

**Troyat, Henri** 1911- ............................ **CLC 23**
See also CA 45-48; CANR 2, 33, 67; GFL 1789 to the Present; MTCW 1

**Trudeau, G(arretson) B(eekman)** 1948-
See Trudeau, Garry B.
See also CA 81-84; CANR 31; SATA 35

**Trudeau, Garry B.** ............................ **CLC 12**
See Trudeau, G(arretson) B(eekman)
See also AAYA 10; AITN 2

**Truffaut, Francois** 1932-1984 ... **CLC 20, 101**
See also CA 81-84; CANR 34

**Trumbo, Dalton** 1905-1976 ................ **CLC 19**
See also CA 21-24R; CANR 10; DLB 26; IDFW 3, 4; YAW

**Trumbull, John** 1750-1831 ............. **NCLC 30**
See also DLB 31; RGAL 4

**Trundlett, Helen B.**
See Eliot, T(homas) S(tearns)

**Truth, Sojourner** 1797(?)-1883 ....... **NCLC 94**
See also DLB 239; FW; LAIT 2

**Tryon, Thomas** 1926-1991 ................ **CLC 3, 11**
See also AITN 1; BPFB 3; CA 29-32R; CANR 32, 77; CPW; DAM POP; HGG; MTCW 1

**Tryon, Tom**
See Tryon, Thomas

**Ts'ao Hsueh-ch'in** 1715(?)-1763 ............ **LC 1**

**Tsushima, Shuji** 1909-1948
See Dazai Osamu

**Tsvetaeva (Efron), Marina (Ivanovna)** 1892-1941 ................... **PC 14; TCLC 7, 35**
See also CA 128; CANR 73; EW 11; MTCW 1, 2; RGWL 2, 3

**Tuck, Lily** 1938- ................................ **CLC 70**
See also CA 139; CANR 90

**Tu Fu** 712-770 ........................................ **PC 9**
See Du Fu
See also DAM MULT; TWA; WP

**Tunis, John R(oberts)** 1889-1975 ..... **CLC 12**
See also BYA 1; CA 61-64; CANR 62; DLB 22, 171; JRDA; MAICYA 1, 2; SATA 37; SATA-Brief 30; YAW

**Tuohy, Frank** ................................. **CLC 37**
See Tuohy, John Francis
See also DLB 14, 139

**Tuohy, John Francis** 1925-
See Tuohy, Frank
See also CA 5-8R; CANR 3, 47; CN 7

**Turco, Lewis (Putnam)** 1934- ..... **CLC 11, 63**
See also CA 13-16R; CAAS 22; CANR 24, 51; CP 7; DLBY 1984

**Turgenev, Ivan (Sergeevich)** 1818-1883 ..... **DC 7; NCLC 21, 37, 122; SSC 7, 57; WLC**
See also DA; DAB; DAC; DAM MST, NOV; DFS 6; DLB 238; EW 6; NFS 16; RGSF 2; RGWL 2, 3; TWA

**Turgot, Anne-Robert-Jacques** 1727-1781 ............................ **LC 26**

**Turner, Frederick** 1943- ..................... **CLC 48**
See also CA 73-76; CAAS 10; CANR 12, 30, 56; DLB 40

**Turton, James**
See Crace, Jim

**Tutu, Desmond M(pilo)** 1931- .. **BLC 3; CLC 80**
See also BW 1, 3; CA 125; CANR 67, 81; DAM MULT

**Tutuola, Amos** 1920-1997 ..... **BLC 3; CLC 5, 14, 29**
See also AFW; BW 2, 3; CA 9-12R; CANR 27, 66; CDWLB 3; CN 7; DAM MULT; DLB 125; DNFS 2; MTCW 1, 2; RGEL 2; WLIT 2

**Twain, Mark** .. **SSC 34; TCLC 6, 12, 19, 36, 48, 59; WLC**
See Clemens, Samuel Langhorne
See also AAYA 20; AMW; AMWC 1; BPFB 3; BYA 2, 3, 11, 14; CLR 58, 60, 66; DLB 11; EXPN; EXPS; FANT; LAIT 3; NFS 1, 6; RGAL 4; RGSF 2; SFW 4; SSFS 1, 7; SUFW; TUS; WCH; WYA; YAW

**Tyler, Anne** 1941- . **CLC 7, 11, 18, 28, 44, 59, 103**
See also AAYA 18; AMWS 4; BEST 89:1; BPFB 3; BYA 12; CA 9-12R; CANR 11, 33, 53, 109; CDALBS; CN 7; CPW; CSW; DAM NOV, POP; DLB 6, 143; DLBY 1982; EXPN; MAWW; MTCW 1, 2; NFS 2, 7, 10; RGAL 4; SATA 7, 90; TUS; YAW

**Tyler, Royall** 1757-1826 .................... **NCLC 3**
See also DLB 37; RGAL 4

**Tynan, Katharine** 1861-1931 ............ **TCLC 3**
See also CA 167; DLB 153, 240; FW

**Tyutchev, Fyodor** 1803-1873 .......... **NCLC 34**

**Tzara, Tristan** 1896-1963 ...... **CLC 47; PC 27**
See also CA 153; DAM POET; MTCW 2

**Udall, Nicholas** 1504-1556 .................... **LC 84**
See also DLB 62; RGEL 2

**Uhry, Alfred** 1936- ............................ **CLC 55**
See also CA 133; CAD; CANR 112; CD 5; CSW; DAM DRAM, POP; DFS 15; INT CA-133

**Ulf, Haerved**
See Strindberg, (Johan) August

**Ulf, Harved**
See Strindberg, (Johan) August

**Ulibarri, Sabine R(eyes)** 1919- ........ **CLC 83; HLCS 2**
See also CA 131; CANR 81; DAM MULT; DLB 82; HW 1, 2; RGSF 2

**Unamuno (y Jugo), Miguel de** 1864-1936 . **HLC 2; SSC 11; TCLC 2, 9**
See also CA 131; CANR 81; DAM MULT, NOV; DLB 108; EW 8; HW 1, 2; MTCW 1, 2; RGSF 2; RGWL 2, 3; TWA

**Undercliffe, Errol**
See Campbell, (John) Ramsey

**Underwood, Miles**
See Glassco, John

**Undset, Sigrid** 1882-1949 ..... **TCLC 3; WLC**
See also CA 129; DA; DAB; DAC; DAM MST, NOV; EW 9; FW; MTCW 1, 2; RGWL 2, 3

**Ungaretti, Giuseppe** 1888-1970 ... **CLC 7, 11, 15**
See also CA 19-20; CAP 2; DLB 114; EW 10; RGWL 2, 3

**Unger, Douglas** 1952- ......................... **CLC 34**
See also CA 130; CANR 94

**Unsworth, Barry (Forster)** 1930- .... **CLC 76, 127**
See also BRWS 7; CA 25-28R; CANR 30, 54; CN 7; DLB 194

**Updike, John (Hoyer)** 1932- . **CLC 1, 2, 3, 5, 7, 9, 13, 15, 23, 34, 43, 70, 139; SSC 13, 27; WLC**
See also AAYA 36; AMW; AMWC 1; AMWR 1; BPFB 3; BYA 12; CA 1-4R; CABS 1; CANR 4, 33, 51, 94; CDALB

1968-1988; CN 7; CP 7; CPW 1; DA; DAB; DAC; DAM MST, NOV, POET, POP; DLB 2, 5, 143, 218, 227; DLBD 3; DLBY 1980, 1982, 1997; EXPP; HGG; MTCW 1, 2; NFS 12; RGAL 4; RGSF 2; SSFS 3; TUS

**Upshaw, Margaret Mitchell**
See Mitchell, Margaret (Munnerlyn)

**Upton, Mark**
See Sanders, Lawrence

**Upward, Allen** 1863-1926 ............... **TCLC 85**
See also CA 187; DLB 36

**Urdang, Constance (Henriette)**
1922-1996 ................... **CLC 47**
See also CA 21-24R; CANR 9, 24; CP 7; CWP

**Uriel, Henry**
See Faust, Frederick (Schiller)

**Uris, Leon (Marcus)** 1924- .......... **CLC 7, 32**
See also AITN 1, 2; BEST 89:2; BPFB 3; CA 1-4R; CANR 1, 40, 65; CN 7; CPW 1; DAM NOV, POP; MTCW 1, 2; SATA 49

**Urista, Alberto H.** 1947- ...... **HLCS 1; PC 34**
See Alurista
See also CA 45-48, 182; CANR 2, 32; HW 1

**Urmuz**
See Codrescu, Andrei

**Urquhart, Guy**
See McAlmon, Robert (Menzies)

**Urquhart, Jane** 1949- .................. **CLC 90**
See also CA 113; CANR 32, 68; CCA 1; DAC

**Usigli, Rodolfo** 1905-1979 ................ **HLCS 1**
See also CA 131; HW 1; LAW

**Ustinov, Peter (Alexander)** 1921- ....... **CLC 1**
See also AITN 1; CA 13-16R; CANR 25, 51; CBD; CD 5; DLB 13; MTCW 2

**U Tam'si, Gerald Felix Tchicaya**
See Tchicaya, Gerald Felix

**U Tam'si, Tchicaya**
See Tchicaya, Gerald Felix

**Vachss, Andrew (Henry)** 1942- ....... **CLC 106**
See also CA 118; CANR 44, 95; CMW 4

**Vachss, Andrew H.**
See Vachss, Andrew (Henry)

**Vaculik, Ludvik** 1926- ......................... **CLC 7**
See also CA 53-56; CANR 72; CWW 2; DLB 232

**Vaihinger, Hans** 1852-1933 ............. **TCLC 71**
See also CA 166

**Valdez, Luis (Miguel)** 1940- ..... **CLC 84; DC 10; HLC 2**
See also CA 101; CAD; CANR 32, 81; CD 5; DAM MULT; DFS 5; DLB 122; HW 1; LAIT 4

**Valenzuela, Luisa** 1938- ........... **CLC 31, 104; HLCS 2; SSC 14**
See also CA 101; CANR 32, 65; CDWLB 3; CWW 2; DAM MULT; DLB 113; FW; HW 1, 2; LAW; RGSF 2; RGWL 3

**Valera y Alcala-Galiano, Juan**
1824-1905 ................... **TCLC 10**

**Valery, (Ambroise) Paul (Toussaint Jules)**
1871-1945 ................ **PC 9; TCLC 4, 15**
See also CA 122; DAM POET; DLB 258; EW 8; GFL 1789 to the Present; MTCW 1, 2; RGWL 2, 3; TWA

**Valle-Inclan, Ramon (Maria) del**
1866-1936 ................... **HLC 2; TCLC 5**
See also CA 153; CANR 80; DAM MULT; DLB 134; EW 8; HW 2; RGSF 2; RGWL 2, 3

**Vallejo, Antonio Buero**
See Buero Vallejo, Antonio

**Vallejo, Cesar (Abraham)**
1892-1938 ............. **HLC 2; TCLC 3, 56**
See also CA 153; DAM MULT; HW 1; LAW; RGWL 2, 3

**Valles, Jules** 1832-1885 ................ **NCLC 71**
See also DLB 123; GFL 1789 to the Present

**Vallette, Marguerite Eymery**
1860-1953 ........................... **TCLC 67**
See also CA 182; DLB 123, 192

**Valle Y Pena, Ramon del**
See Valle-Inclan, Ramon (Maria) del

**Van Ash, Cay** 1918- ......................... **CLC 34**

**Vanbrugh, Sir John** 1664-1726 ........... **LC 21**
See also BRW 2; DAM DRAM; DLB 80; IDTP; RGEL 2

**Van Campen, Karl**
See Campbell, John W(ood, Jr.)

**Vance, Gerald**
See Silverberg, Robert

**Vance, Jack** ........................... **CLC 35**
See Vance, John Holbrook
See also DLB 8; FANT; SCFW 2; SFW 4; SUFW 1, 2

**Vance, John Holbrook** 1916-
See Queen, Ellery; Vance, Jack
See also CA 29-32R; CANR 17, 65; CMW 4; MTCW 1

**Van Den Bogarde, Derek Jules Gaspard Ulric Niven** 1921-1999 ............. **CLC 14**
See Bogarde, Dirk
See also CA 77-80

**Vandenburgh, Jane** ......................... **CLC 59**
See also CA 168

**Vanderhaeghe, Guy** 1951- ................. **CLC 41**
See also BPFB 3; CA 113; CANR 72

**van der Post, Laurens (Jan)**
1906-1996 ........................... **CLC 5**
See also AFW; CA 5-8R; CANR 35; CN 7; DLB 204; RGEL 2

**van de Wetering, Janwillem** 1931- ... **CLC 47**
See also CA 49-52; CANR 4, 62, 90; CMW 4

**Van Dine, S. S.** ........................... **TCLC 23**
See Wright, Willard Huntington
See also MSW

**Van Doren, Carl (Clinton)**
1885-1950 ................... **TCLC 18**
See also CA 168

**Van Doren, Mark** 1894-1972 ........ **CLC 6, 10**
See also CA 1-4R; CANR 3; DLB 45; MTCW 1, 2; RGAL 4

**Van Druten, John (William)**
1901-1957 ................................ **TCLC 2**
See also CA 161; DLB 10; RGAL 4

**Van Duyn, Mona (Jane)** 1921- ...... **CLC 3, 7, 63, 116**
See also CA 9-12R; CANR 7, 38, 60; CP 7; CWP; DAM POET; DLB 5

**Van Dyne, Edith**
See Baum, L(yman) Frank

**van Itallie, Jean-Claude** 1936- ............ **CLC 3**
See also CA 45-48; CAAS 2; CAD; CANR 1, 48; CD 5; DLB 7

**Van Loot, Cornelius Obenchain**
See Roberts, Kenneth (Lewis)

**van Ostaijen, Paul** 1896-1928 ........ **TCLC 33**
See also CA 163

**Van Peebles, Melvin** 1932- ........... **CLC 2, 20**
See also BW 2, 3; CA 85-88; CANR 27, 67, 82; DAM MULT

**van Schendel, Arthur(-Francois-Emile)**
1874-1946 ................................ **TCLC 56**

**Vansittart, Peter** 1920- ...................... **CLC 42**
See also CA 1-4R; CANR 3, 49, 90; CN 7; RHW

**Van Vechten, Carl** 1880-1964 ... **CLC 33; HR 3**
See also AMWS 2; CA 183; DLB 4, 9, 51; RGAL 4

**van Vogt, A(lfred) E(lton)** 1912-2000 . **CLC 1**
See also BPFB 3; BYA 13, 14; CA 21-24R; CANR 28; DLB 8, 251; SATA 14; SATA-Obit 124; SCFW; SFW 4

**Vara, Madeleine**
See Jackson, Laura (Riding)

**Varda, Agnes** 1928- ........................... **CLC 16**
See also CA 122

**Vargas Llosa, (Jorge) Mario (Pedro)**
1936- .... **CLC 3, 6, 9, 10, 15, 31, 42, 85; HLC 2**
See Llosa, (Jorge) Mario (Pedro) Vargas
See also BPFB 3; CA 73-76; CANR 18, 32, 42, 67; CDWLB 3; DA; DAB; DAC; DAM MST, MULT, NOV; DLB 145; DNFS 2; HW 1, 2; LAIT 5; LAW; LAWS 1; MTCW 1, 2; RGWL 2; SSFS 14; TWA; WLIT 1

**Vasiliu, George**
See Bacovia, George

**Vasiliu, Gheorghe**
See Bacovia, George
See also CA 189

**Vassa, Gustavus**
See Equiano, Olaudah

**Vassilikos, Vassilis** 1933- ................. **CLC 4, 8**
See also CA 81-84; CANR 75

**Vaughan, Henry** 1621-1695 ................. **LC 27**
See also BRW 2; DLB 131; PAB; RGEL 2

**Vaughn, Stephanie** ........................... **CLC 62**

**Vazov, Ivan (Minchov)** 1850-1921 . **TCLC 25**
See also CA 167; CDWLB 4; DLB 147

**Veblen, Thorstein B(unde)**
1857-1929 ................................ **TCLC 31**
See also AMWS 1; CA 165; DLB 246

**Vega, Lope de** 1562-1635 .... **HLCS 2; LC 23**
See also EW 2; RGWL 2, 3

**Vendler, Helen (Hennessy)** 1933- ... **CLC 138**
See also CA 41-44R; CANR 25, 72; MTCW 1, 2

**Venison, Alfred**
See Pound, Ezra (Weston Loomis)

**Verdi, Marie de**
See Mencken, H(enry) L(ouis)

**Verdu, Matilde**
See Cela, Camilo Jose

**Verga, Giovanni (Carmelo)**
1840-1922 ................... **SSC 21; TCLC 3**
See also CA 123; CANR 101; EW 7; RGSF 2; RGWL 2, 3

**Vergil** 70B.C.-19B.C. ... **CMLC 9, 40; PC 12; WLCS**
See Virgil
See also AW 2; DA; DAB; DAC; DAM MST, POET; EFS 1

**Verhaeren, Emile (Adolphe Gustave)**
1855-1916 ................................ **TCLC 12**
See also GFL 1789 to the Present

**Verlaine, Paul (Marie)** 1844-1896 .. **NCLC 2, 51; PC 2, 32**
See also DAM POET; DLB 217; EW 7; GFL 1789 to the Present; RGWL 2, 3; TWA

**Verne, Jules (Gabriel)** 1828-1905 ... **TCLC 6, 52**
See also AAYA 16; BYA 4; CA 131; DLB 123; GFL 1789 to the Present; JRDA; LAIT 2; MAICYA 1, 2; RGWL 2, 3; SATA 21; SCFW; SFW 4; TWA; WCH

**Verus, Marcus Annius**
See Aurelius, Marcus

**Very, Jones** 1813-1880 ..................... **NCLC 9**
See also DLB 1, 243; RGAL 4

**Vesaas, Tarjei** 1897-1970 ................. **CLC 48**
See also CA 190; EW 11; RGWL 3

**Vialis, Gaston**
See Simenon, Georges (Jacques Christian)

**Vian, Boris** 1920-1959 .................. **TCLC 9**
See also CA 164; CANR 111; DLB 72; GFL 1789 to the Present; MTCW 2; RGWL 2, 3

**Viaud, (Louis Marie) Julien** 1850-1923
See Loti, Pierre

**Vicar, Henry**
See Felsen, Henry Gregor

**Vicker, Angus**
See Felsen, Henry Gregor

**Vidal, Gore** 1925- ...... **CLC 2, 4, 6, 8, 10, 22, 33, 72, 142**
See Box, Edgar
See also AITN 1; AMWS 4; BEST 90:2; BPFB 3; CA 5-8R; CAD; CANR 13, 45, 65, 100; CD 5; CDALBS; CN 7; CPW; DAM NOV, POP; DFS 2; DLB 6, 152; INT CANR-13; MTCW 1, 2; RGAL 4; RHW; TUS

**Viereck, Peter (Robert Edwin)** 1916- ........................... **CLC 4; PC 27**
See also CA 1-4R; CANR 1, 47; CP 7; DLB 5; PFS 9, 14

**Vigny, Alfred (Victor) de** 1797-1863 ............. **NCLC 7, 102; PC 26**
See also DAM POET; DLB 119, 192, 217; EW 5; GFL 1789 to the Present; RGWL 2, 3

**Vilakazi, Benedict Wallet** 1906-1947 ................................ **TCLC 37**
See also CA 168

**Villa, Jose Garcia** 1914-1997 .... **AAL; PC 22**
See also CA 25-28R; CANR 12; EXPP

**Villarreal, Jose Antonio** 1924- ........... **HLC 2**
See also CA 133; CANR 93; DAM MULT; DLB 82; HW 1; LAIT 4; RGAL 4

**Villaurrutia, Xavier** 1903-1950 ...... **TCLC 80**
See also CA 192; HW 1; LAW

**Villaverde, Cirilo** 1812-1894 ........ **NCLC 121**
See also LAW

**Villehardouin, Geoffroi de** 1150(?)-1218(?) ....................... **CMLC 38**

**Villiers de l'Isle Adam, Jean Marie Mathias Philippe Auguste** 1838-1889 ... **NCLC 3; SSC 14**
See also DLB 123, 192; GFL 1789 to the Present; RGSF 2

**Villon, Francois** 1431-1463(?) . **LC 62; PC 13**
See also DLB 208; EW 2; RGWL 2, 3; TWA

**Vine, Barbara** .................................. **CLC 50**
See Rendell, Ruth (Barbara)
See also BEST 90:4

**Vinge, Joan (Carol) D(ennison)** 1948- ............................. **CLC 30; SSC 24**
See also AAYA 32; BPFB 3; CA 93-96; CANR 72; SATA 36, 113; SFW 4; YAW

**Viola, Herman J(oseph)** 1938- ........... **CLC 70**
See also CA 61-64; CANR 8, 23, 48, 91; SATA 126

**Violis, G.**
See Simenon, Georges (Jacques Christian)

**Viramontes, Helena Maria** 1954- .... **HLCS 2**
See also CA 159; DLB 122; HW 2

**Virgil**
See Vergil
See also CDWLB 1; DLB 211; LAIT 1; RGWL 2, 3; WP

**Visconti, Luchino** 1906-1976 ............. **CLC 16**
See also CA 81-84; CANR 39

**Vittorini, Elio** 1908-1966 .......... **CLC 6, 9, 14**
See also CA 133; DLB 264; EW 12; RGWL 2, 3

**Vivekananda, Swami** 1863-1902 .... **TCLC 88**

**Vizenor, Gerald Robert** 1934- ....... **CLC 103; NNAL**
See also CA 13-16R; CAAE 205; CAAS 22; CANR 5, 21, 44, 67; DAM MULT; DLB 175, 227; MTCW 2; TCWW 2

**Vizinczey, Stephen** 1933- ................... **CLC 40**
See also CA 128; CCA 1; INT 128

**Vliet, R(ussell) G(ordon)** 1929-1984 ........................... **CLC 22**
See also CA 37-40R; CANR 18

**Vogau, Boris Andreyevich** 1894-1937(?)
See Pilnyak, Boris

**Vogel, Paula A(nne)** 1951- ... **CLC 76; DC 19**
See also CA 108; CAD; CD 5; CWD; DFS 14; RGAL 4

**Voigt, Cynthia** 1942- ........................... **CLC 30**
See also AAYA 3, 30; BYA 1, 3, 6, 7, 8; CA 106; CANR 18, 37, 40, 94; CLR 13, 48; INT CANR-18; JRDA; LAIT 5; MAICYA 1, 2; MAICYAS 1; SATA 48, 79, 116; SATA-Brief 33; WYA; YAW

**Voigt, Ellen Bryant** 1943- .................. **CLC 54**
See also CA 69-72; CANR 11, 29, 55; CP 7; CSW; CWP; DLB 120

**Voinovich, Vladimir (Nikolaevich)** 1932- ............................. **CLC 10, 49, 147**
See also CA 81-84; CAAS 12; CANR 33, 67; MTCW 1

**Vollmann, William T.** 1959- ............... **CLC 89**
See also CA 134; CANR 67; CPW; DAM NOV, POP; MTCW 2

**Voloshinov, V. N.**
See Bakhtin, Mikhail Mikhailovich

**Voltaire** 1694-1778 ......... **LC 14, 79; SSC 12; WLC**
See also BYA 13; DA; DAB; DAC; DAM DRAM, MST; EW 4; GFL Beginnings to 1789; NFS 7; RGWL 2, 3; TWA

**von Aschendrof, Baron Ignatz**
See Ford, Ford Madox

**von Chamisso, Adelbert**
See Chamisso, Adelbert von

**von Daeniken, Erich** 1935- ................ **CLC 30**
See also AITN 1; CA 37-40R; CANR 17, 44

**von Daniken, Erich**
See von Daeniken, Erich

**von Hartmann, Eduard** 1842-1906 ................................ **TCLC 96**

**von Hayek, Friedrich August**
See Hayek, F(riedrich) A(ugust von)

**von Heidenstam, (Carl Gustaf) Verner**
See Heidenstam, (Carl Gustaf) Verner von

**von Heyse, Paul (Johann Ludwig)**
See Heyse, Paul (Johann Ludwig von)

**von Hofmannsthal, Hugo**
See Hofmannsthal, Hugo von

**von Horvath, Odon**
See von Horvath, Odon

**von Horvath, Odon**
See von Horvath, Odon

**von Horvath, Odon** 1901-1938 ....... **TCLC 45**
See von Horvath, Oedoen
See also CA 194; DLB 85, 124; RGWL 2, 3

**von Horvath, Oedoen**
See von Horvath, Odon
See also CA 184

**von Kleist, Heinrich**
See Kleist, Heinrich von

**von Liliencron, (Friedrich Adolf Axel) Detlev**
See Liliencron, (Friedrich Adolf Axel) Detlev von

**Vonnegut, Kurt, Jr.** 1922- . **CLC 1, 2, 3, 4, 5, 8, 12, 22, 40, 60, 111; SSC 8; WLC**
See also AAYA 6, 44; AITN 1; AMWS 2; BEST 90:4; BPFB 3; BYA 3, 14; CA 1-4R; CANR 1, 25, 49, 75, 92; CDALB 1968-1988; CN 7; CPW 1; DA; DAB; DAC; DAM MST, NOV, POP; DLB 2, 8, 152; DLBD 3; DLBY 1980; EXPN; EXPS; LAIT 4; MTCW 1, 2; NFS 3; RGAL 4; SCFW; SFW 4; SSFS 5; TUS; YAW

**Von Rachen, Kurt**
See Hubbard, L(afayette) Ron(ald)

**von Rezzori (d'Arezzo), Gregor**
See Rezzori (d'Arezzo), Gregor von

**von Sternberg, Josef**
See Sternberg, Josef von

**Vorster, Gordon** 1924- ...................... **CLC 34**
See also CA 133

**Vosce, Trudie**
See Ozick, Cynthia

**Voznesensky, Andrei (Andreievich)** 1933- ............................ **CLC 1, 15, 57**
See also CA 89-92; CANR 37; CWW 2; DAM POET; MTCW 1

**Wace, Robert** c. 1100-c. 1175 ........ **CMLC 55**
See also DLB 146

**Waddington, Miriam** 1917- ............... **CLC 28**
See also CA 21-24R; CANR 12, 30; CCA 1; CP 7; DLB 68

**Wagman, Fredrica** 1937- .................... **CLC 7**
See also CA 97-100; INT 97-100

**Wagner, Linda W.**
See Wagner-Martin, Linda (C.)

**Wagner, Linda Welshimer**
See Wagner-Martin, Linda (C.)

**Wagner, Richard** 1813-1883 ..... **NCLC 9, 119**
See also DLB 129; EW 6

**Wagner-Martin, Linda (C.)** 1936- .... **CLC 50**
See also CA 159

**Wagoner, David (Russell)** 1926- .... **CLC 3, 5, 15; PC 33**
See also AMWS 9; CA 1-4R; CAAS 3; CANR 2, 71; CN 7; CP 7; DLB 5, 256; SATA 14; TCWW 2

**Wah, Fred(erick James)** 1939- ......... **CLC 44**
See also CA 141; CP 7; DLB 60

**Wahloo, Per** 1926-1975 ....................... **CLC 7**
See also BPFB 3; CA 61-64; CANR 73; CMW 4; MSW

**Wahloo, Peter**
See Wahloo, Per

**Wain, John (Barrington)** 1925-1994 . **CLC 2, 11, 15, 46**
See also CA 5-8R; CAAS 4; CANR 23, 54; CDBLB 1960 to Present; DLB 15, 27, 139, 155; MTCW 1, 2

**Wajda, Andrzej** 1926- ........................ **CLC 16**
See also CA 102

**Wakefield, Dan** 1932- .......................... **CLC 7**
See also CA 21-24R; CAAS 7; CN 7

**Wakefield, Herbert Russell** 1888-1965 ............................... **TCLC 120**
See also CA 5-8R; CANR 77; HGG; SUFW

**Wakoski, Diane** 1937- ...... **CLC 2, 4, 7, 9, 11, 40; PC 15**
See also CA 13-16R; CAAS 1; CANR 9, 60, 106; CP 7; CWP; DAM POET; DLB 5; INT CANR-9; MTCW 2

**Wakoski-Sherbell, Diane**
See Wakoski, Diane

**Walcott, Derek (Alton)** 1930- ... **BLC 3; CLC 2, 4, 9, 14, 25, 42, 67, 76, 160; DC 7**
See also BW 2; CA 89-92; CANR 26, 47, 75, 80; CBD; CD 5; CDWLB 3; CP 7; DAB; DAC; DAM MST, MULT, POET; DLB 117; DLBY 1981; DNFS 1; EFS 1; MTCW 1, 2; PFS 6; RGEL 2; TWA

**Waldman, Anne (Lesley)** 1945- .......... **CLC 7**
See also BG 3; CA 37-40R; CAAS 17; CANR 34, 69; CP 7; CWP; DLB 16

**Waldo, E. Hunter**
See Sturgeon, Theodore (Hamilton)

**Waldo, Edward Hamilton**
See Sturgeon, Theodore (Hamilton)

**Walker, Alice (Malsenior)** 1944- ........ **BLC 3; CLC 5, 6, 9, 19, 27, 46, 58, 103, 167; PC 30; SSC 5; WLCS**
See also AAYA 3, 33; AFAW 1, 2; AMWS 3; BEST 89:4; BPFB 3; BW 2, 3; CA 37-40R; CANR 9, 27, 49, 66, 82; CDALB 1968-1988; CN 7; CPW; CSW; DA; DAB; DAC; DAM MST, MULT, NOV, POET, POP; DLB 6, 33, 143; EXPN; EXPS; FW; INT CANR-27; LAIT 3; MAWW; MTCW 1, 2; NFS 5; RGAL 4; RGSF 2; SATA 31; SSFS 2, 11; TUS; YAW

**Walker, David Harry** 1911-1992 ...... **CLC 14**
See also CA 1-4R; CANR 1; CWRI 5; SATA 8; SATA-Obit 71

**Walker, Edward Joseph** 1934-
See Walker, Ted
See also CA 21-24R; CANR 12, 28, 53; CP 7

**Walker, George F.** 1947- ............. **CLC 44, 61**
See also CA 103; CANR 21, 43, 59; CD 5; DAB; DAC; DAM MST; DLB 60

**Walker, Joseph A.** 1935- .................... **CLC 19**
See also BW 1, 3; CA 89-92; CAD; CANR 26; CD 5; DAM DRAM, MST; DFS 12; DLB 38

**Walker, Margaret (Abigail)** 1915-1998 ........ **BLC; CLC 1, 6; PC 20; TCLC 129**
See also AFAW 1, 2; BW 2, 3; CA 73-76; CANR 26, 54, 76; CN 7; CP 7; CSW; DAM MULT; DLB 76, 152; EXPP; FW; MTCW 1, 2; RGAL 4; RHW

**Walker, Ted** ........................................ **CLC 13**
See Walker, Edward Joseph
See also DLB 40

**Wallace, David Foster** 1962- ..... **CLC 50, 114**
See also AMWS 10; CA 132; CANR 59; MTCW 2

**Wallace, Dexter**
See Masters, Edgar Lee

**Wallace, (Richard Horatio) Edgar** 1875-1932 ................................ **TCLC 57**
See also CMW 4; DLB 70; MSW; RGEL 2

**Wallace, Irving** 1916-1990 ............ **CLC 7, 13**
See also AITN 1; BPFB 3; CA 1-4R; CAAS 1; CANR 1, 27; CPW; DAM NOV, POP; INT CANR-27; MTCW 1, 2

**Wallant, Edward Lewis** 1926-1962 ... **CLC 5, 10**
See also CA 1-4R; CANR 22; DLB 2, 28, 143; MTCW 1, 2; RGAL 4

**Wallas, Graham** 1858-1932 ............. **TCLC 91**

**Waller, Edmund** 1606-1687 ................. **LC 86**
See also BRW 2; DAM POET; DLB 126; PAB; RGEL 2

**Walley, Byron**
See Card, Orson Scott

**Walpole, Horace** 1717-1797 ............. **LC 2, 49**
See also BRW 3; DLB 39, 104, 213; HGG; RGEL 2; SUFW 1; TEA

**Walpole, Hugh (Seymour)** 1884-1941 ...................... **TCLC 5**
See also CA 165; DLB 34; HGG; MTCW 2; RGEL 2; RHW

**Walser, Martin** 1927- .......................... **CLC 27**
See also CA 57-60; CANR 8, 46; CWW 2; DLB 75, 124

**Walser, Robert** 1878-1956 ..... **SSC 20; TCLC 18**
See also CA 165; CANR 100; DLB 66

**Walsh, Gillian Paton**
See Paton Walsh, Gillian

**Walsh, Jill Paton** .............................. **CLC 35**
See Paton Walsh, Gillian
See also CLR 2, 65; WYA

**Walter, Villiam Christian**
See Andersen, Hans Christian

**Walther von der Vogelweide** c. 1170-1228 ................................ **CMLC 56**

**Walton, Izaak** 1593-1683 .................... **LC 72**
See also BRW 2; CDBLB Before 1660; DLB 151, 213; RGEL 2

**Wambaugh, Joseph (Aloysius, Jr.)** 1937- ............................................. **CLC 3, 18**
See also AITN 1; BEST 89:3; BPFB 3; CA 33-36R; CANR 42, 65; CMW 4; CPW 1; DAM NOV, POP; DLB 6; DLBY 1983; MSW; MTCW 1, 2

**Wang Wei** 699(?)-761(?) ...................... **PC 18**
See also TWA

**Ward, Arthur Henry Sarsfield** 1883-1959
See Rohmer, Sax
See also CA 173; CMW 4; HGG

**Ward, Douglas Turner** 1930- ............ **CLC 19**
See also BW 1; CA 81-84; CAD; CANR 27; CD 5; DLB 7, 38

**Ward, E. D.**
See Lucas, E(dward) V(errall)

**Ward, Mrs. Humphry** 1851-1920
See Ward, Mary Augusta
See also RGEL 2

**Ward, Mary Augusta** 1851-1920 ... **TCLC 55**
See Ward, Mrs. Humphry
See also DLB 18

**Ward, Peter**
See Faust, Frederick (Schiller)

**Warhol, Andy** 1928(?)-1987 ............... **CLC 20**
See also AAYA 12; BEST 89:4; CA 89-92; CANR 34

**Warner, Francis (Robert le Plastrier)** 1937- ............................................. **CLC 14**
See also CA 53-56; CANR 11

**Warner, Marina** 1946- ......................... **CLC 59**
See also CA 65-68; CANR 21, 55; CN 7; DLB 194

**Warner, Rex (Ernest)** 1905-1986 ...... **CLC 45**
See also CA 89-92; DLB 15; RGEL 2; RHW

**Warner, Susan (Bogert)** 1819-1885 ................................ **NCLC 31**
See also DLB 3, 42, 239, 250, 254

**Warner, Sylvia (Constance) Ashton**
See Ashton-Warner, Sylvia (Constance)

**Warner, Sylvia Townsend** 1893-1978 .. **CLC 7, 19; SSC 23; TCLC 131**
See also BRWS 7; CA 61-64; CANR 16, 60, 104; DLB 34, 139; FANT; FW; MTCW 1, 2; RGEL 2; RGSF 2; RHW

**Warren, Mercy Otis** 1728-1814 ..... **NCLC 13**
See also DLB 31, 200; RGAL 4; TUS

**Warren, Robert Penn** 1905-1989 .. **CLC 1, 4, 6, 8, 10, 13, 18, 39, 53, 59; PC 37; SSC 4, 58; WLC**
See also AITN 1; AMW; BPFB 3; BYA 1; CA 13-16R; CANR 10, 47; CDALB 1968-1988; DA; DAB; DAC; DAM MST, NOV, POET; DLB 2, 48, 152; DLBY 1980, 1989; INT CANR-10; MTCW 1, 2; NFS 13; RGAL 4; RGSF 2; RHW; SATA 46; SATA-Obit 63; SSFS 8; TUS

**Warshofsky, Isaac**
See Singer, Isaac Bashevis

**Warton, Joseph** 1722-1800 ........... **NCLC 118**
See also DLB 104, 109; RGEL 2

**Warton, Thomas** 1728-1790 .......... **LC 15, 82**
See also DAM POET; DLB 104, 109; RGEL 2

**Waruk, Kona**
See Harris, (Theodore) Wilson

**Warung, Price** ................................ **TCLC 45**
See Astley, William
See also DLB 230; RGEL 2

**Warwick, Jarvis**
See Garner, Hugh
See also CCA 1

**Washington, Alex**
See Harris, Mark

**Washington, Booker T(aliaferro)** 1856-1915 ................... **BLC 3; TCLC 10**
See also BW 1; CA 125; DAM MULT; LAIT 2; RGAL 4; SATA 28

**Washington, George** 1732-1799 ........... **LC 25**
See also DLB 31

**Wassermann, (Karl) Jakob** 1873-1934 .................................. **TCLC 6**
See also CA 163; DLB 66

**Wasserstein, Wendy** 1950- .. **CLC 32, 59, 90; DC 4**
See also CA 129; CABS 3; CAD; CANR 53, 75; CD 5; CWD; DAM DRAM; DFS 5; DLB 228; FW; INT CA-129; MTCW 2; SATA 94

**Waterhouse, Keith (Spencer)** 1929- . **CLC 47**
See also CA 5-8R; CANR 38, 67, 109; CBD; CN 7; DLB 13, 15; MTCW 1, 2

**Waters, Frank (Joseph)** 1902-1995 .. **CLC 88**
See also CA 5-8R; CAAS 13; CANR 3, 18, 63; DLB 212; DLBY 1986; RGAL 4; TCWW 2

**Waters, Mary C.** ................................ **CLC 70**

**Waters, Roger** 1944- .......................... **CLC 35**

**Watkins, Frances Ellen**
See Harper, Frances Ellen Watkins

**Watkins, Gerrold**
See Malzberg, Barry N(athaniel)

**Watkins, Gloria Jean** 1952(?)-
See hooks, bell
See also BW 2; CA 143; CANR 87; MTCW 2; SATA 115

**Watkins, Paul** 1964- .......................... **CLC 55**
See also CA 132; CANR 62, 98

**Watkins, Vernon Phillips** 1906-1967 ................................. **CLC 43**
See also CA 9-10; CAP 1; DLB 20; RGEL 2

**Watson, Irving S.**
See Mencken, H(enry) L(ouis)

**Watson, John H.**
See Farmer, Philip Jose

**Watson, Richard F.**
See Silverberg, Robert

**Waugh, Auberon (Alexander)** 1939-2001 ................................... **CLC 7**
See also CA 45-48; CANR 6, 22, 92; DLB 14, 194

**Waugh, Evelyn (Arthur St. John)** 1903-1966 .. **CLC 1, 3, 8, 13, 19, 27, 44, 107; SSC 41; WLC**
See also BPFB 3; BRW 7; CA 85-88; CANR 22; CDBLB 1914-1945; DA; DAB; DAC; DAM MST, NOV, POP; DLB 15, 162, 195; MTCW 1, 2; NFS 13; RGAL 4; RGSF 2; TEA; WLIT 4

**Waugh, Harriet** 1944- .......................... **CLC 6**
See also CA 85-88; CANR 22

**Ways, C. R.**
See Blount, Roy (Alton), Jr.

**Waystaff, Simon**
See Swift, Jonathan

**Webb, Beatrice (Martha Potter)** 1858-1943 ................................ **TCLC 22**
See also CA 162; DLB 190; FW

**Webb, Charles (Richard)** 1939- ......... **CLC 7**
See also CA 25-28R; CANR 114

**Webb, James H(enry), Jr.** 1946- ...... **CLC 22**
See also CA 81-84

**Webb, Mary Gladys (Meredith)** 1881-1927 .................................. **TCLC 24**
See also CA 182; DLB 34; FW

**Webb, Mrs. Sidney**
See Webb, Beatrice (Martha Potter)

**Webb, Phyllis** 1927- .......................... **CLC 18**
See also CA 104; CANR 23; CCA 1; CP 7; CWP; DLB 53

**Webb, Sidney (James)** 1859-1947 .. **TCLC 22**
See also CA 163; DLB 190

**Webber, Andrew Lloyd** ............... **CLC 21**
See Lloyd Webber, Andrew
See also DFS 7

**Weber, Lenora Mattingly**
1895-1971 ......................... **CLC 12**
See also CA 19-20; CAP 1; SATA 2; SATA-Obit 26

**Weber, Max** 1864-1920 ................ **TCLC 69**
See also CA 189

**Webster, John** 1580(?)-1634(?) ...... **DC 2; LC 33, 84; WLC**
See also BRW 2; CDBLB Before 1660; DA; DAB; DAC; DAM DRAM, MST; DLB 58; IDTP; RGEL 2; WLIT 3

**Webster, Noah** 1758-1843 ............. **NCLC 30**
See also DLB 1, 37, 42, 43, 73, 243

**Wedekind, (Benjamin) Frank(lin)**
1864-1918 .......................... **TCLC 7**
See also CA 153; CDWLB 2; DAM DRAM; DLB 118; EW 8; RGWL 2, 3

**Wehr, Demaris** ....................... **CLC 65**

**Weidman, Jerome** 1913-1998 ........... **CLC 7**
See also AITN 2; CA 1-4R; CAD; CANR 1; DLB 28

**Weil, Simone (Adolphine)**
1909-1943 ......................... **TCLC 23**
See also CA 159; EW 12; FW; GFL 1789 to the Present; MTCW 2

**Weininger, Otto** 1880-1903 ............ **TCLC 84**

**Weinstein, Nathan**
See West, Nathanael

**Weinstein, Nathan von Wallenstein**
See West, Nathanael

**Weir, Peter (Lindsay)** 1944- ............ **CLC 20**
See also CA 123

**Weiss, Peter (Ulrich)** 1916-1982 .. **CLC 3, 15, 51**
See also CA 45-48; CANR 3; DAM DRAM; DFS 3; DLB 69, 124; RGWL 2, 3

**Weiss, Theodore (Russell)** 1916- ... **CLC 3, 8, 14**
See also CA 9-12R; CAAE 189; CAAS 2; CANR 46, 94; CP 7; DLB 5

**Welch, (Maurice) Denton**
1915-1948 ......................... **TCLC 22**
See also BRWS 8; CA 148; RGEL 2

**Welch, James** 1940- ... **CLC 6, 14, 52; NNAL**
See also CA 85-88; CANR 42, 66, 107; CN 7; CP 7; CPW; DAM MULT, POP; DLB 175, 256; RGAL 4; TCWW 2

**Weldon, Fay** 1931- . **CLC 6, 9, 11, 19, 36, 59, 122**
See also BRWS 4; CA 21-24R; CANR 16, 46, 63, 97; CDBLB 1960 to Present; CN 7; CPW; DAM POP; DLB 14, 194; FW; HGG; INT CANR-16; MTCW 1, 2; RGEL 2; RGSF 2

**Wellek, Rene** 1903-1995 ............... **CLC 28**
See also CA 5-8R; CAAS 7; CANR 8; DLB 63; INT CANR-8

**Weller, Michael** 1942- ................. **CLC 10, 53**
See also CA 85-88; CAD; CD 5

**Weller, Paul** 1958- .................... **CLC 26**

**Wellershoff, Dieter** 1925- ............. **CLC 46**
See also CA 89-92; CANR 16, 37

**Welles, (George) Orson** 1915-1985 .. **CLC 20, 80**
See also AAYA 40; CA 93-96

**Wellman, John McDowell** 1945-
See Wellman, Mac
See also CA 166; CD 5

**Wellman, Mac** ........................ **CLC 65**
See Wellman, John McDowell; Wellman, John McDowell
See also CAD; RGAL 4

**Wellman, Manly Wade** 1903-1986 ... **CLC 49**
See also CA 1-4R; CANR 6, 16, 44; FANT; SATA 6; SATA-Obit 47; SFW 4; SUFW

**Wells, Carolyn** 1869(?)-1942 ......... **TCLC 35**
See also CA 185; CMW 4; DLB 11

**Wells, H(erbert) G(eorge)**
1866-1946 ....... **SSC 6; TCLC 6, 12, 19; WLC**
See also AAYA 18; BPFB 3; BRW 6; CA 121; CDBLB 1914-1945; CLR 64; DA; DAB; DAC; DAM MST, NOV; DLB 34, 70, 156, 178; EXPS; HGG; LAIT 3; MTCW 1, 2; RGEL 2; RGSF 2; SATA 20; SCFW 1; SFW 4; SSFS 3; SUFW; TEA; WCH; WLIT 4; YAW

**Wells, Rosemary** 1943- ................ **CLC 12**
See also AAYA 13; BYA 7, 8; CA 85-88; CANR 48; CLR 16, 69; CWRI 5; MAICYA 1, 2; SAAS 1; SATA 18, 69, 114; YAW

**Wells-Barnett, Ida B(ell)**
1862-1931 ........................ **TCLC 125**
See also CA 182; DLB 23, 221

**Welsh, Irvine** 1958- ................... **CLC 144**
See also CA 173; DLB 271

**Welty, Eudora (Alice)** 1909-2001 .. **CLC 1, 2, 5, 14, 22, 33, 105; SSC 1, 27, 51; WLC**
See also AMW; AMWR 1; BPFB 3; CA 9-12R; CABS 1; CANR 32, 65; CDALB 1941-1968; CN 7; CSW; DA; DAB; DAC; DAM MST, NOV; DLB 2, 102, 143; DLBD 12; DLBY 1987, 2001; EXPS; HGG; LAIT 3; MAWW; MTCW 1, 2; NFS 13, 15; RGAL 4; RGSF 2; RHW; SSFS 2, 10; TUS

**Wen I-to** 1899-1946 .................. **TCLC 28**

**Wentworth, Robert**
See Hamilton, Edmond

**Werfel, Franz (Viktor)** 1890-1945 ... **TCLC 8**
See also CA 161; DLB 81, 124; RGWL 2, 3

**Wergeland, Henrik Arnold**
1808-1845 ......................... **NCLC 5**

**Wersba, Barbara** 1932- ................ **CLC 30**
See also AAYA 2, 30; BYA 6, 12, 13; CA 29-32R, 182; CAAE 182; CANR 16, 38; CLR 3, 78; DLB 52; JRDA; MAICYA 1, 2; SAAS 2; SATA 1, 58; SATA-Essay 103; WYA; YAW

**Wertmueller, Lina** 1928- ............... **CLC 16**
See also CA 97-100; CANR 39, 78

**Wescott, Glenway** 1901-1987 .. **CLC 13; SSC 35**
See also CA 13-16R; CANR 23, 70; DLB 4, 9, 102; RGAL 4

**Wesker, Arnold** 1932- ................ **CLC 3, 5, 42**
See also CA 1-4R; CAAS 7; CANR 1, 33; CBD; CD 5; CDBLB 1960 to Present; DAB; DAM DRAM; DLB 13; MTCW 1; RGEL 2; TEA

**Wesley, Richard (Errol)** 1945- ........... **CLC 7**
See also BW 1; CA 57-60; CAD; CANR 27; CD 5; DLB 38

**Wessel, Johan Herman** 1742-1785 ........ **LC 7**

**West, Anthony (Panther)**
1914-1987 ......................... **CLC 50**
See also CA 45-48; CANR 3, 19; DLB 15

**West, C. P.**
See Wodehouse, P(elham) G(renville)

**West, Cornel (Ronald)** 1953- .... **BLCS; CLC 134**
See also CA 144; CANR 91; DLB 246

**West, Delno C(loyde), Jr.** 1936- ........ **CLC 70**
See also CA 57-60

**West, Dorothy** 1907-1998 .. **HR 3; TCLC 108**
See also BW 2; CA 143; DLB 76

**West, (Mary) Jessamyn** 1902-1984 ... **CLC 7, 17**
See also CA 9-12R; CANR 27; DLB 6; DLBY 1984; MTCW 1, 2; RGAL 4; RHW; SATA-Obit 37; TCWW 2; TUS; YAW

**West, Morris L(anglo)** 1916-1999 ..... **CLC 6, 33**
See also BPFB 3; CA 5-8R; CANR 24, 49, 64; CN 7; CPW; MTCW 1, 2

**West, Nathanael** 1903-1940 .. **SSC 16; TCLC 1, 14, 44**
See also AMW; AMWR 2; BPFB 3; CA 125; CDALB 1929-1941; DLB 4, 9, 28; MTCW 1, 2; NFS 16; RGAL 4; TUS

**West, Owen**
See Koontz, Dean R(ay)

**West, Paul** 1930- ..................... **CLC 7, 14, 96**
See also CA 13-16R; CAAS 7; CANR 22, 53, 76, 89; CN 7; DLB 14; INT CANR-22; MTCW 2

**West, Rebecca** 1892-1983 ... **CLC 7, 9, 31, 50**
See also BPFB 3; BRWS 3; CA 5-8R; CANR 19; DLB 36; DLBY 1983; FW; MTCW 1, 2; NCFS 4; RGEL 2; TEA

**Westall, Robert (Atkinson)**
1929-1993 ......................... **CLC 17**
See also AAYA 12; BYA 2, 6, 7, 8, 9; CA 69-72; CANR 18, 68; CLR 13; FANT; JRDA; MAICYA 1, 2; MAICYAS 1; SAAS 2; SATA 23, 69; SATA-Obit 75; WYA; YAW

**Westermarck, Edward** 1862-1939 . **TCLC 87**

**Westlake, Donald E(dwin)** 1933- . **CLC 7, 33**
See also BPFB 3; CA 17-20R; CAAS 13; CANR 16, 44, 65, 94; CMW 4; CPW; DAM POP; INT CANR-16; MSW; MTCW 2

**Westmacott, Mary**
See Christie, Agatha (Mary Clarissa)

**Weston, Allen**
See Norton, Andre

**Wetcheek, J. L.**
See Feuchtwanger, Lion

**Wetering, Janwillem van de**
See van de Wetering, Janwillem

**Wetherald, Agnes Ethelwyn**
1857-1940 ......................... **TCLC 81**
See also CA 202; DLB 99

**Wetherell, Elizabeth**
See Warner, Susan (Bogert)

**Whale, James** 1889-1957 ............... **TCLC 63**

**Whalen, Philip** 1923-2002 ............. **CLC 6, 29**
See also BG 3; CA 9-12R; CANR 5, 39; CP 7; DLB 16; WP

**Wharton, Edith (Newbold Jones)**
1862-1937 ... **SSC 6; TCLC 3, 9, 27, 53, 129; WLC**
See also AAYA 25; AMW; AMWR 1; BPFB 3; CA 132; CDALB 1865-1917; DA; DAB; DAC; DAM MST, NOV; DLB 4, 9, 12, 78, 189; DLBD 13; EXPS; HGG; LAIT 2, 3; MAWW; MTCW 1, 2; NFS 5, 11, 15; RGAL 4; RGSF 2; RHW; SSFS 6, 7; SUFW; TUS

**Wharton, James**
See Mencken, H(enry) L(ouis)

**Wharton, William (a pseudonym)** . **CLC 18, 37**
See also CA 93-96; DLBY 1980; INT 93-96

**Wheatley (Peters), Phillis**
1753(?)-1784 ... **BLC 3; LC 3, 50; PC 3; WLC**
See also AFAW 1, 2; CDALB 1640-1865; DA; DAC; DAM MST, MULT, POET; DLB 31, 50; EXPP; PFS 13; RGAL 4

**Wheelock, John Hall** 1886-1978 ....... **CLC 14**
See also CA 13-16R; CANR 14; DLB 45

**White, Babington**
See Braddon, Mary Elizabeth
**White, E(lwyn) B(rooks)**
1899-1985 .................. **CLC 10, 34, 39**
See also AITN 2; AMWS 1; CA 13-16R; CANR 16, 37; CDALBS; CLR 1, 21; CPW; DAM POP; DLB 11, 22; FANT; MAICYA 1, 2; MTCW 1, 2; RGAL 4; SATA 2, 29, 100; SATA-Obit 44; TUS
**White, Edmund (Valentine III)**
1940- ................... **CLC 27, 110**
See also AAYA 7; CA 45-48; CANR 3, 19, 36, 62, 107; CN 7; DAM POP; DLB 227; MTCW 1, 2
**White, Hayden V.** 1928- .................. **CLC 148**
See also CA 128; DLB 246
**White, Patrick (Victor Martindale)**
1912-1990 ...... **CLC 3, 4, 5, 7, 9, 18, 65, 69; SSC 39**
See also BRWS 1; CA 81-84; CANR 43; DLB 260; MTCW 1; RGEL 2; RGSF 2; RHW; TWA
**White, Phyllis Dorothy James** 1920-
See James, P. D.
See also CA 21-24R; CANR 17, 43, 65, 112; CMW 4; CN 7; CPW; DAM POP; MTCW 1, 2; TEA
**White, T(erence) H(anbury)**
1906-1964 .................. **CLC 30**
See also AAYA 22; BPFB 3; BYA 4, 5; CA 73-76; CANR 37; DLB 160; FANT; JRDA; LAIT 1; MAICYA 1, 2; RGEL 2; SATA 12; SUFW 1; YAW
**White, Terence de Vere** 1912-1994 ... **CLC 49**
See also CA 49-52; CANR 3
**White, Walter**
See White, Walter F(rancis)
**White, Walter F(rancis)** 1893-1955 ... **BLC 3; HR 3; TCLC 15**
See also BW 1; CA 124; DAM MULT; DLB 51
**White, William Hale** 1831-1913
See Rutherford, Mark
See also CA 189
**Whitehead, Alfred North**
1861-1947 .................. **TCLC 97**
See also CA 165; DLB 100, 262
**Whitehead, E(dward) A(nthony)**
1933- .................. **CLC 5**
See also CA 65-68; CANR 58; CBD; CD 5
**Whitehead, Ted**
See Whitehead, E(dward) A(nthony)
**Whitemore, Hugh (John)** 1936- ....... **CLC 37**
See also CA 132; CANR 77; CBD; CD 5; INT CA-132
**Whitman, Sarah Helen (Power)**
1803-1878 .................. **NCLC 19**
See also DLB 1, 243
**Whitman, Walt(er)** 1819-1892 .. **NCLC 4, 31, 81; PC 3; WLC**
See also AAYA 42; AMW; AMWR 1; CDALB 1640-1865; DA; DAB; DAC; DAM MST, POET; DLB 3, 64, 224, 250; EXPP; LAIT 2; PAB; PFS 2, 3, 13; RGAL 4; SATA 20; TUS; WP; WYAS 1
**Whitney, Phyllis A(yame)** 1903- ....... **CLC 42**
See also AAYA 36; AITN 2; BEST 90:3; CA 1-4R; CANR 3, 25, 38, 60; CLR 59; CMW 4; CPW; DAM POP; JRDA; MAICYA 1, 2; MTCW 2; RHW; SATA 1, 30; YAW
**Whittemore, (Edward) Reed (Jr.)**
1919- .................. **CLC 4**
See also CA 9-12R; CAAS 8; CANR 4; CP 7; DLB 5
**Whittier, John Greenleaf**
1807-1892 .................. **NCLC 8, 59**
See also AMWS 1; DLB 1, 243; RGAL 4
**Whittlebot, Hernia**
See Coward, Noel (Peirce)

**Wicker, Thomas Grey** 1926-
See Wicker, Tom
See also CA 65-68; CANR 21, 46
**Wicker, Tom** .................. **CLC 7**
See Wicker, Thomas Grey
**Wideman, John Edgar** 1941- ... **BLC 3; CLC 5, 34, 36, 67, 122**
See also AFAW 1, 2; AMWS 10; BPFB 4; BW 2, 3; CA 85-88; CANR 14, 42, 67, 109; CN 7; DAM MULT; DLB 33, 143; MTCW 2; RGAL 4; RGSF 2; SSFS 6, 12
**Wiebe, Rudy (Henry)** 1934- .. **CLC 6, 11, 14, 138**
See also CA 37-40R; CANR 42, 67; CN 7; DAC; DAM MST; DLB 60; RHW
**Wieland, Christoph Martin**
1733-1813 .................. **NCLC 17**
See also DLB 97; EW 4; RGWL 2, 3
**Wiene, Robert** 1881-1938 .................. **TCLC 56**
**Wieners, John** 1934- .................. **CLC 7**
See also BG 3; CA 13-16R; CP 7; DLB 16; WP
**Wiesel, Elie(zer)** 1928- ....... **CLC 3, 5, 11, 37, 165; WLCS**
See also AAYA 7; AITN 1; CA 5-8R; CAAS 4; CANR 8, 40, 65; CDALBS; DA; DAB; DAC; DAM MST, NOV; DLB 83; DLBY 1987; INT CANR-8; LAIT 4; MTCW 1, 2; NCFS 4; NFS 4; RGWL 3; SATA 56; YAW
**Wiggins, Marianne** 1947- .................. **CLC 57**
See also BEST 89:3; CA 130; CANR 60
**Wiggs, Susan** .................. **CLC 70**
See also CA 201
**Wight, James Alfred** 1916-1995
See Herriot, James
See also CA 77-80; SATA 55; SATA-Brief 44
**Wilbur, Richard (Purdy)** 1921- ..... **CLC 3, 6, 9, 14, 53, 110**
See also AMWS 3; CA 1-4R; CABS 2; CANR 2, 29, 76, 93; CDALBS; CP 7; DA; DAB; DAC; DAM MST, POET; DLB 5, 169; EXPP; INT CANR-29; MTCW 1, 2; PAB; PFS 11, 12, 16; RGAL 4; SATA 9, 108; WP
**Wild, Peter** 1940- .................. **CLC 14**
See also CA 37-40R; CP 7; DLB 5
**Wilde, Oscar (Fingal O'Flahertie Wills)**
1854(?)-1900 ..... **DC 17; SSC 11; TCLC 1, 8, 23, 41; WLC**
See also BRW 5; BRWR 2; CA 119; CANR 112; CDBLB 1890-1914; DA; DAB; DAC; DAM DRAM, MST, NOV; DFS 4, 8, 9; DLB 10, 19, 34, 57, 141, 156, 190; EXPS; FANT; RGEL 2; RGSF 2; SATA 24; SSFS 7; SUFW; TEA; WCH; WLIT 4
**Wilder, Billy** .................. **CLC 20**
See Wilder, Samuel
See also DLB 26
**Wilder, Samuel** 1906-2002
See Wilder, Billy
See also CA 89-92
**Wilder, Stephen**
See Marlowe, Stephen
**Wilder, Thornton (Niven)**
1897-1975 .. **CLC 1, 5, 6, 10, 15, 35, 82; DC 1; WLC**
See also AAYA 29; AITN 2; AMW; CA 13-16R; CAD; CANR 40; CDALBS; DA; DAB; DAC; DAM DRAM, MST, NOV; DFS 1, 4, 16; DLB 4, 7, 9, 228; DLBY 1997; LAIT 3; MTCW 1, 2; RGAL 4; RHW; WYAS 1
**Wilding, Michael** 1942- ...... **CLC 73; SSC 50**
See also CA 104; CANR 24, 49, 106; CN 7; RGSF 2
**Wiley, Richard** 1944- .................. **CLC 44**
See also CA 129; CANR 71

**Wilhelm, Kate** .................. **CLC 7**
See Wilhelm, Katie (Gertrude)
See also AAYA 20; CAAS 5; DLB 8; INT CANR-17; SCFW 2
**Wilhelm, Katie (Gertrude)** 1928-
See Wilhelm, Kate
See also CA 37-40R; CANR 17, 36, 60, 94; MTCW 1; SFW 4
**Wilkins, Mary**
See Freeman, Mary E(leanor) Wilkins
**Willard, Nancy** 1936- .................. **CLC 7, 37**
See also BYA 5; CA 89-92; CANR 10, 39, 68, 107; CLR 5; CWP; CWRI 5; DLB 5, 52; FANT; MAICYA 1, 2; MTCW 1; SATA 37, 71, 127; SATA-Brief 30; SUFW 2
**William of Malmesbury** c. 1090B.C.-c. 1140B.C. .................. **CMLC 57**
**William of Ockham** 1290-1349 ..... **CMLC 32**
**Williams, Ben Ames** 1889-1953 ..... **TCLC 89**
See also CA 183; DLB 102
**Williams, C(harles) K(enneth)**
1936- .................. **CLC 33, 56, 148**
See also CA 37-40R; CAAS 26; CANR 57, 106; CP 7; DAM POET; DLB 5
**Williams, Charles**
See Collier, James Lincoln
**Williams, Charles (Walter Stansby)**
1886-1945 .................. **TCLC 1, 11**
See also CA 163; DLB 100, 153, 255; FANT; RGEL 2; SUFW 1
**Williams, (George) Emlyn**
1905-1987 .................. **CLC 15**
See also CA 104; CANR 36; DAM DRAM; DLB 10, 77; MTCW 1
**Williams, Hank** 1923-1953 ............. **TCLC 81**
See also Williams, Hiram King
**Williams, Hiram Hank**
See Williams, Hank
**Williams, Hiram King**
See Williams, Hank
See also CA 188
**Williams, Hugo** 1942- ................. **CLC 42**
See also CA 17-20R; CANR 45; CP 7; DLB 40
**Williams, J. Walker**
See Wodehouse, P(elham) G(renville)
**Williams, John A(lfred)** 1925- . **BLC 3; CLC 5, 13**
See also AFAW 2; BW 2, 3; CA 53-56; CAAE 195; CAAS 3; CANR 6, 26, 51; CN 7; CSW; DAM MULT; DLB 2, 33; INT CANR-6; RGAL 4; SFW 4
**Williams, Jonathan (Chamberlain)**
1929- .................. **CLC 13**
See also CA 9-12R; CAAS 12; CANR 8, 108; CP 7; DLB 5
**Williams, Joy** 1944- .................. **CLC 31**
See also CA 41-44R; CANR 22, 48, 97
**Williams, Norman** 1952- .................. **CLC 39**
See also CA 118
**Williams, Sherley Anne** 1944-1999 ... **BLC 3; CLC 89**
See also AFAW 2; BW 2, 3; CA 73-76; CANR 25, 82; DAM MULT, POET; DLB 41; INT CANR-25; SATA 78; SATA-Obit 116
**Williams, Shirley**
See Williams, Sherley Anne
**Williams, Tennessee** 1911-1983 . **CLC 1, 2, 5, 7, 8, 11, 15, 19, 30, 39, 45, 71, 111; DC 4; WLC**
See also AAYA 31; AITN 1, 2; AMW; AMWC 1; CA 5-8R; CABS 3; CAD; CANR 31; CDALB 1941-1968; DA; DAB; DAC; DAM DRAM, MST; DFS 1, 3, 7, 12; DLB 7; DLBD 4; DLBY 1983; GLL 1; LAIT 4; MTCW 1, 2; RGAL 4; TUS

**Williams, Thomas (Alonzo)**
1926-1990 .................... CLC 14
See also CA 1-4R; CANR 2

**Williams, William C.**
See Williams, William Carlos

**Williams, William Carlos**
1883-1963 .... CLC 1, 2, 5, 9, 13, 22, 42, 67; PC 7; SSC 31
See also AAYA 46; AMW; AMWR 1; CA 89-92; CANR 34; CDALB 1917-1929; DA; DAB; DAC; DAM MST, POET; DLB 4, 16, 54, 86; EXPP; MTCW 1, 2; NCFS 4; PAB; PFS 1, 6, 11; RGAL 4; RGSF 2; TUS; WP

**Williamson, David (Keith)** 1942- ..... CLC 56
See also CA 103; CANR 41; CD 5

**Williamson, Ellen Douglas** 1905-1984
See Douglas, Ellen
See also CA 17-20R; CANR 39

**Williamson, Jack** .................... CLC 29
See Williamson, John Stewart
See also CAAS 8; DLB 8; SCFW 2

**Williamson, John Stewart** 1908-
See Williamson, Jack
See also CA 17-20R; CANR 23, 70; SFW 4

**Willie, Frederick**
See Lovecraft, H(oward) P(hillips)

**Willingham, Calder (Baynard, Jr.)**
1922-1995 .................... CLC 5, 51
See also CA 5-8R; CANR 3; CSW; DLB 2, 44; IDFW 3, 4; MTCW 1

**Willis, Charles**
See Clarke, Arthur C(harles)

**Willy**
See Colette, (Sidonie-Gabrielle)

**Willy, Colette**
See Colette, (Sidonie-Gabrielle)
See also GLL 1

**Wilmot, John** 1647-1680 .................... LC 75
See Rochester
See also BRW 2; DLB 131; PAB

**Wilson, A(ndrew) N(orman)** 1950- .. CLC 33
See also BRWS 6; CA 122; CN 7; DLB 14, 155, 194; MTCW 2

**Wilson, Angus (Frank Johnstone)**
1913-1991 . CLC 2, 3, 5, 25, 34; SSC 21
See also BRWS 1; CA 5-8R; CANR 21; DLB 15, 139, 155; MTCW 1, 2; RGEL 2; RGSF 2

**Wilson, August** 1945- ... BLC 3; CLC 39, 50, 63, 118; DC 2; WLCS
See also AAYA 16; AFAW 2; AMWS 8; BW 2, 3; CA 122; CAD; CANR 42, 54, 76; CD 5; DA; DAB; DAC; DAM DRAM, MST, MULT; DFS 15; DLB 228; LAIT 4; MTCW 1, 2; RGAL 4

**Wilson, Brian** 1942- .................... CLC 12

**Wilson, Colin** 1931- .................... CLC 3, 14
See also CA 1-4R; CAAS 5; CANR 1, 22, 33, 77; CMW 4; CN 7; DLB 14, 194; HGG; MTCW 1; SFW 4

**Wilson, Dirk**
See Pohl, Frederik

**Wilson, Edmund** 1895-1972 .. CLC 1, 2, 3, 8, 24
See also AMW; CA 1-4R; CANR 1, 46, 110; DLB 63; MTCW 1, 2; RGAL 4; TUS

**Wilson, Ethel Davis (Bryant)**
1888(?)-1980 .................... CLC 13
See also CA 102; DAC; DAM POET; DLB 68; MTCW 1; RGEL 2

**Wilson, Harriet**
See Wilson, Harriet E. Adams
See also DLB 239

**Wilson, Harriet E.**
See Wilson, Harriet E. Adams
See also DLB 243

**Wilson, Harriet E. Adams**
1827(?)-1863(?) .......... BLC 3; NCLC 78
See Wilson, Harriet; Wilson, Harriet E.
See also DAM MULT; DLB 50

**Wilson, John** 1785-1854 .................... NCLC 5

**Wilson, John (Anthony) Burgess** 1917-1993
See Burgess, Anthony
See also CA 1-4R; CANR 2, 46; DAC; DAM NOV; MTCW 1, 2; NFS 15; TEA

**Wilson, Lanford** 1937- ... CLC 7, 14, 36; DC 19
See also CA 17-20R; CABS 3; CAD; CANR 45, 96; CD 5; DAM DRAM; DFS 4, 9, 12, 16; DLB 7; TUS

**Wilson, Robert M.** 1944- .................... CLC 7, 9
See also CA 49-52; CAD; CANR 2, 41; CD 5; MTCW 1

**Wilson, Robert McLiam** 1964- .......... CLC 59
See also CA 132; DLB 267

**Wilson, Sloan** 1920- .................... CLC 32
See also CA 1-4R; CANR 1, 44; CN 7

**Wilson, Snoo** 1948- .................... CLC 33
See also CA 69-72; CBD; CD 5

**Wilson, William S(mith)** 1932- .......... CLC 49
See also CA 81-84

**Wilson, (Thomas) Woodrow**
1856-1924 .................... TCLC 79
See also CA 166; DLB 47

**Wilson and Warnke eds.** .................... CLC 65

**Winchilsea, Anne (Kingsmill) Finch**
1661-1720
See Finch, Anne
See also RGEL 2

**Windham, Basil**
See Wodehouse, P(elham) G(renville)

**Wingrove, David (John)** 1954- .......... CLC 68
See also CA 133; SFW 4

**Winnemucca, Sarah** 1844-1891 .... NCLC 79; NNAL
See also DAM MULT; DLB 175; RGAL 4

**Winstanley, Gerrard** 1609-1676 .......... LC 52

**Wintergreen, Jane**
See Duncan, Sara Jeannette

**Winters, Janet Lewis** .................... CLC 41
See Lewis, Janet
See also DLBY 1987

**Winters, (Arthur) Yvor** 1900-1968 .... CLC 4, 8, 32
See also AMWS 2; CA 11-12; CAP 1; DLB 48; MTCW 1; RGAL 4

**Winterson, Jeanette** 1959- .......... CLC 64, 158
See also BRWS 4; CA 136; CANR 58; CN 7; CPW; DAM POP; DLB 207, 261; FANT; FW; GLL 1; MTCW 2; RHW

**Winthrop, John** 1588-1649 .................... LC 31
See also DLB 24, 30

**Wirth, Louis** 1897-1952 .................... TCLC 92

**Wiseman, Frederick** 1930- .................... CLC 20
See also CA 159

**Wister, Owen** 1860-1938 .................... TCLC 21
See also BPFB 3; CA 162; DLB 9, 78, 186; RGAL 4; SATA 62; TCWW 2

**Witkacy**
See Witkiewicz, Stanislaw Ignacy

**Witkiewicz, Stanislaw Ignacy**
1885-1939 .................... TCLC 8
See also CA 162; CDWLB 4; DLB 215; EW 10; RGWL 2, 3; SFW 4

**Wittgenstein, Ludwig (Josef Johann)**
1889-1951 .................... TCLC 59
See also CA 164; DLB 262; MTCW 2

**Wittig, Monique** 1935(?)- .................... CLC 22
See also CA 135; CWW 2; DLB 83; FW; GLL 1

**Wittlin, Jozef** 1896-1976 .................... CLC 25
See also CA 49-52; CANR 3

**Wodehouse, P(elham) G(renville)**
1881-1975 . CLC 1, 2, 5, 10, 22; SSC 2; TCLC 108
See also AITN 2; BRWS 3; CA 45-48; CANR 3, 33; CDBLB 1914-1945; CPW 1; DAB; DAC; DAM NOV; DLB 34, 162; MTCW 1, 2; RGEL 2; RGSF 2; SATA 22; SSFS 10

**Woiwode, L.**
See Woiwode, Larry (Alfred)

**Woiwode, Larry (Alfred)** 1941- ... CLC 6, 10
See also CA 73-76; CANR 16, 94; CN 7; DLB 6; INT CANR-16

**Wojciechowska, Maia (Teresa)**
1927-2002 .................... CLC 26
See also AAYA 8, 46; BYA 3; CA 9-12R, 183; CAAE 183; CANR 4, 41; CLR 1; JRDA; MAICYA 1, 2; SAAS 1; SATA 1, 28, 83; SATA-Essay 104; SATA-Obit 134; YAW

**Wojtyla, Karol**
See John Paul II, Pope

**Wolf, Christa** 1929- ........ CLC 14, 29, 58, 150
See also CA 85-88; CANR 45; CDWLB 2; CWW 2; DLB 75; FW; MTCW 1; RGWL 2, 3; SSFS 14

**Wolf, Naomi** 1962- .................... CLC 157
See also CA 141; CANR 110; FW

**Wolfe, Gene (Rodman)** 1931- .......... CLC 25
See also AAYA 35; CA 57-60; CAAS 9; CANR 6, 32, 60; CPW; DAM POP; DLB 8; FANT; MTCW 2; SATA 118; SCFW 2; SFW 4; SUFW 2

**Wolfe, George C.** 1954- ........ BLCS; CLC 49
See also CA 149; CAD; CD 5

**Wolfe, Thomas (Clayton)**
1900-1938 ...... SSC 33; TCLC 4, 13, 29, 61; WLC
See also AMW; BPFB 3; CA 132; CANR 102; CDALB 1929-1941; DA; DAB; DAC; DAM MST, NOV; DLB 9, 102, 229; DLBD 2, 16; DLBY 1985, 1997; MTCW 1, 2; RGAL 4; TUS

**Wolfe, Thomas Kennerly, Jr.**
1930- .................... CLC 147
See Wolfe, Tom
See also CA 13-16R; CANR 9, 33, 70, 104; DAM POP; DLB 185; INT CANR-9; MTCW 1, 2; TUS

**Wolfe, Tom** .............. CLC 1, 2, 9, 15, 35, 51
See Wolfe, Thomas Kennerly, Jr.
See also AAYA 8; AITN 2; AMWS 3; BEST 89:1; BPFB 3; CN 7; CPW; CSW; DLB 152; LAIT 5; RGAL 4

**Wolff, Geoffrey (Ansell)** 1937- .......... CLC 41
See also CA 29-32R; CANR 29, 43, 78

**Wolff, Sonia**
See Levitin, Sonia (Wolff)

**Wolff, Tobias (Jonathan Ansell)**
1945- .................... CLC 39, 64
See also AAYA 16; AMWS 7; BEST 90:2; BYA 12; CA 117; CAAS 22; CANR 54, 76, 96; CN 7; CSW; DLB 130; INT CA-117; MTCW 2; RGAL 4; RGSF 2; SSFS 4, 11

**Wolfram von Eschenbach** c. 1170-c. 1220 .................... CMLC 5
See Eschenbach, Wolfram von
See also CDWLB 2; DLB 138; EW 1; RGWL 2

**Wolitzer, Hilma** 1930- .................... CLC 17
See also CA 65-68; CANR 18, 40; INT CANR-18; SATA 31; YAW

**Wollstonecraft, Mary** 1759-1797 ...... LC 5, 50
See also BRWS 3; CDBLB 1789-1832; DLB 39, 104, 158, 252; FW; LAIT 1; RGEL 2; TEA; WLIT 3

**Wonder, Stevie** .................... CLC 12
See Morris, Steveland Judkins

**Wong, Jade Snow** 1922- .................... **CLC 17**
See also CA 109; CANR 91; SATA 112

**Woodberry, George Edward**
1855-1930 ................................. **TCLC 73**
See also CA 165; DLB 71, 103

**Woodcott, Keith**
See Brunner, John (Kilian Houston)

**Woodruff, Robert W.**
See Mencken, H(enry) L(ouis)

**Woolf, (Adeline) Virginia** 1882-1941 . **SSC 7; TCLC 1, 5, 20, 43, 56, 101, 123, 128; WLC**
See also AAYA 44; BPFB 3; BRW 7; BRWR 1; CA 130; CANR 64; CDBLB 1914-1945; DA; DAB; DAC; DAM MST, NOV; DLB 36, 100, 162; DLBD 10; EXPS; FW; LAIT 3; MTCW 1, 2; NCFS 2; NFS 8, 12; RGEL 2; RGSF 2; SSFS 4, 12; TEA; WLIT 4

**Woollcott, Alexander (Humphreys)**
1887-1943 ................................ **TCLC 5**
See also CA 161; DLB 29

**Woolrich, Cornell** ......................... **CLC 77**
See Hopley-Woolrich, Cornell George
See also MSW

**Woolson, Constance Fenimore**
1840-1894 ................................ **NCLC 82**
See also DLB 12, 74, 189, 221; RGAL 4

**Wordsworth, Dorothy** 1771-1855 .. **NCLC 25**
See also DLB 107

**Wordsworth, William** 1770-1850 .. **NCLC 12, 38, 111; PC 4; WLC**
See also BRW 4; CDBLB 1789-1832; DA; DAB; DAC; DAM MST, POET; DLB 93, 107; EXPP; PAB; PFS 2; RGEL 2; TEA; WLIT 3; WP

**Wotton, Sir Henry** 1568-1639 ............. **LC 68**
See also DLB 121; RGEL 2

**Wouk, Herman** 1915- ................ **CLC 1, 9, 38**
See also BPFB 2, 3; CA 5-8R; CANR 6, 33, 67; CDALBS; CN 7; CPW; DAM NOV, POP; DLBY 1982; INT CANR-6; LAIT 4; MTCW 1, 2; NFS 7; TUS

**Wright, Charles (Penzel, Jr.)** 1935- .. **CLC 6, 13, 28, 119, 146**
See also AMWS 5; CA 29-32R; CAAS 7; CANR 23, 36, 62, 88; CP 7; DLB 165; DLBY 1982; MTCW 1, 2; PFS 10

**Wright, Charles Stevenson** 1932- ..... **BLC 3; CLC 49**
See also BW 1; CA 9-12R; CANR 26; CN 7; DAM MULT, POET; DLB 33

**Wright, Frances** 1795-1852 ............ **NCLC 74**
See also DLB 73

**Wright, Frank Lloyd** 1867-1959 .... **TCLC 95**
See also AAYA 33; CA 174

**Wright, Jack R.**
See Harris, Mark

**Wright, James (Arlington)**
1927-1980 ....... **CLC 3, 5, 10, 28; PC 36**
See also AITN 2; AMWS 3; CA 49-52; CANR 4, 34, 64; CDALBS; DAM POET; DLB 5, 169; EXPP; MTCW 1; PFS 7, 8; RGAL 4; TUS; WP

**Wright, Judith (Arundell)**
1915-2000 ..................... **CLC 11, 53; PC 14**
See also CA 13-16R; CANR 31, 76, 93; CP 7; CWP; DLB 260; MTCW 1, 2; PFS 8; RGEL 2; SATA 14; SATA-Obit 121

**Wright, L(aurali) R.** 1939- ................. **CLC 44**
See also CA 138; CMW 4

**Wright, Richard (Nathaniel)**
1908-1960 ... **BLC 3; CLC 1, 3, 4, 9, 14, 21, 48, 74; SSC 2; WLC**
See also AAYA 5, 42; AFAW 1, 2; AMW; BPFB 3; BW 1; BYA 2; CA 108; CANR 64; CDALB 1929-1941; DA; DAB; DAC; DAM MST, MULT, NOV; DLB 76, 102; DLBD 2; EXPN; LAIT 3, 4; MTCW 1, 2; NCFS 1; NFS 1, 7; RGAL 4; RGSF 2; SSFS 3, 9, 15; TUS; YAW

**Wright, Richard B(ruce)** 1937- .......... **CLC 6**
See also CA 85-88; DLB 53

**Wright, Rick** 1945- ............................. **CLC 35**

**Wright, Rowland**
See Wells, Carolyn

**Wright, Stephen** 1946- ....................... **CLC 33**

**Wright, Willard Huntington** 1888-1939
See Van Dine, S. S.
See also CA 189; CMW 4; DLBD 16

**Wright, William** 1930- ....................... **CLC 44**
See also CA 53-56; CANR 7, 23

**Wroth, Lady Mary** 1587-1653(?) ....... **LC 30; PC 38**
See also DLB 121

**Wu Ch'eng-en** 1500(?)-1582(?) .............. **LC 7**

**Wu Ching-tzu** 1701-1754 ...................... **LC 2**

**Wurlitzer, Rudolph** 1938(?)- .... **CLC 2, 4, 15**
See also CA 85-88; CN 7; DLB 173

**Wyatt, Sir Thomas** c. 1503-1542 . **LC 70; PC 27**
See also BRW 1; DLB 132; EXPP; RGEL 2; TEA

**Wycherley, William** 1640-1716 ........ **LC 8, 21**
See also BRW 2; CDBLB 1660-1789; DAM DRAM; DLB 80; RGEL 2

**Wylie, Elinor (Morton Hoyt)**
1885-1928 ....................... **PC 23; TCLC 8**
See also AMWS 1; CA 162; DLB 9, 45; EXPP; RGAL 4

**Wylie, Philip (Gordon)** 1902-1971 ... **CLC 43**
See also CA 21-22; CAP 2; DLB 9; SFW 4

**Wyndham, John** .............................. **CLC 19**
See Harris, John (Wyndham Parkes Lucas) Beynon
See also DLB 255; SCFW 2

**Wyss, Johann David Von**
1743-1818 ................................ **NCLC 10**
See also JRDA; MAICYA 1, 2; SATA 29; SATA-Brief 27

**Xenophon** c. 430B.C.-c. 354B.C. ... **CMLC 17**
See also AW 1; DLB 176; RGWL 2, 3

**Xingjian, Gao** 1940- ........................ **CLC 167**
See also CA 193; RGWL 3

**Yakumo Koizumi**
See Hearn, (Patricio) Lafcadio (Tessima Carlos)

**Yamada, Mitsuye (May)** 1923- ............ **PC 44**
See also CA 77-80

**Yamamoto, Hisaye** 1921- ......... **AAL; SSC 34**
See also DAM MULT; LAIT 4; SSFS 14

**Yanez, Jose Donoso**
See Donoso (Yanez), Jose

**Yanovsky, Basile S.**
See Yanovsky, V(assily) S(emenovich)

**Yanovsky, V(assily) S(emenovich)**
1906-1989 ................................ **CLC 2, 18**
See also CA 97-100

**Yates, Richard** 1926-1992 ......... **CLC 7, 8, 23**
See also AMWS 11; CA 5-8R; CANR 10, 43; DLB 2, 234; DLBY 1981, 1992; INT CANR-10

**Yeats, W. B.**
See Yeats, William Butler

**Yeats, William Butler** 1865-1939 ........ **PC 20; TCLC 1, 11, 18, 31, 93, 116; WLC**
See also BRW 6; BRWR 1; CA 127; CANR 45; CDBLB 1890-1914; DA; DAB; DAC; DAM DRAM, MST, POET; DLB 10, 19, 98, 156; EXPP; MTCW 1, 2; NCFS 3; PAB; PFS 1, 2, 5, 7, 13, 15; RGEL 2; TEA; WLIT 4; WP

**Yehoshua, A(braham) B.** 1936- .. **CLC 13, 31**
See also CA 33-36R; CANR 43, 90; RGSF 2; RGWL 2

**Yellow Bird**
See Ridge, John Rollin

**Yep, Laurence Michael** 1948- ........... **CLC 35**
See also AAYA 5, 31; BYA 7; CA 49-52; CANR 1, 46, 92; CLR 3, 17, 54; DLB 52; FANT; JRDA; MAICYA 1, 2; MAICYAS 1; SATA 7, 69, 123; WYA; YAW

**Yerby, Frank G(arvin)** 1916-1991 ..... **BLC 3; CLC 1, 7, 22**
See also BPFB 3; BW 1, 3; CA 9-12R; CANR 16, 52; DAM MULT; DLB 76; INT CANR-16; MTCW 1; RGAL 4; RHW

**Yesenin, Sergei Alexandrovich**
See Esenin, Sergei (Alexandrovich)

**Yevtushenko, Yevgeny (Alexandrovich)**
1933- ...... **CLC 1, 3, 13, 26, 51, 126; PC 40**
See Evtushenko, Evgenii Aleksandrovich
See also CA 81-84; CANR 33, 54; CWW 2; DAM POET; MTCW 1

**Yezierska, Anzia** 1885(?)-1970 .......... **CLC 46**
See also CA 126; DLB 28, 221; FW; MTCW 1; RGAL 4; SSFS 15

**Yglesias, Helen** 1915- ................... **CLC 7, 22**
See also CA 37-40R; CAAS 20; CANR 15, 65, 95; CN 7; INT CANR-15; MTCW 1

**Yokomitsu, Riichi** 1898-1947 .......... **TCLC 47**
See also CA 170

**Yonge, Charlotte (Mary)**
1823-1901 ................................ **TCLC 48**
See also CA 163; DLB 18, 163; RGEL 2; SATA 17; WCH

**York, Jeremy**
See Creasey, John

**York, Simon**
See Heinlein, Robert A(nson)

**Yorke, Henry Vincent** 1905-1974 ..... **CLC 13**
See Green, Henry
See also CA 85-88

**Yosano Akiko** 1878-1942 .... **PC 11; TCLC 59**
See also CA 161; RGWL 3

**Yoshimoto, Banana** ......................... **CLC 84**
See Yoshimoto, Mahoko
See also NFS 7

**Yoshimoto, Mahoko** 1964-
See Yoshimoto, Banana
See also CA 144; CANR 98; SSFS 16

**Young, Al(bert James)** 1939- ... **BLC 3; CLC 19**
See also BW 2, 3; CA 29-32R; CANR 26, 65, 109; CN 7; CP 7; DAM MULT; DLB 33

**Young, Andrew (John)** 1885-1971 ...... **CLC 5**
See also CA 5-8R; CANR 7, 29; RGEL 2

**Young, Collier**
See Bloch, Robert (Albert)

**Young, Edward** 1683-1765 ............... **LC 3, 40**
See also DLB 95; RGEL 2

**Young, Marguerite (Vivian)**
1909-1995 ................................ **CLC 82**
See also CA 13-16; CAP 1; CN 7

**Young, Neil** 1945- ............................. **CLC 17**
See also CA 110; CCA 1

**Young Bear, Ray A.** 1950- ... **CLC 94; NNAL**
See also CA 146; DAM MULT; DLB 175

**Yourcenar, Marguerite** 1903-1987 ... **CLC 19, 38, 50, 87**
See also BPFB 3; CA 69-72; CANR 23, 60, 93; DAM NOV; DLB 72; DLBY 1988; EW 12; GFL 1789 to the Present; GLL 1; MTCW 1, 2; RGWL 2, 3

**Yuan, Chu** 340(?)B.C.-278(?)B.C. .. **CMLC 36**

**Yurick, Sol** 1925- ................................ **CLC 6**
See also CA 13-16R; CANR 25; CN 7

**Zabolotsky, Nikolai Alekseevich**
1903-1958 ................................ **TCLC 52**
See also CA 164

**Zagajewski, Adam** 1945- ..................... **PC 27**
See also CA 186; DLB 232

**Zalygin, Sergei** -2000 .......................... **CLC 59**
**Zamiatin, Evgenii**
See Zamyatin, Evgeny Ivanovich
See also RGSF 2; RGWL 2, 3
**Zamiatin, Evgenii Ivanovich**
See Zamyatin, Evgeny Ivanovich
See also DLB 272
**Zamiatin, Yevgenii**
See Zamyatin, Evgeny Ivanovich
**Zamora, Bernice (B. Ortiz)** 1938- .. **CLC 89; HLC 2**
See also CA 151; CANR 80; DAM MULT; DLB 82; HW 1, 2
**Zamyatin, Evgeny Ivanovich**
1884-1937 ............................ **TCLC 8, 37**
See Zamiatin, Evgenii; Zamiatin, Evgenii Ivanovich
See also CA 166; EW 10; SFW 4
**Zangwill, Israel** 1864-1926 ... **SSC 44; TCLC 16**
See also CA 167; CMW 4; DLB 10, 135, 197; RGEL 2
**Zappa, Francis Vincent, Jr.** 1940-1993
See Zappa, Frank
See also CA 108; CANR 57
**Zappa, Frank** ...................................... **CLC 17**
See Zappa, Francis Vincent, Jr.
**Zaturenska, Marya** 1902-1982 ..... **CLC 6, 11**
See also CA 13-16R; CANR 22
**Zeami** 1363-1443 ........................ **DC 7; LC 86**
See also DLB 203; RGWL 2, 3

**Zelazny, Roger (Joseph)** 1937-1995 . **CLC 21**
See also AAYA 7; BPFB 3; CA 21-24R; CANR 26, 60; CN 7; DLB 8; FANT; MTCW 1, 2; SATA 57; SATA-Brief 39; SCFW; SFW 4; SUFW 1, 2
**Zhdanov, Andrei Alexandrovich**
1896-1948 ................................. **TCLC 18**
See also CA 167
**Zhukovsky, Vasilii Andreevich**
See Zhukovsky, Vasily (Andreevich)
See also DLB 205
**Zhukovsky, Vasily (Andreevich)**
1783-1852 ................................. **NCLC 35**
See Zhukovsky, Vasilii Andreevich
**Ziegenhagen, Eric** ............................ **CLC 55**
**Zimmer, Jill Schary**
See Robinson, Jill
**Zimmerman, Robert**
See Dylan, Bob
**Zindel, Paul** 1936- .............. **CLC 6, 26; DC 5**
See also AAYA 2, 37; BYA 2, 3, 8, 11, 14; CA 73-76; CAD; CANR 31, 65, 108; CD 5; CDALBS; CLR 3, 45, 85; DA; DAB; DAC; DAM DRAM, MST, NOV; DFS 12; DLB 7, 52; JRDA; LAIT 5; MAICYA 1, 2; MTCW 1, 2; NFS 14; SATA 16, 58, 102; WYA; YAW
**Zinov'Ev, A. A.**
See Zinoviev, Alexander (Aleksandrovich)
**Zinoviev, Alexander (Aleksandrovich)**
1922- ......................................... **CLC 19**
See also CA 133; CAAS 10

**Zoilus**
See Lovecraft, H(oward) P(hillips)
**Zola, Emile (Edouard Charles Antoine)**
1840-1902 ...... **TCLC 1, 6, 21, 41; WLC**
See also CA 138; DA; DAB; DAC; DAM MST, NOV; DLB 123; EW 7; GFL 1789 to the Present; IDTP; RGWL 2; TWA
**Zoline, Pamela** 1941- ......................... **CLC 62**
See also CA 161; SFW 4
**Zoroaster** 628(?)B.C.-551(?)B.C. ... **CMLC 40**
**Zorrilla y Moral, Jose** 1817-1893 .... **NCLC 6**
**Zoshchenko, Mikhail (Mikhailovich)**
1895-1958 .................. **SSC 15; TCLC 15**
See also CA 160; RGSF 2; RGWL 3
**Zuckmayer, Carl** 1896-1977 ............. **CLC 18**
See also CA 69-72; DLB 56, 124; RGWL 2, 3
**Zuk, Georges**
See Skelton, Robin
See also CCA 1
**Zukofsky, Louis** 1904-1978 ... **CLC 1, 2, 4, 7, 11, 18; PC 11**
See also AMWS 3; CA 9-12R; CANR 39; DAM POET; DLB 5, 165; MTCW 1; RGAL 4
**Zweig, Paul** 1935-1984 ................ **CLC 34, 42**
See also CA 85-88
**Zweig, Stefan** 1881-1942 ................. **TCLC 17**
See also CA 170; DLB 81, 118
**Zwingli, Huldreich** 1484-1531 ............. **LC 37**
See also DLB 179

# Literary Criticism Series Cumulative Topic Index

This index lists all topic entries in Gale's *Classical and Medieval Literature Criticism* (CMLC), *Contemporary Literary Criticism* (CLC), *Drama Criticism* (DC), *Literature Criticism from 1400 to 1800* (LC), *Nineteenth-Century Literature Criticism* (NCLC), and *Twentieth-Century Literary Criticism* (TCLC). The index also lists topic entries in the Gale Critical Companion Collection, which includes the following publication: *Harlem Renaissance* (HR).

**Aborigine in Nineteenth-Century Australian Literature, The** NCLC 120: 1-88
  overviews, 2-27
  representations of the Aborigine in Australian literature, 27-58
  Aboriginal myth, literature, and oral tradition, 58-88

**Aesopic Fable, The** LC 51: 1-100
  the British Aesopic Fable, 1-54
  the Aesopic tradition in non-English-speaking cultures, 55-66
  political uses of the Aesopic fable, 67-88
  the evolution of the Aesopic fable, 89-99

**African-American Folklore and Literature** TCLC 126: 1-67
  African-American folk tradition, 1-16
  representative writers, 16-34
  hallmark works, 35-48
  the study of African-American literature and folklore, 48-64

**Age of Johnson** LC 15: 1-87
  Johnson's London, 3-15
  aesthetics of neoclassicism, 15-36
  "age of prose and reason," 36-45
  clubmen and bluestockings, 45-56
  printing technology, 56-62
  periodicals: "a map of busy life," 62-74
  transition, 74-86

**Age of Spenser** LC 39: 1-70
  overviews and general studies, 2-21
  literary style, 22-34
  poets and the crown, 34-70

**AIDS in Literature** CLC 81: 365-416

**Alcohol and Literature** TCLC 70: 1-58
  overview, 2-8
  fiction, 8-48
  poetry and drama, 48-58

**American Abolitionism** NCLC 44: 1-73
  overviews and general studies, 2-26
  abolitionist ideals, 26-46
  the literature of abolitionism, 46-72

**American Autobiography** TCLC 86: 1-115
  overviews and general studies, 3-36
  American authors and autobiography, 36-82
  African-American autobiography, 82-114

**American Black Humor Fiction** TCLC 54: 1-85
  characteristics of black humor, 2-13
  origins and development, 13-38
  black humor distinguished from related literary trends, 38-60
  black humor and society, 60-75
  black humor reconsidered, 75-83

**American Civil War in Literature** NCLC 32: 1-109
  overviews and general studies, 2-20
  regional perspectives, 20-54
  fiction popular during the war, 54-79
  the historical novel, 79-108

**American Frontier in Literature** NCLC 28: 1-103
  definitions, 2-12
  development, 12-17
  nonfiction writing about the frontier, 17-30
  frontier fiction, 30-45
  frontier protagonists, 45-66
  portrayals of Native Americans, 66-86
  feminist readings, 86-98
  twentieth-century reaction against frontier literature, 98-100

**American Humor Writing** NCLC 52: 1-59
  overviews and general studies, 2-12
  the Old Southwest, 12-42
  broader impacts, 42-5
  women humorists, 45-58

**American Novel of Manners** TCLC 130: 1-42
  history of the Novel of Manners in America, 4-10
  representative writers, 10-18
  relevancy of the Novel of Manners, 18-24
  hallmark works in the Novel of Manners, 24-36
  Novel of Manners and other media, 36-40

*American Mercury,* **The** TCLC 74: 1-80

**American Popular Song, Golden Age of** TCLC 42: 1-49
  background and major figures, 2-34
  the lyrics of popular songs, 34-47

**American Proletarian Literature** TCLC 54: 86-175
  overviews and general studies, 87-95
  American proletarian literature and the American Communist Party, 95-111
  ideology and literary merit, 111-17
  novels, 117-36
  Gastonia, 136-48
  drama, 148-54
  journalism, 154-9
  proletarian literature in the United States, 159-74

**American Realism** NCLC 120: 89-246
  overviews, 91-112
  background and sources, 112-72
  social issues, 172-223
  women and realism, 223-45

**American Romanticism** NCLC 44: 74-138
  overviews and general studies, 74-84
  sociopolitical influences, 84-104
  Romanticism and the American frontier, 104-15
  thematic concerns, 115-37

**American Western Literature** TCLC 46: 1-100
  definition and development of American Western literature, 2-7
  characteristics of the Western novel, 8-23
  Westerns as history and fiction, 23-34
  critical reception of American Western literature, 34-41
  the Western hero, 41-73
  women in Western fiction, 73-91
  later Western fiction, 91-9

**American Writers in Paris** TCLC 98: 1-156
  overviews and general studies, 2-155

**Anarchism** NCLC 84: 1-97
  overviews and general studies, 2-23
  the French anarchist tradition, 23-56
  Anglo-American anarchism, 56-68
  anarchism: incidents and issues, 68-97

**Animals in Literature** TCLC 106: 1-120
  overviews and general studies, 2-8
  animals in American literature, 8-45
  animals in Canadian literature, 45-57
  animals in European literature, 57-100
  animals in Latin American literature, 100-06
  animals in women's literature, 106-20

**Antebellum South, Literature of the** NCLC 112:1-188
  overviews, 4-55
  culture of the Old South, 55-68
  antebellum fiction: pastoral and heroic romance, 68-120
  role of women: a subdued rebellion, 120-59
  slavery and the slave narrative, 159-85

**The Apocalyptic Movement** TCLC 106: 121-69

**Aristotle** CMLC 31:1-397
   philosophy, 3-100
   poetics, 101-219
   rhetoric, 220-301
   science, 302-397

**Art and Literature** TCLC 54: 176-248
   overviews and general studies, 176-93
   definitions, 193-219
   influence of visual arts on literature, 219-31
   spatial form in literature, 231-47

**Arthurian Literature** CMLC 10: 1-127
   historical context and literary beginnings, 2-27
   development of the legend through Malory, 27-64
   development of the legend from Malory to the Victorian Age, 65-81
   themes and motifs, 81-95
   principal characters, 95-125

**Arthurian Revival** NCLC 36: 1-77
   overviews and general studies, 2-12
   Tennyson and his influence, 12-43
   other leading figures, 43-73
   the Arthurian legend in the visual arts, 73-6

**Australian Literature** TCLC 50: 1-94
   origins and development, 2-21
   characteristics of Australian literature, 21-33
   historical and critical perspectives, 33-41
   poetry, 41-58
   fiction, 58-76
   drama, 76-82
   Aboriginal literature, 82-91

**Beat Generation, Literature of the** TCLC 42: 50-102
   overviews and general studies, 51-9
   the Beat generation as a social phenomenon, 59-62
   development, 62-5
   Beat literature, 66-96
   influence, 97-100

**The Bell Curve Controversy** CLC 91: 281-330

***Bildungsroman* in Nineteenth-Century Literature** NCLC 20: 92-168
   surveys, 93-113
   in Germany, 113-40
   in England, 140-56
   female *Bildungsroman,* 156-67

**Bloomsbury Group** TCLC 34: 1-73
   history and major figures, 2-13
   definitions, 13-7
   influences, 17-27
   thought, 27-40
   prose, 40-52
   and literary criticism, 52-4
   political ideals, 54-61
   response to, 61-71

**The Blues in Literature** TCLC 82: 1-71

**Bly, Robert,** *Iron John: A Book about Men and Men's Work* CLC 70: 414-62

***The Book of J*** CLC 65: 289-311

**British Ephemeral Literature** LC 59: 1-70
   overviews and general studies, 1-9
   broadside ballads, 10-40
   chapbooks, jestbooks, pamphlets, and newspapers, 40-69

**Buddhism and Literature** TCLC 70: 59-164
   eastern literature, 60-113
   western literature, 113-63

**The *Bulletin* and the Rise of Australian Literary Nationalism** NCLC 116: 1-121
   overviews, 3-32
   legend of the nineties, 32-55
   *Bulletin* style, 55-71
   Australian literary nationalism, 71-98
   myth of the bush, 98-120

**Businessman in American Literature** TCLC 26: 1-48
   portrayal of the businessman, 1-32
   themes and techniques in business fiction, 32-47

**The Calendar** LC 55: 1-92
   overviews and general studies, 2-19
   measuring time, 19-28
   calendars and culture, 28-60
   calendar reform, 60-92

**Captivity Narratives** LC 82: 71-172
   overviews, 72-107
   captivity narratives and Puritanism, 108-34
   captivity narratives and Native Americans, 134-49
   influence on American literature, 149-72

**Catholicism in Nineteenth-Century American Literature** NCLC 64: 1-58
   overviews, 3-14
   polemical literature, 14-46
   Catholicism in literature, 47-57

**Celtic Mythology** CMLC 26: 1-111
   overviews and general studies, 2-22
   Celtic myth as literature and history, 22-48
   Celtic religion: Druids and divinities, 48-80
   Fionn MacCuhaill and the Fenian cycle, 80-111

**Celtic Twilight** See **Irish Literary Renaissance**

**Chartist Movement and Literature, The** NCLC 60: 1-84
   overview: nineteenth-century working-class fiction, 2-19
   Chartist fiction and poetry, 19-73
   the Chartist press, 73-84

**Child Labor in Nineteenth-Century Literature** NCLC 108: 1-133
   overviews, 3-10
   climbing boys and chimney sweeps, 10-16
   the international traffic in children, 16-45
   critics and reformers, 45-82
   fictional representations of child laborers, 83-132

**Children's Literature, Nineteenth-Century** NCLC 52: 60-135
   overviews and general studies, 61-72
   moral tales, 72-89
   fairy tales and fantasy, 90-119
   making men/making women, 119-34

**Christianity in Twentieth-Century Literature** TCLC 110: 1-79
   overviews and general studies, 2-31
   Christianity in twentieth-century fiction, 31-78

**The City and Literature** TCLC 90: 1-124
   overviews and general studies, 2-9
   the city in American literature, 9-86
   the city in European literature, 86-124

**Civic Critics, Russian** NCLC 20: 402-46
   principal figures and background, 402-9
   and Russian Nihilism, 410-6
   aesthetic and critical views, 416-45

**The Cockney School** NCLC 68: 1-64
   overview, 2-7
   *Blackwood's Magazine* and the contemporary critical response, 7-24
   the political and social import of the Cockneys and their critics, 24-63

**Colonial America: The Intellectual Background** LC 25: 1-98
   overviews and general studies, 2-17
   philosophy and politics, 17-31
   early religious influences in Colonial America, 31-60
   consequences of the Revolution, 60-78
   religious influences in post-revolutionary America, 78-87
   colonial literary genres, 87-97

**Colonialism in Victorian English Literature** NCLC 56: 1-77
   overviews and general studies, 2-34
   colonialism and gender, 34-51
   monsters and the occult, 51-76

**Columbus, Christopher, Books on the Quincentennial of His Arrival in the New World** CLC 70: 329-60

**Comic Books** TCLC 66: 1-139
   historical and critical perspectives, 2-48
   superheroes, 48-67
   underground comix, 67-88
   comic books and society, 88-122
   adult comics and graphic novels, 122-36

**Commedia dell'Arte** LC 83: 1-147
   overviews, 2-7
   origins and development, 7-23
   characters and actors, 23-45
   performance, 45-62
   texts and authors, 62-100
   influence in Europe, 100-46

**Connecticut Wits** NCLC 48: 1-95
   overviews and general studies, 2-40
   major works, 40-76
   intellectual context, 76-95

**Contemporary Southern Literature** CLC 167: 1-132
   criticism, 2-131

**Crime in Literature** TCLC 54: 249-307
   evolution of the criminal figure in literature, 250-61
   crime and society, 261-77
   literary perspectives on crime and punishment, 277-88
   writings by criminals, 288-306

**The Crusades** CMLC 38: 1-144
   history of the Crusades, 3-60
   literature of the Crusades, 60-116
   the Crusades and the people: attitudes and influences, 116-44

**Cyberpunk** TCLC 106: 170-366
   overviews and general studies, 171-88
   feminism and cyberpunk, 188-230
   history and cyberpunk, 230-70
   sexuality and cyberpunk, 270-98
   social issues and cyberpunk, 299-366

**Czechoslovakian Literature of the Twentieth Century** TCLC 42:103-96
   through World War II, 104-35
   de-Stalinization, the Prague Spring, and contemporary literature, 135-72
   Slovak literature, 172-85
   Czech science fiction, 185-93

**Dadaism** TCLC 46: 101-71
   background and major figures, 102-16
   definitions, 116-26
   manifestos and commentary by Dadaists, 126-40
   theater and film, 140-58
   nature and characteristics of Dadaist writing, 158-70

**Darwinism and Literature** NCLC 32: 110-206
   background, 110-31
   direct responses to Darwin, 131-71
   collateral effects of Darwinism, 171-205

**Death in American Literature** NCLC 92: 1-170
   overviews and general studies, 2-32
   death in the works of Emily Dickinson, 32-72

death in the works of Herman Melville, 72-101
death in the works of Edgar Allan Poe, 101-43
death in the works of Walt Whitman, 143-70

**Death in Nineteenth-Century British Literature** NCLC 68: 65-142
overviews and general studies, 66-92
responses to death, 92-102
feminist perspectives, 103-17
striving for immortality, 117-41

**Death in Literature** TCLC 78:1-183
fiction, 2-115
poetry, 115-46
drama, 146-81

**de Man, Paul, Wartime Journalism of** CLC 55: 382-424

**Detective Fiction, Nineteenth-Century** NCLC 36: 78-148
origins of the genre, 79-100
history of nineteenth-century detective fiction, 101-33
significance of nineteenth-century detective fiction, 133-46

**Detective Fiction, Twentieth-Century** TCLC 38: 1-96
genesis and history of the detective story, 3-22
defining detective fiction, 22-32
evolution and varieties, 32-77
the appeal of detective fiction, 77-90

**Dime Novels** NCLC 84: 98-168
overviews and general studies, 99-123
popular characters, 123-39
major figures and influences, 139-52
socio-political concerns, 152-167

**Disease and Literature** TCLC 66: 140-283
overviews and general studies, 141-65
disease in nineteenth-century literature, 165-81
tuberculosis and literature, 181-94
women and disease in literature, 194-221
plague literature, 221-53
AIDS in literature, 253-82

**El Dorado, The Legend of** See **Legend of El Dorado, The**

**The Double in Nineteenth-Century Literature** NCLC 40: 1-95
genesis and development of the theme, 2-15
the double and Romanticism, 16-27
sociological views, 27-52
psychological interpretations, 52-87
philosophical considerations, 87-95

**Dramatic Realism** NCLC 44: 139-202
overviews and general studies, 140-50
origins and definitions, 150-66
impact and influence, 166-93
realist drama and tragedy, 193-201

**Drugs and Literature** TCLC 78: 184-282
overviews and general studies, 185-201
pre-twentieth-century literature, 201-42
twentieth-century literature, 242-82

**Dystopias in Contemporary Literature** CLC 168: 1-91
overviews and general studies, 2-52
dystopian views in Margaret Atwood's *The Handmaid's Tale* (1985), 52-71
feminist readings of dystopias, 71-90

**Eastern Mythology** CMLC 26: 112-92
heroes and kings, 113-51
cross-cultural perspective, 151-69
relations to history and society, 169-92

**Eighteenth-Century British Periodicals** LC 63: 1-123
rise of periodicals, 2-31

impact and influence of periodicals, 31-64
periodicals and society, 64-122

**Eighteenth-Century Travel Narratives** LC 77: 252-355
overviews and general studies, 254-79
eighteenth-century European travel narratives, 279-334
non-European eighteenth-century travel narratives, 334-55

**Electronic "Books": Hypertext and Hyperfiction** CLC 86: 367-404
books vs. CD-ROMS, 367-76
hypertext and hyperfiction, 376-95
implications for publishing, libraries, and the public, 395-403

**Eliot, T. S., Centenary of Birth** CLC 55: 345-75

**Elizabethan Drama** LC 22: 140-240
origins and influences, 142-67
characteristics and conventions, 167-83
theatrical production, 184-200
histories, 200-12
comedy, 213-20
tragedy, 220-30

**Elizabethan Prose Fiction** LC 41: 1-70
overviews and general studies, 1-15
origins and influences, 15-43
style and structure, 43-69

**Enclosure of the English Common** NCLC 88: 1-57
overviews and general studies, 1-12
early reaction to enclosure, 12-23
nineteenth-century reaction to enclosure, 23-56

**The Encyclopedists** LC 26: 172-253
overviews and general studies, 173-210
intellectual background, 210-32
views on esthetics, 232-41
views on women, 241-52

**English Caroline Literature** LC 13: 221-307
background, 222-41
evolution and varieties, 241-62
the Cavalier mode, 262-75
court and society, 275-91
politics and religion, 291-306

**English Decadent Literature of the 1890s** NCLC 28: 104-200
fin de siècle: the Decadent period, 105-19
definitions, 120-37
major figures: "the tragic generation," 137-50
French literature and English literary Decadence, 150-7
themes, 157-61
poetry, 161-82
periodicals, 182-96

**English Essay, Rise of the** LC 18: 238-308
definitions and origins, 236-54
influence on the essay, 254-69
historical background, 269-78
the essay in the seventeenth century, 279-93
the essay in the eighteenth century, 293-307

**English Mystery Cycle Dramas** LC 34: 1-88
overviews and general studies, 1-27
the nature of dramatic performances, 27-42
the medieval worldview and the mystery cycles, 43-67
the doctrine of repentance and the mystery cycles, 67-76
the fall from grace in the mystery cycles, 76-88

**The English Realist Novel, 1740-1771** LC 51: 102-98
overviews and general studies, 103-22
from Romanticism to Realism, 123-58
women and the novel, 159-175

the novel and other literary forms, 176-197

**English Revolution, Literature of the** LC 43: 1-58
overviews and general studies, 2-24
pamphlets of the English Revolution, 24-38
political sermons of the English Revolution, 38-48
poetry of the English Revolution, 48-57

**English Romantic Hellenism** NCLC 68: 143-250
overviews and general studies, 144-69
historical development of English Romantic Hellenism, 169-91
influence of Greek mythology on the Romantics, 191-229
influence of Greek literature, art, and culture on the Romantics, 229-50

**English Romantic Poetry** NCLC 28: 201-327
overviews and reputation, 202-37
major subjects and themes, 237-67
forms of Romantic poetry, 267-78
politics, society, and Romantic poetry, 278-99
philosophy, religion, and Romantic poetry, 299-324

**The Epistolary Novel** LC 59: 71-170
overviews and general studies, 72-96
women and the Epistolary novel, 96-138
principal figures: Britain, 138-53
principal figures: France, 153-69

**Espionage Literature** TCLC 50: 95-159
overviews and general studies, 96-113
espionage fiction/formula fiction, 113-26
spies in fact and fiction, 126-38
the female spy, 138-44
social and psychological perspectives, 144-58

**European Debates on the Conquest of the Americas** LC 67: 1-129
overviews and general studies, 3-56
major Spanish figures, 56-98
English perceptions of Native Americans, 98-129

**European Romanticism** NCLC 36: 149-284
definitions, 149-77
origins of the movement, 177-82
Romantic theory, 182-200
themes and techniques, 200-23
Romanticism in Germany, 223-39
Romanticism in France, 240-61
Romanticism in Italy, 261-4
Romanticism in Spain, 264-8
impact and legacy, 268-82

**Exile in Literature** TCLC 122: 1-129
overviews and general studies, 2-33
exile in fiction, 33-92
German literature in exile, 92-129

**Existentialism and Literature** TCLC 42: 197-268
overviews and definitions, 198-209
history and influences, 209-19
Existentialism critiqued and defended, 220-35
philosophical and religious perspectives, 235-41
Existentialist fiction and drama, 241-67

**Familiar Essay** NCLC 48: 96-211
definitions and origins, 97-130
overview of the genre, 130-43
elements of form and style, 143-59
elements of content, 159-73
the Cockneys: Hazlitt, Lamb, and Hunt, 173-91
status of the genre, 191-210

**The Faust Legend** LC 47: 1-117

**Fear in Literature** TCLC 74: 81-258
overviews and general studies, 81

pre-twentieth-century literature, 123
twentieth-century literature, 182

**Feminism in the 1990s: Commentary on Works by Naomi Wolf, Susan Faludi, and Camille Paglia** CLC 76: 377-415

**Feminist Criticism in 1990** CLC 65: 312-60

**Fifteenth-Century English Literature** LC 17: 248-334
background, 249-72
poetry, 272-315
drama, 315-23
prose, 323-33

**Film and Literature** TCLC 38: 97-226
overviews and general studies, 97-119
film and theater, 119-34
film and the novel, 134-45
the art of the screenplay, 145-66
genre literature/genre film, 167-79
the writer and the film industry, 179-90
authors on film adaptations of their works, 190-200
fiction into film: comparative essays, 200-23

**Finance and Money as Represented in Nineteenth-Century Literature** NCLC 76: 1-69
historical perspectives, 2-20
the image of money, 20-37
the dangers of money, 37-50
women and money, 50-69

**Folklore and Literature** TCLC 86: 116-293
overviews and general studies, 118-144
Native American literature, 144-67
African-American literature, 167-238
folklore and the American West, 238-57
modern and postmodern literature, 257-91

**Food in Literature** TCLC 114: 1-133
food and children's literature, 2-14
food as a literary device, 14-32
rituals invloving food, 33-45
food and social and ethnic identity, 45-90
women's relationship with food, 91-132

**Food in Nineteenth-Century Literature** NCLC 108: 134-288
overviews, 136-74
food and social class, 174-85
food and gender, 185-219
food and love, 219-31
food and sex, 231-48
eating disorders, 248-70
vegetarians, carnivores, and cannibals, 270-87

**French Drama in the Age of Louis XIV** LC 28: 94-185
overview, 95-127
tragedy, 127-46
comedy, 146-66
tragicomedy, 166-84

**French Enlightenment** LC 14: 81-145
the question of definition, 82-9
le siècle des lumières, 89-94
women and the salons, 94-105
censorship, 105-15
the philosophy of reason, 115-31
influence and legacy, 131-44

**French New Novel** TCLC 98: 158-234
overviews and general studies, 158-92
influences, 192-213
themes, 213-33

**French Realism** NCLC 52: 136-216
origins and definitions, 137-70
issues and influence, 170-98
realism and representation, 198-215

**French Revolution and English Literature** NCLC 40: 96-195
history and theory, 96-123

romantic poetry, 123-50
the novel, 150-81
drama, 181-92
children's literature, 192-5

**Futurism, Italian** TCLC 42: 269-354
principles and formative influences, 271-9
manifestos, 279-88
literature, 288-303
theater, 303-19
art, 320-30
music, 330-6
architecture, 336-9
and politics, 339-46
reputation and significance, 346-51

**Gaelic Revival** See Irish Literary Renaissance

**Gates, Henry Louis, Jr., and African-American Literary Criticism** CLC 65: 361-405

**Gay and Lesbian Literature** CLC 76: 416-39

**German Exile Literature** TCLC 30: 1-58
the writer and the Nazi state, 1-10
definition of, 10-4
life in exile, 14-32
surveys, 32-50
Austrian literature in exile, 50-2
German publishing in the United States, 52-7

**German Expressionism** TCLC 34: 74-160
history and major figures, 76-85
aesthetic theories, 85-109
drama, 109-26
poetry, 126-38
film, 138-42
painting, 142-7
music, 147-53
and politics, 153-8

**The Gilded Age** NCLC 84: 169-271
popular themes, 170-90
Realism, 190-208
Aestheticism, 208-26
socio-political concerns, 226-70

***Glasnost* and Contemporary Soviet Literature** CLC 59: 355-97

**Gothic Novel** NCLC 28: 328-402
development and major works, 328-34
definitions, 334-50
themes and techniques, 350-78
in America, 378-85
in Scotland, 385-91
influence and legacy, 391-400

**The Governess in Nineteenth-Century Literature** NCLC 104: 1-131
overviews and general studies, 3-28
social roles and economic conditions, 28-86
fictional governesses, 86-131

**Graphic Narratives** CLC 86: 405-32
history and overviews, 406-21
the "Classics Illustrated" series, 421-2
reviews of recent works, 422-32

**Graveyard Poets** LC 67: 131-212
origins and development, 131-52
major figures, 152-75
major works, 175-212

**Greek Historiography** CMLC 17: 1-49

**Greek Mythology** CMLC 26: 193-320
overviews and general studies, 194-209
origins and development of Greek mythology, 209-29
cosmogonies and divinities in Greek mythology, 229-54
heroes and heroines in Greek mythology, 254-80
women in Greek mythology, 280-320

**Greek Theater** CMLC 51: 1-58
criticism, 2-58

**Hard-Boiled Fiction** TCLC 118: 1-109
overviews and general studies, 2-39
major authors, 39-76
women and hard-boiled fiction, 76-109

**The Harlem Renaissance** HR 1: 1-563
overviews and general studies of the Harlem Renaissance, 1-137
primary sources, 3-12
overviews, 12-38
background and sources of the Harlem Renaissance, 38-56
the New Negro aesthetic, 56-91
patrons, promoters, and the New York Public Library, 91-121
women of the Harlem Renaissance, 121-37
social, economic, and political factors that influenced the Harlem Renaissance, 139-240
primary sources, 141-53
overviews, 153-87
social and economic factors, 187-213
Black intellectual and political thought, 213-40
publishing and periodicals during the Harlem Renaissance, 243-339
primary sources, 246-52
overviews, 252-68
African American writers and mainstream publishers, 268-91
anthologies: *The New Negro* and others, 291-309
African American periodicals and the Harlem Renaissance, 309-39
performing arts during the Harlem Renaissance, 341-465
primary sources, 343-48
overviews, 348-64
drama of the Harlem Renaissance, 364-92
influence of music on Harlem Renaissance writing, 437-65
visual arts during the Harlem Renaissance, 467-563
primary sources, 470-71
overviews, 471-517
painters, 517-36
sculptors, 536-58
photographers, 558-63

**Harlem Renaissance** TCLC 26: 49-125
principal issues and figures, 50-67
the literature and its audience, 67-74
theme and technique in poetry, fiction, and drama, 74-115
and American society, 115-21
achievement and influence, 121-2

**Havel, Václav, Playwright and President** CLC 65: 406-63

**Historical Fiction, Nineteenth-Century** NCLC 48: 212-307
definitions and characteristics, 213-36
Victorian historical fiction, 236-65
American historical fiction, 265-88
realism in historical fiction, 288-306

**Hollywood and Literature** TCLC 118: 110-251
overviews and general studies, 111-20
adaptations, 120-65
socio-historical and cultural impact, 165-206
theater and hollywood, 206-51

**Holocaust and the Atomic Bomb: Fifty Years Later** CLC 91: 331-82
the Holocaust remembered, 333-52
Anne Frank revisited, 352-62
the atomic bomb and American memory, 362-81

**Holocaust Denial Literature** TCLC 58: 1-110
overviews and general studies, 1-30

Robert Faurisson and Noam Chomsky, 30-52
Holocaust denial literature in America, 52-71
library access to Holocaust denial literature, 72-5
the authenticity of Anne Frank's diary, 76-90
David Irving and the "normalization" of Hitler, 90-109

**Holocaust, Literature of the** TCLC 42: 355-450
historical overview, 357-61
critical overview, 361-70
diaries and memoirs, 370-95
novels and short stories, 395-425
poetry, 425-41
drama, 441-8

**Homosexuality in Nineteenth-Century Literature** NCLC 56: 78-182
defining homosexuality, 80-111
Greek love, 111-44
trial and danger, 144-81

**Humors Comedy** LC 85: 194-324
overviews, 195-251
major figures: Ben Jonson, 251-93
major figures: William Shakespeare, 293-324

**Hungarian Literature of the Twentieth Century** TCLC 26: 126-88
surveys of, 126-47
*Nyugat* and early twentieth-century literature, 147-56
mid-century literature, 156-68
and politics, 168-78
since the 1956 revolt, 178-87

**Hysteria in Nineteenth-Century Literature** NCLC 64: 59-184
the history of hysteria, 60-75
the gender of hysteria, 75-103
hysteria and women's narratives, 103-57
hysteria in nineteenth-century poetry, 157-83

**Image of the Noble Savage in Literature** LC 79: 136-252
overviews and development, 136-76
the Noble Savage in the New World, 176-221
Rousseau and the French Enlightenment's view of the noble savage, 221-51

**Imagism** TCLC 74: 259-454
history and development, 260
major figures, 288
sources and influences, 352
Imagism and other movements, 397
influence and legacy, 431

**Immigrants in Nineteenth-Century Literature, Representation of** NCLC 112: 188-298
overview, 189-99
immigrants in America, 199-223
immigrants and labor, 223-60
immigrants in England, 260-97

**Incest in Nineteenth-Century American Literature** NCLC 76: 70-141
overview, 71-88
the concern for social order, 88-117
authority and authorship, 117-40

**Incest in Victorian Literature** NCLC 92: 172-318
overviews and general studies, 173-85
novels, 185-276
plays, 276-84
poetry, 284-318

**Indian Literature in English** TCLC 54: 308-406
overview, 309-13
origins and major figures, 313-25

the Indo-English novel, 325-55
Indo-English poetry, 355-67
Indo-English drama, 367-72
critical perspectives on Indo-English literature, 372-80
modern Indo-English literature, 380-9
Indo-English authors on their work, 389-404

**The Industrial Revolution in Literature** NCLC 56: 183-273
historical and cultural perspectives, 184-201
contemporary reactions to the machine, 201-21
themes and symbols in literature, 221-73

**The Irish Famine as Represented in Nineteenth-Century Literature** NCLC 64: 185-261
overviews and general studies, 187-98
historical background, 198-212
famine novels, 212-34
famine poetry, 234-44
famine letters and eye-witness accounts, 245-61

**Irish Literary Renaissance** TCLC 46: 172-287
overview, 173-83
development and major figures, 184-202
influence of Irish folklore and mythology, 202-22
Irish poetry, 222-34
Irish drama and the Abbey Theatre, 234-56
Irish fiction, 256-86

**Irish Nationalism and Literature** NCLC 44: 203-73
the Celtic element in literature, 203-19
anti-Irish sentiment and the Celtic response, 219-34
literary ideals in Ireland, 234-45
literary expressions, 245-73

**Irish Novel, The** NCLC 80: 1-130
overviews and general studies, 3-9
principal figures, 9-22
peasant and middle class Irish novelists, 22-76
aristocratic Irish and Anglo-Irish novelists, 76-129

**Israeli Literature** TCLC 94: 1-137
overviews and general studies, 2-18
Israeli fiction, 18-33
Israeli poetry, 33-62
Israeli drama, 62-91
women and Israeli literature, 91-112
Arab characters in Israeli literature, 112-36

**Italian Futurism** See **Futurism, Italian**

**Italian Humanism** LC 12: 205-77
origins and early development, 206-18
revival of classical letters, 218-23
humanism and other philosophies, 224-39
humanism and humanists, 239-46
the plastic arts, 246-57
achievement and significance, 258-76

**Italian Romanticism** NCLC 60: 85-145
origins and overviews, 86-101
Italian Romantic theory, 101-25
the language of Romanticism, 125-45

**Jacobean Drama** LC 33: 1-37
the Jacobean worldview: an era of transition, 2-14
the moral vision of Jacobean drama, 14-22
Jacobean tragedy, 22-3
the Jacobean masque, 23-36

**Jazz and Literature** TCLC 102: 3-124

**Jewish-American Fiction** TCLC 62: 1-181
overviews and general studies, 2-24
major figures, 24-48
Jewish writers and American life, 48-78

Jewish characters in American fiction, 78-108
themes in Jewish-American fiction, 108-43
Jewish-American women writers, 143-59
the Holocaust and Jewish-American fiction, 159-81

**Jews in Literature** TCLC 118: 252-417
overviews and general studies, 253-97
representing the Jew in literature, 297-351
the Holocaust in literature, 351-416

**Journals of Lewis and Clark, The** NCLC 100: 1-88
overviews and general studies, 4-30
journal-keeping methods, 30-46
Fort Mandan, 46-51
the Clark journal, 51-65
the journals as literary texts, 65-87

**Kabuki** LC 73: 118-232
overviews and general studies, 120-40
the development of Kabuki, 140-65
major works, 165-95
Kabuki and society, 195-231

**Kit-Kat Club, The** LC 71: 66-112
overviews and general studies, 67-88
major figures, 88-107
attacks on the Kit-Kat Club, 107-12

**Knickerbocker Group, The** NCLC 56: 274-341
overviews and general studies, 276-314
Knickerbocker periodicals, 314-26
writers and artists, 326-40

**Lake Poets, The** NCLC 52: 217-304
characteristics of the Lake Poets and their works, 218-27
literary influences and collaborations, 227-66
defining and developing Romantic ideals, 266-84
embracing Conservatism, 284-303

**Language Poets** TCLC 126: 66-172
overviews and general studies, 67-122
selected major figures in language poetry, 122-72

**Larkin, Philip, Controversy** CLC 81: 417-64

**Latin American Literature, Twentieth-Century** TCLC 58: 111-98
historical and critical perspectives, 112-36
the novel, 136-45
the short story, 145-9
drama, 149-60
poetry, 160-7
the writer and society, 167-86
Native Americans in Latin American literature, 186-97

**Law and Literature** TCLC 126: 173-347
overviews and general studies, 174-253
fiction critiquing the law, 253-88
literary responses to the law, 289-346

**Legend of El Dorado, The** LC 74: 248-350
overviews, 249-308
major explorations for El Dorado, 308-50

**The Levellers** LC 51: 200-312
overviews and general studies, 201-29
principal figures, 230-86
religion, political philosophy, and pamphleteering, 287-311

**Literary Prizes** TCLC 122: 130-203
overviews and general studies, 131-34
the Nobel Prize in Literature, 135-83
the Pulitzer Prize, 183-203

**Literature and Millenial Lists** CLC 119: 431-67
The Modern Library list, 433
The Waterstone list, 438-439

**Literature of the American Cowboy** NCLC 96: 1-60

overview, 3-20
cowboy fiction, 20-36
cowboy poetry and songs, 36-59

**Literature of the California Gold Rush** NCLC 92: 320-85
overviews and general studies, 322-24
early California Gold Rush fiction, 324-44
Gold Rush folklore and legend, 344-51
the rise of Western local color, 351-60
social relations and social change, 360-385

**Living Theatre, The** DC 16: 154-214

**Madness in Nineteenth-Century Literature** NCLC 76: 142-284
overview, 143-54
autobiography, 154-68
poetry, 168-215
fiction, 215-83

**Madness in Twentieth-Century Literature** TCLC 50: 160-225
overviews and general studies, 161-71
madness and the creative process, 171-86
suicide, 186-91
madness in American literature, 191-207
madness in German literature, 207-13
madness and feminist artists, 213-24

**Magic Realism** TCLC 110: 80-327
overviews and general studies, 81-94
magic realism in African literature, 95-110
magic realism in American literature, 110-32
magic realism in Canadian literature, 132-46
magic realism in European literature, 146-66
magic realism in Asian literature, 166-79
magic realism in Latin-American literature, 179-223
magic realism in Israeli literature and the novels of Salman Rushdie, 223-38
magic realism in literature written by women, 239-326

**The Masque** LC 63: 124-265
development of the masque, 125-62
sources and structure, 162-220
race and gender in the masque, 221-64

**Medical Writing** LC 55: 93-195
colonial America, 94-110
enlightenment, 110-24
medieval writing, 124-40
sexuality, 140-83
vernacular, 185-95

**Memoirs of Trauma** CLC 109: 419-466
overview, 420
criticism, 429

**Metafiction** TCLC 130: 43-228
overviews and general studies, 44-85
Spanish metafiction, 85-117
studies of metafictional authors and works, 118-228

**Metaphysical Poets** LC 24: 356-439
early definitions, 358-67
surveys and overviews, 367-92
cultural and social influences, 392-406
stylistic and thematic variations, 407-38

**Missionaries in the Nineteenth-Century, Literature of** NCLC 112: 299-392
history and development, 300-16
uses of ethnography, 316-31
sociopolitical concerns, 331-82
David Livingstone, 382-91

**Modern Essay, The** TCLC 58: 199-273
overview, 200-7
the essay in the early twentieth century, 207-19
characteristics of the modern essay, 219-32
modern essayists, 232-45
the essay as a literary genre, 245-73

**Modern French Literature** TCLC 122: 205-359
overviews and general studies, 207-43
French theater, 243-77
gender issues and French women writers, 277-315
ideology and politics, 315-24
modern French poetry, 324-41
resistance literature, 341-58

**Modern Irish Literature** TCLC 102: 125-321
overview, 129-44
dramas, 144-70
fiction, 170-247
poetry, 247-321

**Modern Japanese Literature** TCLC 66: 284-389
poetry, 285-305
drama, 305-29
fiction, 329-61
western influences, 361-87

**Modernism** TCLC 70: 165-275
definitions, 166-184
Modernism and earlier influences, 184-200
stylistic and thematic traits, 200-229
poetry and drama, 229-242
redefining Modernism, 242-275

**Muckraking Movement in American Journalism** TCLC 34: 161-242
development, principles, and major figures, 162-70
publications, 170-9
social and political ideas, 179-86
targets, 186-208
fiction, 208-19
decline, 219-29
impact and accomplishments, 229-40

**Multiculturalism in Literature and Education** CLC 70: 361-413

**Music and Modern Literature** TCLC 62: 182-329
overviews and general studies, 182-211
musical form/literary form, 211-32
music in literature, 232-50
the influence of music on literature, 250-73
literature and popular music, 273-303
jazz and poetry, 303-28

**Native American Literature** CLC 76: 440-76

**Natural School, Russian** NCLC 24: 205-40
history and characteristics, 205-25
contemporary criticism, 225-40

**Naturalism** NCLC 36: 285-382
definitions and theories, 286-305
critical debates on Naturalism, 305-16
Naturalism in theater, 316-32
European Naturalism, 332-61
American Naturalism, 361-72
the legacy of Naturalism, 372-81

**Negritude** TCLC 50: 226-361
origins and evolution, 227-56
definitions, 256-91
Negritude in literature, 291-343
Negritude reconsidered, 343-58

**New Criticism** TCLC 34: 243-318
development and ideas, 244-70
debate and defense, 270-99
influence and legacy, 299-315

**New South, Literature of the** NCLC 116: 122-240
overviews, 124-66
the novel in the New South, 166-209
myth of the Old South in the New, 209-39

**The New World in Renaissance Literature** LC 31: 1-51
overview, 1-18
utopia vs. terror, 18-31
explorers and Native Americans, 31-51

**New York Intellectuals and *Partisan Review*** TCLC 30: 117-98
development and major figures, 118-28
influence of Judaism, 128-39
*Partisan Review,* 139-57
literary philosophy and practice, 157-75
political philosophy, 175-87
achievement and significance, 187-97

***The New Yorker*** TCLC 58: 274-357
overviews and general studies, 274-95
major figures, 295-304
*New Yorker* style, 304-33
fiction, journalism, and humor at *The New Yorker,* 333-48
the new *New Yorker,* 348-56

**Newgate Novel** NCLC 24: 166-204
development of Newgate literature, 166-73
*Newgate Calendar,* 173-7
Newgate fiction, 177-95
Newgate drama, 195-204

**Nigerian Literature of the Twentieth Century** TCLC 30: 199-265
surveys of, 199-227
English language and African life, 227-45
politics and the Nigerian writer, 245-54
Nigerian writers and society, 255-62

**Nihilism and Literature** TCLC 110: 328-93
overviews and general studies, 328-44
European and Russian nihilism, 344-73
nihilism in the works of Albert Camus, Franz Kafka, and John Barth, 373-92

**Nineteenth-Century Captivity Narratives** NCLC 80:131-218
overview, 132-37
the political significance of captivity narratives, 137-67
images of gender, 167-96
moral instruction, 197-217

**Nineteenth-Century Euro-American Literary Representations of Native Americans** NCLC 104: 132-264
overviews and general studies, 134-53
Native American history, 153-72
the Indians of the Northeast, 172-93
the Indians of the Southeast, 193-212
the Indians of the West, 212-27
Indian-hater fiction, 227-43
the Indian as exhibit, 243-63

**Nineteenth-Century Native American Autobiography** NCLC 64: 262-389
overview, 263-8
problems of authorship, 268-81
the evolution of Native American autobiography, 281-304
political issues, 304-15
gender and autobiography, 316-62
autobiographical works during the turn of the century, 362-88

**Norse Mythology** CMLC 26: 321-85
history and mythological tradition, 322-44
Eddic poetry, 344-74
Norse mythology and other traditions, 374-85

**Northern Humanism** LC 16: 281-356
background, 282-305
precursor of the Reformation, 305-14
the Brethren of the Common Life, the Devotio Moderna, and education, 314-40
the impact of printing, 340-56

**Novel of Manners, The** NCLC 56: 342-96
social and political order, 343-53
domestic order, 353-73
depictions of gender, 373-83
the American novel of manners, 383-95

**Novels of the Ming and Early Ch'ing Dynasties** LC 76: 213-356

overviews and historical development, 214-45
major works—overview, 245-85
genre studies, 285-325
cultural and social themes, 325-55

**Nuclear Literature: Writings and Criticism in the Nuclear Age** TCLC 46: 288-390
overviews and general studies, 290-301
fiction, 301-35
poetry, 335-8
nuclear war in Russo-Japanese literature, 338-55
nuclear war and women writers, 355-67
the nuclear referent and literary criticism, 367-88

**Occultism in Modern Literature** TCLC 50: 362-406
influence of occultism on literature, 363-72
occultism, literature, and society, 372-87
fiction, 387-96
drama, 396-405

**Opium and the Nineteenth-Century Literary Imagination** NCLC 20:250-301
original sources, 250-62
historical background, 262-71
and literary society, 271-9
and literary creativity, 279-300

**Orientalism** NCLC 96: 149-364
overviews and general studies, 150-98
Orientalism and imperialism, 198-229
Orientalism and gender, 229-59
Orientalism and the nineteenth-century novel, 259-321
Orientalism in nineteenth-century poetry, 321-63

**The Oxford Movement** NCLC 72: 1-197
overviews and general studies, 2-24
background, 24-59
and education, 59-69
religious responses, 69-128
literary aspects, 128-178
political implications, 178-196

**The Parnassian Movement** NCLC 72: 198-241
overviews and general studies, 199-231
and epic form, 231-38
and positivism, 238-41

**Pastoral Literature of the English Renaissance** LC 59: 171-282
overviews and general studies, 172-214
principal figures of the Elizabethan period, 214-33
principal figures of the later Renaissance, 233-50
pastoral drama, 250-81

**Periodicals, Nineteenth-Century British** NCLC 24: 100-65
overviews and general studies, 100-30
in the Romantic Age, 130-41
in the Victorian era, 142-54
and the reviewer, 154-64

**Picaresque Literature of the Sixteenth and Seventeenth Centuries** LC 78: 223-355
context and development, 224-71
genre, 271-98
the picaro, 299-326
the picara, 326-53

**Plath, Sylvia, and the Nature of Biography** CLC 86: 433-62
the nature of biography, 433-52
reviews of *The Silent Woman*, 452-61

**Political Theory from the 15th to the 18th Century** LC 36: 1-55
overview, 1-26
natural law, 26-42
empiricism, 42-55

**Polish Romanticism** NCLC 52: 305-71
overviews and general studies, 306-26
major figures, 326-40
Polish Romantic drama, 340-62
influences, 362-71

**Politics and Literature** TCLC 94: 138-61
overviews and general studies, 139-96
Europe, 196-226
Latin America, 226-48
Africa and the Caribbean, 248-60

**Popular Literature** TCLC 70: 279-382
overviews and general studies, 280-324
"formula" fiction, 324-336
readers of popular literature, 336-351
evolution of popular literature, 351-382

**The Portrayal of Jews in Nineteenth-Century English Literature** NCLC 72: 242-368
overviews and general studies, 244-77
Anglo-Jewish novels, 277-303
depictions by non-Jewish writers, 303-44
Hebraism versus Hellenism, 344-67

**The Portrayal of Mormonism** NCLC 96: 61-148
overview, 63-72
early Mormon literature, 72-100
Mormon periodicals and journals, 100-10
women writers, 110-22
Mormonism and nineteenth-century literature, 122-42
Mormon poetry, 142-47

**Postcolonialism** TCLC 114: 134-239
overviews and general studies, 135-153
African postcolonial writing, 153-72
Asian/Pacific literature, 172-78
postcolonial literary theory, 178-213
postcolonial women's writing, 213-38

**Postmodernism** TCLC 90:125-307
overview, 126-166
criticism, 166-224
fiction, 224-282
poetry, 282-300
drama, 300-307

**Pre-Raphaelite Movement** NCLC 20: 302-401
overview, 302-4
genesis, 304-12
*Germ* and *Oxford and Cambridge Magazine,* 312-20
Robert Buchanan and the "Fleshly School of Poetry," 320-31
satires and parodies, 331-4
surveys, 334-51
aesthetics, 351-75
sister arts of poetry and painting, 375-94
influence, 394-9

**Pre-romanticism** LC 40: 1-56
overviews and general studies, 2-14
defining the period, 14-23
new directions in poetry and prose, 23-45
the focus on the self, 45-56

**Pre-Socratic Philosophy** CMLC 22: 1-56
overviews and general studies, 3-24
the Ionians and the Pythagoreans, 25-35
Heraclitus, the Eleatics, and the Atomists, 36-47
the Sophists, 47-55

**Prison in Nineteenth-Century Literature, The** NCLC 116: 241-357
overview, 242-60
romantic prison, 260-78
domestic prison, 278-316
America as prison, 316-24
physical prisons and prison authors, 324-56

**Protestant Hagiography and Martyrology** LC 84: 106-217
overview, 106-37
John Foxe's *Book of Martyrs*, 137-97
martyrology and the feminine perspective, 198-216

**Protestant Reformation, Literature of the** LC 37: 1-83
overviews and general studies, 1-49
humanism and scholasticism, 49-69
the reformation and literature, 69-82

**Psychoanalysis and Literature** TCLC 38: 227-338
overviews and general studies, 227-46
Freud on literature, 246-51
psychoanalytic views of the literary process, 251-61
psychoanalytic theories of response to literature, 261-88
psychoanalysis and literary criticism, 288-312
psychoanalysis as literature/literature as psychoanalysis, 313-34

**The Quarrel between the Ancients and the Moderns** LC 63: 266-381
overviews and general studies, 267-301
Renaissance origins, 301-32
Quarrel between the Ancients and the Moderns in France, 332-58
Battle of the Books in England, 358-80

**Rap Music** CLC 76: 477-50

**Renaissance Natural Philosophy** LC 27: 201-87
cosmology, 201-28
astrology, 228-54
magic, 254-86

**Representations of the Devil in Nineteenth-Century Literature** NCLC 100: 89-223
overviews and general studies, 90-115
the Devil in American fiction, 116-43
English Romanticism: the satanic school, 143-89
Luciferian discourse in European literature, 189-222

**Restoration Drama** LC 21: 184-275
general overviews and general studies, 185-230
Jeremy Collier stage controversy, 230-9
other critical interpretations, 240-75

**Revenge Tragedy** LC 71: 113-242
overviews and general studies, 113-51
Elizabethan attitudes toward revenge, 151-88
the morality of revenge, 188-216
reminders and remembrance, 217-41

**Revising the Literary Canon** CLC 81: 465-509

**Revising the Literary Canon** TCLC 114: 240-84
overviews and general studies, 241-85
canon change in American literature, 285-339
gender and the literary canon, 339-59
minority and third-world literature and the canon, 359-84

**Revolutionary Astronomers** LC 51: 314-65
overviews and general studies, 316-25
principal figures, 325-51
Revolutionary astronomical models, 352-64

**Robin Hood, Legend of** LC 19: 205-58
origins and development of the Robin Hood legend, 206-20
representations of Robin Hood, 220-44
Robin Hood as hero, 244-56

**Rushdie, Salman, *Satanic Verses* Controversy** CLC 55: 214-63; 59:404-56

**Russian Nihilism** NCLC 28: 403-47
definitions and overviews, 404-17
women and Nihilism, 417-27
literature as reform: the Civic Critics, 427-33

Nihilism and the Russian novel: Turgenev and Dostoevsky, 433-47
**Russian Thaw** TCLC 26: 189-247
   literary history of the period, 190-206
   theoretical debate of socialist realism, 206-11
   *Novy Mir*, 211-7
   *Literary Moscow*, 217-24
   Pasternak, *Zhivago*, and the Nobel prize, 224-7
   poetry of liberation, 228-31
   Brodsky trial and the end of the Thaw, 231-6
   achievement and influence, 236-46
**Salem Witch Trials** LC 38: 1-145
   overviews and general studies, 2-30
   historical background, 30-65
   judicial background, 65-78
   the search for causes, 78-115
   the role of women in the trials, 115-44
**Salinger, J. D., Controversy Surrounding** *In Search of J. D. Salinger* CLC 55: 325-44
**Science and Modern Literature** TCLC 90: 308-419
   overviews and general studies, 295-333
   fiction, 333-95
   poetry, 395-405
   drama, 405-19
**Science in Nineteenth-Century Literature** NCLC 100: 224-366
   overviews and general studies, 225-65
   major figures, 265-336
   sociopolitical concerns, 336-65
**Science Fiction, Nineteenth-Century** NCLC 24: 241-306
   background, 242-50
   definitions of the genre, 251-56
   representative works and writers, 256-75
   themes and conventions, 276-305
**Scottish Chaucerians** LC 20: 363-412
**Scottish Poetry, Eighteenth-Century** LC 29: 95-167
   overviews and general studies, 96-114
   the Scottish Augustans, 114-28
   the Scots Vernacular Revival, 132-63
   Scottish poetry after Burns, 163-66
**Sea in Literature, The** TCLC 82: 72-191
   drama, 73-9
   poetry, 79-119
   fiction, 119-91
**Sea in Nineteenth-Century English and American Literature, The** NCLC 104: 265-362
   overviews and general studies, 267-306
   major figures in American sea fiction—Cooper and Melville, 306-29
   American sea poetry and short stories, 329-45
   English sea literature, 345-61
**Sensation Novel, The** NCLC 80: 219-330
   overviews and general studies, 221-46
   principal figures, 246-62
   nineteenth-century reaction, 262-91
   feminist criticism, 291-329
**Sentimental Novel, The** NCLC 60: 146-245
   overviews and general studies, 147-58
   the politics of domestic fiction, 158-79
   a literature of resistance and repression, 179-212
   the reception of sentimental fiction, 213-44
**Sex and Literature** TCLC 82: 192-434
   overviews and general studies, 193-216
   drama, 216-63
   poetry, 263-87
   fiction, 287-431

**Sherlock Holmes Centenary** TCLC 26: 248-310
   Doyle's life and the composition of the Holmes stories, 248-59
   life and character of Holmes, 259-78
   method, 278-79
   Holmes and the Victorian world, 279-92
   Sherlockian scholarship, 292-301
   Doyle and the development of the detective story, 301-07
   Holmes's continuing popularity, 307-09
**The Silver Fork Novel** NCLC 88: 58-140
   criticism, 59-139
**Slave Narratives, American** NCLC 20: 1-91
   background, 2-9
   overviews and general studies, 9-24
   contemporary responses, 24-7
   language, theme, and technique, 27-70
   historical authenticity, 70-5
   antecedents, 75-83
   role in development of Black American literature, 83-8
**The Slave Trade in British and American Literature** LC 59: 283-369
   overviews and general studies, 284-91
   depictions by white writers, 291-331
   depictions by former slaves, 331-67
**Social Conduct Literature** LC 55: 196-298
   overviews and general studies, 196-223
   prescriptive ideology in other literary forms, 223-38
   role of the press, 238-63
   impact of conduct literature, 263-87
   conduct literature and the perception of women, 287-96
   women writing for women, 296-98
**Socialism** NCLC 88: 141-237
   origins, 142-54
   French socialism, 154-83
   Anglo-American socialism, 183-205
   Socialist-Feminism, 205-36
**Southern Literature** *See* **Contemporary Southern Literature**
**Southern Literature of the Reconstruction** NCLC 108: 289-369
   overview, 290-91
   reconstruction literature: the consequences of war, 291-321
   old south to new: continuities in southern culture, 321-68
**Spanish Civil War Literature** TCLC 26: 311-85
   topics in, 312-33
   British and American literature, 333-59
   French literature, 359-62
   Spanish literature, 362-73
   German literature, 373-75
   political idealism and war literature, 375-83
**Spanish Golden Age Literature** LC 23: 262-332
   overviews and general studies, 263-81
   verse drama, 281-304
   prose fiction, 304-19
   lyric poetry, 319-31
**Spasmodic School of Poetry** NCLC 24: 307-52
   history and major figures, 307-21
   the Spasmodics on poetry, 321-7
   *Firmilian* and critical disfavor, 327-39
   theme and technique, 339-47
   influence, 347-51
**Sports in Literature** TCLC 86: 294-445
   overviews and general studies, 295-324
   major writers and works, 324-402
   sports, literature, and social issues, 402-45
**Steinbeck, John, Fiftieth Anniversary of** *The Grapes of Wrath* CLC 59: 311-54

**Sturm und Drang** NCLC 40: 196-276
   definitions, 197-238
   poetry and poetics, 238-58
   drama, 258-75
**Supernatural Fiction in the Nineteenth Century** NCLC 32: 207-87
   major figures and influences, 208-35
   the Victorian ghost story, 236-54
   the influence of science and occultism, 254-66
   supernatural fiction and society, 266-86
**Supernatural Fiction, Modern** TCLC 30: 59-116
   evolution and varieties, 60-74
   "decline" of the ghost story, 74-86
   as a literary genre, 86-92
   technique, 92-101
   nature and appeal, 101-15
**Surrealism** TCLC 30: 334-406
   history and formative influences, 335-43
   manifestos, 343-54
   philosophic, aesthetic, and political principles, 354-75
   poetry, 375-81
   novel, 381-6
   drama, 386-92
   film, 392-8
   painting and sculpture, 398-403
   achievement, 403-5
**Symbolism, Russian** TCLC 30: 266-333
   doctrines and major figures, 267-92
   theories, 293-8
   and French Symbolism, 298-310
   themes in poetry, 310-4
   theater, 314-20
   and the fine arts, 320-32
**Symbolist Movement, French** NCLC 20: 169-249
   background and characteristics, 170-86
   principles, 186-91
   attacked and defended, 191-7
   influences and predecessors, 197-211
   and Decadence, 211-6
   theater, 216-26
   prose, 226-33
   decline and influence, 233-47
**Television and Literature** TCLC 78: 283-426
   television and literacy, 283-98
   reading vs. watching, 298-341
   adaptations, 341-62
   literary genres and television, 362-90
   television genres and literature, 390-410
   children's literature/children's television, 410-25
**Theater of the Absurd** TCLC 38: 339-415
   "The Theater of the Absurd," 340-7
   major plays and playwrights, 347-58
   and the concept of the absurd, 358-86
   theatrical techniques, 386-94
   predecessors of, 394-402
   influence of, 402-13
**Tin Pan Alley** *See* **American Popular Song, Golden Age of**
**Tobacco Culture** LC 55: 299-366
   social and economic attitudes toward tobacco, 299-344
   tobacco trade between the old world and the new world, 344-55
   tobacco smuggling in Great Britain, 355-66
**Transcendentalism, American** NCLC 24: 1-99
   overviews and general studies, 3-23
   contemporary documents, 23-41
   theological aspects of, 42-52
   and social issues, 52-74
   literature of, 74-96
**Travel Writing in the Nineteenth Century** NCLC 44: 274-392

the European grand tour, 275-303
the Orient, 303-47
North America, 347-91

**Travel Writing in the Twentieth Century** TCLC 30: 407-56
conventions and traditions, 407-27
and fiction writing, 427-43
comparative essays on travel writers, 443-54

**Tristan and Isolde Legend** CMLC 42: 311-404

**True-Crime Literature** CLC 99: 333-433
history and analysis, 334-407
reviews of true-crime publications, 407-23
writing instruction, 424-29
author profiles, 429-33

*Ulysses* **and the Process of Textual Reconstruction** TCLC 26:386-416
evaluations of the new *Ulysses,* 386-94
editorial principles and procedures, 394-401
theoretical issues, 401-16

**Utilitarianism** NCLC 84: 272-340
J. S. Mill's Utilitarianism: liberty, equality, justice, 273-313
Jeremy Bentham's Utilitarianism: the science of happiness, 313-39

**Utopianism** NCLC 88: 238-346
overviews: Utopian literature, 239-59
Utopianism in American literature, 259-99
Utopianism in British literature, 299-311
Utopianism and Feminism, 311-45

**Utopian Literature, Nineteenth-Century** NCLC 24: 353-473
definitions, 354-74
overviews and general studies, 374-88
theory, 388-408
communities, 409-26
fiction, 426-53
women and fiction, 454-71

**Utopian Literature, Renaissance** LC 32: 1-63
overviews and general studies, 2-25
classical background, 25-33
utopia and the social contract, 33-9
origins in mythology, 39-48
utopia and the Renaissance country house, 48-52
influence of millenarianism, 52-62

**Vampire in Literature** TCLC 46: 391-454
origins and evolution, 392-412
social and psychological perspectives, 413-44
vampire fiction and science fiction, 445-53

**Vernacular Bibles** LC 67: 214-388
overviews and general studies, 215-59
the English Bible, 259-355
the German Bible, 355-88

**Victorian Autobiography** NCLC 40: 277-363
development and major characteristics, 278-88
themes and techniques, 289-313
the autobiographical tendency in Victorian prose and poetry, 313-47
Victorian women's autobiographies, 347-62

**Victorian Fantasy Literature** NCLC 60: 246-384
overviews and general studies, 247-91
major figures, 292-366
women in Victorian fantasy literature, 366-83

**Victorian Hellenism** NCLC 68: 251-376
overviews and general studies, 252-78
the meanings of Hellenism, 278-335
the literary influence, 335-75

**Victorian Illustrated Fiction** NCLC 120: 247-356
overviews and development, 128-76
technical and material aspects of book illustration, 276-84
Charles Dickens and his illustrators, 284-320
William Makepeace Thackeray, 320-31
George Eliot and Frederic Leighton, 331-51
Lewis Carroll and John Tenniel, 351-56

**Victorian Novel** NCLC 32: 288-454
development and major characteristics, 290-310
themes and techniques, 310-58
social criticism in the Victorian novel, 359-97
urban and rural life in the Victorian novel, 397-406
women in the Victorian novel, 406-25
Mudie's Circulating Library, 425-34
the late-Victorian novel, 434-51

**Vietnamese Literature** TCLC 102: 322-386

**Vietnam War in Literature and Film** CLC 91: 383-437
overview, 384-8
prose, 388-412
film and drama, 412-24
poetry, 424-35

**Violence in Literature** TCLC 98: 235-358
overviews and general studies, 236-74
violence in the works of modern authors, 274-358

**Vorticism** TCLC 62: 330-426
Wyndham Lewis and Vorticism, 330-8
characteristics and principles of Vorticism, 338-65
Lewis and Pound, 365-82
Vorticist writing, 382-416
Vorticist painting, 416-26

**Well-Made Play, The** NCLC 80: 331-370
overviews and general studies, 332-45
Scribe's style, 345-56
the influence of the well-made play, 356-69

**Women's Autobiography, Nineteenth Century** NCLC 76: 285-368
overviews and general studies, 287-300
autobiographies concerned with religious and political issues, 300-15
autobiographies by women of color, 315-38
autobiographies by women pioneers, 338-51
autobiographies by women of letters, 351-68

**Women's Diaries, Nineteenth-Century** NCLC 48: 308-54
overview, 308-13
diary as history, 314-25
sociology of diaries, 325-34
diaries as psychological scholarship, 334-43
diary as autobiography, 343-8
diary as literature, 348-53

**Women in Modern Literature** TCLC 94: 262-425
overviews and general studies, 263-86
American literature, 286-304
other national literatures, 304-33
fiction, 333-94
poetry, 394-407
drama, 407-24

**Women Writers, Seventeenth-Century** LC 30: 2-58
overview, 2-15
women and education, 15-9
women and autobiography, 19-31
women's diaries, 31-9
early feminists, 39-58

**World War I Literature** TCLC 34: 392-486
overview, 393-403
English, 403-27
German, 427-50
American, 450-66
French, 466-74
and modern history, 474-82

**Yellow Journalism** NCLC 36: 383-456
overviews and general studies, 384-96
major figures, 396-413

**Yiddish Literature** TCLC 130: 229-364
overviews and general studies, 230-54
major authors, 254-305
Yiddish literature in America, 305-34
Yiddish and Judaism, 334-64

**Young Playwrights Festival**
1988 CLC 55: 376-81
1989 CLC 59: 398-403
1990 CLC 65: 444-8

# *CLC* Cumulative Nationality Index

## ALBANIAN

Kadare, Ismail **52**

## ALGERIAN

Althusser, Louis **106**
Camus, Albert **1, 2, 4, 9, 11, 14, 32, 63, 69, 124**
Cixous, Hélène **92**
Cohen-Solal, Annie **50**

## AMERICAN

Abbey, Edward **36, 59**
Abbott, Lee K(ittredge) **48**
Abish, Walter **22**
Abrams, M(eyer) H(oward) **24**
Acker, Kathy **45, 111**
Adams, Alice (Boyd) **6, 13, 46**
Addams, Charles (Samuel) **30**
Adler, C(arole) S(chwerdtfeger) **35**
Adler, Renata **8, 31**
Ai **4, 14, 69**
Aiken, Conrad (Potter) **1, 3, 5, 10, 52**
Albee, Edward (Franklin III) **1, 2, 3, 5, 9, 11, 13, 25, 53, 86, 113**
Alexander, Lloyd (Chudley) **35**
Alexie, Sherman (Joseph Jr.) **96, 154**
Algren, Nelson **4, 10, 33**
Allen, Edward **59**
Allen, Paula Gunn **84**
Allen, Woody **16, 52**
Allison, Dorothy E. **78, 153**
Alta **19**
Alter, Robert B(ernard) **34**
Alther, Lisa **7, 41**
Altman, Robert **16, 116**
Alvarez, Julia **93**
Ambrose, Stephen E(dward) **145**
Ammons, A(rchie) R(andolph) **2, 3, 5, 8, 9, 25, 57, 108**
L'Amour, Louis (Dearborn) **25, 55**
Anaya, Rudolfo A(lfonso) **23, 148**
Anderson, Jon (Victor) **9**
Anderson, Poul (William) **15**
Anderson, Robert (Woodruff) **23**
Angell, Roger **26**
Angelou, Maya **12, 35, 64, 77, 155**
Anthony, Piers **35**
Apple, Max (Isaac) **9, 33**
Appleman, Philip (Dean) **51**
Archer, Jules **12**
Arendt, Hannah **66, 98**
Arnow, Harriette (Louisa) Simpson **2, 7, 18**
Arrick, Fran **30**
Arzner, Dorothy **98**
Ashbery, John (Lawrence) **2, 3, 4, 6, 9, 13, 15, 25, 41, 77, 125**
Asimov, Isaac **1, 3, 9, 19, 26, 76, 92**
Attaway, William (Alexander) **92**
Auchincloss, Louis (Stanton) **4, 6, 9, 18, 45**
Auden, W(ystan) H(ugh) **1, 2, 3, 4, 6, 9, 11, 14, 43, 123**
Auel, Jean M(arie) **31, 107**

Auster, Paul **47, 131**
Bach, Richard (David) **14**
Badanes, Jerome **59**
Baker, Elliott **8**
Baker, Nicholson **61, 165**
Baker, Russell (Wayne) **31**
Bakshi, Ralph **26**
Baldwin, James (Arthur) **1, 2, 3, 4, 5, 8, 13, 15, 17, 42, 50, 67, 90, 127**
Bambara, Toni Cade **19, 88**
Banks, Russell **37, 72**
Baraka, Amiri **1, 2, 3, 5, 10, 14, 33, 115**
Barber, Benjamin R. **141**
Barbera, Jack (Vincent) **44**
Barnard, Mary (Ethel) **48**
Barnes, Djuna **3, 4, 8, 11, 29, 127**
Barondess, Sue K(aufman) **8**
Barrett, Andrea **150**
Barrett, William (Christopher) **27**
Barth, John (Simmons) **1, 2, 3, 5, 7, 9, 10, 14, 27, 51, 89**
Barthelme, Donald **1, 2, 3, 5, 6, 8, 13, 23, 46, 59, 115**
Barthelme, Frederick **36, 117**
Barzun, Jacques (Martin) **51, 145**
Bass, Rick **79, 143**
Baumbach, Jonathan **6, 23**
Bausch, Richard (Carl) **51**
Baxter, Charles (Morley) **45, 78**
Beagle, Peter S(oyer) **7, 104**
Beattie, Ann **8, 13, 18, 40, 63, 146**
Becker, Walter **26**
Beecher, John **6**
Begiebing, Robert J(ohn) **70**
Behrman, S(amuel) N(athaniel) **40**
Belitt, Ben **22**
Bell, Madison Smartt **41, 102**
Bell, Marvin (Hartley) **8, 31**
Bellow, Saul **1, 2, 3, 6, 8, 10, 13, 15, 25, 33, 34, 63, 79**
Benary-Isbert, Margot **12**
Benchley, Peter (Bradford) **4, 8**
Benedikt, Michael **4, 14**
Benford, Gregory (Albert) **52**
Bennett, Jay **35**
Benson, Jackson J. **34**
Benson, Sally **17**
Bentley, Eric (Russell) **24**
Berendt, John (Lawrence) **86**
Berger, Melvin H. **12**
Berger, Thomas (Louis) **3, 5, 8, 11, 18, 38**
Bergstein, Eleanor **4**
Bernard, April **59**
Bernstein, Charles **142,**
Berriault, Gina **54, 109**
Berrigan, Daniel **4**
Berry, Chuck **17**
Berry, Wendell (Erdman) **4, 6, 8, 27, 46**
Berryman, John **1, 2, 3, 4, 6, 8, 10, 13, 25, 62**
Bessie, Alvah **23**
Bettelheim, Bruno **79**
Betts, Doris (Waugh) **3, 6, 28**

Bidart, Frank **33**
Birkerts, Sven **116**
Bishop, Elizabeth **1, 4, 9, 13, 15, 32**
Bishop, John **10**
Blackburn, Paul **9, 43**
Blackmur, R(ichard) P(almer) **2, 24**
Blaise, Clark **29**
Blatty, William Peter **2**
Blessing, Lee **54**
Blish, James (Benjamin) **14**
Bloch, Robert (Albert) **33**
Bloom, Harold **24, 103**
Blount, Roy (Alton) Jr. **38**
Blume, Judy (Sussman) **12, 30**
Bly, Robert (Elwood) **1, 2, 5, 10, 15, 38, 128**
Bochco, Steven **35**
Bogan, Louise **4, 39, 46, 93**
Bogosian, Eric **45, 141**
Bograd, Larry **35**
Bonham, Frank **12**
Bontemps, Arna(ud Wendell) **1, 18**
Booth, Philip **23**
Booth, Wayne C(layson) **24**
Bottoms, David **53**
Bourjaily, Vance (Nye) **8, 62**
Bova, Ben(jamin William) **45**
Bowers, Edgar **9**
Bowles, Jane (Sydney) **3, 68**
Bowles, Paul (Frederick) **1, 2, 19, 53**
Boyle, Kay **1, 5, 19, 58, 121**
Boyle, T(homas) Coraghessan **36, 55, 90**
Bradbury, Ray (Douglas) **1, 3, 10, 15, 42, 98**
Bradley, David (Henry) Jr. **23, 118**
Bradley, John Ed(mund Jr.) **55**
Bradley, Marion Zimmer **30**
Bradshaw, John **70**
Brady, Joan **86**
Brammer, William **31**
Brancato, Robin F(idler) **35**
Brand, Millen **7**
Branden, Barbara **44**
Branley, Franklyn M(ansfield) **21**
Brautigan, Richard (Gary) **1, 3, 5, 9, 12, 34, 42**
Braverman, Kate **67**
Brennan, Maeve **5**
Bridgers, Sue Ellen **26**
Brin, David **34**
Brodkey, Harold (Roy) **56**
Brodsky, Joseph **4, 6, 13, 36, 100**
Brodsky, Michael (Mark) **19**
Bromell, Henry **5**
Broner, E(sther) M(asserman) **19**
Bronk, William (M.) **10**
Brooks, Cleanth **24, 86, 110**
Brooks, Gwendolyn (Elizabeth) **1, 2, 4, 5, 15, 49, 125**
Brooks, Mel **12**
Brooks, Peter **34**
Brooks, Van Wyck **29**
Brosman, Catharine Savage **9**
Broughton, T(homas) Alan **19**
Broumas, Olga **10, 73**

Brown, Claude **30**
Brown, Dee (Alexander) **18, 47**
Brown, Rita Mae **18, 43, 79**
Brown, Rosellen **32**
Brown, Sterling Allen **1, 23, 59**
Brown, (William) Larry **73**
Brownmiller, Susan **159**
Browne, (Clyde) Jackson **21**
Browning, Tod **16**
Bruccoli, Matthew J(oseph) **34**
Bruce, Lenny **21**
Bryan, C(ourtlandt) D(ixon) B(arnes) **29**
Buchwald, Art(hur) **33**
Buck, Pearl S(ydenstricker) **7, 11, 18, 127**
Buckley, Christopher **165**
Buckley, William F(rank) Jr. **7, 18, 37**
Buechner, (Carl) Frederick **2, 4, 6, 9**
Bukowski, Charles **2, 5, 9, 41, 82, 108**
Bullins, Ed **1, 5, 7**
Burke, Kenneth (Duva) **2, 24**
Burnshaw, Stanley **3, 13, 44**
Burr, Anne **6**
Burroughs, William S(eward) **1, 2, 5, 15, 22, 42, 75, 109**
Busch, Frederick **7, 10, 18, 47, 166**
Bush, Ronald **34**
Butler, Octavia E(stelle) **38, 121**
Butler, Robert Olen (Jr.) **81, 162**
Byars, Betsy (Cromer) **35**
Byrne, David **26**
Cage, John (Milton Jr.) **41**
Cain, James M(allahan) **3, 11, 28**
Caldwell, Erskine (Preston) **1, 8, 14, 50, 60**
Caldwell, (Janet Miriam) Taylor (Holland) **2, 28, 39**
Calisher, Hortense **2, 4, 8, 38, 134**
Cameron, Carey **59**
Cameron, Peter **44**
Campbell, John W(ood Jr.) **32**
Campbell, Joseph **69**
Campion, Jane **95**
Canby, Vincent **13**
Canin, Ethan **55**
Capote, Truman **1, 3, 8, 13, 19, 34, 38, 58**
Capra, Frank **16**
Caputo, Philip **32**
Card, Orson Scott **44, 47, 50**
Carey, Ernestine Gilbreth **17**
Carlisle, Henry (Coffin) **33**
Carlson, Ron(ald F.) **54**
Carpenter, Don(ald Richard) **41**
Carpenter, John **161**
Carr, Caleb **86**
Carr, John Dickson **3**
Carr, Virginia Spencer **34**
Carroll, James P. **38**
Carroll, Jim **35, 143**
Carruth, Hayden **4, 7, 10, 18, 84**
Carson, Rachel Louise **71**
Carver, Raymond **22, 36, 53, 55, 126**
Casey, John (Dudley) **59**
Casey, Michael **2**
Casey, Warren (Peter) **12**
Cassavetes, John **20**
Cassill, R(onald) V(erlin) **4, 23**
Cassity, (Allen) Turner **6, 42**
Castaneda, Carlos (Cesar Aranha) **12, 119**
Castedo, Elena **65**
Castillo, Ana (Hernandez Del) **151**
Catton, (Charles) Bruce **35**
Caunitz, William J. **34**
Chabon, Michael **55, 149**
Chappell, Fred (Davis) **40, 78, 162**
Charyn, Jerome **5, 8, 18**
Chase, Mary Ellen **2**
Chayefsky, Paddy **23**
Cheever, John **3, 7, 8, 11, 15, 25, 64**
Cheever, Susan **18, 48**
Cheney, Lynne V. **70**
Chester, Alfred **49**
Childress, Alice **12, 15, 86, 96**
Chin, Frank (Chew Jr.) **135**

Choi, Susan **119**
Chomsky, (Avram) Noam **132**
Chute, Carolyn **39**
Ciardi, John (Anthony) **10, 40, 44, 129**
Cimino, Michael **16**
Cisneros, Sandra **69, 118**
Clampitt, Amy **32**
Clancy, Tom **45, 112**
Clark, Eleanor **5, 19**
Clark, Walter Van Tilburg **28**
Clarke, Shirley **16**
Clavell, James (duMaresq) **6, 25, 87**
Cleaver, (Leroy) Eldridge **30, 119**
Clifton, (Thelma) Lucille **19, 66, 162**
Coburn, D(onald) L(ee) **10**
Codrescu, Andrei **46, 121**
Coen, Ethan **108**
Coen, Joel **108**
Cohen, Arthur A(llen) **7, 31**
Coles, Robert (Martin) **108**
Collier, Christopher **30**
Collier, James Lincoln **30**
Collins, Linda **44**
Colter, Cyrus **58**
Colum, Padraic **28**
Colwin, Laurie (E.) **5, 13, 23, 84**
Condon, Richard (Thomas) **4, 6, 8, 10, 45, 100**
Connell, Evan S(helby) Jr. **4, 6, 45**
Connelly, Marc(us Cook) **7**
Conroy, (Donald) Pat(rick) **30, 74**
Cook, Robin **14**
Cooke, Elizabeth **55**
Cook-Lynn, Elizabeth **93**
Cooper, J(oan) California **56**
Coover, Robert (Lowell) **3, 7, 15, 32, 46, 87, 161**
Coppola, Francis Ford **16, 126**
Corcoran, Barbara (Asenath) **17**
Corman, Cid **9**
Cormier, Robert (Edmund) **12, 30**
Corn, Alfred (DeWitt III) **33**
Cornwell, Patricia (Daniels) **155**
Corso, (Nunzio) Gregory **1, 11**
Costain, Thomas B(ertram) **30**
Cowley, Malcolm **39**
Cozzens, James Gould **1, 4, 11, 92**
Crane, R(onald) S(almon) **27**
Crase, Douglas **58**
Creeley, Robert (White) **1, 2, 4, 8, 11, 15, 36, 78**
Crews, Harry (Eugene) **6, 23, 49**
Crichton, (John) Michael **2, 6, 54, 90**
Cristofer, Michael **28**
Cronenberg, David **143**
Crow Dog, Mary (Ellen) **93**
Crowley, John **57**
Crumb, R(obert) **17**
Cryer, Gretchen (Kiger) **21**
Cudlip, David R(ockwell) **34**
Cummings, E(dward) E(stlin) **1, 3, 8, 12, 15, 68**
Cunningham, J(ames) V(incent) **3, 31**
Cunningham, Julia (Woolfolk) **12**
Cunningham, Michael **34**
Currie, Ellen **44**
Dacey, Philip **51**
Dahlberg, Edward **1, 7, 14**
Daitch, Susan **103**
Daly, Elizabeth **52**
Daly, Maureen **17**
Dannay, Frederic **11**
Danvers, Dennis **70**
Danziger, Paula **21**
Davenport, Guy (Mattison Jr.) **6, 14, 38**
Davidson, Donald (Grady) **2, 13, 19**
Davidson, Sara **9**
Davis, Angela (Yvonne) **77**
Davis, H(arold) L(enoir) **49**
Davison, Peter (Hubert) **28**
Dawson, Fielding **6**
Deer, Sandra **45**

Delany, Samuel R(ay) Jr. **8, 14, 38, 141**
Delbanco, Nicholas (Franklin) **6, 13, 167**
DeLillo, Don **8, 10, 13, 27, 39, 54, 76, 143**
Deloria, Vine (Victor) Jr. **21, 122**
Del Vecchio, John M(ichael) **29**
de Man, Paul (Adolph Michel) **55**
DeMarinis, Rick **54**
Demby, William **53**
Denby, Edwin (Orr) **48**
De Palma, Brian (Russell) **20**
Deren, Maya **16, 102**
Derleth, August (William) **31**
Deutsch, Babette **18**
De Vries, Peter **1, 2, 3, 7, 10, 28, 46**
Dexter, Pete **34, 55**
Diamond, Neil **30**
Dick, Philip K(indred) **10, 30, 72**
Dickey, James (Lafayette) **1, 2, 4, 7, 10, 15, 47, 109**
Dickey, William **3, 28**
Dickinson, Charles **49**
Didion, Joan **1, 3, 8, 14, 32, 129**
Dillard, Annie **9, 60, 115**
Dillard, R(ichard) H(enry) W(ilde) **5**
Disch, Thomas M(ichael) **7, 36**
Dixon, Stephen **52**
Dobyns, Stephen **37**
Doctorow, E(dgar) L(aurence) **6, 11, 15, 18, 37, 44, 65, 113**
Dodson, Owen (Vincent) **79**
Doerr, Harriet **34**
Donaldson, Stephen R(eeder) **46, 138**
Donleavy, J(ames) P(atrick) **1, 4, 6, 10, 45**
Donovan, John **35**
Doolittle, Hilda **3, 8, 14, 31, 34, 73**
Dorn, Edward (Merton) **10, 18**
Dorris, Michael (Anthony) **109**
Dos Passos, John (Roderigo) **1, 4, 8, 11, 15, 25, 34, 82**
Douglas, Ellen **73**
Dove, Rita (Frances) **50, 81**
Dowell, Coleman **60**
Drexler, Rosalyn **2, 6**
Drury, Allen (Stuart) **37**
Duberman, Martin (Bauml) **8**
Dubie, Norman (Evans) **36**
Du Bois, W(illiam) E(dward) B(urghardt) **1, 2, 13, 64, 96**
Dubus, André **13, 36, 97**
Duffy, Bruce **50**
Dugan, Alan **2, 6**
Dumas, Henry L. **6, 62**
Duncan, Lois **26**
Duncan, Robert (Edward) **1, 2, 4, 7, 15, 41, 55**
Dunn, Katherine (Karen) **71**
Dunn, Stephen (Elliott) **36**
Dunne, John Gregory **28**
Durang, Christopher (Ferdinand) **27, 38**
Durban, (Rosa) Pam **39**
Dworkin, Andrea **43, 123**
Dwyer, Thomas A. **114**
Dybek, Stuart **114**
Dylan, Bob **3, 4, 6, 12, 77**
Eastlake, William (Derry) **8**
Eberhart, Richard (Ghormley) **3, 11, 19, 56**
Eberstadt, Fernanda **39**
Eckert, Allan W. **17**
Edel, (Joseph) Leon **29, 34**
Edgerton, Clyde (Carlyle) **39**
Edmonds, Walter D(umaux) **35**
Edson, Russell **13**
Edwards, Gus **43**
Ehle, John (Marsden Jr.) **27**
Ehrenreich, Barbara **110**
Eigner, Larry **9**
Eiseley, Loren Corey **7**
Eisenstadt, Jill **50**
Eliade, Mircea **19**
Eliot, T(homas) S(tearns) **1, 2, 3, 6, 9, 10, 13, 15, 24, 34, 41, 55, 57, 113**

Elkin, Stanley L(awrence) **4, 6, 9, 14, 27, 51, 91**
Elledge, Scott **34**
Elliott, George P(aul) **2**
Ellis, Bret Easton **39, 71, 117**
Ellison, Harlan (Jay) **1, 13, 42, 139**
Ellison, Ralph (Waldo) **1, 3, 11, 54, 86, 114**
Ellmann, Lucy (Elizabeth) **61**
Ellmann, Richard (David) **50**
Elman, Richard (Martin) **19**
L'Engle, Madeleine (Camp Franklin) **12**
Ephron, Nora **17, 31**
Epstein, Daniel Mark **7**
Epstein, Jacob **19**
Epstein, Joseph **39**
Epstein, Leslie **27**
Erdman, Paul E(mil) **25**
Erdrich, Louise **39, 54, 120**
Erickson, Steve **64**
Eshleman, Clayton **7**
Estleman, Loren D. **48**
Eugenides, Jeffrey **81**
Everett, Percival L. **57**
Everson, William (Oliver) **1, 5, 14**
Exley, Frederick (Earl) **6, 11**
Ezekiel, Tish O'Dowd **34**
Fagen, Donald **26**
Fair, Ronald L. **18**
Faludi, Susan **140**
Fante, John (Thomas) **60**
Farina, Richard **9**
Farley, Walter (Lorimer) **17**
Farmer, Philip José **1, 19**
Farrell, James T(homas) **1, 4, 8, 11, 66**
Fast, Howard (Melvin) **23, 131**
Faulkner, William (Cuthbert) **1, 3, 6, 8, 9, 11, 14, 18, 28, 52, 68**
Fauset, Jessie Redmon **19, 54**
Faust, Irvin **8**
Fearing, Kenneth (Flexner) **51**
Federman, Raymond **6, 47**
Feiffer, Jules (Ralph) **2, 8, 64**
Feinberg, David B. **59**
Feldman, Irving (Mordecai) **7**
Felsen, Henry Gregor **17**
Ferber, Edna **18, 93**
Ferlinghetti, Lawrence (Monsanto) **2, 6, 10, 27, 111**
Ferrigno, Robert **65**
Fiedler, Leslie A(aron) **4, 13, 24**
Field, Andrew **44**
Fierstein, Harvey (Forbes) **33**
Fish, Stanley Eugene **142**
Fisher, M(ary) F(rances) K(ennedy) **76, 87**
Fisher, Vardis (Alvero) **7**
Fitzgerald, Robert (Stuart) **39**
Flanagan, Thomas (James Bonner) **25, 52**
Fleming, Thomas (James) **37**
Foote, Horton **51, 91**
Foote, Shelby **75**
Forbes, Esther **12**
Forché, Carolyn (Louise) **25, 83, 86**
Ford, John **16**
Ford, Richard **46, 99**
Foreman, Richard **50**
Forman, James Douglas **21**
Fornés, María Irene **39, 61**
Forrest, Leon (Richard) **4**
Fosse, Bob **20**
Fox, Paula **2, 8, 121**
Fox, William Price (Jr.) **22**
Francis, Robert (Churchill) **15**
Frank, Elizabeth **39**
Fraze, Candida (Merrill) **50**
Frazier, Ian **46**
Freeman, Judith **55**
French, Albert **86**
French, Marilyn **10, 18, 60**
Friedan, Betty (Naomi) **74**
Friedman, B(ernard) H(arper) **7**
Friedman, Bruce Jay **3, 5, 56**

Frost, Robert (Lee) **1, 3, 4, 9, 10, 13, 15, 26, 34, 44**
Frye, (Herman) Northrop **24, 70**
Fuchs, Daniel **34**
Fuchs, Daniel **8, 22**
Fukuyama, Francis **131**
Fuller, Charles (H. Jr.) **25**
Fulton, Alice **52**
Fuson, Robert H(enderson) **70**
Fussell, Paul **74**
Gaddis, William **1, 3, 6, 8, 10, 19, 43, 86**
Gaines, Ernest J(ames) **3, 11, 18, 86**
Gaitskill, Mary **69**
Gallagher, Tess **18, 63**
Gallant, Roy A(rthur) **17**
Gallico, Paul (William) **2**
Galvin, James **38**
Gann, Ernest Kellogg **23**
Garcia, Cristina **76**
Gardner, Herb(ert) **44**
Gardner, John (Champlin) Jr. **2, 3, 5, 7, 8, 10, 18, 28, 34**
Garrett, George (Palmer) **3, 11, 51**
Garrigue, Jean **2, 8**
Gass, William H(oward) **1, 2, 8, 11, 15, 39, 132**
Gates, Henry Louis Jr. **65**
Gay, Peter (Jack) **158**
Gaye, Marvin (Pentz Jr.) **26**
Gelbart, Larry (Simon) **21, 61**
Gelber, Jack **1, 6, 14, 79**
Gellhorn, Martha (Ellis) **14, 60**
Gent, Peter **29**
George, Jean Craighead **35**
Gertler, T. **134**
Ghiselin, Brewster **23**
Gibbons, Kaye **50, 88, 145**
Gibson, William **23**
Gibson, William (Ford) **39, 63**
Gifford, Barry (Colby) **34**
Gilbreth, Frank B(unker) Jr. **17**
Gilchrist, Ellen (Louise) **34, 48, 143**
Giles, Molly **39**
Gilliam, Terry (Vance) **21, 141**
Gilroy, Frank D(aniel) **2**
Gilstrap, John **99**
Ginsberg, Allen **1, 2, 3, 4, 6, 13, 36, 69, 109**
Giovanni, Nikki **2, 4, 19, 64, 117**
Glasser, Ronald J. **37**
Gleick, James (W.) **147**
Glück, Louise (Elisabeth) **7, 22, 44, 81, 160**
Godwin, Gail (Kathleen) **5, 8, 22, 31, 69, 125**
Goines, Donald **80**
Gold, Herbert **4, 7, 14, 42, 152**
Goldbarth, Albert **5, 38**
Goldman, Francisco **76**
Goldman, William (W.) **1, 48**
Goldsberry, Steven **34**
Goodman, Paul **1, 2, 4, 7**
Gordon, Caroline **6, 13, 29, 83**
Gordon, Mary (Catherine) **13, 22, 128**
Gordon, Sol **26**
Gordone, Charles **1, 4**
Gould, Lois **4, 10**
Gould, Stephen Jay **163**
Goyen, (Charles) William **5, 8, 14, 40**
Grafton, Sue **163**
Graham, Jorie **48, 118**
Grau, Shirley Ann **4, 9, 146**
Graver, Elizabeth **70**
Gray, Amlin **29**
Gray, Francine du Plessix **22, 153**
Gray, Spalding **49, 112**
Grayson, Richard (A.) **38**
Greeley, Andrew M(oran) **28**
Green, Hannah **3**
Green, Julien **3, 11, 77**
Green, Paul (Eliot) **25**
Greenberg, Joanne (Goldenberg) **7, 30**
Greenberg, Richard **57**
Greenblatt, Stephen J(ay) **70**

Greene, Bette **30**
Greene, Gael **8**
Gregor, Arthur **9**
Griffin, John Howard **68**
Griffin, Peter **39**
Grisham, John **84**
Grumbach, Doris (Isaac) **13, 22, 64**
Grunwald, Lisa **44**
Guare, John **8, 14, 29, 67**
Gubar, Susan (David) **145**
Guest, Barbara **34**
Guest, Judith (Ann) **8, 30**
Guild, Nicholas M. **33**
Gunn, Bill **5**
Gurganus, Allan **70**
Gurney, A(lbert) R(amsdell) Jr. **32, 50, 54**
Gustafson, James M(oody) **100**
Guterson, David **91**
Guthrie, A(lfred) B(ertram) Jr. **23**
Guy, Rosa (Cuthbert) **26**
Hacker, Marilyn **5, 9, 23, 72, 91**
Hailey, Elizabeth Forsythe **40**
Haines, John (Meade) **58**
Haldeman, Joe (William) **61**
Haley, Alex(ander Murray Palmer) **8, 12, 76**
Hall, Donald (Andrew Jr.) **1, 13, 37, 59, 151**
Halpern, Daniel **14**
Hamill, Pete **10**
Hamilton, Edmond **1**
Hamilton, Virginia (Esther) **26**
Hammett, (Samuel) Dashiell **3, 5, 10, 19, 47**
Hamner, Earl (Henry) Jr. **12**
Hannah, Barry **23, 38, 90**
Hansberry, Lorraine (Vivian) **17, 62**
Hansen, Joseph **38**
Hanson, Kenneth O(stlin) **13**
Hardwick, Elizabeth (Bruce) **13**
Harjo, Joy **83**
Harlan, Louis R(udolph) **34**
Harling, Robert **53**
Harmon, William (Ruth) **38**
Harper, Michael S(teven) **7, 22**
Harris, MacDonald **9**
Harris, Mark **19**
Harrison, Barbara Grizzuti **144**
Harrison, Harry (Max) **42**
Harrison, James (Thomas) **6, 14, 33, 66, 143**
Harrison, Kathryn **70, 151**
Harriss, Will(ard Irvin) **34**
Hart, Moss **66**
Hartman, Geoffrey H. **27**
Haruf, Kent **34**
Hass, Robert **18, 39, 99**
Haviaras, Stratis **33**
Hawkes, John (Clendennin Burne Jr.) **1, 2, 3, 4, 7, 9, 14, 15, 27, 49**
Hayden, Robert E(arl) **5, 9, 14, 37**
Hayman, Ronald **44**
H. D. **3, 8, 14, 31, 34, 73**
Hearne, Vicki **56**
Hearon, Shelby **63**
Hecht, Anthony (Evan) **8, 13, 19**
Hecht, Ben **8**
Heifner, Jack **11**
Heilbrun, Carolyn G(old) **25**
Heinemann, Larry (Curtiss) **50**
Heinlein, Robert A(nson) **1, 3, 8, 14, 26, 55**
Heller, Joseph **1, 3, 5, 8, 11, 36, 63**
Hellman, Lillian (Florence) **2, 4, 8, 14, 18, 34, 44, 52**
Helprin, Mark **7, 10, 22, 32**
Hemingway, Ernest (Miller) **1, 3, 6, 8, 10, 13, 19, 30, 34, 39, 41, 44, 50, 61, 80**
Hempel, Amy **39**
Henley, Beth **23**
Hentoff, Nat(han Irving) **26**
Herbert, Frank (Patrick) **12, 23, 35, 44, 85**
Herbst, Josephine (Frey) **34**
Herlihy, James Leo **6**
Herrmann, Dorothy **44**
Hersey, John (Richard) **1, 2, 7, 9, 40, 81, 97**
L'Heureux, John (Clarke) **52**

Heyen, William **13, 18**
Higgins, George V(incent) **4, 7, 10, 18**
Highsmith, (Mary) Patricia **2, 4, 14, 42, 102**
Highwater, Jamake (Mamake) **12**
Hijuelos, Oscar **65**
Hill, George Roy **26**
Hillerman, Tony **62**
Himes, Chester (Bomar) **2, 4, 7, 18, 58, 108**
Hinton, S(usan) E(loise) **30, 111**
Hirsch, Edward **31, 50**
Hirsch, E(ric) D(onald) Jr. **79**
Hoagland, Edward **28**
Hoban, Russell (Conwell) **7, 25**
Hobson, Laura Z(ametkin) **7, 25**
Hochman, Sandra **3, 8**
Hoffman, Alice **51**
Hoffman, Daniel (Gerard) **6, 13, 23**
Hoffman, Stanley **5**
Hoffman, William **141**
Hoffman, William M(oses) **40**
Hogan, Linda **73**
Holland, Isabelle **21**
Hollander, John **2, 5, 8, 14**
Holleran, Andrew **38**
Holmes, John Clellon **56**
Honig, Edwin **33**
Horgan, Paul (George Vincent O'Shaughnessy) **9, 53**
Horovitz, Israel (Arthur) **56**
Horwitz, Julius **14**
Hougan, Carolyn **34**
Howard, Maureen **5, 14, 46, 151**
Howard, Richard **7, 10, 47**
Howe, Fanny (Quincy) **47**
Howe, Irving **85**
Howe, Susan **72, 152**
Howe, Tina **48**
Howes, Barbara **15**
Hubbard, L(afayette) Ron(ald) **43**
Huddle, David **49**
Hughart, Barry **39**
Hughes, (James) Langston **1, 5, 10, 15, 35, 44, 108**
Hugo, Richard F(ranklin) **6, 18, 32**
Humphrey, William **45**
Humphreys, Josephine **34, 57**
Hunt, E(verette) Howard (Jr.) **3**
Hunt, Marsha **70**
Hunter, Evan **11, 31**
Hunter, Kristin (Eggleston) **35**
Hurston, Zora Neale **7, 30, 61**
Huston, John (Marcellus) **20**
Hustvedt, Siri **76**
Huxley, Aldous (Leonard) **1, 3, 4, 5, 8, 11, 18, 35, 79**
Hwang, David Henry **55**
Hyde, Margaret O(ldroyd) **21**
Hynes, James **65**
Ian, Janis **21**
Ignatow, David **4, 7, 14, 40**
Ingalls, Rachel (Holmes) **42**
Inge, William (Motter) **1, 8, 19**
Innaurato, Albert (F.) **21, 60**
Irving, John (Winslow) **13, 23, 38, 112**
Isaacs, Susan **32**
Isler, Alan (David) **91**
Ivask, Ivar Vidrik **14**
Jackson, Jesse **12**
Jackson, Shirley **11, 60, 87**
Jacobs, Jim **12**
Jacobsen, Josephine **48, 102**
Jakes, John (William) **29**
Jameson, Fredric (R.) **142**
Janowitz, Tama **43, 145**
Jarrell, Randall **1, 2, 6, 9, 13, 49**
Jeffers, (John) Robinson **2, 3, 11, 15, 54**
Jen, Gish **70**
Jennings, Waylon **21**
Jensen, Laura (Linnea) **37**
Jin, Xuefei **109**
Joel, Billy **26**
Johnson, Charles (Richard) **7, 51, 65, 163**

Johnson, Denis **52, 160**
Johnson, Diane **5, 13, 48**
Johnson, Joyce **58**
Johnson, Judith (Emlyn) **7, 15**
Jones, Edward P. **76**
Jones, Gayl **6, 9, 131**
Jones, James **1, 3, 10, 39**
Jones, LeRoi **1, 2, 3, 5, 10, 14**
Jones, Louis B. **65**
Jones, Madison (Percy Jr.) **4**
Jones, Nettie (Pearl) **34**
Jones, Preston **10**
Jones, Robert F(rancis) **7**
Jones, Thom (Douglas) **81**
Jong, Erica **4, 6, 8, 18, 83**
Jordan, June **5, 11, 23, 114**
Jordan, Pat(rick M.) **37**
Just, Ward (Swift) **4, 27**
Justice, Donald (Rodney) **6, 19, 102**
Kadohata, Cynthia **59, 122**
Kahn, Roger **30**
Kaletski, Alexander **39**
Kallman, Chester (Simon) **2**
Kaminsky, Stuart M(elvin) **59**
Kanin, Garson **22**
Kantor, MacKinlay **7**
Kaplan, David Michael **50**
Kaplan, James **59**
Karl, Frederick R(obert) **34**
Katz, Steve **47**
Kauffman, Janet **42**
Kaufman, Bob (Garnell) **49**
Kaufman, George S. **38**
Kaufman, Sue **3, 8**
Kazan, Elia **6, 16, 63**
Kazin, Alfred **34, 38, 119**
Keaton, Buster **20**
Keene, Donald **34**
Keillor, Garrison **40, 115**
Kellerman, Jonathan **44**
Kelley, William Melvin **22**
Kellogg, Marjorie **2**
Kemelman, Harry **2**
Kennedy, Adrienne (Lita) **66**
Kennedy, William **6, 28, 34, 53**
Kennedy, X. J. **8, 42**
Kenny, Maurice (Francis) **87**
Kerouac, Jack **1, 2, 3, 5, 14, 29, 61**
Kerr, Jean **22**
Kerr, M. E. **12, 35**
Kerr, Robert **55**
Kerrigan, (Thomas) Anthony **4, 6**
Kesey, Ken (Elton) **1, 3, 6, 11, 46, 64**
Kesselring, Joseph (Otto) **45**
Kessler, Jascha (Frederick) **4**
Kettelkamp, Larry (Dale) **12**
Keyes, Daniel **80**
Kherdian, David **6, 9**
Kienzle, William X(avier) **25**
Killens, John Oliver **10**
Kincaid, Jamaica **43, 68, 137**
King, Martin Luther Jr. **83**
King, Stephen (Edwin) **12, 26, 37, 61, 113**
King, Thomas **89**
Kingman, Lee **17**
Kingsley, Sidney **44**
Kingsolver, Barbara **55, 81, 130**
Kingston, Maxine (Ting Ting) Hong **12, 19, 58, 121**
Kinnell, Galway **1, 2, 3, 5, 13, 29, 129**
Kirkwood, James **9**
Kissinger, Henry A(lfred) **137**
Kizer, Carolyn (Ashley) **15, 39, 80**
Klappert, Peter **57**
Klein, Joe **154**
Klein, Norma **30**
Klein, T(heodore) E(ibon) D(onald) **34**
Knapp, Caroline **99**
Knebel, Fletcher **14**
Knight, Etheridge **40**
Knowles, John **1, 4, 10, 26**
Koch, Kenneth **5, 8, 44**

Komunyakaa, Yusef **86, 94**
Koontz, Dean R(ay) **78**
Kopit, Arthur (Lee) **1, 18, 33**
Kosinski, Jerzy (Nikodem) **1, 2, 3, 6, 10, 15, 53, 70**
Kostelanetz, Richard (Cory) **28**
Kotlowitz, Robert **4**
Kotzwinkle, William **5, 14, 35**
Kozol, Jonathan **17**
Kozoll, Michael **35**
Kramer, Kathryn **34**
Kramer, Larry **42**
Kristofferson, Kris **26**
Krumgold, Joseph (Quincy) **12**
Krutch, Joseph Wood **24**
Kubrick, Stanley **16**
Kumin, Maxine (Winokur) **5, 13, 28, 164**
Kunitz, Stanley (Jasspon) **6, 11, 14, 148**
Kushner, Tony **81**
Kuzma, Greg **7**
Lancaster, Bruce **36**
Landis, John **26**
Langer, Elinor **34**
Lapine, James (Elliot) **39**
Larsen, Eric **55**
Larsen, Nella **37**
Larson, Charles R(aymond) **31**
Lasch, Christopher **102**
Latham, Jean Lee **12**
Lattimore, Richmond (Alexander) **3**
Laughlin, James **49**
Lear, Norman (Milton) **12**
Leavitt, David **34**
Lebowitz, Fran(ces Ann) **11, 36**
Lee, Andrea **36**
Lee, Chang-rae **91**
Lee, Don L. **4**
Lee, George W(ashington) **52**
Lee, Helen Elaine **86**
Lee, Lawrence **34**
Lee, Manfred B(ennington) **11**
Lee, (Nelle) Harper **12, 60**
Lee, Shelton Jackson **105**
Lee, Stan **17**
Leet, Judith **11**
Leffland, Ella **19**
Le Guin, Ursula K(roeber) **8, 13, 22, 45, 71, 136**
Leiber, Fritz (Reuter Jr.) **25**
Leimbach, Marti **65**
Leithauser, Brad **27**
Lelchuk, Alan **5**
Lemann, Nancy **39**
Lentricchia, Frank (Jr.) **34**
Leonard, Elmore (John Jr.) **28, 34, 71, 120**
Lerman, Eleanor **9**
Lerman, Rhoda **56**
Lester, Richard **20**
Levertov, Denise **1, 2, 3, 5, 8, 15, 28, 66**
Levi, Jonathan **76**
Levin, Ira **3, 6**
Levin, Meyer **7**
Levine, Philip **2, 4, 5, 9, 14, 33, 118**
Levinson, Deirdre **49**
Levitin, Sonia (Wolff) **17**
Lewis, Janet **41**
Leyner, Mark **92**
Lieber, Joel **6**
Lieberman, Laurence (James) **4, 36**
Lifton, Robert Jay **67**
Lightman, Alan P(aige) **81**
Ligotti, Thomas (Robert) **44**
Lindbergh, Anne (Spencer) Morrow **82**
Linney, Romulus **51**
Lipsyte, Robert (Michael) **21**
Lish, Gordon (Jay) **45**
Littell, Robert **42**
Loewinsohn, Ron(ald William) **52**
Logan, John (Burton) **5**
Lopate, Phillip **29**
Lopez, Barry (Holstun) **70**
Lord, Bette Bao **23**

Lorde, Audre (Geraldine) **18, 71**
Louie, David Wong **70**
Lowell, Robert (Traill Spence Jr.) **1, 2, 3, 4, 5, 8, 9, 11, 15, 37, 124**
Loy, Mina **28**
Lucas, Craig **64**
Lucas, George **16**
Ludlam, Charles **46, 50**
Ludlum, Robert **22, 43**
Ludwig, Ken **60**
Lurie, Alison **4, 5, 18, 39**
Lynch, David (K.) **66, 162**
Lynn, Kenneth S(chuyler) **50**
Lytle, Andrew (Nelson) **22**
Maas, Peter **29**
Macdonald, Cynthia **13, 19**
MacDonald, John D(ann) **3, 27, 44**
MacInnes, Helen (Clark) **27, 39**
Maclean, Norman (Fitzroy) **78**
MacLeish, Archibald **3, 8, 14, 68**
MacShane, Frank **39**
Madden, (Jerry) David **5, 15**
Madhubuti, Haki R. **6, 73**
Mailer, Norman **1, 2, 3, 4, 5, 8, 11, 14, 28, 39, 74, 111**
Major, Clarence **3, 19, 48**
Malamud, Bernard **1, 2, 3, 5, 8, 9, 11, 18, 27, 44, 78, 85**
Malcolm X **82, 117**
Maloff, Saul **5**
Malone, Michael (Christopher) **43**
Malzberg, Barry N(athaniel) **7**
Mamet, David (Alan) **9, 15, 34, 46, 91, 166**
Mamoulian, Rouben (Zachary) **16**
Mano, D. Keith **2, 10**
Manso, Peter **39**
Margulies, Donald **76**
Markfield, Wallace **8**
Markson, David M(errill) **67**
Marlowe, Stephen **70**
Marquand, John P(hillips) **2, 10**
Marqués, René **96**
Marshall, Garry **17**
Marshall, Paule **27, 72**
Martin, Steve **30**
Martin, Valerie **89**
Maso, Carole **44**
Mason, Bobbie Ann **28, 43, 82, 154**
Masters, Hilary **48**
Mastrosimone, William **36**
Matheson, Richard (Burton) **37**
Mathews, Harry **6, 52**
Mathews, John Joseph **84**
Matthews, William (Procter III) **40**
Matthias, John (Edward) **9**
Matthiessen, Peter **5, 7, 11, 32, 64**
Maupin, Armistead (Jones Jr.) **95**
Maxwell, William (Keepers Jr.) **19**
May, Elaine **16**
Maynard, Joyce **23**
Maysles, Albert **16**
Maysles, David **16**
Mazer, Norma Fox **26**
McBrien, William (Augustine) **44**
McCaffrey, Anne (Inez) **17**
McCall, Nathan **86**
McCarthy, Mary (Therese) **1, 3, 5, 14, 24, 39, 59**
McCauley, Stephen (D.) **50**
McClure, Michael (Thomas) **6, 10**
McCorkle, Jill (Collins) **51**
McCourt, James **5**
McCourt, Malachy **119**
McCullers, (Lula) Carson (Smith) **1, 4, 10, 12, 48, 100**
McDermott, Alice **90**
McElroy, Joseph **5, 47**
McFarland, Dennis **65**
McGinley, Phyllis **14**
McGinniss, Joe **32**
McGrath, Thomas (Matthew) **28, 59**

McGuane, Thomas (Francis III) **3, 7, 18, 45, 127**
McHale, Tom **3, 5**
McInerney, Jay **34, 112**
McIntyre, Vonda N(eel) **18**
McKuen, Rod **1, 3**
McMillan, Terry (L.) **50, 61, 112**
McMurtry, Larry (Jeff) **2, 3, 7, 11, 27, 44, 127**
McNally, Terrence **4, 7, 41, 91**
McNally, T. M. **82**
McNamer, Deirdre **70**
McNeal, Tom **119**
McNickle, (William) D'Arcy **89**
McPhee, John (Angus) **36**
McPherson, James Alan **19, 77**
McPherson, William (Alexander) **34**
Mead, Margaret **37**
Medoff, Mark (Howard) **6, 23**
Mehta, Ved (Parkash) **37**
Meltzer, Milton **26**
Mendelsohn, Jane **99**
Meredith, William (Morris) **4, 13, 22, 55**
Merkin, Daphne **44**
Merrill, James (Ingram) **2, 3, 6, 8, 13, 18, 34, 91**
Merton, Thomas **1, 3, 11, 34, 83**
Merwin, W(illiam) S(tanley) **1, 2, 3, 5, 8, 13, 18, 45, 88**
Mewshaw, Michael **9**
Meyers, Jeffrey **39**
Michaels, Leonard **6, 25**
Michener, James A(lbert) **1, 5, 11, 29, 60, 109**
Miles, Jack **100**
Miles, Josephine (Louise) **1, 2, 14, 34, 39**
Millar, Kenneth **14**
Miller, Arthur **1, 2, 6, 10, 15, 26, 47, 78**
Miller, Henry (Valentine) **1, 2, 4, 9, 14, 43, 84**
Miller, Jason **2**
Miller, Sue **44**
Miller, Walter M(ichael Jr.) **4, 30**
Millett, Kate **67**
Millhauser, Steven (Lewis) **21, 54, 109**
Milner, Ron(ald) **56**
Miner, Valerie **40**
Minot, Susan **44, 159**
Minus, Ed **39**
Mitchell, Joseph (Quincy) **98**
Modarressi, Taghi (M.) **44**
Mohr, Nicholasa **12**
Mojtabai, A(nn) G(race) **5, 9, 15, 29**
Momaday, N(avarre) Scott **2, 19, 85, 95, 160**
Monette, Paul **82**
Montague, John (Patrick) **13, 46**
Montgomery, Marion H. Jr. **7**
Moody, Rick **147**
Mooney, Ted **25**
Moore, Lorrie **39, 45, 68, 165**
Moore, Marianne (Craig) **1, 2, 4, 8, 10, 13, 19, 47**
Moraga, Cherrie **126**
Morgan, Berry **6**
Morgan, (George) Frederick **23**
Morgan, Robin (Evonne) **2**
Morgan, Seth **65**
Morris, Bill **76**
Morris, Wright **1, 3, 7, 18, 37**
Morrison, Jim **17**
Morrison, Toni **4, 10, 22, 55, 81, 87**
Mosher, Howard Frank **62**
Mosley, Walter **97**
Moss, Howard **7, 14, 45, 50**
Motley, Willard (Francis) **18**
Mountain Wolf Woman **92**
Moyers, Bill **74**
Mueller, Lisel **13, 51**
Mull, Martin **17**
Mungo, Raymond **72**
Murphy, Sylvia **34**
Murray, Albert L. **73**

Muske, Carol **90**
Myers, Walter Dean **35**
Nabokov, Vladimir (Vladimirovich) **1, 2, 3, 6, 8, 11, 15, 23, 44, 46, 64**
Nash, (Fredric) Ogden **23**
Naylor, Gloria **28, 52, 156**
Neihardt, John Gneisenau **32**
Nelson, Willie **17**
Nemerov, Howard (Stanley) **2, 6, 9, 36**
Neufeld, John (Arthur) **17**
Neville, Emily Cheney **12**
Newlove, Donald **6**
Newman, Charles **2, 8**
Newman, Edwin (Harold) **14**
Newton, Suzanne **35**
Nichols, John (Treadwell) **38**
Niedecker, Lorine **10, 42**
Nin, Anaïs **1, 4, 8, 11, 14, 60, 127**
Nissenson, Hugh **4, 9**
Nixon, Agnes Eckhardt **21**
Norman, Marsha **28**
Norton, Andre **12**
Nova, Craig **7, 31**
Nunn, Kem **34**
Nyro, Laura **17**
Oates, Joyce Carol **1, 2, 3, 6, 9, 11, 15, 19, 33, 52, 108, 134**
O'Brien, Darcy **11**
O'Brien, (William) Tim(othy) **7, 19, 40, 103**
Ochs, Phil(ip David) **17**
O'Connor, Edwin (Greene) **14**
O'Connor, (Mary) Flannery **1, 2, 3, 6, 10, 13, 15, 21, 66, 104**
O'Dell, Scott **30**
Odets, Clifford **2, 28, 98**
O'Donovan, Michael John **14**
O'Grady, Timothy **59**
O'Hara, Frank **2, 5, 13, 78**
O'Hara, John (Henry) **1, 2, 3, 6, 11, 42**
O Hehir, Diana **41**
Olds, Sharon **32, 39, 85**
Oliver, Mary **19, 34, 98**
Olsen, Tillie **4, 13, 114**
Olson, Charles (John) **1, 2, 5, 6, 9, 11, 29**
Olson, Toby **28**
Oppen, George **7, 13, 34**
Orlovitz, Gil **22**
Ortiz, Simon J(oseph) **45**
Ostriker, Alicia (Suskin) **132**
Otto, Whitney **70**
Owens, Rochelle **8**
Ozick, Cynthia **3, 7, 28, 62, 155**
Pack, Robert **13**
Pagels, Elaine Hiesey **104**
Paglia, Camille (Anna) **68**
Paley, Grace **4, 6, 37, 140**
Palliser, Charles **65**
Pancake, Breece D'J **29**
Paretsky, Sara **135**
Parini, Jay (Lee) **54, 133**
Parker, Dorothy (Rothschild) **15, 68**
Parker, Robert B(rown) **27**
Parks, Gordon (Alexander Buchanan) **1, 16**
Pastan, Linda (Olenik) **27**
Patchen, Kenneth **1, 2, 18**
Paterson, Katherine (Womeldorf) **12, 30**
Peacock, Molly **60**
Pearson, T(homas) R(eid) **39**
Peck, John (Frederick) **3**
Peck, Richard (Wayne) **21**
Peck, Robert Newton **17**
Peckinpah, (David) Sam(uel) **20**
Percy, Walker **2, 3, 6, 8, 14, 18, 47, 65**
Perelman, S(idney) J(oseph) **3, 5, 9, 15, 23, 44, 49**
Perloff, Marjorie G(abrielle) **137**
Pesetsky, Bette **28**
Peterkin, Julia Mood **31**
Peters, Joan K(aren) **39**
Peters, Robert L(ouis) **7**
Petrakis, Harry Mark **3**
Petry, Ann (Lane) **1, 7, 18**

Philipson, Morris H. **53**
Phillips, Jayne Anne **15, 33, 139**
Phillips, Robert (Schaeffer) **28**
Piercy, Marge **3, 6, 14, 18, 27, 62, 128**
Pinckney, Darryl **76**
Pineda, Cecile **39**
Pinkwater, Daniel Manus **35**
Pinsky, Robert **9, 19, 38, 94, 121**
Pirsig, Robert M(aynard) **4, 6, 73**
Plante, David (Robert) **7, 23, 38**
Plath, Sylvia **1, 2, 3, 5, 9, 11, 14, 17, 50, 51, 62, 111**
Platt, Kin **26**
Plimpton, George (Ames) **36**
Plumly, Stanley (Ross) **33**
Pohl, Frederick **18**
Poitier, Sidney **26**
Pollitt, Katha **28, 122**
Polonsky, Abraham (Lincoln) **92**
Pomerance, Bernard **13**
Porter, Connie (Rose) **70**
Porter, Katherine Anne **1, 3, 7, 10, 13, 15, 27, 101**
Potok, Chaim **2, 7, 14, 26, 112**
Pound, Ezra (Weston Loomis) **1, 2, 3, 4, 5, 7, 10, 13, 18, 34, 48, 50, 112**
Povod, Reinaldo **44**
Powell, Adam Clayton Jr. **89**
Powell, Dawn **66**
Powell, Padgett **34**
Power, Susan **91**
Powers, J(ames) F(arl) **1, 4, 8, 57**
Powers, John R. **66**
Powers, Richard (S.) **93**
Prager, Emily **56**
Price, (Edward) Reynolds **3, 6, 13, 43, 50, 63**
Price, Richard **6, 12**
Prince **35**
Pritchard, William H(arrison) **34**
Probst, Mark **59**
Prokosch, Frederic **4, 48**
Prose, Francine **45**
Proulx, E(dna) Annie **81, 158**
Pryor, Richard (Franklin Lenox Thomas) **26**
Purdy, James (Amos) **2, 4, 10, 28, 52**
Puzo, Mario **1, 2, 6, 36, 107**
Pynchon, Thomas (Ruggles Jr.) **2, 3, 6, 9, 11, 18, 33, 62, 72, 123**
Quay, Stephen **95**
Quay, Timothy **95**
Queen, Ellery **3, 11**
Quinn, Peter **91**
Rabe, David (William) **4, 8, 33**
Rado, James **17**
Raeburn, John (Hay) **34**
Ragni, Gerome **17**
Rahv, Philip **24**
Rakosi, Carl **47**
Rampersad, Arnold **44**
Rand, Ayn **3, 30, 44, 79**
Randall, Dudley (Felker) **1, 135**
Ransom, John Crowe **2, 4, 5, 11, 24**
Raphael, Frederic (Michael) **2, 14**
Rechy, John (Francisco) **1, 7, 14, 18, 107**
Reddin, Keith **67**
Redmon, Anne **22**
Reed, Ishmael **2, 3, 5, 6, 13, 32, 60**
Reed, Lou **21**
Remarque, Erich Maria **21**
Rexroth, Kenneth **1, 2, 6, 11, 22, 49, 112**
Reynolds, Jonathan **6, 38**
Reynolds, Michael S(hane) **44**
Reznikoff, Charles **9**
Ribman, Ronald (Burt) **7**
Rice, Anne **41, 128**
Rice, Elmer (Leopold) **7, 49**
Rich, Adrienne (Cecile) **3, 6, 7, 11, 18, 36, 73, 76, 125**
Richter, Conrad (Michael) **30**
Riding, Laura **3, 7**
Ringwood, Gwen(dolyn Margaret) Pharis **48**

Rivers, Conrad Kent **1**
Robbins, Harold **5**
Robbins, Trina **21**
Robinson, Jill **10**
Robinson, Kim Stanley **34**
Robinson, Marilynne **25**
Robinson, Smokey **21**
Robison, Mary **42, 98**
Roddenberry, Gene **17**
Rodgers, Mary **12**
Rodman, Howard **65**
Rodriguez, Richard **155**
Roethke, Theodore (Huebner) **1, 3, 8, 11, 19, 46, 101**
Rogers, Thomas Hunton **57**
Rogin, Gilbert **18**
Roiphe, Anne (Richardson) **3, 9**
Rooke, Leon **25, 34**
Rose, Wendy **85**
Rosen, Richard (Dean) **39**
Rosenthal, M(acha) L(ouis) **28**
Rossner, Judith (Perelman) **6, 9, 29**
Roth, Henry **2, 6, 11, 104**
Roth, Philip (Milton) **1, 2, 3, 4, 6, 9, 15, 22, 31, 47, 66, 86, 119**
Rothenberg, Jerome **6, 57**
Rovit, Earl (Herbert) **7**
Royko, Mike **109**
Ruark, Gibbons **3**
Rudnik, Raphael **7**
Rukeyser, Muriel **6, 10, 15, 27**
Rule, Jane (Vance) **27**
Rush, Norman **44**
Russ, Joanna **15**
Russell, Jeffrey Burton **70**
Ryan, Cornelius (John) **7**
Ryan, Michael **65**
Sachs, Marilyn (Stickle) **35**
Sackler, Howard (Oliver) **14**
Sadoff, Ira **9**
Safire, William **10**
Sagan, Carl (Edward) **30, 112**
Said, Edward W. **123**
Saint, H(arry) F. **50**
Salamanca, J(ack) R(ichard) **4, 15**
Sale, Kirkpatrick **68**
Salinas, Luis Omar **90**
Salinger, J(erome) D(avid) **1, 3, 8, 12, 55, 56, 138**
Salter, James **7, 52, 59**
Sanchez, Sonia **5, 116**
Sandburg, Carl (August) **1, 4, 10, 15, 35**
Sanders, (James) Ed(ward) **53**
Sanders, Lawrence **41**
Sandoz, Mari(e Susette) **28**
Saner, Reg(inald Anthony) **9**
Santiago, Danny **33**
Santmyer, Helen Hooven **33**
Santos, Bienvenido N(uqui) **22**
Sapphire, Brenda **99**
Saroyan, William **1, 8, 10, 29, 34, 56**
Sarton, (Eleanor) May **4, 14, 49, 91**
Saul, John (W. III) **46**
Savage, Thomas **40**
Savan, Glenn **50**
Sayers, Valerie **50, 122**
Sayles, John (Thomas) **7, 10, 14**
Schaeffer, Susan Fromberg **6, 11, 22**
Schell, Jonathan **35**
Schevill, James (Erwin) **7**
Schisgal, Murray (Joseph) **6**
Schlesinger, Arthur M(eier) Jr. **84**
Schnackenberg, Gjertrud (Cecelia) **40**
Schor, Sandra (M.) **65**
Schorer, Mark **9**
Schrader, Paul (Joseph) **26**
Schulberg, Budd (Wilson) **7, 48**
Schulz, Charles M(onroe) **12**
Schuyler, James Marcus **5, 23**
Schwartz, Delmore (David) **2, 4, 10, 45, 87**
Schwartz, John Burnham **59**
Schwartz, Lynne Sharon **31**

Scoppettone, Sandra **26**
Scorsese, Martin **20, 89**
Scott, Evelyn **43**
Scott, Joanna **50**
Sebestyen, Ouida **30**
Seelye, John (Douglas) **7**
Segal, Erich (Wolf) **3, 10**
Seger, Bob **35**
Seidel, Frederick (Lewis) **18**
Selby, Hubert Jr. **1, 2, 4, 8**
Selzer, Richard **74**
Serling, (Edward) Rod(man) **30**
Seton, Cynthia Propper **27**
Settle, Mary Lee **19, 61**
Sexton, Anne (Harvey) **2, 4, 6, 8, 10, 15, 53, 123**
Shaara, Michael (Joseph Jr.) **15**
Shacochis, Bob **39**
Shange, Ntozake **8, 25, 38, 74, 126**
Shanley, John Patrick **75**
Shapiro, Jane **76**
Shapiro, Karl (Jay) **4, 8, 15, 53**
Shaw, Irwin **7, 23, 34**
Shawn, Wallace **41**
Shea, Lisa **86**
Sheed, Wilfrid (John Joseph) **2, 4, 10, 53**
Shepard, Jim **36**
Shepard, Lucius **34**
Shepard, Sam **4, 6, 17, 34, 41, 44, 169**
Sherburne, Zoa (Lillian Morin) **30**
Sherman, Jonathan Marc **55**
Sherman, Martin **19**
Shields, Carol **91, 113**
Shields, David **97**
Shilts, Randy **85**
Showalter, Elaine **169**
Shreve, Susan Richards **23**
Shue, Larry **52**
Shulman, Alix Kates **2, 10**
Shuster, Joe **21**
Sidhwa, Bapsi **168**
Siegel, Jerome **21**
Sigal, Clancy **7**
Silko, Leslie (Marmon) **23, 74, 114**
Silver, Joan Micklin **20**
Silverberg, Robert **7, 140**
Silverstein, Alvin **17**
Silverstein, Virginia B(arbara Opshelor) **17**
Simak, Clifford D(onald) **1, 55**
Simic, Charles **6, 9, 22, 49, 68, 130**
Simmons, Charles (Paul) **57**
Simmons, Dan **44**
Simon, Carly **26**
Simon, (Marvin) Neil **6, 11, 31, 39, 70**
Simon, Paul (Frederick) **17**
Simpson, Louis (Aston Marantz) **4, 7, 9, 32, 149**
Simpson, Mona (Elizabeth) **44, 146**
Sinclair, Upton (Beall) **1, 11, 15, 63**
Singer, Isaac Bashevis **1, 3, 6, 9, 11, 15, 23, 38, 69, 111**
Singleton, John **156**
Sissman, L(ouis) E(dward) **9, 18**
Slaughter, Frank G(ill) **29**
Slavitt, David R(ytman) **5, 14**
Smiley, Jane (Graves) **53, 76, 144**
Smith, Anna Deavere **86**
Smith, Betty (Wehner) **19**
Smith, Clark Ashton **43**
Smith, Dave **22, 42**
Smith, Lee **25, 73**
Smith, Martin Cruz **25**
Smith, Mary-Ann Tirone **39**
Smith, Patti **12**
Smith, William Jay **6**
Snodgrass, W(illiam) D(e Witt) **2, 6, 10, 18, 68**
Snyder, Gary (Sherman) **1, 2, 5, 9, 32, 120**
Snyder, Zilpha Keatley **17**
Soderbergh, Steven **154**
Sokolov, Raymond **7**
Sommer, Scott **25**

Sondheim, Stephen (Joshua) **30, 39, 147**
Sontag, Susan **1, 2, 10, 13, 31, 105**
Sorrentino, Gilbert **3, 7, 14, 22, 40**
Soto, Gary **32, 80**
Southern, Terry **7**
Spackman, W(illiam) M(ode) **46**
Spacks, Barry (Bernard) **14**
Spanidou, Irini **44**
Spencer, Elizabeth **22**
Spencer, Scott **30**
Spicer, Jack **8, 18, 72**
Spiegelman, Art **76**
Spielberg, Peter **6**
Spielberg, Steven **20**
Spinrad, Norman (Richard) **46**
Spivack, Kathleen (Romola Drucker) **6**
Spoto, Donald **39**
Springsteen, Bruce (F.) **17**
Squires, (James) Radcliffe **51**
Stafford, Jean **4, 7, 19, 68**
Stafford, William (Edgar) **4, 7, 29**
Stanton, Maura **9**
Starbuck, George (Edwin) **53**
Steele, Timothy (Reid) **45**
Stegner, Wallace (Earle) **9, 49, 81**
Steinbeck, John (Ernst) **1, 5, 9, 13, 21, 34, 45, 75, 124**
Steinem, Gloria **63**
Steiner, George **24**
Sterling, Bruce **72**
Stern, Gerald **40, 100**
Stern, Richard (Gustave) **4, 39**
Sternberg, Josef von **20**
Stevens, Mark **34**
Stevenson, Anne (Katharine) **7, 33**
Still, James **49**
Stitt, Milan **29**
Stolz, Mary (Slattery) **12**
Stone, Irving **7**
Stone, Oliver (William) **73**
Stone, Robert (Anthony) **5, 23, 42**
Storm, Hyemeyohsts **3**
Stout, Rex (Todhunter) **3**
Strand, Mark **6, 18, 41, 71**
Straub, Peter (Francis) **28, 107**
Stribling, T(homas) S(igismund) **23**
Stuart, Jesse (Hilton) **1, 8, 11, 14, 34**
Sturgeon, Theodore (Hamilton) **22, 39**
Styron, William **1, 3, 5, 11, 15, 60**
Sukenick, Ronald **3, 4, 6, 48**
Summers, Hollis (Spurgeon Jr.) **10**
Susann, Jacqueline **3**
Swados, Elizabeth (A.) **12**
Swados, Harvey **5**
Swan, Gladys **69**
Swarthout, Glendon (Fred) **35**
Swenson, May **4, 14, 61, 106**
Talese, Gay **37**
Tallent, Elizabeth (Ann) **45**
Tally, Ted **42**
Tan, Amy (Ruth) **59, 120, 151**
Tartt, Donna **76**
Tate, James (Vincent) **2, 6, 25**
Tate, (John Orley) Allen **2, 4, 6, 9, 11, 14, 24**
Tavel, Ronald **6**
Taylor, Eleanor Ross **5**
Taylor, Henry (Splawn) **44**
Taylor, Mildred D(elois) **21**
Taylor, Peter (Hillsman) **1, 4, 18, 37, 44, 50, 71**
Taylor, Robert Lewis **14**
Terkel, Studs **38**
Terry, Megan **19**
Tesich, Steve **40, 69**
Tevis, Walter **42**
Theroux, Alexander (Louis) **2, 25**
Theroux, Paul (Edward) **5, 8, 11, 15, 28, 46, 159**
Thomas, Audrey (Callahan) **7, 13, 37, 107**
Thomas, Joyce Carol **35**
Thomas, Lewis **35**
Thomas, Piri **17**

Thomas, Ross (Elmore) **39**
Thompson, Hunter S(tockton) **9, 17, 40, 104**
Thompson, Jim (Myers) **69**
Thurber, James (Grover) **5, 11, 25, 125**
Tilghman, Christopher **65**
Tillich, Paul (Johannes) **131**
Tillinghast, Richard (Williford) **29**
Toffler, Alvin
Tolson, Melvin B(eaunorus) **36, 105**
Tomlin, Lily **17**
Toole, John Kennedy **19, 64**
Toomer, Jean **1, 4, 13, 22**
Torrey, E(dwin) Fuller **34**
Towne, Robert (Burton) **87**
Traven, B. **8, 11**
Trevanian **29**
Trilling, Diana (Rubin) **129**
Trilling, Lionel **9, 11, 24**
Trow, George W. S. **52**
Trudeau, Garry B. **12**
Trumbo, Dalton **19**
Tryon, Thomas **3, 11**
Tuck, Lily **70**
Tunis, John R(oberts) **12**
Turco, Lewis (Putnam) **11, 63**
Turner, Frederick **48**
Tyler, Anne **7, 11, 18, 28, 44, 59, 103**
Uhry, Alfred **55**
Ulibarrí, Sabine R(eyes) **83**
Unger, Douglas **34**
Updike, John (Hoyer) **1, 2, 3, 5, 7, 9, 13, 15, 23, 34, 43, 70, 139**
Urdang, Constance (Henriette) **47**
Uris, Leon (Marcus) **7, 32**
Vachss, Andrew (Henry) **106**
Valdez, Luis (Miguel) **84**
Van Ash, Cay **34**
Vandenburgh, Jane **59**
Van Doren, Mark **6, 10**
Van Duyn, Mona (Jane) **3, 7, 63, 116**
Van Peebles, Melvin **2, 20**
Van Vechten, Carl **33**
Vaughn, Stephanie **62**
Vendler, Helen (Hennessy) **138**
Vidal, Gore **2, 4, 6, 8, 10, 22, 33, 72, 142**
Viereck, Peter (Robert Edwin) **4**
Vinge, Joan (Carol) D(ennison) **30**
Viola, Herman J(oseph) **70**
Vizenor, Gerald Robert **103**
Vliet, R(ussell) G(ordon) **22**
Vogel, Paula A(nne) **76**
Voigt, Cynthia **30**
Voigt, Ellen Bryant **54**
Vollmann, William T. **89**
Vonnegut, Kurt Jr. **1, 2, 3, 4, 5, 8, 12, 22, 40, 60, 111**
Wagman, Fredrica **7**
Wagner-Martin, Linda (C.) **50**
Wagoner, David (Russell) **3, 5, 15**
Wakefield, Dan **7**
Wakoski, Diane **2, 4, 7, 9, 11, 40**
Waldman, Anne (Lesley) **7**
Walker, Alice (Malsenior) **5, 6, 9, 19, 27, 46, 58, 103, 167**
Walker, Joseph A. **19**
Walker, Margaret (Abigail) **1, 6**
Wallace, David Foster **50, 114**
Wallace, Irving **7, 13**
Wallant, Edward Lewis **5, 10**
Wambaugh, Joseph (Aloysius Jr.) **3, 18**
Ward, Douglas Turner **19**
Warhol, Andy **20**
Warren, Robert Penn **1, 4, 6, 8, 10, 13, 18, 39, 53, 59**
Wasserstein, Wendy **32, 59, 90**
Waters, Frank (Joseph) **88**
Watkins, Paul **55**
Webb, Charles (Richard) **7**
Webb, James H(enry) Jr. **22**
Weber, Lenora Mattingly **12**
Weidman, Jerome **7**
Weiss, Theodore (Russell) **3, 8, 14**

Welch, James **6, 14, 52**
Wellek, Rene **28**
Weller, Michael **10, 53**
Welles, (George) Orson **20, 80**
Wellman, Mac **65**
Wellman, Manly Wade **49**
Wells, Rosemary **12**
Welty, Eudora **1, 2, 5, 14, 22, 33, 105**
Wersba, Barbara **30**
Wescott, Glenway **13**
Wesley, Richard (Errol) **7**
West, Cornel (Ronald) **134**
West, Delno C(loyde) Jr. **70**
West, (Mary) Jessamyn **7, 17**
West, Paul **7, 14, 96**
Westlake, Donald E(dwin) **7, 33**
Whalen, Philip **6, 29**
Wharton, William (a pseudonym) **18, 37**
Wheelock, John Hall **14**
White, Edmund (Valentine III) **27, 110**
White, E(lwyn) B(rooks) **10, 34, 39**
White, Hayden V. **148**
Whitney, Phyllis A(yame) **42**
Whittemore, (Edward) Reed (Jr.) **4**
Wicker, Tom **7**
Wideman, John Edgar **5, 34, 36, 67, 122**
Wieners, John **7**
Wiesel, Elie(zer) **3, 5, 11, 37, 165**
Wiggins, Marianne **57**
Wilbur, Richard (Purdy) **3, 6, 9, 14, 53, 110**
Wild, Peter **14**
Wilder, Billy **20**
Wilder, Thornton (Niven) **1, 5, 6, 10, 15, 35, 82**
Wiley, Richard **44**
Willard, Nancy **7, 37**
Williams, C(harles) K(enneth) **33, 56, 148**
Williams, John A(lfred) **5, 13**
Williams, Jonathan (Chamberlain) **13**
Williams, Joy **31**
Williams, Norman **39**
Williams, Sherley Anne **89**
Williams, Tennessee **1, 2, 5, 7, 8, 11, 15, 19, 30, 39, 45, 71, 111**
Williams, Thomas (Alonzo) **14**
Williams, William Carlos **1, 2, 5, 9, 13, 22, 42, 67**
Willingham, Calder (Baynard Jr.) **5, 51**
Wilson, August **39, 50, 63, 118**
Wilson, Brian **12**
Wilson, Edmund **1, 2, 3, 8, 24**
Wilson, Lanford **7, 14, 36**
Wilson, Robert M. **7, 9**
Wilson, Sloan **32**
Wilson, William S(mith) **49**
Winters, (Arthur) Yvor **4, 8, 32**
Winters, Janet Lewis **41**
Wiseman, Frederick **20**
Wodehouse, P(elham) G(renville) **1, 2, 5, 10, 22**
Woiwode, Larry (Alfred) **6, 10**
Wojciechowska, Maia (Teresa) **26**
Wolf, Naomi **157**
Wolfe, Gene (Rodman) **25**
Wolfe, George C. **49**
Wolfe, Thomas Kennerly Jr. **147**
Wolff, Geoffrey (Ansell) **41**
Wolff, Tobias (Jonathan Ansell) **39, 64**
Wolitzer, Hilma **17**
Wonder, Stevie **12**
Wong, Jade Snow **17**
Woolrich, Cornell **77**
Wouk, Herman **1, 9, 38**
Wright, Charles (Penzel Jr.) **6, 13, 28, 119, 146**
Wright, Charles Stevenson **49**
Wright, James (Arlington) **3, 5, 10, 28**
Wright, Richard (Nathaniel) **1, 3, 4, 9, 14, 21, 48, 74**
Wright, Stephen **33**
Wright, William **44**
Wurlitzer, Rudolph **2, 4, 15**

Wylie, Philip (Gordon) **43**
Yates, Richard **7, 8, 23**
Yep, Laurence Michael **35**
Yerby, Frank G(arvin) **1, 7, 22**
Yglesias, Helen **7, 22**
Young, Al(bert James) **19**
Young, Marguerite (Vivian) **82**
Young Bear, Ray A. **94**
Yurick, Sol **6**
Zamora, Bernice (B. Ortiz) **89**
Zappa, Frank **17**
Zaturenska, Marya **6, 11**
Zelazny, Roger (Joseph) **21**
Ziegenhagen, Eric **55**
Zindel, Paul **6, 26**
Zoline, Pamela **62**
Zukofsky, Louis **1, 2, 4, 7, 11, 18**
Zweig, Paul **34, 42**

## ANGOLAN

Wellman, Manly Wade **49**

## ANTIGUAN

Edwards, Gus **43**
Kincaid, Jamaica **43, 68, 137**

## ARGENTINIAN

Bioy Casares, Adolfo **4, 8, 13, 88**
Borges, Jorge Luis **1, 2, 3, 4, 6, 8, 9, 10, 13, 19, 44, 48, 83**
Cortázar, Julio **2, 3, 5, 10, 13, 15, 33, 34, 92**
Costantini, Humberto **49**
Dorfman, Ariel **48, 77**
Guevara, Che **87**
Guevara (Serna), Ernesto **87**
Mujica Lainez, Manuel **31**
Puig, Manuel **3, 5, 10, 28, 65, 133**
Sabato, Ernesto (R.) **10, 23**
Valenzuela, Luisa **31, 104**

## ARMENIAN

Mamoulian, Rouben (Zachary) **16**

## AUSTRALIAN

Anderson, Jessica (Margaret) Queale **37**
Astley, Thea (Beatrice May) **41**
Brinsmead, H(esba) F(ay) **21**
Buckley, Vincent (Thomas) **57**
Buzo, Alexander (John) **61**
Carey, Peter **40, 55, 96**
Clark, Mavis Thorpe **12**
Clavell, James (duMaresq) **6, 25, 87**
Conway, Jill K(er) **152**
Courtenay, Bryce **59**
Davison, Frank Dalby **15**
Elliott, Sumner Locke **38**
FitzGerald, Robert D(avid) **19**
Greer, Germaine **131**
Grenville, Kate **61**
Hall, Rodney **51**
Hazzard, Shirley **18**
Hope, A(lec) D(erwent) **3, 51**
Hospital, Janette Turner **42, 145**
Jolley, (Monica) Elizabeth **46**
Jones, Rod **50**
Keneally, Thomas (Michael) **5, 8, 10, 14, 19, 27, 43, 117**
Koch, C(hristopher) J(ohn) **42**
Lawler, Raymond Evenor **58**
Malouf, (George Joseph) David **28, 86**
Matthews, Greg **45**
McAuley, James Phillip **45**
McCullough, Colleen **27, 107**
Murray, Les(lie Allan) **40**
Porter, Peter (Neville Frederick) **5, 13, 33**
Prichard, Katharine Susannah **46**
Shapcott, Thomas W(illiam) **38**
Slessor, Kenneth **14**
Stead, Christina (Ellen) **2, 5, 8, 32, 80**
Stow, (Julian) Randolph **23, 48**
Thiele, Colin (Milton) **17**
Weir, Peter (Lindsay) **20**
West, Morris L(anglo) **6, 33**
White, Patrick (Victor Martindale) **3, 4, 5, 7, 9, 18, 65, 69**
Wilding, Michael **73**
Williamson, David (Keith) **56**
Wright, Judith (Arundell) **11, 53**

## AUSTRIAN

Adamson, Joy(-Friederike Victoria) **17**
Bachmann, Ingeborg **69**
Bernhard, Thomas **3, 32, 61**
Bettelheim, Bruno **79**
Frankl, Viktor E(mil) **93**
Gregor, Arthur **9**
Handke, Peter **5, 8, 10, 15, 38, 134**
Hochwaelder, Fritz **36**
Jelinek, Elfriede **169**
Jandl, Ernst **34**
Lang, Fritz **20, 103**
Lind, Jakov **1, 2, 4, 27, 82**
Perloff, Marjorie G(abrielle) **137**
Sternberg, Josef von **20**
Wellek, Rene **28**
Wilder, Billy **20**

## BARBADIAN

Brathwaite, Edward (Kamau) **11**
Clarke, Austin C(hesterfield) **8, 53**
Kennedy, Adrienne (Lita) **66**
Lamming, George (William) **2, 4, 66, 144**

## BELGIAN

Crommelynck, Fernand **75**
Ghelderode, Michel de **6, 11**
Lévi-Strauss, Claude **38**
Mallet-Joris, Françoise **11**
Michaux, Henri **8, 19**
Sarton, (Eleanor) May **4, 14, 49, 91**
Simenon, Georges (Jacques Christian) **1, 2, 3, 8, 18, 47**
van Itallie, Jean-Claude **3**
Yourcenar, Marguerite **19, 38, 50, 87**

## BOTSWANAN

Head, Bessie **25, 67**

## BRAZILIAN

Amado, Jorge **13, 40, 106**
Boff, Leonardo (Genezio Darci) **70**
Cabral de Melo Neto, João **76**
Castaneda, Carlos (Cesar Aranha) **12, 119**
Dourado, (Waldomiro Freitas) Autran **23, 60**
Drummond de Andrade, Carlos **18**
Lispector, Clarice **43**
Ribeiro, Darcy **34**
Ribeiro, Joao Ubaldo (Osorio Pimentel) **10, 67**
Rosa, João Guimarães **23**

## BULGARIAN

Belcheva, Elisaveta Lyubomirova **10**
Canetti, Elias **3, 14, 25, 75, 86**
Kristeva, Julia **77, 140**

## CAMEROONIAN

Beti, Mongo **27**

## CANADIAN

Acorn, Milton **15**
Aquin, Hubert **15**
Atwood, Margaret (Eleanor) **2, 3, 4, 8, 13, 15, 25, 44, 84, 135**
Avison, Margaret **2, 4, 97**
Barfoot, Joan **18**
Bellow, Saul **1, 2, 3, 6, 8, 10, 13, 15, 25, 33, 34, 63, 79**
Berton, Pierre (Francis Demarigny) **104**
Birney, (Alfred) Earle **1, 4, 6, 11**
Bissett, Bill **18**
Blais, Marie-Claire **2, 4, 6, 13, 22**
Blaise, Clark **29**
Bowering, George **15, 47**
Bowering, Marilyn R(uthe) **32**
Brossard, Nicole **115, 169**
Buckler, Ernest **13**
Buell, John (Edward) **10**
Callaghan, Morley Edward **3, 14, 41, 65**
Campbell, Maria **85**
Carrier, Roch **13, 78**
Child, Philip **19, 68**
Chislett, (Margaret) Anne **34**
Clarke, Austin C(hesterfield) **8, 53**
Cohen, Leonard (Norman) **3, 38**
Cohen, Matt(hew) **19**
Coles, Don **46**
Cook, Michael **58**
Cooper, Douglas **86**
Coupland, Douglas **85, 133**
Craven, Margaret **17**
Cronenberg, David **143**
Davies, (William) Robertson **2, 7, 13, 25, 42, 75, 91**
de la Roche, Mazo **14**
Donnell, David **34**
Ducharme, Rejean **74**
Dudek, Louis **11, 19**
Egoyan, Atom **151**
Engel, Marian **36**
Everson, R(onald) G(ilmour) **27**
Faludy, George **42**
Ferron, Jacques **94**
Finch, Robert (Duer Claydon) **18**
Findley, Timothy **27, 102**
Fraser, Sylvia **64**
Frye, (Herman) Northrop **24, 70**
Gallant, Mavis **7, 18, 38**
Garner, Hugh **13**
Gibson, William (Ford) **39, 63**
Gilmour, David **35**
Glassco, John **9**
Gotlieb, Phyllis Fay (Bloom) **18**
Govier, Katherine **51**
Gunnars, Kristjana **69**
Gustafson, Ralph (Barker) **36**
Haig-Brown, Roderick (Langmere) **21**
Hailey, Arthur **5**
Harris, Christie (Lucy) Irwin **12**
Hébert, Anne **4, 13, 29**
Highway, Tomson **92**
Hillis, Rick **66**
Hine, (William) Daryl **15**
Hodgins, Jack **23**
Hood, Hugh (John Blagdon) **15, 28**
Hyde, Anthony **42**
Jacobsen, Josephine **48, 102**
Jiles, Paulette **13, 58**
Johnston, George (Benson) **51**
Jones, D(ouglas) G(ordon) **10**
Kelly, M(ilton) T(errence) **55**
King, Thomas **89**
Kinsella, W(illiam) P(atrick) **27, 43, 166**
Klein, A(braham) M(oses) **19**
Kogawa, Joy Nozomi **78, 129**
Krizanc, John **57**
Kroetsch, Robert **5, 23, 57, 132**
Kroker, Arthur (W.) **77**
Lane, Patrick **25**
Laurence, (Jean) Margaret (Wemyss) **3, 6, 13, 50, 62**
Layton, Irving (Peter) **2, 15, 164**
Levine, Norman **54**
Lightfoot, Gordon **26**
Livesay, Dorothy (Kathleen) **4, 15, 79**
MacEwen, Gwendolyn (Margaret) **13, 55**
MacLennan, (John) Hugh **2, 14, 92**
MacLeod, Alistair **56, 165**
Macpherson, (Jean) Jay **14**
Maillet, Antonine **54, 118**
Major, Kevin (Gerald) **26**

Marlatt, Daphne **168**
McFadden, David **48**
McLuhan, (Herbert) Marshall **37, 83**
Metcalf, John **37**
Mistry, Rohinton **71**
Mitchell, Joni **12**
Mitchell, W(illiam) O(rmond) **25**
Moore, Brian **1, 3, 5, 7, 8, 19, 32, 90**
Morgan, Janet **39**
Moure, Erin **88**
Mowat, Farley (McGill) **26**
Mukherjee, Bharati **53, 115**
Munro, Alice **6, 10, 19, 50, 95**
Musgrave, Susan **13, 54**
Newlove, John (Herbert) **14**
Nichol, B(arrie) P(hillip) **18**
Nowlan, Alden (Albert) **15**
Ondaatje, (Philip) Michael **14, 29, 51, 76**
Page, P(atricia) K(athleen) **7, 18**
Pollock, (Mary) Sharon **50**
Pratt, E(dwin) J(ohn) **19**
Purdy, A(lfred) W(ellington) **3, 6, 14, 50**
Quarrington, Paul (Lewis) **65**
Reaney, James **13**
Ricci, Nino **70**
Richards, David Adams **59**
Richler, Mordecai **3, 5, 9, 13, 18, 46, 70**
Ringwood, Gwen(dolyn Margaret) Pharis **48**
Ritter, Erika **52**
Rooke, Leon **25, 34**
Rosenblatt, Joe **15**
Ross, (James) Sinclair **13**
Roy, Gabrielle **10, 14**
Rule, Jane (Vance) **27**
Ryga, George **14**
Scott, F(rancis) R(eginald) **22**
Shields, Carol **91, 113**
Skelton, Robin **13**
Škvorecký, Josef (Vaclav) **15, 39, 69, 152**
Slade, Bernard **11, 46**
Smart, Elizabeth **54**
Smith, A(rthur) J(ames) M(arshall) **15**
Souster, (Holmes) Raymond **5, 14**
Suknaski, Andrew **19**
Theriault, Yves **79**
Thesen, Sharon **56**
Thomas, Audrey (Callahan) **7, 13, 37, 107**
Thompson, Judith **39**
Tremblay, Michel **29, 102**
Urquhart, Jane **90**
Vanderhaeghe, Guy **41**
van Vogt, A(lfred) E(lton) **1**
Vizinczey, Stephen **40**
Waddington, Miriam **28**
Wah, Fred(erick James) **44**
Walker, David Harry **14**
Walker, George F. **44, 61**
Webb, Phyllis **18**
Wiebe, Rudy (Henry) **6, 11, 14, 138**
Wilson, Ethel Davis (Bryant) **13**
Wright, L(aurali) R. **44**
Wright, Richard B(ruce) **6**
Young, Neil **17**

## CHILEAN

Alegria, Fernando **57**
Allende, Isabel **39, 57, 97**
Donoso (Yañez), José **4, 8, 11, 32, 99**
Dorfman, Ariel **48, 77**
Neruda, Pablo **1, 2, 5, 7, 9, 28, 62**
Parra, Nicanor **2, 102**

## CHINESE

Chang, Jung **71**
Ch'ien, Chung-shu **22**
Ding Ling **68**
Lord, Bette Bao **23**
Mo, Timothy (Peter) **46, 134**
Pa Chin **18**
Peake, Mervyn **7, 54**
Wong, Jade Snow **17**

## COLOMBIAN

García Márquez, Gabriel (Jose) **2, 3, 8, 10, 15, 27, 47, 55, 68**

## CONGOLESE

Tchicaya, Gerald Felix **101**

## CUBAN

Arenas, Reinaldo **41**
Cabrera Infante, G(uillermo) **5, 25, 45, 120**
Calvino, Italo **5, 8, 11, 22, 33, 39, 73**
Carpentier (y Valmont), Alejo **8, 11, 38, 110**
Fornés, María Irene **39, 61**
Garcia, Cristina **76**
Guevara, Che **87**
Guillén, Nicolás (Cristobal) **48, 79**
Lezama Lima, José **4, 10, 101**
Padilla (Lorenzo), Heberto **38**
Sarduy, Severo **6, 97**

## CZECH

Forman, Milos **164**
Friedlander, Saul **90**
Havel, Václav **25, 58, 65, 123**
Holub, Miroslav **4**
Hrabal, Bohumil **13, 67**
Klima, Ivan **56**
Kohout, Pavel **13**
Kundera, Milan **4, 9, 19, 32, 68, 115, 135**
Lustig, Arnost **56**
Seifert, Jaroslav **34, 44, 93**
Škvorecký, Josef (Vaclav) **15, 39, 69, 152**
Vaculik, Ludvik **7**

## DANISH

Abell, Kjeld **15**
Bodker, Cecil **21**
Dreyer, Carl Theodor **16**
Hoeg, Peter **95, 156**

## DOMINICAN REPUBLICAN

Alvarez, Julia **93**

## DUTCH

Bernhard, Thomas **3, 32, 61**
Buruma, Ian **163**
de Hartog, Jan **19**
Mulisch, Harry **42**
Ruyslinck, Ward **14**
van de Wetering, Janwillem **47**

## EGYPTIAN

Chedid, Andree **47**
Mahfouz, Naguīb (Abdel Azīz Al-Sabilgi) **153**

## ENGLISH

Ackroyd, Peter **34, 52, 140**
Adams, Douglas (Noel) **27, 60**
Adams, Richard (George) **4, 5, 18**
Adcock, Fleur **41**
Aickman, Robert (Fordyce) **57**
Aiken, Joan (Delano) **35**
Aldington, Richard **49**
Aldiss, Brian W(ilson) **5, 14, 40**
Allingham, Margery (Louise) **19**
Almedingen, E. M. **12**
Alvarez, A(lfred) **5, 13**
Ambler, Eric **4, 6, 9**
Amis, Kingsley (William) **1, 2, 3, 5, 8, 13, 40, 44, 129**
Amis, Martin (Louis) **4, 9, 38, 62, 101**
Anderson, Lindsay (Gordon) **20**
Anthony, Piers **35**
Archer, Jeffrey (Howard) **28**
Arden, John **6, 13, 15**
Armatrading, Joan **17**
Arthur, Ruth M(abel) **12**
Arundel, Honor (Morfydd) **17**

Atkinson, Kate **99**
Auden, W(ystan) H(ugh) **1, 2, 3, 4, 6, 9, 11, 14, 43, 123**
Ayckbourn, Alan **5, 8, 18, 33, 74**
Ayrton, Michael **7**
Bagnold, Enid **25**
Bailey, Paul **45**
Bainbridge, Beryl (Margaret) **4, 5, 8, 10, 14, 18, 22, 62, 130**
Ballard, J(ames) G(raham) **3, 6, 14, 36, 137**
Banks, Lynne Reid **23**
Barker, Clive **52**
Barker, George Granville **8, 48**
Barker, Howard **37**
Barker, Pat(ricia) **32, 94, 146**
Barnes, Julian (Patrick) **42, 141**
Barnes, Peter **5, 56**
Barrett, (Roger) Syd **35**
Bates, H(erbert) E(rnest) **46**
Beer, Patricia **58**
Bennett, Alan **45, 77**
Berger, John (Peter) **2, 19**
Berkoff, Steven **56**
Bermant, Chaim (Icyk) **40**
Betjeman, John **2, 6, 10, 34, 43**
Billington, (Lady) Rachel (Mary) **43**
Binyon, T(imothy) J(ohn) **34**
Blunden, Edmund (Charles) **2, 56**
Bolt, Robert (Oxton) **14**
Bond, Edward **4, 6, 13, 23**
Booth, Martin **13**
Bowen, Elizabeth (Dorothea Cole) **1, 3, 6, 11, 15, 22, 118**
Bowie, David **17**
Boyd, William **28, 53, 70**
Bradbury, Malcolm (Stanley) **32, 61**
Bragg, Melvyn **10**
Braine, John (Gerard) **1, 3, 41**
Brenton, Howard **31**
Brittain, Vera (Mary) **23**
Brooke-Rose, Christine **40**
Brookner, Anita **32, 34, 51, 136**
Brophy, Brigid (Antonia) **6, 11, 29, 105**
Brunner, John (Kilian Houston) **8, 10**
Bunting, Basil **10, 39, 47**
Burgess, Anthony **1, 2, 4, 5, 8, 10, 13, 15, 22, 40, 62, 81, 94**
Byatt, A(ntonia) S(usan Drabble) **19, 65, 136**
Caldwell, (Janet Miriam) Taylor (Holland) **2, 28, 39**
Campbell, (John) Ramsey **42**
Carter, Angela (Olive) **5, 41, 76**
Causley, Charles (Stanley) **7**
Caute, (John) David **29**
Chambers, Aidan **35**
Chaplin, Charles Spencer **16**
Chapman, Graham **21**
Chatwin, (Charles) Bruce **28, 57, 59**
Chitty, Thomas Willes **11**
Christie, Agatha (Mary Clarissa) **1, 6, 8, 12, 39, 48, 110**
Churchill, Caryl **31, 55, 157**
Clark, (Robert) Brian **29**
Clarke, Arthur C(harles) **1, 4, 13, 18, 35, 136**
Cleese, John (Marwood) **21**
Colegate, Isabel **36**
Comfort, Alex(ander) **7**
Compton-Burnett, I(vy) **1, 3, 10, 15, 34**
Cooney, Ray **62**
Copeland, Stewart (Armstrong) **26**
Cornwell, David (John Moore) **9, 15**
Costello, Elvis **21**
Coward, Noël (Peirce) **1, 9, 29, 51**
Crace, Jim **157**
Creasey, John **11**
Crispin, Edmund **22**
Dabydeen, David **34**
D'Aguiar, Fred **145**
Dahl, Roald **1, 6, 18, 79**
Daryush, Elizabeth **6, 19**
Davie, Donald (Alfred) **5, 8, 10, 31**
Davies, Rhys **23**

Day Lewis, C(ecil) **1, 6, 10**
Deighton, Len **4, 7, 22, 46**
Delaney, Shelagh **29**
Dennis, Nigel (Forbes) **8**
Dickinson, Peter (Malcolm) **12, 35**
Drabble, Margaret **2, 3, 5, 8, 10, 22, 53, 129**
Duffy, Maureen **37**
du Maurier, Daphne **6, 11, 59**
Durrell, Lawrence (George) **1, 4, 6, 8, 13, 27, 41**
Dyer, Geoff **149**
Eagleton, Terence (Francis) **63, 132**
Edgar, David **42**
Edwards, G(erald) B(asil) **25**
Eliot, T(homas) S(tearns) **1, 2, 3, 6, 9, 10, 13, 15, 24, 34, 41, 55, 57, 113**
Elliott, Janice **47**
Ellis, A. E. **7**
Ellis, Alice Thomas **40**
Empson, William **3, 8, 19, 33, 34**
Enright, D(ennis) J(oseph) **4, 8, 31**
Ewart, Gavin (Buchanan) **13, 46**
Fairbairns, Zoe (Ann) **32**
Farrell, J(ames) G(ordon) **6**
Feinstein, Elaine **36**
Fenton, James Martin **32**
Ferguson, Niall **134**
Fielding, Helen **146**
Figes, Eva **31**
Fisher, Roy **25**
Fitzgerald, Penelope **19, 51, 61, 143**
Fleming, Ian (Lancaster) **3, 30**
Follett, Ken(neth Martin) **18**
Forester, C(ecil) S(cott) **35**
Forster, E(dward) M(organ) **1, 2, 3, 4, 9, 10, 13, 15, 22, 45, 77**
Forster, Margaret **149**
Forsyth, Frederick **2, 5, 36**
Fowles, John (Robert) **1, 2, 3, 4, 6, 9, 10, 15, 33, 87**
Francis, Dick **2, 22, 42, 102**
Fraser, George MacDonald **7**
Frayn, Michael **3, 7, 31, 47**
Freeling, Nicolas **38**
Fry, Christopher **2, 10, 14**
Fugard, Sheila **48**
Fuller, John (Leopold) **62**
Fuller, Roy (Broadbent) **4, 28**
Gardam, Jane (Mary) **43**
Gardner, John (Edmund) **30**
Garfield, Leon **12**
Garner, Alan **17**
Garnett, David **3**
Gascoyne, David (Emery) **45**
Gee, Maggie (Mary) **57**
Gerhardie, William Alexander **5**
Gilliatt, Penelope (Ann Douglass) **2, 10, 13, 53**
Glanville, Brian (Lester) **6**
Glendinning, Victoria **50**
Gloag, Julian **40**
Godden, (Margaret) Rumer **53**
Golding, William (Gerald) **1, 2, 3, 8, 10, 17, 27, 58, 81**
Graham, Winston (Mawdsley) **23**
Graves, Richard Perceval **44**
Graves, Robert (von Ranke) **1, 2, 6, 11, 39, 44, 45**
Gray, Simon (James Holliday) **9, 14, 36**
Green, Henry **2, 13, 97**
Greenaway, Peter **159**
Greene, Graham (Henry) **1, 3, 6, 9, 14, 18, 27, 37, 70, 72, 125**
Griffiths, Trevor **13, 52**
Grigson, Geoffrey (Edward Harvey) **7, 39**
Gunn, Thom(son William) **3, 6, 18, 32, 81**
Haig-Brown, Roderick (Langmere) **21**
Hailey, Arthur **5**
Hall, Rodney **51**
Hamburger, Michael (Peter Leopold) **5, 14**
Hamilton, (Anthony Walter) Patrick **51**
Hampton, Christopher (James) **4**

Hare, David **29, 58, 136**
Harris, (Theodore) Wilson **25, 159**
Harrison, Tony **43, 129**
Hartley, L(eslie) P(oles) **2, 22**
Harwood, Ronald **32**
Hastings, Selina **44**
Hawking, Stephen W(illiam) **63, 105**
Headon, (Nicky) Topper **30**
Heppenstall, (John) Rayner **10**
Hibbert, Eleanor Alice Burford **7**
Hill, Geoffrey (William) **5, 8, 18, 45**
Hill, Susan (Elizabeth) **4, 113**
Hinde, Thomas **6, 11**
Hitchcock, Alfred (Joseph) **16**
Hitchens, Christopher **157**
Hocking, Mary (Eunice) **13**
Holden, Ursula **18**
Holdstock, Robert P. **39**
Hollinghurst, Alan **55, 91**
Hooker, (Peter) Jeremy **43**
Hopkins, John (Richard) **4**
Household, Geoffrey (Edward West) **11**
Howard, Elizabeth Jane **7, 29**
Hughes, David (John) **48**
Hughes, Richard (Arthur Warren) **1, 11**
Hughes, Ted **2, 4, 9, 14, 37, 119**
Huxley, Aldous (Leonard) **1, 3, 4, 5, 8, 11, 18, 35, 79**
Idle, Eric **21**
Ingalls, Rachel (Holmes) **42**
Isherwood, Christopher (William Bradshaw) **1, 9, 11, 14, 44**
Ishiguro, Kazuo **27, 56, 59, 110**
Jacobson, Dan **4, 14**
Jagger, Mick **17**
James, C(yril) L(ionel) R(obert) **33**
James, P. D. **18, 46, 122**
Jellicoe, (Patricia) Ann **27**
Jennings, Elizabeth (Joan) **5, 14, 131**
Jhabvala, Ruth Prawer **4, 8, 29, 94, 138**
Johnson, B(ryan) S(tanley William) **6, 9**
Johnson, Pamela Hansford **1, 7, 27**
Johnson, Paul (Bede) **147**
Jolley, (Monica) Elizabeth **46**
Jones, David (Michael) **2, 4, 7, 13, 42**
Jones, Diana Wynne **26**
Jones, Mervyn **10, 52**
Jones, Mick **30**
Josipovici, Gabriel (David) **6, 43, 153**
Kavan, Anna **5, 13, 82**
Kaye, M(ary) M(argaret) **28**
Keates, Jonathan **34**
King, Francis (Henry) **8, 53, 145**
Kirkup, James **1**
Koestler, Arthur **1, 3, 6, 8, 15, 33**
Kops, Bernard **4**
Kureishi, Hanif **64, 135**
Lanchester, John **99**
Larkin, Philip (Arthur) **3, 5, 8, 9, 13, 18, 33, 39, 64**
Leavis, F(rank) R(aymond) **24**
Lee, Laurie **90**
Lee, Tanith **46**
Lehmann, Rosamond (Nina) **5**
Lennon, John (Ono) **12, 35**
Lessing, Doris (May) **1, 2, 3, 6, 10, 15, 22, 40, 94**
Levertov, Denise **1, 2, 3, 5, 8, 15, 28, 66**
Levi, Peter (Chad Tigar) **41**
Lewis, C(live) S(taples) **1, 3, 6, 14, 27, 124**
Lively, Penelope (Margaret) **32, 50**
Lodge, David (John) **36, 141**
Loy, Mina **28**
Luke, Peter (Ambrose Cyprian) **38**
MacInnes, Colin **4, 23**
Mackenzie, Compton (Edward Montague) **18**
Macpherson, (Jean) Jay **14**
Maitland, Sara (Louise) **49**
Manning, Olivia **5, 19**
Mantel, Hilary (Mary) **144**
Masefield, John (Edward) **11, 47**
Mason, Nick **35**

Maugham, W(illiam) Somerset **1, 11, 15, 67, 93**
Mayle, Peter **89**
Mayne, William (James Carter) **12**
McEwan, Ian (Russell) **13, 66, 169**
McGrath, Patrick **55**
Mercer, David **5**
Middleton, Christopher **13**
Middleton, Stanley **7, 38**
Mitford, Nancy **44**
Mo, Timothy (Peter) **46, 134**
Moorcock, Michael (John) **5, 27, 58**
Mortimer, John (Clifford) **28, 43**
Mortimer, Penelope (Ruth) **5**
Mosley, Nicholas **43, 70**
Motion, Andrew (Peter) **47**
Mott, Michael (Charles Alston) **15, 34**
Murdoch, (Jean) Iris **1, 2, 3, 4, 6, 8, 11, 15, 22, 31, 51**
Naipaul, V(idiadhar) S(urajprasad) **4, 7, 9, 13, 18, 37, 105**
Newby, P(ercy) H(oward) **2, 13**
Nichols, Peter (Richard) **5, 36, 65**
Noon, Jeff **91**
Norfolk, Lawrence **76**
Nye, Robert **13, 42**
O'Brien, Richard **17**
O'Faolain, Julia **6, 19, 47, 108**
Olivier, Laurence (Kerr) **20**
Orton, Joe **4, 13, 43**
Osborne, John (James) **1, 2, 5, 11, 45**
Osborne, Lawrence **50**
Page, Jimmy **12**
Page, Louise **40**
Page, P(atricia) K(athleen) **7, 18**
Palin, Michael (Edward) **21**
Parkin, Frank **43**
Parks, Tim(othy Harold) **147**
Paton Walsh, Gillian **35**
Paulin, Tom **37**
Peake, Mervyn **7, 54**
Perry, Anne **126**
Phillips, Caryl **96**
Pinter, Harold **1, 3, 6, 9, 11, 15, 27, 58, 73**
Plant, Robert **12**
Poliakoff, Stephen **38**
Potter, Dennis (Christopher George) **58, 86, 123**
Powell, Anthony (Dymoke) **1, 3, 7, 9, 10, 31**
Pownall, David **10**
Powys, John Cowper **7, 9, 15, 46, 125**
Priestley, J(ohn) B(oynton) **2, 5, 9, 34**
Prince, F(rank) T(empleton) **22**
Pritchett, V(ictor) S(awdon) **5, 13, 15, 41**
Pym, Barbara (Mary Crampton) **13, 19, 37, 111**
Quin, Ann (Marie) **6**
Raine, Craig (Anthony) **32, 103**
Raine, Kathleen (Jessie) **7, 45**
Rathbone, Julian **41**
Rattigan, Terence (Mervyn) **7**
Raven, Simon (Arthur Noel) **14**
Read, Herbert Edward **4**
Read, Piers Paul **4, 10, 25**
Reading, Peter **47**
Redgrove, Peter (William) **6, 41**
Reid, Christopher (John) **33**
Rendell, Ruth (Barbara) **28, 48**
Rhys, Jean **2, 4, 6, 14, 19, 51, 124**
Rice, Tim(othy Miles Bindon) **21**
Richard, Keith **17**
Richards, I(vor) A(rmstrong) **14, 24**
Roberts, Keith (John Kingston) **14**
Roberts, Michele (Brigitte) **48**
Rowling, J(oanne) K(athleen) **137**
Rudkin, (James) David **14**
Rushdie, (Ahmed) Salman **23, 31, 55, 100**
Rushforth, Peter (Scott) **19**
Russell, (Henry) Ken(neth Alfred) **16**
Russell, William Martin **60**
Sacks, Oliver (Wolf) **67**
Sansom, William **2, 6**

Sassoon, Siegfried (Lorraine) **36, 130**
Scammell, Michael **34**
Scannell, Vernon **49**
Schama, Simon (Michael) **150**
Schlee, Ann **35**
Schumacher, E(rnst) F(riedrich) **80**
Scott, Paul (Mark) **9, 60**
Shaffer, Anthony (Joshua) **19**
Shaffer, Peter (Levin) **5, 14, 18, 37, 60**
Sharpe, Tom **36**
Shaw, Robert **5**
Sheed, Wilfrid (John Joseph) **2, 4, 10, 53**
Shute, Nevil **30**
Shuttle, Penelope (Diane) **7**
Silkin, Jon **2, 6, 43**
Sillitoe, Alan **1, 3, 6, 10, 19, 57, 148**
Simonon, Paul **30**
Simpson, N(orman) F(rederick) **29**
Sinclair, Andrew (Annandale) **2, 14**
Sinclair, Iain **76**
Sisson, C(harles) H(ubert) **8**
Sitwell, Edith **2, 9, 67**
Slaughter, Carolyn **56**
Smith, Stevie **3, 8, 25, 44**
Smith, Zadie **158**
Snow, C(harles) P(ercy) **1, 4, 6, 9, 13, 19**
Spender, Stephen (Harold) **1, 2, 5, 10, 41, 91**
Spurling, Hilary **34**
Stannard, Martin **44**
Stewart, J(ohn) I(nnes) M(ackintosh) **7, 14, 32**
Stewart, Mary (Florence Elinor) **7, 35, 117**
Stoppard, Tom **1, 3, 4, 5, 8, 15, 29, 34, 63, 91**
Storey, David (Malcolm) **2, 4, 5, 8**
Streatfeild, (Mary) Noel **21**
Strummer, Joe **30**
Summers, Andrew James **26**
Sumner, Gordon Matthew **26**
Sutcliff, Rosemary **26**
Swift, Graham (Colin) **41, 88**
Swinfen, Ann **34**
Swinnerton, Frank Arthur **31**
Symons, Julian (Gustave) **2, 14, 32**
Szirtes, George **46**
Taylor, Elizabeth **2, 4, 29**
Tennant, Emma (Christina) **13, 52**
Teran, Lisa St. Aubin de **36**
Thomas, D(onald) M(ichael) **13, 22, 31, 132**
Thubron, Colin (Gerald Dryden) **163**
Tindall, Gillian (Elizabeth) **7**
Tolkien, J(ohn) R(onald) R(euel) **1, 2, 3, 8, 12, 38**
Tomalin, Claire **166**
Tomlinson, (Alfred) Charles **2, 4, 6, 13, 45**
Townshend, Peter (Dennis Blandford) **17, 42**
Treitel, Jonathan **70**
Tremain, Rose **42**
Tuohy, Frank **37**
Turner, Frederick **48**
Unsworth, Barry (Forster) **76, 127**
Ustinov, Peter (Alexander) **1**
Van Den Bogarde, Derek Jules Gaspard Ulric Niven
Vansittart, Peter **42**
Wain, John (Barrington) **2, 11, 15, 46**
Walker, Ted **13**
Walsh, Jill Paton **35**
Warner, Francis (Robert le Plastrier) **14**
Warner, Marina **59**
Warner, Rex (Ernest) **45**
Warner, Sylvia Townsend **7, 19**
Waterhouse, Keith (Spencer) **47**
Waters, Roger **35**
Waugh, Auberon (Alexander) **7**
Waugh, Evelyn (Arthur St. John) **1, 3, 8, 13, 19, 27, 44, 107**
Waugh, Harriet **6**
Webber, Andrew Lloyd **21**
Weldon, Fay **6, 9, 11, 19, 36, 59, 122**
Weller, Paul **26**
Wesker, Arnold **3, 5, 42**

West, Anthony (Panther) **50**
West, Paul **7, 14, 96**
West, Rebecca **7, 9, 31, 50**
Westall, Robert (Atkinson) **17**
White, Patrick (Victor Martindale) **3, 4, 5, 7, 9, 18, 65, 69**
White, T(erence) H(anbury) **30**
Whitehead, E(dward) A(nthony) **5**
Whitemore, Hugh (John) **37**
Wilding, Michael **73**
Williams, Hugo **42**
Wilson, A(ndrew) N(orman) **33**
Wilson, Angus (Frank Johnstone) **2, 3, 5, 25, 34**
Wilson, Colin **3, 14**
Wilson, Snoo **33**
Wingrove, David (John) **68**
Winterson, Jeanette **64, 158**
Wodehouse, P(elham) G(renville) **1, 2, 5, 10, 22**
Wright, Rick **35**
Yorke, Henry Vincent **13**
Young, Andrew (John) **5**

### ESTONIAN

Ivask, Ivar Vidrik **14**

### FIJI ISLANDER

Prichard, Katharine Susannah **46**

### FILIPINO

Santos, Bienvenido N(uqui) **22**

### FINNISH

Haavikko, Paavo Juhani **18, 34**
Salama, Hannu **18**
Sillanpaa, Frans Eemil **19**

### FRENCH

Adamov, Arthur **4, 25**
Anouilh, Jean (Marie Lucien Pierre) **1, 3, 8, 13, 40, 50**
Aragon, Louis **3, 22**
Arp, Jean **5**
Audiberti, Jacques **38**
Aymé, Marcel (Andre) **11**
Barthes, Roland (Gérard) **24, 83**
Barzun, Jacques (Martin) **51, 145**
Bataille, Georges **29**
Baudrillard, Jean **60**
Beauvoir, Simone (Lucie Ernestine Marie Bertrand) de **1, 2, 4, 8, 14, 31, 44, 50, 71, 124**
Beckett, Samuel (Barclay) **1, 2, 3, 4, 6, 9, 10, 11, 14, 18, 29, 57, 59, 83**
Blanchot, Maurice **135**
Bonnefoy, Yves **9, 15, 58**
Bresson, Robert **16**
Breton, André **2, 9, 15, 54**
Butor, Michel (Marie François) **1, 3, 8, 11, 15, 161**
Camus, Albert **1, 2, 4, 9, 11, 14, 32, 63, 69, 124**
Carrere, Emmanuel **89**
Cayrol, Jean **11**
Chabrol, Claude **16**
Char, René(-émile) **9, 11, 14, 55**
Chedid, Andree **47**
Cixous, Hélène **92**
Clair, Rene **20**
Cocteau, Jean (Maurice Eugène Clément) **1, 8, 15, 16, 43**
Cousteau, Jacques-Yves **30**
del Castillo, Michel **38**
Derrida, Jacques **24, 87**
Destouches, Louis-Ferdinand **9, 15**
Duhamel, Georges **8**
Duras, Marguerite **3, 6, 11, 20, 34, 40, 68, 100**
Ernaux, Annie **88**

Federman, Raymond **6, 47**
Foucault, Michel **31, 34, 69**
Fournier, Pierre **11**
Francis, Claude **50**
Gallo, Max Louis **95**
Gao Xingjian **167**
Gary, Romain **25**
Gascar, Pierre **11**
Genet, Jean **1, 2, 5, 10, 14, 44, 46**
Giono, Jean **4, 11**
Godard, Jean-Luc **20**
Goldmann, Lucien **24**
Gontier, Fernande **50**
Gray, Francine du Plessix **22, 153**
Green, Julien **3, 11, 77**
Guillevic, (Eugene) **33**
Ionesco, Eugène **1, 4, 6, 9, 11, 15, 41, 86**
Irigarary, Luce **164**
Japrisot, Sebastien **90**
Josipovici, Gabriel (David) **6, 43, 153**
Jouve, Pierre Jean **47**
Kristeva, Julia **77, 140**
Lacan, Jacques (Marie Emile) **75**
Laurent, Antoine **50**
Le Clézio, J(ean) M(arie) G(ustave) **31, 155**
Leduc, Violette **22**
Leger, (Marie-Rene Auguste) Alexis Saint-Leger **4, 11, 46**
Leiris, Michel (Julien) **61**
Lévi-Strauss, Claude **38**
Mallet-Joris, Françoise **11**
Malraux, (Georges-)André **1, 4, 9, 13, 15, 57**
Mandiargues, Andre Pieyre de **41**
Marcel, Gabriel Honore **15**
Mauriac, Claude **9**
Mauriac, François (Charles) **4, 9, 56**
Merton, Thomas **1, 3, 11, 34, 83**
Modiano, Patrick (Jean) **18**
Montherlant, Henry (Milon) de **8, 19**
Morand, Paul **41**
Nin, Anaïs **1, 4, 8, 11, 14, 60, 127**
Perec, Georges **56, 116**
Pinget, Robert **7, 13, 37**
Ponge, Francis **6, 18**
Poniatowska, Elena **140**
Prévert, Jacques (Henri Marie) **15**
Queneau, Raymond **2, 5, 10, 42**
Quoirez, Francoise **9**
Renoir, Jean **20**
Resnais, Alain **16**
Reverdy, Pierre **53**
Rio, Michel **43**
Robbe-Grillet, Alain **1, 2, 4, 6, 8, 10, 14, 43, 128**
Rohmer, Eric **16**
Romains, Jules **7**
Sachs, Nelly **14, 98**
Sarraute, Nathalie **1, 2, 4, 8, 10, 31, 80**
Sartre, Jean-Paul **1, 4, 7, 9, 13, 18, 24, 44, 50, 52**
Sauser-Hall, Frederic **18**
Schwarz-Bart, André **2, 4**
Schwarz-Bart, Simone **7**
Simenon, Georges (Jacques Christian) **1, 2, 3, 8, 18, 47**
Simon, Claude **4, 9, 15, 39**
Soupault, Philippe **68**
Steiner, George **24**
Tournier, Michel (édouard) **6, 23, 36, 95**
Troyat, Henri **23**
Truffaut, Francois **20, 101**
Tuck, Lily **70**
Tzara, Tristan **47**
Varda, Agnes **16**
Wittig, Monique **22**
Yourcenar, Marguerite **19, 38, 50, 87**

### FRENCH GUINEAN

Damas, Leon-Gontran **84**

# CUMULATIVE NATIONALITY INDEX

## GERMAN

Amichai, Yehuda **9, 22, 57, 116**
Arendt, Hannah **66, 98**
Arp, Jean **5**
Becker, Jurek **7, 19**
Benary-Isbert, Margot **12**
Bienek, Horst **7, 11**
Boell, Heinrich (Theodor) **2, 3, 6, 9, 11, 15, 27, 32, 72**
Buchheim, Lothar-Guenther **6**
Bukowski, Charles **2, 5, 9, 41, 82, 108**
Eich, Guenter **15**
Ende, Michael (Andreas Helmuth) **31**
Enzensberger, Hans Magnus **43**
Fassbinder, Rainer Werner **20**
Figes, Eva **31**
Grass, Guenter (Wilhelm) **1, 2, 4, 6, 11, 15, 22, 32, 49, 88**
Habermas, Juergen **104**
Hamburger, Michael (Peter Leopold) **5, 14**
Handke, Peter **5, 8, 10, 15, 38, 134**
Heidegger, Martin **24**
Hein, Christoph **154**
Herzog, Werner **16**
Hesse, Hermann **1, 2, 3, 6, 11, 17, 25, 69**
Heym, Stefan **41**
Hildesheimer, Wolfgang **49**
Hochhuth, Rolf **4, 11, 18**
Hofmann, Gert **54**
Jhabvala, Ruth Prawer **4, 8, 29, 94, 138**
Johnson, Uwe **5, 10, 15, 40**
Juenger, Ernst **125**
Kissinger, Henry A(lfred) **137**
Kroetz, Franz Xaver **41**
Kunze, Reiner **10**
Lenz, Siegfried **27**
Levitin, Sonia (Wolff) **17**
Maron, Monika **165**
Mueller, Lisel **13, 51**
Nossack, Hans Erich **6**
Preussler, Otfried **17**
Remarque, Erich Maria **21**
Riefenstahl, Leni **16**
Sachs, Nelly **14, 98**
Schmidt, Arno (Otto) **56**
Schumacher, E(rnst) F(riedrich) **80**
Seghers, Anna **7**
Strauss, Botho **22**
Sueskind, Patrick **44**
Tillich, Paul (Johannes) **131**
Walser, Martin **27**
Weiss, Peter (Ulrich) **3, 15, 51**
Wellershoff, Dieter **46**
Wolf, Christa **14, 29, 58, 150**
Zuckmayer, Carl **18**

## GHANIAN

Armah, Ayi Kwei **5, 33, 136**

## GREEK

Broumas, Olga **10, 73**
Elytis, Odysseus **15, 49, 100**
Haviaras, Stratis **33**
Karapanou, Margarita **13**
Nakos, Lilika **29**
Ritsos, Yannis **6, 13, 31**
Samarakis, Antonis **5**
Seferis, George **5, 11**
Spanidou, Irini **44**
Vassilikos, Vassilis **4, 8**

## GUADELOUPEAN

Condé, Maryse **52, 92**
Schwarz-Bart, Simone **7**

## GUATEMALAN

Asturias, Miguel Ángel **3, 8, 13**

## GUINEAN

Laye, Camara **4, 38**

## GUYANESE

Dabydeen, David **34**
Harris, (Theodore) Wilson **25**

## HAITIAN

Danticat, Edwidge **94, 139**

## HUNGARIAN

Faludy, George **42**
Koestler, Arthur **1, 3, 6, 8, 15, 33**
Konrád, György **4, 10, 73**
Lengyel, József **7**
Lukacs, George **24**
Nagy, Laszlo **7**
Szirtes, George **46**
Tabori, George **19**
Vizinczey, Stephen **40**

## ICELANDIC

Gunnars, Kristjana **69**

## INDIAN

Alexander, Meena **121**
Ali, Ahmed **69**
Anand, Mulk Raj **23, 93**
Desai, Anita **19, 37, 97**
Ezekiel, Nissim **61**
Ghosh, Amitav **44, 153**
Mahapatra, Jayanta **33**
Mehta, Ved (Parkash) **37**
Mistry, Rohinton **71**
Mukherjee, Bharati **53, 115**
Narayan, R(asipuram) K(rishnaswami) **7, 28, 47, 121**
Rao, Raja **25, 56**
Ray, Satyajit **16, 76**
Rushdie, (Ahmed) Salman **23, 31, 55, 100**
Sahgal, Nayantara (Pandit) **41**
Sealy, I(rwin) Allan **55**
Seth, Vikram **43, 90**
Singh, Khushwant **11**
Tharoor, Shashi **70**
White, T(erence) H(anbury) **30**

## INDONESIAN

Lee, Li-Young **164**

## IRANIAN

Modarressi, Taghi (M.) **44**
Shamlu, Ahmad **10**

## IRISH

Banville, John **46, 118**
Beckett, Samuel (Barclay) **1, 2, 3, 4, 6, 9, 10, 11, 14, 18, 29, 57, 59, 83**
Behan, Brendan **1, 8, 11, 15, 79**
Binchy, Maeve **153**
Blackwood, Caroline **6, 9, 100**
Boland, Eavan (Aisling) **40, 67, 113**
Bowen, Elizabeth (Dorothea Cole) **1, 3, 6, 11, 15, 22, 118**
Boyle, Patrick **19**
Brennan, Maeve **5**
Brown, Christy **63**
Carroll, Paul Vincent **10**
Clarke, Austin **6, 9**
Colum, Padraic **28**
Day Lewis, C(ecil) **1, 6, 10**
Dillon, Eilis **17**
Donleavy, J(ames) P(atrick) **1, 4, 6, 10, 45**
Doyle, Roddy **81**
Durcan, Paul **43, 70**
Friel, Brian **5, 42, 59, 115**
Gébler, Carlo (Ernest) **39**
Hanley, James **3, 5, 8, 13**
Hart, Josephine **70**
Heaney, Seamus (Justin) **5, 7, 14, 25, 37, 74, 91**
Johnston, Jennifer (Prudence) **7, 150**
Jordan, Neil (Patrick) **110**
Kavanagh, Patrick (Joseph) **22**
Keane, Molly **31**
Kiely, Benedict **23, 43**
Kinsella, Thomas **4, 19, 138**
Lavin, Mary **4, 18, 99**
Leonard, Hugh **19**
Longley, Michael **29**
Mac Laverty, Bernard **31**
MacNeice, (Frederick) Louis **1, 4, 10, 53**
Mahon, Derek **27**
McCabe, Patrick **133**
McGahern, John **5, 9, 48, 156**
McGinley, Patrick (Anthony) **41**
McGuckian, Medbh **48**
Montague, John (Patrick) **13, 46**
Moore, Brian **1, 3, 5, 7, 8, 19, 32, 90**
Morrison, Van **21**
Morrissy, Mary **99**
Muldoon, Paul **32, 72, 166**
Murphy, Richard **41**
Murphy, Thomas (Bernard) **51**
Nolan, Christopher **58**
O'Brian, Patrick **152**
O'Brien, Edna **3, 5, 8, 13, 36, 65, 116**
O'Casey, Sean **1, 5, 9, 11, 15, 88**
O'Doherty, Brian **76**
O'Faolain, Julia **6, 19, 47, 108**
O'Faolain, Sean **1, 7, 14, 32, 70**
O'Flaherty, Liam **5, 34**
Paulin, Tom **37**
Rodgers, W(illiam) R(obert) **7**
Simmons, James (Stewart Alexander) **43**
Toibin, Colm **162**
Trevor, William **7, 9, 14, 25, 71, 116**
White, Terence de Vere **49**
Wilson, Robert McLiam **59**

## ISRAELI

Agnon, S(hmuel) Y(osef Halevi) **4, 8, 14**
Amichai, Yehuda **9, 22, 57, 116**
Appelfeld, Aharon **23, 47**
Bakshi, Ralph **26**
Friedlander, Saul **90**
Grossman, David **67**
Kaniuk, Yoram **19**
Levin, Meyer **7**
Megged, Aharon **9**
Oz, Amos **5, 8, 11, 27, 33, 54**
Shammas, Anton **55**
Sobol, Joshua **60**
Yehoshua, A(braham) B. **13, 31**

## ITALIAN

Antonioni, Michelangelo **20, 144**
Bacchelli, Riccardo **19**
Bassani, Giorgio **9**
Bertolucci, Bernardo **16, 157**
Bufalino, Gesualdo **74**
Buzzati, Dino **36**
Calasso, Roberto **81**
Calvino, Italo **5, 8, 11, 22, 33, 39, 73**
De Sica, Vittorio **20**
Eco, Umberto **28, 60, 142**
Fallaci, Oriana **11, 110**
Fellini, Federico **16, 85**
Fo, Dario **32, 109**
Gadda, Carlo Emilio **11**
Ginzburg, Natalia **5, 11, 54, 70**
Giovene, Andrea **7**
Landolfi, Tommaso **11, 49**
Levi, Primo **37, 50**
Luzi, Mario **13**
Montale, Eugenio **7, 9, 18**
Morante, Elsa **8, 47**
Moravia, Alberto **2, 7, 11, 27, 46**
Ortese, Anna Maria **89**
Palazzeschi, Aldo **11**
Pasolini, Pier Paolo **20, 37, 106**
Piccolo, Lucio **13**
Pincherle, Alberto **11, 18**

Quasimodo, Salvatore 10
Ricci, Nino 70
Sciascia, Leonardo 8, 9, 41
Silone, Ignazio 4
Ungaretti, Giuseppe 7, 11, 15
Visconti, Luchino 16
Vittorini, Elio 6, 9, 14
Wertmueller, Lina 16

## JAMAICAN

Bennett, Louise (Simone) 28
Cliff, Jimmy 21
Cliff, Michelle 120
Marley, Bob 17
Thelwell, Michael Miles 22

## JAPANESE

Abe, Kōbō 8, 22, 53, 81
Enchi, Fumiko (Ueda) 31
Endō, Shūsaku 7, 14, 19, 54, 99
Ibuse, Masuji 22
Ichikawa, Kon 20
Ishiguro, Kazuo 27, 56, 59, 110
Kawabata, Yasunari 2, 5, 9, 18, 107
Kurosawa, Akira 16, 119
Murakami, Haruki
Oe, Kenzaburo 10, 36, 86
Oshima, Nagisa 20
Ozu, Yasujiro 16
Shiga, Naoya 33
Tanizaki, Jun'ichirō 8, 14, 28
Whitney, Phyllis A(yame) 42
Yoshimoto, Banana 84

## KENYAN

Ngugi, James T(hiong'o) 3, 7, 13
Ngũgĩ wa Thiong'o 36

## MALIAN

Ouologuem, Yambo 146

## MARTINICAN

Césaire, Aimé (Fernand) 19, 32, 112
Fanon, Frantz 74
Glissant, Edouard 10, 68

## MEXICAN

Arreola, Juan José 147
Castellanos, Rosario 66
Esquivel, Laura 141
Fuentes, Carlos 3, 8, 10, 13, 22, 41, 60, 113
Ibarguengoitia, Jorge 37
Lopez Portillo (y Pacheco), Jose 46
Lopez y Fuentes, Gregorio 32
Paz, Octavio 3, 4, 6, 10, 19, 51, 65, 119
Poniatowska, Elena 140
Rulfo, Juan 8, 80

## MOROCCAN

Arrabal, Fernando 2, 9, 18, 58

## NEW ZEALANDER

Adcock, Fleur 41
Ashton-Warner, Sylvia (Constance) 19
Baxter, James K(eir) 14
Campion, Jane 95
Gee, Maurice (Gough) 29
Grace, Patricia Frances 56
Hilliard, Noel (Harvey) 15
Hulme, Keri 39, 130
Ihimaera, Witi 46
Marsh, (Edith) Ngaio 7, 53
Sargeson, Frank 31

## NICARAGUAN

Alegria, Claribel 75
Cardenal, Ernesto 31, 161

## NIGERIAN

Achebe, (Albert) Chinua(lumogu) 1, 3, 5, 7, 11, 26, 51, 75, 127, 152
Clark Bekedermo, J(ohnson) P(epper) 38
Ekwensi, Cyprian (Odiatu Duaka) 4
Emecheta, (Florence Onye) Buchi 14, 48, 128
Nwapa, Flora 133
Okigbo, Christopher (Ifenayichukwu) 25, 84
Okri, Ben 87
Saro-Wiwa, Ken(ule Beeson) 114
Soyinka, Wole 3, 5, 14, 36, 44
Tutuola, Amos 5, 14, 29

## NORTHERN IRISH

Deane, Seamus (Francis) 122
Simmons, James (Stewart Alexander) 43
Wilson, Robert McLiam 59

## NORWEGIAN

Friis-Baastad, Babbis Ellinor 12
Heyerdahl, Thor 26
Vesaas, Tarjei 48

## PAKISTANI

Ali, Ahmed 69
Ghose, Zulfikar 42

## PARAGUAYAN

Roa Bastos, Augusto (Antonio) 45

## PERUVIAN

Allende, Isabel 39, 57, 97
Arguedas, José María 10, 18
Goldemberg, Isaac 52
Vargas Llosa, (Jorge) Mario (Pedro) 3, 6, 9, 10, 15, 31, 42, 85

## POLISH

Agnon, S(hmuel) Y(osef Halevi) 4, 8, 14
Becker, Jurek 7, 19
Bermant, Chaim (Icyk) 40
Bienek, Horst 7, 11
Brandys, Kazimierz 62
Dabrowska, Maria (Szumska) 15
Gombrowicz, Witold 4, 7, 11, 49
Herbert, Zbigniew 9, 43
John Paul II, Pope 128
Kieslowski, Krzysztof 120
Konwicki, Tadeusz 8, 28, 54, 117
Kosinski, Jerzy (Nikodem) 1, 2, 3, 6, 10, 15, 53, 70
Lem, Stanislaw 8, 15, 40, 149
Milosz, Czeslaw 5, 11, 22, 31, 56, 82
Mrozek, Slawomir 3, 13
Polanski, Roman 16
Rozewicz, Tadeusz 9, 23, 139
Singer, Isaac Bashevis 1, 3, 6, 9, 11, 15, 23, 38, 69, 111
Skolimowski, Jerzy 20
Szymborska, Wisława 99
Wajda, Andrzej 16
Wittlin, Jozef 25
Wojciechowska, Maia (Teresa) 26

## PORTUGUESE

Migueis, Jose Rodrigues 10
Saramago, José 119

## PUERTO RICAN

Ferré, Rosario 139
Marqués, René 96
Piñero, Miguel (Antonio Gomez) 4, 55
Sánchez, Luis Rafael 23

## ROMANIAN

Celan, Paul 10, 19, 53, 82
Cioran, E(mil) M. 64

Codrescu, Andrei 46, 121
Ionesco, Eugène 1, 4, 6, 9, 11, 15, 41, 86
Rezzori (d'Arezzo), Gregor von 25
Tzara, Tristan 47
Wiesel, Elie(zer) 3, 5, 11, 37

## RUSSIAN

Aitmatov, Chingiz (Torekulovich) 71
Akhmadulina, Bella Akhatovna 53
Akhmatova, Anna 11, 25, 64, 126
Aksyonov, Vassily (Pavlovich) 22, 37, 101
Aleshkovsky, Yuz 44
Almedingen, E. M. 12
Asimov, Isaac 1, 3, 9, 19, 26, 76, 92
Bakhtin, Mikhail Mikhailovich 83
Bitov, Andrei (Georgievich) 57
Brodsky, Joseph 4, 6, 13, 36, 100
Deren, Maya 16, 102
Ehrenburg, Ilya (Grigoryevich) 18, 34, 62
Eliade, Mircea 19
Gary, Romain 25
Goldberg, Anatol 34
Grade, Chaim 10
Grossman, Vasily (Semenovich) 41
Iskander, Fazil 47
Kabakov, Sasha 59
Kaletski, Alexander 39
Krotkov, Yuri 19
Leonov, Leonid (Maximovich) 92
Limonov, Edward 67
Nabokov, Vladimir (Vladimirovich) 1, 2, 3, 6, 8, 11, 15, 23, 44, 46, 64
Olesha, Yuri (Karlovich) 8
Pasternak, Boris (Leonidovich) 7, 10, 18, 63
Paustovsky, Konstantin (Georgievich) 40
Rahv, Philip 24
Rand, Ayn 3, 30, 44, 79
Ratushinskaya, Irina 54
Rybakov, Anatoli (Naumovich) 23, 53
Sarraute, Nathalie 1, 2, 4, 8, 10, 31, 80
Shalamov, Varlam (Tikhonovich) 18
Shatrov, Mikhail 59
Sholokhov, Mikhail (Aleksandrovich) 7, 15
Sinyavsky, Andrei (Donatevich) 8
Solzhenitsyn, Aleksandr I(sayevich) 1, 2, 4, 7, 9, 10, 18, 26, 34, 78, 134
Strugatskii, Arkadii (Natanovich) 27
Strugatskii, Boris (Natanovich) 27
Tarkovsky, Andrei (Arsenyevich) 75
Trifonov, Yuri (Valentinovich) 45
Troyat, Henri 23
Voinovich, Vladimir (Nikolaevich) 10, 49, 147
Voznesensky, Andrei (Andreievich) 1, 15, 57
Yanovsky, V(assily) S(emenovich) 2, 18
Yevtushenko, Yevgeny (Alexandrovich) 1, 3, 13, 26, 51, 126
Yezierska, Anzia 46
Zaturenska, Marya 6, 11
Zinoviev, Alexander (Aleksandrovich) 19

## SALVADORAN

Alegria, Claribel 75
Argueta, Manlio 31

## SCOTTISH

Banks, Iain M(enzies) 34
Brown, George Mackay 5, 48, 100
Cronin, A(rchibald) J(oseph) 32
Dunn, Douglas (Eaglesham) 6, 40
Graham, W(illiam) S(idney) 29
Gray, Alasdair (James) 41
Grieve, C(hristopher) M(urray) 11, 19
Hunter, Mollie 21
Jenkins, (John) Robin 52
Kelman, James 58, 86
Laing, R(onald) D(avid) 95
MacBeth, George (Mann) 2, 5, 9
MacCaig, Norman (Alexander) 36
MacInnes, Helen (Clark) 27, 39
MacLean, Alistair (Stuart) 3, 13, 50, 63

McIlvanney, William **42**
Morgan, Edwin (George) **31**
Smith, Iain Crichton **64**
Spark, Muriel (Sarah) **2, 3, 5, 8, 13, 18, 40, 94**
Taylor, C(ecil) P(hilip) **27**
Walker, David Harry **14**
Welsh, Irvine **144**
Young, Andrew (John) **5**

## SENEGALESE

Ousmane, Sembene **66**
Senghor, Léopold Sédar **54, 130**

## SOMALIAN

Farah, Nuruddin **53, 137**

## SOUTH AFRICAN

Abrahams, Peter (Henry) **4**
Breytenbach, Breyten **23, 37, 126**
Brink, André (Philippus) **18, 36, 106**
Brutus, Dennis **43**
Coetzee, J(ohn) M(ichael) **23, 33, 66, 117, 161, 162**
Courtenay, Bryce **59**
Fugard, (Harold) Athol **5, 9, 14, 25, 40, 80**
Fugard, Sheila **48**
Gordimer, Nadine **3, 5, 7, 10, 18, 33, 51, 70, 123, 160, 161**
Harwood, Ronald **32**
Head, Bessie **25, 67**
Hope, Christopher (David Tully) **52**
Kunene, Mazisi (Raymond) **85**
La Guma, (Justin) Alex(ander) **19**
Millin, Sarah Gertrude **49**
Mphahlele, Ezekiel **25, 133**
Mtwa, Percy **47**
Ngema, Mbongeni **57**
Nkosi, Lewis **45**
Paton, Alan (Stewart) **4, 10, 25, 55, 106**
Plomer, William Charles Franklin **4, 8**
Prince, F(rank) T(empleton) **22**
Smith, Wilbur (Addison) **33**
Tolkien, J(ohn) R(onald) R(euel) **1, 2, 3, 8, 12, 38**
Tutu, Desmond M(pilo) **80**
van der Post, Laurens (Jan) **5**
Vorster, Gordon **34**

## SPANISH

Alberti, Rafael **7**
Alfau, Felipe **66**
Almodovar, Pedro **114**
Alonso, Damaso **14**
Arrabal, Fernando **2, 9, 18, 58**
Benet, Juan **28**
Buero Vallejo, Antonio **15, 46, 139**
Bunuel, Luis **16, 80**
Casona, Alejandro **49**
Castedo, Elena **65**
Cela, Camilo José **4, 13, 59, 122**
Cernuda (y Bidón), Luis **54**
del Castillo, Michel **38**
Delibes, Miguel **8, 18**
Espriu, Salvador **9**
Gironella, José María **11**
Gomez de la Serna, Ramon **9**
Goytisolo, Juan **5, 10, 23, 133**
Guillén, Jorge **11**
Matute (Ausejo), Ana María **11**
Otero, Blas de **11**
Rodriguez, Claudio **10**
Ruiz, Jose Martinez **11**
Saura (Atares), Carlos **20**
Sender, Ramón (José) **8**

## SRI LANKAN

Gunesekera, Romesh **91**

## ST. LUCIAN

Walcott, Derek (Alton) **2, 4, 9, 14, 25, 42, 67, 76, 160**

## SWEDISH

Beckman, Gunnel **26**
Bergman, (Ernst) Ingmar **16, 72**
Ekeloef, (Bengt) Gunnar **27**
Johnson, Eyvind (Olof Verner) **14**
Lagerkvist, Paer (Fabian) **7, 10, 13, 54**
Martinson, Harry (Edmund) **14**
Sjoewall, Maj **7**
Spiegelman, Art **76**
Transtroemer, Tomas (Goesta) **52, 65**
Wahlöö, Per **7**
Weiss, Peter (Ulrich) **3, 15, 51**

## SWISS

Canetti, Elias **3, 14, 25, 75, 86**
Duerrenmatt, Friedrich **1, 4, 8, 11, 15, 43, 102**
Frisch, Max (Rudolf) **3, 9, 14, 18, 32, 44**
Hesse, Hermann **1, 2, 3, 6, 11, 17, 25, 69**
King, Francis (Henry) **8, 53, 145**
Kung, Hans **130**
Pinget, Robert **7, 13, 37**
Sauser-Hall, Frederic **18**
Sterchi, Beat **65**
von Daeniken, Erich **30**

## TRINIDADIAN

Guy, Rosa (Cuthbert) **26**
James, C(yril) L(ionel) R(obert) **33**
Lovelace, Earl **51**
Naipaul, Shiva(dhar Srinivasa) **32, 39**
Naipaul, V(idiadhar) S(urajprasad) **4, 7, 9, 13, 18, 37, 105**
Rampersad, Arnold **44**

## TURKISH

Hikmet, Nazim **40**
Kemal, Yashar **14, 29**
Seferis, George **5, 11**

## UGANDAN

p'Bitek, Okot **96**

## URUGUAYAN

Galeano, Eduardo (Hughes) **72**
Onetti, Juan Carlos **7, 10**
Peri Rossi, Cristina **156**

## WELSH

Abse, Dannie **7, 29**
Arundel, Honor (Morfydd) **17**
Clarke, Gillian **61**
Dahl, Roald **1, 6, 18, 79**
Davies, Rhys **23**
Francis, Dick **2, 22, 42, 102**
Hughes, Richard (Arthur Warren) **1, 11**
Humphreys, Emyr Owen **47**
Jones, David (Michael) **2, 4, 7, 13, 42**
Jones, Terence Graham Parry **21**
Levinson, Deirdre **49**
Llewellyn Lloyd, Richard Dafydd Vivian **7, 80**
Mathias, Roland (Glyn) **45**
Norris, Leslie **14**
Roberts, Kate **15**
Rubens, Bernice (Ruth) **19, 31**
Thomas, R(onald) S(tuart) **6, 13, 48**
Watkins, Vernon Phillips **43**
Williams, (George) Emlyn **15**

## YUGOSLAVIAN

Andrić, Ivo **8**
Cosic, Dobrica **14**
Kǐ, Danilo **57**
Krlěa, Miroslav **8, 114**
Pavic, Milorad **60**
Popa, Vasko **19**
Simic, Charles **6, 9, 22, 49, 68, 130**
Tesich, Steve **40, 69**

# CLC-169 Title Index

"Acte sexuel" (Brossard) **169**:17
Action (Shepard) **169**:259, 270-71, 277, 286-89, 301, 306
The Aerial Letter (Brossard)
  See La Lettre aérienne
Alternative Alcott (Showalter) **169**:341
Amantes (Brossard) **169**:12, 14-16, 20, 25, 58-59, 64
L'Amèr ou le chapitre effrité (Brossard) **169**:12, 19, 25, 27, 47
"American Experimental Theatre—Then and Now" (Shepard) **169**:272
"American Questions" (Showalter) **169**:337, 340
Amsterdam (McEwan) **169**:192-96, 210-11, 220, 224
Angel City (Shepard) **169**:245, 258, 261, 264, 269, 277, 298, 306-7
Atonement (McEwan) **169**:220, 222, 224, 226
Aube à la saison (Brossard) **169**:25
Die Ausgesperrten (Jelinek) **169**:69, 71-72, 121, 129-30, 135
L'Aviva (Brossard) **169**:48, 64
Back Bog Beast Bait (Shepard) **169**:243, 306
Baroque at Dawn (Brossard)
  See Baroque d'aube
Baroque d'aube (Brossard) **169**:24-26, 28-40
"Beyond the Female Aesthetic: Contemporary Women Novelists" (Showalter) **169**:316-17
Die Bienenkönige (Jelinek) **169**:77-78, 82-84
Black Bog Beast Bait (Shepard) **169**:259
Black Dogs (McEwan) **169**:158-65, 184, 186, 196, 212, 216-20, 226
A Book (Brossard)
  See Un livre
Bringing up a Vampire (Jelinek)
  See Erziehung eines Vampirs
Burgtheater (Jelinek) **169**:98
Buried Child (Shepard) **169**:232, 234-36, 242-43, 258-62, 267, 273, 282-86, 289-91, 293, 295-96, 298, 300-301, 306
"Butterflies" (McEwan) **169**:166
The Cement Garden (McEwan) **169**:158, 166, 169, 172, 181, 185, 187-88, 194, 210
Le Centre blanc (Brossard) **169**:9-12
"Chapitre" (Brossard) **169**:18
Chicago (Shepard) **169**:241, 287-88
The Child in Time (McEwan) **169**:158-59, 161-62, 166, 168, 170-72, 174-75, 177, 179-80, 185-87, 189, 193-94, 196, 210-12, 216, 226
The Children of the Dead (Jelinek)
  See Die Kinder der Toten
Clara S. (Jelinek) **169**:122-23, 125, 127-28
The Comfort of Strangers (McEwan) **169**:158-59, 166, 181, 183-85, 188, 194, 196-97, 199, 207, 220
"Common Threads" (Showalter) **169**:346, 348
Cowboy Mouth (Shepard) **169**:243, 259, 301, 307
Cowboys (Shepard) **169**:270
Cruising Paradise (Shepard) **169**:283-84, 286, 298

Curse of the Starving Class (Shepard) **169**:232, 234, 261-62, 266-68, 273, 283, 286-87, 306, 308
Daughters of Decadence (Showalter) **169**:344, 346
The Daydreamer (McEwan) **169**:173, 182, 185, 221
"De radical á intágrales" (Brossard) **169**:45
"The Death of the Lady (Novelist): Wharton's House of Mirth" (Showalter) **169**:348
Demise of a Diver (Jelinek)
  See Untergang eines tauchers
Le Désert mauve (Brossard) **169**:18, 23-27, 48, 59-64
"The Devouring Lion" (Shepard) **169**:284
"The Double Critical Standard and the Feminine Novel" (Showalter) **169**:317
"E Muet Mutant" (Brossard) **169**:27, 29-30, 39
L'Echo bouge beau (Brossard) **169**:10
The Echo Moves Beautiful (Brossard)
  See L'Echo bouge beau
Ein Sportstück (Jelinek) **169**:120-21
Enduring Love (McEwan) **169**:183-89, 191-92, 194, 196, 210-17, 220, 224
"Energy" (Brossard) **169**:29
"Entretien" (Brossard) **169**:28
Erziehung eines Vampirs (Jelinek) **169**:80, 82
Far North (Shepard) **169**:238, 265, 267-68, 270
The Female Malady: Women, Madness, and English Culture, 1830-1980 (Showalter) **169**:323-25, 327, 329, 343-44, 350-52, 356, 363, 369, 374
"The Feminine Novelists and the Will to Write" (Showalter) **169**:317
First Love, Last Rites (McEwan) **169**:158, 181, 188, 194, 212
"First Love, Last Rites" (McEwan) **169**:172
"Flight into Androgyny" (Showalter) **169**:317
Fool for Love (Shepard) **169**:232, 234, 246, 251, 254, 262-63, 266, 276, 282, 291, 298, 301, 306
For Some, the Setting Sun Means the End of a Working Day (Jelinek)
  See Wenn die sonne sinkt ist für manche auch noch büroschluss!
Forensic and the Navigators (Shepard) **169**:271
Fourteen Hundred Thousand (Shepard) **169**:262
French Kiss (Brossard) **169**:12, 20, 23-24, 48
Geography of a Horse Dreamer (Shepard) **169**:2 **169**:59, 258, 261, 282
Gier (Jelinek) **169**:154
"Hail from Nowhere" (Shepard) **169**:284
Hawk Moon (Shepard) **169**:241-42
The Holy Ghostly (Shepard) **169**:263, 298
"Homemade" (McEwan) **169**:194
Hystories: Hysterical Epidemics and Modern Culture (Showalter) **169**:348-52, 354-55, 359-63, 375
Icarus's Mother (Shepard) **169**:241, 260, 271
Illness or the Modern Woman (Jelinek)
  See Krankheit oder Moderne Frauen
The Imitation Game (McEwan) **169**:181-82

In Between the Sheets (McEwan) **169**:158, 194, 212
"In Between the Sheets" (McEwan) **169**:172
Inacoma (Shepard) **169**:298
The Innocent (McEwan) **169**:158-59, 161-62, 181-82, 185, 194, 210-11, 214
"Installation" (Brossard) **169**:17
Installations (Brossard) **169**:17-18, 25
Inventing Herself: Claiming a Feminist Intellectual Heritage (Showalter) **169**:364, 366, 369-73, 375
Jack Flea's Birthday Celebration (McEwan) **169**:169, 182
Journal intime (Brossard) **169**:20
"Just Space" (Shepard) **169**:284
Kasperl and the Chubby Princess or Kasperl and the Skinny Peasants (Jelinek)
  See Kasperl und die dicke Prinzessin oder Kasperl und die dünnen bauren
Kasperl und die dicke Prinzessin oder Kasperl und die dünnen bauren (Jelinek) **169**:78-79
Killer's Head (Shepard) **169**:287-89
"Kind Skin My Mind" (Brossard) **169**:32, 34, 39
Die Kinder der Toten (Jelinek) **169**:104
The King Bees (Jelinek)
  See Die Bienenkönige
Die Klavierspielerin (Jelinek) **169**:69-70, 74-75, 87-90, 93-94, 121, 129-31, 133-36
Krankheit oder Moderne Frauen (Jelinek) **169**:84, 98, 104, 121, 125, 148-49
"Language, Visualization and the Inner Library" (Shepard) **169**:302-3
The Late Henry Moss (Shepard) **169**:297-300
Das Lebewohl (Jelinek) **169**:137-38
La Lettre aérienne (Brossard) **169**:26-27, 44, 46, 62
A Lie of the Mind (Shepard) **169**:232-35, 237-41, 243, 245, 253, 262-63, 266, 268, 271, 276, 282-83, 287, 291, 296, 298, 301, 306
Die Liebhaberinnen (Jelinek) **169**:105-6, 110-11, 121, 123, 130-31, 133-35
A Literature of Their Own: British Women Novelists from Brontë to Lessing (Showalter) **169**:314-15, 317-21, 333-35, 337-38, 341, 343, 363, 366, 369, 371, 374-75
"Little Women: The American Female Myth" (Showalter) **169**:347
Un livre (Brossard) **169**:9-10, 12-16
Logical Consequences/Succession (Brossard)
  See Suite logique
Lovhers (Brossard)
  See Amantes
Lust (Jelinek) **169**:69, 75, 98, 102, 123, 129-30, 142
Machismo Sagas (Shepard) **169**:242
Mad Dog Blues (Shepard) **169**:258, 261
The Mauve Desert (Brossard)
  See Le Désert mauve
Me and My Brother (Shepard) **169**:243-44

*Michael: A Children's Book for the Infantile Society* (Jelinek)
   See *Michael: Ein jugendbuch für manche auch noch büroschluss!*
*Michael: Ein jugendbuch für manche auch noch büroschluss!* (Jelinek) **169**:77-78
"Miranda's Story" (Showalter) **169**:342, 348
*Motel Chronicles* (Shepard) **169**:244, 251, 288
"Mourir" (Brossard) **169**:18
*A Move Abroad* (McEwan) **169**:181-82
*La Nef des sorcières* (Brossard) **169**:16, 19
*The New Feminist Criticism* (Showalter) **169**:321, 328-29, 339, 347
"New Women" (Showalter) **169**:343
"Nicole Brossard" (Brossard) **169**:48
"Odd Women" (Showalter) **169**:335, 343
*Oh Wildnis, oh Schutz vor ihr* (Jelinek) **169**:129
*Operation Sidewinder* (Shepard) **169**:242, 258-59, 261
*Or Shall We Die?* (McEwan) **169**:182, 211-12
"The Other Lost Generation" (Showalter) **169**:342
"The Package Man" (Shepard) **169**:286
*Paris, Texas* (Shepard) **169**:244, 246, 248-49, 251-54, 256, 269, 276
"Partie des fesses" (Brossard) **169**:18
"Pays" (Brossard) **169**:18
*Picture Theory* (Brossard) **169**:10, 12, 14, 16, 23-25, 27-29, 44-48
"Piecing and Writing" (Showalter) **169**:346
*The Ploughman's Lunch* (McEwan) **169**:182
"Poetic Politics" (Brossard) **169**:33, 63-64
"Pornography" (McEwan) **169**:166, 188
"Pré(e)" (Brossard) **169**:44
"The Real Gabby Hayes" (Shepard) **169**:284, 298
*Red Cross* (Shepard) **169**:242, 296
"Reflections of a Kept Ape" (McEwan) **169**:194
"Réplique" (Brossard) **169**:17
*The Rock Garden* (Shepard) **169**:241-42, 259, 270

*Rolling Thunder Logbook* (Shepard) **169**:289
*The Sad Lament of Pecos Bill on the Eve of Killing His Wife* (Shepard) **169**:287-89
*Das Schweigen* (Jelinek) **169**:138
*Seduced* (Shepard) **169**:258, 260
"The Self-Made Man" (Shepard) **169**:283
*Le Sens apparent* (Brossard) **169**:16, 25
*Sexual Anarchy: Gender and Culture at the Fin-de-Siècle* (Showalter) **169**:330-31, 333-38, 341, 343-45, 363, 374
*Silent Tongue* (Shepard) **169**:265
*Simpatico* (Shepard) **169**:281-83, 287, 292
*Sister's Choice* (Showalter) **169**:334-36, 339, 341-42, 346-47
"A Small Circle of Friends" (Shepard) **169**:284
*Solid Geometry* (McEwan) **169**:181-82
*Some American Feminists* (Brossard) **169**:19
*Speaking of Gender* (Showalter) **169**:343
*States of Shock* (Shepard) **169**:265, 269-77, 279, 281, 287, 291
"Subverting the Feminine Novel: Sensationalism and Feminine Protest" (Showalter) **169**:318, 320
*Suicide in B-Flat* (Shepard) **169**:261, 290
*Suite logique* (Brossard) **169**:9, 11-12
*Superstitions* (Shepard) **169**:288
"Talkin' 'Bout My Generation: The 1970s" (Showalter) **169**:372
"Teaching Dangerous Subjects" (Showalter) **169**:376
*Teaching Literature* (Showalter) **169**:375
*These Our Mothers* (Brossard)
   See *L'Amèr ou le chapitre effrité*
*Der Tod und das Mädchen II* (Jelinek) **169**:138
*Tongues* (Shepard) **169**:266-67, 306
*Tooth of Crime (Second Dance)* (Shepard) **169**:290-92
*The Tooth of Crime* (Shepard) **169**:242, 245, 261, 270, 283, 285-87, 289-92, 306-7
*Totenauberg* (Jelinek) **169**:97-99

"Towards a Feminist Poetics" (Showalter) **169**:340
*True West* (Shepard) **169**:232, 234, 239-40, 242, 252, 258, 262, 264, 267-68, 273, 276, 279, 282, 286, 290-92, 296, 298, 300
*La Turista* (Shepard) **169**:242, 258, 261
*The Unseen Hand* (Shepard) **169**:261, 271, 283, 307
*Untergang eines tauchers* (Jelinek) **169**:78
"Vaseline" (Brossard) **169**:36
"Virginia Woolf and the Flight into Androgyny" (Showalter) **169**:318, 341
*The War in Heaven* (Shepard) **169**:287
*Was geschah, nachdem Nora ihren mann verlassen hatte oder Stutzen der Gesellschaften* (Jelinek) **169**:80, 113-15, 121
*Wenn die sonne sinkt ist für manche auch noch büroschluss!* (Jelinek) **169**:80
*We're Decoys, Baby!* (Jelinek)
   See *Wir sind lockvögel baby!*
*What Happened after Nora Left Her Husband or the Pillars of Society* (Jelinek)
   See *Was geschah, nachdem Nora ihren mann verlassen hatte oder Stutzen der Gesellschaften*
*When the World Was Green (A Chef's Fable)* (Shepard) **169**:287-88
*The White Center* (Brossard)
   See *Le Centre blanc*
*Wir sind lockvögel baby!* (Jelinek) **169**:78, 123, 129
*Wolken.Heim* (Jelinek) **169**:98, 130
"The Woman's Case" (Showalter) **169**:335-36, 343
"Women and the Literary Curriculum" (Showalter) **169**:372
*Wonderful, Wonderful Times* (Jelinek) **169**:68, 75, 87
"Zenobia on the Hudson" (Showalter) **169**:372

ISBN 0-7876-6342-5